FORGETFUL REMEMBRANCE

Forgetful Remembrance

Social Forgetting and Vernacular Historiography of a Rebellion in Ulster

GUY BEINER

Dear Eamon,
May you stay radical and
organise, keep up the good
work with Reclaim the
Enlightenment.

Guy Beiner
Belfast 29.5.19

OXFORD
UNIVERSITY PRESS

OXFORD
UNIVERSITY PRESS

Great Clarendon Street, Oxford, OX2 6DP,
United Kingdom

Oxford University Press is a department of the University of Oxford.
It furthers the University's objective of excellence in research, scholarship,
and education by publishing worldwide. Oxford is a registered trade mark of
Oxford University Press in the UK and in certain other countries

© Guy Beiner 2018

The moral rights of the author have been asserted

First Edition published in 2018
Impression: 3

Published in the United States of America by Oxford University Press
198 Madison Avenue, New York, NY 10016, United States of America

British Library Cataloguing in Publication Data
Data available

Library of Congress Control Number: 2018944470

ISBN 978–0–19–874935–6

Printed and bound by
CPI Group (UK) Ltd, Croydon, CR0 4YY

Acknowledgements

At six foot four, I may well be the tallest historian of Ireland, but if I have seen further, it is by standing on the shoulders of giants. Ian McBride was well ahead of me in following the trail that Tony Stewart had blazed. Many other great minds had already worked out much that needed to be understood so that, in more than one case, all that remained was to connect the dots. Their names can be traced through the bibliographical references.

Writing this book has been a long and arduous journey and to name each and every person who helped me along way would require another volume. A couple of trusty travel guides, who kept me on the path, cannot go unmentioned: the mentorship of David Fitzpatrick at an early stage and of Roy Foster towards the conclusion was in both cases instrumental. En route, I have incurred debts to numerous academics from around the world, as well as to archivists, librarians, and museum curators. Among the archives and specialist libraries consulted, I am particularly grateful for permission to publish material from the Francis Joseph Bigger collection at the Belfast Central Library, the Richard Robert Madden papers at Trinity College Dublin, and the National Folklore Collection at University College Dublin. Local historians and many other good people in Northern Ireland (some of whom are acknowledged in footnotes) generously shared their knowledge and offered wise counsel. I hope that they will all recognize their particular contributions in the text.

The research benefitted from the support of the Irish Research Council for the Humanities and Social Sciences (which sponsored a fellowship at Trinity College Dublin), the National Endowment for the Humanities (through a fellowship at the Irish Studies Center in the University of Notre Dame), the Israel Science Foundation (grant 810/07), the Balassi Institute (which facilitated a scholarship to attend the Central European University), and the Gerda Henkel Foundation (which funded a Marie Curie fellowship at the University of Oxford). For assistance in reproducing images and for permission to include them in the book, I am grateful to the Deputy Keeper of the Records at the Public Record Office of Northern Ireland, National Museums of Northern Ireland, National Library of Ireland, Office of Public Works, CAIN (Conflict Archive on the Internet), Ohio State University Billy Ireland Cartoon Library & Museum, University College Dublin Digital Library, Hesburgh Libraries of the University of Notre Dame, Digital Library at Villanova University, Brown Digital Repository at the Brown University Library, *County Down Spectator*, *Mourne Observer*, *Belfast News-Letter*, and the *Irish Independent*. Matthew Stout kindly provided the cartography. This book was published with the support of the Israel Science Foundation.

One can too easily become dizzy from the arithmetic of memory. Special thanks are due to Cathryn Steele at Oxford University Press for never losing her patience, though it was taxed to the very limit. Having narrowly avoided the fate of Philitas of Cos, my final tribute must go to Jorge Luis Borges, who knew all too well what he meant when, paraphrasing Alfonso Reyes, he remarked that 'one publishes a book in order to forget it'.

Contents

List of Figures

List of Maps

List of Abbreviations

BBC	British Broadcasting Corporation
BCL	Belfast Central Library
BNL	*Belfast News-Letter*
BL	British Library
BMH	Bureau of Military History
BNFC	Belfast Naturalists' Field Club
BOD	Bodleian Library, Oxford
CRC	Community Relations Council
DUP	Democratic Unionist Party
GAA	Gaelic Athletic Association
IRA	Irish Republican Army
KHLC	Kent History and Library Centre
NAI	National Archives of Ireland
NFC	National Folklore Collection, University College Dublin
NLI	National Library of Ireland
NMI	National Museum of Ireland
NMNI	National Museums of Northern Ireland
PRONI	Public Record Office of Northern Ireland
PSNI	Police Service of Northern Ireland
PUP	Progressive Unionist Party
QUB	Queen's University Belfast
RIA	Royal Irish Academy
RIC	Royal Irish Constabulary
RTÉ	Raidió Teilifís Éireann
SDLP	Social Democratic and Labour Party
SVV	*Shan Van Vocht*
TCD	Trinity College Dublin
TNA	The National Archives, UK [formerly PRO]
UCD	University College Dublin
UFTM	Ulster Folk and Transport Museum
UICS	United Irishmen Commemoration Society
UJA	*Ulster Journal of Archaeology*
UUP	Ulster Unionist Party

Mrs. Malaprop: . . . But the point we would request of you is, that you will promise to forget this fellow—to illiterate him, I say, quite from your memory.

Lydia: Ah, madam! our memories are independent of our wills. It is not so easy to forget.

Mrs. Malaprop: But I say it is, miss; there is nothing on earth so easy as to forget, if a person chooses to set about it.

Richard Brinsley Sheridan, *The Rivals* (1775), act I, scene II

Large are the treasures of oblivion, and heaps of things in a state next to nothing almost numberless; much more is buried in silence than recorded, and the largest volumes are but epitomes of what hath been. The account of time began with night, and darkness still attendeth it. Some things never come to light; many have been delivered; but more hath been swallowed in obscurity and the caverns of oblivion.

Thomas Browne[1]

[1] Comments possibly related to *Hydriotaphia* (1658), BL Sloane MS 1848, f. 194; reproduced in *Sir Thomas Browne's Works, Including His Life and Correspondence*, edited by Simon Wilkin, vol. 3 (London: William Pickering, 1835), p. 493n2.

Preface: Forgetful Remembrance

> I prefer to see historians as the guardians of the skeletons in the cupboard of the social memory.
>
> Peter Burke, 'History as Social Memory'[1]

This book pursues a modest task with dogged ambition. The scope is limited to an exploration of how an episode in provincial history, in a peripheral corner of Europe, was paradoxically both forgotten and remembered locally. The investigation naively aspires to comprehensiveness, yet accepts that the realization of such a goal is ultimately unattainable. In choosing to focus on what seemed to be a classic example of collective amnesia, a shorter and tighter book was originally envisaged, one that would have amounted to a meditative, albeit speculative, reflection on gaps of silence. However, meticulous research uncovered thousands of sources that offer access to voices that have been muffled and cloaked behind a perceived veil of silence. Reticence is shown to be quite verbal, even multivocal. These supposedly hidden sources were found by poring through manuscripts, close reading of partially obscure publications, combing of provincial newspapers, and undertaking ethnographic oral history fieldwork. Each and every account was carefully transcribed, catalogued, contextualized, and analysed, and the results of this pedantic examination yielded a self-constructed archive of vernacular historiography. Additional research would, no doubt, have yielded even more sources.

Making sense of a puzzle of thousands of fragmented pieces in order to put together a coherent picture proved to be no mean task. Among the voluminous publications on history and memory that have come out in the last three decades, I am not aware of another study that has charted the vicissitudes of memory over more than two hundred years in such high resolution. In writing up the findings, the intention has been to accommodate a range of readerships, from researchers coming from the diverse disciplines that are broadly interested in how societies deal with problematic episodes in their past, through to amateur aficionados of local history, while also appealing to a gamut of more specialist scholars in various fields of European, British, and Irish studies. Juggling the demands of such a varied clientele is a devilishly tricky task and I can only hope that the particular curiosities of various readers will be rewarded as they peruse the pages of this book.

For those perplexed by the sheer amount of local minutiae through which the arguments are demonstrated, it is worth pointing out that studies of cultural and social memory have too often made sweeping claims that have not been fully substantiated. It is therefore necessary to lay out the nuts and bolts of remembrance in order to closely examine the mechanics of how social forgetting actually works. The same can be said

---

[1] Peter Burke, 'History as Social Memory', in *Varieties of Cultural History*, edited by Peter Burke (Cambridge: Polity, 1997), p. 59.

for studies of history that tend to overlook provincial discourses. Once folklore and other vernacular accounts are treated with the same respect normally given to more conventional historical sources, the past begins to look very different indeed. Admittedly, the analysis could have patterned the materials otherwise, leading to different results. Unsatisfied readers are therefore invited to take the book apart and rewrite it anew.

At its most ambitious goal, the book aspires to offer a new model for the study of memory, as well as an alternative way of approaching history. With so many sources, including a substantial volume of published literary works, the inevitable question arises as to whether it is at all still possible to speak of forgetting? The answer depends on what we mean by forgetting and its relationship to history. Accordingly, this book proposes a rethinking of the relationship between remembering and forgetting, in terms of social forgetting, and of the study of history, in terms of vernacular historiography. This seems to work well for the northern Irish province of Ulster and, I am convinced, should be equally applicable to places elsewhere.

Over the course of this exploration, I have become keenly aware of some of the pitfalls that await those who dare to venture into the Borgesian labyrinths of Mneme and to navigate the river Lethe. Something strange seems to happen to the poor wayfarers who spend many years in pursuit of memory. Oftentimes, they go slightly mad and begin to imagine that the recollections of others, with which they have intimately familiarized themselves, are their own. Even doctors are not immune to this psychosis. Richard Robert Madden, a physician by training, who was born in 1798, devoted himself to documenting the memories of United Irishmen. He became so engrossed in this task that he ended up writing poetry as if he had been one of them. Twenty years earlier, something similar happened to another physician, John Gamble, who toured the Ulster countryside collecting recollections of those that had witnessed the recent United Irish rebellion. He then wrote a novel in which the protagonist is a younger version of himself, traversing the very same landscape at the time of the rebellion, as if this had been his own personal experience. Twenty years after Madden, another physician, T. C. S. Corry, wrote a long poetic reminiscence of 1798, though he was born much later. The journalist W. G. Lyttle and the antiquarian Francis Joseph Bigger, among many others, were similarly affected. Their writings demonstrate the irresistibly fixating power of memory, which can possess, like a *dybbuk*, even the scholarly mind.

As an outsider, I would like to believe that I am inoculated to this peculiar syndrome, though somehow, I doubt that this is truly the case. Over the course of repeated visits to Northern Ireland, I could not help myself from viewing present-day surroundings through the prism of stories that were told and retold over two centuries in muted forms, oftentimes behind closed doors. Visits to places like Ballynahinch, Saintfield, Antrim, Templepatrick, Randalstown, Ballymena, Toome, Coleraine, Greyabbey, and even the very modern city of Belfast seemed to bring back disturbing memories of events that I had not personally experienced. Is it normal to be troubled by recollections of people that one has never known? Some memories are probably best forgotten. But what does that mean?

Introduction

Sites of Oblivion

My intention was not to write the history of that language, but rather draw up the archaeology of that silence.

Michel Foucault, History of Madness[1]

But, first of all, is there a history of silence? Further, is not an archaeology, even of silence, a logic, that is, an organized language, a project, an order, a sentence, a syntax, a work?

Jacques Derrida, 'Cogito and the History of Madness'[2]

Fascination with the Emerald Isle—a name first bestowed on Ireland by the United Irish poet William Drennan—has been a source of endless inspiration, both for its own people and for outsiders.[3] In the 1830s, Gustave de Beaumont—lifelong companion and alter ego of Alexis de Tocqueville—found reason to tour the island on two occasions and to inspect closely its social, political, and religious features. He concluded that 'Ireland is a little country which raises the greatest questions of politics, morals and humanity'.[4] Irish writers of all sorts—novelists, poets, and playwrights—have risen to the challenge and, in asking daring questions, have reached for the stars. The questions posed by historians of Ireland, however, have been constrained by concerns that irresponsible explorations of the past may have harmful ramifications, in particular when it comes to the province of Ulster—perceived by some as 'The Black North'.[5]

---

[1] Michel Foucault, *History of Madness*, translated by Jonathan Murphy and Jean Khalfa (London and New York: Routledge, 2006), p. xxviii; the quotation is taken from Foucault's original preface to *Folie et Déraison: Histoire de la Folie à l'âge Classique* (Paris: Plon, 1961), which was removed from subsequent French editions.

[2] Jacques Derrida, *Writing and Difference*, translated by Alan Bass (London: Routledge, 2001), p. 41; originally published as Jacques Derrida, 'Cogito et histoire de la folie', in *L'écriture et la différence* (Paris: Seuil, 1967), pp. 51–97.

[3] 'The Emerald Isle' first appeared in the poem 'Erin', described as 'a party song, written without the rancour of party, in the year 1795'; William Drennan, *Fugitive Pieces, in Verse and Prose* (Belfast: printed by F. D. Finlay, 1815), pp. 1–4. Originally published in the United Irish newspaper the *Press* in 1797, it featured as the opening song for a 1798 edition of the United Irish songbook 'Paddy's Resource'; *The Irish Harp (Attun'd to Freedom): A Collection of Patriotic Songs; Selected for Paddy's Amusement* (Dublin: s.n., 1798), pp. 1–3.

[4] 'L'Irlande est une petite contrée sur laquelle se débattent les plus grandes questions de la politique, de la morale et de l'humanité'; Gustave de Beaumont, *L'Irlande sociale, politique et réligieuse*, 3rd edn (Paris: Librairie de Charles Gosselin, 1839), vol. 1, p. ii.

[5] 'The Black North' was noted in print in the early nineteenth century and by the 1830s and 1840s was in wide use in newspapers and magazines. For an early example see Edward Wakefield, *An Account*

The shirking away from pondering the more tricky conundrums of memory is a telling indicator. Although Irish culture has generated a dazzling panoply of complex mnemonic practices, which can be found among other places in Ireland's rich folklore traditions, for a long time Irish disciples of Cleo were hesitant to engage creatively with the mysteries of Mnemosyne and rarely ventured beyond conventional conceptions of how the past can be studied.

On the year of his retirement from the Erasmus Smith's chair of modern history at Trinity College Dublin, the Belfast-born historian Theodore William ('Theo') Moody delivered in May 1977 a presidential address to the Dublin University History Society, which opened with a grandiloquent statement: 'The past is dead. Nothing, for good or ill, can change it; nothing can revive it.' Moody qualified this truism by adding that 'there is a sense in which the past lives on: in works of human hands and minds, in beliefs, institutions, and values, and in us all, who are its living extension. It lives on in us, both for good and ill, shaping our lives and helping to determine our action, whether or not we know how our present is related to our past.' He argued that 'just as individuals cannot exist as complete persons without knowledge of their past, so human societies must have their self-knowledge if they are to preserve their corporate identity and their distinctive patterns of living'. Although he was convinced that it was the duty of historians 'to supply this knowledge', Moody conceded that 'nations derive their consciousness of their past not only—and not mainly—from historians. They also derive it from popular traditions, transmitted orally, in writing, and through institutions'.

Moody's lecture was delivered against the backdrop of a bloody conflict raging in Northern Ireland—known locally as 'the Troubles'. This was a time when historians became particularly self-conscious about appropriations of history that could be used to justify political violence. Accordingly, Moody drew a clear distinction between popular 'received views', which he labelled 'mythology', and the more dispassionate 'knowledge that the historian seeks to extract by the application of scientific methods to his evidence', which in his eyes was history proper. The two were deemed to be inevitably at odds with each other: 'history is a matter of facing the facts of the Irish past, however painful some of them may be; mythology is a way of refusing to face the historical facts.' Historians, he concluded, must be committed to 'demythologising', even if 'the effect on the public mind appears to be disappointingly slow'.[6]

Moody did not bother to precisely define what he meant by myths, but explained that they 'combine elements of fact and of fiction; they are part of the dead past that historians study, as well as being part of the living present in which we all, historians included, are involved'. Less interested in the ancient and medieval legends of Celtic mythology than in current popular beliefs about the past, he touched on a subject that would preoccupy English historians some years later, as evident in the collections of essays *The Myths We Live By* (1990), edited by Raphael Samuel and Paul Thompson,

of Ireland, Statistical and Political, vol. 2 (London: printed for Longman, Hurst, Rees, Orme, and Brown, 1812), p. 737.

    6 T. W. Moody, 'Irish History and Irish Mythology', *Hermathena*, 124 (1978), pp. 7–24; reproduced in *Interpreting Irish History: The Debate on Historical Revisionism, 1938–1994*, edited by Ciaran Brady (Blackrock, Co. Dublin: Irish Academic Press, 1994), pp. 71–86.

and *Myths of the English*, edited by Roy Porter in (1992).[7] Moody's insistence on an opposition between history and mythology mirrored, albeit without the continental suave, the distinction between history and memory espoused by the French historian Pierre Nora. Whereas a generation of so-called 'revisionist' Irish historians, mentored by Moody and his equally influential peer Robert ('Robin') Dudley Edwards, chair of modern Irish history at University College Dublin, obstinately denied the historical value of myths and shied away from memory, Nora assembled 125 leading historians of France to collaborate on an innovative interrogation of the interface of memory and history. The produce of their labour, the multi-volume *Les Lieux de mémoire* (1984–1992), signalled the advent of a worldwide 'memory boom', which would reshape historiography.[8]

In subsequent years, similar collaborative studies of national memory were undertaken in all five of the other founding member states of the European community, as the concept of *Lieux de mémoire* was adapted to Italy (*Luoghi della memoria*, edited by Mario Isnenghi), Germany (*Erinnerungsorte*, edited by Hagen Schulze and Étienne François), the Netherlands (*Lieux de mémoire et identités nationales*, edited by Pim den Boer and Willem Frijhoff, and *Plaatsen van herinnering*, edited by H. L. Wesseling et al.), Belgium (*Belgie, een parcours van herinnering*, edited by Johan Tollebeek et al.), and Luxemburg (*Lieux de mémoire au Luxembourg*, edited by Kmec et al.). The concept was also tried out on a provincial scale in various areas of France, at a transnational regional level in Central Europe and even as an all-European project.[9] It would take a while before historians of Ireland caught up with this trend. The publication in 2001 of *History and Memory in Modern Ireland*, edited by Ian McBride, heralded the belated arrival of memory studies to the forefront of Irish history.[10] A decade later, the interdisciplinary four-volume collection *Memory Ireland* (2011–14), edited by Oona Frawley, signalled the coming of age of Irish memory studies.[11]

[7] Raphael Samuel and Paul Thompson, eds, *The Myths We Live By* (London and New York: Routledge, 1990); Roy Porter, ed., *Myths of the English* (Cambridge: Polity Press, 1992). Subsequent studies have examined in greater detail the history of historical myths; for a Dutch example see Laura Cruz and Willem Frijhoff, eds, *Myth in History, History in Myth* (Leiden and Boston: Brill, 2009).

[8] Pierre Nora, *Les Lieux de mémoire* (Paris: Galimard, 1984–1992), 3 vols. For a reappraisal see Patrick H. Hutton, *The Memory Phenomenon in Contemporary Historical Writing: How the Interest in Memory Has Influenced Our Understanding of History* (New York: Palgrave Macmillan, 2016), pp. 29–48.

[9] See Pim Den Boer, 'Loci memoriae—Lieux de mémoire', in *Cultural Memory Studies: An International and Interdisciplinary Handbook*, edited by Astrid Erll and Ansgar Nünning (Berlin and New York: Walter de Gruyter, 2008), pp. 22–4; Benoît Majerus, '*Lieux de Mémoire*—A European Transfer Story', in *Writing the History of Memory*, edited by Stefan Berger and William John Niven (London: Bloomsbury Academic, 2014), pp. 157–71; Benoît Majerus, 'The "Lieux de Mémoire": A Place of Remembrance for European Historians?', in *Erinnerungsorte: Chancen, Grenzen und Perspektiven eines Erfolgskonzeptes in den Kulturwissenschaften*, edited by Stefan Berger and Joana Seiffert (Essen: Klartext, 2014), pp. 117–30.

[10] Ian McBride, ed., *History and Memory in Modern Ireland* (Cambridge and New York: Cambridge University Press, 2001); see also Guy Beiner, 'History and Memory in Modern Ireland', *Irish Historical Studies*, 32, no. 128 (2001): pp. 600–2.

[11] Oona Frawley, ed., *Memory Ireland* (Syracuse, N.Y.: Syracuse University Press, 2011), vol. 1: *History and Modernity* (2011); vol. 2: *Diaspora and Memory Practices* (2012); vol. 3: *The Famine and the Troubles* (2014); vol. 4 (co-edited with Katherine O'Callaghan): *James Joyce and Cultural Memory* (2014).

Writing in 2001, at a time when it seemed that the extreme violence of the Troubles may be over, the Northern Irish historian Anthony Terence Quincey ('Tony') Stewart revisited Moody's dictum 'The past is dead, and nothing that we choose to believe about it can either harm or benefit those who were alive in it', adding a warning that 'it has the power to harm us'. Stewart took issue with historians committed to demythologizing—those 'who would persuade us that if only we could discover the truth about our history, some of that harm might be neutralised'—and pointed out that 'the myth is often more potent than the reality, and perhaps a different kind of truth.' He pragmatically realized that 'academic historians must resign themselves to the fact that they have little real influence on a nation's view of its past' and should accept that 'what a nation thinks of its history is shaped rather by colourful narrative and the need for a political myth.' Keenly aware—if not apprehensive—of the potency of memory, Stewart sensed that vernacular historical traditions suggested other ways of looking at the past which did not sit well with the way Irish historians have written history.[12]

In a characteristically quirky historiosophical reflection, Stewart opined that 'there is something wrong with the shape of Irish history . . . it is very difficult to see where the past ends and the present begins.' For some, he discerned, history 'is a burden, to be cast aside as soon as possible', while for others it is 'a problem to which one day some clever person will find the answer'. Yet, 'for most Irish people', Stewart observed, 'it is simply a family heirloom, a fine old painting in a gilt frame, which they would miss if it was no longer there.'[13] The likening of popular historical consciousness to the possession of a treasured inherited painting is both suggestive and elusive. Heirlooms are often kept in private possession and little is known of how they have been regarded behind closed doors.

Rev. Robert Lyons Marshall, a Presbyterian minister and professor of History and English at Magee College in Londonderry, recalled how he was once allowed rare access to such a painting. Upon visiting 'a house where Toryism is a religion', Marshall, who—as a unionist and member of the Orange Order—was greeted as a trusted ally, happened to mention that one of his maternal ancestors had 'carried a pike in '98', that is to say that he had been among the United Irishmen who rebelled against the Crown in 1798. This confidential disclosure unlocked a secret:

> I was taken to an upstairs room and there from its covering of many wrappers I was shown a small worn oil painting of the direct progenitor of the family who was hanged as a rebel in '98. But the portrait is never shown to any except those whose forbears also carry the taint.[14]

Like the portrait of Dorian Gray, locked away in an attic to hide its record of unspeakable sins, the awkward recollection of a loyalist family having a republican rebel ancestor was kept out of sight and was only furtively revealed to those who could be trusted.

Concerns that the discovery of such compromising heirlooms might cause embarrassment gave them a haunting presence, which could not be simply discarded and done with. The Ulster poet Mary Florence Wilson penned an insightful short story that told of a young lady who had killed herself upon hearing that her lover 'was hanged as a

---

[12] A. T. Q. Stewart, *The Shape of Irish History* (Belfast: Blackstaff, 2001), p. 185.
[13] Ibid., p. 2.
[14] R. L. Marshall, 'Maghera in '98', in *Presbyterianism in Maghera: A Social and Congregational History*, edited by S. Sidlow McFarland (Maghera: Presbyterian Church, 1985), p. 174.

rebel sometime in the dark days after '98'. The lady's father, 'a man who prided himself on his unanswering loyalty to the British throne', was intent on wiping out this blemish on the family's reputation and had her picture destroyed. Nonetheless, a century later, the ghosts of the rebel and of his sweetheart were reportedly seen in the area clutching to the portrait. Upon hearing of an encounter with these shunned apparitions, a descendant of the loyalist household insisted that it must not be talked about in the open: 'best, we should forget all about it.' But, as Wilson remarked, the advice to forget was 'easier said than done'.[15]

By listening to such stories, we have moved away from *History* (capitalized and in the singular), as it has been normally studied in the halls of the academy, and find ourselves in the realm of *histories* (in lower case and inevitably in the plural), which reflect the myriad ways in which the past is routinely recalled in discreet social and cultural interactions, some of which are barely noticeable to outsiders.[16] We have also moved beyond *lieux de mémoire* and stumbled into the unfamiliar domain of *lieux d'oubli*, which have been defined as 'sites that public memory has expressly avoided because of the disturbing affect that their invocation is still capable of arousing'.[17] These realms of forgetting, where individuals and communities anxiously try to conceal discomforting skeletons in their cupboards, are still, by and large, *terra incognita*. New terminology and conceptual frameworks are required in order to help us find our bearings and to try and understand the denizens of these strange places. Let us first turn our gaze upon what we mean by 'histories' and then consider what we mean by 'forgetting'.

VERNACULAR HISTORIOGRAPHY

It is enlightening to rethink our relationship with the past in terms of *mythistory* and to question a steadfast conviction, which has been upheld dogmatically by many histor- ians, that History (seen as a truthful representation of facts) must be irreconcilably divorced from Myth (considered a fictional fabrication). The iconoclast urge for demythologizing is an expression of a modern 'hermeneutics of suspicion', which harks back to the classical differentiation between symbolic *mythos* and critical *logos*, through which generations of scholars have devalued traditions, regardless of the vital role they continue to play in society and culture.[18] By insisting that Irish historians turn their back on myths, Theo Moody not only reiterated the tenets of an empiricist historiography, associated with the disciples of Leopold von Ranke, but also elicited a time-old debate on whether historical inquiry should disregard popular traditions. After

---

[15] Florence Mary Wilson, 'The Man at the Well' (unpublished typescript); Florence Mary Wilson Papers, Irish Linen Centre and Lisburn Museum.

[16] For the distinction between official history and 'histories', in the context of 'the way that silences and commemorations lie in different kinds of relationship to one another', see Gerald M. Sider and Gavin A. Smith, eds, *Between History and Histories: The Making of Silences and Commemorations* (Toronto: University of Toronto Press, 1997), pp. 8–17.

[17] Nancy Wood, *Vectors of Memory: Legacies of Trauma in Postwar Europe* (Oxford: Berg, 1999), p. 10; see also Yosef Hayim Yerushalmi, 'Réflexions sur l'oubli', in *Usages de l'oubli* (Paris: Seuil, 1988), pp. 7–21.

[18] Richard Kearney, 'Myth and the Critique of Tradition', in *Reconciling Memories*, edited by Alan Falconer and Joseph Liechty (Blackrock, Co. Dublin: Columba Press, 1998; orig. edn 1988), pp. 37–56.

all, Ranke was an admirer of Thucydides, who had taken to task Herodotus for his use of myths and, in doing so, had narrowed the scope of history.

Herodotus had written his *Histories* 'in the hope of thereby preserving from decay the remembrance of what men have done'. He considered it his duty 'to report all that is said', though he did not feel 'obliged to believe it all alike'.[19] Evaluating the greater contribution of this open-minded approach, Arnaldo Momigliano perceptively observed that 'when Herodotus took the recording of tradition as his primary duty, he was in fact doing something more than simply saving facts from oblivion. He was guiding historical research towards the exploration of the unknown and the forgotten.'[20] Conversely, Thucydides, in writing a contemporary account of the *History of the Peloponnesian War*, was wary of 'imperfect memory', as well as of 'undue partiality for one side or the other', and took pride in the 'absence of romance' in his work.[21] In dismissing oral traditions as unreliable fictions, Thucydides steered the study of history towards a focus on political, diplomatic, and military affairs. Nevertheless, his writing of history was inevitably shaped by prevalent cultural conventions and reflected the myths of his day. Despite its promise to provide 'exact knowledge of the past', the historical account written by Thucydides was perspicaciously labelled, in a somewhat neglected critique by Francis Macdonald Cornford, 'mythistoria'.[22]

An Herodotean interest in historical traditions persevered into modern times through the scholarly writings of a long line of antiquarians, whose erudite studies were regularly belittled by historians for their tendency to collect seemingly trivial details.[23] The Enlightenment's inherent aversion of superstition reintroduced doubts about the value of popular belief. Use of the term 'mythistory' in English was first recorded in 1737 by Nathan Bailey in a supplementary volume added to the third edition of his *Universal Etymological English Dictionary*, where it was defined as 'an history mingled with false fables and tales'.[24] Romanticism overturned this dismissive attitude. With the rise of historicism, a number of philologists, philosophers, and historians—who were indirectly influenced by Giambattista Vico's *Scienza Nuova* (1725) and more directly by the writings of Johann Gottfried Herder—rediscovered the historical value of popular traditions. Best typified by the Brothers Grimm, collectors of traditions operated within a budding environment of cultural nationalism, to which they contributed vernacular resources, while rekindling the study of mythology and establishing the study of folklore.[25] Their contribution to the study of history, labelled by Donald R. Kelley 'mythistory', can be seen as a historiographical

---

[19] *The History of Herodotus*, translated by George Rawlinson, vol. 1 (1858), p. 121 [*Histories*, Book 1, intro] and vol. 2 (1860), p. 129 [*Histories*, Book 7, 152].

[20] Arnaldo Momigliano, *The Classical Foundations of Modern Historiography* (Berkeley: University of California Press, 1990), p. 37.

[21] Thucydides, *History of the Peloponnesian War*, translated by Richard Crawley (London: J. M. Dent and Sons, 1910), p. 15 [Book 1, 22].

[22] Francis Macdonald Cornford, *Thucydides Mythistoricus* (London: Edward Arnold, 1907).

[23] Arnaldo Momigliano, 'Ancient History and the Antiquarian', *Journal of the Warburg and Courtauld Institutes*, 13, no. 3/4 (1950): pp. 285–315; Momigliano, *Classical Foundations of Modern Historiography*, pp. 54–79.

[24] Nathan Bailey, *The Universal Etymological English Dictionary Containing an Additional Collection of Words (Not in the First Volume)*, 3rd edn, vol. 2 (London: Thomas Cox, 1737).

[25] Peter Burke, *Popular Culture in Early Modern Europe*, 3rd edn (Farnham and Burlington: Ashgate, 2009; orig. edn 1978), pp. 23–48; Joep Leerssen, 'Oral Epic: The Nation Finds a Voice',

counter-movement that was largely excluded from the professionalization of the discipline of history and was sidelined by the rise to dominance of the Rankean school of history.[26]

Another form of mythistory, marked by 'the recognition of myth', has been iden- tified by Joseph Mali as a distinctly modernist historiography, which can be found in the exceptional historical writings of Jacob Burckhardt, Aby Warburg, Ernst Kantorowicz, Walter Benjamin, and, not least, in the fiction of James Joyce.[27] Indeed, as already noted, Irish creative writers have been ahead of historians in developing innovative approaches to the past and Joyce, more than any other author, has been recognized—even by historians—for his insights into cultural memory.[28] Mainstream historiography has been reluctant to pursue such directions.

Never afraid to raise big questions, William McNeill, in his 1985 presidential address to the American Historical Society, reconsidered the fraught relationship between 'truth, myth, history, and historians' and offered an appraisal of mythistory. Acknowledging 'the elastic, inexact character of truth', he shrewdly pointed out that 'one person's truth is another's myth, and the fact that a group of people accepts a given version of the past does not make that version any truer for outsiders.' He soberly cautioned that 'mythical, self-flattering versions of rival groups' pasts simply serve to intensify their capacity for conflict'. Yet, he maintained that the study of historical myths was 'a high and serious calling' and that the historian must strive to understand 'what a group of people knows and believes about the past', as this was a significant factor in shaping both views and actions. In calling upon historians to overcome their engrained inhibitions and embrace the study of mythistory, McNeill candidly admitted that he did 'not expect the term to catch on in professional circles'.[29]

McNeill's prediction has fulfilled itself. Although the portmanteau 'mythistory' aptly captures the synthesis of facts and imagination that is characteristic of more creative forms of engaging with the past, it is a cumbersome term and apart from a few notable examples, such as Gary Dickson's examination of how the medieval Children's Crusade evolved into modern mythistory, it has not entered into common usage.[30] There is a need for a more suitable label, which can better describe the wider range of activities through which the past is recalled outside of mainstream-official history. Consideration of alternative terminology opens a range of possibilities for the study of other histories.

in *Folklore and Nationalism in Europe during the Long Nineteenth Century*, edited by Timothy Baycroft and David M. Hopkin (Leiden and Boston: Brill, 2012), pp. 11–26.

[26] Donald R. Kelley, 'Mythistory in the Age of Ranke', in *Leopold Von Ranke and the Shape of the Historical Discipline*, edited by Georg G. Iggers and James M. Powell (Syracuse, N.Y.: Syracuse University Press, 1990), pp. 3–20; see also Peter Burke, 'Ranke the Reactionary', in ibid., pp. 36–44.

[27] Joseph Mali, *Mythistory: The Making of a Modern Historiography* (Chicago: University of Chicago Press, 2003).

[28] See the collected essays on 'James Joyce and Cultural Memory', in Frawley and O'Callaghan, *Memory Ireland*, vol. 4.

[29] William H. McNeill, 'Mythistory, or Truth, Myth, History, and Historians', *The American Historical Review*, 91, no. 1 (February 1986): pp. 1–10; see also Chris Lorenz, 'Drawing the Line: "Scientific" History between Myth-Making and Myth-Breaking', in *Narrating the Nation: Representations in History, Media, and the Arts*, edited by Stefan Berger, Linas Eriksonas, and Andrew Mycock (New York: Berghahn Books, 2008), pp. 35–55.

[30] See Gary Dickson, *The Children's Crusade: Medieval History, Modern Mythistory* (Houndmills and New York: Palgrave Macmillan, 2008).

Calling attention to an essential quality of mythistory, Mali described historical myths 'as those stories that are not merely told but actually lived'.[31] Whereas professional historians, such as Moody and Stewart, typically insist that 'the past is dead', outside the halls of academia the past appears to be alive and well. The detachment assumed by academics gives the impression, in the famous words of L. P. Hartley, that 'the past is a foreign country', a concept which has been thoughtfully interrogated by David Lowenthal.[32] Other forms of engaging with history reject this sense of remoteness and identify closely with the past, making it a *living history*. The evocative term 'living history', however, is already spoken for. It has been claimed by heritage enthusiasts for a variety of performative activities which seek to reconstruct and re-enact the past for the benefit of modern-day consumers.[33]

In recent decades, living history has been commodified and commercialized through a wide range of popular cultural productions that increasingly avail of new media and technologies to facilitate mass consumption of history.[34] Whereas pageantry and theatre have always offered a way of reliving history, the mushrooming of the heritage industry in the late twentieth century seems to have been driven by an anxiety that a supposedly authentic link with past has been severed and the belief that this connection can only be regained in artificial forms, or, as critics would have it, though fabrication.[35] This perception does not give full credit to more traditional historical practices—such as storytelling and ballad singing—that are not only still rampant, but are now widely disseminated through use of modern technologies. Moreover, the term 'living history' gives a misleading sense of interminable vitality, akin to eternal life, which fails to acknowledge that mythistory can go through periods of stagnation and even cease to exist. When taking into account the ebbs and flows of historical curiosity, as preoccupation with certain episodes falls in and out of fashion over time, it is possible to identify life cycles that chart how historical interest lapses into neglect but may later be revived, or to use other terms—remembered, forgotten, and regenerated.

Such unconventional history is distinguished not only by its vivacity, which makes the past seem to come alive, but also by its preoccupation with subjects that were long neglected in mainstream historiography. The 1960s signalled newfound interest in *history from below*, a term popularized by E. P. Thompson and associated in its initial stages with George Rudé's studies of the historical agency of crowds.[36] This direction

---

[31] Mali, *Mythistory*, p. 6.

[32] David Lowenthal, *The Past is a Foreign Country* (Cambridge and New York: Cambridge University Press, 1985).

[33] Raphael Samuel, *Theatres of Memory: Past and Present in Contemporary Culture* (London and New York: Verso, 2012; orig. edn 1994), pp. 169–202. See also Jay Anderson, *Time Machines: The World of Living History* (Nashville, Tenn.: American Association for State and Local History, 1984); Scott Magelssen, *Living History Museums: Undoing History through Performance* (Lanham, Md.: Scarecrow Press, 2007).

[34] Jerome de Groot, *Consuming History: Historians and Heritage in Contemporary Popular Culture*, 2nd edn (London and New York: Routledge, 2016; orig. edn 2009).

[35] David Lowenthal, *The Heritage Crusade and the Spoils of History* (Cambridge and New York, 1998).

[36] E. P. Thompson, 'History from Below', *Times Literary Supplement*, no. 3345 (7 April 1966), pp. 279–80; George Rudé, *The Crowd in the French Revolution* (London, Oxford, and New York: Oxford University Press, 1967; orig. edn 1959). See also Jim Sharpe, 'History from Below', in *New Perspectives on Historical Writing*, edited by Peter Burke (University Park, Pa.: Pennsylvania State

was developed in the 1970s and '80s by the History Workshop movement, which was committed to 'democratising the act of historical production, enlarging the constituency of historical writers, and bringing the experience of the present to bear upon the interpretation of the past'. Its adherents promoted *people's history*, which, as noted by Raphael Samuel, was a term that 'has had a long career, and covers an ensemble of different writings', though its 'remote origins' could supposedly be traced back to 'that no-man's land of ballad tradition where myth and historicity cross'. Intent on 'bringing the boundaries of history closer to those of people's lives', writers of people's history sought 'an alternative to "dry as dust" scholarship'. People's history was directed 'towards the recovery of subjective experience'. Contrary to the privileging of dominant elites in conventional historiography, sights were set on uncovering the lesser-known experiences of the disenfranchised, the oppressed, and the poor.[37]

The ideological thrust of 'people's history' chimed with the politics of the New Left. This outlook is particularly apparent in *A People's History of the United States* (originally published in 1980), a best-selling book by the radical historian Howard Zinn, who openly professed that he was 'sceptical of governments and their attempts, through politics and culture, to ensnare ordinary people in a giant web of nationhood pretending to a common interest'. Rejecting the notion of a homogenous national collective memory—'we must not accept the memory of states as our own'—Zinn retold the history of North America from the point of view of Native Americans, African Americans, factory workers, immigrant labourers, the working poor, and women.[38] This approach shares a common interest with Subaltern studies, a field that was developed in the 1980s by South Asian postcolonial scholars—most notably Ranajit Guha—and has since taken root in other areas, including Latin America and the Middle East, as well as making an impact on Irish studies. *Subaltern history* denounced colonial 'elitist historiography' and took upon itself to uncover the 'politics of the people'.[39]

Both people's history and subaltern history aim for a *democratic history*, which will faithfully represent the historical experiences of common people (*demos*) and give recognition to how they themselves chose to recall their history. The inherently democratic nature of people's history is only fully revealed when taking into account the many mediators and audiences through which history has been narrated by 'the people', about 'the people', and for 'the people'. However, the Neo-Marxist flag-bearers of history from below have at times resorted to idealized and insufficiently sophisticated notions of 'the people', unduly ascribing to them innate progressive values. In practice, democratic history is by no means egalitarian—it has its own hierarchies and multilayered power structures that give an advantage to certain people who are better

University Press, 1992), pp. 24–41; E. J. Hobsbawm, *On History* (London: Abacus, 1998), pp. 266–96.

[37] Raphael Samuel, 'People's History', in *People's History and Socialist Theory*, edited by Raphael Samuel (London and Boston: Routledge & Kegan Paul, 1981), pp. xv–xxxix.

[38] Howard Zinn, *A People's History of the United States* (London and New York: Longman, 1980), quotations from pp. 9–11; see also Howard Zinn, *Howard Zinn on History*, 2nd edn (New York: Seven Stories Press, 2011), pp. 211–13 ('The New History').

[39] See Ranajit Guha, 'On Some Aspects of the Historiography of Colonial India', in *Subaltern Studies I: Writings on South Asian History and Society*, edited by Ranajit Guha (Delhi: Oxford University Press), pp. 1–8. For Irish history and Subaltern studies see Eóin Flannery, *Versions of Ireland: Empire, Modernity and Resistance in Irish Culture* (Newcastle: Cambridge Scholars Press, 2006), pp. 37–54.

equipped to exploit the cultural capital that can be gained by narrating their pasts, to the neglect of others, who are either left outside of history or relegated to its margins.

The exclusion of non-literate societies from conventional document-driven history has been partly redressed by *ethnohistory*, a field that combines methodologies from history and anthropology, with contributions from other disciplines, such as archaeology. Emerging out of the study of Native American communities in the post-Second World War era of the Indian Claims Commission, ethnohistory has since expanded beyond North America to Mesoamerica and South America, as well as Africa and Polynesia. Ethnohistorians have made use of folklore and oral traditions for emic fieldwork that aims to reveal how indigenous societies perceive their pasts. Pioneering figures in the development of ethnohistory, such as Nancy Oestreich Lurie and William C. Sturtevant, have argued that this approach could be fruitfully applied to the study of Western societies, but such initiatives have not picked up and very few explicitly designated ethnohistories of European communities have been written to date.[40]

Since the 1980s, history of 'ordinary people' has been increasingly referred to as *popular history*. The adoption of this term rides on the back of the flourish of innovative historical studies of European popular culture written by early modernists. In these works, vulgar (in the original sense of the word, stemming from *vulgus*—the common people) 'popular culture' is vaguely conceptualized in opposition to a more refined elite 'high culture', while accepting that no clear boundaries separate the two. The favoured method to broach the subject has been microhistory, an approach developed in the 1970s in Italy (*microstoria*), with correlatives in France (*microhistoire*), and the English-speaking world. In Germany, it took a slightly different direction in the 'history of everyday life' (*Alltagsgeschichte*).[41] Microhistories have produced such seminal books as Emmanuel Le Roy Ladurie's *Montaillou, village Occitan* (1975) and *Le Carnaval de Romans, 1579–1580* (1980), Carlo Ginzburg's *Il formaggio e i vermi* (1976; translated in 1980 as *The Cheese and the Worms*), Natalie Zemon Davis's *The Return of Martin Guerre* (1983), and Robert Darnton's *The Great Cat Massacre* (1983). In such works the great questions of history have been brought to bear on close examinations of small communities, or even individuals, by applying anthropological-ethnographic tools, most notably the concept of 'thick description' introduced by Clifford Geertz.[42]

Historians of popular history have been faulted for the empathy—bordering on unbridled sympathy—that they have shown for their subjects, which can lean towards

[40] Nancy Oestreich Lurie, 'Ethnohistory: An Ethnological Point of View', *Ethnohistory*, 8, no. 1 (1961): pp. 78–92; William C. Sturtevant, 'Anthropology, History, and Ethnohistory', *Ethnohistory*, 13, no. 1/2 (1966): pp. 1–51; see also Michael E. Harkin, 'Ethnohistory's Ethnohistory: Creating a Discipline from the Ground Up', *Social Science History*, 34, no. 2 (2010): pp. 113–28.

[41] Alf Lüdtke, 'What Is the History of Everyday Life and Who Are Its Practitioners?', in *The History of Everyday Life: Reconstructing Historical Experiences and Ways of Life*, edited by Alf Lüdtke, translated by William Templer (Princeton: Princeton University Press, 1995), pp. 3–40.

[42] Levi Giovanni, 'On Microhistory', in *New Perspectives on Historical Writing*, edited by Peter Burke (University Park, Pa.: Pennsylvania State University Press, 1992), pp. 93–113; Sigurður Gylfi Magnússon and István M. Szíjártó, *What Is Microhistory?: Theory and Practice* (Abingdon and New York: Routledge, 2013); see also John Brewer, 'Microhistory and the Histories of Everyday Life', *Cultural and Social History*, 7, no. 1 (2010): pp. 87–109.

valorization.[43] However, the use of the adjective 'popular' is somewhat misleading. It is too readily assumed that celebrations of plebeian culture were popular, in the sense of generally liked and admired, without due attention to the opinions of those who were ill at ease with the revelries. The historical experience of conflicted regions demonstrates how the so-called popular culture of one group can provoke antagonism and incur hostility from an adversary group. In Northern Ireland, for example, the parades of the Orange Order have frequently been met with antipathy in Catholic communities and, similarly, the celebrations of nationalists have often aggravated Protestant communities. In other words, popular history needs to take into account that popular culture can be downright unpopular for some people.

Another sense of popular history, which relates to the ways in which interpretations of the past are made accessible to broad general publics, has been labelled *public history*.[44] As an organized field of studies, public history first emerged in the United States, where the journal *The Public Historian* was founded in 1978 and the National Council on Public History was established in 1979. Within a few years, the growing impact of this development was noticeable in Western Europe, before spreading elsewhere.[45] The participation of professionally trained historians in a wide range of activities outside of academia, whether as consultants, archivists, preservationists, film producers, or policy advisors, has also been referred to as *applied history*, though, ironically, the applicability of this term has in itself been debated.[46]

Non-professionals have demanded equal recognition for their contributions to understanding the past, manifested through such activities as community-based oral history projects and various local history programmes. The involvement of amateurs alongside professional historians, and the desire to encourage partnerships with members of the public, suggests a 'major redefinition of the role of the historian'.[47] The feasibility of 'shared authority', a concept popularized by Michael H. Frisch, has been debated by oral historians and museum curators, but has been greeted with suspicion by the scholarly historical establishment.[48] In any case, public history is generally seen to be performed in the open, without concealment, in a public sphere which allows free

[43] See Gerald Strauss, 'The Dilemma of Popular History', *Past & Present*, no. 132 (1991): pp. 130–49; for a rebuttal see William Beik, 'The Dilemma of Popular History', *Past & Present*, no. 141 (1993): pp. 207–15.
[44] John Tosh, *Why History Matters* (Houndmills and New York: Palgrave Macmillan, 2008), pp. 99–199; Faye Sayer, *Public History: A Practical Guide* (London and New York: Bloomsbury Academic, 2015), pp. 1–19.
[45] For 'Public History: State of the Art, 1980' see the articles in *The Public Historian*, vol. 1, no. 2 (Autumn 1979). For the expansion overseas see Anthony R. Sutcliffe, 'Gleams and Echoes of Public History in Western Europe: Before and after the Rotterdam Conference', *The Public Historian*, 6, no. 4 (1984): pp. 7–16.
[46] Henry Rousso, 'Applied History, or the Historian as Miracle-Worker', *The Public Historian*, 6, no. 4 (1984), pp. 65–85.
[47] Ronald J. Grele, 'Whose Public? Whose History? What Is the Goal of a Public Historian?', *The Public Historian*, 3, no. 1 (1981): pp. 40–8; cf. Peter Novick, *That Noble Dream: The 'Objectivity Question' and the American Historical Profession* (Cambridge: Cambridge University Press, 1988), pp. 510–21.
[48] Michael H. Frisch, *A Shared Authority: Essays on the Craft and Meaning of Oral and Public History* (Albany: State University of New York Press, 1990). For constructive debates see *Oral History Review*, 30, no. 1 (Winter–Spring, 2003), pp. 23–113; Bill Adair, Benjamin Filene, and Laura Koloski, eds, *Letting Go?: Sharing Historical Authority in a User-Generated World* (Philadelphia: The Pew Center for Arts & Heritage, 2011).

discussion. This conception does not adequately take on board the countless intimate spheres in which history is retold surreptitiously. The complex relationships between private and public forms of history await to be teased out.

The philosopher David Carr rejected the misconception, too readily upheld in studies of historiography, whereby the 'only real connection to the historical past is the result of historical inquiry, whether we carry it out ourselves or are provided with it second-hand by reading the results of the historians' work'. Carr pointed out the simple truism that 'we have a connection to the historical past, as ordinary persons, prior to and independently of adopting the historical-cognitive interest.'[49] Taking to heart this critique, the Finnish historian Jorma Kalela floated the term *everyday history* (*jokapäiväinen historia*), which incorporates the 'interplay of public, popular and scholarly histories'. He maintained that the 'social process of history making' is evident in *shared histories*, through which communities and groups negotiate their reconstructions of the past in consultation with professional historians. Kalela noted that 'the trouble with shared histories is simply the lack of research on them.'[50]

Raphael Samuel, seeking to acknowledge the 'invisible hands' behind the production of history, astutely remarked that 'if history was thought of as an activity rather than a profession, then the number of its practitioners would be legion.'[51] While the notion of 'shared history' hints at the communal dimension of public histories, 'everyday history' gives the impression that preoccupation with the past is commonplace. At some level this is undoubtedly true, as references to the past often crop up in mundane contexts. Yet quotidian evocations of history in traditional societies were not necessarily routine daily activities, on par with eating, working, or praying.

Within folklore, it is possible to discern a sub-field of *folk history* to which devoted enthusiasts were attracted. Among storytellers and ballad singers, there were those who had a reputation for being 'history-tellers', akin to the African *griots*. For example, among the *seanchaí*—the traditional storytellers of Ireland—one can distinguish *staireolaigh*, who were specifically skilled in narrating history. Alongside history-tellers, there were designated folk historians, who became informal archivists by assuming the role of custodians of oral communal records. They processed these historical sources for the benefit of the community, and therefore rightly deserved the epithet 'historians'. In addition, certain folklore collectors were primarily interested in documenting historical traditions (*seanchas*) and in doing so gave these local accounts external recognition.[52] To a large degree, everyday history was placed in the hands of local specialists. Their work typically took place in specific contexts but was then shared with wider audiences, who participated in its dissemination and reinterpretation.

There is a geographical dimension to people's history, which has been primarily 'used to denote a history which is local in scale, taking as its subject the region, the

[49] David Carr, *Time, Narrative, and History* (Bloomington: Indiana University Press, 1986), pp. 2–3.
[50] Jorma Kalela, *Making History: The Historian and Uses of the Past* (Basingstoke: Palgrave Macmillan, 2012), pp. 50–81.
[51] Raphael Samuel, *Theatres of Memory: Past and Present in Contemporary Culture* (London and New York, 2012; orig. edn 1994), p. 17.
[52] Guy Beiner, *Remembering the Year of the French: Irish Folk History and Social Memory* (Madison: University of Wisconsin Press, 2006), pp. 115–23.

township or the parish'.[53] *Local history* has a pedigree that goes back to the antiquarians of the nineteenth century (if not earlier) but was introduced into the modern academy by William George Hoskins, who established in 1948 a department of English Local History at University College, Leicester. In his work, Hoskins broadened the scope of local history and referred to it also as *provincial history*.[54] While local history provides fertile ground for undertaking microhistories, the broader concept of provincial history offers a corrective to the prejudiced metropolitan perspective through which national history has been mostly written. Even so, a more complex conceptualization of local and provincial history needs to scrupulously address the multifaceted relationships between centre and peripheries. It may seem that the production of local history stems from *grass-roots history*, a term that seems to be understood intuitively, but has not yet been properly defined.[55] The distinctiveness of provincial history, however, is negotiated through the reception, rejection, or adaptation of metropolitan discourses. It is therefore not simply a history from below, but rather a history written from 'in between'. The work of local historians can be better appreciated by considering their essential role as mediators between *grass-roots history* and national history.

Our brief survey of the available nomenclature that can contribute to a better understanding of general uses of mythistory has yielded a mind-boggling array of compatible, though not identical, terms: living history, history from below, people's history, subaltern history, democratic history, ethnohistory, popular history, public history, applied history, everyday history, shared history, folk history, grass-roots history, as well as local and provincial history. Wishing to avail of the advantages of each and every one of these concepts, yet also weary of subscribing blindly to their predilections and being saddled with unwarranted baggage, this study has opted to introduce a different term: *vernacular historiography*.

Vernacular historiography has been considered in studies of the Middle Ages in its most rudimentary sense, namely the writing of chronicles in vernacular languages, as opposed to Latin—the standard language of the clerical and aristocratic elite.[56] This conceptualization of vernacular history can be broadened to incorporate the various types of unconventional history listed above, while retaining an interest in accounts that appear in native languages, regional dialects, and colloquial registers. At times, vernacular historiography—when thought of in this wider sense—may seem very close, almost synonymous, to folk history. However, use of the term consciously steers clear of the artificial divides between oral and literary cultures that lie at the heart of conceptualizations of oral tradition.

---

[53] Samuel, 'People's History', p. xvii.

[54] W. G. Hoskins, *Local History in England*, 3rd edn (London and New York: Longman, 1984; orig. edn 1959); W. G. Hoskins, *Provincial England: Essays in Social and Economic History* (London: Macmillan and New York: St Martin's Press, 1963); see also Charles Phythian-Adams, 'Hoskins's England: A Local Historian of Genius and the Realisation of His Theme', *Local Historian*, 22, no. 4 (1992): pp. 170–83.

[55] See for example David Hey, *The Grass Roots of English History: Local Societies in England before the Industrial Revolution* (London: Bloomsbury Academic, 2016).

[56] Gabrielle M. Spiegel, *Romancing the Past: The Rise of Vernacular Prose Historiography in Thirteenth-Century France* (Berkeley and Oxford: University of California Press, 1993); Peter Damian-Grint, *The New Historians of the Twelfth-Century Renaissance: Inventing Vernacular Authority* (Rochester, N.Y.: Boydell Press, 1999); Charity Urbanski, *Writing History for the King: Henry II and the Politics of Vernacular Historiography* (Ithaca, N.Y.: Cornell University Press, 2013).

Oral accounts, when inspected carefully, often show signs of subtle interplay with written sources. Moreover, oral testimonies were either documented in writing or recorded orally and then converted into transcripts. Therefore, the reclamation from scholarly history of the term 'historiography', which has a Greco-Latin etymology combining history (*historia*) and writing (*graphia*), is apposite. Thinking in the more fluid terms of historiography puts an emphasis on a diachronic awareness of how constructions of vernacular history were repeatedly reconstructed over time. The adjective 'vernacular' refers to the documentation of various informal expressions, including the seemingly oxymoronic combination of 'oral historiography', alongside literary and also non-textual historical representations.

At a first glance, vernacular historiography tries to recover a 'hidden history', one which seems extremely hard to track down, as by definition it refers to what has been left outside of official history. There is however nothing really hidden about vernacular historiography, one just has to look outside of the conventional repositories of historical sources. The study of vernacular historiography necessitates the compilation of a wide range of sources, effectively creating an alternative custom-made archive. This does not obviate the need to consult standard archives, in which the researcher is required, in the famous words of Walter Benjamin, 'to brush history against the grain' in an effort to pick up on echoes of demotic voices that were suppressed or overlooked by the ruling establishment.[57] That said, most of the sources for such an investigation are to be found outside of state and institutional archives.

Benedict Anderson called attention to how 'the convergence of capitalism and print technology' standardized vernacular languages so that they could be more widely shared within national frameworks, and in doing so became the main medium of historical documentation.[58] Newspapers and magazines regularly discussed matters that were not officially recorded by the authorities. Searches for sources for vernacular history in the journalism of the late modern era must look beyond the national press and also trawl through provincial newspapers, where the cultural negotiations between the metropolitan government and the regional population were more thoroughly mediated and debated.[59] Such an exploration needs to be extended more generally to popular print, with its plethora of extensively read ephemeral pamphlets and chapbooks. In Ireland, for example, a study of the cheap books widely sold by itinerant pedlars throughout the countryside from the mid-eighteenth into the mid-nineteenth century noted that 'many of the texts of printed popular literature contain a strong historical dimension.'[60]

---

[57] Walter Benjamin, *Illuminations*, translated by Harry Zohn and edited by Hannah Arendt (New York: Shocken Books, 2007; orig. edn 1968), p. 266.

[58] Benedict Anderson, *Imagined Communities: Reflections on the Origin and Spread of Nationalism*, rev. edn (London and New York: Verso, 2006; orig. edn 1983), pp. 33–46.

[59] Andrew Walker, 'The Development of the Provincial Press in England *c.*1780–1914', *Journalism Studies*, 7, no. 3 (2006): pp. 373–86. For Ireland see Marie-Louise Legg, *Newspapers and Nationalism: The Irish Provincial Press, 1850–1892* (Dublin: Four Courts Press, 1999); Jim Mac Laughlin, *Reimagining the Nation State: The Contested Terrains of Nation-Building* (London and Sterling, Va.: Pluto Press, 2001), pp. 187–226.

[60] Niall Ó Ciosáin, *Print and Popular Culture in Ireland, 1750–1850*, 2nd edn (Dublin: Lilliput Press, 2010), p. 112; see also Niall Ó Ciosáin, 'Oral Culture, Literacy and Reading', in *Oxford History of the Irish Book*, edited by James H. Murphy (Oxford: Oxford University Press, 2011), vol. 4: *The Irish Book in English, 1800–1891*, pp. 177–91.

For a better understanding of the formation of popular historical consciousness, the examination of historical references in popular print should follow closely the social process of reading in order to try and determine how texts were received and shared. The spread of mass literacy, which in the nineteenth century was extended in the West to the lower classes, as well as to women and children, requires what has been referred to as a 'history of the common reader'.[61] The dynamics of cultural transmission can be charted through discourse analysis that follows the re-adaptation of ideas and motifs—or, to use the neologism coined by Richard Dawkins, 'memes'—through the dissemination of texts over space and time.

Oral history offers access to unwritten discourses. Subaltern studies have demanded recognition of the fact that 'in addition to the narratives of state officials, of newspaper editors, and those to be found in institutional collections of "private papers", historians have available to them the narratives of storytellers, and balladeers, and folk memories available in oral accounts.'[62] Once purist aversions of 'fakelore'—defined by Richard M. Dorson as 'the presentation of spurious and synthetic writings under the claim that they are genuine folklore'—are overcome, folklore accounts can also be used to appreciate the creative, and often ingenious, reception and recycling of print which reveals reflexive interactions between print and oral culture.[63]

Long before oral history received academic recognition, antiquarians were busy documenting vernacular traditions that were overlooked by historians. The historical value of antiquarian writings, although characteristically eclectic and overflowing with excessive minutiae, is particularly apparent in provincial districts which sustained local cultures that did not conform to the official culture of the ruling elites. For example, the publications and unpublished papers of antiquarians from the Celtic Fringe of the British Isles—located, in the words of Colin Kidd, on 'the western periphery of the European Enlightenment'—contain a wealth of information on historical traditions which were mined by national and regional revivalists as a resource for cultural regeneration.[64] Antiquarianism was left out of the rigidly defined academic disciplines and by the beginning of the twentieth century had been largely discredited

[61] Martin Lyons, 'New Readers in the Nineteenth Century: Women, Children, Workers', in *A History of Reading in the West*, edited by Guglielmo Cavallo and Roger Chartier, translated by Lydia G. Cochrane (Amherst: University of Massachusetts Press, 1999), pp. 313–44; Jonathan Rose, 'Altick's Map: The New Historiography of the Common Reader', in *The History of Reading*, edited by Rosalind Crone and Shafquat Towheed (Houndmills and New York: Palgrave Macmillan, 2011), vol. 2: *Methods, Strategies, Tactics*, pp. 15–26.

[62] Gyanendra Pandey, 'Voices from the Edge: The Struggle to Write Subaltern Histories', in *Mapping Subaltern Studies and the Postcolonial*, edited by Vinayak Chaturvedi (London: Verso, 2000), p. 284.

[63] Richard M. Dorson, 'Folklore and Fake Lore', *American Mercury*, 70 (March 1950): pp. 335–43; see also Alan Dundes, *Folklore Matters* (Knoxville: University of Tennessee Press, 1989), pp. 40–56 ('The Fabrication of Folklore').

[64] Colin Kidd, 'Gaelic Antiquity and National Identity in Enlightenment Ireland and Scotland', *The English Historical Review*, 109, no. 434 (1994): pp. 1197–1214; Clare O'Halloran, *Golden Ages and Barbarous Nations: Antiquarian Debate and Cultural Politics in Ireland, c.1750–1800* (Cork: Cork University Press in association with Field Day, 2004), pp. 127–86; Joseph Th. Leerssen, *Mere Irish & Fíor-Ghael: Studies in the Idea of Irish Nationality, Its Development, and Literary Expression Prior to the Nineteenth Century* (Amsterdam and Philadelphia: John Benjamins Pub. Co., 1986), pp. 356–78; Joseph Th. Leerssen, *Remembrance and Imagination: Patterns in the Historical and Literary Representation of Ireland in the Nineteenth Century* (Cork: Cork University Press in association with Field Day, 1996), pp. 68–156.

by professional academic history. In its place, amateur scholarship continued through the work of dedicated local historians and genealogists, whose papers—when they can be found—are well worth inspecting.

Historical traditions were occasionally listed in surveys carried out by agents working for the state bureaucracy. More often, they were described in diaries and memoirs of local residents and recorded in the travelogues of passing visitors. Vernacular history also appears in other genres, not least in songs and ballads. Literary reworking of traditions can be found in historical fiction, drama, and poetry. Going beyond texts, ethnographic observation of folklife—otherwise known as ethnology—has looked at ritual performances of traditions and their tangible representations. Museums and art galleries host collections of material and visual culture that are essential sources for vernacular historiography. Yet, local folk artefacts are rarely treated with the same respect given to exhibits that fall within the national cultural canon, and documentation on their prior history and provenance is lacking. As noted in the opening of this chapter, many relics and souvenirs remain in private possession and are only discovered in rare circumstances, through serendipitous rummaging of attics and basements.

Apart from scribbled notes written on dusty leaves of yellow paper and the odd curiosity, there are also more up-to-date sources. Vernacular historiography has evolved and availed of new media. Over the twentieth century, modern communication technologies—namely radio, television, and cinema—created platforms for the broadcasting of history to the general public and have become leading agents in shaping popular perceptions of the past. In this process, public history, while still appealing to local constituencies, has become increasingly transnational. Since the end of the century, the cyber revolution has created new forms of 'digital history' that can be accessed online and shared through social media.[65] Concurrently, folklore has partly shed its old-fashioned image, with the Internet facilitating the dissemination of 'virtual folklore' and opening new possibilities for oral history.[66] Overall, at a time when enrolment to history studies at universities is in decline, history outside of academia is actually flourishing.[67]

The detection of vernacular historiography in virtually all aspects of popular culture requires from the researcher the kind of 'promiscuous mix of sources', which has been identified as the 'most singular characteristic' of antiquarianism.[68] This does not necessitate a return to the outdated antiquarianism of the nineteenth century, or a repeat of its flowery and often tedious excesses, but suggests the need to develop a more sophisticated neo-antiquarianism. To some extent, this challenge has been addressed by

[65] de Groot, *Consuming History*, pp. 67–104 and 165–309; Meg Foster, 'Online and Plugged In?: Public History and Historians in the Digital Age', *Public History Review*, 21 (2014): pp. 1–19.

[66] Simon J. Bronner, 'Digitizing and Virtualizing Folklore', in *Folklore and the Internet: Vernacular Expression in a Digital World*, edited by Trevor J. Blank (Logan, Utah: Utah State University Press, 2009), pp. 21–66; William Schneider, 'Oral History in the Age of Digital Possibilities', in *Oral History and Digital Humanities: Voice, Access, and Engagement*, edited by Douglas A. Boyd and Mary Larson (Houndmills and New York: Palgrave Macmillan, 2014), pp. 19–34.

[67] See Niall Ferguson, 'The Decline and Fall of History', *Remarks Accepting the Philip Merrill Award for Outstanding Contributions to Liberal Arts Education* (ACTA; Washington, DC, 2016), pp. 9–22.

[68] Philippa Levine, *The Amateur and the Professional: Antiquarians, Historians, and Archaeologists in Victorian England, 1838–1886* (Cambridge and New York: Cambridge University Press, 1986), p. 71.

the emergence of memory studies, which have introduced new interdisciplinary approaches to the study of how societies recall their pasts.

The historical turn to memory in the late twentieth century signifies, according to François Hartog, a presentist 'regime of historicity', in which the past is evoked entirely for present purposes.[69] A similar argument has also been made for current preoccupation with heritage, which is seen as an obsession with the concerns of the present time, as opposed to antiquarian interest in memorials as remnants from the past.[70] However, consideration of instances of social forgetting, whereby communities seemingly suppress public remembrance of historical episodes that do not correspond to present interests, and yet tenaciously find subtle ways to continue to remember these discomfiting memories, calls this assumption into question. If the study of social memory offers another way of looking at mythistory, the study of social forgetting reveals that there is more to vernacular historiography than meets the eye.

While it is commonly acknowledged that memory involves both remembering and forgetting, studies of social and cultural memory have mostly focused on remembering and overlooked forgetting, as if it is simply memory's negative other and, as such, does not require sustained analysis in its own right. Let us therefore consider the value of paying attention to forgetting, in particular the notion of wilful forgetting, for a deeper understanding of vernacular historiography.

SOCIAL FORGETTING

The paradox of intentional forgetting is embodied in the proverbial courtroom scenario, in which a judge determines that certain evidence is inadmissible and instructs that it should be disregarded and 'forgotten'. As explained by Avishai Margalit in *The Ethics of Memory*, such a ruling does not achieve oblivion. On the contrary, 'if the judge asks the jurors to forget this evidence, this request would merely guarantee that they would remember it.' Margalit insisted that 'forgetting cannot be voluntary', but pointed out that while 'the request to forget makes remembering more likely, the request to disregard does not'.[71] The evocation of a subject in order to sanction its effacement, effectively ensuring that it will be remembered in an obscured form, deserves further attention as a peculiar cultural practice that pairs memory with forgetting.

Umberto Eco once amused himself with reflections on the contradictions of an imaginary *ars oblivionalis*, which, in contrast to the *ars memoriae*, would elaborate on techniques that facilitate forgetting. By classifying all forms of mnemotechnics as a sub-branch of semiotics, designed to call attention to their subject, he argued that such a discipline was a logical impossibility and concluded that recollections could at best be

---

[69] François Hartog, *Regimes of Historicity: Presentism and Experiences of Time*, translated by Saskia Brown (New York: Columbia University Press, 2015), pp. 97–205; see also Hutton, *The Memory Phenomenon*, pp. 169–75.

[70] Anne Eriksen, *From Antiquities to Heritage: Transformations of Cultural Memory* (New York and Oxford: Berghan, 2014).

[71] Avishai Margalit, *The Ethics of Memory* (Cambridge, Mass. and London: Harvard University Press, 2002), pp. 200–3. For the legal practicalities of such rulings see Linda J. Demaine, 'In Search of an Anti-Elephant: Confronting the Human Inability to Forget Inadmissible Evidence', *George Mason Law Review*, 16, no. 1 (2008): pp. 99–140.

obscured, but not intentionally forgotten. Having introduced the concept of an 'Art of Forgetting', Eco advised, tongue in cheek, to 'forget it!'.[72]

Unencumbered by such philosophical stipulations, cognitive psychologists went ahead and investigated the practicalities of 'directed forgetting', starting with the early work of Robert Allen Bjork in the late 1960s. The paradigms developed for laboratory studies of 'goal-directed forgetting' of individuals have since been tried out in group situations in order to examine the ways in which social interactions, such as conversations with other people, might influence forgetting.[73] While intentional forgetting has been shown to be feasible, Eco was not entirely wrong. The results of empirical research suggest that such exercises do not result in total obliteration of memory, but in its diminution. A conscious effort to forget produces an altered form of memory, and this 'forgetful memory' needs to be better understood. However, consideration of forgetting has always been overshadowed by the study of memory.

Refutation of an 'art of forgetting' has a long pedigree. The classical art of memory was attributed to the poet Simonides of Ceos, who supposedly could recall the precise seating of each and every one of the many guests of a banquet thrown by Scopas of Thessaly so that, after the building in which they dined collapsed, their mangled bodies could be identified for burial and memorialization. Simonides allegedly went on to found the mnemonic method of *loci* (later developed into 'memory palaces'), a classical tradition that would eventually inspire Pierre Nora when developing his more modern concept of *lieux de mémoire*. Cicero prefaced his telling of this foundation myth of mnemonics with an anecdote about Themistocles of Athens, who refused to be taught how 'to remember everything' and preferred, in the words of Mark Anthony (who related the tale), 'the science of forgetting to that of remembering'. Cicero, an advocate of the importance of memory for rhetoric, disapproved of this choice and professed that it 'must not cause us to neglect the training of the memory'. Even though the apocryphal story of Themistocles' preference for learning about forgetting was later repeated by the early Renaissance poet Petrarch, Frances Yates in *The Art of Memory* dismissed it as no more than a 'frivolous remark'.[74]

Nonetheless, Harald Weinrich, in *Lethe: Kunst und Kritik des Vergessens* (originally published in 1997), traced a fragmented history of illuminating, and far from inconsequential, contemplations on forgetting in the writings of Homer, Ovid, Plato,

---

[72] Umberto Eco, 'An Ars Oblivionalis? Forget It!', *PMLA*, 103, no. 3 (1988): pp. 254–61.

[73] Celia B. Harris, John Sutton, and Amanda J. Barnier, 'Autobiographical Forgetting, Social Forgetting and Situated Forgetting: Forgetting in Context', in *Forgetting*, edited by Sergio Della Sala (Hove: Psychology Press, 2010), pp. 253–84; Elizabeth L. Bjork, Robert A. Bjork, and Malcolm D. MacLeod, 'Types and Consequences of Forgetting: Intended and Unintended', in *Memory and Society: Psychological Perspectives*, edited by L. G. Nilsson and N. Ohta (New York: Psychology Press, 2006), pp. 134–58. For a concise overview see Karen R. Brandt, 'Directed Forgetting', in *Memory in the Twenty-First Century: New Critical Perspectives from the Arts, Humanities, and Sciences*, edited by Sebastian Groes (Houndmills and New York: Palgrave Macmillan, 2016), pp. 263–7; for earlier work in the field see Colin M. MacLeod, 'Directed Forgetting', in *Intentional Forgetting: Interdisciplinary Approaches*, edited by Colin M. MacLeod and Jonathan M. Golding (Mahwah, N.J.: L. Erlbaum Associates, 1998), pp. 1–57.

[74] Frances A. Yates, *The Art of Memory* (London and New York: Routledge, 1999; orig. edn 1966), pp. 17 and 103. For the original text see Cicero, *De oratore*, 2.74.299–300 and 2.86.351–4; reproduced in Cicero, *On the Orator*, Books 1–2, translated by E. W. Sutton, H. Rackham, Loeb Classical Library 348 (Cambridge, Mass.: Harvard University Press, 1942), pp. 427 and 464–7.

Augustine, and a host of other illustrious philosophers. Weinrich followed the 'art and critique of forgetting' from its classical origins, through the Middle Ages, Renaissance, Enlightenment, Romanticism, and Modernism. His survey ends with more recent writers, such as Jean-Paul Sartre, Primo Levi, Elie Weisel, Jorge Semprún, and, not least, Jorge Luis Borges, whose '*Funes el memorioso*' ['Funes the Memorious']—the fictional tale of a dysfunctional man suffering from an inability to forget—is a classic in its own right.[75] It is now clear that forgetting has always been a subject of intellectual preoccupation, even if it failed to gain wide recognition.

One of the more striking cases examined by Weinrich pertains to the elderly Immanuel Kant, who was determined to rid himself of the memory of his long-time manservant Martin Lampe and wrote a memorandum that 'the name Lampe must now be completely forgotten.' Ironically, the discovery of this note by Kant's amanuensis, Ehregott Andreas Wasianski, ensured that the otherwise obscure name of Lampe would be remembered by posterity. Wasianski assumed that this curious reminder to forget was a sign of infirmity and that, in his old age, the great thinker was losing his faculties, but this does not have to be the case.[76] When trying to forget unneeded information, the mnemonist Solomon V. Shereshevsky ('S.'), a real-life Funes who was the subject of a famous study by the Soviet psychologist Alexander Romanovich Luria, similarly reasoned that 'writing something down means I'll know I won't have to remember it.'[77] If taken seriously, this practice challenges the intuitive understanding of writing—and by extension all artificial records of memory—as an *aide-mémoire*, rather than an *aide d'oubli*.[78]

In Plato's *Phaedrus*, Socrates recounts how the king of Upper Egypt Thamus rejected the gift of writing offered to him by the god Theuth, despite the promise that it 'will make the Egyptians wiser and will improve their memories'. Unconvinced, Thamus declared that 'this invention will produce forgetfulness in the minds of those who learn to use it, because they will not practise their memory.'[79] This ancient argument seems all the more current now, in an age in which we readily consign the information that we need to remember to digital appliances and refrain from exercising our own memory.

Describing writing as a *pharmakon*—a drug that is both 'the remedy and the poison'—Jacques Derrida's commentary on Plato's passage highlights the inherent ambiguity of memory aids:

> it is this life of the memory that the *pharmakon* of writing would come to hypnotize: fascinating it, taking it out of itself by putting it to sleep in a monument. Confident of the

[75] Harald Weinrich, *Lethe: The Art and Critique of Forgetting*, translated by Steven Rendall (Ithaca: Cornell University Press, 2004). For 'Funes the Memorious' (translated by James E. Irby) see Jorge Luis Borges, *Labyrinths: Selected Stories & Other Writings* (New York: New Directions, 1964), pp. 69–75.
[76] Weinrich, *Lethe*, pp. 67–77; see also Wasianski's account of 'The Last Days of Immanuel Kant', in Thomas De Quincey, *Narrative and Miscellaneous Papers*, vol. 2 (Boston: Ticknor, Reed, and Fields, 1853), p. 267.
[77] A. R. Luria, *The Mind of a Mnemonist: A Little Book About a Vast Memory*, translated by Lynn Solotaroff (New York and London: Basic Books, 1968), p. 70.
[78] For a discussion of how *aides-mémoire* can serve as *aides d'oubli* (with reference to photographs) see Gunnthórunn Gudmundsdóttir, *Representations of Forgetting in Life Writing and Fiction* (London: Palgrave Macmillan, 2017), pp. 147–61.
[79] Plato, *Euthyphro. Apology. Crito. Phaedo. Phaedrus*, translated by Harold North Fowler, Loeb Classical Library 36 (Cambridge, Mass.: Harvard University Press, 1914), pp. 562–3.

permanence and independence of its types (*tupoi*), memory will fall asleep, will not keep itself up, will no longer keep to keeping itself alert, present, as close as possible to the truth of what is. Letting itself get stoned [*médusée*] by its own signs, its own guardians, by the types committed to the keeping and surveillance of knowledge, it will sink down into *lēthē*, overcome by non-knowledge and forgetfulness.[80]

Studies of cultural memory too readily assume that any representation of the past—whether appearing in writing or as a monument—is an indication of memory. Yet, memory is not actually stored in these lifeless artefacts. Historical remembrance is generated by the interactions of readerships and audiences with such representations, so that an examination of a memorial that is disregarded can tell us more about forgetting than about remembering. Hence a comprehensive appreciation of the dynamics of memory necessitates an 'amnesiology', defined by Liedeke Plate as an exploration of 'forgetfulness and the state or condition of being forgotten', which is seen as 'a made condition, produced and reproduced, that requires being studied in and for itself, and, consequently, needs its own set of tools'.[81]

Scientific breakthroughs seem to promise a new understanding of forgetting. Twenty-first-century advances in the neuroscience of memory have moved beyond the study of consolidation, which looks at the processes through which memory traces—labelled 'engrams' by the German zoologist Richard Semon—are stabilized and become long-term memories. New research has increasingly focused on reconsolidation, which is the process whereby previously consolidated memories are recalled and reinforced or, if unsuccessful, forgotten. Experimenting with pharmacological interventions (administering 'amnesic agents' such as propranolol) and behavioural interventions (using various techniques to condition reactions to certain recollections), recent research on reconsolidation suggests that it may be possible to remove painful memories and perhaps even replace them with more satisfying alternative memories.[82] It would seem that science has all but caught up with the science fiction of *Total Recall*, *Eternal Sunshine of the Spotless Mind*, and other such movies that have toyed with erasing and implanting memories. As of yet, however, scientific experiments test reactions to a narrow range of sensory stimuli, which is a far cry from the complexity of the communally shared narratives that are examined in studies of history and memory.

A variety of metaphors for memory have been adopted throughout history, each going in and out of fashion in turn, partly because they referred to the technologies of the time. The currently prevailing metaphor in psychology and neuroscience likens memory to a computer. Despite the shared terminology, whereby information stored

[80] Jacques Derrida, *Dissemination*, translated by Barbara Johnson (London: The Athlone Press, 1981), p. 105.

[81] Liedeke Plate, 'Amnesiology: Towards the Study of Cultural Oblivion', *Memory Studies*, 9, no. 2 (April 2016): pp. 143–55.

[82] Elizabeth A. Phelps and Daniela Schiller, 'Reconsolidation in Humans', in *Memory Reconsolidation*, edited by Cristina M. Alberini (London and New York: Elsevier Academic Press, 2013), pp. 185–211; Almut Hupbach et al., 'Memory Reconsolidation', in *The Wiley Handbook on the Cognitive Neuroscience of Memory*, edited by Donna Rose Addis et al. (Malden, Mass., Oxford, and Chichester: Wiley Blackwell, 2015), pp. 244–64; Michael Treanor et al., 'Can Memories of Traumatic Experiences or Addiction Be Erased or Modified? A Critical Review of Research on the Disruption of Memory Reconsolidation and Its Applications', *Perspectives on Psychological Science*, 12, no. 2 (2017): pp. 290–305.

on computer hardware is referred to as 'memory', the assumption that the human mind computes in digital fashion is questionable.[83] The comparison to a computer, like all the earlier metaphors, perceives memory as a recording and storage device. Forgetting, as Douwe Draaisma points out, has to make do with a 'reversal of metaphors for memory', as if its sole purpose is to delete memories.[84] For all the impressive developments in recent years, and the troubling ethical questions that they raise, scientists admit that 'the mechanism of memory remains one of the great unsolved problems of biology.'[85]

Laboured attempts to adapt clinical research findings into models of collective remembering, with reference to an illusory 'social hippocampus', have, at least for the moment, little to offer towards advancing our understanding of what Paul Connerton described in 1989 as 'how societies remember'.[86] Moreover, the focus of inquiry is in need of recalibration. As noted by Ann Rigney, 'after several decades of research in the field of cultural memory it has become apparent that the key issue is not really how societies remember but how societies (learn to) forget.'[87]

Keeping up with the times, Connerton has since moved on to contemplate 'how modernity forgets' and has outlined a typology that calls attention to seven different types of forgetting: repressive erasure, prescriptive forgetting, forgetting that is constitutive in the formation of a new identity, structural amnesia, forgetting as annulment, forgetting as planned obsolescence, and forgetting as humiliated silence.[88] Other critics have suggested additional typologies. Frank Ankersmit wrote of four types of forgetting, with particular attention to 'when a civilization "commits suicide" by exchanging a previous identity for a new one', and Aleida Assmann has drawn a distinction between two forms of forgetting—active (intentional acts of destruction) and passive (disregard and loss).[89] Although these different categories are neither definitive nor mutually exclusive, thinking in more precise terms is a significant step forward towards a more meaningful appreciation of the roles of forgetting in society.

---

[83] Bridget N. Queenan et al., 'On the Research of Time Past: The Hunt for the Substrate of Memory', *Annals of the New York Academy of Sciences*, 1396, no. 1 (2017): pp. 108–25; see also Douwe Draaisma, *Metaphors of Memory: A History of Ideas about the Mind* (Cambridge and New York: Cambridge University Press, 2000), pp. 151–61.

[84] Douwe Draaisma, *Forgetting: Myths, Perils and Compensations* (New Haven and London: Yale University Press, 2015), pp. 1–4.

[85] Poo et al., 'What Is Memory? The Present State of the Engram', in *BMC Biology*, 14 (2016), p. 40. For consideration of the ethical issues and their legal implications see Christoph Bublitz and Martin Dresler, 'A Duty to Remember, a Right to Forget? Memory Manipulations and the Law', in *Handbook of Neuroethics*, edited by Jens Clausen and Neil Levy (Dordrecht: Springer, 2015), pp. 1279–1307.

[86] See Thomas J. Anastasio et al., *Individual and Collective Memory Consolidation: Analogous Processes on Different Levels* (Cambridge, Mass.: MIT Press, 2012).

[87] Ann Rigney, *The Afterlives of Walter Scott: Memory on the Move* (Oxford: Oxford University Press, 2012), p. 221.

[88] Paul Connerton, *How Modernity Forgets* (Cambridge and New York: Cambridge University Press, 2009); Paul Connerton, 'Seven Types of Forgetting', *Memory Studies*, 1, no. 1 (January 2008): pp. 59–71. Cf. Paul Connerton, *How Societies Remember* (Cambridge and New York: Cambridge University Press, 1989).

[89] F. R. Ankersmit, 'The Sublime Dissociation of the Past: Or How to Be(Come) What One Is No Longer', *History and Theory*, 40, no. 3 (2001): pp. 295–323; Aleida Assmann, 'Canon and Archive', in *Cultural Memory Studies: An International and Interdisciplinary Handbook*, edited by Astrid Erll and Ansgar Nünning (Berlin and New York: Walter de Gruyter, 2008), pp. 97–107.

If traditionally forgetting was considered in negative terms, as an impairment of memory, cognitive psychologists now realize that 'the study of forgetting cannot be separated from the study of memory'.[90] Similarly, memory studies from within the humanities have come to understand, in the words of Aleida Assmann, that 'on all of its levels, memory is defined by an intricate interaction between remembering and forgetting.' Assmann has sharpened this point and argued that 'when thinking about memory, we must start with forgetting.'[91] Although the subject of memory is still much more valued than forgetting, it has become more common to encounter such statements as those made in an examination of late twentieth-century struggles over memory of the Second World War, which notes that 'remembering always already entails forgetting and forgetting is possible only where there is remembering in the first place.'[92] Ann Whitehead concluded a guide book to the study of memory with the observation that 'forgetting, paradoxical as it may seem, constitutes a crucial if not essential element in the future trajectory and direction of "memory" studies.'[93] This openness to forgetting should not be taken for granted. Maurice Halbwachs—the founding father of the study of collective memory—had little to say about forgetting even though he himself engaged in a remarkable act of wilful forgetting.

Writing in the interwar period, Halbwachs ignored the historical memory of the event that loomed most heavily on his generation, that of the First World War. Having worked throughout the war in the French Ministry of Armaments, he was keenly aware of the scale of suffering and devastation. On a personal level, his brother was injured and taken prisoner and many of Émile Durkheim's former students, alongside whom he had studied, died in the war. Moreover, when developing his theory of memory, Halbwachs first looked at the condition of aphasia among war veterans suffering from head wounds, as studied by the English neurologist Herbert Head. His reluctance to refer to the memory of the war is therefore all the more glaring. After noting that 'now twelve to fifteen years separate me from the Great War', Halbwachs elaborated on how he still felt connected to the pre-war period and avoided any mention of his experiences between 1914 and 1918.[94] By implicitly marking the war as a topic to be forgotten, he subconsciously flagged the shortfall in his study of memory. In the words of Annette Becker, his biographer and an historian of the Great War, Halbwachs 'chooses to

[90] Roberto Cubelli, 'A New Taxonomy of Memory and Forgetting', in *Forgetting*, edited by Sergio Della Sala (Hove and New York: Psychology Press, 2010), p. 42. For the negative image of forgetting in earlier studies of memory see Jens Brockmeier, 'Remembering and Forgetting: Narrative as Cultural Memory', *Culture & Psychology*, 8, no. 1 (March 2002), pp. 15–17.

[91] Aleida Assmann, 'Memory, Individual and Collective', in *The Oxford Handbook of Contextual Political Analysis*, edited by Robert E. Goodin and Charles Tilly (Oxford and New York: Oxford University Press, 2006), p. 220; Assmann, 'Canon and Archive', p. 97.

[92] Maja Zehfuss, 'Remembering to Forget / Forgetting to Remember', in *Memory, Trauma and World Politics: Reflections on the Relationship between Past and Present*, edited by Duncan Bell (Basingstoke and New York: Palgrave Macmillan, 2006), pp. 213–30.

[93] Anne Whitehead, *Memory* (London and New York: Routledge, 2009), p. 157.

[94] Maurice Halbwachs, *The Collective Memory*, translated by Francis J. and Vida Yazdi Ditter (New York: Harper & Row, 1980), pp. 67–8. For the consultation of the work of Henry Head see Maurice Halbwachs, *Les cadres sociaux de la mémoire* (Paris: Félix Alcan, 1925), pp. 95–196. For his experiences during the war years see Annette Becker, *Maurice Halbwachs: Un intellectuel en guerres mondiales 1914–1945* (Paris: Agnès Viénot, 2003), pp. 33–147.

forget, and to be sure of forgetting he almost completely forgets the process of forgetting itself'.[95]

The influential theory of collective memory which Halbwachs presented emphasized the overriding importance of the social frameworks which shape individual memories (*les cadres sociaux de le mémoire*). Forgetting, which for Halbwachs was simply the opposite of remembering and therefore seemed to require little clarification, was explained as the 'disappearance of these frameworks or of a part of them' and this could result from the fact that 'these frameworks change from one period to another'.[96] Although he endorsed the term 'collective memory' (*mémoire collective*), Halbwachs was equally at ease with 'social memory' (*mémoire sociale*).[97] More recent scholarship, which moved on to develop an 'historical sociology of mnemonic practices', shows a preference for referring to *social*, rather than *collective*, memory.[98] At the same time, collective memory has not fallen out of use and often appears interchangeably with social memory, as evident, for example, in the multiple references to social memory in *The Collective Memory Reader*.[99] Although the terms, when applied unreflectively, may appear to be synonymous, a clearer distinction between the two has significance for how memory is approached, and consequently for how forgetting is conceptualized.

Wary of giving an impression of collective homogeneity, studies of social remembrance are at pains to show that constructions of memory are not uniform and cannot be simply imposed from above and passively adopted by subservient communities. Even in the totalitarian conditions of the Soviet Union, where memory was regimented in the public sphere through 'state-imposed univocality', alternative memories were sustained through 'internal emigration' into private spheres.[100] With such considerations in mind, the historian Chris Wickham and the anthropologist James Fenton maintained that the term 'social memory' is better suited for 'a conception of memory which, while doing full justice to the collective side of one's conscious life, does not render the individual a sort of automaton, passively obeying the interiorized collective will'.[101]

Peter Burke was quick to realize the value of social memory for historical studies and pointed out that 'if we refuse to use such terms, we are in danger of failing to notice the

---

[95] See Annette Becker, 'Memory Gaps: Maurice Halbwachs, Memory and the Great War', *Journal of European Studies*, 35, no. 1 (March 2005): pp. 102–13 (quotation on p. 108); see also Becker, *Maurice Halbwachs*, pp. 211–19.

[96] Maurice Halbwachs, *On Collective Memory*, translated by Lewis A. Coser (Chicago and London: University of Chicago Press, 1992), pp. 172–3. Brief clarifications can be found in scattered references elsewhere; see Halbwachs, *The Collective Memory*, pp. 28–30, 75–6, and 82. For an attempt to find 'the outlines of a multidimensional concept of social forgetting in Halbwachs' writings' see Oliver Dimbat and Peter Wehling, 'Exploring the Dark Side of Social Memory: Towards a Social Theory of Forgetting', in *Theorizing Social Memories: Concepts and Contexts*, edited by Gerd Sebald and Jatin Wagle (Abingdon and New York: Routledge, 2016), pp. 140–3.

[97] Halbwachs, *Les cadres sociaux*, pp. xi, 320, and 391; Maurice Halbwachs, *La mémoire collective* (Paris: Presses universitaires de France, 1968; orig. edn 1950), pp. 37 and 68.

[98] Jeffrey K. Olick and Joyce Robbins, 'Social Memory Studies: From "Collective Memory" to the Historical Sociology of Mnemonic Practices', *Annual Review of Sociology*, 24 (1998): pp. 105–40.

[99] Jeffrey K. Olick, Vered Vinitzky-Seroussi, and Daniel Levy, eds, *The Collective Memory Reader* (New York and Oxford: Oxford University Press, 2011).

[100] James V. Wertsch, *Voices of Collective Remembering* (Cambridge: Cambridge University Press, 2002), pp. 72–86 and 138–47.

[101] James Fentress and Chris Wickham, *Social Memory* (Oxford and Cambridge, Mass.: Blackwell, 1992), p. ix.

different ways in which the ideas of individuals are influenced by the groups to which they belong.' Bringing his characteristic perceptiveness to bear, Burke observed that 'it is often illuminating to approach problems from behind, to turn them inside out' and suggested that 'to understand the workings of the social memory it may be worth investigating the social organization of forgetting, the rules of exclusion, suppression or repression, and the question of who wants whom to forget what, and why.' Burke referred to this direction as the study of 'social amnesia', which he considered to be 'the complementary opposite' of social memory.[102] In order to avoid confusion with a less-relevant concept of social amnesia, previously employed by Russell Jacoby in an intellectual history of neo-Marxist neglect of psychoanalytical theory, this study has opted for using the term *social forgetting* to redress the continued neglect of forgetting in studies of social memory.[103]

Theories of social remembering have referred to forgetting, but the term 'social forgetting' has only been picked up on at a late stage, with reference to the 'outcome of society's need to eliminate segments of its social memory which are interfering with the society's present functions'.[104] Social forgetting has also appeared in writings inspired by the systems theory developed by the German sociologist Niklas Luhmann. Followers of Luhman regard social memory as a system of communication in which forgetting is essential in order to prevent overload of information.[105] This theoretical approach, which rejects Halbwachs's presumption that 'the memory of the group realizes and manifests itself in individual memories,'[106] seems to show little interest in the historical recollections of individuals and so fails to make clear what social forgetting actually means on a ground level.

Crucially, social forgetting is not 'collective amnesia', which is too readily taken to mean that specific historical episodes can be completely expurgated at will from the collective memory of an entire society. In a thought-provoking book, David Rieff enumerated the harmful excesses of historical memory in today's culture and advocated the need for forgetting, without going into the practicalities of how memory can be terminated and disposed of.[107] Appealing as it may seem, the conviction that memory can be turned off on command (presumably at the whim of politicians, with the help of

[102] Burke, 'History as Social Memory', pp. 43–59.

[103] Cf. Russell Jacoby, *Social Amnesia: A Critique of Contemporary Psychology* (New Brunswick, N.J.: Transaction Publishers, 1997; orig. edn 1975).

[104] Barbara A. Misztal, 'Collective Memory in a Global Age: Learning How and What to Remember', *Current Sociology*, 58, no. 1 (January 2010): pp. 24–44. Misztal's earlier survey of the field includes numerous references to forgetting, without referring explicitly to 'social forgetting'; see Barbara A. Misztal, *Theories of Social Remembering* (Maidenhead and Philadelphia: Open University Press, 2003).

[105] Elena Esposito, 'Social Forgetting: A Systems-Theory Approach', in *Cultural Memory Studies: An International and Interdisciplinary Handbook*, edited by Astrid Erll and Ansgar Nünning (Berlin and New York: Walter de Gruyter, 2008), pp. 181–9. See also Dimbat and Wehling, 'Exploring the Dark Side', pp. 149–51.

[106] Halbwachs, *On Collective Memory*, p. 40. For a study that considers systems theory alongside personal narratives see Kristof Van Assche, Patrick Devlieger, Petruta Teampau, and Gert Verschraegen, 'Forgetting and Remembering in the Margins: Constructing Past and Future in the Romanian Danube Delta', *Memory Studies*, 2, no. 2 (May 2009): pp. 211–34.

[107] David Rieff, *In Praise of Forgetting: Historical Memory and Its Ironies* (New Haven and London: Yale University Press, 2016); for an earlier version see David Rieff, *Against Remembrance* (Carlton, Vic.: Melbourne University Press, 2011).

historians) derives from a simplistically conceived notion of collective memory, which assumes that if memory is constructed and malleable it can be easily annulled. This reasoning echoes the critique of nationalism that came to the fore in the 1980s and its corresponding post-nationalist historiography, in consequence of which some academics seemed to expect that popular myths and the political structures which they sustain could be dismissed with the stroke of a pen.

In qualifying the constructivist approach to nationalism, Benedict Anderson took issue with Ernest Gellner's use of 'invention'—as opposed to 'imagining' and 'creation'—in order to signify 'fabrication' and 'falsity', an interpretation that was developed to great effect by Eric Hobsbawm. Anderson argued that 'all communities larger than primordial villages of face-to-face contact (and perhaps even these) are imagined' and that they 'are to be distinguished, not by their falsity/genuineness, but by the style in which they are imagined'. Branding this process as 'invention' failed to properly acknowledge that it involves creative re-use of already existing traditions, retaining—as Gellner himself admitted—'some links with the earlier local folk styles and dialects'.[108] Hobsbawm's influential thesis on the 'invention of tradition' sees collective memory (a term that he avoided using) in modern national states as the product of 'mass-generation of traditions', which occurred throughout Europe (and the United States) in between 1870 and 1914.[109] The ethno-symbolism approach to the study of nationalism, most prominently advanced by Anthony D. Smith, argued that the agents of nationalism could draw on the 'deep resources' of older memories and ethno-history, so that the traditions of national memory were effectively re-invented rather than invented *ex nihilo*. Surprisingly, Smith said little about forgetting.[110] Anderson, on the hand, made it clear that national identities are 'imagined' through a combination of remembering and forgetting.[111]

In a famous lecture, delivered at the Sorbonne in 1882, on 'What Is a Nation?' [*Qu'est-ce qu'une nation?*], the Breton philosopher Ernest Renan identified forgetting as 'a crucial factor in the creation of a nation'. For Renan, 'the essence of a nation is that all individuals have many things in common, and also that they have forgotten many things.' His point was that if nations are at least partly bound together by 'possession in common of a rich legacy of memories', then the embarrassing legacy of the 'deeds of violence which took place at the origin of all political formations' had to be deliberately forgotten. Hence 'every French citizen has to have forgotten the massacre of Saint Bartholomew or the massacres that took place in the Midi in the thirteenth century.' Renan therefore advised the members of his Parisian audience, who just a decade earlier had experienced humiliating defeat in the Franco-Prussian war and the brutal violence

---

[108] Anderson, *Imagined Communities*, p. 6. Cf. Ernest Gellner, *Nations and Nationalism* (Ithaca: Cornell University Press, 1983), pp. 48–9 and 56–7; E. J. Hobsbawm, *Nations and Nationalism since 1780: Programme, Myth, Reality*, 2nd edn (Cambridge and New York: Cambridge University Press, 1992), pp. 91–2.

[109] Eric Hobsbawm, 'Mass-Producing Traditions: Europe, 1870–1914', in *The Invention of Tradition*, edited by Eric Hobsbawm and Terence Ranger (Cambridge and New York: Cambridge University Press, 1983), pp. 263–307.

[110] Anthony D. Smith, *Myths and Memories of the Nation* (Oxford: Oxford University Press, 1999), pp. 163–281; see also John Hutchinson, 'Warfare, Remembrance and National Identity', in *Nationalism and Ethnosymbolism: History, Culture and Ethnicity in the Formation of Nations*, edited by Athena S. Leoussi and Steven Grosby (Edinburgh: Edinburgh University Press, 2007), pp. 47–50.

[111] Anderson, *Imagined Communities*, pp. 187–206.

of the suppression of the Paris Commune, that 'it is good for everyone to know how to forget' ['*pour tous il est bon de savoir oublier*'].[112]

Anderson provided insightful commentary on this exhortation to forget, showing that it implies the persistence of memory:

> Nor did Renan find anything queer about assuming 'memories' in his readers' minds even though the events themselves occurred 300 and 600 years previously. One is also struck by the peremptory syntax of *doit avoir oublié* (not *doit oublier*)—'obliged already to have forgotten'—which suggests, in the ominous tone of revenue-codes and military conscription laws, that 'already having forgotten' ancient tragedies is a prime contemporary civic duty. In effect, Renan's readers were being told to 'have already forgotten' what Renan's own words assumed that they naturally remembered![113]

The relationship between remembering and forgetting is not a straightforward dialectic between opposing forces and, as Aleida Assmann put it, these 'are rarely mutually exclusive practices, which is why we should pay more attention to crossovers'. The philosopher Paul Ricoeur persuasively argued that 'forgetting can be so closely tied to memory that it can be considered one of the conditions for it,' suggesting an 'imbrication of forgetting in memory'.[114]

Halbwachs likened memory to small pools left in between the rocks when the sea recedes ('*lacs minuscules demeurés dans les rochers après que la mer s'est retirée*'). Inverting this maritime metaphor, the ethnographer Marc Augé proposed that 'memories are crafted by oblivion as the outlines of the shore are created by the sea.' If it had not been for forgetting, clearing away the sheer volume of clutter, 'our memory would be "saturated" rapidly.' Therefore, according to Augé, 'oblivion is the life force of memory and remembrance is its product.'[115] It is wrong to think of forgetting as a malfunction of memory. If anything, remembrance is the abnormal exception, which is only made possible thanks to the pervasiveness of forgetting. The vast majority of human experiences are irredeemably forgotten and the recovery of all but a select few of the countless lost details is neither achievable nor desirable. Funes the Memorious, who 'not only remembered every leaf on every tree of every wood, but even every one of the times he had perceived or imagined it', was incapable of thinking properly for, as Borges reminds us, 'to think is to forget differences, generalize, make abstractions.'[116] Or, as Friedrich Nietzsche famously put it in his 1874 essay 'On the Uses and Disadvantages of History for Life', 'forgetting is essential to action of any kind.'[117]

---

[112] Ernest Renan, *Qu'est-Ce Qu'une Nation? Conférence Faite En Sorbonne, Le 11 Mars 1882* (Paris: Calmann Lévy, 1882); translated and annotated by Martin Thom in *Nation and Narration*, edited by Homi K. Bhabha (London and New York: Routledge, 1990), pp. 8–22.

[113] Anderson, *Imagined Communities*, p. 200.

[114] Aleida Assmann, 'To Remember or to Forget: Which Way out of a Shared History of Violence?', in *Memory and Political Change*, edited by Aleida Assmann and Linda Shortt (New York: Palgrave Macmillan, 2012), p. 68; Paul Ricoeur, *Memory, History, Forgetting*, translated by Kathleen Blamey and David Pellauer (Chicago: University of Chicago Press, 2004), p. 426.

[115] Halbwachs, *Les cadres sociaux de la mémoire*, p. 24 (this passage was omitted in the English translation); Marc Augé, *Oblivion*, translated by Marjolijn de Jager (Minneapolis: University of Minnesota Press, 2004), pp. 20–1.

[116] Borges, *Labyrinths*, 74–5; see also Rodrigo Quian Quiroga, *Borges and Memory: Encounters with the Human Brain* (Cambridge, Mass.: MIT Press, 2012), pp. 37–50.

[117] Friedrich Wilhelm Nietzsche, *Untimely Meditations*, edited by Daniel Breazeale and translated by R. J. Hollingdale (Cambridge: Cambridge University Press, 1997), p. 62.

Out of the great mass of everyday experiences that are swept into oblivion by the river Lethe, certain episodes are rescued and pulled out to be remembered. Nietzsche, who came to realize the importance of memory in the Second Essay of his 1884 book *On the Genealogy of Morality*, wrote that 'a thing must be burnt in so that it stays in the memory: only something that continues to hurt stays in the memory.'[118] That said, hurtful memories are often the prime target of wilful forgetting. Sigmund Freud, reflecting in *The Psychopathology of Everyday Life* on his own personal experiences, maintained that 'forgetting in all cases is proved to be founded on a motive of displeasure.' He concluded that 'painful memories merge into motivated forgetting with special ease.' Freud supported his thesis by stating that 'it is universally admitted that in the origin of the traditions and folklore of a people care must be taken to eliminate from memory such a motive as would be painful to the national feeling.'[119] Believing that this common knowledge is beyond doubt, Freud did not find it necessary to consider how a society can collectively forget.

Freud's main contribution to the study of memory and forgetting was the assertion that the repressed recollections of individuals are stored in the unconscious mind and that they can be retrieved through the 'talking cure' of psychoanalysis. Carl Gustav Jung, who—following Freud—wrote a number of articles on forgetting, went on to develop the controversial concept of a collective unconscious (*kollektive Unbewusste*), which is mystifyingly inherited from primordial times.[120] One of the reasons given by Wickham and Fentress in favour of using the term social (rather than collective) memory was 'to avoid the image of a Jungian collective unconscious'.[121] Accordingly, this historical study of social forgetting does not follow a psychoanalytical path and instead identifies traces of forgetting within social memory.

Significantly, social forgetting is not 'total oblivion'. Episodes in the past that have been completely erased and cannot be retrieved in any way are of limited interest to historians of memory, who can at best note the gaps and comment on the absences. Conversely, the study of social forgetting closely examines what happens behind the scenes when communities try, or profess to try, to forget discomfiting historical episodes, but actually retain muted recollections. In *States of Denial*, Stanley Cohen discussed the 'blocking out' of inconvenient personal memories (in particular regarding atrocities) and their exclusion from public histories.[122] Psychological research seems to confirm that public silence encourages forgetting, both at an individual and collective

---

[118] Friedrich Wilhelm Nietzsche, *On the Genealogy of Morality*, edited by Keith Ansell-Pearson, translated by Carol Diethe (Cambridge and New York: Cambridge University Press, 2007), p. 38. For the shift in Nietzsche's thoughts on memory and forgetting see Joshua Foa Dienstag, *'Dancing in Chains': Narrative and Memory in Political Theory* (Stanford: Stanford University Press, 1997), pp. 111–25.

[119] Sigmund Freud, *Psychopathology of Everyday Life*, translated by A. A. Brill (New York: The Macmillan Company, 1914), pp. 138 and 154.

[120] *The Collected Works of C. G. Jung*, 2nd edn, translated by R. F. C. Hull (Princeton University Press: Princeton, 1980), vol. 9, part 1: *The Archetypes and the Collective Unconscious*. For references to Jung's essays on forgetting see Hans J. Markowitsch and Matthias Brand, 'Forgetting: An Historical Perspective', in *Forgetting*, edited by Sergio Della Sala (Hove and New York: Psychology Press, 2010), pp. 26 and 28.

[121] Fentress and Wickham, *Social Memory*, p. ix.

[122] Stanley Cohen, *States of Denial: Knowing About Atrocities and Suffering* (Cambridge: Polity; Malden, Mass.: Blackwell, 2001), pp. 117–39.

level (though this has been tested in very limited circumstances).[123] However, rhetoric that advocates 'public forgetting', as discussed by Bradford Vivian, provokes resistance and ultimately results in the formation of counter-memory.[124] Social forgetting is to be found in the interface of public silence and more private remembrance, which sustains subdued memories that are occasionally allowed to re-surface into the public sphere.

If 'addressing the role of silence' has been identified as 'the key for understanding not only collective amnesia but also collective memory',[125] then penetrating reticence suggest the possibility of unlocking social forgetting. A much-needed 'shift of emphasis in discussions of the general themes of memory and forgetting' has been proposed 'by privileging a third element, that surrounding silence and silencing in the way individuals and groups reconfigure the past'.[126] In this context, Jay Winter explained that silence can be seen as:

> a socially constructed space in which and about which subjects and words normally used in everyday life are not spoken. The circle around this space is described by groups of people who at one point in time deem it appropriate that there is a difference between the sayable and the unsayable, or the spoken and the unspoken, and that such a distinction can and should be maintained and observed over time. Such people codify and enforce norms which reinforce the injunction against breaking into the inner space of the circle of silence.

There is a creative tension between 'agents of silencing, intent on keeping the lid on certain topics or words', and 'memory agents equally dedicated to blowing the lid off'. Most interesting of all are the breakers of silence, those 'who live in a special space accorded to risky speech, one which can offend and provoke by saying things which everyone knows but no one says in public'. Discovering the unacknowledged stories of such 'liminal figures' offers a glimpse of those who 'live their lives surrounded by a cloud of socially produced silence, a cloud which can be opaque or vanish in a flash'.[127]

The work of Eviatar Zerubavel on 'social organization of silence and denial' reveals yet another paradox of social forgetting by showing how a 'conspiracy of silence', whereby 'people collectively ignore something of which each one of them is personally aware', actually serves to accentuate the 'elephant in the room'. It appears that silence can be a powerful mnemonic device, reminding those in the know of what they are supposed to forget. Zerubavel pertinently remarks that 'silence is more than simply absence of sound' and 'often speaks louder than words'.[128] Silence, in itself, can be seen as a rhetoric and, at the same time, references to silence can be metaphorical and allude

[123] Charles B. Stone and William Hirst, '(Induced) Forgetting to Form a Collective Memory', *Memory Studies*, 7, no. 3 (July 2014): pp. 314–27.

[124] Bradford Vivian, *Public Forgetting: The Rhetoric and Politics of Beginning Again* (University Park, Pa.: Pennsylvania State University Press, 2010), pp. 39–60.

[125] Vered Vinitzky-Seroussi and Chana Teeger, 'Unpacking the Unspoken: Silence in Collective Memory and Forgetting', *Social Forces*, 88, no. 3 (March 2010), pp. 1118–19.

[126] Efrat Ben-Ze'ev, Ruth Ginio, and J. M. Winter, eds, *Shadows of War: A Social History of Silence in the Twentieth Century* (Cambridge and New York: Cambridge University Press, 2010), Preface, p. ix.

[127] Jay Winter, 'Thinking About Silence', in Ben-Ze'ev et al., *Shadows of War*, pp. 3–31.

[128] Eviatar Zerubavel, *The Elephant in the Room: Silence and Denial in Everyday Life* (Oxford and New York: Oxford University Press, 2006), p. 8; for a concise distillation of his arguments see Eviatar Zerubavel, 'The Social Sound of Silence: Toward a Sociology of Denial', in Ben-Ze'ev et al., *Shadows of War*, pp. 32–44.

to various discreet communications that are considered less audible and yet are very effective when put to political use.[129] We are therefore required to follow the lead of Simon and Garfunkel, peer into what may first appear to be darkness, and tune into the 'sounds of silence'.

Louisa Passerini observed that 'silences, oblivions and memories are aspects of the same process, and the art of memory cannot but be also an art of forgetting.' It is no chance that this insightful observation was made by an oral historian, whose work on the popular memory of Italian fascism breached a culture of silence and censorship to collect and study previously undocumented personal testimonies.[130] Mainstream historiography has a disconcerting record of collaboration with social forgetting. Indeed, when it comes to censoring marginalized voices, official history, as shown by Marc Ferro, as well as by Michel-Rolph Trouillot, has often been deployed for the purposes of 'silencing the past'.[131] New sensibilities are therefore required for unravelling the history of social forgetting.

To denote a history of memory, Jan Assmann coined the term *mnemohistory* [*Gedächtnisgeschichte*], defined as a sub-branch of history 'which is concerned not with the past as such, but only with the past as it is remembered. It surveys the story-lines of tradition, the webs of intertextuality, the diachronic continuities and discontinuities of reading the past.' Assmann described mnemohistory as 'reception theory applied to history', adding that reception should be understood in its broadest sense, so as to reveal how 'the present is "haunted" by the past and the past is modeled, invented, reinvented, and reconstructed by the present.'[132] Mnemohistory has since been conceptualized in greater depth and applied to a variety of European case studies to explore the 'afterlife of events'.[133] An awareness of social forgetting demands a similar *lethehistory*. Forgetting deserves to be treated with the same rigour as remembering. There is an evident need for major historical studies of *lieux d'oubli* to counterbalance the studies of *lieux de mémoire*.

The search for sources that can uncover the muffled voices behind social forgetting leads us back to vernacular historiography. If forgetting—*pace* Renan—can be observed at a national level, it is even more interesting to examine forgetting in a provincial context, where the negotiations of memory between centre and periphery are at play and vernacular history is particularly prominent. While the uses of folklore in

---

[129] Cheryl Glenn, *Unspoken: A Rhetoric of Silence* (Carbondale: Southern Illinois University Press, 2004), pp. 1–19; Adam Jaworski, *The Power of Silence: Social and Pragmatic Perspectives* (Newbury Park and London: Sage, 1993), pp. 98–137. For a discussion of theories of silence see Colum Kenny, *The Power of Silence: Silent Communication in Daily Life* (London: Karnac Books, 2011), pp. 67–86.

[130] Louisa Passerini, 'Memories between Silence and Oblivion', in *Contested Pasts: The Politics of Memory*, edited by Katharine Hodgkin and Susannah Radstone (London and New York: Routledge, 2003), p. 250; Luisa Passerini, *Fascism in Popular Memory: The Cultural Experience of the Turin Working Class*, translated by Robert Lumley and Jude Bloomfield (Cambridge and New York: Cambridge University Press, 1987).

[131] Marc Ferro, *L'Histoire sous surveillance: Science et conscience de l'histoire* (Paris: Calmann-Lévy, 1985); Michel-Rolph Trouillot, *Silencing the Past: Power and the Production of History* (Boston: Beacon Press, 1995).

[132] Jan Assmann, *Moses the Egyptian: The Memory of Egypt in Western Monotheism* (Cambridge, Mass. and London: Harvard University Press, 1997), p. 9.

[133] Marek Tamm, 'Beyond History and Memory: New Perspectives in Memory Studies', *History Compass*, 11, no. 6 (2013): pp. 458–73; Marek Tamm, ed., *Afterlife of Events: Perspectives on Mnemohistory* (Houndmills: Palgrave Macmillan, 2015).

nation-building have been studied, David Hopkin's argument that in France folklorists were engaged in 'province-building', rather than nation building, can also be extended to other areas of Europe, including Ireland.[134] Each country has its own geography of mythistory, which privileges certain regions as 'authentic' heartlands. Irish folklorists have traditionally looked to the West for inspiration, but it is in the North where conflicted provincial identities most vocally challenged the imagining of an homogenous Irish nation.[135]

Writing at the turn of the nineteenth century, the Irish historian Cæsar Litton Falkiner believed that 'no one is entitled to theorise about Ireland until he has made some progress towards understanding Ulster.'[136] Ireland's northern province—Ulster—is a particularly suitable setting for a study of social forgetting. It is a transnational frontier zone, located at the interface of British and Irish cultures with an additional home-grown Ulster-Scots sub-culture. This conflicted melange—with its ingrained sectarian tensions, propped up by bitter religious and political divides—has cultivated noteworthy vernacular traditions of *disremembering*.

Unlike postmodern contributions to memory studies, which tend to fetishize the wordsmithery of hyphens and brackets through references to 're-membering' and '(re) membering', the verb 'disremember' is a vernacular term for forgetting, recorded by the Belfast antiquarian William Hugh Patterson in a late-nineteenth-century *Glossary of Words in Use in the Counties of Antrim and Down*. It may have its origins in 'good old English', but, as noted by the linguistically minded folklore collector Patrick Western Joyce, by the early twentieth century, the term was 'out of fashion in England, but common in Ireland'. A glossary of Ulster speech, compiled in 1910 by the Belfast folklore scholar Sir John William Byers, mentions that the use of disremember 'often implies a disinclination to remember' and as such could be taken to signify 'pretend to forget'.[137] Practices of disremembering bury secrets, which can only be excavated with difficulty. Let us then finally turn to identifying a suitable case study in Ulster for utilizing vernacular historiography in order to undertake an archaeology of social forgetting.

THE TURN-OUT

The art of forgetting is not new to Ulster, which has its own mythological version of Funes. According to a local legend that first appeared in the medieval Irish vernacular manuscript *Auraicept na n-Éces* [The Scholars' Primer], the warrior Cenn Faeladh Mac

---

[134] David Hopkin, *Voices of the People in Nineteenth-Century France* (Cambridge and New York: Cambridge University Press, 2012), p. 21.

[135] A survey of the role of Irish folklore in nation building overlooked provincialism but noted that the early pioneers of folklore were northerners; see Diarmuid Ó Giolláin, *Locating Irish Folklore: Tradition, Modernity, Identity* (Cork: Cork University Press, 2000), pp. 63–100.

[136] Cæsar Litton Falkiner, *Studies in Irish History and Biography, Mainly of the Eighteenth Century* (London: Longmans & Co., 1902), p. 57.

[137] William Hugh Patterson, *A Glossary of Words in Use in the Counties of Antrim and Down* (London: English Dialect Society, 1880), p. 30; P. W. Joyce, *English as We Speak It in Ireland* (London: Longmans, Green & Co. and Dublin: M. H. Gill & Son, 1910), p. 248; Michael Montgomery, *From Ulster to America: The Scotch-Irish Heritage of American English* (Belfast: Ulster Historical Foundation, 2006), p. 52.

Aillela sustained a head injury at the Battle of Magh Rath (which took place in Moira, county Down, in 636). Unlike better-known cases of patients who suffered brain damage and lost their ability to remember, such as the much-studied Henry Gustave Molaison ['H. M.'],[138] Cenn Faeladh was said to have 'lost his brain of forgetting' [*inchind dermaid*]. This condition enabled him to become a famed scholar, who preserved his erudition by committing it to writing.[139] In the interpretation of Eoin MacNeill, the Ulster-born Gaelic scholar and nationalist revolutionary, this story signifies the transition from oral to written tradition, marking a symbolic moment in the development of Irish vernacular historiography.[140]

Throughout the late modern period, the inhabitants of Ulster have shown relatively high literacy rates. By the end of the nineteenth century, according to census figures, 79 per cent of the province's population aged 5 and older could read and write and another 9 per cent could only read. Significantly for this study, the highest literacy rates were in the north-east counties of Antrim and Down (these were the highest for all of Ireland, outside of Dublin). The figures were particularly impressive among Ulster's substantial Presbyterian communities, of whom 88.1 per cent could read and write and 6.9 per cent could only read (putting the rate of illiteracy at only 5 per cent).[141] Already half a century earlier, the 1841 census (the first to provide figures on reading and writing) found the highest literacy rates in Ireland in Antrim and Down.[142] Popular print was distributed through such networks as libraries, newspapers, local booksellers, travelling chapmen, and hawkers of broadside ballads, which catered for the readership of the 'common man'.[143] Even at its grass roots, this was a provincial vernacular culture that combined orality with literacy.

Upon inspection, it turns out that there is remarkably rich ethnographic documentation of Ulster's vernacular historical traditions. It seems as if accounts of local folk history were collected or noted in intervals of every few years, either by interested locals or by visitors to the area. Whether these opportune circumstances can be credited to the value attributed to literacy by the province's large Protestant population (stemming perhaps from the Reformation doctrine of *sola scriptura*), or to a more general appreciation of education, which may have been motivated by economic interests, is of less importance here. Compared to areas with lower literacy, such as the western province of Connacht, where oral traditions were less frequently recorded in writing, the abundant source material available for Ulster makes it possible to follow in greater resolution the development of vernacular historiography over time. Social remembering can therefore be closely examined to see how it evolved, without having to resort to the leaps of faith

---

[138] Suzanne Corkin, *Permanent Present Tense: The Unforgettable Life of the Amnesic Patient, H.M.* (London: Allen Lane, 2013).

[139] David Georgi, 'A Stunning Blow on the Head: Literacy and the Anxiety of Memory in the Legend of Cenn Faelad's Brain of Forgetting', *Proceedings of the Harvard Celtic Colloquium*, 16/17 (1996), 195–205; Hildegard L. C. Tristram, 'Warum Cenn Faelad sein "Gehirn des Vergessens" verlor', in *Deutsche, Kelten und Iren: 150 Jahre deutsche Keltologie*, edited by Hildegard L. C. Tristram (Hamburg: Buske, 1990), pp. 207–48.

[140] Eoin MacNeill, 'A Pioneer of Nations', *Studies*, 11, no. 41 (March 1922): pp. 13–28.

[141] *Census of Ireland 1901*, General Report, Detailed Tables (Second Series), tables 152–4, pp. 524–6 [British Parliamentary Papers 1902, vol. CXXIX, Cd.1190].

[142] See Ó Ciosáin, *Print and Popular Culture*, pp. 37–45.

[143] J. R. R. Adams, *The Printed Word and the Common Man: Popular Culture in Ulster 1700–1900* (Belfast: Institute of Irish Studies, 1987), pp. 23–41, 119–35, and 159–72.

that are to be found in studies of memory that try to cover extended periods but make do with patchy access to the 'voices of the people'.

And yet, the sources for vernacular historiography in Ulster do not make easy reading, as the accounts need to be carefully scrutinized in order to uncover what has been omitted and obscured through social forgetting. Whereas the Irish are renowned for their loquacity, with exoticized descriptions of the colourful volubility of Hiberno-English speech featuring in travel literature and quasi-ethnographic fiction, Ulstermen gained a reputation for their taciturnity and aversion to such garrulousness. The Presbyterian minister and poet William Robert ('Bertie') Rodgers put this attitude in verse, describing the people of Ulster as those

> Who bristle into reticence at the sound
> Of the round gift of the gab in Southern mouths.[144]

Oral history in Ulster has had to contend with what is often described as 'a culture of avoidance', whereby people prefer to steer clear of controversial topics when having conversations in mixed company, or in the presence of strangers. A study of the recollections of farming families noticed that the testimonies of interviewees showed 'very little discussion of the communal divisions within Northern Ireland', although these conflicts had impacted their lives. Accordingly, the interviewers were obliged to 'respect the reticence of the people interviewed'.[145]

Cautiousness and fears instilled by years of conflict have inhibited people in Northern Ireland from speaking out openly and putting their historical experiences on record.[146] The northern poet Seamus Heaney was particularly attentive to Ulster's vernacular culture of silence. In a poem that takes as its title the local aphorism 'Whatever You Say, Say Nothing', Heaney referred to 'Northern reticence, the tight gag of place', and described Ulster as a 'land of password, handgrip, wink and nod ... Where tongues lie coiled' and communications are transmitted in 'whispering morse'.[147] James C. Scott explained, in an anthropological study of 'hidden transcripts, that 'whenever one encounters euphemism in language it is a nearly infallible sign that one has stumbled on a delicate subject. It is used to obscure something that is negatively valued or would prove to be an embarrassment if declared more forthrightly.'[148] In Ulster's culture of discretion, evasive euphemisms and opaque allusions need to be attentively deciphered.

There is a case to be made for an examination of 'Forgetting Ulster' on similar scale to Frawley's *Memory Ireland*. Frawley maintained that certain historical episodes function as 'cruxes' of memory, which are 'analogous to "reminiscence bumps" found in individuals, but occur on a cultural level'—'reminiscence bumps' being

---

[144] W. R. Rodgers, *Poems* (Oldcastle, Co. Meath: Gallery Books, 1993), p. 106.

[145] Jonathan Bell, *Ulster Farming Families 1930–1960* (Belfast: Ulster Historical Foundation, 2005), pp. 12–13.

[146] Anna Bryson, '"Whatever You Say, Say Nothing": Researching Memory and Identity in Mid-Ulster, 1945–1969', *Oral History*, 35, no. 2 (Autumn 2007): pp. 45–56; Hastings Donnan and Kirk Simpson, 'Silence and Violence among Northern Ireland Border Protestants', *Ethnos*, 72, no. 1 (March 2007): pp. 5–28; Claire Hackett and Bill Rolston, 'The Burden of Memory: Victims, Storytelling and Resistance in Northern Ireland', *Memory Studies*, 2, no. 3 (September 2009): pp. 355–76.

[147] Seamus Heaney, *North* (London: Faber and Faber, 1975), pp. 52–5.

[148] James C. Scott, *Domination and the Arts of Resistance: Hidden Transcripts* (New Haven: Yale University Press, 1990), p. 53.

'periods of time during the lifespan for which an individual has a disproportionate amount of memories'. These memory cruxes 'center around perceived traumatic historical spaces that pose questions and offer conflicting, oppositional and sometimes intensely problematic answers about the way that a culture considers its past, and that are crucial in the shaping of social identities'.[149] Frawley identified the Troubles in Northern Ireland as such a memory crux. When taking into account local reluctance to speak about the period, it could also be seen as a 'forgetting crux', but acknowledgement of social forgetting still needs to find its due place in the growing literature on the traumatic memories of the Troubles.

Subtle practices of disremembering have been noticed on occasion. Literary critics, for example, have commented on the role of silence in Seamus Deane's prize-winning novel *Reading in the Dark* (1996). The child narrator, who grows up in a Catholic household in Derry in the years leading up to the outbreak of the Troubles, encounters 'suppressions, omissions, withholdings and evasions'. He eventually comes 'to respect and understand his mother's desire for "forgetfulness", her desire to keep things secret, to forget the past' in a society in which 'traumatic family secrets' are encoded in oral storytelling and folklore.[150] 'Dealing with the Past' is still a very heated topic in Northern Ireland and, in absence of consensus on what to remember in public, consideration of forgetting becomes an even more loaded and sensitive issue.

Disagreements on remembrance in Northern Ireland feed on traditions of 'deep memory' that reflect distinct mythistories, cultivated separately by Catholic nationalists and Protestant unionists. These traditions are celebrated in a variety of commemorative practices that, for all their differences, share common themes of trauma and triumph, but seem to leave little room for forgetting.[151] The annual 12 July Orange festivities, widely celebrated by Protestants, triumphantly commemorate the iconic victory of King William III over James II at the Battle of the Boyne in 1690, and often also evoke traumatic memories of earlier sectarian massacres in the 1641 rebellion. The Anglican clergyman Rev. John Frederick MacNeice (father of the poet Louis MacNeice), when serving as rector of St. Nicholas Church in Carrickfergus, county Antrim, kept himself at arm's length from these events. Speaking out in July 1909, MacNeice wished 'to God he had the wisdom not only to remember but to forget. Surely there is no true wisdom in recalling year after year the story of wrongs inflicted upon Protestants in 1641, or any other rebellion'.[152]

Whereas the events of the seventeenth century were incessantly remembered in public, it would seem that the participation of Protestants in a rebellion at the end of the eighteenth century was largely forgotten. This is partly because its memory defied

---

[149] Oona Frawley, 'Cruxes in Irish Cultural Memory', in Frawley, *Memory Ireland*, vol. 3, pp. 1–14.

[150] See Elmer Kennedy-Andrews, 'The Language of Memory: Translation, Transgression, Transcendence' and Stefanie Lerner, 'The Irreversible and the Irrevocable: Encircling Trauma in Contemporary Northern Literature', in Frawley, *Memory Ireland*, vol. 3, pp. 256–62 and 278–85 (respectively).

[151] Guy Beiner, 'Between Trauma and Triumphalism: The Easter Rising, the Somme, and the Crux of Deep Memory in Modern Ireland', *Journal of British Studies*, 46, no. 2 (2007): pp. 366–89.

[152] *Carrickfergus Advertiser*, 16 July 1909; cited in David Fitzpatrick, '"I Will Acquire an Attitude Not Yours": Was Frederick MacNeice a Home Ruler and Why Does This Matter?', *Field Day Review*, 4 (2008): p. 160. For the persistence of local memories of 1641 see Naomi McAreavey, 'Portadown, 1641: Memory and the 1641 Depositions', *Irish University Review*, 47, no. 1 (2017): pp. 15–31.

stereotypical divisions between Protestant loyalists and Catholic rebels. Prolonged disremembering of the northern arena of the rebellion of 1798 can therefore offer an ideal case study for social forgetting in Ulster.

The Secret Society of the United Irishmen was founded in Belfast in 1791 by a cabal of Protestant radicals, who were inspired by the revolution in France. Another main branch was soon set-up in Dublin, with the intention of opening clubs across Ireland. That year, self-styled Jacobins openly commemorated the anniversary of the fall of the Bastille in the streets of Belfast, and these festivities were repeated once again the following year. Upon visiting the town, the Dublin radical Theobald Wolfe Tone— who would later be venerated as the 'father of Irish republicanism'—hailed Thomas Paine's recently published *Rights of Man* as 'the Koran of Blefescu' (using the name of a fictional island in Jonathan Swift's *Gulliver's Travels* as a code name for Belfast).[153] An indication of the rapid spread of the United Irishmen can be found in their organ the *Northern Star*, which was established by Samuel Neilson in Belfast in 1792 and soon achieved an impressive circulation of 4,000 copies, with distribution concentrated particularly in Ulster.[154]

The United Irishmen started off as a reformist movement, demanding emancipation for Catholics, but evolved within a few years into a fully fledged revolutionary organization. In 1795, Tone travelled to America, intending from there 'to set off instantly for Paris and apply in the name of my country for the assistance of France to enable us to assert our independence'. Before leaving, he assembled a core group of conspirators—including the Ulstermen Samuel Neilson, Robert Simms, and Henry Joy McCracken, as well as his close friend Thomas Russell, a southerner (from county Cork) who was resident in Belfast. Together they climbed Cave Hill and from its summit on McArt's fort, they looked over Belfast and 'took a solemn obligation . . . never to desist in our efforts, until we have subverted the authority of England over our country and asserted her independence'.[155]

The northern United Irishmen were predominantly Dissenters [Presbyterians] of Scottish descent. Their founding leaders were from the middle class, but, in building a mass-revolutionary movement, they made an effort to reach out to the working classes and peasants and to bring into their ranks Catholics, as well as more well-off Anglican Protestants from the established church [Episcopalians]. By May 1797, government surveillance put the membership of the United Irishmen in Ulster at 117,917, of which 48,869 came from the more-concentrated Presbyterian counties of Antrim and Down.[156] The republican ideal of bringing together people from different social and religious backgrounds carried a deliberate agenda of forgetting historical conflicts. They were committed, in the words of Tone, to 'unite the whole people of Ireland, to abolish the memory of all past dissentions, and to substitute the common name of Irishman, in place of the denominations of Protestant, Catholic and Dissenter'.[157]

---

[153] William Theobald Wolfe Tone, ed., *Life of Theobald Wolfe Tone*, vol. 1 (Washington: printed by Gales & Seaton, 1826), p. 141 (a key to the code names appears on p. 137).

[154] Nancy J. Curtin, *The United Irishmen: Popular Politics in Ulster and Dublin, 1791–1798* (Oxford: Clarendon Press, 1998), pp. 202–11; Gillian O'Brien, ' "Spirit, Impartiality and Independence": *The Northern Star*, 1792–1797', *Eighteenth-Century Ireland*, 13 (1998): pp. 7–23.

[155] *Life of Theobald Wolfe Tone*, pp. 125 and 128. For the transition from reform to revolution see Curtin, *United Irishmen*, pp. 38–66.

[156] Curtin, *United Irishmen*, p. 125.   [157] *Life of Theobald Wolfe Tone*, pp. 51–2.

Like the Jacobins in France, who set a new calendar to restart history, the revolutionaries in Ireland aspired to wipe the slate clean. At a meeting in Dublin at the end of 1791, United Irishmen declared that 'we have thought little about our ancestors—much of our posterity. Are we for ever to walk, like beasts of prey, over fields which these ancestors stained with blood?'. Preferring not to dwell on a long history of violence ('we see this, and are silent'), they resolved to 'look forward to brighter prospects—to a People united in the fellowship of freedom'.[158] As in France, they too brought the 'republic to the village' by appealing to popular culture and developing alternative commemorative celebrations, such as planting trees of liberty and composing subversive songs.[159] Under the banner of republicanism, memory was supposed to take on a new life, but memorable events soon changed things.

In December 1797, a tempest scattered the ships of a sizeable French invasion force, commanded by Lazare Hoche, and prevented them from landing on the shores of Bantry Bay, in the south of Ireland, and supporting a United Irish insurrection. Wolfe Tone, who was on board one of the vessels, wrote in his journal that 'England has not had such an escape since the Spanish Armada.'[160] This fiasco alerted the authorities to the imminent danger of rebellion and a clampdown on the United Irishmen was ordered. Counter-revolutionary measures were particularly harsh in the north, where the 'dragooning of Ulster' under General Gerard Lake aimed to crush the rebel spirit. Disillusion set in among some of the Presbyterian radicals. They observed from afar how the Helvetic Republic, which had been forcefully created by the French in Switzerland, was resisted by popular armed uprisings in the spring of 1798 and they became concerned that a revolution along French lines could deteriorate into terror, which in Ireland's case would inflame sectarian violence. After the principal ringleaders of the United Irish conspiracy were arrested, an attempt to go ahead with the original plans and kick-off a nation-wide rebellion in Dublin was easily thwarted. When in May 1798 an unforeseen uprising erupted in county Wexford, in the south-east of Ireland, the hesitance of the revolutionaries in Ulster allowed the military to secure Belfast.

Nevertheless, in June 1798, rebellion broke out in the north-east counties of Antrim and Down. Robert Simms, a Belfast Presbyterian businessman who had been reluctantly appointed United Irish adjutant-general for Antrim, wavered and insisted on waiting for French military aid. Simms resigned from his post and was replaced by Henry Joy McCracken, a Belfast Presbyterian manager of a cotton mill. Left with hardly any time to prepare plans, McCracken issued orders to 'The Army of Ulster' on 6 June of what was designated 'The First Year of Liberty': 'To-morrow we march on Antrim—drive the garrison of Randalstown before you, and haste to form a junction with

---

[158] 'Extracts from the Proceedings of the Society of United Irishmen of Dublin, Meeting of the Society, 5th December, 1791'; reproduced in Richard Robert Madden, *The United Irishmen: Their Lives and Times*, 1st ser., vol. 2 (London: J. Madden & Co., 1842), p. 316.

[159] Kevin Whelan, *The Tree of Liberty: Radicalism, Catholicism and the Construction of Irish Identity 1760–1830* (Cork: Cork University Press & Field Day, 1996), pp. 59–96. Cf. Mona Ozouf, *Festivals and the French Revolution* (Cambridge, Mass.: Harvard University Press, 1988); Laura Mason, *Singing the French Revolution: Popular Culture and Politics, 1787–1799* (Ithaca: Cornell University Press, 1996).

[160] *Life of Wolfe Tone*, vol. 2, p. 266.

the commander-in-chief.'[161] Armed mostly with pikes and assorted improvised weapons, United Irishmen mobilized throughout east Antrim, rallying in Glenarm, Islandmagee, Ballycarry and staging an attack on the garrison in Larne. Thousands of rebels from villages along the Sixmilewater valley and from around the wider area assembled, as instructed, at Donegore Hill, while other insurgents seized control of Ballymena and Randalstown. Rebels also gathered in Maghera, county Derry, hoping to cross the river Bann at Toome and join the insurgent forces in Antrim. However, McCracken's attempt to take Antrim town on 7 June, in what was to be known as the Battle of Antrim, failed and the rebellion in county Antrim was soon quelled (Fig. I.1).

Meanwhile, United Irishmen also mobilized in great numbers in north county Down, where it was noted that 'the rebels came from the eastern parts of the Country, as the plague of locusts came in Egypt.'[162] The commander of the United Irish army in Down, the Presbyterian minister Rev. William Steel Dickson, was arrested on 5 June, effectively decapitating the local organization at a crucial moment (his predecessor, Thomas Russell, had been arrested two years earlier and was still being held in prison

Fig. I.1. '"Stand to the Guns!" Henry Joy McCracken's last rally of the United Irishmen at the Battle of Antrim, June 7, 1798'

Nationalist illustration by Walter C. Mills, gratis supplement to the *Irish Weekly Independent*, December 1895. Courtesy of the National Library of Ireland.

---

[161] Madden, *The United Irishmen*, 2nd ser., vol. 2 (London: J. Madden & Co., 1843), p. 435.
[162] John Moore Johnston, *Heterogenea, or Medley: For the Benefit of the Poor* (Downpatrick: James Parks, 1803), p. 144.

without trial). Thousands, nonetheless, rallied to the United Irish cause throughout the Ards peninsula, attacking Newtownards in the north and Portaferry at the southern tip. They were encouraged by a minor victory on 9 June at Saintfield, where a detachment of York fencibles was ambushed and forced to retreat after sustaining heavy losses. The following day—which was known as 'Pike Sunday'—the Croppies (a common soubriquet for rebels, named after their typically cropped hairstyles that imitated the fashion of French revolutionaries) assembled at Creevy Rocks, just outside Saintfield.

In preparation for an attack on Ballynahinch, the county Down rebels elected as their commander Henry Munro, an Anglican linen draper from Lisburn, who like his counterpart in Antrim had no prior combat experience (Fig. I.2). They were finally routed at the Battle of Ballynahinch on 12 June, after which military mopping-up operations ruthlessly disposed of the remaining insurgent bands. Both McCracken and Munro were arrested and executed, as were many of the other rebel leaders. In total, the brief insurrection in Ulster lasted only a week and was confined to the north-eastern parts of the province. All the same, it was the most lethal eruption of violence the area would see in the late modern period. Forgetting such a memorable event, if at all possible, required concerted efforts.

1798 is engrained as an iconic date in Irish *mentalité* and is recognized simply as 'Ninety-Eight'. Broadly speaking, it is possible to distinguish between three distinct modes of remembrance, each of which was prevalent in a different district of what has come to be known as the Great Irish Rebellion of 1798. The extensive insurrection in the south-east, around county Wexford, as argued by Kevin Whelan, 'never passed into history, because it never passed out of politics'.[163] Ninety-Eight in Wexford

Fig. I.2. 'Henry Munro chief of the Irish rebels' (1798)

Contemporary loyalist drawing by Thomas Rowlandson (1757–1827).

Anne S. K. Brown Military Collection, Brown University Library, courtesy Brown Digital Repository.

[163] Whelan, *The Tree of Liberty*, p. 133.

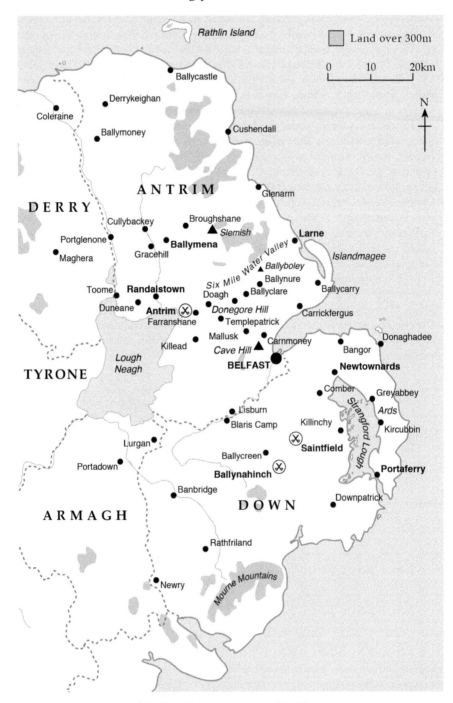

Map I.1. Main sites mentioned in Ulster

consequently became a cornerstone of national collective memory and has dominated metropolitan commemorations of the rebellion. The rebellion's western theatre saw an invasion of the province of Connacht by a small French expeditionary force, which generated a significant body of folklore about '*Bliain na bfFrancach*' [The Year of the French] that was mostly overlooked in national discourse, but was central to local social memory. In contrast to these two different types of *lieux de mémoire*, the northern rebellion in Ulster was subject to social forgetting and became a *lieu d'oubli*.[164]

Following the suppression of the rebellion and the passing of the Act of Union in 1800, which created the United Kingdom of Great Britain and Ireland, the Presbyterian communities of Antrim and Down that had been implicated in the republican rebellion realigned their political affiliations. Over the long nineteenth century, Presbyterians increasingly identified with unionism and loyalism. They vocally opposed the rise of nationalism amongst Catholics and their communities became to be seen as bastions of Orangeism. This apparent instant conversion from radicalism to conservatism has puzzled historians.

Tony Stewart, in an unpublished Master's dissertation written in 1956, was the first to critically dwell on 'The Transformation of Presbyterian Radicalism' and others have since followed his lead to show that progressive attitudes were still held by many northern Presbyterians in the decades following the rebellion. It could be said that liberal Ulster suffered a slow death, and perhaps never fully died at all.[165] Another way of looking at this problem is through the prism of memory. This shift in identity towards unionism created what may appear to be classic conditions for collective amnesia, encouraging public effacement of recollections of the mass participation of Protestants in a republican insurrection alongside Catholics. Indeed, it has often been claimed that the memory of this episode was completely erased.

While recognizing that the airbrushing of 1798 out of Ulster Protestant memory was the outcome of a deliberate 'process of remembering to forget', Ian McBride suggested that it is possible to uncover 'the survival of a "hidden" history of the '98 in the Ulster countryside'.[166] It is this vernacular historiography that this study sets out to reveal in order to lay bare the dynamics of social forgetting. It proves to be a very different kind of history, though not one that conforms to a simplistic folk pattern of valiant rebels facing brutal soldiers. Its single most defining feature is that it is riddled with ambiguities.

The collectors, who devotedly documented traditions of the rebellion over the years, came from different ideological persuasions—including conservatives, liberals, and radicals—and their conflicting politics encouraged diverging attitudes to the rebellion. Similarly, the many narrators, who were interviewed at different times about their recollections, included both supporters and opponents of the rebellion, and in some cases hybrid family ancestries could be traced to people from both sides of the conflict.

---

[164] For elaboration on these distinctions see Guy Beiner, 'Modes of Memory: Forgetting and Remembering 1798', in Frawley, *Memory Ireland*, vol. 1, pp. 66–82.

[165] A. T. Q. Stewart, 'The Transformation of Presbyterian Radicalism in the North of Ireland, 1792–1825' (M.A. thesis: Queen's University, Belfast, 1956). See also Gerald R. Hall, *Ulster Liberalism, 1778–1876: The Middle Path* (Dublin: Four Courts Press, 2011); Julie Louise Nelson, '"Violently Democratic and Anti-Conservative"?: An Analysis of Presbyterian "Radicalism" in Ulster, *c.*1800–1852' (PhD: Department of History, University of Durham, 2005).

[166] Ian McBride, 'Memory and Forgetting: Ulster Presbyterians and 1798', in *1798: A Bicentenary Perspective*, edited by Thomas Bartlett, David Dickson, Dáire Keogh, and Kevin Whelan (Dublin: Four Courts Press, 2003), p. 479.

For those who looked back at Ninety-Eight, censure was often tinged with empathy, just as reverence was tainted by regret. The inherent ambivalence of these memories made sure that they would be concealed, but at the same time preserved.

In vernacular historiography, the events of Ninety-Eight in Ulster were often referred to by other names. Samuel McSkimin of Carrickfergus in county Antrim, a local antiquarian who had lived through the events and subsequently took down recollections from those that had participated in the rebellion, even though he was a staunch loyalist, found that people 'happened to have a rooted aversion to calling it an insurrection or rebellion'. McSkimin noted that 'in speaking of this insurrection it is very rarely called a rebellion, but commonly the "turn out"; the call used at the time, to those who appeared tardy to come forth to the ranks.'[167] The subtle allusion to reluctant rebels touches on the characteristic ambivalence of these local traditions.

The name the Turn-Out (which can appear with or without a hyphen, and sometimes as one word) has a distinct vernacular flavour. It was pronounced 'Turn-Oot' in the local Ulster-Scots dialect, as noted for example in verses written in the early twentieth century by a local poet, Adam Lynn of Cullybackey in county Antrim:

> Few o' us min' the turn-oot fecht
> That taen place here in ninety-eicht.[168]
>
> [few of us remember the fighting of the Turn-Out
> that had taken place here in Ninety-Eight.]

A mid-nineteenth-century 'Stranger's Guide' to 'Belfast and its Environs' mentioned in passing 'the disastrous turn-out of 1798' but skipped over this episode, preferring to dwell on a more positive history, seen as 'a series of advances—increasing rapidity in imports, in manufacturing, commercial, and literary celebrity'.[169] There are numerous examples of such telling omissions but, at the same time, many writers who felt uneasy with the topic often found themselves drawn into its orbit and became fascinated with its traditions.

Other names in popular use included euphemistic references to 'the Hurry' or 'the Hurries' (referring to the brevity of the rebellion), 'the Ruction' (apparently a colloquial allusion to insurrection), and 'the Battles' (evoking the military engagements).[170] The year 1798 could be referred to as 'pike time' (recalling the standard weapon of the insurgents) or the 'Time of the Burning' (bringing to mind the destruction).[171] The rebellion was even referred to as 'the Troubles', a name that could also appear as the 'Year

---

[167] Samuel McSkimin, 'Secret History of the Irish Insurrection of 1803', *Fraser's Magazine for Town and Country*, 14, no. 83 (November 1836), p. 554; Samuel McSkimin, *Annals of Ulster; or, Ireland Fifty Years Ago* (Belfast: John Henderson, 1849), p. 112n.

[168] Adam Lynn, *Random Rhymes Frae Cullybackey* (Belfast: printed by W. & G. Baird, 1911), p. 46.

[169] *Belfast & Its Environs: Or, Stranger's Guide*, new edn (Belfast and Dublin: John Henderson (Belfast) and James McGlashan (Dublin), 1855), p. 15.

[170] For nineteenth-century examples see: Mary Damant, *Peggy: A Tale of the Irish Rebellion* (London: W. H. Allen & Co., 1887), p. 124 ['the Hurry']; Robert M. Young, *Ulster in '98: Episodes and Anecdotes* (Belfast: Marcus Ward & Co., 1893), p. 74 ['the Hurries']; *The McIlwham Papers: In Two Letters from Thomas McIlwham, weaver, to his friend Mr. James McNeight, Editor of the Belfast Newsletter*, edited by John Morrison (Belfast: William McComb, 1838), p. 12 ('the Ruction'); Alexander McCreery, *Presbyterian Ministers of Killileagh: A Notice of Their Lives and Times* (Belfast: William Mullan, 1875), p. 161 ['the Battles'].

[171] *BNL*, 26 September 1867, p. 2 ['pike time']; Francis Davis, *Earlier and Later Leaves: Or an Autumn Gathering* (Belfast: W. H. Greer; Dublin: W. H. Gill & Son; London: H. Washbourne, 1878), p. 161 ['Time of the Burning'].

of the Troubles', the 'Troubled Times', or, in another variant, 'the Troublous Times'.[172] Ulster was apparently preoccupied with the memory of Troubles long before the renewed eruption of violence in the late twentieth century. Denoting local attitudes to the problematic memory of the rebellion, these names distinguish vernacular history from official history. They show how people found inexplicit ways to refer to 1798, which were understood by locals, but were less noticeable to outsiders. Through such practices of forgetful remembrance, the Turn-Out could be both forgotten and remembered.

Though supposedly a 'hidden history', for those willing to make the effort and look under the surface, the sources for vernacular historiography of the Turn-Out are ubiquitous. In the early twentieth century, when it seemed that the episode might have been finally forgotten, provincial newspapers claimed that 'there must be many family papers lying in old libraries and muniment rooms in Down and Antrim bearing on the story of those June days in 1798.'[173] Rev. R. L. Marshall, the Presbyterian minister who—as mentioned earlier—was shown a portrait secretly kept by a loyalist family as a souvenir of their rebel ancestor, observed that:

> In almost every country district there are stories and traditions of the 'turn out' in '98 which are rapidly disappearing. The rising tide of loyalty which reached its zenith in the last quarter of a century deliberately covered with the waters of oblivion family histories which portrayed their ancestry in the role of rebels; and even where knowledge survives among our own people it is retailed with a reticence which reveals as little as possible. Sometimes, however in a burst of confidence the veil is drawn aside and one is shown a glimpse of old unhappy far off things.[174]

The notion that historical traditions that had been cultivated in conditions of social forgetting were on the verge of disappearing echoes the 'poetics of disappearance' characteristic of 'salvage folklore' and 'eleventh hour ethnography', which purport to document the last vestiges of tradition before they sink into oblivion.[175] This assumption turns out to be surprisingly misleading.

Social forgetting can be regenerated and transmitted over several generations. Rather than leading to amnesia, it is a way of preserving under the radar sensitive memories, which cannot be openly remembered. When these memories emerge to be celebrated in public, commemoration is often met with a violent response of decommemorating, which drives them back into the private sphere, but in turn may trigger initiatives for re-commemorating. These dynamics can only be observed through close inspection over a long period, and this requires an extension of micro-history so that it covers an entire region and stretches over centuries. In short, social forgetting has a long and complex history waiting to be unveiled.

---

[172] For example, Mr & Mrs S. C. Hall, *Ireland: Its Scenery, Character, Etc.*, vol. 3 (London: Jeremiah How, 1843), p. 147 ['the Troubles' and 'the Ruction']; Gerald Griffin, *Talis Qualis, or, Tales of the Jury Room*, vol. 3 (London: Maxwell & Co., 1842), p. 73 ('year of the troubles'); W. J. McMullan, 'Belfast as It Was, and as It Is', *Ulster Magazine and Monthly Review of Science and Literature*, 2, no. 17 (May 1861): p. 239 ['Troubled Times']; Letitia M'Clintock, 'Beasts, Birds, and Insects in Irish Folk-Lore', *Belgravia*, 40, no. 157 (November 1879), p. 91 and *The Belfast and Province of Ulster Directory* (Belfast: James Alexander Henderson, 1892), p. 220 ['Troublous Times'].

[173] *Northern Whig*, 11 December 1911, p. 8; *County Down Spectator and Ulster Standard*, 15 December 1911.

[174] Marshall, 'Maghera in '98', p. 174.

[175] Barbara Kirshenblatt-Gimblett, 'Folklore's Crisis', *Journal of American Folklore*, 111, no. 441 (1998): pp. 281–327; Bruce Jackson, *Fieldwork* (Urbana: University of Illinois Press, 1987), pp. 37–9.

The historical events of the 1798 rebellion in Ulster have been thoroughly surveyed in monographs by Charles Dickson, Thomas Pakenham, and Tony Stewart, as well as in chapters of more general historical studies by the likes of Marianne Elliot and Jonathan Bardon, and in numerous local histories.[176] What remains to be clarified is the troubled afterlife of the rebellion. However, this historical study starts before the rebellion, with a chapter on 'Pre-Forgetting', that shows how memories of 1798 were influenced by earlier events. It argues that concerns of forgetting were already embedded into this prememory. The following chapter on 'Amnesty and Amnesia' skips to the immediate aftermath of the rebellion and shows how military suppression undermined reconciliation and drove resentful memories underground, creating conditions for social forgetting. A chapter on 'The Generation of Forgetting' looks at how a culture of social forgetting took shape over the first half of the nineteenth century and a chapter on 'Regenerated Forgetting' follows the fluctuations of remembering and forgetting though the second half of the nineteenth century, showing how memories of the Turn-Out could gradually emerge into the open.

A chapter on 'Decommemorating' focuses on the fin de siècle, when the centenary of 1798 was controversially celebrated in Ulster. Despite an outburst of violent opposition to public remembrance, the commemorations initiated a short-lived cultural revival, which came to an end in consequence of the partition of Ireland. 'Restored Forgetting' looks at how the devolved regime in Northern Ireland tried to keep a lid on remembrance of the United Irishmen, which did not suit the unionist ethos of the state. 'Post-Forgetting' evaluates the impact of the bicentenary of 1798, which coincided with the signing of a peace agreement in Belfast (the Good Friday Agreement) and its promise of 'parity of esteem' that seemed to remove all prohibitions on public remembrance. Although a commemorative flourish would seem to suggest that forgetting had run its course, various incidents in subsequent years reveal that social forgetting has not been completely eradicated. The concluding chapter briefly reflects on the current state of remembering and forgetting in Northern Ireland and broadens the scope to consider the wider relevance of this study of social forgetting, with reference to other areas. The sub-sections in each of the chapters present in-depth examinations of a wide variety of public and private memorial practices that existed in conditions of social forgetting.

In 1998, during the bicentenary of the rebellion, Edna Longley criticized the outpour of 'destructive, irresponsible forms of memory', which she diagnosed as '"memophilia"—a near-relation to necrophilia' and mordantly proposed that 'we should build a statue to Amnesia and forget where we put it.'[177] This seemingly flippant comment has a Borgesian quality, which touches on the paradoxical essence of the notion of wilful forgetting. The singling out of a subject for forgetting makes it all the more memorable. For two centuries, the Turn-Out in Ulster was purposely shrouded in obscurity and buried in silence. By undertaking an archaeology of social forgetting, this study is an excavation of a monument to amnesia.

---

[176] Charles Dickson, *Revolt in the North: Antrim and Down in 1798* (London: Constable, 1997; orig. edn 1960); Thomas Pakenham, *The Year of Liberty: The Story of the Great Irish Rebellion* (London: Weidenfeld and Nicholson, 1997; orig. edn 1969), pp. 170–86 and 215–31; A. T. Q. Stewart, *The Summer Soldiers: The 1798 Rebellion in Antrim and Down* (Belfast: Blackstaff Press, 1995). See also Marianne Elliott, *The Catholics of Ulster: A History* (London: Allen Lane, 2000), pp. 213–66; Jonathan Bardon, *A History of Ulster* (Belfast: Blackstaff, 1992), pp. 218–39.

[177] *Belfast Telegraph*, 17 February 1998.

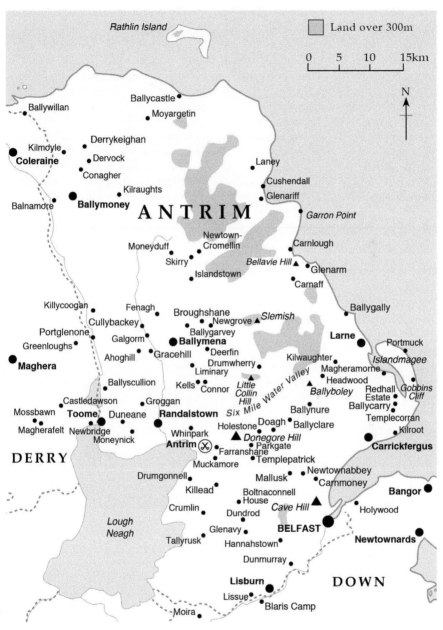

Map I.2. Sites mentioned in county Antrim

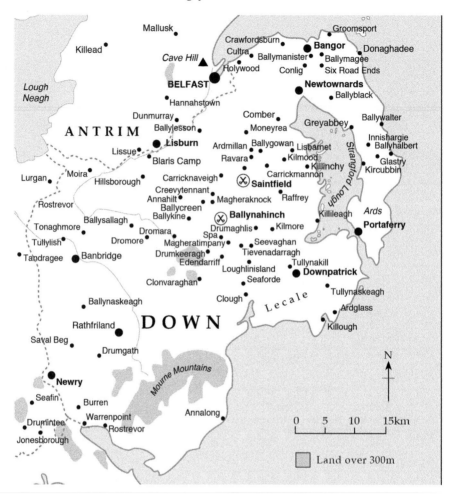

Map I.3. Sites mentioned in county Down

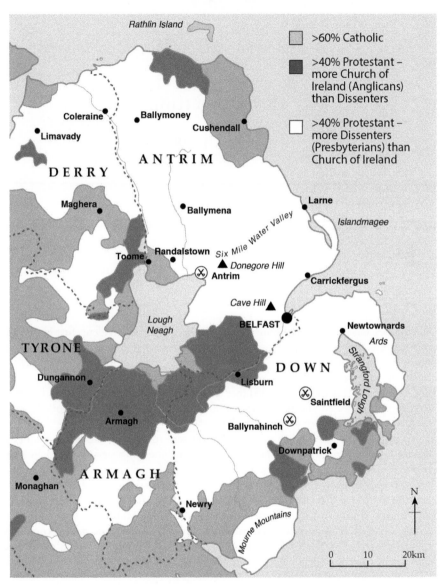

Map I.4. Religious divides in east Ulster

1

Pre-Forgetting

Before 1798

We move into the future backwards.

Paul Valéry, *Variété IV*[1]

one's memory works both ways... It's a poor sort of memory that only works backwards.

Lewis Carroll, *Through the Looking Glass
and What Alice Found There*[2]

When does social forgetting begin? The sequence appears self-evident: first events are experienced, then they are remembered, and ultimately they are forgotten. Hence, history is followed by memory, which wanes with time, so that, after due delay, forgetting sets in. On further thought, the notion of a neat linear succession may prove misleading. It could be argued that remembrance commences much earlier than is intuitively expected and that concerns of forgetting, though often unnoticed, may even be raised in advance of the unravelling of historical events.

To begin with, the a priori assumption that remembrance is launched at a delay cannot be taken for granted. There is actually no inherent necessity for an interval between historical occurrences and the construction of memory. On the contrary, the anthropologist Edwin Ardener incisively pointed out that 'there are, indeed, plenty of grounds for saying that "memory" of history begins when it is registered.'[3] Similarly, in an overview of history and memory in modern Ireland, Ian McBride observed that 'the arrangement of experience through narrative frames is such a basic part of cognition that events are encoded with meaning as they actually occur.'[4] Certain events are immediately deemed by their contemporaries to be worthy of being remembered. The simultaneous construction of memory ensures that such events will indeed become historically significant. David Fitzpatrick has shown, for example, how the key events of

---

[1] 'Nous entrons dans l'avenir à reculons'; Paul Valéry, *Variété IV* (Paris: Gallimard, 1938), p. 139.

[2] Lewis Carroll, *Through the Looking Glass and What Alice Found There* (London: Macmillan & Co., 1871), p. 95.

[3] Edwin Ardener, 'The Construction of History: "Vestiges of Creation"', in *History and Ethnicity*, edited by Elizabeth Tonkin, Maryon McDonald, and Malcolm Chapman (London and New York: Routledge, 1989), p. 25.

[4] Ian McBride, 'Memory and National Identity in Modern Ireland', in *History and Memory in Modern Ireland*, edited by Ian McBride (Cambridge and New York: Cambridge University Press, 2001), p. 8.

the Irish Revolution were theatrically staged as 'instant history' in real-time performances that made them memorable.[5] Instead of the axiom that memory is constructed out of history, we are faced with a perplexing *mise en abîme* in which the two seem to construct each other.

Instantaneous formation of the memory of historical events is even sometimes apparent in the work of public institutions charged with curating official memorialization. The Imperial War Museum was established to commemorate the Great War not after the war, but during the war. On 5 March 1917, the War Cabinet in London approved the proposal of Sir Alfred Mond for the creation of a national museum which would record and exhibit the civilian and military sacrifice that was taking place at the time. Already before that date, local museums had begun to collect exhibits. More generally, public demand for the war to be chronicled and remembered was evident in a crop of memorial publications that appeared from its early stages. This seemingly spontaneous outburst of remembrance was encouraged by wartime propaganda. The press baron Sir Max Aitken (subsequently Lord Beaverbrook), who was appointed Minister of Information towards the end of the war, played a seminal role in shaping memorable popular perceptions. In addition to his dominance of newspaper coverage, in 1916 he established in Canada the War Records Office, responsible for documenting and publicizing the war effort, and he also established a War Memorials Fund, which sponsored an artistic record of the visual memory of the war. Effectively, commemoration of what would come to be known as the First World War commenced before the war was over and the enormity of the casualties could be fathomed.[6]

A similar dynamic can be found behind the scenes of another paradigm of twentieth-century memorialization, remembrance of the Holocaust. Mordechai Shenhavi, who would become the inaugural director of the Yad Vashem Remembrance Authority in Jerusalem, envisioned the construction of a memorial site in Mandatory Palestine for the Jewish victims of the Nazis already in 1942, just as the first reports arrived of the mass extermination that was happening at the time in Europe. The plan he submitted to the Jewish National Fund for a 'national project' was to be tied in with a designated memorial day. The Jewish Agency organized three days of remembrance from 30 November to 2 December 1943 and shortly afterwards an additional thirty days of mourning were proclaimed. Towards the end of the Second World War, several other Jewish institutions in Mandatory Palestine, including the Hebrew University in Jerusalem, considered plans for memorialization to mark the catastrophe. It turns out that the *Shoah* was already being commemorated before the extent of the genocide was revealed and prior to the establishment of the state of Israel.[7] Evidently, history and memory are entwined and develop in tandem.

---

[5] David Fitzpatrick, 'Instant History: 1912, 1916, 1918', in *Remembering 1916: The Easter Rising, the Somme and the Politics of Memory in Ireland*, edited by Richard S. Grayson and Fearghal McGarry (Cambridge: Cambridge University Press, 2016), pp. 65–85. For the formation of 'instant memory' see Iwona Irwin-Zarecka, *Frames of Remembrance: The Dynamics of Collective Memory* (New Brunswick, N.J.: Transaction Publishers, 1994), pp. 161–74.
[6] Gaynor Kavanagh, 'Museum as Memorial: The Origins of the Imperial War Museum', in *Journal of Contemporary History*, 23, no. 1 (1988), pp. 77–97; Gaynor Kavanagh, *Museums and the First World War: A Social History* (London: Leicester University Press, 1994), pp. 103–43.
[7] Mooli Brog, 'In Blessed Memory of a Dream: Mordechai Shenhavi and Initial Holocaust Commemoration Ideas in Palestine, 1942–1945', *Yad Vashem Studies*, 30 (2002): pp. 297–336.

An understanding of how memory is constructed at a cognitive level suggests that the origins of remembrance can be pushed back even further, beyond the contemporaneity of history and memory. In a famous series of experiments conducted in Cambridge in the early twentieth century, the pioneer of cognitive psychology Charles Frederic Bartlett followed repeated retellings of an unusual folk narrative and demonstrated that memory, at the time of its formation, is structured so as to correspond with knowledge derived from previous experiences. Bartlett went on to develop a theory of remembering as an 'effort after meaning', through which memories are fit to pre-existing schemata.[8] Schema theory has since been fruitfully developed in the cognitive sciences, with numerous studies showing that new experiences are normally perceived and remembered in accordance with familiar scripts.[9] By applying this insight to the study of the past, it becomes clear that historical events were invariably understood and remembered in their time through reference to memories of previous events. In other words, there is a *prememory* to history, which influences the development of subsequent memory. Paradoxical as it may seem, memory can pre-date history!

Prememory was manifest, for example, in 1914. Memories of the Franco-Prussian War pre-conditioned the respective perceptions of Germans and Frenchmen of the Great War and the ways in which it would be remembered. Based on their previous success, the German military entered the war with expectations of a swift and total victory, which were soon frustrated.[10] The circulation of mythologized recollections of encounters with *francs-tireurs* in 1870–1 resulted in the perpetration of outrages against unarmed civilians during the occupation of Belgium and northern France and in the subsequent denial of the memory of these atrocities.[11] On the other side, the *mentalité* of the French soldiers who fought in the trenches of the Western Front was moulded by revanchist memories of '*l'année terrible*', which had been instilled by the republican education system over the previous four decades. Moreover, the cult of the dead that was officially endorsed and cultivated after 1871 laid the foundations for the commemorative culture of *les monuments aux morts* after 1918.[12] There were many other available schemata from previous conflicts, including recent colonial struggles. In addition, as memory is not confined only to factual events, the fin de

[8] F. C. Bartlett, 'Some Experiments on the Reproduction of Folk-Stories', in *Folklore*, 31, no. 1 (1920), pp. 30–47; F. C. Bartlett, *Remembering: A Study in Experimental Social Psychology* (Cambridge: Cambridge University Press, 1932).
[9] See William F. Brewer, 'Bartlett's Concept of The Schema and Its Impact on Theories of Knowledge Representation in Contemporary Cognitive Psychology', in *Bartlett, Culture and Cognition*, edited by Akiko Saito (London and New York: Psychology Press, 2000), pp. 69–89.
[10] Stig Förster, 'Dreams and Nightmares: German Military Leadership and the Images of Future Warfare, 1871–1914', in *Anticipating Total War: The German and American Experiences, 1871–1914*, edited by Manfred F. Boemeke, Roger Chickering, and Stig Förster (Washington, D.C., Cambridge, and New York: German Historical Institute and Cambridge University Press, 1999), pp. 343–76.
[11] John Horne and Alan Kramer, *German Atrocities, 1914: A History of Denial* (New Haven and London: Yale University Press, 2001), esp. 140–74.
[12] Karine Varley, *Under the Shadow of Defeat: The War of 1870–71 in French Memory* (Houndmills and New York: Palgrave Macmillan, 2008), esp. 11, 75, and 230–1. Cf. Annette Becker, 'Monuments aux morts après la Guerre de Sécession et la Guerre de 1870–1871: Un legs de la Guerre Nationale?', in *Guerres mondiales et conflits contemporains*, no. 167 (1992), pp. 23–40; Antoine Prost, 'Mémoires locales et mémoires nationales: Les monuments de 1914–1918 en France', in ibid., pp. 41–50.

siècle vogue for popular fiction that imagined a future war fed into the prememory of the Great War.[13]

Elements of prememory can be inserted in retrospect to reshape historical narratives and make them more familiar in popular reception. An examination for the popular memory of the Great Irish Famine, as reflected in folklore collections collected in the mid-twentieth century, reveals that 'informants draw on a repertoire of images, motifs and short narratives, many of which predate the Famine.'[14] Recognizing the formative role of such mnemonic traditions, McBride argued, in the vein of F. C. Bartlett, that 'memories take root most successfully when they are patterned in accordance with the culture's accepted customs of telling stories about itself.'[15] Close examination of the recycling of previous memories in the construction of historical memory can also expose less-noticed appearances of early forgetting. But can an event be forgotten before it is properly remembered? To answer this puzzle, we must delve into the formation of prememory.

RECYCLING MEMORY

In June 1798, it was reported that 'the Chiefs of the Rebels were dressed in green jackets, turned up with white or yellow, white vest, buckskin breeches, half boots, hats with white cockneck feathers, and green cockades.'[16] When Henry Joy McCracken set out to lead the insurgent army in the attack on Antrim town, he had a choice of clothing—he could have donned an all-green dress uniform coat, but instead it was recalled that he wore an undress uniform jacket of coarse green cloth with yellow facings and fringe epaulets (Fig. 1.1). He had acquired both these items some years beforehand, upon following his elder brother's example and joining Belfast's First Volunteer Company.[17] Membership of the Volunteers had been a formative moment in McCracken's ideological and political development and was an equally influential experience for many other Ulstermen. In organizing for rebellion, United Irishmen could draw on recollections of previous paramilitary activity.

Twenty years earlier, on St Patrick's Day 1778, the Belfast First Volunteer company had been formed, ostensibly in order to defend Ireland from a possible French invasion at a time when regular troops were being redeployed to combat the American Revolution. Soon after, in a mass display of popular patriotism that engulfed Ulster and spread throughout the rest of Ireland, able Protestants rushed to enrol in local voluntary

---

[13] See I. F. Clarke, *The Tale of the Next Great War, 1871–1914: Fictions of Future Warfare and of Battles Still-to-Come* (Liverpool: Liverpool University Press, 1995); I. F. Clarke, *The Great War with Germany, 1890–1914: Fictions and Fantasies of the War-to-Come* (Liverpool: Liverpool University Press, 1997).

[14] Niall Ó Ciosáin, 'Famine Memory and the Popular Representation of Scarcity', in *History and Memory in Modern Ireland*, edited by Ian McBride (Cambridge and New York: Cambridge University Press, 2001), p. 102.

[15] McBride, 'Memory and National Identity', p. 36.

[16] *BNL*, 12 June 1798, p. 2.

[17] The two coats are described in detail in *BNL*, 3 February 1892, p. 7. For colour photographs see W. A. Maguire, *Up in Arms* (Belfast: Ulster Museum, 1998), pp. 57 (green and yellow coat) and 241 (all green coat).

Fig. 1.1. McCracken's uniform

Regimental undress uniform jacket of an officer in Belfast's First Volunteer Company, worn by Henry Joy McCracken at the Battle of Antrim in 1798.

© National Museum NI, Collection Ulster Museum, BELUM.O474.1914.

defence units. In the words of their commander, Lord Charlemont, the Volunteers constituted:

> A great army, wholly independent of the crown, self-raised in times of grievance and of universal complaint, in a country deemed and affectedly styled subordinate, when England was weak beyond all former example, beset on every side by enemies whom her own arbitrary follies had brought into action.[18]

[18] John Thomas Gilbert, ed., *The Manuscripts and Correspondence of James, First Earl of Charlemont* (London: H.M.S.O., 1891), vol. 1, p. 51.

Volunteer membership was reported in 1782 to have reached a peak of 88,827 men, of whom over a third (34,152) were from Ulster.[19] The organization subsequently fell into decline and two years later its numbers were put at 18,469.[20] Even then, their enrolment was greater than the strength of the regular army in Ireland.[21]

In the early 1790s, self-styled Irish Jacobins endeavoured to revive the Volunteers in Ulster and invited into their ranks Catholics. On 14 July 1792, a crowd of thousands gathered in Belfast to watch several hundred Volunteers from Antrim and Down parade through the town in an anniversary celebration of the fall of the Bastille. It is not coincidental that the contingents from county Down in this procession came from areas that would be heavily implicated in rebellion six years later. In addition, among the civilians who joined the procession, a considerable number came from Antrim parishes that would be agitated in 1798.[22] Volunteers subsequently held celebrations in Antrim and Down to mark the 'glorious triumph of liberty in France', upholding the French Revolution as a model for Ireland.[23]

The secret society of the United Irishmen emerged out of this radicalized sub-culture.[24] Later in 1792, the attendants of a meeting of United Irishmen in the village of Doagh, county Antrim, toasted 'May every United Irishman become a volunteer, and every volunteer a United Irishman.'[25] The following year, when a 'military mob' of regular troops went on a rampage in the streets of Belfast, smashing windows and damaging the property of residents identified as radicals, they were confronted by a formidable body of the town's Volunteers, who restored order.[26] The administration in Dublin Castle became increasingly alert to the subversive potential of this independent and highly politicized armed body. In 1793, the Volunteers were suppressed and in

[19] 'Abstract of the effective Men in the different Volunteer Corps, whose Delegates met at Dungannon, and those who acceded to their Resolutions, and to the requisitions of the House of Commons of Ireland, the 16th of April, 1782'; reproduced in Thomas MacNevin, *The History of the Volunteers of 1782* (New York: R. Martin & Co., 1845), pp. 106–7.

[20] 'Return of the Volunteers of Ireland 1784'; reproduced in James Kelly, 'Select Documents xliii: A Secret Return of the Volunteers of Ireland in 1784', *Irish Historical Studies*, 26, no. 103 (1989): pp. 277–92.

[21] See Peter Smyth, ' "Our Cloud-Cap't Grenadiers": The Volunteers as a Military Force', *Irish Sword*, 13, no. 52 (1978–9): p. 196.

[22] The loyalist historian Samuel McSkimin maintained that the Volunteers who marched in the parade amounted to 790 (of which 194 came from Belfast and were joined by county Down companies from Moira, Dromore, Villa, Ballynahinch, Downpatrick, and Dromore) and that another 180 joined the procession from the Antrim parishes of Templepatrick and Carnmoney; McSkimin, *Annals of Ulster*, pp. 14–15. Wolfe Tone, who was one of the main speakers at the event, estimated the total number of attendance at 6,000; William Theobald Wolfe Tone, ed., *Memoirs of Theobald Wolfe Tone* (London: Henry Colburn, 1827), vol. 1, pp. 90–1.

[23] See reports in the *Northern Star*, 27 October, 10 and 14 November 1792; reproduced in Brendan Clifford, *Belfast in the French Revolution* (Belfast: Belfast Historical and Educational Association, 1989), pp. 72–4.

[24] See Nancy J. Curtin, *The United Irishmen: Popular Politics in Ulster and Dublin, 1791–1798* (Oxford: Clarendon Press, 1998), pp. 51–5 and 166.

[25] McSkimin, *Annals of Ulster*, p. 21.

[26] Letter to Wolfe Tone signed R. S. [probably Robert Simms], reproduced in William Theobald Wolfe Tone, ed., *Life of Theobald Wolfe Tone* (Washington: Gales & Seaton, 1826), vol. 1, pp. 271–2. The *BNL* report on the 'military riot' of 9 March 1793 is reproduced, alongside accounts of similar affrays on 15 April and 25 May, in Madden, *The United Irishmen*, 2nd edn, 1st ser., vol. 1 (Dublin: James Duffy, 1857), pp. 190–2.

their stead a new Irish militia was introduced.[27] Lord Lieutenant Westmoreland issued on 11 March 1793 a proclamation authorizing 'the magistrates, sheriffs, bailiffs, and other peace officers, having jurisdiction within the said town of Belfast, and other several districts adjacent thereto, to be careful in preserving the peace within the same, and to disperse all seditious and unlawful assemblies'. Although not mentioned by name, the target of the prohibition was obvious and it was soon reported that 'in compliance with the proclamation, the Volunteers ceased to parade or any longer to appear in military array.'[28]

More than anywhere else, in north-east Ulster, where the members of the corps had been primarily Presbyterians, the Volunteers left a legacy of militarized politicization, which anticipated revolutionary mobilization.[29] This background featured in the social memory of the 1798 rebellion. The sister-in-law of Henry Munro—the commander of the United Irish army at the Battle of Ballynahinch—recalled in 1842 that the rebel general had acquired his military training as a member of the Volunteers in Lisburn, and this family tradition was repeated and shared with acquaintances.[30] James Hope, who was elevated in the memory of Ninety-Eight into an iconic 'man of no property', reminisced in the mid-nineteenth century that his 'connection with politics began in the ranks of the Volunteers'. En route to the Battle of Antrim, Hope encountered his erstwhile comrades—'a small body of the Roughforth Volunteers'—leading the rebel vanguard, and at Ballymena he recognized the rebel commander as 'an officer of the Volunteers of 1784'.[31]

Francis McCracken, Henry Joy's elder brother, was known in his old age for recalling the Volunteers with 'ardour and enthusiasm'. On his death in 1842, at the age of 80, he was hailed 'the last of the old volunteers'.[32] After the veterans had all passed away, recollections of United Irishmen who had previously been Volunteers were retold by their descendants. The granddaughter of Robert Lennon of Ballygowan—the leader of a rebel contingent in the Antrim parish of Ballynure—noted that he had formerly been an ensign in the Volunteers.[33] Oral tradition recounted that the United Irish Captain Jack Fullarton [Fullerton] of McTrusterystown, who in 1798 commanded a group of

---

[27] K. P. Ferguson, 'The Volunteer Movement and the Government, 1778–1793', *Irish Sword*, 13, no. 52 (1978–9): pp. 208–16.

[28] William Bruce and Henry Joy, *Belfast Politics* (Belfast: H. Joy, 1794), pp. 138–40.

[29] See Ian McBride, *Scripture Politics: Ulster Presbyterians and Irish Radicalism in the Late Eighteenth Century* (Oxford and New York: Clarendon Press, 1998), pp. 123–34.

[30] 'Memoir of Henry Munro', in Madden, *The United Irishmen*, 3rd ser. (1846), 1, p. 400. The informant, described as Munro's 'nearest surviving relative', can be identified as Katherine Templeton of Cranmore; Madden Papers, TCD 873/317 (letter dated 13 December 1842). This account was repeated in the late nineteenth century by the local historian Hugh McCall, who was a friend of the family, see Young, *Ulster in '98*, pp. 81–2.

[31] 'Autobiographical Memoir of James Hope', in Madden, *The United Irishmen*, 3rd ser., vol. 1 (1846), pp. 229–30, 262, and 266.

[32] R. R. Madden to William Tennent, 28 December 1842, Tennent Papers, PRONI D1748/G/426/3. A detailed account of Francis McCracken's death was written by his sister; Mary Ann McCracken to R. R. Madden, 6 January 1843, Madden Papers, TCD 873/96. See also Madden, *The United Irishmen*, 2nd ser. (London: J. Madden & Co., 1843), 2, pp. 505–6.

[33] Family tradition recounted by Mrs Graham Shannon; W. S. Smith, *Memories of '98* (Belfast: Marcus Ward & Co., 1895), p. 28.

rebels in an attack on Ballymena, had previously been a Volunteer captain.[34] It was considered particularly memorable that the cannon manned by the rebels at Antrim was one of two brass six-pounders which had originally belonged to the Blue Battalion of the Belfast Volunteers and had been concealed in the Presbyterian Meeting-house at Templepatrick.[35] In these narratives, the Volunteers were recalled as the forerunners of the insurgents of 1798 and the memory of their activities functioned as a prememory of the rebellion.

The Volunteers can be credited with introducing modern politics into Irish popular culture through a variety of commemorative media. They skilfully staged memorable displays of ceremonial ritual by holding reviews and field days; made extensive use of print to publicize the cause of legislative reform; rejoiced in the orality of patriotic toasts and songs; and created a market for a rich array of symbolic paraphernalia, which ranged from uniform accoutrements and insignia to specially decorated ceramics, such as inscribed jugs, teapots, and bowls.[36] Above all else, the durability of the commemorative material culture that they produced ensured that memory of the Volunteers remained present in Ulster long after their political agenda had lost its immediate relevance.[37]

In 1852, the Belfast Museum put on an exhibition of antiquities collected from individuals throughout Ulster which included Volunteer uniforms and memorabilia, as well as relics from the United Irish rebellion.[38] Forty years later, the museum added to its collections a new wall case, which exhibited 'various relics of the Volunteers and the stirring times of '98'. The artefacts, which had hitherto been carefully preserved in private possession, included various 'interesting badges, pikeheads, and small objects of the time'. Pride of place was given to 'the volunteer uniform of the celebrated Henry Joy M'Cracken; also the coat of green cloth, with yellow facings and gilt buttons, which he wore when in supreme command at the sanguinary battle of Antrim'. These items, which were displayed alongside McCracken's sword—identified by antiquarians as a Volunteer sword, were expected to 'attract much attention'.[39] McCracken's jackets were exhibited once more in Belfast in 1938, a time when nationalists celebrated the one hundred and fortieth anniversary of the 1798 rebellion but were prevented from

[34] Collected by Francis Joseph Bigger from Robert Johnston, whose ancestor, Jack Taylor, had been recruited to the rebel ranks by Fullarton; ibid., p. 54.

[35] McSkimin, *Annals of Ulster*, p. 118; see also Young, *Ulster in '98*, pp. 43–4 (recollections of 91-year-old James Burns, interviewed by Rev. Classon Porter on 24 June 1863).

[36] Padhraig Higgins, *A Nation of Politicians: Gender, Patriotism, and Political Culture in Late Eighteenth-Century Ireland* (Madison: University of Wisconsin Press, 2010); see also Stephen O'Connor, 'The Volunteers 1778–1793: Iconography and Identity' (PhD: Department of History, National University of Ireland, Maynooth, 2008).

[37] See Robert Day, 'The Ulster Volunteers of '82: Their Medals, Badges, &C', *Ulster Journal of Archaeology*, 2nd ser., 4, no. 2 (1898): pp. 73–85.

[38] *Descriptive Catalogue of the Collection of Antiquities and Other Objects, Illustrative of Irish History, Exhibited in the Museum, Belfast on the Occasion of the Twenty-Second Meeting of the British Association for the Advancement of Science, September, 1852* (Belfast: Archer & Sons, 1852), pp. 27, 33, and 46 (Volunteers paraphernalia); 17, 19, 27, 42, and 52 (United Irish relics). For further discussion of the exhibition see Chapter 4, pp. 274–6.

[39] *BNL*, 15 April 1892, p. 7. For identification of the sword see Young, *Ulster in '98*, p. 32 (a drawing of a typical Volunteer sword appears on p. 13). The sword is now kept in the collections of the Ulster Museum; NMNI BELUM.O475.1914.

holding commemorations in Northern Ireland.[40] The coats were shown again in 1967 for the bicentenary of McCracken's birth and in 1998 for the bicentenary of the 1798 Rebellion, and they have since been put by the Ulster Museum on permanent display.[41] However, the deliberate twinning of the Volunteers with the United Irishmen does not do full justice to the complexity of their place in Irish memory.

Historical memory, as famously demonstrated in a Jewish context by Yosef Hayim Yerushalmi, can follow a cyclical pattern. Through memorial rituals, namely penitential prayers [*selichot*], memorial books [*Memorbüch*], dedicated feasts [second Purims], and special fast days, Ashkenazi Jewish communities repeatedly interpreted persecutions, such as the Cossack pogroms led by Bogdan Chmielnicki in 1648, with reference to earlier persecutions.[42] Through such recycling of memory, recollections of events in the past function as a prememory for the recurrence of relatively similar events. This mnemonic process inevitably blurs historical specificity and tends to mask differentiation. Remembrance of historical events with reference to such recycled 'narrative templates', as shown by James Wertsch through examples from the Soviet Union, reaffirms the identity of the communities that mobilize around these memories. Significantly, in situations of conflict, distinct memories are formed by rival groups, who can remember the same event through different prememory schemata.[43]

The founding of the Volunteers in Belfast in 1778 had its own prememory, which harped back to the raising of similar defence corps and independent militia companies to confront Jacobite threats (in 1715, 1719, and 1745) and the fear of a French invasion during the Seven Years War. Particularly vivid memories persisted of the local response to the landing at Carrickfergus of the French privateer François Thurot in 1760.[44] Recollections of previous episodes of civilian mobilization resurfaced at each historical moment of volunteering. For example, an anniversary dinner for the Battle of Culloden held by Volunteers in Belfast in April 1778 honoured veteran volunteers of 1745.[45] These prememories from the past fed into new memories of taking up arms in defence of Ireland, which in turn served as prememories for future memories. In this cycle of recurring episodes, volunteering was essentially an act of loyalism. This conservative connotation did not sit well with the radical transformation of the United Irishmen in the mid-1790s from a reform movement to a revolutionary organization.[46]

---

[40] *Irish News*, 9 May 1938 and 4 December 1939 (reproduced in *Irish News*, 9 May 2007, p. 28 and 4 December 2008, p. 22).

[41] Fergus Pyle, 'McCracken Exhibition in Belfast', in *Irish Times*, 25 August 1967, p. 11; Maguire, *Up in Arms*, pp. 57 and 241. McCracken's coats are listed in the Ulster Museum catalogue as NMNI BELUM.O473.1914 (green) and BELUM.O474.1914 (yellow and green).

[42] Yosef Hayim Yerushalmi, *Zakhor, Jewish History and Jewish Memory* (Seattle: University of Washington Press, 1982), esp. pp. 45–52.

[43] James V. Wertsch, 'Collective Memory and Narrative Templates', *Social Research*, 75, no. 1 (2008): pp. 133–56; see also Wertsch, *Voices of Collective Remembering*, pp. 60–2, 93–7, and 176–7.

[44] See Thomas Crofton Croker, ed., *Popular Songs: Illustrative of the French Invasions of Ireland* (London: reprinted for the Percy Society by T. Richards, 1845–6), parts 1 and 2.

[45] Allan Blackstock, 'Loyal Clubs and Societies in Ulster, 1770–1800', in *Clubs and Societies in Eighteenth-Century Ireland*, edited by James Kelly and Martyn J. Powell (Dublin: Four Courts Press, 2010), p. 451.

[46] For the reconfiguration of the United Irishmen see Nancy J. Curtin, 'The Transformation of the Society of United Irishmen into a Mass-Based Revolutionary Organisation, 1794–6', *Irish Historical Studies*, 24, no. 96 (1985): pp. 463–92.

Unlike the republicanism of the United Irishmen who rebelled against the Crown in 1798, the Volunteer patriotism of the late-1770s and early-1780s was consistent with loyalty to the monarch. Even though families throughout Ulster had relatives in the American colonies and were inclined to sympathize with their struggle for independence, most Ulster Presbyterians re-affirmed their loyalty to King George III.[47] From 1796, when it became apparent that the United Irishmen were planning a rebellion in conjunction with a French invasion of Ireland, many former Volunteers stood by their original conviction to protect home security and joined the yeomanry corps, which were formed to oppose the revolutionary threat. The 'Men of Mourne' Volunteers in county Down, for example, re-embodied as a yeomen company named the 'Loyal Men of Mourne'.[48] The yeoman unit raised in Lisburn in 1798 was styled the 'Troop of Lisburn Volunteer Cavalry'.[49] Like its predecessors, the yeomanry was a locally raised defence force commanded by its own officers. However, in contrast to the Volunteers, who in Ulster declined payment from the Crown and refused to take a military oath, the yeomanry was financed by the government and was subordinate to the regular army chain of command.[50]

Radicals saw themselves as the sole heirs of the Volunteer tradition and, in the words of the United Irishman Charles Hamilton Teeling, considered those Volunteers who became yeomen 'double traitors'—first for their perceived betrayal of the patriotic spirit of the Volunteers and second for their rejection of the seemingly related cause of the United Irishmen. Nonetheless, there was a large degree of continuity between the Volunteers and the recruitment of yeomanry corps in Ulster.[51] Moreover, in 1798, loyalist civilians spontaneously renewed the practice of volunteering in times of emergency and formed local ad hoc defence units. In Coleraine, county Londonderry, one such volunteer—John Galt—noted in his diary that 'the loyal inhabitants of the town' were armed by Lord Henry Murray (the Colonel in command of the Royal Manx Fencibles) and wilfully joined the regular troops in suppressing the rebellion in their area.[52]

Loyalists endorsed an alternative prememory for 1798, which challenged the monopolization of the memory of the Volunteers by the United Irishmen. In a 'Retrospective Memorandum' written *circa* 1844, the county Down liberal politician William Sharman Crawford, whose father William Sharman had been a colonel in the Volunteers and had taken 'a leading part in all the proceedings', described the crisis of the early 1790s as a time when 'a new class of Volunteers got up called the United Irishmen, whereupon the old Volunteers broke up.' In response, according to Sharman

[47] Vincent Morley, *Irish Opinion and the American Revolution, 1760–1783* (Cambridge and New York: Cambridge University Press, 2002), pp. 23–39, 81–5, and 189–92.

[48] Blackstock, 'Loyal Clubs and Societies', p. 464.

[49] *Lisburn Standard*, 13 April 1917 ('Interesting Supplementary Items').

[50] For a register of the yeomanry units at the time of the rebellion see *A List of the Counties of Ireland, and the Respective Yeomanry Corps in Each County* (Dublin: Dublin Castle, 1798), nos. 2 (Antrim) and 17 (Down).

[51] Allan Blackstock, *An Ascendancy Army: The Irish Yeomanry, 1796–1834* (Dublin: Four Courts Press, 1998), pp. 75–92; see also Allan Blackstock, *Double Traitors? The Belfast Volunteers and Yeomen 1778–1828* (Belfast: Belfast Society & Ulster Historical Foundation, 2000).

[52] Diary of John Galt, PRONI D561/1, f. 47 (entries for 11 and 14 June 1798).

Crawford, the 'volunteer yeomanry' of 1798 emulated the 'old volunteers' of 1778.[53] This lineage was proudly recalled in loyalist traditions.

The former Volunteer Thomas Wright of Portadown, who died in 1828 at the reported age of 96, was 'better known by the name of Old Loyalty'. In 1798, 'his well-known loyalty' had 'brought upon him the ill-will of those disaffected persons who were then distracting their unhappy country' and his house was attacked by rebels. Consequently, he joined the yeomanry as a drummer and opposed the rebels.[54] Similarly, when William Ellison of Tievenaderiff [Tievenadarragh] (about 10 km south-west of Ballynahinch) in county Down passed away in 1844, his obituary recalled that he had first been a Volunteer at the time of the American war and had later joined the yeomanry to fight against the United Irishmen at the Battle of Ballynahinch.[55]

An exhibition organized by the Banbridge Literary Society in 1882 featured 'the black and tattered banner of the Loughbrickland Volunteers, who fought on the loyalist side, and with it is associated the active part taken by them in the engagements of the day'. This 'interesting relic of the memorable but troublous times' was displayed together with mementoes dedicated to the Lower Iveagh Yeomen Cavalry, which were 'very interesting[ly] handed down as they are as relics of days when this fine corps distinguished themselves in making loyalty triumphant over the rebellious spirit of the time'.[56] The Belfast Public Art Gallery hosted in 1909 an exhibition of Volunteers and Yeomanry medals from the private collection of a local antiquarian, William Mayes.[57] Two decades later, in 1938, the City of Belfast Museum and Art Gallery (which had moved to a new location in Stranmillis) curated an impressive exhibition of Volunteer, yeomanry, and militia collectibles from around Ulster. In accordance with the unionist culture that prevailed in Northern Ireland at the time, the catalogue eschewed specific mention of the United Irishmen. The exhibition also included several artefacts that had belonged to prominent leaders of the rebellion (including McCracken's uniform), but this connection was purposely not flagged.[58] Whilst republicans claimed exclusive ownership of the memory of the Volunteers, loyalists were intent on obliterating memories that linked Volunteers with revolutionaries.

Although the Volunteer movement was part of a common heritage, shared by radicals, liberals, and some conservatives, it offered an inherently ambivalent pre-memory for 1798, which provoked different responses. A decade earlier, the radical writer William Drennan shared his anxieties about the decline of the Volunteers with his friend, the Presbyterian minister Rev. William Bruce. Disappointed by Charlemont's desertion of reform politics, Drennan's correspondence in 1785 repeatedly

---

[53] Sharman Crawford Papers, PRONI D 856/D/1.

[54] *BNL*, 22 July 1828, p. 4.

[55] *Downpatrick Recorder*, 24 February 1844, p. 3.

[56] *BNL*, 6 April 1882, p. 8.

[57] *Belfast Evening Telegraph*, 26 October 1909, p. 3.

[58] *A Guide to the Irish Volunteer, Yeomanry and Militia Relics (18th and 19th Centuries)* (Belfast: City of Belfast Museum and Art Gallery, 1938); for exhibits relating to 1798 (mostly taken from the collections of Francis Joseph Bigger), see pp. 35, 38, and 43; see also *Irish News*, 9 May 1938 (reproduced in *Irish News*, 9 May 2007, p. 28).

alluded to the 'the ghost of volunteering', which was beset by 'cruel forgetfulness'.[59] Apprehensions that the Volunteers were being forgotten assumed historical agency in Drennan's pamphlet *Letters of Orellana, an Irish Helot*, which appealed to the Volunteers to unite Protestants and Catholics in the common cause of freeing Ireland from English domination. This stirring text, with its implicit concerns of forgetting, was influential in the development of the United Irish ideology.[60]

Rev. Bruce, on the other hand, was a self-described 'alarmed Whig' who did not share Drennan's radical aspirations. He had formerly been a member of the Lisburn True Blues Volunteer company and in 1798 he enrolled as a corporal in the Belfast merchants' yeomanry infantry unit, known as the 'Black Cockades' in order to defend Belfast from rebels.[61] Afterwards, he took a leading part in the Presbyterian Synod's drive to initiate forgetting of Presbyterian involvement in the insurrection. Not all members of his congregation were receptive to this revision of the past. When Bruce denounced the United Irishmen from the pulpit in November 1798, his sermon reputedly met with a mixed response, 'approved of by some, and stabbing others who hardly prevailed on themselves to sit'.[62] Concerns over the memory of the Volunteers had evolved into divisive struggles over forgetting and remembering of 1798.

Beyond recollections of the Volunteers, a more pungent prememory for 1798 stemmed from the processing of experiences that occurred just before the rebellion. The 'dragooning of Ulster' under General Gerard Lake left particularly disturbing memories. In March 1797, Lake was given 'full authority' to take 'immediate and decisive measures' against the United Irishmen and soon after he advocated that 'nothing but terror will keep them in order'.[63] Seeking to break 'the spirit of rebellion', Brigadier-General John Knox, the military commander in central Ulster, likened the situation to the ruthless suppression of opposition to the revolutionary regime in France: 'I look upon Ulster to be a La Vendée, and that it will not be brought into subjection but by the same means adopted by the republicans in power—namely spreading devastation through the most disaffected parts.'[64]

---

[59] Bruce-Drennan letters, William Drennan to William Bruce, 15 May 1785, PRONI D553/43 and August 1785, D553/45; see also A. T. Q. Stewart, *A Deeper Silence: The Hidden Origins of the United Irish Movement* (London: Faber and Faber, 1993), pp. 68–9.

[60] Anon. [William Drennan], *Letters of Orellana, an Irish Helot, to the Seven Northern Counties Not Represented in the National Assembly of Delegates, held at Dublin, October, 1784, for Obtaining a More Equal Representation of the People in the Parliament of Ireland* (Dublin: J. Chambers & T. Heary, 1785); see also Stewart, *A Deeper Silence*, pp. 129–42.

[61] Classon Emmett Porter, *The Seven Bruces: Presbyterian Ministers in Ireland in Six Successive Generations* (Belfast: reprinted from the *Northern Whig*, 1885), pp. 43–6; Rev. Alexander Gordon, 'William Bruce, D. D.', in *Belfast Literary Society, 1801–1901: Historical Sketch, with Memoirs of Some Distinguished Members* (Belfast: McCaw, Stephenson, and Orr, 1902), pp. 29–34; see also W. I. Craig, *Presbyterianism in Lisburn from the Seventeenth Century: First Lisburn Presbyterian Church* (Lisburn: printed by H. MacBride & Son, 1960), ch. 12.

[62] Martha McTier to William Drennan, 30 November 1798 in Jean Agnew, ed., *The Drennan-McTier Letters*, vol. 2 (Dublin: The Women's History Project in association with the Irish Manuscripts Commission, 1999), p. 428.

[63] Thomas Pelham, Dublin Castle, to General Lake, 3 March 1797, Downshire Papers, PRONI D607/E/148; Lake to Pelham, 16 April 1797, Pelham Papers, BL Add. MS 3310/3 [reproduced in Pelham Transcripts, PRONI D755/4/2/268]; also correspondence of Lord Camden with General Lake, Pratt Manuscripts, KHLC U840/O165/1-6.

[64] General John Knox, Dungannon, to Marquess of Abercorn, 21 March 1797, Abercorn Papers, PRONI D623/A/156/10.

The unrestrained measures unleashed by regular troops, militia, and yeomanry on the civilian population in an effort to root out popular support for the United Irishmen indeed amounted to a rampage of state terror. Certain units, such as the Welsh fencible cavalry regiment—known by the nickname the 'Ancient Britons', which was despatched to south county Down, acquired notoriety for their excessive brutality. The French (or, to be more precise, Breton) émigré traveller Chevalier de Latocnaye [Jacques Louis de Bourgenet] correctly predicted that 'Newry will long remember the Ancient Britons' ['les habitans de Newry ne se rappellent longtemps *des anciens Bretons*'].[65]

Among the many horrific displays of brutality that preceded the rebellion, some memorable events stood out more than others. A particularly infamous case was the execution of four soldiers from the Monaghan Militia at the Blaris Moor camp. At their court martial, the four steadfastly denied the charges of having taken the United Irish oath and, when sentenced to death, went to their executions with 'uncommon fortitude'.[66] James Watson, a captain in the Brookhill Yeomanry who was stationed nearby, recalled that 'to render the fatal punishment more exemplary' they were marched in front of their regiment to the tune of the 'Dead March in Saul', forced to kneel in front of their coffins and shot by a firing squad.[67] This poignant scene left a lasting impression.

The executions at Blaris were soon politicized. United Irish poets, including William Drennan, William Sampson, and the lesser-known James Garland of Lurgan, composed songs and elegies in memory of the executed militiamen and it was later asserted that 'the prevalence of those songs did more to increase the numbers of the conspirators than all the efforts of the French emissaries, or the writings and harangues of all the political philosophers, and age-of-reason men of the times.'[68] These compositions were sung and recited in Ulster throughout the nineteenth century and re-appeared in local song collections and nationalist publications.[69] An account of the executions included an anecdote that told how the father of one of the condemned men prohibited his son from informing on his comrades in return for a pardon. The father reputedly declared that 'the life of a son was of great value to a father, but if his son was spared to become

[65]   de Latocnaye, *Rambles through Ireland; by a French Emigrant* (Cork: printed by M. Harris, 1798), vol. 2, p. 225; for the original see de Latocnaye, *Promenade d'un français dans l'Irlande Orné de gravures en taille douce*, troisième volume (Dublin: M. et D. Graisberry, 1797), p. 299. For recollections of the Ancient Britons see Chapter 3, p. 195 and Chapter 6, pp. 478–9.

[66]   *Dublin Evening Post*, 20 May 1797, p. 3; see also Brian MacDonald, 'The Monaghan Militia & the Tragedy of Blaris Moor', *Clogher Record*, 16, no. 2 (1998): pp. 123–43.

[67]   James Watson, *Memorial of James Watson, Esq. Brookhill, with Notices of His Contemporaries* (Belfast: James Alex. Henderson, 1851), p. 28.

[68]   Solomon Secondsight [James McHenry], *O'Halloran; or The Insurgent Chief: An Irish Historical Tale of 1798* (Philadelphia: Carey and Lea, 1824), 1, pp. 62–5.

[69]   Richard Robert Madden, ed., *Literary Remains of the United Irishmen of 1798 and Selections from Other Popular Lyrics of Their Times* (Dublin: James Duffy, 1887), pp. 177–9; P. W. Joyce, *Old Irish Folk Music and Songs* (London and New York: Longmans, Green, and Co., 1909), pp. 107–10; Hugh Shields, 'Some "Songs and Ballads in Use in the Province of Ulster…1845"', *Ulster Folklife*, 17 (1971), p. 10; Georges Denis Zimmerman, *Songs of Irish Rebellion: Irish Political Street Ballads and Rebel Songs, 1780–1900* (Dublin: Four Courts Press, 2002; orig. edn 1966), pp. 129–32; Terry Moylan, *The Age of Revolution: 1776–1815 in the Irish Song Tradition* (Dublin: Lilliput Press, 2000), pp. 35–6. Additional early verses, possibly composed by the poet Mary Balfour, were left unpublished and did not enter into the folk song repertoire; see Robert Magill Young, *Historical Notices of Old Belfast and Its Vicinity* (Belfast: M. Ward & Co., 1896), p. 279.

a traitor, he would shoot him with his own hand.'[70] Such narratives, which reappeared in folk stories of 1798, were recycled in nationalist mythmaking as didactic exemplars of patriotism.

The excesses of the military were denounced by oppositional papers in England, but in Ireland could only be talked about in public with the utmost caution.[71] The hushed memories of 1797 anticipated the suppression of the rebellion in 1798 and prepared the ground for social forgetting. For some, the surge in violence resembled similar outbursts during previous rebellions and could be slotted into a cyclical pattern of memory that recalled recurring atrocities. Conversely, revulsion from the horrors could also trigger 'rejection of the rebellion, or selective amnesia about aspects of it'.[72] The complex dynamics of how recollections of events that immediately preceded the rebellion influenced the ways it would be subsequently remembered and forgotten can be demonstrated through a detailed inspection of the case of the most celebrated victim of pre-rebellion repression in Ulster, William Orr.

INITIATING COUNTER-MEMORY

A century after 1798, when the United Irishmen were widely celebrated by Irish nationalists, one of their number would stand out for having been memorably executed before the rebellion broke out. This was William Orr, the Irish republican protomartyr, whose portrait featured on lithographs among the most notable of 'The Men of '98' and the 'Leaders of the United Irishmen'.[73]

Orr's hallowed place in the national pantheon is exemplified in his appearance on silk handkerchiefs dedicated to 'The Heroes of '98', which were kept in households as cherished mementoes (Fig. 1.2). In these commemorative souvenirs, Orr appears alongside four of the most venerated United Irishmen: Lord Edward Fitzgerald, the designated commander-in-chief of the United Irish army; Theobald Wolfe Tone, who over the course of the nineteenth century became the most revered United Irishman; Henry Joy McCracken, the leader of the rebels in Antrim; and Robert Emmet, the idolized leader of the aborted rising in 1803. Displaying the typical extravagance of romantic-nationalist symbolism, the portraits of the five are bound together by angel-winged harps and bouquets of shamrocks that adorn the symbolic date of '98'.[74]

---

[70] Madden, *The United Irishmen*, 2nd ser., vol. 2 (1843), pp. 399–400. The newspaper report of the execution had the father saying that 'if he [his son] was base enough to involve the lives of innocent men, he would deserve the death which he was about to receive'; *Dublin Evening Post*, 20 May 1797, p. 3.

[71] See Michael De Nie, *The Eternal Paddy: Irish Identity and the British Press, 1798–1882* (Madison: University of Wisconsin Press, 2004), p. 46.

[72] Elizabeth Malcolm, 'A New Age or Just the Same Old Cycle of Extirpation? Massacre and the 1798 Irish Rebellion', *Journal of Genocide Research*, 15, no. 2 (2013): pp. 151–66.

[73] Two examples can be found in the printed drawing collections of the National Library of Ireland: 'The Men of '98', published in Dublin by John Arigho *c.*1901–12; 'Leaders of the United Irishmen, 1798 and 1803', by Thomas O'Bolger, published in New York in 1908.

[74] Two samples of the commemorative handkerchief can be found in the collections of the National Museum and the National Library of Ireland; NMI HH:2013.422 and NLI EPH F224.

(a)

(b)

Fig. 1.2. 'The Heroes of '98'

(a) Silk handkerchief commemorating 'The Heroes of '98', including William Orr (bottom left) and Henry Joy McCracken (top right).

Reproduced courtesy of the National Library of Ireland (EPH F224).

(b) Photograph of Mrs. Sarah Conlan of Portaferry with such a memento (taken by P. Lawson of Portaferry) which originally appeared in *Newtownards Spectator*, 11 November 1960, p. 5.

Reproduced by the National Library of Ireland with permission from the Spectator Group.

Orr's prominence in this hagiographic iconography is somewhat curious. He was neither an ideologue of the revolutionary movement, nor one of its chief organizers. In the reductive terms of a purely factual history, he could be dismissed as a negligible figure, yet his aggrandisement in social memory is in itself a significant historical fact.

The memory of William Orr's arrest, trial, and public execution on the gallows known as 'The Three Sisters' outside Carrickfergus on 14 October 1797 was an essential prememory for 1798. His example demonstrated the value of martyrdom for the revolutionary cause, making it clear that:

> The peasant who is to be shot, or the ploughman who is to be hanged, may feel and sustain his fate with fortitude, and leave behind him an example not to deter, but rather, inspirit others; his memory will be revered, and his name handed down to posterity, in the village or hamlet where he resided, and he suffered, as a political martyr.[75]

Others would consciously follow in Orr's footsteps. The following year, at the trial of the radical Catholic priest Rev. James Coigly, who was arrested when trying to muster support for the United Irishmen in England, the defence counsel explicitly referred to 'the fate of the unfortunate Mr. Orr'.[76] After Coigly was sentenced to death, he issued an 'Address to the People of Ireland' in which he consciously fashioned his execution at Maidstone on 7 June 1798 in imitation of the 'Immortal Orr'.[77]

In light of Orr's example, those who turned out in arms in 1798, knowing that they may have to pay the ultimate sacrifice, could rightfully expect that in their death they too would be remembered. Admittedly, Christian tradition provided an array of worthy exemplars for self-sacrifice, starting with Christ and the martyrs of the early Church. Moreover, there were specifically Irish traditions of martyrdom that stemmed from the early modern struggles of colonization, reformation, and counter-reformation.[78] Orr, however, was to become Ireland's first *republican* martyr, preceding, among others, the so-called 'father of Irish republicanism', Wolfe Tone. He was, in a sense, the 'warm-up act' for the heroes of Ninety-Eight. Peter Burke has argued that the main criteria for achieving recognition as a hero in social memory was the extent to which there was a 'fit' with a pre-existing perception of heroism. As a central figure in the prememory of 1798, Orr signified the archetypal standard for United Irish martyrdom, by which all others would be measured.[79]

Appeals to the memory of Orr were utilized for the purpose of mobilization towards rebellion. United Irishmen toasted 'The memory of ORR, who died a martyr to Irish Freedom' and sang 'Thy blood to our union, more energy gave'.[80] This propaganda was

---

[75] *Press*, 4 November 1797, p. 3.

[76] *The Life of the Rev. James Coigly, an Address to the People of Ireland, as Written by Himself During His Confinement in Maidstone Gaol* (London: s.n., 1798), p. 60.

[77] *The Trial of James O'Coigly . . . Taken in Short-Hand by Joseph Gurney* (London: M. Gurney, 1798), pp. 381–2; see also Dáire Keogh, *A Patriot Priest: A Life of Reverend James Coigly* (Cork: Cork University Press, 1998), p. 1.

[78] See Alan Ford, 'Martyrdom, History and Memory in Early Modern Ireland', in *History and Memory in Modern Ireland*, edited by Ian McBride (Cambridge and New York: Cambridge University Press, 2001), pp. 43–66; Clodagh Tait, 'Catholic Martyrdom in Early Modern Ireland', *History Compass*, 2, no. 1 (2004), unpaginated.

[79] Burke, 'History as Social Memory', pp. 51–2.

[80] The verse appeared in the song 'Oh Union For Ever'; *The Irish Harp*, p. 88. The toast is included in a list of 'Toasts and Sentiments' appended to this songbook. It appeared also on another list, which

apparently effective. In February 1798, the informer John Edward Newell reported to the Lord Lieutenant, Earl Camden:

> My Lord, the people execrate you—your very guards are The Friends of Freedom, and detest you—the[y] look upon you as the executioner of Orr, their friend and brother, and his death is as a call to battle and stirs them up to courage and revenge—they say that blood must have blood.[81]

The United Irishmen John and Henry Sheares, who were arrested in advance of the rebellion in May 1798, were convicted for high treason and sentenced to be executed on the evidence of a handwritten proclamation that had been found in their possession, which read:

> Vengeance, Irishmen, Vengeance on your Oppressors—Remember what thousands of your dearest friends have perished by their [Murders, Cruel plots (scratched out)] Merciless Orders—Remember their burnings, their rackings, their torturings, their Military Massacres, and their legal Murders. Remember ORR.[82]

The son of the notable reformist politician Henry Grattan later recalled the prevalence of this seditious catchphrase: '"*Remember Orr!—Remember Orr!*" were words written every where—pronounced every where. I recollect, when a child, to have read them on the walls—to have heard them spoken by the people.'[83]

The historian of the United Irishmen, Richard Robert Madden, summarized these propaganda efforts:

> Poems were written, sermons were preached; after-dinner speeches, and after supper still stronger speeches, were made, of no ordinary vehemence, about the fate of Orr and the conduct of Lord Camden, which certainly, in the peculiar circumstances of this case, was bad, or rather stupidly base and iniquitously unjust.
>
> The scribes of the United Irishmen wrote up the memory of the man whom Camden had allowed to be executed with a full knowledge of the foul means taken to obtain a conviction, officially conveyed to him by persons every way worthy of credit and of undoubted loyalty.
>
> The evident object of the efforts to make this cry, 'Remember Orr', stir up the people to rebellion, cannot be mistaken—that object was to single out an individual case of suffering for the cause of the Union, for the sympathy of the nation, and to turn that sympathy to the account of the cause.[84]

---

was produced as incriminating evidence at a trial on 5 July 1798; see William Ridgeway, *A Report of the Trial of Michael-William Byrne, Upon an Indictment for High Treason* (Dublin: printed by John Exshaw, 1798), p. 128. Several other United Irish songs referred to Orr, including 'Union's Your Helm' ('O Orr! Who died for all, While we have breath, And in our death we will avenge your fall'); 'Paddy's Demands' ('While they have their Harts and their Orrs for a toast'); 'Fly to Arms—Brave the Field' ('And when on martyred Orr you think'); see Madden, *Literary Remains of the United Irishmen*, pp. 23, 159, 160, 317.

[81] John Edward Newell to Lord Camden, 21 February 1798, Pratt Manuscripts, KHLC U840/O197/3.

[82] *The Report from the Secret Committee of the House of Commons* (Dublin: printed by J. King and A. B. King, 1798), Appendix XX, p. 208.

[83] Henry Grattan, Jr, *Memoirs of the Life and Times of the Rt. Hon. Henry Grattan* (London: Henry Colburn, 1849), 4, p. 319.

[84] Madden, *The United Irishmen*, 2nd ser., 2nd edn, vol. 2 (1858), pp. 253–4.

The persecution of Orr, as noted by James McHenry—an author who lived through the events as a child and later retold the story in a work of historical fiction—inspired many others to fight for the United Irish cause and effectively triggered the insurrection:

> The blood of martyrs has been truly said to be like seed to the cause for which they suffered; and perhaps, in no portion of the history of nations, has this truth been more clearly illustrated than in that we have just recited. The unnecessary, unjust, impolitic, and cruel execution of William Orr, almost instantaneously resulted in thousands of William Orrs, or rather of characters such as he was accused of being, starting into existence, and vowing revenge upon his persecutors.[85]

Above all, his memory was conspicuously present in Ulster in June 1798, when 'Remember Orr' was used as a battle cry by the insurgents of Antrim and Down.

The ritualized practices through which the martyrdom of Orr was constructed offered a template for the remembrance of the celebrated United Irish leaders who died in consequence of partaking in rebellion, such as Bartholomew Teeling and Wolfe Tone (both of whom had taken part in failed French invasion attempts). Seeking to rekindle the embers of 1798, Robert Emmet organized another insurrection and among his papers were found United Irish proclamations, including those previously issued by the Sheares brothers, which ended with the exhortation 'Remember Orr'.[86] After the collapse of Emmet's aborted rising and his execution, the inspiration of Orr's protomartyrdom was particularly noticeable in the ornate commemoration of Emmet, who became to be regarded as the most beloved of Irish republican martyrs.[87] The patterns of memorialization, which were originally established in the lead up to the rebellion, were later revived and magnified by nationalist mythographers. Hence, memory of the 1798 rebellion began before the rebellion.

In truth, the martyrdom of Orr was accidental. His background was fairly unexceptional and it would seem that the sole reason for his elevation to heroic grandeur was his sociability. He was a well-to-do Presbyterian farmer from Farranshane, county Antrim, aptly described by the contemporary historian Rev. James Bentley Gordon as 'a man of good family and connexions'.[88] If zealous revolutionaries seem to be intent on martyrdom from birth, while devotees strive to achieve martyrdom by emulating noble deeds, Orr had martyrdom thrust upon him, and, with the help of his friends and supporters, he rose to the task admirably. The government, in its dogged determination to prevent his glorification, unintentionally contributed to his apotheosis.

---

[85] Solomon Secondsight [James McHenry], *The Insurgent Chief; or, O'Halloran: An Irish Historical Tale of 1798* (Philadelphia: H. C. Carey and London: A. K. Newman & Co., 1824; reprint), 3, pp. 273–4. For McHenry's writings on the rebellion see Chapter 3, pp. 185–6, 191–5 and 200–1.

[86] NLI MS 8079.

[87] For Emmet's memory see Marianne Elliott, *Robert Emmet: The Making of a Legend* (London: Profile Books, 2003); Ruan O'Donnell, *Remember Emmet: Images of the Life and Legacy of Robert Emmet* (Bray: Wordwell, 2003); Kevin Whelan, 'Robert Emmet: Between History and Memory', *History Ireland*, 11, no. 3 (2003): pp. 50–4.

[88] James Gordon, *History of the Rebellion in Ireland, in the Year 1798 &C., Containing an Impartial Account of the Proceedings of the Irish Revolutionists, from the Year 1782 Till the Suppression of the Rebellion* (Dublin: printed by William Porter, 1801), p. 70n.

Orr was first brought to the attention of the authorities by an informer, Samuel Turner (alias Richardson) of Newry.[89] Aware that a warrant had been issued for his arrest, Orr went into hiding in July 1796 but was apprehended after two months of searches, when he paid a visit to his dying father 'Old Sam Orr' of Kilbegs.[90] Many decades later, an old woman from the neighbourhood, who died around 1876 and retained a 'very vivid impression of the closing years of the last century', recalled the exasperation in the locality upon receiving the news of his arrest.[91] Incriminating evidence had been gathered by the magistrate Rev. George Macartney, the Church of Ireland vicar of Antrim. It was alleged that, in April 1796, Orr had suborned into the United Irishmen two soldiers—lance corporal Hugh Wheatley and private John Lindsay—of the Fifeshire Fencibles, a Scottish regiment stationed in Ulster as part of the government's counter-insurgency measures.[92] He was charged under a recently enacted Insurrection Act (36 Geo. II c. 20), which rendered the administering of seditious oaths a felony punishable by death.[93]

The struggle over what would be forgotten and what would be remembered permeates all historical knowledge of Orr. Even accounts of his physical appearance were subject to partisan representations. At the time of his incarceration, he attracted universal sympathy. The *Belfast News-Letter*, though firmly opposed to the United Irishmen, generously noted that he was 'remarkably good looking, and [had] much the appearance of a gentleman'.[94] His supporters elaborated on the virtues of his comeliness.

Sensing that 'the Irish nation feels highly interested in whatever relates to the unfortunate William Orr', one of his visitors in jail subsequently published a detailed 'description of that ever to be venerated martyr' in which he was presented as an ideal image of manliness ('it is a question if a finer fellow could have been found'). Orr was portrayed as perfectly handsome ('nothing can be conceived more completely formed than every part of his body') and impeccably dressed ('his apparel appeared to be all new and fashionable'). In writing this flattering pen portrait, the pseudonymous author 'Humanitas' noted: 'I am the more scrupulous and minute, as I understand some of the Irish artists are meditating an engraving of their countryman.'[95] This deliberate bid to formulate

---

[89] The informer, who is mentioned anonymously by the Victorian historian James Anthony Froude, was identified by W. J. Fitzpatrick. See J. A. Froude, *The English in Ireland in the Eighteenth Century* (New York: Scribner, Armstrong, and Co., 1873), 3, pp. 179–80; W. J. Fitzpatrick, *Secret Service under Pitt* (London and New York: Longmans, Green, and Co., 1892), p. 55.

[90] Robert Macartney to Rev. George Macartney, [15] September 1797, Rebellion Papers, NAI 620/25/132.

[91] W. S. Smith, *Historical Gleanings in Antrim and Neighbourhood* (Belfast: Alex. Mayne & Boyd, 1888), pp. 17–19.

[92] Examination of Hugh Wheatley, Lance Corporal and John Lindsay, a private soldier in his Majesties' Fife Shire Fencible Regiment, 17 July 1796, Rebellion Papers, NAI 620/24/41.

[93] See *An Act More Effectually to Suppress Insurrections, and Prevent the Disturbance of the Publick Peace* (Dublin: printed by George Grierson, 1796), pp. 5–8 (the bill was introduced on 22 February 1796 and given royal assent on 24 March).

[94] *BNL*, 22 September 1797, p. 3.

[95] *Press*, 21 December 1797. A similar adulatory description appeared in a contemporary account of the trial; see *A Brief Account of the Trial of William Orr, of Farranshane, in the County of Antrim* (Dublin: printed by J. Chambers, 1797), p. 35. For the idealization of Orr as 'a widely accessible model of manly behaviour' see Nancy J. Curtin, 'Reclaiming Gender: Transgressive Identities in Modern Ireland', in *'A Nation of Abortive Men': Gendered Citizenship and Early Irish Republicanism*, edited by Marilyn Cohen and Nancy J. Curtin (New York: St Martin's Press, 1999), pp. 40–2.

an iconic visual memory was successful insofar as it was later considered authentic.[96] Its lasting impact is apparent in the artistic portraits of Orr a century later, which would be modelled on this romanticized textual depiction.[97]

However, such valorizing was unacceptable to those loyal to the Crown and was disputed by Arthur Chichester Macartney, the son of Rev. George Macartney, the magistrate who had issued Orr's arrest warrant. Interviewed by Madden some three decades later, Macartney, Jr (who in the meanwhile had succeeded his father as vicar of Belfast) recalled how he had personally arrested Orr and insisted that 'the fact is he was a very ordinary man, [a] wild dissipated young man of very loose morals and very moderate abilities.' Macartney conceded that Orr was 'popular among his class', but attributed this popularity to his being 'a frequenter of cockfights, drinking bouts in public houses and a fair-going boisterous sporting young man' and claimed that, rather than being 'a patriot of great and noble qualities', he was 'irregular in his habits and of very moderate abilities'.[98]

Madden, who regularly consulted personal testimonies and was therefore in a position to assess their credibility, acknowledged the trustworthiness of this account. His impression of Macartney was that 'this gentleman would have served the party to which he unfortunately belonged at the expense of his life, but, to the best of my opinion, not at the expense of truth.'[99] Madden even declared that 'a clearer statement of facts and opinions in reference to this subject I never heard given by any person on either side.'[100] Nonetheless, in preparing his notes for publication, he chose to sanitize this unflattering description and omitted the deprecatory comments.[101] Madden's monumental *The United Irishmen: Their Lives and Times*, which was published over a time frame of twenty-five years, between 1842 to 1867, in multiple series and editions that amounted to a total of eleven volumes, practically defined the pantheon of early republican heroes—including Orr—and elevated them into national idols.[102] Canonization entailed subtle erasure, employing selective editing as an instrument for the intended forgetting of inconvenient information. This form of behind-the-scenes editorial expurgation is less noticeable than the centre-stage struggles between official attempts to impose amnesia and popular determination to remember, which typified social forgetting in its early stages.

Orr was committed to Carrickfergus jail by Lord Castlereagh on 17 September 1796.[103] The authorities availed of the suspension of Habeas Corpus the following month (37 George III c.1) and were in no rush to prosecute, so that he was held in prison without trial for a year. The United Irish organ *The Northern Star* reported on rumours of 'severe treatment' of the many detainees rounded up in Antrim. The public

[96] See 'Notes and Queries', in *Ulster Journal of Archaeology*, 2nd ser., 1, no. 1 (1894), p. 78.

[97] A painting and sketch by Edwin Arthur Morrow (1877–1952) and a drawing by Joseph William Carey (1859–1937) were reproduced in Francis Joseph Bigger, *Remember Orr* (Dublin: Maunsel & Co., 1906), pp. 10 and 78 (Morrow), 41 (Carey).

[98] Madden Papers, TCD 873/267. For the involvement of Arthur Macartney and his father in suppressing the rebellion see Maurice H. Fitzgerald Collis, 'Antrim Parish Church for Three Hundred Years', *UJA*, 2nd ser., 3, no. 2 (January 1897): pp. 90–1.

[99] Madden, *The United Irishmen*, 2nd ser., 2nd edn, vol. 2 (1858), p. 254n.

[100] Madden Papers, TCD 873/267.

[101] The published account reads: 'he was a man of very moderate abilities; athletic in his frame, active, and somewhat of a sporting character among his class'; see Madden, *The United Irishmen*, 2nd ser. (1843), 2, p. 461.

[102] See Chapter 3 below, pp. 220–8.

[103] The warrant of imprisonment is reproduced in *A Brief Account of the Trial of William Orr*, p. 1.

was called upon to come to their aid, as 'when any persons are sent to prison it is necessary for their friends to send to them immediately, a bed with plenty of warm bedclothes, otherwise the prisoners will suffer severely of their health.'[104] In an impressive display of solidarity, the week after Orr's incarceration, a crowd of between five to six hundred of his neighbours gathered on a Friday morning to cut his harvest, professing that they 'would accept of no compensation'.[105]

The French travel writer de Latocnaye, who was travelling in Ulster around that time, was told that it was 'an old custom with the peasantry here to assemble at the end of the autumn and to dig up the potatoes of persons for whom they have any sort of affection'. He observed that the government was disturbed that this traditional practice had been co-opted in support of 'persons who had been arrested for high treason, or of persons who were known to be disaffected'.[106] Indeed, the United Irishmen resourcefully utilized these gatherings to great effect as part of their investment in propaganda by deed.[107] A political prisoner could expect to have 'his harvest reaped —his land tilled, and the wants of his family attended to by a kind and generous hearted peasantry in his absence'.[108] Local custom was politicized as part of what Kevin Whelan, paraphrasing the French historian Maurice Agulhon, labelled 'The Republic in the Village'.[109] At first, the pro-government press 'abstained from mentioning the curious circumstance that has repeatedly happened of late, of multitudes of people assembling to cut down the harvest of different Persons'. But the newspapers soon realized that their obligation 'as faithful historians of public proceedings' required mention of these mass public demonstrations, which were too substantial to be ignored.[110]

The week after the harvest, a vast crowd reassembled on Orr's land to gather the crop. The 'Hasty Shearing' was described in *The Northern Star* with the newspaper's characteristic irony, designed to both mock government reports of rebellious activities and to protect the publisher from charges of sedition:

> On Monday last, about 600 men assembled on the lands of William Orr, near Antrim, and armed themselves each with a sheaf of his oats under their shoulder, and proceeded to the attack of his hagyard, where they deposited their arms, after having got possession of the post without opposition.[111]

[104] *Northern Star*, 30 September to 3 October 1796, p. 3.

[105] *Northern Star*, 23 to 26 September 1796, p. 4.

[106] de Latocnaye, *Rambles through Ireland*, vol. 2, pp. 112–13. In the original: 'On m'a dit, que c'était une ancienne coutume établie parmi les paysans, de s'assembler sur le retour de la saison à la fin de l'automne et de déterrer les pommes de terre des personnes à qui ils veulent du bien'; de Latocnaye, *Promenade d'un français dans l'Irlande*, vol. 3, pp. 236–7.

[107] Curtin, *The United Irishmen*, pp. 241–5; see also Brendan Clifford, *Prison Adverts and Potatoe Diggings: Materials from the Public Life of Antrim and Down during the Years of Government Terror which led to the Rebellion of 1798* (Belfast: Athol, 1992).

[108] Charles Hamilton Teeling, *Sequel to Personal Narrative of the 'Irish Rebellion' of 1798* (Belfast: John Hodgson, 1832), p. 53.

[109] Whelan, *The Tree of Liberty*, pp. 62–74; cf. Maurice Agulhon, *The Republic in the Village: The People of the Var from the French Revolution to the Second Republic* (Cambridge: Cambridge University Press, 1982).

[110] *BNL*, 14 October 1796, p. 3. For a compilation of the reportage see Henry Joy, *Historical Collections Relative to the Town of Belfast from the Earliest Period to the Union with Britain* (Belfast: George Berwick, 1817), pp. 443–4.

[111] *Northern Star*, 3 to 7 October 1796, p. 3.

At the end of October, another mass gathering assembled for a 'hasty digging' of Orr's potatoes, which were raised 'in a short space of time'.[112] The supporters of this well-liked man had turned him into a *cause célèbre* deemed worthy of remembrance. Notably, publicity had been achieved through use of few words.

Words were a cause for concern for the government and its supporters, who were troubled by the radical publications of the *Northern Star*. Under the capable editorship of the United Irishman Samuel Neilson, the paper had developed an extensive distribution network, which was particularly strong in north-east Ulster.[113] Its average print run of over 4,000 copies reached an estimated readership of up to 40,000, surpassing the other Irish newspapers of its day. Repeated prosecution of the management, culminating in a military raid on its offices and the arrest of Neilson in September 1796, failed to put an end to the paper's publication.[114] On the contrary, the proprietor of the rival pro-government *Belfast News-Letter* (which, at its height, reached a print run of only 2,750) found that he was unable to compete with a surge in the popularity of the *Northern Star* and applied for subsidies from the government.[115] The growing popularity of the United Irish newspaper, which in some locations in Ulster was distributed gratis, seemed unstoppable.[116]

The *Northern Star* was finally muzzled on 19 May 1797, when the Monaghan Militia ransacked its offices and 'demolished the whole of the printing apparatus'.[117] General Lake, who was conveniently absent during the riot, expressed his 'extreme satisfaction' at the news of the destruction.[118] The printers claimed that a Sergeant-Major in the militia had told them that 'we are only executing orders of our officers.'[119] This charge was denied by the authorities, who claimed that the militiamen were disciplined for their unruly conduct, yet radicals insisted that they had not seen any proof that punishments had indeed been meted out.[120] Thomas Pelham, the Chief Secretary in Dublin Castle, denounced the destruction of the *Northern Star* as an 'outrage', but his condemnation was mitigated by an explicit understanding that 'the regiment should feel an indignation at the printers of that paper which had been

---

[112] *Northern Star*, 28 to 30 October 1796, p. 3.

[113] Brian MacDonald, 'Distribution of the *Northern Star*', *Ulster Local Studies*, 18, no. 2 (1982): pp. 54–68.

[114] Richard Robert Madden, *The History of Irish Periodical Literature, from the End of the 17th to the Middle of the 19th Century, Its Origins, Progress and Results* (London: T. C. Newby, 1867), vol. 2, pp. 225–35; O'Brien, 'Spirit, Impartiality and Independence'.

[115] George Gordon, Belfast, to Lord Downshire, 26 October 1796, Downshire Papers, PRONI D607/D/257. For the rivalry between the two papers see John Gray, 'A Tale of Two Newspapers: The Contest between the *Belfast News-Letter* and the *Northern Star* in the 1790s', in *An Uncommon Bookman: Essays in Memory of J. R. R. Adams*, edited by John Gray and Wesley McCann (Belfast: Linen Hall Library, 1996), pp. 175–98.

[116] See information from 'Statements to Secret Committee of House of Commons, Dublin', reproduced in John Thomas Gilbert, *Documents Relating to Ireland, 1795–1804* (Dublin: printed by J. Dollard, 1893), p. 108.

[117] Thomas Lane to Lord Downshire, 21 May 1797, Downshire Papers, PRONI D607/E/262; Pelham to Earl of Sheffield, 22 May 1797, Sheffield Papers, PRONI T2965/145.

[118] See Brian Inglis, *The Freedom of the Press in Ireland, 1784–1841* (London: Faber and Faber, 1954), p. 97.

[119] The accusation appeared in an account of the assault on the *Northern Star* office, which was printed on hand-bills soon after the event but was confiscated by the military before it could be distributed; reproduced in *A Brief Account of the Trial of William Orr*, pp. 42–5.

[120] *Press*, 9 December 1797, p. 4.

industriously circulated amongst them and had corrupted so many of their comrades as well as the whole province of Ulster.'[121]

For United Irishmen, the *Northern Star* had 'represented the moral force of Ulster' so that its destruction, as claimed by James Hope, 'silenced moral force for a time, and physical force was then resorted to, by the people, for the preservation of life and liberty'.[122] The liberal Earl of Moira, Francis Edward Rawdon-Hastings, insisted on government responsibility. Moira's vocal criticism of the brutal anti-insurgency policy in Ulster earned him the epithet 'Lord Longbow, the alarmist' in a satirical caricature by James Gillray.[123] The mockery was misguided. Moira's allegation that 'the destruction of the property by the military was done in order to check animadversions in other papers upon the conduct of Government' was not entirely off the mark.[124] From mid-1797 to the spring of 1798, the oppositional press in Ireland was systematically dismantled through repressive legislation and imposition of heavy taxes.[125]

For a short period, the void left by the *Northern Star* was filled by the *Press*, an equally radical newspaper launched in Dublin on 28 September 1797 by a group of United Irishmen headed by Arthur O'Connor. It attained instant success, reaching an unparalleled print-run of 6,000 copies.[126] As seen through the government's eyes:

> This paper, conducted on principles still more licentious than the *Northern Star* (which had contributed so largely to the extension of treason in the North) was distributed throughout all parts of the kingdom, and from the activity of its partisans, had immediately a more extensive circulation than any paper long established.[127]

The authorities were informed that 'it is read with as much avidity' as the *Northern Star* and that its articles were becoming 'more violent and desperate every day'.[128] With official concerns running high, the *Press* unsurprisingly met a similar fate to that of its predecessor. In February 1798, its printer, John Stockdale, was imprisoned. The following month, troops raided the newspaper's offices and destroyed the printing presses.[129] William Drennan who witnessed the remaining equipment being carried away to Dublin Castle likened it to the taking of 'the soul of the Dublin public'

[121] Thomas Pelham, Dublin, 2 November 1797, TNA HO 100/70/182.

[122] Madden, *The United Irishmen*, 3rd ser., vol. 1 (1846), pp. 232–3.

[123] James Gillray, 'Lord Longbow, the alarmist, discovering the miseries of Ireland' (hand-coloured etching, published by Hannah Humphrey, 12 March 1798), National Portrait Gallery, D13092.

[124] *The Parliamentary Register; or, History of the Proceedings and Debates of the Houses of Lords and Commons . . . During the Second Session of the Eighteenth Parliament of Great Britain*, vol. 4 (London: J. Debrett, 1798), p. 241.

[125] See Johanna Archbold, 'Periodical Reactions: The Effect of the 1798 Rebellion and the 1800 Act of Union on the Irish Monthly Periodical', in *Book Trade Connections from the Seventeenth to the Twentieth Centuries*, edited by John Hinks and Catherine Armstrong (New Castle, Del.: Oak Knoll Press; London: British Library, 2008), pp. 147–9.

[126] See Whelan, *The Tree of Liberty*, pp. 70–1.

[127] *Report from the Secret Committee of the House of Commons*, p. 13.

[128] Thomas Lane, Hillsborough, to Lord Downshire, 22 February 1798, Downshire Papers, PRONI D607/F/65; Pelham to Earl of Sheffield, 29 November 1797, Sheffield Papers, PRONI T2965/151.

[129] Madden, *The United Irishmen*, 3rd ser., 2nd edn (London: The Catholic Publishing & Bookselling Company and Dublin: J. Mullany 1860), p. 334 (mistakenly dated to 1797); Inglis, *The Freedom of the Press*, pp. 103–4.

and, in absence of media to chronicle this deed, regretted that 'it is not yet the time for history.'[130]

By the spring of 1798, all critical newspaper journalism had been quashed. Beyond the primary purpose of thwarting the United Irish conspiracy, the silencing of the radical press was an attempt to prevent the formation and circulation of interpretative narratives that disputed the official take on the development of the crisis in Ireland. Loyalist propaganda, such as a contrived *Letter from a Father to His Son, a United Irishman, in the Barony of Ards, in the County of Down*, aimed to discredit revolutionary agitation.[131] When looking back at the build-up towards the 1798 rebellion, the forced cessation of radical reportage on government repression can be seen as a contentious attempt to prevent prememory and initiate pre-forgetting. By recalling the example of William Orr, the United Irishmen defiantly claimed the right to uphold a radical counter-memory.

SILENCING

Apart from the reuse of the memory of William Orr at the time of the rebellion, there is also a more immediate sense in which the case of Orr exhibits workings of prememory. During his lifetime, as the events leading to his tragic death unfolded, several interested parties—including William Orr himself—were engaged in competing attempts to influence the way he would be remembered. Silencing was a main concern for the United Irishmen, who were apprehensive that the counter-memory of Orr would be suppressed before it could develop and that he would be forgotten. The origins of this discourse of pre-forgetting pre-dated his execution, so that Orr was being discussed in terms of forgetting even before he had died. It appears that preoccupation with oblivion can commence before an event has happened. In other words, at some level, forgetting can precede history!

When Orr was finally brought before the Antrim assizes and charged with 'administering unlawful oaths' on 18 September 1797, the United Irishmen recognized an opportunity of turning his court case into a memorable show trial that would expose government repression. He was represented by their most talented attorneys, John Philpot Curran and William Sampson, who mounted a defence that hinged on lack of clarity regarding the validity and expiry date of the Insurrection Act.[132] Despite their energetic legal efforts, the court proceedings were over in a single day and ended in conviction.[133] The tense atmosphere in the gallery was apparent in the muteness of the spectators. An 'exact statement of the trial' taken down by 'an eminent Stenographer' (probably Sampson) noted that 'during the whole of the trial the silence and anxiety of

[130] William Drennan to Martha McTier, Fast Day, March 1798; see Agnew, *Drennan-McTier Letters*, 2, p. 374.

[131] Anon. ['Publicola'], *A Letter from a Father to His Son, a United Irishman, in the Barony of Ards, in the County of Down* (Dublin: n.s., 1797).

[132] W. N. Osborough, 'Legal Aspects of the 1798 Rising, Its Suppression and the Aftermath', in *1798: A Bicentenary Perspective*, edited by Thomas Bartlett et al. (Dublin: Four Courts Press, 2003), p. 438n2. The hopes of United Irishmen that Orr could be acquitted on these grounds are evident in a letter written by William Drennan; see Agnew, *Drennan-McTier Letters*, 2, p. 337.

[133] *BNL*, 22 September 1797, pp. 2–3; *Freeman's Journal*, 28 September 1797, p. 4.

a crowded audience were singularly solemn and striking.'[134] An eyewitness confirmed that, throughout the deliberations, 'the public seemed sunk in silent and torpid suspense.'[135] This inability to talk is significant. Silence would feature as a leimotiv in the remembrance of Orr.

Even the presiding judge Lord Avonmore, Barry Yelverton, was 'scarcely articulate' and, upon pronouncing the sentence, 'burst into tears'.[136] This impassioned display was more than just a nod to the contemporary convention of expressing sorrow when condemning a criminal to death. Yelverton had previously been known as a liberal politician, who championed legislative reforms. He was an old acquaintance of the defence counsellor John Philpot Curran, their friendship going back to when they were both members of a convivial-political club nicknamed 'The Monks of the Screw', established by Yelverton in 1779.[137] He even shared a common significant experience with the defendant, as both of them had been members of the Volunteers. Since then, Yelverton had allied himself with the conservative establishment and was appointed chief baron of the exchequer. Although he was fully committed to the prosecution of United Irishmen, the description of his breakdown at the conclusion of the trial shows that he was genuinely rattled:

> he was so deeply affected as scarcely to be able, articulately, to conclude a very impressive address. The tears gushed down his eyes, and covered his face with both his hands, his Lordship, greatly agitated, remained in the situation for several minutes.[138]

The striking displays of speechlessness in the courtroom demonstrated the unsettling effect of Orr's case.

In determining Orr's guilt, the jury recommended that he should be shown mercy and this request (which, in private, was not supported by Yelverton) was duly submitted to Dublin Castle.[139] Consequently, the execution, originally set for 7 October, was postponed in order to allow for reconsideration. Heightened public interest in this affair was palpable. The publication of the *Belfast News-Letter* was stopped in the press in order to include a last-minute notice of a temporary 'Respite for Mr. Orr'.[140] Additional respites followed and during these intervals Dublin Castle was inundated by petitions on his behalf. It was widely expected that Orr would be pardoned, or that his sentence would be commuted.[141]

---

[134] *Press*, 19 October 1797, p. 1. For Sampson's authorship see Mary Helen Thuente, 'William Sampson: United Irish Satirist and Songwriter', *Eighteenth-Century Life*, 22, no. 3 (1998), p. 29.

[135] 'Extract of a Letter from Carrickfergus', in *Press*, 19 October 1797, p. 2.

[136] *Press*, 19 October 1797, p. 1.

[137] In this society, officially called the Monks of the Order of St Patrick, Yelverton was designated 'Founder' and Curran was the 'Prior'; see James Kelly, 'Elite Political Clubs, 1770–1800', in *Clubs and Societies in Eighteenth-Century Ireland*, edited by James Kelly and Martyn J. Powell (Dublin: Four Courts Press, 2010), pp. 268–74.

[138] *BNL*, 22 September 1797, p. 3.

[139] Lord Yelverton to Lord Camden, 19 September 1797, Pratt Manuscripts, KHLC U840/O31/1.

[140] *BNL*, 6 October 1797, p. 3.

[141] See correspondence and statements concerning William Orr, Pratt Manuscripts, KHLC U840/O31; in particular items numbered 7 (Address to Lord Camden and Lord Yelverton, n.d.), 9 (William John Skeffington to Camden, Chichester Skeffington to W. J. Skeffington, and William Bristow to W. J. Skeffington, 10 October 1797), 10 (Petition to Lord Camden, 12 October 1797), and 11 (George Macartney to W. J. Skeffington, 12 October 1797).

Expressions of sympathy came from far and wide and were not confined to radical cliques. The moderate liberal Dr Alexander Henry Haliday maintained that Orr had 'a character without reproach' and that the pleas for his reprieve were made 'by most respectable people, and on strong grounds'.[142] Lady Londonderry, the stepmother of Lord Castlereagh, tried to intercede and prevent the execution. Reportage in the conservative press avoided the associations of malevolence that were regularly applied to those accused of being United Irishmen and showed unusual sensitivity by referring to Orr as an 'unfortunate' individual. The authorities in Dublin Castle became increasingly troubled by reports of public rejoicings at the prospect that Orr might be set free and were wary of the reactions to the execution.[143] The efforts to spare Orr's life had begun to fashion him as a martyr ahead of his death.

The seemingly clear-cut verdict delivered by the court was undermined by an unofficial trial, which took place in the public sphere and reflected popular rejection of the legitimacy of military repression. Radicals spread allegations of miscarriage of justice and refused to recognize Orr's guilt. William Drennan was informed by his sister, Martha McTier, of the emergence of evidence that seemed to discredit the soldier on whose testimony the conviction had been reached, rendering the case 'the most flagrant breach of it [i.e. justice] ever known in this part of the world'.[144] Rumours circulated that the conspicuously packed jury had been drunk during the deliberations and that intimidation was applied to secure a unanimous conviction. Henry Joy McCracken, who at the time was imprisoned in Kilmainham jail, was told by his sister, Mary Ann McCracken, that a jury member 'was beaten, and threatened with being wrecked, and not left a six-pence in the world, on his refusing to bring in a verdict of guilty'.[145]

Supporters of the government were disturbed by 'gross misrepresentation' of Orr's case in the 'disaffected prints'. The 'scribbling advocates of the unfortunate man' were cautioned that:

> they should recollect the punishment due to those who unjustly expose to suspicion the proceedings of any court of criminal judicature or shall charge such with error or partiality; they should remember also, that unfounded attack against the impartial administration of public justice is a crime of the foulest injury to the judges of the land, that it lessens the public confidence in the laws themselves, and ultimately shakes the foundation of public protection and tranquillity.

The more shrill supporters of Orr may have done him a disservice, as loyalists became convinced that 'an example is necessary' and resolved to thwart the efforts for a reprieve.[146]

---

[142] Alexander Haliday to Lord Charlemont, 6 October 1797; reproduced in Gilbert, *Manuscripts and Correspondence of Charlemont*, 2, pp. 306–7.

[143] Thomas Pelham to Lord Yelverton, 20 September 1797, Pratt Manuscripts, KHLC U840/O31/2. See also reference to letter from Colonel Barber in Bigger, *Remember Orr*, p. 38.

[144] Martha McTier, Belfast, to William Drennan, Dublin, postmarked 9 October 1797; Agnew, *Drennan-McTier Letters*, 2, pp. 340–1. Rev. George Macartney indeed collected a statement from Rev. James Elder, the Presbyterian minister of Finroy parish in county Antrim, which seemed to put in disrepute the character of Wheatley, who was the main witness for the prosecution; KHLC, Pratt Manuscripts, U840/O31/6.

[145] Mary Ann McCracken to Henry Joy McCracken, 27 September 1797; reproduced in Madden, *The United Irishmen*, 3rd ser., vol. 1 (1846), p. 164; also 2nd ser., 2nd edn, vol. 2 (1858), pp. 254–5.

[146] *Freeman's Journal*, 10 October 1797, p. 3.

At the summer assizes of 1797, twenty-seven defendants were found guilty of administering oaths, of whom only four were condemned to death.[147] It was therefore conceivable that Orr's sentence would be remitted. However, accusations of misconduct had pushed the authorities into a corner, from which bestowing a pardon would be seen as an admission of wrongdoing. Moreover, the government was determined to demonstrate its ability to crack down on the United Irish organization in Ulster and prevent rebellion. The Chief Secretary, Pelham, insisted that an example would have to be made and, after giving the matter consideration, the Lord Lieutenant, Earl Camden, decided to uphold the verdict and ruled that 'the law must take its course.'[148]

The execution was rescheduled for 14 October 1796 and, given the extent of public interest, substantial resistance was anticipated. Orr was escorted along the road leading out of Carrickfergus to the Gallows Green by an exceptionally formidable guard:

> A considerable number of military consisting of part of the Fifeshire fencibles, the Monaghan militia, the Reay fencibles, the Carrickfergus invalids, a part of the 22d dragoons, and the Carickfergus yeomen cavalry, as also a party of the artillery, with two pieces of cannon were attending. The High Sheriff, on horseback preceded the carriage, and the Sub-Sheriff, on horseback followed it.[149]

This impressive show of arms was unnecessary, as the local public appeared to be stunned. Once again, popular response to the ordeal was marked by silence.

An eyewitness from Carrickfergus described the sombre scene on the day of the hanging:

> The inhabitants of this town, man, woman, and child, quit the place this day, rather than be present at the execution of their hapless countryman, William Orr. Some removed to a distance of many miles—scarce a sentence was interchanged during the day, and every face presented a picture of the deepest melancholy, horror and indignation.[150]

This pattern of restrained behaviour would be later repeated at the executions that followed the 1798 rebellion. Memories of such horror-struck reactions were noted a half-century later in the area of Ballymena, county Antrim:

> We have heard a friend say that, though he was then a mere child, the impression made on his memory by the cavalcade in escort of the prisoners to execution was indescribable. He knew, he said, from the solemn silence which pervaded the dwelling of his family—the closed doors—the darkened windows—and the whispered communications between the senior member[s], that something extraordinary was about to happen.[151]

Whereas social memory is traditionally transmitted through oral communication, these recollections were part of a memory of silence, which was shared in intimate, less vocal, circumstances.

---

[147] Michael Durey, 'Loyalty in an Age of Conspiracy: The Oath-Filled Civil War in Ireland 1795–1799', in *Unrespectable Radicals?: Popular Politics in the Age of Reform*, edited by Michael T. Davis and Paul A. Pickering (Aldershot and Burlington: Ashgate, 2008), p. 82.

[148] Thomas Pelham to Lord Yelverton, 20 September 1797, Pratt Manuscripts, KHLC U840/O31/2; *BNL*, 13 October 1797, p. 2.

[149] Originally published in *BNL*, 16 October 1797; republished in *Dublin Evening Post*, 19 October 1797, p. 3; *BNL*, 20 October 1797, pp. 2–3 (with additional affidavit); *Freeman's Journal*, 21 October 1797, p. 3.

[150] 'Extract of a Letter from Carrickfergus' (14 October 1797); *Press*, 17 October 1797, p. 3.

[151] *Old Ballymena: A History of Ballymena during the 1798 Rebellion* (Ballymena: Ballymena Observer, 1857), p. 49.

The withdrawal of the public from the scene of the execution had denied Orr an audience for his most significant act of prememory. After engaging in 'devotional exercises' with Rev. William Stavely and Rev. Adam Hill, the two ministers who had accompanied him to the gallows, he drew from his pockets a 'dying declaration', which, in absence of a crowd, could only be read out to the military guard. This statement had been written in the presence of a minister, Rev. John Savage, nine days earlier (5 October). In coming to terms with the inevitability of his death, Orr was primarily concerned with his reputation—'which is dearer to me than Life'—and troubled that he may be remembered unfavourably, or even forgotten. He therefore made a final appeal: 'I trust that all my virtuous countrymen will bear me in kind Remembrance.'[152]

Orr's declaration was intended for distribution. Printed copies had been prepared in advance by Mathew Smith, a nephew of Samuel Neilson who assumed responsibility for publishing the last issues of the *Northern Star* following the arrest of his uncle. The High Sherriff of County Antrim returned from the execution with a copy and believed that urgent measures should be taken to prevent its dessemination.[153] Smith's house was raided by the military and the hand bills with the declaration were confiscated before they could be circulated.[154] However, this attempt at stifling embryonic remembrance—and to forcefully impose pre-forgetting—proved to be futile, as the authorities were unable to prevent further prints.

Three days after the execution, Orr's dying declaration was published in the *Press*. Soon after, it reappeared in partisan accounts of the trial and other associated publications issued by United Irishmen in Dublin, Belfast, and Philadelphia. It was even reproduced in the non-political *Walker's Hibernian Magazine*. In addition, handwritten copies abounded. From beyond the grave, Orr triumphantly continued to declare: 'I glory in my Innocence.'[155] His moving words politicized the popular eighteenth-century genre of gallows speeches and effectively inaugurated a new literary form.[156] Rhetorical addresses by condemned republicans would flourish in the nineteenth century and attain canonical status in the collection *Speeches from the Dock*, first published in 1867 and reissued continuously in numerous editions. The inclusion of Orr's declaration at the beginning of this seminal anthology, which has been acclaimed as 'one of the most influential books in nineteenth-century Irish nationalist literature', affirmed his status as the republican protomartyr.[157]

---

[152] 'The Dying Declaration of William Orr, Ferranshane, Co. Antrim', PRONI T1901/1; also Pratt Manuscripts, KHLC U840/O31/12A.

[153] Chichester Skeffington to Camden, Pratt Manuscripts, KHLC U840/O31/12.

[154] Humphrey Galbraith, D[onagha]dee, to Lord [Downshire], 21 October 1797, Downshire Papers, PRONI D607/E/344; 'Extract of a Letter from Belfast', *Press*, 21 October 1797, p. 3. See also *A Brief Account of the Trial of William Orr*, pp. 41–2.

[155] *Press*, 17 October 1797, pp. 2–3; *A Brief Account of the Trial of William Orr*, pp. 38–40; *Billy Bluff and 'Squire Firebrand; or, a Sample of the Times, as It Periodically Appeared in the Northern Star* (Belfast, 1797), pp. 27–8; *The Trial of William Orr, at Carrickfergus Assizes, for Being an United Irishman; with His Dying Declaration* (Philadelphia, 1798), pp. 15–16; *Walker's Hibernian Magazine, or Compendium of Entertaining Knowledge*, October, pp. 356–7. For a handwritten copy see PRONI D1494/2/11 [MIC 506/1].

[156] Kevin Whelan, 'Introduction to Section V', in *1798: A Bicentenary Perspective*, edited by Thomas Bartlett et al. (Dublin: Four Courts Press, 2003), p. 388. Cf. James Kelly, *Gallows Speeches from Eighteenth-Century Ireland* (Dublin: Four Courts Press, 2001), pp. 40–1.

[157] Out of deference, Orr's declaration appears immediately after the courtroom speech of Wolfe Tone; T. D. Sullivan, A. M. Sullivan, and D. B. Sullivan, *Speeches from the Dock; or, Protests of Irish*

At the time of its original issue, the declaration was part of a struggle for predetermining Orr's public memory. Shortly after the trial, the *Belfast News-Letter* reported that it had heard 'from the best and most respectable authority' that Orr had written a confession of his guilt and this sensational news item soon circulated in the loyalist press.[158] The disclosure was expected to deal a heavy blow to 'the manufacturers of the seditious prints'.[159] It transpired that the source of the information was Dublin Castle, which had acquired a handwritten confession dated 24 September, yet its authenticity was soon called into question. Orr wrote to the Lord Lieutenant on 10 October, seeking 'to contradict a most cruel and injurious publication which has been put into the newspapers' and stated that, even though he had been made to understand that admission of guilt would save his life, he had 'decidedly refused' to sign a confession.[160] At his execution, Orr used his dying declaration as a 'solemn method of contradicting that calumny' and made a point of publicly denouncing the 'false and ungenerous publication' that had tarnished his reputation.

The radical *Press* complained about the 'flagitious persistency' with which newspapers aligned with the government, such as *Faulkiner's Dublin Journal*, were trying 'to murder the fair fame of the martyred Mr. Orr'.[161] Some members of the Ascendancy were willing to accept that they may have been duped by the rumours of 'a spurious confession' after William Tankerville Chamberlain, the second judge at Orr's trial, declared that it was 'totally false'.[162] However, the High Sherriff of Antrim, Chichester Skeffington, and the Sovereign of Belfast, William Bristow, issued public notices, backed by affidavits, which were designed to refute Orr's declaration and confirm the validity of his confession.[163] In response, William's brother—James Orr—revealed that he was in fact the author of the confession, 'the whole transaction being entirely my act, and not that of my brother, as he utterly refused'.[164] This startling revelation was reissued in the *Press*, which also published the letter William Orr had written to Lord Camden in which he resolutely professed his innocence.[165]

The struggle over how Orr would be remembered, which had commenced during his imprisonment, continued in full swing after his death. A fortnight after the execution, on 27 October 1797, the *Press* published on its front page an open letter to the Lord Lieutenant, railing that in 'the death of Mr. Orr, the nation has promoted

---

Patriotism (Providence: H. McElroy, Murphy, and McCarthy, 1878; this 1st US edn corresponds to 23rd Dublin edn), pp. 28–31. For the book's impact see David George Boyce, '"A Gallous Story and a Dirty Deed": Political Martyrdom in Ireland since 1867', in *Ireland's Terrorist Dilemma*, edited by Yonah Alexander and Alan O'Day (Dordrecht, Boston, and Lancaster: Martinus Nijhoff, 1986), p. 14.

[158] *BNL*, 29 September 1797, p. 2. For an example of republication see *Finn's Leinster Journal*, 7 October 1797, p. 3.

[159] *Freeman's Journal*, 7 October 1798, p. 3.

[160] William Orr to Lord Camden, 10 October 1797, Pratt Manuscripts, KHLC U840/O31/8. For the confession document see U840/O31/3.

[161] *Press*, 19 October 1797, p. 2.

[162] Lord Ely, Dublin, to Archbishop Charles Agar, 19 October 1797, Normanton Papers, PRONI T3719/C/31/93.

[163] *BNL*, 20 October 1797, pp. 2–3; *Freeman's Journal*, 21 October 1797, p. 3.

[164] *BNL*, 20 October 1797, p. 2. James Staples, a member of parliament for county Antrim, was named as one of the people who had promised to secure a pardon for Orr in exchange for the false confession but subsequently denied his involvement; *BNL*, 27 October 1797, p. 2.

[165] *Press*, 28 October 1797, p. 2 and 21 November 1797, p. 3.

one of the most sanguinary and savage acts that had disgraced the laws'. Camden was brazenly condemned for not stepping in to save Orr from 'the death that perjury, drunkenness, and reward had prepared for him'. Moreover, Camden's perceived culpability was seen as part of a more general responsibility for 'massacre and rape, military murders, desolation and terror'.[166] The letter was signed 'Marcus'. Its author was later shown to be Deane Theophilus Swift—the 'Dust of Drumcondra', a purported descendant of Jonathan Swift, who had acquired a reputation as an acerbic pamphleteer. On account of this article, he was hounded by the authorities and consequently refrained from writing further pieces on behalf of the United Irishmen. Swift vanished into obscurity until he was traced by Madden sixty years later and was found to be living in Gravesend, London, 'aloof from all factions and ambitions'.[167] The authorities were not satisfied with the silencing of the writer and were intent on also punishing the newspaper. In early November 1797, the printer and nominal proprietor of the *Press*, Peter Finnerty, was taken to court for publishing libel.[168]

The Finnerty trial was an attempt to suppress radical interpretations of the trial of William Orr before they could become public memory. The United Irishmen protested that 'public money is lavished to buy panegyricks on one side, and silence is enjoined upon the other.' In the name of 'liberty of the press', they refused to be silenced.[169] In another open letter to the Lord Lieutenant, an author going by the name of William Caxon reiterated the allegations previously made by Marcus, while he gingerly pretended that he 'can not possibly be supposed to allude to the case of Mr. Orr'. Camden was warned that 'he may take up a Printer every day; he may punish him as he pleases, but he never will stop the voice of truth, or impede the career of Liberty' and 'he never can gag our mouths'.[170]

The *Press* defiantly announced that 'the death of Mr. Orr is a topic that should never be relinquished.' Convinced that 'the public must feel a lively interest in every thing that concerns the suffering of the martyr'd Orr', the United Irish newspaper published affidavits by jurors who testified that they had been plied with 'very strong whiskey spirits' and were pressed upon to reach a verdict of guilty.[171] Publication followed of additional affidavits, which confirmed the rumours that the sole witness against Orr had been found to be unreliable.[172] The Finnerty court case took place on the background of this appeal to public opinion for a radical revision of the official memory of Orr's conviction.

In what appeared like a replaying of Orr's trial, Curran and Sampson once again took up the defence. Curran's long concluding speech, which would later be admired by nationalists as a classic example of Irish rhetoric, meticulously reviewed the details of Orr's trial in order to formulate an indictment of British government in Ireland.[173]

---

[166] *Press*, 26 October 1797, p. 1. A previous article by Marcus 'On the Liberty of the Press' was published on the day of Orr's execution; *Press*, 14 October 1797, p. 1.
[167] Madden, *United Irishmen*, 2nd ser., 2nd edn (1858), pp. 259–62.
[168] *BNL*, 6 November 1797, p. 4.   [169] *Press*, 23 December 1797, p. 3.
[170] *Press*, 5 December 1797, p. 1.   [171] *Press*, 5 December 1797, p. 3.
[172] *Press*, 21 December 1797, p. 3.
[173] *Press*, 30 December 1797, pp. 2–4. See also William Henry Curran, *The Life of the Right Honourable John Philpot Curran: Late Master of the Rolls in Ireland*, 2nd edn (Edinburgh: Archibald Constable & Co. and London: Hurst, Robinson & Co., 1822; orig. edn 1817), 1, pp. 308–24; Thomas Davis, ed., *The Speeches of The Right Honorable John Philpot Curran*, 4th edn (Dublin: James Duffy, 1862; orig. edn 1843), pp. 276–99.

The court could not afford to accept the damning accusation that Camden had acted 'inhumanly, wickedly and unjustly'. Finnerty was convicted of libel and was sentenced to stand in the pillory for an hour, serve in prison for two years, pay a fine of twenty pounds, and provide on his release hefty securities (in total of one thousand pounds) that would guarantee his 'good behaviour for seven years'. The unusually severe punishment was intended to send out a strong message that the dissemination of oppositional interpretations of Orr's trial was unacceptable. In a break of discipline, the Armagh militia violently harassed the 'immense course of people', including 'some most respectable citizens', who gathered to support Finnerty at the pillory.[174] As in previous cases when soldiers were let loose on the population, this unruly display of military force was seen to enforce government repression. Undeterred, the United Irishmen organized subscriptions to cover Finnerty's relief for the period of his imprisonment, making sure to maintain the anonymity of the donors in order to shield them from 'violence or persecution'.[175]

The case of Orr was picked up by radicals in England. The London *Courier* described his execution as 'Murder most Foul'.[176] Toasts at a birthday party for the Whig parliamentarian Charles James Fox included: 'The memory of William Orr, basely murdered' and 'May the Lord Lieutenant, and the Irish Cabinet, be seen in the situation of William Orr.'[177] Responding to criticism voiced by Lord Moira at a debate in the Irish House of Lords on 19 February 1798, the Lord High Chancellor, Lord Clare, was obliged to refute persistent accusations of misconduct at Orr's trial.[178] After the *Press* was closed down and the United Irishmen no longer had their own newspaper, an anthology titled *The Beauties of The Press* republished its most effective items on William Orr.[179] Despite the extensive repressive legislation at their disposal, the authorities were shown to be incapable of effacing the counter-memory that disobediently continued to champion Orr.

On a ground level, United Irishmen refused to forgive those they held responsible for Orr's death. On the night of 27 February 1798, the executioner was dragged naked from his bed and violently assaulted by a party of men who 'feloniously cut the ears out

---

[174] *Trial of Peter Finerty, Late Printer of the Press, for a Libel against His Excellency Earl Camden, Lord Lieutenant of Ireland, in a Letter Signed Marcus, in that Paper* (Dublin: printed by J. Stockdale, 1798). See also Inglis, *Freedom of the Press*, pp. 101–2.

[175] *Press*, 30 December 1797, p. 1.

[176] *Courier*, 25 December 1797; quoted in W. J. Fitzpatrick, *The Life, Times and Cotemporaries of Lord Cloncurry* (Dublin, 1855), p. 126n.

[177] John Gifford, *A History of the Political Life of the Right Honourable William Pitt; Including Some Account of the Times in Which He Lived* (London: T. Cadell and W. Davies, 1809), 6, pp. 434–5. The toasts were recalled in several versions; see for example: W. E. H. Lecky, *A History of Ireland in the Eighteenth Century* (London: Longmans, Green, and Co., 1913; orig. edn 1892), vol. 4, pp. 103–4 ('to the memory of the martyred Orr'); Samuel McSkimin, *The History and Antiquities of the County of the Town of Carrickfergus, from the Earliest Records Till 1839* (Belfast: Mullan & Son, James Cleeland, Davidson, and McCormack, 1909), p. 97n. ('May the Irish Cabinet soon take the place of William Orr'); Grattan, Jr, *Memoirs of the Life and Times*, 4, p. 319 ('May the execution of Orr provide places for the Cabinet of St, James's at the Castle').

[178] *The Debate in the Irish House of Peers on a Motion Made by the Earl of Moira, Monday, February 19, 1798* (Dublin: John Milliken, 1798), pp. 61–9; see also *The Speech of the Right Honourable John, Earl of Clare, Lord High Chancellor of Ireland, in the house of Lords of Ireland, Monday, February 19, 1798* (Dublin: s.n., 1798; re-issued in multiple editions in Dublin, Cork, London, and Oxford).

[179] See *The Beauties of The Press* (London: s.n., 1800), pp. 106–10, 250–5, 275, 312–40, 379–85.

of his head and left him for dead'.[180] The jurors were also subject to intimidation.[181] One of them, George Casement of Larne, recalled how, several days after the 'memorable trial', he was assaulted on the road. With the outbreak of the rebellion in his locality on 7 June 1798, Casement was notified that he had been designated 'the first person to be put to death'.[182] Oral traditions collected in the mid-nineteenth century by the local Presbyterian minister Rev. Classon Porter recounted how a relative, who had received inside information on the intended attack, arranged for Casement to go into hiding 'until the vengeance of the United Irishmen died out'.[183] In turn, Orr's family was targeted by loyalists. On 9 June 1798, their household was attacked by a party of yeomen from Antrim town, who pillaged the place and burnt it down. The widow and her six young children were forced to take shelter in a tenant's barn and, according to a claim filed twenty years later, the damage was evaluated between 2,500 to 3,000 pounds.[184]

The struggle over remembrance of Orr mirrored the conflict between official enforcement of counter-revolutionary emergency legislation and its popular rejection. Public memory, as conceived by the American historian John Bodnar, is situated at 'the intersection of official and vernacular cultural expressions'.[185] A related concept of popular memory, developed in the early 1980s by the Popular Memory Group at the University of Birmingham, pivots on two sets of dialectical relations—'between dominant memory and oppositional forms', as well as between 'public discourses in their contemporary state of play and the more privatized sense of the past which is generated within a lived culture'.[186] A fuller appreciation of these tensions requires awareness of a corresponding dynamic of 'popular forgetting', which is the outcome of struggles over silencing. In seeking legitimization for partisan interpretations of Orr's trial and execution, each side sought to invalidate, essentially to consign to oblivion, the opponent's claim on truth and justice. Silencing signalled an attempt to remove memory from the public sphere. However, the absence of speech, as argued by Eviatar Zerubavel, can demarcate the presence of a particularly salient issue, leaving an unavoidable 'elephant in the room'.[187] In effect, silence can function as a subtle mnemonic device.

Although the government's attempt to impose complete silence was unsuccessful, legal and military recrimination had impressed upon radicals the necessity for caution. As a result, early literary efforts to remember Orr reflected reticence. Under the

[180] Dickson, *Revolt in the North*, p. 182.

[181] See Durey, 'Loyalty in an Age of Conspiracy', p. 82.

[182] George Casement to George Anson McClevirty, 20 July 1798, Massereene-Foster Papers, PRONI D562/3038. See also see Rob Davison, 'George Casement and the United Irishmen', *North Irish Roots*, 9, no. 2 (1998), p. 12.

[183] Young, *Ulster in '98*, p. 50.

[184] J. Orr to Lord Castlereagh, 18 January 1819, NAI CSO/RP/1819/656.

[185] John E. Bodnar, *Remaking America: Public Memory, Commemoration, and Patriotism in the Twentieth Century* (Princeton: Princeton University Press, 1992), pp. 13–15.

[186] See Popular Memory Group, 'Popular Memory: Theory, Politics, Method', in *Making Histories: Studies in History-Writing and Politics*, edited by R. Johnson, G. McLennan, B. Schwartz, and D. Sutton (London: Hutchinson in association with the Centre for Contemporary Cultural Studies, University of Birmingham, 1982), pp. 205–52 [quotation from p. 211].

[187] See introduction chapter, p. 28.

pseudonym 'The Minstrel', William Drennan published in the *Press* his poem 'William, an Elegy', in which he commented on the silence that had followed Orr's death:

> Are your springs, Oh! ye Muses run dry?
> Has horror suspended their source!
> That yet nor a tear nor a sigh,
> Oh William! has hallow'd thy cor[p]se.[188]

The poet William Hamilton Drummond was subsequently inspired to compose an 'Elegiac Ode to the Honored Memory of William Orr'.[189] But it was Drennan who would return to write the definitive tribute to Orr in another poem, which he penned around the time of the execution and published three months later.

Drennan's poetic masterpiece first appeared under the lightly disguised title 'Wake of W——M. O——R.' and was later republished in a collection of Drennan's poems with the unspecific title 'The Wake'. It called for restrained and muted remembrance:

> Here our brother worthy lies,
> Wake not *him* with women's cries;
> Mourn the way that mankind ought;
> Sit, in silent trance of thought.

This appeal for silence was not a submission to censorship, but a form of clandestine vigilance:

> Here we watch our brother's sleep,
> Watch with us; but do not weep;
> Watch with us thro' dead of night,
> But expect the morning light.[190]

William Orr was to be commemorated guardedly, through feigned silence.

With this formulation, Drennan had created a poetic genre of veiled mourning that was distinct from the flagrantly sentimental expressions of grief in contemporary English literature.[191] Drennan's evocation of silence inspired Thomas Moore, an avid reader of the *Press* who would become the most celebrated Irish poet of the early nineteenth century. Moore famously perfected this style in his poem 'Oh! Breathe Not His Name', which depicted a hidden ritual of mourning through which Robert Emmet's execution in 1803 was commemorated:

> And the tear that we shed, though in secret it rolls,
> Shall long keep his memory green in our souls.[192]

The subversive political content of these poems was outwardly hidden. Yet, the implicit references to the identity of the commemorated United Irish heroes were recognizable to the intended readership and did not need to be spelt out.

---

[188] *Press*, 31 October 1797, p. 3. The poem was mainly recalled in a touched-up version published by Madden; see Madden, *Literary Remains of the United Irishmen*, pp. 43–4.

[189] *Press*, 23 November 1797, p. 2.

[190] *Press*, 13 January 1798, p. 3; Drennan, *Fugitive Pieces*, pp. 79–81.

[191] Cf. Esther H. Schor, *Bearing the Dead: The British Culture of Mourning from the Enlightenment to Victoria* (Princeton: Princeton University Press, 1994), esp. pp. 48–52.

[192] Thomas Moore, *A Selection of Irish Melodies* (Dublin: W. Powers, 1808), 1, no. 1, pp. 16–18. Drennan's influence is acknowledged in the poem 'The Farewell to the Harp', in which Moore notes that he borrowed from him a reference to 'the cold chain of silence'; see Thomas Moore, *Irish Melodies* (Philadelphia: M. Carey, 1815), p. 147n. For Moore's involvement with the *Press* see Mary Helen Thuente, *The Harp Restrung: The United Irishmen and the Rise of Irish Literary Nationalism* (Syracuse: Syracuse University Press, 1994), pp. 117–18.

Madden considered Drennan's poem 'a piece written with great power, and which, probably, had more effect on the public mind than any production of the day in prose or verse'.[193] In the mid-nineteenth century, it was enthusiastically endorsed by the romantic nationalists of Young Ireland and appeared in the multiple editions of Charles Gavan Duffy's popular anthology *The Ballad Poetry of Ireland*.[194] It was later described by a northern nationalist as 'that heart-quickening work which we, as youngsters of the early-nineteen-hundreds, were ever ambitious to recite'.[195] The poetic call for silence—not actual silence—embedded a discourse of omissions into the cultural memory of the United Irishmen.

Reserve was also apparent in local vernacular poetry. Writing mainly for an Antrim audience, the poet James Orr of Ballycarry in county Antrim composed 'The Execution', which appeared in print in 1804. It tells of a condemned man, who was lead to his hanging 'Thro' Carrickfergus' far-fam'd wall', and it dwells on his final stirring words, in what appears to be a reference to William Orr's dying declaration:

His last address had power to reach
Ev'n scornful hearts, tho' void of art:
Affecting still must be the speech
That simply leaves a feeling heart.

According to a biographical memoir written in the early nineteenth century, the poet was a nephew and intimate acquaintance of William Orr.[196] Regardless of this uncorroborated claim, James Orr was undoubtedly aware of William Orr's execution. The poem's ambivalence about the circumstances of the hanging—'I blame his deeds, but mourn his death'—appear to reflect the personal experience of the poet as a former United Irishmen. James Orr was among the rebels at the Battle of Antrim in 1798 and was obliged to flee for his life to America. He later returned to live in his home area, harbouring bitter memories of the rebellion. At the time when the poem was published, United Irishmen could not be lamented openly in public and the guarded verses, which refrain from naming the executed man, are yet another example of masked remembrance.[197]

Silent remembrance was not merely a figment of poetic imagination. Commemorative practices did not necessarily require words. For this purpose, fashion could be pressed in the use of counter-memory. The portrayal of Orr during his imprisonment complemented his stylish clothing and noted that he wore a green ribbon, as was the custom among United Irish prisoners.[198] It was later noted that 'the colour of his coat at the time he suffered became a kind of uniform dress.'[199] Imitative dressing-up was adopted as a non-verbal memorial practice.

[193] See Madden, *United Irishmen*, 1st ser. (1842), 2, p. 45; also 2nd ser., 2nd edn (1858), 2, p. 262 [dated mistakenly to 1791].
[194] *Nation*, 25 March 1843, p. 378; Charles Gavan Duffy, *The Ballad Poetry of Ireland*, 40th edn (Dublin: James Duffy, 1869; orig. edn 1845), pp. 70–2.
[195] F. P. Carey, 'The Shrines of the Patriot Dead', in *Ninety-Eight*, edited by Seamus McKearney (Belfast: The 1798 Commemoration Committee, 1948), pp. 59–61.
[196] George Pepper, 'Literary and Biographical Notices of Irish Authors and Artists: James Orr', in *Irish Shield and Monthly Milesian*, 1, no. 12 (1829), p. 450–2.
[197] James Orr, *Poems on Various Subjects* (Belfast: Smyth & Lyons, 1804), pp. 96–8. For the poetry of James Orr and the wider post-rebellion context in which it appeared see Chapter 3 below, pp. 180–2.
[198] *Press*, 21 December 1797, p. 3.   [199] McSkimin, *Annals of Ulster*, p. 91.

Orr's fashionable dress was mocked by loyalists, who formulated an alternative understanding of the execution, which presented Orr as a gullible pawn who had fallen prey to revolutionary scheming, rather than an ideologically committed victim of state oppression. The lengthy poetic composition *Orange: A Political Rhapsody*, which was probably written by John Giffard—a militant opponent of the United Irishmen—and was dedicated to the ultra-conservative politician John Claudius Beresford, put this interpretation in verse:

> Might farmer Orr have run his humble race,
> And never changed, or wish to change his place—
> But strong persuasion flowed from Grattan's tongue,
> And Orr believed—grew indiscreet—and hung.

The poem was first published in 1798 and its reissue in nine editions is indicative of the enthusiasm with which it was received in loyalist circles.[200] The notion that Orr had been misled was another aspect of prememory that fed into an ambiguous memory of 1798, in which the defeated United Irishmen of Ulster would be remembered by their loyalist descendants as reluctant rebels.

Another form of coded remembrance, which did not have to be spoken about and was practised in everyday circumstances, is apparent in the naming of children after Orr. This custom may have been inspired by the christening of his own daughter Wilhelmina, who was born shortly after the execution. It was soon adopted as a popular form of memorialization. For example, in 1798, Joseph McGaw and Laetitia Thoburn of Sunnyside in the parish of Carnmoney, county Antrim, expressed their indignation at the execution by calling their new-born son William Orr.[201] The tradition of naming children after Orr, which would continue into the twentieth century, was shared across the political divide, as noticed by the historian of the Orange Order Robert Mackie Sibbett, who hailed from Portglenone, county Antrim (near Ballymena): 'To this day the name is popular among those who are in sympathy with sedition, notwithstanding the fact that it also belongs to men conspicuous for loyalty.' Sibbett repeated the loyalist interpretation, explaining that Orr 'had unfortunately been duped, and he paid the penalty which worse than he escaped'. The fact that loyalists continued, however inadvertently, to remember Orr spoke for itself.[202]

A more esoteric practice of nonverbal memory may have been associated with the daily use of a set of corn-mill scales from Straid, near Gracehill, county Antrim, which was inscribed with William Orr's name. This artefact was dated 1803—the year of Robert Emmet's unsuccessful attempt to mobilize remaining United Irishmen—and a time when awareness of the prememory left over from 1798 was very much in the air. Philip Robinson, the former Head of Collections at the Ulster Folk and Transport

---

[200] *Orange: A Political Rhapsody* (Dublin: s.n., 1798), Canto II, p. 16 (verses 267–70). The commentary, which refers to Orr's clothing, may have been added by the printer, George Faulkner, Jr. For the historical context of this publication see Allan Blackstock, 'Politics and Print: A Case Study', in *The Oxford History of the Irish Book*, edited by Raymond Gillespie and Andrew Hadfield (Oxford and New York: Oxford University Press, 2006), vol. 3: *The Irish Book in English, 1550–1800*, pp. 234–49.
[201] William Orr McGaw, 'Notes on the Parish of Carnmoney, Co. Antrim', *Ulster Folklife*, 1 (1955), p. 56.
[202] R. M. Sibbett, *Orangeism in Ireland and Throughout the Empire* (Belfast: Henderson, 1914), 2, pp. 27–8.

Museum (which acquired the item in the mid-1980s) ventured an explanation of its secret commemorative function:

> In 1803 the metaphorical symbolism of this inscription would have been evident to most men using the Straid Mill: the scales of 'justice', with the inscription of a heart motif and the name of William Orr on a beam which would jerk with scaffold-like violence each time a sack of grain was thrown on.

Reference to a cipher that was in use in the area at the time suggests that the mention of the date may have also implied an encrypted religious allusion to I.N.R.I., thus evoking archetypal Christian martyrdom in association with Orr's execution.[203] For a long while, the rebellion could not be talked about openly in public, and yet silence was evidently making a strong sound.

ANTICIPATING FORGETTING

'Death is the most powerful agent of forgetting. But it is not all-powerful.' In reminding us of this simple truth, Harald Weinrich commented on the memorial limitations of funerary rites. Weinrich observed that 'gravestones always also serve as "monuments" warning the living not to forget their dead—and yet people often forget all too easily.'[204] Following his execution for treason, William Orr could not be memorialized freely. After the hanging, the corpse was removed by his friends and an unsuccessful attempt at resuscitation was made in a nearby house. The body was then taken on a hearse to the Presbyterian meeting house in Ballynure, where it was waked. The minister Rev. Adam Hill was subsequently arrested for hosting this forbidden event but was soon released, as nobody could be found to testify against him.[205] The government was made to realize that silence could also be used in defiance.

Orr's body was taken for burial to the graveyard in Templepatrick. An eyewitness later recalled seeing 'immense crowds, of both sexes, hurrying to witness the melancholy scene'.[206] A party of dragoons assigned to police the funerary procession encountered difficulties in dispersing the 'amazing concourse of people' that gathered along the road and surrounding hills.[207] In the sardonic account of the contemporary loyalist historian Sir Richard Musgrave, it was 'a most splendid funeral, which was attended by a numerous body of united Irishmen, who lamented in doleful accents the fate of this martyr to republican liberty, and bedewed his hearse with tears of sympathetick civism [sic]'.[208]

---

[203] UFTM L2403/1; Philip Robinson, 'Hanging Ropes and Buried Secrets', *Ulster Folklife*, 32 (1986): pp. 7–8. For the debacle of 1803 in Ulster and its resonance in social memory see Chapter 2 below, pp. 140–3.

[204] Weinrich, *Lethe*, p. 24.

[205] Account collected *c*.1906 by Alexander W. Forysthe of Ballynure from William Scott, whose father had attended the wake; Bigger Papers, Z401/6 [William Scott of Bryantang, Ballynure, is described in the 1901 census as an 80-year-old Unitarian farmer]. See also David Hume, *'To Right Some Things That We Thought Wrong': The Spirit of 1798 and Presbyterian Radicalism in Ulster* (Lurgan: Ulster Society, 1998), pp. 40–1.

[206] William Grimshaw, *Incidents Recalled; or, Sketches from Memory* (Philadelphia: G. B. Zieber, 1848), p. 24.

[207] *A Brief Account of the Trial of William Orr*, p. 41.

[208] Richard Musgrave, *Memoirs of the Different Rebellions in Ireland, from the Arrival of the English*, 3rd edn (Dublin: Robert Parchbank, 1802), 1, p. 217.

Not only United Irishmen attended the funeral. Orr was generally well liked in the area and his loyalist friends also came to pay their respects.[209] Much to the chagrin of the authorities, the execution had aroused widespread popular sympathy which could not be contained.

Orr was buried in a family plot, but his name was not inscribed on the grave. The tombstone only mentions Ally Orr, who is believed to have been his sister but may have actually been his mother or an aunt.[210] By early 1798, the *Press* noted that 'there is now in preparation, a monument to the memory of William Orr.'[211] The attempt by the United Irishmen to erect a memorial in advance of the rebellion epitomizes prememory. But conditions of repression and silencing made open commemoration impossible. The site of Orr's grave was tenaciously preserved in local memory and yet, being unmarked, it was always susceptible to forgetting. A century later, in 1896, visiting nationalists from Belfast found the grave covered in yew branches and wild roses. They realized that ever since the burial, 'in the long years that followed when men feared to speak of 'ninety-eight, his name was not cut on the stone.'[212] Although nationalists were committed to rectifying this situation, and returned the following year to decorate the grave, a proper memorial was not erected during the centennial commemorations of 1798.[213] It would take another century before the grave of William Orr was marked in 1998 with a modest plaque during the bicentenary of the rebellion.[214] Social forgetting of the United Irishmen, initiated in advance of the rebellion, would have a long life.

In absence of a monument, a furtive vernacular memorial culture developed immediately after Orr's death. The cap which had been placed over his head at the execution was cut up into pieces that were distributed among his friends, who 'cherished it as a most precious relick', and these revered mementoes were carefully preserved over the nineteenth century.[215] A range of purposely designed commemorative artefacts served as potent *aides-mémoire*. 'Remember Orr' was inscribed on 'mourning rings', some of which had Orr's hair set in them while others were wrought with silk. United Irishmen presented these memorial tokens to each other. The Belfast antiquarian Francis Joseph

---

[209] In the late nineteenth century, the antiquarian Rev. W. S. Smith heard from James Kirk of Whinpark, county Antrim, how his father Samuel Kirk—'a warm, Loyalist friend of the condemned man'—attended the execution and burial; Smith, *Memories of '98*, pp. 42–3.

[210] Bigger maintained that the inscription on the grave referred to his 'favourite sister'; Bigger, *Remember Orr*, p. 51. A party of nationalists from Belfast who visited the grave in 1896 were lead to believe that 'it is his mother's grave'; *SVV*, 1, no. 7 (July 1896), p. 140. In the early twentieth century, it was noted that 'some of the old people say that this Ally Orr was the aunt of William, and some say that she was his sister'; Robert Johnston, Lisnaveane, Antrim Road, Belfast, to [Henry] Dixon, 26 June 1913, Robert Johnston Papers, NLI MS 35,262/1. See also R. H. Foy, *Remembering All the Orrs: The Story of the Orr Families of Antrim and Their Involvement in the 1798 Rebellion* (Belfast: Ulster Historical Foundation, 1999), p. 33n14.

[211] *Press*, 8 February 1798, p. 2.   [212] *SVV*, 1, no. 7 (3 July 1896), p. 140.

[213] *SVV*, 2, no. 7 (5 July 1897), p. 129. For a sketch of the grave at the time see the publication of the '98 Centenary Committee, *The Story of William Orr* (Dublin: James Duffy, 1898), p. 13; for an early photograph see Fig. 3.1a, p. 154.

[214] See Chapter 7 below, p. 577.

[215] Musgrave, *Memoirs of the Different Rebellions*, 1, p. 217; see also McSkimin, *History and Antiquities*, p. 97n. Madden retained one of these cloths, which was given to him by Robb McGee of Belfast; Madden Papers, TCD 873/336. Another piece was kept by a member of the Orr family; Young, *Ulster in '98*, p. 89.

Bigger described one such ring, which had been originally presented by a relative of the deceased, Robert Orr:

> a little thin finger or scarf ring, hand-made, of gold. On one side is a round plate enclosing a green enamelled shamrock, with white enamel surrounding it. On the opposite side in an oval are the words, 'Remember Orr', and on each side of the plate in gaelic letters '*Erin go bragh*'.[216]

Henry Joy McCracken had a similar ring (presented to him by his friend Thomas Richardson) and, before his execution in July 1798, he bequeathed it to his mother. This act, which took place in Carrickfergus jail, the same prison in which Orr had been previously held, was essentially a gesture of prememory, which signified McCracken's readiness to imitate Orr's martyrdom.[217]

An assortment of memorial cards, silk rosettes, and custom-made watch-paper featured commemorative texts that were dedicated 'Sacred to the Memory of William Orr' and entreated 'Let us bear him in steadfast memory' (Fig. 1.3).[218] Medals were struck in his honour. One of these souvenirs was described by a respected nineteenth-century local historian, Hugh McCall of Lisburn:

> It is made of copper, and about the size of a penny piece of the old coinage. On one side is a figure of the Irish harp with spear and cap of freedom and the motto 'Liberty—remember William Orr'. On the obverse are the words 'May Orr's fate nerve the impartial arm to avenge the wrongs of Erin.'[219]

This overtly seditious memorabilia had to be carefully concealed. A search of the residence of Father Duffy in Drogheda—a radical Catholic priest, later described as a 'zealous patriot'—uncovered 'a laboured complimentary epitaph to the late William Orr' that had been hidden in a secret compartment in his desk.[220]

Oral traditions recalled the dangers of being caught in possession of these commemorative items. Hugh McCall would recount 'with great animation' the story of how a man was hanged in Hillsborough, county Down, after the medal described above was found concealed in his shoe.[221] He also noted that Tom Armstrong, a United Irishman who was executed in Lisburn after the rebellion, had been identified by a

---

[216] Bigger acquired the ring from a descendant of William Stevenson, of Springfield, Belfast, who had received it from Orr's widow and daughter; Bigger, *Remember Orr*, pp. 56–7.

[217] Madden, *United Irishmen*, 2nd ser. (1843), 2, p. 485.

[218] Young, *Ulster in '98*, pp. 89–90; Bigger, *Remember Orr*, pp. 55–8; *Guide to the Irish Volunteer, Yeomanry and Militia Relics*, p. 43; Maguire, *Up in Arms*, pp. 167–8.

[219] Anon. [Hugh McCall], *Ireland and Her Staple Manufactures: Being Sketches of the History and Progress of the Linen and Cotton Trades More Especially in the Northern Province*, 2nd edn (Belfast: Henry Greer, George Phillips & Son, 1865; orig. edn 1855), pp. 142–3; reproduced as 'Episodes of Ninety-Eight', in *Northern Whig*, 8 October 1867, p. 4. For an almost identical description see W. G. Lyttle, *Betsy Gray; or, Hearts of Down: A Tale of '98* (Newcastle, Co. Down: Mourne Observer, 1968; orig. edn 1888), p. 134. In the early twentieth century, such a medal was in the possession of the London coin dealers Messrs. Spink & Son; see R. D., 'A Memorial of 1798', *Journal of the Cork Historical and Archaeological Society*, ser. 2, 12 (1906), pp. 102–3. A silver 'Remember Orr' medal was put on display at the Belfast Museum in 1852; *Descriptive Catalogue of the Collection of Antiquities*, p. 27.

[220] *BNL*, 12 July 1798, p. 2; see also Richard Hayes, 'Priests in the Independence Movement of '98', in *The Irish Ecclesiastical Record*, 66 (1945), p. 264.

[221] McCall, *Ireland and Her Staple Manufactures*, pp. 142–3; see also *Some Recollections of Hugh McCall, Lisburn* (Lisburn: J. E. Reilly, 1899), p. 16. The medal was later kept in the possession of a conservative unionist; *Nation*, 18 February 1843, p. 296.

(a)

(b)

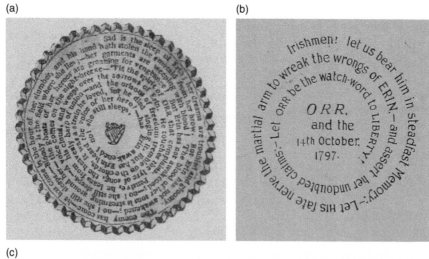

(c)

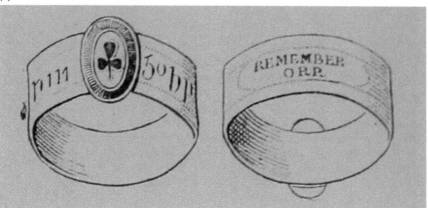

Fig. 1.3. William Orr memorabilia

(a) memorial silk rosette (pink); (b) memorial silk rosette (white); (c) memorial ring; (d) memorial card.
From the collections of Francis Joseph Bigger; reproduced in Bigger, *Remember Orr* (1906).

cockade inscribed 'Remember Orr', which was found in the lining of his hat.[222]
Travelling with 'a manuscript copy of verses written on the death of William Orr' in
his pocket and a cockade concealed in his hat, James Standfield of Lisburn was
stopped at a military station outside Ballymena and came within a hair's breadth of
being searched. Realizing that 'the discovery of such emblems of disaffection might
have been fatal', he made sure to dispose of them the moment he was out of sight.[223]
Bigger noticed that the commemorative ring in his possession had been repaired in
several places, 'the explanation being that it was smashed in pieces by Orr's daughter,
and then thrown away to hide it from the eyes of the soldiers, who were on the look
out for such "treasonable" articles, as its possession was made an offence punishable by

---

[222] Young, *Ulster in '98*, pp. 80–1.   [223] *Northern Whig*, 7 January 1867, p. 3.

(d)

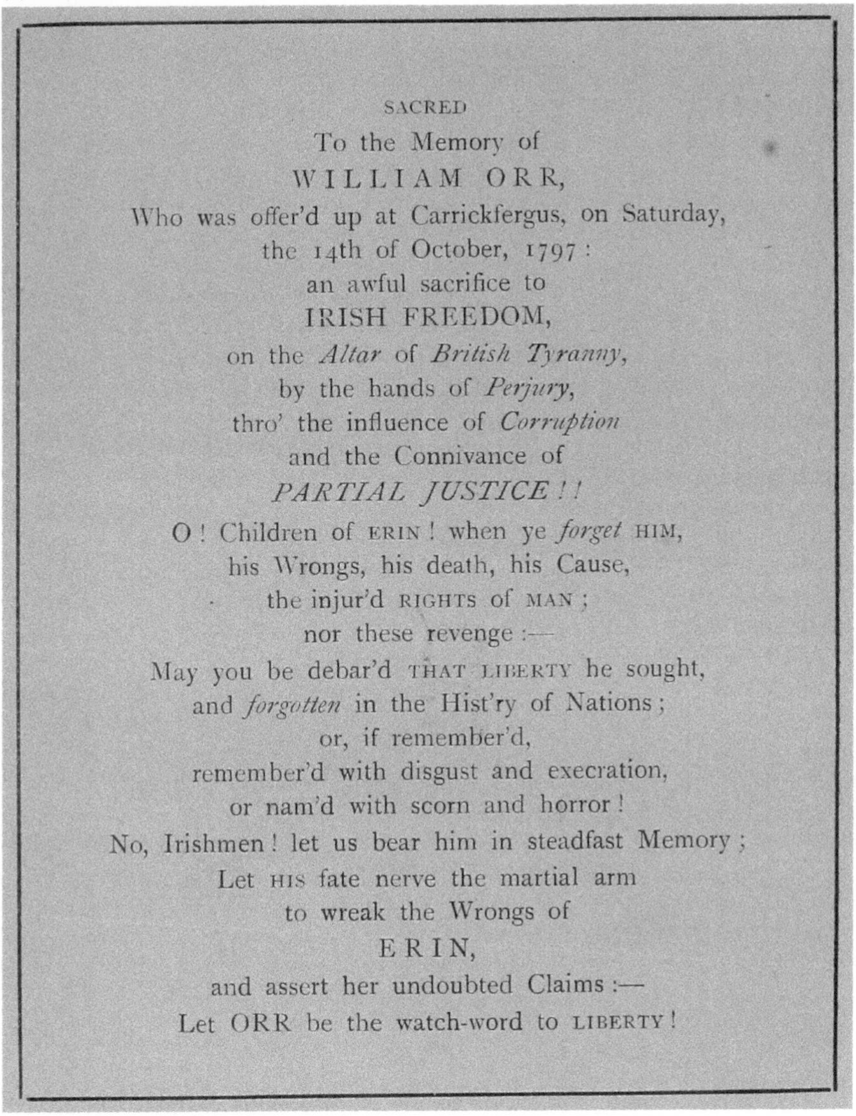

SACRED
To the Memory of
WILLIAM ORR,
Who was offer'd up at Carrickfergus, on Saturday,
the 14th of October, 1797 :
an awful sacrifice to
IRISH FREEDOM,
on the *Altar* of *British Tyranny,*
by the hands of *Perjury,*
thro' the influence of *Corruption*
and the Connivance of
PARTIAL JUSTICE !!
O ! Children of ERIN ! when ye *forget* HIM,
his Wrongs, his death, his Cause,
the injur'd RIGHTS of MAN ;
nor these revenge :—
May you be debar'd THAT LIBERTY he sought,
and *forgotten* in the Hist'ry of Nations ;
or, if remember'd,
remember'd with disgust and execration,
or nam'd with scorn and horror !
No, Irishmen ! let us bear him in steadfast Memory ;
Let HIS fate nerve the martial arm
to wreak the Wrongs of
E R I N,
and assert her undoubted Claims :—
Let ORR be the watch-word to LIBERTY !

Fig. 1.3. Continued

death.[224] By necessity, initial remembrance of Orr developed through an extremely cautious culture of clandestine commemoration.

Even when boldly announcing the imperative to 'Remember Orr', the wording on these souvenirs reflected concerns that his memory would be forsaken. A memorial card with an evocative text, which was believed to have originated as an epitaph composed by Wolfe Tone for Orr's tomb, included a pre-emptive denunciation of forgetting:

[224] Bigger, *Remember Orr*, p. 57.

'when YE *forget* HIM ... May you be debar'd THAT LIBERTY he sought, and *forgotten* in the Hist'ry of Nations; or, if remember'd, remember'd with disgust and execration, or nam'd with scorn and horror!'—the emphases on forgetting appeared in the original text.[225] A popular memorial poem, which first appeared in the *Press* as a 'fragment' (fashioned after the style of Macpherson's *Ossian*), was then circulated on commemorative rosettes, and even migrated with United Irishmen to America, portrayed Erin—a female representation of Ireland—in a tragic state of deep slumber ('sad is the sleep of Erin'), beset by enemies and drenched in the blood of her children. The inability of the ghostly 'spirit of Orr' to awaken Ireland in this poem appears to echo apprehensions that even determined remembrance might not triumph over forgetful indifference.[226] Remembrance of Orr was perforated with anxieties about forgetting.

Orr's attorney, William Sampson, was repeatedly penalized for his attempts to expose the excesses of the military and defend his fellow United Irishmen. In 1806, after a series of arrests and forced exiles, he finally gave in and relocated to America, where he enjoyed a successful legal career. Twenty-five years later, at a dinner held in his honour in Philadelphia's Congress Hall, he was toasted 'the defender of William Orr'. Sampson exhorted his audience to 'Remember Orr', adding 'may you remember me when you remember Orr.'[227] What seemed like a display of confident remembrance was actually an expression of angst. The memory of Orr was evoked as a means for veteran United Irishmen to address their own anxieties of being forgotten. Although phrased in the imperative, 'Remember Orr' was more of a plea than a command, and concerns of forgetting were always close at hand.

With the rise of Irish nationalism, from the middle of the nineteenth century, public silence on the legacy of the United Irishmen was broken. The memory of the republican protomartyr could now be publicly celebrated as part of an increasingly assertive counter-memory that openly challenged the hegemony of British-Imperial memory. Young Ireland extolled the martyrdom of Orr in their organ *The Nation* and it featured prominently in a popular history of political trials by Thomas MacNevin.[228] Above all, Madden's history of *The United Irishmen*, which included a detailed account of the 'case of William Orr' (published in 1858), influenced other popular nationalist histories, such as John Mitchel's *The History of Ireland* and Mary Francis Cusack's *The Illustrated History of Ireland* (both published in 1868 and re-issued in multiple editions), so that the memory of Orr's martyrdom became common knowledge.[229] In popular

---

[225] For facsimile reproductions see Young, *Ulster in '98*, p. 90; Bigger, *Remember Orr*, p. 58. The supposed authorship of Wolfe Tone was first noted by Mary Ann McCracken; Madden Papers, TCD 873/33. This claim was subsequently endorsed in social memory; see '98 Centenary Committee, *The Story of William Orr* (Dublin: James Duffy, 1898), pp. 13–14.

[226] *Press*, 20 February 1798, p. 3. For the poem's appearance on memorial cards see Bigger, *Remember Orr*, pp. 55–6; *Maguire, Up in Arms*, p. 167. For its circulation in America see David A. Wilson, *United Irishmen, United States: Immigrant Radicals in the Early Republic* (Dublin: Four Courts Press, 1998), p. 162.

[227] *Hazard's Register of Pennsylvania*, 8, no. 19 (1831), pp. 299–303.

[228] *Nation*, 16 September 1843, p. 778; Thomas MacNevin, *The Lives and Trials of Archibald Hamilton Rowan, the Rev. William Jackson, the Defenders, William Orr, Peter Finnerty, and Other Eminent Irishmen* (Dublin: J. Duffy, 1846), pp. 481–96.

[229] Madden, *United Irishmen*, 2nd ser., 2nd edn (1858), 2, pp. 253–63; John Mitchel, *The History of Ireland, from the Treaty of Limerick to the Present Time* (New York: D. J. Sadlier & Co., 1868), p. 277;

culture, the injustice of Orr's trial was encapsulated in the folk song 'By Memory Inspired', which was hawked on broadsides from the early 1860s:

> In October Ninety-Seven,
> May his soul find rest in Heaven!
> William Orr to execution was led on;
> The jury, drunk, agreed
> That Irish was his creed,
> For perjury and threats drove them on, boys, on.[230]

'Remember Orr' was put to effective use as a prememory template in the construction of the memory of the 'Manchester Martyrs'—three Fenians, whose conviction for the killing of a policeman in a rescue operation of republican prisoners following the failed insurrection attempt of 1867 was presented by nationalists as a similar miscarriage of justice.[231]

A typically stirring appeal to the memory of Orr was expressed at the end of nineteenth century by the Irish-American Fenian Rev. George W. Pepper of Cleveland, Ohio. Born in 1833 in Ballinagarrick, county Down, to a loyalist Episcopalian father, who was master of the local Orange lodge, and a republican Presbyterian mother, whose family had been United Irishmen, Pepper considered the martyrdom of William Orr to be 'one of the noblest incidents in history'. At a nationalist demonstration in Philadelphia in 1895, Pepper addressed 'an immense audience' and declared in liturgical fashion:

> We will remember Orr! When we think of the hallowed name of the United Irishmen, we will remember Orr! When we think of the persecutions which have deluged earth in the holy name of religion, and which was the work of England, we will remember Orr! When we think of the outrages perpetrated by a brutal soldiery, we will remember Orr! When we think of the howl of intolerance raised by the landlords to continue the foul demonstration of tyranny, we will remember Orr! When we think of the disgraceful bigotry and virulence which would chill the warm hearts of the Irish Presbyterians towards their Catholic countrymen, we will remember Orr! When we think that all popular modes of coercion have been bred, the scaffold, the gaol, in famine and exile; when we think of the horrible inhumanity in the trial and execution of the gallant Manchester martyrs, we will remember Orr![232]

For zealous nationalists, such as Pepper, the memory of Orr was a generic marker for resistance to oppression and, as such, it functioned as a prememory for all nationalist remembrance.

Mary Francis Cusack, *The Illustrated History of Ireland from the Earliest Period* (London: Longmans, Green, and Co., 1868), pp. 548–9.

[230] Confusingly, a reference to 'the memory of John Mitchel that is gone!' refers to Mitchel's exile (as the ballad antedates his death in 1875) and was already hawked on broadsides in 1864; see Duncathail [Ralph Varian], ed., *Street Ballads, Popular Poetry and Household Songs of Ireland*, 2nd edn (Dublin: McGlashan & Gill Co., 1865), p. 88n.

[231] *Irishman*, 23 November 1867; *Nation*, 30 November 1867, p. 281. See also references to 'Remember Orr' in the speech for the defence at the trial of Alexander Martin Sullivan, the editor of the *Weekly News* who was charged for sedition in his coverage of the Manchester Martyrs; *Nation*, 22 February 1868, p. 422.

[232] George Whitfield Pepper, *Under Three Flags; or, The Story of My Life as Preacher, Captain in the Army, Chaplain, Consul, with Speeches and Interviews* (Cincinnati: Curts & Jennings, 1899), pp. 524–5.

As a familiar prememory of 1798, remembrance of Orr periodically kick-started commemorations of the United Irishmen. The centenary of 1798 was launched with a commemoration of William Orr at St Mary's Hall in Belfast on 14 October 1897 and the first publication of the '98 Centenary Committee was a penny pamphlet on *The Story of William Orr*, issued in January 1898.[233] Similarly, in 1938, William Orr was the subject of the first in the series of leaflets *Who Fears to Speak of '98?*, which was published in London by the bookseller Joseph Hilary Fowler 'at a price and in a form that would reach the humblest of people' to mark the hundred-and-fortieth anniversary of 1798.[234] Once more, on 14 October 1997, a memorial event at the Templepatrick Old Presbyterian Church signalled the opening of the bicentenary of 1798.[235] There is something misleading in the brimming assertiveness of all these commemorations, which belie an almost imperceptible insecurity. Time and time again, nationalists would confidently proclaim 'Remember Orr' and yet fail to raise a major public monument that would recognize the primacy of his standing in memory. To decipher this commemorative paralysis requires a deeper understanding of the social forgetting of the 1798 rebellion in Ulster and how it developed over the course of two centuries.

Social remembering is dependent on mediation. In a study of the memory of the Indian Mutiny of 1857, Astrid Erll re-adapted terms developed for media studies by Richard Grusin: 'premediation' and 'remediation'. When applied to history, premediation refers to how 'existent media which circulate in a given society provide schemata for new experience and its representation'; and remediation follows how historical memory is 'represented again and again, over decades and centuries, in different media'.[236] Prememory—the recycling of memories of early events in the construction of memory—clearly relies on premediation. But what is often left unnoticed is the subtle role of pre-forgetting, which embeds into the very earliest stage of memory formation anxieties of forgetting. Similarly, the study of the remediation of social memory can too easily miss out on the remediation of social forgetting.

Social forgetting of the Turn-Out in Ulster was premediated by earlier memories. Rival interpretations of the memory of the Volunteers offered alternative models for rebels and for supporters of the Crown and framed remembrance of 1798 as a conflict between loyalist memory and republican counter-memory, which tried to annul each other. The repressive counter-revolutionary measures that preceded the rebellion further complicated the contestations over memory. Silencing precipitated muted remembrance, which was suppressed in public and recalled in private. The continued remediation of the protomartyrdom of William Orr over two centuries exemplifies the sustained role of prememory in the development of social forgetting. From the very beginning, remembrance of the United Irishmen in Ulster would be troubled by anxieties of forgetting, which could not be shaken off.

---

[233] See Chapter 5 below, pp. 360–1 and 365–6.

[234] J. H. Fowler, *William Orr* (London: Joseph H. Fowler, 1938).

[235] See Chapter 7 below, pp. 541–2.

[236] Astrid Erll, 'Remembering across Time, Space, and Cultures: Premediation, Remediation and the "Indian Mutiny"', in *Mediation, Remediation, and the Dynamics of Cultural Memory*, edited by Astrid Erll and Ann Rigney (Berlin and New York: Walter de Gruyter, 2009), pp. 109–38. For the original context of the terms see Richard A. Grusin, *Premediation: Affect and Mediality after 9/11* (Basingstoke and New York: Palgrave Macmillan, 2010); J. David Bolter and Richard A. Grusin, *Remediation: Understanding New Media* (Cambridge, Mass.: MIT Press, 1999).

2

Amnesty and Amnesia

The Aftermath of 1798

In Lethe be the past forever sunk!

Friedrich Schiller, *The Maid of Orleans* (act III, scene II)[1]

Know how to forget ... The things that should most be forgotten are the ones most easily remembered ... Sometimes the best remedy for troubles is to forget them, but we forget the remedy.

Baltasar Gracián y Morales, *The Art of Worldly Wisdom*[2]

The buds of social forgetting can be found in the unfolding of contentious historical events. This is particularly true of attempts to encourage oblivion after violent outbursts of conflict through policies of pacification, which are challenged by residual pockets of discontent. The ensuing competition between stifling and persistence of memory lays the conditions for disremembering as a contested form of remembrance. Close re-examination of the immediate aftermath of rebellion can therefore uncover the growth of an inherently ambiguous hidden mnemonic culture.

In order to avert the feelings of rancour on which memories of the vanquished normally thrive, following the defeat of the 1798 rebellion, an attempt was made at reconciliation. This seemed to raise the possibility of burying troublesome recollections. Prime Minister William Pitt, who was eager to resolve the crisis in Ireland and advance a long-term solution to the Anglo-Irish conflict through a political union with Great Britain, nominated marques Charles Cornwallis—at the time master-general of the ordnance and a member of cabinet—to replace the dysfunctional governance of Lord Camden. Cornwallis was a distinguished general who had also proved himself as an accomplished colonial administrator in India, and was now appointed both Lord Lieutenant and Commander-in-Chief of the army in Ireland. Although armed with unrivalled administrative and military authority, he was well aware of the limitations of relying solely on might to counter a popular uprising.

---

[1] 'Versenkt im Lethe sei auf ewig das Vergangene'; Friedrich Schiller, *Die Jungfrau von Orleans: Eine romantische Tragödie* (Berlin: Johann Friedrich Unger, 1802), dritter Aufzug, zweiter Auftritt.

[2] 'Saber olvidar ... Las cosas que son más para olvidadas son las más acordadas. ... Consiste a veces el remedio del mal en olvidarlo, y olvídase el remedio'; Baltasar Gracián y Morales, *Oráculo manual y arte de prudencia* (1647), cclxii; for a modern translation by Christopher Maurer see *The Art of Worldly Wisdom: A Pocket Oracle* (New York: Doubleday, 1992), p. 148.

In 1781, Cornwallis had surrendered to George Washington's army at Yorktown. During that conflict, he had learned the necessity of winning over a disaffected rebellious population, amongst which, as John Adams later observed, 'the Revolution was in the minds and hearts of the people'.[3] In America, he had also seen how pandering to hard-line loyalists could exacerbate revolutionary hostility. With past experience in mind, Cornwallis was determined to pacify Ireland through clemency.[4] The many common people who had espoused militant republicanism, and in particular radical Presbyterians in Ulster, were to be invited to surrender their arms and declare loyalty in exchange for a pardon. The promise of forgiveness implied an incentive to forget the rebellion. Amnesty was to be employed as an agent of amnesia.

WILFUL FORGETTING

Just as Cornwallis prepared to set out for his new appointment, news of the outbreak of rebellion in Antrim confirmed apprehensions that the insurrection could not be contained in the south-east of Ireland. The conservative Anglo-Irish ascendancy, which dominated domestic government in Ireland, felt increasingly threatened by the republican advocacy of a 'fellowship of freedom' and 'brotherhood of affection'.[5] Whereas the upheaval in Leinster, if disassociated from the largely Protestant leadership of the United Irishmen, could be contentiously portrayed as an essentially Catholic affair, it was not as easy to dismiss the predominance of Presbyterians amongst the rebel rank and file in Ulster. In the attempts to disrupt the United Irish radical alliance between 'Protestant, Catholic and Dissenter', particular effort was devoted to winning over disaffected northern Protestants. For this purpose, loyalists soon realized the value of spreading 'dreadful accounts' of sectarian killings committed by rebels in county Wexford. Advocating the benefits of 'horrid use' of atrocity reports, the Irish member of parliament John Beresford informed Pitt's close advisor Lord Auckland that 'for now there is a flying off of many Protestant men who were united, and the North consider it [the Rebellion] as a religious war, and, by many letters this day, have resolved to be loyal.'[6]

Most notably, Ambrose Hardinge Giffard, a member of the Lawyers' Corps of yeomanry and son of the former High Sheriff of Dublin—John Giffard (a prominent

---

[3] John Adams, Quincy, Massachusetts to Dr Jedidiah Morse, 29 November 1815; John Adams, Quincy, Massachusetts to Hezekiah Niles, 13 February 1818; see *The Works of John Adams, Second President of the United States: with a Life of the Author, Notes and Illustrations, by his Grandson Charles Francis Adams* (Boston: Little, Brown and Co., 1856), vol. 10, pp. 182 and 282.

[4] For Cornwallis's reflections on his experience in America and Ireland see Dermot Dix, 'A Settled Question? Charles, Lord Cornwallis, the Loss of America and the Mind of Empire', in *Studies in Settler Colonialism: Politics, Identity and Culture*, edited by Fiona Bateman and Lionel Pilkington (Houndmills and New York: Palgrave Macmillan, 2011), pp. 63–74.

[5] The term 'fellowship of freedom' appears in a United Irish resolution passed in Dublin on 30 December 1791; reproduced in anon. [James Gordon], *The History of the Irish Rebellion, in the Year 1798* (Alston, Cumberland: printed by John Harrop, 1809), 2, p. 263. For United Irish uses of 'brotherhood of affection' see *The Report from the Secret Committee of the House of Commons* (Dublin: printed by J. King and A. B. King, 1798), pp. 78, 110–11, 236–7, and 240.

[6] John Beresford to Lord Auckland; 31 May 1798; William Eden, *The Journal and Correspondence of William, Lord of Auckland* (London: R. Bentley, 1861), vol. 3, p. 439. See also Lecky, *A History of Ireland in the Eighteenth Century*, vol. 4, p. 413.

figure in ultra-conservative cliques), documented a notorious sectarian atrocity committed in Wexford on 5 June 1798, when, following defeat at New Ross, rebels set fire to a barn in Scullabogue, burning alive the mostly Protestant prisoners who were locked inside. Giffard's printed affidavit on the massacre was widely distributed in Ulster, with a mind to 'detach the dissenters in the north from the general conspiracy'.[7] These exertions appeared to bear fruit. Lord William Bentinck, the military commander in Armagh, observed on 21 June that 'The Dissenters, whom I knew to be the most disaffected a year and a half ago, are now ready to support the existing Government . . . They prefer a Protestant to a Popish Establishment.'[8] In July, Rev. Edward Hudson, the Church of Ireland rector of Ahoghill in county Antrim, wrote 'The brotherhood of affection is over; rancor and animosity to an incredible degree have succeeded.'[9] Within a year, he maintained that 'the word "Protestant," which was becoming obsolete in the north, has regained its influence, and all of that description seem drawing closer together.'[10]

The contemporary loyalist historian Sir Richard Musgrave asserted that the circulation of news about massacres in the South effectively 'extinguished the flame of rebellion in the North'. Musgrave, whose prejudiced writings augmented this propaganda drive, brought attention to the embittered words of a rebel leader named James Dickey, who at his execution allegedly declared that 'the presbyterians of the North perceived too late, that, if they succeeded in subverting the constitution, they would ultimately have to contend with the Roman catholicks.'[11] This anecdote may be apocryphal, as it is not mentioned in the contemporary report of Dickey's hanging in Belfast on 26 June 1798 and first appeared in a newspaper account a month later.[12] Loyalists had previously attributed a similar saying to William Orr, alleging—without any foundation—that before his execution in October 1797 he had said that 'it was not material wither they had gained the day now or not, yet if they ever had they must have fought it over again with the papists.'[13]

At some level, accounts of gullible republicans relinquishing their revolutionary false consciousness when confronted by the reality of sectarian violence may reflect wishful thinking on behalf of loyalist Protestants. Prior to the outbreak of the rebellion in his county Down diocese, Bishop Thomas Percy of Dromore was convinced that 'the North is perfectly safe.' Writing to his wife from Dublin on 29 May 1798, he

---

[7] 'Report from the Select Committee Appointed to Inquire into the Nature, Character, Extent and Tendency of Orange Lodges, Associations or Societies in Ireland; with the Minutes of Evidence, and Appendix', *British Parliamentary Papers: House of Commons* 1835, vol. XV (377), evidence of Rev. Mortimer O'Sullivan, p. 82 (article 1054). For the troublesome place of the Scullabogue massacre in Irish history and memory see Tom Dunne, *Rebellions: Memoir, Memory and 1798* (Dublin: Lilliput Press, 2004), ch. 13 ('The Killings at Scullabogue').

[8] See Lecky, *A History of Ireland in the Eighteenth Century*, vol. 4, p. 415n.

[9] E. Hudson to Lord Charlemont, 18 July 1798; John T. Gilbert (ed.), *The Manuscripts and Correspondence of James, First Earl of Charlemont* (London, 1894), 2, p. 327.

[10] Hudson to Charlemont, 5 July 1799; ibid., p. 354.

[11] Musgrave, *Memoirs of the Different Rebellions*, 3rd edn (1802), vol. 2, p. 108.

[12] For the immediate report of Dickey's trial and execution see *BNL*, 29 June 1798, p. 2 (the reproduction of this account a half-century later is indicative of renewed interest; *BNL*, 10 January 1851). A later account has Dickey saying that 'he well knew that had the *North* been successful, *they* would have had to fight the battle over again with the Catholics of the *South*'; *BNL*, 24 July 1798, p. 3.

[13] Diary of John Galt, PRONI D561/1 f. 45 (entry for 20 May 1798).

argued that 'the Protestants being here in some places murdered by the Irish Papists, has turned all the Dissenters against them [the United Irishmen].' On 8 June, oblivious to the battle the rebels had just fought in Antrim town and the magnitude of the rebellion in north-east Ulster, Percy wrote that 'a wonderful change has taken place among republicans in the North', professing that they 'are grown quite loyal'. Three days later, with rebels taking over Saintfield and preparing for the attack on Ballynahinch, Percy reassured his panicked wife, who was living in mortal fear of insurgents arriving at their estate in Dromore, that 'the better sort of republicans' were defecting and 'separating from the Papish Defenders who are only bent on mischief'.[14] In reality, as pointed out by Frank Wright, 'the arsenal of fear' exploited by loyalist propaganda did not result in Presbyterians turning against Catholics in Antrim and Down.[15]

Although the extent to which atrocity reports actually dissuaded rebels is unclear, this theme resonated in loyalist memory. It offered Presbyterian loyalists solid justification for having taken a stand against radicals from their own communities. Henry Joy, junior (a cousin of Henry Joy McCracken), who had previously been a prominent northern liberal but disagreed with the United Irishmen on the issue of Catholic emancipation, joined the yeomanry shortly after the outbreak of the rebellion in Ulster. Joy found vindication for his own shift in politics by recounting a historical narrative of appalled Protestant conspirators who 'experienced a mortifying disappointment' when they realized that 'no sooner had the rebellion exploded, than the Roman Catholics displayed all the bigotry and intolerance of the middle ages.'[16] The story of last-minute Protestant awakening would be repeatedly recalled by loyalists. Speaking at a demonstration in Belfast on 21 January 1841, the conservative Presbyterian leader Rev. Henry Cooke declared to a cheering audience (who clearly recognized the reference) that the Protestants who died in 1798 in Wexford 'live in our remembrance—their deaths opened the political eyes of the many thousands of Ulster.'[17]

In comparison to other arenas of the 1798 rebellion, it seems that a greater effort was made in Ulster to win over hesitant insurgents. Even as masses of armed men assembled to partake in rebellion, rebels in Antrim were coaxed to sign a 'paper of submission and repentance'.[18] It was soon reported that 'the disaffected in the County of Antrim were delivering up their arms, and shewing every symptom of contrition.'[19] At the same time, no quarter was offered on the battlefields. At Antrim town, Colonel James Durham, the commander of the Fifeshire Fencibles, 'hanged many of the rebels, who

---

[14] 'Letters of Bishop Percy to His Wife', BL Add. MS 32,335; see also Lecky, *A History of Ireland in the Eighteenth Century*, vol. 4, pp. 414–15.

[15] Frank Wright, *Two Lands on One Soil: Ulster Politics before Home Rule* (Dublin: Gill & Macmillan, 1996), pp. 42–3.

[16] Joy, *Historical Collections*, pp. x–xii.

[17] William McComb, *The Repealer Repulsed! A Correct Narrative of the Rise and Progress of the Repeal Invasion of Ulster* (Belfast: W. M'Comb, 1841), pp. 103–4.

[18] Lord Lieutenant Camden to Duke of Portland, n.d. (*c.*12 June 1798), TNA HO 100/77/141–143; *BNL*, 12 June 1798, p. 2.

[19] 'Accounts Received from General Nugent', Dublin Castle, 13 June 1798 (printed bulletin; Dublin, 1798). Reports of rebels surrendering their arms also appear in the letters of the Lord Lieutenant Camden to the Duke of Portland from 10 to 12 June 1798; TNA HO 100/77/141–143, 100/81/59–60, and 74–75. James McKey of Belfast informed Lord Downshire on 11 June 1798 that 'the flogging we gave them at Antrim h[as] had the good effect to make the survivors beg for mercy, and they are all giving up their arms'; Downshire Papers, PRONI D607/F/222.

were left on trees as a comfort to their brethren, and every other put to the bayonet'.[20] The dispatches that reported on military victories made repeated reference to wholesale slaughter of insurgents.[21]

When clemency was offered, it was extended through a combination of carrot and stick. After defeating the rebels of county Down at Ballynahinch, Major-General George Nugent promised to accept their petition for a pardon on the condition that they hand in the 'principal traitors who had instigated them to their wicked practices' (including their leader, Henry Munro).[22] While offered the same concessions 'that have been eagerly and gratefully accepted by many of their equally deluded neighbours in the county of Antrim', the rebels of Down were given twenty-four hours to comply with the terms of 'submission and atonement', which were backed up with an ominous threat:

> Should the above injunctions not be complied with in the time specified, Major-General Nugent will proceed to set fire to and totally destroy, the towns of Killinchy, Killeleagh, Ballynahinch, Saintfield, and every cottage and farmhouse in the vicinity of those places, carry off the stock and cattle, and put every one to the sword who may be found in arms.

The defeated rebels were notified that this was to be 'the only opportunity there will be of rescuing themselves and properties from indiscriminate vengeance of an army necessarily let loose on them'.[23] News that 'the town of Ballynahinch was completely destroyed, and many of the houses of the Insurgents at Saintfield, and on the road between the two places' left little doubt about the cold-blooded sincerity of this ultimatum. Shortly after Nugent's announcement, it was reported that 'in every town and village throughout the county Down, the people are coming in and delivering up their arms, heartily sorry for their late conduct, and promising every amendment in future'; some of them were even willing to provide a list of the leaders and of 'those people who supplied them with money and who were to join them if they made any impression'.[24]

The intimidation through which this compliance had been achieved was remembered with unease by loyal supporters of the military. An Orange history, published a century later, wrote of Nugent's proclamation: 'It was a cruel order, and many innocent people suffered', noting that 'it has never been concealed or attempted to be justified by the loyalists.'[25] Allegations also emerged of misconduct in the administration of amnesty in Antrim. The commander of the forces that defeated the rebels in Randalstown, Colonel Henry Mordaunt Clavering, was remembered in the mid-nineteenth

---

[20] 'Extract of a Letter from Belfast, Dated June 8th, 1798'; published as government bulletin, Londonderry, 10 June 1798. The number of rebels killed by Colonel Durham at Antrim was estimated to have been between 500 and 600; Downshire Papers, John Patrickson to Lord Downshire, 9 June 1798, PRONI, D607/F/213.

[21] Examples can be readily found in the bulletins of Dublin Castle printed by George Grierson; see 9 June 1798 ('the rebels, who were pursued to Shane's Castle and Randalstown, with much slaughter'); 12 June 1798 ('Colonel Stapleton had attacked a body of rebels near Saintfield and . . . entirely defeated them with great slaughter'); 14 June 1798 ('The rebels attacked impetuously . . . and even jumped into the road from the Earl of Moira's demesne . . . but they were repulsed with slaughter').

[22] Camden to Portland, Dublin Castle, 16 June 1798, TNA HO 100/81/92–93; see also 'Advices Received from Major-General Nugent', Dublin Castle, 16 June 1798 (official print; Dublin, 1798).

[23] See Nugent's proclamation from 11 June 1798 in *BNL*, 12 June 1798, p. 3; *Freeman's Journal*, 16 June 1798, p. 2.

[24] *BNL*, 15 June 1798, p. 3; see also Northern Intelligence report in *BNL*, 23 June 1798, p. 3.

[25] Anon., *The History of the Orange Order* (Toronto: William Banks, 1898), p. 26.

century as 'an unprincipled and a merciless man'. It was resentfully recalled that when the local inhabitants complied with his terms of surrender, willingly turning in their arms, Clavering nonetheless allowed his troops to plunder and burn the town, after which he proceeded to Ballymena, where he staged wanton executions.[26]

By the time Cornwallis arrived in Dublin, on 20 June 1798, the insurrection in Ulster had already been quelled and on the following day the remaining rebels in Wexford were defeated at the Battle of Vinegar Hill.[27] Despite the promised pardon, brutal punitive measures had continued on the ground. A report from Lieutenant-Colonel Atherton in Newtownards, county Down, reads like an inventory of retributive destruction:

> We have burned Johnston's house at Crawford's Bourn-Mills, at Bangor, destroyed the furniture of Pat. Agnew; James Francis, and Gibbison, and Campbell's not finished yet, at Ballyholme; burned the house of Johnston at the Demesnes, near Bangor; the houses of Jas. Richardson and John Scott at Ballymaconnell-Mills; burned the house of M'Connell, miller, and James Martin, a Captain and a friend of M'Cullock's [McCullough's], hanged at Ballynahinch.[28]

At this stage, the main threat of violence was clearly from loyalist retribution. Rebecca Leslie, the wife of Colonel David Leslie of the Tay Fencibles, observed that in Antrim 'whenever a prisoner comes in there is a great shout and hundreds of voices cry out "kill them, kill them." '[29]

Upon applying himself to restoring normality, Cornwallis soon recognized the need to 'soften the ferocity of our troops'. Voicing concerns that 'any man in a brown coat who is found within several miles of the field of action, is butchered without discrimination', he instructed the generals in the districts that had seen military action to offer 'the deluded wretches' terms that would allow them the possibility of 'returning quietly to their homes'.[30]

Accordingly, Major-General Nugent, who realized that 'it is most desirable that the lower classes of people should return to their homes and follow their usual occupations,' issued a notice in Belfast on 24 June that invited 'all persons to return quietly to their respective abodes for that purpose, where they shall remain unmolested, and their property be secured to them as long as they continue to be peaceable subjects'.[31] A more detailed proclamation, issued on 29 June, gave remaining rebels fourteen days to surrender and submit their arms to designated officers, stationed in a list of specified towns. Justices of the Peace were on hand to register their names, accept an acknowledgement of guilt and

---

[26] Recollections of Dr McGee of Belfast, who 'was arrested in 1798, on a charge of high treason, being then a resident at Randalstown, and had an intimate acquaintance with the matters of which he spoke'; Madden, *The United Irishmen*, 2nd ser., vol. 1 (1843), p. 470. A more forgiving local account of Clavering's amnesty appears in *Old Ballymena*, pp. 44–50.

[27] Cornwallis to Major-General Ross, Whitehall, 12 June 1798 and Cornwallis to Portland, Dublin Castle, 21 June 1798; Charles Ross (ed.), *Correspondence of Charles, First Marquis Cornwallis* (London, 1859), vol. 2, pp. 350–2.

[28] Asherton, Newtownards, to Nugent, 20 June 1798; reproduced in Madden, *The United Irishmen*, 2nd ser., vol. 2 (1843), pp. 429–30. Madden was given access to the letter by the radical journalist John Lawless, who had received it from a county Down magistrate.

[29] Mrs Leslie to Mrs Stewart, 7 June 1798, Leslie Papers, PRONI D3167/3/A/9.

[30] Cornwallis to Portland, Dublin Castle, 28 June 1798; Ross, *Correspondence of Cornwallis*, pp. 354–5.

[31] Musgrave Papers, NLI 4156; *BNL*, 26 June 1798, p. 3.

a promise of good behaviour, and to administer an oath of allegiance, following which they would be issued 'a certificate which will entitle them to protection so long as they demean themselves as becomes good subjects'.[32] It was noted that these certificates, 'were, by the lower classes, commonly called "Cornys"' in acknowledgement of the conciliatory policy introduced by Cornwallis.[33]

Witnessing a change of heart among Presbyterians of property following the rebel defeat at Ballynahinch, James McKey of Mount Collyer reassured Lord Downshire that republicans 'will become loyal subjects'.[34] Another correspondent noted that 'the poor people . . . profess themselves ready to take any oath, to undertake any duty.'[35] Vernacular parlance reflected the disillusionment that had set in among many of the disaffected in Ulster:

> it is now a common saying among the folk in the Ardes, county Down, with that shrewdness for which our northerns are remarkable—that no body will ever prevail on them to go *to catch cannon-balls on the points of pikes and pitchforks again.*[36]

In an effort to encourage former rebels to apply for pardon, Lord Dunsany, a liberal member of parliament, made a public address 'to the People of Ireland' in which he promised that all would be forgotten:

> My Countrymen, I beseech you, to avail yourselves of that lenity of that which is again willing to receive you into the bosom of the community, to pass an act of oblivion on all your past errors, and to restore you to that peace and tranquility, which you have so rashly forsaken.[37]

The *Belfast News-Letter*, praising the 'wise and merciful policy' of amnesty, reported: 'great numbers, we hear, have every where submitted under it and returned to their allegiance.'[38]

Beyond individual pardons, whole communities were offered collective certificates of protection, which guaranteed that upon affirming their loyalty 'the inhabitants of such townland may remain unmolested at their respective houses, and their property be secured to them.'[39] Taking their cue from a 'general declaration of loyalty and fidelity to His Majesty and the Constitution' issued by the Belfast yeomanry on 18 June 1798, a spate of declarations of loyalty ensued across Ulster, as residents of communities in formerly unruly areas rushed to disassociate themselves in public from the 'savage and unnatural rebellion'.[40] In county Down, 980 Presbyterians signed such a declaration in the parish of Killinchy, 940 in Drumbo, 700 in Knockbreda, 600 in Comber, 306 in Holywood, 272 in Portaferry; in county Antrim, 814 'respectable inhabitants' signed in Carnmoney, 766 in the area of Donagore, 486 in Ballyeaston, and 340 in Rasharkin, to name but some of the localities that participated in what seems to have been a

---

[32] *BNL*, 3 July 1798, p. 2.   [33] Ross, *Correspondence of Cornwallis*, vol. 2, p. 357.

[34] James McKey, Belfast, to Lord Downshire, 14 June 1798, Downshire Papers, PRONI D607/F/244.

[35] Thomas Lane, Hillsborough, to Lord Downshire, 3 July 1798, Downshire Papers, PRONI D607/F/298.

[36] *BNL*, 29 June 1798, p. 2.

[37] Speech delivered at Dunsany Castle on 2 July 1798, first published in the *Dublin Evening Post*, 3 July 1798, and republished in *BNL*, 6 July 1798, p. 4.

[38] *BNL*, 13 July 1798, p. 4.   [39] *BNL*, 26 June 1798, p. 2.

[40] Several of the civilian declarations took their wording from the initial declarations issued by the Belfast Troop of Yeoman Cavalry and the First Corps of Belfast Supplementary Yeoman Infantry; *BNL*, 18 June 1798, p. 3.

ubiquitous trend.[41] Opportunities were offered for late-comers to join the growing current. The declaration of the residents of the town and suburbs of Belfast was first advertised in the press and then displayed in a shop in the centre of the city so as to facilitate additional signatures.[42] As an alternative to the collecting of individual names, some declarations were endorsed collectively by a local magnate, such as Squire Edward Jones Agnew, who signed on behalf of the entire Kilwaughter congregation in Antrim.[43]

With no less than sixty-three ministers and probationers suspected of involvement in the rebellion, of whom three were executed and others went into exile, the Presbyterian leadership in Ulster was under particular scrutiny.[44] Seeking to obliterate this embarrassing memory, the General Synod, under the influence of the loyalist ministers Rev. William Bruce and Rev. Robert Black, issued its own declaration of loyalty, which included an expression of 'sorrow and indignation' at 'the late attempts that have been made by some to subvert our Government'.[45] At a grass-roots level, local ministers, such as Rev. Rentoul of Tamlaghtfinlagan, county Londonderry, rallied their congregations to unanimously approve loyalty statements.[46] Catholics were not to be outdone and they too professed their loyalty in droves, with 4,000 signing a declaration in the area of Newry, county Down, and another 400 in the nearby parish of Seagoe, county Armagh; shortly after, 800 signed in parishes around Antrim, followed by 400 in the parish of Derriaghy, 800 in the parish of Layd and Ardclines, 900 in the parish of Culfaghtrin and Grange, and another 500 in the parishes of Ramoan, Armoy, and Ballintoy.[47]

Communities were anxious that their declarations would be noticed and often resubmitted them to the same newspaper for repeated publication. For wider exposure, the inhabitants of Macosquin in county Londonderry resolved that their declaration would be published in a variety of prominent provincial and national newspapers, including the *Belfast News-Letter*, *Londonderry Journal*, *Dublin Journal*, and *Dublin*

---

[41] *BNL*, 26 June 1798, p. 3 (Rasharkin); 29 June 1798, p. 3 (Carnmoney); 3 July 1798, p. 3 (Comber; Killinchy, Tullynakill, and Kilmud); 10 July 1798, p. 3. (Portaferry; Drumbo; Donagore, Killbride, and the Grange of Nilteen), 17 July 1798, p. 3 (Ballyeaston); 20 July 1798, p. 4 (Knock-Breda and Holywood).

[42] *BNL*, 22 June 1798, p. 3.

[43] *BNL*, 10 July 1798, p. 1 (Kilwaughter). For additional communal declarations of loyalty see *BNL*, 22 June 1798, p. 3 (town and suburbs of Belfast); 26 June 1798, p. 3 (district between Belfast and Lisburn); 10 July 1798, p. 3 (Glendermot); 20 July 1798, p. 3 (Killead and Ballyclare); 27 July 1798, p. 3 (Dundonald, Dromara, and Antrim town).

[44] See list of 'Presbyterian Ministers and Probationers Suspected of Involvement in the 1798 Rebellion', in McBride, *Scripture Politics*, pp. 232–6. See also William McMillan, 'Presbyterian Ministers and the Ulster Rising', in *Protestant, Catholic and Dissenter: The Clergy and 1798*, edited by Liam Swords (Blackrock: Columba Press, 1997), pp. 81–117.

[45] *BNL*, 18 September 1798, p. 3 (signed 28 August 1798); published also in the *Dublin Evening Post* and the *Dublin Journal*. A pastoral letter, denouncing the rebellion and professing loyalty, was distributed to Presbyterian congregations and read out from every pulpit; *Records of the General Synod of Ulster, from 1691 to 1820*, vol. 3 (Belfast: Presbyterian Church in Ireland, 1898), pp. 210–12.

[46] *BNL*, 26 June 1798, p. 3.

[47] *BNL*, 18 June 1798, p. 3 (Seagoe); 26 June 1798, p. 3 (Newry, Dromore, Garvaghy, Clonallalen, Donaghmore, Kilbroney, Drumgooland, Dromgath, and Clonuff); 17 July 1798, p. 3 (Drumaul, Antrim, Donegore, Templepatrick, and Conner); 24 July, p. 3 (Derriaghy); 1 January 1799, p. 1 (Culfaghtrin and Grange) and p. 3 (Layd and Ardclines); 8 January 1799, p. 1 (Ramoan, Armoy, and Ballintoy).

Evening Post.[48] Occasionally, the statements were supplemented by additional demonstrations of loyalty. For instance, a public subscription was undertaken in Coleraine to repay the costs incurred in the defence of the town and the inhabitants of Donegore, Kilbride, and Grange of Nilteen raised twenty guineas 'for the benefit and support of the 22d Dragoons as suffered by the conduct of the misled insurgents at Antrim'.[49] As a stamp of recognition, letters of acknowledgement from senior figures in the civil and military authorities were typically appended to the published declarations and the press credited the 'spirited and constitutional declarations' with contributing to the restoration of tranquillity.[50]

The declarations were supposedly signed exclusively by those who had remained loyal throughout the rebellion. In order to ensure that only 'pure and uncorrupted signatures' endorsed their statement, the Presbyterian congregation of Killinchy formed an organizing committee of certified 'men of known and approved loyalty', carefully selected from the different townlands of the parish. Each committee member took an oath 'that he would not receive the signature of any person whom he either knew or believed to be engaged in the late rebellion'; whenever in doubt, an individual signatory could be required to take an oath 'that he was not concerned in the late rebellion, by force or otherwise.' The purpose of outlining this pedantic method was to assert that 'the great mass of the people are yet uncorrupted; that the unfound few are secluded, and that they have procured a large list of men of perfectly pure, good and loyal principles.'[51] However, the names on these documents far exceed those that appeared on declarations of loyalty issued prior to the rebellion.[52]

From the high numbers of signatures collected in Antrim and Down, which often correspond to the majority of the adult male population in areas that had raised large parties of rebels, it is evident that the signatories were not solely long-standing loyalists. William Grimshaw, who had lived through the events as a 16-year-old boy and later emigrated to Philadelphia, recalled that in his home parish of Carnmoney, county Antrim: 'I never knew a man, born within its precincts, who was not a United Irishman, and, moreover, of the Protestant religion, almost wholly Presbyterians,' and yet 'in that single parish, not less than seven hundred persons, of adult age, took the oath of allegiance, before a magistrate, in the Presbyterian meeting-house.'[53] Declarations of loyalty were effectively a platform for former republicans to proclaim their political conversion and for communities to renounce their recent involvement in rebellion. As such they were a high-profile vehicle for publicly disowning, if not quite forgetting, the recent past.

Espousal of loyalism was not merely declaratory. As Musgrave noted, 'numbers of presbyterians, who had been united, deserted their associates, joined the yeomanry, and

---

[48] *BNL*, 17 July 1798, p. 4.   [49] *BNL*, 17 July 1798, p. 4 and 14 August 1798, p. 3.
[50] *BNL*, 4 July 1798, p. 3.   [51] *BNL*, 6 July 1798, p. 2.
[52] For examples of early declarations see PRONI, D1494/2/24 (Newtownards, November 1796); TNA HO 100/72/206–276 (Antrim, May 1797). A declaration of loyalty published as the rebellion broke out in Antrim, but dated a week earlier to 29 May 1798, was tellingly signed by the 'major part of landholders and principal inhabitants', rather than the entire population of the parish; *BNL*, 8 June 1798, p. 1; see also Dixon Donaldson, *Historical, Traditional, and Descriptive Account of Islandmagee* (s. l.: s.n., 1927), pp. 59–60.
[53] Grimshaw, *Incidents Recalled*, p. 32.

became orangemen.'[54] It was subsequently noted that the ranks of the yeomanry 'were now swelled by multitudes, eager to evince their reawakened fidelity to the government'.[55] To an onlooker, it appeared that 'every man in Belfast has now a red coat on.'[56] Allan Blackstock, an historian of Irish loyalism, has described this mass conversion as a 'rite of passage'.[57] In addition to its immediate functional purpose as a means of reintegration into society, the renouncing of involvement in rebellion also showed determination to forget for the sake of assuming a new identity. However, doubts arose about the sincerity of the transformation and its implications.

The yeomanry—labelled contemptuously an 'ascendancy army' by the liberal parliamentarian Henry Grattan—originated in the counter-insurgency measures that were introduced in the autumn of 1796 to confront the imminent threat of United Irish rebellion. Cavalry and infantry units were recruited and commanded by local gentry but were financed by the government. In order to purge the corps of infiltrators with United Irish sympathies, Major-General John Knox, the military commander in central Ulster, introduced in 1797 a public 'test oath' to be taken in addition to the standard oath of allegiance. As an Irish loyalist force, the yeomanry played a major role in suppressing the insurrection, showing vehemence in hunting down rebels. Their presence was particularly felt in the North, where it was recalled that large bodies of yeomanry were stationed in every village.[58] There is evidence to suggest that they regularly violated letters of protection issued by officers and killed people indiscriminately, regardless of whether they had taken up arms in the rebellion.[59]

In response to the rebellion, Ulster, and in particularly Antrim and Down, became the most dense area in Ireland in its recruitment of yeomanry corps.[60] Bemoaning pervasive defection to the ranks of the yeomanry, the United Irishman Charles Hamilton Teeling of Lisburn observed that 'these corps increased in proportion to the disappointed hopes or the personal fears of the men who had most strenuously opposed their formation.' Yet, he claimed that the disillusioned United Irishmen who became yeomen 'were viewed with evident marks of suspicion and distrust'.[61] The upsurge in born-again loyalism was shrouded in ambiguity. After an incident in which a member of the Seaforde yeomanry called into question the loyalty of an official and

---

[54] Musgrave, *Memoirs of the Different Rebellions*, 3rd edn (1802), vol. 2, p. 109. Musgrave heard from General John Knox that at the end of June, after news arrived of atrocities in Wexford, the flow of Presbyterian former rebels who 'affirmed their services and received arms' doubled the number of yeomen; R. Musgrave to Bishop Percy, postmarked 16 May 1799, Musgrave Papers, NLI 4157/71–72.

[55] James McHenry, *The Insurgent Chief; or, The Pikemen of '98: A Romance of the Irish Rebellion* (Belfast: John Henderson, 1847; orig. edn 1824), p. 125.

[56] James McKey, Mount Collyer, to Lord Downshire, London, 1 July 1798, Downshire Papers, PRONI, D507/F/293.

[57] Allan Blackstock, *Loyalism in Ireland 1789–1829* (Woodbridge: Boydell Press, 2007), pp. 98–105.

[58] See Blackstock, *An Ascendancy Army*; Allan Blackstock, 'The Irish Yeomanry and the 1798 Rebellion', in *1798: A Bicentenary Perspective*, edited by Thomas Bartlett et al. (Dublin: Four Courts Press, 2003), pp. 331–44. For the deployment of yeomen in suppressing the northern rebellion see William Richardson, *History of the Origin of the Irish Yeomanry* (Dublin: printed by R. E. Mercier, 1802), pp. 41–2.

[59] Letter received by Col. Littlehales, March 1800; NAI, SOC 1019/6.

[60] See Blackstock, *An Ascendancy Army*, pp. 117–22.

[61] Charles Hamilton Teeling, *Personal Narrative of the 'Irish Rebellion' of 1798* (London: Henry Colburn, 1828), pp. 207–10.

assaulted him, another member of the corps—Robert Browne of Clough—complained to his commander that 'this mussroom [mushroom] loyalty in Downe is the cause of all this.'[62]

For those seeking to dispel doubts about their allegiance, embracing Orangeism was an even more extreme way of professing loyalty to the Crown. The Orange Society originated in the 1790s in sectarian clashes between rival agrarian secret societies in mid-Ulster, which reached a climax in a skirmish between Protestant Peep o' Day Boys and Catholic Defenders at the so-called Battle of the Diamond in Loughall, county Armagh, on 21 September 1795. This event, which became the founding myth of the Orange Order, would controversially be described in later loyalist polemics as a confrontation with United Irishmen.[63] Orangemen, who ardently sported their loyalty to the monarchy, were prominent in the yeomanry. Moreover, in anticipation of rebellion, Orange lodges were armed so that they could be employed as a supplementary paramilitary force.[64] By June 1798, the undersecretary in Dublin Castle Edward Cooke noted that in Ulster 'the force of Orange yeomanry is really formidable'.[65] After the rebellion broke out, it was reported that 'upwards of 400 Orangemen have got arms, and been upon duty, under the command of Mr. William Atkinson, Grand Master for the County Antrim.'[66] Inflated rumours of unrestrained Orangemen being unleashed on the Catholic population enhanced their notoriety as feared shock troops, known to be predisposed to sectarian violence.[67]

In the months after the northern insurrection was suppressed, Presbyterian loyalists were reputedly beset by an 'Orange mania', which was initiated by yeomen rushing to join the order. Rev. Edward Hudson claimed in October 1798 that the number of Orangemen in Ballymena trebled within a forty-eight hour period.[68] A year after the rebellion, the chief secretary in Dublin Castle, Lord Castlereagh, boasted to the Home Secretary, the Duke of Portland, that 'the Protestant Dissenters in Ulster have in a great

---

[62] Robert Brown, Clough, to Mathew Forde, Rutland Square, Dublin, 7 July 1798; Down County Museum, Seaforde Documents; reproduced in Allan Blackstock, 'Pictures of the Past: Some Forde Documents', in *Down Survey 1998: The Yearbook of Down County Museum*, edited by Brian S. Turner (Downpatrick: Down County Museum, 1998), pp. 31–2.

[63] 'By-Ways of Irish History', in *Dublin University Magazine*, 10, no. 58 (1837), pp. 467 and 480. For the attribution of this text to the Church of Ireland clergymen and polemicists Rev. Mortimer O'Sullivan and Rev. Samuel O'Sullivan see Wayne E. Hall, *Dialogues in the Margin: A Study of the Dublin University Magazine* (Washington, D.C.: Catholic University of America Press, 1999), p. 66. Their accusation that the sectarian violence in Armagh had been deliberately provoked by United Irishmen was refuted by James Hope and Charles Hamilton Teeling; see statement by James Hope, Belfast, 8 January 1838, Leon Ó Broin Papers, NLI MS 27,950; C. H. Teeling, *Observations on the 'History and Consequences' of the 'Battle of the Diamond'* (Belfast: John Hodgson, 1838).

[64] Cecil Kilpatrick, ed., *The Formation of the Orange Order, 1795–1798: The Edited Papers of Colonel William Blacker and Colonel Robert H. Wallace* (Belfast: Education Committee of the Grand Orange Lodge of Ireland, 1994), pp. 83–7. The government and the military were apparently concerned about the mobilization and arming of Orange lodges in Ulster; see Blackstock, *Loyalism in Ireland*, pp. 92–5.

[65] Edward Cooke to William Wickham, 2 June 1798; TNA HO 100/77/21.

[66] *BNL*, 15 June 1798, p. 3. The early historian of the Orange Order Ogle Robert Gowan compiled a list of armed Orange corps in Antrim and Down, which amounts to 1,500 men; Ogle Robert Gowan, *Orangeism; Its Origin and History* (Toronto: printed by Lovell and Gibson, 1859), p. 183.

[67] See James Wilson, 'Orangeism in 1798', in Thomas Bartlett, David Dickson, Dáire Keogh, and Kevin Whelan (eds), *1798: A Bicentenary Perspective* (Dublin: Four Courts Press, 2003), pp. 345–62.

[68] E. Hudson to Charlemont; 6 October 1798; Gilbert, *Correspondence of Charlemont*, 2, p. 336.

degree withdrawn themselves from the Union [i.e. the Society of the United Irishmen], and become Orangemen'[69] A revealing story told in Antrim in the late nineteenth century, recalled how 'a staunch United Irishman' named Jack Gibb of Kilmakee, near Dunadry, 'after studying carefully the characters of his neighbours, also United Irishmen, solemnly declared it was his conviction that, after the rising had taken place, most of them would turn their coats and become Orangemen'. It was recalled with due irony that Gibb 'was made an Orangeman almost immediately afterwards'.[70]

Letters in the Ulster-Scots dialect published in the mid-1830s and attributed to a county Down weaver named Thomas McIlwham noted that at 'the time o' the ruction' [the insurrection] he was 'a united man frae simple secrecy' but, after he 'saw the folly an' the danger o' that', he 'became staunch loyal, an amaist a kin' o' an Orangeman'. This supposed admission, which appeared in a Conservative satire directed against James McKnight, the liberal unionist editor of the *Belfast News-Letter*, would have seemed plausible to a local readership.[71] In the decade following the rebellion, the numbers of Orange societies increased significantly. Speaking to a Select Committee appointed by parliament to investigate the Orange Order in 1835, William Sharman Crawford, an MP for county Down, testified that it was common knowledge that 'many men who have been United Irishmen have become Orangemen.'[72]

Familiarly known as 'Orange Croppies', rehabilitated rebels displayed zeal for their new allegiance and it was claimed that 'no insults—no barbarities towards their recent friends and comrades, were too great to evince their staunch loyalty to their new masters.'[73] Joining the Orange Order—an institution dedicated to the 'glorious and immortal memory' of William III—was more than a categorical demonstration of loyalty, it was also an act of wilful forgetting that entailed perjury. The Orange oath in that period stipulated that 'I was not, am not nor never will be an United Irishman, and that I never took an oath of secrecy to that society.'[74] In administering this oath leniently, masters and brethren of Orange lodges in Ulster apparently turned a blind

---

[69] Castlereagh to Portland, 3 June 1799; Charles Vane, ed., *Memoirs and Correspondence of Viscount Castlereagh, Second Marquess of Londonderry*, 12 vols (London: Henry Colburn, 1850), vol. 2, p. 326.

[70] Recounted by James Boyd of Antrim, who heard it from his grandfather; W. S. Smith, *Memories of '98*, pp. 45–6.

[71] *Ulster Times*, 27 December 1836, p. 3 (republished in John Morrison, *The McIlwham Papers*, p. 12). For the contemporary literary context of 'polemical faux-letters in Scots' published in Belfast see Frank Ferguson, 'Ulster-Scots Literature', in *The Oxford History of the Irish Book*, vol. 4: *The Irish Book in English 1800–1891*, edited by James H. Murphy (Oxford: Oxford University Press, 2011), p. 427.

[72] 'Report from the Select Committee . . . of Orange Lodges', evidence of William Sharman Crawford, pp. 404 (article 5912), 405 (6011), 410 (6069–71). The post-rebellion increase in numbers was noted by Lieutenant-Colonel William Verner, MP and Orange grand master for Armagh, p. 20 (305–6).

[73] John A. Crozier, *The Life of the Rev. Henry Montgomery L. L. D., Dunmurry, Belfast; with Selections from His Speeches and Writings*, vol. 1 (London: Simpkin, Marshall and Co. and Belfast: W. H. Greer, 1875), p. 12n.

[74] 'Rules and Regulations of the Orange Society', 20 November 1798; PRONI, D3815/D/5, Aiken McClelland papers (from the minute book of the Grand Orange Lodge of Ireland found in the papers of Bro. McRobert of Rademon, Crossgar, member of L.O.L. 1607; transcribed by J. D. Rice of Saintfield; November 1938). See also *Rules and Regulations for the Use of All Orange Societies: Revised and Corrected by a Committee of the Grand Orange Lodge of Ireland and Adopted by the Grand Orange Lodge, Jan. 10, 1800* (Dublin: J. J. Stockdale, 1800), pp. 3, 6, 7, and 8; reproduced in Francis Plowden, *The History of Ireland from Its Union with Great Britain, in January 1801, to October 1810*, vol. 1 (Dublin: John Boyce, 1811). This stipulation was renewed in Orange oaths over the next decade and a half; see *The Orange Institution; a Slight Sketch* (London: J. J. Stockdale, 1813), pp. 22, 26, and 27.

eye on the shady past record of their new members, prompting the perceptive Belfast letter writer Martha McTier to figuratively write: 'The Orangemen I hear have got green in their hats, blue and orange with forget and forgive on their breasts.'[75]

Some former rebels felt betrayed by erstwhile comrades reneging on past commitments. William Grimshaw recalled how in his neighbourhood in Carnmoney, 'about a year after the country became tranquil', violent reprisals were taken against a man named Kelsy who had supported the rebels and then joined an Orange lodge, and another man named McKelvey was killed. Such cases show reluctance on the part of die-hard republicans to accommodate political conversions and to permit renunciation and forgetting of the rebel past.[76] Dread of being seen as a defector was so ingrained that when Thomas Hunter of Killinchy, who had fought with the rebels at Saintfield and Ballynahinch, was asked by the woman attending him on his deathbed if he would like to be turned over, he instinctively replied: 'No; I will never turn, or take a bribe.'[77]

For supporters of the government, declarations of loyalty were not only considered redemptive, but were also seen as confirmation that republicanism lacked popular support. In loyalist eyes, the rebellion had been forced on an unwilling population. According to a report in the *Belfast News-Letter*, 'It is a melancholy fact, that the insurgents greatly increased their numbers by a system of terror, wherever they could exercise it. Many of the people now with them had either the choice of instant death, and their houses and families destroyed, or to go along with them.'[78] A letter sent to Lord Downshire just before the Battle of Ballynahinch claimed that the rebels 'are hanging and shooting all that will not join them'.[79] James McKey of the Belfast Yeoman Cavalry, who was preoccupied with hunting down fugitive rebels fleeing Ballynahinch, maintained that 'thousands of these creatures were driven to join through fear' and was told that all the inhabitants of a townland near Saintfield had been 'forced into the crowd'.[80] Writing shortly after the events, John Moore Johnston, the agent of the Montalto estate, on which the Battle of Ballynahinch was fought, stated that the 'professed patriots' had:

> forced a great number of People to take united oaths in order to obtain reform; those who refused were threatened with assassination and burnings, and some loyal men were actually murdered: many honest men, friends to their King and Country, who had no idea of rebellion or revolution, took tests, some from curiosity, others from fear, and afterwards the oath of allegiance and kept it.[81]

Depositions collected after the rebellion from individuals who had been spotted in the United Irish camp regularly claimed that they had been bullied into joining the rebels.[82]

---

[75] Martha McTier, Belfast, to William Drennan, Dublin, 30 January 1799; Agnew, *Drennan-McTier Letters*, 2, p. 465.

[76] Grimshaw, *Incidents Recalled*, pp. 35–7.

[77] Recounted by James Hope; Madden, *The United Irishmen*, 3rd ser., vol. 1 (1846), p. 248.

[78] *BNL*, 23 June 1798, p. 3.

[79] George Stephenson, Downpatrick, to Lord Downshire, 12 June 1798, Downshire Papers, PRONI D507/F/226.

[80] James McKey, Belfast, to Lord Downshire, 14 June 1798, Downshire Papers, PRONI D607/F/244.

[81] John Moore Johnston, *Heterogenea, or Medley: For the Benefit of the Poor* (Downpatrick: James Parks, 1803), pp. 142–3.

[82] For example, in depositions sworn before the magistrate Captain James Clealand and produced at courts martial in Newtownards, James Robinson of Rathgill stated that he had been 'stopt on the

Records of courts martial held in Ulster show that a number of men were convicted for intimidating people into joining the rebel ranks. In other historical circumstances, such forced recruitment might have been recognized as a reason to exonerate and win over disenchanted rebels.[83] However, the claims of defendants who pleaded that they had been compelled to join the insurrection in 1798 were routinely dismissed and their sentences were not mitigated, which suggests that—for all their propaganda value—narratives of unwilling rebels were not fully believed by the authorities.[84] The stories were repeated nonetheless.

'Memories of '98' documented in the late nineteenth century by Rev. William Sunderland Smith, the minister of the Old Presbyterian Congregation of Antrim, are replete with accounts of attempts to force unwilling locals to partake in the rebellion. Mrs Thomas Hunter of Ardmore had heard her father Arthur McConnell of Corbally, who died in 1879 at age of 103, tell how he was 'impressed into the service of the band of United Irishmen, and a pitchfork put into his hand, with the injunction that he was to make good use of it', but he managed to escape from their camp under cover of darkness. Mrs Adam Gray of Dunadry recounted how a United Irish recruiter, who could not persuade her grandfather—John Baird of Ballywee (near Holestone)—to join the rebels, 'proceeded to compel him by taking forcible possession of his person'. According to Richard Fleming of Antrim, a passing band of yeomen rescued the Donegore farmer Samuel Skelton from being hanged by rebels after he resisted their call to arms. Similarly, 84-year-old John Ingram recalled that in his home area an army officer from Antrim had saved James Greer of Summerhill, Shanoguestown, from being murdered by United Irishmen for refusing to join their cause.[85]

On the one hand, such stories may recall actual incidents of coercion and popular opposition to the rebellion. At the same time, the prevalence in local folk history of accounts about reluctant rebels, who were forced to 'turn out', offered a convenient explanatory narrative for those who wished to repress recollections of their motivations for joining the United Irishmen. These narratives began to formulate at the time of the rebellion, as noted by an eyewitness in county Down, who met an insurgent deserter fleeing an engagement in Newtown and was told that 'it was with the greatest reluctance they went into the engagement and that great numbers broke their pikes and ran away.'[86] A year after the rebellion, Nugent observed that:

A manifested change has taken place in the sentiments of many former persons of all classes since the suppression of the rebellion as they have thereby considered themselves absolved

---

road . . . by a number of men' who sent him to join a rebel party commanded by Archibald Wilson of Conlig, and William Clark, Jr of Conlig stated that he was similarly accosted and 'ordered to join the Rebels'; Cleland Papers, PRONI D714/3/6 and 13.

[83] Anthony James Joes, *Resisting Rebellion: The History and Politics of Counterinsurgency* (Lexington, Ky.: University Press of Kentucky, 2004), pp. 166–70.

[84] Rebellion Papers, NAI 620/2/8/1–15; 620/2/9/1–29 and 34–36; 620/2/15/1–64; see also Patrick C. Power, *The Courts Martial of 1798–9* (Kilkenny: Irish Historical Press, 1997), pp. 137–72; Thomas Bartlett, 'Repressing the Rebellion in County Down', in *1798 Rebellion in County Down*, edited by Myrtle Hill, Brian Turner, and Kenneth Dawson (Newtownards: Colourpoint, 1998), pp. 187–210.

[85] See Smith, *Memories of '98*, pp. 27–31.

[86] John Catherwood, Balgown, to David Ker, 12 June 1798, Ker Papers, PRONI D2651/2/145.

from the treasonable oaths which they had taken either by compulsion or by the persuasive acts of designing villains.[87]

The flux in allegiance encouraged reconstruction of biographical and social memory through a blanket denial of ever having shown enthusiasm for republicanism and wilfully taking up arms in rebellion. Political conversion was an incentive for wilful forgetting of a past that had become an embarrassment.

UNFORGIVINGNESS

A great many people, who were unable to make a convincing transition into loyalism, were not allowed to put the past behind them. The pardon that had been authorized by Cornwallis and proclaimed by Nugent did not include 'the Principals who may have been very active in fomenting the present Rebellion', and this proviso was interpreted broadly by military officials so as to exclude many from clemency.[88] Even though a magistrate testified before a court martial in Coleraine on 13 July 1798 that John Gunning of Ballymoney had surrendered to him and taken an oath of allegiance in accordance with the proclamation, and the receipt of a certificate of protection was confirmed by another witness, Gunning was found guilty of having led rebels in his locality and punished accordingly.[89]

When suppressing the rebellion in the area of Ballymena, Colonel Clavering had issued a proclamation that offered amnesty to rebels who handed in their weapons. In Dublin Castle it was noted that this 'unwarrantable proclamation fetters Government extremely' and questions were raised as to 'how far it would compromise the faith of Government were they to proceed against those who have availed themselves of its offer of Pardon.'[90] Such compunction, however, was easily overcome. At a court martial on 1 July 1798, Thomas and James Montgomery, brothers from Broughshane in county Antrim, claimed that they had delivered their arms in compliance with Clavering's proclamation. Regardless, the court determined that they were rebel officers and sentenced them to death, a verdict which was approved by Clavering.[91] In such cases, the wider public was affronted by what was perceived as a breach of faith perpetuated by arbitrary enforcement of martial law. There was widespread sympathy for the condemned, whose fate was remembered as a grievance. A young eyewitness observed that the spectators were appalled by the execution of the Montgomery brothers and recalled it as an 'event that impressed my memory'.[92]

---

[87] Nugent, Armagh, 3 June 1799; TNA HO 100/89/47.

[88] *BNL*, 26 June 1798, p. 2.

[89] Initially condemned to be hanged, Gunning's sentence was mitigated by Colonel Henry Murray, the commanding officer in Coleraine, to transportation for life to Botany Bay; Rebellion Papers, NAI 620/2/8/10/13; see also Power, *The Courts Martial*, pp. 141–2.

[90] Edward Cooke, Dublin 16 July 1798, McCance Family Papers, PRONI D272/4.

[91] Rebellion Papers, NAI 620/2/9/28; see also Power, *The Courts Martial*, pp. 143–4. The brothers are mistakenly listed as Charles and John Montgomery in newspaper accounts; see *BNL*, 10 July 1798, p. 2; *Freeman's Journal*, 14 July 1798, p. 2. A half-century later, the facts had been slightly distorted in local social memory, which recalled that they were uncle and nephew and were executed for assaulting a local magistrate, Rev. William McCleverty, on the first day of the rebellion; see *Old Ballymena*, pp. 48–9.

[92] Robert Magill, 'Recollections of '98 in Broughshane', in Young, *Ulster in '98*, pp. 16–17.

Aware that 'several of the Principals concerned in the Rebellion in the county of Down have secreted themselves to evade the punishment which their crimes do truly deserve, and which must in the end inevitably overtake them', Major-General Nugent issued on 18 July 1798 a list of individuals for whom a reward of fifty guineas was offered. On 23 July, a similar notice followed for county Antrim. The wider population was cautioned that all those caught 'harbouring one or more of those persons, or knowing where they are' would 'suffer as capital offenders, and their property be destroyed'.[93] Lists of proscribed rebels were not restricted to the upper echelons of the United Irish leadership and were constantly revised and augmented.

The pursuit after wanted men was etched into social memory so that in the mid-twentieth century it was noted that 'the term "fifty-pounder" is still a familiar one in the north.'[94] Lieutenant-Colonel Atherton circulated in county Down a notice which demanded, as proof of loyalty, assistance in tracking down outlaws on the run. In order to 'ensure the Tranquillity of the Country', residents were required to remain at home under curfew and were alerted that 'the military have orders to burn the tenements of all those who are absent'. Blacksmiths and associated tradesmen were targeted for additional surveillance and prohibited from practising their trade, so as to prevent manufacture of weapons, and any offender caught violating the strict regulations was to be 'executed at his own door'.[95] In the Catholic parish of Ballinascreen, county Derry, a saying entered into popular Gaelic parlance: '*Cha rabh a léitheid aimsire againn ó dhóghadh tigh Chormaic Uí Dhuibhlin*' [we had not such times as these since Cormac O Devlin's house was burned], recalling the torching of the house of the local blacksmith by the yeomanry.[96]

Martial law had already been proclaimed as a preventative measure on 30 March 1798, in advance of the rebellion. Even prior to that, on 5 March, Sir Lawrence Parsons, a critic of the policy of repression, spoke out in the Irish parliament against how 'the North has been rendered quiet through the presence and immediate terror of a military force.'[97] The anxieties caused by the emergency regulations and the harsh punishments they carried would be recalled years later. A 'true narrative' published in the *Dublin Penny Journal* in 1834 told of a woman named Nannie Boyd from the area of Slemish, county Antrim, who sheltered an injured rebel officer. In doing so, she was aware that at any moment her house could be raided and inspected by troops, in which case her offense would be immediately discovered, as 'orders had been issued by the military, who then had the administration of the law, that a paper containing the names of all the family, males and females, should be posted on the outside door of every inhabited house.'[98]

---

[93] *BNL*, 20 July 1798, p. 3; 24 July 1798, pp. 3–4. A copy of Nugent's proclamation is held at the National Museum of Ireland; NMI HH:1997.3.

[94] Dickson, *Revolt in the North*, p. 158.

[95] Richard Musgrave Papers, NLI MS 4156; Notice to Blacksmiths & C., 24 June 1798, PRONI D277/2; *BNL*, 26 June and 10 July 1798, pp. 2 and 4 (respectively). Colonel James Durham, Commandant of Belfast, issued a similar warning against anybody caught assisting the concealment of an escaped prisoner; *BNL*, 3 July 1798, p. 3.

[96] H. Morris, 'Some Ulster Proverbs', *Journal of the County Louth Archaeological Society*, 4, no. 3 (1918), p. 272.

[97] *BNL*, 9 March 1798, p. 2.

[98] J. G., 'Old Nanny Boyd—a True Narrative', in *Dublin Penny Journal*, 2, no. 91 (1834), pp. 310–11.

With the outbreak of rebellion on 24 May 1798, Lieutenant-General Gerard Lake, the commander of the army in Ireland, declared his intention 'to punish Rebels in the most summary manner according to Martial Law' and, over the following weeks and months, this notice was repeatedly republished in newspapers.[99] Suspects dragged before drumhead courts martial around the time of the insurrection were subjected to unsparing retributive justice, which amounted to 'white terror'.[100] An example that happened to be noted in the local press was the execution of William Magill of Loughbrickland, county Down (16 km north of Newry), who was accused of 'swearing soldiers from their allegiance' and hanged on a lamp post opposite the Market House in Belfast on 9 June 1798.[101]

Captured rebels were often put to the sword without question, and, if treated to a rushed trial and found guilty, they were executed on the spot.[102] The injured United Irish colonel Hugh McCullough [McCulloch] of Bangor, county Down (whose brother was serving in the Downshire yeomanry) was taken prisoner at the Battle of Ballynahinch and, after 'a court martial was instantly held upon him', was hanged from the sails of the windmill perched on the summit of the hill on which the rebels had camped.[103] Captain-Lieutenant John Henry Slessor commented in his diary on the 'greatest difficulty' officers encountered in trying to restrain their men from 'committing all kinds of excesses' and Thomas Lane of Hillsborough informed Lord Downshire that 'the horrid acts of the rebels created such a paroxysm of revenge that even General Nugent could not restrain the Monaghan Militia.'[104] These excesses, which remain largely off the official record, were remembered in oral accounts.

Collecting traditions in Antrim towards the end of the nineteenth century, the antiquarian W. S. Smith met an old man named John Kilpatrick of Rathmore, who, prior to his death in 1874, recalled having witnessed in 1798 an officer shoot a deserter in cold blood, while he was waiting outside a court house for his trial. Kilpatrick himself had narrowly escaped being killed by a party of soldiers, who accused him of being a rebel and were about to shoot him in a field by the side of the road but were stopped by the fortuitous intervention of the local magistrate, Rev. Macartney.[105]

---

[99] *BNL*, 25 May 1798, p. 2.

[100] Thomas Bartlett, 'Clemency and Compensation: The Treatment of Defeated Rebels and Suffering Loyalists after the 1798 Rebellion', in *Revolution, Counter-Revolution, and Union: Ireland in the 1790s*, edited by Jim Smyth (Cambridge: Cambridge University Press, 2000), pp. 106–8.

[101] *BNL*, 12 June 1798, p. 2. William Magill was tried by court martial in Belfast on 2 June 1798; Rebellion Papers, NAI 620/28/1; see also Bartlett, 'Repressing the Rebellion', p. 191; Power, *The Courts Martial*, pp. 169–70.

[102] George Stephenson, Downpatrick, to Lord Downshire, 12 June 1798, Downshire Papers, PRONI D607/F/226.

[103] George Stephenson, Hillsborough, Co. Down, to the Marquess of Downshire, 13 June 1798, Downshire Papers, PRONI D607/F/236; William Hartigan, Dublin, to Lord Downshire, London, 16 June 1798, Downshire Papers, PRONI D607/F/250; Thomas Ledlie Birch, *A Letter from an Irish Emigrant, to His Friend in the United States* (Philadelphia: s.n., 1799), p. 14. For the depiction of McCullough's arrest in a contemporary painting of the battle by Thomas Robinson see Chapter 7, pp. 553–5.

[104] Entry for 8 June 1798; reproduced in Alethea Hayter, *The Backbone: Diaries of a Military Family in the Napoleonic Wars* (Edinburgh: Pentland, 1993), p. 42; Thomas Lane, Hillsborough, to Lord Downshire, 19 June 1798, Downshire Papers, PRONI D607/F/255.

[105] W. S. Smith, *Historical Gleanings in Antrim and Neighbourhood* (Belfast: Alex. Mayne & Boyd, 1888), pp. 24–6.

It was recalled locally that, after repelling the rebels in Antrim town, the military 'had orders to shoot every person in coloured clothes' and killed fugitives indiscriminately. One such case was the death of a resident named Quin and his 16-year-old daughter, who were shot when trying to flee their house, which had come under fire. They 'were buried where they fell, and it was said that the beautiful long hair of the girl was partly above the ground waving in the wind for many days'. In the 1840s, 'a gentleman of that town, one who had a personal knowledge of the circumstance, and in some of the matters connected with it' told the historian Richard Madden that 'this was the fact, and I recollect it excited more sympathy among the poor people than many horrid barbarities of the time.'[106]

Appalled by the 'wretched situation', Cornwallis wrote his confidant Major-General Ross to vent his exasperation:

> there is no law either in town or country but martial law, and you know enough of that to see all the horrors of it, even in the best administration of it, judge then how it must be conducted by Irishmen heated with passion and revenge. But all this is trifling compared to the numberless murders that are hourly committed by our people without any process or examination whatever. The yeomanry are in the style of the Loyalists in America, only much more numerous and powerful, and a thousand times more ferocious. These men have saved the country, but they now take the lead in rapine and murder. The Irish militia, with few officers, and those chiefly of the worst kind, follow closely on the heels of the yeomanry in murder and every kind of atrocity, and the Fencibles take a share, although much behindhand with the others[107]

Seeking to put an end to 'this system of blood', in early July 1798 Cornwallis requested royal approval for a general pardon, which would 'exclude from security of life, only those who have been guilty of cool and deliberate murder'. He proposed extending clemency even to the leaders of the rebellion, preferring banishment for fixed periods (and in some cases for life) over executions.[108] The Duke of Portland wrote back to convey the king's approbation of 'those lenient and conciliatory means you propose to employ for bringing back his deluded people of Ireland to a proper sense of their duty'. In turn, Cornwallis requested that an amnesty bill 'with the royal sign manual' would be issued with as little delay as possible.[109]

In its ancient Greek etymology, amnesty [*amnēstia*] is related to amnesia [*amnēsia*]. Early modern peace treaties in the civil wars of religion on the continent offered amnesty as a means of dissolving bitter memories that threatened to perpetuate conflict. Edicts of pacification in France, from the end of the first civil war in 1563 through to the Edict of Nantes in 1598, included amnesty clauses purposely intended to accommodate *oubliance*.[110] During the suppression of the Dutch revolt by the Spanish

---

[106] Madden, *The United Irishmen*, 2nd ser., vol. 2 (1843), pp. 472–3.

[107] Cornwallis to Major-General Ross, Dublin Castle, 24 July 1798; Ross, *Correspondence of Cornwallis*, vol. 2, p. 369.

[108] Cornwallis to Portland, Dublin Castle, 8 July 1798; Ross, *Correspondence of Cornwallis*, vol. 2, pp. 356–9.

[109] Portland to Cornwallis, Whitehall, 13 July 1798; Ross, *Correspondence of Cornwallis*, vol. 2, p. 364.

[110] See Philip Benedict, 'Shaping the Memory of the French Wars of Religion: The First Centuries', in *Memory before Modernity: Practices of Memory in Early Modern Europe*, edited by Erika Kuijpers et al. (Leiden and Boston: Brill, 2013), pp. 112–13.

Habsburgs (1578–1592), governor-general Alexander Farnese granted cities that capitulated a pardon with a stipulation of *oubli du passé*, which promised to forgive and forget in the sake of reconciliation.[111] Article 2 of the Treaty of Osnabrück of 1648, which formulated the Peace of Westphalia that brought an end to the Thirty Years War, stipulated that 'there shall be on the one side and the other a perpetual Oblivion, Amnesty, or Pardon of all that has been committed since the beginning of these Troubles' and decreed that 'all that has pass'd shall be bury'd in eternal Oblivion.'[112]

In seeking to ameliorate the bitter legacy of 1798, the policy of Cornwallis might have benefitted from an amnesty along the lines of the 1660 Restoration, which had passed 'An Act of Free and General Pardon, Indemnity, and Oblivion' (12 Cha. II c. 11) that decreed public forgetting of the Interregnum in order to cast aside the tensions of civil war in England.[113] In Ireland, however, the concept of introducing amnesia through amnesty did not fit well with already entrenched traditions, which relished in vindictive remembrance of rebellion. The version of the Indemnity and Oblivion Act put before the Irish parliament in 1664, as argued a century and a half later by the Irish-American radical polemicist Mathew Carey, included fifty categories of exceptions, 'embracing almost every conceivable crime of which the Statute-Book takes cognizance'.[114] Once again in 1798, the intention to promote forgetting in Ireland was predictably undermined.

On 17 July 1798, Castlereagh read to the Irish House of Commons a message from Cornwallis:

> that notwithstanding the abhorrence which his majesty justly entertained for the present unnatural Rebellion raging in this country, yet wishing to exercise his royal prerogative of mercy, and by lenient means to bring back a sense of their duty to those deluded from their allegiance, his majesty held forth free pardon and oblivion to all past offences, with such exceptions as should be deemed necessary to the public safety.

Castlereagh made it clear that this proposal required immediate attention and a similar announcement was made to the House of Lords two days later. Regardless of the need for urgency, legislation of the amnesty bill was dragged over several months. It was brought before parliament at the end of August and only received royal assent on 6 October.[115]

On the face of it, the legislation of 'An Act for the King's Most Gracious, General and Free Pardon' (38 Geo. III c. 55) seemed to be inclusive:

> all and every [of] his Majesty's subjects of this his Majesty's kingdom of Ireland, their heirs, successors, executors and administrators, and every of them, shall be, by the authority of

---

[111] Violet Soen, 'Reconquista and Reconciliation in the Dutch Revolt: The Campaign of Governor-General Alexander Farnese (1578–1592)', in *Journal of Early Modern History*, 16, no. 1 (2012), pp. 10–11.

[112] 'Treaty of Westphalia: Peace Treaty between the Holy Roman Emperor and the King of France and their Respective Allies', available in translation through the Yale Law School's Avalon Project; <http://avalon.law.yale.edu/17th_century/westphal.asp>. For contemporary 'Acts of Oblivion' see also Judith Pollmann, *Memory in Early Modern Europe, 1500–1800* (Oxford and New York: Oxford University Press), pp. 140–58.

[113] Jonathan Scott, *England's Troubles: Seventeenth-Century English Political Instability in European Context* (Cambridge and New York: Cambridge University Press, 2000), pp. 393–4 and 410.

[114] Mathew Carey, *Vindiciæ Hibernicæ; or, Ireland Vindicated* (Philadelphia: M. Carey & Son, 1819), pp. 274–88.

[115] *Walker's Hibernian Magazine*, August 1798, p. 575; *Journals of the House of Lords* (Dublin: printed by William Sleater, 1800), 8, pp. 116, 136, 138, and 187.

this present parliament, acquitted, pardoned, released and discharged against the king's most excellent Majesty, his heirs and successors, and every one of them, of and from all such treasons, misprisions of treasons and seditious words or libels, and also of and from all such riots, routs, offences, contempts, trespasses, pains of death, pains corporal, and pains pecuniary, and generally of and from all such other things, causes, quarrels, suits and executions which have been had, made, done, committed, perpetrated, incurred, or forfeited in prosecution or furtherance of the said rebellion, or in suppressing, counteracting, or in any manner putting down the same.

However, the bill incorporated a long list of exceptions, which included anyone charged or suspected of treason who had been detained anytime since 1795, all manner of murder or petty treason, soldiers (including militiamen and yeomanry) who had deserted to join the rebels or administered United Irish oaths, anybody involved in conspiring for a foreign invasion or corresponding with a hostile power, members of United Irish committees (at national, provincial, and county levels), all rebel officers, any person who failed to deliver arms and ammunition in their possession, those who had been attainted of high treason, those convicted by court martial since 24 May 1798, and all offences committed against any of the extensive Mutiny Acts.[116] In effect, despite the promised pardon, it was still practically possible to prosecute anyone involved in the rebellion.

Moreover, the bill named thirty individuals—half of them from Ulster—who were explicitly excluded from pardon. The extent of amnesty was even further curtailed by additional repressive legislation passed around the same time. This included a bill indemnifying the retributive actions of loyalists (38 Geo. III c. 74), a renewed bill to suspend *habeas corpus* in order to detain suspects of conspiracy (38 Geo. III c. 14), an insurrection bill that reinforced punitive measures for preventing disturbances of the public peace (38 Geo. III c. 21), a 'Banishment bill' preventing the return of rebels that had been transported or exiled (38 Geo. III c. 78), and a 'Fugitive bill' aimed at bringing to trial outlawed rebels (38 Geo. III c. 80).[117] Evidently, the proposals for a comprehensive amnesty put forward by Cornwallis had been substantially diluted.

Appeals for clemency encouraged displays of feigned forgetting, designed to downplay the extent of participation in the rebellion. A petition submitted to the Lord Lieutenant by William Russell of Ballymagee (near Bangor), county Down, is typical in its omissions:

> I, your humble supplicant, do freely confess that I was so unhappy as [to go] to Bangor that day of the Rebellion, along with a number more boys from our neighbourhood, and when they saw that the rest of the people had [orders] they cried out on the street of Bangor that they would have me for their leader. So I went away with them not thinking of my danger till too late.

By not mentioning what he actually did in the rebellion, Russell was hoping that his leadership role would be overlooked and that his plea for forgiveness—submitted 'as

---

[116] *The Statutes at Large, Passed in the Parliaments Held in Ireland: From the Third Year of Edward the Second, A.D. 1310, to the Thirty-Eighth Year of George the Third, A.D. 1798 Inclusive* (Dublin: printed by George Grierson, 1798), vol. 18, pp. 1054–9.

[117] See *Statutes at Large*, pp. 442–3, 777, 793–5, 1129–35, and 1138–40; see also *BNL*, 12 October 1798, p. 4. Fourteen individuals from Ulster are listed in the Banishment bill and another fifteen in the Fugitive bill. For accessible lists of the names see Madden, *The United Irishmen*, 2nd ser., vol. 2 (1843), appendix II, pp. 521–2.

upon the knees of my heart'—would be rewarded with a pardon.[118] For many proscribed rebels that option was not possible.

Following military defeat, the main leaders of the rebellion in Antrim and Down made desperate attempts to go into hiding but were soon apprehended, tried, and publicly executed. It has been repeatedly suggested in historiography that the defeated rebels in Ulster were treated more mercifully than elsewhere, but this claim is questionable. Thomas Pakenham—whose classic *The Year of Liberty* (first published in 1969) still stands out as a comprehensive modern history of the 1798 rebellion in all its arenas—rightfully pointed out that according to official statistics 'it was the Presbyterian North that suffered most executions.'[119] Northern rebels were not let off the hook lightly.

Henry Joy McCracken, the leader of the rebels at the Battle of Antrim town, was hanged in Belfast on 17 July at the Market House on High Street (Fig. 2.1).[120] He would subsequently be elevated to heroic martyrdom in nationalist-republican hagiography.[121] Likewise, Henry Munro, the Anglican leader of the county Down rebels at the Battle of Ballynahinch, was brought before a garrison court martial on 16 July and hanged that afternoon opposite the door of his own house in the centre of Lisburn.[122] Although he features less prominently than McCracken in republican commemoration, he became the subject of several popular folk songs, most notably 'General Munroe' (which has been collected in several versions).[123] Munro's head was severed from his body, fixed on a spike, and put on public display at the Market House, alongside the heads of other executed rebels. Several months later, Lord Bredelbane, the commander of a Scottish regiment quartered in Lisburn, ordered to remove these offensive exhibits, observing that 'it was a bad way to conciliate the people.'[124]

Conciliation was apparently not the order of the day. McCracken's corpse had been spared the indignity of decapitation and was handed over to his family on condition that it would be buried immediately, but this seemingly humane gesture was less indicative of compassion on behalf of General Nugent than of his concerns that the beheading of McCracken would provoke renewed agitation.[125] At the time, the heads of other United Irishmen—James Dickey, John Storey, Hugh Grimes and Henry Byers—were on display at the Market House in Belfast and would remain there for

---

[118] A Petition from William Russel[l] of Ballymagee to the Lord Lieutenant, 1799, Russell Papers, PRONI T3055/3. See also Sandra A. Millsop, 'Ballymagee, County Down', in W. H. Crawford and R. H. Foy (eds), *Townlands in Ulster: Local History Studies* (Belfast: Ulster Historical Foundation, 1998), pp. 108–9.

[119] Pakenham, *The Year of Liberty*, p. 284.   [120] *BNL*, 20 July 1798, p. 2.

[121] The most significant landmark in the canonization of Henry Joy McCracken is Richard Robert Madden's near-hagiographical biography; Madden, *The United Irishmen*, 2nd ser., vol. 2 (1843), pp. 399–506. A biography written in a similar vein half a century later by Francis Joseph Bigger, who collected additional local sources, remains unpublished; 'Life of the United Irishman Henry Joy McCracken (1767–1798)', Bigger Papers, BCL K2.

[122] Rebellion Papers, NAI 620/2/9/2; *Freeman's Journal*, 23 June 1798, p. 2.

[123] See Chapter 3, pp. 243–4.

[124] Madden, *The United Irishmen*, 3rd ser., vol. 1 (1846), p. 399. A vivid account of the execution of Munro and other rebels in Lisburn was written in the mid-nineteenth century by the local historian Hugh McCall; see anon. [McCall], *Ireland and Her Staple Manufactures*, pp. 129–35.

[125] Madden, *The United Irishmen*, 2nd ser., vol. 2 (1843), pp. 494–5; Mary McNeill, *The Life and Times of Mary Ann McCracken 1770–1866: A Belfast Panorama* (Belfast: Blackstaff Press, 1988; orig. edn 1960), p. 187.

Fig. 2.1. 'The Execution of Henry Joy McCracken'

Drawing by Joseph William Carey (1859–1937), who specialized in historical illustrations for antiquarian publications.

From Robert Magill Young, *Historical Notices of Old Belfast and Its Vicinity* (1896).

another month.[126] John Caldwell, an incarcerated United Irishmen who was brought to Belfast by coach in mid-July, later recalled the terror these severed heads produced on onlookers.[127] Similar gruesome sights were common in many other towns and were remembered for many years later. The display of the heads of two rebels named Cochron [Cochrane] and Lowans on spikes above the News Room in Newry was still recalled in the mid-twentieth century.[128]

---

[126] The heads were removed from the Market House on 17 August 1798; see 'Chronological List of Events in Belfast and Neighbourhood: 1797–98', in Young, *Ulster in '98*.

[127] John Caldwell, 'Particulars of History of a North County Irish Family', PRONI T3541/5/3, p. 106. The memoir was written in 1849 and drew on Caldwell's autobiographical writings from the 1820s; see David A. Wilson, 'John Caldwell's Memoir: A Case Study in Ulster-American Radicalism', in *Ulster Presbyterians in the Atlantic World: Religion, Politics and Identity*, edited by David A. Wilson and Mark G. Spencer (Dublin: Four Courts Press, 2006), pp. 104–27.

[128] Writing in the mid-twentieth century about these 'ghastly relics of the insurrection', the local nationalist journalist and politician Joseph Connellan relied on 'a tradition mentioned by Mr. Peter Fox, of Hill Street, some years ago'; *Fermanagh Herald*, 1 March 1948, p. 3; see also *Frontier Sentinel*, 4 November 1967. Recollection of the execution of Lowans in the nineteenth century is apparent in a letter written in 1897 that mentions reminiscences originally recounted 'more than fifty odd years ago'; *Newry Reporter*, 19 January 1898.

Fig. 2.2. 'Watty Graham's Beech', Maghera

Photograph by W. A. Green of a tree (uprooted in 1945) in Maghera, county Derry, on which it was recalled that Walter (Watty) Graham was hanged.

© National Museum NI, Collection Ulster Museum (HOYFM.WAG.1688).

According to local tradition, the Catholic servant of Walter Graham [known locally as Watty Grimes], who was executed on 15 June 1798 in Maghera, county Londonderry, was 'compelled by the soldiery to carry the head of his master up and down the street saying, "This is the head of a traitor"'. It was said that he was not up for the harsh task and in his sorrow fell back on a Hiberno-English expression of empathy, calling out instead: 'This is the head of a *craythur*'.[129] The manner of Graham's execution aroused considerable sympathy and was remembered in a ballad that gained wide popularity. Thomas Reid, who was a 5-year-old child at the time, would talk about the execution up until his death at the purported age of 105 in 1898. The place of the hanging was identified to surveyors in 1836 and the tree was for generations pointed out, until it was uprooted in a storm in September 1945 (Fig. 2.2). A mark on

[129] The execution of 'Walter Graham, otherwise Grimes' was noted in the press; *Londonderry Journal*, 19 June 1798; *Freeman's Journal*, 3 July 1798, p. 2. An early account of his involvement in the rebellion appears in McSkimin, *Annals of Ulster*, pp. 105–6 and 117. The story of his execution was recounted in the late nineteenth century by Thomas Witherow; see *BNL*, 12 May 1888, p. 6. See also Nora Ni Chathain, 'Watty Graham—The Maghera Patriot', in *Ninety-Eight*, edited by Seamus McKearney (Belfast: The 1798 Commemoration Committee, 1948), pp. 53–6; Eoin Walsh, *Watty Graham: Maghera Martyr* (Celbridge: printed by A. S. Donaldson, *c.*1955); R. L. Marshall, 'Maghera in '98', in *Presbyterianism in Maghera: A Social and Congregational History*, edited by S. Sidlow McFarland (Maghera: Presbyterian Church, 1985), pp. 175–6. A portrait of Graham was presented in 1949 by one of his descendants to the Belfast Museum; John Hewitt, 'Portrait of a United Irishman', *Belfast Municipal Museum and Art Gallery Bulletin*, 1, no. 2 (1949): pp. 29–30.

the nearby church wall was long believed, into the late twentieth century, to have been left when soldiers callously played ball with the severed head.[130]

In Ballymena, it was recalled that residents of the town were ordered to undertake the 'revolting operation' of cutting off the heads of hanged rebels:

> The humiliating office thus imposed upon them was submitted to as a matter of necessity, for they were unable to raise the exempting funds, and in order that the odium might be distributed extensively, a large number of the inhabitants put their hands to the knife in turn, and the heads were finally severed by a man excited by intoxication to the required act. The heads were then firmly fixed upon pitchforks, and elevated upon the tower of the market-house, where they remained a public and ghastly spectacle for many months.[131]

Thirty years later, the Presbyterian minister Rev. Robert Magill distinctly remembered having encountered as a 10-year-old boy 'the awful spectacle of human heads fastened on spikes and placed on the Market-house of Ballymena. When I looked up and saw the hair of the heads waving to and fro in the wind, I felt sensations indescribable.'[132]

Ellen Orr née Killen of Newgrove (near Broughshane, 5 km north-east of Ballymena), who passed away in 1871, would enthral her nephews by repeating her mother's accounts of

> the ghastly heads of some of these rebels swaying on poles which were set on the battlemented roof of the old Town Hall in Ballymena. On clear, frosty nights they would rattle and clink together ... and scraps of fraying flesh would come floating down to the street below.[133]

Such memorats fed into folklore and were vividly recalled in social memory. In 1955, an 80-year-old man in the glens of Antrim repeated to Michael J. Murphy—a collector for the Irish Folklore Commission—the stories he had heard from a grand-uncle, who 'remembered distinctly seeing the skulls on the spires in Ballymena and the hair still blowing in the wind on the skulls, he could never forget it'.[134]

Each community remembered the dead of its locality. The names of numerous executed rebels, by and large lost to national history, were discreetly preserved locally. Reactions to what was perceived as a 'reign of terror' were recalled through reminiscences of such instances as the 'solemn impression' left by the hanging of Daniel English, a Presbyterian-Covenanter accused of leading a party of United Irishmen in an attack on the house of Samuel Redmond of Thornhill, near the village of Connor in

---

[130] For the recollections of Thomas Reid see 'More Than a Centenarian', in *Derry Journal*, 21 January 1898, p. 8. The execution was listed among 'remarkable circumstances', in Fair Sheets by J. Bleakly (June 1836); Angélique Day and Patrick McWilliams, eds, *Ordnance Survey Memoirs of Ireland*, vol. 18: *Parishes of County Londonderry V, 1830, 1833, 1836–7, Maghera and Tamlaght O'Crilly* (Belfast: Institute of Irish Studies in association with the Royal Irish Academy, 1993), p. 74. R. H. Marshall noted in 1986 that the bloody mark on the old abbey wall 'was until recently shown'; Marshall, 'Maghera in '98', p. 176. For the song 'Watty Grimes' see Chapter 3 above, p. 244.

[131] *Old Ballymena*, p. 50.

[132] PRONI, D2930/9/15, Robert Magill, autobiography (*c.*1831); reproduced in Young, *Ulster in '98*, p. 17.

[133] The story told by 'Aunt Orr' (who died in 1871) about 1798 was recalled by her nephew Rev. George Wilson (who died in 1897) and appeared in a memoir compiled by his daughter in 1935; see James G. Kenny, *As the Crow Flies over Rough Terrain* (Ballymena: s.n., 1988), p. 186.

[134] Collected in March 1955 from John McAuley of High Street, Cushendall; NFC 1387/230.

county Antrim.[135] The approval of his court-martial sentence at Ballymena on 7 March 1800 merely lists the charge and states the verdict.[136] Social memory recalled the missing details, omitted from official documentation, on how such executions were carried out.

The execution of Daniel English featured in an account received 'from one who had it from an eye-witness', which was collected at the end of the nineteenth century by Rev. Samuel Ferguson of Waterside, Londonderry. This oral tradition described how English—with his arms pinioned and 'dressed in his grave clothes'—was accompanied on the long march from the guardhouse in Ballymena to the gallows on the bridge of Connor by a massive crowd of sympathizers, who were convinced that the evidence brought against him had been insufficient to secure his conviction. Additional consternation was caused by the denial of a proper burial. Relatives were determined to redeem this humiliation and retrieved the corpse, which had been interred under the gallows in an unconfined grave.[137] Such defiant acts of removing the bodies of condemned men have been recognized as expressions of 'public dissatisfaction with the administration of justice and an increased disposition to demonstrate discontent'.[138] In the early twentieth century, it was noted that the memory of this execution 'still lingers in local tradition'.[139]

Whereas historical documentation is sparse on many of the common rebels that were condemned to die, folklore fills in the gaps. The execution of Thomas Coulter of Ringbane, near Lecale in county Down, appears in a brief note appended to the record of his court martial at Downpatrick on 10 July 1798, where he was found guilty of 'treason, forcing people into rebellion, having a command and for seditious practices'. Local traditions collected from the mid-nineteenth century provided information on Coulter's failed attempt to escape arrest by swimming across a river near Strangford Lough and hiding in a wheat field. It was recalled that after his execution 'many a long and weary night his widowed mother mourned in loneliness over the remains of her beloved and only child.'[140]

The record of the trial of William Cuddy, who was convicted by a drumhead court martial in Maghera, county Derry, on 20 June 1798, does not mention any evidence brought against him and dryly notes that he was to be hanged and beheaded, with the instruction that the severed head should be put on public display at a place to be designated by Colonel James Leith, the commanding officer of the local garrison.[141] Oral tradition, recorded in the late nineteenth century by the Presbyterian historian

---

[135] James Seaton Reid and William D. Killen, *History of the Presbyterian Church in Ireland, Comprising the Civil History of the Province of Ulster, from the Accession of James the First*, 2nd edn (London: Whittaker, 1853), vol. 3, p. 424n35.

[136] Kilmainham Papers, NLI 1200/299–300.

[137] Samuel Ferguson, *Brief Biographical Sketches of Some Irish Covenanting Ministers Who Laboured During the Latter Half of the Eighteenth Century* (Londonderry: James Montgomery, 1897), pp. 55–6.

[138] Kelly, *Gallows Speeches*, p. 39.

[139] James Winder Good, *Ulster and Ireland* (Dublin and London: Maunsel & Co., 1919), p. 135.

[140] Rebellion Papers, NAI 620/2/15/14. Local recollections of Coulter's attempt to escape were first collected by the Downpatrick antiquarian J. W. Hanna; *Ulsterman*, 23 June 1858, p. 4 (republished in *UJA*, 2nd ser., 11, no. 2 [1905]: pp. 73–4); see also McCreery, *Presbyterian Ministers of Killileagh*, pp. 174–5. Colin Johnston Robb collected traditions about Coulter in the mid-twentieth century; *Irish News*, 4 March 1957 [name mistakenly given as Cotter].

[141] See Power, *The Courts Martial*, pp. 150–1.

Thomas Witherow, who had been a minister in Maghera for twenty years, maintained that 'an unseasonable jest cost him his life.' The story told locally was that 'he had been employed by somebody to insert a pane of glass in a leaden window-frame, and while doing the job he remarked jocularly that it would not be difficult to turn the lead into bullets.' It was said that this harmless comment was produced, at the insistence of the Protestant rector, as the grounds for his sentence. Cuddy went to his death professing his innocence and it was remembered that this 'case excited much commiseration at the time'. As befits a local folk hero, rumours spread that 'Billy Cuddy, cut down when halfhanged, was revived and smuggled to America.' In order to mislead the authorities, a mock funeral was supposedly held and the deception was kept up by the erection of a tombstone with his name at the local graveyard of St Lurach.[142]

Appalled perceptions of public executions were preserved in minute detail. Three quarters of a century after the rebellion, Rev. Alexander McCreery, minister of the second Presbyterian church of Killileagh, repeated from local tradition an account of the execution of five rebels from Killinchy on the Gallows' Hill at Downpatrick: 'It was an appalling spectacle. They were conducted from the prison to the place of execution with white caps on their heads and the fatal ropes fastened round their necks, and coiled up behind their backs.'[143] Clearly, the horrors of capital punishment were not forgotten.

The way in which memorable executions undermined amnesty and prevented amnesia was palpably demonstrated in the case of William Neilson [often spelt locally as Nelson], who was brought before a court martial in Carrickfergus on 25th June 1798 and charged with forcing a private in the Royal Invalids Regiment to join the rebels on 7 June. Although it could hardly be claimed that Neilson, who was aged only sixteen, was a principal leader of the rebellion, he was convicted of 'treason and rebellion' and sentenced to death.[144] The time and place of the execution was left to the discretion of the commanding officer of the district, who opted for a forceful demonstration of martial justice and ordered to hang the youth in his home village of Ballycarry in early July.[145]

The personal tragedy that befell the Neilson family was later recounted by William's sister and additional details were provided by his widowed mother, who was left destitute after her other sons were banished abroad.[146] The story was repeated in family and local traditions and later retold by William Neilson's niece, Miss Reid, to the Rev. Classon Porter of Larne, who also collected additional details in 1865 from 91-year-old

---

[142] *BNL*, 12 May 1888, p. 6; see also Marshall, 'Maghera in '98', p. 177. The story of the 'half hanging' and false burial was collected in the mid-twentieth century; see Ni Chathain, 'Watty Graham', p. 56.

[143] McCreery, *Presbyterian Ministers of Killileagh*, p. 174.

[144] William Colman, who was tried alongside Neilson for the same offence but had mitigating circumstances in his favour, was sentenced to 1,500 lashes and transportation for life; Rebellion Papers, NAI 620/2/9/16; see also Power, *The Courts Martial*, pp. 147–8.

[145] *BNL*, 6 July 1798, p. 2.

[146] Communicated by William Neilson's sister and mother to Mary Ann McCracken; TCD MS 873/694; published in Madden, *The United Irishmen*, 2nd ser., vol. 2 (1843), pp. 475–8. One of the brothers, Samuel Neilson, died on a transatlantic voyage and the other, John Neilson, was transported to the West Indies but escaped to America, where he became a noted architect; see also David Hume, *Far from the Green Fields of Erin: Ulster Emigrants and Their Stories* (Newtownards: Colourpoint Books, 2005), pp. 94–7.

Alex Service. The hanging tree was later considered an offensive sight and was chopped down.[147] Even after the tree's removal, it was said that the spot was 'often viewed with horror and indignation, by travellers as well as by the surrounding population'.[148] In social memory, Willie Nelson achieved apotheosis as 'the Ballycarry martyr', who was purportedly put to death because he refused to inform on his comrades. By the end of the nineteenth century, the hyperbolic rhetoric of the preparations for the 1798 centenary in Ulster declared: 'let us search the annals of our country from page to page, we cannot find one to compare with that brave young rebel soul.'[149] There was to be no oblivion of those believed to be wrongfully killed in what were perceived as acts of arbitrary retribution perpetrated by merciless authorities.

Military tribunals in the north-east often decreed vicious floggings, sometimes in addition to the main sentence. James Caldwell of Limavaddy, who impenitently professed at his court martial to be a United Irishman, was to receive 1,000 lashes for his outspokenness before being sent abroad for life in His Majesty's service.[150] Rulings of hundreds of lashes exceeded human capability for suffering and often could not be carried out in full. The death sentence of a rebel from Maghera named Grey, who was convicted on the confession of his own brother, was 'mercifully' mitigated by the Earl of Cavan to 1,500 lashes, of which 300 were inflicted.[151]

Spectators at these public floggings were left with horrific memories. Rev. Magill recalled:

> I saw Samuel Bones, of Lower Broughshane, receive 500 lashes, 250 on the back, and 250 on the buttocks. I saw Samuel Crawford, of Ballymena, receive 500 lashes. The only words he spoke during the time were 'Gentlemen, be pleased to shoot me.' I heard him utter them. I saw Hood Haslet, of Ballymena, receive 500 lashes. I believe he was only then about 19 years of age. Before he had received 100 lashes, I heard him exclaiming 'I'm a-cutting through.'[152]

Sixty-five years after the rebellion, 91-year-old James Burns of Templepatrick, who in 1798 had deserted from the Royal Irish Artillery to join the rebels, reminisced about the escapades of a fellow deserter, William Murphy of Armagh. Murphy had supplied the United Irishmen with ammunition taken from Carrickfergus Castle, for which he was to be sentenced to death, but was instead transported to the West Indies. Burns recited a song about Murphy, which included verses that recalled an additional whipping ordered by Colonel Lucius Barber of the Royal Irish Artillery:

> It was by a Court-Martial this hero they did try,
> And by his false accusers he was condemned to die.
> At length, the 1000 lashes he was for to sustain
> 'Twas more than double punishment for any in the crime!

---

[147] Young, *Ulster in '98*, pp. 25–7.
[148] McHenry, *The Insurgent Chief* (1844 edn), p. 466.
[149] *Northern Patriot*, 1, no. 8 (5 June 1896): p. 123. See also Chapter 5, pp. 415–16.
[150] Rebellion Papers, NAI 620/2/8/5; cited in Power, *The Courts Martial*, p. 138.
[151] *Freeman's Journal*, 3 July 1798, p. 2. Another example is Adam Millar of Cardy, who was sentenced by Rev. Cleland at a court martial at Newtownards to 500 lashes and was discharged after 425; Rebellion Papers, NAI 620/2/15/43; reproduced in Bartlett, 'Repressing the Rebellion', p. 194.
[152] Magill, 'Recollections of '98', p. 17.

> When they took him from the guard-house to the halberts he was bound,
> Where all those cruel officers brave Murphy did surround.
> Besides there were ten drummers stripped in a line did stand
> To flog this noble hero, as Barber gave command.
> There being one among the rest to him did mercy shew,
> For which the tyrant Barber gave him a deadly blow,
> And sixty-seven lashes he was to receive besides.[153]

Another case of a bystander punished for showing compassion at a flogging was recalled in the late nineteenth century. Thomas Given of Markstown told how a young man named James Giffen of Cullybackey had offered to take upon himself the remaining lashes of an old man named Esler, who had fainted during the course of his flogging at Clough (11 km north of Ballymena). In consequence, Giffen was arrested as a rebel sympathizer and hanged.[154]

These memories persisted in local storytelling traditions. Mary O'Hare of Saval Beg, near Newry, who was said to have died in 1886 at the age of 104, recalled the flogging to death in Rathfriland of a captured rebel who had attempted to escape from Downpatrick jail, noting that 'residents of the district stated that so mercilessly was he beaten that his intestines protruded through his flesh.'[155] Sometime shortly before 1885, the aged Catholic former rebel Paddy O'Heany from the Glen of Banagher in county Londonderry, who claimed to be 103 years old, recounted to the folklorist Letitia McClintock how at the 'the time o' the Uniting' he had witnessed in Dungiven the merciless flogging of the Presbyterian rebel Jack McSparron, who was fortified by his mother not to give in and inform on his comrades: 'They gave him a great many lashes . . . I dinna mind how many hundred it was, an' each time they stopped he was asked if he would tell, an' his mother still bid him die like a man, an' his answer was still the same.'[156]

In 1889, at the well-attended funeral of Quintan O'Kane of Swateragh at the Catholic cemetery in Granaghan, county Derry, the ministering priest Father Gallen stated that 'it was well known to the people of the neighbourhood that the father of the old gentleman whose remains was before them, was, in common with many of his countrymen, a sufferer in fatal '98'. It had become 'a well known fact' that Jack O'Kane had been stripped and flogged on the Diamond of Kilrea and after receiving 125 lashes took upon himself also half of the strokes of an old man who was too feeble to bear the flogging to which he had been sentenced.[157] The public flogging of David Matthews of Lurgancahone in the square of Rathfrilan was still recalled locally in the early twentieth century.[158] Such harrowing displays of cruel punishment, pitilessly meted out in public on former rebels, would not be readily forgotten.

---

[153] Collected by Rev. Classon Porter on 5 September 1863; see Young, *Ulster in '98*, pp. 48–50.

[154] Smith, *Memories of '98*, p. 60 (for additional recollections of floggings in the area of Coleraine and Ballymena see pp. 62–3).

[155] Joseph Connellan, 'Newry District and the Men of "Ninety-Eight": Seaver's Killeavey Yeomanry', in *Frontier Sentinel*, 9 September 1967.

[156] Letitia McClintock, 'An Actor in the Rebellion of 1798', *Belgravia*, 55 (1885): pp. 185–9.

[157] 'Funeral of Mr Quintan O'Kane, Swateragh: A Reminiscence of '98', in *Derry Journal*, 15 August 1889; extract in Bigger Papers, BCL K4/J.

[158] Andrew Morrow, 'The Rev. Samuel Barber. A.M., and the Rathfrilan Volunteers (Continued)', *UJA*, 2nd ser., 16, nos. 1/2 (1910), pp. 39–40.

EXILING MEMORY

There were many signs that the trials of former rebels were not conducted with impartiality and that convictions were pursued with excessive fervour. A revision of the court martial proceedings of Henry Fleming confirmed that he was not guilty of the charge of 'being very active in the Rebellion' and yet, in disregard of the conditions of amnesty promised by Major-General Nugent, he was still condemned for being 'too far implicated in it'.[159] Joseph Irvine was sentenced to be hanged at a military tribunal, which considered any involvement in the rebellion in Antrim whatsoever a 'breach of the articles of war'.[160] Judges at a court martial in Ballymena vented their inquisitorial zeal when they unwarily denounced Francis Shields and John Martin for 'being men of wicked principles, not having the fear of God before their eyes and being moved and seduced by the Devil' and a similar accusation appeared in the trial of John Bayans. Repulsion from the violence of the rebellion was augmented by the identification of republicanism with evil, evident in a contemporary loyalist poem titled 'Satan Unmasked'.[161]

In an effort to ensure the integrity of judicial procedures and prevent vindictive excesses, Cornwallis personally revised the minutes of courts martial, devoting, according to the Lord Chancellor, 'five hours each day in that laborious and humane office'.[162] Whenever it was deemed acceptable, he opted for remitting death sentences in favour of sending former rebels abroad. Expulsion was sanctioned through sentences of 'general service' in the army, transportation to the penal colony in Botany Bay, or banishment to a country that was not at war with Britain.[163] Castlereagh instructed the commanders in Ulster that 'in case any persons are convicted Capitally before the Court Martials now sitting within your District that you will respite their execution, and communicate with me, for the Lord Lieutenant's information, before the sentence is put in force.'[164] In practice, verdicts of courts martial in Ulster were vetted by the top military command and, as a rule, Cornwallis refrained from overturning their decisions.

Major-General Nugent quickly realized that indiscriminate rulings of capital sentences were not in favour and that 'we had therefore better endeavour to send as many abroad, either at their own expense or to serve.'[165] This preference was upheld by local commanding officers, such as Lord Murray, who repeatedly overturned death sentences at the courts martial in Coleraine, opting instead to transport condemned rebels to

[159] Rebellion Papers, NAI 620/2/9/17.   [160] Rebellion Papers, NAI 620/2/9/20.

[161] Kilmainham Papers, NLI 1200/258–26 (Shields and Martin) and 302–4 (Bayans). 'Satan Unmasked' was written on 15 July 1798 and published the following year; *BNL*, 21 June 1799, p. 4.

[162] *Freeman's Journal*, 20 March 1800, p. 2.

[163] See Michael Durey, 'Marquess Cornwallis and the Fate of Irish Rebel Prisoners in the Aftermath of the 1798 Rebellion', in *Revolution, Counter-Revolution, and Union: Ireland in the 1790s* edited by Jim Smyth (Cambridge: Cambridge University Press, 2000), pp. 128–45.

[164] Letter from Castlereagh dated 30 July [1798]; McCance Family Papers, PRONI D272/2. Castlereagh later acted on behalf of the Lord Lieutenant and approved death sentences ruled by court martials held in Ballymena, county Antrim, in February and March 1800; Kilmainham Papers, NLI 1200/250–253 (Alexander Stewart), 1200/257–258 (James McCarthy and William Linn), 1200/299–300 (Daniel English), 1200/301–302 (Samuel Dunlop).

[165] Nugent to Leslie, 9 August 1798, National Archives of Scotland, Leslie Family Papers, GD 26/9/527/1/7; cited in Bartlett, 'Clemency and Compensation', p. 112.

Botany Bay.[166] In numerous cases, such as batches of rebels who were court martialled in Lisburn in July 1798, trial proceedings were suspended in accession to requests by the accused for permission to serve abroad for life.[167]

Moreover, the incarceration of thousands of suspected rebels awaiting trial proved to be a heavy burden on an overstretched prison system. A yeoman officer professed his frustration with the situation after the Battle of Ballynahinch:

> We are tormented by the number of prisoners here. I wish from my heart they were all
> hanged, for such a set of rascals I never heard of. Indeed, I think it was wrong to make them
> prisoners. They should have been shot at once, and then one would not have been plagued
> with them.[168]

Financial considerations surfaced in court-martial verdicts. John Crawford of Toome was acquitted of the charge of being a rebel leader in July 1798 after he and his family paid substantial securities to the total of 4,000 pounds.[169] The approval of the decision to release Charles McAuley from the guard house in Ballymena in February 1800 was dependent on whether 'his situation and circumstances will enable him to obtain bail to the extent adjudged by the court'.[170] Contemplating the fate of the prisoners, Castlereagh came to realize that:

> It would be very desirable, for many reasons, to get rid of them as speedily as possible, as it is
> difficult to confine them with the necessary precaution; and the expence of this regiment of
> traitors exceeds five-fold that of the best regiment in the King's service.[171]

In order to cut costs and rid the country of United Irishmen, many inmates were released on the condition that they would leave the country permanently.

This policy was informally introduced on a ground level at an early stage and was declared officially in Belfast on 23 August 1798, when Major-General Nugent issued a proclamation that offered 'state prisoners' (a term that generally referred to United Irish leaders who had been arrested before the outbreak of the rebellion and therefore could not be easily convicted), as well as 'others whom it may concern' in the Northern District, the same conditions that had been negotiated in a special arrangement with the high-profile state prisoners in Dublin. This meant that they would be allowed 'to emigrate to such country as should be agreed upon between them and Government, giving security not to return to this country without the permission of Government and not to pass into an enemy's country'.[172]

---

[166] The sentences of at least three Antrim rebels (Hugh Boyd and James Well of Ballycastle and John Gunning of Ballymoney), who were condemned to be hanged after which their severed heads were to be publicly displayed, were commuted by Murray to transportation; Rebellion Papers, NAI 620/2/8/10, 11, and 13. Lord Henry Murray, who arrived in Ireland with the Royal Manx Fencibles, played a key role in suppressing the rebellion in north Antrim as the commander of the garrison at Coleraine.

[167] Rebellion Papers, NAI 620/2/8/14 and 15.

[168] George Stephenson, Hillsborough, to Lord Downshire, 27 June 1798, Downshire Papers, PRONI D607/F/283.

[169] Rebellion Papers, NAI 620/2/9/19.

[170] Kilmainham Papers, NLI 1200/258–261; Littlehales, Dublin Castle, to Gen. Drummond, 24 February 1800, NLI 1200/256.

[171] Castlereagh to Wickham, Dublin Castle, 29 October 1798; Vane, *Correspondence of Castlereagh*, vol. 1, p. 414.

[172] Rebellion Papers, NAI 620/4/55 (includes an annotated list of prisoners entitled to this benefit, compiled in Belfast on 24 August 1798); *Freeman's Journal*, 28 August 1798, p. 2.

More often than not, the commuting of a sentence to banishment was the privilege of United Irishmen who had influential relatives and friends who could intercede on their behalf.[173] On the other hand, the economic rationale for allowing rebels to independently relocate with their families to a foreign country was made clear following the conviction of John McCreery of Ballymanister in county Down. He was sentenced in Newtownards to transportation for fourteen years to New South Wales, but the court requested General Nugent in earnest to allow the prisoner 'to transport himself to America as he has a wife and eleven children who otherwise must remain a burthen on their country'.[174]

The use of such arrangements by the authorities to remove troublesome radicals is apparent in the case of the Caldwell family of Harmony Hill, Balnamore (near Ballymoney) in county Antrim. Eighteen-year-old Richard Caldwell was wanted for having commanded, together with John Gunning, a contingent of rebels that assembled at Kilraughts and attacked the nearby town of Ballymoney. After the rebellion, the two 'Fifty Pounders' crossed the Glens of Antrim, took a boat from Cushendall to the Mull of Kintyre and went into hiding in Scotland, where they were arrested by Rev. Alexander Campbell, the minister of Kilcalmonell, and returned to Ireland. On 13 July 1798, Caldwell was brought before a court-martial and sentenced to death but his father, John Caldwell, Sr, who was a well-connected merchant from a respected Ulster-Scots family, appealed to Cornwallis for clemency.

Richard's elder brother, John Caldwell, Jr, had been a leading fundraiser for the United Irish organization in Ulster. He was arrested prior to the outbreak of rebellion in the North and held outside Belfast aboard the Postlethwaite prison ship, known as the 'floating Bastille'. The magistrate Edmund McNaghten of Beardiville commented that 'all his family and connections are notoriously disaffected. Altho [sic] I cannot bring any proof against any one of them.' Cornwallis took advantage of the opportunity to rid the country of a troublesome family. Richard Caldwell's death sentence was remitted in exchange for a bond, which guaranteed that the father, both sons and their families would leave Ireland for 'the term of their natural lives and never more to return to any part of his Majesty's European dominions'. After some delays, they all emigrated to the United States, carrying with them resentful memories. Years later, at the age of 81 John Caldwell still bitterly recalled how the house of his father, who had abstained from involvement in the rebellion, was burnt to the ground and his dependents were forced to take shelter under a carpet thrown over two hedges before moving to live in their bleaching house.[175]

---

[173] See, for example, a letter by Castlereagh requesting that the sentence of James Long of Magilligan, whose brother was 'a very respectable officer', in the Londonderry regiment, be commuted to banishment to America, Castlereagh Papers, PRONI T424/4 (copy also found in McCance Family Papers, PRONI D272/2/8).

[174] Rebellion Papers, NAI 620/21/15/18.

[175] John Caldwell, 'Particulars of History of a North County Irish Family', PRONI T3541/5/3, pp. 107–9. The Caldwell Family Papers and correspondence testify to the repercussions of their involvement in the rebellion and to their forced emigration; PRONI T3541/1–6. Copies of letters also appear in Rev. D. Stewart Papers, D1759/3/B/6, and extracts from John Caldwell's memoir can be found in J. B. Hamilton Papers, PRONI D1518/1/1. The Rebellion Papers provide additional information: NAI 620/2/8/8 and 620/3/51/5 (court martial record of Richard Caldwell); 620/37/132 (Edmund A. McNaghten to Castlereagh, 23 May 1798). See also T. H. Mullin, *Coleraine in Georgian Times* (Belfast: printed by Century Services, 1977) p. 158–71; David A. Wilson, 'John

Numerous local traditions recollected how rebels who could not benefit from amnesty became outlaws and went 'on their keeping', making every effort to avoid arrest and escape overseas. The chorus of a song described in the late nineteenth century as 'an old ballad' included the verse 'For I'm a Fifty Pounder, and am obliged to flee.'[176] John Nevin of Kilmoyle, near Dervock in county Antrim (8 km north of Ballymoney), who had commanded rebels in the area of Ballymena, was one such fugitive. A ballad toasted 'Captain Nevin, God bless his lovely eyes' and recalled that the 'gallant hero' had overcome yeomen who tried to arrest him.[177] Family traditions recounted how Nevin, after hiding in various locations, was smuggled out of Coleraine hidden in a barrel and sailed to America from Magilligan in county Derry.[178]

After finding a living as a trader with Indians in the frontier of east Tennessee, Nevin wrote his family to say that he was 'Now in this Country Under a Real Republickan Government and the Best in the Woreld [sic]'. Nonetheless, like many of the exiles of 1798, he was beset by homesickness. Prohibited from fulfilling his desire to return to Ulster, he died abroad, bequeathing his property in America and land in Antrim to his siblings, 'who suffered persecution with me in Ireland for my political Opinions'.[179] His family made sure that he would not be forgotten by commissioning the manufacture of a number of commemorative china jugs, which were dedicated:

> To the memory of John Nevin of Kilmoyle, who was by the Foes of Reform Banished from his Native Home in June, 1798. He lived in the state of Exile seven years, eleven months, eight days, and departed this Life in Knoxville, Tennessee, 19th of May, 1806, Much lamented by all his Friends, Acquaintances, and Friends to their Country.

These 'memorials' were kept as treasured heirlooms.[180] One of the souvenir jugs was acquired in the 1960s by the Ulster Folk Museum. Previously to that another jug was exhibited in the Ballymoney town hall and was later put on permanent display alongside Nevin's sword in the Ballymoney museum, which received in 2015 yet another jug that

Caldwell's Memoir', pp. 114–19. According to the military, Caldwell's house was destroyed 'in consequence of his having forced his son to join the rebels'; Abercorn Papers, PRONI D623/A/90/23.

[176] Young, *Ulster in '98*, p. 39n.

[177] Collected in the late nineteenth century by Thomas Camac from John Ferguson of Carnaff, county Antrim; Thomas Camac, 'The Parish of Derrykeighan (County Antrim) for Three Centuries', *UJA*, 2nd ser., 5, no. 3 (1899): p. 154. Another local historian, Rev. Hugh McNeill, collected in the late nineteenth century a verse of the ballad from the oldest inhabitant of the area, 90-year-old John Ross, of Crofthead; reproduced in Hugh McNeill, *The Annals of the Parish of Derrykeighan: From A. D. 453 to A.D. 1890* (Ballymena: Mid-Antrim Historical Group, 1993; orig. edn 1910). See also Keith Beattie, *Ballymoney and the Rebellion 1798*, 2nd edn (Ballymoney: Ballymoney Borough Council, Leisure & Amenities Dept., 1998), 15–17.

[178] Collected in the late nineteenth century from John Nevin's grand-nephew, Captain John Nevin, and from Mrs Thomas Bryson of Antrim, a descendant of Nevin's companion-in-arms Peter Lyle; Smith, *Memories of '98*, pp. 64–5 and 67–9; see also Mullin, *Coleraine in Georgian Times*, pp. 158–60, 168, and 170. These traditions are rooted in stories told already in the aftermath of the rebellion, see *Journal of a Tour in Ireland . . . Performed in August 1804* (London: printed for Richard Phillips, 1806), p. 22.

[179] John Nevin, Knoxville, Tennessee, to James Nevin, Kilmoyle, Ballyrashane Parish, County Antrim, 10 April 1804; PRONI T3727; reproduced with reference to Nevin's will in Kerby A. Miller, *Irish Immigrants in the Land of Canaan: Letters and Memoirs from Colonial and Revolutionary America, 1675–1815* (New York and Oxford: Oxford University Press, 2003), pp. 603–8. See also T. H. Mullin, *Families of Ballyrashane: A District in Northern Ireland* (Belfast: printed by News Letter Printing, 1969), pp. 310–13.

[180] Smith, *Memories of '98*, pp. 68–9.

had hitherto been thought lost.[181] Forced exile was long remembered by the families that stayed at home and their communities.

Fugitives on the run often aspired to sail for America, but actually fled to wherever they could find asylum, sometimes arriving in remote corners. It was recalled both in Antrim and in Down that a few individuals found shelter in faraway Norway.[182] The free German towns of Altona and Hamburg, viewed as a gateway to continental Europe, were preferred destinations. Hamburg served as a temporary stop for many United Irishmen, who were unaware that their activities were being monitored by an informer, Samuel Turner, who had previously resided in Newry, county Down and had infiltrated United Irish circles in Ulster.[183] The prominent Belfast United Irishman Samuel Neilson, who was arrested before the outbreak of the rebellion in the North and held at Fort George in Scotland as a state prisoner, was exiled in July 1802 to Altona and forbidden to return to Ireland. In 1889, his granddaughter, Elizabeth Thomson, recalled from family tradition how he had paid a secret visit to arrange for the emigration of his family to America, 'but after being one night at home, he was warned to fly again having been warned that the authorities knew he was there. This visit, then, was the only time my mother ever saw her father and she must then have been about seven years old.' Neilson's plans to be re-united with his family remained unfulfilled. He made it to Poughkeepsie, New York, but died there of sickness in August 1803.[184]

A Banishment bill passed in 1798 to prevent the return of exiled rebels was extended and renewed in 1799 (39 Geo. III c.36) and again in 1800 (40 Geo. III c. 44).[185] Although some minor rebels quietly made their way home unperceived by the authorities, the repatriation of proscribed rebels was officially prevented for many years. William Putnam McCabe, who was listed among the proscribed United Irishmen excluded from the amnesty, went into hiding in Scotland and fled to France in 1799. Known as a master of disguise, he used his resourcefulness to travel incognito and pay visits home, during which he narrowly avoided capture on several occasions, until he

[181] James B. Hamilton, *Ballymoney and District in the County of Antrim, Prior to the 20th Century* (Ballycastle: J. S. Scarlett & Son, 1958), p. 87; Aiken McClelland, 'A Link with the '98', in *Ulster Folk Museum Year Book 1966–67* (Cultra, Co. Antrim: Ulster Folk Museum, 1968), pp. 14–15; Bill Murray and John Cullen, *Epitaph of 1798: A Photographic Record of 1798 Memorials on the Island of Ireland and Beyond* (Enniscorthy: Carrigbyrne Film Productions Ltd and The Carrigbyrne Pikegroup, 2002), p. 8; 'Rare United Irishmen Nevin Jug Donated to Museum', in *BNL*, 25 June 2015. For Nevin's sword see <www.visitballymoney.com/captain-john-nevins-sword.aspx>; <www.bbc.co.uk/ahistoryoftheworld/objects/yGTdMIZsQgSdClsgni38vg>.

[182] In county Antrim it was remembered that James Hunter of Gallaugh escaped to Norway, taking with him Bob Major of Belfast; Young, *Ulster in '98*, p. 40; Smith, *Memories of '98*, p. 59. In county Down it was recalled that John Robb and Alexander Lowry, who fought at the Battle of Ballynahinch, made their way to Norway; Colin Johnston Robb, 'Insurgent Colonel John Robb', in *Irish Independent*, 19 July 1946, p. 4; Colin Johnston Robb, 'Fate of an Irish Patriot of '98', in *Down Recorder*, 6 June 1971, p. 3.

[183] See Paul Weber, *On the Road to Rebellion: The United Irishmen and Hamburg, 1796–1803* (Dublin: Four Courts Press, 1997); see also Thomas Bartlett, *Revolutionary Dublin, 1795–1801: The Letters of Francis Higgins to Dublin Castle* (Dublin: Four Courts Press, 2004), pp. 50–2.

[184] Copy of notes dictated by Elizabeth Thomson and written by her daughter Bessie Thomson (written *c*.1889–91; copy made 1913), F. J. Bigger Papers, NLI 35,143. In 1880, Irish-American nationalists placed a marble slab memorial on Samuel Neilson's grave in Poughkeepsie and in 1905 a monument was unveiled; Bigger Papers, BCL K4/J.

[185] See *Statutes Passed in the Parliaments Held in Ireland: From the Thirty-Ninth Year of George the Third, A.D. 1799 to the Fortieth Year of George the Third, A.D. 1800 Inclusive* (Dublin, 1801), vol. 12, pp. 10–12 and 152.

was arrested in 1814 and deported to Portugal. McCabe later returned to Belfast to try
and regain his property but was denounced by his step-mother and imprisoned in
Kilmainham gaol for a year and a half, after which he was again obliged to go into exile.
Following McCabe's death in 1821, his daughter (who had joined him in prison) was
left destitute in Paris.[186]

When the question of the fate of the United Irish exiles was raised in 1832, the
Home Secretary, Lord Melbourne, admitted to the Lord Lieutenant of Ireland, the
Marquess of Anglesey, that only rarely had people that 'were deeply implicated in
the rebellion of 1798' been allowed to return to Ireland.[187] As late as 1834, the
London Observer reported that a pardon had just been given to a former rebel named
McKan [McCann], who had been residing in Germany. That same year, Arthur
O'Connor, a former senior United Irishman living in exile in France, was permitted
to return only for a limited period in order to address some urgent 'private affairs'.[188]
The sense that escape abroad meant a lifetime of separation was captured in a poetic
'sorrow song of 1798' from the early twentieth century in which a woman laments
the loss of a lover who fled the country as a punishment worse than death:

> Wud God he'd fallen at Antrim toon!
> Wud God the Redcoats had shot me doon!
> Far bether the ane grave for him an' me.
> Than both o' us dhramin' dhrames that can niver be.[189]

For many United Irishmen, exile became a permanent condition.

In addition to those compelled to leave by decree, large numbers of radicals who
could not reconcile themselves with the state of the country after the rebellion
voluntarily opted for emigrating to the United States, following patterns of Ulster-
Scot Presbyterian migration that were already well established by the end of the
eighteenth century.[190] An unpublished history of Irish Presbyterianism, written in
1803 by the Rev. William Campbell of Armagh, noted that after the rebellion:

> Presbyterians went in thousands to America. And if ships had been found, thousands
> more would have sought a peaceful asylum in that land of Liberty—a happy refuge from
> the despotism of England—far removed from the violence of her satellites and legal
> assassins.[191]

To a newspaper in Massachusetts, it seemed in September 1798 that 'every ship vomited
United Irishmen on the American shore.'[192] Though nowhere near as torturous as

---

[186] Account collected by R. R. Madden from McCabe's daughter, Mrs Nesbitt, in Paris, October
1843; Madden, *The United Irishmen*, 3rd ser., vol. 1 (1846), pp. 355–9.
[187] Lord Melbourne to Lord Anglesey, 5 October 1832, Anglesey Papers, PRONI D619/29/A/90.
[188] *BNL*, 2 May 1834, p. 4 (McKan) 28 March 1834, p. 4 (O'Connor).
[189] 'Molly Asthoreen', in Padric Gregory, *Ulster Songs and Ballads* (Dublin: Talbot Press and
London: Fisher Unwin, 1920), pp. 30–1.
[190] See Michael Durey, *Transatlantic Radicals and the Early American Republic* (Lawrence: University Press of Kansas, 1997), esp. pp. 134–73; Wilson, *United Irishmen, United States*.
[191] Presbyterian Historical Society of Ireland, MS William Campbell, 'Sketches of the History of
Presbyterians in Ireland', p. 100; cited in Wilson, *United Irishmen, United States*, pp. 33–4.
[192] *Salem Gazette*, 18 September 1798; see Kevin Whelan 'The Green Atlantic: Radical Reciprocities between Ireland and America in the Long Eighteenth Century', in *A New Imperial History:
Culture, Identity, and Modernity in Britain and the Empire, 1660–1840*, edited by Kathleen Wilson
(Cambridge: Cambridge University Press, 2004), p. 227.

the dehumanizing 'rough crossings' endured by African slaves, the transatlantic voyages of United Irish exiles were nonetheless remembered as extremely unpleasant experiences. The poet James Orr of Ballycarry, a proscribed rebel who fled to America, depicted in vernacular Ulster-Scots verse the tribulations of the passengers of 1798 as they endured stomach-churning gales, 'frae gulph to gulph we're tumble't', which left them panic-stricken, 'win's, wives, an' weans, rampage an' rave'. Upon docking in Newfoundland, they faced quite literal rites of passage, as seaman forcefully extracted 'the poll-tax' of 'a pint, or else a shillin' a piece' and shaved without soap those who could not pay.[193]

Not all of those who emigrated were able to resettle in the New World. In a memoir written some forty years after the events, Aynsworth Pilson of Downpatrick recalled how the surgeon Samuel Johnston of Seaforde in county Down had accompanied Mathew Forde, the commander of the Seaforde and Kilmore Yeomanry, to the Battle of Ballynahinch and yet was obliged to emigrate on account of the discovery that his brother-in-law and nephew, Ambrose and Samuel Cramer, were United Irishmen. Johnston sailed to America with his family in July 1800 but, faced with 'an inglorious exile and prospective poverty', he soon 'yielded to remorse'. Within a year and a half, Johnston succumbed to 'chagrin and the cruel extinction of his hopes' and, following his untimely death, his widow and children had to make their own way back to county Down.[194]

The wholesale departure of Presbyterian radicals seems to have been encouraged by the government, which was interested in clearing Ulster of subversive elements. The removal of 'a large and disproportionate number' of politically disaffected people, as argued by the Kerby Miller, helped secure unionist hegemony.[195] Visiting Ireland a decade later, the English writer Edward Wakefield commented on the noticeable effects of politically motivated emigration: 'In Ulster there is a very strong republican party . . . but many who would have formed their most daring and zealous partisans, finding their principles disliked, and their views little encouraged, emigrated to America.'[196]

Commenting on the dispersal of his rebel comrades, James Hope remarked: 'The few who were neither to be intimidated nor corrupted, were thus sacrificed in one way or the other, either put to death or banished, or pursued, and forced to fly to foreign countries.'[197] Ultimately, the export of United Irishmen became the defining feature of the 1798 amnesty policy. Between those who left by stealth, those who emigrated freely, those who were sentenced to leave, and the released prisoners who undertook to remove themselves, there was an exodus of thousands of Ulstermen who had been involved with republicanism and insurrection.[198] This mass migration had far-reaching

---

[193] 'The Passengers', in James Orr, *Poems on Various Subjects* (Belfast: Smyth & Lyons, 1804), pp. 114–20. Cf. Simon Schama, *Rough Crossings: Britain, the Slaves, and the American Revolution* (New York: Ecco, 2006); Marcus Rediker, *The Slave Ship: A Human History* (New York: Viking, 2007).

[194] 'Memoirs of Notable Inhabitants of Downpatrick', Aynsworth Wilson Papers, PRONI D365/7.

[195] Whelan, 'The Green Atlantic', pp. 230–1; Kerby A. Miller, ' "Heirs of Freedom" or "Slaves to England"? Protestant Society and Unionist Hegemony in Nineteenth-Century Ulster', *Radical History Review*, no. 104 (Spring 2009): pp. 17–40.

[196] Wakefield, *An Account of Ireland*, vol. 2, p. 493.

[197] Madden, *The United Irishmen*, 3rd ser., vol. 1 (1846), p. 269.

[198] Trevor Parkhill, 'The Wild Geese of 1798: Emigrés of the Rebellion', in *Seanchas Ardmhacha*, 19, no. 2 (2003): pp. 118–35.

consequences for the remembering and forgetting of 1798 in Antrim and Down. Memory has often been studied in relation to place, as in Jay Winter's seminal study of the sites of mourning that commemorate the dead of the First World War in Europe.[199] Such an approach is especially inviting in rural Ireland, where the retention over long periods of family names in specific localities gives an impression of long-term continuity. However, remembrance is first and foremost tied to people and follows their migration patterns. Even though local folk histories recalled the names of some of the rebels who left and the circumstances in which they were obliged to depart, when taken as a whole, their withdrawal signalled a drain of memory from Ulster.

The dispersal of rebels to remote locations, where they had to eke out a living, shattered the social frameworks ('*les cadres sociaux*'), which, as Maurice Halbwachs demonstrated, are essential for maintaining collective memory.[200] An act passed to augment the amnesty bill and prevent former rebels from returning declared it forbidden under penalty of transport for life to 'directly or indirectly hold any communication or correspondence by writing or otherwise, with any person who shall be so transported, exiled, or banished' (38 Geo. III c. 78).[201] Even though such a sentence of social excommunication could not be comprehensively policed, the government was intent on severing ties between those who were forced to leave Ireland and those who remained.

The conditions of service abroad were unsparing. In accordance with a special request from the King of Prussia, which the government was pleased to oblige, three hundred and fifty of the sturdiest rebel prisoners—among them many from Ulster—were handpicked for service in the Prussian army and sent to Emden.[202] A story was later told of a Mrs O'Neill, who bribed a jailer at the New Geneva barracks in a desperate last attempt to pay a visit to her son, before his departure for Prussia, but, after being cruelly tormented by the guards, was prevented from meeting him.[203] Once the prisoners had been dispatched, it was practically impossible for their friends and relations to contact them. In the case of James McCambridge, a loyalist from Ulster who was erroneously convicted and sent to Prussia on the basis of perjured evidence, even official efforts made by the authorities to locate his whereabouts were unsuccessful.[204]

When not in action, the Irish recruits were compelled to labour 'like slaves' in Prussian mines. A number of them fell captive at the Battle of Jena in 1806 and were permitted to join the Irish Legion of the French army, where they fought alongside

---

[199] Jay M. Winter, *Sites of Memory, Sites of Mourning: The Great War in European Cultural History* (Cambridge: Cambridge University Press, 1995), pp. 78–116 ('War Memorials and the Mourning Process').

[200] Halbwachs, *Les cadres sociaux de la mémoire*.   [201] *Statutes at Large*, pp. 1129–35.

[202] See Wickham to Castlereagh, Whitehall, 18 March 1799; Vane, *Correspondence of Castlereagh*, vol. 2, p. 215; Wickham to Castlereagh, Whitehall, 29 April 1799, ibid., p. 292; Wickham to Castlereagh, Whitehall, 8 May 1799, ibid. p. 300. For reports on rebel prisoners in Ulster offered for Prussian service see *BNL*, 16 April 1799, p. 3; 7 May 1799, p. 2; 31 May 1799, p. 3; 18 June 1799, p. 3; 13 August 1799, p. 3.

[203] Constance Markievicz, 'The Women of '98', in *Irish Citizen*, 6 November 1915, p. 150. The claim in oral tradition that women visitors to New Geneva 'were always subject to terrible insults and indignities' is partly confirmed by an inmate's recollections of the brutal punishment inflicted on wives suspected of smuggling in clothes to facilitate an escape; see *Andrew Bryson's Ordeal: An Epilogue to the 1798 Rebellion*, edited by Michael Durey (Cork: Cork University Press, 1998), p. 66.

[204] See also Durey, 'Marquess Cornwallis', p. 137.

United Irish émigrés, among them the Ulsterman Rev. Arthur MacMahon, the former Presbyterian minister of Kilrea and Holywood, who was listed as proscribed on the amnesty bill and had fled to France via Hamburg.[205] Another group deserted and escaped to Austria. Prussian demands for their return were refused and, through the intercession of the sympathetic Anglo-Irish peer Lord Cloncurry, they were repatriated and allowed to resettle in Ulster.[206] Despite such reunions, there are no surviving records of the recollections of rebels who were drafted into Prussian service.

Prisoners of lesser stature, who were considered too unruly or unsuitable for service in the army, were transported aboard convict ships to the penal colony in New South Wales. Court martial sentences of transportation for life often stipulated that the convict would be hanged in the event that he returned to Ireland or, for that matter, to 'any of his Majesty's European dominions'.[207] The precise numbers of rebels who were transported cannot be determined, as in many cases the surviving records do not make clear distinctions between political prisoners and common criminals. A conservative calculation estimated that 350, about a third of all the Irish convicts who landed in Australia between 1800 and 1806, had been rebels.[208] The presence of hardened United Irishmen amongst the convicts was apparent in the many conspiracies that were uncovered and it appears that northerners were prominent in these schemes. Peter McClean from Ulster was hanged on 14 December 1800 for his role as one of the ringleaders of a plot to take over the convict settlement on Norfolk Island with crudely manufactured pikes.[209] Samuel Humes of Moneyduff near Cloughmills in county Antrim, who had left Ireland in 1801 aboard the *Hercules*—a ship which experienced a mutiny on its voyage to Australia—was one of the leaders of the convict uprising known as the Castle Hill rebellion, for which he was executed and hung in chains at Parramatta on 8 March 1804.[210] Evidently, military defeat, imprisonment, and transportation had not broken their spirit of defiance.

Despite these outbreaks of violence, once the former rebels served their terms, they usually settled down and were integrated into Australian colonial society. Commenting on the lack of archival documentation, the historian George Rudé noted that 'most rebel-convicts, like the convicts in general, melt into the crowd after the first few years

---

[205] *Memoirs of Miles Byrne: Chef de Bataillon in the Service of France, Officer of the Legion of Honour, Knight of Saint-Louis, etc.*, edited by Fanny Byrne (Paris and New York: Gustave Bossange et Cie, 1863), vol. 1, pp. 40–1 and vol. 3, pp. 163–4. For Arthur MacMahon see W. A. Maguire, 'Arthur McMahon, United Irishman and French Soldier', in *Irish Sword*, no. 9 (1969–70), pp. 207–15; also *UJA*, 2nd ser., 15, no. 1 (1909), pp. 36–41 and nos. 2/3 (1909), pp. 134–8.

[206] See *Personal Recollections of the Life and Times, with Extracts from the Correspondence, of Valentine, Lord Cloncurry* (Dublin: James McGlashan, 1849), pp. 207–8. Francis Joseph Bigger issued an appeal in the early twentieth century for 'personal details of these Ulster exiles' in an unsuccessful attempt to uncover their traces; 'Ulster Exiles on the Continent after '98', in *UJA*, 2nd ser., 12, no. 1 (1906), p. 46.

[207] Examples of the explicit denial of possibility of return can be found in sentences given at courts martial in Ballymena in March 1800; Kilmainham Papers, NLI 1200/302–304 (John Bayans); 1200/352–354 (John Gamble); 1200/354–355 (Alexander Sheerer).

[208] George Rudé, 'Early Irish Rebels in Australia', in *Historical Studies*, 16, no. 62 (1974), pp. 17–35.

[209] Robert Hughes, *The Fatal Shore* (London: Vintage, 2003), pp. 116–17.

[210] Anne-Marie Whitaker, *Unfinished Revolution: United Irishmen in New South Wales, 1800–1810* (Sydney: Crossing Press, 1994), p. 103. For the mutiny on the *Hercules* see Charles Bateson, *The Convict Ships, 1787–1868* (Sydney: Reed, 1974; orig. edn 1959), pp. 179–82.

from their arrival and tend to disappear from view.'[211] The assimilation of former convicts from Ulster left few traces of historical memory. Over the nineteenth century, the 1798 rebellion became a founding myth for Irish-Australians, which would receive broader public recognition at the centennial commemorations in Sydney in 1898. Commemorative attention in Australia focused on Catholic rebels from the South, in particular the 'Wicklow Chief' Michael Dwyer, largely overlooking the memory of northern Presbyterians.[212]

An eye-opening glimpse into the personal experiences of a transported Ulsterman can be found in a 'Diary of an Irish Rebel', which was deposited in Sydney's Mitchell Library in the early twentieth century. Initial consideration of the text maintained that it contained 'nothing of startling interest'.[213] It later transpired that the journal was written by William Orr of Creavery, a namesake and relative of the celebrated United Irish martyr. He was arrested in a post-rebellion sweep of United Irishmen in Antrim on 16 April 1799 and imprisoned at the Provot jail in Belfast. At his court martial, on 9 May 1799, Orr was charged with 'treason and rebellion, in aiding and assisting in taking up arms, and making ball cartridges, and being out of his house after sunset and before sunrise'. Orr professed his innocence, declaring: 'I found that several of my relatives had been charged with some of the crimes which then disgraced the country, and I profited by the melancholy examples I saw before me and studiously avoided entering into any Society or Schemes whatsoever.' Indeed, among his kin were Samuel Orr of Kilbegs, a rebel commander at Randalstown who saved himself by becoming an informer, and John Orr of the Folly, who was sentenced to death for his part in the Battle of Antrim. In addition, his brother, John Orr of Creavery, had escaped to America after participating in the rebellion, in consequence of which the family's home was destroyed by the military. William Orr offered to banish himself to America, but was sentenced to 'serve the King of Prussia'.[214]

A petition for the release of William Orr was submitted to Dublin Castle by his widowed mother, Elizabeth Orr, and was supported by the Rev. George Macartney, the magistrate responsible for his arrest, who later became convinced of his innocence. However, the petition was processed too late. Orr, who apparently did not meet the standards of the Prussian draft, was transported to Australia, sailing out of Cork harbour aboard the *Friendship* on 24 August 1799 and arriving after an arduous voyage at Botany Bay on 16 February 1800. In a cryptic memo labelled 'a vision', which outlined the key dates of his ordeals, Orr allegorically referred to his arrest as a time when he 'grew sick', to the verdict of transportation as having 'died & sailed for unknown regions', and to his journey to the Antipodes as having 'crossed Styx and arrived at

[211] Rudé, 'Early Irish Rebels in Australia', p. 28. Rudé tracked down information on the fortunes of several former rebel-convicts, including three from Ulster: Patrick Mason, a shoemaker from Saintfield, county Down, who was a farmer in Richmond; Robert Chambers, an elderly weaver from Londonderry, who was a servant in Windsor; Tristram Moore from Broughton, in county Derry who became a farmer in Wilberforce (pp. 32–5).

[212] *Sydney Morning Herald*, 23 May 1898, p. 3; *Evening News* (Sydney), 23 May 1898, p. 7; *Freeman's Journal*, 28 May 1898, pp. 6–9; see also Patrick J. O'Farrell, *The Irish in Australia* (Kensington: New South Wales University, 1987), pp. 29–34 and 51–3.

[213] 'Diary of an Irish Rebel', State Records New South Wales, 13697 (Microfilm SR Reel 2504; see also *Sydney Morning Herald*, 27 February 1932, p. 9.

[214] Account of William Orr's court-martial, *BNL*, 17 May 1799, p. 3; Orr's defence statement, Col. J. B. Wilson (depositor) Papers, PRONI T1956/3.

purgatory'. By 1805, when Mrs Orr finally succeeded in convincing Castlereagh that her son had been wrongly convicted, William Orr was working in his profession as a watchmaker in the colony. The letter with his pardon arrived after he had escaped aboard an American ship, which took him to Calcutta, where he spent two years before moving on to Penang, living in both places incognito, under the alias of William Jamieson. Orr returned to Ireland in 1822 and settled in Newgrove, near Broughshane in county Antrim, where he married and lived in obscurity till the age of 86.[215]

William's brother John Orr, who had returned from exile in America, concealed the memory of his involvement in the insurrection and upon his death in 1840 was considered to have been 'an old reformer', rather than a former rebel.[216] William Orr's tombstone at Kirkinriola cemetery alludes vaguely to 'various vicissitudes in early life', without actually mentioning the heavy price he had paid in consequence of the rebellion. Although his presence in Newgrove was known in 1843 to Richard Robert Madden, the biographer of the United Irishmen, he was not interviewed and did not merit more than a passing comment in Madden's canonical history.[217] Recollections of Orr's time away did not survive as family traditions and his remarkable life story had to be pieced together from fragmentary archival sources at the end of the twentieth century by a diligent local historian, Bob Foy of the Antrim and District Historical Society.[218] As this case demonstrates, Ulster folk history did not preserve memories of those who were transported.

A large number of rebel prisoners, estimated by Michael Durey at 3,200, were sent to the West Indies and drafted into British regiments, which were emaciated by disease and in need of constant reinforcements.[219] A rare personal account of such a typically unpleasant post-rebellion experience was written by Andrew Bryson from Ballysallagh, county Down (near Downpatrick). Bryson, who had commanded rebels in Newtownards, was proclaimed a 'Fifty Pounder' and explicitly excluded from pardon in the amnesty bill. Following the rebellion, he went into hiding but was caught, tried, and sentenced to service aboard. Bryson was then taken to the prisoner depot in New Geneva, near Waterford, and confined in the 'Belfast Barrack', where he had the 'melancholy pleasure' of meeting many northern acquaintances who had met a similar fate.[220]

After several weeks, marked by witnessing prisoner escape attempts and displays of disobedience that were severely punished, Bryson sailed to Martinique, where the commanding officer insisted that the 'Belfast People' should be dispersed in different units. He was one of ten Ulster rebels assigned to the 43rd regiment. They suffered from fever and several of them died on the isle. Together with a friend named Sibbett, Bryson succeeded in escaping from St Pierre aboard an American ship, which brought

[215] 'A Vision', William Orr Papers, PRONI D4391/2/1 (also found in T1956/2); correspondence concerning William Orr's release, PRONI D4391/1/1–4 and T1956/4–10; petition of Elizabeth Orr, 21 January 1805, NAI Prisoner Petitions and Cases 1140; see also Foy, *Remembering all the Orrs*.
[216] Dr John Paul, Carrickfergus, to William Orr, Newgrove, 10 May 1840; PRONI T1956/12.
[217] See Madden, *The United Irishmen*, 2nd ser., vol. 2 (1843), p. 464.
[218] See Foy, *Remembering all the Orrs*.
[219] See Michael Durey, 'White Slaves: Irish Rebel Prisoners and the British Army in the West Indies 1799–1804', in *Journal of the Society for Army Historical Research*, 80 (2002), pp. 296–312.
[220] PRONI T1373/5; reproduced in Durey, *Andrew Bryson's Ordeal*, pp. 21–59.

him to New York. There he met his father, who had been imprisoned during the rebellion and was then forced to emigrate, as well as his brother and other United Irish acquaintances.[221] On behalf of the exiled family members, Daniel Robb, Andrew Bryson's brother-in-law, applied for a reprieve that would allow them to return to their homes in county Down, but, although Robb was recognized as 'a good and peaceable subject', his request was denied.[222]

Bryson's memoir, written in New York on 28 May 1801 as a long letter to his sister Nelly Robb née Bryson of Ballysallagh, glosses over the details of his participation in the rebellion and dwells on the hardships of imprisonment and the transatlantic voyage. In contrast to the undocumented recollections of the many other United Irishmen who were sent to the West Indies and are now unrecoverable, the composition of Bryson's narrative shows how the United Irish emigrant networks in the United States provided a context for the formulation of diasporic memories. Such letters were essentially expressions of private remembrance and Bryson entreated his sister 'not to expose the writer by letting any person see it'.[223] Once United Irish émigrés had established themselves in the United States, their recollections could become public. Ninety-Eight was recognized as a central episode in Irish-American collective memory, which in time would be overshadowed by the Famine. This reservoir of memory in North America would later offer a resource for re-charging memory in Ireland.[224]

IMPENITENCE

If, outside of America, the exiling of memory largely resulted in amnesia, the deliberate attempt to introduce forgetting through amnesty in Ireland encountered recalcitrance. Cornwallis's course of action was applauded by Castlereagh for its 'mixture of firmness and leniency'.[225] Serjeant Stanely, a member of parliament who spoke out in support of 'the general measures', argued that Cornwallis:

> had wisely tempered justice with clemency—at the same time that he held forth oblivion and pardon to the repentant and deluded, he had selected the most active characters as objects of public justice[226]

Conversely, ultra-conservatives dubbed the Lord Lieutenant 'Croppy Wallis', ridiculing his policy of placating rebels, who were commonly referred to as 'Croppies'.[227] Driven by revanchist urges, loyalists clamoured for indiscriminate punitive repression of disaffected areas.

---

[221] Durey, *Andrew Bryson's Ordeal*, pp. 59–105.
[222] Robb family correspondence, PRONI, T1454/3/1.
[223] Durey, *Andrew Bryson's Ordeal*, p. 103.
[224] For further discussion of emigrant letters and the influence of recollections from America see Chapter 3, pp. 171–3.
[225] Castlereagh Papers, PRONI, T424/4.
[226] Speech of Irish House of Commons, 26 February 1799; *BNL*, 5 March 1799, p. 4.
[227] Robert Ross to Lord Downshire, 29 October 1798, Downshire Papers, PRONI D607/F/502; see also William Sampson, *Memoirs of William Sampson: An Irish Exile* (London: Whittaker, Treacher and Arnot, 1832), p. 22n.

Robert Ross, an associate of Lord Downshire, registered the seething resentment among loyalists who were convinced that 'overtures have been made to the rebel chiefs.'[228] After the Battle of Ballynahinch, Ross expressed the frustration aroused by Cornwallis's insistence on proper legal procedures:

> For God sake, let the innocents be hanged, and then when the rebellion is extinguished, a bill of indemnity cures all. Any other proceeding is rank insanity, and common sense tells you, if the hydra head is not taken off, it will produce shortly a second rebellion.[229]

Hardliners opposed any form of appeasement. The conservative politician Patrick Duigenan (who would become the grand secretary of the Orange Order in 1801) complained to Castlereagh about 'the unaccountable conduct of the present Lord-Lieutenant, which has rendered him not only an object of disgust, but of abhorrence, to every loyal man'.[230] Amnesty was a red flag for stalwarts of the Ascendancy.[231] The spymaster William Wickham (at the time a superintendent in the Home Office) observed that 'at present there is a general, I may say universal, persuasion that lenient measures have been carried too far.'[232]

The concern that amnesty would cast a veil on the memory of atrocities committed by insurgents encouraged vocal enumeration of the grievances of 'Suffering Loyalists'. At the same time, victory over the rebels was celebrated gloatingly. The chorus of the popular loyalist song 'Croppies Lie Down' revelled in the humiliation of the United Irishmen. One of its versions mocks the rebellion in Ulster, with a stanza on the victory in Antrim, in which 'The Northerns display'd the merciless steel,' and another on Ballynahinch, where 'The innocent croppies were thrown on their back.'[233] This triumphalist rhetoric thwarted efforts for reconciliation.

Loyalists, who firmly opposed dispensations for former rebels, demanded blanket absolution for the brutal excesses committed by unrestrained troops and vindictive vigilantes. As a concession, the amnesty bill granted pardon for any deeds that had been done 'in suppressing, counteracting, or in any matter manner putting down' the rebellion.[234] In addition, a separate bill promised those on the government's side who had committed 'acts not justifiable by law' that they would receive indemnity from 'all personal actions, suits, indictments, informations, attachments, molestations, prosecutions and proceedings'.[235] Consequently, loyalists were not obliged to confront

---

[228] Ross to Downshire, 12 July and 26 July 1798, Downshire Papers, PRONI D607/F/314 and D607/F/339 (respectively).

[229] Ross to Downshire, 16 June 1798, Downshire Papers, PRONI, D607/F/249.

[230] Dr Duigenan to Castlereagh, Dublin, 20 December 1798, Vane, *Correspondence of Castlereagh*, vol. 2, pp. 52–3.

[231] A typical northern example can be found in a long letter written by Sir George Fitzgerald Hill, MP for Londonderry City arguing against the government's policy of amnesty; see G. F. Hill, 5 July 1798, Hill of Brook Hall Papers, PRONI D642/A/15.

[232] William Wickham to Castlereagh, London, 4 March 1799, cited in Ross, *Correspondence of Cornwallis*, vol. 3, p. 90.

[233] *A Collection of Loyal Songs, as Sung at All the Orange Lodges in Ireland* (Dublin: printed by W. McKenzie, 1798), no. 1.

[234] 38 Geo. III c. 55; see *Statutes at Large*, p. 1054.

[235] 38 Geo. III c. 74; see *Statutes at Large*, pp. 442–3. Indemnity for acts committed 'for the preservation of the public peace, and the suppression of the insurrections prevailing in some parts of this kingdom' was extended in additional legislation in 1799 (39 George III c. 3), 1800 (40 George III c. 89), and 1801 (41 Geo. III c. 49).

their misconduct in 1798. When translated into the cultural politics of memory, the triumphalism of loyalists, who doggedly reminded republicans of their crushing defeat, entailed tacit forgetting of their own wrongdoings.

Cornwallis complained that 'the ferocity of the loyalists will not for a long time permit the restoration of perfect tranquillity,' yet bloodthirsty loyalists were not alone in destabilizing his efforts to put the conflict to rest.[236] When the Northern District remained 'perfectly quiet' during the French invasion of Connacht in August 1798, it seemed that Ulster had been completely subdued.[237] It soon transpired that many unrepentant rebels were still active in Ulster, regardless of the declared amnesty. The reasoning behind their obstinacy was explained by James Hope:

> I felt bound to that cause to which I had pledged my life along with my countrymen, and I considered to surrender under that proclamation, was not only a recantation of one's principles, but a tacit acquiescence in the justice of the punishment which had been inflicted on thousands of my unfortunate associates. To hold up my hands for pardon to those who had imbrued theirs in the blood of my associates, seemed to me to carry with it a participation in the guilt of the blood of my brethren. Thinking a clear conscience of all things most necessary, and looking to the Most High alone for protection, I could not join in any written or verbal acknowledgment of guilt, or solicitation for pardon to any human being. I resolved never to be taken alive [238]

Committed United Irishmen evidently felt obliged to honour the memory of their dead comrades and refused to submit.

Diehards from the lower classes, who could not afford the heavy costs of emigration, found an outlet for continued resistance in brigandage. Widespread disaffection was evident in the return of Defenderism. The Defenders was a secret society that in the early 1790s had been associated with Catholic agrarian violence, particularly in south-east Ulster. When mobilizing for the rebellion, the United Irishmen had invested effort into subsuming this subversive organization. Ulster was considered fertile ground for such a merger. The Catholic United Irishman Charles Hamilton Teeling was active in the smaller towns of Ulster, swearing in Defenders, and in December 1795 Henry Joy McCracken was 'sent round the northern counties in order to unite the Defenders with the United Irishmen'.[239] After the United Irishmen had been dealt a fatal blow in 1798, the Defenders re-emerged with a vengeance.

---

[236] Cornwallis to Major-General Ross, Phoenix Park, 8 June, 1799; Ross, *Correspondence of Cornwallis*, vol. 3, p. 102.

[237] General Nugent, Enniskillen, to General Hewitt, 30 August 1798; TNA HO 100/78/308–309. The attorney John Pollock, who was effectively a government spymaster in Belfast, informed William Wickham, after news arrived of the French landing in Mayo, that 'so perfectly loyal and quiet is this part of the country'; John Pollock, Belfast to Wickham, 26 August 1798; TNA HO 100/81/339–340. In spite of subsequent news that General Lake had been defeated at Castlebar, Pollock re-affirmed that 'this country continues firm, peacable, and in a state of perfect quiet'; Pollock, Belfast to Wickham, 31 August 1798; TNA HO 100/81/377.

[238] Madden, *The United Irishmen*, 3rd ser., vol. 1 (1846), pp. 268–9.

[239] For recollection of Teeling's activities see Madden, *The United Irishmen*, 3rd ser., vol. 1 (1846), p. 231. For information collected by Dublin Castle on McCracken's mission see Edward Cooke to Lord Pelham, 4 December 1795, Pelham Papers, BL Add. MS 33101 f. 359 (copy found also in Pelham Transcripts, PRONI, T755/2, p. 254). For pre-rebellion Defenderism see Marianne Elliott, 'The Defenders in Ulster', in *The United Irishmen: Republicanism, Radicalism and Rebellion*, edited by David Dickson, Dáire Keogh, and Kevin Whelan (Dublin: The Lilliput Press, 1993), pp. 222–33;

The revived Defenders in post-rebellion Ulster changed their composition, bridging sectarian divides that had previously excluded Presbyterians. Rev. Snowden Cupples, the Anglican rector of Lisburn and a prominent county Down loyalist, reported that Defenderism had been 'modified as to comprehend such Protestants as prefer revolution and plunder'.[240] While expressing satisfaction at the decline of the United Irishmen, Castlereagh observed that in their place:

> Defenderism was introduced, and it is principally under that organization, into which the most profligate of the Dissenters have been prevailed on to enter, that whatever there is of treason in the North is at present associated. They are destitute of leaders; and the people of substance, manufacturers as well as farmers, have withdrawn from them.[241]

Alarmed by the daily increase in rebellious activities in Antrim, Rev. Edward Hudson noted that 'the name of United Irishman is never heard, it is merged in that of Defender' and 'The "D[efende]rs" oath has taken place of the "United" one, and this is taken not only by Catholics but P[resbyterian]s.'[242] The reconfiguration and resurgence of this secret society, which the authorities could only comprehend to a very limited extent, was recalled in local folk history.[243]

A version of a ballad on the rebel general Henry Munro, collected by the antiquarian Samuel McSkimin in the first half of the nineteenth century, addresses an audience of 'all you Defenders wherever you be'. Some years later, Rev. Classon Porter was told that 'The Defenders' oath, as at first proposed, was of such a kind that no true-bred Presbyterian or Protestant could take it. But it was afterwards modified, and generally taken in this neighbourhood.' In 1863 he found that there were still a number of elderly Presbyterians in the area of Larne, county Antrim, who professed to have been Defenders. Among them was 91-year-old James Burns from the parish of Ballynure, who could repeat a Defenders' song.[244] In the late nineteenth century, Robert Johnston, formerly of Deerfin (5 km west of Ballymena), county Antrim, repeated to the antiquarian Francis Joseph Bigger family traditions which recalled how, after the insurrection, the United Irish 'intrepid captain' Jack Fullarton [Fullerton] of McTrusterystown, Liminary (nearby Ballymena) invited his neighbours to an illegal 'Defender's Dance'.[245]

In open defiance of the government clampdown on rebels, parties of 'armed banditti' raided unwary military patrols and houses of gentry for their weapons and assaulted

Jim Smyth, *The Men of No Property: Irish Radicals and Popular Politics in the Late Eighteenth Century* (Basingstoke: Macmillan, 1992), esp. pp. 45–51, 66–78, 100–20, and 157–8.

[240] Rev. Cupples, Lisburn, 19 March 1799; TNA HO 100/86/247–248.

[241] Castlereagh to Portland, Dublin Castle, 3 June 1799; Vane, *Correspondence of Castlereagh*, vol. 2, p. 326.

[242] E. Hudson to Charlemont; 9 March and 17 October 1799; Gilbert, *Correspondence of Charlemont*, 2, pp. 347 and 398 (respectively).

[243] The limited ability of the authorities to collect information on the newly configured Defenders is apparent in examinations of individuals willing to testify on their activities in Antrim. For example: examinations of Daniel McFaddin and Daniel Curry, 15 January 1799, Rebellion Papers, NAI 620/46/38; Proceedings of General Court Martial at Ballymena, 12 March 1800, and Examinations of Witnesses NAI 620/49/12.

[244] Apart from Burns, former Defenders still alive in 1863 included Henry Johnston and the brothers Jamey and Billy McMullan from the village of Glynn; Willy Nelson of the Whins, Willy Nelson of Rory's Glen and Willy Humphries of the Bogtown in the parish of Kilwaughter; Young, *Ulster in '98*, p. 44; see also pp. 52 (Defenders' song) and 65 ('Henry Munro' song).

[245] Smith, *Memories of '98*, pp. 54–6.

loyalists who were known to have collaborated in the conviction of rebels, audaciously flogging them in public or murdering them in their homes. These outrages crudely mirrored the brutality of state violence under military law. The Antrim magistrate Rev. Macartney reported on the prevalence of 'nocturnal parties of rebels', who 'flog the loyal inhabitants and give them from 50 to 200 lashes and where resistance is made they shoot the persons who resist'.[246] In a particularly gruesome incident, Andrew Swan, a farmer from near Ballymena, died from wounds inflicted on the night of 24 April 1799, when he was dragged from his house by 'some villains', tied to a tree and given 500 lashes, the assailants taking turns in giving him twenty-five lashes each.[247] These acts of violence were glamorized in local folklore. George Dixon [spelt locally Dickson] of Crumlin, county Antrim, was executed on 17 May 1799 for 'robbing his majesty's soldiers of their arms when on duty, aiding and administering unlawful oaths, flogging and threatening to destroy the property of his Majesty's loyal subjects, and plundering them of their arms'. His escapades were recounted thirty years later as a tale of a daring rebel, who with the aid of a single companion disarmed a sergeant, a corporal, and twenty-four privates of the Tay Fencibles, while their captain was distracted in a public house.[248]

The most notorious of the dreaded outlaws active in Ulster in the immediate aftermath of the rebellion was Thomas Archer from Ballymena, who commanded a band of outlaws that consisted mainly of Presbyterians (but also included several Catholics). In local tradition, it was said that 'the sight of "God save the King" upon the door of an Orange lodge-room always drove him into the wildest and most dangerous paroxysms of excitement.' Alongside a burning hatred of loyalists, ineligibility for amnesty was apparently a key motive for becoming a 'contumacious rebel'. Archer had deserted from the Antrim militia and it was said that his followers were 'chiefly deserters from the militia regiments', so that their lives were 'doubly forfeited'.[249]

In spite of his contemporary reputation for terrorizing the locality and committing heinous acts of savage torture, murder, and rape, Archer achieved lasting fame in the mould of a 'social bandit', which has been classified by the historian Eric Hobsbawm as a form of 'primitive rebel'.[250] The government repeatedly declared its determination to bring Archer and his associates 'to speedy and condign punishment'. A reward of one hundred pounds was offered for the first three members of his gang to be apprehended as well as a pardon to any of his followers who could provide information leading to

[246] Dr McCartney, Antrim, 3 May 1799, TNA HO 100/86/355–357.

[247] Two men were court-martialled and convicted for participating in the flogging of Swan: John Eggleson was executed on the Moat outside Ballymena and Robert McDonnell was condemned to Prussian military service. See *BNL*, 14 May 1799, p. 3; 31 May 1799, p. 3; 7 June 1799, p. 3; 18 June 1799, p. 3.

[248] *BNL*, 17 May 1799, p. 3; Q., 'Incident on Dromadaragh Mountain: Disarming of an Escort Party', in *Ulster Magazine*, 1, no. 10 (1830), pp. 635–7.

[249] *BNL*, 4 February 1800, pp. 2–3; Rev. Arthur Chichester Macartney, vicar of Belfast; Madden Papers, TCD 873/267; *Old Ballymena*, pp. 51–6.

[250] See E. J. Hobsbawm, *Primitive Rebels: Studies in Archaic Forms of Social Movement in the 19th and 20th Centuries*, 3rd edn (Manchester: Manchester University Press, 1971), pp. 13–29; E. J. Hobsbawm, *Bandits* (New York: Pantheon Books, 1981; rev. edn). For the labelling of the Archer gang's resort to rape as 'political acts of terror' see Michael Durey, 'Abduction and Rape in Ireland in the Era of the 1798 Rebellion', *Eighteenth-Century Ireland*, 21 (2006): p. 45.

their arrest.[251] In open defiance of his proscription, Archer drafted his own list of wanted loyalists and it was reported that he 'had the audacity in open day to stand singly on the high road and armed with two large pistols examined the passengers returning from market, to see if any of his proscribed list were to be found'.[252] For almost two years after the rebellion, Archer eluded the long arms of the authorities and brazenly continued to commit outrages, clearly benefitting from some level of popular support.

The arrest of 'the rebel Archer' in a dramatic gun battle and his court martial in March 1800 caused sensation.[253] After the execution, his corpse was gibbeted in irons on the moat of Ballykeel, outside Ballymena. The wife of an officer stationed in the town wrote: 'I can take no walk that I do not see the wretched Archer hanging in chains; the moat where he is hung is so high, it is seen in every direction.'[254] The fact that his body remained on display over the next two years was recalled decades later, when he was spoken about as 'the most courageous' of those who had been executed there.[255] When several youth from the town put an end to the 'unwonted and horrible exhibition' by removing Archer's remains and burying them in the family's grave plot in churchyard, it was apparent that he still had local sympathizers.[256]

The execution of the members of Archer's gang was supposed to have launched them into oblivion.[257] In practice, the public example that was made of Archer only strengthened his standing, which flourished in social memory and over time transcended political divides. In the townland of Leighinmohr (just outside Ballymena), a seventeen-inch-long pistol with a brass mounted stock pistol, which was said to have been taken from the outlaw at the time of his capture, was preserved through the nineteenth century in loyalist households as a treasured souvenir.[258] Similarly, what was believed to be his blunderbuss was kept over several generations in the house of a local farmer, until it was purchased in the mid-twentieth century by the Ulster Folk Museum.[259] A quarter of a century after the execution, James McHenry recalled with reference to biblical analogies how, as a youth living in nearby Larne, he had been enthralled by the news of Archer's exploits:

[251] 'By the Lord Lieutenant and Council of Ireland: A Proclamation', *Freeman's Journal*, 4 January 1800, p. 4; repeatedly republished over the next three months, even after Archer's arrest and execution: 9 January, p. 4; 11 January, pp. 3 and 7; 21 January, p. 4; 4 February, p. 4; 13 February, p. 7; 15 February, p. 3; 20 March, p. 4; 22 March, p. 8; 1 April, pp. 3, 4, and 5.

[252] *BNL*, 21 January 1800, p. 3.

[253] *BNL*, 7 March 1800, p. 3. Also Rebecca Leslie to Elizabeth Stewart, 8 March 1800, Leslie Papers, PRONI, D3167/3/B/24; *The 1798 Rebellion as Recorded in the Diaries of Gracehill Moravian Church* (Newtownabbey Moravian History Magazine, 1998), p. 20 (entry from 4 March 1800).

[254] Leslie to Stewart, 22 March 1800, PRONI, D3167/3/B/25. For the execution see also *BNL*, 11 March 1800, p. 3.

[255] Fair Sheets on the Parish of Ahoghill by John Bleakly (May–July 1837) in Day and McWilliams, *Ordnance Survey Memoirs of Ireland*, vol. 23: *Parishes of County Antrim VIII, 1831–5 and 1837–8, Ballymena and West Antrim* (1993), p. 34.

[256] *Old Ballymena*, pp. 55–6.   [257] *BNL*, 25 February 1800, p. 3.

[258] The antiquarian W. S. Smith inspected the pistol in 1894. He was informed that it had been kept by Captain Dickey, the militia officer who arrested Archer, then passed on to his son John Dickey, and following his death was given by his widow to Samuel Miller of Laymore [Leighinmohr]; W. S. Smith to F. J. Bigger, 18 September 1894, Bigger Papers, BCL SM 8/14; Smith, *Memories of '98*, pp. 50–1 (mentioned in an account of the 'Betrayal of Thomas Archer', pp. 46–52).

[259] Aiken McClelland, 'Thomas Archer and His Gang', in *Ulster Folk and Transport Museum Year Book 1969–70* (Cultra Manor: Ulster Folk and Transport Museum Year Book, 1971), pp. 15–17.

Well do I remember the impression of wonder, mingled with terror, which the relations of this man's actions made on my young mind. I was then about twelve years of age, and resided not far from the scene of his achievements. I looked upon his escapes from his pursuers as almost superhuman; and could not avoid resembling them to those which delivered the persecuted and heroic David from the vengeful power of Saul.

In 1828, McHenry published anonymously in Philadelphia 'The Outlaw of Slimish', a romanticized short story about Archer, in which the outlaw's death and the defeat of his followers represented 'the last embers of the terrible rebellion of 1798, completely extinguished throughout the north of Ireland'.[260]

At the end of the century, Archer was described glowingly by a popular nationalist author from Antrim, Margaret T. Pender, as 'a very daring and remarkable character, handsome, generous, bold and gay, ready of wit, light of foot, and heavy of hand, he had all the qualities that go to make a popular hero'.[261] In preparation for the centenary commemoration in 1898, an Archer '98 Club was named in his honour.[262] Archer would continue to be recalled as a republican hero into the late twentieth century. The Antrim memorial in the republican plot of Milltown cemetery in Belfast, which is in the custody of the National Graves Association of Belfast, lists him in its roll of honour of United Irishmen.[263] In response to the co-option of Archer's memory by militant nationalists, he would be later reclaimed as a local hero by unionists, despite his pathological aversion of Orangeism.[264] By the turn of the millennium, his memory had crossed the standard cleavages of Northern Ireland's politics, with a ballad on 'Tam Archer' featuring as part of an Ulster-Scots revival associated with unionism.[265] His reputation has since been depoliticized in Ballymena, where he is remembered as a 'leader of a band of social outcasts'.[266]

The memorable case of Thomas Archer calls attention to the extent of post-rebellion disaffection and its lasting popular appeal. By the end of February 1799, Cornwallis found that 'there is reason to believe that parts of the counties of Down and Antrim are again ready for insurrection.'[267] Major-General Nugent sent alarmed reports that rebels were gathering in anticipation of a French landing and was instructed to 'act with vigour'.[268] Cornwallis was obliged to admit the failings of amnesty and to concede that 'the lenient measures'—namely 'the pardons and protections which were held out to

[260] Mc [James McHenry], 'The Outlaw of Slimish: A Tale of the United Irishmen', in *Philadelphia Monthly Magazine*, 2nd ser., v. 1, no. 1 (1828), pp. 36–57 (quotations on pp. 37 and 57).

[261] Mrs M. T. Pender, 'Men and Episodes of Nine-Eight: Antrim Tales', in *SVV*, 2, no. 10 (October 1897), pp. 183–4.

[262] *SVV*, 3, no. 4 (4 April 1898), p. 75.   [263] See Murray and Cullen, *Epitaph of 1798*, p. 4.

[264] John Brown, *Orangeism around Ballymena* (Ballymena: Mid-Antrim Historical Group, 1990), Part I, p. 36.

[265] Ulster-Scots Collective of Performing Artists, *A Clatter O Fowk: A Collection of Poetry, Music and Song from the Ulster Scots Tradition* (Belfast: FowkGates, 2000); see also Katrin Pietzonka, *And the Healing Has Begun: A Musical Journey Towards Peace in Northern Ireland* (Bloomington: Author House, 2013), pp. 112–13.

[266] *Ballymena Times*, 14 September 2007.

[267] Cornwallis to the Duke of Portland, 23 February 1799; Ross, *Correspondence of Cornwallis*, vol. 3, p. 67.

[268] Marquis of Buckingham to Lord Grenville, 11 March 1799; Walter Fitzpatrick, ed., *The Manuscripts of J. B. Fortescue, Esq., Preserved at Dropmore*, vol. 4 (London: H.M.S.O., 1892), p. 497; Edward Cooke to William Wickham, 28 February 1799, TNA HO 100/85/287–288.

those of inferior note'—'had not been productive of the good effects expected from them'.[269] The administration in Dublin Castle, as advocated by the hardliner attorney-general John Toler, argued for the need to continue 'the summary punishment of offenders by martial law, without being subject to the interference of the civil power, or the operation of Habeas Corpus Law'.[270] Consequently, martial law was reintroduced in March 1799 with the passing of an act 'for the suppression of the rebellion which still unhappily exists within this kingdom' (39 Geo. III c.11). This allowed for streamlined prosecution of rebels at courts martial, as well as at civil assizes.[271]

Outrages were reported in county Down, but they were noticeably rampant in county Antrim. Following instructions from Dublin, Major-General Nugent convened in Carrickfergus a meeting of magistrates from around the county to deliberate 'the most effectual measures to be pursued for the restoration of peace and good order'. The magistrates maintained that 'the act for suppressing rebellion supercedes the civil power' and unanimously resolved that as 'the whole of the County of Antrim & c. were in a state of disturbance; that they required the intervention of martial law'. Castlereagh informed Nugent that the Lord Lieutenant 'can no longer forbear directing that the most summary punishment be inflicted' and authorized him 'to repress the Rebellious disturbances within your district', adding that it was hoped that by making 'some striking examples' the 'mischief' would be contained in Antrim.[272] Accordingly, on 12 March 1799, Nugent re-introduced to the Northern District the harsh regulations that had been previously used to suppress insurgency, making it clear that violators would 'suffer such punishment as a court martial shall inflict'.[273] Half a year later, Cornwallis could only note with regret that 'the same wretched business of courts-martial, hanging, transporting, &c., attended by all the dismal scenes of wives, sisters, fathers, kneeling and crying, is going on as usual.'[274]

Although Castlereagh expressed confidence that 'the authority of the Military Tribunals, under the late act, no longer impeded by the clashing jurisdiction of the civil courts' would 'keep the country in a tolerable state of tranquillity', renewed repression did not yield the desired results.[275] Initial reports seemed promising for the government. Following the arrest of a gang of outlaws in Antrim lead by George Dickson, who was known locally as 'the Northern Holt' (presumably after the well-known rebel outlaw General Joseph Holt in county Wicklow), Nugent believed that 'the business is almost wholly at an end'. Rev. Cupples noticed in county Down 'a decline in disaffection or at least a despair of success from it and an impression of the

[269] Cornwallis to Portland, Dublin Castle, 11 March 1799; Ross, *Correspondence of Cornwallis*, vol. 3, p. 73.

[270] *BNL*, 26 February 1799, p. 3.

[271] *The Statutes at Large, Passed in the Parliaments Held in Ireland: From the Third Year of Edward the Second, A.D. 1310, to the Thirty-Ninth Year of George the Third, A.D. 1799 Inclusive* (Dublin: printed by George Grierson, 1799), vol. 19, pp. 176–80.

[272] Letters from Castlereagh to Nugent, March 1799, McCance Family Papers, PRONI D272/42 (A) and (D); Castlereagh Papers, PRONI T424/2.

[273] *BNL*, 12 March 1799, pp. 2 and 3.

[274] Cornwallis to Castlereagh, Phoenix Park, September 26, 1799; Ross, *Correspondence of Cornwallis*, vol. 3, p. 135.

[275] Castlereagh to Wickham, 22 May 1799, TNA HO 100/86/415–417.

strength and resources of Government.'[276] But in early June 1799, even as he reported that 'the disposition of the inhabitants in general throughout the province of Ulster is loyal', Nugent disclosed that he 'cannot disguise that a spirit of discontent still exists in some counties of the North' and that 'the counties of Antrim, Down, and Londonderry in which alone the people rose in rebellion last year are still in different degrees disturbed.'[277] Just when it seemed that the Belfast court martial, which had convened in the Donegall Arms since March, had completed its duties, it became apparent that the lull in rebellious activities was momentary.[278]

General Lake returned from an inspection of the North in October 1799 and reported that 'the people in that part of the kingdom never appeared more ripe for mischief.'[279] In January 1800, troops were rushed to Ballymoney in response to news that '12,000 rebels are in arms and have assumed the name of Knights of the Black Garter.'[280] Although such scares may have been overstated, they are symptomatic of the general sense of alarm and insecurity. In this case, the name given to the armed grouping appears to have derived from masonic ritual, which reflects a common practice of attributing rebel activities after the insurrection to freemasonry in order to mask United Irish and Defender resurgence.[281]

The turbulent situation showed no signs of abating. By 17 March 1800, Cornwallis officially recognized 'the revival of internal commotion and disquietude', noting that 'some outrages and barbarous murders have been lately perpetuated with peculiarly aggravating circumstances of atrocity and guilt.' Brigadier General Drummond was dispatched to Antrim with a considerable force to combat 'a formidable banditti of the association of Defenders' and, even after the ringleaders were apprehended, it was feared that 'this system has however taken a deep root, and some of the better kind of farmers are supposed to be implicated.'[282]

On the tail of the executions of thirteen rebels in Antrim, in March 1800 a Rebellion Bill was re-enacted, which prolonged martial law (40 Geo. III c. 2).[283] This was part of a large corpus of repressive legislation which remained in effect after 1798 in order to pacify Ireland.[284] In the two years after the rebellion had officially ended, low-intensity conflict was sustained in Ulster through continued insurgency and counter-insurgency.[285] This cycle of violence breathed new life into remembrance of the United

---

[276] Reports from Nugent in county Antrim (10 and 13 May 1799) and Rev. Cupples in Lisburn (14 May 1799), TNA HO 100/88/340–341.

[277] Nugent, Armagh, 3 June 1799; TNA HO 100/89/47–48.

[278] In the same week, two houses in the parish of Glenarm were set on fire and the owners flogged; *BNL*, 14 June 1799, p. 3.

[279] Elliot to Castlereagh, Dublin Castle, October 17, 1799; Vane, *Correspondence of Castlereagh*, vol. 2, p. 428.

[280] James Hamilton, Jr, Strabane to Marquis of Abercorn, 22 January 1800; Abercorn Papers, PRONI D623/A/92/4.

[281] James G. Patterson, *In the Wake of the Great Rebellion: Republicanism, Agrarianism and Banditry in Ireland after 1798* (Manchester and New York: Manchester University Press, 2008), 71–2.

[282] Cornwallis to Portland, 17 March 1800, TNA HO 100/93/188–190.

[283] *Freeman's Journal*, 20 March 1800, p. 2.

[284] Abstract of some of the Principal Laws for maintaining the Public Peace in Ireland, with remarks by Lord Kilwarden, 15 January 1802; Charles Abbot, 1st Baron Colchester Papers, TNA 30/9/133.

[285] See Patterson, *In the Wake of the Great Rebellion*, pp. 25–70.

Irishmen. For many, the rebellion could not be forgotten as it was still reflected in current reality. Sustained repression eventually eroded popular resistance. In April 1800, military reports from the North claimed that 'from the vigour and energetic means that have been adopted, the deluded people are strongly inclining to return to a sense of their duty, and some strong instances of contrition have manifested themselves.'[286] The formerly disaffected were to be given another opportunity to embrace loyalism and forget 1798.

THE CHIMERA OF OBLIVION

Even as pockets of insurgency remained unpacified and small-scale violence continued to rage, Cornwallis shifted his sights towards what was conceived as a permanent British solution for the Anglo-Irish conflict in the form of a legislative union between the two kingdoms, loosely modelled on the union with Scotland of 1707. Whereas Pitt was in a position of passing this constitutional change in Westminster, it was up to the administration in Dublin Castle to ensure its ratification in the exclusively Protestant Irish parliament (which had to effectively annul itself). As part of a comprehensive effort to overcome opposition from conservative ascendancy politicians, the pro-Union campaign solicited the support of the predominantly Presbyterian constituencies in north-east Ulster, which had just recently been the centres of rebellion.

Returning from a tour of the North in October 1799, Cornwallis noted with satisfaction that it had met his 'most sanguine expectations'. He had found that 'throughout the whole counties of Antrim and Derry the cry for an Union is almost unanimous' and that the case in favour was making 'rapid progress through the Province of Ulster'.[287] A petition in support of the Union was signed by 1,520 'noblemen, gentlemen, and freeholders of the county of Antrim' and published in the *Belfast News-Letter*.[288] Similar addresses, issued by 'principal inhabitants' and endorsed by the corporations, were presented to Cornwallis in towns across Antrim, although he made a tactful decision to avoid county Down so as not to antagonize Castlereagh's political rival, Lord Downshire.[289] The canvassing for the Union enjoyed particular success in Belfast, where the corporation and merchants declared their enthusiastic support. The tokens of respect lavished on Cornwallis by 'all classes and descriptions of persons' were 'generally and indeed unequivocally considered as a pledge to support the measures of his Excellency's administration'.[290]

---

[286] Col. Littlehales to Cooke, 5 April 1800 (report based on an inspection of the Northern District by Lieutenant General Gardiner), TNA HO 100/93/260–261.

[287] Cornwallis to Major-General Ross, 24 October 1799, in Ross, *Correspondence of Cornwallis*, vol. 3, pp. 140–1; Cornwallis to Lord Gosford, Phoenix Park, 31 October 1799, Gosford Papers PRONI, D1606/1/1/225A.

[288] Alexander Marsden [assistant secretary in Dublin Castle] to Castlereagh, Dublin, 28 September 1799, in Vane, *Correspondence of Castlereagh*, vol. 2, p. 406; *BNL*, 11 October 1799, p. 1.

[289] Cornwallis to Portland, 22 October 1799, *Correspondence of Cornwallis*, vol. 3, pp. 138–40.

[290] Henry Alexander to Castlereagh, 7 October 1799, Castlereagh Papers, PRONI, D3030/1005; Col. Littlehales to Castlereagh, Belfast, 9 October 1799, Castlereagh Papers, PRONI D3030/1006 (reproduced in Vane, *Correspondence of Castlereagh*, vol. 2, pp. 414–15).

Ulster Presbyterians, as a whole, shied away from public debate on the Union.[291] Yet, one undeterred radical stood out for his outspokenness. The former United Irishman William Drennan wrote three pamphlets against the Union in which he held the government accountable for the devastation of the rebellion and also referred in passing to the 'new course of coercion, preparing its prongs to rake up the fresh embers of rebellion'.[292] Drennan's arguments, which were informed by liberal ideas of the Enlightenment, fell on deaf ears. When it came to voting in 1800, a majority of members of parliament representing Antrim and Londonderry supported the Act of Union. The picture was more chequered in Down, where Lord Downshire eventually came out in opposition and exercised his patronage to secure votes in parliament against the act, though this had nothing to do with radical politics.[293]

The rivalry between the two magnates who dominated electoral politics in county Down—the Marquess of Downshire Arthur Hill and the Marquess of Londonderry Robert Stewart—would inadvertently create a new context for remembrance of 1798. In the by-elections of 1805, the recently widowed Lady Downshire sponsored the successful campaign of Colonel John Meade, who defeated Castlereagh. The election-eering propaganda made much use of the fact that Castlereagh had begun his political career as a supporter of reform. Satirical squibs included repeated reference to his former association with the radical cliques behind the rebellion:

> A friend to the Gallican light,
> Against Kings he most gallantly talked,
> Then leaving the croppies to fight,
> Away he most prudently walked.

In the charged political debates in county Down, 1798—'When dark rebellion stai't this lan'—was evoked and it was suggested that 'there are now several gentlemen in Belfast, outrageously loyal, who were concerned in the matters which produced the catastrophe of 1798.'[294] Although this Whig rhetoric was overtly hostile to the rebellion, it appealed to residues of bitterness amongst former radicals who felt betrayed. Travelling through Down in 1812, the writer John Gamble found that Castlereagh was despised locally 'on account of his having turned renegado' by forsaking former United Irish associates and supporting the Union with England.[295]

---

[291] Ian McBride, 'Ulster Presbyterians and the Passing of the Act of Union', in *The Irish Act of Union, 1800: Bicentennial Essays*, edited by Patrick M. Geoghegan, Michael Brown, and James Kelly (Dublin: Irish Academic Press, 2003), pp. 68–83.

[292] *A Second Letter to the Right Honorable William Pitt* (Dublin, 1799), p. 31; see also *A Letter to the Right Honorable William Pitt* (Dublin, 1799), esp. pp. 22, 28, and 33; *A Protest from One of the People of Ireland, Against an Union with Great Britain* (Dublin, 1800).

[293] Geoffrey Bolton, *The Passing of the Irish Act of Union: A Study in Parliamentary Politics* (London: Oxford University Press, 1966), pp. 135–9.

[294] See *County of Down Election, 1805: The Patriotic Miscellany: Or Mirror of Wit, Genius, and Truth, Being a Correct Collection of All the Publications During the Late Contested Election, between the Hon. Colonel John Meade, and the Right Hon. Lord Viscount Castlereagh* (London: n.p., 1805), pp. 36, 40, 41, 54, 74, and 77. For the politics of patronage in the 1805 elections in Down see Brian Walker, 'Landowners and Parliamentary Elections in County Down, 1801–1921', in Lindsay Proudfoot, ed., *Down: History & Society* (Dublin: Geography Publications, 1997), p. 303.

[295] John Gamble, *A View of Society and Manners in the North of Ireland, in the Summer and Autumn of 1812* (London: C. Cradock and W. Joy, 1813), pp. 57–8.

In theory, the creation of the United Kingdom of Great Britain and Ireland in 1801 promised to usher in an age of reconciliation in which the troubled history of Irish rebellions could be put in the past. Several years later, the restoration of the Bourbon monarch Louis XVIII in France was introduced as a similar moment of '*union et oubli*', which attempted to wipe out the memory of the French Revolution and Bonapartism without resorting to recrimination. The *Charte constitutionnelle* of 1814 included an amnesty clause which forbid 'all investigations of opinions and votes given prior to the restoration', specifically promising juristic 'oblivion'.[296] While an initial moderate policy of reconciliation in France seemed to show some success, it was soon undermined in 1820 by reactionary ultra-royalists, who, like Irish ultra-loyalists, rejected the sanctioning of forgiveness for revolutionaries.[297]

In its classic form, implementation of post-conflict amnesty accommodates a fresh start, founded on wilful amnesia. In order to bring together warring factions into a united citizenry, the paradigmatic amnesty which ended the *stasis* in Athens after the fall of the Thirty Tyrants in 403 BC required all people to take an oath which explicitly forbid the remembrance of past wrongs [*mē mnēsikakein*]. This 'mindful forgetfulness', in the words of Andrew Wolpert, achieved a non-triumphalist victory in which the painful past was obliquely recalled but not flaunted.[298] In the twentieth century, amnesty has assumed a range of different forms so that it is difficult now to speak about it without generalization, and in more recent times it has moved away from its traditional association with amnesia.[299]

Following the downthrow of regimes responsible for horrendous crimes, amnesty has offered impunity from what has become to be known as 'transitional justice'. Precedents were set following the Second World War. Konrad Adenauer's policy of 'integration through amnesty' was a founding principle of the Federal Republic of Germany, which lead to the shelving of denazification in the amnesty law of 1954.[300] Similarly, the French Fourth Republic legislated acts of amnesty in 1951 and 1953 that exonerated collaborators with Nazi Germany. The philosopher Jacques Derrida observed that the reconstitution of national unity through amnesty can be considered 'a *leitmotiv* of all the French heads of state and Prime Ministers since the Second World War'.[301] Somewhat closer to the Irish case, amnesty has also been used by governments to reintegrate insurrectionists and diffuse social unrest. When it

---

[296] 'Toutes recherches des opinions et votes émis jusqu'à la restauration sont interdites. Le même oubli est commandé aux tribunaux et aux citoyens'; *Charte constitutionnelle du 4 juin 1814*, Article 11.

[297] See David Skuy, *Assassination, Politics and Miracles: France and the Royalist Reaction of 1820* (Montreal and Ithaca: McGill-Queen's University Press, 2003), pp. 67–99.

[298] Andrew Wolpert, *Remembering Defeat: Civil War and Civic Memory in Ancient Athens* (Baltimore: Johns Hopkins University Press, 2002), pp. 75–99; see also Nicole Loraux, *The Divided City: On Memory and Forgetting in Ancient Athens* (New York: Zone Books, 2006), esp. pp. 145–71.

[299] For an inclusive definition see Mark Freeman, *Necessary Evils: Amnesties and the Search for Justice* (Cambridge and New York: Cambridge University Press, 2009), pp. 12–17. A study of 506 amnesty processes introduced in 130 countries since the Second World War reveals that 'the traditional conception of amnesty as "amnesia" is increasingly becoming outdated'; Louise Mallinder, *Amnesty, Human Rights and Political Transitions: Bridging the Peace and Justice Divide* (Oxford and Portland, Ore.: Hart Publishing, 2008), p. 14.

[300] Norbert Frei, *Adenauer's Germany and the Nazi Past: The Politics of Amnesty and Integration* (New York: Columbia University Press, 2002), esp. pp. 67–91.

[301] Jacques Derrida, *On Cosmopolitanism and Forgiveness* (London and New York: Routledge, 2001), p. 44.

became apparent that the traumatic memory of the brutal suppression of the Paris Commune in 1871 undermined the unity of the French Third Republic, Léon Gambetta famously advocated the need to 'place the tombstone of oblivion over the crimes and vestiges of the Commune'. The passing of an amnesty bill in July 1880 was tied in with the introduction of unifying national commemorative symbols (the anthem, flag, and national day) that obviated remembrance of civil conflict in France.[302]

Ireland, as it entered into a Union with Great Britain, failed to come up with a framework through which the divisive legacies of 1798 could be neutralized and dissolved. Prosecution of rebels was still an active concern and on 20 March 1801, three months after the Act of Union came into effect, the House of Commons approved, yet again, the continuation of martial law in Ireland.[303] Moreover, key political issues remained unresolved. Reformist liberals were disappointed that the Union did not fulfil the implicit promise of Catholic emancipation, which had been a core demand of the United Irishmen since Theobald Wolfe Tone published his celebrated pamphlet *An Argument on Behalf of the Catholics of Ireland* (1791). Even more embittered, revolutionary radicals could not accept that their vision of a separate republic founded on an Irish union of Catholics, Protestants, and Dissenters had been supplanted by a United Kingdom, which preserved traditional hierarchies.

The commitment of remaining republicans was put to test in the summer of 1803 during the failed attempt of a further United Irish rising led by Robert Emmet. Three northern emissaries—Thomas Russell, James Hope, and William Henry Hamilton—traversed the former Presbyterian rebel heartland in north-east Ulster in an unsuccessful effort to foment popular support for another rebellion. James Hope, who had fought in Antrim during the rebellion, was immediately recognized and had to flee the area and go into hiding in Drogheda.[304] Hamilton appealed to republicans in county Antrim, where 'some even talked of wiping off the disgrace incurred at Antrim' in 1798. Unable to assemble a significant body of rebels, he went into hiding in the area of Monaghan. A reward of 300 pounds was offered for his capture, and Hamilton was subsequently arrested and imprisoned without trial in Kilmainham jail until 1806.[305] It was later recalled in the area of Ballynure that 'in 1798 they were almost all United Irishmen but in the insurrection of 1803 showed every symptom of loyalty to the government.'[306]

Russell focussed his attention on rousing county Down. Dressed in 'a very splendid green uniform', he issued on 23 July a proclamation addressed to 'Men of Ireland, once more in arms to assert the rights of mankind and liberate your country', which he signed as 'Member of the Provisional Government and General-in-Chief of the Northern District'. In spite of the impressive apparel and the issue of bold declarations,

---

[302] Colette E. Wilson, *Paris and the Commune, 1871–78: The Politics of Forgetting* (Manchester and New York: Manchester University Press, 2007), pp. 9–10. For the passing of the Amnesty Bill of 1880 see J. P. T. Bury, *Gambetta's Final Years: 'The Era of Difficulties', 1877–1882* (London and New York: Longman, 1982), pp. 149–70.

[303] *Freeman's Journal*, 26 March 1801, p. 2.

[304] Madden, *The United Irishmen*, 3rd ser., vol. 1 (1846), p. 283.

[305] Samuel McSkimin, 'Secret History of the Irish Insurrection of 1803', in *Fraser's Magazine for Town and Country*, 14, no. 83 (1836), pp. 556–7; Madden, *The United Irishmen*, 3rd ser., vol. 2 (1846), pp. 216–17; *BNL*, 11 October 1803, p. 3 and *Freeman's Journal*, 11 October 1803, p. 1.

[306] Memoir of Parish of Rashee by James Boyle (August 1835) with insertions from draft memoir of J. R. Ward; Day and McWilliams, *Ordnance Survey Memoirs of Ireland*, vol. 32, *Parishes of County Antrim XII, 1832–3 and 1835–40, Ballynure and District* (1995), p. 140.

the meetings that Russell convened were poorly attended. After failing to rally a substantial rebel force in Down, he too went into hiding with a reward of 500 pounds on his head. Russell then headed for Dublin with the intention of trying to free Emmet, whose attempt to take over the capital—like the fiasco in Ulster—had ended in failure.[307]

Russell was arrested on 9 September 1803, and sent to Downpatrick to be tried before one of the two Special Commissions that were appointed to prosecute the new wave of rebels in counties Down and Antrim. At his trial, held on 20 October, Russell appealed to the 'gentlemen who have all the wealth and power of the country in their hands' and exhorted them

> to pay attention to the poor, by the poor, I mean the labouring class of the community, their tenantry and dependants. I advise them, for their good, to look into their grievances, to sympathize in their distresses, and to spread comfort and happiness around their dwellings.[308]

The nationalist historian Richard Robert Madden, who wrote a biographical memoir of Russell in the mid-nineteenth century, envisaged that these potent words would 'not be forgotten by his countrymen; they will be remembered when the names and the acts of hundreds of the distinguished apostates of his cause, when it was that of the landed and mercantile aristocracy of the north, shall be buried in oblivion.'[309] Baron George, who presided over the court, was determined that this would not be the case and avowed in advance: 'let no man who be convicted of High Treason, and is sentenced to be executed, think he is going to suffer martyrdom.'[310] Nonetheless, contemporary accounts of the trial noted courtroom audience's manifest sympathy for the defendant and the execution ultimately launched Russell into republican martyrdom.[311]

Russell's memory aside, the debacle of 1803 demonstrated that there was no longer mass support for rebellion in Ulster. By then, many of the rebels of 1798 had been killed or dispersed, the numbers of survivors had been depleted by exile, and most of the population, if not altogether wholeheartedly converted to unionism, seemed to have

---

[307] Edward Baynes, Lisburn, to Lord Hardwicke, 25 July 1803, reproduced in Michael MacDonagh, *The Viceroy's Post-Bag; Correspondence, Hitherto Unpublished, of the Earl of Hardwicke, First Lord Lieutenant of Ireland, after the Union* (London: J. Murray, 1904), pp. 413–14; James McClelland, the Solicitor General, Carrickfergus, Co. Antrim, to Alexander Marsden, 9 August 1803, TNA HO 100/112/202–4 (reproduced in MacDonagh, *The Viceroy's Post-Bag*, pp. 416–18); *BNL*, 30 July 1803, p. 1 (republished on 2, 5, and 23 August 1803, p. 1); Russell's proclamation was reproduced in *BNL*, 28 October 1803, p. 3. See also James Quinn, 'Pursuing the Millennium: Thomas Russell's Attempt to Raise Antrim and Down in 1803', in *Down Survey 2003*, edited by Linda McKenna (Downpatrick: Down County Museum, 2003), pp. 6–14.

[308] 'Notes of the Trial of Thomas Russell, Found Among the Papers of His Law Agent, Mr. Ramsey, of Belfast', reproduced in Madden, *The United Irishmen*, 3rd ser., vol. 2 (1846), pp. 260–4 (quotation on p. 263). See also 'The King v. Thomas Russell: Brief on Behalf of the Prisoner in Indictment for High Treason, Special Commission at Downpatrick, County Down'; PRONI D1494/2/22 (MIC 506/1).

[309] Madden, *The United Irishmen*, 3rd ser., vol. 2 (1846), pp. 266–7.

[310] *Freeman's Journal*, 13 October 1803, p. 3.

[311] *BNL*, 25 October 1803, pp. 2–3; *Walker's Hibernian Magazine*, October, pp. 577–83. Whereas Russell's failed attempt to stir rebellion in Ulster has been comprehensively covered, the history of his popular memory remains mostly unstudied; see Denis Carroll, *The Man from God Knows Where: Thomas Russell 1767–1803* (Blackrock, Co. Dublin: Gartan, 1995), pp. 208–23; James Quinn, *Soul on Fire: A Life of Thomas Russell, 1767–1803* (Dublin: Irish Academic Press, 2002), pp. 302–9. For key developments in the remembrance of Russell see below, pp. 163, 178, 205–6, 218, 417–18, 473, 567, 569, and 579.

found a place for themselves in the new order. The overall official impression of county Down was that:

> a high spirit of loyalty, and zealous attachment to the King and Constitution pervades the breasts of the great bulk and majority of the inhabitants of the country; and from the late feeble and unavailing efforts of the disaffected, such wicked and presumptuous projects are more to be wondered at than dreaded.[312]

Declarations of loyalty were once again issued by Presbyterian communities in Antrim and subsequently Catholic parishes also made a point of publicly reaffirming their loyalty.[313] It is telling that Russell recognized in his courtroom 'many, who, during the last years of my life, have disseminated principles for which I now am to die', apparently referring to six jury members who had previously been United Irishmen before converting to loyalism.[314] The *Belfast News-Letter* pointed out that at the time of his failed attempt to persuade Presbyterians to partake in rebellion, 'their Ministers from the Pulpit were preaching Loyalty to their flocks, and exhorting them to gird on their armour to meet the foe.'[315]

Information collected by the authorities suggests that there actually was some level of insurgent organization in response to Russell's appeal. It was noted that parties of rebels that had been active in 1798 had once again 'gone out'.[316] The following month, in August 1803, 'strong symptoms of disaffection' were observed in Antrim and Down. General Campbell claimed that unrest was particularly noticeable in the areas of Ballynahinch and Saintfield, which had been centres of rebellion five years earlier.[317] While registering an overall increase in the 'spirit of loyalty', Rev. Snowden Cupples, who was considered by Dublin Castle a reliable source of information on the state of county Down, conceded that 'it must not at the same time be denied that there are agitators and rebels among us.'[318] Numerous people were arrested and their prosecution at the Special Commission trials held at Downpatrick and Carrickfergus in October 1803 reawakened memories of 1798. The presiding judge, Justice Charles Osborne noted: 'we must lament the repetition of those crimes in the present year,

---

[312] *BNL*, 30 July 1803, p. 1. An unpublished history of Downpatrick written in the early twentieth century notes that 'on looking over an old Nominal Roll of the Down Yeomen of 1803, we find that those who had been "United" men in 1798, had then become "King's Men" and were serving there as such'; R. H. Wallace, 'Historical Collections Relating to Downpatrick', Wallace Family Papers, PRONI D1889/8/4 (p. 100).

[313] *BNL*, 29 July 1803, p. 2 (inhabitants of Larne, Carncastle, and Kilwaughter); 9 December 1803, p. 4 (Catholics in the parishes of Ballymoney, Rasharkin, and Finvoy); 14 February 1804, p. 3 (Catholics in the parishes of Glenarm, Tickmackrevin, Ardcliness, and Carncastle).

[314] Jas. D. Rose Cleland, Bangor, to Mary Ann McCracken, 18 November 1843, Madden Papers, TCD 873/626 (reproduced in Madden, *The United Irishmen*, 3rd ser., vol. 2, pp. 265–6).

[315] *BNL*, 25 October 1803, p. 4.

[316] Information obtained by Lieutenant George Stephenson of Lower Iveagh Yeomanry and communicated to Sir Edward Littlehales, 28 July 1803, State of the Country Papers, NAI SOC 1025/2; notes of secret information collected by Rev. Thomas Beatty, Vicar General and Magistrate of County Down, Garvaghy, 17 August 1803, TNA HO 100/112/402. See also Patterson, *In the Wake of the Great Rebellion*, pp. 73–4.

[317] Gen. Campbell, Armagh to Sir Edward Littlehales, Dublin Castle, 1 August 1803, State of the Country Papers, NAI SOC 1024/2; Campbell, Belfast, to Wickham, 31 August 1803, NAI SOC 1024/4.

[318] Rev. Cupples, Lisburn to Rev. Archer, Inspector General of Prisons, 26 September 1803, State of the Country Papers, NAI SOC 1025/3.

which has nearly involved the country again in such scenes of blood, as, but a few years ago, we unhappily experienced.' Osborne reported with satisfaction that 'the rebellious spirit has not gained any ground,' but was reluctant to 'go so far as to say that all engaged in the former rebellion are converts in principle'. Although the trial proceedings had shown that the rising was not driven by 'any religious animosities', he admitted that Presbyterian loyalty had been attained by manipulating sectarian tensions and spreading the false impression that 'the country is in danger from the Catholics.'[319]

A year later, as Defender raids continued in the area of Ballymoney, information arrived from Antrim that 'shortly one other attempt will be made against the government.'[320] In July 1804, inflammatory notices were posted in Belfast. Former rebels were put under surveillance in October, as the authorities sensed that 'the great bulk of the people are as much inclined to be led astray by designing persons as ever.'[321] At the Carrickfergus assizes in 1804, former rebels were still being charged with crimes committed in 1798.[322] In 1816, during the depression that followed the Napoleonic War, violence erupted once again in the areas of the former rebellion in Antrim and Down. The judge addressing the Grand Jury at the county Antrim assizes that summer expressed his 'great concern and surprise on opening the calendar, at finding a list of so many unprecedented and atrocious crimes, accumulated in so short a space of time' and complained of at least seventy cases that were 'written in characters of blood'. The *Belfast News-Letter*, reporting on the county Down assizes, was 'sorry to find that in the neighbourhood of Ballynahinch there is no prospect of returning tranquillity'. Although it was expected that 'the good sense of a country, visited so lately as the year 1798 with all the miseries of war and rebellion, would have triumphed,' the newspaper lamented that 'we are under the necessity of recording fresh outrages.'[323] Amnesty and the Union had failed to make a clean break with the past and the legacy of the rebellion lingered on into the nineteenth century.

Countless studies of social memory have exposed the limitations of a state's capacity to construct and impose a homogenous collective memory. Similarly, attempts to decree collective amnesia from above are subject to contestation. Looking at the failure of the amnesties introduced in France after the Second World War 'to close that chapter of French history', Susan Rubin Suleiman concluded that 'they demonstrate the difficulty, if not the downright impossibility, of prescribed forgetting on a national scale.'[324] The term 'amnesty', as it was used at the time of the 1798 rebellion, was

---

[319] *BNL*, 14 October 1803, p. 2 and 18 October 1803, pp. 2–3; see also Fitzpatrick, *The Manuscripts of J. B. Fortescue*, vol. 7, p. 196.

[320] John Lee, Carrickfergus, to William Taylor, Dublin Castle, 20 August 1804, State of the Country Papers, NAI SOC 1028/4.

[321] Report from Maj.-Gen. Wanchope, Belfast, 24 July 1804, State of the Country Papers, NAI SOC 1028/3; extract of a letter by Mr Skeffington, Belfast, 10 October 1804, State of the Country Papers, NAI SOC 1028/19.

[322] *BNL*, 3 March 1804, p. 2 and 6 April 1804, p. 2.

[323] *BNL*, 9 August 1816, pp. 2 (Down) and 4 (Antrim). See also Kerby A. Miller, 'Forging the "Protestant Way of Life": Class Conflict and the Origins of Unionist Hegemony in Early Nineteenth-Century Ulster', in *Ulster Presbyterians in the Atlantic World: Religion, Politics and Identity*, edited by David A. Wilson and Mark G. Spencer (Dublin: Four Courts Press, 2006), p. 141.

[324] Susan Rubin Suleiman, *Crises of Memory and the Second World War* (Cambridge, Mass.: Harvard University Press, 2006), p. 224.

defined as 'an act of oblivion'.[325] There is a noticeable gap between what was intended and what was achieved. The philosopher Paul Ricoeur argued that 'commanded forgetting' decreed by amnesty is a 'denial of memory' (not to be confused with oblivion), which, by 'condemning competing memories to an unhealthy underground existence', actually presents an obstacle to making peace with the past. Behind the scenes of amnesty, according to Ricoeur, there is a persistent tension between an 'unforgetting memory' [*l'inoublieuse mémoire*] and an excluded 'forgetful memory' [*l'oublieuse mémoire*].[326]

Amnesty was only partially introduced in Ireland. There were many people in Ulster, in particularly those who benefitted from pardons and publicly converted to loyalism, who were keen on disremembering 1798 and putting the memory of rebellion behind them. In addition, thousands had been forced to leave Ulster, withdrawing their painful recollections of the rebellion from the repertoire of local social memory. On the other hand, ultra-loyalists demanded indemnity for themselves but opposed amnesty for rebels. Excluded from amnesty and subject to repression, steadfast radicals were determined not to forget. In the first years of its aftermath, the rebellion could not be freely discussed in public, but the official semblance of silence was misleading, as various expressions of remembrance in private encouraged the development of a tensely ambiguous culture of social forgetting.

[325] See 'amnesty', in James Barclay, *A Complete and Universal English Dictionary* (London, 1799; new edn).
[326] Ricoeur, *Memory, History, Forgetting*, pp. 452–6 and 501.

3

The Generation of Forgetting

The First Half of the Nineteenth Century

When we awake each morning, we hold in our hands, usually weakly and loosely, but a few fringes of the tapestry of lived life, as loomed for us by forgetting. However, with our purposeful activity and, even more, our purposive remembering each day unravels the web and the ornaments of forgetting.

Walter Benjamin, 'The Image of Proust'[1]

No one knows whether it is better to remember or to forget, memory is sad and forgetting on the other hand usually repairs and heals.

Camilo José Cela, *San Camilo, 1936*[2]

Social forgetting is generated through discreet processing of troublesome, often humiliating, historical experiences that cannot be openly expressed in official representations of public memory. Military defeat, in itself, does not necessarily entail forgetting. In fact, defeat can be translated into a vigorous (albeit highly selective) culture of remembrance and put to use for the purposes of national resurgence. Noteworthy nineteenth-century examples include the mythologizing of 'The Lost Cause' in the former Confederate South after the American Civil War, and the memorialization of *La Débâcle* of 1870–1 in the French Third Republic.[3] Different types of defeat, depending on particular historical conditions, trigger various responses and some defeats cannot be commemorated in the open. Loss in a rebellion, or in a civil war that denies any autonomy to the defeated side, is typically followed by a demand for silent conformity, enforced through repression.[4] After the Spanish Civil War, Franco's autocratic regime ruthlessly stamped out dissent and prohibited republican remembrance. The use of

---

[1] Benjamin, *Illuminations*, p. 202.

[2] Camilo José Cela, *Vísperas, Festividad Y Octava de San Camilo Del Año 1936 En Madrid* (Madrid: Alfaguara, 1969), p. 67. For translation to English by J. H. R. Polt see Camilo José Cela, *San Camilo, 1936: The Eve, Feast, and Octave of St Camillus of the Year 1936 in Madrid* (Durham: Duke University Press, 1991), p. 57.

[3] Wolfgang Schivelbusch, *The Culture of Defeat: On National Trauma, Mourning, and Recovery* (New York: Metropolitan Books, 2003), esp. pp. 37–187. See also Gaines M. Foster, *Ghosts of the Confederacy: Defeat, the Lost Cause, and the Emergence of the New South, 1865 to 1913* (New York: Oxford University Press, 1987); Karine Varley, *Under the Shadow of Defeat: The War of 1870–71 in French Memory* (Houndmills and New York: Palgrave Macmillan, 2008).

[4] See John Horne, 'Defeat and Memory in Modern History', in *Defeat and Memory: Cultural Histories of Military Defeat in the Modern Era*, edited by Jenny Macleod (Basingstoke and New York: Palgrave Macmillan, 2008), pp. 11–29 (esp. 14–15 and 20).

prisoners in the erection of the monumental *Valle de los Caídos* [Valley of the Fallen], with the declared intention of perpetuating '*desafío al tiempo y al olvido*' [defiance of time and oblivion], forcefully demonstrated the dominance of the victors in the construction of public memory.[5]

In a pioneering essay on 'History as Social Memory', Peter Burke took issue with the hackneyed adage that history is necessarily written by the victors, and its implied correlative that the history of the vanquished is doomed to oblivion. Burke suggested that 'the losers are unable to accept what happened and are condemned to brood over it, relive it, and reflect how different it might have been.'[6] Recollections of defeated rebels are often sustained underground and this subaltern remembrance can eventually emerge and develop into a counter-memory that contests the official collective memory, instilled by those in power. There are, however, reasons for non-compliant memories to remain concealed, even when the prohibitions imposed by the state are gradually relaxed. After tranquillity has been restored, the airing of grievances from the past can be perceived as counterproductive and unwelcome. Rebellions, which at some level are also civil wars, leave an ambivalent legacy. Recollections of the complex relationships between rebels and loyalists tend to complicate the formation of clear-cut narratives and are therefore uneasy topics to discuss in public. Moreover, once a popular rebellion is suppressed, those left on the defeated side are obliged to come to terms with the new reality and to re-adjust their lives through compromises with the authorities. These incentives make conducive conditions for obscuring ambiguous memories that are at odds with the dominant collective memory. Silencing is not simply imposed from above by the victors but also adopted from below by the vanquished. Consequently, social forgetting thrives on the conscious withholding of private recollections from the public domain.

Looking back at the defeat of the rebels in 1798, James Hope, who had fought at the Battle of Antrim, recalled:

> The people's cause was finally lost, (at least in that struggle). It now only remained for the enemy to attack the memory of the dead, and the characters of the living, and to slander all who had dared to resist their cruelty.

Many of Hope's acquaintances were executed, among them Henry Joy McCracken. He himself 'was a marked man, and was compelled for years to wander from place to place', lying low to avoid arrest.[7] The survivors of the rebellion were in no position to speak out and were unable to defend in print the memory of the United Irishmen from defamation. More generally, the experience of the rebellion had been distressful for all those concerned. Local opponents of the rebellion in Ulster, although they had come out on the winning side, were also disinclined to talk in public about their actions and experiences. The construction of official memory would therefore be left in the hands of external agents.

---

[5] Michael Richards, *A Time of Silence: Civil War and the Culture of Repression in Franco's Spain, 1936–1945* (Cambridge: Cambridge University Press, 1998); Paloma Aguilar Fernández, *Memory and Amnesia: The Role of the Spanish Civil War in the Transition to Democracy* (New York: Berghahn Books, 2002), pp. 71–91; Álex Bueno, 'Valle de Los Caídos: A Monument to Defy Time and Oblivion', in *Memory and Cultural History of the Spanish Civil War: Realms of Oblivion*, edited by Aurora G. Morcillo (Leiden and Boston: Brill, 2014), pp. 51–109.

[6] Burke, 'History as Social Memory', p. 54.

[7] Madden, *The United Irishmen*, 3rd ser., vol. 1 (1846), pp. 258 and 270.

Protestant loyalist memory found a formidable spokesman in the ultra-conservative political writer Sir Richard Musgrave, grand master of the Orange Order in county Waterford, whose near-contemporary *Memoirs of the Different Rebellions in Ireland*, despite its sweeping title, focused exclusively on 1798. When compiling source materials for his seminal history, Musgrave realized that he knew 'little of the origins and progress of the rebellion in the north' and conceded that he was 'very ignorant of the events which occurred in Down and Antrim'.[8] He expected that 'suffering loyalists' would readily furnish him with witness statements, as they had done elsewhere. But, much to his dismay, Musgrave discovered that people in Ulster were tight-lipped about the events of the recent rebellion. His dissatisfaction was exacerbated by the content of the few testimonies he received from northern informants, which failed to match his expectations.

Based on his understanding of the rebellion in Wexford, Musgrave had already formed an interpretation of the northern insurrection. He was convinced that a clique of 'Jacobinical' United Irishmen, allied with Catholic Defenders, had unsuccessfully attempted to mislead a guileless Presbyterian public and that this conspiracy had inevitably deteriorated into an outburst of wanton sectarian violence. In the spring of 1799, Musgrave wrote to the county Londonderry landowner and magistrate George Lenox-Conyngham of Springhill (near Moneymore) seeking confirmation for his preconceived notions:

> I have been assured that the Presbyterians quitted the Papists as soon as they discovered that they were impelled by that sanguinary spirit which was ever peculiar to their religion. Any anecdotes of atrocities committed by the United Irishmen and Defenders will be very acceptable.[9]

Contrary to these assumptions, in his reply, Lenox-Conyngham insisted that in his locale 'few or none of the Papists appeared in arms.' Apart from the exception of a single Catholic, the rebels taken prisoner and tried at Maghera were 'all Presbyterians except one Church of England man'.[10] This was not what Musgrave wanted to hear. He was an avowed 'zealous Protestant', who acknowledged that he 'could not resist the opportunity of showing the public the origin of Popery, and the struggles which the Saxon and English Churches made against Papal encroachment'. Musgrave therefore chose to ignore such noncompliant testaments and even contemplated leaving Ulster entirely out of his historical account.[11]

The model for Musgrave's history of 1798 was Sir John Temple's history of the 1641 rebellion, originally published in 1646 and re-issued in numerous editions, which wallowed in detailed descriptions of the 'barbarous cruelties and bloody massacres'

---

[8] Richard Musgrave to Bishop Percy, undated [c.Autumn 1798] and 2 July 1799, Musgrave Papers, NLI 4157/93 and 47–8 (respectively).

[9] Musgrave to George Lenox-Conyngham, 27 April 1799; PRONI D1449/12/292. For Musgrave's ideological prejudices see Jim Smyth, 'Anti-Catholicism, Conservatism, and Conspiracy: Sir Richard Musgrave's *Memoirs of the Different Rebellions in Ireland*', in *Eighteenth-Century Life*, 22, no. 3 (1998), pp. 62–73.

[10] Lenox-Conyngham to Musgrave, c.April–May 1799; Musgrave Papers, PRONI D1449/12/292A.

[11] Musgrave to Bishop Percy, undated [c.March 1799], Musgrave Papers, NLI 4157/40.

committed by Catholics.[12] In reformulating this familiar narrative to cover the United Irish rebellion, Musgrave glossed over the complexities of 1798 that did not suit his thesis. Accordingly, his *Memoirs of the Different Rebellions in Ireland* downplayed the participation of Protestants in the rebellion and mostly ignored the excessive punitive violence meted out by the Crown's forces on the local population. It first appeared in London in March 1801 and was soon sold out, with a Belfast newspaper noting 'unprecedented' demand.[13] In preparing a revised edition, which came out later in 1801, Musgrave banked on the interest of 'the Protestants of the north', whom he believed would 'purchase the whole of the second edition in a short time from its publication', though he did not add any material on the rebellion in the North.[14] An expanded third edition, spread over two volumes but without any additions on Ulster, was issued in Dublin in 1802. The overall print run of 3,850 is indicative of significant sales, in spite of the book's daunting length and costly price.[15] Yet, within less than two decades, it had become a rarity and only few copies could be found in the stocks of booksellers in the United Kingdom.[16]

Even in his own day, Musgrave's tome was contested. In a sensational incident, he was challenged to a duel by William Todd Jones, a former member of parliament for Lisburn, county Antrim, who Musgrave had accused of having had 'sinister motives' for supporting Catholic emancipation.[17] The controversy contributed to enhancing the book's reputation among loyalists. With his lesser-known writings also taken into account, Musgrave has been recognized as the 'chief ideologist and pre-eminent propagandist of Irish ultra-Protestant loyalism in the early years of the nineteenth century' and it has even been suggested that his magnum opus was a foundational text of British conservatism. As a canonical history of the 1798 rebellion it cast a long shadow over Irish historiography and remained at the heart of Irish Protestant polemics for over a century. Musgrave's arguments were repeatedly cited and, although the *Memoirs of the Different Rebellions* remained out of print, passages were regurgitated in numerous publications.[18]

---

[12] John Temple, *The Irish Rebellion... Together with the Barbarous Cruelties, and Bloody Massacres Which Ensued Thereupon* (London: printed by R. White for Samuel Gellibrand, 1646). See also Kelly, *Sir Richard Musgrave, 1746–1818: Ultra-Protestant Ideologue* (Dublin: Four Courts Press, 2009), pp. 91–3; John Gibney, *The Shadow of a Year: The 1641 Rebellion in Irish History and Memory* (Madison: University of Wisconsin Press, 2013), pp. 56–60.

[13] *BNL*, 19 June 1801.

[14] Musgrave to John Stockdale (his publisher), 18 May 1801; reproduced by F. S. Bourke in *Irish Sword*, 2 (1954–6), p. 298.

[15] Kelly, *Sir Richard Musgrave*, pp. 120–5.

[16] *BNL*, 29 August 1815, p. 3 and 1 September 1815, p. 1. A fourth edition was only issued at the end of the twentieth century; Sir Richard Musgrave, *Memoirs of the Different Rebellions in Ireland* (Fort Wayne: Round Tower Books and Enniscorthy: Duffry Press, 1995), edited by Delores E. McKnight and Steven W. Myers and introduced by David Dickson.

[17] William Todd Jones, *Authentic Detail of an Affair of Honour between William Todd Jones, esq., and Sir Richard Musgrave* (Dublin: s.n., 1802); see also Kelly, *Sir Richard Musgrave*, pp. 135–7; Patrick Rogers, 'A Protestant Pioneer of Catholic Emancipation', *Down and Connor Historical Society Journal*, 6 (1934), pp. 14–23.

[18] Kelly, *Sir Richard Musgrave*, p. 183; James J. Sack, *From Jacobite to Conservative: Reaction and Orthodoxy in Britain, c.1760–1832* (Cambridge: Cambridge University Press, 1993), pp. 240–2. See also Stuart Andrews, *Irish Rebellion: Protestant Polemic, 1798–1900* (Basingstoke and New York: Palgrave Macmillian, 2006), esp. pp. 39–41, 84, 104, and 171.

Musgrave touched on what he assumed were the causes of Ulster rebelliousness and briefly covered the principal engagements in Antrim and Down, but these sections, if combined, span only twenty-six out of a total of 1,135 pages, just above 2 per cent of the entire historical account as it appeared in the third edition. Such a cursory depiction effectively dismissed the rebellion in the North.[19] In this case, Musgrave's depreciatory terms of reference were accepted by his liberal critics. A contemporary history written by the Anglican clergyman Rev. James Bentley Gordon was willing to accept that the 'very short and partial' affair in Ulster had been an 'active and vigorous insurrection', yet devoted to it few pages.[20] Gordon's brief section on Ulster was abridged even further when it was reproduced without credit in another popular contemporary history, written by the Catholic historian Francis Plowden.[21]

In 1815, it was announced that an Ulster author, Rev. Samuel Burdy, the Anglican curate of Ardglass in county Down, was preparing a history of Ireland which would include an account of the 1798 rebellion. Burdy, however, did not put much effort into his study, which, as noted by Donald MacCartney, was 'for all practical purposes a re-edition of Gordon (1805), even to the very sentences and marginal indications of the contents of paragraphs'. Although he was born in Dromore, county Down, and had lived through the events of 1798, Burdy only allocated a few pages to the northern rebellion, essentially rephrasing Gordon's account.[22]

All in all, the northern rebellion was repeatedly framed as an insignificant side arena of 1798. If, in the words of Kevin Whelan, Musgrave's history defined the 'matrix of memory' at the heart of 'the shifting and contested meaning of 1798 after 1798',[23] it promoted disregard of the rebellion in Ulster and can therefore also be seen as a 'matrix of oblivion'. Marginalization of Ulster within a hierarchy of national memory, which denied the full scale of the northern insurrection and stripped it of its peculiarities, served to enforce social forgetting. The loyalist metanarrative of 1798 downplayed the extent of cooperation between Protestants and Catholics. It did not properly acknowledge the mass participation of Presbyterians and also ignored local instances of mutual aid across the republican-loyalist divide. The endorsement of this partisan interpretation of the rebellion by the establishment inhibited public recollection of non-compliant memories.

---

[19] Musgrave, *Memoirs of the Different Rebellions*, 3rd edn (1802), vol. 1, pp. 184–92 and vol. 2, pp. 93–110. See also Whelan, *The Tree of Liberty*, p. 138; Kelly, *Sir Richard Musgrave*, pp. 115 and 119.

[20] Gordon, *History of the Rebellion in Ireland*, pp. 158–63. The section on Ulster remained unchanged in editions issued in 1803 and 1808. A lightly retouched version appeared in James Gordon, *A History of Ireland, from the Earliest Account, to the Accomplishment of the Union with Great Britain in 1801* (London: Longman, Hurst, Rees, and Orme, 1806), vol. 2, pp. 418–22.

[21] Francis Plowden, *An Historical Review of the State of Ireland, from the Invasion of That Country under Henry II to Its Union with Great Britain on the 1st of January, 1801*, vol. 2 (London: C. Roworth for T. Egerton, 1803), part 2, pp. 768–9. Plowden's history was re-issued in several editions over the next decade.

[22] Samuel Burdy, *The History of Ireland, from the Earliest Ages to the Union* (Edinburgh: Doig and Sterling, 1817), pp. 529–33; for the advance publicity see *Newry Magazine; or, Literary & Political Register*, 1, no. 2 (May & June 1815): p. 201. See also Donald MacCartney, 'The Writing of History in Ireland 1800–30', *Irish Historical Studies*, 10, no. 40 (1957): pp. 347–8.

[23] See ''98 After '98: The Politics of Memory', in Whelan, *The Tree of Liberty*, pp. 133–75 (esp. 135–45).

Following the failure of the insurrection, many radicals were forced into exile and those who stayed at home were obliged to reconcile with the Union. This, however, did not mean that they completely renounced their ideological convictions. A good number of former United Irishmen in Ulster channelled their radicalism into liberal unionism and became prominent supporters of reformist causes. Notable examples of what Sean Connolly has termed 'quiet rehabilitation' can be found in the careers of the poet William Drennan and the businessman William Tennent, both founding members of the United Irishmen. Drennan had not taken part in the insurrection, but vocally opposed the Act of Union. Upon retiring from his Dublin medical practice in 1807, he became a leading figure in Belfast literary and cultural life and was known for his support of parliamentary reform and Catholic emancipation. Tennent was imprisoned for almost four years after the rebellion and following his return to Belfast became a prosperous merchant and banker who supported numerous municipal reforms. Within the social circles of progressive activists, memories could be recalled in private. Yet, in absence of designated public spaces for memorialization, the living memory of Ninety-Eight was mediated through practices of social forgetting.[24]

According to a story told in the area of Saintfield, county Down, a tombstone of a United Irishman, which was said to have been discovered on the site of Model Farm (a nineteenth-century agricultural school in the townland of Lisdoonan), was believed to have been interred with the corpse.[25] This anecdote most probably derives from a misunderstanding and yet, the very thought of a sunken memorial—pre-dating the subterranean counter-monuments [*Gegendenkmal*] to the Holocaust, introduced by radical German artists in the late twentieth century—is striking.[26] The notion that people would go to the effort of constructing a monument and then purposely bury it, so as to conceal it from view, is an apt metaphor for the dialectic of preserving and erasing memory that derived from the inability to openly remember insurgents in public during the first decades after the Turn-Out in Ulster. Memory had gone underground.

UNINSCRIBED EPITAPHS

Towards the beginning of the nineteenth century, cemeteries began to emerge across Europe, offering an alternative to church graveyards. These modern gardens of remembrance accommodated public expressions of personal grief and also served as civic

---

[24] For the 'quiet rehabilitation' of United Irishmen and the continuation of conflict 'beneath the apparently tranquil surface of post-Union Belfast politics' see S. J. Connolly, 'Improving Town, 1750–1820', in *Belfast 400: People, Place and History*, edited by S. J. Connolly (Liverpool: Liverpool University Press, 2012), pp. 190–5. For the championing of progressive ideals in the first half of the nineteenth century under the aegis of liberal unionism see John Bew, *The Glory of Being Britons: Civic Unionism in Nineteenth-Century Belfast* (Dublin: Irish Academic Press, 2009), pp. 52–125; Gerald R. Hall, *Ulster Liberalism, 1778–1876: The Middle Path* (Dublin: Four Courts Press, 2011), pp. 49–124; Jonathan Wright, *The 'Natural Leaders' and Their World: Politics, Culture and Society in Belfast, c.1801–32* (Liverpool: Liverpool University Press, 2012); see also Nelson, 'Violently Democratic and Anti-Conservative'.

[25] Interview with Martyn Todd, Saintfield Heritage Society (Saintfield, 21 September 2011).

[26] See James E. Young, *The Texture of Memory: Holocaust Memorials and Meaning* (New Haven and London: Yale University Press, 1993), pp. 27–48.

spaces for communal commemoration.[27] Such open memorialization was not available for the fallen United Irishmen. The rebels who died on the battlefields of 1798 were mostly buried in mass graves and consigned to oblivion through the collective anonymity of careless interment.

The diary entry of an army officer for 8 June 1798, the day following the Battle of Antrim, impassively notes: 'sent a party to throw the dead bodies into the lake.'[28] The daughter of Ezekiel Vance, a yeoman who fought at Antrim, later recalled that her father had witnessed the car-loads leaving the Market House and 'found to his consternation that what he at first mistook for pigs were no other than the naked bodies of dead peasants on their way to burial'.[29] Samuel Skelton, the agent of Lord Massereene, would relate how he had witnessed the corpses of the rebels heaped on carts and brought down to be buried in the wet sandy ground by Lough Neagh. He poignantly recalled that among them was an unfortunate man, who was still barely alive:

> the driver seated on the top was asked by the yeomanry officer commanding the burying party, 'Where the devil did these rascals come from?' A poor wretch raised his gory head from the cart and feebly answered, 'I come frae Ballyboley.' He was buried with the others.[30]

A decade later, local residents could identify for interested visitors the unmarked graves of rebels by the shores of the lake.[31]

Collective burial was also prevalent in county Down. A rebel who arrived in Saintfield the day after the battle recalled his dismay: 'to see a number of my fellow-men thrown on a car like dead dogs and cast carelessly into a large pit, filled my mind with gloomy reflections.'[32] The locations of mass graves near Ballynahinch, 'where hundreds of bodies were thrown after being taken there in block wheel cars', were remembered in oral traditions into the twentieth century.[33]

Shortly after the rebellion, Mary Ann McCracken, who had lost her beloved brother and other close friends, commented on the unfeasibility of rallying support for communal remembrance:

> At this disastrous period, when death and desolation are around us, and the late enthusiasm of the public mind seems sinking into despair, when human sacrifices are become so

[27] See Thomas W. Laqueur, 'Spaces of the Dead', *Ideas from the National Humanities Center*, 8, no. 2 (2001): pp. 3–16; Thomas W. Laqueur, 'The Places of the Dead in Modernity', in *The Age of Cultural Revolutions: Britain and France, 1750–1820*, edited by Colin Jones and Dror Wahrman (Berkeley: University of California Press, 2002), pp. 17–32. For the role of cemeteries as sites of familial remembrance see Doris Francis, Leonie A. Kellaher, and Georgina Neophytou, *The Secret Cemetery* (Oxford and New York: Berg, 2005).

[28] Alethea Hayter, ed., *The Backbone: Diaries of a Military Family in the Napoleonic Wars* (Edinburgh: Pentland, 1993), p. 42.

[29] Collected in the late nineteenth century from Mrs Graham Shannon, Antrim; Smith, *Memories of '98*, pp. 34–5.

[30] The account was written down by Samuel Skelton's great-grandson, the Belfast antiquarian Robert Magill Young; Young, *Ulster in '98*, p. 68.

[31] S. M. S., 'Sketch of a Ramble to Antrim', *Belfast Monthly Magazine*, 3, no. 12 (1809), pp. 5–6.

[32] Unidentified personal narrative reproduced in *McComb's Guide to Belfast... with an Account of the Battle of Ballynahinch* (Belfast: William McComb, 1861), p. 128.

[33] Collected by the local historian Colin Johnston Robb; *Mourne Observer*, 12 July 1968, p. 5. See also Robb's article in *Irish News*, 18 June 1942 (reproduced in *Irish News*, 18 June 2011, p. 18).

frequent as scarcely to excite emotion, it would be a folly to expect that the fate of a single individual should excite any interest beyond his own unhappy circle.[34]

In this discouraging atmosphere, family members made covert efforts to locate and maintain the graves of their loved ones. A 76-year-old man in the townland of Ballykine (1 km east of Ballynahinch) recalled in 1861 how as a youth of 13 he had helped his father bury a fugitive who had been killed by soldiers in their field and noted that, over the next thirty years, the relatives of the dead rebel frequently visited the grave, which was crudely marked with a stone at both ends.[35] A 'lonely grave' by an earthen ringfort at Ballylone, on the outskirts of Ballynahinch, was identified as the burial place of John Whinton, who died of a gunshot wound while escaping the battle. His sweetheart waited for years until she could decorate the gravesite with a bunch of white primroses.[36] A half-century after the rebellion, it was remembered in county Down that 'after the Battle of Ballynahinch, a dog lay for several days and nights on his master's grave on the hill of Ednavady, and could with difficulty be removed.' This touching story of a faithful pet honouring a grave of a rebel at a time when open memorialization was not feasible for relatives and friends was 'treasured up in memory'.[37]

Whenever it was possible, the bodies of dead rebels were retrieved by their kin and reinterred in local graveyards. An oral tradition in the townland of Magheratimpany, county Down (4 km south of Ballynahinch), told how two rebels, who had been 'ruthlessly slain' and were buried on a hillside, 'were later removed to the old burial place'.[38] The reclamation of rebel corpses raised difficulties. After the execution on 21 July 1798 of John Skelly of Creevytennant (4 km north of Ballynahinch), who was found guilty at a court martial in Downpatrick of 'having a command in the Rebel Army, and for seditious practices', his family was left to find the means of removing the dead body.[39] It was remembered locally that his wife, who was thought to have been responsible for having encouraged him to join the United Irishmen in the first place, took a horse and cart and transported the body by herself to the Presbyterian meeting house in Saintfield so that it could be buried in the graveyard. The tombstone (which now lays fallen on the family plot) gives no hint to this ordeal and simply mentions that 'he departed this life in July 1798 aged 34 years', without specifying his date of execution.[40]

---

[34] Extract of a letter from Mary Ann McCracken, Belfast, 22 August 1798; reproduced in Madden, *The United Irishmen*, 2nd ser., vol. 2 (1843), pp. 500–1.

[35] *McComb's Guide to Belfast*, p. 139.

[36] John Cardwell, 'The Legend of Ballylone Fort, in the County of Down', *UJA*, 2nd ser., 10, no. 2 (1904): p. 91.

[37] *Downpatrick Recorder*, 11 November 1854, p. 2.

[38] Collected by Colin Johnston Robb from 'different people who remembered the Insurrection' and believed to have been 'handed down by one who talked to those who were there'; *Down Recorder*, 9 October 1970.

[39] Rebellion Papers, NAI 620/2/15/12; Bartlett, 'Repressing the Rebellion', pp. 196–7. See also the newspaper report in *BNL*, 26 July 1798; reproduced in Martyn Todd, 'The Aftermath of 1798', *Saintfield Heritage*, 8 (2010): p. 19.

[40] Recollections of John Skelly's involvement in the rebellion were first collected in the area of Tonaghmore (near Saintfield), county Down in the late nineteenth century by the local historian John Cardwell, who passed the information on to Francis Joseph Bigger; Bigger Papers BCL K3/102–9; see also ''Ninety-Eight in County Down', in *SVV*, 2, no. 11 (1 November 1897), p. 203. These traditions were still recalled locally in the mid-twentieth century, when Skelly's pike was preserved in Belfast

Leave to reclaim corpses was not easily granted to families of rebels. A local tradition in Newry claimed that permission to bury a rebel named Cochron [Cochrane], who had been executed and beheaded, was given to his father on the condition that he carry the severed head through the streets of the town and proclaim his son a traitor.[41] In their intent to demonstrate that rebels would be severely punished, the authorities often prevented the retrieval of corpses. Lord Cavan decreed that the body of Mickey O'Donnell, who had been killed in a skirmish with yeomen in Fannet [Fanad], county Donegal, should be hung in chains from Knockalla Fort, but the body was then stolen in a raid and brought back to his townland of Ballywhoriskey so that it could be waked. The son of Anthony Gallagher, a member of the party of yeomen sent to retrieve the corpse, later recalled how 'The women cried an' lamented, an' went on their knees to the officer to leave the poor corpse where it was to get Christian burial.'[42]

Court-martial sentences sometimes specified that executed rebels should be buried under the gallows, purposely denying them burial in consecrated ground.[43] Oral tradition recalled that William Dunlop of Priestlands, who was hanged in Coleraine on 11 June 1798, lay buried by the side of the road 'till his friends came by night, "attired" as ghosts, and so, frightening the sentinel, carried away the corpse and buried it in old Derrykeighan'.[44] The reburial was remembered in the late nineteenth century, when the local historian Thomas Camac was told by 'a man of a most retentive memory' that he 'remembered the stone being several times painted green'. Such rituals of vernacular commemoration substituted for normal funerary customs, when they could not be performed.[45]

At the furtive reburials, names were usually not added to the gravestones. As mentioned in a previous chapter, the republican protomartyr William Orr of Farranshane, who was a cause célèbre at the time of his execution, was laid to rest in Templepatrick, county Antrim, under a tombstone that only named his relative Ally Orr, who had passed away in 1791.[46] Although the motto 'Remember Orr' had been repeated at countless United Irish meetings and was shouted out as a battle cry during the rebellion, his grave remained forlorn. It was clearly not possible at the time to inscribe in stone the memory of a popular republican hero (Fig. 3.1).

---

by a family that originated in the Saintfield area; *Mourne Observer*, 19 April 1968, p. 3 and 3 May 1968, p. 9.

[41] *Fermanagh Herald*, 1 March 1948, p. 3; see also Tony Canavan, *Frontier Town: An Illustrated History of Newry* (Belfast: Blackstaff Press, 1989), p. 114.

[42] McClintock, 'An Actor in the Rebellion of 1798', pp. 191–3.

[43] Examples from county Antrim include Hugh Boyd and James Well, who were convicted in Ballycastle in early July 1798; Rebellion Papers, NAI 620/2/8/10/10 and 11 (respectively). This stipulation was prevalent in the executions of those who continued the resistance after the rebellion, as evident in sentences passed in Ballymena in February, March 1800 for John Ryan, Daniel English, Samuel Dunlop, and John Stewart; Kilmainham Papers, NLI 1200/253–5, 299–300, 301–2, and 350–1 (respectively).

[44] Collected in the late nineteenth century by the local historian Rev. Hugh McNeill (d. 1893); McNeill, *Annals of the Parish of Derrykeighan*, p. 47. For Dunlop's gravestone, which does not mention that he died in 1798, see Dorothy Arthur, *Derrykeighan Old Church Graveyard* (Ballycastle, Impact Printing, 2012); Murray and Cullen, *Epitaph of 1798*, p. 8; Beattie, *Ballymoney and the Rebellion 1798*, pp. 23 and 26.

[45] Thomas Camac, 'A '98 Gravestone', in *UJA*, 2nd ser., 2, no. 3 (1896), p. 207.

[46] See Chapter 1 above, p. 82.

(a)

(b)   (c)

Fig. 3.1. Obscured graves of United Irishmen

(a) The grave of William Orr at the turn of the nineteenth century. Illustration after a photograph reproduced in Bigger, *Remember Orr* (1906). William Orr's name was not inscribed on the family grave in Templepatrick, county Antrim, in which he was buried. (b) Recent photograph of Orr's grave (with plaque). A plaque was added in 1997 for the bicentenary. (c) The grave of John Lowry in Saintfield. The inscription dates Lowry's death to 19 (instead of 9) June 1798.

Photographs by Guy Beiner (2011).

The same constraint was also true for many common rebels, who were buried unnamed in family plots or unmarked graves. Family tradition recalled that the beheaded corpse of Watty Graham, who was executed in Maghera, county Londonderry, was retrieved and buried temporarily at a nearby site and 'when times became more tranquil, it was exhumed and stealthily re-interred in "The Old Churchyard"'. It was noted that 'fear of discovery, prevented the erection of a headstone over the slab which is said to be marked by an uninscribed slab.'[47]

---

[47] Walsh, *Watty Graham*, p. 11.

A story still told in the 1960s in the area of Newtownards, county Down, recalled the efforts to find and bury 21-year-old John McWilliam of Lisbarnet (9 km north-west of Saintfield), who died at the Battle of Ballynahinch. His mother, Mary née McCullough, travelled to the battlefield and brought the corpse home by pony and trap for burial in the family grave, located in Tullynakill graveyard (6 km south-east of Comber). His name, however, was only added to the gravestone much later.[48] It could indeed take many years for names of rebels to appear on headstones and, even then, the rebellious activities in which they had engaged, or the violent circumstances which had caused their death, were rarely mentioned.

A demonstrative example of the absence of vital information at burial sites of United Irishmen can be found at the grave of the radical Presbyterian minister Rev. James Porter in Greyabbey, county Down, which is located adjacent to the serene ruins of a twelfth-century Cistercian monastery. The standard formulaic inscription—which simply notes that he 'departed this life'—gives no indication of the magnitude of shock and horror that had marked his execution. The significance of this omission can only be appreciated through an understanding of Porter's standing in folk memory. Prior to the rebellion, Porter had been one of the chief propagandists of the United Irishmen. He had a reputation as a popular speaker and his public lectures on natural philosophy, which were apparently a cover for recruitment, and his sermons, which often discussed political matters, were still remembered by members of the audience decades later.[49]

Porter gained renown for his compositions of songs and satire that were published in the *Northern Star* under various pseudonyms, and in particular for *Billy Bluff and Squire Firebrand*, which lampooned the corrupt behaviour of magnates in county Down. Written as a series of letters, serialized in 1796, *Billy Bluff* was soon re-issued as a pamphlet that enjoyed immense popularity, with 3,000 copies printed in Dublin alone and a northern edition published in Belfast.[50] In Antrim, the text was said to have been 'almost committed to memory by the entire peasantry of the district'.[51] It was re-published in numerous editions and in the late nineteenth century was still read with enthusiasm, according to Charles Gavan Duffy, even 'by northern farmers who call themselves Orangemen and Unionists'. With such renown, he was unlikely to be easily forgotten.[52]

---

[48] Typescript of recollections of Ernest Lowry (c.1960–6); Lowry Papers, PRONI T2794/2, p. 4; see also Bill Wilsdon, *The Sites of the 1798 Rising in Antrim and Down* (Belfast: Blackstaff, 1997), pp. 147–8.

[49] W. S. Smith, *Doagh and the 'First' Sunday School in Ireland* (Belfast: Alex, Mayne, and Boyd, 1890), pp. 2–3; Young, *Ulster in '98*, p. 59.

[50] *Northern Star*, 27–30 May 1796, p. 3; 15–18 July 1796, p. 4; 12–15 August 1796, p. 2; 29 August–2 September 1796, p. 2; 19–23 September 1796, p. 3; 7–11 November 1796, p. 3; 28 November–2 December 1796, p. 2; collated as James Porter, *Billy Bluff and 'Squire Firebrand; or, a Sample of the Times, as It Periodically Appeared in the Northern Star* (Belfast: s.n., 1797). For a modern edition see Brendan Clifford, ed., *Billy Bluff and The Squire and Other Writings by Rev. James Porter* (Belfast: Athol Books, 1991). See also Francis Joseph Bigger, 'James Porter (1753–1798), with Some Notes on "Billy Bluff" and "Paddy's Resource"', *Irish Book Lover*, 13, nos. 7/8 (1922), pp. 126–31; Thuente, *The Harp Re-Strung*, pp. 12–13 and 235; Mary Helen Thuente, '"The Belfast Laugh": The Context and Significance of United Irish Satires', in Jim Smyth, ed., *Revolution, Counter-Revolution, and Union: Ireland in the 1790s* (Cambridge and New York: Cambridge University Press, 2000), pp. 79–82.

[51] Montgomery, 'Outlines of the History of Presbyterianism', *Irish Unitarian Magazine, and Bible Christian*, 2, no. 10 (1847) p. 331.

[52] Charles Gavan Duffy, *The Revival of Irish Literature* (London: T. Fisher Unwin, 1894), p. 15.

Porter was well aware that writing a text as powerful as *Billy Bluff* would not go unpunished and presciently wrote in the preface: 'I am in danger of being hanged or put in gaol, perhaps both.'[53] Even though he probably refrained from taking an active part in the rising, he was nonetheless brought before a court martial in Newtownards on 28–9 June 1798 and accused of 'treason rebellion and sedition and with being concerned in divers [sic] treasonable rebellious and seditious acts contrary to his majesty's peace, his crown and dignity'. The official record of the trial, which claims that Porter threw himself on the mercy of the court, omitted his address to the court, in which (according to a manuscript account allegedly 'written very shortly after the event') he protested against the irregularities of the 'mock trial' and professed his innocence.[54] To the general public, it seemed that the conviction relied on dubious testimony and the verdict of a death sentence was widely denounced as an arbitrary demonstration of injustice. Suspicions were further aroused when a public request to inspect the minutes of the trial revealed that they could not be found.[55] Four decades later, local allegations of 'gross perfidy and unblushing perjury connected with his trial' were repeated to the historian Richard Robert Madden, who was left with 'the impression, that the proceedings in his case, made on the minds of some of those who were present, is not yet removed'.[56]

Entreaties for a repeal made by Porter's wife were turned down by Lord Londonderry, who was seen to be resentful for having been caricatured in *Billy Bluff* as 'Lord Mountmumble'. The only concession granted was that the corpse would be spared beheading and, in response, the condemned minister was said to have consoled his wife with characteristic wit, remarking 'then my dear, I shall lie at home tonight.' The *Belfast News-Letter* matter-of-factly noted that Porter was 'put in execution yesterday at the rear of his own Meeting-house at Greyabbey; head not severed.'[57] The terse newspaper reportage failed to acknowledge what the Presbyterian minister Rev. Henry Montgomery of Killead, county Antrim, would later describe as 'circumstances of extreme cruelty towards both himself and his family, which were altogether unnecessary for any purpose of public example'.[58]

Charles Hamilton Teeling, who maintained that the execution 'was a wanton display of cruelty', observed that 'the fate of this highly gifted individual was one of peculiar interest, and excited more than ordinary regret.'[59] An account based on the recollections of family members and acquaintances captured local resentment of what was seen as a calculated display of vindictiveness:

> With cruel cleverness the place of his execution was selected so as to add as much as possible to the poignancy of the event. It was on a rising ground a short distance from

[53] *Northern Star*, 27 to 30 May 1796, p. 3.
[54] Rebellion Papers, NAI 620/2/15/54; cf. Classon Porter, *Irish Presbyterian Biographical Sketches* (Belfast: Northern Whig, 1883), p. 18.
[55] *Irishman*, 12 October 1821, p. 2.
[56] 'Queries Respecting the Revd James Porter, Grey Abbey'; Madden Papers, TCD 873/51; Madden, *The United Irishmen*, 3rd ser., vol. 1 (1846), p. 373.
[57] *BNL*, 3 July 1798, p. 3.
[58] Montgomery, 'Outlines of the History of Presbyterianism', p. 331.
[59] Teeling, *Sequel to Personal Narrative*, pp. 35–9.

the village of Greyabbey and from it the unfortunate man as he took his last look around him, could see in one direction the meeting-house in which for eleven years he had ministered to an attached people and in the other direction, the hitherto happy home in which for the same period he had lived in peace with a loving wife and an affectionate family. A member of his congregation, who was a carpenter, was compelled to erect the scaffold on which he was to die, and many others of his hearers were also compelled to attend and witness the execution of their beloved minister. Altogether, not a drop of gall appears to have been omitted which could add to the bitterness of his cup of death.[60]

In consequence of this display of 'fiendish cruelty, unnecessarily wanton, and outrageous to the feelings of the family and the congregation', Madden was told that 'the fate of the minister of Grey Abbey excited universal sympathy.'[61]

Rumours circulated that Porter had been hanged 'on the account of the love a great official entertained for his wife' and the execution was remembered in song and story.[62] The contemporary poet Andrew McKenzie from nearby Dunover incorporated into one of his poems a reference to a touching anecdote about one of Porter's young sons discovering the body after it was brought into the house and not comprehending why his father would not wake from his sleep.[63] For many years afterwards, Sally Boal of Ballywalter, county Down (5 km west of Greyabbey), who died in 1875 at the reputed age of 103, would point out to interested passers-by the tree on which the beloved minister (mistakenly referred to as *William* Porter) had been hanged.[64] On a visit to Belfast in the mid-nineteenth century, the Scottish newspaper editor Alexander Russel was startled by the extent to which these embittered memories were retained, having witnessed a grandson of James Porter blatantly confront a local county gentleman with the accusation: 'Your grandfather hanged my grandfather.'[65]

The inability to mark this traumatic memory at the grave resulted in cognitive dissonance. Visitors, who made pilgrimages to the 'graveyard where the first Presbyterian minister, hanged for his connection with the United Irishmen, sleeps', were left

---

[60] Porter, *Irish Presbyterian Biographical Sketches*, p. 19. Classon Porter's memoir was reproduced in slightly edited form in *Lyttle's North Down Almanac and Directory* (Bangor, Co. Down: North Down Herald, 1892), pp. 9–16. For notes on Rev. James Porter and his family written by his son James, see PRONI D3579.

[61] Madden, *The United Irishmen*, 3rd ser., vol. 1, p. 375.

[62] Thomas MacKnight, *Ulster as It Is; or, Twenty-Eight Years' Experience as an Irish Editor* (London and New York: Macmillan, 1896), vol. 1, p. 84. A song on the death of James Porter, sung to the tune of 'The Wounded Hussar', was collected by Rev. Classon Porter in 1863 from 91-year-old James Burns; Young, *Ulster in '98*, pp. 57–8. Classon Porter also took down recollections of the executed minister from 80-year-old Mr Andrew Stilly of Ballindrait, county Donegal; Young, *Ulster in '98*, pp. 58–60. For a poem written in the twentieth century see Ormonde D. P. Waters, 'The Rev. James Porter: Dissenting Minister of Greyabbey, 1753–1798', in *Seanchas Ardmhacha*, 14, no. 1 (1990): pp. 99–100.

[63] Andrew McKenzie, *Poems and Songs on Different Subjects* (Belfast: Andrew Mackay, 1810), pp. 89–91 and 173. The story of the child finding the corpse appears in Porter, *Irish Presbyterian Biographical Sketches*, p. 19; it is repeated in W. T. Latimer, *Ulster Biographies, Relating Chiefly to the Rebellion of 1798* (Belfast: James Cleeland, William Mullan & Son, 1897), p. 72.

[64] *Downpatrick Recorder*, 18 September 1875, p. 3. The misnaming of the executed Rev. *James* Porter recalls an error that stems back to some of the reports in 1798, which probably derived from confusion with a contemporary Presbyterian minister, Rev. William Porter of Newtownlimavaddy.

[65] MacKnight, *Ulster as It Is*, vol. 1, p. 23.

disappointed by the unimpressive sight of the grave.[66] The historian of Irish Presbyterianism Thomas Witherow voiced a prevalent conviction, when he wrote that Porter's 'true epitaph' should have been: 'Murdered by martial law for the crime of writing "Billy Bluff"'.[67] Instead, the actual writing on the ledger simply reads 'Sacred to the memory of the Rev. James Porter, who departed this life July 2d, 1798 aged 45 years'. As with other gravestones of United Irishmen, a common formulaic memorial inscription served to obscure, rather than preserve, memory.

A similar inscription at Movilla Abbey, on the outskirts of Newtownards, marks the family grave of Archibald Warwick, 'who departed this life October the 15th 1798 aged 29 years'.[68] Warwick, a probationer [Presbyterian clerical student] who was mistakenly referred to by the authorities as Reverend, was listed among the most wanted rebels and was arrested a month after the rebellion. He was brought before a court martial in Newtownards on 15 August 1798 and was convicted of 'acting as a traitor and rebel and endeavouring to excite treason and rebellion in Ireland', but the death sentence was not carried out immediately and his incarceration for two months in Newtownards Gaol raised expectations of a reprieve. The execution was then held deliberately outside the Kircubbin meeting house (5 km south of Greyabbey), where he had ministered, and only warranted scant reference in the newspaper.[69]

The stirring 'scene often witnessed' of Warwick's bereaved mother visiting his grave every day for the rest of her life was described by an observer: 'The frail old woman, with wrinkled features and white hair, kneeling upon the grave, her hands clasped, her weeping eyes turned up to Heaven, and her quivering lips moving in silent prayer.'[70] Forty-five years after the execution, the travel writers Samuel and Anna Maria Hall visited the churchyard, where they met an elderly Presbyterian, who had attended the hanging. He referred to 1798 as 'a wicked rebellion to God's will', but remembered Warwick with admiration and recalled how his death had instantly turned him into a popular hero among Presbyterians:

> those who held the same political faith regarded him as a martyr, and thousands had assembled from all parts of the country to take the last farewell of so extra ordinary a man. Mothers held up their children, hoping that his eyes might rest upon them. And strong men, who would have been ashamed of tears, hung down their heads, and wept yet there he stood, in the sight of the people who looked more like a congregation than a multitude come to view an execution erect before the God he was to meet within the hour erect in mind and body. He was, literally, in the centre of his church, dying a shameful death in the presence of hundreds to whom he had taught humility, charity, and peace their duty to God and their duty to their neighbour.[71]

[66] Charles Gavan Duffy, *My Life in Two Hemispheres*, vol. 1 (London: T. Fisher Unwin, 1898), p. 118.

[67] Thomas Witherow, *Historical and Literary Memorials of Presbyterianism in Ireland (1731–1800)* (London and Belfast: William Mullan and Son, 1880), 2nd ser., pp. 297–8.

[68] For the grave's location see Wilsdon, *Sites of the 1798 Rising*, pp. 132–4.

[69] *BNL*, 24 July 1798, p. 4 and 16 October 1798, p. 2; Rebellion Papers, NAI 620/2/15/32 (reproduced in part in Bartlett, 'Repressing the Rebellion', p. 206; Power, *Courts Martial of 1798–9*, pp. 157–8); McCreery, *Presbyterian Ministers of Killileagh*, pp. 167–8; see also Dickson, *Revolt in the North*, pp. 202–4.

[70] Lyttle, *Betsy Gray*, 3rd edn (1894), ch. 42.

[71] Mr & Mrs S. C. Hall, *Ireland: Its Scenery, Character, Etc.* (London: Jeremiah Howe, 1843), 3, pp. 16–18.

Another eyewitness, Thomas Stevenson of nearby Innishargie, would recount his recollections of 'that eventful period' up until his death at the purported age of 102 in 1878.[72]

Although the execution was remembered long afterwards, Archibald Warwick's name was subject to forgetting. Henry Montgomery mistakenly referred to him as *James* Warwick.[73] More significantly, Teeling named him *William* Warwick and this error filtered into social memory.[74] The error was propagated in the late nineteenth century by the local journalist and author Wesley Greenhill Lyttle, whose best-selling novel *Betsy Gray; or, Hearts of Down: A Tale of '98* featured a colourful account of Warwick's arrest and an 'almost hagiographical' depiction of the execution. The pervasive influence of the sensationalist writing of Lyttle, who maintained that 'the name of Warwick will be remembered in Down as long as that of Orr will be recollected in Antrim', is apparent in local traditions.[75] By the turn of the century, the misnamed *William* Warwick was recognized by nationalists as a 'Martyr to Injustice' and the hanging of 'young Warwick' appeared in Florence Wilson's much-recited poem 'The Man from God Knows Where' (1918) as a memorable landmark. In the middle of the twentieth century, the nationalist public was finally re-introduced to *Archibald* Warwick's real name in a newspaper article by the popular writer Cathal O'Byrne.[76] This intense preoccupation with remembrance is not reflected on Warwick's gravestone, which does not draw any connection between his untimely death and the rebellion that had taken place four months earlier.

It appears that some families falsified dates of death on gravestone inscriptions in order to conceal the involvement of their relatives in the rebellion. John Lowry of Bellymaron [Ballymartin], near the village of Ardmillan in county Down (7 km south-west of Comber), died commanding a company of rebels from the parish of Killinchy at the engagement in Saintfield on 9 June 1798.[77] The rebels who died at the battle were mostly interred communally, without a tombstone, on the grounds of Saintfield First Presbyterian Church, yet Lowry was among the few rebels for whom individual gravestones were raised. The date of death engraved on the slab is 19 June 1798, signifying a remove of ten days from the battle (Fig. 3.1)[78] A grave inscription in Bangor Abbey is similarly misleading. James Dunlap [Dunlop] was convicted at a court martial in Newtownards and hanged, alongside two other United Irishmen, in

[72] 'Kircubbin—Death of a Centenarian', in *BNL*, 28 January 1878, p. 4.

[73] Montgomery, 'Outlines of the History of Presbyterianism', p. 332.

[74] Teeling, *Sequel to Personal Narrative*, p. 41.

[75] Lyttle, *Betsy Gray*, chs 12–17, 23, and 42; see also Colin Walker, 'A Bibliography of Presbyterianism in Irish Fiction, 1780–1920', in *Revising Robert Burns and Ulster: Literature, Religion and Politics, c.1770–1920*, edited by Frank Ferguson and Andrew R. Holmes (Dublin: Four Courts Press, 2009), p. 183. An example of the influence of the literary text can be detected in a local account of the ostracizing of James Dillon of Drumawhey, who was identified by Lyttle as the informer who had turned Warwick into the authorities; John Q. Graham Papers, NLI 41,664.

[76] *Northern Patriot*, 1, no. 1 (15 October, 1895), pp. 6 and 9; Wilson, *The Coming of the Earls*, p. 9; *Irish News*, 4 December 1943 (reproduced by Eamon Phoenix in *Irish News*, 4 December 2012).

[77] Birch, *A Letter from an Irish Emigrant*, p. 11.

[78] Inspection of the gravestone shows what appears to be a later attempt to correct the date and strike out the first digit.

Bangor on 10 July 1798. His gravestone, however, lists the date of death as 24 July, two weeks after the execution.[79]

Francis McKinley of Conagher, county Antrim (5 km north of Ballymoney), an ancestor of the United States president William McKinley, was hanged in Coleraine and local tradition recalled that his wife obtained the body and had it buried in the family burying-ground of Derrykeighan. The gravestone gave his date of death as 7 July 1798. When the family emigrated to America over a decade later, another stone, to which were added the names of his deceased wife and daughter, was put up. Curiously, the second memorial dated his death to 24 June 1798.[80] The local historian Thomas Camac realized that 'his wife would hardly be likely to forget the date of her husband's execution' and feebly tried to attribute this discrepancy to the change from the Julian to the Gregorian calendar, but had to concede that this explanation was unsatisfactory. Not only did the difference between the dates on the two memorials exceed the eleven-day adjustment, but the New Style calendar, which was officially approved by the Irish parliament in 1782, had already been in effect since 1752, so that Old Style dates were no longer in local use by 1798.[81]

On other gravestones, dates of death that would have hinted towards humiliating ways in which rebels met their deaths appear to have been purposely obfuscated by the bereaved family. One of two rebel graves outside Killinchy parish church may be indicative of such an effort at clouding public remembrance. James McCann of Killinchy, county Down, was found guilty at a court martial in Downpatrick of 'being active in forcing persons into the rebellion and instigating others to rise, and bearing the appearance of a leader', for which he was hanged on 27 June 1798. Unlike the nearby grave of the apothecary Dr James Chorde [Cord], which clearly states that he died on 23 June 1798 (in accordance with a court-martial sentence for 'having a command in the rebel army and instigating the people of Killinchy to rise'), no date is specified on McCann's grave. The inscription on the recumbent slate headstone laid by his son, John McCann of Carragullin, vaguely mentions that he died in June 1798.[82] Numerous occurrences of such misleading listings on graveside memorials for rebels in counties Antrim and Down suggest that the modification, or concealment, of dates

---

[79] *BNL*, 17 July 1798, p. 3; Rebellion Papers, NAI 620/2/15/20; see also Bartlett, 'Repressing the Rebellion', p. 195; Power, *Courts Martial of 1798–9*, pp. 163–4. For information on the gravestone see Wilsdon, *Sites of the 1798 Rising*, p. 128.

[80] Thomas Camac, 'The M'Kinleys of Conagher, Co. Antrim, and Their Descendants', in *UJA*, 2nd ser., 3, no. 3 (1897), pp. 167–70; McNeill, *Annals of the Parish of Derrykeighan*, pp. 46–7. For an embroidered version of local traditions of Francis McKinley's execution see Edward T. Roe, *The Life of William McKinley, Twenty-Fifth President of the United States, 1897–1901* (Chicago: Laird & Lee, 1913), p. 13. Around the time of the '98 centenary, *Francis* McKinley was mistakenly referred to as *William* McKinley, conflating the name of the ancestor with his illustrious descendant; see for example *Weekly Freeman*, 5 March 1898, p. 1; *Derry Journal*, 18 September 1901, p. 2.

[81] Camac, 'The M'Kinleys of Conagher', p. 169. This explanation was later endorsed by another local historian, Rev. Thomas Hugh Mullin; see Mullin, *Coleraine in Georgian Times*, p. 168. For the change of calendar in Ireland see Hiram Morgan, 'Calendars in Conflict: Dating the Battle of Kinsale', *History Ireland*, 10, no. 2 (2002): pp. 16–20.

[82] Rebellion Papers, NAI 620/2/15/10 (McCann) and 620/2/15/15 (Cord); *BNL*, 26 June 1798, p. 2 and 29 June 1798, p. 2; Bartlett, 'Repressing the Rebellion in County Down', p. 192; Wilsdon, *Sites of the 1798 Rising*, pp. 148–9. Due to the worn-out state of the inscription on McCann's gravestone, the possibility that it may have included a precise date cannot be ruled out with certainty, however there does not appear to be adequate space for insertion of numerals.

mark deliberate attempts to obliterate recollection of individual participation in the rebellion from the public sphere, while still allowing for discreet remembrance in private.

The grave of Archibel [Archibald] Wilson in the churchyard of Bangor Abbey offers an example of how a reference to death in consequence of the rebellion could be coded. At a court martial in Newtownards 26-year-old Wilson was found guilty of having been a rebel captain at the engagements in Ballynahinch and Saintfield, for which he was executed in his home village of Conlig, county Down (between Newtownards and Bangor), on 26 June 1798.[83] A contemporary account noted the grisly conduct of the troops at the execution: 'after he had been hanged for the space of eight-minutes, he was took down, and his head cut-off by one of the Lancashire Light Dragoons, and left upon the spot, sticking upon the point of one of there [sic] own invented spikes.'[84] Family tradition, as recalled by his descendant, the unionist politician and writer Ian Adamson, claimed that it was not Archibald but his sisters who were involved with the United Irishmen. Local folklore recalled that he 'went to the gallows on his bare knees, singing psalms, and died declaring his innocence'. The belief that Wilson was a victim of injustice is expressed in the poetic inscription on his grave:

> Morn not, dear frends, tho I'm no more
> Tho I was martred, your eyes before
> I am not dead, but do sleep hear
> And yet once more I will appeer.
> That is when time will be no more
> When thel be judged who falsely sore
> And them that judged will judged be
> Whither just or on just, then thel see.
> Purpere, deer frends, for that grate day
> When death dis sumance you away
> I will await you all with due care
> In heven with joy to meet you there.[85] [sic]

The evocation of martyrdom in demotic verse echoes the local perception of an unjust execution. However, the epitaph does not specifically refer to the rebellion.

Only in rare cases do memorial stones explicitly associate deaths with the rebellion, as in graves found in the remote cemetery of Whitechurch, on the outskirts of the village of Ballywalter, on the eastern sea coast of the Ards Peninsula in county Down.

---

[83] *BNL*, 29 June 1798, p. 2; Rebellion Papers, NAI 620/2/15/41; deposition of Jas. Robinson of Rathgill, Hackler, 19 June 1798, Cleland Papers, PRONI D714/3/6; see also Bartlett, 'Repressing the Rebellion', p. 193.

[84] This account, which appears in notes on the Lancashire Light Dragoons written on the fly leaf of a copy of 'Aristotles Discourses of Government' claims that the execution was held in Newtownards; PRONI T2286/1.

[85] Ian Adamson heard the story from his grandmother, Granny Kerr née Sloan; Ian Adamson, *Bangor, Light of the World* (Belfast: Pretani, 1987). This family tradition is partly confirmed by the deposition of William Clark, Jr, of Conlig, who testified before Rev. John Cleland (the Judge Advocate in Archibald Wilson's trial) that 'he was ordered to join the Rebels by Archibald Wilson Sister (Betty Wilson)'; Cleland Papers, PRONI D714/3/13. For local traditions see Francis Joseph Bigger and Herbert Hughes, 'Some Notes on the Architectural and Monumental Remains of the Old Abbey Church of Bangor, in the County of Down', in *UJA*, 2nd ser., 7, no. 1 (1901), p. 33. For the grave see Wilsdon, *The Sites of the 1798 Rising*, pp. 128–9.

The *Freeman's Journal* referred to the nine deaths and thirteen injuries amongst the inhabitants of the 'trifling village' of Ballywalter as an example of 'the magnitude of the punishment of many districts of the county of Down'.[86] The headstone for the brothers Hugh and David Maxwell of Ballywalter openly states that 'They fell in an attack made on the town of Newtownards the 10th of June 1798.' This detail is followed by an epitaph, composed by the local poet Andrew McKenzie:

> Lo! Erin's genius hov'ring o'er their tomb,
> With mournful eye surveys the hallow'd sod,
> Where sleep her bravest sons in earth's dark womb:
> She weeps . . . Hope whispers, 'cease, they dwell with God.'[87]

The roll of names on a nearby family grave mentions 'James Kain who was killed at Newtownards on 10th June 1798 aged 47'.[88] The singularity of these overt references, which appear in a somewhat isolated location, underlines the general pattern of omission on memorials that were more exposed to the public gaze.

A list of names engraved on a stone marking the burying ground of the Storeys of Island Lodge in the graveyard of Muckamore, county Antrim (2 km south-east of Antrim town), includes: 'John Storey who for his country died 1798.'[89] Storey was a printer at the *Northern Star* and was arrested and imprisoned in Carrickfergus in February 1798, for having administered a United Irish oath to a private in the Monaghan Militia, but was acquitted in April. He was re-arrested after the rebellion and convicted by court martial of having commanded a company of rebels at the Battle of Antrim, for which he was hanged and beheaded.[90] The memorial through which his family endeavoured to discreetly rehabilitate his memory was erected over a half-century later, sometime after 1852, in accordance with the wishes of his youngest brother James.[91]

Previously, the execution of John Storey and the macabre display of his decapitated head on Belfast Market House, alongside that of the rebel general James Dickey, was remembered in a song, which included the stanza:

[86] *Freeman's Journal*, 10 August 1798, p. 4.

[87] William J. Roulston, *Researching Scots-Irish Ancestors: The Essential Genealogical Guide to Early Modern Ulster, 1600–1800* (Belfast: Ulster Historical Foundation, 2005), p. 43. For the poetic epitaph see Bigger Papers, BCL K3/H/61; Francis Joseph Bigger, 'Andrew MacKenzie, the Bard of Dunover', *Irish Book Lover*, 3, no. 12 (1912), p. 198. McKenzie included the poem in a collection of his works, where it is introduced as an 'epitaph, engraven on the tombstone of two brothers who fell in the field of battle'; McKenzie, *Poems and Songs*, p. 166.

[88] Wilsdon, *Sites of the 1798 Rising*, pp. 136–7. The Maxwell brothers and James Kain are named in an account of the attack on Newtownards written by Humphrey Galbraith, the revenue officer at Groomsport (at the north tip of the Ards Peninsula); H. Galbraith, Belfast, to Edward Hull, Stranraer, 13 June 1798, Downshire Papers, PRONI D607/F/235. David Maxwell was named as the commander of the Ballywalter contingent in the deposition of William Wallace of Ballyferis, collected by Rev. John Cleland on 17 July 1798; Cleland Papers, PRONI D714/3/18.

[89] 'The Silent Land: Muckamore Burial-Ground', in *Belfast Evening Telegraph*, 9 April 1907; also *Larne Times*, 13 April 1907, p. 7.

[90] *BNL*, 23 February 1798, p. 3; 6 April 1798, p. 3; 3 July 1798, pp. 2–3. See also Young, *Ulster in '98*, pp. 12–13.

[91] Information provided in the late nineteenth century by Ellen McNally of Antrim, a relative of the Storey family; Smith, *Memories of '98*, pp. 37–9. As a child of 12 in 1798, James Storey reputedly assisted another brother, Thomas, to escape from prison and flee to America, where he remained in exile for sixteen years before receiving a pardon.

> When Dickey called for justice they all shook their heads,
> When Story called for vengance the sentrys all fled
> Declareing to their officers that they were obludged to fly
> For the *Heads* called for vengance aloud from the sky. [sic]

In another version, the demand for retribution attributed to the severed heads becomes a call for renewed rebellion:

> While *Story* lay martyred, and *Dickey* lay dead,
> And the hands of oppressors on spires placed their heads,
> Their spirits in glory triumphed to the skies,
> And proclaimed through the air that the Croppies would rise.

This explicitly seditious counter-memory could only be expressed orally within tightly knit radical circles. When Storey's death eventually received recognition on the family memorial, the inscription alluded to martyrdom indirectly.[92]

The disparity between vivid oral recollections and the nondescript epitaphs on the graves of the United Irishmen sustained the dynamics of social forgetting as a form of muted remembrance through times when public commemoration was not feasible. The mnemonic potential of feigned oblivion was foreseen by Robert Emmet at his 'departure from this world' in his request for 'the charity of its silence', as famously encapsulated in his speech from the dock:

> Let no man write my epitaph; for as no man who knows my motives dare now vindicate them, let not prejudice or ignorance asperse them. Let them rest in obscurity and peace, my memory be left in oblivion, and my tomb remain uninscribed, until other times and other men can do justice to my character.

Emmet was remembered but the location of his unmarked grave was lost. Absence of external recognition clearly endangered the preservation of rebel graves.[93]

In Downpatrick, the grave of Thomas Russell, which was marked by a tombstone paid for by Mary Ann McCracken, became a contested site. It was noted that 'the front of this stone has been several times turned down to the ground, and as often again replaced in its proper position.'[94] The nationalist politician Charles Gavan Duffy recalled that when he visited the site in the 1845 with other northern members of Young Ireland, who wished to pay tribute to 'the Protestant patriot of '98', they found that 'the reputed grave of the Irish Apostle is shamefully neglected. No monument, no railing, no cross, and the naked sod scratched into holes, doubtless by the piety of the poor people who love to carry a fragment of the clay to their homes.'[95]

The most infamous case of memorial desecration related to the rebellion in Ulster was the destruction of the grave of Henry Joy McCracken—and possibly other graves of rebels—at the Parish Church of St George in Belfast a few years after the rebellion.

---

[92] The reference to Storey's execution appears in the song 'Henry's Ghost', also known as 'McCracken's Ghost'; see Young, *Ulster in '98*, 52–4 and 94; Hugh Shields, 'Some "Songs and Ballads in Use in the Province of Ulster . . . 1845": Texts', *Ulster Folklife*, 18 (1972): p. 39.

[93] Madden, *The United Irishmen*, 3rd ser., vol. 3 (1846), p. 246.

[94] *Fraser's Magazine for Town and Country*, 14, no. 83 (November 1836): p. 567. For Mary Ann McCracken's financing of Russell's gravestone see Madden, *The United Irishmen*, 2nd ser., vol. 2 (1846), p. 274.

[95] Duffy, *My Life in Two Hemispheres*, vol. 1, p. 118.

The demolition was part of a building development scheme put forward by the Vicar of Belfast, Rev. Edward May, who was a close associate of the senior Orangeman Thomas Verner and had little regard for the memory of the United Irishmen. For the relatives and friends of the deceased, this 'sacrilege' was intolerable, yet they were not in a position to mount effective opposition. May, who was a former sovereign of Belfast, enjoyed the patronage of his brother-in-law, the influential Lord Donegal, and had strong connections with the city's Tory establishment. Four decades later, Mary Ann McCracken, still seething with 'painful and indignant feelings', shared with Madden her recollections of this 'most daring outrage', in which 'the graves were levelled, the ashes of the dead were scandalously disturbed, and the tombstones torn up'.[96]

The incompatibility between what could be said orally, albeit with due caution, in private spheres and what could be written publicly about the dead rebels of 1798 is apparent in the inability to publish obituaries, a genre which has been recognized as an important medium for the formation of modern social memory.[97] The oppositional press had been suppressed prior to the rebellion and there was no question of the exclusively pro-government newspapers showing any form of tribute in the coverage of the executions of United Irishmen. In later years, death notices purged recollections of the period from the biographies of the deceased, as noted by Breandán Mac Suibhne:

> Only seldom in the first decades of the century did an obituary in the regional press even hint at a respectable person having been a rebel or a republican in former days. Those few that did were for men who died abroad, suggesting that their politics was not only not of this time, but also not of this place: the past was *in* a different country.[98]

In fact, references to the rebellious activities of veteran United Irishmen who passed away in America were also understated. After his death in Washington, Pennsylvania, in 1827, Rev. Thomas Ledlie Birch was politely described as 'formerly a zealous Minister', without clarifying that this was a circumspect allusion to his having preached to the rebels before the Battle of Ballynahinch.[99] On the death of Rev. John Glendy of Maghera in Philadelphia in 1833, it was elusively noted that 'in the unfortunate distraction of 1798, he was obliged to leave his native country.'[100] Such euphemisms epitomize the essence of social forgetting, which avoids explicit mention in the public sphere of a troubling past.

In listing praises for the merchant and banker William Tennent, who died of cholera in 1832, a memorial tablet erected in the First Belfast Presbyterian Church in 1854 stated that he was 'a consistent advocate of free inquiry and rational liberty', adding that he was 'moderate in times of popular excitement and firm when exposed to the reaction of power'. Apparently, this was an obscure allusion to Tennent's involvement in the United Irishmen. Tennent was arrested on 6 June 1798 and, despite his denial of 'ever having been a member of the Secret Association', was held as a state prisoner till 1802. Previously, an obituary for his father, Rev. John Tennent—minister of the Seceding Presbyterian congregation of Roseyards in Ballymoney, which appeared in 1837 in

---

[96] Madden, *The United Irishmen*, 2nd ser., vol. 2 (1843), pp. 495–6. For Rev. Edward May's political connections see Wright, *The 'Natural Leaders'*, pp. 81–4.

[97] See Bridget Fowler, *The Obituary as Collective Memory* (New York: Routledge, 2007).

[98] Breandán Mac Suibhne, 'Afterworld: The Gothic Travels of John Gamble (1770–1831)', *Field Day Review*, 4 (2008): p. 80.

[99] *BNL*, 2 December 1828, p. 2. For Birch see below, pp. 172–3.

[100] *BNL*, 23 April 1833, p. 3; see also Hume, *Far from the Green Fields of Erin*, p. 96.

several newspapers, had included an outright rejection of the validity of the 'suspicion' of William's connection to the rebellion. The family was evidently keen on obfuscating public memory of involvement in 1798.[101]

Conflict between the wishes of family members to maintain a public façade of forgetfulness and the aspirations of radicals to air personal recollections was apparent in controversy over the memory of the Presbyterian minister Rev. Samuel Barber of Rathfriland in county Down, who died at the age of 74 in 1811. Barber's gravestone obliquely notes that he was a 'Steady friend of Civil and Religious liberty'. An obituary in the *Belfast News-Letter* alluded to his association with the Volunteers and his regard for 'patriotism and the natural rights and liberties of mankind' but glossed over his involvement with the United Irishmen.[102] The article avoided mentioning that Barber had been arrested on 3 June 1798, convicted for sedition at a court martial on 14 July, and imprisoned for a period of two years. His appeal for an early release was turned down by Lord Castlereagh, who considered him 'a turbulent spirit' and decreed that 'he must stay till he cools.'[103] Barber's implication in the rebellion was remembered orally in an account of the arrest that was transmitted into the late nineteenth century.[104] However, two decades after Barber's death, the request of the United Irish historian Charles Hamilton Teeling for permission to consult his papers was refused by family members, who were intent on preventing mention of Barber in a published memoir on the rebellion.

In a sequel volume to his *Personal Narrative*, Teeling recalled that Barber, who was 60 years old at the time, actively supported the rebels but declined an offer of a senior command in the United Irish army on account of his advanced age.[105] Following the book's publication in 1832, Barber's 90-year-old widow, Eliza, issued a forthright denial 'that he took any part in that unfortunate affair, either in council or action'. She tried to invalidate Teeling's personal recollections, stating that he 'was not at all acquainted with Mr. Barber till many years after the year '98; and, even then, instead of enjoying his confidence and friendship, the intercourse was exceedingly slight.' Teeling responded to the 'formidable attack' on his 'veracity as an historian' with a public reply that asserted that he 'was acquainted, intimately acquainted, with Mr. Barber during and prior to the year 98' and insisted on the accuracy of his statements, which were founded on 'personal knowledge'.[106]

---

[101] Wright, *The 'Natural Leaders'*, pp. 1–2 and 21–33. The obituary, which was published in the *BNL*, 1837, p. 1 and the *Northern Whig*, 7 March 1837, had originally appeared in the *Christian Liberator*. For William Tennent's denial of his membership in the United Irishmen see Madden, *The United Irishmen*, 3rd ser., vol. 2 (1846), p. 54.

[102] *BNL*, 10 September 1811, p. 3; see also Morrow, 'The Rev. Samuel Barber', p. 39.

[103] Samuel Barber, Downpatrick Jail, to Lord Castlereagh, November 1798, Morrow Papers, PRONI D3696/A/1A; Samuel Barber to Stewart, Downpatrick, c.August 1805, Castlereagh Papers, PRONI D3030/N/51.

[104] Robert M. Young received the information from the Belfast antiquarian Miss Carruthers, who was the daughter of the well-known antiquarian James Carruthers of Glenravel, Belfast; Young, *Ulster in '98*, pp. 91–2.

[105] Teeling, *Sequel to Personal Narrative*, pp. 31–2. An informer notified a local magistrate in early 1798 that Barber was considered a candidate for the position of commander of the rebel army in county Down; Nicholas Mageann [Magin] to Rev. John Cleland, 23 March 1798, Cleland Papers, PRONI D714/2/16.

[106] *BNL*, 7 December 1832, p. 2 (Eliza Barber's letter) and 14 December 1832, p. 1 (Teeling's rebuttal).

In contrast to the family's unease with recollections of involvement with the United Irishmen appearing in print, Teeling recounted that in 1798 Barber's daughter had proudly defended her father before the conservative magistrate Lord Annesley, the former parliamentary representative for Newtownards in county Down, defiantly declaring: 'If attachment to his country, constitute a Rebel, my father is one: and the dungeon, my Lord, is now the seat of honor.'[107] This anecdote was preserved in social memory through a poem known as 'Mary Barber's Rejoinder', which was well known in the Rathfriland area in the early twentieth century, when it was collected by the antiquarian Andrew Morrow.[108] It would seem that Presbyterians did not acknowledge this memory in public. During the centennial of the rebellion, the nationalist journalist Hugh Digenan of Drumgath (near Newry) in county Down found Barber's grave in a state of neglect and concluded that 'the memory of this popular and patriotic Presbyterian pastor' was 'finally forgotten by the members of his own communion', so that it was left to Catholics to 'keep his memory green among the hills of Down'.[109] It was not that Presbyterians had completely forgotten, but rather that they refrained from speaking out and practising remembrance in public.

WILFUL MUTENESS

In the wake of the rebellion, Ulster was left in a state of utter devastation. Newspapers reported that 'the town of Antrim has suffered very considerably. Most of the town is destroyed' and that 'besides Antrim, the towns and townlands of Ballymanure, Ballyclare, Templepatrick, Killeade, Doagh, Randalstown, and Ballymoney have suffered severely by disturbances, both by fire and sword.'[110] A Quaker later recalled the carnage visited on Antrim town: 'the bodies of men and horses were lying in the blood-stained streets; and the people were to be seen here and there saluting their neighbours—like those who survived a pestilence or an earthquake—as if they were glad to see each other alive, after the recent calamity.'[111]

In a 'sanguinary Proclamation', issued on 11 June 1798 and reputedly 'circulated throughout the country, with almost telegraphic despatch', Major-General Nugent threatened 'to set fire to, and totally destroy the towns of Killinchy, Killeleagh, Ballynahinch, Saintfield, and every cottage and farmhouse in the vicinity of those places'.[112] In quelling the insurrection in county Down, Nugent blatantly disregarded the compliance of many disenchanted insurgents with his ultimatum and unleashed indiscriminate destruction on the inhabitants. The general public was appalled by this 'awful example' of destruction: 'behold the town of Saintfield in a considerable part

---

107 Teeling, *Sequel to Personal Narrative*, pp. 58–9.

108 *UJA*, 2nd ser., 15, no. 4 (1909), p. 157 and 16, nos. 1–2 (1910), p. 39.

109 Hugh Digenan, 'A South Down Hero: The Rev. Samuel Barber, A. M.', in *Donegal News*, 24 March 1906, p. 6 (also published in *Frontier Sentinel* and *Ulster Herald*).

110 *BNL*, 14 June 1798, p. 2; *Freeman's Journal*, 16 June 1798, p. 2.

111 Thomas Hancock, *The Principles of Peace Exemplified in the Conduct of the Society of Friends in Ireland, During the Rebellion of the Year 1798* (London: William Phillips, 1825), pp. 136–7.

112 *BNL*, 12 June 1798, p. 3; Teeling, *Sequel to Personal Narrative*, p. 26.

destroyed—the dwellings on the road from thence to Ballynahinch in the same fate—Ballynahinch itself an undistinguished heap of ruins.'[113]

The day after the Battle of Ballynahinch, an associate of Bishop Percy of Dromore 'went down to see the appearance of the place which is very near burned down but three houses', and likened the scene to the annihilation of Sodom and Gomorrah.[114] John Armstrong, the postmaster of Ballynahinch, lamented that the 'once flourishing and happy little town' had become 'a complete scene of wretchedness' and that even the houses that had escaped demolition were 'completely plundered, gutted and wrecked'.[115] Reflecting a quarter of a century later on the 'barbarous procedure' of indiscriminate torching of farm houses, an eye-witness, who had been a child at the time, recalled that 'a feeling of execration and horror against the perpetrators was produced in the minds of all who beheld the conflagration.'[116] Another youth who had been on the scene, William Grimshaw of Carnmoney (9 km north of Belfast), county Antrim, remembered that: 'As far as the eye could reach, the ridge, intervening between Saintfield and Belfast, presented an almost continuous blaze; and, throughout the kingdom, entire villages were destroyed by the military, which were never afterwards rebuilt.' [117]

Charles Hamilton Teeling was one of many outlawed fugitives that escaped the carnage at Ballynahinch and went into hiding. Availing of the 'native generosity' of sympathetic locals, who put themselves and their families at risk by assisting him in his flight, he headed first south towards Slieve Donard in the Mourne Mountains and then turned westward, crossed into county Armagh and moved on to the relative safety of county Fermanagh. While on the run through Ulster, Teeling witnessed the burning of cottages by soldiers, who 'had scoured the country, and committed great devastation in their route'. Unable to contain his 'feelings of horror and indignation', he protested that 'this infernal system of outrage has been carried to such an effect, that in some places, whole districts were nearly depopulated.'[118]

It was believed by the inhabitants that 'a whole century would elapse, before the country could recover from the destructive effects of the rebellion', but economic recovery came sooner than expected. Within a short period, 'trade had resumed more than its usual vigour; money became again abundant, and the people were fully employed at their usual vocations.'[119] Notwithstanding the recommencement of everyday commercial life, the marks of the devastation remained to be seen all over. William Gregory, an itinerant Calvinist preacher who stopped in Saintfield in July 1800 and preached 'in the green where the Rebels were buried', found the town still 'much destroyed by the rebellion'.[120] The old Anglican parish church in Ballymena,

---

[113] *BNL*, 15 and 22 June 1798, pp. 3 and 2 (respectively).

[114] Letter from Dromore House, dated 13 June 1798; BL Add. MS 32,335.

[115] John Armstrong to Lady Moira, 25 June 1798, PRONI, Granard Papers, T3765/M/3/6/35; cited in Bartlett, 'Clemency and Compensation', p. 99.

[116] 'Recollections of the Battle of Ballynahinch by an Eye Witness', in *Belfast Magazine and Literary Journal*, 1, no. 1 (1825), p. 60.

[117] Grimshaw, *Incidents Recalled*, p. 31.

[118] Teeling, *Sequel to Personal Narrative*, pp. 46–80 (esp. pp. 65–8).

[119] Grimshaw, *Incidents Recalled*, p. 31.

[120] William Gregory, *The Second Edition of a Visible Display of Divine Providence; or, the Journal of a Captured Missionary. To Which Is Added, the Journal or Tour of the Author through the North of Ireland* (London: printed by J. Skirvern, 1801), p. 166. For the Evangelical Society of Ulster and Gregory's

which had been used as a barracks and 'every particle of timber contained in it was broken up and used as fire-wood', remained in a state of dilapidation till 1802 and the repairs were only completed at great expense the following year.[121]

Renovation could take a long time, especially in peripheral areas. Ten years after the rebellion, a visitor to the village of Templepatrick found that 'many of the houses have never been rebuilt.'[122] A guide for 'the Northern tourist' published in 1830 noted that the village of Jonesborough, county Armagh (10 km south of Newry), which had been burnt to the ground in 1798, 'has been, up to this time, only partially rebuilt'.[123] In the parish of Derrykeighan, where it was said that 'the Insurrection was rather a tame affair here; the signs of the fray being soon afterwards obliterated,' there were still 'a few roofless houses with their charred beams' to be seen at the end of the nineteenth century.[124] A late nineteenth-century history of parishes in south Antrim noted the lasting damage caused to Glenavy, which had 'suffered much in the rebellion of 1798', acknowledging that the village 'for a long time was in a declining condition'.[125]

Rebuilding was more noticeable in towns. A traveller who passed through Bally-money in 1813 realized that 'in the memorable year 1798' many of the houses had been destroyed but noted that 'a considerable part of the town is new'.[126] Yet, memory of the ruination lingered on even after the damages had been mostly repaired. During a visit to Ballynahinch in 1822, the surgeon Thomas Reid, who had many relatives and friends in the Orange Order but was not a member of 'the party', found himself reflecting on 'the occurrences of 1798' and admitted that 'the unfortunate inhabitants must have suffered severely: their town was reduced to ashes, and what property they had was entirely destroyed.'[127] In the 1830s, the field workers of the Ordnance Survey in Antrim were made aware of the extent of the damage that had been caused to such places as Randalstown, where 'more than one-half of the town was burned by the king's troops,' and Doagh, where 'a portion of the village was burned by the king's troops.'[128] Rev. Henry Montgomery maintained in 1847 that 'even now, at the expiration of fifty years, there are still some living hearts whose deep wounds might be opened' by memories of 'the awful spectacle of public executions, the entire destruction of peaceful

mission see David Hempton and Myrtle Hill, *Evangelical Protestantism in Ulster Society 1740–1890* (London and New York: Routledge, 1992), pp. 37–9.

[121] *Old Ballymena*, p. 71.

[122] S. M. S., 'Sketch of a Ramble to Antrim', *Belfast Monthly Magazine*, 3, no. 12 (1809): p. 6.

[123] Philip Dixon Hardy, *The Northern Tourist; or, Stranger's Guide to the North and North West of Ireland* (Dublin: William Curry, Jr, 1830), p. 32.

[124] Camac, 'Parish of Derrykeighan', p. 155.

[125] Charles Watson, *The Story of the United Parishes of Glenavy, Camlin, and Tullyrusk; Together with Short Accounts of the History of the Different Denominations in the Union* (Belfast: M'Caw, Stevenson & Orr, 1892); available online: www.lisburn.com/books/Glenavy_past_present/glenavy_past–1.html

[126] *Belfast Monthly Magazine*, 11, no. 64 (1813), p. 351.

[127] Thomas Reid, *Travels in Ireland in the Year 1822, Exhibiting Brief Sketches of the Moral, Physical, and Political State of the Country* (London: Longman, Hurst, Rees, Orme, and Brown, 1823), p. 184 (for the author's background see pp. i–v).

[128] Memoir of the Parish of Drummaul by James Boyle (June 1838) in Day and McWilliams, *Ordnance Survey Memoirs*, vol. 19: *Parishes of County Antrim VI, 1830, 1833, 1835–8, South-West Antrim* (1993), p. 41; Statistical Report on the Grange of Doagh by Lt. Edward Durnford (October 1832) in Day and McWilliams, *Ordnance Survey Memoirs of Ireland*, vol. 29: *Parishes of County Antrim XI, 1832–3 and 1835–9, Antrim town and Ballyclare* (1995), p. 68.

villages, the wide-spread burning of extended rural districts, the hopeless miseries of thousands of widows, and orphans, and desolate homes'.[129]

One might have expected that this sorry state of affairs would have been a topic of heated debate; however, the unavoidable reminders of the rebellion scattered ubiquitously throughout the Ulster landscape, were only rarely mentioned in public discourse. An envoy who visited the Presbyterian community in Saintfield in 1804 was blind to the devastation and, finding the place 'evidently actuated by a spirit of virtuous industry', he considered it to be an ideal 'flourishing little town'. He had previously 'heard it said, that this parish furnished some malcontents in the last wicked rebellion', but concluded that 'if so, they must have been some of its foolish young men; for that the heads of families, and all the wiser part of its inhabitants, were always loyal in their principles.' The envoy left satisfied that the people of Saintfield 'were now universally the friends of government'.[130]

An obstinate determination to overlook the remnants of the destruction was typical of the Presbyterian communities that had been shattered in 1798. The enactment of the Act of Union would be configured as a historical watershed, which ushered in prosperity and tranquillity. A writer in the *Belfast Monthly Magazine* boasted in 1813 that Great Britain and Ireland were fortunate to have been spared the ravages of the revolutionary wars:

> The fierce tempest, that has swept the extended continent, and poured death and destruction around, has there spent its fury; whilst these two highly favoured islands have enjoyed a clear unclouded atmosphere, and basked undisturbed in the sunbeams of peace

The editor of the journal, which was a main platform for liberal Presbyterians, gently pointed out that 'our correspondent has surely forgotten that this unclouded sky was obscured in 1798, when Ireland suffered the actual miseries of war,' but conceded that it was 'not the place to discuss' the matter further.[131] When referring in passing to residues of 'the disturbances in 1798', writers would make do with vague references, such as alluding to 'the embers, not yet altogether extinguished'.[132]

In the period immediately following 1798, Catholics, who had also participated in the insurrection in large numbers, were equally silent about the devastation. For a number of years, mass services were celebrated at the sites of ruined chapels which had been burned to the ground in 1798 by Orangemen and loyalists, generically identified as 'Rackers' [wreckers], in an outburst of vigilante violence that may have emerged out of a sectarian secret society known as the Break-of-Day Men.[133] And yet, in Irish language manuscripts written between 1798 and 1806 by the scribe Eóin Ó Gribpean [Ó Gripín] from Ballymagreehan, Drumgooland, county Down, there is no reference

---

[129] Montgomery, 'Outlines of the History of Presbyterianism', p. 334.

[130] Aglaus, 'Sketches of a Journey to Saintfield', *Walker's Hibernian Magazine* (December 1804): pp. 745–8.

[131] *Belfast Monthly Magazine*, 10, no. 57 (1813): p. 275.

[132] *Belfast Monthly Magazine*, 4, no. 18 (1810): p. 4.

[133] James O'Laverty, *An Historical Account of the Diocese of Down and Connor, Ancient and Modern*, vol. 2 (Dublin: M. H. Gill and Son, 1880), pp. 292, 329, 332, and 352; see also Marianne Elliott, *The Catholics of Ulster: A History* (London: Allen Lane, 2000), p. 261. For association with the Break-of-Day Men see Fair Sheets on the Parish of Aghagallon by Thomas Fagan (January–February 1838) in Day and McWilliams, *Ordnance Survey Memoirs*, vol. 21, *Parishes of County Antrim VII, 1832–8: South Antrim* (1993), pp. 18–19.

to the recent calamity.[134] As a whole, Catholics, who were hoping to improve their situation under the Union and achieve emancipation, were not interested in stirring up disquieting recollections of 1798. In an open letter to 'The Catholics of Ulster', published in 1813, a Church of Ireland supporter of Catholic emancipation from Lambeg, county Antrim cautioned against the danger of responding to Orange provocations. His advice to 'remember the disturbances in 1798' was actually a call to put the past behind them.[135]

Inhibition was shared across the board and the reticence of the formerly rebellious communities was mirrored by Church of Ireland Anglicans, who had been mostly loyal. In writing his history of the rebellion immediately after the events, Richard Musgrave was assisted in the South by Anglican bishops, who 'materially served me by stating certain queries to some of their most intelligent of their clergy'. He approached Bishop Percy of Dromore, expecting to utilize the same channels in the North to procure a 'lively description of the fermentation which took place at Ballymena, Ballynahinch and Antrim, and an account of any curious incidents which the actors there must have must have produced'.[136] However, a year later he found that he could not complete his history because he was still insufficiently 'acquainted with the events which occurred in Down and Antrim'. He complained to Rev. William Sturrock, the archdeacon of Armagh, about the lack of cooperation he encountered in Ulster from Church of Ireland clergymen, who were mostly 'unwilling to communicate to me what has come to their knowledge', even though he had made it clear that he was 'writing in defence of the constitution in church and state'. Musgrave applied to Sturrock, who had been previously stationed in the county Down diocese of Dromore and had served as a justice of the peace, for 'a relation of the most material transactions'. At the same time, he confessed to Bishop Percy that he had come to terms with his inability to acquire detailed information from local informants and was willing to make do with a skeleton 'description of the battles of Saintfield, Ballynahinch and Antrim, and the characters of the Presbyterian ministers who were banished or hanged in them'.[137]

The difficulties Musgrave encountered in persuading northern Protestants to put their personal testimonies of 1798 on record are telling. A decade later, at the behest of the Chief Secretary Robert Peel, William Shaw Mason—the 'remembrancer or receiver of the first-fruits' in Dublin—undertook a statistical survey of Ireland, for which he compiled detailed reports on parishes that were written by Church of Ireland clergymen. In contrast to reports from other areas, contributors from Antrim and Down, with hardly any exceptions, avoided mentioning 1798.[138] This omission was also replicated in the substantial surveys of counties Antrim and Down written by Rev. John Dubourdieu,

---

[134] McAdam and Bryson Papers, BCL MS 13; see also Breandán Ó Buachalla, *Clár na Lámhsríbhinní Gaeilge i Leabharlainn Phoiblí Bhéal Feirste* (Dublin: An Clóchamhar Tta, 1962), pp. 9–10.

[135] M. D., 'To the Catholics of Ulster', *Belfast Monthly Magazine*, 11, no. 62 (1813): pp. 255–7.

[136] R. Musgrave to Bishop Percy, undated [*c.*Autumn 1798], Musgrave Papers, NLI 4157/93.

[137] R. Musgrave to Bishop Percy and to Archdeacon Sturrock, 2 July 1799; Musgrave Papers, NLI 4157/47–50.

[138] William Shaw Mason, *A Statistical Account; or, Parochial Survey of Ireland, Drawn up from the Communications of the Clergy* (Dublin: J. Cumming and N. Mahon, 1814–19), 3 vols. Rev. John Graham of Maghera in county Londonderry mentioned local happenings during the rebellion; vol. 1 (1814), pp. 579 and 608. Rev. Stewart Dobbs, the curate of Aclinis and Laid, in the glens of Antrim, claimed that, in absence of bigotry, he could recruit after the rebellion both Protestants and Catholics into the local yeomanry; vol. 3 (1819), p. 28.

the rector of Annahilt in county Down, who included passing references to 1641 but refrained from making allusions to the rebellion of 1798.[139]

Silence should not be mistaken for ignorance. Dubourdieu had experienced the turmoil of the rebellion at first hand. The Huguenot community in Lisburn, of which his father—Rev. Saumarez Dubourdieu—was minister, had suffered at the hands of rebels, their industries were badly damaged and the workers were forcibly dispersed.[140] Moreover, John Dubourdieu was married to the sister of William Sampson, a senior northern United Irishman. Sampson was arrested prior to the outbreak of the rebellion and spent most of 1798 in prison. He was then exiled to the continent, only to be re-arrested and incarcerated in Portugal at the request of the English authorities. Dubourdieu appealed to the Marquis of Downshire on behalf of his brother-in-law and was curtly rebuffed by the Home Secretary, the Duke of Portland.[141] Troubled by unpleasant recollections and aware that talk of the United Irishmen was discouraged, Dubourdieu refrained from explicitly mentioning 1798 in his official reports.

Nonetheless, Dubourdieu found a subtle way to alert his local readers that he was in the know. In a display of *faux naif* buried in the midst of one of his thick volumes, he complained about the 'often erroneous relations given of places in works, which profess to describe them'. As an example, he cited an obscure reference to the small town of Ballycastle on the north Antrim coastline, where it was allegedly claimed that 'a volcano broke out there in 1798, which did infinite mischief, devastating the country to a considerable extent.'[142] People in Ballycastle retained strong memories of the rebellion throughout the nineteenth century and into the late twentieth century.[143] By subtly slipping into his text a coded reference to the destruction of 1798, Dubourdieu revealed that his obliviousness was feigned. Silence on the rebellion perpetuated a masquerade of forgetting.

At a time when recollections of the rebellion could not be discussed openly in public or committed to print, private letters to relatives abroad offer occasional glimpses of raw memories. For example, in May 1800, Henry Johnston of Loughbrickland, county Down, wrote to his brother Moses in Northumberland, Pennsylvania, about 'the Troubles' in which 'many lost thier Lives, and many [innoce]nt People lost thier all, by plundering House burning & desolations'.[144] [sic] As articulations of private memory, such personal communications were not circulated at home and did not

---

[139] John Dubourdieu, *Statistical Survey of the County of Down, with Observations on Means of Improvement* (Dublin: The Dublin Society, 1802); John Dubourdieu, *Statistical Survey of the County of Antrim, with Observations on Means of Improvement* (Dublin: The Dublin Society, 1812).

[140] Samuel Smiles, *The Huguenots: Their Settlements, Churches, & Industries in England and Ireland* (London: J. Murray, 1867), pp. 365–6.

[141] William Sampson, *Memoirs of William Sampson* (New York: George Forman, 1807), p. 177.

[142] Dubourdieu, *Statistical Survey of the County of Antrim*, p. 455.

[143] See McSkimin, *Annals of Ulster* (1849 edn), p. 137; Smith, *Memories of '98*, 71–2; Cathal Dallat, ed., *M'Cahan's Local Histories: A Series of Pamphlets on North Antrim and the Glens* (Coleraine: Glens of Antrim Historical Society, 1988; orig. publ. 1923), pp. 1–5; Cathal Dallat, 'A Ballycastle Story of the 1798 Rebellion', *The Glynns*, 26 (1998): pp. 83–6; Cathal Dallat, 'Ballycastle in the 1798', *The Glynns*, 27 (1999): pp. 61–7; John Beattie, 'The "Turn out" in Ballycastle, 8–9 June 1798', *The Glynns*, 42 (2014): pp. 41–8.

[144] Henry Johnston, Loughbrickland, Co. Down, to Moses Johnston, Northumberland, Pennsylvania, 11 May 1800, Johnston Family Papers, PRONI, T3578/7; reproduced in Miller, *Irish Immigrants in the Land of Canaan*, pp. 37–8.

generate a communal discourse of social memory in Ulster. Alongside the emigration of many Presbyterian radicals, memory had effectively been exported abroad.[145]

The rebellion could be discussed more freely in the Irish-American diaspora and references to these conversations occasionally appeared in emigrant letters home. Writing in 1820 from Birmingham, Alabama, to a friend in Dunmurry, county Antrim (5 km north-east of Lisburn, on the road to Belfast), Robert Craig, related how he had met a Mr Cloaky [Clokey], who 'had a son that lost his life in Lisburn with Monroe in the unfortunate year Ninety-eight'.[146] John Houston wrote in 1836 from Madison, Indiana, to his mother in Larne, county Antrim, and mentioned that he was staying at the house of a Mr McClean, described as 'a native of Newry who was deeply engaged in the Rebellion and had to leave Ireland then'.[147] The letters typically do not offer much detail on how the rebellion was recalled abroad.

The personal epistolary genre was co-opted in the immediate aftermath of the rebellion by Rev. Thomas Ledlie Birch, whose detailed memoir—styled in the form of an anonymous 'letter from an Irish Emigrant'—was published in 1799 in Philadelphia.[148] The radical Presbyterian minister, who had been unkindly nicknamed 'Blubbering Birch' by a loyalist informant, had already twice been brought before the assizes at Downpatrick prior to the rebellion, in September 1797 and April 1798, but could not be convicted. During the insurrection, he was the chaplain of the United Irish rebel army in county Down, for which he was brought before a court martial in Lisburn on 18 June 1798 but was acquitted, largely thanks to the intercession of his brother George, the commander of the Newtownards yeomanry. He was permitted to emigrate and only narrowly escaped being lynched at the hands of vindictive Orangemen from the Lisburn yeomanry, who were infuriated by his release.[149]

Writing after his arrival in America, Birch carefully phrased his recollections so as not to implicate himself in treasonable offenses that he had categorically denied at his trial. It was later recalled that he had preached at the rebel camp in Creevy Rocks on 'Pike Sunday', just prior to the Battle of Ballynahinch, but his published memoir prudently omitted reference to direct involvement in the insurrection. Even from the safety

---

[145] Kerby A. Miller, 'Ulster Presbyterians and the "Two Traditions" in Ireland and America', in *Making the Irish American: History and Heritage of the Irish in the United States*, edited by Joseph Lee and Marion R. Casey (New York: New York University Press, 2006), p. 266.

[146] Robert Craig, Birmingham [Ala.], to James McBride, Dunmurry near Lisburn, 30 December 1820, McBride Papers, PRONI T2613/4.

[147] John Houston, Madison, Indiana to Mrs Houston, Larne, Co. Antrim, 24 April 1836, PRONI T439/1.

[148] Thomas Ledlie Birch, *A Letter from an Irish Emigrant, to His Friend in the United States: Giving an Account of the Rise and Progress of the Commotions in Ireland, of the United Irishmen, and Orange Societies, and of Several Battles and Military Executions* (Philadelphia: s.n., 1799), esp. pp. 9–24; for an annotated edition see Kenneth Robinson, ed., *Thomas Ledlie Birch: A Letter from an Irish Emigrant (1799): A Vindication of The United Irish Rebellion in The North* (London: Athol Books, 2005).

[149] For the earlier trials see *BNL*, 17 November 1797, p. 4 and 29 June 1798, p. 2. For the court martial record see Rebellion Papers, NAI 62012/9/5; reproduced in Robinson, *Thomas Ledlie Birch*, pp. 69–84; see also *BNL*, 29 June 1798, p. 2. For the attempt on his life see Birch, *Letter from an Irish Emigrant*, pp. 22–4; see also the account of William Blacker, commander of the Seagoe yeomanry; reproduced in T. G. F. Paterson, 'Lisburn and Neighbourhood in 1798', *UJA*, 3rd ser., 1 (1938): p. 198. The nickname 'Blubbering Birch' appears in a letter from Thomas Lane, Hillsborough, to Lord Downshire, 19 June 1798, Downshire Papers, PRONI D607/F/255.

of America, the retelling of memory was compromised by selective masking of inconvenient details.[150]

Similarly, David Bailie Warden of Ballycastle, county Down (near Greyabbey), a Presbyterian probationer and student of Rev. James Porter, wrote pseudonymously in America 'A Narrative of the Principal Proceedings of the Republican Army of the County of Down, during the late Insurrection', which was apparently sent to Ireland, where it was intercepted by the authorities. The manuscript offers a detailed personal account of the preparations for the insurrection in Down and how rebels from the Ards peninsular rallied with hesitation and eventually went to join the United Irish army in Ballynahinch.[151] Warden, who surrendered himself after the rebellion, was initially imprisoned in Downpatrick and was then held for several weeks in crowded conditions aboard a prison ship outside Belfast. In absence of sufficient evidence for his conviction by trial, he accepted an offer of exile for life and emigrated to America, where he had a distinguished scholarly and diplomatic career.

In *A Farewell Address to the Junto of the Presbytery of Bangor*, which he published in 1798, Warden referred to the period 'before the late unfortunate rebellion', stating that he 'dreaded the horrors of a revolution'. He then described his situation 'since the rebellion', purposely avoiding any admission of what he had actually done during the rebellion.[152] As noted by the local historian Harry Allen, the narrative Warden eventually penned in America at an unspecified date in the early nineteenth century 'is very careful, through the use of initials and aliases, not to incriminate any of the principals who might have escaped detection and punishment'. Moreover it is attributed to a fictional rebel named William Fox and even signed with his name.[153] Although he was writing from abroad at a remove from the events, Warden took considerable care to mask his memoir. If to judge by the notices in the Ulster press of his death in Paris in 1847, which made no mention to his rebellious past, Warden's involvement in 1798 was apparently forgotten locally. It was only thanks to information provided by a friend in Paris that the *Nation* could publish a half year later a detailed obituary, which credited Warden for having been a United Irish colonel.[154]

The early decades of the nineteenth century introduced a vogue for travel writing that encouraged explorations of Ireland as a relatively remote part of the newly formed

---

[150] Day and McWilliams, *Ordnance Survey Memoirs*, vol. 17: *Parishes of County Down IV, 1833–7, East Down and Lecale* (1992), p. 120; Young, *Ulster in '98*, p. 66. See also: Aiken McClelland, 'Thomas Ledlie Birch, United Irishman', in *Proceedings and Reports of the Belfast Natural History and Philosophical Society*, 2 ser., vol. 7 (1965), pp. 30–3; Wilson, *United Irishmen, United States*, pp. 118–19; Peter Gilmore, '"Minister of the Devil": Thomas Ledlie Birch, Presbyterian Rebel in Exile', in *Ulster Presbyterians in the Atlantic World: Religion, Politics and Identity*, edited by David A. Wilson and Mark G. Spencer (Dublin: Four Courts Press, 2006), pp. 69–70.

[151] William Fox [D. B. Warden], 'A Narrative of the Principal Proceedings of the Republican Army of the County of Down, During the Late Insurrection, Rebellion Papers', NAI 620/4/41; partly reproduced in Dickson, *Revolt in the North*, pp. 221–3. For Warden's authorship see A. T. Q. Stewart, *The Summer Soldiers: The 1798 Rebellion in Antrim and Down* (Belfast: Blackstaff Press, 1995), p. 271n2. Warden's admiration of James Porter is evident in his keeping for over four decades the notebook of his lecture notes, which he later sent to Porter's son; PRONI D3579/2.

[152] D. B. Warden, *A Farewell Address to the Junto of the Presbytery of Bangor, which met in Belfast, on The Sixth Of November, 1798* (Glasgow, 1798); reproduced in W. T. Latimer, 'David Bailie Warden, Patriot 1798', *UJA*, 2nd ser., 13, no. 1 (1907): pp. 33–8.

[153] Harry Allen, *The Men of the Ards* (Donaghdee, Co. Down: Ballyhay Books, 2004), pp. 149–59.

[154] *BNL*, 17 October 1845, p. 3; *Vindicator*, 18 October 1845, p. 3; cf. *Nation*, 25 April 1846.

United Kingdom. The sites of the recent rebellion, which had featured in news reportage, aroused particular curiosity. The entries for Ulster in *The Traveller's New Guide through Ireland*, published in 1815, included a couple of passing allusions to the 'great body of rebels' defeated at Ballynahinch and to the 'furious battle' fought at Antrim town.[155] Descriptions of popular tourist routes sometimes referred incidentally to 1798, as in *A Guide to the Giant's Causeway* (first published in 1823 and reissued in 1834), which mentioned the 'dreadful engagement' in Antrim.[156] These characteristically brief references did not offer much detail.

Travel writers who showed sufficient persistence could occasionally penetrate northern reticence and uncover local recollections of the rebellion. An Englishman travelling to the Giant's Causeway in 1804 asked his guide about the presence of former United Irishmen in the area and was told 'if there are, they keep quiet'. Nonetheless, he cajoled the guide into revealing that 'in the rebellion two companies went from Bushmills to join the rebel army at Balynahinch [sic], and *fought like men.*' Once the local guide's tongue had been loosened, he recounted that their leader, Captain McNeven [John Nevin], 'had a purse of guineas as long as my arm, and intrusted one to each private, lest he should himself be killed or taken'. He also recalled how Nevin was later smuggled out of Coleraine in a barrel and escaped to America.[157]

Travellers seeking local curiosities were particularly fascinated by stories that identified caves along the Antrim coast as the hiding places of fugitive rebels. The Anglican clergyman and travel writer Rev. George Newenham Wright was informed in Islandmagee that at the base of cliffs known as the Gobbins there 'are several small caves, now used as boat-houses; but in 1798 they were the retreats of outlaws'.[158] Remote hideaways could still be pointed out to visitors over the next decades. A fieldworker of the Ordnance Survey noted in 1835 that two caves at the base of Garron Point (9 km north of Glenarm) were 'much used as a place of refuge in the rebellion of 1798 by many of the present inhabitants of the parish' and in the early 1840s, a local guide showed Samuel and Maria Hall a 1798 hideaway in a cave known locally as the 'Priest Hole'.[159] The locations of such underground places of shelter would be remembered into the twentieth century.[160] In the 1920, the local historian Dixon Donaldson of Islandmagee heard local traditions of how, after the Battle of Antrim, William McClelland of Portmuck hid in a 'small and almost inaccessible

---

[155] Anon., *The Traveller's New Guide through Ireland Containing, a New and Accurate Description of the Roads, with Particulars of All the Different Towns* (Dublin: J. Cumming, 1815), pp. 506 (Ballynahinch) and 519 (Antrim).

[156] George Newenham Wright, *A Guide to the Giant's Causeway, and the North East Coast of the County of Antrim* (London: Baldwin, Cradock, and Joy, 1823), p. 130.

[157] *Journal of a Tour*, p. 22; emphasis in the original. For traditions remembering John Nevin of Kilmoyle see Chapter 2 above, pp. 120–1.

[158] Wright, *Guide to the Giant's Causeway*, p. 30. See also S. M. S., 'An Account of Island Magee, Taken in 1809', in *Belfast Monthly Magazine*, 3, no. 13 (1809), p. 105; S. M. S., 'A Statistical Account of Island Magee', in *Newry Magazine*, 3, no. 18 (1818), p. 508.

[159] Memoir of the Parish of Dunaghy by James Boyle (September 1835) in Day and McWilliams, *Ordnance Survey Memoirs*, vol. 13: *Parishes of County Antrim IV, 1830–8, Glens of Antrim* (1992), p. 6; Hall, *Ireland*, 3, p. 175.

[160] Mary Hobson, 'Some Ulster Souterrains', *Journal of the Royal Anthropological Institute of Great Britain and Ireland*, 39 (1909): p. 227; Robert M'Cahan, *Tales from the Glens of Antrim* (Coleraine: Northern Constitution, 1923), p. 2 [reproduced in *M'Cahan's Local Histories* (Coleraine: Glens of Antrim Historical Society, 1988)].

cave' in the cliffs by his farm, where friends provided for him in 'great secrecy'.[161] Under the veil of public silence, there were evidently many local recollections, which were discussed in confidence and passed on to next generations.

Some travel writers, like the Englishman John Barrow who toured Ireland in the autumn of 1835, made a conscious decision to try and avoid 'the all-engrossing topics of Religion and Politics', though it was soon apparent that these subjects 'have become so intimately intermixed' in everyday life that they were inescapable. In Antrim, Barrow's guide, a Captain Skinner who had fought on the government side in the rebellion, took him to Shane's Castle, where they met an old house-keeper. It turned out that in 1798 both the housekeeper and Skinner had witnessed the 'memorable event' of the killing of Lord O'Neill by rebels. Barrow found himself fascinated as he 'listened to the tale of their recollections with great attention'.[162] It seems that specific recollections of the rebellion were to be found everywhere and yet many, if not most, standard travel guides remained oblivious to these local memories or refused to engage with them. A typical example can be found in John Borbridge Doyle's *Tours in Ulster* (1854), which includes numerous references to the rebellion of 1641 but says very little about 1798, apart from noting that 'Belfast was reduced to silence' and mentioning in a few words the defeat of the rebels at Antrim.[163]

Local travellers were better placed to solicit oral recollections and were more attuned than outsiders to muted utterances of social memory. 'A Ramble to Antrim' written a decade after the rebellion was serialized in the *Belfast Monthly Magazine*, a journal associated with the former United Irishman William Drennan and Presby-terian Whig circles.[164] The author was most probably the Carrickfergus shopkeeper Samuel McSkimin, a noted antiquarian. Unlike most of the journal's contributors, who typically came from a radical background, McSkimin was a conservative loyalist, but was nonetheless fascinated by the rebellion. Over the course of his travels, he visited sites of major engagements at Antrim town and Ballymena as well as the lesser-known site of a skirmish at Larne, and the hiding places of fugitive rebels in Islandmagee and at the Skirry, near Broughshane. At Donegore Hill, he was par-ticularly 'curious to see the post of the insurgents of this quarter'. In the village of Templepatrick, he commented on the ruined houses that were still visible. The landlady of a public house in Antrim Town and her husband accompanied his party to Lough Neagh, where they 'pointed to several places, and informed us they were the graves of the unfortunate people who fell in the action of the 7th of June, 1798'. McSkimin was profoundly moved by this sight, admitting that 'several of

---

[161] Donaldson, *Historical, Traditional, and Descriptive Account*, p. 58; see also Donald Harman Akenson, *Between Two Revolutions: Islandmagee, County Antrim 1798–1920* (Hamden, Conn.: Archon Books, 1979), p. 20.

[162] John Barrow, *A Tour Round Ireland, through the Sea-Coast Counties, in the Autumn of 1835* (London: John Murray, 1836), pp. ii–iii and 19–20.

[163] See John Borbridge Doyle, *Tours in Ulster: A Hand-Book to the Antiquities and Scenery of the North of Ireland* (Dublin: Hodges and Smith, 1854), pp. 11–12 and 119–20.

[164] For the *Belfast Monthly Magazine* as the organ of Belfast's liberal reformers see Wright, *The 'Natural Leaders'*, pp. 62–80; Nelson, 'Violently Democratic and Anti-Conservative', pp. 35–7; Hall, *Ulster Liberalism*, pp. 56–7.

them had been my acquaintances.'[165] Throughout his travelogue, as noted by Norman Vance, 'landscape recalls the conflict of 1798'.[166]

The depiction of the post-rebellion countryside as a mnemonic is even more evident in the travel writing of the Presbyterian physician John Gamble, which has been characterized by Breandán MacSuibhne as 'gothic' for its ghostly representations of living people, in a manner that conveys a strong impression that early-nineteenth-century Ulster was pervaded by haunting memories of the suppression of the United Irishmen.[167] Gamble was born and raised in Strabane, county Tyrone and belonged to the congregation of Rev. William Crawford, a liberal and former member of the Volunteers. Strabane was considered by the authorities 'a nest of the United Irishmen'. Although Crawford was averse to republicanism, many of his congregation (including the minister's brother) supported the revolutionary cause. In 1798, Crawford moved to the congregation of Holywood, county Down, to succeed Rev. Arthur McMahon, who had joined the rebels and then fled to France. Meanwhile, Crawford's successor in Strabane, Rev. William Dunlop, actively assisted the United Irishmen.[168] Gamble left home in the early 1790s to study at the University of Edinburgh and was not around at the time of the rebellion. He had since served in the British army on the continent. Over return visits to Ulster in 1810, 1812, and 1818, he closely observed the 'society and manners in the North of Ireland' and often picked up on traces of 'the late unfortunate rebellion'.[169]

In 1812, Gamble sailed on a ship from Liverpool that was wrecked near Skerries on the north Antrim coast and he ended up travelling extensively through counties Antrim and Down. At the market house of Banbridge, county Down, he witnessed a 'genteel-looking man' being taunted with a boisterous rendition of the loyalist tune 'Croppies Lie Down' by a party of yeomen, who suspected that he had been a United Irishman. On the road from Dromore to Hillsborough, Gamble registered the popular

[165] *The Belfast Monthly Magazine*, 2, no. 11 (1809), pp. 424–5 (Donegore Hill); 3, no. 12 (1809), pp. 5–6 (Lough Neagh); 3, no. 13 (1809), p. 105 (Island Magee); 6, no. 32 (1811), p. 183 (Larne); 8, no. 45 (1812), p. 265 (Skirry); 8, no. 46 (1812), p. 369 (Ballymena). Elizabeth J. McCrum, McSkimin's great-granddaughter, confirmed that 'Ramble to Antrim' was 'taken by Samuel M'Skimin and a friend'; Samuel McSkimin, *The History and Antiquities of the County of the Town of Carrickfergus, from the Earliest Records Till 1839*, new edn, with notes and appendix by E. J. McCrum (Belfast: Mullan & Son, James Cleeland, Davidson, and McCormack, 1909), p. 525.
[166] Norman Vance, *Irish Literature since 1800* (London: Routledge, 2002), p. 38.
[167] Mac Suibhne, 'Afterworld', pp. 62–113.
[168] See Breandán Mac Suibhne, 'Politicization and Paramilitarism: North-West and South-West Ulster *c.*1772–98', in *1798: A Bicentenary Perspective*, edited by Thomas Bartlett et al. (Dublin: Four Courts Press, 2003), p. 268; Norman Vance, 'Volunteer Thought: William Crawford of Strabane', in *Political Discourse in Seventeenth- and Eighteenth-Century Ireland*, edited by David George Boyce, Robert Eccleshall, and Vincent Geoghegan (Houndmills and New York: Palgrave, 2001), p. 267; Porter, *Irish Presbyterian Biographical Sketches*, pp. 20–1; A. Albert Campbell, *Notes on the Literary History of Strabane* (Omagh: Tyrone Constitution, 1902), pp. 68–9.
[169] John Gamble, *Sketches of History, Politics and Manners, Taken in Dublin, and the North of Ireland, in the Autumn of 1810* (London: C. Cradock and W. Joy, 1811); John Gamble, *A View of Society and Manners in the North of Ireland, in the Summer and Autumn of 1812* (London: C. Cradock and W. Joy, 1813); John Gamble, *Views of Society and Manners in the North of Ireland, in a Series of Letters Written in 1818* (London: Longman, Hurst, Rees, Orme, and Brown, 1819). For a critical edition of Gamble's travel writings see Breandán Mac Suibhne, ed., *Society and Manners in Early Nineteenth-Century Ireland by John Gamble* (Dublin: Field Day, 2011).

resentment of the tenants of the Marquis of Downshire against Lord Castlereagh, who in their eyes had 'turned renegado' in 1798. Near Belfast, he breakfasted at the house of Robert Simms, who had been appointed the insurgent adjutant general for county Antrim but was imprisoned in Fort St George for the duration of the rebellion, alongside 'other misguided heads of the United Irish'. Visiting Larne, he observed that the town had been attacked by insurgents during the rebellion. In the vicinity of Ballymena, which had been overrun by rebels, Gamble heard long tales about 1798 from his hosts at places called Vale and Violet-Bank. Crossing into county Tyrone, near Strabane he met an eye-witness to the murder of Rev. William Hamilton, the loyalist rector of Fánaid [Fanad], who was killed by an insurgent mob in 1797.[170]

On the way to Ballymena, Gamble encountered lasting residues of sectarian embitterment within the rebel camp. A Catholic wayfarer referred to Presbyterians as the 'black-hearted breed' and, when asked for the reason of this bitterness, explained 'didn't they *sell the pass* upon us at Ballinahinch.' Gamble understood this idiom to signify an accusation of 'abandoning, deserting, betraying'. He noted that 'the feeling which dictated the expression, is common, perhaps universal, among the Catholics. They accuse the Presbyterians of leading them into the rebellion, and when they had got them fairly engaged in, it, leaving them to shift for themselves.'[171] Indeed, a song collected a few decades later in the nearby area of Glenarm and attributed to a Catholic 'rustic poet' named McKay encapsulated this sentiment:

> Treachery, treachery, damnable treachery!
> Put the poor Catholics all in the front,
> The Protestants next was the way they were fixed,
> And the black-mouthed Dissenters they skulked at the rump.[172]

Gamble also discovered expressions of lingering animosity towards Church of Ireland clergymen, who were 'accused of great harshness and severity in their office of magistrates during the late rebellion'.[173]

According to Gamble, people were left shattered by the rebellion and 'several who were concerned in it, turned drinkers, and others died mad.' He also noted that there were those who turned towards evangelical faith (in particular Methodism, which more than doubled its membership in Ulster in the three years after the rebellion), their 'enthusiasm of politics, gave place to the enthusiasm of religion'. On the other hand, he was weary of a tendency to exaggerate in attributing too much to the rebellion. At the seat of the Marquis of Abercorn in Barons-Court, a fire was wrongly blamed on the United Irishmen, as were many other unrelated faults. Gamble joked that 'a judicious old lady once remarked, that the climate of the country had changed, as well as the morals of the people, ever since the rebellion.' Nevertheless, he concluded his 1812 tour

---

[170] See Gamble, *View of Society and Manners ... in the Summer and Autumn of 1812*, pp. 40 (Banbridge), 55 (Bishop Percy and 'the late unfortunate rebellion'), 69 ('the late unfortunate rebellion' and 'the late most unnatural rebellion'), 71 (breakfast with Simms), 83 (Larne), 123–86 (Ballymena), 201 (concealing gold during 'the late rebellion'), 227 (story set in 'harvest of 1798' concerning 'desperadoes, who had been concerned in the rebellion'), 269–73 (murder of Rev. Hamilton).

[171] Ibid., pp. 116–20.

[172] Collected by Classon Porter of Larne and reproduced in Young, *Ulster in '98*, p. 51.

[173] Gamble, *View of Society and Manners ... 1812*, pp. 290–2.

with sombre ruminations on the legacy of 'the rebellions, the insurrections, and murders, which have disgraced and desolated Ireland'.[174]

Meeting an old acquaintance near Strabane in 1818, Gamble acidly reflected on 'our rebellion', remarking 'how little we have gained by it; and how we have only drawn the chain round our necks the closer'. Although he would have personally preferred to have seen this episode completely forgotten, the conversations Gamble conducted over the course of his travels repeatedly turned towards 'the late rebellion, of which the memory still is green'. Private communication clearly revealed that Ninety-Eight was remembered, even though it was not a topic of open discussion in public.[175]

VERSIFIED RECALL

A sentimental poem titled 'The Grave of Russell', which has been dated to 1804 and attributed to a lesser-known Ulster poet—James Gilland from Dungannon, county Tyrone (who was just 17 years old at the time), mourns the death of Thomas Russell. It decries the absence of a fitting monument to the noted United Irishman, who was executed in Downpatrick in 1803:

> No sculptor has chiselled thine actions in stone
> Nor reared the tall column, nor moulded the bust.

This lament 'for a hero laid low', presented as a martyr, was deemed too subversive to be printed in Ulster in close proximity to the events.[176] It was initially published in provincial American newspapers, such as the *Supporter* in Chillicothe, Ohio, and the *Reporter* in Washington, Pennsylvania, which catered for an eager readership of United Irish émigrés.[177] In 1812, the poem appeared in the *Irish Magazine*, a sensationalist anti-government newspaper edited by the controversial Walter ('Watty') Cox, who had been both a supporter of the rebellion and an informer. The authorities were weary of the seditious influence of Cox, who was imprisoned for libel. Although an extended term in Newgate prison (1811–14) did not put an end to the publication of the *Irish Magazine*, Cox was obliged to emigrate to New York, where his attempts to

---

[174] Ibid., 343–4 (drunks, madmen, and Methodists), 353 (Barons-Court), and 386 (general observations). For the post-rebellion spread of Methodism see Hempton and Hill, *Evangelical Protestantism*, pp. 30–6.

[175] Gamble, *Views of Society and Manners . . . in 1818*, pp. 198 and 368; for additional references to the 1798 rebellion see pp. 13, 92, 373, and 418.

[176] Madden Papers, TCD 873/675; published in Madden, *Literary Remains of the United Irishmen*, pp. 289–91. For Gilland's authorship see D. J. O'Donoghue, *The Poets of Ireland: A Biographical and Bibliographical Dictionary of Irish Writers of English Verse* (Dublin: Hodges Figgis and London: Henry Frowde, 1912), pp. 162 and 408.

[177] *Supporter* (Chillicothe, Ohio), 11 May 1809. For the poem's publication in the Washington, Pennsylvania, *Reporter*, 3 September 1810, see Peter Gilmore and Kerby A. Miller, 'Searching for "Irish" Freedom—Settling for "Scotch-Irish" Respectability: Southwestern Pennsylvania, 1780–1810', in *Ulster to America: The Scots-Irish Migration Experience, 1680–1830*, edited by Warren R. Hofstra (Knoxville: University of Tennessee Press, 2011), p. 176.

continue the publication of anti-British writings in a journal named *Exile* (1817–18) were unsuccessful.[178]

Poets had to be constantly on their guard. Prior to the rebellion, the authorities became aware that the United Irishmen had 'established clandestine societies who are well supplied with inflammatory publications, some calling themselves Book Clubs, Literary Societies and Reading Societies'.[179] In an attempt to silence dissident voices and prevent the dissemination of subversive texts, rural reading societies were raided by yeomanry in June 1798 and dispersed through such brutal acts as the breaking up of the Newry Literary Society (during which 'many of the books were carried away or destroyed') and the ransacking and destruction of the Doagh Book Club.[180] Shortly after the Battle of Antrim, the Presbyterian clerical student William Hamilton Drummond, who had previously published poems in United Irish newspapers, was stopped in the streets of Larne by a cavalry officer, who put a pistol to his head and exclaimed: 'You young villain, it is you and the like of you that have brought this upon us, with your infernal poetry!'[181]

The poet Mary Balfour was at first a schoolteacher in Newtown Limavaddy, an area in county Londonderry that had seen action in 1798.[182] She later opened a school for young ladies in Belfast, where she became a close friend of the McCracken family. Deeply affected by the death of Henry Joy McCracken, Balfour composed verses in his memory. One of her poems, 'The Seventeenth of July' commemorates the date of his execution. The aftermath of the rebellion is portrayed as a time of oppression and desolation, in which 'the despot triumphs and the patriot weeps', though 'some lips yet dare the hero's worth to tell.' Another poem opens "Twas thus the cause the Hero fell', but claims that 'the spark remains' and promises that, despite the 'black clouds and stormy wind', 'the sun will rise.' Such defiance could not be uttered openly and these poems remained unpublished.[183]

Poetic compositions were targeted for confiscation. The early works of the poet James Campbell of Ballynure, county Antrim, were seized at the time of his arrest in

---

[178] *The Irish Magazine, and Monthly Asylum for Neglected Biography*, January 1812, pp. 45–6.

[179] Mentioned under 'General Object and Views', in 'Extracts from Letters etc. in the Office of the Chief Secretary Relative to the Society of the United Irishmen'; TNA HO 100/58/171–190; reproduced in Bartlett, *Revolutionary Dublin*, pp. 337–46 (quotation on p. 341). See also Johanna Archbold, 'Book Clubs and Reading Societies in the Late Eighteenth Century', in *Clubs and Societies in Eighteenth-Century Ireland*, edited by James Kelly and Martyn J. Powell (Dublin: Four Courts Press, 2010), pp. 138–62 (esp. 151–2).

[180] For Newry see *Newry Magazine; or, Literary & Political Register*, 1, no. 1 (1815), p. 20n. For Doagh see Statistical Report on the Grange of Doagh by Lt Edward Durnford (October 1832) in Day and McWilliams, *Ordnance Survey Memoirs of Ireland*, vol. 29, p. 69; 'Doagh Book-Club County Antrim', *Larne Literary and Agricultural Journal* (1 November 1838) [reproduced in *UJA*, 2nd ser., 15, no. 4 (1909), pp. 158–60]; Smith, *Doagh and the 'First' Sunday School*, p. 7.

[181] See the biographical memoir written by Rev. John Scott Porter in *Sermons by the Late Rev. W. H. Drummond, D. D., M. R. I. A.* (London: E. T. Whitfield and Edinburgh: Williams and Norgate, 1867), pp. vi–vii.

[182] A skirmish in Newtown Limavaddy, in which a party of yeomen prevented a large United Irish force from Belfast spreading the rebellion in to Derry, was subsequently recalled for having given a 'death-blow in the North to that fraternity'; *The Belfast and Province of Ulster Directory* (Belfast: James Alexander Henderson, 1865), p. 165.

[183] Young, *Historical Notices of Old Belfast*, p. 279.

1798 and were never returned.[184] A decade and a half later, Campbell disparagingly
looked back at the rebellion in 'Willie Wark's Song' (1814):

> In Ninety-eight we arm'd again
> To right some things we thought wrang
> We gat sae little for our pains
> It's no worth mindin' in a sang.

'Minding' in Ulster-Scots refers to remembering and the paradoxical assertion in verse
that the rebellion need not be remembered in a song exhibits a characteristic coupling
of professed forgetting with continued remembrance. The poem goes on to caution
against speaking about the rebellion, advising a former United Irishmen that he 'should
silent been, for ance ye war' a crappy loon' [once you were a Croppy boy]. Nonetheless,
disregarding his own admonition, Campbell wrote poetic epitaphs in memory of
comrades who had died as patriots in 1798.[185] His conflicted approach echoes William
Drennan's call for silent commemoration of William Orr in 'The Wake'.[186]

James Orr, 'the bard of Ballycarry', probably the most renowned of the local country
poets, was the secretary of the Antrim Association of the United Irishmen in the 1790s,
when he composed songs to further the revolutionary cause.[187] After participating in the
rebellion, in 1799 he escaped to America with a price on his head, 'to seek sad refuse in some
kindred place'.[188] On his return home in 1800, he professed his loyalty and volunteered for
the Broadisland yeomanry. Although similar requests of returning United Irish exiles to join
the yeomanry, even in that very parish, were approved, Orr's offer was turned down.[189] This
snub, which denied Orr the rehabilitative rite of passage from proscribed rebel to credited
loyalist, prompted James Campbell to compose a song titled 'The Rejected Yeoman'.[190]

Poetic verses, often written in the Ulster-Scots vernacular, offered a medium for
remembering local experiences of 1798 in a register which was less noticeable to
outsiders. In his poetry, James Orr soberly recalled the rebellion in Antrim. His masterpiece 'Donegore Hill' was phrased in the Christis Kirk style, a traditional Scottish genre
mostly used to satirize happenings at county fairs.[191] Orr vividly described from personal
experience how common folk 'Turn'd out *en masse*, as soon as ax'd', but, when faced with
'Nugent's red-coats, bright in arms', their courage failed them, 'An' rush! the pa'e-fac'd

---

[184] John Fullarton, 'Memoir of James Campbell', in *The Poems and Songs of James Campbell of Ballynure* (Ballyclare; S. Corry, 1870), p. iv.
[185] *The Poems and Songs of James Campbell of Ballynure* (Ballyclare: S. Corry, 1870; orig. edn 1820), pp. 100–1, see also 13–15. The expression 'crappy loon' ['Croppy boy'] evokes a common nickname for rebels.
[186] See Chapter 1 above, pp. 78–9.
[187] George Pepper, 'Literary and Biographical Notices', pp. 449–57.
[188] A. McDowell, 'Sketch of the Author's Life', in *The Posthumous Works of J. Orr* (Belfast: Francis D. Finlay, 1817), p. vii.
[189] In referring to an insurgent leader from Ballycarry who escaped to America, Samuel McSkimin noted that, 'after his return', he 'even acted sergeant in a corps of yeomen raised in this parish!'; *Newry Magazine*, 3, no. 18 (1818), p. 511. Similarly, it was remembered that William McClelland of Portmuck had been a proscribed rebel and, on his return from exile, became a lieutenant in the Island Magee yeomanry; see Young, *Ulster in '98*, p. 41; Donaldson, *Historical, Traditional, and Descriptive Account*, p. 59.
[190] Young, *Ulster in '98*, p. 41.
[191] Liam McIlvanney in 'Across the Narrow Sea: The Language, Literature and Politics of Ulster Scots', in Liam McIlvanney and Ray Ryan, eds, *Ireland and Scotland: Culture and Society, 1700–2000* (Dublin: Four Courts Press, 2005), pp. 216–20.

randies [pale-faced beggars], Took leg, that day.' In addition to recalling the misfortunes of the combatants, he dwelt on the anxieties of the family members, who nervously awaited the outcome of the rebellion:

> The leuks o' wheens wha stay'd behin',
> Were mark'd by monie a passion;
> By dread to staun, by shame to rin,
> By scorn an' consternation.[192]
> [The looks on some, who stayed behind
> Were marked by many a passion
> By dread to stay, by shame to run
> By scorn and consternation.]

The poem was published in 1804 in a collected volume of Orr's work, which was circulated locally. Of 559 copies sold by subscription, 150 copies were acquired by Belfast printers for commercial distribution, another ten copies were purchased by a book club, and 380 individuals—mostly from Orr's home area in Antrim—took out subscriptions and in some instances ordered multiple copies, presumably to pass on to acquaintances.[193]

Several other poems in the volume relate to 1798, including 'A Prayer' written on the eve of the Battle of Antrim, verses on 'the notorious informer' John Edward Newell, 'The Wanderer' about the flight of fugitive rebels, and 'The Passengers' about forced emigration in consequence of the rebellion.[194] Apart from these explicit references, Orr's poetry also has many indirect associations with the time of the rebellion. It is possible that an elegy 'On the Death of A. M'Cracken', with its epithet 'Basely Murdered', is a lightly disguised allusion to the execution of Henry Joy McCracken, in which the call to 'Avenge him, Erin! firm he fought for you' had to be obscured so as not to be seen as incitement.[195] 'The Penitent', written in 1800, was inscribed to the Reverend J. Bankhead, the Presbyterian minister of Broadisland who had interceded with the authorities on behalf of his parishioners that had taken part in the rebellion.[196] The choice of stark metaphors for the description of a desolate landscape in 'A Winter Piece' seems to recall the outcome of the rebellion:

> How would her soul shudder, if fear, flight and slaughter,
> Should add tenfold horrors to rude winter's reign!
> If her brethren were buthcher'd and raz'd their lov'd village,

---

[192] James Orr, *Poems on Various Subjects* (Belfast: Smyth & Lyons, 1804), pp. 13–17. Literal readings of the poem emphasize the tone of disillusionment, but awareness to the poetic technique suggests that Orr showed empathy to the rebel cause; see Stephen Dornan, 'Beyond the Milesian Pale: The Poetry of James Orr', *Eighteenth-Century Ireland*, 20 (2005): p. 150; cf. Stewart, *Summer Soldiers*, pp. 77–8.

[193] Orr, *Poems on Various Subjects*, pp. v–xiii.

[194] Orr, *Poems on Various Subjects*, pp. 26–7, 114–21, and 151. See also Donald Harman Akenson and W. H. Crawford, *Local Poets and Social History: James Orr, Bard of Ballycarry* (Belfast: PRONI, 1977), pp. 13 and 43; Linde Connolly Lunney, 'Attitudes to Life and Death in the Poetry of James Orr, an Eighteenth-Century Ulster Weaver', *Ulster Folklife*, 31 (1985): p. 5; Carol Baraniuk, 'James Orr: Ulster-Scot and Poet of the 1798 Rebellion', in *Scottish Studies Review*, 6 (2005), pp. 22–32.

[195] Orr, *Poems on Various Subjects*, pp. 72–3; see also Fred Heatley, *Henry Joy McCracken and His Times*, 2nd edn (Belfast: Wolfe Tone Society, 1967), pp. 54–5.

[196] Orr, *Poems on Various Subjects*, pp. 153–9; see also Jane Gray, 'Folk Poetry and Working Class Identity in Ulster: An Analysis of James Orr's "The Penitent"', in *Journal of Historical Sociology*, 6, no. 3 (1993), p. 264.

> From the red reeking soil they improv'd by their tillage,
> And herself, stript of all by the ruffians of pillage,
> An outcast forlorn 'mong a poor homeless train![197]

Similarly, reference to the 'land's devastation' in a poem about the Haitian slave's revolt in Saint Domingo would have been read, in all likelihood, with the outcome of Ninety-Eight in mind.[198]

The publication of such inexplicit poetic references, which conjured up connotations of the rebellion, was a relatively safe way to remember 1798 in public, yet some poets were careful to disguise even further their references to the rebellion. Samuel Thomson, 'the bard of Carngranny', near Templepatrick in county Antrim, had supported the United Irish movement in its early days and contributed poetry in support of radical reform, but his writing after 1798 became much more guarded. When his poem 'To the Cuckoo'—originally published in 1797 in the *Northern Star*—was republished in 1799, a stanza that praised the 'True United Irishmen' was prudently omitted.[199] Although Thomson's late poetry seems to be devoid of its former radicalism, subtle political commentary can be detected in his animal fables, mostly written in Ulster-Scots.[200] 'To a Hedge-hog', published in 1799, ends with a warning reminiscent of the recent rebellion:

> It might be fatal,
> For you, wi' a' the pikes ye claim,
> Wi' him to battle.

The depiction of the hedgehog's spines as pikes, which were the main weapon associated with the rebels of 1798, is unavoidably redolent.[201]

In his seminal work on the 'rhyming weavers' of Ulster, the twentieth-century Northern Irish poet John Hewitt characterized the country poets as intrinsically radical. Subsequent research has shown that not all of them were political radicals.[202] And yet,

---

[197] A. McDowell, *The Posthumous Works of James Orr of Ballycarry, with a Sketch of His Life* (Belfast: Francis D. Finlay, 1817), pp. 12–14; see also Akenson and Crawford, *Local Poets and Social History*, p. 12.

[198] 'Toussaint's Farewell to St Domingo', in McDowell, *The Posthumous Works*, pp. 31–3; see also Dornan, 'Beyond the Milesian Pale', p. 154.

[199] Jennifer Orr, *The Correspondence of Samuel Thomson (1766–1816): Fostering an Irish Writers' Circle* (Dublin: Four Courts Press, 2012), pp. 218–19.

[200] Jennifer Orr, '1798, Before, and Beyond: Samuel Thomson and the Poetics of Ulster-Scots Identity', in *Revising Robert Burns and Ulster: Literature, Religion and Politics, c.1770–1920*, edited by Frank Ferguson and Andrew R. Holmes (Dublin: Four Courts Press, 2009), pp. 106–26. For the wider context of caution in post-rebellion vernacular poetry see Jennifer Orr, *Literary Networks and Dissenting Print Culture in Romantic-Period Ireland* (Houndmills and New York: Palgrave Macmillan, 2015), pp. 122–61.

[201] Samuel Thomson, *New Poems on a Variety of Different Subjects* (Belfast: Doherty and Simms, 1799), pp. 126–9. For the uncovering of another example, in which Thomson may have included a coded reference to 1798 in the pastoral poem 'Allan, Damon, Sylvander and Edwin', see Jennifer Orr, 'Constructing the Ulster Labouring-Class Poet: The Case of Samuel Thomson', in *Class and the Canon: Constructing Labouring-Class Poetry and Poetics, 1750–1900*, edited by Kirstie Blair and Mina Gorji (Basingstoke: Palgrave Macmillan, 2013), pp. 47–53.

[202] John Hewitt, *Rhyming Weavers and Other Country Poets of Antrim and Down* (Belfast: Blackstaff Press, 1974), pp. 33–4. For the influence of Hewitt's thesis see Ivan Herbison, *Presbyterianism, Politics and Poetry in Nineteenth-Century Ulster: Aspects of an Ulster-Scots Literary Tradition* (Belfast: Queen's University, Institute of Irish Studies, 2000), pp. 13–17. For a critique see Andrew R. Holmes,

also those who held conservative views were troubled by memories of 1798. Francis Boyle [also known as Frank Boal], a loyalist Covenanter from Gransha, near Comber in county Down, published the poem 'The Colonel's Retreat' a decade after the rebellion. In it he reminded the audience of the dire results of taking up arms against the government:

> My friends, be admonished no more to rebel,
> Its dreadful effects there's no Poet can tell,
> It desolates countries, proves nations' o'erthrow,
> Brings men to the scaffold, like General Munro.

Although the thrust of the poem ridicules an unnamed rebel officer for deserting the United Irishmen at the Battle of Ballynahinch, Boyle's sympathetic portrayal of Henry Munro, the commander-in-chief of the county Down rebels, shows an ambiguous attitude to the uprising.[203] Joseph Carson, 'the bard of Kilpike' (from Seapatrick, near Banbridge in county Down), wrote a scornful epitaph 'On a Noted Wrecker of 1798', referring probably to a loyalist perpetrator of sectarian atrocities but without making it clear why his subject was doomed 'with fiends infernal to dwell for ever'.[204] Even poets whose oeuvre was typically non-political were deeply affected by the rebellion. Andrew McKenzie, 'the bard of Dunover' (near Ballywalter, county Down), confessed that he often wept over 'a scene of horror and bloodshed' in 1798 and furtively composed epitaphs for young rebels in his area.[205]

Local memory was jogged by external cultural stimuli. Sympathetic British poets encouraged a transition towards sentimental writing, which provided evocative imagery through which recollections of 1798 could be articulated. One of the most influential of these romantic poets was the blind radical abolitionist Edward Rushton of Liverpool. Rushton composed 'Jemmy Armstrong' about a northern United Irishman who was executed, after declining an offer to save his life by informing on his comrades. Thomas Ledlie Birch had previously mentioned this incident in his memoir from 1799. The original telling praised the condemned rebel's young wife for showing a 'remarkable example of female fortitude' by stoically witnessing the execution and then exclaiming 'God be thanked! He died like a man and has not dishonoured his Family.' In Rushton's poetic adaptation the wife entreats Armstrong 'for Christ's sake comply'. Clearly, romantic poets availed of their licence to reformulate memory.[206]

Already a decade before its posthumous publication in 1824, Rushton's poem was familiar to readers in Ulster and was recognized as 'an anecdote indelibly impressed in

---

'Presbyterian Religion, Poetry and Politics in Ulster, *c.*1770–1850', in *Revising Robert Burns and Ulster: Literature, Religion and Politics, c.1770–1920*, edited by Frank Ferguson and Andrew R. Holmes (Dublin: Four Courts Press, 2009), pp. 37–63.

[203] Francis Boyle, *Miscellaneous Poems* (Belfast: printed by D. & S. Lyons, 1811), pp. 154–8. The poem was dated by Francis Joseph Bigger to *c.*1799; Bigger Papers, BCL K2/H/51–53. See also F. J. Bigger, 'Francis Boyle, the poet of Comber Granshaw', *Northern Whig*, 27 April 1916.

[204] Joseph Carson, *Poems, Odes, Songs, and Satires* (Newry: Morgan and Stevenson, 1831), p. 85.

[205] McKenzie, *Poems and Songs*, p. 173. For McKenzie's response to the death of Rev. James Porter and the epitaph he wrote for Hugh and David Maxwell see above, pp. 157 and 162 (respectively).

[206] Edward Rushton, *Poems and Other Writings* (London: Effingham Wilson, 1824), pp. 98–101; Birch, *Letter from an Irish Emigrant*, p. 19.

the memories of those who feel interest in the events of the memorable year 1798'.[207] Charles Hamilton Teeling claimed personal knowledge of the story of the death of 'the brave and dauntless Armstrong', who had apparently been executed in his home town of Lisburn. He can therefore be identified as *William* Armstrong, who was tried and executed in Lisburn on 10 July 1798. Teeling considered Rushton a 'valued friend' and was an ardent admirer of his 'simple and beautiful lays'. In the sequel to his memoir (1832), Teeling recounted the story of Armstrong in line with the way it was 'affectionately recorded' in the poem, allowing imaginative poetry to dictate historical memory.[208]

In the mid-nineteenth century, the local historian Hugh McCall retold the story of *Tom* Armstrong. McCall later repeated the story to the Belfast antiquarian Robert M. Young, who in turn included it in his collection of memories of *Ulster in '98* (1893).[209] Through these transmissions the poetic version permeated into local memory. By the early twentieth century, not only was the name Tom Armstrong familiar in local history, but the radical nationalist Constance Markievicz would castigate his wife as the only 'one woman who was weak enough to implore her husband to save his own life, at the cost of his friends', unwittingly showing how social memory had steered away from the original casting of the wife as a model advocate of self-sacrifice.[210] The Christian name *Jemmy* (a common nickname for James), which may have been invented by Rushton, had also filtered into local folklore, as evident in a story and a fragment of a song about *James* Armstrong collected in 1909.[211]

Showing even greater influence, a series of poems written by Rushton about Mary Le More, a woman driven insane after she was raped and forced to witness the killing of her father, established an iconic trope for recalling horrific atrocities committed in the suppression of the rebellion.[212] Another archetypal trope for recalling the consequences of the rebellion was provided by the Scottish poet Thomas Campbell. Inspired by a meeting in Hamburg in 1800 with Anthony McCann, a refugee United Irishman from

[207] Edward Rushton, Jr, 'Biographical Sketch of Edward Rushton', in *Belfast Monthly Magazine*, 13, no. 77 (1814), p. 477.

[208] Teeling, *Sequel to Personal Narrative*, pp. 44–5. The court-martial record of William Armstrong appears in the Rebellion Papers, NAI 620/2/8/11.

[209] Anon. [McCall], *Ireland and Her Staple Manufactures*, 2nd edn (Belfast: Henry Greer, George Phillips & Son, 1865), p. 135; Young, *Ulster in '98*, pp. 80–1. In an earlier version, McCall related the story to another United Irishman executed in Lisburn, named Crabbe, but seems to have been subsequently corrected by local informants; see *Our Staple Manufactures* (1855), p. 63.

[210] Constance Markievicz, 'The Women of '98', Part V, in *Irish Citizen*, 4 December 1915, p. 183. The execution of Tom Armstrong is mentioned in W. G. Green, *A Concise History of Lisburn and Neighbourhood* (Belfast: T. H. Jordan, 1906). Both the earlier account of Robert M. Young and that of W. G. Green were reprinted in a local newspaper; *Lisburn Standard*, 28 December 1917 and 18 July 1919 (respectively).

[211] An account written by William Mullholland of Tullyrusk on 3 February 1909; Bigger Papers, BCL K3/H/10.

[212] 'Mary Le More', 'The Maniac', and 'Mary's Death', in Edward Rushton, *Poems* (London: printed by J. M'Creery, 1806), pp. 52–63; see also Mary Helen Thuente, 'Liberty, Hibernia and Mary Le More: United Irish Images of Women', in *The Women of 1798*, edited by Dáire Keogh and Nicholas Furlong (Dublin: Four Courts Press, 1998), pp. 9–25; Bill Hunter, *Forgotten Hero: The Life and Times of Edward Rushton: Liverpool's Blind Poet, Revolutionary Republican & Anti-Slavery Fighter* (Liverpool: Living History Library, 2002), pp. 78–80; Franca Dellarosa, *Talking Revolution: Edward Rushton's Rebellious Poetics, 1782–1814* (Liverpool: Liverpool University Press, 2014), 75–97.

Ulster, Campbell composed 'The Exile of Erin'. It soon became a popular ballad that shaped the image of the émigré rebels who were obliged to live abroad.[213]

James McHenry was one of the budding writers at the time, whose early work shows the influences of these poets. Primarily an admirer of the local poet James Orr, he penned his first verses in 1798, as a child of 12. Although he came from Larne, an area in Antrim that was affected by the insurrection, McHenry passed that year in 'harmless mirth and joy serene' in the sheltered home of Rev. John Nicholson at nearby Black-Cave Shore, where he studied to become a Presbyterian minister.[214] He later recalled his 'wonder, mingled with terror' upon receiving news about the dramatic current events from which he was spared.[215]

McHenry's first book of 'mostly national' poetry, published in Belfast in 1808, avoided direct mention of the rebellion, but its patriotic sentiments intimated sympathy for the legacy of the United Irishmen. The title poem 'The Bard of Erin' includes the verse 'O! then her sons in brotherhood shall join', which is clarified in a note as a statement in support of the politics of 'liberality, patriotism and union'.[216] The poem 'The Exile of Erin's Return', set to the tune of 'Erin go Bragh', is written as a follow-up to Campbell's 'Exile of Erin' and also echoes the popular United Irish song 'The Exiled Irishman's Lamentation'.[217] A review in the *Belfast Monthly Magazine* recognized in McHenry 'a good deal of poetic genius', yet chided him for not having 'spoken more boldly and explicitly' in the poem 'Caithalore', which recounted 'an Irish historical tale' about an Ulster chieftain who died as a 'glorious martyr' when he stood up to face a tyrant king. The poet's reluctance to dwell on the 'thousand heart-rending recollections' inspired by the poem suggested to the reviewer a 'want of true knowledge of the state of Ireland, of studying the disposition of its inhabitants, and of conciliation in the treatment of them'.[218]

McHenry seems to have taken this criticism to heart. His next composition was the long narrative poem 'Patrick', which featured graphic depictions of the devastation incurred by the suppression of the insurrection in Antrim that were clearly inspired by Rushton's 'Mary Le More'.[219] Written in 1810, when he was a student of medicine in

---

[213] See Madden, *Literary Remains of the United Irishmen*, pp. 329–54; Frank Molloy, 'Thomas Campbell's "Exile of Erin": English Poem, Irish Reactions', in *Back to the Present, Forward to the Past: Irish Writing and History since 1798*, edited by Brian Coates, Joachim Fischer, and Patricia A. Lynch (Amsterdam and New York: Rodopi, 2006), 1, pp. 43–52.

[214] For McHenry's admiration of James Orr see Pepper, 'Literary and Biographical Notices', p. 457. For recollections of his youth in 1798 see notes to the poem 'Black-Shore Cave' (1802) in James McHenry, *The Bard of Erin; and Other Poems, Mostly National* (Belfast: Smyth and Lyons, 1808), p. 76; see also the appendix to McHenry, *The Insurgent Chief* (1844 ed.), pp. 461–3.

[215] *Philadelphia Monthly Magazine*, 2nd ser. v. 1, no. 1 (1828), p. 37; see also Robert E. Blanc, 'James McHenry (1785–1845): Playwright and Novelist' (PhD thesis: University of Pennsylvania, 1939), p. 8.

[216] McHenry, *The Bard of Erin*, pp. 7 and 19.

[217] ibid., pp. 71–5. 'The Exiled Irishman's Lamentation', attributed to George Nugent Reynolds, was popularized in the *Northern Star* (27 July 1796), and included in United Irish songbooks; see *The Irish Harp* (Dublin: s.n., 1798), pp. 5–6; *Paddy's Resource* (New York, 1798), pp. 1–2; see also Mary Helen Thuente, 'United Irish Poetry and Songs', in *A Companion to Irish Literature*, edited by Julia M. Wright (Chichester and Malden: Wiley-Blackwell, 2010), 1, pp. 264–5.

[218] *Belfast Monthly Magazine*, 2, no. 7 (28 February 1809), pp. 136–8.

[219] James McHenry, *Patrick: A Poetical Tale Founded on Incidents Which Took Place in Ireland During the Unhappy Period of 1798* (Glasgow: D. McKenzie, 1810).

Glasgow, it attained instant success, with 700 copies sold in less than a month. A critic from county Down—probably the Presbyterian minister Rev. Samuel Edgar of Ballynahinch—objected to its sympathetic portrayal of rebels and argued that such recollections were 'unseasonable':

> The summer of ninety-eight has elapsed; better times have ensued; being an unhappy period, it would seem more prudent, and more congenial to the spirit of an Irishman to cast a veil over it, than by a tragical detail of our follies and our woes to revive, especially in another country, what is partly forgotten.[220]

In face of this open call for forgetting, fellow students—many of whom were Presbyterians from Ulster—came to McHenry's defence, as did several readers of the liberal *Belfast Monthly Magazine*, which was a favoured journal among former United Irishmen. Even though the re-awakening of memories of the rebellion in print was considered controversial, there was apparently an eager readership for remembrance.[221]

This interest was noted by the editors of the *Belfast Magazine and Literary Journal*, a periodical established in 1825 and 'chiefly occupied with Literary Subjects and topics of general interest connected with Life and Manner'. Their call for 'contributions from literary characters' was answered enthusiastically by correspondents and the editors promised to publish articles on a variety of topics, including 'Scenes of the rebellion of 1798'.[222] Indeed, the very first issue featured 'Recollections of the Battle of Ballynahinch by an Eye Witness'. The author, who used the pseudonym Iota, was James Thomson, originally from the village of Annaghmore, county Down (2 km south of Ballynahinch). He had visited the rebel encampment as a boy of 12 and had viewed the battle from a nearby hill.[223] A decade later, as a student at the University of Glasgow, Thomson was probably the author of a letter (signed T.) in support of the publication of James McHenry's poem on 1798.[224]

Thomson (whose son William would achieve fame as the renowned physicist Lord Kelvin), was appointed professor of mathematics at the college department of Belfast Academical Institution, which provided him with a suitable social surrounding for maintaining his memories of the rebellion.[225] The foundation in 1810 of this school and university, locally known as 'Inst', brought together Presbyterian radicals, who were determined to prevent government intervention in its management. The original board of directors was effectively a hub of former United Irishmen, foremost among them the poet William Drennan. They were accused by Sir George Hill, MP for Londonderry City, of being 'men, some of whom had figured in the horrible transactions of 1798; but who having failed in that more prompt experiment to upset the constitution by rebellion, were now attempting the slower, but surer, means of

---

[220] 'The Rejoinder of S. E.', in *Belfast Monthly Magazine*, 5, no. 24 (1810), pp. 2–3.
[221] See *Belfast Monthly Magazine*, 4, no. 19 (1810), pp. 95–9; 4, no. 21 (1810), pp. 275–6; 4, no. 22 (1810), pp. 347–50; 5, no. 24 (1810), pp. 1–4; 5, no. 27 (1810), pp. 260–1.
[222] *Belfast Magazine and Literary Journal*, 1, no. 1 (1 February 1825), 'Prospectus' (i–ii) and note 'To Correspondents' (n.p.).
[223] *Belfast Magazine and Literary Journal*, 1, no. 1 (1825), pp. 56–64.
[224] *Belfast Monthly Magazine*, 4, no. 21 (1810), pp. 275–6.
[225] Crosbie Smith and M. Norton Wise, *Energy and Empire: A Biographical Study of Lord Kelvin* (1989), pp. 3–12. For a more nuanced analysis see Andrew R. Holmes, 'Professor James Thomson Sr. and Lord Kelvin: Religion, Science, and Liberal Unionism in Ulster and Scotland', in *Journal of British Studies*, 50, no. 1 (2011), pp. 100–24.

revolution, by inculcating and infusing into early youth the religious and political precepts of Paine and Priestly', a charge which Drennan vigorously denied.[226]

Thomson admitted that he had often heard stories of the aftermath of the rebellion, concerning 'the occurrences of the flight, and the perils and exertions of the fugitives in endeavouring to conceal themselves, or to get safely out of their native land to America or other places, with the numerous privations and hairbreadth escapes of many'. However, he confined his published account of 1798 to his own personal reminiscences, which he recalled with clarity:

> These impressions were formed at that time of life, when the traces may be expected to be stronger and more vivid than at a more advanced age, and especially when the events are of a striking character; and this expectation has been fully realised in the present instance. Some of the lighter, shades are no doubt worn away and defaced in a considerable degree, by the busy scenes and various cares of more than a quarter of a century; still, however, not only the grand outline of events, but in many instances even the minuter traces, retain such, a freshness and strength as to seem to be stamped in indelible characters on the very substance of the mind, and to be apparently as durable as itself.

Public interest in this narrative was apparent in its immediate reproduction in the *Belfast News-Letter*. It would later be reprinted in other publications and in Thomson's obituary, following his death in 1849, would be recognized as 'an exceedingly interesting account'.[227]

Rev. Samuel Edgar, Thomson's former schoolteacher, wrote to the editors in praise of the account of the Battle of Ballynahinch. He claimed that it 'was interesting to many of your readers' because 'it introduced various minute circumstances which could only present themselves to an eye-witness, and which were calculated to give a more vivid conception of the whole scene, than the general descriptions of history.' Asserting that 'the recollection of troublesome periods should not be forgotten', Edgar submitted for publication his own 'Recollections of 1798', describing 'a few circumstances connected with the battles of Saintfield and Ballynahinch, which came within my own observation, and are similar to those which are yet fresh in the recollection of others'.

As a Presbyterian minister in Ballynahinch in 1798, Edgar had tried to dissuade people in his locality from joining the rebels. He found that responses to the rebellion were influenced by unreliable rumours, 'wild as imagination could conceive in her highest flights, and false as fame had ever circulated' and he recalled the emotions of terror and anxiety roused by the violence of the rebels and of the military. Edgar believed that remembrance should serve a moral instructive purpose. He therefore ended his narrative with a description of how Presbyterian services were conducted

---

[226] *The Parliamentary Debates from the Year 1803 to the Present Time*, 1st ser., vol. 34 (London: T. C. Hansard, 1816), p. 428; William Drennan, *A Retort Courteous to the Remarks of 'Presbyter' Relative to the Belfast Academical Institution, Published in the BNL, July 26, 1816* (Belfast: Francis D. Finlay, 1816). See also Stewart, 'The Transformation of Presbyterian Radicalism', pp. 141–76; Peter Brooke, *Ulster Presbyterianism: The Historical Perspective, 1610–1970* (Dublin: Gill and Macmillan and New York: St Martin's Press, 1987), pp. 139–45; McBride, *Scripture Politics*, pp. 211–13; Nelson, 'Violently Democratic and Anti-Conservative', pp. 37–47; Wright, *The 'Natural Leaders'*, pp. 160–1.

[227] *BNL*, 1 February 1825, p. 2. For subsequent republications see Madden, *The United Irishmen*, 3rd ser., vol. 1 (1846), pp. 385–7; *McComb's Guide to Belfast* (1861), pp. 126–7. For the obituary see *Freeman's Journal*, 17 January 1849, p. 1.

during the rebellion, regardless of the surrounding perils, and suggested to the editors of the journal that 'many of your readers may take an interest in this simple record of my own experience, and that of my Christian friends who were involved in the same difficulties.'

Just fifteen years earlier, Edgar had objected to McHenry's poetic recollection of the rebellion, but as he approached the end of his life, he had come to realize that 'unless such particulars be recorded now, by those who had opportunities of witnessing them, they will soon be entirely forgotten. Yet they seem on many accounts to be worthy of preservation.'[228] Despite its promising start, the *Belfast Magazine and Literary Journal* was a short-lived enterprise and its publication was discontinued after 1825. Nonetheless, the appearance of personal recollections of 1798 in a local literary magazine opened the way for representations of the repressed social memory of the rebellion in Ulster to appear in works of literature.

FICTIONALIZED MEMORY

With United Irish exiles pouring into the United States, it is perhaps no surprise that the first Irish-American novel *The Irish Emigrant*, subtitled *An Historical Tale Founded on Fact*, is preoccupied with the 1798 rebellion. Writing under the pseudonym 'An Hibernian', the author was most probably Adam Douglass, who joined the publisher in 1817 to register the book at the office of the Virginia state clerk.[229] Douglass was born in Belfast in 1790 and as a young boy was taken to America by an uncle shortly after the rebellion. He came back to Ireland in 1812, joined the army and participated in the Napoleonic wars. He then returned to America and settled down in New Market, Virginia, where he worked as a school master and surveyor.[230] The novel was 'written with a view to perpetuate in the memory of the writer . . . the country that gave him birth'. It opens on 'the banks of the Majestic Potowmac' with the reminiscences of Owen McDermott from county Antrim, who

> had been obliged (in consequence of his political sentiments together with the persecution he had to sustain in consequence of his religious opinions) to leave his native country after the unfortunate termination of the revolution, in favour of the British Government, during the year one thousand seven hundred and ninety eight.[231]

The story of the protagonist's involvement in the rebellion is then recounted in mawkish prose over two volumes.

Although liberties were taken in readapting historical information to a crude romantic plot, the text is littered with actual figures and events from the time of the rebellion.

---

[228] *Belfast Magazine and Literary Journal*, 1, no. 4 (1825), pp. 540–8.

[229] An Hibernian, *The Irish Emigrant: An Historical Tale Founded on Fact*, 2 vols. (Winchester, Va.: John T. Sharrocks, 1817). See also Charles Fanning, *The Irish Voice in America: 250 Years of Irish-American Fiction* (Lexington: University Press of Kentucky 2000; orig. edn 1990), pp. 39–43.

[230] For brief biographical information on Adam Douglass see Ella Hazel Spraker, *The Boone Family . . . Containing Many Unpublished Bits of Early Kentucky History* (Rutland, Vt.: The Tuttle Company, 1922), p. 518; John Walter Wayland, *A History of Shenandoah County, Virginia* (Baltimore: Regional Pub. Co., 1980; orig. edn 1927), p. 598.

[231] *The Irish Emigrant*, 1, pp. iii and 6.

An informer named Billy Newell (based on the notorious informer Edward Newell) brings to the knowledge of the authorities that Owen's father, a liberal Catholic landowner from near Lough Neagh, is a member of the United Irishmen. After his father and sister are killed in a brutal military raid, Owen rallies the tenants of his demesne and assumes the position of commander-in-chief of the rebels in the Northern District. Among his subordinates are Munroe (based on Henry Munro, the actual commander-in-chief of the rebels in county Down), McCance (based on Samuel McCance, who commanded a party of pikemen at Ballynahinch), and Keane (based on William Keane, a former printer at the *Northern Star*, who accompanied Henry Munro on his attempted escape after the defeat at Ballynahinch). Lord O'Neill, who was killed by the rebels in Antrim, is renamed in the novel Sir Phelim Oniall of Shane Castle.

The Irish Emigrant sentimentally recalled the memory of 1798 for the benefit of the republican exile community, recognizing that in the wake of the rebellion 'the emigration from Ireland to the United States had been vast.' The admission that 'those emigrants took every opportunity that offered to inform their relatives of the change they had made so much for the better' suggests that the novel was also directed to acquaintances and relatives at home, where it was still inexpedient to publish such a sympathetic literary account of the recent rebellion.[232] While the author exploited the freedom of speech in America, he also glossed over some of the more sensitive features of the rebellion in Ulster. On the one hand, the ruthlessness of the government's counter-insurgency measures is revealed:

> the enemy were now resorting to the most barbarous expedients they could devise to quell the revolution; nothing was to be heard from all quarters, but that of dreadful excesses being committed by the English army on all descriptions of persons; the innocent suffered with the guilty, neither age nor sex spared, but delivered up to the brutal ferocity of the soldiers, who were permitted to glut their sanguinary and cruel propensities, as they thought proper, with impunity.[233]

And yet, Douglass, who had just two years earlier sustained injuries when fighting in the ranks of the British army at the Battle of Waterloo, could not bring himself to unequivocally denounce the military command. In contrast to the sadistic junior officers and their henchmen, General Nugent is sympathetically depicted as 'a republican at heart'.[234] More strikingly, the protagonist of *The Irish Emigrant* is a Catholic insurgent, the other main characters belong to the Anglican circles of the Anglo-Irish ascendancy, and there is no explicit mention of the mass participation of Presbyterians in the rebellion in Antrim and Down. The deliberate obfuscation of the defining character of the northern rebellion, which was well known to the author on account of his own Ulster-Scot background, reveals how a seemingly unapologetic expression of cultural memory could mask deliberate public forgetting.[235]

Unlike Douglass, the travel writer John Gamble maintained that it is 'among the Presbyterians of Ulster, that the provincial character is to be sought' and did not shy

---

[232] Ibid., 2, pp. 176–7.   [233] Ibid., 2, pp. 124–5.   [234] Ibid., 1, pp. 30 and 36.

[235] For an attempt to explain the bafflement caused by the Catholic identity of the hero see Jim Shanahan, 'Tales of the Time: Early Fictions of the 1798 Rebellion', in *Irish University Review*, 41, no. 1 (2011), p. 164.

from writing about their involvement in the rebellion. Gamble used the many fresh recollections of 1798 that he had heard during his tours in Ulster to write *Charlton; or, Scenes in the North of Ireland*, a three-volume novel first published in 1823 and re-issued in 1827.[236] A review disapproved of the novel's dwelling on the 'heartless, yet heart-breaking subject' and questioned 'whether it is likely to fulfil any good purpose thus to renew, as it were, the horrors of that period'.[237] Anticipating this criticism, Gamble stated that 'the period of my story is that of the late rebellion, a period of such horror in many parts of Ireland, as perhaps to make it an unfit subject for a tale; yet happily a variety of circumstances combined to make it often a scene of wonder, sometimes of admiration, and always one of interest.'[238]

Gamble outlined his interpretation of the historical events in an exegesis at the opening of the second volume:

> It was in the North of Ireland that the late rebellion may be said to have originated; it was there that insurrection was most dreaded; and doubtless from the greater intelligence of the people, it would there, if extensive, have been most formidable; except in a few districts, however, this part, of the country may be said to have remained undisturbed. It is creditable to the Presbyterians of the North of Ireland likewise, that in the highest exaltation of revolution, they rarely lost their humanity; and though they often enough spoke daggers, they never, or at least seldom (except in battle) used them. The truth is, they were by this time heartily tired of the business, and . . . had pretty generally discovered that there was a wide difference between a revolt, and the planning of it.

Gamble maintained that the Presbyterian commitment to revolutionary republicanism was only skin-deep. In contrast, he argued that 'the constancy of the Catholic was not so easily shaken. His opposition to government was, in some degree, his settled habit; it was in a great measure his ordinary and habitual movement.' Protestants played for 'the counter of speculative freedom', while Catholics joined the insurrection out of 'a zeal, a fidelity, a devotedness'.[239]

In a style laden with literary references and classical quotations, the narrative is structured around the exploits of a young liberal-minded Presbyterian doctor who travels around the area of county Down in 1798. The lively retelling of conversations conducted with people from all classes and backgrounds presents a panoramic showcase of a wide range of local opinions and views on the politics of the day. The circumstances in which the protagonist finds himself 'might make him a democrat, but, in his heart, he was an aristocrat'.[240] Although Charlton ends up dressed in the uniform of a United Irish officer at the Battle of Ballynahinch, he is at best a reluctant rebel. Charlton's character therefore personifies the apologetic narratives that were in circulation after the rebellion, which claimed that United Irish recruitment was founded on coercion of the populace. These claims, which appeared in loyalist propaganda and were voiced to no effect in defence pleas at court-martial trials, would later feature prominently in folklore.[241]

---

[236] John Gamble, *Charlton; or, Scenes in the North of Ireland, a Tale* (London: Baldwin, Cradock, and Joy, 1823), 3 vols (the quotation is taken from the preface, vol. 1, p. ix). The title of the second edn was slightly amended to *Charlton; or, Scenes in Ireland* (1827).

[237] *Monthly Review*, 103 (February, 1824), pp. 215–17.

[238] Gamble, *Charlton*, 1, pp. vi–vii (preface).   [239] Ibid., 2, pp. 181–2.

[240] Ibid., 1, p. 106.   [241] See Chapter 2 above, pp. 101–3.

A sense of historical authenticity is enhanced by the inclusion of long extracts from United Irish publications and the reproduction of political ballads, which Gamble vouched are 'real songs which were then sung; and they exerted such an influence, that it would be unpardonable to have overlooked them, in a narrative founded on the transactions of those days'.[242] Yet, for all his use of historical materials and local reminiscences, Gamble was uncomfortable with the social memory of the rebellion. A central character in the novel is unmistakably modelled on the radical Presbyterian minister Rev. James Porter, who is renamed Dimond. Brushing aside the common belief that Porter had been wrongly convicted, the novel endorses the government's version of events and presents him as a zealot who leads a party of rebels into battle at Ballynahinch. Gamble refrained from recreating the disturbing scene of Porter's execution, in full view of his family and congregation. In its stead, the fictional rebel minister commits suicide by taking poison, replaying a scenario which is borrowed from the death of the revolutionary Anglican clergyman Rev. William Jackson, who famously took poison during his trial for high treason in 1795.[243]

Charlton ends with reflections on the transience of remembrance. After the rebellion, the hero is still troubled by the recent painful events and contemplates emigration to America, but is reassured that 'the memory of those things soon passes away. Our people . . . do not long remember'. This prediction ultimately fulfils itself and, looking back at the events years later, he 'regarded the Rebellion in which he had so strangely got entangled, its idle hopes and wishes, as a phantom that had vanished, or a tale that was told'.[244] Gamble, who discovered in his travels that recollections of the rebellion still haunted the Ulster countryside, maintained that this episode had best be forgotten in the grander scheme of historical developments. Despite its ethnographic semblance, his work was devoted to subtly laying to rest the unsettling legacy of Presbyterian radicalism. *Charlton* was intended to be a work of cultural forgetting, rather than cultural memory.

The author most widely associated with the memory of 1798 in Ulster was James McHenry. Since his graduation in Glasgow, he had returned to Ulster to work as a doctor, first in Larne and then in Belfast, and had also tried his hand at editing a literary journal. In 1817, he emigrated to the United States and eventually settled in Philadelphia, where he resumed his literary pursuits.[245] From across the Atlantic, McHenry revisited the topic of his early 1798 poem 'Patrick', which had provoked controversy in 1810, and composed the poem 'The Star of Love', which is also set in the bloody aftermath of the rebellion:

> The fight was o'er on Antrim's plain,
> And thousands mourn'd for thousands slain
>
> . . .
>
> Deep then the wounds that Erin felt,

---

[242] Gamble, *Charlton* 1, p. vii (preface).

[243] Jackson's manner of death was well known to the author, who as a young man had been impressed by the 'magnanimity, unshaken fortitude, and contempt of death' shown by United Irishmen who died in prison; see Gamble, *Sketches of History, Politics and Manners*, pp. 63–4.

[244] Gamble, *Charlton*, 3, pp. 229, 236, and 244.

[245] See the biographical memoir of McHenry in *The Poems of the Pleasures* (Philadelphia: J. B. Lippincott & Co., 1841), pp. 273–82. McHenry later claimed that he moved to the United States in 1816; see Blanc, 'James McHenry', pp. 10–12.

> For strong th' avenging sword was dealt;
> Death, drench'd in blood, stalk'd o'er the plain,
> And scaffolds quiver'd with the slain.

On the background of the devastation, the long poem tells the story of a romance between Eliza, the daughter of a 'firm supporter of the law', and a proscribed rebel named Fergus, who is forced to flee abroad. After a long separation, the former rebel receives a pardon in reward for his military service in the Napoleonic wars and is allowed to return home.[246] Although McHenry's poetry was generally well received in America and was re-issued in multiple editions, this particular poem did not attract critical attention. It was ultimately through the writing of prose that his literary endeavours to present the memory of the rebellion would make an impact.

After gaining recognition as an author by writing two novels set in pre-independence America, McHenry established in 1824 the *American Monthly Magazine*. In the first issues he published anonymously the opening chapters of his novel *O'Halloran; or the Insurgent Chief*, subtitled *An Historical Tale of 1798*.[247] Serialization was disrupted by the discontinuation of the journal and in its place an advertising campaign heralded the novel's appearance in book form. In mid-1824, *The Insurgent Chief* was published in Philadelphia, as well as in London, where it was said to 'have attracted much attention'. Reprints were issued before the year was over and by 1825 the novel had already come out in three editions, of which two were unauthorized, and a French translation was reputedly published in Paris.[248] McHenry felt unsatisfied with the 'mutilated form' in which his novel had been issued and considered the title too romantic 'for the matter-of-fact statements it contains'. Its runaway success, however, prevented the author from pursuing his plans to revise the text and produce 'a more complete edition, under the more appropriate title of "The United Irishmen"'.[249]

McHenry has been credited with taking the Irish national tale—a genre that aspired to familiarize British readerships in the newly formed United Kingdom with the idiosyncrasies of Ireland—and adapting this literary form to the regionalism of Ulster. Dialogues in *The Insurgent Chief* exhibit familiarity with the Ulster-Scots vernacular and the plot dwells on the distinct composition of the northern United Irish movement, 'nine-tenths of their number being Presbyterians'. Novels in the national tale genre typically culminate with a marriage between an Englishman and an Irishwoman, as exemplified in *The Wild Irish Girl* (1806) by Lady Morgan (Sydney Owenson). Instead, *The Insurgent Chief* ends with an all-Protestant union, in which Edward Barrymore, the son of a loyalist Dublin aristocrat, weds Ellen Hamilton, the grand-daughter of the leader of the northern rebels, in a ceremony conducted 'according to

---

[246] James McHenry, *The Pleasures of Friendship, and Other Poems* (Philadelphia: Grigg & Elliott, 1836), pp. 89–99. The poem was originally published in James McHenry, *The Feelings of Age, to Which Is Added The Star of Love*, 2nd edn (Philadelphia: Banks & Brother, 1830).

[247] *American Monthly Magazine*, 1, no. 1 (1824), pp. 30–9 and no. 2 (1824), pp. 147–58.

[248] *National Gazette*, 2 May 1825; cited in Blanc, 'James McHenry', p. 16.

[249] See preface to James McHenry, *The Hearts of Steel: An Irish Historical Tale of the Last Century* (Philadelphia, 1825), vol. 1, pp. iv–v. For notice of the novel's success in London see *Cincinnati Literary Gazette*, 2, no. 24 (1824), p. 191. For the report of the French translation (of which no copies can be traced) see *National Gazette*, 2 May 1825; cited in Blanc, 'James McHenry', p. 16.

the form observed by the reverend ministers of the Synod of Ulster'.[250] This tale of Ulster-Scot Presbyterian reconciliation with the Anglo-Irish Anglican elite signified the 'Ulsterization' of 1798.[251]

McHenry claimed to have been motivated by an elderly aunt, who 'was much chagrined, with the carelessness with which even professed travellers through Ireland have uniformly mentioned its northern province' and was particularly 'displeased at the very partial and inaccurate accounts which have been given to the world of the motives, designs, and transactions of the Northern United Irishmen'. This 'aunt', who was actually modelled on a Jane Houston of Larne, encouraged him to write 'a fair statement of the manners of the people of Ulster, and of the part they had taken in the late rebellion'.[252] In addressing the sensitive topic of 1798, McHenry was aware that 'many of the actors in the scenes we have described, are yet living' and that their 'prejudices either for, or against the principles which occasioned the contest, may induce them to expect either a defence or reprehension of their doctrines and conduct'. He therefore committed himself to 'strict impartiality not only in relating, the events, but in detailing the opinions, and delineating the characters of the different parties. The United Irishmen and the loyalists, are permitted to express their sentiments with equal force and freedom.' Despite his professed neutrality, the author had a distinct take on the historical events, favouring moderate unionism, while shunning republicanism and extreme loyalism: 'The fanatical and the fierce on either side, are painted as such, while the moderate and lenient, we hope, have ample justice done to the rationality of their views.'[253]

In McHenry's view, the rebellion was caused by the 'coercive system of government' of Lord Camden, whose excesses were exemplified by the 'unnecessary, unjust, impolitic, and cruel execution of William Orr'. The crisis was effectively resolved with the appointment of Lord Cornwallis, described as 'a man of a more enlightened understanding and a more humane temper'. The 'adoption of healing measures' accommodated reconciliation so that: 'in the course of a few months, rebellion was converted into submission, and disaffection into loyalty. With the restoration of the ordinary laws, confidence in the government, tranquillity, industry, and national prosperity, were also restored.' McHenry conceded that 'the flames of the civil war had been too extensive for its dying embers to be all at once extinguished' and that 'the government, comparatively mild and merciful as it was, still displayed, in some instances, a harshness towards several proscribed individuals, which kept alive, for a considerable time, a

---

[250] James McHenry, *The Insurgent Chief; or, The Pikemen of '98: A Romance of the Irish Rebellion. To Which Is Added an Appendix, Containing Biographical Memoirs of the Principle Characters and Descriptive of the Scenery of the Work* (Belfast: John Henderson, 1847; orig. edn 1824), p. 449. In order to avoid inconsistencies in pagination between the many editions of this work, the citations refer to this authoritative edition, first produced in Belfast in 1844.

[251] McBride, 'Memory and Forgetting', pp. 492–3; Fanning, *The Irish Voice in America*, pp. 46–50; Stephen Dornan, 'Irish and American Frontiers in the Novels of James McHenry', *Journal of Irish and Scottish Studies*, 3, no. 1 (2009): pp. 139–56. For the use of Ulster-Scots as a regional marker see Stephen Dornan, 'Scots in Two Early Ulster Novels', in *Scots: Studies in Its Literature and Language*, edited by John M. Kirk and Iseabail Macleod (Amsterdam and New York: Rodopi, 2013), pp. 171–82; Frank Ferguson, ed., *Ulster-Scots Writing: An Anthology* (Dublin: Four Courts Press, 2008), p. 166.

[252] McHenry, *The Insurgent Chief* (1847 edn), pp. 11–14. For identification of the aunt see p. 464.

[253] Ibid., pp. 7–8. For McHenry's authorial voice see Ina Ferris, *The Romantic National Tale and the Question of Ireland* (Cambridge and New York: Cambridge University Press, 2002), pp. 135–6.

soreness in the minds of many, who would otherwise have returned at once to their former habits and feelings of loyalty.' However, he maintained that 'this course of irritation and danger' ended within a year. In the fashion of Walter Scott's treatment of Jacobitism in the *Waverly* novels, overtones of ideological radicalism and lingering traces of bitterness were purposely subdued in order to produce a domesticated cultural memory of the rebellion, which was deemed more suitable for public consumption.[254]

McHenry considered *The Insurgent Chief* a work of history and asserted that it 'contains numerous *facts* that have never yet appeared in print' (emphasis in the original). A preface, written in 1820, noted that 'many of the actors in the scenes we have described, are yet living' and that 'these characters are drawn nearly as we knew them in life; and with respect to the events, it was our lot, although then in our childhood, personally to, witness many of them.' To supplement personal recollections, historical information was obtained from 'sources of unquestionable authenticity'. In the author's view, there was only limited scope for the 'colouring of romance', as 'during the singular period that has supplied our subject, numberless exploits and transactions took place highly enough coloured of themselves, and requiring no embellishment from fancy to suit them to the appetite of the most choice admirer of extraordinary facts that ever derived gratification from novel-reading.'[255] Twenty years later, a local historian writing the 'Annals of the Parish and Town of Larne' found that local testimonies confirmed that McHenry's account of the events in Larne during the rebellion 'may be relied on as authentic'.[256]

Nonetheless, casting aside factual history, McHenry chose to put a fictional character at the head of the northern 'United Irish confederacy'. In the novel, O'Halloran appears as the commander-in-chief at the Battle of Antrim, presiding over the actual United Irish leader McCracken and other historical insurgent officers, including Samuel Orr and Rev. James Porter (who appears as a senior commander). O'Halloran's character was loosely based on the county Antrim landowner James Agnew Farrell of Magheramorne (4 km south of Larne). McHenry recalled that at the age of 7 he had seen Farrell in 1792 command the Larne company of the 'Independent Irish Volunteers' at a review in Ballygally.[257]

Farrell joined the United Irishmen and was appointed a colonel, but, unlike O'Halloran, he went into hiding in Scotland during the insurrection. The author may not have known that, prior to taking flight, Farrell betrayed his republican comrades by communicating his fighting orders to General Nugent.[258] After the rebellion, he returned and benefited from the amnesty. By 1803, Farrell was a captain in the Magheramorne yeomanry and in 1815 he was appointed the High Sheriff of Antrim.[259] This example of successful rehabilitation suited McHenry's view on the outcome of 1798:

---

[254] McHenry, *The Insurgent Chief* (1847 edn), pp. 124–5.   [255] Ibid., p. 8.

[256] *Larne Literary and Agricultural Journal*, no. 9 (1839): p. 1. This article, part of a local history series, was probably written by Rev. Classon Porter of Larne.

[257] McHenry, *The Insurgent Chief* (1847 edn), pp. 454–5.

[258] For Farrell's treachery see the account of James Hope in Madden, *The United Irishmen*, 3rd ser., vol. 1 (1846), p. 263. See also 'The Oakboys, the Hearts of Steel the Volunteers and the United Irishmen of Larne and Neighbourhood', C. J. Robb Papers, PRONI D2095/18.

[259] *A List of the Officers of the Militia and of the Yeomanry Cavalry and Volunteer Cavalry of the United Kingdom* (London, 1820), p. 263; 'Fifteenth Report on the Office of Sheriff', Appendix no. 5:

so evidently had the majority of the North became loyal, that it seemed, by their conduct and expressions, as if a species of reaction had taken place in their feelings, and the government appeared so much convinced that these professions were sincere, that it scrupled not to entrust arms into the hands of thousands who had been active in the rebellion.[260]

In the novel, O'Halloran is sentenced to death by a court martial for his part in the rebellion but receives a pardon. He is restored to his property and lives to an old age, 'leaving behind him a memory which will be long honoured by the warm-hearted people of the romantic country, for whose independence he had, in vain, contended so bravely, and suffered so much.' Such a happy ending was more amenable to the author's political outlook than the dire fate of the actual leadership of the rebellion.[261]

The literary critic Norman Vance commented on McHenry's adroitness in conveying 'sympathy for his Irish insurgents while avoiding direct endorsement of their causes'. Deeds such as the martyrdom of William Orr are registered 'as a point at which local history is just about to pass over into national myth, the kind of myth which was the stock in trade of romantic novelists and the ancient bards alike.'[262] McHenry did not altogether avoid local painful memories of the rebellion. However, his choices of what to highlight from the repository of local recollections were highly selective. The executions of McCracken and Porter are only alluded to in passing and no indication is given of the social memory of resentment that these prominent demonstrations of capital punishment engendered. Behind the scenes of this literary endeavour to make the memory of the United Irishmen palatable to a popular readership lurked a deliberate effort at forgetting troubling aspects of 1798.

The flourish of northern historical fiction in the 1820s was not confined to the writings of Gamble and McHenry. A two-volume novel about the rebellion in Ulster entitled *O'Hara; or, 1798*, was published anonymously in 1825.[263] It was written by the aspiring novelist William Hamilton Maxwell, who at the time was a nominal Church of Ireland clergyman in Balla, county Mayo, and was staying at the hunting lodge of the Marquess of Sligo, to whom the book is dedicated. Maxwell had grown up in Newry, in south county Down, an area that had been subject to severe government repression in the year leading up to the rebellion. The populace was outraged by the conduct of a notorious Welsh cavalry regiment known as the Ancient Britons, which, under the pretext of searches for arms, committed brutal atrocities, killing unarmed civilians and burning houses.[264] Even though the insurrection did not spread to Newry,

---

[260] McHenry, *The Insurgent Chief* (1847 edn), p. 125.   [261] Ibid., p. 450.

[262] Vance, *Irish Literature since 1800*, pp. 62–3.

[263] William Hamilton Maxwell, *O'Hara; or, 1798*, 2 vols (London: J. Andrews and Dublin: Miliken, 1825); the author's name does not appear in the original edition.

[264] An appalled officer in the Dublin militia described the barbaric conduct of the Ancient Britons in the area of Newry; John Giffard to Edward Cooke, 5 June 1797, Rebellion Papers, NAI 620/31/36; partly reproduced in Lecky, *A History of Ireland in the Eighteenth Century*, vol. 4, pp. 40–2. Contemporary information also appears in Plowden, *An Historical Review of the State of Ireland*, vol. 4 (Philadelphia: William F. McLaughlin, 1806), p. 268. These atrocities were recalled in the area into the mid-twentieth century; see NFC 1470/195–202; Joseph Connellan, 'Newry District and the Men of 'Ninety-Eight: The Ancient Britons', in *Frontier Sentinel*, 16 September 1967.

its consequences were strongly felt there. Maxwell witnessed as a 6-year-old boy the hanging of two United Irishmen. The gruesome sight of the executions at 'Gallows Hill' and the impaling of the severed heads over the entrance to Newry's News Room in 1798 were long remembered by the residents of the town and were even carried abroad by emigrants.[265] A century later, the Cloakey and Cochrane '98 club was named in their honour and a plaque marking their execution was erected for the sesquicentenary in 1948.[266]

Maxwell, like McHenry, chose to put at the head of the rebellion a fictional Presbyterian landed gentleman. Whereas the actual leaders of the United Irishmen in Antrim and Down came from the middle classes and were mostly employed in the linen industry, the O'Hara family are presented as the owners of a vast estate at Castle Carra, borrowing the name of a medieval fort in north Antrim that had long been in ruins.[267] The protagonist, Henry O'Hara, joins the rebels seeking vengeance for the execution of his father, Major Frederic O'Hara, a veteran of the British army in the American War who had espoused the United Irish demand for reform. The death of O'Hara Sr. is modelled on the popular memory of the martyrdom of William Orr. He is found guilty by a 'drunken jury' and sentenced to death by a 'heartless judge'; a footnote clues in less-knowledgeable readers: 'vide William Orr's speech at his execution.'[268] In response to this act of injustice, the enraged Henry O'Hara leads the rebels at Antrim and participates in the Battle of Ballynahinch. He then goes into hiding and, with assistance from a loyalist friend, escapes abroad to take up arms in the service of the French (and ultimately dies at Waterloo).

Maxwell seems to have mined Richard Musgrave's ultra-loyalist account of the rebellion for historical information, but he may also have supplemented this source with local hearsay received from acquaintances in Ulster. The defeat at Antrim is attributed to the panicked retreat of the insurgent colonel Orr, who, according to Musgrave, 'frightened on hearing the cannon, marched his column, which was one thousand five hundred strong, back to Randalstown'. This accusation echoes recollections of participants in the battle who recalled the cowardly conduct of Samuel Orr (a brother of the famous William Orr).[269] The defeat at Ballynahinch is blamed on the 'imbecility' of the rebel commander Munro, who 'imagined he possessed military talents, and only when it was too late discovered his mistake'. Despite this criticism, Munro is given credit for his show of 'calmness and intrepidity' at the

---

[265] In a letter written in 1897, Allen MacDonnell of Laredo, Texas, retold recollections of the execution that he heard 'more than fifty odd years ago' from his grand-uncle Christy Marmion; 'Newry and Mourne Recollections of 1796–98', in *Newry Reporter*, 19 January 1898; also PRONI D3337/2 (re-publication from the 1960s).

[266] *Newry Reporter*, 25 May and 13 June 1898; *Fermanagh Herald*, 1 March 1948, p. 3. See also Joseph Connellan, 'Newry District and the Men of 'Ninety-Eight: Executions in Newry', in *Frontier Sentinel*, 4 November 1967.

[267] Wright, *Guide to the Giant's Causeway*, p. 58.

[268] Maxwell, *O'Hara*, vol. 2, pp. 147–67 (reference to Orr's speech on p. 155).

[269] Musgrave, *Memoirs of the Different Rebellions*, 3rd edn, vol. 2 (1802), p. 100; cf. Maxwell, *O'Hara*, vol. 2, p. 205. James Hope recalled that 'Samuel Orr behaved like a coward at Antrim'; Madden, *The United Irishmen*, 2nd ser., vol. 2 (1846), p. 455. A yeoman known as 'Ekey V.' (probably Ezekiel Vance) recalled that when his force engaged with the rebels under Orr, both parties retreated: 'They ran and we ran, and they all ran away'; Young, *Ulster in '98*, p. 69.

execution. Maxwell's endorsement of the epithet 'the unfortunate Munro' is faithful to recollections that were told by Henry Munro's family and their friends.[270]

Although Maxwell was a loyalist, in an effort to portray the United Irishmen in good faith, he undertook 'to view the opposite party in their progress, and though it may be a painful task, yet it shall be performed with impartiality'.[271] He drew a distinction between what he considered a less malignant uprising in Ulster and the insurrection in the south, where 'murder and rapine marked the progress of the rebel armies'. The depictions of the northern United Irishmen are generally sympathetic and condemnation is reserved for the sectarian animosities that flared between Presbyterians and Catholics in the rebel camp at Ballynahinch.[272] The novel acknowledges the suffering of 'many rebels of lesser name', as well as the harsh punishments meted out to Presbyterian ministers, and ends with a plea for Catholic emancipation, support of which was the shibboleth that distinguished liberals from conservatives in the mid-1820s.[273]

Maxwell subsequently achieved literary recognition as a writer of military and adventure novels, with the publication of *Stories of Waterloo* (1829), which was re-issued in multiple editions. It included a story of an officer in the Royal Irish Artillery who returns to Ireland from overseas service in 1798 and is appalled by the unrestrained violence of loyalists, who 'visited the inoffensive and the aggressing peasantry with indiscriminate vengeance'.[274] This was yet another expression of the author's liberalism in his youth. Maxwell's politics hardened over time and in following years he became increasingly conservative, assuming editorship of the Tory newspaper the *Mayo Constitution*. His understanding of the rebellion changed accordingly and in 1845 he published a popular loyalist history of 1798, which emphasized the misconduct of rebels.[275]

O'Hara, which has been described as 'a scarce book', failed as a literary debut.[276] It was not reviewed and for a long time Maxwell's authorship remained unknown.[277] From a query sent to the *Irish Book Lover* in 1910, it would seem that even the antiquarian Francis Joseph Bigger, considered in his day to be the most knowledgeable

---

[270] Maxwell, *O'Hara*, vol. 2, pp. 244–5; cf. Thomas Thompson, 'Memoir of the Late Mrs. Thompson, of Heworth-Moor, near York', *The Wesleyan-Methodist Magazine*, 19 (1840): p. 992; *Some Recollections of Hugh McCall*, p. 15.

[271] Maxwell, *O'Hara*, vol. 1, p. 133. Maxwell was later credited for giving 'a strangely impartial picture'; Stephen J. Brown, 'Irish Historical Fiction', in *Studies*, 4, no. 15 (1915), p. 450.

[272] Maxwell, *O'Hara*, vol. 2, pp. 173 and 217–19. Maxwell was again drawing on Musgrave; see Musgrave, *Memoirs of the Different Rebellions*, 3rd edn, vol. 2 (1802), p. 107. The book was later praised for shedding 'some light on the nature of the friction between the Catholic and Protestant commanders'; Horatio Sheafe Krans, *Irish Life in Irish Fiction* (New York: Macmillan, 1903), p. 59; Stephen J. M. Brown, *Ireland in Fiction; a Guide to Irish Novels, Tales, Romances, and Folk-Lore* (Dublin and London: Maunsel & Co., 1916), p. 175.

[273] Maxwell, *O'Hara*, vol. 2, pp. 245 and 291.

[274] 'The Story of Colonel Hilson', in anon. [W. H. Maxwell], *Stories of Waterloo, and Other Tales*, vol. 1 (London: H. Colburn and R. Bentley, 1829), pp. 283–5.

[275] For Maxwell's turn towards conservatism see Jim Shanahan, 'Fearing to Speak: Fear and the 1798 Rebellion in the Nineteenth Century', in *Fear: Essays on the Meaning and Experience of Fear*, edited by Kate Hebblethwaite and Elizabeth McCarthy (Dublin: Four Courts Press, 2007), p. 43. For Maxwell's *History of the Irish Rebellion in 1798* see Chapter 4 below, pp. 288–9.

[276] Anon. [Charles Lever], 'Our Portrait Gallery, No. XXI: William Hamilton Maxwell', *Dublin University Magazine*, 18, no. 114 (1841): p. 224; see also Colin McKelvie, 'Notes towards a Bibliography of William Hamilton Maxwell (1792–1850)', in *Irish Booklore*, 3, no. 1 (1976), pp. 32–42.

[277] See *Notes and Queries*, 4th ser., vol. 11 (1873), pp. 135 and 451.

authority on the northern United Irishmen, was not aware that Maxwell had written a novel on 1798.[278] *O'Hara* might be considered to be an early work of *cultural* memory, but its failure to attract readers meant that it did not make a noticeable impact on *social* memory in Ulster.

The rebellion in the North was also used as a setting for historical fiction by writers who were not from Ulster. The journalist and aspiring historian Eyre Evans Crowe published anonymously in 1829 the collection *Yesterday in Ireland* (1829), which included the tale 'The Northerns of 1798'.[279] The title may have been inspired by a passage in Lady Morgan's *Wild Irish Girl*, which noted that one 'will find in the Northerns of this island much to admire and more to esteem'.[280] Crowe, who was born in Southampton in 1799 and educated in Carlow and at Trinity College Dublin, did not have direct access to people with personal recollections of the rebellion in Antrim and Down. He selected the historical experience of Ulster in order to draw political analogies to the present. The book was dedicated to the Whig home secretary Lord Lansdowne (Henry Petty), who is praised as 'Ireland's warmest friend', and its contents were designed to be 'illustrative of her political state'. Crowe, who had previously written *To-Day in Ireland* (1825) to criticize agrarian violence, used 1798 to denounce sectarianism. This was part of a polemical drive he led against Orangeism, which would eventually lead to an investigation of the Orange Order by a special parliamentary committee in 1835.

In 'The Northerns of 1798', the rebellion breaks out in Ulster after the arrest of William Orde, a Presbyterian man of property. Orde's character is loosely based on William Orr except that, in a break from history, he is not executed. Presbyterians and Catholics join together to take over Antrim town and release Orde, who is then appointed a general in the United army. He is joined by his brother-in-law, Theobald Winter, a radical Dublin lawyer modelled on Theobald Wolfe Tone. The Catholic rebels are infuriated by sectarian atrocities committed by the Orange yeomanry, headed by the villainous Captain Dick Kinsella, known as 'Orange Dick'. Their victories in the field deteriorate into vengeful killing and as a result the Presbyterians, commanded by an entirely fictional Belfast republican named Theodosius Snelling, desert the United army and are pardoned under the amnesty. While Orde is captured and sent for trial in Dublin, Winter leads the Catholic rebels southwards, where they are defeated at Tara in county Meath (the site of a minor engagement that in reality occurred on 26 May 1798, two weeks before the rising in the North). Realizing that the government desired 'to make an example of a dissenting leader of insurrection' and were 'determined that one of the Northern leaders should suffer', Winter surrenders himself in exchange for the release of Orde and then commits suicide.[281] This story, which has been rightly characterized as a 'highly imaginative treatment of the rebellion', was not reviewed favourably and does not seem to have

---

[278] *Irish Book Lover*, 1, no. 11 (1910), p. 152.

[279] Anon. [E. E. Crowe], *Yesterday in Ireland* (London: Henry Colburn, 1829), vol. 2, pp. 293–327, and vol. 3.

[280] Sydney Owenson, *The Wild Irish Girl: A National Tale*, 5th London edn, vol. 3 (London: Longman Hurst Rees Orme and Brown, 1813; orig. edn 1806), pp. 74–5 (letter XXVII).

[281] Crowe, *Yesterday in Ireland*, vol. 3, pp. 287 and 296–7.

attracted notice in Ulster, where it would have seemed far-fetched to a readership that was closely familiar with the actual historical events.[282]

Several shorter stories were also set on the background of the rebellion in Ulster. The liberal journalist Robert Bell, who was born in Cork in 1800 and educated at Trinity College Dublin, wrote in 1827 'The Heart and the Altar'. It tells of a romance occurring after 'the unhappy rebellion, which at that period devastated the face of the country', between Mary Wynham, the daughter of a staunch Protestant loyalist, and Charles Keller, a Catholic who joins the rebels.[283] Extracts were published in the *Belfast News-Letter*, which praised 'this beautiful and affecting tale', while calling attention to the fact that 'the scene is laid amongst the memorable disturbances of 1798 in Ireland'.[284] 'The Curate's Daughter', published in 1835 in a collection of stories by the Scottish physician and antiquarian Alexander Maxwell Adams, tells the story of a vulnerable Protestant girl from 'one of the northern provinces of Ireland', who falls victim to a predatory English colonel after her father's house is destroyed by Catholic rebels. During her ordeal, she witnesses 'the wanton cruelties of the soldiers', who burn down houses and shoot indiscriminately at defenceless civilians.[285] In these stories, the northern rebels are depicted as exclusively Catholic.

Whereas writers from outside Ulster may have been misinformed about the religious identity of the northern United Irishmen, having perhaps derived their knowledge of 1798 from accounts of the rebellion in the South, this cannot be said to be the case for 'The Wet Wooing: A Narrative of Ninety-Eight' by Samuel Ferguson, who was born in Belfast in 1810 to an Antrim family of Scottish descent and was schooled at the Belfast Academical Institution. Published in *Blackwood's Edinburgh Magazine* in 1832, this story was one of the early writings that launched the distinguished literary career of Ferguson, whose antiquarian pursuits exemplified the fascination of Protestant unionist scholars in the Gaelic past. Taking place in the Glens of Antrim in the autumn of 1798, when 'many of the heads of the rebellion were still lurking with their families among the mountains of Ulster', the story tells of a romance between Willie Macdonnell, a Protestant loyalist, and Madeline O'More, the daughter of one of 'the chief Catholic rebels in the North'. Although the outlawed rebels are sheltered by speakers of Ulster-Scots, they are identified as Catholic. Ferguson's poetry and antiquarian writings showed interest in the history and folklore of Ulster and a keen awareness of its Scottish heritage, and yet his story of 1798, which was praised by the *Belfast News-Letter* and

---

[282] See Walker, 'A Bibliography of Presbyterianism', p. 173. A contemporary review dismissed the writing as 'deficient in freshness and vitality', refusing to engage with 'the political or religious feelings of the writer'; *La Belle Assembée, or Court Fashionable Magazine*, vol. 9, new ser. no. 52 (April 1829), p. 171. The claim of a literary scholar that the scenes of warfare 'accurately mark the course of the rebellion' does not hold water; see introduction by Robert Lee Wolff to modern edition: Eyre Evans Crowe, *Yesterday in Ireland*, vol. 1 (New York: Garland, 1979), pp. xxiii–xxiv.

[283] Robert Bell, 'The Heart and the Altar', in *Tales and Selections from the English Souvenirs for MDCCCVIII* (Philadelphia: James Kay, Jr, 1828), pp. 58–72; republished from *Forget Me Not* (1828), pp. 177–202. Not to be confused with a collection of stories by Bell with a similar title, which does not include this narrative of 1798, see Robert Bell, *Hearts and Altars* (London: Colburn and Co., 1852), 3 vols.

[284] *BNL*, 6 November 1827, p. 4.

[285] 'The Curate's Daughter; Or, the Victim of Irish Anarchy and English Despotism', in *A Physician* [Alexander Maxwell Adams], *Sketches from Life* (Glasgow: W. R. McPhum and London: Simpkin, 1835), pp. 1–63 (for atrocities committed by soldiers see pp. 41–3).

would later be republished and circulated locally, endorses cultural forgetting in its conscious neglect of Ulster-Scot Presbyterian involvement in rebellion.[286]

The emergence of historical fiction on 1798 in Ulster a quarter of a century after the rebellion is somewhat misleading. The number of commercial publications indicates that there was an eager readership. Yet, for many of the stories there is little evidence of local popularity, which may have been limited to a refined literary audience. Behind a façade of cultural memory lies a strain of social forgetting that covered up aspects of the rebellion, which were considered less savoury. Some writers overlooked the extent of Presbyterian involvement and others diverted attention away from remaining sediments of bitterness. The anonymous and pseudonymous publication suggests that authors were weary of being publicly identified with writing on this sensitive topic.

Among all the literary works on the northern rebellion, the writing of James McHenry, who would be hailed 'the bard of Larne', stands out for its popular reception.[287] His attention to 1798 earned him the respect of the Irish republican émigré community in Philadelphia and on the death of the prominent United Irish exile Thomas Addis Emmet in 1827 he was approached to draft a letter of condolence to the family. In 1828, he published anonymously 'The Outlaw of Slimish', a little-noticed short story about post-rebellion banditry in Antrim. A review, which confirmed McHenry's authorship, described it as a 'mawkish sentimental story . . . nothing more, we presume, than a record of some Irish squabble, aided by a little sprinkling of fancy'.[288] Meanwhile, the popularity of *The Insurgent Chief* continued to soar and unauthorized editions were published in Dublin, Glasgow and New York.[289] The novel had originally appeared under the pseudonym Solomon Secondsight and some editions did not name an author. Troubled by 'the innumerable inaccuracies which have crept into several of the metropolitan editions', in 1838 McHenry permitted the London publisher Joseph Smith to acknowledge his authorship. He also expressed his intention 'as soon as leisure will permit, to superintend personally a revised and improved impression of the work.'[290]

In 1843, McHenry returned to his native country as the American consul in Londonderry. Soon after, he was approached by John Henderson—a Belfast printer,

---

[286] Samuel Ferguson, 'The Wet Wooing: A Narrative of Ninety-Eight', *Blackwood's Edinburgh Magazine*, 31, no. 193 (1832): pp. 624–45; for contemporary praise see *BNL*, 6 April 1832, p. 4. Later republished in *Tales from 'Blackwood'*, vol. 7 (London and Edinburgh: William Blackwood and Sons, 1860), pp. 1–65; republished also in the local press, see *Downpatrick Recorder*, 21 January 1860, p. 4. See also Peter Denman, 'Ferguson and *Blackwood's*: The Formative Years', *Irish University Review*, 16, no. 2 (1986): p. 143.

[287] W. Clarke-Robinson, 'James MacHenry, Author of "O'Halloran," "Hearts of Steel," Etc., Etc', in *UJA*, 2nd ser., 14, nos. 2/3 (1908), pp. 127–32 (epithet appears on p. 131); also *Larne Times*, 29 March 1951, p. 4

[288] Mc, 'The Outlaw of Slimish'; *The Ariel: A Literary and Cultural Gazette*, vol. 2, no. 16 (29 November 1828), p. 126.

[289] Glasgow editions were published by R. Griffin in 1848 and 1858 and by Cameron and Ferguson *circa* 1895. The first Dublin edition was issued by Tegg and Co. in 1838. A later edition published by M. H. Gill probably in the early twentieth century was considerably abridged. A New York edition published by P. M. Haverty was advertised in 1871. For the book's publishing history see Rolf Loeber and Magda Loeber, *A Guide to Irish Fiction, 1650–1900* (Dublin, 2005), pp. 824–5; Walker, 'A Bibliography of Presbyterianism', pp. 183–4.

[290] James McHenry to Joseph Smith, 30 October 1838; reproduced in McHenry, *The Insurgent Chief* (1847 ed.).

publisher, bookseller, general newsagent and proprietor of the Northern Circulating Library—with a request to publish an authorized edition of *The Insurgent Chief*, which would include an appendix, 'elucidating the scenery and characters' in order to satisfy 'the desire to view the scenes or the stirring events narrated in your work'.[291] There was a demand for the historical references in the novel to be spelt out for the benefit of the unknowledgeable. Ballygally Castle (5 km north of Larne on the coastal road), which was identified as the residence of the novel's hero, had become to be known locally as O'Halloran's Castle.[292] O'Halloran would later be referred to as if he had been an actual historical personage.[293] The new edition was published in Belfast in 1844 and included an appendix 'containing biographical memoirs of the principle characters and descriptive of the scenery of the work', which was designed to affirm that the novel was 'rigidly historical'. The local popularity of this enhanced edition, which was sold for just one shilling and marketed as the first volume of the 'Irish Standard Library', is evident in its reissue in 1847 and 1853.

At the time of McHenry's death in 1845, it was asserted that the leading characters in *O'Halloran* 'are easily recognised by those who are conversant with the events and scenes of that memorable period'.[294] Yet, there was an implicit understanding that this local knowledge could not be voiced openly in public. In 1842, an ill-informed drama group announced in Belfast the 'intended production of a new, local, historical drama, founded upon the tale "O'Halloran, the Irish Insurgent Chief, or the Battle of Antrim", into which several characters, who were unfortunately involved in the troubles of that stormy period, were about to be introduced'. The players were clearly 'unaware of the local interest likely to be excited' and 'the piece was withdrawn at the request of the magistrates, who apprehended a disturbance.'[295] A play adapted from the novel was eventually published in Belfast in 1867, but there is no record of it ever being staged in Ulster.[296] This minor, yet telling incident demonstrates that, despite the publication of historical novels, the taboo on public displays of remembrance of 1798 had not been lifted.

[291] John Henderson to James McHenry, 22 September 1843; reproduced in McHenry, *The Insurgent Chief* (1847 ed.). For Henderson's professional preoccupations see *Henderson's New Belfast and Northern Repository for 1843–1844* (Belfast: John Henderson, 1844), p. 311; see also Roger Dixon, 'Ulster-Scots Literature', in *Oxford History of the Irish Book*, edited by James H. Murphy (Oxford: Oxford University Press, 2011), 4, pp. 73–80. Henderson was interested in publishing the novel even though, as publisher of the *Ulster Conservative* newspaper (which ran from 4 January 1845 to 27 June 1846), he also catered for readerships that were critical of the United Irishmen.
[292] Porter Classon, 'Ballygally Castle' (edited by Francis Joseph Bigger) in *UJA*, 2nd ser., 7, no. 2 (1901), p. 74 (originally published in the *Larne Reporter* in 1884). See also Felix McKillop, *History of Larne and East Antrim* (Belfast: Ulster Journals, 2005), pp. 67–8.
[293] At a debate of the Carrickmacross Catholic Literary and Debating Society in 1907 on 'was the Insurrection of 1798 justified?', one of the speakers against the motion matter-of-factly declared that 'Even at the battle of Ballynahinch, O'Halloran, the Irish Chieftain, shouted "hurrah for Presbyterian Government."'; *Dundalk Democrat*, 23 December 1907, p. 8.
[294] *Freeman's Journal*, 26 July 1845, p. 2.
[295] *Freeman's Journal*, 20 May 1842, p. 4; originally reported in *Dublin Evening Packet and Correspondent*, 19 May 1842, p. 3.
[296] James Allen, *O'Halloran; or, The Insurgent Chief, a Drama in Three Acts* (Belfast: D. Allen, 1867).

HESITATIONS IN COMING OUT

In the late 1820s, the London publisher Henry Colburn, who was known for having 'a very keen perception as to what the public required', capitalized on a ready market for literature on the 1798 rebellion.[297] In addition to Eyre Evans Crowe's *Yesterday in Ireland*, Colburn published a number of novels on 1798 in the South, most notably Michael Banim's *The Croppy: A Tale of the Irish Rebellion of 1798* (1828), as well as personal accounts of prominent United Irishmen, starting with the *Memoirs of Theobald Wolfe Tone* (1827). In 1828, Colburn published a *Personal Narrative of the 'Irish Rebellion' of 1798* by the northern United Irishman Charles Hamilton Teeling. The book was soon sold out and it was rumoured that plans to issue a second edition had been quashed by the government, which allegedly paid a subvention to the publisher in order to prevent publication. Local enthusiasm was evident in Ulster and a sequel appeared in Belfast four years later.[298] The *Northern Whig*, a newspaper established in 1824 and which, according to a later editor, 'expressed to a great degree the convictions held at the time and long afterwards by the sons and grandsons of many who had taken part in the rebellion of '98, and who were called United Irishmen', acknowledged that Teeling's work 'abounds with passages of deep interest'.[299]

The *Belfast News-Letter* described Teeling's writings as 'romance, not veritable history'. His entry in the *Dictionary of Irish Biography* notes that 'though often cited, they are circumspect, imprecise and disappointing on important questions.' In contrast, the literary critic Julia Wright has argued that they should not be read as a work of history but rather as 'a polemic which draws heavily on sensibility and nationalism not to relay historical facts but to change hearts and minds'.[300] Teeling, however, was very much concerned with asserting his 'veracity as an historian'.[301] Kevin Whelan perceptively noticed 'a palpable nervousness' in the *Personal Narrative*, which is typical also of other early memoirs of 1798. In writing about the rebellion, Teeling had to confront a record of intimidation and social forgetting in which he himself was implicated.[302]

The Teelings were a well-connected liberal middle-class Catholic family and as such were targeted by the government. Already at a young age, Charles Hamilton Teeling

---

[297] For Henry Colburn's publishing enterprise see Henry Curwen, *A History of Booksellers, the Old and the New* (London: Chatto & Windus, 1873), pp. 279–95 (quotation from p. 292).

[298] For the claim that the government had tried to discourage publication of the sequel see Alibi Norman, 'The Teelings', *The Gentleman's Magazine*, 299, Part II (October 1905): p. 349n. A second 'cheap edition' (advertised as 'within reach of all') was issued in Glasgow by Cameron and Ferguson in 1876 under a slightly revised title, which presented the 'personal narrative' as a work of history; *BNL*, 17 December 1876, p. 1; for a facsimile reproduction see Charles Hamilton Teeling, *History of the Irish Rebellion of 1798 and Sequel to the History of the Irish Rebellion of 1798* (Shannon: Irish University Press, 1972).

[299] *Northern Whig*, 20 September 1832, p. 4. For the association of the newspaper with descendants of United Irishmen see MacKnight, *Ulster as It Is*, vol. 1, p. 17.

[300] *BNL*, 16 January 1844, p. 2; C. J. Woods, 'Teeling, Charles Hamilton', in *Dictionary of Irish Biography* (Cambridge University Press and Royal Irish Academy, 2009), online: <http://dib.cambridge.org/viewReadPage.do?articleId=a8486>. For Wright, Teeling's accounts of 1798 articulated 'sentimental nationalism'; see Julia M. Wright, *Ireland, India, and Nationalism in Nineteenth-Century Literature* (Cambridge and New York: Cambridge University Press, 2007), pp. 29–52 (esp. 43–9).

[301] Letter to the editor by C. H. Teeling; *BNL*, 14 December 1832, p. 1.

[302] Kevin Whelan, 'Introduction to Section VI', in *1798: A Bicentenary Perspective*, edited by Thomas Bartlett et al. (Dublin: Four Courts Press, 2003), p. 475.

made acquaintance with leading figures in the United Irish northern leadership and was instrumental in forging ties between Presbyterian radicals and Catholic Defenders. He was arrested in person by Castlereagh on 16 September 1796—a day before the arrest of William Orr—and, like Orr, was accused of high treason and held in prison without trial for a year. Released on bail, with broken health and loss of property, he remained free during 1798. His elder brother, Bartholomew, also joined the United Irishmen, took part in the French invasion of the western province of Connacht in August 1798 and was captured after the Battle of Ballinamuck (8 September 1798). The family's petition for a reprieve was denied and Bartholomew was executed for treason on 24 September 1798. The father, Luke Teeling, a wealthy linen merchant, had represented Ulster in the Catholic convention of 1792. Even though he did not join the United Irishmen, Luke was arrested in the summer of 1798 and held in prison for four years. The authorities were aggravated by his refusal to accept an offer for banishment of the entire family, which was a preferred means for getting rid of radicals.[303]

Following the execution of his brother and arrest of his father, and realizing that it was left to him 'to give bread to many indignant fellow creatures, and support to a numerous family of younger brothers and sisters', Charles Hamilton Teeling wrote Lord Lieutenant Cornwallis in November 1798 and categorically stated that he 'neither acted nor aided in the late rebellion'.[304] Such feigned forgetfulness was common in petitions for clemency from those who had been involved with the United Irishmen.[305] The Teeling family were subject to surveillance and harassment in following years. Luke Teeling, who was released from prison in 1802, set up a linen shop in Belfast. It was later recalled that the house was raided by loyalists, spurred on by a Mrs Murdoch of Mill Street, who was described as 'a sort of leader among the low ascendancy party', and its contents were looted: 'his window curtains were seen in Murdoch's and his cuckoo clock was heard in the house. When Mrs. Murdoch saw Mr. Teeling passing and the clock happened to sound she insultingly said, "thank you croppy."'[306] With the family subjected to such intimidation, Charles prudently distanced himself from radical causes. In 1803, when Thomas Russell tried to rekindle rebellion in the north, the informer Samuel Turner (writing under the code name 'Belfast') reported that Teeling abstained from getting involved.[307] It was only after three decades had passed since the rebellion that he could safely return to reclaim the memory of his association with the United Irishmen.

Teeling's *Personal Narrative* and its *Sequel* attributed central significance to the insurrection in Ulster. He cast responsibility on the government for a 'reign of terror' and detailed excesses committed by troops against civilians. The memoir presented

---

[303] Madden, *The United Irishmen*, 3rd ser., vol. 1 (1846), pp. 189–96 and 231.

[304] C. H. Teeling to Marquis Cornwallis, 4 November 1798; Teeling Family Correspondence, NLI 17863/10.

[305] See for example the petition submitted by William Russel[l] of Ballymagee to the Lord Lieutenant, discussed in Chapter 2 above, pp. 108–9.

[306] B. [Francis Joseph Bigger], 'Belfast in Ninety-Eight', in *SVV*, 1, no. 6 (5 June 1896), pp. 105–6.

[307] 'Belfast' [Samuel Turner] to under-secretary Alexander Marsden of Dublin Castle, 4 June 1803; reproduced in Michael MacDonagh, *The Viceroy's Post-Bag: Correspondence, Hitherto Unpublished, of the Earl of Hardwicke, First Lord Lieutenant of Ireland, after the Union* (London: J. Murray, 1904), pp. 275–6.

a counter-memory that challenged the early historiography of the rebellion, which had been dominated by the intentional forgetting propagated by Richard Musgrave, whose ultra-loyalist bias underplayed these very features of 1798 and marginalized the rebellion in Ulster. A review in the nationalist *Irish Monthly Magazine* praised Teeling's commitment 'to rescue from oblivion' a 'testimony of Irish greatness' and 'to place before the public candid impartial statements'. It was felt that the 'Rebellion'—which, following Teeling's cue, was placed in inverted commas to signify rejection of its illegitimacy—'has not yet had its true history written' and that 'it is only recently that men competent to give authentic details of its most important circumstances have ventured to lay them fearlessly before the public.'[308]

The stimulation that Teeling's narrative offered readers in Ulster, who had grown up on muted memories of 1798, is evident in the memoirs of Charles Gavan Duffy. Born in 1818 to a Catholic family in the south Ulster county of Monaghan, Duffy recognized that 'the fraternal doctrines of '98 had few friends in Ulster in the first quarter of the present century' and yet, he observed that 'survivors of that era were still plentiful in the north'. He was raised on 'legends and traditions' of the rebellion told by an old servant, who ignited his boyhood imagination with the promise of revealing 'where the Croppies hid their arms when the troubles were over'. Duffy's next door neighbour, a Presbyterian 'old democrat' named John Sloan, had been a United Irishman and shared his recollections of the time. A close friend, Mat Trumble, was the son of a lieutenant in the British army but preferred to identify with the ideals of his grandfather, who had been 'a notable United Irishman'. Having grown up immersed in stories of the United Irishmen, Duffy was deeply moved when he was introduced to Teeling, whom he considered 'an historic man, one of the surviving leaders in 1798'. He was given a copy of the *Personal Narrative* from the author and recalled that 'it was the first book dealing frankly with the aims and hopes of Irish Nationalists which I had read, and it thrilled me with a new emotion.'[309]

Following the success of his *Personal Narrative*, Teeling established two radical newspapers—the *Ulster Magazine* (1830–1) and the *Northern Herald* (1833–6)—for which he recruited the help of Duffy (who would move on in 1839 to become the editor of the Belfast *Vindicator*) and other talented young Catholics, including his future son-in-law Thomas O'Hagan (who thirty-five years later would become the Lord Chancellor of Ireland). In the first issue of the *Ulster Magazine*, James Morgan of Newry (writing under his initials) contributed the poem 'The Rebel's Grave', which 'alludes to the unfortunate transactions of Ninety-Eight'. It had been written ten years earlier, but till then had not found a place in a Belfast newspaper. Although Morgan claimed that the poem was based on recollections that he had heard from an 'aged narrator' and had 'the merit of being "owre true a tale"', its depiction of a woman called Mary who was driven insane by the sight of the beheading of a beloved rebel shows the continuing influence of Rushton's 'Mary Le More'.[310]

The *Ulster Magazine* also ventured into publishing an episode of folk memory of the rebellion, which was retold as an entertaining tale of social banditry. The story 'Incident

[308] *Irish Monthly Magazine of Politics and Literature*, 1, no. 7 (November, 1832), pp. 479–83.
[309] Duffy, *My Life in Two Hemispheres*, vol. 1, pp. 7, 14–16, 19–21.
[310] J. M., 'The Rebel's Grave', *Ulster Magazine*, 1, no. 1 (January 1830): pp. 9–12; later republished in Madden, *Literary Remains of the United Irishmen*, pp. 180–3.

on Dromadaragh Mountain' recounted the adventures of a 'remarkably strong and muscular' rebel outlaw, who single-handedly disarmed a party of Tay Fencibles.[311] Although written in a seemingly fictional literary style, it was based on historical recollections. The account referred to George Dickson [also spelt Dixon] of Crumlin, county Antrim, who had commanded rebels at an engagement in Randalstown and in the aftermath of the rebellion gained notoriety as an outlaw known as 'General Holt' [also appears as Halt]. He was apprehended in May 1799 and court-martialled at Belfast, where he was found guilty of 'treason and rebellion, robbing his majesty's soldiers of their arms when on duty, aiding and administering unlawful oaths, flogging and threatening to destroy the property of his Majesty's loyal subjects, and plundering them of their arms', for which he was executed.[312] Dickson's memory was celebrated in a song, which explained that his nickname derived from soldiers exclaiming 'here is the man who made us all halt' (though the authorities believed that it was a northern tribute to the Wicklow rebel outlaw Joseph Holt).[313] Under the guise of historical fiction, the *Ulster Magazine* found a way of bringing oral recollections to a wider readership. Narratives that claimed to be based on memories of Ninety-Eight also appeared in Teeling's other newspaper, the *Northern Herald*, which was credited for having 'the old fraternal spirit of the United Irishmen', and were occasionally re-issued in local Papers.[314]

In Teeling's newspapers, notices that announced the death of former United Irishmen showed less reserve in referring to the past. For example, Archibald Hamilton Rowan, who had fled abroad to avoid capture in advance of the rebellion, was described as a 'venerable patriot, patriarch of liberty'.[315] Keen on publicly exculpating the memory of executed rebels, Teeling entrusted the writer James Morgan with the papers of Thomas Russell and commissioned him to write a biography, which was to be published in the *Ulster Magazine*.[316] Although Morgan did not concur with Teeling's apologia for the rebellion, admitting that 'my sentiments upon this subject are not altogether in unison with your own', he was nonetheless bent on speaking out against 'the opinions of those who speak with unnecessary harshness of the men who loved their country "not wisely, but too well"'.[317] However, this attempt to counter the defamation of the United Irishmen in a popular provincial magazine was marked by hesitance. Teeling's journalist enterprise proved to be short-lived and the intended

---

[311] Q., 'Incident on Dromadaragh Mountain: Disarming of an Escort Party', *Ulster Magazine*, 1, no. 10 (October 1830): pp. 635–7.

[312] *BNL*, 17 May 1799, p. 3. See also Patterson, *In the Wake of the Great Rebellion*, p. 33.

[313] Recounted in 1863 to Rev. Classon Porter by 91-year-old James Burns, who was 'almost an eye-witness of the entire occurrence'; Young, *Ulster in '98*, pp. 47–8. At the time of the execution, Castlereagh referred to Dickson as 'the Northern Holt'; Castlereagh to Wickham, 22 May 1799, TNA HO 100/86/415–417.

[314] A. Albert Campbell, *Belfast Newspapers, Past and Present* (Belfast: W. & G. Baird, 1921), p. 9. For an example of re-circulation of traditions published in the *Northern Herald* see 'Ninety-Eight', in *Newry Examiner and Louth Advertiser*, 11 January 1834, p. 4.

[315] *Northern Herald*, 8 November 1834, p. 2.

[316] J. M., 'Sketch of the Life of Thomas Russell, Who Was Executed for High Treason at Down-patrick, 21st October, 1803', *Ulster Magazine*, 1, no. 1 (1830): pp. 39–60. In an effort to trace the whereabouts of Russell's papers, Mary Ann McCracken informed Madden that they had been 'contained in a red leather portfolio', which 'Mr. Teeling allowed Morgan to carry with him to Newry'; M. A. McCracken, Belfast, 2 July 1844; Madden Papers, TCD 873/155.

[317] *Ulster Magazine*, 1, no. 1 (January 1830): p. 9.

serialization of the biography of Thomas Russell, which was halted after the initial instalment in 1830, had, as noted by a reviewer, 'unfortunately, been forgotten'.[318]

The 1831 elections in county Down, in which the liberal candidate William Sharman Crawford unsuccessfully contested the Tory MPs Lord Castlereagh and Lord Arthur Hill, showed that 1798 was still a very sensitive political issue. Campaign squibs mocked reformists by linking them to the rebellion. A 'Revolutionary Alphabet' listed prominent Belfast radicals and concluded: 'To this 98 set, we could many add.' In a satirical piece, radicals were presented as horses on auction and labelled with such mock descriptions as 'he was got by Radical, on Reform, out of Democrat . . . grand damn Revolution, by Croppy. For performance, see Racing Calendar of 1798 and 1803.' These damning insinuations caused particular offense.[319]

John Barnett, a tanner and merchant from Belfast who was on Sharman Crawford's campaign committee, sued Henry Lanktree, the publisher of the squibs, for libel. He had been described as: 'Tanner—An old Hack . . . This Horse particularly distinguished himself in 1798; ran for the Saintfield Stakes under the name of INFORMER, and distanced all competitors.' At the trial in the county Antrim assizes, witnesses for the prosecution testified that this text was understood to mean that Barnett had participated in the rebellion and had then become a government informer. Unknown to the court, archival records of depositions taken in 1799 by the Newtownards magistrate John Cleland reveal that Barnett was probably associated with the United Irishmen. But in 1831, any involvement with the rebellion was vehemently denied. The allegations were considered extremely harmful. Barnett explained to the judge that 'he was advanced in life, and being both a father and grandfather, he did not like, after his removal from the present scene, that any malicious persons would have it in their power to say to his family your ancestor was charged with such infamous crimes.' Fear that the stigma of implication in the rebellion would carry on to future generations was an incentive to repress memory.[320]

An exchange of accusations between rival newspapers in Londonderry revealed how recollections of former membership in the United Irishmen could be used for vilification. When conservatives were criticized in 1838 for not attending a commemorative dinner to mark the anniversary of the relief of the Siege of Derry, the conservative *Londonderry Sentinel* lashed back with coded insinuations: 'Shades of 1798 where are you? Where is now the Chancellor of Exchequer of the United Irishmen's Exchequer, who were [sic] plotting the surrender of the City to the rebels'. This was taken as a jibe directed against the more liberal *Londonderry Standard*, which replied accordingly:

> Well, then it is certain that a relative of one of the proprietors of the *Derry Standard* was a United Irishman in 1798; and although among the United Irishmen were to be found many men of honourable feeling, and high and even chivalrous notions of patriotism—yet,

[318] *Dublin Literary Gazette*, 15 (April 1830): p. 282.

[319] *The Down Squib-Book, Containing an Impartial Account of the Contested Election for the County of Down, in May 1831, between Lord Arthur Hill, W. S. Crawford, Esq., and Lord Viscount Castlereagh. Also, the Addresses and Squibs which were Issued During this Interesting Struggle* (Belfast: Henry Lanktree, 1831), pp. 61 and 63.

[320] 'Libel Case: John Barnett, *Versus* Henry Lanktree', in *BNL*, 2 August 1831, p. 1 and 4 August 1831, p. 4. John Barnett was named in depositions taken from Robert Moorhead of Saintfield (6 July 1799) and James Dougherty of Ballyblack (10 September 1799); Cleland Papers, PRONI D714/3/42 and 43 (respectively).

it must be, that the having belonged to such a body is a blot upon the memory of every one of them, and it must be that the sin of the father shall be visited upon the children until the third and fourth generation.

Association with the memory of 1798 continued to cause discomfiture and could be used as a defamatory political weapon.[321]

In the 1830s, recollections of 1798 were not openly discussed in the Ulster countryside. If to judge by the observations of the field workers of the Ordnance Survey, who were instructed to supplement cartographic data with detailed memoirs on local customs and history, it might seem as if there was scant popular interest in recollecting local involvement with the United Irishmen. It has been claimed that this detailed ethnographic documentation project 'turned the entire countryside of Ireland into one vast *lieu de mémoire*.'[322] When it came to 1798, it would seem that many places remained a *lieu d'oubli*. However, it should also be acknowledged that, although the parishes of Ulster were surveyed systematically, the ability to access memories screened by social forgetting was a matter of hit and miss.

The Ordnance Survey map for the area of Ballynahinch marked Edenavaddy and Windmill hills as 1798 battle sites, yet, remarkably, the historical section of the memoir for the district does not mention at all the major battle of the northern rebellion. At the same time, an account was written of the much smaller engagement in nearby Saintfield.[323] In many areas of Down that had been heavily involved in the rebellion, such as the north part of the county and the Ards peninsula, memoirists avoided mentioning 1798 altogether.[324] The entry on 'Remarkable Events' for the town of Lisburn lists a victory over rebels in 1641 but overlooks the executions in 1798 of United Irishmen, including the hanging of the rebel general Henry Munro. A section on 'Longevity' refers to a 107-year-old widow named Margaret McCurry and only incidentally notes that she had previously lived in Kilwarlin, county Down, 'up to the last rebellion of Ireland, at which event her husband was killed and his place and chattels consumed by fire'.[325]

The memoir for Antrim town describes in detail the major battle that was fought there in 1798. The memoir for the Grange of Doagh notes that 'In 1798 a portion of the village was burned by the king's troops, in consequence of the part which its inhabitants took in the insurrection of that year.' The memoir for the neighbouring parish of Drummaul refers to an encounter between rebels and the yeomanry at Randalstown, in consequence of which 'more than one-half of the town was burned by the king's troops' and the Market House was used as a stable by the cavalry.[326]

[321] *Londonderry Sentinel*, 25 August 1838, p. 2; *Londonderry Standard*, 29 August 1838, p. 2.
[322] Leerssen, *Remembrance and Imagination*, p. 102.
[323] 'Miscellaneous Papers, County Down', in Day and McWilliams, *Ordnance Survey Memoirs*, vol. 17: *Parishes of County Down IV, 1833–7, East Down and Lecale* (1992), pp. 100 and 120.
[324] Day and McWilliams, *Ordnance Survey Memoirs*, vol. 7: *Parishes of County Down II, 1832–4 and 1837, North Down and the Ards* (1991). There is also an absence of references to 1798 in the memoirs for south Down, as well as in the parishes of mid-Down, which include the areas of Blaris, Hillsborough, and Dormara that had seen extensive repression; ibid., vol. 3: *Parishes of County Down I, 1834–6, South Down* (1990) and vol. 12: *Parishes of County Down III, 1833–8, Mid Down* (1992).
[325] Day and McWilliams, *Ordnance Survey Memoirs*, vol. 8: *Parishes of County Antrim II, 1832–8, Lisburn and South Antrim* (1991), pp. 15 and 47.
[326] Memoir of the Parish of Antrim by James Boyle (May 1848) in Day and McWilliams, *Ordnance Survey Memoirs*, vol. 29: *Parishes of County Antrim XI, 1832–3 and 1835–9, Antrim town and Ballyclare* (1995), pp. 5–6 (Antrim) and 68–9 (Doagh). A Draft Memoir by J. Fleming Tait (April 1835)

However, memoirs of other parishes in Antrim are conspicuously silent on the turmoil that had devastated those localities during the rebellion.[327] The same is mostly true for the adjacent areas in county Londonderry in which the United Irishmen had been very active, though the memoir for Maghera inadvertently used 1798 as a memorable marker, noting that 'since the last rebellion no remarkable circumstances worthy of record have taken place in this district.'[328] The tribute to James Orr—the 'Bard of Ballycarry'—in the memoir for the parish of Templecorran ignores the recollections of 1798 that featured prominently in his poetry.[329]

James Boyle, who wrote memoirs for most of county Antrim, repeatedly asserted that the Ulster-Scot Presbyterian communities had distanced themselves from their United Irish past. He determined that the inhabitants of the parish of Kilraghts 'were all, except about 6, deeply engaged in the rebellion' and added that 'since this time they have never interfered with any political occurrence.'[330] In the parish of Dunaghy, where the Presbyterians 'were, with very few exceptions, deeply implicated in the rebellion of 1798' and three people had been hung on the same day, Boyle inferred that 'these examples, with the harassing effects of billeting, free quarters, etc., gave them a surfeit of rebellion and produced a very desirable change in their conduct and politics.' The 'descendants of the Scottish Presbyterians' in the neighbouring parish of the Grange of Dundermot 'were almost to a man implicated in the rebellion of 1798, but the examples made of them by hanging gave them a distaste for such proceedings and has since had a salutary effect on them, besides effecting a total change in their political sentiments.'[331] Similarly, Boyle noted that the Presbyterians of the parish of Ballymartin 'during the rebellion of 1798 took conspicuous part in the troubles of that period, but now they never think of interfering in such matters.'[332]

mentions 'the murder of the Earl of O'Neill in 1798, in the rebellion of this year'; ibid., p. 48. References to the events of 1798 in Randalstown appear in the Memoir of the Parish of Drummaul by James Boyle (June 1838) in Day and McWilliams, *Ordnance Survey Memoirs*, vol. 19, pp. 41 and 43.

[327] Day and McWilliams, *Ordnance Survey Memoirs*, vol. 2: *Parishes of County Antrim I, 1838–9, Ballymartin, Ballyrobert, Ballywalter, Carnmoney, Mallusk* (1990); vol. 24: *Parishes of County Antrim IX, 1830–2, 1835, 1838–9, North Antrim coast and Rathlin* (1994).

[328] Memoir of the Parish of Maghera by J. Stokes with sections by C. W. Ligar (January 1837) in Day and McWilliams, *Ordnance Survey Memoirs*, vol. 18: *Parishes of County Londonderry V, 1830, 1833 and 1836–7, Maghera and Tamlaght O'Crilly* (1993), p. 22. Similarly, it was noted that in 'the year after the rebellion of '98' land had been obtained from a United Irishman who had fled the country; Fair Sheets by John Bleakly, with sections by Thomas Fagan (July 1836–February 1837) in ibid., p. 54. The overall silence on 1798 in the surrounding areas is also apparent in Day and McWilliams, *Ordnance Survey Memoirs*, vol. 6: *Parishes of County Londonderry I, 1830, 1834, 1836, Arboe, Artrea, Ballinderry, Ballyscullion, Magherafelt, Termoneeny* (1990).

[329] Day and McWilliams, *Ordnance Survey Memoirs*, vol. 26: *Parishes of County Antrim X, 1830–1, 1833–5, 1839–40, East Antrim, Glynn, Inver, Kilroot and Templecorran* (1994).

[330] Memoir of the Parish of Kilraghts by James Boyle (August 1835) in Day and McWilliams, *Ordnance Survey Memoirs*, vol. 16: *Parishes of County Antrim V, 1830–5 and 1837–8, Giant's Causeway and Ballymoney* (1992), p. 128.

[331] Memoirs of the Parishes of Dunaghy and Grange of Dundermot by James Boyle (September 1835) in Day and McWilliams, *Ordnance Survey Memoirs*, vol. 13: *Parishes of County Antrim IV, 1830–8, Glens of Antrim* (1992), pp. 14 and 32 (respectively).

[332] Memoir of Ballymartin by James Boyle (9 December 1838) in Day and McWilliams, *Ordnance Survey Memoirs*, vol. 1, p. 11.

Boyle's observation that the Presbyterians of Islandmagee had 'in 1798 distinguished themselves by the active part they took in the rebellion, but since they have not interfered in politics' was confirmed by his assistant John Bleakly. Noting that 'there are at present residing in the parish many persons who were United Irishmen during the rebellion of '98', Bleakly found that 'the inhabitants of Island Magee have little or no spirit for politics and are less enthusiastic than any other parish in the district.'[333] Templepatrick, where William Orr was buried, had reputedly been 'the hotbed of mischief for the neighbourhood' and its inhabitants were 'among the most disaffected in the kingdom', but 'since the lesson they got in 1798 they have meddled but little with party politics.'[334]

Along these lines, the entry on 'Habits of the People' for the village of Kells notes that:

> They were almost to a man engaged in the rebellion of 1798. This, however, may not be wondered at, as most of the rich and respectable persons in the neighbourhood and some of the ministers were deeply concerned in it. However, since that time, their politics have changed and they now seem indifferent and careless on the subject.

By hammering home this observation, Boyle tried to show that political dissent had been completely eradicated, a conclusion which would have suited his government employers. Yet, he tellingly prefaced his comments with the admission that the Presbyterian population, 'like their Scottish forefathers, are canny and cautious in their dealings and in expressing their opinion'. The unwillingness of local inhabitants in tight-knit communities to disclose their private thoughts to strangers would suggests that their professed disinterest in politics need not necessarily be taken at face value.[335]

There were indications that suggested that the Presbyterian radicalism of 1798 had not passed away. When a military surveyor noted that 'during the rebellion of '98 the inhabitants of Glynn village are said to have been very zealous in the cause of United Irishmen', Boyle was delighted to receive what seemed to be additional confirmation of the general pattern that he was promoting and he scribbled his approval in the margin. However, the report went on to reveal that an absence of Orange lodges in the parish signified that the population 'are still opposed to conservative principles'.[336] In the parish of Kilbride, county Antrim, Boyle was shocked to discover that the obedience of the populace was only skin-deep and could quickly revert to insubordination. The

---

[333] Memoir of Parish of Island Magee by James Boyle (January 1835–April 1840) and Fair Sheets by John Bleakly (September–December 1839) in Day and McWilliams, *Ordnance Survey Memoirs*, vol. 10: *Parishes of County Antrim III, 1833, 1835 and 1839–40, Larne and Island Magee* (1991), pp. 41 and 93 (respectively). Already in 1817, it was noted of the people of the parish that 'they meddle little with parties or politicks, though in 1798; they had a full portion of the political leaven of that time'; S. M. S. [Samuel McSkimin], 'A Statistical Account of Island Magee', *The Newry Magazine; or, Literary & Political Register*, 3, no. 17 (November–December 1817): pp. 433–8.

[334] Memoir of the Parish of Templepatrick by James Boyle (November 1838) in Day and McWilliams, *Ordnance Survey Memoirs*, vol. 35: *Parishes of County Antrim XIII, 1833, 1855 and 1838* (1996), p. 123.

[335] Memoir of the Parish of Connor by James Boyle (November 1835) in Day and McWilliams, *Ordnance Survey Memoirs*, vol. 19, pp. 24–5.

[336] Parish of Glynn Statistical Account by Lieutenant R. Stotherd (with marginal comments by James Boyle) in Day and McWilliams, *Ordnance Survey Memoirs*, vol. 26, p. 42. An elderly veteran of 1798 later noted that 'all the young fellows in the Glynn village were Defenders' and that a number of them were still alive in 1863; Young, *Ulster in '98*, p. 44.

refusal of Presbyterians to pay increased tithes to a non-resident Anglican clergyman, who lived in county Down, resulted in a lawsuit that provoked widespread resentment: 'The very worst feelings, which since 1798 (when to a man the people of this parish were actively engaged as rebels) had slumbered and were beginning to be forgotten by the passing, and had as yet been unknown to the rising generation, were aroused.' Faced with an outbreak of unrest, Boyle contradicted his usual statements and concluded that 'the general character of the people is that of a bigoted race of republicans.'[337]

Upon further inspection, it appears that Presbyterian disengagement did not signify total oblivion. *A Topographical Dictionary of Ireland*, compiled by the London publisher Samuel Lewis around the same time as the Ordnance Survey, includes numerous references to local events in Ulster during 'the disturbances of 1798'. A list of corrections that appeared in the *Northern Whig* reveals detailed knowledge of these incidents, backed up with a concern that they should be properly represented.[338] Recollections of specific events in 1798, while not discussed in depth, frequently crop up in the ordnance survey memoirs in listings of memorable incidents, such as the destruction of bridges at Kells and Toome by rebels, who tried 'to retard the pursuit of the king's troops',[339] or the humiliating admission that Ballymena church had been used as a barrack and was 'very much injured by all the woodwork being used for fuel'.[340] Unnerving memories of outrages remained unforgiven, as in the torching of Catholic chapels by loyalists in Aghagallon, Glenavy, and at Aghalee, where forty years later many people were still aggrieved over '4 persons burned to death and 1 shot in the house'.[341]

There were those who felt that outsiders could not be trusted with private memories. Despite the intentions of Lieutenant-Colonel Thomas Colby, the director of the Ordnance Survey, to play down the military character of the project with the hiring of civilian staff, the inquiries of surveyors accompanied by armed guards were often viewed as a government reconnaissance scheme. Deeply ingrained suspicions were

---

[337] Memoir of the Parish of Kilbride by James Boyle (June 1836 to February 1839) in Day and McWilliams, *Ordnance Survey Memoirs of Ireland*, vol. 29, pp. 141 and 144.

[338] Samuel Lewis, *A Topographical Dictionary of Ireland: Comprising the Several Counties, Cities, Boroughs, Corporate, Market, and Post Towns, Parishes, and Villages, with Historical and Statistical Descriptions*, 2nd edn (London: S. Lewis, 1847; orig. edn 1837), vol. 1: 38 (Antrim), 108 (Ballynahinch), 200 (Belfast), 270 (Carrickfergus); vol. 2: 154 (Kilmood, county Down), 207 (Larne), 292 (Maghera), 294 (Magheradroll, county Down), 306 (Markethill, county Armagh), 400 (Newtown-Cromellin, county Antrim), 520 (Saintfield), 592 (Toome). For errors (which remained uncorrected in the 2nd edn) see *Northern Whig*, 9 June 1838, p. 4.

[339] Day and McWilliams, *Ordnance Survey Memoirs*, vol. 19, pp. 25 (Kells) and 99 (Toome).

[340] Memoir of the Parish of Kirkinriola by James Boyle (October 1835) in Day and McWilliams, *Ordnance Survey Memoirs*, vol. 23: *Parishes of County Antrim VIII, 1831–5 and 1837–8, Ballymena and West Antrim* (1993), p. 116.

[341] Fair Sheets on the Parish of Aghagallon (January–February 1838) and on the Parish of Aghalee (December 1837–January 1838) by Thomas Fagan, and Memoir of the Parish of Glenavy by James Boyle (January 1836) in Day and McWilliams, *Ordnance Survey Memoirs*, vol. 21: *Parishes of County Antrim VII, 1832–8, South Antrim* (1993), pp. 9, 37, and 85 (respectively). Rev. Philip Johnson, the Anglican vicar of Derriaghy, denied the allegations of the Catholic historian Francis Plowden that he had incited Orangemen to commit these crimes and claimed that he had in fact raised funds for rebuilding the burned chapels and offered a reward for the discovery of those responsible; *A Plain Statement of Facts, in Answer to Certain Charges Adduced by Francis Plowden, Esq. in His History of Ireland against the Rev. Philip Johnson, Vicar of the Parish of Derriaghy, and the Orangemen of That Parish* (Dublin: Thomas Courtney, 1814), pp. 40–2.

apparent in reluctance to share local knowledge. The outright refusal in the parish of Banagher, county Londonderry, to reveal the whereabouts of hiding places used in 1798 seems to reflect a general pattern that contrasted with more open communications with travel writers, who were sometimes privy to these secret locations.[342] Several instances of non-cooperation were recorded in county Down. Most strikingly, after visiting the village of Bryansford in the parish of Kilbroney (between Castlewellan and Newcastle, county Down), a memoirist complained that 'every person seems to have the most decided objection of giving information relative to any part or portion of the place.'[343]

Exceptional field workers, such as the Gaelic scholar John O'Donovan, succeeded in infiltrating local reticence. In the area of Garvagh, county Londonderry, O'Donovan visited a peasant dwelling, which he courteously described as the 'lowly residence of the oldest branch of the celebrated sept of the O'Mullans', earning the confidence of the former United Irishman Brian O'Mullan, whom he referred to as a 'warlike patriot, Ireland's friend for ever'.[344] Few surveyors could establish such a rapport with the people they interviewed. When speaking with the caretaker of an estate in the parish of Ahoghill, John Bleakly learned that the encampment site of the Tay Fencibles by the townland of Ballea, near Ballymena, was known locally as the Camp Hill.[345] This was just one of several place names that recalled military presence in 1798, most of which were not recorded by the Ordnance Survey. The collective burial site of the York Fencibles who died at the Battle of Saintfield was since called York Island.[346] A lane by a house at Mile Cross, near Newtownards, which had been occupied by yeomen in 1798, was known as the Soldiers' Walk.[347] Many more place names recalled episodes relating to the rebels. For all their efforts, the field workers were only partially able to penetrate the unofficial toponymy that mapped the vernacular landscape of 1798 in Ulster.[348]

---

[342] Fair Sheets on Parish of Banagher by J. Bleakly, with Sections by J. Stokes (October–December 1834) in Day and McWilliams, *Ordnance Survey Memoirs*, vol. 30: *Parishes of County Londonderry X, 1833–35 and 1838, Mid-Londonderry* (1995), p. 36; see also Gillian Smith, '"An Eye on the Survey": Perceptions of the Ordnance Survey in Ireland 1824–1842', *History Ireland*, 9, no. 2 (2001): p. 41. An exception is the identification of a beech tree on the grounds of Moneyglass House, near Toome, country Antrim, which was 'said to have been a hiding place for many persons during the rebellion of '98'; Memoir of Parish of Duneane by James Boyle (May 1836) in Day and McWilliams, *Ordnance Survey Memoirs*, vol. 19, p. 118.

[343] Memoir of the Parish of Kilbroney by J. Hill Williams (October 1836) in Day and McWilliams, *Ordnance Survey Memoirs*, vol. 3, p. 44. See also Patrick S. McWilliams, 'Reactions to the Ordnance Survey: A Window on Prefamine Ireland', *New Hibernia Review*, 13, no. 1 (2009): pp. 65–6; Stiofán Ó Cadhla, *Civilizing Ireland: Ordnance Survey 1824–1842: Ethnography, Cartography, Translation* (Dublin: Irish Academic Press, 2007), pp. 135–6.

[344] Gillian M. Doherty, *The Irish Ordnance Survey: History, Culture and Memory* (Dublin: Four Courts Press, 2006), p. 183.

[345] Fair Sheets on Parish of Ahoghill by John Bleakly (May–July 1837); Day and McWilliams, *Ordnance Survey Memoirs*, vol. 23, p. 34.

[346] For an early reference to this place name see Alexander Knox, *A History of the County of Down from the Most Remote Period to the Present Day Including an Account of Its Early Colonization, Ecclesiastical, Civil, and Military Polity, Geography, Topography, Antiquities and Natural History* (Dublin: Hodges, Foster & Co., 1875), p. 518.

[347] Francis Joseph Bigger, *Four Shots from Down* (Belfast: William Sweeney, 1918), p. 9.

[348] For the concept of 'vernacular landscape' with reference to memory sites of 1798 in the West of Ireland see Beiner, *Remembering the Year of the French*, pp. 208–30.

Local histories and antiquarian writings published from the mid-nineteenth century show that oral traditions preserved numerous commemorative place names. The 'Drilly Knowe', near the village of Derrykeighan (8 km north-west of Ballymoney), identified the site where the United Irish captain John Nevin had trained his men in advance of the rebellion.[349] The assembly place of rebels from mid-Antrim on the hill of Drumlurg was subsequently known as 'Pike-Hill'.[350] 'McCracken's Well' in Slemish marked the place where the remnants of the United Irish army, headed by Henry Joy McCracken, took refuge after their defeat at Antrim town.[351] A cliff at the top of the Old Mill Glen in the Redhall demesne near Ballycarry, county Antrim, was known as 'Madman's Leap' in memory of the impressive feat of a fugitive rebel who jumped over the gorge to escape his pursuers.[352] 'Dickey's Field' was named after the insurgent general James Dickey, who went into hiding there after the rebellion, but was betrayed, arrested, and executed shortly afterwards.[353] Harper's Bridge marked the place on the road from Saintfield to Belfast where the informer Richard Harper was said to have been murdered by United Irishmen in order to prevent him from giving away information that would lead to the conviction of suspected rebels, including Rev. Ledlie Birch.[354]

The celebrated Irish poet Thomas Moore, who had befriended many United Irishmen as a student at Trinity College Dublin, described in romantic verse how sites of death served as an *aide mémoire*, in absence of proper memorials:

> Forget not the field where they perish'd,
> The truest, the last of the brave,
> All gone and the bright hope we cherish'd
> Gone with them, and quench'd in their grave![355]

The locations of these unrecognized graves were often identified through commemorative place names. A short story written in the early twentieth century refers to a place on the Antrim coast that was known with dread as 'the Moanin' Sands', recalling an

---

[349] Camac, 'The Parish of Derrykeighan', p. 154. For Nevin see Chapter 2 above, pp. 120–1.

[350] McSkimin, *Annals of Ulster*, p. 132.

[351] McSkimin, *Annals of Ulster*, p. 135; *Old Ballymena*, p. 45; Young, *Ulster in '98*, p. 32. Mary Ann Millar of Deerfin (near Ballymena), county Antrim, who was born in 1866, recalled in the 1930s that her grandmother 'had a lot to relate about Slemish' and the well; Reiltín Murphy, ed., 'Memories of My Irish Home by Mary Ann Millar née Laverty' (2014), ch. 12; <www.reiltinmurphy.ie/Memories_of_My_Irish_Home.html>.

[352] *Annual Reports and Proceedings of the Belfast Naturalists' Field Club for the Year Ending 31st March 1877*, vol. 1, Part 4 (Belfast: Belfast Naturalists' Field Club, 1878), pp. 226–7. This tradition of 1798 may have been grafted on an earlier tradition that referred to the escape of a seventeenth-century rapparee; see Stewart, *Summer Soldiers*, p. 95.

[353] From the notes of Canon McEvoy, who collected local traditions in the 1930s; see Patrick Joseph McKavanagh, *Glenavy: The Church of the Dwarf 1868–1968* (Belfast: Irish News Ltd, 1968), p. 38.

[354] Samuel McSkimin to R. R. Madden, n.d. (*c*.1842), Madden Papers, TCD 873/301; published in Madden, *The United Irishmen*, 2nd edn, 1st ser., vol. 1 (1857), p. 535. Information on the plans to murder Harper was included in the deposition of John Barnett and Robert Reid; Papers of the Lowry, Cleland, Steele and Nicholson families, PRONI MIC 506/1. For the connection between the killing of the informer and the trial of Rev. Birch see Aiken McClelland, *History of Saintfield and District* (Saintfield: Anderson Trust, 1972), p. 7.

[355] 'Forget Not the Field' in Thomas Moore, *Irish Melodies* (London: J. Power, 1821), p. 176; originally appeared in *A Selection of Irish Melodies*, no. 7 (London: J. Power, 1818).

incident in which yeomen massacred fleeing rebels and buried the wounded alive in a mass grave. The Belfast author professed to rely on local historical information, but did not specify his sources.[356] Such an atrocity was historically plausible. A late nineteenth-century account of the aftermath of the Battle of Antrim, based on local tradition, noted that 'large holes were dug in the sand beds near the lake, and the bodies; many, it is asserted, still alive, shot into them.'[357] Even if the legend of the 'The Moaning Sands' happens to be a literary invention, the place name aptly captures the haunting character of the vernacular landscape through which memory of 1798 maintained a daily presence. It required dedicated collectors of oral traditions to record these folk memories.

COLLECTING RECOLLECTIONS

Without official venues for commemoration, in the first decades after the rebellion, social memory in Ulster was mainly communicated orally and, for the large part, remained out of sight. However, a number of dedicated antiquaries were interested in uncovering this hidden memory for the sake of its preservation. Much antiquarian work remained unknown, as findings were often left unpublished. For example, the Catholic antiquarian John William Hanna of Downpatrick, seems to have interviewed in the mid-nineteenth century a number of elderly residents of county Down on their recollections of local incidents in 1798. The only reference in print to this fieldwork appeared incidentally in his article 'An Inquiry into the True Landing Place of St. Patrick in Ulster'. Hanna had heard stories about a fugitive rebel named Coulter, who crossed a river near Strangford Lough in an attempt to avoid arrest, but the essay focused on the curious name used locally for the river, which may have had ancient origins, and made little of the historical memories from the time of the rebellion.[358] Following Hanna's death in 1879, his reputation fell into obscurity and three decades later a member of the Royal Society of Antiquaries of Ireland would complain that he had 'sought in vain for any bibliographical notices of him or his work'.[359] For all intents and purposes, the oral traditions of 1798 that he had collected were lost.

Above all others, three individuals played a key role in confronting social forgetting of 1798, each from a different perspective: the conservative loyalist Samuel McSkimin, the liberal nationalist Richard Robert Madden, and the liberal unionist Classon Emmett Porter. They shared an antiquarian interest in history, but came from diverse

---

[356] Andrew James [James Andrew Strahan], 'Nabob Castle: A Legend of Ulster', *Blackwood's Magazine*, 181, no. 1096 (February 1907): p. 199. The author repeatedly referred to 'The Moaning Sands'; see Andrew James, *The Nabob: A Tale of Ninety-Eight* (Dublin: Four Courts Press, 2006; orig. publ. 1911 as *Ninety-Eight and Sixty Years After*), pp. 14–15, 23–4, 113, and 117.

[357] W. S. Smith, *Historical Gleanings in Antrim and Neighbourhood* (Belfast: Alex. Mayne & Boyd, 1888), p. 22.

[358] *UJA*, 2nd ser., 11, no. 2 (1905): pp. 73–4 (orig. published in *Ulsterman*, 23 June 1858, p. 4); *Larne Times*, 16 October 1926, p. 10.

[359] *Irish Book Lover*, 4 (December 1912), p. 92. For biographical information see William Stranney, 'The Editor and the Antiquarian (J. J. M. Kenney and J. W. Hanna)', *Lecale Review*, no. 10 (2012): pp. 64–74.

backgrounds. McSkimin was a Presbyterian shopkeeper in Carrickfergus; Madden was a Catholic physician from Dublin, who became a colonial administrator, journalist, and author; and Classon Porter was a Presbyterian minister in Larne. Although they had different motivations and operated independently of each other, the fruit of their combined labour offers remarkable insight into the mediations of remembering and forgetting among the generation that had lived through the rebellion (Fig. 3.2).

When collecting accounts of 1798, Samuel McSkimin, who attained recognition as a leading authority on the history of Antrim, was battling the demons of his own past. He had unsettling personal recollections of the rebellion, which he had experienced as a young man of 23 years of age. In 1797, McSkimin was obliged to abruptly leave his home in Ballyclare, county Antrim, where he had been employed as a weaver, and to take refuge in the garrison town of Carrickfergus. He had apparently been identified as a suspected informer on account of his association with a government agent, Sergeant John Lee of the Royal Irish Invalids, a unit that was stationed in Carrickfergus. Convinced that he was a victim of slander, he was clearly shaken by this experience and became fixated with exposing the existence of a secret United Irish committee responsible for the assassination of informers.[360] A confidante, Adam Dickey, of Cullybackey, observed that he 'was constantly in fear of being murdered' and another acquaintance described his anxieties as 'a sort of monomania'.[361] McSkimin took an active part in suppressing the rebellion, which was no easy task, as he was familiar with people on the opposite side and would later grieve over acquaintances that were killed in the Battle of Antrim fighting in the rebel ranks.[362] Among his comrades in the Carrickfergus Invalids (who were popularly referred to as 'Old Fogies'), there were individuals who tried to help rebel friends escape capture.[363]

One particular incident haunted the bookish McSkimin for the rest of his life. In June 1798, he was among a party of soldiers from Carrickfergus who ransacked the Doagh book club, of which he had previously been a member. To his horror, a routine mission of searching for arms and arresting wanted men deteriorated into an 'unprovoked act of devastation'. It was only shortly before his death in 1843 that he could bring himself to relate in a private conversation the barbaric conduct that he had witnessed that day:

> We entered the village, but not finding the objects searched for, those in command of
> the party ordered the doors of the Club Room to be burst open; and the work of demolition

---

[360] The allegation that McSkimin was a spy was put forward by James Hope; Madden, *The United Irishmen*, 3rd ser., vol. 1 (1846), p. 223. Upon visiting Ballyclare a decade after the rebellion, McSkimin complained that: 'slander had driven me hence'; *Belfast Monthly Magazine*, 2, no. 11 (1809), p. 422. His allegations on assassinations of suspected informers are detailed in Madden Papers, TCD 873/300–302; see also Madden, *The United Irishmen*, 2nd ser, 1st ser., vol. 1 (Dublin, 1857), pp. 533–8. Madden's impression was 'that at some period he had been apprehensive of personal violence at the hands of the United Irishmen'; Madden, *The United Irishmen*, 3rd ser., vol. 2 (1846), p. 139.

[361] William John Fitzpatrick, *The Sham Squire; and the Informers of 1798, with Jottings About Ireland Seventy Years Ago*, 6th edn (Dublin: W. B. Kelley and London: Simpkin, Marshall & Co., 1872), p. 340 (testimony of Adam Dickey); *Banner of Ulster*, 6 November 1849, p. 4.

[362] *Belfast Monthly Magazine*, 3, no. 12 (1809): p. 6.

[363] In 1863, 91-year-old James Burns, who was among the fugitive rebels that hid on Little Collin hill, near Glenwherry, recalled that an 'old Fogy, called John Magill . . . a private in "The Veterans"' had sent them a warning to avoid capture; Young, *Ulster in '98*, p. 33.

(a)

(b)

SAMUEL M'SKIMIN.

(c)

Fig. 3.2. Early collectors of '98 traditions: Samuel McSkimin, R. R. Madden, and Rev. Classon Emmett Porter

The collectors who documented the recollections of the generation that had participated or witnessed the 1798 rebellion in Ulster came from contrasting backgrounds. (a) Samuel McSkimin (1775–1843) was a Presbyterian conservative loyalist; (b) Richard Robert Madden (1798–1886) was a Catholic liberal nationalist; and (c) Presbyterian minister Rev. Classon Emmett Porter (1814–85) was a liberal unionist.

Sources: Samuel McSkimin, *The History and Antiquities of the County of the Town of Carrickfergus* (1909 edn); Richard Robert Madden, *The United Irishmen: Their Lives and Times*, 2nd edn, vol. 1 (1858); Classon Porter, *Congregational Memoirs: Old Presbyterian Congregation of Larne and Kilwaughter* (1929).

at once commenced. The windows and the entire furniture of the house were broken in pieces; a pair of elegant new globes smashed to atoms; the library shutters enclosing the books and papers, beaten in with musket ends, and the books thrown into the street, forming a huge pile were set fire to and burned.

Still ridden with guilt and shame in his old age, he confessed to John Rowan (a relative of the United Irishman Archibald Hamilton Rowan): 'never, either before or since did I return home with a heavier heart than from the disgraceful proceedings at the edifice wherein I received the first rudiments of education.'[364] Whereas acts of suppression were intended to silence dissent, troubling recollections of participation in violence could also serve to silence the perpetrators.

Over the following decade, McSkimin made a point of visiting sites of the rebellion in his 'Ramble to Antrim'.[365] Yet in 1811, when he first published his magnum opus— *The History and Antiquities of the County of the Town of Carrickfergus*, in which he made extensive use of local traditions collected from 'old inhabitants', he deferred to the conventions of public silence on the topic. Despite the book's promise to provide a historical review up 'to the present time', McSkimin refrained from writing about the events of 1798. An evasive statement that Carrickfergus Castle was converted into a state prison at the time did not refer to the political prisoners that had been incarcerated there (including William Orr). Ignoring the courts martial that had been held in the town, McSkimin blatantly wrote that 'no capital conviction has taken place here since 1772.' Claiming that 'no where in this kingdom are religious or political distinctions less known', he disingenuously argued that 'in 1798 and some years preceding, when party distinctions ran high in most places, fewer excesses were committed within this district than, perhaps, in any other place in Ireland.'[366] In subsequent editions this somewhat embarrassing passage was carefully touched up and tucked away at the end of the book.[367]

McSkimin's historical survey was greatly expanded in 1823, in a revised edition of *History and Antiquities*, for which he 'studiously engaged in collecting materials'. An added section on the United Irishmen and the tumultuous events of 1796–9 addressed previous omissions. McSkimin now admitted that the first members of the republican secret society to be arrested in Ireland were confined in the county Antrim gaol and enumerated the harsh acts of counter-insurgency that had been undertaken in the area, giving due recognition to the significance of the execution of William Orr. In referring to the 'dreadful flagellation' and executions of rebels, he pedantically pointed out that 'none of these persons were inhabitants of Carrickfergus: nor was a house burned or destroyed in the county of the town, during the rebellion.'[368] This short section, which

---

[364] R. [John Rowan], 'The Doagh Book Club and Sunday School', in *Northern Whig*, 17 April 1874, p. 3; see also p. 179.

[365] See above, pp. 175–6.

[366] Samuel McSkimin, *The History and Antiquities of the County of the Town of Carrickfergus, from the Earliest Records to the Present Time, in Four Parts* (Belfast: printed by Hugh Kirk Gordon, 1811), p. 85. It was later claimed that McSkimin was responsible for 'gathering information and procuring original documents to copy', while 'a schoolmaster named O'Beirney, and another friend called Hagan, lent their aid in putting his material into a literary form'; Young, *Historical Notices of Old Belfast*, p. 279.

[367] McSkimin, *History and Antiquities*, new edn (1909), based on 1839 edition, p. 338.

[368] McSkimin, *History and Antiquities*, 2nd edn (1823), pp. 95–100.

was not enhanced in later editions that came out in 1829, 1833, and 1839, did not make use of the large amount of material that McSkimin had amassed on the rebellion in the North.

McSkimin's unparalleled knowledge of local history was widely acknowledged. In the 1830s he assisted the investigations of the Ordnance Survey and was praised by John O'Donovan as a 'worthy man', who 'has laboured so assiduously to throw light upon the history of the district in which he lives'.[369] According to anecdotal evidence attributed to O'Donovan, McSkimin suffered from a heavy speech impediment.[370] This did not prevent him from enthusiastically collecting oral testimonies. One of his areas of interest was the 1641 rebellion, on which he was recognized as 'a first-rate authority on all local matters connected with the events of that memorable year' and was credited by other antiquarians for having 'recorded the oral history'—a remarkably early use of the term—in specific localities.[371]

Although McSkimin's historical interests were varied, by the time of his death in 1843, it became clear that 'his traditions were chiefly clustered about '98'. An obituary in the nationalist organ the *Nation* noted that:

> His store of traditions was great; he used to go walking about the county of Antrim, gossiping with the people. The only way in his opinion, to come at the truth from the poorer people who were "up" in '98 was to make them free with drink, and in this way he said he laid out a good deal of money for his information.[372]

The scope of his fieldwork covered traditions of both loyalists and rebels. The ballads that he collected included United Irish songs, still recalled from the 1790s, and subsequently composed folk songs on rebel heroes, as well as Orange songs, which denounced the United Irishmen.[373] The *Belfast News-Letter* maintained that:

> In regard to the history of the Irish Insurrection of 1798, he possessed more information than is to be found in all the works that have ever been published, or that will be published for perhaps half a century to come.[374]

It turned out that he had tirelessly collected memories of Ninety-Eight for decades, but somehow could not bring himself to complete a history of the rebellion.[375] The prospect that McSkimin's writings on the topic would eventually come out in print became a matter of concern for those who believed that his work was tainted by loyalist bias.

---

[369] Letters written by John O'Donovan to the Ordnance Survey headquarters dated 16 September 1834 and 9 October 1834; quoted in James Seery, 'Samuel McSkimin (*c.*1774–1843) Author of the History of Carrickfergus and Annals of Ulster 1790–1798', *Bulletin of the Presbyterian Historical Society of Ireland*, 27 (1998–2000): pp. 1–13. McSkimin's help is credited in Day and McWilliams, *Ordnance Survey Memoirs*, vol. 12, pp. 27 and 72; vol. 17, p. 116; vol. 37, p. 173.

[370] Fitzpatrick, *The Sham Squire*, p. 312n. [371] *UJA*, ser. 1, vol. 9 (1861/2): p. 241.

[372] 'Samuel McSkimmin, Historian of Carrickfergus', in *Nation*, 4 March 1843, p. 329 [reproduced in *Irish Book Lover*, 6, no. 6 (1915): pp. 85–7].

[373] The songs collected by McSkimin were later published in Young, *Ulster in '98*, pp. 60–5.

[374] 'Death of Mr. Sam. McSkimmin, the Historian of Carrickfergus', in *BNL*, 21 February 1843, p. 3.

[375] Samuel McSkimin Papers, RIA 12 F 36. For McSkimin's notes on recollections of 1795–9 in county Antrim see in particular ff. 13–23 (insurgency in 1797) and ff. 23–32 (the 1798 rebellion).

Unease over McSkimin's partiality was aroused by an article he published in 1836 in *Fraser's Magazine* on the 'Secret History of the Irish Insurrection of 1803', which, according to the *Nation*, was 'marked throughout with bitterness against the United Irishmen' and showed that his historical judgement relied on 'mere prejudice'.[376] Captain John A. Russell, Thomas Russell's nephew, took offence from 'different statements' in McSkimin's narrative and visited Downpatrick and Belfast in order to dig up evidence that could counter the arguments.[377] In response to the unfavourable account, Nelly Rabb of Ballysallagh, county Down, whose husband had been involved in the insurrection alongside Russell, resolved to write down her recollections in which 'many particulars will be found which dispose a fair portion of the mass of fabrication concerning Russell's movements in the North in McSkimmin's statement.'[378] Mary Ann McCracken corresponded with James D. Rose Cleland of Rathgael House, Bangor, county Down, who had been a juror at Russell's trial, and received from him 'a memorandum made from recollection' of the court proceedings. This document was passed on for verification to the veteran United Irishmen James Hope, who had assisted Russell in 1803. Hope insisted that an allegation made against Russell, who was accused of having spread false rumours of a French landing at Ballywalter, was untrue. Hope's personal recollections were cross-checked with those of another follower of Russell, John Douglas of Belfast, described as 'a man of a taintless spirit and unimpeachable integrity', who confirmed that 'he had never heard of it before, and was certain it was a falsehood.'[379] The former rebels and their families were determined to challenge McSkimin's hostile account.

James Hope, who had been interviewed by McSkimin, complained that the 'entire article is a misrepresentation of my answers'. He claimed that his testimony had been 'mixed with calumnious assertions of some person' and were then embellished with the help of another loyalist antiquarian known for his partisan interest in traditions of 1798, Thomas Crofton Croker.[380] In turn, these charges were denied by McSkimin, who insisted that he had verified his historical account by reference to several sources. Professing that 'I never in my life made a secret of my opinions,' he pertinently pointed out to Hope that 'there is [sic] indeed two ways of telling a story and of course I adopted one of them.'[381] Memory of the rebellion was open for contestation.

---

[376] Samuel McSkimin, 'Secret History of the Irish Insurrection of 1803', *Fraser's Magazine for Town and Country*, 14, no. 83 (November 1836): pp. 546–67; *Nation*, 4 March 1843, p. 329.

[377] Madden Papers, TCD 873/674. Additional letters by J. A. Russell can be found in TCD 873/662–6.

[378] Nelly Rabb, Ballysallagh, to Mary Ann McCracken, 18 November 1843, Madden Papers, TCD 873/627.

[379] James D. Rose Cleland, Rath Gael House, Bangor, to Mary Ann McCracken, 18 November 1843 and M. A. McCracken, Belfast, to R. R. Madden, 2 July 1844; Madden Papers, TCD 873/626 and 155 (respectively). Rose Cleland's memorandum of Russell's trial is reproduced in Madden, *The United Irishmen*, 3rd ser., vol. 2 (1846), pp. 265–6. In 1895, F. J. Bigger made a transcript of a more detailed account of Russell's life, written by Rose Cleland on 17 September 1838; Bigger Papers, BCL K6/2–9.

[380] James Hope, Belfast, 8 January 1838, Leon Ó Broin Papers, NLI 27,950.

[381] Samuel McSkimin, Carrickfergus, to James Hope, Belfast, around the end of November–beginning of December 1836, Madden Papers, TCD 873/652; published in Madden, *The United Irishmen*, 3rd ser., vol. 2 (1846), pp. 139–42.

The remaining old guard of the northern United Irishmen were intent that the story of 1798 would be told otherwise. By the 1840s, the former republicans, now in their seventies and eighties, were mostly reconciled with the rule of the United Kingdom but obstinately refused to accept the dominance of conservatism in unionist circles. They had weathered the years after the rebellion, unable to openly commemorate their lost loved ones, and, realizing that soon they too would pass away, were more intent than ever to bequeath a heroic memory of the rebellion. James McDonnell, aged 81 in 1844, 'wished much for the possession of McSkimmin's papers . . . fearing they might contain facts derogatory to the Irish character, particularly regarding the assassination of informers, which he wished to suppress'. Mary Ann McCracken objected to any form of censorship and professed more noble intentions:

> my motive in wishing for the papers was that truth and falsehood might be separated while there were living witnesses competent to do so; I do not think it would be consistent with truth (the legitimate object of history) to suppress any well authenticated fact, let the blame rest where it may, the run of history being to promote the knowledge of mankind, and the service of governing.

The 74-year-old McCracken endeavoured to acquire the papers of McSkimin in order to have them checked by 80-year-old Hope, so that 'all the falsehoods and misrepresentations therein contain may not go down to posterity as historical truth.' As it was, she worried that Russell's papers might have fallen into the hands of William Hamilton Maxwell, who was writing a history of 1798, which, in light of the writer's turn towards conservatism, was likely to be a 'villainous publication'.[382] The last survivors had a strong personal investment in how the United Irishmen would be recalled by the next generations, knowing that the memory of Ninety-Eight would reflect also on how they themselves would be remembered by posterity.

Much to their annoyance, McSkimin's unsympathetic draft history of the rebellion was published in unexpurgated form. In 1849, the Belfast publisher John Henderson, who just a few years earlier had produced an authoritative edition of McHenry's 1798 novel *The Insurgent Chief*, printed McSkimin's unfinished narrative under the evasive title *Annals of Ulster; or, Ireland Fifty Years Ago*. A review in the conservative *Downpatrick Recorder* was satisfied with McSkimin's loyalist perspective—disingenuously claiming that 'a spirit of impartiality pervades the whole'—but duly pointed out that it is 'an unfinished production' and that 'the title of this volume is a misnomer'.[383] Four years later, another Belfast publisher, John Mullan, re-issued the book with a more precise heading: *History of the Irish Rebellion in the Year 1798; Particularly in Antrim, Down and Derry* (1853).[384] A critical review in the liberal *Banner of Ulster*, probably written by James McKnight, described the book as 'a sort of connected narrative', which was cobbled out of 'fragmentary, and traditional facts, anecdotes, local histories, and other queerly miscellaneous information', and complained that McSkimin had deliberately left out many of the recollections that he had documented over the years.

---

[382] M. A. McCracken, Belfast, to R. R. Madden, 2 July and 15 October 1844, Madden Papers, TCD 873/155 and 156 (respectively).

[383] *Downpatrick Recorder*, 17 November 1849, p. 4.

[384] For a modern edition see Samuel McSkimin, *Annals of Ulster: From 1790 to 1798*, edited by Elizabeth J. McCrum (Belfast: J. Cleeland and William Mullan, 1906).

He was specifically faulted for 'his very defective notice of the battle of Antrim', which omitted all reference to the reminiscences of James Hope, who had provided 'the most valuable information which McSkimin possessed on the subject of the affairs of '98'. McKnight, who claimed that he was 'acquainted with very much, both of the public and secret history of the period in question', condemned the book for its 'total want of candour, even to a positively ludicrous degree' and concluded that it 'ought never to have seen the light'.[385]

McSkimin's narrative was evidently informed by oral accounts, which it chose to overlook. Meanwhile, Richard Robert Madden had also begun to collect testimonies from people who had lived through the events of 1798, as well as oral traditions that had been passed on to family members. Out of respect, Madden paid a visit to the elderly McSkimin, shortly before his death, and 'observed, with regret' the limitations of his prejudices:

> the political atmosphere in which he lived, had given a very strong bias to his opinions, and had disposed him to turn his attention chiefly, indeed I might say wholly, to the faults and follies of the unfortunate Northern leaders of the United Irishmen, and to with-draw his consideration from the qualities of another kind, for which many of them were remarkable.[386]

In contrast, Madden intended to write a history of the lives of the United Irishmen that would allow them to tell their stories and would valorize their memory.

Unlike McSkimin, Madden did not have his own personal recollections of the rebellion. Somewhat akin to Thomas Hobbes, who attributed significance to having been born at the time of the Spanish Armada and famously wrote 'fear and I were born twins', Madden found particular meaning in his having been born in 1798. His birth had occurred on the day that his father's house in Dublin was searched by the notorious town major Charles Henry Sirr, the man responsible for the arrest of many of the principal United Irishmen. This incident, Madden believed, provided the motive for his lifelong 'interest in the affairs of the Irish Insurrectionary movement of 1798, and of those that figured therein, whose memory I have endeavoured to preserve and vindicate'.[387] Madden was a prolific writer (his son claimed that he wrote over forty books) and the way he approached the history of 1798 was nothing short of monumental. In several spurts—from 1842 to 1843, in 1846, 1857 to 1858 and in 1860—he published eleven volumes (issued, somewhat misleadingly, as three 'series' and two 'editions') and, according to the auction records of his 'valuable library', he also wrote manuscripts for an additional two unpublished volumes.[388]

Madden's *The United Irishmen: Their Lives and Times* was not written as a narrative history. It is a series of biographical memoirs of leading figures and additional shorter

[385] *Banner of Ulster*, 6 November 1849, p. 4.
[386] Madden, *The United Irishmen*, 3rd ser., vol. 2 (1846), pp. 138–9. In another account of this meeting, Madden referred to McSkimin's 'rabid Orange feelings of bitter hatred to the leaders and others of 1798'; Madden, *The United Irishmen*, 2nd edn, 1st ser., vol. 1 (1857), pp. 535–6.
[387] Thomas More Madden, ed., *The Memoirs (Chiefly Autobiographical) from 1798 to 1886 of Richard Robert Madden, M.D., F.R.C.S.* (London: Ward & Downey, 1891), p. 2. See also Andrew Boyd, 'The Life and Times of R. R. Madden', *Seanchas Ardmhacha*, 20, no. 2 (2005): pp. 133–5.
[388] *Catalogue of the Valuable Library of the Late Dr. R. R. Madden* (Dublin: T. C. Newby, 1886), pp. 46–7.

notices of those considered to be of lesser importance, with an overall total of seventy-three people covered.[389] The principal memoirs of the northern United Irishmen were later republished in Glasgow as a separate volume titled *Antrim and Down in '98*. This included chapters on Henry Joy McCracken, James Hope, William Putnam McCabe, Rev. James Porter, and Henry Munro, but left out references to a number of additional Ulstermen who had appeared in the original publications.[390]

Madden began collecting information on 1798 in between colonial postings in Jamaica and Cuba. In 1835–6, he visited the United States, where he met distinguished United Irish émigrés. Madden was particularly taken with William James MacNevin, who in 1806 had sent out a circular, asking for people in Ireland and America to send him 'the facts and documents they possess, which their avocations or safety may not allow themselves to make public'. This appeal was used to collect materials for his *Pieces of Irish History* (1807), which was influential in shaping nationalist perceptions of 1798.[391] MacNeven convinced Madden of the need to collect memories of United Irishmen. Concerned with the deterioration in MacNeven's health, Madden met with him again in 1839 to prepare 'a memorandum of the subjects of conversation on which he expressed any opinion respecting the events of '98, or communicated any interesting information'.[392] As the remaining United Irishmen reached old age, Madden realized that he was working against time and that collecting memories had become an urgent imperative.

In Madden's eyes, a parallel could be drawn between the political oppression in Ireland at the close of the eighteenth century and the injustices of colonial rule, which he was struggling to rectify as a liberal colonial administrator, who was deeply committed to the abolition of slavery.[393] While serving abroad, he gathered materials on 1798 from afar through extensive correspondence, drawing on the help of his family and friends. During intervals between colonial posts in Africa and Australia and his many world travels, Madden perseveringly continued to trace the biographies of former United Irishmen in Ireland, on the continent and in America. He was assisted by their relatives, who were appreciative of his 'labours to rescue the memory of the United Irishmen from oblivion and obloquy'.[394] Temporary redundancy during the Tory government of Sir Robert Peel allowed him, from 1841, to spend more time in Ireland

---

[389] For an overview, with synopses of the volumes and an index of the memoirs and notices, see C. J. Woods, 'R. R. Madden, Historian of the United Irishmen', in *1798: A Bicentenary Perspective*, edited by Thomas Bartlett, David Dickson, Dáire Keogh, and Kevin Whelan (Dublin: Four Courts Press, 2003), pp. 497–511. For an unauthorized complete edition see Richard Robert Madden, *The United Irishmen: Their Lives and Times*, edited with notes bibliography, and index by Vincent Fleming O'Reilly, 12 vols (New York: The Catholic Publication Society, 1916).

[390] Richard Robert Madden, *Antrim and Down in '98* (Glasgow: Cameron, Ferguson & Co., c.1900).

[391] William James MacNeven, *Pieces of Irish History, Illustrative of the Condition of the Catholics of Ireland; of the Origins and Progress of the Political System of the United Irishmen; and of Their Transactions with the Anglo-Irish Government* (New York: Bernard Dornin, 1807); the circular is reproduced on pp. 254–6.

[392] Madden, *The United Irishmen*, 2nd edn, 3rd ser. (1860), pp. 239–42.

[393] Madden, *The United Irishmen*, 2nd edn, 1st ser., vol. 1 (1857), preface, pp. ix–xvi.

[394] Robert Emmet [son of the United Irishman Thomas Addis Emmet], New York, to R. R. Madden, November 1843; reproduced in Madden, The United Irishmen, 3rd ser., 2nd edn (1860), pp. 2–3.

to further his research and a permanent position in Dublin as secretary of the Loan Fund Board, from 1850, brought him closer to his sources. Madden cast his net wide and followed the lives of United Irishmen from all over the isle. By the end of 1842, after the first two volumes of *The United Irishmen* were out and the third was about to go to press, he was intent on directing his attention more specifically towards the 'subject of the Northern movement'.[395]

To Madden's good fortune, he was able to access a coterie of remaining northern radicals, to which he was introduced by a person of slightly dubious credentials— Dr James McDonnell, a prominent Belfast physician. McDonnell had been an associate of the United Irishmen but did not support their participation in armed insurrection. In 1803, he turned against his erstwhile close friend Thomas Russell and contributed funds for his arrest. This deed was denounced as 'foul falsehood' in the contemporary poem 'The Grave of Russell' and earned McDonnell the nickname 'The Brutus of Belfast' in a scathing poem by the United Irish poet William Drennan. Consequently, McDonnell was ostracized in republican circles for some time.[396] By the 1840s, this animosity had been patched and McDonnell was able to direct Madden to a number of key people, central among them was Mary Ann McCracken.[397]

In search of records that might be 'rescued from oblivion' Madden found that:

> the preservation of them in most instances which have come to our knowledge had been owing to the fidelity of female friendship, or affection on the part of their surviving relatives, the sisters and daughters of the men who were engaged in the struggle of 1798, which neither time, nor obloquy, nor new ties and interests had estranged, nor had been able to extinguish.

Mary Ann McCracken's devotion to the memory of her brother, Henry Joy, proved to be exemplary in this regard: 'The recollection of every act of his seems to have been stored up in her mind, as if she felt the charge of his reputation had been committed to her especial care.'[398]

Although shattered by the execution of her brother in 1798, Mary Ann remained faithful to the ideals of the United Irishmen. She sheltered Russell during the aborted rising of 1803, upon his arrest she paid for his defence, and after he was executed she was responsible for putting up a tombstone on his grave at Downpatrick. When the United Irishmen went underground, she fearlessly kept the republican flame alive. Fugitives, such as David Lyons, who 'lived obscure, thinking it preferable to remain ignorant of events, then risque [sic] the safety of my friends', turned to her for information on the fate of those who had been 'charged in the county of Down and

---

[395] R. R. Madden to R. J. Tennent, 10 November and 28 December 1842, Tennent Papers, PRONI D1748/G/426/2 and 3 (respectively).

[396] Madden, *Literary Remains of the United Irishmen*, p. 290. Drennan's denigration of McDonnell appears in the poem 'Epitaph—on the Living', which was attached to an undated letter to Martha McTier (c.1803); Agnew, *Drennan-McTier Letters*, 3, p. 170. McDonnell was repeatedly referred to with scorn in letters written by McTier, see ibid., pp. 139, 144–5, 156, 158, 159–61, 165, 167, 258, 269, and 427.

[397] Dr McDonnell, Belfast, to R. R. Madden, 8 October 1840; reproduced in Madden, *The Memoirs*, pp. 205–6. McDonnell's account of his conduct in 1803 is reproduced in Madden, *The United Irishmen*, 3rd ser., vol. 2 (1846), pp. 230–1.

[398] Madden, *The United Irishmen*, 2nd ser., vol. 2 (1843), p. 389.

Antrim'.[399] United Irish emigrants in America sent her money so that she could pass it on to their relatives at home.[400] In subsequent decades, she engaged in a range of philanthropic and educational activities and her home on Rosemary Lane continued to function as a meeting place for Belfast radicals, as it had done in the 1790s. Madden's impressive credentials as an abolitionist earned him deep respect in these circles.[401]

McCracken found in Madden a kindred spirit and a trustworthy friend. She was soon convinced that he would not let her down like McSkimin, whose failure to return manuscripts given on loan was a lingering sore.[402] They corresponded over a period of twenty years (1840–59), from when she was aged 70 to 90. Though she was concerned about mental decline—'there is no loss I regret so much as the loss of memory, but I must think more of what I enjoy and am allowed to retain, than of what I have lost'— she maintained a 'vigorous and highly cultivated intellect' almost up to her death at the age of 96 in 1866.[403] Aware that 'there are few now living who took an active part in that unfortunate period in Ireland's history and those who are in general have defective memories', McCracken took upon herself to help Madden in his investigations, openly sharing with him her knowledge, passing on to him her memorabilia and remaining papers, and putting him in contact with other knowledgeable persons.[404]

Some of the leads that McCracken provided turned out to be less fruitful than desired. It was expected, for example, that John McAdam of Belfast, who had married the daughter of Samuel Neilson, 'must of course take a deep interest in these matters' and that he 'may remember or be able to direct to some person who has a recollection of these old affairs'.[405] But when approached by Madden, McAdam revealed that he could not offer useful information: 'I know the matters merely from the history of the times; I was but 14 years old when I witnessed the fight in Antrim, too young to understand the nature of the contest.'[406] Probably the most meaningful contact McCracken furnished Madden was when she introduced him to James ('Jemmy') Hope, who had commanded 'The Spartan Band' of Roughfort Volunteers in the rebel vanguard at the Battle of Antrim and was Russell's 'right arm' in 1803.[407]

[399] David Lyons, London, to M. A. McCracken, Rosemary Lane, Belfast, 26 January 1804, Young Papers, PRONI D2930/3/2/1.
[400] McNeill, *Life and Times of Mary Ann McCracken*, p. 301.
[401] For Madden's abolitionist activities see David R. Murray, 'Richard Robert Madden: His Career as a Slavery Abolitionist', *Studies*, 61, no. 241 (1972): pp. 41–53; Nini Rodgers, 'Richard Robert Madden: An Irish Anti-Slavery Activist in the Americas', in *Ireland Abroad: Politics and Professions in the Nineteenth Century*, edited by Oonagh Walsh (Dublin: Four Courts Press, 2003), pp. 119–31.
[402] Anna McCleery, 'Life of Mary Ann M'Cracken, Sister of Henry Joy M'Cracken', in *Historical Notices of Old Belfast*, edited by Robert M. Young (Belfast: Marcus Ward & Co., 1896), p. 197.
[403] M. A. McCracken, Belfast, to R. R. Madden, 13 November 1857, Madden Papers, TCD 873/70; *Nation*, 4 August 1866, p. 796; *Belfast Morning News*, 30 July 1866, p. 3.
[404] M. A. McCracken, Belfast, to R. R. Madden, 16 December 1853, Madden Papers, TCD 873/73. See also McNeill, *Life and Times of Mary Ann McCracken*, pp. 297–307.
[405] M. A. McCracken to R. R. Madden, 16 December 1853; Madden Papers, TCD 873/73.
[406] John McAdam, Belfast to M. A. McCracken, 29 December 1853, Madden Papers, TCD 873/160.
[407] Hope testified that his comrades called him 'the Spartan'; Madden, *The United Irishmen*, 3rd ser., vol. 1 (1846), p. 23. Teeling noted that Henry Joy McCracken referred to the unit commanded by Hope at Antrim as 'The Spartan Band'; Teeling, *Personal Narrative*, p. 227. The Wicklow United Irishman Miles Byrne recalled that, when Robert Emmet requested that Hope would stay with him in Dublin, Russell remarked 'you certainly take off my right arm'; Byrne, *Memoirs of Miles Byrne*, vol. 1, p. 357.

The liberal journalist James McKnight, who around that time also met Hope ('or "Hoop", as the country people pronounced his name'), described him as:

> a little man, but a most extraordinary character, remarkable for talent, and though he must have been nearly 80 years of age when I went to meet him, he became animated with an almost terrific energy, whenever he got into the spirit of the times, and his eyes literally blazed like balls of lightening.[408]

Having previously been scathed by his experience with McSkimin, Hope was at first 'extremely anxious' about how 'the North' would be addressed in Madden's work, 'lest there should be any inaccuracy or anything admitting of misinformation'.[409] His worries were soon put to rest. After reading the initial two volumes of *The United Irishmen*, Hope appreciatively wrote to thank Madden: 'you could not have sent anything to me of equal value: it refreshes my memory . . . I am so well convinced of the impartiality of your intentions, and their accordance with my own, to be fair and faithful, that my notes are at your service.'[410]

Madden arranged to meet Hope in the house of Israel Milliken, a veteran United Irishman who had been incarcerated for the duration of the rebellion, yet was still said to have 'been "out" in '98. Madden noted that 'his recollections of that period were of most interesting kind, and he enjoyed greatly to recite the adventures in which he took part to his visitors and friends.' Milliken was a steadfast supporter of Catholic emancipation, which, alongside abolition, was another liberal cause shared by Madden and many of the former United Irishmen. His house was a regular gathering place for radicals and was therefore a perfect venue.[411] From their first meeting, Madden was enthralled by Hope—a weaver who lived 'in very humble circumstance' and a 'self-taught man, of the most clear and vigorous intellect'. Madden encouraged him to write down his recollections. There were moments when Hope was flooded by reminiscences. At the end of a letter, written on the eve of an anniversary day of the Battle of Antrim, he wistfully noted 'This day 45 years past, I had other work before me.'[412]

The two corresponded up until 1846, at which time 82-year-old Hope informed his 'dear friend' that he was still working on his 'Deathbed book', not knowing if 'ever it will be read'.[413] Over three years, Madden collected from Hope notes, which amounted to 'a mass of unconnected materials, piled on one another in reference to events, not in the order of their succession, but as passing circumstances or topics of conversation

---

[408] James McKnight, Newry, to George Benn, Ballymena, 12 September 1874, Benn Papers, PRONI D3113/7/100.

[409] M. A. McCracken, Belfast, to R. R. Madden, 6 January 1843, Madden Papers, TCD 873/96.

[410] Undated letter from Hope to Madden; reproduced in *The United Irishmen*, 3rd ser., vol. 1 (1846), p. 221.

[411] *Belfast Mercury*, 10 January 1857, p. 2. Milliken's name appears alongside the signatures of many other former Belfast United Irishmen on the 'Petition of the Protestants of Ireland in Favour of Catholic Emancipation' presented to parliament in 1812; *Belfast Monthly Magazine*, 8, no. 44 (1812): pp. 237–9. He was subsequently a steadfast supporter in Belfast of Daniel O'Connell's reform campaigns; see *BNL*, 20 December 1839, p. 4 and 21 March 1843, p. 4; *Freeman's Journal*, 24 March 1843, p. 3.

[412] J. Hope to R. R. Madden, 6 June 1843, Leon Ó Broin Papers, NLI 27,950.

[413] J. Hope to R. R. Madden, 23 January 1846, Leon Ó Broin Papers, NLI 27,950. Hope's 'Death Bed Book' (which ran to almost one hundred folio pages) was committed to Mary Ann McCracken, who gave it to Madden; *Catalogue of the Valuable Library of the Late Dr. R. R. Madden*, p. 27.

chanced to recall them'. These were edited and published as an 'autobiographical memoir' that would eventually gain Hope recognition as a working class hero among socialist republicans, who found inspiration in his unstinting critique of social inequality and economic exploitation.[414] Six years after Hope's death in 1847, Madden fulfilled the wishes of his remaining friends, McCracken and Milliken, and saw to the erection of a memorial over his grave in Mallusk cemetery. Half a century had passed since the rebellion and it now seemed possible to commemorate a United Irishman in the open. Yet Hope's epitaph—which read 'in the best era of his country's history a soldier in her cause; and in the worst of times still faithful to it'—refrained from explicitly mentioning his involvement in rebellion.[415]

When compiling the materials for his biographical memoirs, Madden sent detailed lists of queries to his informants. A questionnaire on Rev. James Porter included seventy-two questions and a questionnaire on Henry Munro had eighty.[416] He explained the purpose for the large number of questions to Robert John Tennent, a liberal MP for Belfast, who was approached for information on his uncle John Tennent, a United Irishman who went on to serve with distinction in the Irish Legion of the French army:

> Many of the queries in the accompanying paper may seem to imply a total ignorance on the points to which they refer. My object however is to corroborate what I already know as well as to obtain collateral information which bears on other matters I am less acquainted with.[417]

By feigning ignorance, Madden solicited as much information as he could gather. This method allowed the facts to be cross-checked and constantly expanded the scope of Madden's familiarity with the past. Like other informants, Tennent felt that 'there was much more to be told' and provided Madden with family papers that uncovered additional information.[418]

The private papers given to Madden revealed, among other things, that former United Irishmen maintained networks of mutual support in the decades after the rebellion. When in 1821 it was discovered that a niece of Thomas Russell was 'in great distress', Tennent was asked by his father to approach the 'Gentlemen of 1798' still living in Belfast 'with a view of getting her admitted to some charitable

---

[414] 'Autobiographical Memoir of James Hope', in Madden, *The United Irishmen*, 3rd ser., vol. 1 (1846), pp. 218–95. For a modern edition see John Newsinger, ed., *United Irishman: The Autobiography of James Hope* (London: Merlin Press, 2001). For an example of Hope's iconic status in modern-day left-wing circles see Sean Cronin, *A Man of the People* (Dublin: The Worker's Party, 1998; orig. edn 1964).

[415] M. A. McCracken to R. R. Madden, 29 November and 16 December 1853, Madden Papers, TCD 873/72 and 73. Eighty-two-year-old Milliken, though frail and unable to leave his house, was responsible for raising funds by subscription for Hope's monument; *Belfast Mercury*, 11 March 1853, p. 3. The tombstone was restored at the turn of the century by Francis Joseph Bigger; 'The James Hope Monument', *UJA*, 2nd ser., 7, no. 1 (1901): p. 64.

[416] Madden Papers, TCD 873/51 (Porter) and 317 (Munro).

[417] R. R. Madden to R. J. Tennent, 13 September 1842, Tennent Papers, PRONI D1748/G/426/1. R. J. Tennent's answers appear in the 'Memoir of John Tennent', in Madden, *The United Irishmen*, 3rd ser., vol. 2 (1846), pp. 51–63. See also Eileen Black, 'John Tennent, 1798–1813, United Irishman and Chevalier de la Legion d'Honneur', *Irish Sword*, 13 (1977–9): pp. 157–9.

[418] R. J. Tennent, Belfast, to R. R. Madden, 7 October 1842, Madden Papers, TCD 873/403.

institution'.[419] Madden subsequently learned that Thomas Russell's sister, Margaret, had also been rescued from destitution by a similar subscription, which was organized by Mary Ann McCracken some years earlier. In her efforts to provide for the bereaved dependents of executed rebels, McCracken declined warnings 'to keep out of the way' and refused to be intimidated by loyalists, who tried to put an end to the fundraising among former United Irishmen by spreading malicious rumours that she was raising money to buy arms.[420]

Comparison between Madden's original notes and the published work shows that interviews were treated to editorial polishing and were not necessarily reproduced verbatim. Delicate issues had to be broached with care. Mary Ann McCracken confessed that she 'felt considerable regret and self reproach at my injudicious and imprudent communication of private matters, particularly the names of ladies' and asked, 'might not these ladies names be omitted in the ensuing edition and the particulars more lightly touched on?'[421] Discretion was needed in writing about people who had lived their lives without talking in public about their previous involvement with the United Irishmen. Some of Madden's informants specifically stipulated that their name should not be mentioned. He also encountered people who objected to the airing of their recollections of 1798 and refused to cooperate with him. Thomas Corbitt of Belfast, who had been for a while the nominal editor of the United Irish newspaper the *Northern Star*, was said to be 'averse to any publication on the subject at the present time'.[422] Although Madden was referred to Robert Simms, the United Irish adjutant-general of Antrim who had resigned his command prior to the outbreak of the rebellion, Simms apparently declined to meet him. Robert Holmes, a brother-in-law of Robert Emmet who was imprisoned in 1798 and 1803 even though he had not participated in the insurrections, turned down Madden's request for information, forthrightly stating his opposition to the publication of a memoir on the rebellion: 'as I greatly disapprove of such an attempt, I must be excused from aiding its execution in any way whatsoever.'[423]

Madden's collecting of memory rubbed against the grain of the prevailing culture of social forgetting, bringing out into the public domain recollections that had previously only been discussed in private. It confronted an official construction of memory that was overtly hostile to the United Irishmen and was heavily influenced by the ultra-conservative historical interpretation of Richard Musgrave, who had presented the rebellion as a Jacobin conspiracy driven by sectarian hatred. In its place, Madden promoted a nationalist narrative that blamed the government for having 'fomented a rebellion, and, in the words of Lord Castlereagh, caused it "to explode prematurely," in

---

[419] Dr Robert Tennent, Belfast to R. J. Tennent, 14 February 1821, Tennent Papers, PRONI D1748/G/667/11.

[420] Madden, *The United Irishmen*, 2nd ser., vol. 2 (1846), pp. 274–6. Madden noted that McCracken was reluctant to provide information on her 'noble conduct' in support of former United Irishmen and their dependents.

[421] M. A. McCracken to Madden, 13 November 1857, Madden Papers, TCD 873/70. In a previous letter, McCracken had asked for a name of a woman to be omitted 'as when living she would have shrunk from publicity'; M. A. McCracken to Madden, 27 October 1853, Madden Papers, TCD 873/72.

[422] John Scott Porter, Belfast, to R. R. Madden, 19 April 1842, Madden Papers, TCD 873/53.

[423] Robert Holmes to R. R. Madden, 22 November 1842, Madden Papers, TCD 873/325.

order to break down the strength and spirit of the country, to enable its agents in the Irish parliament to effect an union'.[424] Unsurprisingly, this forceful configuration of counter-memory was strongly criticized in the unionist press. The *Dublin University Magazine*, the most significant Irish conservative journal at the time, published long articles (probably written by Rev. Samuel O'Sullivan) with scathing reviews of each series of *The United Irishmen*, bluntly stating that Madden could not be trusted with 'doing honour to the memory of the dead'. An essay on 'Seditious Literature in Ireland', which was mainly devoted to lambasting Madden's historical writings, described him as 'a perverter of the uses of history' and labelled his biographies of the United Irishmen a 'martyrology of treason'.[425]

Madden complained to the military historian Sir William Napier that even the liberal press in London considered 'the act of referring to the atrocities of "'98" as a renewal of painful recollections that ought to be buried in oblivion'.[426] To counter this dismissive attitude, he made an appeal to the predominantly liberal Presbyterian readers of the *Northern Whig*, arguing that 'the time has arrived when this history may be written without provoking rancour of party or lacerating the feelings of surviving relatives.' The newspaper's review of the first edition of *The United Irishmen* commended Madden's work, but opined that 'his ardour is almost too great, leading him occasionally to transgress beyond the limits of historic narrative and to indulge more in declamation than befits the sober historian.'[427]

The cultural nationalists of Young Ireland expressed unreserved admiration for Madden's *The United Irishmen*. Thomas Davis, their literary kingpin, published in the *Nation* an article full of praise for the initial volumes, and subsequent volumes were treated to equally glowing reviews. James McCormick, one of their publishers, produced an anthology on 1798 in which the section on Ulster was entirely based on Madden. James Duffy, another publisher favoured by Young Ireland, stepped in to continue publication of *The United Irishmen*, after the London publisher found that he was unable to finance the production of the later volumes.[428]

Madden, however, was a liberal nationalist in the constitutionalist tradition of Daniel O'Connell and not a republican. In order that his work would not be read as

[424] Richard Robert Madden, *The Connexion between the Kingdom of Ireland and the Crown of England* (Dublin: James Duffy, 1845), p. 116.

[425] For the review essays see *Dublin University Magazine*, 20, no. 118 (October 1842): pp. 485–508 (quotation on p. 497); 22, no. 132 (December 1843): pp. 685–700; 28, no. 167 (November 1846): pp. 535–50. See also 'Seditious Literature in Ireland', *Dublin University Magazine*, 31, no. 182 (1848): pp. 159–72 (quotations from pp. 159 and 161).

[426] Madden to Sir W. Napier, 28 August 1842; published in Madden, *The Memoirs*, p. 169. Napier was a supporter of Madden's work, even though as a youth of 12 in 1798 he and his brothers had been armed to defend the family house in Castleton, county Kildare, from insurgents; H. A. Bruce, *Life of General Sir William Napier*, vol. 1 (London: John Murray, 1864), pp. 6–7.

[427] Madden attempted to convince liberal readers of the value of his work by placing a promotional advertisement in the *Northern Whig*, which first appeared on 29 March 1842, p. 3 (repeated on 5, 19, and 26 of April and 3 and 12 July 1842). For the review see *Northern Whig*, 9 July 1842, p. 4.

[428] Nation 22 October 1842, p. 24 (for examples of praise for subsequent volumes see *Nation*, 18 July 1846, p. 634 and 16 April 1859, p. 523); James McCormick, ed., *The 'Irish Rebellion of 1798', with Numerous Historical Sketches, Never before Published*, 2nd edn (Dublin: James McCormick, 1844), pp. 11–18 (originally published in the *Weekly Chronicle*, 2 March 1844). For the publication of *The United Irishmen* and contemporary reviews see León Ó Broin, *An Maidíneach: Staraí na nÉireannach Aontaithe* (Dublin: Sáirséal agus Dill, 1971), 152–95 and 319–42; Leon Ó Brion, 'R. R. Madden, Historian of the United Irishmen', *Irish University Review*, 2, no. 1 (1972): pp. 20–33.

a call for armed insurrection, he declared in the preface of a volume published in 1846 his absolute belief 'in the abstinence from physical force proceedings, and the employment only of moral means'. This statement was originally intended as a rejection of Young Ireland's preparations for a rebellion and was republished in a later volume as a rebuke of Fenianism.[429] Madden's liberal-nationalist world view shaped the way he presented the memory of 1798. In a reversal of loyalist historiography, the United Irishmen were presented as reformist ideologues, their faults were airbrushed and their revolutionary republicanism was downplayed. The less savoury aspects of the 1798 rebellion, namely the sectarian excesses, were purposely hidden. For all the rhetoric of rescue from oblivion, Madden's self-censorship balanced counter-memory with counter-forgetting.

Mary Ann McCracken expressed her fear that the publication of Madden's books 'will be a losing concern', as 'the politics of half a century back is little thought of.' Her friend John McAdam doubted if the sales would even cover the costs in light of the 'sad falling off among our present population of all feeling of patriotism, and love of country'.[430] These gloomy thoughts, which say little about actual interest among readers, reflect the apprehensions of the generation that had personal recollections of the rebellion and were riddled with concerns that the stories they had long kept to themselves would not be appreciated. Although Madden incurred financial losses, *The United Irishmen* went on to become a classic of Irish nationalist literature. All available copies were soon bought out and unauthorized editions were printed abroad to meet an unstoppable demand. At the same time, the unbridled enthusiasm shown by nationalists for Madden's writings made them unappealing to potentially interested readers among Ulster's unionists.

Apart from blanket denunciations from conservatives, more specific criticism was also voiced by liberal unionists. The *Northern Whig* maintained that 'Madden's forte consists more in industry as a collector, than skill as an author.'[431] In retrospect, it was felt that the scope of his recovery of memory was insufficient:

> If the unwritten annals of the Irish insurrection had been carefully collected from the mouths of credible witnesses the most graphic episodes of those events would have been rescued from utter oblivion. A few of these have been chronicled, but how much have been lost. Madden's history abounds in valuable reminiscences, yet even his work fails to give full particulars of many interesting occurrences connected with the part taken by Ulster in the wild conflict.[432]

Madden concentrated his efforts on the leadership of the United Irishmen and was less concerned with the rank and file. Recollections of common Presbyterian rebels, which were mutedly preserved within unionist communities throughout Ulster, were mostly out of bounds to a southern Catholic nationalist.

Thomas MacKnight, the editor of the *Northern Whig*, insisted that he had 'never been able to find that the Presbyterians in the North of Ireland, and others who might

---

[429] Madden, *The United Irishmen*, 3rd ser., vol. 1 (1846), p. 10; Madden, *The United Irishmen*, 2nd edn, 1st ser., vol. 1 (1857), p. 211.

[430] M. A. McCracken to R. R. Madden, 27 October 1853; John McAdam to M. A. McCracken, 29 December 1853; Madden Papers, TCD 873/72 and 160 (respectively).

[431] *Northern Whig*, 5 November 1846, p. 4.　　[432] *Northern Whig*, 8 October 1867, p. 4.

be considered United Irishmen or sympathizers with them entertained what are now called Irish national views.' He observed that 'the Protestant Liberals of Ulster, whose fathers and grandfathers were United Irishmen, had generally become warm supporters of the Liberal party' and, even though they opposed Catholic nationalism, they were still 'rather proud than otherwise of their ancestors for having been rebels'. From his experience, the painful events of 1798:

> were vividly present to the descendants of those who had suffered in that dreadful insurrection, or rather series of insurrections. The wounds, though healed, left scars still visible. The scenes of the battles, as at Ballynahinch, and of the executions, as of McCracken in Belfast, were still pointed out.

For many people in Ulster, 'personal and detailed associations with the terrible events of '98' were 'a vivid reality, and not merely a tale that had been so often told by poets, historians, romance writers, and Irish rhetoricians'.[433] It would take a liberal Presbyterian unionist to be able to tap into these recollections. Another northern liberal journalist, James McKnight, editor of the *Londonderry Standard* (and former editor of the *Banner of Ulster*), dismissed Madden's work as 'meagre and imperfect' and advised the historian of Belfast George Benn to turn instead to a local historian—Classon Porter of Larne, who 'possesses large stores of historic information relative to the 17th and 18th centuries and he is no churl about the communication of any knowledge he possesses.'[434]

Rev. Classon Emmett Porter, the non-subscribing minister of the Old Presbyterian Congregation of Larne and Kilwaughter in county Antrim from 1834 to 1875, had previously acquired some of the manuscripts of Samuel McSkimin, ahead of Mary Ann McCracken and her friends.[435] These contained many oral traditions about the rebellion that had not been included in McSkimin's published history. However, as a liberal clergyman, he was obliged, to pursue his interest in 1798 with care. The struggle over memory of the rebellion had remained a divisive issue within the Presbyterian Church and Porter had to take heed of a history of several decades of tense ambivalence. His approach to collecting traditions about the United Irishmen can best be understood on the background of attempts over several decades to silence and obscure recollections of the participation of Presbyterians in the insurrection.

In 1799, the Synod of Ulster announced with satisfaction that a 'solemn enquiry', conducted internally among the presbyteries, had found that:

> the general conduct of its Members and Probationers has been conformable to order and good government, in the late afflicting circumstances of the country. It appears, that of the comparatively small number who have been implicated in treasonable or seditious practices, two only, one a Minister, the other a Probationer, have been executed; two are still in confinement, some have expressed their sincere contrition; others are no longer connected with the Synod, and the remainder have, either voluntarily or by permission of Government, removed from the kingdom.[436]

---

[433] MacKnight, *Ulster as It Is*, vol. 1, pp. 18–24.

[434] James McKnight, Newry, to George Benn, Ballymena, 12 September 1874, Benn Papers, PRONI D3113/7/100.

[435] M. A. McCracken, Belfast, to R. R. Madden, 2 July 1844, Madden Papers, TCD 873/155.

[436] *Records of the General Synod of Ulster*, vol. 3, p. 221.

This was a palpable attempt to downplay the extent of the involvement of Presbyterian clergymen in the rebellion and to disown those that had been implicated. It was hoped that 'this afflicting subject would be permitted to rest, and to sink gradually into oblivion' and for the next few years, according to Rev. Robert Black of Derry, who assumed a dominant role in the Synod, 'all allusion to the events of 1798 was wisely and liberally avoided.'[437]

The policy of disavowal was pursued pitilessly. The widow of the executed minister Rev. James Porter was at first denied on a technicality pension payments from the church widows' fund.[438] When the probationer David Bailie Warden, who was implicated in the rebellion and obliged to go into exile in America, applied for a certificate to confirm that he had been licensed to preach, he was notified that the Presbytery of Bangor, for 'motives of prudence, unanimously refused to grant it'. Infuriated by this response, which harmed his prospects of finding employment abroad, Warden wrote a scathing pamphlet in which he reminded the members of the Presbytery that prior to the rebellion 'every one of you has both publickly [sic] and privately circulated republican morality' and claimed that in repudiating their own radical past they were effectively acting as an 'ecclesiastical Court Martial'.[439]

In order to ensure 'efficient protection and support given on the part of Government to those who have committed themselves in support of the State against a democratic party in the Synod, several of whom, if not engaged in the Rebellion, were deeply infected with its principles', Castlereagh arranged for substantial increases in the *Regium Donum*—the annual grant paid by the state to the clergy. Entitlement for funding required each minister to provide 'satisfactory testimonials' from his congregation 'of his being a loyal subject'. The subvention was administered by Rev. Black, whose staunch loyalism was rewarded by his appointment as a regulator on behalf of the government. Three tiers of stipend were offered and eligibility was supposed to be determined solely on the basis of the size of the congregation, though suspicions soon arose that personal considerations were also applied.[440] The extent of government intervention caused considerable controversy within the Synod. One of the outspoken critics of the new arrangement was Rev. Henry Henry, the minister of Connor in country Antrim, who had been imprisoned for his support of the United Irishmen and was admonished by Black.[441] These contentions undermined the aspiration of the loyalist Presbyterian leadership that the 'events which unfortunately took place in our bounds, in the fatal year of 1798' would be 'permitted to rest in forgetfulness'.[442]

The use of the *Regium Donum* for recrimination became apparent in 1803, when, the Presbyterian congregation of Second Keady in county Armagh was denied its share

[437] Robert Black, *Substance of Two Speeches, Delivered in the General Synod of Ulster at Its Annual Meeting in 1812* (Dublin: printed by Stewart & Hopes, 1812), pp. 3–5.

[438] William Steel Dickson, *A Narrative of the Confinement and Exile of William Steel Dickson, D. D., Formerly Minister of the Presbyterian Congregations of Ballyhalbert and Portaferry, in the County of Down, and Now of Keady, in the County of Armagh* (Dublin: printed for the author, by J. Stockdale, 1812), p. 269; Black, *Substance of Two Speeches*, pp. 44–9.

[439] Warden, *Farewell Address to the Junto of the Presbytery of Bangor*; Latimer, 'David Bailie Warden'.

[440] Lord Castlereagh to prime minister Henry Addington, 21 July 1802 and Alexander Knox to Lord Castlereagh, 15 July 1803; Vane, *Correspondence of Castlereagh*, vol. 4, pp. 224–6 and 284–9 (respectively). See also Brooke, *Ulster Presbyterianism*, pp. 133–5; McBride, *Scripture Politics*, p. 218.

[441] Witherow, *Historical and Literary Memorials*, p. 288.

[442] Black, *Substance of Two Speeches*, p. 15.

on a technicality following the appointment of the radical minister Rev. William Steel Dickson, who was then obliged to live in discomfort.[443] Dickson had previously been a minister at Ballyhalbert and afterwards at Portaferry (both in county Down), where he had consistently advocated political reform. In 1776, he criticized the British government's conduct during the American Revolution, in 1778 he joined the Volunteers and in 1792 he came out in support of the French Revolution. In three influential sermons on 'Scripture Politics', published in 1793, he adapted Christian millenarianism to political radicalism. These texts, in conjunction with political sermons delivered by Rev. Samuel Barber and Rev. Thomas Ledlie Birch, made republicanism more appealing to many Presbyterians.[444]

Dickson was arrested at Ballynahinch on 5 June 1798, just prior to the outbreak of the rebellion, and imprisoned initially in Belfast and afterwards at Fort George in the Scottish Highlands, where he was held until January 1802. The government received information that the 'rascally parson of Portaferry' had 'some days been sowing sedition' and an investigative committee of the House of Lords heard testimony that Dickson had been appointed adjutant-general of the United Irish forces of county Down. However, the reluctance of a key informer—Nicholas Mageean of Saintfield—to testify in court meant that no charges were brought against him. The release of a prominent figure that had been so closely associated with the United Irishmen inconvenienced the Presbyterian leadership, which was intent on distancing the Synod from the rebellion.[445]

From 1805, Dickson began contesting the sanctions that he believed the Synod had placed against him and demanded that his name be cleared of any insinuations of treason in 1798. His exertions to achieve full rehabilitation were frowned upon. A request for Synodical documents to back up his claims was denied by the clerk, Rev. Thomas Cuming (who happened to be Black's brother-in-law).[446] Dickson was violently assaulted on 9 September 1811, when returning from a reform meeting in support of Catholic emancipation in Armagh, and was afterwards subjected to harassment from loyalists in what could be seen as an effort to silence him.[447] He remained determined to speak out and the following year published *A Narrative of the Confinement and Exile of William Steel Dickson* in which he unapologetically revealed that he had taken the United Irish test in December 1791. Even though he categorically refuted specific allegations made against him by informers, he did not explicitly deny having had any connection with the United Irish movement during the preparations for the rebellion, so that the extent of his involvement remained vague.

---

[443] W. T. Latimer, 'The Rev. Dr. Wm. S. Dickson at Keady', *UJA*, 2nd ser., 17, nos. 1/4 (1911): pp. 95–6.

[444] Dickson, *Narrative of the Confinement and Exile*, pp. 8–29; 'Scripture Politics' and other key sermons are reproduced in the appendix. For a modern edition see Brendan Clifford, *Scripture Politics: Selections from the Writings of William Steel Dickson, the Most Influential United Irishman of the North* (Belfast: Athol Books, 1991). See also McBride, *Scripture Politics*, pp. 197–200.

[445] George Stephenson, Hillsborough, to Lord Downshire, 6 June 1798, Downshire Papers, PRONI D607/F/200; 'Examination of John Hughes' (3 August 1798) in *Report from the Committee of Secrecy, of the House of Lords of Ireland* (London: John Stockdale, 1798), p. 31. For Mageean's refusal to act as witness see Bartlett, *Revolutionary Dublin*, p. 57. For Dickson's response see Dickson, *Narrative of the Confinement and Exile*, pp. 62–75 and 190–238.

[446] *Records of the General Synod*, pp. 302 and 373.

[447] Dickson, *Narrative of the Confinement and Exile*, 317–52.

Dickson recalled visiting the members of his congregation that were incarcerated in Downpatrick in 1796–7, as well as several others from Belfast, who were sent to Kilmainham Gaol in Dublin. He looked back at 'July 1798—the awful month of terror, rage and blood' as a time when northerners were imprisoned on ships outside Belfast in harsh conditions, without 'proceedings of any kind instituted against them'. At the heart of his memoir, was the accusation that the Synod's denunciation in 1799 of ministers implicated in 'treasonable and seditious practices' was a 'groundless and malicious calumny' that had been used by supporters of the government as pretence to withhold payments due to him.[448] A review in the *Belfast Monthly Magazine* found that 'the reading of this interesting narrative by recalling the scenes of 1798, and the two preceding years, furnishes many subjects for serious reflection.'[449]

Dickson's *Narrative* caused a furore at the Synod's meeting in July 1812, where it was decided to issue a clarification that the minutes from 1799 referred to individuals who at the time were 'under suspicion' and did not determine that they were actually guilty of wrongdoing. Despite this concession, Dickson was denounced by Black and called upon to 'publicly retract his misstatements and misrepresentations' or face suspension. Instead, Dickson defiantly re-issued another edition of the *Narrative*, supplemented by additional commentary on the present debate, and published *Retractations*, which reiterated his accusations. In its following meeting in 1813, the Synod reaffirmed its 'attachment to the principles of the British constitution' and this renewed declaration of loyalty was supposed to put the debate to rest.[450] The memory of 1798, however, had been shown to be a divisive issue that could not be simply dismissed. Black's rebuff of Dickson's *Narrative* was challenged by a writer in the *Belfast Monthly Magazine*, who argued that 'the cant of permitting the events of 1797, 1798, and the few succeeding years "to sink into oblivion," is common, but the wish is vain.'[451]

Dickson's insistence on speaking out did not play in his favour. If prior to 1798, he was 'a courted and honoured guest in the most splendid mansions of Belfast', after he resigned his ministry in 1815 he was left impoverished. For his remaining years, Dickson resided in Belfast, where he was sustained by a weekly allowance raised by old friends, who were mostly former United Irishmen (among them William Drennan, William Tennent, and Francis McCracken), in yet another example of a veteran support network. Despite his illustrious past, Dickson's funeral in 1824 at Belfast's Clifton Street cemetery was attended by only a handful of acquaintances and he was buried in an unmarked pauper's grave. Thanks to his publications, his involvement with the United Irishmen could not be covered up and an obituary in the *Northern Whig* briefly mentioned his ordeal 'in Erin's evil day, at the period of the insurrection of 1798'.[452]

---

[448] Ibid., *passim*.   [449] *Belfast Monthly Magazine*, 8, no. 46 (1812): p. 397.

[450] Black, *Substance of Two Speeches*; Dickson, *Narrative of the Confinement and Exile*, 2nd edn (Dublin: J. Stockdale, 1812); William Steel Dickson, *Retractations* (Belfast: Joseph Smyth, 1813); *Belfast Monthly Magazine*, 9, no. 49 (1812): pp. 158–62; vol. 10, no. 58 (1813): pp. 433–4; vol. 11, no. 60 (1813): pp. 55–60.

[451] *Belfast Monthly Magazine*, 9, no. 52 (1812): p. 404. The commentaries and reviews of the debate on Dickson were signed 'K', which was a pseudonym used by John Hancock of Belfast.

[452] Montgomery, 'Outlines of the History of Presbyterianism', pp. 333–4; *Northern Whig*, 30 December 1824 (reproduced in Clifford, *Scripture Politics*, pp. 145–6). For an overview of his life see W. D. Bailie, 'William Steel Dickson', in *Protestant, Catholic and Dissenter: The Clergy and 1798*, edited by Liam Swords (Blackrock: Columba Press, 1997), pp. 45–80.

Memory of 1798 became inadvertently embroiled in the Presbyterian theological debates that divided the Synod in the 1820s, when Rev. Henry Cooke lead a campaign in the name of Trinitarian orthodoxy against what was labelled heterodox Arianism. Evangelicalism had revived Presbyterianism along Calvinist lines and when Cooke moved in 1818 from a ministry in Donegore, county Antrim, to Killyleagh, county Down, he came under the influence of Captain Sidney Hamilton Rowan (the son of the United Irishman Archibald Hamilton Rowan), who was an ardent evangelical. Cooke was determined to remove from the Synod the minority of ministers who did not subscribe to the Westminster Confession and mostly held Unitarian beliefs. Cooke's main opponent was Rev. Henry Montgomery, the minister of Dunmurry in county Antrim, who was elected moderator of the Synod in 1818. Under the dominant influence of Cooke, the Synod introduced in 1828 a theological examination to test the orthodoxy of ordinands. When a remonstrance protesting this decision was rejected, Montgomery lead a withdrawal of seventeen ministers and their congregations, who set up in 1830 the Remonstrant Synod of Ulster, which united in 1835 with the Non-Subscribing Presbytery of Antrim and the Synod of Munster.[453]

This religious conflict had a political subtext, which entailed historical revision. Cooke was a conservative and, in taking a firm stand against liberalism, aligned himself with Orangeism (although he never actually joined the Orange Order).[454] The New Light beliefs of the Non-Subscribing ministers, which Cooke wished to purge, were seen as associated with the United Irishmen, while orthodox Old Light Presbyterians were regarded as steadfastly loyalist. This misleading dichotomy was endorsed in the seminal history of Irish Presbyterianism started by James Seaton Read (who succeeded Cooke to the ministry of Donegore) and completed in 1853 by William Dool Killen. The ecclesiastical historians argued that 'many of the Presbyterians were, no doubt, implicated in the [United Irish] movement, but they were acting in opposition to the authority of the Church to which they belonged.'[455] In reality, the Presbyterian clergymen who supported the United Irishmen were both New Light (such as Samuel Barber, James Porter, and William Steel Dickson) and Old Light (such as Ledlie Birch). A thorough examination of a list prepared by Musgrave of sixty-three ministers and probationers suspected of being United Irishmen at the time of the rebellion identified twenty-two as New Light, twenty-two as Old Light, and noted that 'the remainder cannot be classified, though it seems likely that the majority were orthodox'. Similarly, lay Presbyterians in the rebel ranks were both New Light Non-Subscribers, as well as Old Light Covenanters (such as James Hope). Moreover, among the opponents of the rebellion there were several prominent New Light ministers (such as William Bruce and Robert Black). It was clearly impossible to distinguish between Presbyterian rebels and loyalists on the sole basis of theological beliefs.[456]

Both Cooke and Montgomery were born in 1788 and their childhood experiences during the rebellion had left them with formative recollections, which would influence

---

[453] P. E. C. Brooke, 'Controversies in Ulster Presbyterianism 1790–1836' (PhD: Faculty of Divinity, University of Cambridge, 1981), ch. 5.

[454] Finlay Holmes, *Presbyterians and Orangeism 1795–1995* (Belfast: Presbyterian Historical Society of Ireland, 1996), pp. 4–5.

[455] Reid and Killen, *History of the Presbyterian Church*, vol. 3, pp. 415–31 (quotation on p. 416).

[456] McBride, *Scripture Politics*, pp. 203, 232–6, and 296.

their politics in very different ways.[457] Cooke was left with a bitter aversion to the rebellion. He was raised in Maghera, where the minister was the radical Rev. John Glendy, who joined the United Irishmen. After the rebellion, Glendy's house was burnt by troops and Colonel James Leith, commander of the Aberdeenshire Fencibles, allowed him to emigrate to America (where he became minister to the Second Presbyterian Church in Baltimore and was appointed chaplain to the US congress).[458] During the rebellion, the Tipperary militia was quartered in the Presbyterian meeting house and the soldiers were said to have 'burned everything in it except the Bible'.[459] Cooke's family were loyalists and lived in fear of rebel reprisals. They were obliged to take refuge in open fields, sheltering in barns, cowsheds, and caves, and he recalled that 'during the summer of '98 I never slept in my father's house.' He saw houses set on flame by soldiers, among them the house of Walter (Watty) Graham, who would be remembered as a local United Irish hero. Looking back at this time, he later wrote:

> It was then and thus I learned my political principles. I was taught in a hard school—the school of care and suffering. Unceasing watchfulness made me prematurely old. In early boyhood I was taught to think and act as a man. My personal safety required it. Impressions were then left on my mind which I have never forgotten, and which I never wish to forget.[460]

The inability to forget 1798 became a driving force behind Cooke's conservatism and his struggle against the liberals, whom he held responsible for the harmful rebellion.

In reaction to Cooke's 'historical misrepresentation of those Irish Presbyterians who were mixed up in the events of 1798', a number of prominent Presbyterian writers tried to obscure the memory of Presbyterian involvement in the United Irishmen and argued that the rebellion had been instigated primarily by Anglicans.[461] Rev. Alexander Porter Goudy, the minister of Strabane's First Presbyterian Church, was the grandson of the executed United Irishman Rev. James Porter and was therefore well aware of the dominant Presbyterian presence in 1798; yet, in an essay on 'Irish Presbyterian Politics' published in 1852, he claimed that 'Episcopalian brethren were far more directly and extensively implicated.'[462] In a lecture on 'Our Covenanting Forefathers' delivered in 1857, Rev. John Rogers, the minister of Comber, stated that only towards the end of the insurrection a small number of Presbyterians 'were mixed up in it' and that they

---

[457] Andrew Boyd, *Montgomery and the Black Man: Religion and Politics in Nineteenth-Century Ulster* (Blackrock, Co. Dublin: Columba, 2006), pp. 9–10.

[458] *Records of the General Synod of Ulster*, vol. 3, p. 205; Thomas Holmes Walker, *One Hundred Years of History, 1802–1902, Second Presbyterian Church, Baltimore, Maryland* (Baltimore, Md.: Sun Printing Office, 1902), pp. 43–9 [republished in *UJA*, 2nd ser., 13, no. 3 (1907): pp. 101–5].

[459] Witherow, *Historical and Literary Memorials*, p. 314.

[460] Josias Leslie Porter, *The Life and Times of Henry Cooke* (London: John Murray, 1871), p. 14. See also the account of Maghera in 1798 given by the Presbyterian historian Thomas Witherow in a tribute to the centenary of Cooke's birth in *BNL*, 12 May 1888, p. 6 [reproduced Eull Dunlop, *Henry Cooke's Centenary* (Draperstown, Co. Londonderry and Ballymena, Co. Antrim: Moyola Books and Braid Books, 1993), pp. 17–19].

[461] See letter to the editor by 'a Presbyterian elector of Down', who took offence that 'a Minister of the Presbyterian Church [Cooke] has dared to insinuate that Presbyterian Ministers and Presbyterian people alone were implicated in the unfortunate struggle of 1798', in *Northern Whig*, 29 July 1852, p. 1.

[462] A. P. Goudy, *Right versus Might; or, Irish Presbyterian Politics Discussed in Five Letters* (Londonderry: Londonderry Standard, 1852), p. 21.

'were seduced chiefly by those in communion with the Church of England'.[463] W. D. Killen's continuation of J. S. Read's *History of the Presbyterian Church* also claimed that 'the majority of the leading conspirators were nominally connected with the Established Church.'[464] This historical revision was unacceptable to Montgomery, who found that it contradicted his own memory of 1798.

In contrast to Cooke's loyalist background, Montgomery's family at Boltnaconnell House, in the parish of Killead (9 km south-east of Antrim town), had radical sympathies. As a child in 1798, he viewed from the vantage point of a nearby hill the Battle of Antrim, in which his two elder brothers—John and William—participated as rebels. The brothers went into hiding but were both captured and eventually released. In a punitive raid, yeomen looted the Montgomery residence and burnt it down, leaving the family homeless and destitute.[465] A half-century later, he rejected the efforts to erase traces of Presbyterian involvement in the United Irishmen and firmly professed 'the truth ought not to be concealed: the Rebellion, at the close of the last century was, in its origin and almost to its end, an Ulster rebellion and a Presbyterian rebellion. I remember it very well.' Although he conceded that the Presbyterian rebels 'undoubtedly erred in judgment', he affirmed a sincere belief that 'they were truly honest and patriotic—merely seeking to attain a right end by wrong means.' In face of the conservative repudiation of former associations with republicanism, Montgomery declared:

> I am not, therefore, ashamed to acknowledge that some of my own 'kith and kin' fought in the ranks of their country: and I am proud to say that, during the last forty years, I have found my best, my clearest-headed, and my warmest hearted friends, amongst the United Irishmen of 1798.[466]

The social networks of liberal Presbyterians allowed them to continue to hold on to their memory of the rebellion even when it was being disavowed in public. Yet, the conservative interpretation of the rebellion would be the one officially endorsed by mainstream publications such as the *Belfast News-Letter*, which rejected Montgomery's claims of 'a Presbyterian rebellion' and pointed out that Cooke 'has given us, a different version of the history of the period, and of the part which the Presbyterian Church played in 1798.'[467]

After Daniel O'Connell refused a challenge to publicly debate Cooke during his visit to Belfast in 1841, Cooke was celebrated as 'the "Cock of the North," the "Cook who dished Dan," and the champion of Unionists'.[468] O'Connell made overtures to liberal Presbyterians, referring to the experience of 1798 in Ulster in order to ask for their support for the repeal of the Act of Union. Cooke in turn evoked the sectarian atrocities committed against Protestants in Wexford, which had become engrained in loyalist

---

[463] *Northern Whig*, 3 February 1857, p. 1; see also A. R. Holmes, 'Covenanter Politics: Evangelicalism, Political Liberalism and Ulster Presbyterians, 1798–1914', *English Historical Review*, 125, no. 513 (2010): pp. 358–9.

[464] Reid and Killen, *History of the Presbyterian Church*, vol. 3, p. 416.

[465] Crozier, *The Life of the Rev. Henry Montgomery*, pp. 11–14.

[466] Montgomery, 'Outlines of the History of Presbyterianism', pp. 330–5.

[467] *BNL*, 27 February 1875, p. 3.

[468] W. T. Latimer, *A History of the Irish Presbyterians* (Belfast: James Cleeland and Edinburgh: R. W. Hunter, 1893), p. 211. See also Finlay Holmes, *Henry Cooke* (Belfast: Christian Journals, 1981), pp. 150–86.

memory, and asked 'why will you not permit us to forget?'[469] Although Cooke
succeeded in expelling Non-Subscribers from the General Synod, he was less successful
in enforcing his conservative politics. The liberal Presbyterians who opposed his hard-
line conservatism remained moderate unionists. They favoured Catholic emancipation
and were even willing to cooperate with O'Connellites in struggles for tenant
rights, but were apprehensive of the aggressive mass politics displayed in Catholic
nationalist campaigns and stopped short of supporting Repeal. Liberal unionists were
typically reluctant to accept loyalist determination to forget Protestant participation
in the rebellion.[470]

Classon Porter had grown up on the background of these struggles within Ulster
Presbyterianism. His father, Rev. William Porter, minister of Newtownlimavaddy in
county Derry, was a probationer in 1798 and did not take part in the rebellion, yet he
remained a liberal. In 1813, William Porter supported William Steel Dickson in the
Synod debates over his *Narrative*. In the split of 1830, he resigned his position as clerk
of the General Synod and followed Montgomery, joining the Remonstrant Synod, of
which he was elected the first moderator. Classon Porter's half-brother, Rev. John Scott
Porter was the minister of Rosemary Street Non-Subscribing Presbyterian church and
assisted Madden in his inquiries on memories of the United Irishmen, but prudently
stipulated that his name should not be mentioned.[471]

Classon Porter was an enthusiastic amateur historian and published many articles in
local newspapers, such as the *Larne Reporter*, and church newspapers, such as the
Unitarian Christian. His research on Ulster Presbyterianism resulted in written memoirs of the nearby congregation of Ballycarry, as well as the memoirs of his own
congregation of Larne and Kilwaughter, and biographical sketches of prominent
Presbyterian ministers. Porter had no intention of stirring up political controversy in
his historical writing. He self-deprecatingly referred to his antiquarian pursuits by
styling himself, with a nod to Walter Scott and Thomas Carlyle, 'Dryasdust'.[472] That
said, he did not shy away from mentioning connections with the United Irishmen.
His pen-portraits of Rev. William Steel Dickson and Rev. James Porter show marked
sympathy for their subject, and he also mentioned that Rev. William Dunlop of
Strabane was involved with the United Irishmen, but Porter was careful not to condone
the rebellion. At the same time, he faulted Rev. Robert Black for his excessive loyalty
that 'led him in those stirring times to say and to do things which cannot be now
commended'.[473]

---

[469] From Cooke's speech at a demonstration in Belfast on 21 January 1841; reproduced in
McComb, *The Repealer Repulsed*, p. 103. For an example of O'Connell's rhetorical use of the 1798
rebellion in Ulster see *Northern Whig*, 13 May 1843, p. 2. In private conversation, O'Connell was less
appreciative and told an Irish-American from Ulster that 'the Presbyterians fought badly at Ballinahinch'; William Joseph O'Neill Daunt, *Personal Recollections of the Late Daniel O'Connell, M.P.*, vol. 2
(London: Chapman & Hall, 1848), p. 7.
[470] Hall, *Ulster Liberalism*, pp. 144–5; Wright, *Two Lands on One Soil*, pp. 50–1.
[471] Rev. John Scot Porter, Belfast, to R. R. Madden, 19 and 20 April 1842, Madden Papers, TCD
873/52–3.
[472] Classon Porter, *Congregational Memoirs: Old Presbyterian Congregation of Larne and Kilwaughter*
(Larne: n.p., 1929), p. 86
[473] Classon Porter, *Irish Presbyterian Biographical Sketches*, pp. 6 (Black), 10–15 (Dickson), 16–19
(Porter) and 20–21 (Dunlop). Elsewhere, the loyalism of Rev. William Bruce was portrayed in a more
positive light; see Porter, *The Seven Bruces*, p. 45.

When writing about matters closer to home, Porter was far more careful. A biographical entry for one of his predecessors at Larne—Rev. James Worrall, who had joined the United Irishmen and had consequently spent time in Carrickfergus Gaol—made it clear that 'Mr. Worrall's conduct in '98 seriously and permanently injured his Congregation.' As 'a recognized leader of the insurgents in this neighbourhood', Worrall stood accused of having been 'cognizant of measures contemplated, if not perpetrated, against hearers of his own, which should never have been connived at, or silently observed, by a minister of the Gospel of peace.' The ramifications of his association with the rebels were spelt out so that there would be no doubts about the damage done to the congregation: 'he drove away from it, at this time, and for ever, some of the most intelligent and influential families, who had for generations been connected with it, but who, being irreconcilably displeased by the political conduct of their minister on this occasion, left our meeting-house never to return.' Porter evidently felt the need to make it clear to his congregation that in writing about United Irishmen he was not taking their side.[474]

It has been noted that Porter, who was a liberal, 'had decided views on national politics, but generally held his tongue, though he spoke up when he had to'.[475] One such instance was in May 1848, when he addressed a public meeting in Larne about the dangers of a Young Ireland insurrection. Encouraging his audience to take a stand against the attempted rebellion, he recognized that 'many of the people in Ulster having been engaged, in their early days, in the great rebellion of '98, knew the evils of civil warfare so well.' As a historian, Porter suggested that 'if they only read Dr. Madden's book, they would see that the whole scheme of the United Irishmen was full of rottenness, and that there was treachery at its very heart.'[476]

This public persona shows little of Classon Porter's personal fascination with local memories of 1798. Not only did he acquire the manuscripts that contained early oral traditions of the rebellion collected by McSkimin, but from at least as early as the 1840s he also began collecting first hand stories and anecdotes from elderly people who still recalled the events. At first, this pursuit may have been incidental to his historical research. When meeting in November 1841 with the minister of the neighbouring congregation of Cairncastle, Rev. Thomas Alexander, Porter took notes of his experience in 1798, when Alexander was briefly jailed at the Carrickfergus Market House for assisting a rebel to escape. On a visit in January 1845 to Ballindrait, county Donegal, to collect information on Rev. James Porter, he met with a cousin of the executed minister, 81-year-old Andrew Stilley, 'who had been deeply implicated in the affairs of '98' and willingly shared his recollections. The majority of oral testimonies that Porter collected on the rebellion were documented in the summer of 1863, when he gathered materials for a history of the neighbouring congregation of Ballycarry, and supplementary notes on 1798 were taken over the next five years. Even at this late date, Porter found several survivors in their eighties and nineties and met with relatives of rebels, who recounted numerous memories of the 'Turn-Out'.[477]

---

[474] Classon Porter, *Congregational Memoirs*, p. 75.

[475] R. H. McIlrath, 'Classon Porter: A Short Account of the Life and Work of a Nineteenth Century Non-Subscribing Minister in Larne', *Ulster Local Studies*, 15, no. 1 (1993): p. 19.

[476] 'Meeting at Larne', in *BNL*, 5 May 1848, p. 2.

[477] Classon Porter's notes, alongside materials collected by McSkimin, were later reproduced verbatim by the antiquarian Robert M. Young; see Young, *Ulster in '98*, pp. 18–65.

The term Turn-Out had been noted previously by McSkimin, who observed that it was 'commonly given by the Irish people to the rebellion of 1798; who happened to have a rooted aversion to calling it an insurrection or rebellion' and suggested that it implied an ambivalence, as 'the call used at the time, to those who appeared tardy to come forth to the ranks'.[478] McSkimin, however, did not take precise notes of his conversations in the countryside and his sources were not identified. The common name for the rebellion may have originated at the time of the events, when the act of joining the rebels was popularly designated 'to turn out'. Already then, it showed uncertainty. For example, a man named Beatty was heard to exclaim in the area of Saintfield in 1799 that 'he never would again turn out, unless an Invasion.'[479] Several early documented recollections refer to the Turn-Out. In a letter published in 1821 in the Belfast Whig newspaper *The Irishman*, 'An Old Inhabitant of the County Down' referred to the 'turn-out at Antrim'. Samuel Edgar recalled in 1825 that the rebels had sent recruitment parties around Ballynahinch calling on the people 'in the name of the nation, to turn out, and fight for their country's rights'.[480] Use of the term seems to have been distinct to the northern rebellion.[481] It appears in local references to the rebellion in Ulster and is not found in official reports, or in early written histories. It therefore functioned as a signifier of vernacular historiography. As such, it was completely missed by Madden and its notice in conversation is a credit to the care Classon Porter took to ensure that his interviews were 'taken down almost verbatim', with 'only a few alterations'.[482] In today's terms, he was doing oral history par excellence.

Porter's most remarkable informant was James Burns, who was born in 1772 and styled himself 'the old croppy'. He was 91 years old when he was first invited to Porter's house in Larne on 24 June 1863. This meeting was followed with another interview three days later and a final meeting in September that year. Porter discovered that Burns quite literally carried the scars of the rebellion on his body: 'he showed me the marks of a sabre cut on the back of his head, and of a bullet wound in one of his legs.' His life story proved to be remarkable.

Burns was a Presbyterian from Templepatrick, who had enlisted in the army at a young age and became a gunner in the Royal Irish Artillery, but deserted to join the Defenders, after which he took the United Irish oath. At the age of 26, he fought with the insurgents at the Battle of Antrim and, after the defeat, he only narrowly avoided falling into the hands of pursuing cavalrymen. He was among a small group of surviving rebels, alongside Henry Joy McCracken and James Hope, who took refuge on top of Slemish Mountain, near Ballymena. He then hid on Little Collin hill, near Drumwherry, county Antrim, and escaped for a short while to Scotland, but was arrested on his return. When in jail, he received modest financial support

---

[478] McSkimin, 'Secret History', p. 554n; McSkimin, *Annals of Ulster* (1849 edn), p. 112n.

[479] Letter from Belfast, 11 October 1799, State of the Country Papers, NAI SOC 3363/1 (possibly written by the informer James McGucken).

[480] *Irishman*, 12 October 1821, p. 2; *Belfast Magazine and Literary Journal*, 1, no. 4 (1825), pp. 541–2.

[481] A rare instance from elsewhere appears in a letter from pardoned rebels in Wexford, who wrote Major-General Hunter in August 1798 to declare their loyalty, stating: 'We the Macamore boys was in the turn out against the orrange-men' [sic]; Edward Hay, *History of the Insurrection of the County of Wexford, A.D. 1798* (Dublin: John Stockdale, 1803), appendix X, p. xxvi.

[482] Young, *Ulster in '98*, pp. 52 and 57.

from Mary Ann McCracken. Sentenced to transportation, Burns was sent to New Geneva, county Waterford, where he volunteered for the army in order to escape the harsh fate of a convict. He served in the 3rd Buffs till he was discharged in 1802, after the Peace of Amiens. On his release, he found that he could no longer live in his native area of Templepatrick, 'where all the people became Orangemen round about him'. Unable to settle down, Burns moved about and found employment as a gardener, weaver, pedlar, and ended his life as an itinerant mendicant. In old age, his memory remained sharp and he could recite to Porter numerous stories and songs about the Turn-Out. There were moments when Porter suspected that Burns subtly modified his recollections, as when he told of a comrade killing two soldiers, though his tone suggested that he was too ashamed to admit that he had killed one of them himself.[483]

Burns died at the Larne poor house a year after meeting Porter. He had arranged in advance for a headstone in Templecorran graveyard (just outside Ballycarry) to be inscribed with an enigmatic text:

> Chr3st wis th2 w4rd thlt splk2 3t,
> H2 t44k th2 Br21d lnd brlk2 3t,
> lnd whit thlt w4rd d3d mlk2 3t,
> Thlt 3 b2132v2 lnd tlk2 3t.[484]

This script was not, as Porter initially assumed, taken from Freemasonic ritual, but was a cypher known to agrarian secret societies. In 1839, a magistrate from county Down, working for a Select Committee of the House of Lords on the state of crime in Ireland, encountered communications of 'Ribandmen' [Ribbonmen] in Mullingar, county Westmeath, that had been similarly encrypted.[485] Once made legible, with the help of a key provided by Burns, the tombstone inscription read:

> Christ was the word that spake it,
> He took the Bread and brake it,
> And what that word did make it
> That we believe and take it.

To his regret, Porter failed to ascertain how and where Burns had learned these antiquated verses on the Eucharist, which originated in the early modern period and have been attributed to Queen Elizabeth I.[486] The choice of a veteran rebel to encrypt his epitaph demonstrates the tenacity of practices of social forgetting, which had long dictated that rebel graves remain uninscribed. Although sixty-five years had passed since 1798, the epitaph does not mention the rebellion, though it was the defining event in the life of the 'old croppy'.

When it came to formal memorialization, recollections of 1798 were left unspoken. Like his informants, Classon Porter was weary of sharing in public the traditions of the Turn-Out that he had recorded and refrained from publishing his collections. After

---

[483] Ibid., pp. 28–60.   [484] Ibid., pp. 36–8.

[485] Testimony of Hill Wilson Rowan, 4 May 1839 in *Report from the Select Committee of the House of Lords, Appointed to Enquire into the State of Ireland in Respect of Crime*, Part I (London: House of Commons, 1839), p. 179.

[486] *Notes and Queries*, 3rd ser., XI (16 February 1867): p. 140. For the attribution to Elizabeth see Leah S. Marcus, Janel M. Mueller, and Mary Beth Rose, eds, *Elizabeth I: Collected Works* (Chicago and London: University of Chicago Press, 2000), p. 47.

his death, Porter's papers were acquired by the Belfast antiquarian Robert Magill Young. The recollections of the rebellion that Porter took down from elderly survivors were only published towards the end of the nineteenth century in Young's book *Ulster in '98: Episodes and Anecdotes* (1893). By then, the generation that had lived through the events was no longer alive.

POSTMEMORY ANXIETIES

On 26 November 1798, Squire Edward Jones Agnew of Kilwaughter, up until recently a parliamentary representative for county Antrim, wrote down his recollections of the rebellious activities that he had witnessed in his area a few months earlier. On 7 June, he had helped broker an exchange between loyalists that were held hostage by rebels and a number of prisoners held by the Tay Fencibles. Thanks to the good relations he maintained with his tenants, Agnew was permitted the following morning to visit the rebel camp on Bellavie [Bellair] Hill near Glenarm (18 km north-west of Larne). There he saw the Presbyterian minister Rev. Robert Acheson, who had been among the exchanged prisoners, 'in full regimentals, green jacket faced with yellow, white breeches, black hose and silver buckled shoes' presiding over 2,000 men 'and there were many women on the field, some cooking an early meal on the camp fires and others moving around with jugs of fresh milk and oat cake for the citizen army.' Agnew recalled that he left the scene concerned with 'the fate that lay ahead of these worthy common people'. Subsequently, at his house and in the nearby house of his cousin, Henry Shaw of Ballygally, 'hunted rebels were given shelter and many afforded a safe passage to America.' Upon completing the memorandum, Agnew decided that 'this account I shall put away from the eyes of man for a generation, when no one can come to any harm thereby.' He died in 1834, without bringing out his memoir. Memory was quite literally locked away for the duration of a lifetime and was later neglected. Many others took their memories to the grave, without leaving a written account.[487]

Rev. Acheson, who had been spotted by Agnew in the rebel camp at Bellair, negotiated terms of surrender and survived the rebellion. Depositions collected in the area testified that he had fulfilled his side of the arrangement and encouraged the rebels under his command to deliver their arms. A letter of support from the commander of the Glenarm yeomanry, Captain George Stewart, confirmed that Acheson and the other leaders had been promised forgiveness 'without any reserve'. Nonetheless, he was dragged before a court martial in Belfast on 25 July 1798 and accused of having been a leader of the rebels in Glenarm. Over a three-day trial he successfully defended himself. After his acquittal, Acheson did not return to his post as assistant minister to his uncle, Rev. Thomas Reid, in Glenarm. The following year, he became minister of the Donegall Street Congregation in Belfast, where he remained till his death in 1824. As could be expected, in 1813 he was among the supporters in the Synod of Rev. Steel

---

[487] Edward Jones Agnew, 'What Happened in the Late Rebellion as I Saw It on the 7th and 8th June 1798', 26 November 1798; McClelland transcription reproduced in Dickson, *Revolt in the North*, pp. 223–4.

Dickson, during the controversy over the publication of his *Narrative*. Life in Belfast placed Acheson within networks of former United Irishman.[488]

Veteran United Irishmen residing in Belfast rallied to help old friends who found themselves in situations of financial need, as when they contributed to the welfare of Thomas Russell's niece in 1821 or sustained Steel Dickson from 1815 to 1821. They met in social gatherings at such favoured haunts as the house of Mary Ann McCracken on Rosemary Lane and later at her new home on Donegall Street. Their liberal views were expressed in articles for the *Belfast Monthly Magazine* (to which Acheson also contributed) and they were prominent in the management of the Belfast Academical Institution. The many facets of this milieu provided social frameworks, to use Maurice Halbwachs' term, for sustaining collective memory within the group. However, they also served as a framework for accommodating the dynamics of social forgetting. Intimate forums, which allowed for the sharing of recollections in private, obviated the need to come out in public. To all appearances, memories kept in silence were outwardly forgotten.

The directors of the Belfast Academical Institution discovered the danger of dropping their guard, even among themselves, in 1816, when the *Belfast Commercial Chronicle* revealed that disloyal toasts had been made at a Saint Patrick's Day dinner. Among many radical utterances proclaimed that night, the revellers had allowed themselves to lapse into nostalgia by toasting 'The memorable 14 July 1789', a salute that harped back to the United Irish commemorations in Belfast of the fall of the Bastille. Another toast paid homage to their former United Irish comrades that had left for America: 'The Exiles of Erin—may they find that protection under the wing of the republican eagle, which was denied them by the monarchical lion.' The scandal that ensued following the exposure of this incident was exploited by Castlereagh to push for government intervention in the management of the Institution. The Synod was threatened that the *regium donum* would be rescinded if it did not bow down to the demands. This pressure from above was resisted at the price of losing government funding for the Institution and the resignation of several members of its joint Board of Managers and Visitors. It was evidently unwise to speak out indiscreetly.[489]

Whereas Acheson could share his recollections with like-minded associates behind closed doors, and while Agnew chose to store away his memory of that same event, local tradition preserved a song that openly recalled the local insurrection in the Glens of Antrim:

> 'Twas in the days of '98
> In a place they call Glenarm
> On the 7th of June at Bellavie
> The United men were up in arms.[490]

Drawing on an expansive knowledge of Irish street songs, the modern-day Dublin folk singer Frank Harte aphorized that 'those in power write history, those who suffer write

---

[488] Depositions collected on 12 July 1798; Capt. George Stewart, Glenarm to Edward McNaghton, 18 June 1798; McCance Family Papers, PRONI D272/22 and 32 (respectively). The trial proceedings and outcome appear in *BNL*, 27 and 31 July 1798, p. 2. For Acheson's support of Dickson in 1813 see *Records of the General Synod*, p. 399.

[489] *Belfast Commercial Chronicle*, 20 March 1816, p. 2. See also McBride, *Scripture Politics*, 212–12; Wright, *The 'Natural Leaders'*, pp. 85–8.

[490] Felix McKillop, *Glenarm: A Local History* (Belfast: Ulster Journals, 1987), p. 31; "'98 Rebellion in Glenarm and Glencoy', *The Glynns*, 27 (1999): pp. 22–3 (unnamed author).

the songs.'[491] Singing was a powerful media for performing counter-memory. Yet, tracing the development of memory through folk songs is a tricky task. The historical record is fragmentary and authorship is generally unknown. Even when variations of texts were taken down, notes on performances are few and far between and the different audiences that partook or listened to the singing are rarely registered.

Madden had a particular interest in songs and poetry, which did not find a place in the many volumes of his magnum opus. Charles Patrick Meehan, a Catholic priest and historian associated with Young Ireland, was aware that Madden 'went on rescuing from oblivion street ballads' and edited these papers, which were originally intended as a supplementary volume to *The United Irishmen*, but were published posthumously as the *Literary Remains of the United Irishmen of 1798* (1887). Madden believed that the songs of 1798 no longer posed a threat and deserved recognition as cultural artefacts:

> I can see no good reason why the Jacobite relics of Scotch song should be in high repute with loyal men throughout the kingdom, and old songs of '98 and other Tyrtaean lyrics of the people called 'United Irishmen', should be held unworthy of the attention of literary curiosity. It is very possible to be gratified at hearing an old song, however political its tendencies, well sung, or to find it rescued from oblivion in a modern collection, without having one's spirit excited to the frenzy of a passion for rebellion by the poetry, which stimulated the souls of our fathers and grandfathers to acts of violence and desperation.

In compiling the songs, Madden drew on the propaganda publications of the United Irishmen, published poem collections and the personal papers of some of the leaders, as well as 'several written by persons in the lower ranks of life—with few claims to literary excellence'. He made sure that the selection had 'ceased to be of a mischievous tendency', purposely leaving out 'many cleverly written pieces of an irreligious tendency, and others bearing the stamp of French political philosophy of the Revolutionary period'. For Madden, songs were literary relics from the past and not living memory. The later compositions of William Drennan, James Orr, and James Hope were dated to the time of the events and not recognized as reflections that looked back at that time, and as such were actually expressions of remembrance in the early nineteenth century.[492]

It is apparent that songs recalling the rebellion were composed from an early stage, yet they could not be systematically collected till much later. Edward Bunting, the pioneering collector of Irish traditional music, was a close friend of the McCracken family and stayed at their house whenever he was in Belfast. Although ideally placed to take note of early ballads, he refrained from collecting songs or tunes associated with the recent rebellion and was careful not to acknowledge in his published work the support he had received from the McCrackens. When Madden asked him for information on a pamphlet from the time of the rebellion, Bunting evasively replied that he had no recollection of 'anything of the kind'.[493] The Belfast antiquarian Robert M. Young

---

[491] Accompanying notes to a CD of traditional songs of the rebellion of 1798 performed by Frank Harte and Donal Lunny; *1798: The First Year of Liberty* (Hummingbird, 1998).

[492] Madden, *Literary Remains of the United Irishmen*. Charles Patrick Meehan's comments appear in the publisher's introduction (pp. v–viii); Madden's comments appear in his editorial preface (pp. ix–xii). See also *Catalogue of the Valuable Library of the Late Dr. R. R. Madden*, pp. 23–4.

[493] Edward Bunting to R. Madden, 31 March 1843, Madden Papers, TCD 873/428. See also Robert M. Young, 'Edward Bunting's Irish Music and the McCracken Family', *UJA*, 2nd series, 4, no. 3 (1898): pp. 175–8.

published in 1893 songs that had been collected earlier by Samuel McSkimin and Classon Porter and maintained that they were 'of special value, as they have died out in oral tradition'.[494] This claim, which reflects the prevalent concern of folklorists that living tradition inevitably faces imminent death, is not altogether grounded. Songs that touched their listeners gained popularity and were repeated in different versions, so that they were more likely to survive.

McSkimin collected a song about Henry Munro and the Battle of Ballynahinch. It tells how, after the battle, Munro paid a woman to keep his hiding place secret but was betrayed and sent to his execution. The concluding verses exhort the audience to learn a lesson, with implications for silence and remembrance:

> Never trust your secrets wherever you go,
> And I hope you'll remember the fate of Munroe.[495]

Madden wrote down a different version of 'General Munroe', which ends with an appeal to memory that places the local hero among renowned national heroes:

> Remember the martyrs were slain by the foe
> Brave Emmet, Fitzgerald, and General Munroe.[496]

In this rendition, Munro's sister appears after the execution, dressed in green and brandishing a sword, to demand revenge, in what appears to be an embroidered version of an incident that was recalled in local tradition. Margaret Munro was known to be a radical and after her brother's execution fled the country, only to be imprisoned in Carrickfergus Gaol on her return. The local historian Hugh McCall recalled that 'not many days after his execution', she stood in front of her brother's severed head, which was displayed on the Lisburn Market House, and declared 'Ah, Harry, you will be revenged for all yet!'.[497]

Father Alexander MacMullan, the parish priest of Kirkinriola in Ballymena from 1889, had grown up in the townland of Seevaghan, county Down (7 km south-east of Ballynahinch), and recalled hearing Madden's version of the ballad sung in the streets of Ballynahinch 'in the earlier part of the century'.[498] The tune was sufficiently familiar in the 1840s to be designated by the Ulster-Scot poet Robert Huddleston, the 'bard of Moneyrea' (10 km south-east of Belfast), as the air for one of his compositions.[499]

From the middle of the nineteenth century, variations of the two versions of the ballad of General Munro appeared on broadsides that were printed in Dublin, Cork, London, and Glasgow, showing that the song had a wide circulation.[500] In some of the versions,

[494] Young, *Ulster in '98*, preface.   [495] Ibid., pp. 64–5.

[496] Madden, *Literary Remains of the United Irishmen*, pp. 237–9.

[497] Anon. [McCall], *Ireland and Her Staple Manufactures*, p. 133; account of Margaret Munro written by the yeoman Poynz Stewart (November 1804), reproduced in Dickson, *Revolt in the North*, p. 251; see also Madden, *The United Irishmen*, 3rd ser., vol. 1 (1846), p. 400.

[498] *SVV*, 2, no. 6 (June 1897), p. 102. Fr. MacMullan was born in 1827 in Seavaghan, in the parish of Loughinislan; *Ballymena Observer*, 15 October 1909, p. 7.

[499] Huddleston used the tune in order to associate with the rebellion his song 'Erin go Bragh', which does not explicitly mention 1798; Robert Huddleston, *A Collection of Poems and Songs on Different Subjects*, vol. 2 (Belfast: self-published, 1846), pp. 117–18.

[500] Fourteen copies are held in the Bodleian Library Broadside Collection: 2806 b.10(8) [additional copy: 2806 b.10 (9)]; 2806 c.13 (96); 2806 c.15(185) [additional copies: 2806 b.9(267); Harding B 19(9)]; 2806 c.14(70); Harding B 11 (1297); Harding B 11(1298) [another edition: Harding B 11 (3562)]; Harding B 40 (14); Johnson Ballads 614 [additional copy: Firth b.25(315)]; Firth b.26(204). Four copies can be found in the University of Cambridge, Madden Ballads: reel 5, frame 3801; reel 6, frame 3975; reel 12, frames 8339 and 8639. See also Zimmerman, *Songs of Irish Rebellion*, pp. 156–7.

Munro fights at Ballynahinch alongside another rebel leader named Clokey. As the United Irish colonel Joseph Clokey of Ballynahinch was arrested just prior to the rebellion, this may be a reference to one of the Clokey brothers from nearby Spa—either William, who at the battle was decked in a Volunteers uniform (complete with sash and epaulets) and was afterwards transported to Botany Bay, or his sibling Andrew, who was banished to America, from where he later returned and was known locally as 'the last of the rebels'.[501]

In most versions of the song, the story of Munro is told from the point of view of a young unknown rebel named George Campbell (and in other versions, the narrator merges with the reference to Clokey, or is assigned a similar name). In this way, the memory recalled in the song was just as much about the experience of common rebels as it was about their general. The ballad would persist into the twentieth century. In 1904, the folk song collector Herbert Hughes took down a version in London from his brother Frederick Cairns Hughes, who was a well-known Ulster folk singer and had 'heard it sung on the Falls Road, Belfast, quite recently'. Later in the century, the song was performed and recorded by traditional song revivalists.[502]

A number of 'common' rebels, on whom the official historical record is mostly silent, were revered as local heroes and, as acknowledged by the poet John Hewitt, subsequently 'became part of the folklore and balladry of the North'. One such example is Watty Graham [also known as Grimes], who was executed in Maghera on 15 June 1798. In a ballad collected by McSkimin, Grimes blames his misfortune on the leader of the insurgents in south Derry, William McKeiver, who had compelled him to join the rebels but at the moment of truth McKeiver and his associates 'like cowardly villains they took their heels'. Contrary to Young's conviction, the song did not pass away. It appears in a manuscript of 'Songs and Ballads in use in the Province of Ulster' collected in 1845 by John Hume of Kilwarlin, county Down, and annotated by his brother, the antiquarian Rev. Abraham Hume. By the mid-nineteenth century, a version of the song was sold as a broadsheet at the 'Poet's Box' in Belfast.[503] Former rebels could identify experiences that were reminiscent of their own recollections of 1798 in songs that honoured other individuals. James Burns recited to Porter a long ballad on William Murphy, who, like himself, had been an artillery gunner and deserted to join the rebels in the Turn-Out. The merciless flogging of 1,000 lashes inflicted on Murphy, who was then transported to the West Indies, offered Burns a salutary reminder of what might have been his own fate had he been less fortunate.[504]

Burns dictated to Porter two variations of a song titled 'McCracken's Ghost' or 'Henry's Ghost', in which the shade of the executed rebel leader appears at night-time

[501] For the court martial records of the Clokeys see Rebellion Papers, NAI 620/2/15/16 (William) and 620/3/28/19 (Andrew); *BNL*, 27 July 1798, p. 2; see also Bartlett, *Repressing the Rebellion*, pp. 202 and 209. Colin Johnston Robb collected in the mid-twentieth century local folklore on 'Clokey of the Spa'; *Mourne Observer*, 19 July 1968, p. 9. Another possibility is that the ballad refers to Joseph Clokey's son, who was allegedly executed for refusing to renege on his United Irish convictions; Birch, *Letter from an Irish Emigrant*, p. 18.

[502] *Journal of the Irish Folk Song Society*, 1, no. 1 (April 1904): p. 18. For more renditions see Chapter 6 below, pp. 507–9.

[503] Young, *Ulster in '98*, pp. 60–1; John Hewitt, 'Portrait of a United Irishman', *Belfast Municipal Museum and Art Gallery Bulletin*, 1, no. 2 (1949): pp. 29–30; Shields, 'Some Songs and Ballads', p. 56; Broadside Ballads, BOD Harding B 26(666); see also Moylan, *Age of Revolution*, pp. 64–5. For the involvement of McKeiver and Graham in the rebellion see McSkimin, *Annals of Ulster*, pp. 101, 105–6, 117. For folklore relating to Watty Graham's execution see, p. 154 and Chapter 2, pp. 111–12.

[504] Young, *Ulster in '98*, pp. 48–50.

'in green garments clad' and promises that the executions of United Irishmen will be avenged and the wrongdoings redressed. John Hume collected another version (spelt 'Henrey's Song') two decades earlier in north county Down, showing that it had a popular distribution. Burns stated that the song was 'made' by James Hope in collaboration with the poet James Orr, after his return from America. The text, however, does not appear among Hope's poetic compositions, which were entrusted to Madden. It is neither found in the published works of Orr nor does it match the poet's peculiar linguistic or aesthetic style. Later in the century, Young collected another version from Mrs Thomas L'Estrange, a prominent member of the First Presbyterian Church in Belfast, who claimed that the song was written in 1799 by Thomas Russell. These apocryphal attributions, which cannot be corroborated, show a desire to authenticate the song.[505]

Hugh Shields, an authority on Irish traditional narrative singing maintained that all of the versions of 'Henry's Ghost' are 'characterized by a sort of literary pretension unsuited to popular song'.[506] Such purist criticism misses the point of vernacular history, which indiscriminately blends between orality and literacy. This was a literary text that could not be written. Oral recitals of a subversive song, which could not be safely sung in public, let alone appear in print, were meaningful performances of hidden remembrance that took place among confidants. Society and politics had moved on since 1798 and yet many of the generation that had witnessed torching of houses, imprisonment, floggings, executions, beheadings, transportation, and other brutal acts of oppression were still haunted by the ghosts of the Turn-Out.

It was only in their old age that some of the people who had lived their lives in conditions of social forgetting were willing to speak openly with collectors. Mary Ann McCracken had given on loan some of her papers to Charles Hamilton Teeling when he wrote his *Personal Narrative* in the late 1820s, knowing that Teeling was one of the in-group and could be trusted. She regretted, however, sharing information with McSkimin, who had betrayed her confidence. When she eventually opened up to Madden, McCracken was in her seventies and eighties. At his first meeting with Madden, Hope was 79. Till then, their stories had been mostly kept to themselves and only voiced in private (Fig. 3.3).

In absence of being able to mourn in public, the generation of 1798 had to make do with expressing pain in masked forms. Such silent rituals of lament for an executed rebel were described in a song in memory of David Woods of Connor, which Burns shared with Porter:

> As ye walk the Shore Road, leading into Belfast,
> Pause and sigh at the place where the Yeos held him fast.
> As you're walking through Doagh, shed a tear at the place
> Where he mounted the tree with a smile on his face.[507]

---

[505] Ibid., pp. 52–4 (Burns) and 94 (L'Estrange); Shields, 'Some Songs and Ballads', p. 39 (Hume). An attempt to take the attribution to Orr and Hope at face value conceded that the song does not correspond with Orr's renowned 'gentleness and his abhorrence for violence'; Carol Baraniuk, *James Orr, Poet and Irish Radical* (London: Pickering & Chatto, 2014), pp. 40–1 and 49–50.

[506] Shields, 'Some Songs and Ballads', p. 40; see also Hugh Shields, *Narrative Singing in Ireland: Lays, Ballads, Come-All-Yes and Other Songs* (Blackrock: Irish Academic Press, 1993), p. 107.

[507] Young, *Ulster in '98*, pp. 56–7. It was later recalled that David Woods was hanged at his mother's door in Doagh; George Warnock to F. J. Bigger, 21 August 1908, Bigger Papers, BCL K1/A/4 [the informant is probably 84-year-old George Warnock of Clifton Ward, Belfast; listed in the 1901 Census as a Unitarian retired farmer].

(a)

(b)

Fig. 3.3. Custodians of memory: Mary Ann McCracken and James Hope

In their old age, the people who had dedicated their lives to remembering those who had died in the Turn-Out faced postmemory anxieties that their efforts might be forgotten.

(a) Photograph of Mary Ann McCracken (1770–1866).

Photograph taken by John Gibson in the last decade of her life. © National Museum NI, Collection Ulster Museum (BELUM.P475.1932).

(b) Portrait by T. W. Huffam of James Hope (1764–1847), reproduced from an original portrait in his possession.

Published by Madden and Company. Courtesy of National Library of Ireland.

Relatives of rebels were prevented from erecting monuments and the few epitaphs inscribed on graves had to be obfuscated. Vernacular poetry was carefully phrased to both reveal and conceal glimpses of memory, sharing with the readers the inherent conflict of forbidden representation. Early literary accounts typically display hesitancy, leaving discernible gaps of silence. Memory was enveloped in a shroud of forgetting.

Literary texts have been discussed as mediums of cultural memory or, to use Ann Rigney's term, 'portable monuments'.[508] Less noticed is their function as agents of social forgetting. The publication from the 1820s of a significant volume of texts on 1798 may seem to signal an outpouring of cultural remembrance, but further inspection reveals that the early novels subtly avoided key issues that had made the rebellion ambivalent, either denying the extent of Presbyterian involvement or glossing over residual resentment. Walter Scott successfully employed such a literary strategy to domesticate the memory of Jacobite revolts in Scotland, showing that the Forty-Five (1745) no longer posited a real

---

[508] Astrid Erll, *Memory in Culture* (Houndmills and New York: Palgrave Macmillan, 2011), pp. 144–71; Rigney, *The Afterlives of Walter Scott*, pp. 17–48.

threat and could therefore be integrated into British cultural memory. This manoeuvre could not be implemented for Ninety-Eight in Ulster, which was riddled with ambiguity and remained unsettled. There were limits to what could be written and the literary works did not produce agreed terms or create a safe atmosphere through which memory could be openly discussed in public. Paradoxically, historical novels contributed to social forgetting, ensuring that uneasy memories would stay at home.

In a poem published in 1846 on 'Thoughts of a Volunteer of Ninety-Eight'—which was written by Andrew McEwen, an apothecary in Downpatrick and the son of the former professor of elocution at the Royal Belfast College—an old Ulster veteran rebel professes 'I well remember Ninety-eight', yet admits that:

> Few of its strong men now can tell
> The sufferings of that year.[509]

The dread of passing away without having had the opportunity to tell their story was the main stimulant for elderly survivors to share their recollections in the hope that they would be remembered by the next generations. Although their aspirations for the future were phrased in reference to the past, their angst was primarily about the present, reflecting the yearnings of the elderly survivors to find meaning in their own life as it approached its end.

The ghost of McCracken was not just Henry's ghost, but was equally a premonition of the spectre of Mary Ann McCracken and her generation, who wanted to ensure that their life of muted remembrance had not been spent in vain. The fear that their death would signify the end of the memory of 1798 was shared by the collectors and, at some level, by Ulster society at large. A comparable dread of loss was felt in Britain with the demise of Harry Patch and the last Tommies of the Great War, or similarly in Australia with the last Anzac, in France with the last Poilu, and America with the last Doughboys. This anxiety is often articulated in reference to the remaining survivors of Nazi death camps, implying that their passing away will lead to the decline of Holocaust remembrance.[510]

The term 'postmemory' has come into vogue, marking a shift of scholarly interest from the memory of those who experienced historical events to the inherited memories of a second generation. It was first introduced by Marianne Hirsch in a book on family photographs in order to characterize the 'experience of those who grew up dominated by narratives that preceded their birth, whose own belated stories are evacuated by the stories of the previous generation shaped by the traumatic events that can be neither understood nor recreated'. Postmemory has since been widely adopted in Memory

---

[509] Andrew McEwen, *Zayda, and Other Poems* (Belfast: Lamont Brothers 1846), pp. 116–20. Contemporary reviews of this collection failed to notice the 1798 poem; *BNL*, 28 July 1846, p. 4; *Belfast Protestant Journal*, 8 August 1846, p. 4; *Belfast Commercial Chronicle*, 5 August 1846, p. 4; *Morning Post*, 8 August 1846, p. 6; *Londonderry Standard*, 28 August 1846, p. 3. Advertisements in the *Downpatrick Reporter* identify Andrew McEwen as an apothecary and his parentage was noted by the *Londonderry Standard*.

[510] The reverential discourse around the passing away of the last veterans of the First World War was apparent in extensive media coverage and is evident in a number of books. See Jonathan King, *Gallipoli: Our Last Man Standing. The Extraordinary Life of Alec Campbell* (Milton, Qld.: John Wiley, 2003); Peter Parker, *The Last Veteran: Harry Patch and the Legacy of War* (London: Fourth Estate, 2009); Richard Rubin, *The Last of the Doughboys: The Forgotten Generation and Their Forgotten World War* (New York: Houghton Mifflin Harcourt, 2013); see also the television documentary series *The Last Tommy* (dir. Harvey Lilly, BBC, 2005). The discourse of anxieties over the passing away of Holocaust survivors has yet to be studied.

Studies without sufficient attention to its essentialist conceptualization, which does not fully take on board the social dynamics of remembrance or properly appreciate the transmission of oral traditions. According to Hirsch, postmemory can supposedly be distinguished from memory proper in that 'its connection to its object or source is mediated not through recollection but through an imaginative investment and creation.' The same, however, is largely true for first generation social memory, which is repeatedly reconstructed, remediated, and imaginatively reinvented, so that immediate proximity to the historical events is not its defining feature. It follows that the concept of postmemory is in need of redefinition.[511]

The discussion in a previous chapter of the execution of William Orr in 1797 as a prememory of the rebellion, which was already constructed in advance of 1798, reveals a contemporary fear of pre-forgetting: the very people who were most determined that their actions, and their actions of their loved ones, would be remembered also harboured anxieties that they might end up being forgotten. Towards the end of their lives, these self-appointed custodians of memory would face postmemory anxieties. In these terms, postmemory angst reflects the concerns of people in their twilight that the fruits of a lifetime devoted to cultivating memory would ultimately be forgotten.

When McCracken, Hope and their friends vehemently expressed their disapproval of McSkimin's work, it was because he was seen to debase the memory of 1798 that they had faithfully constructed. In Madden's work they found a platform that promised to respectfully preserve their version of memory. Others were alienated by the privileging of the United Irish elite in Madden's work and its association with nationalism. Presbyterians in the countryside felt more comfortable putting their memory on record by confiding with Classon Porter. In all of these cases, postmemory angst motivated people to speak out in order that the recollections that they had constructed in conditions of social forgetting would be passed on to a next generation.

'Generation' here has two meanings. It is both a collective of people for whom the rebellion was a memorable event and also the act of generating, through which the memory of the rebellion was given meaning. The concept of generation is central to understanding memory and Pierre Nora even defined it as a *lieu de mémoire*.[512] It is also a *lieu d'oubli*. The memories transmitted by those who had witnessed 1798 were shaped through practices of concealment and were replete with hesitations, so that, unwittingly, the generation of the Turn-Out also bequeathed traditions of forgetting to future generations.

---

[511] Marianne Hirsch, *Family Frames: Photography, Narrative and Postmemory* (Cambridge, Mass.: Harvard University Press, 1997), pp. 17–40 (esp. 22); see also Marianne Hirsch, *The Generation of Postmemory: Writing and Visual Culture after the Holocaust* (New York and Chichester: Columbia University Press, 2012), pp. 29–52. For a critique and rethinking of the term 'postmemory' see Guy Beiner, 'Probing the Boundaries of Irish Memory: From Postmemory to Prememory and Back', *Irish Historical Studies*, 39, no. 154 (2014): pp. 296–307.

[512] Pierre Nora, 'Generation', in *Realms of Memory: The Construction of the French Past*, edited by Pierre Nora, translated by Arthur Goldhammer (New York: Columbia University Press, 1996), vol. 1, pp. 499–531; see also Astrid Erll, 'Generation in Literary History: Three Constellations of Generationality, Genealogy, and Memory', *New Literary History*, 45, no. 3 (2014): pp. 385–409.

4

Regenerated Forgetting

The Second Half of the Nineteenth Century

> ...forgetfulness is retained in the memory.
>
> St Augustine, *Confessions*[1]
>
> One is not ignorant of what is forgotten.
>
> Søren Kierkegaard, *Works of Love*[2]

How does generation change affect social forgetting? The muted practices of memorialization cultivated by the generation of the Turn-Out were passed on to their children and grandchildren after them. Over time, it seemed that remembrance could emerge into the public sphere in broad daylight and yet, social forgetting was sustained by various forms of restraint. Romantic nationalism, and corresponding variations of regionalism, built on an already-existing fascination with folklore and encouraged throughout Europe the collecting of vernacular historical traditions, which were repackaged and reintroduced into popular culture. This rediscovery of regenerated echoes from the past was eventually overtaken by a more general vogue for commemoration. In Ulster as well, traditions of Ninety-Eight were collected, re-adapted and remediated. Towards the end of the nineteenth century, a flourish of antiquarianism fed into a cultural revival that was intent on publicly commemorating the United Irishmen. Nonetheless, reverberations of forgetting were always close at hand.

Painful family traditions could be conveyed silently. Matilda Goudy née Porter had witnessed at a very young age the execution in 1798 of her father, Rev. James Porter of Greyabbey, and, as noted by the Presbyterian ministers Rev. Thomas Croskery and Rev. Thomas Witherow (both professors at Magee College in Derry), 'in after life she seldom talked about him to her children.' For her son, Rev. Alexander Porter Goudy, 'the unjust death of his grandfather' was a 'painful subject'. In public, Rev. Goudy rejected the politics of the United Irishmen and was inclined to disremember Presbyterian involvement in the rebellion. Yet, when this 'unwelcome subject' was brought up 'in private talks of the fireside with his brethren', he would allude to his family's memory and cryptically remark that 'my grandfather was suspended.'[3]

---

[1] '*memoria retinetur oblivio*'; *St Augustine's Confessions* (Loeb Classical Library, No. 27), translated by William Watts (1631), vol. 2 (London: Heineman and New York: Macmillan Co., 1912), bk 10, ch. 16, p. 119.

[2] Søren Kierkegaard, *Works of Love*, edited and translated by Howard V. Hong and Edna H. Hong (Princeton, N.J.: Princeton University Press, 1995), p. 295.

[3] Thomas Croskery and Thomas Witherow, *Life of the Rev. A. P. Goudy, D. D.* (Draperstown, Co. Londonderry and Ballymena, Co. Antrim: Moyola Books and Braid Books, 1994; orig. edn 1887), pp. 12–14.

First-hand memories of the veterans of 1798 were mostly transmitted to the next generations behind closed doors. The example of the Belfast Fenian Frank Roney, who was born in 1841 and would go on to make a name as a trade union organizer in California, is instructive. His maternal grandfather John [Jack] Thompson, who was 'a rigid Presbyterian and hereditary Covenanter', had been a United Irish captain at the Battle of Ballynahinch and after the rebellion retained strong republican views, going so far as to disown one of his sons for joining the Orange Order. A grand-aunt, Alice Small, had witnessed in 1798 the summary hanging of her fiancée and her 'long life afterwards was spent between prayer for his soul and in heaping maledictions upon his murderers'. Roney recalled that, in his youth, stories of the execution of Henry Joy McCracken 'were recited to me time and time again, and made such an impression on my young mind.' His mother, who converted to Catholicism, would take him on annual visits to the McCracken household on Donegall Street, where he met Mary Ann McCracken and 'the descendants of the old rebel stock that remained in Belfast', all of whom were Presbyterian. The favoured date for these valued visits was St Patrick's Day, which was celebrated as a 'solemn festival' by Mary Ann McCracken, who on that day wore a green dress and would open the blinds of her house, which were usually kept shut as a sign of perpetual mourning for her executed brother. Attendance at these gatherings was confined to an inner circle of former United Irishmen. The reminiscences of Ninety-Eight that were retold in such cloistered forums were shrouded in secrecy. These surreptitious encounters left an imprint on the young Roney, who later wrote that 'the impressions made upon me became permanent.'[4]

Fragmented recollections of the Turn-Out were retold to children as anecdotal stories. Before moving to England in 1802, Patrick Brontë—the father of the famous authors Charlotte, Emily, and Anne Brontë—had witnessed the consequences of the 1798 rebellion in his native parish of Drumballyroney in county Down. His father, Hugh Prunty, was a known radical Presbyterian, whose house in Ballynaskeagh (8 km south of Banbridge) was nearly burnt down by the 'Welsh Horse' cavalry unit. Patrick's brother William was among the rebels at Ballynahinch and had to go into hiding.[5] Brontë's experiences during the period of the rebellion were not discussed openly or written down. Nevertheless, Agnes Mary Frances Robinson, an early biographer of Emily Brontë, noted that in their home in Yorkshire the children were 'nursed on grisly Irish horrors, tales of 1798, tales of oppression and misery'.[6] The progeny of veterans and eyewitnesses across Ulster and in the diaspora often picked up snippets of memories that were not told in public.

---

[4] *Frank Roney, Irish Rebel and California Labor Leader: An Autobiography*, edited by Ira B. Cross (Berkeley: University of California Press, 1931), pp. 3–13 and 65–9. See also Kerby A. Miller and Breandán Mac Suibhne, 'Frank Roney and the Fenians: A Reappraisal of Irish Republicanism in 1860s Belfast and Ulster', *Éire-Ireland*, 51, nos. 3 & 4 (Fall–Winter 2016), p. 25.

[5] Cathal O'Byrne, *As I Roved Out: A Book of The North, Being a Series of Historical Sketches of Ulster and Old Belfast*, 3rd edn (Belfast: Blackstaff, 1982; orig. edn 1946), pp. 366–7; William Wright, *The Brontës in Ireland; or, Facts Stranger Than Fiction* (London: Hodder and Stoughton, 1893), pp. 136–7, 150–1, and 160. See also Brian Wilks, 'Patrick Brontë: The Man Who Arrived at Cambridge University', *Brontë Studies*, 39, no. 2 (2014): pp. 93–105; Edward Chitham, *The Brontës' Irish Background* (New York: St Martin's Press, 1986), pp. 20, 27, 103, and 137–40; Edward Chitham, *Western Winds: The Brontës' Irish Heritage* (Stroud: The History Press, 2015), chs 14–15.

[6] A. Mary F. Robinson, *Emily Brontë* (Boston: Roberts Brothers, 1883), p. 215.

When passed on to a second generation, the narratives of Ninety-Eight retained their characteristic ambivalence, which could appear in subtle forms. The poet James Munce, who was born in 1817 to a Presbyterian farming family in Carrickmannon, county Down (4 km east of Saintfield), and later moved to Donaghadee (8 km east of Bangor), where he was dubbed the 'The Rabbie Burns of Donaghadee', composed a long narrative poem 'Honest John: A Tale of 1798', published in Glasgow, to where he emigrated in 1845. While telling a generic tale of a rebel commander who participated in the battles of Saintfield and Ballynahinch, after which he was sentenced to death but instead goes into exile and has to wait many years before he can return to his wife and child, the poem includes numerous unknown details about the rebellion. Such specifics as the meeting of insurgents at Malcolm's Glen near Saintfield, or the executions of James Morrison of Donaghadee and of a man named Breeze from Killinchy, who were designated 'warners', charged with spreading news about the rebellion, evidently derived from local traditions that Munce had heard when residing in the area. Although the poet's sympathies are clearly on the side of the United Irishmen, the rebels are presented as 'misguided men', who had been 'led astray'. Caution was required when writing about 1798 for a local readership in what had become a predominantly unionist area.[7]

Recollections of the Turn-Out were passed on to third and fourth generations. The journalist and author William Stavely Armour, for some time editor of the *Northern Whig*, was born in Ballymoney in 1883. He was the son of the radical Presbyterian minister Rev. J. B. Armour and through his mother was related to Rev. William Stavely, who had been implicated in 1798. He recalled having 'heard many a detail of events in the Northern Protestant Rebellion from men who were but a generation removed from them and could recount what they had heard with the greatest and most minute accuracy'. Such memories of rebels, however, were overshadowed by loyalist 'reports spread by the oppressors of the time to blacken Irish adversaries'. According to Stavely Armour, these 'were much more readily believed than the sufferings of their own fellows which many must have witnessed and are still a living tradition'. The result of propagated defamation was the silencing of radical voices: 'so effective were they in putting down the Rebellion in the North that there has been no real opinion since.'[8] At the same time as traditions of social memory were passed on from generation to generation, social forgetting was also being regenerated.

Mrs E. Higginson née Campbell of Larne was the great-granddaughter of William Campbell (known as 'Big Billy Campbell'), a United Irish captain from Killead who had served under Henry Joy McCracken and was shot at the Battle of Antrim. In the early twentieth century, she recalled the stealth with which she was told family traditions of 1798 as a child growing up in Muckamore, county Antrim (2 km south-east of Antrim town):

My poor mother used to tell us the story considerable over 30 years ago [*c*.1875] and would only tell it to us when the light was lit and the windows blinden [sic] how her grandfather

---

[7] James Munce, *Poems*, 2nd edn (Glasgow: George Gallie, 1881; orig. edn 1863), pp. 99–117. Whereas the insurgents are treated with ambiguity, Munce had unequivocal scorn for informers; see his poem 'Epitaph on a Notorious Informer of 1798', ibid., p. 396. For biographical information see *Words Fae Hearth an' Hame: Ulster-Scots: The 'Heart Language' of Ards and North Down* (Belfast: Ulster-Scots Agency, 2016), p. 14.

[8] W. S. Armour, *Facing the Irish Question* (London: Duckworth, 1935), p. 99.

was shot dead and would rehearse it under her breath and almost swaired [sic] us never to repeat it or say we had a friend a rebel for we never knew what would happen.

Although Higginson dismissed the apprehensions of her mother, Eliza Jane Campbell, as 'the ideas of a simple country women', the fear to speak of Ninety-Eight evidently persisted even after the passing away of the generation that had lived through the events.[9]

'The Memory of the Dead', by far the most famous poetic composition written about 1798, was first published in the *Nation* in April 1843, a generation after the rebellion. It caught the public's attention in January the following year, when it was produced as evidence of the nationalist newspaper's treasonable sympathies in the trial of one of the founding editors, Charles Gavan Duffy, and its meaning was contested in court. The implication that it was still forbidden to recite poetry in memory of 1798 became a cause célèbre among nationalists. 'The Memory of the Dead' was soon adapted into a song. At first sung to the air of 'Auld Lang Syne', it was assigned an original tune—probably composed by William Elliott Hudson—and republished in the extremely popular song collection *The Spirit of the Nation* (which by 1870 was already in its fiftieth edition), as well as on broadsheets and countless song books. At the meetings of the Young Ireland confederate clubs in 1848, it was hailed as 'The Irish Marseillaise', a hallowed status that would be retained within nationalist culture at least up to the turn of the century.

The anthemic poem opens with striking verses that address the unease of remembering the rebellion:

> Who fears to speak of Ninety-Eight?
> Who blushes at the name?
> When cowards mock the patriot's fate,
> Who hangs his head for shame?

These rhetorical questions amounted to a call for speaking out in memory of the United Irishmen, in defiance of the embarrassment—manifested in fear, blushing, mockery, and shame—that such open remembrance incurred.[10] Joep Leerssen has attributed the poem's outstanding popularity to its encapsulation of 'a remarkable combination of attitudes':

> on the one hand, the 1798 rebellion (and Irish history and politics generally) became unmentionable almost, in a rictus of discreet 'don't mention the war' avoidance, while on the other hand, there was much eloquent preoccupation with the painful topic.[11]

---

[9] E. Higginson, Dunluce St., Larne, to F. J. Bigger, 15 and 20 March 1906; Bigger Papers, BCL K2/A/15–16. The death of 'Big Billy Campbell' at Antrim was recalled in 1863 by 9-year-old James Burns; Young, *Ulster in '98*, pp. 30–1.

[10] *Nation*, 1 April 1843, p. 393 and 27 January 1844, p. 253; *The Spirit of the Nation by the Writers of The Nation Newspaper*, 2nd edn (Dublin: James Duffy, 1844), pp. vii and 48–50; for the score of the tune see *The Spirit of the Nation: Ballads and Songs of the Writers of 'The Nation', with Original and Ancient Music, Arranged for the Voice and Piano-Forte* (Dublin: James Duffy, 1845), pp. 44–7. See also Zimmerman, *Songs of Irish Rebellion*, pp. 226–7. For a typical reference to 'The Irish Marseillaise' see *United Irishman*, 18 March 1848, p. 5.

[11] Joep Leerssen, '1798: The Recurrence of Violence and Two Conceptualizations of History', *Irish Review*, 22 (1998): pp. 39–40.

This ambivalence touches on the dilemma at the heart of social forgetting: the fraught distinction between what was discreetly remembered in private and what could be overtly commemorated in public.

The anonymous publication of the celebrated poem seems to reflect an apprehension to own up in public to a call for the right to speak without fear about Ninety-Eight. The poem was written by the young scholar John Kells Ingram, who went on to a distinguished academic career in Trinity College Dublin. Ingram's family background made him particularly attune to the difficulties of openly remembering 1798. Although a member of the established Protestant church, his family had Ulster-Scot Presbyterian origins and he attended school in Newry, county Down, an area that had a strong nationalist presence. In his politics, Ingram was known as a unionist, though he has been more thoughtfully described as a 'hypothetical nationalist'.[12] It has often been assumed that he was a 'reluctant author' and later regretted having written the poem. This charge was repudiated by Ingram, who insisted in including it in his collected poems, published in 1900. Already previously, he had considered claiming authorship of the poem for the centenary of 1798 but was discouraged by his brother, who argued that an explicit association with nationalist commemoration might do harm to his children, 'who live and move chiefly among Conservatives'. On both a personal and collective level, 'The Memory of the Dead' was a call to overcome the taboo of social forgetting and to speak out about Ninety-Eight.[13]

CONTINUED DISREMEMBRANCE

The second half of the nineteenth century was a time in which the memory of Ninety-Eight was coming out all over Ireland, but there were a number of factors that reinforced disremembering in Ulster and provided contexts for continued social forgetting of the northern United Irishmen. Foremost amongst them was the rise of Orangeism in the very areas in which the United Irishmen had mobilized in great numbers. The republican idealists of Young Ireland imagined that that could appeal to Presbyterian Orangemen and even entertained far-fetched fantasies that 'the young men of Ulster who have been taught to "remember Orr," who have read the songs of Drennan, and heard the story of Ballynahinch' might join their ranks.[14] But in actuality, Orangeism represented hard-line loyalism and uncompromising opposition to nationalism. Since collective memory is often characterized as an embodiment of present concerns about identity, the impression that Presbyterians had forsaken the Green and taken up the Orange might seem to present convincing grounds for total collective amnesia.

---

[12] G. K. Peatling, 'Who Fears to Speak of Politics? John Kells Ingram and Hypothetical Nationalism', *Irish Historical Studies*, 31, no. 122 (1998): pp. 202–21.

[13] T. D. Ingram to J. K. Ingram, 6 April 1898, PRONI, Ingram Papers, D2808/C/2E; John K. Ingram, *Sonnets and Other Poems* (London: Adam and Charles Black, 1900), pp. 6–7 and 104–6. For the common belief that Ingram was a 'reluctant author' see for example William O'Brien, 'Who Fears to Speak of Ninety-Eight?', *Contemporary Review*, 73 (January 1898): p. 14.

[14] *Nation*, 15 September 1849, p. 296.

In the decade and a half after the rebellion, the number of Orange societies in Ulster had markedly increased. However, the notion of an instant sweeping transformation from revolutionary republicanism to militant loyalism is misleading. It is well worth taking into account the admission of Lieutenant-Colonel William Verner, the Orange grand master of county Armagh, that 'there were many more that were not Orangemen.'[15] Presbyterian membership fluctuated, as the fortunes of the Orange Order rose and fell. In reality, the transition was gradual and chequered, creating conditions which better suited the more complex dynamics of social forgetting, in which memories are preserved in private, rather than completely erased.[16]

The Orange Order played on concerns of Catholic empowerment shared by Anglicans and Presbyterians and purported to offer a common sense of Protestant community.[17] From the time of the rebellion, Orangeism infiltrated the yeomanry and militia and became a driving force within conservative politics in Ulster, yet it was greeted with suspicion and hostility from successive Irish administrations and it alienated liberal Protestants. The Orange Order was dissolved and reconstituted following a ban in 1823 on oath-bound societies (4 Geo. IV c. 87). Its activities were further curtailed by the passing in 1825 of an Unlawful Societies Act (6 Geo. 4 c. 4). Moreover, in 1832, a Party Processions Act (2 & 3 Will. 4 c. 118) prohibited the celebration of commemorative processions, which were a central ritual of Orange popular politics.[18] Orangemen failed to acknowledge that these prohibitions were also applied against Catholic nationalist organizations and felt aggrieved that they were 'persecuted and placed in the felon's dock should they attempt to wear an orange lily, while the sons whom their fathers subdued are fondled and caressed.'[19] Despite the restrictions, Orangeism continued to spread and in 1835 the number of lodges in north-east Ulster was put at 229 in county Antrim and upwards of 200 in Down.[20]

The main impetus for Orange resurgence was a vigorous 'non-popery' campaign in response to Catholic Emancipation, which was legislated in the Roman Catholic Relief Act of 1829 (10 Geo. 4 c. 7). A mass meeting on 30 October 1834 at Hillsborough, county Down, was attended by an estimated 60,000 people, who heard Rev. Henry Cooke advocate that differences between the Protestant faiths should be put aside in favour of 'agreement in the great and stupendous truths' shared by Presbyterians

---

[15] 'Report from the Select Committee ... of Orange Lodges', evidence of Lieutenant-Colonel William Verner, MP, p. 20 (304–6).

[16] For the limited reach of Orangeism see Andrew R. Holmes, 'Presbyterians, Loyalty, and Orangeism in Nineteenth-Century Ulster', in *Loyalism and the Formation of the British World 1775–1914*, edited by Allan Blackstock and Frank O'Gorman (Woodbridge: Boydell Press, 2014), pp. 125–44.

[17] Daragh Curran, *The Protestant Community in Ulster, 1825–45: A Society in Transition* (Dublin: Four Courts Press, 2014).

[18] For infiltration of military see David Fitzpatrick, *Descendancy: Irish Protestant Histories since 1795* (Cambridge: Cambridge University Press, 2014), pp. 21–34; for political restrictions see Hereward Senior, *Orangeism in Ireland and Britain 1795–1836* (London: Routledge & Kegan Paul, 1966), pp. 177–284. See also Kevin Haddick-Flynn, *Orangeism: The Making of a Tradition* (Dublin: Wolfhound Press, 1999), pp. 203–71.

[19] Robert Young, *The Ulster Harmonist, Consisting of Constitutional Songs, with Notes* (Derry: Sentinel, 1840), pp. 198–9.

[20] 'Report from the Select Committee ... of Orange Lodges', evidence of Stewart Blacker, Grand Secretary of the Grand Orange Lodge, p. 113 (article 1751).

and Anglicans.[21] This vision of pan-Protestant solidarity had to overcome ingrained religious and class animosities among Protestants. The *Northern Whig* pointed out that no mention was made at the 1834 Orange gathering in county Down of the 'ticklish topic' of the requirement to pay tithes to the Established Church. This issue, together with grievances over high rents, had long been a cause of Presbyterian resentment against the Anglican Ascendancy, as was noted in 1812 by the visiting Englishman Edward Wakefield.[22]

Around the same time as Cooke called for Protestant unity, the fieldworkers of the Ordnance Survey observed in the Antrim parish of Kilbride—where 'in the year 1798 the people of this neighbourhood signalized themselves by the active part which they took in the proceedings of that period'—that Presbyterians expressed 'a very violent and general prejudice to episcopacy, but more especially to the Established Church'. Apparently, 'political feeling, which had for a long time lain dormant, was lately aroused by the increased applotment of their tithe, and at the present moment the great bulk of the population are in a state of rancorous excitation.'[23] Rev. Henry Montgomery testified before a parliamentary Select Committee, assigned with investigating complaints against the collection of tithes in Ireland, that one of the principal reasons that Presbyterians had rebelled in 1798 was 'their hostility to tithes'. He stated, 'on authority which I deem to be quite as good as any authority possible', that this resentment was still in place in the formerly rebellious counties of Derry, Antrim, and Down.[24] Animosities between Presbyterians and Anglicans were the theme of 'The Rector and the Barber', a poem by the Antrim rhyming-weaver Samuel Walker, published in the *Belfast Penny Journal* in 1845.[25] Despite Orange claims of Protestant unity, rifts that stemmed back to the time of the rebellion remained unhealed.

Tensions between Protestants were overshadowed by the more noticeable outbreaks of violence around the 12 July annual celebrations of the victory of William of Orange at the Battle of the Boyne. Although the demonstrations benefitted from the patronage of a refined leadership, drawn from the landed and educated classes, Orange events were mainly attended by the working class and farming brethren, who frequently displayed unruly behaviour. These riots, which became ritualized as a form of popular politics, have mostly been mapped along the religious fault lines that divided Protestants and Catholics.[26] Yet the micro-geography of violence was more nuanced. Instances

---

[21] For the 'non-popery' response to Daniel O'Connell's political gains see Gilbert A. Cahill, 'Some Nineteenth-Century Roots of the Ulster Problem, 1829–1848', *Irish University Review*, 1, no. 2 (1971): pp. 215–37 (esp. 226–7).

[22] For the liberal critique of the Hillsborough meeting see *Northern Whig*, 3 November 1834, pp. 1, 2, and 4 and 10 November 1834, p. 1. For Presbyterian opposition to tithes in Ulster see Wakefield, *An Account of Ireland*, vol. 2, pp. 483, 493, and 547.

[23] Memoir of the Parish of Kilbride by James Boyle (June 1836 to February 1839) in Day and McWilliams, *Ordnance Survey Memoirs of Ireland*, vol. 29, pp. 141 and 144.

[24] Evidence of Rev. Hugh Montgomery before the Select Committee of the House of Commons on Tithes in Ireland (10 March 1832), reproduced in *Northern Whig*, 12 July 1832, p. 1.

[25] See Holmes, 'Presbyterian Religion, Poetry and Politics', p. 54.

[26] For the ritualization of sectarian violence see Sean Farrell, *Rituals and Riots: Sectarian Violence and Political Culture in Ulster, 1784–1886* (Lexington: University Press of Kentucky, 2000), pp. 102–24; see also Sybil E. Baker, 'Orange and Green: Belfast, 1832–1912', in *The Victorian City: Images and Realities*, edited by H. J. Dyos and Michael Wolff, vol. 2 (London and Boston: Routledge & Kegan Paul, 1973), pp. 789–814.

of local resistance to Orangeism in Presbyterian areas, which appear to have retained traditions of radicalism that stemmed back to the 1790s, suggest that social memory of the United Irish rebellion may have also played a subtle role in local conflicts.

At least forty people died in riots on 13 July 1829, when Orange lodges across Ulster came out in force to voice their displeasure with the Roman Catholic Relief Act.[27] In the coverage of the many violent incidents that day, the loyalist and English press reported that the parade of the Kircubbin Orange lodge through the village of Greyabbey—the site of the memorable hanging of Rev. James Porter in 1798—had been assailed by a 'party of Romanists'. A local correspondent, however, pointed out that 'there is not, within several miles of Greyabbey, on any side a Roman Catholic family except one.' At the Down assizes it transpired that Orangemen had in fact assaulted local Presbyterians, who opposed the parade.[28]

The area of Greyabbey remained a flashpoint. Slogans at an Orange parade a couple of years later targeted Catholicism as well as Presbyterian liberalism: 'No Pope', 'No O'Connell', 'No Montgomery', 'No New-Light', and 'No Surrender'. In an outburst of rioting, in 1832, Orangemen assaulted the houses of people in Greyabbey known to be 'friendly to Reform, both in Church and State, and the Emancipation of their Catholic fellow-countrymen'.[29] A local ballad applauded the resolute stand of 'The Green Boys of Greba', a name which recalled previous support of the United Irishmen. One of the versions included the verse:

> In Greyabbey town there lived men of renown
> Who ne'er were afraid to wear green.

Opposition to Orange attacks was seen as a continuation of a tradition that stemmed back to 1798. The Green Boys, who were considered a 'relic of the United Irishmen', were later affiliated with the Irish Republican Brotherhood. The incursion of Orangeism into the locality was resisted for another three decades and an Orange lodge was only established in Greyabbey as late as 1863.[30]

The growth of Orangeism was curbed by sustained government disapproval. In 1835, the Orange Order was subject to an investigation by a Select Committee appointed by parliament and the following year it was charged with conspiracy to influence the succession to the throne. Consequently, the Grand Lodge of Ireland was obliged to disband. Nominal dissolution did not put an end to Orangeism, which continued to maintain a presence on the ground, and in 1846 the Grand Lodge was revived. Henry Montgomery expressed his anguish that 'the degenerate descendants of the illustrious Volunteers of 1783, of the United Irishmen of 1798, now swell the

---

[27] Ibid., pp. 96–8.

[28] *Belfast Commercial Chronicle*, 18 July 1829, p. 1 and 20 July 1829, p. 2; *Morning Post*, 20 July 1829, p. 4; *Dublin Evening Mail*, 26 August 1829, p. 3.

[29] *Northern Whig*, 23 July 1832, p. 4.

[30] Robinson, 'Hanging Ropes and Buried Secrets', p. 8; Kenneth Robinson, *North Down and Ards in 1798* (Bangor: North Down Heritage Centre, 1998), p. 107. The cited verse was recalled by Rev. Thomas M. Johnstone, minister of Newington Church in Belfast and a Moderator of the General Assembly of the Presbyterian Church, whose great-grandfather John Patterson came from Greyabbey; Thomas M. Johnstone, *The Vintage of Memory*, 2nd edn (Belfast: Quota Press, 1943), p. 17. For the association of the Green Boys with Fenianism see Cross, *Frank Roney*, pp. 60–5; Miller and Mac Suibhne, 'Frank Roney and the Fenians', pp. 34–5.

Orange Societies and Processions of Ulster; and are, at every election, the most confidential supporters of religious and political intolerance.'[31] The ire of the authorities, however, was re-awakened in 1849, after a 12 July procession in south county Down resulted in a number of deaths at a violent sectarian clash near Castlewellan. This incident would attain iconic status in Orange memory as the 'Battle of Dolly's Brae'. Consequently, a new Party Processions Act, enacted in 1850 (13 & 14 Vict. c. 2), banned further Orange parades.[32]

Further evidence of localized opposition to the spread of Orangeism can be found in ritualized demarcation of territory. Green arches were occasionally erected in response to the decoration of the routes of Orange procession with arches, adorned with Orange lilies and loyalist iconography.[33] Whereas early examples of such symbolic conflicts in Stewartstown, county Tyrone, Newry, and Belfast correspond to a segregated urban geography that separated Protestant and Catholic areas, this was not the case in the predominantly Presbyterian area of Newtownards. The Orange celebrations in 1852, which were held during elections that resulted in the triumph of Conservative candidates across Ulster, compounded in Newtownards the familiar rhetoric of anti-popery with a denunciation of the local Presbyterian liberal candidate: 'To hell with Sharman Crawford and the Pope.' After several Orange arches were put up in the town, a riot broke out at the site of a Green arch, in what appears to be another example of obstinate resistance to Orangeism in a former United Irish stronghold in north Down.[34]

Rev. William Gibson—minister of the Rosemary Street congregation in Belfast, a professor at the Presbyterian Assembly's College, and a founder of the liberal organ *The Banner of Ulster*—refused to accept that 'the Orange organisation universally prevailed in Ulster.' He insisted in 1860 that 'there are many districts into which it [the Orange Order] never entered' and claimed that, as a result of 'the vigorous enforcement of the laws against processions' and a more general distaste of Orangeism, 'it has been falling to pieces even in those parts of the country where formerly it exercised its baneful influence.'[35] This assessment reflected a momentary surge in the confidence of liberals. An editorial in the *Banner of Ulster* asserted in 1856 that 'the recollection of what was called the Rebellion in Ireland has lost its power to call forth animosity between parties of different shades of feeling on the great subjects that were at issue' and argued that, in 'the age of sweeping reforms', the aspirations of 'Harry Munroe and the other leaders of the wild campaign of Ninety-eight' had effectively

---

[31] Montgomery, 'Outlines of the History of Presbyterianism', pp. 335–6.

[32] Christine Kinealy, 'A Right to March? The Conflict at Dolly's Brae', in Problems and Perspectives in Irish History since 1800, edited by D. George Boyce and Roger Swift (Dublin: Four Courts Press, 2003), pp. 54–79; Sean Farrell, 'Writing an Orange Dolly's Brae', in *Shadows of the Gunmen: Violence and Culture in Modern Ireland*, edited by Danine Farquharson and Sean Farrell (Cork: Cork University Press, 2008), pp. 90–106.

[33] Neil Jarman, 'The Orange Arch: Creating Tradition in Ulster', *Folklore*, 112, no. 1 (2001): pp. 1–21 (esp. 4–7).

[34] *BNL*, 14 July 1852, p. 2 and 19 July 1852, p. 4. Early appearances of Green arches at counter-demonstrations to Orange parades were noted in Stewartstown (13 July 1829), see *BNL*, 21 July 1829, p. 1; *Belfast Commercial Chronicle*, 29 August 1829, p. 1; *Enniskillen Chronicle*, 8 April 1830, p. 1; Newry (13 July 1829), see *BNL*, 9 April 1830, p. 1; and Belfast (12 July 1835), see *Belfast Commercial Chronicle*, 13, 15, and 18 July 1835 (pp. 2, 2, and 4 respectively); *BNL*, 14 and 17 July 1835, pp. 1–2. See also Farrell, *Rituals and Riots*, pp. 107 and 137.

[35] William Gibson, *The Year of Grace: A History of the Ulster Revival of 1859* (Edinburgh: Andrew Elliot, 1860), p. 155.

been achieved. The writer—who was probably the liberal journalist Hugh McCall of Lisburn—posed a rhetorical question: 'under such signs of regeneration, Who fears to speak of Ninety-eight?'[36] However, the self-perceived triumph of liberalism was overstated and the notion that memory of 1798 could now emerge into the open proved to be illusory, as Orangeism made a comeback.

In the mid-1860s, a populist campaign against the prohibition of processions headed by William Johnston of Ballykilbeg (near Downpatrick) reinvigorated Orangeism. A two-month prison sentence, handed out to Johnston for organizing on 12 July 1867 a massive parade of 117 lodges from Newtownards to Bangor, turned him into a political martyr of sorts. This prestige secured Johnston's election as a member of parliament for Belfast in 1868 and Orange protests continued till the ban on processions was repealed in 1872. Consequently, the Orange Order re-emerged in the 1870s as a revitalized movement, which attracted many northern Protestants. Notwithstanding tentative attempts to find common cause with liberals, Orangeism ultimately consolidated its alliance with conservative politics.[37] As Orangemen were determined to efface the memory of Protestant participation in the rebellion, the gradual spread of Orangeism contributed to the conditions for social forgetting. Although Presbyterian liberals retained memories of the United Irishmen, as unionists, their remembrance of 1798 was inevitably reserved. Often qualified by statements that expressed disapproval of rebellion in general, liberal recollections were couched in an ambivalence that inhibited commemoration in public of Ninety-Eight.

Concerns over the rise of Irish nationalism united most Ulster Protestants in opposition to the Home Rule bills of 1886, 1893, and 1912. Unionism formed alliances between Tory Anglican landowners and liberal middle-class and tenant-farmer Presbyterians, who were brought within the fold of British conservatism. In this political constellation, Orangeism assumed the role of a militant vanguard. In times of crisis, when Home Rule was on the table, the conservative leadership could, in the famous words of Lord Randolph Churchill, play the 'Orange card' and issue threats that concessions to nationalists would result in an uncontainable escalation of violence.[38] And yet, vocal Presbyterian liberalism persisted into the 1870s and '80s, when it championed tenant rights, and was revived in the early twentieth century under the independent-liberal leadership of Thomas Wallace Russell.[39] When Russell assembled

[36] *Banner of Ulster*, 14 October 1856, p. 2.

[37] For the campaign to repeal the Party Processions Act see Aiken McClelland, *William Johnston of Ballykilbeg* (Lurgan, Co. Armagh: Ulster Society, 1990); Farrell, *Rituals and Riots*, pp. 154–73. For the popular revival of Orangeism and its political alignment with conservatism see K. Theodore Hoppen, *Elections, Politics, and Society in Ireland, 1832–1885* (Oxford: Clarendon Press, 1984), pp. 324–9.

[38] For the consolidation of Ulster unionism see Gibbon, *The Origins of Ulster Unionism*, pp. 112–42; Graham Walker, *A History of the Ulster Unionist Party: Protest, Pragmatism and Pessimism* (Manchester and New York: Manchester University Press, 2004), pp. 1–21; Alvin Jackson, *Ireland, 1798–1998: War, Peace and Beyond*, 2nd edn (Chichester and Malden, Mass.: Wiley-Blackwell, 2010), pp. 212–41. For the original context of Randolph Churchill's use of the phrase 'Orange card' see R. F. Foster, *Paddy & Mr Punch: Connections in Irish and English History* (London and New York: Penguin Books, 1995), pp. 233–61.

[39] For the recrudescence of liberalism under Russell see Alvin Jackson, 'Irish Unionism and the Russellite Threat, 1894–1906', *Irish Historical Studies*, 25, no. 100 (1987): pp. 376–404; James Loughlin, 'T.W. Russell, the Tenant-Farmer Interest and Progressive Unionism in Ireland, 1886–1900', *Eire-Ireland*, 25, no. 1 (1990): pp. 44–63; see also Richard McMinn, 'Presbyterianism and Politics in Ulster, 1871–1906', *Studia Hibernica*, no. 21 (1981): pp. 127–46.

a well-attended convention in June 1901 with the support of the Presbyterian Unionist Voters' Association, an alarmed Belfast unionist wrote to a local Antrim newspaper that this was a 'meeting of the United Irishmen' and cautioned that 'the Rebellion of 1798 is to be fought again.'[40] Following Russellite gains in by-elections in 1903 and faced with the threat of a devolution scheme, an Ulster Unionist Council was established in 1905. Its aim was to organize unionists in the province into a disciplined mass movement that rallied behind the Ulster Unionist Party and its alliance with the Conservative party, leaving little room for alternative liberal politics.[41]

To the chagrin of the conservative unionist establishment, liberal mavericks continued to express interest in the memory of Ninety-Eight and refused to let it pass into oblivion. The eccentric lawyer and populist agitator John Rea, a Presbyterian from west Belfast, was described in an obituary as a 'Young Irelander, Liberal, Cromwellian, and Orange Conservative, by turns'.[42] Rea was notorious for his provocative oratory, which frequently included references to the memory of the United Irishmen. When representing complainants in a lawsuit against the Marquis of Londonderry at the Newtownards petty session in 1854, Rea coaxed an elderly witness to declare in court that he 'recollected the '98 rebellion'.[43] At a St Patrick's Day banquet in the Belfast Music Hall in 1856, Rea's announcement that 'he revered the memory of '98' was met with 'vociferous cheers'.[44] In 1857, when defending Denis Holland—the editor of the Catholic newspaper the *Ulsterman*, in a libel case against the county Down landlord John Waring Maxwell of Finnebrogue (whose father had commanded the Inch parish yeomanry corps during the rebellion), Rea received applause from the courtroom audience for suggesting that the treatment of Ulster Catholic tenants at the hands of landlords and their agents was reminiscent of the oppression in 1798.[45] In an address that year to an electoral gathering of the Liberal party at the Belfast Corn Exchange, Rea stated that he 'would like to see the gallant Presbyterians, who fought in Ulster in perilous times, have monuments erected in their memory and to their deeds'. Refusing to comply with the taboos of social forgetting, he declared that he 'would never consent, when addressing an Ulster audience, to omit mentioning the deeds which their fathers performed fifty years ago'.[46]

Rea made provocative comments on the conditional nature of 'Presbyterian loyalty', which he justified by referring to his pedigree, as a grandson of United Irishmen.[47] In return, his political opponents tried to use this lineage against him. A booklet titled *Memoirs of the Rea Family* described John Rea's paternal grandfather, John (Jack) Rea of Tamaghmore, near Saintfield, as the 'terror of the neighbourhood'. It claimed that

[40] *Larne Times*, 29 June 1901, p. 6. For the extended life of Ulster liberalism see Hall, *Ulster Liberalism*, pp. 180–249; Frank Thompson, *The End of Liberal Ulster: Land Agitation and Land Reform, 1868–1886* (Belfast: Ulster Historical Foundation, 2001).

[41] F. S. L. Lyons, 'The Irish Unionist Party and the Devolution Crisis of 1904–5', *Irish Historical Studies*, 6, no. 21 (1948): pp. 1–22.

[42] *Northern Whig*, 21 May 1881; reproduced in <www.thesilverbowl.com/biographies/Rea_John.html>. A collection of excerpts from obituaries appears in *BNL*, p. 8.

[43] *Banner of Ulster*, 21 February 1854, p. 4.

[44] *BNL*, 26 March 1856, p. 2.

[45] *Derry Journal*, 4 March 1857, p. 4. The involvement of the plaintiff's father, Captain John Waring Maxwell, as 'an active and energetic magistrate' in the suppression of the rebellion was remembered locally; *Downpatrick Recorder*, 14 September 1861, p. 4.

[46] *Ulsterman*, 9 March 1857, p. 3.   [47] *Ulsterman*, 9 April 1856, p. 3.

Jack Rea had first been a rebel and then turned into a corrupt informer, passing false evidence on to the government that led to the execution of innocent men from county Down. In all likelihood, the author of the defamatory memoir was the Belfast Tory Arthur Hill Thornton, who at the age of 84 claimed to be 'the oldest living witness probably in existence'. Upon repeating the allegations in a letter published in the *Northern Whig*, Thornton professed that his 'object in writing is simply to put the public right in a matter of fact, and, at the same time, suggest that it were better to let the deplorable circumstances connected with the year in question sink into oblivion'.[48] Understandably, John Rea's father, Francis Rea of Holywood, county Down, could not let the matter lie and issued a public denial of the charges made against his father's conduct in 1798.[49]

At a meeting of the Belfast Town Council, John Rea responded to the taunts of Alderman Robert Lindsay that 'some of the best men in County Down have been hanged by the oath of a near relative of Mr Rea', by defending the honour of his grandfather and reminding the other councillors that they too were 'the grandsons of Volunteers and United Irishmen, whose relatives on one side or the other took part in the fight... in the battles with the Royal troops at Antrim and Ballynahinch'. The admission that many loyalists had rebel ancestors touched on a raw nerve. The conservative mayor, who chaired the meeting, promptly silenced Rea and demanded that he withdraw his controversial comments.[50]

Although Rea was idolized by liberals on account of his successful campaign to break Tory dominance in the Belfast corporation, in what became known as the 'Chancery suit', there were few, if any, takers for his oxymoronic blend of 'Fenian Orangeism'. In 1867, when justifying the Fenian rebellion, Rea professed that he revered the memory of the United Irishmen and referred to Belfast as 'the town where Henry Joy McCracken gave up his noble life'.[51] Yet, the following year he campaigned for the Orangeman William Johnston in the elections of 1868. This fusion of republicanism and Orangeism was symbolically represented in Rea's residence on Donegall street, popularly known as 'the Old Orange Hall', where he reputedly slept in 'the bed in which Henry Joy McCracken used to rest'.[52] Rea's outrageous antics attracted publicity but did not bridge the entrenched political divides. On the contrary, his exuberant evocations of the United Irishmen were a cause of embarrassment for many liberal unionists, who preferred that their rebel lineage would not be made public.

Somewhat less quixotic than Rea, several Presbyterian ministers also upheld the legacy of the United Irishmen and even came out in support of nationalism. Rev. Isaac Nelson, originally a minister at First Comber in county Down (a former United Irish stronghold) and subsequently a long-standing minister at Donegall Street (Cliftonville)

[48] *Northern Whig*, 4 December 1863, p. 3; A Belfast Man [A. H. Thornton], *Memoirs of the Rea Family: From the Period of the Irish Rebellion in 1798 Till the Year 1857* (London: s.n., n.d.), pp. 5–16; for Thornton's authorship see D. J. Owen, *History of Belfast* (Belfast and London: W. & G. Baird, 1921), p. 393. Thornton passed away just several days after writing the letter and an obituary stated that at the age of 84 'his memory was as tenacious when he lay on his death-bed as it was in his youth'; *BNL*, 8 December 1863, p. 2; *Belfast Morning News*, 9 December 1863, p. 2.

[49] *BNL*, 3 December 1863, p. 3.

[50] *Belfast Morning News*, 2 December 1863, p. 3; *BNL*, 2 December 1863, p. 3.

[51] *Derry Journal*, 27 November 1867, p. 3.

[52] *Belfast Morning News*, 18 May 1881, p. 3.

Belfast, was a stalwart champion of liberal causes. His support for the Land League and Home Rule lead to his election as a member of parliament for the Irish nationalist party. In 1878, he delivered lectures on 'Ulster and Its Battlefields in 1798' to Irish nationalist audiences in Scotland. In an appeal to the Mayo nationalist electorate in 1880, Nelson presented himself as a living link to 1798. Stating that he had a lifelong commitment 'to carry out the policy of the Volunteers of '82 or that of the United Irishmen of '98', he made it known that his father had been a United Irishman at a time when 'Belfast had given birth to the noblest of organisations'.[53] These declarations were well received by Catholic nationalists. But, after Nelson spoke in 1873 at a Home Rule Conference in Dublin on the topic of 1798 and 'the healthy Republicanism of Ulster Presbyterians' and introduced himself as a 'Presbyterian minister from the North', Rev. William Johnston, the Moderator of the General Assembly of the Presbyterian Church in Ireland, rushed to declare that all other Presbyterian ministers and laymen 'have no sympathy whatever with either Republicanism or rebellion'.[54] Visitations of the Donegall Street congregation conducted by the Belfast Presbytery in 1873 and 1880 revealed a sharp decline in membership, which seemed to indicate that Nelson's politics had alienated many of his Presbyterian communicants.[55]

Popular struggles for tenant rights nurtured a strain of radical liberalism, which was regarded by some Presbyterians as a continuation of the anti-establishment tradition of their United Irish ancestors. In county Antrim, Rev. James Brown Armour of Ballymoney, an outspoken critic of landlord excesses, acknowledged that he grew up in an area in which 'the hanging of alleged rebels . . . was still a living memory to some of the inhabitants'. He took particular pride in the ancestry of his wife, Jennie Adams Stavely Hamilton, the great-granddaughter of the reformed Presbyterian minister Rev. William Stavely, who had ministered to condemned United Irishmen before their execution (including William Orr) and was jailed in 1798. Armour came to endorse Home Rule, for which he was ostracized by unionists. Although he found some support among Antrim liberals, his congregation remained loyalist and in 1893 the Presbyterian general assembly rejected his contention that 'the principle of home rule is a Presbyterian principle.'[56]

In county Down, Rev. Richard Lyttle, the non-subscribing Presbyterian minister of Moneyrea (near Comber), came from a unionist family from near Dromore, but at an early age converted to nationalism and subsequently became an Irish language enthusiast. The tenant-farmer radicalism of his congregation (which had been encouraged by his equally radical predecessor, Rev. Harold Rylett) could be traced back to 1798, when John Miles, a Presbyterian probationer in Moneyrea, was imprisoned and obliged to

---

[53] In 1878, Nelson lectured in Glasgow and Dumbarton; *Nation*, 6 and 20 April 1878, pp. 13 and 4 (respectively). In appealing to Mayo nationalists, Nelson repeatedly alluded to his connections with the United Irishmen; *Connaught Telegraph*, 1 and 15 May 1880, pp. 2 and 3 (respectively); *Belfast Morning News*, 10 August 1880, p. 4 (Mayo electoral campaign); see also Paul Bew, *Land and the National Question in Ireland, 1858–82* (Atlantic Highlands, N.J.: Humanities Press, 1979), p. 98.

[54] *Downpatrick Recorder*, 29 November 1873, p. 3.

[55] Daniel Ritchie, 'Evangelicalism, Abolitionism, and Parnellism: The Public Career of the Revd Isaac Nelson' (PhD: School of History and Anthropology, Queen's University, Belfast, 2014), pp. 189–90.

[56] W. S. Armour, *Armour of Ballymoney* (London: Duckworth, 1934), esp. pp. 28 and 51. For Rev. Stavely's involvement with the United Irishmen see the memoir written by his great-grandson, a Presbyterian minister in Waterside, county Derry; Ferguson, *Brief Biographical Sketches*, pp. 42–58.

emigrate to America, and James Hamilton of Moneyrea, a brigadier-general in the insurgent army, was listed among the most wanted rebels.[57] Lyttle cultivated his community's Ninety-Eight heritage and was considered by his nationalist contemporaries 'a beautiful representative of that type of justice-loving class who once thrilled the manhood of the North in that ever-memorable movement associated with such beautiful men as the Rev. Steele Dickson, Rev. James Porter, Samuel Neilson, the Orrs, M'Crackens'.[58]

Lyttle was later described as 'a true spiritual descendant of those Protestant clergymen who worked and fought with the United Irishmen in 1798' and the mentor 'of the older generation of farmers, grandsons of men who had fought at Ballynahinch and Antrim'.[59] Most notably, he organized in 1896 a party of ladies from Moneyrea to decorate the graves of rebels in county Down in preparation for the centenary of 1798.[60] The unorthodox activities of exceptional individuals like Nelson, Armour, and Lyttle preserved pockets of radicalism in north-east Ulster in which remembrance of the Turn-Out was not entirely washed away by the rising tide of Orangeism.

The entanglement of political affiliations within Ulster families is apparent in the biography of the Belfast-born land reformer and nationalist John Ferguson. His grandfather, a substantial Antrim farmer, supported the republican cause in 1798. In contrast, the father, Leonard Ferguson, was a Presbyterian Tory and married Charlotte Ferris, an Anglican whose family were Orangemen, so that John was raised in a staunchly loyalist Protestant household. When as a youth he came out in support of the northern Young Irelander John Mitchel, his mother, 'who felt bitterly grieved by the apostasy of her son', reputedly remarked: 'Your father's family held these views: they were connected with William Orr, the rebel, and had to fly in '98, so there's rebel blood in your veins.'[61]

At the age of 24, Ferguson moved to Scotland and in 1871 founded the Glasgow Home Government branch of what would become the Home Rule Confederation of Great Britain, which in turn stimulated the Irish Home Rule and land reform movements of the 1870s and '80s. In Glasgow, Ferguson also established, in partnership with the local publisher Duncan Cameron, a press for the publication of Irish nationalist literature. Cameron and Ferguson's 'cheap editions for the people' of key works on 1798 featured several titles on Ulster, including a single-volume edition of Teeling's *Personal Narrative* and *Sequel*—renamed *History of the Irish Rebellion of 1798* (1876), a reprint of McHenry's novel *The Insurgent Chief* (1898), and a compilation of

---

[57] John Miles was among the signatories of a Petition of Sixteen Prisoners at Belfast, 31 January 1799, McCance Family Papers, PRONI D272/23; see also William McMillan, *A History of the Moneyreagh Congregation, 1719–1969* (Moneyreagh: The Church Committee, 1969), pp. 27–8; McMillan, 'Presbyterian Ministers', p. 110. James Hamilton was listed as attending a meeting of United Irish senior military commanders at Saintfield on 31 May 1798 and after the rebellion was wanted as a 'Fifty Pounder'; Rebellion Papers, NAI 620/54/30; *BNL*, 24 July 1798, p. 4.

[58] Seaghan O'Cleírigh, 'Benmore' [John Clarke], *Thoughts from the Heart* (Belfast: Irish News and Dublin: M. H. Gill and Sons, 1907), pp. 113–15.

[59] Bulmer Hobson, *Ireland Yesterday and Tomorrow* (Tralee: Anvil Books, 1968), p. 24.

[60] *SVV*, 1, no. 3 (3 July 1896): pp. 139–40; see also Flann Campbell, *The Dissenting Voice: Protestant Democracy in Ulster from Plantation to Partition* (Belfast: Blackstaff Press, 1991), pp. 377–8; A. C. Hepburn, *A Past Apart Studies in the History of Catholic Belfast 1850–1950* (Belfast: Ulster Historical Foundation, 1996), pp. 177–8.

[61] *Nation*, 17 January 1880, p. 6.

Madden's biographies of northern United Irishmen titled *Antrim and Down in '98* (*c.*1900). These affordable publications contributed to recharging the memory of Ninety-Eight around the time of the centenary of the rebellion.[62]

Historical remembrance, however, was not always at the forefront of public attention. In everyday life, it was often overshadowed by religious devotion. Evangelical Protestantism first spread in Ulster at the end of the eighteenth century. It responded to the crisis of 1798 with intensive missionary activities, which were evident in a steep growth of Methodism in the 'Linen Triangle of Ulster' (the region on the southern side of Lough Neagh, between Lisburn, Dungannon, and Newry), as well as in the area of Lough Erne. The 'Second Reformation', which invigorated Protestantism from the 1820s, mainly affected Anglicans in the south of Ulster, though it was a stimulus for revival elsewhere and a cause for exacerbating sectarian tensions between Protestants and Catholics.[63] These early Protestant awakenings were surpassed by the spectacular evangelical revival that swept Ulster in 1859, which, as noted by Peter Gibbon, 'involved larger numbers of people in sustained common activity than any movement in rural Ulster between 1798 and 1913'. Gibbon pointed out that 'the area to which the revival was primarily confined was none other than that where sixty years before the radicalism of the United Irishmen had flourished' and argued that 'its effects were to displace this ideology and to prepare its bearers for one that allowed their incorporation into an ethnocentric Conservative regionalism.'[64] Nonetheless, many evangelical Presbyterians rejected Henry Cooke's attempt to compound evangelical revival with conservative politics.

In an official account of the evangelical revival of 1859, Rev. William Gibson maintained that religious devotion tamed the excesses of Orangemen by engaging brethren with preaching and prayer and directing them away from 'party spirit'.[65] A diversion of attention was also noticed in regard to radicalism. The visiting English Presbyterian minister Rev. John Weir, described a night-time display of pietism outside Coleraine:

> This was a band of 'United Irishmen,' indeed. In 1798 such a band might have been seen marching in military order, with firm tread, with gleaming pikes, in silence, under the stimulus of mistaken love of country. But now the Author of peace and Giver of concord had been welding all hearts together by the grace of his Holy Spirit, and inspiring these hymns of praise.[66]

Despite these contemporary impressions, it is unclear if the revival actually changed social behaviour in the long term. It is also difficult to positively determine if the religious revival carried explicit political implications. At the very least, it boost Protestant self-confidence,

---

[62] *Nation*, 10, 17, 24, and 31 1880; *Belfast Morning News*, 29 May 1884, p. 5; see also E. W. McFarland, *John Ferguson 1836–1906: Irish Issues in Scottish Politics* (East Linton: Tuckwell Press, 2003). For an advertisement for Cameron & Ferguson 'Books relating to 1798' see *Derry Journal*, 15 April 1898, p. 2.

[63] Hempton and Hill, *Evangelical Protestantism*, pp. 19–60 and 84–92; see also Irene Whelan, *The Bible War in Ireland: The 'Second Reformation' and the Polarization of Protestant-Catholic Relations, 1800–1840* (Madison: University of Wisconsin Press, 2005), p. 166.

[64] Peter Gibbon, *The Origins of Ulster Unionism: The Formation of Popular Protestant Politics and Ideology in Nineteenth-Century Ireland* (Manchester: Manchester University Press, 1975), pp. 44 and 51.

[65] Gibson, *The Year of Grace*, pp. 154–65.

[66] John Weir, *Irish Revivals. The Ulster Awakening: Its Origin, Progress, and Fruit, with Notes of a Tour of Personal Observation and Inquiry* (London: Arthur Hall, Virtue & Co., 1860), p. 111.

which in turn triggered a response from Catholics and increased sectarian hostility.[67] When Catholics began to embrace the memory of 1798 *en masse*, the tense rivalry between the communities contributed towards social forgetting among Protestants.

At first, many Catholics were reluctant to remember Ninety-Eight. The 1790s politicized the Catholics of Ulster and left them with a bitter sense of rejection by the state.[68] The turmoil of the rebellion had been a divisive experience. Catholics were recruited to militia units and sent to quell the insurrection in other provinces, where they were pitted against Catholic rebels. The Hierarchy, which had been placated by the establishment of a seminary at Maynooth in 1795, strongly opposed the rebellion. Advocacy of loyalty was also noticeable on a local level. Parish priests backed communal declarations of loyalty, which were endorsed by most middle-class Catholics. In some cases, it appears that the loyalty of priests was won by applying pressure. Rev. Patrick MacArtan, the parish priest of Loughinisland (near Downpatrick), was brutally assaulted by a party of Orange yeomen and coerced into giving evidence against the United Irishman Thomas Russell. Obliged to profess his loyalty, in 1803 MacArtan sent the local landlord, Mathew Forde of Seaforde, a declaration on behalf of his parishioners which affirmed their 'abhorrence of every attempt towards Rebellion or Anarchy'.[69] The radical Presbyterian minister Rev. Ledlie Thomas Birch, who considered Dissenting clergymen 'well-disposed to Catholic liberty', found that 'the Catholic clergymen are bad friends to liberty.' Yet, calls for loyalty issued by priests were sometimes openly rejected by their parishioners. When Father William Taggart of Saintfield denounced the United Irishmen from the altar, he 'was immediately rebuked in the chapel by one of his congregation'.[70]

Catholic priests were actively recruited by the agents of the government's secret service. Over a period of three years, the Dominican friar Rev. James Mathew McCary, who served as the parish priest of Carrickfergus and Larne, received payments for information he sent Edward Cooke, the undersecretary at Dublin Castle. McCary, who was handled during the rebellion by Sergeant John Lee of the Royal Irish Invalids, discouraged the members of his congregation from joining the United Irishmen, warning them in a sermon of the 'sins and wickedness' of those who take 'illegal and unjust oaths'. In folklore, it was later said that he 'would go to hell for money'.[71] Indeed, the treachery of Catholic clergymen who informed on United Irishmen was

---

[67] Hempton and Hill, *Evangelical Protestantism*, pp. 155–6; Andrew R. Holmes, 'The Experience and Understanding of Religious Revival in Ulster Presbyterianism, *c.*1800–1930', *Irish Historical Studies*, 34, no. 136 (2005): p. 374; Andrew R. Holmes, 'The Ulster Revival of 1859: Causes, Controversies and Consequences', *Journal of Ecclesiastical History*, 63, no. 3 (2012): p. 512.

[68] Elliott, *The Catholics of Ulster*, pp. 227–66.

[69] For MacArtan see O'Laverty, *Historical Account of the Diocese of Down*, vol. 1 (1878), pp. 98–102. See also Oliver Rafferty, *Catholicism in Ulster, 1603–1983: An Interpretative History* (Columbia, S.C.: University of South Carolina Press, 1994), p. 95. For Catholic declarations of loyalty see Chapter 2, pp. 96 and 142; see also Daire Keogh, 'Christian Citizens: The Catholic Church and Radical Politics 1790–1800', in *Protestant, Catholic and Dissenter: The Clergy and 1798, edited by Liam Swords* (Blackrock: Columba Press, 1997), p. 16.

[70] *Memoirs of Theobald Wolfe Tone*, vol. 2, p. 398; see also McClelland, *History of Saintfield and District*, p. 9.

[71] O'Laverty, *Historical Account of the Diocese of Down*, vol. 3 (1884), p. 111; Dickson, *Revolt in the North*, pp. 173–4; John Gray, 'A Loyal Catholic Sermon of 1798' *Linen Hall Review* 4, no. 4 (Winter 1987): pp. 12–13; *Mourne Observer*, 30 August 1968, p. 3 [mistakenly referred to as MacCrory].

recalled locally. In the 1860s, Classon Porter was told that 'old Father Devenny', the parish priest of Ballygowan (near Larne), was 'commonly supposed to have been an informer in 1798'. The 'old croppy' James Burns was convinced that Devenny was responsible for the capture of the fugitive rebel William Murphy, claiming that although he 'did not inform personally himself, he got his mother to do so, but he got the reward'.[72]

Very few northern Catholic priests were involved in the United Irishmen and, unlike other arenas of the 1798 rebellion, none of them became folk heroes. The remote death of the most militant among them, Rev. James Coigly (also spelt Coigley, Quigley, O'Coigley), who was intercepted in England and executed in Maidstone, near Kent, just as the rebellion broke out in Ulster, removed him from local memory, despite his attempt to emulate the martyrdom of William Orr. Wolfe Tone wrote in his diary: 'If ever I reach Ireland, and we establish our liberty, I will be the first to propose a monument to his memory.' In actuality, as noted by Daire Keogh, Coigly was left 'forgotten in the general narrative history of 1798'.[73] Following the centenary of the rebellion, attempts were made to revive and politicize his memory in 1899 and 1900, when pilgrimages were organized to Maidstone and addressed by members of the Irish Parliamentary Party. These events were organized by the London branches of the Irish National League and do not seem to have attracted particular interest in Ulster.[74]

Coigly and Charles Hamilton Teeling were instrumental in forging an alliance with the agrarian secret society of the Defenders, which brought over to the United Irishmen the support of the scions of once prominent Catholic families who still carried considerable influence in the countryside, such as John Magennis and Alexander Lowry in county Down.[75] Disaffection was widespread among lower-class Catholics and many of them rallied to the rebel cause, fighting alongside Presbyterians and other Protestants, though their exact number is unknown. Fears of impending sectarian atrocities played a major role in mobilizing Catholics. McSkimin noted that they were motivated to take up arms by widespread rumours that 'Orangemen were coming at night to massacre them in their beds, having entered into a compact to wade knee-deep in their blood.'[76]

The extent of Catholic involvement in the rebellion was obscured by loyalist propaganda, which circulated claims of Catholic untrustworthiness and sectarian animosity within the United Irish camp. Musgrave stated that around 2,000 Catholics, mainly from the area of Loughinisland, deserted the rebel camp at Ballynahinch and viewed the battle

---

[72] For Fr Devenney see Young, *Ulster in '98*, pp. 44 and 48; also Andrew James Blair, Ballynure, to F. J. Bigger, 8 September 1908, Bigger Papers, BCL K1/A/Z.

[73] *Memoirs of Theobald Wolfe Tone*, vol. 2, p. 324; Dáire Keogh, 'Coigly (Coigley, Quigley, O'Coigley), James', in James McGuire and James Quinn (eds), *Dictionary of Irish Biography* (Cambridge University Press and Royal Irish Academy, 2009), online: <http://dib.cambridge.org/viewReadPage.do?articleId=a1814>. See also Brendan McEvoy, 'Father James Quigley: Priest of Armagh and United Irishman', *Seanchas Ardmhacha*, 5, no. 2 (1970): pp. 247–68; Réamonn Ó Muirí, 'Father James Coigly', in *Protestant, Catholic and Dissenter: The Clergy and 1798*, edited by Liam Swords (Blackrock: Columba Press, 1997), pp. 118–64; Denis Carroll, *Unusual Suspects: Twelve Radical Clergymen* (Blackrock, Co. Dublin: Columba Press, 1998), pp. 23–39. For Coigly's execution see Chapter 1 above, p. 61. Cf. remembrance of priests in other arenas: Nicholas Furlong, *Fr. John Murphy of Boolavaogue 1753–1798* (Dublin: Geography Publications, 1991); Beiner, *Remembering the Year of the French*, pp. 176–8.

[74] *London Daily News*, 15 July 1899, p. 3; *Dover Express*, 13 July 1900, p. 2. See also Ó Muirí, 'Father James Coigly', pp. 159–60.

[75] Elliott, 'The Defenders in Ulster'.   [76] McSkimin, *Annals of Ulster* (1849 edn), p. 99.

from a distance, 'expressing their satisfaction that the Protestants were mutually destroying each other'.[77] Whereas the rebel forces undoubtedly suffered from mass defections, it is difficult to ascertain the veracity of accusations that pinned the desertions primarily on Catholics. A half-century later, James Hope argued that this allegation originated in a 'false report', which had been 'industriously spread' and that in reality 'the Catholics that were there were mixed with the Dissenters, and fought side by side with them, in a common cause.'[78] Nonetheless, Catholic perfidy became a key theme in polemical accounts of the rebellion, such as McSkimin's loyalist history, which stressed discord between United Irishmen and Defenders. Politicized narratives that originated in anti-Catholic propaganda were more readily believed than oral traditions, which recalled shared suffering.[79] Catholics for their part cultivated memories of betrayal at the hands of 'black-hearted', or 'black-mouthed', Presbyterians, who had incited them to take up arms in 1798 and had then left them to bear the brunt of government repression.[80] Accordingly, the memory of the United Irishmen was disunited and split into separate competing memories, leaving Catholics with uneasy recollections.

In the nineteenth century, Catholic nationalists gradually reclaimed the legacy of Ninety-Eight. This appropriation was the outcome of a delayed process, which was particularly stalled in Ulster. Daniel O'Connell, the leader of Catholic nationalism in the first half of the century, rejected the revolutionary tactics of the United Irishmen and yet was constantly accused of subversion by loyalists. In 1828, when John Lawless ('Honest Jack')—the former editor of the nationalist *Ulster Register* and the *Belfast Magazine*—tried to campaign on behalf of O'Connell in Ulster, Catholics were warned by the *Belfast News-Letter* against paying the 'Catholic rent', as O'Connell's member-ship dues were known, with reference to memories of the suffering caused by the 1798 rebellion: 'Let them recollect the subscription of ninety-eight and the purpose to which they were applied in the long run.'[81] When addressing northern audiences during the campaign to repeal the Act of Union between Great Britain and Ireland, O'Connell appealed to memories of Presbyterian rebels in an attempt to win the support of Presbyterian liberals, without acknowledging Catholic involvement in the rebellion.[82]

An early history of Irish republicanism by the nationalist writer John Savage accused the Catholic middle classes and clergy, who supported O'Connell, of forsaking the memory of 1798:

> In the self-created excitement, they forgot the past. Forgot, or seemed to forget the Protestants and Presbyterians who died for them the United Irishmen, whose lives were devoted to them upon a grander issue. The priests apparently forgot those of their own order, who left them the scaffold as well as the altar for a legacy.[83]

---

[77] Musgrave, *Memoirs of the Different Rebellions*, 3rd edn, vol. 2, p. 107.
[78] Madden, *The United Irishmen*, 3rd ser., vol. 1 (1846), p. 393.
[79] McSkimin, *Annals of Ulster* (1849 edn), pp. 117 and 133.
[80] See Gamble, *A View of Society and Manners in the North of Ireland*, pp. 116–20 ('the black-hearted breed'); Young, *Ulster in '98*, p. 51 ('the black-mouthed Dissenters they skulked at the rump').
[81] *BNL*, 12 August 1828, p. 2.
[82] See for example O'Connell's speech at a Repeal meeting in May 1843 at the Belfast Corn Exchange; *Northern Whig*, 13 May 1843, pp. 1–2.
[83] John Savage, *'98 and '48: The Modern Revolutionary History and Literature of Ireland*, 4th edn (Chicago: Union Catholic Pub. Co., 1882; orig. edn 1856), p. 253.

On a local level, however, there were occasions in which Catholic priests found cause to recall the rebellion. For example, at a demonstration held in front of the Ballynahinch Catholic church on 26 April 1840 to protest Lord Stanley's Irish Voters Registration Bill, the parish priest Rev. D. Sharkey referred to the 'scenes of former sanguinary conflict', where 'misguided men have fallen into an unhonoured grave' in an implicit reference to 1798.[84]

Teeling's *Personal Narrative* and *Sequel* presented the recollections of a Catholic United Irishman, yet his account of 1798 in Ulster did not focus in particular on the experiences of Catholics. Although Madden was determined to rehabilitate the memory of Catholic involvement in the United Irishmen, his biographical memoirs and notices overlooked northern Catholics. The only exception was Rev. Coigly. However, unlike his tolerance for Presbyterian ministers associated with the United Irishmen, Madden felt obliged to censure the involvement of Coigly as a priest in military affairs: 'it cannot be forgotten that it is more incumbent on the ministers of religion, than on all other men, to abstain.'[85] The writers of Young Ireland, among them the Catholic Ulsterman Charles Gavan Duffy, lionized the United Irishmen. As pluralist republicans, they strove to de-sectarianize the memory of the rebellion and so did not call particular attention to Catholics.[86] Consequently, for over half a century, remembrance of Catholic participation in 1798 was mostly neglected in printed accounts.

The first substantial attempt to articulate a specifically Catholic cultural memory of the northern rebellion was made outside of Ireland by Peter McCorry, a Fenian journalist of Ulster Catholic background. McCorry lived for a while in Scotland, where he worked as editor of the *Glasgow Free Press* and the *Irish Catholic Banner*. Under the pseudonym Shandy McSherry, he published an early novel titled *Randal M'Cartin: A Story of Ninety-Eight*, which was serialized in the *Free Press* from December 1863 to April 1864. In this work of historical fiction, the northern rebels are Catholics, though this is not explicitly emphasized.[87] In 1868, McCorry emigrated to the United States, where he edited a number of Irish-American newspapers, most notably the *Catholic Herald* in Boston, the *Catholic World* in New York, and the Fenian organ the *Irish People*, and also authored several notable works of Irish-American nationalist fiction. Shortly after arriving in America, McCorry showed his knowledge of the history of the rebellion in Ulster in a lecture on 'The Irish Patriot Martyrs from 1798 to 1866', delivered to a Fenian audience at the Cooper Institute in New York on 8 January 1869.[88] That year he wrote, under the pseudonym Con O'Leary, a novel titled *The Irish Widow's Son; or, The Pikemen of Ninety-Eight*, which was published by Patrick Donohue, editor of the main Irish-American Catholic newspaper the *Boston Pilot*, with the descriptive

---

[84] *Vindicator*, 29 April 1840, p. 2.

[85] Madden, *The United Irishmen*, 3rd ser., vol. 3 (1846), pp. 1–50.

[86] Sean Ryder, 'Speaking of '98: Young Ireland and Republican Memory', *Éire-Ireland*, 34, no. 2 (1999): pp. 51–69; James Quinn, *Young Ireland and the Writing of Irish History* (Dublin: University College Dublin Press, 2015), pp. 84–7.

[87] *Randal M'Cartin: A Story of Ninety-Eight* appeared in the *Glasgow Free Press* in thirteen weekly instalments from 12 December 1863 to 16 April 1864 (with a break between 19 March to 9 April 1864).

[88] *Irishman*, 9 January 1869, p. 435.

subtitle *A Story of the Irish Rebellion, Embracing an Historical Account of the Battles of Antrim and Ballinahinch.*[89]

The preface of *The Irish Widow's Son* professes that 'the facts related in this story will be readily recognized by many who are acquainted with the local history, or traditions of the places mentioned'. Rather than writing a scholarly history, McCorry emulated the narrative storytelling style of folk history in order 'to direct the mind of the reader through the pleasing channel of narrative to the knowledge of a few things connected with the Rebellion of Ninety-Eight', as 'it is well known, that the mass of our people retain historical facts received in this manner, with greater tenacity than when presented to them in the dry order of chronology.' McCorry seems to have supplemented information found in Madden's history with oral traditions, noting that forty years after 'the memorable year of Ninety-Eight' (when he presumably collected his sources in Ulster) 'there are those still living who can recall to mind the yet unwritten stories' and 'there are others whose fathers and mothers were eye-witnesses of strange scenes, sufferers in the "troublous times"'. This history of 'song and story', which could 'not be written at the time of its occurrence', had previously been transmitted 'with hushed voice and bated breath' and 'repeated by the turf fire on a winter's evening'. McCorry's novel was therefore styled as a written representation of a muted oral history.[90]

The choice of title *The Irish Widow's Son; or, The Pikemen of Ninety-Eight* may have been a riposte to James McHenry's popular *The Insurgent Chief; or, The Pikemen of '98*, which centred on the Ulster-Scot Presbyterian experience of 1798 in Antrim. McCorry instead focused on Antrim Catholics driven to rebellion by atrocities committed by Orange 'Wreckers'. A fictional patriotic priest, Father John McAuley, encourages Catholics to become insurgents. The protagonist is a young farmer from the townland of Ballygrooly, near Randlastown, named Cormac Rogan. He is the son of a widow, who dies when her house is torched in a shocking outrage, apparently modelled on an actual incident that occurred in March 1798 in the townland of Fenagh, county Antrim (5 km north-west of Ballymena).[91] Rogan becomes a leader of local rebels and meets the northern United Irish Protestant leaders, including Rev. Porter, McCracken, and Munro. Israel Milliken, a Belfast Presbyterian radical who helped Madden in his investigation, is scripted into a central role as a liaison between the United Irish leadership and the Catholic Defenders, even though in reality Milliken was in prison for the duration of the rebellion.

Rogan ultimately emigrates to America and is joined by friends from home. The book ends with a young clergyman interviewing the Ulster veterans in a depiction of transmission of historical tradition in the diaspora. The setting is not altogether implausible. Among the wave of Presbyterian rebels who left for America, there were also some Catholics. For example, John O'Raw [O'Rawe] of Ballymena, county Antrim, arrived in Charlestown, South Carolina, in 1806. He had fought with the

---

[89] Con O'Leary [Peter McCorry], *The Irish Widow's Son; or, The Pikemen of Ninety-Eight* (Boston: Patrick Donahoe, 1869). See also Loeber and Loeber, *A Guide to Irish Fiction*, p. 809; O'Donoghue, *The Poets of Ireland*, p. 272. For McCorry's activities in Scotland see Terence McBride, 'Fenianism and Irish Associational Culture in Glasgow, 1863–91', in *Romantic Ireland: From Tone to Gonne; Fresh Perspectives on Nineteenth-Century Ireland*, edited by Patrick Lyons et al. (Newcastle-upon-Tyne: Cambridge Scholars Publishing, 2013), p. 100.

[90] O'Leary, *The Irish Widow's Son*, pp. 5–9.   [91] Ibid., p. 97n.

rebels at Antrim as a youth of 15 and was captured, but escaped execution. He was then spared further punishment, thanks to the intervention of his loyalist father, Bryan O'Raw, who had joined yeomen in opposing the rebels at Ballymena. A letter to his parents written in 1809 shows that John O'Raw associated in the American South with other former Antrim United Irishmen, such as William Bones, a Presbyterian from Ballygarvey (3 km north-east of Ballymena), who settled in Savannah, Georgia.[92] However, *The Irish Widow's Son* was not intended for the generation of United Irish emigrants. Like McCorry's other works of fiction, it was primarily aimed at strengthening the Irish identity of the large wave of Catholic immigrants that came to America after the Great Famine. There is no record of the novel's reception in Ireland.[93]

Around the same time as McCorry—writing in America—likened the rebellion in Ulster to that in Wexford, back in Ireland the Franciscan priest Father Patrick Fidelis Kavanagh wrote *A Popular History of the Insurrection of 1798* (1870). Kavanagh made use of oral traditions to write a history of the rebellion in Wexford in which Catholic priests, rather than republican revolutionaries, were placed at the centre of the uprising, unwittingly offering a mirror image of Musgrave's sectarian interpretation. A revised and enlarged version of Kavanagh's work, issued in 1878, claimed to have drawn on 'every available written record and reliable tradition', but deliberately ignored sources that focused on the politics and organization of the United Irishmen (including Madden's volumes). Republished in several editions, Kavanagh's *Popular History* popularized a 'faith and fatherland' interpretation of 1798 that reflected the struggle between Catholic nationalism and Fenianism over the legacy of Ninety-Eight. The rebellion in Ulster did not fit this model. Kavanagh's two short chapters on Antrim and Down tactfully neglect to note the different religious composition of the Ulster rebels. An admission that 'the northerns were, almost without exception, Protestants or Presbyterians' is buried in a footnote in one of many chapters on Wexford.[94]

From the 1870s, just as a rejuvenated Orange Order was expanding in Ulster and alienating Presbyterians from their radical past, nationalists increasingly engaged with the memory of 1798. Significantly, they did not reclaim the neglected and problematic memories of Catholic-Defender participation in the northern rebellion, but appropriated the wider heritage of 1798 in Ulster, with its Presbyterian predominance. Following the repeal of the Party Processions Act in 1872, Catholic nationalists organized annual nationalist parades throughout Ulster to mark Lady Day (the Feast of the Assumption of the Virgin Mary) on 15 August. These processions, which came out in support of Home Rule, mirrored the Orange processions of 12 July. Instead of waving Union flags and decorating themselves in Orange, the participants waved green

---

[92] John O'Raw, Charleston, to Bryan and Nellie O'Raw, Ballymena, 1 April 1809; emigrant letters, PRONI D3613/1/2; Miller, *Irish Immigrants in the Land of Canaan*, pp. 94–103 (information on John O'Raw's experiences in 1798 collected from Brian Moore O'Hara of Ballylesson, county Antrim). Bryan O'Raw's opposition to the rebels was recalled in local tradition; see *Old Ballymena*, p. 27; Smith, *Memories of '98*, p. 54.

[93] Fanning, *The Irish Voice in America*, pp. 79–80.

[94] Patrick F. Kavanagh, *A Popular History of the Insurrection of 1798: Derived from Every Available Written Record and Reliable Tradition*, 3rd edn (Dublin: M. H. Gill & Son, 1880), pp. 41–57 and 153n. See also Anna Kinsella, '1798 Claimed for Catholics: Father Kavanagh, Fenians and the Centenary Celebrations', in *The Mighty Wave: The 1798 Rebellion in Wexford*, edited by Dáire Keogh and Nicholas Furlong (Dublin: Four Courts Press, 1996), pp. 139–55; Whelan, *The Tree of Liberty*, pp. 169–72.

flags and wore green accoutrements. Rather than commemorating King William III, nationalist banners celebrated Irish national heroes and commemorated United Irishmen through such slogans as 'Remember Orr'.[95]

In addition, St Patrick's Day parades in Ulster were co-opted and effectively turned into nationalist demonstrations in which 1798 was frequently mentioned. This incurred a rebuke by the controversial Catholic judge and Tory politician William Nicholas Keogh. At a speech in Londonderry in 1878, Keogh railed against 'retaliatory commemoration', which, as the *Belfast News-Letter* explained to its unionist readers, was a denunciation of 'commemoration of rebellions'.[96] An outburst of riots in Belfast, in response to the inaugural Lady Day celebrations of 1872, showed that loyalist antagonism to nationalist demonstrations was likely to result in sectarian violence.[97]

Despite a large police and military presence at the Lady Day parade of 1876, rioting in Belfast resulted in a number of injuries. The procession, which began in the Catholic area of Smithfield and concluded with a gathering in a field in Hannahstown, a Catholic suburb on the south-western outskirts of the city, performed en route a symbolic memorial gesture in city centre that infuriated Protestant loyalists:

> When they reached the Albert Memorial, the Emmet Band, which accompanied a contingent from Dundalk, commenced to play the 'Dead March.' This change in the musical programme was on account of their proximity to St George's Church, where Henry Joy McCracken was buried, and the band kept up the melancholy strain till past the corner of Corn Market, at which place it is believed McCracken was executed.

In response, an editorial in the *Belfast News-Letter* asked: 'What did Henry Joy McCracken ever do for Ireland that the place at which he was executed in High Street should be dignified as a shrine...?'[98] An offended Belfast loyalist residing in Manchester wrote to protest that the memory of McCracken had been 'dragged from obscurity'.[99] Nationalists repeated this memorial gesture at a Saint Patrick's parade in 1878. Upon passing the site of McCracken's execution, once again the bands played the 'Dead March'. This political appropriation of the national festival provoked rioting of 'Orange rowdies'.[100] A seemingly innocuous non-verbal ritual of remembering 1798 was considered an offensive violation of the status quo of social forgetting, which avoided commemoration in public.

The assertive nature of the nationalist processions and the aggressive response of loyalists served to obscure an ironic transformation of historical memory: at nationalist events, the Protestant leaders of the United Irishmen were being commemorated by northern Catholics, many of whose ancestors had been loyal; this memorialization was vigorously opposed by northern Protestants, many of whose ancestors had been rebels. The brazen co-option of the memory of Ninety-Eight by Catholic nationalists discouraged Protestant unionists from acknowledging in public their own United Irish lineage.

---

[95] Neil Jarman and Dominic Bryan, *From Riots to Rights: Nationalist Parades in the North of Ireland* (Belfast: Centre for the Study of Conflict, University of Ulster, 1997), ch. 2.

[96] *BNL*, 19 and 22 March 1878, pp. 4 and 5 (respectively).

[97] Baker, 'Orange and Green', pp. 798–9; Andrew Boyd, *Holy War in Belfast: A History of the Troubles in Northern Ireland* (New York: Grove Press, 1972), pp. 89–119.

[98] *BNL*, 16 August 1876, p. 3.

[99] *BNL*, 23 August 1876, p. 3 (signed D. Vernon, Broughton, Manchester).

[100] *Freeman's Journal*, 18 March 1878, p. 6.

In the polarized sectarian politics of Ulster, reaction to partisan remembrance was a powerful stimulant for social forgetting.

It is less noticed that the northern Catholics who actually had family traditions from the time of rebellion, as opposed to those who later claimed the cause of Presbyterian rebels, often kept this memory to themselves. Such an example can be found in Charles Arthur Russell, who would become lord chief justice and was raised to the peerage as Baron Russell of Killowen. Russell came from a well-off Catholic family in Newry, county Down, and in his childhood, around the middle of the nineteenth century, had heard from his mother 'stories of those terrible times'. She would often recount how in 1798 her grandmother was assaulted by a soldier, who savagely killed a baby that she held in her arms, and that her husband was incarcerated for lodging a complaint against this atrocity. Later, as a nationalist politician, Russell appealed to Ulster Orangemen that 'they should be in the van of the national movement, as their fathers had been in 1782 and 1798.' Yet, he himself refrained from sharing his painful family recollections and avoided mentioning Ninety-Eight in his public statements. In his most celebrated role as the counsellor for the pre-eminent nationalist leader Charles Stewart Parnell at his examination before a Special Inquiry in 1889, Russell opened the defence with a survey of Irish history in which he decided to 'pass by the hapless story of the Rebellion of 1798'.[101] Personal memory was evidently withheld through self-censorship.

Modernization was also a factor in the reconfiguring of social forgetting. The area of north-east Ulster, more than any other part of Ireland, was drastically altered by the industrial revolution. In the eighteenth century, the manufacture of linen brought rapid economic growth to the region. Following the introduction of industrialized wet spinning from the 1820s, domestic hand spinning and handloom weaving were gradually replaced by machinery. This development would eventually oust the local culture of rhyming weavers, whose vernacular poetry had offered a medium for remembrance of the Turn-Out within their local communities. In addition to the impact of the booming linen industry, urbanization was also accelerated by the development of shipbuilding. With the displacement of timber sailing vessels by iron ships in the second half of the nineteenth century and the establishment of two major shipyards—Harland and Wolff (1861) and Workman Clark and Co. (1879)—Belfast emerged as one of the United Kingdom's major centres of shipbuilding.[102]

Belfast's transformation into a 'workshop of the Empire' made it a very different place from the small town in which the United Irishmen plotted the rebellion and where McCracken was hanged.[103] Most of the new residents of the rapidly growing provincial metropolis came from counties Antrim and Down.[104] Amongst the customs

[101] R. Barry O'Brien, *The Life of Lord Russell of Killowen* (London: Smith, Elder, & Co., 1901), pp. 24–5 and 133; Charles Russell, *The Parnell Commission: The Opening Speech for the Defence Delivered*, 3rd edn (London and New York: Macmillan, 1889), p. 31.

[102] See Andy Bielenberg, *Ireland and the Industrial Revolution: The Impact of the Industrial Revolution on Irish Industry, 1801–1922* (London and New York: Routledge, 2009), pp. 9–52 (linen) and 128–40 (shipping).

[103] Stephen A. Royle, 'Workshop of the Empire, 1820–1914', in Connolly, *Belfast 400*, pp. 199–236.

[104] 'Birthplaces of the Persons Enumerated in the City of Belfast as Constituted at Each of the Census from 1841 to 1911, Together with their Percentages to the Total Population Thereof' (Table XXV) in *Census of Ireland, 1911: Area Houses and Population Province of Ulster, City of Belfast* (Belfast: H. M. Stationary Office, 1912), p. 31. See also S. J. Connolly and Gillian McIntosh, 'Whose City? Belonging and Exclusion in the Nineteenth-Century Urban World', in Connolly, *Belfast 400*, p. 268.

and traditional practices of everyday rural life that were inevitably disrupted by the move to the city, as peasants became Belfastmen, the covert ways in which the Turn-Out had been remembered in the countryside were now subject to erosion. Belfast was perceived as a forward-looking city with little interest in historical traditions. The nationalist politician and writer Stephen Gwynn observed in the early twentieth century that 'Belfast does not dwell much on these memories to-day, nor indeed on any memories; her interest is in the prosperous present, the growing future.'[105]

EXCAVATING MEMORY

In the latter part of the nineteenth century, there was a growing sense of disconnection with the past, which was noticed by contemporaries. Writing in 1877, George Benn, a non-subscribing Presbyterian historian of Belfast, lamented that the radicalism of the late eighteenth century 'has been pushed into the well of forgetfulness', since:

> The men who could speak personally of the sights which they had seen or the deeds which they had done as Volunteers or United Irishmen have all passed away, and it is hardly to be now expected that, among the majority in this young, busy, commercial community, the eloquent and passionate appeals of either body should find an echo.[106]

Benn, who was born in 1801, was among the first alumni of the Belfast Academical Institution, which was founded by former United Irishmen. As a student he had received the commendation of the college's faculty, upon winning in 1819 a gold medal for an essay on 'The history of the parish of Belfast'. This text was expanded into *The History of the Town of Belfast with an Accurate Account of the Former and Present State*, which he published anonymously in 1823 at the age of 22. In this book, Benn covered the rebellion in Ulster in just a few sentences and concluded that 'it will be sufficient to observe that the spirit of political opposition which has so long distinguished the town of Belfast . . . has by no means evaporated.' Clearly, it was inexpedient at the time to elaborate on this sensitive subject. Although he acquiesced to the norms of social forgetting, Benn was confident that in the distant future 'the herald of antiquity must long and faithfully commemorate' these events.[107]

Three decades later, Benn acknowledged that Belfast had dramatically changed and argued that:

> those who remember what this town was fifty or sixty, or even twenty or thirty years ago, should, for the information of the present new generation of inhabitants, and for that of those who in time will push them from their seats, detail what they recollect or have heard

---

[105] Stephen Lucius Gwynn, *Ulster*, illustrated by Alexander Williams (London and Glasgow: Blackie and Son limited, 1911), p. 15.

[106] George Benn, A History of the Town of Belfast: *From the Earliest Times to the Close of the Eighteenth Century*, vol. 1 (London: Marcus Ward, 1877), p. 666.

[107] Anon. [George Benn], *The History of the Town of Belfast With an Accurate Account of the Former and Present State; to which is added A Statistical Survey of the Parish of Belfast, and a Description of Some Remarkable Occurrences* (Belfast: A. Mackay, 1823), pp. 62–6 (actual coverage of the northern rebellion is limited to p. 63). See also Séamas Ó Saothraí, 'Two Ulster Historians', *Books Ireland*, no. 15 (1977): p. 131.

of its past condition. If all the old inhabitants would simply relate what they know for publication, some very important and interesting information would be obtained.

He insisted that recollections should be recorded 'as the changes for some time past have been so marked that the necessary knowledge of the juvenile days of our town may be otherwise, in a great measure, swept into oblivion'.[108] In 1871, Benn began to work on an expanded new edition of his history of Belfast, for which he consulted other local historians, including Classon Porter, and mined all available sources, incidentally uncovering oral traditions that related to 1798.[109] Benn, who was 76 when the first volume of his magnum opus came out in 1877, had come to realize that 'the spirit and enthusiasm of those distant days have long died out in the meaning of the last century' and felt compelled to include an extended section of over twenty-five pages on the rebellion. The concern that modernization detached people from their historical roots had driven him to overcome the inhibitions of social forgetting, to which he had succumbed in his earlier work, and relate the past in greater detail.[110] This impulse was shared by other local scholars.

The sweeping changes in Ulster triggered a revival of antiquarianism, which had been frowned upon in the early nineteenth century. Writing in 1817, Henry Joy, junior, aspired to distinguish his *Historical Collections Relative to the Town of Belfast* from earlier publications, which he lambasted:

> The object of their compilers, who are in general, of the tribe emphatically called *Antiquaries*—a race, partial, narrow-minded and blind to the real interests of mankind—is, for the most part, confined to the deciphering of dilapidated tombstones and worm-eaten charters, the restoring of heraldic shields and obsolete genealogies, and other matters of equal importance; while the great cause of historic truth is thrown contemptuously into the shade.

Buying into the promise that the Act of Union would usher in a new era and brush away the conflicts of the past, Joy maintained that 'Belfast is a town of modern creation and contains not a single object deserving the notice of the antiquary.'[111] By the mid-nineteenth century, scholarly sensibilities had changed and there was growing appreciation for uncovering historical relics, which were perceived to be endangered and in need of preservation.

To cater for this need, the *Ulster Journal of Archaeology* was established as a house publication for local antiquarianism. Its founding editor, Robert Shipboy Macadam (another of the early graduates of the Belfast Academical Institution), rejected disciplinary boundaries and promised that the journal would engage with 'ethnology, topography, philology, music, history both civil and ecclesiastical, and Irish antiquities'. Showing a keen appreciation of folklore, he added that:

---

[108] G. B. [George Benn], 'Reminiscences of Belfast', *UJA*, 1st ser., 3 (1855): pp. 260–4 (quotation from p. 260).

[109] Benn was informed about how a fugitive named Kane, who was 'conspicuous for activity in 1798', hid under an iron plate on the river bank off Castle Street, near the Donegal Arms; George Benn to William Pinkerton, *c.*1873, Benn Papers, PRONI D3113/6/130. Benn had previously heard that the old market house had been used as a prison in 1798; *UJA*, 1st ser., 3 (1855): p. 262.

[110] Benn, *A History of the Town of Belfast*, 2nd edn, vol. 1, pp. 642–68 (comments on forgetting in pp. 646–8).

[111] Joy, *Historical Collections*, pp. iii–iv.

it is worth noting, also that the taste for such subjects is not confined to one class of the community; but exists in a much lower grade of society than would be anticipated. It is not, by any means, rare in Ulster, to meet with men in the humbler walks of life who possess considerable knowledge of history and of local antiquarian lore.

The impetus for collecting records of the past derived from an apprehension that 'that which conquest and colonization failed to effect in centuries, steam and education are now accomplishing peacefully and rapidly; so that, erelong, the traces of the olden time will have faded from our view.' Macadam was convinced that 'almost every townland in Ulster retains memorials of its singularly chequered history' and that 'the whole Province, in fact, at this moment teems with the most varied and remarkable memorials of successive phases of society, still accessible, and still capable of complete elucidation.' However, he feared that time was running out in a race against forgetting: 'The tangled web of Northern Irish History can yet be unravelled by existing aids; but in twenty years more the case will be different' and so 'the present is a fitting opportunity for endeavouring to rescue from oblivion what remains of the History of Ulster.'[112]

In 1852, members of the Belfast Natural History and Philosophical Society, which had encouraged antiquarian work since its establishment in 1821, resolved to curate an historical exhibition to mark the occasion of Belfast hosting a convention of the British Association for the Advancement of Science. A call for donations of artefacts from around Ulster received an overwhelmingly enthusiastic response, which resulted in 'a collection of Irish Antiquities, as has, perhaps, never been brought together before, and such as may hardly be seen again in one place'. Visitors were astonished 'by the number and variety of these relics' and it was believed that the exhibition 'will long be remembered by those who have had an opportunity of visiting it.'[113] Already some years earlier, the society had received a pike that was used in 1798, in a donation that showed that the rebellion was recognized as a memorable historical episode.[114] Although the emphasis of the exhibition at the Belfast Museum in September 1852 was on prehistoric archaeology, a number of more recent artefacts were also accepted, including several items from the rebellion.

As the circulars requesting artefacts had been sent out 'to all the leading noblemen and gentlemen in Ulster', the respondents came mainly from the Ascendancy and therefore most of the 1798 exhibits had been originally acquired as trophies taken from rebels. By the mid-nineteenth century, such triumphal acquisitions were not easily found. Around 1807, when the Scottish travel writer Rev. James Hall visited Bishop Thomas Percy of Dromore—a literary antiquarian renowned for his *Reliques of Ancient English Poetry* (1765)—he was shown 'some curious instruments of death, taken from the rebels in the late rebellion' (including bludgeons, bloodied pikes, and a sawn-off musket). Yet, after Percy died in 1811, the episcopal palace fell into decay and its

[112] M. [Robert Shipboy MacAdam], 'The Archæology of Ulster', *UJA*, 1st. ser., 1 (1853): pp. 1–8 (quotations from pp. 6 and 7); see also the Prospectus for this inaugural issue of the journal (most probably also written by Macadam).

[113] *Descriptive Catalogue of the Collection of Antiquities*, preface. See also *BNL*, 13 September 1852, p. 2; 'Proposed Exhibition of Objects of Antiquity', 'Preparations, Guidelines and Rules for Exhibition', and 'Memorandum of the Antiquities Shown at the Belfast Exhibition'; Young Papers, PRONI 2930/4/4 and 20.

[114] For the earlier donation of the pike see *BNL*, 28 November 1845, p. 2.

contents were dispersed. A prized possession—the green and white plume that had adorned the hat of Henry Munro at the Battle of Ballynahinch—was reclaimed by Percy's agent, Crane Brush, who as captain of the Dromore Yeomanry had taken custody of the rebel general after he was captured. The Brush family, which preserved the relic into the twentieth century, did not see fit to put it on public display.[115]

Souvenirs of Ninety-Eight shown at the Belfast exhibition in 1852 included pikes donated by the Marquis of Downshire and by John Caldwell Bloomfield, of Castle Caldwell, county Fermanagh (whose maternal grandfather, Sir John Caldwell, had been a lieutenant-colonel in the Fermanagh militia and was the county Sheriff in 1798), as well as a ribbon that had been worn by a rebel at the engagement in Randalstown, which was donated by another prominent Fermanagh landowner, Folliet Warren Barton of Clonelly. A more obvious loyalist souvenir was provided by the Belfast merchant Robert Batt, who donated the stands of the colours of the Belfast Yeomanry Corps, a force that had been deployed to suppress the rebellion.[116]

The provenance of other exhibits from the rebellion is less clear and may have been preserved by families associated with the United Irishmen. The Belfast antiquarian James Carruthers of Glencregagh, county Down (near Belfast), donated to the exhibition an 'iron pike of 1798' without explaining how he had acquired this weapon, which stood out from the rest of his impressive collection of ancient antiquities. The family, who were non-subscribing Presbyterians, had an interest in the rebellion. His daughter, Rose Anne Carruthers, collected traditions of 1798 in Ulster and remained involved in Belfast antiquarian circles into the latter part of the century, specializing in making drawings of antiquities.[117] Other rebel arms eluded the antiquarian gaze.

When the rebellion was suppressed, reports were given of 'car-loads of pikes' and arms delivered by the 'thousands, of all kinds'. In the parishes of Broadisland and Island Magee, for example, people came 'voluntarily in large bodies, and delivered up all their arms, consisting of musquets, bayonets, pitch-forks, and pikes'. In Ballymena alone, fifty muskets and eight hundred pikes were given up to the magistrates.[118] Although all remaining weapons were supposed to have been confiscated under martial law, some were secretly retained at great personal risk. For example, the Clements family of Headwood, county Antrim (8 km south-west of Larne), sheltered the fugitive United Irishman and former artilleryman William Murphy and, after his arrest, kept his

---

[115] Rev. James Hall, *Tour through Ireland; Particularly the Interior & Least Known Parts*, vol. 2 (London: R. P. Moore, 1813), p. 210. Crane Brush had presented Munro's plume to Percy and Meredith Darby, the bishop's steward, 'brought home two of the Pikes used by the Rebbles, all bloody, for to be put along with your Lordship's other Curiosities'; Alice C. C. Gaussen, *Percy: Prelate and Poet* (London: Smith, Elder, & Co., 1908), pp. 254–5. In 1906, Francis Joseph Bigger was shown by a descendant of the Brush family 'all that now remains of Munro's plume'; Bigger Papers, BCL K3/69.

[116] *Descriptive Catalogue of the Collection of Antiquities*, pp. 19 (Barton), 42 (Bloomfield), 46 (Batt), and 52 (Downshire).

[117] *Descriptive Catalogue of the Collection of Antiquities*, p. 17. For James Carruthers see Mary Cahill, Raghnall Ó Floinn and Aideen M. Ireland, 'James Carruthers: A Belfast Antiquarian Collector', in *Irish Art Historical Studies in Honour of Peter Harbison*, edited by Peter Harbison and Colum Hourihane (Dublin: Four Courts Press, 2004), pp. 219–60. His collection of antiquities was sold by auction in 1857; *Journal of the Royal Society of Antiquaries of Ireland*, 6th ser., vol. 12, no. 1 (June 1922), pp. 81–2. For traditions of 1798 collected by Miss Carruthers see Young, *Ulster in '98*, pp. 71–2 and 91–3.

[118] Downshire Papers, PRONI D607/F/245 and 251 (Ballynahinch); *BNL*, 12 June 1798, p. 3 (Broadisland and Island Magee); TNA HO 100/81/74–75 (Ballymena).

flintlock musket, which remained in their possession for several generations.[119] Similarly, the "98 flint gun' of James Russell, the innkeeper at Groomsport, county Down (4 km north-east of Bangor), was known to have been 'long preserved' in his pub.[120]

The difficulties entailed in keeping such mementoes can be learned from the history of a gun brought home from the battlefield of Ballynahinch by the wife of a wounded rebel named Anderson. It was given to a hired man named Robb, 'who, in dread of being detected with arms in his possession, destroyed the stock of the gun, plugged the barrel up inside with lard, smeared it outside with tar, and stuck it in the eaves of a thatched dwelling, where it remained concealed and forgotten.' The gun was later discovered by a thatcher and passed into the hands of a tenant farmer named John Tilly, who had it re-stocked so that it could be used for fowling. Tilly was evicted from his holding a decade after the Great Famine and in 1863 emigrated to New Zealand, but upon arrival in Auckland the firearm was seized by customs. Following an appeal, the antiquated weapon was returned to its owner in 1868 and thirty years later, at the time of the centenary of the rebellion, was publicly recognized as 'a relic of '98'.[121] Having gone to such lengths, few families were willing to part with their venerated keepsakes.

A 'Remember Orr' medallion exhibited at the 1852 exhibition was contributed by Miss Getty, a Belfast philanthropist and sister of the antiquarian Edmund Getty. As secretary to the Belfast harbour commissioners and a well-known public figure, Edmund apparently did not want to be directly associated with the memory of the United Irishmen and instead contributed from the family's possessions a Volunteer uniform. Their father, Robert Getty, had been a member of the original Belfast Volunteers and in 1798 was arrested for arming the rebels with two Volunteer canons, though this charge may have been based on false information provided by the informer James McGucken. Under the Union, Robert Getty remained an unrepentant Presbyterian liberal, who supported Catholic emancipation and was among the founders of the Belfast Academical Institution. His radical past was remembered by the family but was not talked about publicly.[122] The display of 1798 relics at the 1852 antiquities exhibition demonstrated a willingness to display in public for the first time mementoes of the rebellion, which had been previously preserved in the private possession of both liberal and conservative unionist Protestant families.

By this time, some nationalists were also ready to openly attest to their ownership of such historical souvenirs. In protesting the controversial Irish Arms Act (6 & 7 Vict. c. 74) put forward in 1843 by the chief secretary Lord Edward Granville Eliot, a reader of the *Nation* mentioned that he had in his possession a sword that his uncle had used at Ballynahinch and declared that 'such a legacy I would not like to lose.'[123] Unlike Protestant unionist antiquarians, it was difficult for nationalists to publicly exhibit relics of rebellion in mid-nineteenth-century Ireland. This could be done with more

---

[119] C. J. Robb Papers, PRONI D2095/18. Murphy had worked as a weaver at the house of Henry Clements of Headwood, county Antrim, until his whereabouts were discovered; Young, *Ulster in '98*, p. 48.

[120] *Irish Book Lover*, 3, no. 12 (1912): p. 197.

[121] *New Zealand Tablet*, 27 May 1898, p. 37.

[122] *Descriptive Catalogue of the Collection of Antiquities*, pp. 43 ('Remember Orr' token) and 46 (Volunteers uniform). For Robert Getty's experience in 1798 see Madden, *The United Irishmen*, 1st ser., vol. 1 (1842), p. 330.

[123] *Nation*, 16 September 1843, p. 10.

ease in the Irish-American diaspora. In 1864, when Fenians organized in Chicago a 'Great Irish National Fair' and appealed to people in Ireland to send 'reliques of Ireland's past history', among the items sent from Belfast were a couple of relics from the Battle of Ballynahinch, including a bayonet that had been taken 'from a redcoat at Ballinahinch' and a blunderbuss that had been used at the battle and had since accrued additional significance through repeated use 'in many a local fight', including the notorious 1849 clash with Orangemen at Dolly's Brae. Other contributions from Ulster sent to the Fenian exhibition were souvenirs that had been specifically crafted in places of significance associated with the memory of Ninety-Eight, including a blackthorn stick cut at one of the first meeting places of the United Irishmen in Belfast and a piece of stone taken from McArt's Fort on Cave Hill, where the United Irish leaders had committed themselves by oath to the revolutionary struggle.[124]

Commenting on how objects can elicit a 'sense of the past', the poet Seamus Heaney perceptively observed that they 'suggest obligations to and covenants with generations who have been silenced'.[125] Relics could be recycled. The antiquarian Robert M. Young noted that 'for years afterwards' school-boys around Antrim collected lead bullets in the fields, which were later sold, and that concealed pikes, when found, were often 'converted to peaceful purposes, the long oak shafts forming capital rungs for ladders'.[126] A late nineteenth-century history of Presbyterian churches in mid-Antrim noted that weapons from 1798 had been refashioned into souvenirs that could be more easily kept in a domestic context: 'Even to this day in some houses in the district may be seen relics of the Rebellion, in the shape of knives made out of swords used at that crisis.'[127] This combination of preservation and redesign reflected the silent regeneration of memory in the private sphere, very little of which was exhibited in public.

The collections of the Belfast Natural History and Philosophical Society that were first displayed in 1852 formed the nucleus of the collections of the Belfast Museum, which would evolve into the Belfast Municipal Museum and Art Gallery, to be renamed in 1962 the Ulster Museum. Over the nineteenth century, the 1798 collection was supplemented with additional items, most notably the uniforms and sword of Henry Joy McCracken, which were donated by Christopher Aitchison, a Belfast publisher and bookseller who married a descendant of the McCracken family and later moved back to his ancestral home in Loanhead, in the Midlothian region of Scotland. These historical artefacts were exhibited in a dedicated display case in a room named after the historian George Benn.[128] After the museum moved to its present location in Stranmillis, it was hailed 'Belfast Rebel's Store House' by a nationalist visitor, who was taken by its

---

[124] *Irish People*, 20 and 27 February and 12 March 1864, pp. 204, 222, and 254 (respectively); see also Brian Griffin, '"Scallions, Pikes and Bog Oak Ornaments": The Irish Republican Brotherhood and the Chicago Fenian Fair, 1864', *Studia Hibernica*, no. 29 (1995): pp. 91–2. The exhibition of these relics was mocked as 'nonsense' in the local Ulster unionist press; see for example *Ballymena Observer*, 1 October 1864, p. 3.

[125] Seamus Heaney, 'The Sense of the Past', *Ulster Local Studies*, 20, no. 20 (1985), p. 109.

[126] Young, *Ulster in '98*, p. 68.

[127] Rev. A. H. Dill, Rev. James B. Armour, Rev. D. D. Boyle, and Rev. John Ramsay, *A Short History of the Presbyterian Churches of Ballymoney County Antrim* (Bradford and London: Percy Lund, Humphries & Co., 1898), p. 30.

[128] For the donation of McCracken's uniform and sword see *Report and Proceedings of the Belfast Natural History and Philosophical Society for the Session 1891–1892* (Belfast: Alexander Mayne & Boyd, 1893), pp. 4 and 11; *BNL*, 3 February 1892, p. 7, 15 April 1892, p. 7 and 22 June 1892, p. 7.

remarkable 1798 collections.[129] However, the museum hosted only a small share of the memorabilia of the Turn-Out.

The Catholic antiquarian Rev. James O'Laverty, who had been a curate in Ahoghill and Portglenone, county Antrim, and was parish priest for thirty years in Holywood, county Down, noted that 'during what were called the bad times, families were afraid to keep such articles, as they were sure to draw upon them the anger of their neighbours.' By the late nineteenth century, the danger had receded and 'any family who now possessed such relics naturally wished to keep them.'[130] Although Aitchison was praised by O'Laverty for 'the great public spirit' he had shown in parting with the valuable heirlooms of the McCracken family, his wife Mary née McCleery—the granddaughter of Henry Joy McCracken and grandniece of Mary Ann McCracken—had chosen to hold on to several mementoes, including various 'Remember H. Joy McCracken' tokens, which reveal that the leader of the Antrim rebels had been commemorated in secret, after the fashion of William Orr.[131] The coat MacCracken was believed to have worn at his execution was preserved by the family of a woman who worked in the household.[132] Similarly, most relics of Ninety-Eight remained stowed away in private possession so that reverence of the rebellion in Ulster was largely kept out of the public domain.

A county Down family history acknowledged that, at the turn of the nineteenth century, relics were to be widely found in the homes of descendants of rebels and loyalists: 'Abundant memories of "98" are still treasured in the minds of the old inhabitants of the Ards, and pikes of the insurgents and relics of the militiamen and yeomanry are reverently preserved as heirlooms in many a homestead.'[133] Even furniture that had been damaged during the rebellion could serve as a domestic *aide mémoire*. The Stavely family preserved a table with sword marks that were left when the house of Rev. William Stavely in Annsborough, county Down (1 kilometre north-east of Castlewellan), was searched and pillaged by the military on 13 June 1798.[134] Similarly, family tradition recalled the origin of a groove left on an old table in a house at Parkgate, county Antrim (7 km south-west of Ballyclare):

> A sergeant having been placed on guard in the house where the table in 1798 was, and being desirous of relieving himself of the weight of his musket, to which a bayonet was attached, rested the point on the table in question, and, to aid in whiling away the time, gently drew the weapon backward and forward, thus leaving 'his mark' on the table, if not elsewhere.[135]

---

[129] *Irish Press*, 2 November 1932, p. 6.   [130] *BNL*, 3 February 1892, p. 7.

[131] Mary Ann McCracken had previously shared the items in her possession with Madden and in the early twentieth century they were shared with the antiquarian Francis Joseph Bigger; A. Penny Francis (Loanhead Town Clerk and agent for the Aitchison family) to F. J. Bigger, 6 April 1907; Bigger Papers, BCL K2/B/13.

[132] In 1948, the coat was owned by 75-year-old Catherine McPeake of Belfast, who had inherited it from her aunt Sarah Dowds, who in turn had received it from her sister Nellie; *Irish News*, 18 September 1948, p. 3.

[133] George Francis Savage-Armstrong, ed., *A Genealogical History of the Savage Family in Ulster* (London: Chiswick Press, 1906), pp. 155–6.

[134] Armour, *Armour of Ballymoney*, p. 51. Rev. Stavely's account of the raid on his house and his subsequent imprisonment (written on 24 August 1798, when he was held at the Artillery Barrack in Belfast), is reproduced in Ferguson, *Brief Biographical Sketches*, pp. 46–51.

[135] Smith, *Memories of '98*, p. 46.

Bullet marks were another enduring reminder of the rebellion. At the end of the nineteenth century, holes left from shots fired in a punitive loyalist attack were still to be seen in the oak beam on the ceiling of a house on the north side of Main Street in Antrim. On the old Market House of Ballymena, the marks of bullets were noticeable on a pillar in what had since been designated as the Town Commissioners' rooms. The bullet-scarred oak door of the Anglican church in Antrim town was kept in the castle of Lord Massereene (where it served as a background panel for the display of a more dignified historical souvenir—the old speaker's chair of the Irish House of Commons).[136] These visible reminders of the rebellion were mostly inaccessible to the general public.

Any item considered by its owners to have sentimental value could imaginatively become a souvenir of the rebellion. Joseph Joy Dean Magee, a constable at Belfast Harbour Police for almost sixty years since his appointment in 1848, cherished as his 'most treasured possession and almost lifelong companion' a walking-stick, 'crooked in a fearful and wonderful manner', which had formerly belonged to Henry Joy McCracken. At the age of 94, in 1907, Magee could 'spin a yarn of bygone days in Belfast with the best of them'. Born sixteen years after the rebellion, the 'stirring events of the troublous times of '98 were kept fresh in his memory as he grew up' and he was known to have an 'immense fund' of anecdotes about the rebellion. The valued walking stick had been presented by McCracken to Rowland Kerr, an employee in his father's cotton mill, and was passed on to his son, Constable Pat Kerr, who bequeathed the heirloom to Magee on his deathbed. Magee fixed to it a silver band with 'a lengthy but suitable historical description', which served as a kind of certificate that vouched for the relic's provenance.[137]

Whereas some souvenirs were cherished continuously from the time of the rebellion, others were discovered at a later date. For example, a pike head found in a bog at Ballyhay, near Donaghadee, county Down, was given to Rev. John Walker, the minister of the nearby Millisle Presbyterian Church. In 1838, Walker gave the relic as 'a small token of his great esteem' to his prize pupil Robert Maxwell Hanna, who would go on to become a minister of the Free Church of Scotland.[138] These findings were generally authenticated by supposition and popular belief. When an old rusty metal pot with lead bullets was uncovered in 1867, during the preparatory excavations for the cemetery on Falls Road in Belfast, it was assumed that it had been there 'since pike time (1798)'.[139] A bullet found in 1885 lodged in an elm tree that had been brought to the Downpatrick Saw Mills from Ballynahinch was believed to have been fired at the Battle of Ballynahinch and was 'preserved as an interesting relic of that memorable encounter'.[140]

Attitudes to these artefacts changed over time. In 1894, a farmer named John Scott found three pikes in 'a fairly good state of preservation' buried in his farm adjoining Ballylintagh Park, halfway between Ballynahinch and Hillsborough. Scott's elderly

---

[136] Smith, *Memories of '98*, pp. 24–5 (house on Main Street, Antrim); *UJA*, 2nd ser., 4, no. 2 (1898): p. 102 (Ballymena Market House); *UJA*, 2nd ser., 10, no. 3 (1904): pp. 97–8 (Antrim church door).

[137] *Larne Times*, 6 April 1907, p. 12; *Belfast Evening Telegraph*, 17 December 1907, p. 6.

[138] Thomas Kilpatrick, *Millisle and Ballycopeland Presbyterian Church: A Short History* (Newtownards: Henry Bros., 1934); p. 86.

[139] *BNL*, 26 September 1867, p. 2.   [140] *Downpatrick Recorder*, 4 April 1885, p. 3.

father, 'who was a very old man, but possessed all his mental faculties', recalled his own father 'pointing out to him the very spot where the spears were buried, the day after the battle of Ballynahinch, when the rebels were routed and the King's troops were scouring the country, and it was certain death to any person in whose possession these weapons were found'. It was 'conjectured that many relics of those stirring times are concealed in the neighbourhood of Ballylintagh'. By the late nineteenth century it had become possible to exhibit such weapons. Accordingly, the discovered pikes were acquired by the local ironmonger, W. J. Gillespie, and displayed in his shop window.[141]

More than anything else, the excavation of human remains and associated objects captured popular imagination and palpably demonstrated how skeletons could come back to haunt loyalist communities with a rebel past. Every once in a while, unionist newspapers reported on instances in which labourers cutting turf in bogs discovered remains that were immediately associated with local traditions of 1798. A skeleton found in 1848 on Ballyboley Mountain, near Ballynure in county Antrim (10 km south-west of Larne), was believed to have belonged to a schoolmaster named McClure, who had been a United Irishman and was suspected of passing information to the government, for which he was 'taken to a lonely house on the mountain and murdered'. Near Ballyna-hinch, labourers found in 1858 a skeleton of a man with 'a green silk handkerchief, in a perfect state of preservation' round his neck and it was maintained that he had belonged to 'one of a party of five or six rebels who were cut down by the troopers while attempting to escape from the battle of Ballynahinch'. Human remains uncovered in 1865 at Cule's Long Bog, near Irvenstown in county Fermanagh, were related to a tradition of a skirmish that had taken place there in 1798 'and the people believe that the remains are those of a rebel slain on that occasion.'[142]

A grave discovered in a field in Ballykine, outside Ballynahinch, sometime around the early 1860s was identified locally as belonging to a rebel named Adair from Greyabbey. The skeleton was found with clothes 'in a perfect state of preservation'. The hat was sent to the museum in Belfast, while the rest of 'the clothing was cut into small pieces, and, with the buttons, distributed among the people of the district.' A quarter of a century later, it was noted that local inhabitants 'still preserve them as interesting souvenirs of the terrible struggle'.[143]

Once identified with the help of local traditions, human remains could be reclaimed and honoured by interested parties. In September 1883, workmen laying water pipes in Ballymoney unearthed at the tower by the old Town Hall a coffin with the remains of 'a stalwart man'. Based on the recollections of the town's oldest inhabitant, the corpse was believed to be that of Alexander Gamble, who had been found guilty at a court martial of Treason and Rebellion and was executed near that spot on 25 June 1798. This discovery 'excited the greatest interest'. Gamble's three grandchildren showed up to provide a new coffin and arranged for the reinterment of the remains in the old Ballymoney churchyard, in the presence of 'a number of respectable inhabitants'. Twenty-five years later, in 1908, the new burial site was marked with a granite tombstone memorial, which acknowledged that he had been 'an insurgent of '98'.

[141] *Lisburn Herald and Antrim and Down Advertiser*, 21 April 1894, p. 4.
[142] *Belfast Protestant Journal*, 24 June 1848, p. 4; *Downpatrick Recorder*, 19 June 1858, p. 3; *Londonderry Standard*, 24 June 1865, p. 3.
[143] Lyttle, *Betsy Gray*, ch. 36.

The original report of the execution at the time of the rebellion observed that Gamble 'was extremely penitent—confessed his crime—and acknowledged the justice of his sentence', but, over a century later, this contrition was not acknowledged on the gravestone, which quoted a verse from 'The Memory of the Dead' as a triumphant epitaph: 'They rose in dark and evil days to right their native land.'[144] Whereas Gamble was relatively unknown, the discovery of graves associated with more famous rebel heroes caused greater sensation.

On 23 November 1843, construction works on a family vault in the Lisburn Cathedral cemetery uncovered remains, which were brought for identification to Rev. Edward Cupples, the Rector of Glenavy and Vicar General of Down and Connor, who was known to be 'profoundly erudite, and rich in traditional and antiquarian lore'. After inspecting fragments of a coat and buttons that were found by the corpse, Cupples ascertained that this was the grave of the rebel general Henry Munro. As a youth, he had attended the execution of Munro with his father, Rev. Snowden Cupples, who had been called upon to minister the last sacrament to the famous rebel. Although both father and son were staunch loyalists and prominent Orangemen, they maintained a fascination with the rebellion. The obituary of Edward Cupples noted that 'of the days of '98 he had many exciting recollections, and his descriptions of some scenes which took place in Lisburn between the authorities and several of the condemned insurgents were of the most melancholy character, and, at the same time, the most graphic.' Cupples held on to the buttons and coins that had been retrieved from the grave and these remained as heirlooms in his family to be shown by his niece to the antiquarian Francis Joseph Bigger in the early twentieth century.[145]

The finding of Munro's corpse stirred 'considerable excitement' in Lisburn. Examination of the severed head showed that 'part of the hair was found on his skull and his brains entire', which was taken as evidence that 'the head had been covered with a pitched cap when put on the Market House' ('pitchcapping' the heads of rebels with hot tar was recalled as a notorious form of torture in 1798). Nationalist newspapers expressed disapproval of the 'unmanly outrage', in which the remains of 'one of the most celebrated leaders of the Irish rebellion' were 'shamefully exposed', and pointed out that 'even to this day his memory is spoken of with the utmost respect.'[146]

---

[144] The execution was reported in the *BNL*, 29 June 1798, p. 2. News of the discovery of the remains appeared in local and national newspapers: *Coleraine Constitution*, 15 and 22 September 1883, p. 5; *Ballymoney Free Press and Northern Counties Advertiser*, 22 September 1883, p. 2; *Freeman's Journal*, 18 September 1883, p. 7 (reported also in provincial newspapers throughout Britain). The testimony of two of Alexander Gamble's grandsons appears in Smith, *Memories of '98*, pp. 63–4. For the erection of the memorial see *UJA*, 2nd ser., 14, no. 4 (1908): p. 158; for a photo see Murray and Cullen, *Epitaph of 1798*, p. 8; see also Beattie, *Ballymoney and the Rebellion 1798*, pp. 24–5.

[145] *BNL*, 2 December 1857, p. 1; also *Belfast Mercury*, 27 November 1857, p. 2. In 1838, McSkimin collected from Edward Cupples his recollections of Henry Munro and what he had heard from his father. In the early twentieth century this information was retrieved by F. J. Bigger, who traced the whereabouts of the souvenir buttons and coins in the possession of the surviving relatives; Bigger Papers, BCL K3/H/15–17, 58, 76, and 79.

[146] The news of the discovery was first announced in *Dublin Monitor*, 29 November 1843, p. 2; soon after, it appeared in *Freeman's Journal*, 30 November 1843, p. 3 and *Cork Examiner*, 1 December 1843, p. 3; for a notice in the northern press see *Vindicator*, 2 December 1843, p. 3. The manuscript in which Edward Cupples described his examination of the remains was copied by F. J. Bigger in 1906; Bigger Papers, BCL K3/H/126.

Local tradition recalled the details of Munro's beheading at the hands of a pardoned rebel:

> The morning was wet, and the handle of the axe was so slippery, that the man said he could not hold it properly, so one of the dragoons who was in attendance pulled a piece of chamois out of his wallet and threw it to him. He wrapped it round the handle and used it, but the handle was broken by the force of the blow. The axe, handle and all, were put in the grave with the headless corpse.[147]

An axe was indeed found alongside the corpse and it immediately became a coveted object. It was possessed by a local solicitor with antiquarian interests, George Stephenson, who was said to have also acquired Munro's blunderbuss. On Stephenson's death in 1868, his 'rare and well-known collection of antiquities' was put up for sale by the Belfast auctioneer Hugh Hamilton and the axe fetched 3 shillings (just slightly less than a wig that had belonged to Daniel O'Connell). It was subsequently kept in the house of a respectable merchant and justice of the peace, James Theodore Richardson, in nearby Lissue (3 km west of Lisburn).[148]

In contrast to this record of genteel transactions, the preservation of the gruesome relic was given an alternative folkloric history, which was taken down in the late nineteenth century by the Newtownards journalist and author W. G. Lyttle:

> A soldier's hands held the axe by which Monro's head was struck off. With the blood still reeking on its blade, the soldier rushed into a marine store kept in Lisburn by a Mrs. Griffin, and, throwing down the weapon, demanded for it the price of a naggin of whiskey. The woman regarded the bloody instrument with feelings of horror, but knowing how dangerous it was in those days to refuse compliance to the demands of a soldier, she gave threepence to the man, who left with her the hatchet and departed. On the same day a Glassdrummond farmer, named Thomas Murray, was in Lisburn selling peats. He called on Mrs. Griffin, and the poor woman begged him to take away the hatchet, as neither luck nor grace could follow the house that gave it shelter. Murray gave her a bag of turf in exchange for the axe, and sold the latter for seven and sixpence to Hugh Duncan, a carpenter in Glassdrummond. His son, James Duncan, had the axe long in his possession, showing it to the writer of this story. It is now in the possession of the Richardsons, of Lissue.[149]

Unlike McCracken's exquisite Volunteer sword, which was wrought of silver and had a bone handle, and was even the subject of poems,[150] the crude axe was not donated to the Belfast museum or put on public display (Fig. 4.1). Even more significantly, after

---

[147] R. Nevin, Chrome Hill, Lisburn, to R. M. Young; Young, *Ulster in '98*, pp. 83–4 (reproduced also in *BNL*, 19 June 1893, p. 3).

[148] The whereabouts of the axe were tracked down by F. J. Bigger in 1904–5; Bigger Papers, BCL K3/H/16–17, 56, 59, and 72. For the sale of the axe see *Northern Whig*, 30 April 1868, p. 3 and *Belfast Morning News*, 1 May 1868, p. 3. A photograph taken a half-century later by late T. McNeilly of Ballynahinch appeared in *Mourne Observer*, 28 June 1968, p. 10 [reproduced in Lyttle, *Betsy Gray* (1968 edn), appendix, p. 164].

[149] Lyttle, *Betsy Gray*, ch. 39. Belfast nationalist Robert Hanna claimed in 1897 that the axe was 'still kept by a farmer at Glassdrummond, near Ballynahinch', but was probably misinformed; *Nation*, 24 April 1897, p. 10.

[150] The poem 'Harry's Sword', attributed to 'a distinguished Presbyterian clergyman', was first published in Samuel Lover, ed., *The Lyrics of Ireland* (London: Houlston and Wright, 1858), pp. 295–6. It had previously inspired the poet Mary Balfour to compose another poem sometime shortly after the rebellion; see Young, *Historical Notices of Old Belfast*, p. 279.

(a)

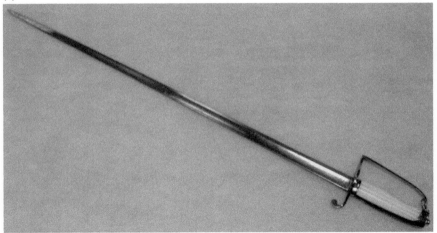

(b)

Fig. 4.1. Relics of two Henrys: Henry Joy McCracken's sword and the axe that beheaded Henry Munro

(a) Volunteer sword of Henry Joy McCracken.

Photograph courtesy of the National Museum of Northern Ireland, Ulster history collection (BELUM.O475.1914).

(b) Photograph of the axe which was believed to have been used for the beheading of the insurgent general Munro. Taken sometime in the early twentieth century by Mr McNeilly of Mourneview, Ballynahinch and published in *Mourne Observer*, 28 June 1968.

Reproduced by the National Library of Ireland with the newspaper's permission.

Munro's remains were reinterred in the churchyard, the location of the grave was once again forgotten. Memory had been momentarily resuscitated but soon after was quite literally put to rest, so that social forgetting was effectively renewed.

In 1853, extensive drainage works on Lough Neagh necessitated the replacement of the bridge over the river Bann at Toome. Unexpectedly, 'the scenes of 1798 were resumed' at the site of the old bridge following the discovery of a skeleton that was believed to belong to a local rebel named Rodger (Roddy) McCorley. Remarkably, the bones were found to be 'quite fresh and nothing decayed after fifty-five years'.[151] McCorley was a local folk hero, who had eluded the official historical record. His name does not appear in the government's Rebellion Papers and is not listed in the 'Black Book of the North of Ireland'—a register of some two hundred northern United Irishmen—or in any other report from 1798, so that the extent of his actual involvement in the insurrection is unknown. He was reputedly a member of Thomas Archer's 'desperate gang of villains', most of whom were apparently deserters from the military and could therefore not avail of amnesty. For nearly two years after the insurrection, these 'desperadoes' continued to commit acts of violence in the mid-Antrim area of Ballymena, keeping the district in 'alarm and terror' and extracting 'vengeance' from 'such as were notorious for having deserted the good cause of rebellion'.[152]

McCorley's engagement in post-rebellion low-scale insurgency ended with his arrest in early February 1800, as part of a clampdown on Archer's gang. McCorley was bought before a court martial in Ballymena on 20 February and was 'charged with being a rebel never having surrendered appearing in arms in furtherance of the Rebellion, socializing with rebels and committing many wanton acts of cruelty and depredation on His Majesty's peaceable subjects', for which he was sentenced 'to be hanged at Toomebridge for his great atrocities until he is dead, and his body to be buried under the gallows'. As an additional gesture of degradation, his corpse was to 'be given to the surgeon of the Tay fencibles for dissection'. A letter published in the *Belfast News-Letter* confirmed that this sentence was indeed carried out in 'a most awful procession' on 28 February 1800.[153]

McCorley seems to have been considered a 'social bandit' and his execution was long recalled in the locality, appearing in an entry on 'Remarkable Circumstances' in the parish memoir compiled by James Boyle for the Ordnance Survey in 1836.[154] Yet his memory was also subject to social forgetting. In 1833, the distinguished antiquarian and music collector George Petrie took down in nearby county Derry the score of a 'pleasing melody' associated with a ballad that 'was composed to preserve in remembrance the acts and fate of a certain Roddy M[c]Curley'. Petrie was not given the lyrics of the ballad. He gathered that it related to someone who 'was hanged at Toomebridge',

---

[151] *Catholic Telegraph*, 10 December 1853, p. 2. For the construction works at Toome see *Twenty-First Report from the Board of Public Works, Ireland* (H. M. Stationary Office: Dublin, 1853), pp. 178 and 183.

[152] *BNL*, 21 January and 4 February 1800, pp. 3 and 2 (respectively). The 'Black Book of the North' is found in McCance Family Papers, PRONI D272/1 and 42. For Thomas Archer see Chapter 2 above, pp. 132–3.

[153] Confirmation by Lord Castlereagh of the Court Martial Sentence of Roger McCorley, 23 February 1800, Kilmainham Papers, NLI MS 1200/262–3; *BNL*, 4 February 1800, pp. 2–3 and 4 March 1800, p. 3. See also Patterson, *In the Wake of the Great Rebellion*, p. 62.

[154] Memoir of Parish of Duneane by James Boyle (May 1836) in Day and McWilliams, *Ordnance Survey Memoirs*, vol. 19, p. 118.

but was unable to ascertain 'at what time, or for what reason, he so suffered', even though he had 'taken more trouble with a view to acquire information on these points, than, perhaps, the inquiry deserved'. He was left to surmise that McCorley 'was a person of the peasant class who had been implicated in the "troubles" of "Ninety-eight"'. Evidently, outsiders were not privy to the details of local folk memory.[155]

The old bridge of Toome functioned as a local site of memory, which was commonly associated with the rebellion. In 1798, insurgents had destroyed one of its arches in an attempt to prevent military reinforcements from crossing into Antrim but the army soon regained control over the area and the rebels were dispersed.[156] The construction of a new bridge in 1852 seemed to be 'evidence of old things passing away and new objects taking their places' and it was recalled that over the old bridge 'many a loyalist as well as many a rebel has passed in times more troublous than now'. The discovery of McCorley's skeleton 'invigorated again into life' stories that were 'long lost in oblivion'. A local witness observed the reawakening of memory:

> The aged persons were telling the tales of by-gone feuds and their consequences, and of chiefs who fell victims to their own folly. They were telling of the valiant youths hanged at Toome in those days, and pointed to the very trees on which they had atoned for their rebellious crimes. The young, with the interest peculiar to their years, were listening attentively, and gazed with awe as the stones were removed and the bones presented to view, of him who has been the subject of song, which has kept fresh in his country's memory.

Relatives of 'the notorious rebel' McCorley, who was now hailed 'a leader in the late rebellion of '98', reclaimed his 'crumbling remains' and had them buried in the nearby Protestant churchyard of Duneane.[157] It was later recalled that 'the Protestant or Orange element resented this' and that 'the great concourse at Rody's burial headed by the navvys from the bridge building forced their rights.'[158] Tellingly, Roddy McCorley was reinterred in a family grave without his name being added to the tombstone.[159]

Within twenty years of this contested moment of revival, the memory of McCorley was again clouded in obscurity. In 1872, Adam Dickey of Cullybackey, county Antrim (17 km north-east of Toome), made inquiries about recollections of Thomas Archer's gang of outlaws, but found that people in the area could not properly recall the name of 'Roderick or Roddy, or Royce McCurley (McGorley, or McSorley)'.[160] Roddy McCorley

---

[155] George Petrie, *Ancient Music of Ireland*, vol. 2 (Dublin: M. H. Gill and Son, 1882), p. 37. For a modern scholarly edition see David Cooper and Lillis O Laoire, eds, *The Petrie Collection of the Ancient Music of Ireland* (Cork: Cork University Press, 2002), p. 239.

[156] Diary entry of Captain-Lieutenant John Henry Slessor for 9 June 1798, reproduced in Hayter, *The Backbone*, p. 42; Lord Lieutenant Camden to Duke of Portland, Dublin Castle, 12 June 1798, TNA HO 100/81/74–75; Dublin Castle bulletin, dated 12 June 1798 (printed by George Grierson).

[157] *Northern Whig*, 13 December 1853, p. 1. This account was later reproduced by the historian of Orangeism Robert Mackie Sibbett, a loyalist Presbyterian from Portglenone, county Antrim (16 km north of Toome), who maintained a keen interest in the heritage of 1798; Robert M. Sibbett, *On the Shining Bann: Records of an Ulster Manor* (Belfast: Baird, 1928), p. 181.

[158] Statement by Francis Joseph Bigger (c.1907); Bigger Papers, BCL Z271.

[159] Francis Joseph Bigger, *Rody MacCorly: 'Who Fears to Speak of '98?'* (Belfast: s.n., 1907), pp. 8–9. Also buried in Duneane is the man who according to local tradition hung McCorley from the bridge at Toome, Sergeant William Dallas of the Dunbartonshire Fencibles; see McClelland, 'Thomas Archer and His Gang', p. 17.

[160] Fitzpatrick, *The Sham Squire*, 6th edn, pp. 351–2.

would ultimately become a household name among nationalists and aficionados of Irish folk song, thanks to an extremely popular song written for the 1798 centenary by the Belfast poet Ethna Carbery (pseudonym of Anna Johnston) and published in the beginning of the twentieth century. Through a dynamic similar to what experimental researchers of memory have labelled 'retrieval-induced forgetting', whereby newly acquired information inadvertently supplants earlier memories, this new composition eclipsed an older traditional song, which was still recalled in the locality but was generally unknown to outsiders and remained obscure.[161]

The practice of 'invention of tradition', which has attracted considerable scholarly attention since it was conceptualized by the historian Eric Hobsbawm and the anthropologist Terence Ranger, has not been sufficiently interrogated: as can be learned from the discovery of relics, which are imaginatively re-invested with meaning but can then lapse into obscurity, reinvention of memory also entailed regeneration of social forgetting.

COUNTERING NEGLECT

It was less difficult to speak, and write, openly of Ninety-Eight abroad than in Ireland. The subject was covered in popular nationalist publications that came out in America in the mid-nineteenth century. For example, William Lyon Mackenzie's biographical compendium *The Sons of the Emerald Isle* included several references to northern United Irishmen. The original edition (1844) had entries on Henry Munro and Henry Joy McCracken and a second edition (1845) added an entry on Rev. Porter (mistakenly listed as William, and not James, Porter). It also noted that the linen merchant Alexander Brown emigrated in consequence of the rebellion and it was recognized that the mathematician Robert Adrain had formerly been a rebel commander.[162]

Nonetheless, a history of *The Irish Confederates, and the Rebellion of 1798* (1851) written by the American Presbyterian minister Henry Martyn Field allocated only a single paragraph to Ulster, effectively dismissing the northern rebellion.[163] A sympathetic history of the 1798 rebellion published in London by the English Unitarian minister and journal editor Philip Harwood included a nine-page section on Ulster, which recycled information from Teeling and Madden. Harwood's history was later praised in a nationalist newspaper for 'a tone by no means "loyalist" or "English"', but, when it first appeared, it does not seem to have attracted particular attention in Ulster.[164]

---

[161] See Chapter 5 below, pp. 413–15. For 'retrieval-induced forgetting' see E. L. Bjork, R. A. Bjork, and M. D. MacLeod, '7 Types and Consequences of Forgetting: Intended and Unintended', in *Memory and Society: Psychological Perspectives*, edited by L. G. Nilsson and N. Ohta (New York: Psychology Press, 2006), pp. 331–54.

[162] William Lyon Mackenzie, *The Sons of the Emerald Isle; or, Lives of One Thousand Remarkable Irishmen Including Memoirs of Noted Characters of Irish Parentage or Descent*, 2nd edn (New York: Burgess, Stringer, and Company, 1845), pp. 36–7, 45, 65–7, 70–3, and 83–5.

[163] Henry M. Field, *The Irish Confederates, and the Rebellion of 1798* (New York: Harper & Brothers, 1851), pp. 250–1.

[164] Philip Harwood, *History of the Irish Rebellion of 1798* (London: Chapman & Elcoate, 1844); *Freeman's Journal*, 27 March 1886, p. 5.

The thrust of Musgrave's seminal *Memoirs of the Different Rebellions in Ireland*, which deliberately downplayed the northern rebellion, continued to dominate Irish historiography and to a large extent shaped public discourse on 1798. An article published in the *Downpatrick Recorder* on 9 June 1838 to mark the fortieth anniversary of the rebellion featured an account of the insurrection in county Down, which was lifted without attribution from Musgrave, under the assumption that it 'may not be uninteresting to many of our readers'.[165] The influence of Musgrave's belittling of the insurrection of Ulster was pervasive.

A chapter on the insurrection in a *History of the Civil Wars of Ireland* published in 1831 by the Whig historian William Cooke Taylor—a Protestant from county Cork who was educated in Trinity College Dublin—reflected liberal memories of loyalist atrocities in 1798, yet covered the events in Ulster in a single paragraph.[166] Patrick O'Kelly, a former rebel from county Kildare, wrote a *General History of the Rebellion of 1798*, which was published in Dublin in 1842. During a period of exile in France, O'Kelly had renounced his support for militant republicanism but was still determined to present the insurrection in a heroic light. His history included a very short section on Ulster, which reached similar conclusions to those of Musgrave:

> the terrible examples which had been made during the short period of the people's struggle in the two counties of Down and Antrim, deterred them effectually to make any further attempt at insurrection.... The awful massacres which occurred on both sides, the army and the people, in the county of Wexford alone, operated on the minds both of Presbyterians and Protestants, so as to influence them to join the ranks of the yeomanry corps throughout Ulster, under the general name of the Orangemen of the North, who thus form to this day, a body of people in compact alliance against the Catholic population of Ireland.[167]

A New and Improved History of the Rebellion, written by S. L. Corrigan and published in Belfast in 1844 to loyalist acclaim, purported to be 'abridged from the most authentic sources', but mainly relied on Musgrave, reproducing entire passages, and accordingly allocated few pages to Ulster.[168] A history of Belfast and county Antrim by James Adair Pilson, published in 1846, briefly presented the key events of 1798 as an insignificant diversion that preceded the era of progress under the Union.[169] Although written from different perspectives, all these works followed Musgrave in attributing little consequence to the northern arena of the rebellion.

---

[165] *Downpatrick Recorder*, 9 June 1838, p. 2; for the original see Musgrave, *Memoirs of the Different Rebellions*, 3rd edn, vol. 2, pp. 103–7.

[166] W. C. Taylor, *History of the Civil Wars of Ireland, from the Anglo-Norman Invasion till the Union of the Country with Great Britain*, vol. 2 (Edinburgh: Constable, 1831), p. 318.

[167] Patrick O'Kelly, *General History of the Rebellion of 1798: With Many Interesting Occurrences of the Two Preceding Years: Also, a Brief Account of the Insurrection in 1803* (Dublin: J. Downes, 1842), pp. 268–76. For the historiographical context see Liam Chambers, 'Patrick O'Kelly and the Interpretation of the 1798 Rebellion in County Kildare', in *Kildare: History and Society*, edited by William Nolan and Thomas McGrath (Templeogue, Dublin: Geography Publications, 2006), pp. 439–59.

[168] S. L. Corrigan, *A New and Improved History of the Rebellion in Ireland in the Year 1798, Abridged from the Most Authentic Sources* (Belfast: James Wilson, 1844), pp. 82–95; cf. Musgrave, *Memoirs of the Different Rebellions*, 3rd edn, vol. 2 (1802), pp. 93–110. For an example of loyalist acclaim see *Belfast Protestant Journal*, 1 and 22 June 1844, p. 4.

[169] James Adair Pilson, *History of the Rise and Progress of Belfast, and Annals of the County Antrim* (Belfast: Hodgson, 1846), pp. 21–3 and 148–51.

The most popular history of 1798 to come out of the mid-nineteenth century was written by the novelist William Hamilton Maxwell, who was born in Newry, county Down, and had personal recollections from his childhood of the rebellion in Ulster. Maxwell's *History of the Irish Rebellion in 1798* was initially issued in serial form, appearing in 1844 in fifteen parts and twelve numbers. The *Belfast News-Letter* took issue with its portrayal of the insurgent leadership as 'untalented fools' and maintained that they 'were very far from being the silly characters depicted by Mr. Maxwell, and if he wish his history to *live*, he will take a very different view of the men engaged in that tremendous undertaking.'[170] However, the negative light in which the United Irishmen were cast did not hinder the success of Maxwell's history, which was praised in the English press for its riveting style.[171] In 1845, it was issued as a single volume, which was republished in multiple editions into the early twentieth century: the London publisher Henry George Bonn published five editions between 1852 and 1864 and, after his firm was taken over by George Bell (originally in partnership with Frederick Daldy), another eleven editions came out between 1866 and 1903.

Maxwell, in his preface to the *History of the Irish Rebellion in 1798*, took pride in having consulted a wide range of sources, including early historical accounts, as well as 'manuscripts for the first time printed' and 'private details of men still living, and who themselves enacted a leading part during that troubled era'. The promise of 'strict impartiality' masked a distinct loyalist bias, which was denounced in the nationalist *Freeman's Journal* as a 'tissue of vile and despicable falsehood'. Maxwell's coverage of the rebellion in Ulster was more thoughtful than that of other contemporary writers. He was well aware of the scale of the rebellion's northern arena, having written twenty years earlier his first historical novel, *O'Hara* (1825), on the topic. Nevertheless, he accepted Musgrave's frame of reference and allocated only one out of thirty-one chapters to the rebellion in Antrim and Down.[172] The Presbyterian minister Rev. Alexander P. Goudy branded Maxwell 'an Orange squire . . . steeped in narrow-souled bigotry, and hatred of the people' and lambasted his account of the rebellion in Ulster as an 'historical falsehood'. This harsh judgement, however, derived from Goudy's desire to completely bury the memory of Presbyterian involvement in 1798 and to disingenuously rewrite history as if Anglicans had been 'far more directly and extensively implicated'.[173]

In describing the insurrection in Ulster, Maxwell's narrative was more nuanced than his categorically negative accounts of the other arenas of the rebellion. He deployed excerpts from McSkimin, Musgrave, Teeling, and Madden, as well as a less familiar manuscript journal of a field officer, in order to demonstrate 'the folly of precipitating into action tumultuary masses of men, under chiefs incompetent to direct their movements'. Unlike his depictions of the rebels in Wexford as primitive savages, the 'cannie Northerns' were credited for their 'great determination' and for having

---

[170] *BNL*, 16 January 1844, p. 2 (emphasis in the original).

[171] See for example *Era*, 18 May 1845, p. 5.

[172] William Hamilton Maxwell, *History of the Irish Rebellion in 1798; with Memoirs of the Union, and Emmett's Insurrection in 1803* (London: Baily Brothers, 1845), preface and ch. 20; a previous chapter looks at the political background in Ulster and several additional sections refer to the northern rebellion, see pp. 290–2, 324–5, and 331–2. For its negative reception in the nationalist press see *Freeman's Journal*, 17 April 1844, p. 2; also *Cork Examiner*, 12 January 1844, p. 4.

[173] Goudy, *Right versus Might*, p. 21.

assembled 'very superior materiel to the insurgents of the South'. Maxwell reproduced snippets of interviews he claimed to have had with former 'discomfited insurgents' in order to show that the rank and file were disillusioned by the misconduct of their 'affishers' [officers] and that this resulted in mass defections, so that 'the hale airmy had melted away, like snaw aft a dyke' [the whole army had melted away like snow off a dyke]. The unsympathetic assessment of the defeat of the rebels, which is attributed to the 'imbecility or cowardice of their leaders', is tempered by a measure of ambiguity. Though Henry Munro is first presented as an 'imbecile commander', he is also portrayed as a 'romantic character'. A hostile account of Munro's execution is subsequently retold in a more favourable light, so as to emphasize 'the terrible visitations on both the guilty and the innocent, which were unfortunately too common in those turbulent times of civil warfare'. Acknowledging that excesses were committed by the military in Ulster (and giving credit to Madden's 'startling revelations' of these deeds), Maxwell asserted that the rebellion was ultimately suppressed by 'the terrible severity fulminated not only against the actual insurgents, but also those who resetted or assisted them' and claimed that 'on the Northerns the lesson was not lost'.[174]

Maxwell's ambivalent, and somewhat befuddled, description of the rebellion in the North made it less memorable than his distinctly negative account of the rebellion in the South, which received the lion share of his attention. The historical narrative was illustrated with twenty-one drawings by the renowned caricaturist and book illustrator George Cruikshank (who had famously drawn the artwork for the original edition of Dickens's *Oliver Twist*). On the original cover design, Cruikshank presented Maxwell's history as a monument to the rebellion, at the foot of which both Britannia and Hibernia (the female allegorical depictions of England and Ireland) pay solemn tribute. Cruikshank's graphic depictions of Catholic rebels engaged in wanton violence became iconic representations of loyalist memory. As none of the images portrayed scenes from Antrim and Down, visual disregard of Ulster rendered the rebellion's northern arena less noticeable and contributed to social forgetting.[175]

For most of the nineteenth century, Irish historiography continued to discourage remembrance of the northern rebellion in Ulster. The extent of historical neglect is evident for example in Martin Haverty's *The History of Ireland, Ancient and Modern*. This lengthy book, first published in 1860 and advertised as a 'school history of Ireland', was re-issued in multiple reprints and editions (which repeatedly updated the historical narrative, so that it caught up with recent events) and was adopted as a favoured textbook for teaching Irish history. Out of forty-nine pages in a chapter on the 1798 Rebellion and the Act of Union, less than two pages were given to the insurrection in Ulster.[176]

---

[174] Maxwell, *History of the Irish Rebellion in 1798*, pp. 194–203 and 290–2.

[175] For Cruikshank's illustrations see C. E. M. Mewburn, 'Representing the Irish Body in England and France the Crisis of Pauperism Rebellion and International Exchange, 1844–1855' (PhD: Art History, University of British Columbia, 2005), pp. 17–69; C. E. M. Mewburn, 'Imaging the Body Politics the Social and Symbolic Spaces of Citizenship in Maxwell's History of the Irish Rebellion' (MA: Department of Fine Arts, University of British Columbia, 1996). The original cover design is reproduced in Maguire, *Up in Arms*, p. 233.

[176] Martin Haverty, *The History of Ireland, Ancient and Modern: Derived from Our Native Annals, from the Most Recent Researches of Eminent Irish Scholars, from the State Papers, and from All the Resources of Irish History Now Available. With Copious Topographical and General Notes* (Dublin: James Duffy,

In 1872, the Dublin historian William John Fitzpatrick, author of a popular history of informers in 1798, was contacted by Adam Dickey of Cullybackey, county Antrim, who was unsatisfied with the neglect of local history. Dickey was a lesser-known antiquarian, who approached descendants of United Irishmen in Antrim in search of local traditions that could provide historical details that had not appeared in print. For example, he wrote Charles Duffin of Aughnadore, Broughshane, and, after stating that he had amassed 'copious details of the parties implicated in the so called rebellion', inquired for 'particulars in addition to what I possess' about his uncle, William Duffin, who had been a rebel commander in Ballymena. Fitzpatrick noted that 'in the course of his correspondence and interviews with us, [Dickey] frequently asserts that the History of the Rebellion in Ulster has never been written.' Dickey, who was interested in discovering the identity of the informer responsible for the arrest and execution in 1798 of his ancestor, the rebel general James Dickey, furnished Fitzpatrick with a narrative based on family tradition.[177] Such folk history was mainly left outside of the remits of scholarly history.

Official historiography primarily catered for metropolitan and national readerships and could afford to neglect provincial experiences. In contrast, the traditions of folk memory that are characteristic of vernacular historiography found expression in local publications, despite initial reluctance of editors to address the rebellion in print. In 1857, the mid-Antrim unionist newspaper the *Ballymena Observer* published 'Walks about Ballymena', a series of articles on the history of the neighbourhood, which was subsequently issued in a separate volume titled *Old Ballymena*. Over the previous half-century, the area had seen a rapid rise of Orangeism. An historian of the local Orange Order claimed that 'many a Presbyterian "Croppy" who had marched into Ballymena as a rebel in 1798 was soon marching on the Twelfth of July with an Orange Lodge.'[178] Even if recollections of involvement in rebellion had become a cause of embarrassment for loyalists, widespread conversion to unionism failed to erase these memories.

After an introductory chapter, *Old Ballymena* shortly 'arrived at the memorable year of 1798, at which time Ballymena became the scene of some stirring events'. Although the author insisted that he was 'not writing a history of the insurrection', he unwittingly became engrossed with 'this exciting subject'. After four chapters, he realized that he had 'much exceeded the space originally intended for occupation by this subject' and yet was unable to desist, devoting no less than seven chapters to the rebellion. He was spurred on by additional information received from correspondents, who had 'taken much interest in our recent notices of the "Turn-Out"'. The unintentional result was that Ninety-Eight stole the show and the collected essays of *Old Ballymena*, which also looked at other topics, were billed as a 'History of Ballymena during the 1798

1860), pp. 753–5. New editions came out in Dublin (1860, 1861, 1865, 1867, 1872, 1880, 1882, 1886, and 1906); New York (1867, 1869, 1871, 1873, 1884, and 1885), Chicago (1885), Sydney (1867, 1881, 1882, and 1883), and Melbourne (1881).

[177] Fitzpatrick, *The Sham Squire*, 6th edn, pp. 337–52; Adam Dickey to Charles Duffin, 3 May 1874, Duffin Family Papers, PRONI D2109/2/2C.

[178] Brown, *Orangeism around Ballymena*, Part I, p. 7. This local history of Orangeism, written by a county grand master of Antrim and District Master of Ballymena, originally appeared as a series of articles in *the Ballymena Weekly Telegraph*, running from 1 November 1962 to 13 August 1964.

Rebellion'. Unlike standard history books, this was a vernacular history, rich in local folk memory.[179]

Old Ballymena was probably written by George White, the founding editor and proprietor of the *Ballymena Observer*. White was a conservative unionist. His wife Ida, on the other hand, was a radical poet, who advocated for the advancement of women's rights and has been described as 'a staunch republican'.[180] Their personal alliance hints to the complexity of unionist identity. His negative account of 1798, in which 'the more reflective and intelligent classes of the community' refrain from joining the United Irishmen, is riddled with ambivalence. An awkward ambiguity marks the explanation given for why 'the rebellion was very seldom spoken of as an insurrection' and 'was almost invariably designated a "Turn Out"':

> This arose from the fact that many persons became connected with the United Irishmen without criminal intention, and at a period when political reform, to be effected by lawful means, was the only acknowledged object of the association. Thousands joined the society under the influence of an all pervading mania, but without any design of arraying themselves in armed hostility to the government. These misguided, but comparatively innocent individuals, soon found themselves upon the horns of a dilemma, and in a position from which a retreat was justly reckoned to be quite as hazardous as an advance, and, although most unwilling to appear in absolute rebellion, or to further co-operate with the southern politico-religious confraternity of their associates, they were compelled, under threat of immediate vengeance in the event of their refusal, to obey the mandate of their leaders, conveyed at the appointed day in a brief but imperative order to 'Turn Out.'[181]

The predicament of the 'misguided, but comparatively innocent individuals' ends with disillusion and renunciation of revolutionary republicanism:

> The deluded people now crowded homeward upon all the thoroughfares, many of them actually rejoicing at the speedy though humiliating conclusion of their campaign; others abusing their ill-luck; some bewailing their infatuation, and heartily denouncing the political imposture of which they had been made the tools.[182]

This narrative, and its conclusion that those who died in the rebellion were 'deluded victims of an epidemical insanity', is in line with the dominant loyalist interpretation of Ninety-Eight, as shaped by Musgrave. In order to accommodate the political climate of a unionist public sphere, folk recollections of rebellion were couched in hostility. In this formulation, memory was both evoked and covered-up, so that social forgetting was reinforced even as the past was being recalled.

The antagonistic re-framing of local folk memory provided colourful material for deriding republicanism. The conservative *Belfast News-Letter* entertained its readers in 1857 with the anecdote of a 'poor lunatic' named Timothy (Tim) Corry, whose impression of the rebellion was that the foolish people were dancing to the devil's

---

[179] *Old Ballymena*, chs 2–10, pp. 13–56.

[180] Catherine W. Reilly, *Mid-Victorian Poetry, 1860–1879: An Annotated Biobibliography* (London and New York: Mansell, 2000), p. 492. Ida's early poetry, some of which was published in the *Ballymena Observer*, was largely apolitical and her 'very advanced opinions' only came to the fore in her second collection *The Three Banquets and Prison Poems* (London: Sonnenschein & Co., 1890); see O'Donoghue, *The Poets of Ireland*, p. 478; see also *Ballymena Observer*, 11 January 1889, p. 11; *Freeman's Journal*, 30 May 1890, p. 2.

[181] *Old Ballymena*, pp. 41–2.   [182] Ibid., p. 45.

tune: 'I dinna ken the richts o' it; but it jeest seems to me as if the muckle deevil wor skirlin ane o' his tunes in Ballymena, an' that the daft folk wor a' dancin' tae it' [I don't know the rights of it, but it just seems to me as if the great devil was shouting one of his tunes and the daft folk were dancing to it']. Later, in response to Fenian insurgency in 1865, the newspaper turned to stories of peasants that in 1798 had claimed for themselves the estates of the gentry, including an anecdote of a cobbler's wife who went to blows with a tailor's wife over the mansion of the Dickey family at Hill Head, which she demanded for 'hersel' an' her ain gude man' [herself and her own good man].[183] Folklore, which had originally reflected mixed attitudes, was plucked out of context and cast in an entirely negative light.

A decade after the publication of *Old Ballymena*, Sir Robert Alexander Shafto Adair, a former high sheriff of county Antrim and liberal MP for Cambridge (soon to be ennobled as Baron Waveney), gave a talk to 'a very large and respectable' audience on the historical development of the town and its neighbourhood. Adair had consulted the series in the *Ballymena Observer*, which he regarded 'a work composed with rare industry and astonishing accuracy, and written with a vigour of style which entitled it to take a high place in local history'. Yet, in reviewing the history of the locality, he consciously decided to avoid the 'dreadful time' of 'civil war' (a purposely obscured reference to 1798). After describing the decade of 1782 to 1792 as 'the most glorious period in Irish history', Adair skipped straight over to 'the march of improvement' in the fifty years after the passing of the Union.[184] Although the events of 1798 appeared prominently in his source, the topic was deemed unsuitable for public discourse and excluded from the presentation. It seems appropriate that one of the many local traditions recounted in *Old Ballymena* refers to the 'remarkable fact' that blood stains left on the floor of a house in 1798 could not be washed away and 'remained visible for more than forty years afterwards'. Similarly, ambiguous recollections of the Turn-Out could not be entirely brushed aside and persisted behind closed doors.[185]

The negative portrayal of the memory of the rebellion did not curb interest in its folk memory. Due to popular demand, the *Ballymena Observer* repeatedly republished *Old Ballymena*. When serialized for a second time, between January and June 1883, the parish priest Rev. John Lynch complained about the anti-Catholic bias of one of the articles (which did not relate to the rebellion), but was informed by the newspaper editor that the series was re-published as it had originally appeared 'at the request of many of the readers of the *Observer* (Catholic as well as Protestant)'.[186] After a third serialization, between February to May 1910, the local history was re-issued as a cheap booklet (priced at 4½d), which received praise from numerous local Ulster newspapers, who all shared the belief that the articles, and in particular those about 1798, would be of great interest to readers across the province. A long-time resident of Ballymena

[183] *BNL*, 9 October 1857, p. 3 and 2 October 1865, p. 4; taken from *Old Ballymena*, p. 36. Another version of the Timothy Corry story (in which he is named Tim Corr) appeared in a humorous polemic against Daniel O'Connell, written as a letter in Ulster-Scots and attributed: James Anderson, Ballintrae, N. B. to John Hill, Belfast, 1 February 1841; published in McComb, *The Repealer Repulsed*, p. 158.
[184] *Northern Whig*, 2 January 1867, p. 2.   [185] *Old Ballymena*, p. 53.
[186] Letter to editor, *Ballymena Observer*, 24 April 1883, p. 3. The chapters on 1798 appeared weekly between 3 January to 3 March 1883.

suggested that 'every father and mother should have one of them for the benefit of their sons to enable them to know the past history of their town.'[187]

In the winter of 1937/8, between November to March, the *Ballymena Observer* serialized the local history for the fourth time, following 'numerous requests for its re-appearance in our columns'. Upon completion, 'in response to many requests from our readers', the series was once again issued as an affordable book, which was sold for two shillings.[188] The new edition was denounced by the southern nationalist *Irish Press* as the product of 'a venomous pen'. The reviewer, who was apparently not *au fait* with the inherent ambivalence of social forgetting in Ulster, was unable to make sense of how 'the booklet presents the Presbyterian patriots as a drunken, blood-thirsty rabble, but curiously enough refers in complimentary terms to the members of that denomination towards the end.'[189] The repeated re-issue of *Old Ballymena* at intervals of a quarter of a century made this vernacular local history of 1798 available for each new generation, effectively regenerating a local formulation of social forgetting.

The conflicted position of unionist popular print, which could not resist the allure of local traditions of rebellion even though they were not politically acceptable, is evident in the popular writings and publications of the Belfast publisher and book seller William McComb, whose annual *Presbyterian Almanac* showed a knack for identifying information of interest to local readers. McComb was an evangelical Presbyterian and an ardent loyalist. He published the monthly *Orthodox Presbyterian* (1829–40), which assisted Henry Cooke in his campaign against Unitarianism. Moreover, McComb's satirical compilation *The Repealer Repulsed*, which celebrated the withdrawal of Daniel O'Connell from a public debate with Cooke in 1841, was instrumental in establishing Cooke's reputation as the champion of northern unionism.[190] McComb's poetry earned him the accolade of 'the Laureate of the [Presbyterian] Church'.[191] His abhorrence of revolution was made clear in a response to the European 'Spring of Nations', which took the form of a long poem—'The Voice of a Year, or, Recollections of 1848'—that berated the 'Reign of Terror'. He rejoiced that Britain was largely 'unshaken by the tossings of the age' and that Ulster, with its 'people schooled in Bible loyalty', was spared the ravages of 'Irish anarchy'.[192]

McComb's politics were distinctly averse to the republicanism of those who admired the United Irishmen. Upon arriving in Belfast as a young apprentice draper from

[187] Letter to editor, *Ballymena Observer*, 2 September 1910, p. 6. Praise from regional newspapers is reproduced in *Ballymena Observer*, 23 September 1910, p. 11. The 1798 chapters appeared between 25 February to 8 April 1910.

[188] *Old Ballymena: A History of Ballymena during the 1798 Rebellion*, 2nd edn (Ballymena: Ballymena Observer, 1938). Advance notices on the re-publication of the series and the book appeared in *Ballymena Observer*, 29 October 1937, p. 10 and 16 December 1938, p. 7. The chapters on 1798 appeared in the *Ballymena Observer* from 12 November to 24 December 1937.

[189] *Irish Press*, 31 January 1939, p. 6; see also *Irish Times*, 25 February 1939, p. 7.

[190] W. D. Killen, *History of Congregations of the Presbyterian Church in Ireland and Biographical Notices of Eminent Presbyterian Ministers and Laymen, with the Signification of Names of Places* (Belfast: J. Cleeland and Edinburgh: J. Gemmell, 1886), pp. 274–5; see also biographical note in William McComb, *The Repealer Repulsed*, edited by Patrick Maume (Dublin: University College Dublin Press, 2003; orig. edn 1841), pp. vii–ix.

[191] Robert Jeffrey, *The Indian Mission of the Irish Presbyterian Church* (London: Nisbet, 1890), p. 63.

[192] William McComb, *The Voice of a Year; or, Recollections of 1848* (London: Hamilton, Adams, 1849); republished in *The Poetical Works of William McComb* (London: Hamilton Adams, 1864), pp. 123–47 (see esp. 142–4).

Coleraine, over a decade after the rebellion, McComb was infuriated by the sight of radicals, who gathered on Sundays in Belfast's Smithfield neighbourhood for the purpose of 'disseminating, by lectures and small publications, the infidel and demo-cratic principles taught by Tom Payne [Paine] and others during the rebellion in America and France'. In response, he established a Sunday school to 'teach the pure Gospel', with the intention of rooting out lingering remnants of United Irish ideol-ogy.[193] McComb's experiences as a politically driven schoolteacher were reflected in his long poem 'The School of the Sabbath', which railed against the harm of the secular French Revolution (in contrast to the more beneficial Protestant character of the American Revolution) and complained that 'the state of ignorance, and of consequent immorality and mental degradation of the lower classes of the community in Ireland' had 'proved, in the late unfortunate rebellion of 1798, a fruitful source of mischief and misery'. However, verses that briefly allude to the devastation wrecked by the suppres-sion of the rebellion show that he was affected by the early poetical representations of Rushton's 'Mary Le More' and McHenry's 'Patrick', which expressed compassion for the suffering that had been caused in the suppression of the rebellion. This offered a first indication that McComb was not devoid of empathy for the plight of those who had rebelled.[194]

In 1855, McComb was responsible for the publication of *Our Staple Manufactures*, a collection of articles on 'the history and progress of the linen and cotton trades in the North of Ireland' that had been serialized the previous year in the liberal newspaper the *Banner of Ulster*. It included an extended account of Henry Munro and his execution, which stirred a reader from Yorkshire, who was 'present at the awful scene, within a few yards of the fatal gallows', to send the newspaper his personal recollections of the event and insist that Munro's final words, which professed the rebel general's willingness to die for his country, 'should never be omitted in any statement where his execution is introduced'.[195]

The author of the essays (which were written under the pseudonym 'A Mechanic') was the liberal unionist journalist Hugh McCall of Lisburn. McCall was born in 1805 and his mother had been a neighbour and intimate friend of the Munro family. He became renowned for 'the interest with which he told the many stories of the Rebellion he had heard from those who had taken a very prominent part in that disastrous attempt', and in particular for telling 'with great animation the story of Harry Munroe and his betrayer'.[196] Prior to his death in 1897, at the age of 93, McCall was recognized by antiquarians and historians to be 'more knowledgeable of these matters than any

---

[193] *BNL*, 15 September 1873, p. 4.
[194] William McComb, *The School of the Sabbath, and Other Poems*, 2nd edn (Edinburgh: W. Oliphant, 1825; orig. edn 1822), pp. 28–39 and 151–2 (1798), 109–11 (French Revolution), and 114–17 (American Revolution).
[195] 'Our Staple Manufactures, Past and Present—No. X', in *Banner of Ulster*, 2 February 1854, p. 2; letter to the editor from Joseph Livingstone, Brighouse, Yorkshire, 20 February 1854 on 'The Execution of Henry Munro', in *Banner of Ulster*, 28 February 1854, p. 1. Originally serialized from December 1853 to October 1854, the collected essays were published anonymously as *Our Staple Manufactures* (Belfast: William McComb and Shepherd & Aitcheson, 1855); a revised, and substan-tially enhanced, edition was issued a decade later with the title *Ireland and Her Staple Manufactures* (Belfast: Henry Greer, George Phillips & Son, 1865) and a third edition appeared in 1870.
[196] *Some Recollections of Hugh McCall*, pp. 15–16.

person now alive'.[197] Hailed as 'The Wizard of Ulster' for the lively way he 'conjured up the scenes and actions of ancient times' in a fashion that resembled Walter Scott (the 'Wizard of the North'), extractions from McCall's writings were 'paraded in works that have had a wide celebrity' and he was quoted as a highly regarded authority on local history in provincial newspapers, such as the *Lisburn Herald* and *Lisburn Standard*. He therefore not only preserved, but also reinforced, traditions of Ninety-Eight.[198] In publishing McCall's unapologetically sympathetic recollections of the United Irishmen, McComb was willing to put aside his own loyalist prejudice and pamper to popular interest in the Turn-Out. He soon realized that there was great demand for such accounts (Fig. 4.2).

McComb's Guide to Belfast, the Giant's Causeway and the Adjoining Districts of the Counties of Antrim and Down, published in 1861, catered for a growing local tourist market, following the launch of the Belfast and County Down Railway (which commenced passenger traffic in 1848) and in particular the opening of its Ballynahinch line in 1858.[199] Hailed by the *London Examiner* as 'one of the most readable and interesting guide books we have ever seen', it was commended both by the conservative *Belfast News-Letter* and the liberal *Northern Whig*, and was also praised by local newspapers as 'an admirable guide book'.[200] 1798 was given a prominent place in this text. In the historical background on Belfast, *McComb's Guide* dwells on the circumstances that lead to the outbreak of the rebellion and admits that in the previous two years 'unprovoked assaults upon private individuals, in the streets, by parties of armed military, were of frequent occurrence.' A description of the 'memorable and sanguinary' engagement at Antrim includes references to the executions of McCracken and other prominent United Irishmen. McComb made a point of stating that 'the Rebellion was soon extinguished in this part of Ulster, and, indeed, in every other portion of the province where civil war had commenced, or wide-spread disaffection shown itself.' His emphatic conclusion is that 'the insurrection was entirely unsuccessful, and most unfortunate for the majority of those who were engaged in it, of whatever rank or creed.'[201]

Although *McComb's Guide* opens with what reads like an attempt to discourage further debate on the sensitive topic of the rebellion, this sanction is soon overcome. Additional information on 1798 appears in entries for different localities, including Antrim town, Randalstown, and Ballymena, and the Battle of Saintfield is treated to a full account. When writing about the Battle of Ballynahinch, McComb became

[197] Bigger Papers, BCL MA 17 (Hugh McCall to F. J. Bigger, 10 June 1895) and K3/H/111–118 (copy of the contents of a letter from Hugh McCall to W. T. Latimer, 1897); Latimer, *Ulster Biographies*, p. 33; *BNL*, p. 7; *SVV*, 2, no. 5 (3 May 1897), p. 95. See also obituaries in the *Ulster Echo* and *Northern Whig*, reproduced in *Some Recollections of Hugh McCall, Lisburn*, pp. 50–5.

[198] *Ballymena Observer*, 9 April 1870, p. 3. For examples of recycling of McCall's writings on 1798 see *Lisburn Herald and Antrim and Down Advertiser*, 11 June 1898; *Lisburn Standard*, 1 June and 29 June 1917 and 4 January 1918.

[199] See Desmond Coakham, *The Belfast & County Down Railway* (Newtownards: Colourpoint, 2010), p. 22.

[200] Snippets of laudatory reviews appear in advertisements; see for example *Northern Whig*, 15 June 1864, p. 2. For an example of praise in the local press see *Newry Herald and Down, Armagh, and Louth Journal*, 5 June 1861, p. 3.

[201] William McComb, *McComb's Guide to Belfast, the Giant's Causeway and the Adjoining Districts of the Counties of Antrim and Down, with an Account of the Battle of Ballynahinch, and the Celebrated Mineral Waters of That Neighbourhood* (Belfast: William McComb, 1861), pp. 10–16.

(a)   (b)

Fig. 4.2. Unionist Collectors of '98 traditions: William McComb and Hugh McCall

(a) William McComb; (b) Hugh McCall. Although a conservative unionist, William McComb (1793–1873) became fascinated with collecting traditions of Ninety-Eight. Putting aside his own loyalist prejudices, he also published sympathetic traditions of 1798 collected by the local historian Hugh McCall of Lisburn (1805–97), who was a liberal unionist.

Sources: William McComb, *The Poetical Works of William McComb* (1864); *Some Recollections of Hugh McCall, Lisburn* (1899).

unexpectedly engrossed in the subject. He studied numerous sources, including several previously unpublished accounts by unnamed authors. These include a 'stirring narrative' by a writer with whom McComb had been 'well acquainted' and could vouch for his 'authenticity, impartiality, and intelligence', as well as 'another account of the memorable proceedings'. In addition, he made use of detailed information 'collected by a friend interested in our publication who received the statements from the lips of several aged persons now residing in the town and neighbourhood of Ballynahinch, some of whom at the time of the "Rebellion" were themselves eye-witnesses of the distressing events'.[202]

After presenting his readers 'with an account of one of the most interesting passages in the history of Ireland', enriched with 'a variety of curious and important facts, which have never before been brought under the notice of the public', McComb realized that

[202] Ibid., pp. 49 (Antrim town), 62 (Randalstown), 63 (Ballymena), 109 (Comber), 111–13 (Saintfield), 113 (Portaferry and Newtownards), and 121–41 (Ballynahinch).

he may have got carried away. He therefore felt obliged to subjoin 'a few practical reflections', which stressed that 'the Irish Rebellion of 1798 was a melancholy exhibition of folly and recklessness.' He was intent to make it clear that the United Irishmen suffered terribly for 'their impiety and insubordination' by affirming that 'some of them fell by the hand of the executioner; some lost their property, and their posterity have never since recovered the social position which their families once occupied; others were driven into exile; and not a few were consigned to lingering imprisonment.' *McComb's Guide* presented 1798 as 'a turning point in the history of Ireland' and argued that revolutionary radicalism had since lost all relevance: 'intelligent Irishmen now wonder how their fathers could have been so befooled as to think of a separation from England' and 'grandmothers may entertain children in the nursery with stories of '98, but we trust that there will never be a repetition of the scenes of that awful year.'[203]

And yet, McComb, for all his instinctive animosity to the ideology of the United Irishmen, could not let go of the memory of the rebellion. He became besotted with local remembrance of the county Down rebel heroine Elizabeth Grey [Gray], commonly known as Betsy Gray [also appearing as Bessie and Bessy]. He was enthralled to discover that 'a rough map representing the battle scene with our heroine mounted on a pony and bearing a green flag, was to be seen hung up in many a cottage.' He also found that she was the subject of 'many rude ballads', such as:

> They murdered a beautiful lady.
> Her name it was Miss Bessie Grey,
> And for doing that barbarous action,
> We'll reward them on some other day.[204]

According to local tradition, Betsy Gray followed her brother, George, and her lover, William Boal, to the rebel camp at Ballynahinch and after the battle, upon trying to make their way home, all three of them were brutally killed by yeomen. This episode, which was not recognized in official history, featured prominently in vernacular historiography.

The local heroine had previously been the subject of a romantic poem, which told how *Bessy* Gray:

> With fond affection swelling,
> To learn a lover's, brother's fate,
> Forsook her peaceful dwelling;
> With them to share her simple store,
> On all their griefs a balm to pour,
> The field of death she dared explore,
> Each selfish thought repelling.

And related how, after the battle (which is unnamed), her companions had tried to protect her from the pursuing victors:

> But lover's, brother's sighs are vain,
> Even in their sight the maid is slain,
> And now on Erin's ruined plain,
> Their mingled blood is flowing.

---

[203] Ibid., pp. 141–3.   [204] Ibid., p. 132.

The verses were written by Mary Balfour, who was associated with the McCracken household in Belfast, where she was introduced to the song collector Edward Bunting. Balfour's poem about Bessy Gray was included in a volume of her writings, published in 1810. It was, however, prudently placed in a section devoted to translation of Gaelic songs that had been collected by Bunting and was evasively named 'Nancy of the Branching Tresses', after the traditional air '*Cuil Chraobaigh Anna*'. The masked allusion to the recent rebellion was virtually unnoticeable to outsiders.[205]

A decade later, a long poem titled *Ednavady; a Poetical Tale, founded on the Battle of Ballynahinch*, published anonymously in Belfast in 1822, featured another obscured version of the legend. In this rendition, *Eliza*, the daughter of a fictitious rebel chief named O'Nial, is courted by Henry, a soldier on the side of the Crown. After the battle, the two lovers unite, but the stragglers are attacked and killed by a party of loyalist vigilantes; Eliza is shot and Henry dies trying to protect her:

> Thus fell the lovers, and their ashes now
> Mingle beneath the heathy mountain's brow
> And tho' amidst the numerous dead forgot,
> No sculptur'd marble marks the scared spot.

A postscript reveals the poet's nervousness of being seen as a sympathizer of the rebels, which lead him to stress that he:

> condemns those visionary ideas of liberty entertained by the promoters of the rebellion of 1798: The principal design of the piece being to impress more strongly on the public mind a sense of the unhappy consequences of that undertaking.

The poem does not seem to have attracted attention and its author remains unknown.[206]

Several early historical accounts mention Betsy Gray. Thirty years after the rebellion, the story of this 'young and interesting female' was recounted by Teeling in his *Personal Narrative*. Two decades later, Madden included in his memoir of Henry Munro a graphic description of the death of *Elizabeth* Grey, provided to him by Mary Ann McCracken from a man 'whose friends had been at the battle, and who lived in the neighbourhood of the yeomen'.[207] McComb was intrigued by these sources. He quoted Balfour's poem and Teeling's account, but, as a unionist, he felt unease at citing the nationalist historian Madden and so he deceptively attributed Mary Ann McCracken's account to the loyalist historian McSkimin. McComb's fascination with the folk memory of the rebellion, however, went a step beyond collecting and publishing traditions. He too composed a poem about 'bonnie Bessie Grey', which would

---

[205] Mary Balfour, *Hope, a Poetical Essay; with Various Other Poems* (Belfast: Smyth and Lyons, 1810), pp. 181–2. For the air 'Nancy's Branching Tresses' see *O'Neill's Music of Ireland . . . Collected from All Available Sources and Edited by Capt. Francis O'Neill, Arranged by James O'Neill* (Pacific, Mo.: Mel Bay Publications, 1996; orig. edn Chicago, 1903), p. 65 (tune 374).

[206] Anon., *Ednavady; a Poetical Tale, Founded on the Battle of Ballynahinch* (Belfast: printed by A. Mackay, 1822).

[207] Teeling, *Personal Narrative*, pp. 258–60. M. A. McCracken's Account of Elizabeth Grey of Killinchey (undated), Madden Papers, TCD 873/163 was slightly touched-up and published in Madden, *The United Irishmen*, 3rd ser., vol. 1 (1846), pp. 397–8.

prove to be one of his few poems that would stand the test of time.[208] A half-century later, following the poem's re-publication in a local newspaper, it was criticized as 'misleading, and not all accurate'.[209] Although McComb was intent on laying to rest the memory of 1798, in yet another manifestation of the puzzling dynamic of social forgetting, like other unionist producers of popular print, he paradoxically ended up contributing to its regeneration.

IMAGINED REMINISCENCE

In August 1845, four northern Young Irelanders—Charles Gavan Duffy, John O'Hagan, John Mitchel, and John Martin—all born more than a decade after the rebellion, went on a walking tour of their native Ulster and visited sites of historical interest. At Ballynahinch, they toured the battlefield and were guided by a veteran rebel named Innes, 'who had carried a pike that day' and furnished them with a detailed first-hand account of the battle. His personal testimony made history come to life.[210] When James Standfield, who 'was a witness of most of the terrible scenes of 'Ninety-eight', passed away in 1867, the *Northern Whig* lamented that 'the death of this venerable gentleman breaks another of the few links still remaining that connect the Belfast merchants of a past generation with the present.'[211]

Personal reminiscences gave the impression that the past was still present, yet, for all their vividness, there was no guarantee for the veracity of the recollections. An unnamed Ulster Protestant, who in 1798 had been 'one of a small party who set out to join Munroe's army, but were not in time to share in the defeat of the patriot forces at Ballinahinch', was said to have died at the age of 97 in 1874. An acquaintance later recalled how 'after a most interesting conversation about old times, he would gradually forget me and all around us, and, with his eyes closed, talk earnestly with friends of seventy years before' so that it seemed as if 'the spirits of the dead' were still alive in his presence. The claim of this 'interesting veteran' to have known 'William Boal, the sweetheart of the heroine, Betsy Grey, who fought at Ballinahinch, and was foully murdered by British soldiery thereafter' can be taken either as personal testimony that validates a local legend, or as evidence of the influence of folklore on personal recollections.[212]

A direct link with the past seemed to be still in place in 1875, when a long poem titled 'The Battle of Antrim: A Reminiscence of 1798' was published by the Belfast publisher John Henderson. It followed Henderson's previous issue of works by authors with personal recollections of the Turn-Out, namely James McHenry's novel *The Insurgent Chief* and Samuel McSkimin's *Annals of Ulster*. Not all such publications left an imprint on cultural memory. In 1842, Henderson published the poem 'The

---

[208] *McComb's Guide to Belfast*, pp. 129–32; republished in *The Poetical Works of William McComb*, pp. 357–8.

[209] *Lisburn Standard*, 20 September 1918. McComb's poem 'Bessie Grey' had been previously reproduced in *Lisburn Standard*, 11 January 1918; *Newtownards Chronicle*, 4 May 1918, p. 6.

[210] Charles Gavan Duffy, *Young Ireland: A Fragment of Irish History, 1840–1850*, final revision edn, (London: T. Fisher Unwin, 1896), 2, p. 195; Duffy, *My Life in Two Hemispheres*, pp. 118–19.

[211] *Northern Whig*, 7 January 1867, p. 3. [212] *Ulster Herald*, 8 July 1905, p. 3.

Battle of Ballynahinch, a Tale of 1798', which was the title piece in a collection by James Byers of the Ards Peninsula. Byers, who also wrote under the pseudonym Dominick Dunwoody, was dubbed 'the boy bard of Ballyblack' (6 km south-east of Newtownards). The poem was advertised in various Ulster newspapers and was listed in the *Downpatrick Recorder* among 'interesting local works'. Originally priced at a shilling and shortly afterwards reissued in an even cheaper edition, which sold for sixpence, 'The Battle of Ballynahinch' was intended to appeal to the remaining members of the generation that could still recall witnessing the events. The *Nation* apparently considered Byer's poem of inferior quality, declining to publish it, and whatever success the poem enjoyed was ephemeral. By the early twentieth century, copies could not be found and the poet, who died from consumption in 1845 in Donaghadee, had become obscure.[213]

In contrast to the neglect of 'The Battle of Ballynahinch' in the mid-nineteenth century, the publication three decades later of the 'The Battle of Antrim', which had a public reading at the Belfast Elocution Class in March 1875, did make a mark. The poem opened with the verse: 'Tho' old, I still remember well the year of ninety eight.' Although presented in first person, as a personal recollection, it was written by the Belfast physician Thomas Charles Steuart Corry, who was actually born a quarter of a century after the rebellion. Around the same time, the northern Young Ireland poet Francis Davis, popularly known by his soubriquet 'The Belfast Man', included in a collection of his works the poem 'The Burning', which vividly described how the desolation of 1798 was remembered among the peasantry as 'The Time of the Burning'.[214] Unlike Davis, whose maternal uncle—Daniel McFee—had been a United Irishman, Corry did not come from a republican background. In fact, Corry's father, an MP for Monaghan, had been a county grand master of the Orange Order. Written seventy-seven years after 1798, Corry's reminiscence of the rebellion was entirely imagined.[215]

Considering the problem of memory and generation change, Pierre Nora remarked that 'the past never passes; those who took part in it linger on the scene, even as newcomers crowd their way in.'[216] It is difficult to pinpoint when exactly the generation of Ninety-Eight came to an end. Some of the veterans and witnesses of the rebellion were said to have lived exceptionally long lives. It was reported that John Anderson, who fought in the insurrection and emigrated to the United States, died in Cincinnati in 1853, as he was about to turn 101. A widow named Mary Kelly from near Downpatrick died in 1860 at the stated age of 106, and the people of the area insisted that she was actually 114 on her death. It was recalled that of her eight children, 'nearly all had been adults when the battle of Ballynahinch was fought, now 62 years ago'. A supposedly 115-year-old man named McCormick, living in 1865 in New Windsor,

[213] *Northern Whig*, 26 November 1842, p. 3; *Ulster Times*, 17 December 1842; *Coleraine Chronicle*, 4 May 1844, p. 3; *Belfast Commercial Chronicle*, 2 July 1845, p. 3; *Nation*, 5 July and 27 September 1845, pp. 639 and 824 (respectively); *Downpatrick Recorder*, 24 July 1847, p. 3. Arcane queries about the poem in the early twentieth century reveal the extent to which it had become a rare item and the bibliographer D. J. O'Donoghue mistakenly gave the name of the poet as Bryce, instead of Byers; *Irish Book Lover*, vol. 5 (June 1914), p. 202 and vol. 11 (March 1920), pp. 85–6; O'Donoghue, *The Poets of Ireland*, pp. 45 and 496.

[214] Davis, *Earlier and Later Leaves*, pp. 161–2.

[215] Thomas Charles Stewart Corry, *The Battle of Antrim: A Reminiscence of 1798* (Belfast: John Henderson, 1875). For the public reading see *BNL*, 19 March 1875, p. 3.

[216] Nora, 'Generation', p. 530.

New York, could show two wounds in his leg from his days as a rebel in 1798. Even after seven decades had passed, a number of aged eyewitnesses to the rebellion were reported to be still alive.[217]

Jimmy Cavan, who was 'proud to be considered one of the pikemen of '98', passed away in a cottage on the shore of Strangford Lough in 1872, at the reputed age of 104, and was known locally as 'the last of the croppies'. Thomas Stevenson, a farmer from Innishargie, near Kircubbin in county Down, died in 1878, allegedly aged 102, 'in full possession of his mental faculties' and well 'acquainted with many of the circumstances connected with that eventful period'. Sally Boal, who died in 1875 in Ballywalter, county Down, at the supposed age of 103, 'could also tell many an interesting story of the doings about Greyabbey at the time of the Rebellion'.[218] Shortly before her death in 1874, Anne Given of Ballymena, who was presumed to be 102 years old, recounted her reminiscences of visiting a man sentenced to death in 1798. Her son, John Given, Secretary of Ballymena National District Model School, could 'well remember' how his father, who was a youth of about 16 in 1798, would talk about 'the morning of the "Turn Out", when the Cullybackey and Craigs contingent, with others, marched into Ballymena with a view to take the town, [and] he and a number of lads ran after them to see what was going on.'[219]

Even more incredibly, individuals who claimed to have lived through the rebellion were still to be found in the last two decades of the nineteenth century. Bigger maintained that 'the last of the real croppies in the North' was James Haslett of Killinchy, county Down, a veteran of the Battle of Saintfield, who was said to have died in 1880 aged 106. He was outlived by several other people who claimed to have recollections of 1798. 'An old veteran' from Ballyclare named Alexander Courtenay had turned 100 and in 1883 could still remember 'quite distinctly the battle of Antrim in '98', in which he had taken part at the age of 15. Sometime before 1885, the folklore collector Letitia McClintock paid a visit to the glen of Banagher, a remote part of county Londonderry, where she met 103-year-old Paddy O'Heany, who had joined the United Irish rebels at the age of 19 and could 'relate graphic tales of adventures in which he took part'. Mary O'Hare of Savalbeg, near Newry in county Down, who died in 1886 at the reputed age of 104, recounted to the local historian Francis Clements Crossle her recollections of an incident in which rebels ambushed soldiers of the notorious Welsh Horse. John Steele, who was interred in 1886 in Seaforde Churchyard in county Down and was said to have been born in 1781, remembered that 'prior to the great battle of Ballynahinch in 1798, his father had to state on oath that he (his son) was under eighteen to prevent him being pressed into the services of the Royalists, who were raising a heavy conscription.' An old lady named McManus, who was interred at the old Boho burial-ground, near Derrygonnelly in county Fermanagh, supposedly at

---

[217] *BNL*, 26 January 1853, p. 2 (Anderson); *Downpatrick Recorder*, 3 March 1860, p. 2 (Kelly); *Enniskillen Advertiser*, 19 October 1865 (McCormick).

[218] *BNL*, 28 January 1878, p. 4 (Cavan and Stevenson); *Downpatrick Recorder*, 18 September 1875, p. 3 (Boal). For Cavan see also Robinson, *North Down and Ards in 1798*, p. 107.

[219] *Ballymena Observer*, 7 March 1874, p. 3; see also *Memento of 'an Old Disciple': Notes of a Discourse by the Rev. S. J. Moore on the Death of Mrs. Anne Given, Ballymena (in her 102nd Year) with Appendices by her Son* (Ballymena: W. Erwin and Belfast: W. Mullan & C. Aitchison, 1874), p. 17; preserved in Classon Porter Papers, PRONI D2009/2/37.

the age of 105, was known to have 'had a clear recollection of the '98 period, and [she] retained her faculties to the last'.[220]

The antiquarian Robert Magill Young interviewed on 29 June 1891 an 'old lady of 105', who recalled witnessing the execution of Henry Joy McCracken and could also recount how an inmate named Campbell Sweeny escaped from the Prevôt jail that year. The notice that a 110-year-old Mrs Todd had passed away in 1893 in Donaghmore, county Down (10 km north of Newry), stated that 'she remembered the scenes of the Rebellion in 1798.' In 1895, when Margaret McVey was buried in Ballykinlar, near Downpatrick, her age was given as 105, but it was believed locally that she was 115. She 'remembered the battle of Ballynahinch well, and often told her neighbours about seeing the dead and wounded carried off the field'. Perhaps the very last of that generation, Samuel Reid of Greenloughs, county Antrim (16 km west of Ballymena), who died in 1898 at the presumed age of 105, was said to have retained recollections of the rebellion in the area of Maghera from when he was 5 years old.[221] The attributed age of the centenarians cannot be positively verified in any of these cases.

Remarkable longevity fascinated the antiquarians of the late nineteenth century. Classon Porter, who recorded in 1863 the recollections of the 91-year-old 'Old Croppy' James Burns, compiled a list of centenarians, nonagenarians, and octogenarians living in the area of Larne. In 1881, he encountered a notice from further afield of a reputedly 117-year-old widow from Seafin, county Armagh (7 km from Newry), named Anne McSherry, who was married in 1798 and had 'a very vivid recollection of the stirring events of that remarkable year, and can tell wonderful stories with reference to the rising and its exciting incidents'.[222] Personal recollection of the rebellion was in itself considered proof of old age. Rev. Alexander McCreery, the minister of the second Presbyterian church of Killileagh in county Down, observed that 'the old people amongst us reckon their ages from the time of "The Battles"' and Robert M. Young noted that 'for a long time after the Rebellion a witty question was asked of ladies who wished to be thought young—What age were you at "the Hurries"'.[223]

The Belfast antiquarian Seaton Forrest Milligan proposed in 1891 to the Royal Society of Antiquaries of Ireland that its members 'should in their respective districts record the death of any person who lived one hundred years or upwards, together with any details as to their mode of life and surroundings that might be of interest' and that the society's journal should include obituaries of centenarians, as these 'vital statistics are of considerable interest'.[224] Ninety years after the rebellion, Milligan maintained that 'the present is an opportune time to take the rising of 1798 as a milestone on the highway of life, from which centenarians may calculate their years.' Over the course of

[220] *BNL*, 14 June 1883, p. 5 (Courtenay) and 13 December 1886, p. 3 (Steele); *Morning News*, 25 February 1997, p. 6 (McManus); McClintock, 'An Actor in the Rebellion of 1798', pp. 185–93 (O'Heany); Joseph Connellan, 'Newry District and the Men of 'Ninety-Eight: Seaver's Killeavey Yeomanry', in *Frontier Sentinel*, 9 September 1967 (O'Hare); *Irish News*, 22 June 2013 [reprint of item published in 1944] (Haslett).

[221] Young, *Ulster in '98*, pp. 54 and 86–7 (unnamed lady); *Lisburn Herald*, 15 April 1893, p. 2 (Todd); *Freeman's Journal*, 7 March 1895, p. 3 (McVey); *Derry Journal*, 21 January 1898, p. 8 (Reid).

[222] *Northern Whig*, 1 September 1881; cited in Classon Porter Papers, PRONI D2009/2/35.

[223] McCreery, *Presbyterian Ministers of Killileagh*, p. 161; Young, *Ulster in '98*, p. 74.

[224] Seaton F. Milligan, 'Longevity', *Journal of the Royal Society of Antiquaries of Ireland*, 1, no. 5 (1891): p. 409.

his investigations, he discovered no less than thirteen centenarians who in 1889 were known to have personal recollections of the Turn-Out in Ulster.[225] Yet, the validity of such claims, which relied solely on the authority of personal memory, was a subject of debate.

The English politician and scholar George Cornewall Lewis questioned the veracity of the alleged age of centenarians, whenever it could not be corroborated by documents. His essay on the topic planted doubts in the mind of William John Thoms, the antiquary who coined the term 'folklore'. In his journal *Notes and Queries*, which was a standard reference for Victorian amateur scholars, Thoms had previously published without question notices of centenarians but, after reading Lewis, he reconsidered his position and wrote a book-length study on *The Longevity of Man*, which argued that most cases cannot pass the test of critical scrutiny. Of all the methods used to validate old age in absence of official documentation, Thoms considered personal recollection 'the most fallible, unsatisfactory, and difficult to deal with'. He pointed out that an examination of one's earliest recollection makes it 'difficult to decide whether he really recollected such event, or having heard it much talked of in his youth did not actually recollect it, but had it impressed upon his memory by what he had heard others say of it'.[226]

By this logic, elderly people who claimed to personally recall 1798 in the late nineteenth century may have inadvertently demonstrated that in their childhood in the early nineteenth century—when the rebellion was not spoken about in public—the recent events of the Turn-Out were recalled vividly in families around Ulster and that these recollections were passed on to impressionable children. Regardless of whether the stated ages of elderly veterans and witnesses of the rebellion in Ireland were indeed authentic, it is apparent that in the second half of the nineteenth century people were willing to be identified in public with 1798. A family tradition from the area of Ballymena, county Antrim, recalled the destruction of 'an ancient Celtic Cross' that had marked the family grave of an old man named John Thomson, who 'was one of the few old people who lived through the '98 times and who was looked on by his Orange neighbours as a

---

[225] Milligan Seaton's notes from 1889 of centenarians in Ulster who distinctly recalled 1798 list: 106-year-old Peggy Elliott of Trasna, near Enniskillen; 100-year-old Bridget Brennan of Rostrevor, county Down; 107-year-old Nancey Branney of Downpatrick; 106-year-old Mrs Mac Donnell of Ballymore, near Tandragee in county Armagh; 102-year-old Mrs McFetridge of Deer Park, Glenarm; 103-year-old Belle Rowley, a resident of the Belfast Union Workhouse; 102-year-old Martha McMullan of Castleroe, near Coleraine; 106-year-old Margaret Howard of Keenagh, near Desertmartin in county Derry; 102-year-old Hugh Morrison of Coleraine; 107-year-old John Jenkinson of Drumnahee, near Markethill in county Armagh; 100-year-old Samuel Crowe of Straidland, near Ballyclare; 103-year-old Henry Walsh of Leemish, near Rathfriland in county Down; 103-year-old Arthur McConnell of Drumgonnell, on the shore of Lough Neagh in county Antrim. See F. Milligan Seaton, 'Some Recent Cases of Remarkable Longevity', *Journal of the Royal Society of Antiquaries of Ireland*, 1, no. 3 (1890): pp. 232–9; see also *Ballymena Observer*, 19 December 1890, p. 7; Smith, *Memories of '98*, pp. 27–8. A follow-up essay added another name: Samuel Shields of Molenan, near Derry, who died in 1891 at the age 'at the authenticated age of 108 years'; Seaton F. Milligan, 'Some Recent Cases of Remarkable Longevity (Second Paper)', *Journal of the Royal Society of Antiquaries of Ireland*, 2, no. 3 (1892), p. 227.

[226] George Cornewall Lewis, 'Centenarians', *Notes and Queries*, 3rd ser., 2 (1862): pp. 281–2; William John Thoms, *The Longevity of Man: Its Facts and Its Fictions* (London: Frederic Norgate, 1879), p. 53.

"Croppy"'.[227] This act of vandalism had occurred sometime in the first half of the nineteenth century, when public remembrance of rebels was a taboo. By contrast, a Celtic cross memorial in the Drumbeg parish churchyard (5 km north-east of Lisburn), county Down, inscribed 'In memory of William Gouldie, an Irish Volunteer of '98. Died April 8th 1873 aged 104 years,' demonstrates that by the late nineteenth century it had become possible to openly memorialize Ninety-Eight, without fear of recrimination.[228]

T. C. S. Corry's poem 'The Battle of Antrim: A Reminiscence of 1798', written in 1875, at a time when almost all, if not all, of the generation of Ninety-Eight had passed away, adopted their voice and remembered in their name. The second part of the poem dwells on the execution of Henry Joy McCracken. Corry had met Mary Ann McCracken and was touched by how she had devotedly mourned for her executed brother for over a half-century and perpetuated his memory. Following her death at the age of 96, Corry wrote an 'Ode to the Memory of Mary McCracken' that described the sense of loss left by her passing away:

> Now she is gone, and severed is the chain
> Which linked our generation to the past.

By masquerading as a personal reminiscence, the 'Battle of Antrim' was an attempt to bridge this gap. After its initial publication as a booklet, it was included in a volume of Corry's collected poems, which came out in two editions (1879 and 1884) and brought the poem to the attention of a wider readership.[229]

In addition to attending his medical practice and writing poetry, Corry was also a thriving businessman and a cultural entrepreneur, who pioneered the commercialized presentation of heritage to a general public. He gained renown with a diorama show on 'Ireland: Its Scenery, Music, and Antiquities', which was lauded by the *Ulster Observer* as 'the most popular entertainment ever given in Belfast'. Performances commenced at the Belfast's Victoria Hall in the end of December 1864. After a couple of months, the show travelled to Dublin, where it was staged at the Rotundo, and, over the next decade and a half, it toured England, Scotland, America, and Australia, with periodical return visits to Belfast. In Corry's diorama, fifty large canvas paintings of sites around Ireland were illuminated and used as the background for performances of songs and recitations. The original accompanying texts for this heritage extravaganza included a reference to 1798 in Wicklow but omitted any allusion to the northern rebellion. In later years, performances aboard would include a recital of Corry's poem 'The Battle of Antrim'. A new diorama created in 1869 on 'Ireland in Shade and Sunshine' added to the depiction of Belfast 'scenes of the executions in 1798'. These shows attracted large audiences and Corry's references to the rebellion, which were praised by nationalists, do not seem to have alienated unionists or harmed his business interests.[230]

---

[227] Memoir written in the 1930s by Mary Ann Millar née Laverty (born 1866), recalling stories told by her mother Rose Ann (Mary) née Johnston (born *c.*1840) about her mother Mary O'Hara (born *c.*1810); Murphy, 'Memories of My Irish Home', ch. 12.

[228] Murray and Cullen, *Epitaph of 1798*, p. 42. The grave was restored around the time of the 1798 bicentenary; *Glasgow Herald*, 17 November 1998, p. 19.

[229] Thomas Charles Stuart Corry, *Irish Lyrics, Songs & Poems* (Belfast: D. & J. Allen, 1879), pp. 17–24 ('The Battle of Antrim') and 113–14 ('Ode to the Memory of Mary McCracken').

[230] Thomas Charles S. Corry, *Ireland; Its Scenery, Music, and Antiquities*, 3rd edn (Dublin: Hodges, Smith & Co., 1866), extracts from newspaper reviews of the original show appear on p. 27. See also

Corry dedicated his collected volume of poetry to Madden, who had inspired a younger generation with imaginings of the rebellion. Madden was also caught up in such flights of fancy. In compiling the *Literary Remains of the United Irishmen*, a collection of poetry written by the men of Ninety-Eight, he included in the manuscript 'some pieces of a later date, illustrative of some leading occurrences in the lives, or remarkable traits of the characters of the United Irishmen'. These more recent poems were attributed to IERNE, an ancient name for Ireland which often appeared in United Irish poetry. In fact, they were written by Madden himself. Some of the pieces had been previously published in the *Nation*, but had not been selected for republication in the popular song anthology *The Spirit of the Nation* (1843), and so had become obscure.

Madden invented for his alter ego an entirely fictional persona, which blended moments from his own biography with elements taken from the many stories that he had collected from former rebels. Ierne was presented as:

> one of 'the Boys of '98', who was confined several months in that year, and was indebted to Major Sirr for some polite attentions, in the midst of the Rebellion, when his father's house was searched for arms, and his family frightened out of their wits by the ransacking duties of a yeomanry rabble.

This account reconfigures the actual circumstances of Madden's birth, which had occurred during a raid in 1798 lead by Major Sirr on his father's house. Instead of a new-born baby, Madden re-imagined himself as a 'young Croppy', who became enraged by the incursion and 'was not long at large before he was up in arms, and began to make some noise, in the autumn of "The Troubles."' The fictional Ierne refrained from participating in Emmet's rebellion in 1803 and subsequently renounced violence. He chose to 'discard the pike' in order:

> to devote the remainder of his days to the task of looking after the graves of the United Irishmen, driving away the beasts that browse in security in neglected church-yards, and trample on the ashes of those who have few to care for their remains, of picking the mould out of the letters of the tomb-stones, of setting up slabs, where there were none before, covering the earth, that 'caught' the poor United brothers, 'to her breast,' with green sods, and, from time to time, pulling up the weeds that had no business to grow there, and pitching them to the devil.[231]

Madden consciously fashioned himself after Walter Scott's famous Old Mortality, an aged eccentric devoted to memorialization (Fig. 4.3). The romantic image of an antiquarian obsessed with preserving the memory of a failed rebellion was a source of inspiration for writers in the nineteenth century, though its appeal later waned in the twentieth century.[232] In the convergence of history and fiction, the boundary between social remembrance and more imaginative literary representations of cultural memory was blurred.

Cathal O'Byrne, *As I Roved Out*, 2nd edn reprint (Wakefield: S. R. Publishers, 1970; orig. edn 1957), pp. 190–2; John Gray, 'Popular Entertainment', in *Belfast: The Making of the City, 1800–1914*, edited by J. C. Beckett et al. (Belfast: Appletree Press, 1983), pp. 99–110. For a reading of 'The Battle of Antrim', in the original diorama show see *Sheffield and Rotherham Independent*, 20 April 1875, p. 7. For the inclusion of 1798 executions in the new diorama see *BNL*, 13 December 1869, p. 3. For nationalist praise of Corry's 1798 poem see *Nation*, 8 May 1875, p. 10.

231 Madden, *Literary Remains of the United Irishmen*, pp. xii and 243–5.
232 Rigney, *The Afterlives of Walter Scott*, pp. 218–21.

Fig. 4.3. R. R. Madden searching for Robert Emmet's grave

Richard Robert Madden (1778–1886), who dedicated his life to preserving the memory of the United Irishmen, was passionate about locating and restoring their graves. At the age of over 80, the elderly Madden pointed out to Dr Thomas Addis Emmet of New York what he believed to be the grave of his illustrious rebel uncle in the Protestant churchyard in Glasnevin, Dublin.

Source: Thomas Addis Emmet, *The Emmet Family, with Some Incidents Relating to Irish History* (1898).

CULTURAL MEMORY AND SOCIAL FORGETTING

In the mid-Victorian era, a number of Anglo-Irish women authors wrote novels set on the background of the rebellion in Ulster. In these books, which were published in London with the intent of appealing to a general British readership, the female novelists preferred to avoid explicit association with current debates about Ireland's politics and its troubled history. When writing in 1868 a novel about the fortunes of an Ulster-Scot Presbyterian family in eighteenth-century Antrim in which the final chapters take place in 1798, Mrs Ward, the author of *Waves on the Ocean of Life*, felt obliged to dispel suspicions that she might entertain 'any sympathy with the present Fenian movement'. To make the point that the rebellion could now be safely remembered by writers belonging to a second or third generation after the events, without being tainted with support of republicanism, she quoted from the preface to the opening volume of Madden's *The United Irishmen*:

> While Scotland preserves the memory of those who fell in the Rebellion of 1745, while their lives and actions are recorded by loyal Scotchmen, and read by loyal Englishmen, there can be no reason why the reminiscences of the Irish Rebellion of 1798, and of those

who were unfortunately engaged in it, should not be faithfully recorded, without prejudice to the loyalty of the writer or the reader of their history. We have out-lived the wrongs which made rebels of these men. In our times their descendants are possessed of rights for the enjoyment of which they have reason to be good and loyal subjects.

Tellingly, Ward refrained from naming the source of this quotation, so as not to be explicitly associated with a nationalist historian.[233]

Mrs Ward was the owner of a bookselling and stationary business in Coleraine and had a vested interest in appealing to a local market. The literary reviewer of the *Coleraine Chronicle*, who was acquainted with the author and had read the book in manuscript form, maintained that 'its contents entitle it to a proud placed in the literary shelf of the student of Irish customs and the traditions of the past and present centuries.'[234] The study of historical folklore had been constructed by antiquarians as a neutral terrain that could be shared by Protestants and Catholics. Accordingly, the nationalist *Belfast Morning News* believed the book would be 'perused with pleasure and profit by all who take an interest in Irish history and specially by natives of Ulster' and the unionist *Dublin Evening Mail* was 'agreeably surprised to find the character of the book less gloomy than we anticipated'.[235] The desire to reach readers from both camps of Ireland's polarized politics necessitated that the more controversial aspects of historical memory would be glossed over. Accordingly, Ward clarified that 'it is not our place to enter into a minute history of the time preceding, and the rebellion of 1798, but merely to narrate sufficient to make our story understood.'[236]

However, the historical details, which were supposed to be left in the background, unintentionally took over the centre stage. The most dramatic scenes in the novel occur towards its ending, when 'the embers of discontent which had smouldered for so long in Ireland now burst into the lurid flames of disloyalty and open rebellion.' In reaction to the horrific lashing of his son, a formerly loyal Presbyterian minister named Gordon becomes a zealous United Irishman and is apprehended by the Crown forces. Castlereagh's rejection of the heart-rending appeal of the minister's wife 'to spare the father of her children and the husband of her love' and the minister's subsequent execution on the green in front of his own meeting house is clearly modelled on the popular memory of Rev. James Porter.[237] Although treated gingerly, memories of Ninety-Eight proved to be uncontainable. And yet, despite promotion of the book in advertisements in local newspapers and its availability in local reading venues, such as the Omagh Circulating Library, the little-known novel does not seem to have made much of an impact.[238]

---

[233] Mrs Ward, *Waves on the Ocean of Life: A Dalriadian Tale* (London: Simpkin, Marshall and Dublin: Moffat, 1869), Prefatory Address, pp. vii–viii; taken from Madden, *The United Irishmen*, 1st ser., vol. 1 (1842), Preface, pp. xi–xii.

[234] *Coleraine Chronicle*, 24 October 1868, p. 4. Although little is known of the author, this work cannot be attributed to other notable contemporary women writers with the same name: the Northern Irish microscopist and author Mary [née King] Ward typically signed her books 'The Hon. Mrs Ward'; the British philanthropist and novelist Mary Augusta [née Arnold] Ward adopted the pen-name Mrs Humphry Ward at a slightly later date, after her marriage in 1872.

[235] *Belfast Morning News*, 18 December 1868, p. 3; *Dublin Evening Mail*, 11 December 1868, p. 4.

[236] Ward, *Waves on the Ocean of Life*, p. 275.

[237] Ibid., chs 27–30 (quotations from pp. 288 and 307–8).

[238] *Waves on the Ocean of Life* was available for purchase from mid-October 1868. Advertisements appeared from August 1868 to January 1869 in the *Belfast Morning News*, *Coleraine Chronicle*,

Rosa Mulholland—later known as Lady Gilbert—was the most celebrated of the Ulster women writers. Described by W. B. Yeats in 1891 as 'the novelist of contemporary Catholic Ireland', she wrote over forty novels.[239] *Hester's History*, one of Mulholland's first novels, was serialized in 1868 by Charles Dickens in his magazine *All the Year Round*. A review in the *Pall Mall Gazette* likened it to a second-rate imitation of one of Dickens's weaker novels. Nonetheless, it was published the following year in two volumes. Judging by the novel's contents, Mulholland does not seem to have inherited traditions of Ninety-Eight from her prosperous Catholic Belfast family. Sir Archie Munroe, the owner of the castle of Glenluce in the glens of Antrim (a location based on Dunluce Castle), sympathizes with the ideals of the United Irishmen yet remains loyal to the Crown. He is falsely incriminated as a rebel leader through the machinations of Lady Humphrey, an old adversary of the family, who schemes to take over his estate. When Glenluce is ransacked by military 'hell-hounds', Munroe manages to escape the carnage, but is believed to have perished and so the rebels consider him 'a martyr to their cause'. After his name is finally cleared, he regains ownership of his ancestral home and marries the heroine—Hester Cashel, an orphaned daughter of an Irish political exile, who had been duped into spying and informing on him by the villainous Lady Humphrey.[240]

Mulholland's labelling of government soldiers as 'the enemy' gives away her implicit nationalist sympathies, which in later work progressed into open support of Fenianism. She did not consider herself obliged to take on board historical information and preferred to assume that 'every one knows how the rebellion raged in Ireland in the year ninety-eight.'[241] The narrative, which has been described as a 'sanitized version of the rebellion', ignores the centrality of Presbyterian involvement and has little to do with historical reality or the way it was remembered in Ulster.[242] As noted by the *Freeman's Journal*, Mulholland 'preferred dwelling on fictitious scenes rather than on the historical events themselves'.[243]

Hester's History was listed among 'the hundred best Irish books' by Matthew Russell, the editor of the *Irish Monthly*, but this choice was probably guided more by personal considerations than literary merit. Mulholland, a regular contributor to the literary magazine, was related to Russell by marriage and had modelled the angelic character of Munroe's sister—a nun named Mother Augustine—after one of his siblings, Sister Mary Aquin. A decade and a half after its publication, Russell was obliged to admit that the book was 'not easily procurable' and he strove to counter the apparent lack of public interest by re-serializing *Hester's History* again in the early twentieth century.[244] The novel apparently did not acquire a popular readership in Ireland.

Londonderry Standard, and the *Northern Whig*; its inclusion in the Omagh Circulating Library was advertised in the *Tyrone Constitution* from March to September 1869.

[239] W. B. Yeats, ed., *Representative Irish Tales* (Gerrards Cross: Smythe, 1979; orig. edn 1891), p. 321.

[240] Rosa Mulholland, *Hester's History*, 2 vols (London: Chapman and Hall, 1869). For the less-appreciative review see *Pall Mall Gazette*, 7 April 1869, p. 12.

[241] Mulholland, *Hester's History*, vol. 2, p. 220.   [242] Shanahan, 'Fearing to Speak', p. 44.

[243] *Freeman's Journal*, 4 March 1869, p. 3.

[244] *Freeman's Journal*, 26 March 1886, p. 5. *Hester's History* was serialized in the *Irish Monthly*, volumes 35 (September 1907) to 36 (August 1908). For Mulholland's regular contributions to the literary journal see Declan O'Keefe, 'A Beacon in the Twilight: Matthew Russell, S.J. and the *Irish Monthly*', *Studies*, 99, no. 394 (2010), p. 170. For the identification of the fictional Mother Augustine

Unlike Mulholland's preference for fantasy over history, Mary Damant's *Peggy: A Tale of the Irish Rebellion*, published in 1887, was noted for its 'air of reality', which seemed to impart 'a *vraisemblance* which will convince the reader that he has a faithful picture of the dreadful times referred to'.[245] This verisimilitude can be attributed to the author's familiarity with social memory. Damant, a resident of Cowes, in the Isle of Wight, regularly contributed articles on the folklore and antiquities of Northern Ireland to the *Antiquary* journal. In an error, which has misled a number of scholars, she was misidentified by the bibliographer Stephen James Meredith Brown as the daughter of the famed explorer Francis Radwdon Chesney, who as a child in Annalong, county Down (a seaside village, 30 km east of Newry), assisted his father in opposing rebels.[246] In fact, she was the daughter of a cousin of Chesney, David Wilson of Ballymoney, county Antrim, a well-known figure in mid-nineteenth-century Ulster antiquarian circles.

In the preface to *Peggy*, Damant acknowledged her use of local traditions as a main source for her historical novel:

> The facts of my little tale are not drawn from my own imagination. Many of them were told me in my childhood by those whose recollection of the rising was rendered vivid by desolate homes, and by the loss of relations who had fallen in the field, or found a more dishonourable fate.[247]

The story is narrated by Peggy Thornhill, whose brother Aleck is a United Irishman who falls foul of an informer. Injured on the battlefield, he is sheltered by locals and escapes abroad. The father, a conservative loyalist, disowns his rebel son and moves with Peggy to the Isle of Wight, where, at the very end of the novel, father and son finally reconcile. The conflict within the family highlights the civil war nature of the northern rebellion, which divided Presbyterian families and communities.

Damant eschewed controversy and avowed that she had no intention to 'deal with the complicated historical and political questions involved'.[248] This stance reassured English readers that they could 'take up the book without any dread of being dragged upon any debatable ground'. The author was commended by the *Graphic* for avoiding the pitfall of misleading her readers with 'a stolid political or social pamphlet disguised as fiction'.[249] In Ireland, however, historical fiction could not be detached from political readings. According to the *Belfast News-Letter*, 'though Mrs. Damant does not write a political dissertation in [the] form of a novel, yet she allows her readers to infer a great deal from her graphic and faithful account of some of the incidents of the rebellion.' Reading his own politics into the text, the unionist reviewer maintained that the book offered an apologia for loyalist opposition to Home Rule. Despite the novel's

---

with Sister Aquin see Matthew Russell, *The Life of Mother Mary Baptist Russell, Sister of Mercy* (New York: The Apostleship of Prayer, 1901), pp. 67–9.

[245] Mary Damant, *Peggy: A Tale of the Irish Rebellion* (London: W. H. Allen & Co., 1887). For comments on the novel's realism see *Morning Post*, 9 April 1887, p. 3; *Hampshire Advertiser*, p. 7.

[246] Stephen J. M. Brown, *Ireland in Fiction: A Guide to Irish Novels, Tales, Romances, and Folk-Lore*, 2nd edn (Dublin and London: Maunsel & Co., 1919), p. 82. For Chesney's experience in 1798 see Stanley Lane-Poole, ed., *The Life of the Late General F. R. Chesney . . . By His Wife and Daughter* (London: W. H. Allen & Co., 1885), pp. 41–4.

[247] Damant, *Peggy*, Preface.   [248] Ibid.; see also Brown, *Ireland in Fiction*, p. 82.

[249] *Graphic*, 6 August 1887, p. 150; *Hampshire Advertiser*, 16 April 1887, p. 3.

subtitle promising to deliver *A Tale of the Irish Rebellion*, only a third of the book relates to 1798. It was lavished with praises by the regional newspaper on the Isle of Wight, the location in which most of the plot takes place, but does not seem to have been particularly noticed in Ulster. Indeed, there is no evidence that the prediction of the reviewer in the *Belfast News-Letter* that 'it will delight Ulstermen and Ulsterwomen in every part of the world' actually materialized.[250]

In making use of local traditions of the Turn-Out, Damant stripped folklore accounts of their specificity. In one particularly dramatic scene, two rebels, 'remarkable for extreme youth and dauntless bearing', desperately try to spur on their comrades during a skirmish. They are joined in the mist of the fray by a young women, the sister of one of them, who 'lent the powerful aid of her beauty and her spirited bearing to the appeals of her friends'. All three fall 'in the indiscriminate slaughter that followed'. At the end of the battle, the victorious soldiers encounter 'the saddest sight they had seen in all that dark time of misery':

> For close to each other were the two luckless lads who had been so prominent in the short campaign—one dead, and the other sore wounded and unconscious. And near them lay the poor, brave girl whose zeal and selfless devotion had carried her into the thick of the brief battle—a girl in the sweet bloom of earliest youth, little more than a child.

This episode is a re-rendering of the story of the county Down heroine Betsy Gray, which had previously featured in the works of several writers, most recently in *McComb's Guide to Belfast*. In her literary adaptation, Damant relocated the folk heroine from Ballynahinch to the Glynns in Antrim and changed the names of those involved. She also added a twist, whereby one of the companions happens to be Aleck (the rebel brother of the protagonist), who survives his injuries in the battle and lives on. The story appears in the novel as an incidental anecdote and the female character is just barely mentioned. In this way, elements of popular tradition were subtly woven into the plot in a form that is practically indistinguishable even to those who are familiar with folk history.[251]

A decade earlier, another female author also adapted a version of Betsy Gray's story into a historical novel. Mrs Charles Montague Clarke—a novelist mainly known for Protestant moralist juvenile literature—published in 1875 *Strong as Death*, a three-volume novel set on the background of the rebellion in Ulster. The author, Marion Clarke née Doake, was the daughter of Samuel Doake of Glenlagan, county Down, a Presbyterian landowner from the area of Kinallen, near Dromara, county Down (13 km south-west of Ballynahinch). She dedicated the book to her mother, Eliza, 'from the storehouse of whose traditional lore I have largely drawn'. In dedicating a second edition 'to my countrymen at home and abroad', she described the novel as 'an old story—founded for the most part on oral tradition'.[252]

[250] *BNL*, 17 March 1887, p. 2. Preoccupation with the rebellion is mainly limited to chs 2 to 8 in *Damant, Peggy*, pp. 18–164. For laudatory reviews in the author's area of residence see *Hampshire Advertiser*, 26 February 1887, p. 8; 12 March 1887, p. 7, and 16 April 1887, p. 3.

[251] *Damant, Peggy*, pp. 133–6.

[252] See dedications in Mrs Charles Montague Clarke, *Strong as Death*, 3 vols (London: Tinsley Bros., 1875); Mrs Charles M. Clarke, *Strong as Death: A Story of the Irish Rebellion*, 2nd edn (Aberdeen: Moran, 1898). Marion Clarke's family background can be traced from the notice of her marriage at the First Presbyterian church of Dromara in the *Londonderry Standard*, 18 February 1871, p. 2; her

Clarke's *Strong as Death* received moderate reviews in the London press. The *London Daily News* characterized it as 'overcrowded with detail' and the *Graphic* stated that 'no one can accuse the book of dullness, though we should hardly take it as an example of work of a high order.' A more approving reviewer in the *Morning Post*, who was slightly irritated that the inhabitants of Antrim and Down were 'represented as a little too Scotch', was impressed by the descriptions, 'showing the state of feeling Protestant and Catholic, the bitterness of the Orangemen, the excesses of the soldiery, the extent to which loyal men carried their loyalty, and disloyal ones their spirit of opposition to law and rule, and their unreasoned hatred of the Government.' However, he found the side plot, which features Elizabeth 'Betty' Grey, less convincing. A scene of 'burial and resurrection', in which the heroine simulates her death, was deemed 'unnatural' and 'extremely improbable'. In writing their criticism, the English reviewers were unaware of the extent to which Clarke had deviated from local tradition.[253]

In Clarke's fanciful reworking of the traditional account, Betty Grey [Betsy Gray]— 'the belle of Ednevady'—marries in secret her beloved—a United Irishman named John Holmes—but upon hearing that he was shot by soldiers, she feigns her own death. After discovering that he survived the attack, Grey shows up at the rebel encampment and declares 'I was buried but I am not dead'. Following the routing of the rebels at 'Battle of Ballynahaugh' (a thinly disguised relocation of Ballynahinch), the two exhausted protagonists (unaccompanied by Betty's brother, who chooses not to participate in the battle) are hounded by soldiers. At the fatal moment, when the fugitives are about to be overtaken and killed, they are fortuitously saved and, 'after many escapes', the couple emigrate to America.[254]

This turn of events sharply contradicts local reminiscences and popular traditions, which distinctly recalled that the heroine and her companions were cruelly killed in their attempt to flee the battlefield. Indeed, this tragic outcome is at the heart of the traditional story. It would seem that the far-fetched notion of Betsy Gray surviving 1798 and living a life in exile did not go down well with local readers. There are few signs that the original edition of *Strong as Death* was received with any enthusiasm in Ulster. Applauding the novel's re-issue in 1898 in a 538-page single volume, the *Aberdeen Weekly Journal* claimed, perhaps out of loyalty to the local Scottish publisher, that the book 'in its former three-volume form was widely read and appreciated and there was everything to justify its reproduction in this elegant but bulky volume'. The *Pall Mall Gazette*, however, found the style 'curiously old-fashioned'. Even though the *Irish Monthly* considered it 'a notable contribution to the Centenary literature of 'Ninety-Eight', the second edition, like its predecessor, was barely noticeable and was overshadowed by the many other publications that came out around the time of the centenary of 1798.[255]

mother's death notice appears in *BNL*, 11 March 1862, p. 3; her father's standing as a landowner is evident from his leasing out land in 1857, see Doak Family Papers, PRONI D682/60.

[253] *Graphic*, 9 January 1875, p. 42; *London Daily News*, 22 January 1875, p. 2; *Morning Post*, 22 January 1875, p. 3.

[254] Clarke, *Strong as Death*, 1875 edn, vol. 3, ch. 8 ('The Battle of Ballynahaugh'), pp. 223–56.

[255] *Aberdeen Weekly Journal*, 15 December 1898, p. 2; *Pall Mall Gazette*, 20 September 1898, p. 4; *Irish Monthly*, 26, no. 303 (September 1898): p. 507.

The publication of four novels within a period of two decades—Mrs Ward's *Waves on the Ocean of Life* (1869), Rosa Mulholland's *Hester's History* (1869), Marion Clarke's *Strong as Death* (1875), and Mary Damant's *Peggy* (1887)—would seem to show that memory of 1798 had at last emerged in the open. Official censorship was clearly not an issue, but this had already been the case for the earlier literary input, in the first half of the century. At the time, fear of repression was not the driving factor behind social forgetting in Ulster, which was founded on a peculiar form of self-censorship, manifested in withdrawing of remembrance from the wider public domain while maintaining memory locally. In ignoring actual historical events and the way they were perceived locally, Mulholland wrote a novel which had little relevance to those who retained private recollections of the Turn-Out. The novels of Ward and Damant were more representative of local memories, but in both these narratives the rebellion was deliberately allocated limited space so that it appeared in inverse proportion to its centrality in vernacular historiography.

The extent to which these works of literature actually countermanded social memory, is evident in a throwaway comment in which Clarke revealed her opinion on the remembrance of the event she was writing about: 'May the memory of that time of violence be forgotten by her people, or remembered only as a warning again to those who may ever seek, by stirring up discontent and lawless feeling, to bring back its horrors.'[256] This sentiment corresponds to what has been identified as a general theme of 'paramnesiac history' running through nineteenth-century Anglo-Irish literature, whereby novelists were intent on forgetting the violence of Irish history and replacing it with more amenable memories.[257] Paradoxically, writing about Ninety-Eight could also function, at some level, as an act of forgetting.

All four novels ended up as obscure titles in bibliographical listings of Anglo-Irish literature and the extent of their local readership in Ulster appears to be very small. Attentive consideration of the poor reception of these works can serve to sharpen a critical distinction between social and cultural memory, which has been elided in the scholarly literature of memory studies. It is too readily assumed by modern-day researchers that any cultural representation of the past, however inconspicuous, is inherently an expression of an ill-defined collective-cultural memory. However, the contribution of authors and creative artists to social memory is dependent on the popular reception of their work. It is worth recalling Eric Hobsbawm's thoughtful caveat to his seminal thesis on 'invention of tradition', which noted that 'conscious invention succeeded mainly in proportion to its success in broadcasting on a wavelength to which the public was ready to tune in.'[258] These novels did not correspond to the culture of private remembrance and social forgetting in Ulster. This inaptness becomes clear in comparison to another novel, which was written by a county Down journalist and achieved astonishing success as a vehicle for regenerating social memory.

---

[256] Clarke, *Strong as Death*, 1875 edn, vol. 3, p. 61.

[257] Patrick R. O'Malley, *Liffey and Lethe: Paramnesiac History in Nineteenth-Century Anglo-Ireland* (Oxford: Oxford University Press, 2017).

[258] Eric Hobsbawm, 'Mass-Producing Traditions: Europe, 1870–1914', in *The Invention of Tradition*, edited by Eric Hobsbawm and Terence Ranger, 2nd edn (Cambridge and New York: Cambridge University Press, orig. edn 1983), p. 263.

Wesley Greenhill (oftentimes listed as Guard) Lyttle, the proprietor of the liberal *North Down Herald*, began serializing his most famous novel—*Betsy Gray; or, Hearts of Down: A Tale of Ninety-Eight*—on 7 November 1885. Publication of chapters in the *North Down Herald* continued over the next few months and in 1888 the novel first appeared as a book. Showing a characteristic flair for the overly romantic, Lyttle described the novel's heroine as 'the devoted, beautiful, and noble-hearted Betsy Gray, who headed the patriots at the Battle of Ballynahinch'. Although she was supposed to have been a camp follower and was definitely not a rebel leader, this embroidering was not entirely off the mark. The demotic folk poetry, which had been noted by McComb, and the more refined poems written by Balfour and McComb justify Lyttle's statement that 'her beauty and bravery have been sung of by poets'. He was also right in claiming that her 'chivalry has been recorded by historians' and that her memory was shared 'irrespective of prejudice, politics, or religion'. Early accounts of Betsy Gray had been provided by the Catholic United Irishman Teeling and by the Presbyterian Mary Ann McCracken. She had appeared in the nationalist history written by the Catholic Madden as well as in the loyalist history written by the Anglican Maxwell (who reproduced Teeling's account) and in the travel guide written by William McComb. However, Lyttle's assertion that she was 'revered by countless thousands of the Irish people' applied mainly to interested parties in the heroine's home area in county Down.[259] Betsy Gray was a local heroine and the novel was primarily intended for local readership.

The enthusiastic response was evident in 'numerous letters received by the author during the progress of this story in the columns of the *North Down Herald*'. As serialization was going ahead, readers furnished Lyttle with additional information on local traditions, some of which he worked into the novel. As pointed out by an historian from the area, 'the book was read and no doubt commented on by hundreds of well-informed persons in County Down during the author's life-time.'[260] Lyttle noted in 1894, within six years of the original publication, that the novel's 'success was phenomenal and the demand for its appearance in book form has been such as to warrant the issue of a very large third edition'. After the author's death in 1896, the *North Down Herald* re-printed this edition, which was sold for only sixpence, and was widely marketed during the centenary of the rebellion.[261] A fourth edition was issued in 1899 by his widow and additional editions followed after the turn of the century (Fig. 4.4). The novel's status as a regional best-seller was later acknowledged by Aiken McClelland, the librarian and archivist at the Ulster Folk Museum, who observed, in a preface to a mid-twentieth-century edition, that 'for many years after its first publication, this was a standard book in almost every County Down home.'[262]

---

[259] W. G. Lyttle, *Betsy Gray; or, Hearts of Down: A Tale of Ninety-Eight*, 3rd edn (Bangor: W. G. Lyttle, 1894), ch. 1. As pagination changed in the many different editions of this book, references are given to the number of the short chapters, which were standardized in the third edition. The text of a popular edition from 1968 (Newcastle Co. Down: Mourne Observer Ltd) is available online at a local history website: <http://lisburn.com/books/betsey_gray/betsy-gray1.htm>.

[260] Lyttle, *Betsy Gray*, ch. 27; Dickson, *Revolt in the North Antrim and Down*, p. 232.

[261] Lyttle, *Betsy Gray*, 3rd edn (1894), Preface; *North Down Herald*, 13 May 1898, p. 3. Weekly advertisements for this new edition were placed between April and May 1898.

[262] Aiken McClelland, 'Preface' to Lyttle, *Betsy Gray* (Newcastle, Co. Down: Mourne Observer, 1968), p. x.

Fig. 4.4. W. G. Lyttle, *Betsy Gray* (cover of 9th edn)

Betsy Gray or, Hearts of Down: A Tale of Ninety-Eight (first serialized in the North Down Herald in 1885) by Wesley Greenhill Lyttle (1844–96) became a landmark of provincial vernacular historiography which regenerated social remembrance of Ninety-Eight more than any other work. This cover of a paperback edition of the local bestseller appeared on several of the early twentieth-century editions, based on the text edited and slightly revised by Francis Joseph Bigger (1913).

Photograph courtesy of Mark Thompson.

In the novel, Lyttle offered a sweeping retelling of the entire local 1798 experience. The eponymous heroine Betsy Gray is just one, albeit the most memorable, of many characters, and her presence is limited to only nine out of forty-three chapters, which go on to recount many other stories of the rebellion in Ulster. Additional material, which could not be adequately treated in the novel, was published separately in Lyttle's *North Down Almanac*.[263] The bibliographer and librarian Stephen Brown, who was born in Holywood, county Down, noted that Lyttle 'has gone over every inch of the ground, and has hunted up old documents and old traditions indefatigably'.[264] His account of the martyrdom of William Orr was informed by a history written by the Young Irelander Thomas MacNevin, the depiction of Rev. William Steel Dickson relies on Dickson's autobiographical *Narrative of the Confinement and Exile* and other episodes draw on Teeling's *Personal Narrative*.[265] Beyond his knowledge of printed historical sources, Lyttle's most vital resource, as a local man born in Newtownards in 1842 and well-known throughout the region, was his unfettered access to unpublished social memory.

In affirming the novel's trustworthiness, Lyttle wrote that 'the incidents have been collected from reliable sources, relatives of the sufferers in '98 have been interviewed, and the places written of have all been visited by the author.'[266] From the Byers family of Greyabbey, to whom he was related through his second marriage to Anne Bankhead Byers, Lyttle learned of family traditions that recalled the involvement of two siblings in the United Irishmen: Alexander (Alick) Byers fought and died at Ballynahinch, while his brother William, though obliged to stay at home in Grove Cottage to look after their elderly mother, was arrested. The novel featured their story in a chapter on 'The Greyabbey Insurgents'.[267] Lyttle also visited the house of Hans Gray MacCartney in the village of Six Road Ends (4 km south-east of Bangor), who claimed to be a relative of the heroine and owned possessions that were said to have belonged to her.[268] Upon reading the book, an emigrant relative of Gray Macartney living in the United States—Mrs K. Y. Sanders of Sandwich, Illinois, found that 'it was not new to us', as she could recognize in Lyttle's text family traditions that she had heard as a child.[269]

When writing about the blacksmith of Six Road Ends, Mat McClenaghan, who had manufactured pikes for the rebels in 1798, Lyttle made use of stories that had been repeated to him by the local postmaster, George Moore of Ballygrainey, whose great-grandparents had been acquainted with the smith.[270] Whereas such stories, which cannot be found in official records or in the early works of scholarly history, had previously been remembered by families in private, Lyttle's novel offered an acceptable platform through

---

[263] An article on 'The Execution of Rev. James Porter, of Greyabbey, Co. Down: An Incident of the Irish Rebellion of 1798' appeared in *Lyttle's North Down Almanac and Directory* (Bangor, Co. Down: North Down Herald, 1892), pp. 9–16.

[264] Lyttle, *Betsy Gray*, 3rd edn (1894), Preface; Brown, *Ireland in Fiction*, p. 180.

[265] For an attempt to trace some of Lyttle's sources see Kenneth Robinson, 'Betsy Gray Revisited', *Journal of the Upper Ards Historical Society*, no. 24 (2000): pp. 8–13.

[266] Lyttle, *Betsy Gray*, 3rd edn (1894), Preface.

[267] Lyttle, *Betsy Gray*, ch. 29. The body of Alexander Byers was reclaimed and buried in a family plot in Greyabbey; see Wilsdon, *The Sites of the 1798 Rising*, p. 14; Maeve Friel, *Here Lies: A Guide to Irish Graves* (Dublin: Poolbeg, 1997), p. 225. There is insufficient proof for the claim that he was related to Henry Byers of Saintfield, who was court-martialled and executed in Belfast; Stewart, *Summer Soldiers*, p. 275n73.

[268] Lyttle's visit was still recalled many years later, by the son of the man who had hosted him; *Newtownards Spectator and Donaghadee Review*, 9 September and 7 October 1960, p. 5.

[269] K. Y. Sanders to George (Gray) Macartney, 10 July 1891, Gray Family Papers, PRONI T1296/8.

[270] Lyttle, *Betsy Gray*, ch. 29. George Moore was active in the campaign for tenant rights in his area but eventually lost his lands on the Percival-Maxwell estate and ended up in the workhouse in Bangor, where he reminisced about his meetings with Lyttle; see Robinson, 'Betsy Gray Revisited', p. 10.

which they could be more widely shared. The naming of a commemorative club in east Belfast after Mat Clenaghan during the 1798 centenary celebrations is a clear indication of the novel's influence in gaining wider recognition for local social memory.[271]

The novel *Betsy Gray* became a landmark of provincial vernacular historiography. Its local appeal can be attributed to the interest aroused by the recounting of traditional stories in a narrative style that readapted folk storytelling to the literary sensibilities of a Victorian readership. The register in which the novel was written, which seemed to authenticate the contents as bona fide folk history, was another contributing factor to its remarkable success. Lyttle had a good ear for the Ulster-Scots vernacular of county Down and a talent in rendering spoken idiom in literary form. Assuming the character of a county Down farmer named Robin Gordon from the fictional townland of Ballycuddy, Lyttle entertained audiences across the province with performances of sketches in Ulster-Scots and these enormously popular *Humorous Readings* were published in several volumes and re-issued in multiple editions.[272] His virtuosic use of dialect, however, clouds the provenance of the folklore reproduced in *Betsy Gray*.

Some passages in the novel give the impression of a faithful recollection of early perceptions of the rebellion, as in verses voicing fears of soldiers taken from an 'old song':

> The sodgers ir comin'! rin fast! rin fast!
> Wi' guns an' wi' baynets! rin fast! rin fast!
> They're lukin' fur guns, an' they're lukin' for pikes,
> They'll show ye nae mercy, the bloodthirsty tykes![273]

However, Lyttle moved freely between different types of sources. In the epigraphs at the head of chapters, he quoted poetry from various periods, citing William Drennan's 'The Wake', written after the execution of William Orr, as well as John Kells Ingram's 'The Memory of the Dead' (identified vaguely as an 'Irish ballad') from a half-century later. He was familiar with the work of T. C. S. Corry, having previously been employed as a presenter in Corry's diorama, and quoted verses from 'The Battle of Antrim', which Corry had billed in 1875 as 'a reminiscence of 1798'.[274]

In addition, Lyttle, who had not found success as an amateur poet, wanted to showcase his own compositions.[275] It seems that he was the author of some of the verses that appear in the novel under the label of 'old ballads'. In this practice, he followed in the footsteps of Walter Scott. In an 'Essay on Imitations of the Ancient Ballad', written in 1830 for a new edition of his collection of *Minstrelsy of the Scottish Border* (originally published in 1802–3), Scott observed that it was practically impossible for most readers to distinguish between genuine historical poetry and poetry written in an antiquated style. His literary executor and biographer, John Gibson Lockhart, revealed that Scott would attribute verses that he had written himself to traditional sources and that upon writing *The Antiquary* (1816) he found that

---

[271] *Irish News*, 19 August 1898, p. 6.

[272] Ferguson, *Ulster-Scots Writing*, pp. 281–9; see also Loreto Todd, *The Language of Irish Literature* (Basingstoke: Macmillan, 1989), pp. 134–5. For Robin's *Humorous Readings* see O'Donoghue, *The Poets of Ireland*, p. 261; Loeber and Loeber, *A Guide to Irish Fiction*, pp. 790–2.

[273] Lyttle, *Betsy Gray*, ch. 5.

[274] Lyttle, *Betsy Gray*, chs 7 (Drennan), 24 (Ingram), 27, and 29 (Corry).

[275] For Lyttle's early poetry see *Poetic Lispings by Robin* (Dublin: J. Robertson & Co.; Belfast: C. Aitchison and W. E. Mayne, 1872).

'whenever memory failed to suggest an appropriate epigraph, he had recourse to the inexhaustible mines of "old play" or "old ballad", to which we owe some of the most exquisite verses that ever flowed from his own pen.' In subsequent novels, Scott repeatedly designated quotations taken from his own writings as 'Old Ballad', 'Old Song', 'Old Poem', 'Ancient Drama', and 'Anonymous'.[276]

Lyttle claimed that a 'Ballad of Ninety-Eight', which runs to eighteen stanzas, was 'still familiar in thousands of homes', though its style does not appear to be of old vintage:

> Shame on the cruel, ruthless band,
> Who hunted down to death their prey!
> And palsy strike the murderous hand,
> That slew the lovely Betsy Gray![277]

After the ballad appeared in the novel, it was repeated as folklore, republished in local newspapers and in the early twentieth century was included by the northern writer Richard Hayward in a collection of *Ulster Songs and Ballads*, 'which for generations, have been sung by the people of our Province'.[278] A puristic insistence on distinguishing folklore from 'booklore', which has long plagued folklore studies, would too readily brand the introducing of literary texts into oral history as a fabrication. Lyttle, however considered himself to be renewing tradition.

The origin of another ballad in *Betsy Gray* was attributed to an idealized chain of transmission, which supposedly stemmed back to words spoken by the heroine at Ballynahinch: 'her words have been repeated by father to son, and have been immortalised by a poet.' The poem shows that the transmission of tradition is just as much about those who memorialize as about the heroes of the past:

> An Irish maid in heart and soul
> I love the dear old land;
> Honour those who in her cause
> Lift voice, or pen, or hand.[279]

Agents of regeneration played a cardinal role in the perpetuation and reshaping of memory. The concept of 'invention of tradition' fails to appreciate the subtleties involved in the repackaging of oral traditions in literary forms. Folk memory was not just repeated but recast and augmented with new additions. Through this process of reinvention, rather than straightforward invention, Lyttle strove to counter social forgetting and to air private recollections in the open, where they would be publicly acknowledged.

---

[276] Walter Scott, *The Minstrelsy of the Scottish Border... Introductions, Additions, and the Editor's Notes*, vol. 4 (Edinburgh: Robert Cadell, 1849), pp. 3–78 (esp. 16–21); J. G. Lockhart, *Memoirs of the Life of Sir Walter Scott, Bart.* (Edinburgh: Robert Cadell and London: John Murray and Whittaker, 1837), vol. 1, p. 65 and vol. 4, p. 14; see also Walter Graham, 'Notes on Sir Walter Scott', *Modern Language Notes*, 30, no. 1 (1915): pp. 14–16.

[277] Lyttle, *Betsy Gray*, ch. 40.

[278] Harold Richard Hayward, *Ulster Songs and Ballads of the Town and the Country* (London: Duckworth, 1925), pp. 93–5 (see also 'Prefatory Note', pp. 5–6); John Q. Graham Papers, NLI 41,665; *Irish Weekly and Ulster Examiner*, 7 May 1898, p. 1; *Lisburn Standard*, 20 September 1918.

[279] Lyttle, *Betsy Gray*, ch. 28.

Although Lyttle's self-published novel did not benefit from the distribution networks at the disposal of the larger British presses, copies of *Betsy Gray* found their way outside of Ulster. One of the readers in England was none other than William Gladstone, who after his fall from power, in consequence of the first Home Rule crisis in 1886, spent much of his time reading on Ireland. He read 'with extreme interest' an early edition of the book in July 1889 and immediately wrote the author. Gladstone had just published an essay titled 'Plain Speaking on the Irish Union' that referred to atrocities committed by troops during the suppression of the United Irishmen, for which he had relied on the standard historiography, which neglected Ulster. Finding that he did not have sufficient material on the northern rebellion, apart from Teeling's *Personal Narrative*, Gladstone asked Lyttle for references to some of the episodes recounted in the novel, 'as would enable me to examine their sources, and in case of need to quote from them'.[280] Folk history had acquired new political value.

Gladstone notified Thomas Henry Webb, a proprietor of the organ of the Protestant Home Rule Association *North and South*, that in his opinion 'nothing can be more legitimate than the appeal to the Protestants of Ireland to retain and maintain the tradition of their sires.'[281] Accordingly, upon returning to power, Gladstone's speeches in support of the second Home Rule bill made references to Protestant participation in the rebellion in Antrim and Down.[282] However, in fishing for historical arguments that might help overcome entrenched resistance to Home Rule in Ulster, Gladstone misjudged the dynamics of social forgetting. Picking at errors in Gladstone's account of 1798, an editorial in the *Belfast News-Letter* expostulated: 'we want Mr. Gladstone to mind his own business. He knows nothing about our country's history, and to his rashness may be attributed much of our country's misfortune.'[283] Contrary to his expectations that he would win over the support of Ulster Presbyterians by reminding them of their United Irish ancestry, Gladstone's public appeal to the memory of Ninety-Eight provoked antagonism.

Previously, Lord Randolph Churchill, in an address to Orangemen during a visit to Belfast in February 1886, appealed to loyalist memory and referred to their 'forefathers in '98' opposing the rebellion. Even though some of his audience would most probably have had rebel, rather than loyal, ancestry, Churchill's questionable allusion to memory was not challenged by the conservative public, which preferred to go along with the myth that they were all of pure loyalist stock.[284] Liberals, however, were more sensitive to references to their lineage.

In an open letter to Gladstone, published in the *Northern Whig* in November 1888 and republished by the Liberal Unionist Association as a pamphlet titled *Ulster's Apology for Being Loyal*, Robert McGeagh [MacGeagh] of Knock, county Down (just outside Belfast), took issue with the reproach of 'the men of Belfast and Ulster with political

---

[280] H. C. G. Matthew, ed., *The Gladstone Diaries*, vol. 12 (Oxford: Clarendon Press, 1968), p. 215 (entry for 2 July 1889); W. E. Gladstone, 'Plain Speaking on the Irish Union', *The Nineteenth Century*, 26, no. 149 (July 1889): pp. 1–20. Gladstone's letter to Lyttle (dated 4 July 1889) was subsequently published in the *North Down Herald*; see Jack McCoy, *Ulster's Joan of Arc: An Examination of the Betsy Gray Story* (Bangor, Co. Down: North Down Borough Council Visitors and Heritage Centre, 1987), p. 4.
[281] *Times*, 19 February 1887, p. 7.
[282] See for example Gladstone's speech in Glasgow on 2 July 1892; *Times*, 4 July 1892, p. 4.
[283] *BNL*, 7 June 1889, p. 4.   [284] *BNL*, 23 February 1886, p. 7.

degeneracy and apostasy from the revolutionary principles to their grandfathers.' The author, who was a Presbyterian, acknowledged that 'the grandfathers of many Ulstermen were rebels and Republicans', but stressed that they were a minority. As vice president, soon to become president, of the Ulster Liberal Unionist Association (founded in 1886), McGeagh asserted that 'their grandsons are to-day sincerely loyal to the Throne, and attached to Imperial rule' and that, although 'we cherish the memory of our ancestors and the principles they contended for', the conditions had since changed, so that 'we feel utterly bereft of the incentives to disaffection and disloyalty which goaded them to insurrection.' The rebellion, while not forgotten, was considered no longer relevant to current politics: 'The muskets of '98 have been beaten into ploughshares, and the pikes into pruning hooks, and the cursed arts of civil war have been abandoned for the blessed industries of peace'. If anything, the spirit of rebellion persisted in resistance to the imposition of Home Rule: 'force a Dublin Parliament on Ulstermen anew, and so re-establish a more ignorant and intolerant ascendency, and it will soon be seen that the spirit of the sires yet lives in the sons, and that Ulstermen have still in them the stuff to make rebels.'[285] This view was shared by other Presbyterian liberals.

James Shaw, former professor of political economy at Trinity College Dublin and originally a native of Kirkcubbin, on the Ards peninsular in county Down (16 km south of Newtownards), responded similarly. In a pamphlet styled as an open 'Letter to an Ulster Liberal Elector', Shaw acknowledged that Presbyterian liberals were not 'ashamed of the fact that our ancestors were United Irishmen'. Denying that they 'fear to speak of '98', he expounded:

> We were brought up in the district where Ulster disaffection assumed its acutest form. We have talked in our boyhood with aged relatives who remembered the scenes and incidents of the Rebellion, and whose fathers and brothers were deeply involved in the conflict. We were taught to reverence and respect the memory of those who took up arms against intolerable oppression, and struck a blow for freedom. But, at the same time, we were taught that every object which our forefathers fought for had long since been attained.

Significantly, the transition to unionism that had occurred in the previous generation did not entail renunciation of the memory of the United Irishmen: 'we were taught to love England and England's Queen by those who loved and remembered the rebels of '98, and who loved Ireland as deeply and as ardently as the men who shed their blood at Ballynahinch.'[286]

McGeagh, Shaw, and other prominent Presbyterian liberals, such as the Belfast merchant and politician Thomas Sinclair (first chairman of the Ulster Liberal Unionist Association) and the local historian Hugh McCall of Lisburn, had been enthusiastic supporters of Gladstone's reformist policies in Ireland up to his conversion to Home

---

[285] *Northern Whig*, 5 November 1888; Robert McGeagh, *Ulster's Apology for Being Loyal* (London: Cassell & Company, 1888).

[286] James J. Shaw, *Mr. Gladstone's Two Irish Policies: 1868 and 1886, a Letter to an Ulster Liberal Elector* (London and Belfast: Marcus Ward & Co., 1888), pp. 9 and 11. See also Finlay Holmes, 'From Rebels to Unionists: The Political Transformation of Ulster's Presbyterians', in *The Union: Essays on Ireland and the British Connection*, edited by Ronnie Hanna (Newtownards: Colourpoint, 2001), p. 44; Andrew Holmes, 'Nineteenth-Century Ulster Presbyterian Perspectives on the 1798 Rebellion', *Irish History: A Research Yearbook*, 2 (2003): p. 49; McBride, 'Memory and Forgetting', p. 494.

Rule, which they fiercely opposed.[287] After meeting with Gladstone in 1893, members of the Belfast Chamber of Commerce rejected his interpretation of Ulster history and stated that there was no inconsistency between their past and present politics: 'not the least earnest Unionists among us to-day are the descendants of the rebels of 1798.'[288]

Opposition to Home Rule brought together liberal and conservative unionists. Robert Hugh Wallace, president of the Downpatrick Unionist Club and a devoted Orangeman, recounted in 1894 an anecdote of 'a noted Unionist in Belfast, a Presbyterian, who had been a staunch supporter of Mr. Gladstone until that statesman tried to subvert the constitution', and had subsequently written a letter against the alliance of liberal and nationalists:

> Gladstone replied to him by casting in his teeth that his ancestors had been rebels, as he said the Presbyterians were in '98. 'Yes,' replied the Belfast man, 'they were rebels in '98, and you are doing your utmost to make rebels of them again.'[289]

In their aversion to Gladstone's appeal to the memory of 1798, Presbyterian unionists found new meaning in their rebel ancestry.

During the preparations for a unionist convention in Belfast in 1892, the independent liberal T. W. Russell shared a stage with the conservative Colonel Edward Saunderson and announced that 'the actual lineal descendants of the Volunteers and the United Irishmen' had 'been converted in the meantime'.[290] Liberals somehow found common cause with Orangemen, who also railed against Gladstone's historical references to 1798, though for different reasons. At a 12 July demonstration in Belfast in 1889, Lord Erne, the imperial grand master of the Orange Order, accused Gladstone of ignoring the sectarian atrocities, which were central to loyalist memory.[291] Rev. Richard Rutledge Kane, the grand master of Belfast, showed greater sophistication in a lecture delivered in Gilford, county Down, in 1890 on 'Our Country: Her History, Claims, and Hopes', which faulted Gladstone for failing to realize that 'Ulstermen—even Ulstermen who are sprung from the rebels of 1798'—were committed to unionism.[292]

These heated political controversies over the meaning of the memory of 1798 were a far cry from what Lyttle had intended in his literary representation of local folk history. Aptly described in an obituary as 'a liberal in politics, and in religion a Presbyterian, but neither in politics nor in Church affairs did he give himself much concern', Lyttle deliberately evaded controversy.[293] Aware that Orangemen (some of whose ancestors may have been United Irishmen) might be among the local readers interested in his *Betsy Gray* novel, he took particular care not to cause any offence. A description in the novel of a United Irish initiation ceremony includes a performance of the song 'The Shan Van Vocht' [*An tSeanbhean Bhocht*]. Of the many available variations, Lyttle

---

[287] For Sinclair see Holmes, 'From Rebels to Unionists', p. 45; see also Graham Walker, 'Thomas Sinclair: Presbyterian Liberal Unionist', in *Unionism in Modern Ireland: New Perspectives on Politics and Culture*, edited by Richard English and Graham S. Walker (Houndmills and New York: Macmillan Press, 1996), pp. 19–40. For McCall see Bew, *The Glory of Being Britons*, p. 229.

[288] *Times*, 15 April 1893, p. 6.   [289] *BNL*, 2 March 1894, p. 7.

[290] *BNL*, 9 April 1892, p. 7.

[291] *BNL*, 13 July 1889, p. 6. Erne was reacting to a speech Gladstone had made a month earlier in Cornwall, which claimed that the United Irish alliance between Catholics and Protestants had been disrupted by the Orange Order; *Times*, 13 June 1889, p. 9.

[292] *BNL*, 27 September 1890, p. 7.   [293] *BNL*, 2 November 1896, p. 6.

chose to reproduce a version found in *The Songs of Ireland*, compiled in 1845 by the Young Ireland poet Michael Joseph Barry, making one small, yet significant, change: the verse 'And the Orange will decay' was replaced with 'And tyrants will decay'.[294]

In another scene, Lyttle made a point of retelling a story that was remembered in Lisburn of how the members of an Orange lodge gave shelter to the Catholic parish priest Father Magee, when he was caught outside during a curfew.[295] More generally, the novel avoids mentioning acts of violence committed by the Orange Order in 1798. In referring to the yeomen who killed the heroine and her companions, the novelist noted that 'to the day of their death they were abhorred and avoided as a pestilence, alike by Orange and Green, Protestant and Catholic, saint and sinner'. Memory was purposely depoliticized in order that it could be shared across the region.[296]

Lyttle was very much aware of local sensitivities and refrained from using the real names of certain individuals in order 'not to draw aside too far the veil which has fallen upon incidents connected with the history of many who still reside in districts where these pages are certain to be read'.[297] It was later maintained that he was given the names of the killers of Betsy Gray, two of whom were said to have been yeomen from the village of Annahilt (8 km north-west of Ballynahinch), but purposely omitted publishing this incriminating identification, as he was aware that they had relatives still living in the area who would prefer that it would not be mentioned in public.[298] Although the novel's narrative describes in detail many sorrowful events, the author claimed in the conclusion to have exercised self-restraint:

> I have but little more to tell my readers regarding the struggle of '98 in County Down. Volumes could be filled in recounting deeds of blood; the publication of these, however, might but perpetuate ill-feeling and freshen the recollections of much that had better be forgotten.[299]

Even as he was publicizing the memory of the rebellion, Lyttle acknowledged local interest in curtailing remembrance with conscious forgetting.

The most poignant scene in the *Betsy Gray* novel is the depiction of the burial place of the heroine and her two companions at Ballycreen (3 km north-west of Ballynahinch):

> Neither spade nor plough has ever disturbed that hallow spot. The people of the district regard it with the deepest reverence, and often as they visit the place, they sit upon the emerald sod and recall the story which has been handed down from father to son. A log of black oak thrown across the head of the grave alone marks the spot, and this is so grown over by the grass as to be scarcely noticeable.

---

[294] Lyttle, *Betsy Gray*, ch. 11; Michael Joseph Barry, ed., *The Songs of Ireland* (Dublin: James Duffy, 1845), pp. 49–51.

[295] Lyttle, *Betsy Gray*, ch. 11. The story was previously recalled by Hugh McCall; anon. [McCall], *Ireland and Her Staple Manufactures*, 2nd edn (1865), pp. 143–4. In the late twentieth century, the story was reproduced in a publication issued by the Education Committee of the Grand Orange Lodge of Ireland as an example of 'the behaviour of a true Orangeman'; Kilpatrick, *The Formation of the Orange Order*, p. 81.

[296] Lyttle, *Betsy Gray*, ch. 40. See also Robinson, 'Betsy Gray Revisited', p. 10.

[297] Lyttle, *Betsy Gray*, ch. 13.

[298] Ernest Lowry Papers, PRONI T2794/2. The killers of Betsy Gray, as recalled in local tradition, are named in Madden, *The United Irishmen*, 3rd ser., vol. 1 (1846), p. 398; *McComb's Guide to Belfast*, p. 130.

[299] Lyttle, *Betsy Gray*, ch. 43.

This glaring absence of a memorial on the grave is reiterated in a stanza of a ballad (probably composed by the author):

> No tombstone marks that humble grave,
> No tree nor shrub is planted there;
> And never spade disturbs that spot,
> Where sleeps the brave, where rest the fair.[300]

In the preface to the 1894 edition, Lyttle commented on the overwhelming reactions of readers, who were deeply touched by this account of neglect:

> The mournful fate of the beautiful Betsy Gray has excited universal sympathy. Many letters have been received by the writer of these pages expressing a desire to subscribe towards a suitable monument to be erected at the lonely grave in the vale of Ballycreen, where the ashes of Betsy repose. A movement is on foot to have this object carried out in the year 1898.[301]

By giving birth to a campaign for the erection of a monument, the reception of Lyttle's text unwittingly initiated a grass-roots countdown towards the centennial of 1798. The desire to commemorate Ninety-Eight in public undermined the culture of social forgetting in Ulster. This open challenge would eventually have explosive results.

REVIVALISM AND RE-COLLECTING

The mid-nineteenth-century flourish of antiquarianism, which had resulted in the establishment of the *Ulster Journal of Archaeology* (*UJA*) in 1853, gradually petered out. Within less than a decade, in 1862, the journal ceased publication. Nonetheless, concerns persisted that the progress of modernity would obliterate the historical record. Towards the end of the century, angst over the past being forgotten was once again at the fore. This time, it was expressed by a new generation of antiquarians:

> A very general feeling has lately grown up that the time has now fully come when the Journal should be revived, unless we are prepared to allow records and investigations into the past history and antiquities of our Province to pass into oblivion. At the present time, when the face of the country is changing, and local sources of information gradually dying out, it is the more needful that an effort should be made to provide a means of bringing together, in a permanent form, the immense mass of information still existing in the possession of private persons, ere it be utterly lost.[302]

Accordingly, in 1894 the Belfast solicitor Francis Joseph Bigger, who would gain a reputation as the leading Irish antiquarian of his day, set about reviving the *UJA*.

Bigger was a prominent member of several antiquarian hubs: he joined the Belfast Naturalists' Field Club in 1884, subsequently serving as honorary secretary (1891–7), vice-president (1898–1900), and president (1901–3); he was a shareholding member of the Belfast Natural History and Philosophical Society; in 1894 he was appointed a member of the Royal Irish Academy; and in 1896 he was elected a fellow of the Royal

---

[300] Lyttle, *Betsy Gray*, chs 40 and 41.
[301] Lyttle, *Betsy Gray*, 3rd edn (1894), Preface.
[302] 'Prospectus', *UJA*, 2nd ser., 1, no. 1 (September 1894): p. 1.

Society of Antiquaries of Ireland and went on to serve as its vice-president. Bigger was also the honorary secretary of the Irish class taught by P. J. O'Shea [Pádraig Ó Seaghdha], which would evolve in 1895 into the Belfast Gaelic League; he was elected to the Coiste Gnótha, the Gaelic League's national executive committee, where he became acquainted with Douglas Hyde, Eoin MacNeill, and the other major figures of the Irish language revival. As a member of the governing body of the Belfast Library and Society for Promoting Knowledge—commonly known as the Linen Hall library (an institution that had been associated with the United Irishman Thomas Russell), he encouraged acquisitions of early printed books from across the province, which from 1892 were shelved separately in a designated Irish collection. In all these engagements, Bigger was intent on continuing the enterprise of the previous generation of noted Ulster antiquarians and upheld in particular the example of Sir Samuel Ferguson, in whose honour he organized a centennial celebration in 1910.[303]

Significantly, in reviving the house journal of Ulster antiquarianism, Bigger received the blessing of the original founding editor, 86-year-old Robert Shipboy Macadam, who died shortly after publication recommenced. The few other remaining contributors to the original run of the *UJA* were persuaded to write for the new series. Rev. George Hill of Moyargetin, county Antrim (6 km south-west of Ballycastle), who was the former librarian of Queen's College Belfast and had been the minister of the Presbyterian non-subscribing congregations of Ballymoney and Crumlin, published articles in the journal up until his death, at the age of 90 in 1900. Similarly, Rev. James O'Laverty, the Catholic parish priest of Holywood, county Down (just outside Belfast), continued to publish in the journal till 1905, the year before his death at the age of 78.[304] The involvement of these venerable figures allowed the revival at the end of the century to be presented as a direct continuation of a local tradition of highly respected amateur scholarship.

The editors of the revived *UJA* announced that it would 'deal with various subjects of interest to the Antiquarian and Student of Local History' and that it would accommodate 'any subject helping to elucidate the History or Manners of Ulster'. Contributors were required to ensure that 'their statements, above and beyond all other considerations, shall be absolutely trustworthy', even if 'their impartiality and truth telling' would 'be met by the angry clamourings of would-be critics and reviewers'. While they were not afraid of academic criticism, the editors wished to steer away from the tensions that had just recently been exacerbated during the Second Home Rule Bill crisis. They therefore endorsed a 'peace-preserving arrangement', whereby, it was 'unanimously resolved to exclude all matter tending to excite controversies on present questions of religion and politics'. The editors promised that 'the Poetry, Music, and Folklore of the North of Ireland will not be forgotten,' but when it came to the sensitive topic of the 1798 rebellion, it was evident that these traditions could still provoke disagreement.

---

[303] John S. Crone, 'Memoir', *In Remembrance: Articles & Sketches, Biographical, Historical, Topographical, by Francis Joseph Bigger, M.A., M.R.I.A., F.R.S.A.I., edited by John S. Crone and F. C. Bigger* (Dublin and Cork: Talbot Press and Belfast: Mullan & Son, 1927), pp. xv–xxxviii; see also Guy Beiner, 'Revisiting F. J. Bigger: A Fin-de-Siècle Flourish of Antiquarian-Folklore Scholarship in Ulster', *Béaloideas*, 80 (2012): pp. 142–62.

[304] See obituaries in *UJA*, 2nd ser., vol. 1, no. 2 (January 1895): p. 152 (Macadam); vol. 6, no. 3 (July 1900): pp. 125–7 (Hill); vol. 12, no. 3 (July 1906): pp. 129–31 (O'Laverty).

Nevertheless, at Bigger's insistence, it was stipulated that 'space will be given to the Insurrection of '98'.[305]

Bigger's dedication to antiquarian scholarship was inexhaustible. Starting with an article on the United Irish newspaper *The Northern Star*, which made use of local tradition, he contributed articles, reviews, and notes to every issue of the *UJA*, throughout the entire run of the second series, from 1894 to 1911, and also wrote many other articles, often under pseudonyms, for associated journals.[306] Although his many intellectual pursuits ranged far beyond history and folklore, Bigger was particularly fascinated by the memory of 1798. His interest was first kindled as a child, when he was sent for health reasons to relatives in Carnmoney—the McKinneys of Sentry Hill, where he first encountered traditions of the rebellion that were still circulating in the Antrim countryside. His close friend, the antiquarian and bibliophile John Smyth Crone, editor of the *Irish Book Lover*, recalled that 'the stories of "the turn out" of '98, of Antrim fight and Donegore . . . told to him by the sons and daughters of those who had participated therein, exercised a powerful influence on his youthful mind, and all throughout his career . . . he never lost interest in that painful period.' Remembrance of the northern United Irishmen became Bigger's lifelong obsession.[307]

Bigger could trace a family link to the period. One of his ancestors, James Bigger of Biggerstown, county Antrim, had been among the first patriots to join the Volunteers in 1782 and another relative, Matthew Bigger, was a United Irish colonel at the Battle of Antrim.[308] Around the same time as he relaunched the *UJA*, Bigger declared his intention to write the lives of the 'Northern Leaders of '98'. This initiative was applauded by the pioneering folklorist Douglas Hyde, who solicited the approval of the chairman of the Irish Literary Society, the veteran nationalist politician Sir Charles Gavan Duffy.[309] This endorsement had significant symbolic value. Bigger modelled himself on Madden, whose *Lives of the United Irishmen* had been published with the help of Duffy half a century earlier. He believed that he was in a unique position to go beyond his predecessor's impressive achievements and to redress the shortcomings in Madden's treatment of Ulster:

> It has fallen to me, brought up in the country of the northern leaders of the insurrection of '98, related to several of them, familiar with their homes and haunts, acquainted with the scenes of their deaths, a frequent visitor to their graves, their people and my people known and connected with each other, their names household words—it has fallen to me, after the lapse of a century, to be a chronicler of their lives and actions.[310]

As Bigger saw it, the recovery of the local memory of the Turn-Out was his calling (Fig. 4.5).

[305] *UJA*, 2nd ser., 1, no. 1 (1894): Prospectus and Introduction, pp. 1 and 8–10.
[306] *Sources*, the National Library of Ireland database for Irish research, credits F. J. Bigger with 267 journal articles, of which 186 appeared in the *Ulster Journal for Archaeology*. This enumeration, which omits numerous articles written anonymously or under a pseudonymous, is not comprehensive.
[307] Crone, 'Memoir', pp. xvi–xvii. See also Thomas Joseph Campbell, *Fifty Years of Ulster, 1890–1940* (Belfast: Irish News, 1941), p. 281; Isabel Rosborough Crozier, *William Fee McKinney of Sentry Hill: His Family and Friends* (Coleraine: Impact, 1985), p. 22.
[308] 'The Bigger Family of Belfast and County Antrim', Bigger Family Papers, PRONI D3905/C/2; Robert M. Young, *The Town Book of the Corporation of Belfast, 1613–1816* (Belfast: Marcus Ward & Co., 1892), p. 323.
[309] Douglas Hyde to F. J. Bigger, 7 January, 5 and 13 February 1895; Bigger Papers, NLI 35,456/2.
[310] Bigger, *Remember Orr*, p. 6.

Fig. 4.5. Francis Joseph Bigger

Francis Joseph Bigger (1863–1926) rubbing gravestones (*c.*1903) with the folksong collector Herbert Hughes (1882–1937). Bigger, who was recognized as the leading antiquarian of his day, considered himself the rightful successor of Madden and was dedicated to preserving the memory of the northern United Irishmen.

Courtesy of the National Library of Ireland (MS 21,543).

In reawakening preoccupation with 1798, Bigger could count on already existing interest among local historians, which was evident in talks given at the time to local societies. For example, the Lisburn Cathedral Literary and Debating Society hosted on 7 December 1891 an 'interesting and instructive paper' by Mercer Rice, the 60-year-old local railway station master, on 'Glimpses of Irish History, and 1798 and Its Times'. The lecture, which showed a detailed knowledge of local history and made use of vernacular sources, such as traditions that had been collected by Madden and the recollections of Hugh McCall, was subsequently serialized over four weeks in the local newspaper, the *Lisburn Herald and Antrim and Down Advertiser*. Significantly, Rice was an Anglican and his talk was given in the Church of Ireland cathedral before what would have been a largely unionist audience, which shows that there was a wide interest—not confined only to Presbyterians—in the local history of the rebellion that could be tapped into.[311]

---

[311] *Lisburn Herald and Antrim and Down Advertiser*, 12, 19, 26 December 1891 and 2 January 1892, all on p. 8. The religious affiliation of Mercer Rice is given in the 1901 census. For biographical

Another example can be found in Bigger's friend and distant relative from Carnmoney, the highly respected local historian and antiquarian William Fee McKinney. Sentry Hill, his house near Glengormley (outside Newtownabbey), stored a remarkable collection of curiosities, including a souvenir jug celebrating the fall of the Bastille, as well as pikes and muskets from the time of the rebellion. McKinney was a Presbyterian liberal unionist, who readily acknowledged the involvement of his ancestors in the United Irishmen. His maternal grandfather, Hugh Giffen, was active in trying to spring free United Irish prisoners, but did not take part in the rebellion and ended up swearing an oath of allegiance. His paternal grandfather, John McKinney, had taken part in the Battle of Antrim, at which also his granduncle Samuel George was killed.[312]

Thomas Camac, the local historian of the parish of Derrykeighan in county Antrim, regretted that 'the average Ulsterman's knowledge of the history of his native province is very limited indeed'. Camac asserted that acquaintance with the past of one's district was generally lacking, 'with the exception of a few facts handed down by tradition, which, at the best, are not always reliable, and at the utmost do not extend further back than the "rising" of 1798.'[313] Bigger was intent on salvaging these oral traditions and according them public recognition.

Bigger began to collect sources on the memory of the rebellion in Ulster from at least as early as 1892, when he approached the elderly T. C. S. Corry—who seventeen years earlier had published the poem 'The Battle of Antrim'—in search of a colour illustration of Henry Munro drawn in 1798.[314] In October 1893, the antiquarian, bookplate designer and first president of the Belfast Art Society, John Vinycomb, introduced Bigger to Patrick McFerran [also given as Fearon], an engraver who 'promises a wonderful fund of information about early Belfast'. McFerran fulfilled his promise and three months later furnished Bigger with his notes on 'Belfast in '98', which included oral traditions with recollections of the rebellion that he had collected in the town.[315] In 1895, Bigger corresponded with the venerable local historian Hugh McCall, who was then 90-years-old, to collect from him traditions of Henry Munro.[316]

The following year, Bigger compiled notes on the folk heroine Betsy Gray. This research allowed him later to produce a new (sixth) edition of Lyttle's novel, which would become the authoritative version of text and has since been reproduced in all

information see 'Lisburn Stationmaster Held Office for 55 Years' at the local history website: <www. lisburn.com/history/digger/Digger-2007/digger-16-03-2007.html>.

[312] Crozier, *William Fee McKinney of Sentry Hill*, pp. 89–91 and 99; Brian Mercer Walker, *Sentry Hill: An Ulster Farm and Family* (Dundonald: Blackstaff Press, 1981), esp. pp. 15–16; Maguire, *Up in Arms*, pp. 87–8 and 201. For Hugh Giffen see *UJA*, 2nd ser., 5, no. 3 (1899), p. 178. For a photograph of the room with the pikes and muskets see Sarah Edge, *Traces of Traces: An Exploration of the Albums of William McKinney* (Inishowen: Art Link, 2011). My thanks to custodian Wesley Bonar for facilitating a visit to Sentry Hill on 18 September 2011.

[313] *UJA*, 5, no. 3 (1899), p. 147.

[314] T. C. S. Corry, Glenfield, Belfast, to Francis Joseph Bigger, 11 September 1892, Bigger Papers, BCL K3/H/124. For the illustration see Thomas Rowlandson, *Henry Munro, Chief of the Irish Rebels* (1798); NLI EP MUNR-HE (1) II (also p. 37, Fig. I.2).

[315] Patrick McFerran, via J. Vinycomb, to Bigger, 6 October 1893, Bigger Papers, BCL K2/A/ 12–13; Patrick Fearon (in the presence of J. Vinycomb) to Bigger, 30 January 1894, BCL G 74. The 1901 census identifies Patrick Ferran as a 50-year-old Catholic die sinker and brass engraver living in Belfast.

[316] Hugh McCall to F. J. Bigger, 10 June 1895, F. J. Bigger Papers Collection, BCL MA 17.

subsequent editions of the popular book. In its conclusion, the original text had looked back at 'the participators in the scenes of '98' guardedly: 'they may have been foolish and misguided in their actions, but no ill shall be spoken of the dead. History deals charitably with them; the present generation speaks leniently and reverently of them.' Bigger's subtly revised version removed any sign of ambivalence. It omitted the allusion to 'foolish and misguided' actions, and stated more resolutely that 'history should deal fearlessly with them; the present generation should speak reverently of them.' In his capacity as editor, Bigger was effectively responsible for the canonization of cultural memory along heroic, quasi-hagiographical, lines.[317]

Bigger was ideally suited to uncover sources of vernacular history, as his friend Crone attested:

> No man had a wider circle of friends in all walks of life, than he; the country folk, knowing his tastes, would preserve any old book, paper, antiquarian 'find,' or curio, ancient or modern, for his acceptance; sometimes for years, well-knowing that one day he would pass their way and receive it with pleasure. And later, well-known people would present him with valuable family papers, which they feared might be destroyed or lost by careless relatives.[318]

He was able to access materials that had been collected earlier by interested locals and remained in private possession. One of many examples can be found in his communications with John Cardwell, a Presbyterian farmer from Tonaghmore, county Down (2 km south-west of Saintfield). Cardwell was a local historian, who became acquainted with Bigger through the Belfast Naturalists' Field Club.[319] He showed Bigger relics that had formerly belonged to William Holmes, the man who had betrayed Munro when he took shelter in his house after the Battle of Ballynahinch. These included a 'precious and massive glass mug', from which Munro had supposedly been given a drink when he arrived exhausted at Holmes' door, and a gun that had reputedly belonged to the rebel general. The firearm had been kept in the Holmes family for three generations and was then sold by auction, after the lock had been removed and sold separately. As a token of his appreciation, Cardwell presented Bigger with the souvenir gun, stating that 'many times I have [been] offered money for it but no one shall have it but you.'[320] It joined a remarkable collection of '98 relics, which were displayed in Ardrigh, Bigger's house in Belfast, in a room designated as a 'museum' of the Turn-Out, which included objects

---

[317] D. J. O'Donoghue of the London Celtic Literary Society (who in 1902 wrote a biography of Robert Emmet) mentioned that Bigger sent his notes on 'Betsie Gray' to an O'Keefe, possibly referring to J. G. O'Keefe, an editor for the Irish Texts Society; D. J. O'Donoghue to Bigger, 4 February 1896, F. J. Bigger Papers, BCL OD 6. Bigger's lightly edited version of the novel came out seventeen years later; W. G. Lyttle, *Betsy Gray; or, Hearts of Down: A Tale of Ninety-Eight*, 6th edn (Belfast: R. Carswell & Son, 1913).

[318] Crone, 'Memoir', p. xxxi.

[319] For Cardwell see H.C. Patterson, 'John Cardwell—Local Historian', *Saintfield Heritage*, 2 (1986): pp. 59–60. He is listed in the 1901 census as a 50-year-old Presbyterian farmer living in Tonaghmore. In 1894 Bigger responded to a lecture he gave to the BNFC (which mentioned 'a curious old bridge built by the King's troops in 1798'); *Annual Reports and Proceedings of the Belfast Naturalists' Field Club*, ser. 2, vol. 4, part I (Belfast, 1894), p. 83. Cardwell later wrote about an act of private remembrance at a rebel's grave near Ballynahinch; *UJA*, 2nd ser., 10, no. 2 (1904): pp. 90–1.

[320] Bigger Papers, BCL K3/H/32, 35 and 82. Cardwell also claimed that Munro's sword had been 'thrust up under a mass of stones in Holmes's cow house almost rusted away all but the silver mounted guard' and noted that its subsequent whereabouts were forgotten.

attributed to William Orr, Henry Joy McCracken, and James Hope, with whom Bigger claimed kinship.[321]

Cardwell provided Bigger with a detailed description of Henry Munro that was collected in 1859 from 98-year-old Margaret Simpson, who had been 'perfectly acquainted with him'. In the area of Saintfield, Bigger was retold the reminiscences of Charles Young, a veteran of Ballynahinch, who prior to his death at the age of 86 in 1845, recalled how Patrick Sweeny, a Covenanter from Lecale in east county Down, was known after the battle as 'the Boy in the Gap' for his bravery in holding an opening in the line of defence 'until he was literally cut in pieces'. Bigger was also given an account collected in the mid-nineteenth century from 96-year-old Ellen George of Tonaghmore, whose son had joined the insurgents and then escaped to America. She recalled that 'the soldiers burned my house shot my husband, who was a loyal man, in his own field and also fired at me but I escaped by a miracle to tell the world of the tyranny which drove the Presbyterians of Ulster into taking up arms.' Until Bigger arrived on the scene, these folk history accounts had not attracted interest outside the locality.[322]

Bigger approached individuals, who had previously kept their family memories of 1798 to themselves, and, by earning their respect and admiration, persuaded them to share with him their traditions. A typical informant, the 52-year-old non-subscribing Presbyterian McNeilly Hope of Muckamore, county Antrim (2 km south-east of Antrim town), with whom he corresponded in 1895, was very much impressed by Bigger's 'desire to preserve any thing belonging to the grand old people', just when it seemed that 'there would not be a soul left who cared a fig for the few old things that I have here and it vexed me to think they would be lost'. One contact often led to another. McNeilly Hope informed Bigger that he 'had a long talk' with his uncle, who was 'very proud to think you take such an interest in his old friends and will be glad to supply any information in his power'.[323] Over the next two decades, Bigger diligently pursued every possible lead in search of traditions and artefacts, meeting and corresponding with numerous people across Ulster, as he meticulously compiled sources for a history of 'The Northern Leaders of '98'.

Bigger's boundless enthusiasm was contagious. He inspired other antiquarians, who shared his interest in 1798, and this triggered a flourish of publications on the folk history of the Turn-Out. In producing the first volumes of the renewed *UJA*, Bigger brought on board the architect and local historian Robert Magill Young as co-editor. Young came from a line of antiquarians, which personified the regeneration of antiquarianism in Ulster. His grandfather, Rev. Robert Magill, the staunchly orthodox and conservative minister of the First Presbyterian congregation of Millrow in Antrim town, had compiled genealogical records of his parishioners. Young's father, the eminent Belfast architect Robert Young,

---

[321] 'The Late Francis Joseph Bigger', *Journal of the County Louth Archaeological Society*, 6, no. 2 (1926): p. 104; Hugh A. MacCartan, 'Belfast: Some Backwards Glances', *Capuchin Annual* (1943): pp. 177–8.

[322] Bigger Papers, BCL K3/H/37–39 (Young), 36 and 80–82 (Simpson), 109 (George). Selections form the accounts collected in the area appeared in B. [F. J. Bigger], ''Ninety-Eight in County Down', *SVV*, 2, no. 11 (November 1897): pp. 203–5.

[323] McNeilly Hope to Bigger, 8 and 13 October 1895; F. J. Bigger Papers NLI 35,456/4. The 1901 census lists McNeilly Hope of Shanoguestown, Muckamore, as a 58-year-old Unitarian linen yarn bleacher.

regularly wrote articles for the *UJA*. Traditions of 1798 ran in the family. R. M. Young's great-grandfather, Samuel Skelton, was the agent of Lord Massareene and had vivid recollections of the rebellion. Young's maternal grandfather, Robert Magill, had witnessed executions of United Irishmen as a 10-year-old child in Broughshane, near Ballymena, and the paternal grandmother, Mary Young née Magee of Dundrod, county Antrim (12 km west of Belfast), would often recount recollections from when she was 13 'of the dreadful doings of the "yeos" (yeomen) in the '98 days'.[324]

As a historian of Belfast, who edited the archival manuscripts of the town's corporation, R. M. Young was aware that recollections of 1798 had been left out of the official historical record.[325] Whilst he acknowledged that 'a number of histories of the Rebellion in 1798 have been written, and its political aspects exhaustively treated', Young was concerned that 'the social and local details of the struggle in Ulster are fast dying out with their narrators.' To counter the neglect, he published in 1893 a book titled *Ulster in '98: Episodes and Anecdotes*, which included 'recollections of '98 in Broughshane' that had been written around 1831 by his ancestor Robert Magill, as well as traditions found in the manuscripts of McSkimin and Classon Porter. In addition to publishing for the first time accounts that had been taken down over the previous two generations, Young went on to collect from his relatives 'anecdotes from Antrim'. From other informants he collected 'county Down incidents of '98', which included also traditions about 'Henry Munro and his friends' provided by the local historian Hugh McCall.[326]

Young found that he could address the glaring omission of 1798 in the official records of Belfast by turning to oral history and tradition. He provided a vivid account of 'Belfast under martial law', which was based on information he collected in interviews with an unnamed elderly lady, who at the time of the interview, on 29 June 1891, claimed to be 105 years old, and with the granddaughters of people that had been harassed by the military. In an appendix, he described souvenirs that commemorated William Orr, one of which was in the collections of the Belfast Museum and another was still in the private possession of a relative, the resident magistrate W. Orr. After the book had gone to press, Young continued to receive additional 'material of original value'. Memories of the Turn-Out were evidently still alive and could now appear in public.[327]

Despite the new openness, it transpired that not everything about the past could be aired. Young published in 1896 *Historical Notices of Old Belfast*, in which he included a 'Life of Mary Ann McCracken' that covered her brother's involvement in the United Irishmen and his execution. This early biography was written by Anna McCleery, who was identified as Mary Ann's grand-niece. It was tactfully not mentioned that the author's mother, Maria McCleery, was the illegitimate daughter of the rebel hero. Although Maria was already 4 years old when Henry Joy McCracken was executed, the McCracken family was unaware of her existence until Mary Ann was informed of her niece's whereabouts in a communication from Rev. Steel Dickson (who was in prison

---

[324] Robert Young, Sr, 'Memories of a Nonagenarian'; Young Family Papers, PRONI D2930/9/15 and D2930/1/19/3.

[325] Young, *The Town Book of the Corporation of Belfast*.

[326] Young, *Ulster in '98, passim.*

[327] Ibid., pp. 14–17 (Magill), 1–13 and 60–5 (McSkimin), 18–60 (Classon Porter), 68–72 (anecdotes from Antrim), 73–84 (county Down incidents), 84–7 (Belfast under martial law), 89–91 (William Orr).

at the time). Mary Ann fostered the child and later sent her to boarding school at
Ballycraigy, outside Antrim town, but refrained from making her parentage known.
The girl's mother is believed to have been Mary Bodle, the daughter of David Bodle, a
poor labourer near Cave Hill, in whose house Henry Joy hid when he was on the run
after the Battle of Antrim. Mary Ann financed the family's emigration to America and
vaguely informed Madden that she had 'an opportunity of materially serving' the Bodle
family. When stories of 1798 appeared in print a century after the events, the desire to
bolster Henry Joy McCracken's heroic image demanded that his reputation should
remain without blemish. Inconvenient details, such as the fathering of a child out of
wedlock, were purposely left out of printed accounts. Even in this time of coming out,
not all secrets were to be revealed.[328]

Another antiquarian, Rev. William Sunderland Smith—the pastor of the old non-
subscribing Presbyterian congregation of Antrim town and for many years the clerk of
the Antrim Presbytery—was won over by Bigger's resuscitation of the *UJA*, which he
believed met a need for a magazine that 'would show what Ulster has been and what it
is at present'. Critical of Young's *Ulster in '98*, which he found lacking in its coverage of
local memory, Smith was persuaded by Bigger to contribute articles on the memory of
the rebellion.[329] Smith recalled that when he first arrived in Ulster in 1872, after
holding ministries in Scotland and England, he 'used to know several people who
remembered the "Turn-Out"' and regretted that many of them had since passed
away.[330] In *Historical Gleanings in Antrim and Neighbourhood*, published in 1888,
Smith had included historical traditions of the Battle of Antrim, most of which he had
collected from John Kilpatrick of Rathmore. Prior to his death at an advanced age in
1874, Kilpatrick 'used to relate several incidents connected with the battle, to the truth
of which he could bear personal testimony'.[331] Smith was persuaded by Bigger to return
to the study of the local history of 1798, and to try and collect additional oral accounts.
Although it seemed at first that he could not dig up material, Smith doggedly stuck to
the task, 'dedicating every possible moment', and soon became so '"possessed" with the
subject' that his family believed he was 'becoming Rebellion crazy'.[332] The fruits of his
persistence resulted in a series of essays on 'Memories of '98', which was published over
four issues in the *UJA* from January 1895 to January 1896.[333]

At a remove of two to three generations, Smith salvaged family stories that had not
been previously documented:

> Many of the events of a minor character, hitherto unrecorded, connected with the Insurrection
> of 1798, are fast becoming the merest traditions. Those who personally took part in them, or

---

[328] Madden, *The United Irishmen*, 2nd ser., vol. 2 (1843), pp. 483 and 497; McCleery, 'Life of
Mary Ann M'Cracken' (1896), pp. 175–97. See also McNeill, *Life and Times of Mary Ann McCracken*,
pp. 194–5.
[329] W. S. Smith to F. J. Bigger, 10 February and 28 March 1894; Bigger Papers, BCL SM8/2 and 5.
[330] W. S. Smith to F. J. Bigger, 8 February 1894; Bigger Papers, BCL SM8/1.
[331] Smith, *Historical Gleanings*, pp. 16–26.
[332] W. S. Smith to F. J. Bigger, February 1894 (not dated precisely); Bigger Papers, BCL SM8/3.
[333] W. S. Smith, 'Memories of '98', *UJA*, 2nd ser., 1, no. 2 (January 1895), pp. 133–42; vol. 1, no. 3
(April 1895), pp. 210–17; vol. 1, no. 4 (July 1896), pp. 284–9; vol. 2, no. 2 (January 1896), pp. 86–91.
As late as December 1895 Smith continued to receive accounts, though by then it was no longer possible
to include the information in the published collection; W. S. Smith to F. J. Bigger, 27 December 1895;
Bigger Papers, BCL SM8/33.

were in any way concerned with them and were well acquainted with their details, have all passed away. Only the children of such, or the grandchildren, or still more distant relatives, now survive to hand on, too often with strange indifference, the facts still remembered of what at first may have been incidents of much interest. It is with a view to the preservation of some of these, that at the expenditure of not a little time and patience, the following memories have been gleaned from very varied and widely scattered sources, but at the same time with no slight satisfaction that so interesting a record yet remained to be made.[334]

The text was immediately identified by the *Belfast News-Letter* as the journal's most interesting essay and Smith was commended for having 'taken immense pains to gather from the children and grandchildren of the men who took part in that affray' their accounts of 'incidents that have never before been recorded'.[335] Popular demand was evident when local newspapers reprinted sections from the articles. After they appeared, 'in a very little time not a copy was to be had' of the *Coleraine Chronicle* and the issue of the *Ballymoney Free Press* 'was soon snapped up'.[336] Even before serialization in the *UJA* had concluded, *Memories of '98* was issued as a book and it was expected that 'the volume will find a large number of readers.'[337]

Bigger's predilection for glorifying the United Irishmen was not shared by Smith, who, as 'a pronounced Liberal in politics but a staunch Unionist at heart', was less prone to idealize the memory of 1798.[338] The bulk of the traditions he collected came from the district of Antrim Town, with additional clusters relating to the areas of Ballymena and Ballymoney. Smith was well attuned to the inherent ambivalence with which the Turn-Out—a term that appears repeatedly in his collections—was remembered in these predominantly unionist constituencies. The accounts relate the experiences of both rebels and loyalists and feature descriptions of misdeeds committed on all sides. Numerous accounts recall the coercion of reluctant locals into the insurgent ranks. At the same time, it is acknowledged that the yeomanry also used 'great pressure' in their recruiting efforts. Stories tell of property wantonly destroyed by yeomen, terrified civilians feverishly hiding their valuables, and hapless bystanders shot at their own door by passing soldiers. The arbitrary hangings and brutal floggings of suspected rebels are counterbalanced by a tally of cold-blooded murders committed by rebels. In one instance, it is claimed that the insurgents in Glenarm intended to use female hostages as a human shield: 'they were to be placed in front of the attacking force, so that in case the Yeomen resisted they would have to shoot their own wives before they injured the United Irishmen'. The Turn-Out, although clearly a memorable event, is soberly shown to have been a far cry from a glorious struggle.[339]

The characteristic ambivalence of the narratives of the Turn-Out was also apparent in the hybrid identities of the storytellers, whom Smith interviewed. For example, one of Smith's principal informants was Mrs Eliza Graham Shannon née Vance of Antrim. Her father, Ezekiel Vance, a Methodist yeoman of Quaker background, had displayed bravery in the loyalist defence of Antrim town, after he witnessed the killing of Lord O'Neill by rebels. On the other side of her family, Mrs Shannon's maternal grandfather was Robert Lennon of Ballygowan, who had led a contingent of rebels from Ballynure and afterwards went into hiding to avoid capture. Moreover, one of the family traditions

[334] Smith, *Memories of '98*, pp. 7–8.   [335] *BNL*, 19 January 1895, p. 3.
[336] W. S. Smith to F. J. Bigger, 27 February 1896; Bigger Papers, BCL SM8/38.
[337] *BNL*, 13 February 1896, p. 7.   [338] *Ballymena Observer*, 17 May 1912, p. 3.
[339] Smith, *Memories of '98*, passim.

recounted how Ezekiel Vance, despite being a proven loyalist, was accused of 'being always on the side of the Insurgents', after he interceded with Lord Massereene to spare the lives of a group of twenty-two prisoners who had been wrongly identified as rebel sympathizers. This kind of nuanced complexity, in which families often had ancestors who fought on both sides of the rebellion and could recall experiences that did not necessarily comply with rigid political divides, exemplified the ambiguity of the memory of the Turn-Out, which eschewed simplistic narratives of virtuous rebels boldly taking a stand against villainous redcoats.[340]

Smith observed that the traditions he collected 'have not, it is believed, hitherto come under public notice by means of the printed page'.[341] Names of such local heroes as Ezekiel Vance were not widely known. Although Vance had subsequently lived an uneventful life, his daughter claimed that 'he enjoyed the confidence and esteem of his fellow-townsmen, and died greatly respected when eighty-two years of age'. The *Belfast News-Letter*, probably taking her testimony at face value, stated that 'the old people of Antrim to this day mention with pride the name of Ezekiel Vance, of whom their sires were never done sounding the praises for his valour.'[342] However, the only occasion in Vance's lifetime in which his name appeared in newspapers was when his land was put up on sale at the Encumbered Estates' Court, like those of many other small property owners who sank into irredeemable debt after the Great Famine.[343] By the end of the century, his grandchildren, four of whom had emigrated to New Zealand, were keen on Smith's work being published in order that their ancestor would receive public recognition.[344]

Caught up in the enthusiasm with which his work was received, Smith came to believe that that there was no longer any objection to bringing out the memory of 1798. This assumption proved to be mistaken. When Smith submitted to the *Christian Freeman* an article on the execution of Rev. James Porter, the editor, A. H. Biggs, became 'somewhat alarmed' and treated the submission 'as one would a live coal'. The reluctance of a respected Presbyterian journal to publish an article on this sensitive topic was an indication that the inhibitions of social forgetting had not been entirely overcome.[345]

Smith was not alone in his determination to bring the memory of the United Irishmen into mainstream northern Protestant unionist memory. Rev. William Thomas Latimer, the orthodox-evangelical Presbyterian minister of Eglish, county Tyrone (near Dungannon), was also inspired by the antiquarian rediscovery of 1798. Latimer, who was a member of the Royal Society of Antiquaries of Ireland (serving as its president from 1903 to 1906), gained a reputation as an historian with his *History of the Irish Presbyterians*, first published in 1893 and reissued in a revised and expanded edition in 1902. This widely praised work was used as a textbook for Presbyterian students of theology and its enthusiastic reception by Ulster-Scot communities in the United States earned for the author an honorary membership of the Scottish-Irish Society of America. In his history,

[340] For stories told by Mrs Shannon see Smith, *Memories of '98*, pp. 8–11, 19–22, 28–9, 33–4.
[341] Smith, *Memories of '98*, p. 8.
[342] Ibid., p. 11; *BNL*, 19 January 1895, p. 3.
[343] *London Evening Standard*, 21 January 1851, p. 3; *BNL*, 24 January 1851, p. 1.
[344] W. S. Smith to F. J. Bigger, 12 November 1894; Bigger Papers, BCL SM8/18. Four of Mrs Shannon's sons established families in New Zealand; see Marianne Davis, ed., *A Shannon Family: From Antrim, Ireland to New Zealand, by Family Members* (Feilding, N.Z.: The Shannon Family Reunion and Book Committee, 2000).
[345] W. S. Smith to F. J. Bigger, 5 March 1905, Bigger Papers, BCL SM 8/91.

Latimer incorporated traditions—labelled as 'valuable information regarding this period'—that he had received from the local historian Hugh McCall, who was in his late 80s at the time.[346] In 1897, Latimer compiled various articles on prominent northern United Irishmen, which he had previously published in the popular Presbyterian weekly the *Witness* and other Ulster newspapers. These early writings were 'revised, enlarged, and offered to the public in a more permanent form', as a volume titled *Ulster Biographies, Relating Chiefly to the Rebellion of 1798*. Latimer consulted 'R. M. Young's interesting volume on this rebellion' as well as other local sources and was complimented by Bigger in the *UJA* for having been 'able to add important facts not given by Dr. Madden'.[347]

Latimer could authoritatively affirm that 'in the districts of Antrim and Down that "turned out," in the year 1798, the great majority of the people were Presbyterians', but he misleadingly maintained that the radical ministers that supported the rebellion were all New Light unorthodox Presbyterians, endorsing an ingrained misconception that had been promulgated by Rev. Henry Cooke half a century earlier. Latimer found it 'absolutely necessary to deal with the misgovernment and persecution which drove so many of these loyal Presbyterians into rebellion', however, as a liberal unionist, he advocated that the political demands of the United Irishmen had since been addressed through 'measures of reform' and that therefore 'a strong argument may be drawn for maintaining the supremacy of the Imperial Parliament by which these grievances have been removed.'[348] In order to drive home this point, the biographies of the revolutionary United Irishmen were supplemented by a biography of the more recent agrarian reformer and liberal journalist James MacKnight, who had co-founded the Ulster Tenant Right Association in 1847 and was presented as '"The Grand Old Man of Ulster," whom Presbyterian farmers regarded as their leader and prophet.'[349]

Even though Latimer opposed republicanism, he cherished the memory of the northern United Irish leaders: Henry Joy McCracken 'freely gave his life in a vain effort to save his country from oppression, and if we as Unionists condemn the fatal mistake he made, we must respect his motives, admire his courage, and venerate his memory'; Henry Munro was 'one of the bravest spirits among the Northern rebels—a dauntless patriot, who did not fear to die for what he believed to be the good of his country' and, although 'rash and headstrong', he was 'popular with the people'; James Hope 'exhibited all the determination and uprightness of a true Presbyterian'. Latimer expressed regret for the fate of Rev. William Steel Dickson, who 'as a result of taking that political course which he honestly thought best for his creed and his country, he was cast out of society, forgotten by his friends, and treated with injustice by the leaders of the Church for which he had suffered'.[350] Owning up to this record of denial, Latimer's biographies attempted to make amends for previous neglect in Presbyterian historiography.

The nationalist press disagreed with Latimer 'in some of his prominent conclusions' but was nonetheless delighted by his sympathetic portrayal of the United Irishmen and

---

[346] Latimer, *A History of the Irish Presbyterians*, p. 396n. For the enthusiastic reception of the first edition, see the foreword to the second edition (p. iii). Biographical information on Latimer can be found in his obituaries in the liberal Presbyterian press, see *Northern Whig*, 21 July 1919, p. 7; *Witness*, 25 July 1919 (n.p.).

[347] *UJA*, 2nd ser., 3, no. 4 (1897): p. 279.

[348] Latimer, *Ulster Biographies*, 'To the Reader' [preface].   [349] Ibid., p. 106.

[350] Ibid., pp. 20 (McCracken), 34–5 (Munro), 60 (Hope), 92 (Dickson).

334 *Forgetful Remembrance*

considered his *Ulster Biographies* 'a valuable work of particular attractiveness to Ulster-men', which was 'sure to be widely read'.[351] Latimer's contributions to the *UJA* included additional articles on Presbyterian ministers who suffered in consequence of their involvement of the rebellion, a topic on which he claimed to be the leading author-ity.[352] By insisting that 'the Rev. James Porter was the only Presbyterian clergyman, and Mr. Archibald Warwick the only Licentiate who suffered the extreme penalty of the law in connection with the 1798 rebellion', Latimer picked a quarrel with Bigger, which was fought in the pages of the *Irish Book Lover* till Bigger conclusively proved that there was at least another executed clergyman—Robert Gowdie [appears also as Gowdy and Goudy], a probationer from Dunover, county Down, who was court martialled and executed in Newtownards.[353]

More generally, Latimer's historical approach was criticized by Bigger for its narrow denominational focus, to which Latimer truculently responded that 'the questions in debate concern not only the truth of certain statements, but how some of them ought to be used, and the inferences that might be drawn from others.'[354] Although Latimer has been characterized as 'the epitome of Presbyterian cantankerousness', his retort was to the point.[355] These seemingly personal controversies are indicative of conflicting ideological interpretations of the history of Ulster. Bigger supported the work of Young, Smith, Latimer, and others, yet his purpose in recovering the memory of 1798 was quite different from that of the liberal unionist antiquarians.

Bigger was hailed by an admirer as 'the enthusiastic Apostle of Ireland's Ancient Customs and Traditions, of her Language, Music, and Pastimes, and the earnest and successful Promoter of the development of her Industries'.[356] However, his antiquarian pursuits and the many enterprises of social improvement which he vigorously promoted were not motivated by the same civic unionism espoused by other prominent liberal Protestants. Aptly referred to by the Catholic historian Rev. O'Laverty as 'Everybody's Friend', Bigger's contacts crossed sectarian and political divides. In a thinly disguised fictional depiction, he was described by the writer John Randolph ('Shane') Leslie, as 'a Protestant with Franciscan leanings', who held the politics of a 'United Irishman', insofar as his 'chief solution for the Irish problem was to temper the dreary Orange drum with the Irish war-pipes'.[357] Indeed, Bigger's brand of congenial ecumenical politics and local patriotism signified a romantic, yet nonetheless, radical ideology.

[351] *Derry Journal*, 7 July 1897, p. 5; *SVV*, 2, no. 7 (5 July 1897), p. 121.
[352] *UJA*, 2nd ser., 13, no. 1 (1907): pp. 29–38 ('David Bailie Warden, Patriot 1798') and 17, nos. 1/4 (1911): pp. 95–6 ('The Rev. Dr. Wm. S. Dickson at Keady').
[353] *Irish Book Lover*, 3, no. 12 (1912): pp. 197–9; 4, no. 1 (1912): p. 17; 4, no. 3 (1912): pp. 53–4. The execution was still remembered locally in the early nineteenth century; *Irishman*, 12 October 1821, p. 2. For Gowdie's court martial record see Rebellion Papers, NAI 620/2/15/38; Bartlett, 'Repressing the Rebellion in County Down', pp. 193–4. For contemporary newspaper reports of his trial (27–9 June 1798) and execution (2 July 1798) see *BNL*, 26 June 1798, p. 2 and 3 July 1798, p. 3. He is mentioned in several contemporary reports: Hugh McComb to John Catherwood, 29–30 June 1798, Porter Family Papers, PRONI D3579/1; George Stephenson, Hillsborough, to Lord Down-shire, 4 July 1798, Downshire Papers, PRONI D607/F/299.
[354] *UJA*, 2nd ser., 8, no. 2 (1902): pp. 94–5.
[355] Holmes, 'Covenanter Politics', p. 365.
[356] J. K. Owen, *An Irish Chieftain of To-Day* (Belfast: s. n., c.1910), pp. 4 and 15.
[357] Shane Leslie, *Doomsland* (New York: Scribner's, 1924), p. 171; see also Shane Leslie, *The Film of Memory* (London: Michael Joseph Ltd, 1938), pp. 384–5.

Bigger was at the forefront of a northern cultural revival movement, which blended Ulster regionalism with advanced Irish nationalism. At Ardrigh, his Belfast residence on Antrim Road (located at the foot of Cave Hill and overlooking Belfast Lough), he hosted social gatherings of local *culturati*, which attracted visits of luminaries from further afield. These colourful soirées constituted a remarkable 'fireside school' (a rejoinder to W. B. Yeats's 'Celtic Twilight') at which Ireland's nationalist-minded intelligentsia mingled with the radical youth of the generation that would later participate in the Irish revolution.[358] Bigger infused the flourish of artistic and literary talent in fin-de-siècle Belfast with cultural revivalism and channelled this burst of creativity into the preparations for the centenary of the 1798 rebellion.[359]

With Bigger's support, a Henry Joy McCracken Literary Society was founded in Belfast on 9 February 1895. Within a year it had 140 members, who held bi-weekly meetings on alternate Sunday evenings to hear lectures, primarily on 1798. In spite of the difficulties of operating 'in the heart of Toryism', they perceived themselves as 'the pioneers, in the "Northern Athens," of this important branch of the work of the advanced national literary movement—the celebration of the anniversaries of the men who died for Ireland.' [360] By the end of its first year, the society 'could point back to the many successful anniversary commemorations held during the year'.[361] Most notably, on 7 June 1895, the members marked in Belfast the anniversary of the Battle of Antrim. The event opened with a lecture on Lord Edward Fitzgerald, the intended leader of the rebellion in Leinster, after which 'the rest of the evening was devoted to the celebration of the memory of the men of the North and their gallant stand at Antrim.' The proceedings also included 'a brief address to the women whose devotion and courage entitled them to rank among the patriots of that day', of which the main part was devoted to the memory of Mary Ann McCracken.[362]

In October 1895, the Henry Joy McCracken Literary Society launched its monthly journal, the *Northern Patriot*, which was initially sold for twopence. The cover displayed a romantic image of McCracken, decked in full uniform and sword in hand, standing beside a canon and surrounded by icons of Irish cultural nationalism—a round tower, a Celtic Cross, and a sunburst, all appearing on a shield propped up with two pikes and adorned with wreaths of shamrocks (Fig. 4.7b). The journal's motto 'How is Old Ireland? And how does she stand?' was taken from the popular 1798 song 'The Wearing of the Green', which was already well known in the first half of the nineteenth century and enjoyed a revival after a version appeared in Dion Boucicault's popular melodrama *Arrah-na-Pogue* (first performed in 1864). Ignoring the song's recent fame, it was described in the inaugural editorial as 'an old ballad, which was sung in the streets; nay, I should say, secretly, in the homes of Belfast nearly a

---

[358] See Richard Kirkland, *Cathal O'Byrne and the Northern Revival in Ireland, 1890–1960* (Liverpool: Liverpool University Press, 2006), pp. 87–122.

[359] See Eugene McNulty, 'The Place of Memory: Alice Milligan, Ardrigh, and the 1898 Centenary', *Irish University Review*, 38, no. 2 (2008): pp. 203–21. For personal recollections of the gatherings at Ardrigh see J. Anthony Gaughan, ed., *Memoirs of Senator Joseph Connolly (1885–1961): A Founder of Modern Ireland* (Blackrock, Co. Dublin: Irish Academic Press, 1996), pp. 76–7; MacCartan, 'Belfast', pp. 176–8. See also Campbell, *The Dissenting Voice*, pp. 342–3.

[360] *Northern Patriot*, 1, no. 5 (February 1896), pp. 75 and 78.

[361] *United Ireland*, 11 January 1896, p. 3.

[362] *United Ireland*, 15 June 1895, p. 2.

ANNA JOHNSTON.   ALICE MILLIGAN

Fig. 4.6. Alice Milligan and Ethna Carbery

Alice Milligan (1866–1953)—standing—and Ethna Carbery (Anna Johnston, 1866–1902), the tireless editors of the *Shan Van Vocht*, were central memory activists around the time of the '98 centenary.

From *Donahoe's Magazine*, vol. XXXVIII, no. 6 (Dec. 1897); reproduced from the original held by the Hesburgh Libraries of the University of Notre Dame.

hundred years ago'. In response to the perceived 'shame and sorrow and treachery' that 'within late years has fallen to Ireland's lot', the memory of 1798 was to be used as a resource for the regeneration of Irish nationalism.[363]

---

[363] *Northern Patriot*, 1, no. 1 (October 1895), pp. 1–2. For 'The Wearing of the Green' see *Citizen*, January 1841, pp. 64–6; Zimmermann, *Songs of Irish Rebellion*, pp. 167–70; Moylan, *Age of Revolution*, pp. 26–7.

The title poem 'The Northern Patriot', which appeared on the front page of the first issue, upheld McCracken as the foremost of 'Ireland's martyrs'. Another poem in the same issue identified remembrance of political martyrs as the magazine's key theme:

> Remember most of all the need,
> For hands to strike and hearts to bleed,
> And later martyrs to remember.[364]

Accordingly, the following issues of the *Northern Patriot* featured entries on 'this month's martyrs', starting with the Ulstermen William Orr, William [Archibald] Warwick and Thomas Russell.[365] Another primary purpose of the magazine was to provide historical information on the events of 1798 in Ulster. A series of articles on 'Irish Battlefields' written by John Clarke (under the pseudonym Ben More), the secretary of the Henry Joy McCracken Literary Society, described the engagements at Saintfield, Ballynahinch, and Antrim.[366]

The first three issues of the *Northern Patriot* were edited by two radical women, who were regular members of Bigger's Ardrigh coterie: Alice Leticia Milligan and Anna Isabel Johnston (Fig. 4.6). In January 1896, following a rift within the Henry Joy McCracken Literary Society, they left to establish a rival magazine, the *Shan Van Vocht*, which was also dedicated to the memory of the United Irishmen. Competition between the two publications resulted in the *Northern Patriot* reducing its price to just one penny, yet it could not match the superior literary quality of the new magazine and ceased publication in November 1897, ahead of the centenary year.

The title 'The Shan Van Vocht' is a transliteration of the Irish for 'The Old Poor Woman' [*an tSean-bhean bhocht*]—a reference that was deeply rooted in the cultural memory of Irish popular politics and reflected the fusion of antiquarianism and revivalism that the magazine promoted. The figure of a prophetic elderly woman harked back to the mythological *Cailleach Bhéarra* [Hag of Béarra], whose character appeared in medieval Gaelic texts and was preserved in Irish folklore. It also evoked the *aisling* (vision/dream) genre, prevalent in Irish Jacobite poetry, in which a *spéirbhean* [sky-woman], who could appear as a young beautiful maiden or as a wizened woman, personified Ireland.[367] Significantly, 'The Shan Van Vocht' was associated with the United Irishmen. It was the name of a well-known song that recalled, in its original version, expectations of military aid from revolutionary France ('The French are on the sea! says the Shan Van Vocht') and its provenance was attributed to the time of the failed French expedition to Bantry Bay under Lazare Hoche in December 1796, or possibly the French landing at Killala under Jean Joseph Amable Humbert in August 1798.[368] It had since been recycled and updated to address various national and local causes.

---

[364] *Northern Patriot*, 1, no. 1 (October 1895), pp. 1 and 9.   [365] Ibid., pp. 6–9.

[366] *Northern Patriot*, 1, no. 3 (December 1895), pp. 34–5 [Saintfield and Ballynahinch]; no. 8 (June 1896), pp. 114–15, and no. 9 (July 1896), p. 137 [Antrim].

[367] See Gearóid Ó Crualaoich, 'Continuity and Adaptation in Legends of Cailleach Bhéarra', *Béaloideas*, 56 (1988): pp. 153–78; Breandán Ó Buachalla, *Aisling Ghéar: Na Stíobhartaigh agus an tAos Léinn, 1603–1788* (Dublin: An Clóchomhar Tta, 1996).

[368] Thomas Crofton Croker, ed., *Popular Songs Illustrative of the French Invasions of Ireland*, Parts III–IV: *The Bantry Bay and Killala Invasions* (London: printed for the Percy Society by T. Richards, 1847), pp. 43–6.

The mid-nineteenth-century songwriter and author Samuel Lover noted that 'there are many versions of this song, which has always been a favourite with the people at all times of political excitement, either varied or rewritten, according to circumstances.' Newly written versions (in which the title was sometimes spelt 'Shan van Vough') began to appear in print from the 1820s. Verses were adapted to support the campaign for Catholic Emancipation and later on Daniel O'Connell stirred audiences at Repeal meetings by reciting verses which gained notoriety as seditious texts.[369] The Young Ireland poet Thomas Davis noted that 'the songs to this air are innumerable' and, after a printer in Drogheda was prosecuted in 1842 for printing and circulating the ballad, the *Nation* defiantly published what was believed to be the most authentic of the many available versions.[370]

Over the following decades, countless additional adaptations and variations appeared in newspapers, song books, and broadsides. The journalist and nationalist politician A. M. Sullivan observed that 'in every election the street ballad-singer is as important a power as the platform orator or the village band, and I never knew an Irish election poet that did not invoke the "Shan Van Vocht."'[371] The general public was reminded of the song's original association with the United Irishmen in 1885, when the *Weekly News* serialized James Murphy's novel *The Shan Van Vocht: A Story of the United Irishmen*, which was set on the background of the French expedition to Lough Swilly, county Donegal, in October 1798, and related the circumstances that led to the death of Wolfe Tone. The historical novel was subsequently re-issued as a popular book, which went through several editions.[372] With such a long record of adaptations, this was clearly an apt choice of title for a revivalist journal.

The cover page of the January 1896 inaugural issue of the *Shan Van Vocht* magazine featured a version of the song which clarified, for the benefit of modern readers, that the title alluded to a female personification of the nation: 'For old Ireland is the name of the Shan Van Vocht.' More traditional verses, which expressed the aspirations of republican separatism, were adopted as the paper's motto: 'Yes Ireland shall be free, from the centre to the sea, and hurrah for liberty, says the Shan Van Vocht.' Like the cover art of the *Northern Patriot*, the crest on the original issues of the *Shan Van Vocht* featured an assemblage of nationalist iconography, including a sunburst, a round tower, and shamrocks (Fig. 4.7c).[373] Even though the magazine published articles on a range of subjects, commemoration of the United Irishmen was its *raison d'être*. The intensive

[369] Lover, *The Lyrics of Ireland*, pp. 276–80. For an example of an early adaptation of the ballad to contemporary political concerns see *Captain Rock; or, the Chieftain's Gazette, for the Year 1825*, p. 152. For versions of the ballad used by O'Connell and his supporters, see *Freeman's Journal*, 3 April 1839 and 9 January 1841, p. 3; *Nation*, 27 May 1843, p. 520 and 3 June 1843, p. 15; *BNL*, 19 March 1844, p. 2.

[370] *Freeman's Journal*, 8 July 1842, p. 2; *Nation*, 29 October 1842, p. 40; see also *Thomas Davis: The Memoirs of an Irish Patriot, 1840–1846*, edited by Charles Gavan Duffy (London: K. Paul, Trench, Trübner & Co., 1890), p. 81. Davis composed a new version of the song, which remained unpublished in his lifetime; *Nation*, 22 September 1855, p. 57.

[371] A. M. Sullivan, *New Ireland: Political Sketches and Personal Reminiscences of Thirty Years of Irish Public Life*, 7th edn (Glasgow and London: Cameron & Ferguson, 1882; orig. edn 1877), p. 335; see also Zimmerman, *Songs of Irish Rebellion*, pp. 133–7.

[372] James Murphy, *The Shan Van Vocht: A Story of the United Irishmen*, 2nd edn (Dublin: M. H. Gill & Son, 1889).

[373] *SVV*, 1, n. 1 (January 1896), p. 1. The crest, alongside the motto, appeared in the first two issues and was then replaced, but the original motto was brought back for the centenary.

(a)

Vol. XV. Parts 2 & 3. PUBLISHED QUARTERLY. May, August, 1909.

Yearly Subscription, 5/-; Post Free, 1/- extra. American Subscribers, 1½ Dollars.

CONTENTS.

	Page		Page
The Franciscan Friary at Carrickfergus. Francis Joseph Bigger	49	Memorials of the Patriot Dead. Francis Joseph Bigger	93
The Ulster Civil War, 1641. Thomas Fitzpatrick, LL.D.	61	Ulster Bibliography. John S. Crone	95
The Church of Cool or Carinmony. Francis Joseph Bigger	65	The National Volunteers of Ireland. Francis Joseph Bigger	104
Richard Montgomery	70	Songs on the French Revolution. John S. Crone	119
The Vestry Books of the Parish of Down. Edward Parkinson	78	The Rev. Samuel Barber, A.M., and the Rathfriland Volunteers. A. Morrow, J.P.	125
The MacSuibhne of Banagh and Fanad. Francis Joseph Bigger	85	Rev. Arthur M'Mahon. Rev. David Stewart, B.A.	134

DAVIDSON & M'CORMACK,
The North Gate Printing Works,
Belfast.

Fig. 4.7. Fin-de-siècle revivalist journals

Covers of the *Ulster Journal of Archaeology*, second series (a), the *Northern Patriot* (b), and the *Shan Van Vocht* (c). The journals, which were edited by enthusiastic national revivalists, were key organs for revitalizing remembrance around the time of the '98 centenary.

Source: Internet Archive (*UJA*); British Library (*Northern Patriot*); Joseph McGarrity Collection, Digital Library@Villanova University (*SVV*).

(b)

Fig. 4.7. Continued

(c)

VOL. I.—No. 1.   BELFAST, 15TH JANUARY, 1896.   PRICE TWOPENCE.

The Shan Van Vocht.

THERE is news from o'er the sea,
    Says the Shan Van Vocht;
There is news from o'er the sea,
    Says the Shan Van Vocht;
And this message o'er the sea,
From the land of liberty,
Brings the best of news for me,
    Says the Shan Van Vocht.

Ere the dying of the year,
    Says the Shan Van Vocht;
From a land that's far but dear
    To the Shan Van Vocht;
In a voice that laughed at fear,
There rang forth defiance clear,
Let us send an answering cheer,
    Says the Shan Van Vocht.

And a cloud is glooming now,
    Says the Shan Van Vocht,
O'er our haughty tyrant's brow,
    Says the Shan Van Vocht;
Whilst like thunder bursts afar,
Where her sons and daughters are,
The din of dreadful war,
    Says the Shan Van Vocht.

But there's light behind that cloud
    For the Shan Van Vocht;
And that thunder roaring loud,
    Says the Shan Van Vocht;
Though it strikes the weakling dumb,
Shouts in tones of joy to some
That the dawn of Freedom's come
    To the Shan Van Vocht.

But tell me who is she
    Called the Shan Van Vocht;
And if other name there be
    For the Shan Van Vocht;
Yes! immortal is her fame,
She's the queen no foe could tame,
For old Ireland is the name
    Of the Shan Van Vocht.

The Boy From Barnesmore.

(A STORY OF '67). BY IRIS OLKYRN.

THE train had stopped an unusually long time at Strabane Station. Trains in Ireland are rarely in a hurry; indeed, when you come to think of it why should they be, as some wit remarked "there is more time to spare than there is of anything else in this distressful country." And to-day there was every excuse for delay, and plenty to divert my attention whilst we waited, for that day had been the great spring hiring market in Strabane, and the crowd upon the platform was an interesting and picturesque one.

Here were the wives of strong farmers in all the flaunting bravery of their new spring bonnets, gorgeous in scarlet and purple, and emerald green ribbons with wondrous flowers, fresh from the milliners' hands; whilst in paper bags they carried the head-dresses in which they had come to town that morning. Their crinoline distended skirts, their gay fringed shawls, their loudly creaking boots, were objects of wonder and envy to the simply dressed country girls of Donegal, who had entered into six months service with them that day, and who had left homes among the mountain glens up by Stranorlar and Glenties, and far away in Gweedore, to do housework and field work on farms in Tyrone. I could not help admiring the picturesque simplicity of their plain kilted skirts of grey or dark blue homespun; the bright kerchiefs knotted simply over their neatly braided locks as compared with the tawdry grandeur of their newly found mistresses. The men were shouting and talking excitedly, running this way and that, and calling to their women folk to follow to the seats they had secured in the carriages. Through the swaying, surging crowd, with quiet sauntering step passed two or three straight military looking men, easily recognised as members of the police force in plain clothes. I thought nothing of their passing up and down and

Fig. 4.7. Continued

preoccupation with this theme signified a deliberate co-optation of the memory of 1798 in Ulster for an advanced nationalist agenda.

Decades later, Alice Milligan, a Methodist, who was raised in a liberal unionist household, put forward the claim that her great-grandfather and his five sons had been among the insurgents at the Battle of Antrim, but this apocryphal patriotic genealogy was not mentioned in the late nineteenth century.[374] In 1888 she had co-written with her father, Seaton Forrest Milligan, a successful businessmen and respected antiquarian, *Glimpses of Ireland*, an 'account of the ancient civilization, manners, customs, and antiquities of Ireland', which was soon re-issued in a revised and enlarged edition of ten thousand copies. In this book, the authors opted 'to abstain from talking politics'. 1798 was only touched upon briefly and discussion of its repercussions was deliberately avoided. Milligan's early understanding of the rebellion was influenced by the dominant loyalist interpretation, which distinguished between the idealist pluralism of the United Irishmen in the North and the 'menacing outbreak' in the South, where 'the religious question alone incited the people'. Yet, already at this early stage of her intellectual formation, her attitude to the rebellion was ambivalent and even mildly sympathetic, as evident in two poems that she composed for the volume. In 'Mary Bannan: A Night Scene in '98', a woman by the river Shannon, in the West of Ireland, is enthralled by an encounter with a band of insurgents. 'Mary Bannan' was later adapted into a song by the poet's sister, the ethnomusicologist Charlotte Olivia Fox née Milligan, so that it could be performed in 1898 by the Irish contralto Lucie Johnstone. In another poem, 'Wexford Bridge: A Story of '98', Milligan described one of the notorious sectarian atrocities which were considered cornerstones of Protestant loyalist memory. Contrary to the standard hostile narrative, which depicted the rebellion as an outburst of violence driven by papist religious fanaticism, in Milligan's rendition the involvement of a Catholic priest has a calming presence, so that, after his blessing is given, 'no more blood was shed that night on the bridge.'[375]

Following a conversion to Parnellism in 1891, Milligan made up for the absence of Irish history and culture in the unionist schooling she had received in county Tyrone by taking Irish language lessons at the Royal Irish Academy in Dublin and through avid reading of nationalist newspapers and books.[376] She soon became a spokesperson for radical northern nationalism. Milligan gave her maiden public lecture in February 1893, addressing the Belfast Natural History and Philosophical Society on the topic of 'Historic Ulster'. At first, it seemed that the audience was unresponsive, up until she came to discuss Belfast in 1798. Her argument that 'Henry Joy McCracken and his colleagues might be honoured in their native town even by those who were most opposed to revolutionary methods' was met with applause.[377] Spurred on by this encouraging reaction, she polished her lectures on the northern rebellion and in 1897 delivered a well-received talk to the Celtic Literary Society in Dublin on

---

[374] *Derry Journal*, 25 July 1941, p. 4; see also Catherine Morris, 'Becoming Irish? Alice Milligan and the Revival', *Irish University Review*, 33, no. 1 (2003), p. 98n59.

[375] Seaton F. Milligan and Alice Milligan, *Glimpses of Erin: Containing an Account of the Ancient Civilisation, Manners, Customs, and Antiquities of Ireland* (London: Marcus Ward, 1888), pp. 176–82. For the song adaptation of 'Mary Bannan' see *SVV*, 3, no. 3 (March 1898), p. 56.

[376] Catherine Morris, *Alice Milligan and the Irish Cultural Revival* (Dublin: Four Courts Press, 2012), pp. 24–32 and 124–38.

[377] *BNL*, 18 February 1893, p. 3. Milligan's diary entry is quoted in Morris, *Alice Milligan*, p. 188.

'Ninety-Eight and After', which focused on Ulster.[378] While improving her rhetorical skills, Milligan also honed her writing, often using the pseudonym Iris Olkyrn. In 1895, she began to write a regular column on 'Notes from the North' for the nationalist *Irish Weekly Independent*, setting the tone in a long article on 1798, which appeared as a featured special in the Christmas issue under the title 'The North Is Up!' (after a poem by the northern Young Ireland poet Francis Davis).[379] The United Irishmen became the main theme in her writings during the years leading up to the centenary of the rebellion. These included short stories, plays and poetical compositions, as well as a biography of Theobald Wolfe Tone, which was praised by the *UJA*, for its 'bright and taking manner, well adapted to the multitude'.[380]

Milligan has been faulted for the 'derivative and banal nature of her writing, and a congenial weakness for bathos'.[381] Nonetheless, her poetry was received with acclaim within the nationalist literary circles of her day. George William Russell (Æ) maintained that she had 'indeed written memorable verses, I think the best patriotic poetry written in Ireland in my time' and Thomas MacDonagh praised her as 'the best living Irish poet'.[382] Milligan's poems on 1798 were not considered her finest specimens and none of them were selected for the early anthologies that showcased her poetry. 'The Preaching', subtitled 'A Story of the North in '98', recalled one of the many escapes of the United Irishman William Putnam McCabe, who 'was famous for his skill in assuming various disguises and baffling the vigilance of the authorities'. It appeared in the *Shan Van Vocht* as part of a series of purposely written ''98 ballads', designed to be 'suitable for recitation' at commemorative meetings. Contrary to the author's expectations, the poem did not become a popular recitation.[383]

Milligan's efforts to commemorate the United Irishmen through drama also met with limited success. In a conversation with W. B. Yeats in 1893, she announced her intention of writing a stirring 'bloodthirsty melodrama of the '98 period'. She ended up writing three plays set on the background of the rebellion, of which only one—*The Harp that Once* (set in the West of Ireland)—was actually staged, albeit for just three performances in Dublin. There is no record of her melodrama *The French Are on the Sea*, or of her 'short play for three persons' *The Green Upon My Cape* (about a meeting in Paris between Wolfe Tone and the Belfast United Irishman John Tenant), having been performed. Moreover, Milligan's submission to a competition on '98 plays, advertised by the dramatist J. W. Whitbread in 1902, was unsuccessful and failed to attract attention.[384]

---

[378] *Freeman's Journal*, 30 March 1897, p. 7; *SVV*, 2, no. 4 (April 1897), p. 76.

[379] *Irish Weekly Independent*, 21 December 1895. The death of Francis Davis—'the Belfast Man'—in 1886 was commemorated the following year by the Belfast Young Ireland Society with an erection of a monument; Davis, *Earlier and Later Leaves*, pp. 162–3; *BNL*, 28 October 1886, p. 3.

[380] Alice Milligan, *Life of Theobald Wolfe Tone* (Belfast: J. W. Boyd, 1898); *UJA*, 2nd ser., 4 (1898), p. 263.

[381] R. F. Foster, *Vivid Faces: The Revolutionary Generation in Ireland, 1890–1923* (London: Allen Lane, 2014), pp. 152–3.

[382] AE, ed., *New Songs: A Lyric Selection*, 3rd edn (Dublin and London: O'Donoghue & Co. and A. H. Bullen, 1904), p. 5; Thomas MacDonagh, 'The Best Living Irish Poet', *Irish Review*, 4, no. 42 (September-November 1914): pp. 287–93.

[383] *SVV*, 2, no. 3 (12 March 1897), p. 43.

[384] Morris, *Alice Milligan*, pp. 218–20, 230–1, and 306n10. Staged by Frank and William Fay, *The Harp that Once* was performed by Inghinidhe na hEireann at the Antient Concert Rooms in Dublin on

The romantic fiction on the rebellion that Milligan published in the *Shan Van Vocht* included two stories set in Ulster that followed a formula of romance across the religious divide, which inevitably leads to emigration. The hero of 'A Rebel's Wooing' is Randal McAllister, a United Irishman from Cushendall, in the Glens of Antrim. After the insurgent attack on Ballymena, when 'there were thousands of good men and true fleeing for life and liberty over the hills of Antrim and through the glens', McAllister is pursued by 'blood-thirsty yeos and fierce English soldiers who, day and night followed on his track'. He takes refuge in county Derry, 'hoping to be able to help in a rally there; but nowhere was there a word of cheer, only the track of the destroyer made plain by gibbeted corpses, burning homes, and mangled bodies of the slain.' John Macauley, a Catholic loyalist, had previously forbidden McAllister from courting his daughter, Rosie, but, after the Macauley household is burned in an indiscriminate attack of yeomen, the couple marry and flee the country together. Milligan anchored the story in vernacular history by noting that the fictional McAllister was a cousin of the local rebel hero Roger (Roddy) McCorley and by slipping in references to the execution of William Orr, as well as to the gathering of fugitive rebels under Henry Joy McCracken and James Hope at Slemish.[385]

'The Little Green Slippers', described as 'A Belfast Story of Christmas 1798', was inspired by an actual relic from the time of rebellion—'a dainty pair of emerald green slippers or half boots', which had purportedly been worn by a female sympathizer of the United Irishmen, as a gesture of participation in the mourning over the execution of Henry Joy McCracken. The slippers, as noted by Bigger, had belonged to a Miss Spencer, 'an old lady of Belfast', and had been given to Milligan's brother-in-law, Dr Wheeler, who passed them on to the antiquarian Robert Young. Milligan recreated the story of the wearing of the slippers in a Cinderella-like tale in which Jessica Houston, the orphaned daughter of an associate of the United Irish leaders, thwarts her loyalist stepfather's scheme to marry her off to an army officer and ends up marrying her outlawed lover, Bernard Magennis, a fugitive rebel (presumably a Catholic), with whom she flees the country.[386] These stories, which held up the example of 1798 as a time when radical Protestants—like Milligan—partnered with Catholics to commemorate the rebellion, served a didactic purpose. Remembrance of the United Irishmen was presented as a shared memory, which could bridge sectarian divides and unite the people of Ulster in a common identity.

Fittingly, Milligan's partner in editing the radical magazines associated with the memory of 1798 was a northern Catholic nationalist. Anna Johnston, commonly known by her pseudonym Ethna Carbery, was born in Ballymena and lived most of her life in Belfast. Like Milligan, she was an ardent Parnellite with strong republican sympathies. A local tradition in Donegal claimed that her pen-name was a tribute to a woman who in 1798 had sheltered one of her rebel ancestors, probably on the side of her mother, Margery née Magee, whose father came from Petigo in county Donegal.

26, 28, and 30 August 1901; see Nelson O'Ceallaigh Ritschel, *Productions of the Irish Theatre Movement, 1899–1916: A Checklist* (Westport, Conn.: Greenwood Press, 2001), p. 9. It was based on a short story that had appeared in *SVV*, vol. 3, no. 4 (4 April 1898), pp. 57–9.

[385] *SVV*, 1, no. 8 (7 August 1896), pp. 141–5.

[386] Alice Milligan, 'The Little Green Slippers: A Belfast Story of Christmas, 1798', *SVV*, 2, no. 12 (6 December 1897): pp. 213–18; see also Morris, 'Becoming Irish', p. 98n58.

Even if this claim was apocryphal, Carbery could boast bona fide republican credentials through her father, Robert Johnston, who represented Ulster on the Supreme Council of the Irish Republican Brotherhood and was president of the Belfast Amnesty Association, which campaigned for the release of republican political prisoners. Both his father and grandfather had participated in previous rebellions and by 1937, at the time of his death at the age of 97, 'Johnston of the North' would be revered as the 'last of the Fenian leaders'.[387] Johnston, who was a prosperous timber merchant, contributed financially to his daughter's journalistic enterprise and allocated offices for the *Shan Van Vocht* in his Belfast timber yard.[388]

As Robert Johnston was away in the America when the *Shan Van Vocht* was launched, the funding for the first issue was provided from subscriptions collected in county Down by the Presbyterian minister Rev. Richard Lyttle of Moneyrea. Milligan later recalled that descendants of Presbyterian United Irishmen were prominent amongst the supporters.[389] In dividing responsibilities, Milligan was designated the editor, responsible for literary content, and Carbery was the secretary, in charge of business management. In practice, the production of the magazine was a joint collaboration at all levels. Carbery's future husband, Seumas MacManus, who considered himself the 'most constant contributor' in the years leading up to 1898, described the extent of their personal commitment:

> For three and a half years these two girls edited the magazine, and managed it. They themselves wrote almost all of the magazine . . . they compiled the subscription list. They read the proofs. They kept the books. They sent the bills. They wrote the letters. With their own hands they folded and addressed every copy that was to go out, and licked every stamp that was to carry it on its journey.[390]

Their tenacious dedication bore fruit and the *Shan Van Vocht* became a leading journalist platform for advanced Irish nationalism.

Already at a young age, Carbery had acquired a reputation as a popular poet of patriotic verse. She wrote for the *Shan Van Vocht* both poetry and prose, much of which was inspired by folk traditions that she had heard in her youth. A collection of stories titled 'In the North Countrie', which appeared in the magazine as a series in 1896, included an episode in which old Jack Black, 'who had been through the battle of Antrim, and had wielded his pike with the best of them', regaled a Hallow-Eve gathering with his recollections of the rebellion.[391] The stories that the fictional storyteller told about the United Irish captain Jack Fullerton of McTrusterystown and the informer Andrew [also known as Jack] Swan, who was lynched by his neighbours for giving information on Fullerton to the military authorities, had previously appeared in W. S. Smith's *Memories of '98*. Smith received the information from

---

[387] *Irish Press*, 2 January 1953, p. 4 (recollections of the painter Padraig H. Marrinan, who sketched Robert Johnston's portrait shortly before his death). For Johnston's position in the republican organization see T. W. Moody and Leon Ó Broin, 'The I.R.B. Supreme Council, 1868–78', *Irish Historical Studies*, 19, no. 75 (1975), p. 292.

[388] Sheila Turner Johnston, *Alice: A Life of Alice Milligan* (Omagh: Colourpoint Press, 1994), p. 345.

[389] *Irish Press*, 23 November 1938, p. 10.

[390] Seumas MacManus, 'Memoir', in *The Four Winds of Eirinn: Poems by Anna MacManus (Ethna Carbery)*, new edn (Dublin: M. H. Gill, 1918), pp. 149–50, see also pp. 154–7.

[391] *SVV*, 1, no. 11 (November 1896), pp. 203–4.

Bigger, who, in turn, had collected the traditions from Robert Johnston, Carbery's father. The original source appears to have been Hugh Dempsey of Liminary (4 km south-west of Ballymena), who was related to Johnston's mother, Peg née Dempsey. Dempsey's grandfather, Jack Taylor, had been recruited into the United Irishmen by Fullerton and on his property the informer Swan had been whipped to death and hung on a tree by sympathizers of the United Irishmen.[392] Recollections of these events subsequently reappeared in the *Shan Van Vocht* in colourful literary accounts, which drew upon Smith's work and Carbery's tale in order to retell, in an even more romanticized style, the daring adventures of Captain Jack Fullerton and the gruesome fate of Andy Swan.[393] This chain of transmission and re-adaptation reveals how, a century after the rebellion, social memory recalled in family traditions was collected by antiquarians and re-used by writers as source material for cultural memory.

Several months after the launch of the *Shan Van Vocht*, Carbery informed a meeting of the magazine's supporters in Belfast that she had acquired the manuscript of Madden's memoir of Henry Joy McCracken.[394] Madden's work as a historian of the United Irishmen and early collector of recollections was held in high regard by nationalists and this original version of his published work was serialized in the paper from June 1896 to August 1897.[395] Towards the conclusion of its publication, the editors announced their intention of publishing a 'series of '98 traditions, which we would ask our friends throughout the country to lose no time in collecting', specifying that they were 'especially anxious to publish such stories as are not to be found in the works of Madden or other writers dealing with the period, but which live still upon the lips of the people'.[396] After Madden's memoir had been fully published, a second appeal was issued to 'our friends throughout the country who are acquainted with unpublished traditions of the times, to communicate them to us', asserting that 'it is the sacred duty of all who are in sympathy with the cause of freedom to revive the memory of the humbler and almost forgotten heroes of the strife.'[397] The editors were intent in salvaging undocumented social memory that had been preserved in private circumstances.

The initiative to collect folk memories of 1798 was launched with 'a series of anecdotes', which appeared in three instalments under the heading 'Some Men and Episodes of '98'.[398] These essays were authored by the popular Catholic nationalist writer Margaret Teresa Pender and were based on a lecture that she had given on 6 June 1895, at an event to mark the anniversary of the Battle of Antrim organized by the Irish Women's Association (co-founded by Milligan in 1894). Pender, like Carbery, had first

---

[392] Smith, *Memories of '98*, pp. 54–6.

[393] *SVV*, 2, no. 10 (October 1897), pp. 183–4 (written by M. T. Pender) and 3, no. 5 (May 1898), pp. 90–4 (written by J. P. Dunlevy).

[394] *SVV*, 1, no. 4 (April 1896), p. 76.

[395] *SVV*, 1, no. 6 (June 1896), pp. 108–9, no. 7 (July 1896), pp. 136–7, no. 8 (August 1896), p. 156, no. 9 (September 1896), pp. 173–5, no. 10 (October 1896), pp. 188–9, no. 11 (November 1896), pp. 214–16, no. 12 (December 1896), pp. 232–3; vol. 2, no. 13 [1] (January 1897), pp. 15–16, no. 14 [2] (February 1897), pp. 32–3, no. 3 (March 1897), pp. 44–5, no. 4 (April 1897), pp. 71–3, no. 5 (May 1897), pp. 86–8, no. 6 (June 1897), p. 103, no. 7 (July 1897), pp. 118–20, no. 8 (August 1897), pp. 137–8.

[396] *SVV*, 2, no. 7 (July 1897), p. 123.   [397] *SVV*, 2, no. 9 (September 1897), p. 153.

[398] *SVV*, 2, no. 7 (July 1897), pp. 123–6; no. 9 (September 1897), p. 153; no. 10 (October 1897), pp. 183–4.

acquired a literary reputation writing poetry for nationalist newspapers under pseud-onyms, though she would find even greater success as a writer of prose.[399]

A decade earlier, Pender had written *The Green Cockade: A Tale of Ulster in 'Ninety-Eight*, which was serialized from October 1886 to May 1887 in the *Shamrock* ('A National Weekly Journal of Irish History, Literature, Science, and Arts') and its first episodes were illustrated by John D. Reigh, one of several caricaturists who specialized in drawing iconic images of 1798.[400] The novel was extolled by the magazine's predomin-antly southern-nationalist readership. A reader from Cork believed that 'it has only one equal—Scott's *Ivanhoe*' and a correspondent from Kilkenny claimed that, in the fifteen years in which he had been reading the *Shamrock*, he 'cannot remember ever having been so deeply impressed with any other tale'.[401] Although the enthusiastic responses strongly encouraged the re-issue of the novel in book form, Pender was aware of the sensitivity of writing about Ninety-Eight in Ulster and did not opt for immediate re-publication. When a book edition finally appeared in 1898, it was issued by a Dublin, rather than a Belfast, publisher and was not specifically intended for a northern readership.[402]

The central character in *The Green Cockade* is the United Irishman William Putnam McCabe, who was renowned for his resourcefulness in escaping capture under various disguises. Although McCabe was arrested in Dublin in May 1798 and only managed to escape confinement after the insurrection in Ulster was over, in the novel he partici-pates in the Battle of Antrim. Apart from the historical figures of Lord Edward Fitzgerald, Henry Joy McCracken, Jemmy Hope, and the informer Ned (Edward) Newell, most of the characters in the romantic drama are fictional. Pender, in accordance with her own background, stressed Catholic involvement in the northern insurrection. The liberal Catholic priest Father Hugh O'Donnell, who in reality did not participate in the rebellion, is presented as being involved in the United Irishmen and McCabe's love interest is a Catholic. In contrast, it has been noted that 'Presbyterian aspects are rather underplayed.'[403]

The *Irish Monthly Magazine* pointed out that the story of *The Green Cockade* is 'almost wholly fictitious' and that the author made 'no attempt at impartiality'.[404] A nationalist reviewer in the *Derry Journal* believed that 'it will surely find a hearty welcome from the descendants of the men who took to the field in '98.'[405] As could be expected, the enthusiasm of Catholic nationalists was unbridled. A pupil at a Christian Brothers school later recalled how 'we devoured the books of Mrs Pender' and listed *The Green Cockade* among his favourites.[406] The response of unionists, however, was more circumspect. The *Belfast News-Letter* acknowledged that 'it is a very interesting

---

[399] O'Donoghue, *The Poets of Ireland*, p. 380.

[400] *Shamrock*, 24, no. 1042 (2 October 1886) to no. 1073 (7 May 1887). For Reigh's depictions of 1798 see Lawrence McBride, 'Nationalist Constructions of the 1798 Rebellion: The Political Illus-trations of J. D. Reigh', *Éire-Ireland*, 34, no. 2 (1999): pp. 117–34.

[401] *Shamrock*, 24, no. 1073 (7 May 1887), p. 517 and no. 1076 (28 May 1887), p. 576.

[402] See Chapter 5 below, p. 367.

[403] Walker, 'A Bibliography of Presbyterianism', pp. 187–8.

[404] *Irish Monthly*, 26 (November 1898): p. 622. This assessment was re-affirmed by scholarly critics; see Stephen J. M. Brown, *A Readers' Guide to Irish Fiction* (London: Longmans Green and Co., 1910), p. 28.

[405] *Derry Journal*, 28 October 1898, p. 5.

[406] J. P. Ryan, 'Reminiscences of a Distinguished Past Pupil', in *Centenary Record, 1847–1947* (Portlaoise: St Mary's Christian Brothers, 1947), p. 92; cited in Barry M. Coldrey, *Faith and*

story' and that 'many incidents in the Irish rebellion are eloquently described', but complained about the one-sided 'nationalist point of view'. The reviewer was concerned that 'the story will doubtless have a large circulation in Ireland, but it will not aid in a right understanding of the events of '98.'[407] Protestant unionist readers were uncomfortable with Pender's blatant partisan style.

In writing 'thrilling narratives' of Antrim in 1798 for the *Shan Van Vocht*, Pender drew upon folklore that had been previously collected and published by antiquarians, having realized that this was rich material for historical fiction:

> But over the page of its history, all stained with blood and blackened with crime as it is—crime that, for the most part, did not rest with the people—there are other tales of deeds of almost inconceivable daring, high deeds of patriot love, of splendid chivalry, of sublime sacrifice, of heroic valour, of truth and faith and unshaken constancy, amid a dark gehenna of torture, terror, betrayal, and death, and of glorious strife in freedom's cause—over the chequered page of its history such deeds lie thick as dewdrops in the fields at dawn.[408]

While consulting W. S. Smith's *Memories of '98*, she took exception with the sympathy that many of the narratives showed for the 'loyal and prudent persons' that had abstained from participating in the rebellion. In Pender's retelling of such a story, two Presbyterian brothers, Laird and Hugh Campbell, get their comeuppance for staying at home and rejoicing in the ill-fate of their rebel neighbours when their homestead is inexplicably burned by soldiers.[409]

Having been raised in the townland of Ballytweedy, Killead (6 km south of Antrim town), by a Catholic father (Daniel Doherty) and a Presbyterian mother (Margaret née White), Pender was knowledgeable of traditions of the Turn-Out. She recalled that as a child she would dread passing on her way to school through the fields of a shunned family, whose yeoman ancestor had killed a relative on his return from the rebellion and inherited his property. Pender was aware that the parish of Killead had 'furnished a large contingent to the fighting force that marched to Antrim under Henry Joy McCracken' and she graphically described the destruction wrecked by the government troops in suppressing the rebellion:

> There was death everywhere, everywhere horrors too awful to contemplate—men hung up head downward, in ropes full of twist, while the soldiers flogged them with their belts; bushes by the wayside and in front of the blazing cottages, on which were spread the entrails of human beings who were still alive!

She noted that there were instances of help across the political divide and told the story of how Arthur Beattie, a rebel returning from the battle, was saved by 'a friendly Orangeman'.[410] Although Pender's writing typically sketched cardboard depictions of valiant rebels and villainous loyalists, she could not entirely avoid the inherent ambiguity of social memory, even if she selected and embroidered the narratives to suit nationalist purposes.

Fatherland: The Christian Brothers and the Development of Irish Nationalism 1838–1921 (Dublin: Gill and Macmillan, 1988), p. 138.

[407] *BNL*, 13 October 1898, p. 3.   [408] *SVV*, 2, no. 10 (October 1897), p. 184.
[409] *SVV*, 2, no. 9 (September 1897), pp. 153–5.
[410] Ibid.

The *Shan Van Vocht* joined other nationalist newspapers in facilitating the publication of new poetry on 1798, which vented a popular desire to commemorate the United Irishmen. Many of the compositions were the works of amateur poets, such 'A Dangan Boy'—the pseudonym of Thomas Ryan of Tipperary, a regular contributor of patriotic poetry, whose verses were typical:

> 'Then here is to their memory,' and let us celebrate
> Their holocaust for Ireland, in glorious Ninety-Eight.[411]

Some contributions were from more established poets, such as Lionel Pigot Johnson, a recent convert to Catholicism residing in London and a close associate of W. B. Yeats. In 1894, Johnson delivered a lecture to the Irish Literary Society on 'Poetry and Patriotism', which called upon writers to go beyond the romantic nationalist tradition of Young Ireland and the *Nation*. Yet his poem 'To the Dead' did not stray far from that same hagiographical literary genre:

> God rest you, rest you, rest you, Ireland's dead!
> Peace be upon you shed,
> Peace from the Mercy of the Crucified,
> You, who for Ireland died![412]

Douglas Hyde, the founder of the Gaelic League, contributed a poem in Irish, 'An Sean-Chroppi agus é tinn', which described a poorly veteran of the rebellion lamenting the broken state of his country. Two decades earlier, Hyde had become fascinated with the memory of 1798 and composed, in a style designed to resemble Gaelic folk tradition, several poems in Irish about the rebellion, which appeared in nationalist newspapers under his pseudonym, *An Craoibhin Aoibhinn* ['the pleasant little branch']. Hyde came from a loyalist Protestant background but fancied, somewhat like Milligan, that his grandfather had participated in the rebellion. He availed of the revival of interest in the years leading up to the centennial of 1798 to republish some of his earlier poems.[413]

Very few of the countless nationalist poems written in the 1890s would be remembered in the long term. The ephemerality of most of the patriotic verse reveals the limitations of the deliberate attempt to construct a nationalist cultural memory of 1798. Several poems, however, did make it into social memory and became part of the folklore of Ninety-Eight. Patrick Joseph McCall, who was honorary secretary of the National Literary Society (of which Hyde was president) and of the national music festival Feis Ceoil, contributed to the *Shan Van Vocht* a ballad titled 'The Belfast Mountains: A Story of '98', which recalled the capture and execution of Henry Joy McCracken, as recounted by a heart-broken lover.[414] P. J. McCall had been raised on

---

[411] *SVV*, 2, no. 4 (April 1897), p. 74. For identification of the pseudonym 'A Dangan Boy' see *United Ireland*, 23 April 1887, p. 1; *Irish Independent*, 3 May 1956, p. 10.

[412] *SVV*, 2, no. 6 (June 1897), p. 104. The main text of the lecture 'Poetry and Patriotism' was published in *Poetry and Ireland: Essays by W. B. Yeats and Lionel Johnson* (Dundrum: Cuala Press, 1908), pp. 21–54.

[413] *SVV*, 3, no. 1 (7 November 1898), p. 197. For another of Hyde's '98 poems published in 1898—'Bás an Chroppí', translated to English by William Rooney as 'The Dead Croppy', see Moylan, *Age of Revolution*, p. 105.

[414] *SVV*, 1, no. 6 (5 June 1896), p. 107.

folk stories of 1798 in Leinster, which were told by his father, John McCall—a nationalist antiquarian from county Carlow, and by his mother, Eliza Mary née Newport from county Wexford. His historical understanding was also influenced by Father Kavanagh's Catholic nationalist *Popular History of the Rebellion of 1798*. McCall's patriotic verses enjoyed immense success and two songs on the rebellion in Wexford—'Kelly, the boy from Killanne' and 'Boolavogue'—became popular folk songs.[415]

As McCall did not have a personal connection with the folklore of the rebellion in Ulster, he found the information for his song about Henry Joy McCracken in Robert M. Young's *Ulster in '98* and set the tune to the air of 'an old Northern ballad', which had been collected earlier in the nineteenth century by George Petrie. The authenticity attributed to McCall's composition after it gained popularity as a folk song is apparent in its common misattribution to the northern United Irish poet William Drennan.[416] Evidently, the success of revivalist formulations of tradition depended, at least to some extent, on use of earlier materials and entailed reinvention, rather than straightforward invention, of memory. This regeneration of memory was channelled into commemoration.

The burst of publications in memory of the United Irishmen served the greater purpose of establishing commemorative rituals in anticipation of the centenary of 1798. From its first issue, the *Shan Van Vocht* ran a series on 'The Neglected Shrines and Sepulchres of Ireland's Illustrious Dead', which was devoted to raising awareness to neglected graves of celebrated United Irishmen. It was written by Bigger under the pseudonym ENREI, a name by which he subtly paid tribute to his role model, Madden, who had composed poetry in the style of the United Irishmen under the inverse pseudonym IERNE. The title of the series was taken from Madden's two-volume survey of *The Shrines and Sepulchres of the Old and New World* (a global study which was supposed to have included a third volume with references to graves of United Irishmen in America). Towards the end of his life, Madden had devotedly searched for and restored graves of various figures connected with 1798, including the burial sites of the executed rebels Wolfe Tone, and John and Henry Sheares, and he erected a tombstone for Robert Emmet's 'faithful servant' Anne Devlin. Bigger, who aspired to emulate Madden in Ulster, was intent in enthusing others to join him in similarly honouring the burial sites of the principal United Irishmen of the North.[417]

From the end of 1895, the Henry Joy McCracken Literary Society found cause to cooperate with other radical nationalist associations that were active at the time in Belfast, namely the Young Ireland League (founded in 1891 on the basis of previously existing Young Ireland Societies, of which a Belfast branch was active since 1883), the Amnesty Society (part of a revived Amnesty Association, established in 1892, which set up its Belfast branch in 1893 under the leadership of Robert Johnston), and the Charles J. Kickham Literary Society (which had just been formed by Milligan and Carbery). Together, these organizations, which had a considerable overlap in their membership,

---

[415] Liam Gaul, *Glory O! Glory O!: The Life of P. J. McCall* (Dublin: History Press Ireland, 2011), pp. 135–9.
[416] Charles Villiers Stanford, ed., *The Complete Collection of Irish Music as Noted by George Petrie*, Part II (London: Published for the Irish Literary Society of London by Boosey & Co., 1905), p. 141 [song no. 558]; Moylan, *Age of Revolution*, pp. 81–2.
[417] *SVV*, 1, no. 1 (January 1896), pp. 14–16; no. 2 (February 1896), p. 30; no. 3 (March 1896), p. 55; no. 4 (April 1896), pp. 74–5. Cf. Richard Robert Madden, *The Shrines and Sepulchres of the Old and New World*, 2 vols (London: T. C. Newby, 1851).

promoted an initiative to establish a national Decoration Day, to be celebrated in proximity to the birthday of Wolfe Tone on 20 June.[418] The concept was modelled on the Fenian anniversaries of the Manchester Martyrs, commemorated annually to mark the execution on 23 November 1867 of William Allen, Michael Larkin, and Michael O'Brien for their part in a prisoner rescue operation that had resulted in the death of an English policeman.[419] The choice of name for the event seems to have been taken from the United States, where the outcome of various local initiatives to establish a Decoration Day in commemoration of the Civil War had resulted in an official public holiday, which was familiar in Ulster through regular reports on the memorial ceremonies in Irish newspapers.[420] Decoration Day in Ulster was supposed to facilitate the commemoration of republican heroes, with particular emphasis on the United Irishmen.

At a meeting of the McCracken Literary Society in May 1896, John Clarke, the society's secretary and business manager of the *Northern Patriot*, gave a talk on 'The decoration of the Graves of the Ulster Patriots, a neglected National Work'. He noted that 'Ulster holds to-day almost unknown and forgotten the ashes of many a peasant soldier who fell in '98' and chided those who 'think that it is better to allow the faithful heroes to sleep in oblivion' rather than 'commemorating the anniversaries of our patriots, by visiting and marking their tombs'. To drive home this point, an editorial in the *Northern Patriot* added that 'The country that allows the names of its martyred patriots to sink into oblivion is unworthy of freedom.' [421]

Preparing the ground for the introduction of Decoration Day, the *Shan Van Vocht* published in early June a register of 'the graves of the patriot dead in the North', which mainly listed burial sites of United Irishmen, though a number of graves of Young Irelanders and Fenians were also included. Accordingly, on Sunday, 21 June 1896, parties of nationalists visited the memorial sites of 1798 throughout Antrim and Down and ceremoniously laid floral wreaths at the identified graves.[422] The memorial rituals were repeated the following year, on 20 June 1897, when the graves of Mary Ann McCracken and William Drennan at Belfast's Clifton Street Cemetery and the graves of James Hope in Mallusk and of William Orr in Templepatrick were again adorned.[423] During the planning of these commemorative events, sights were set on preparations for celebrations of the 1798 centenary, which was to be organized by local '98 clubs.[424]

---

[418] *Northern Patriot*, 1, no. 3 (December 1895), p. 49; no. 7 (April 1896), p. 101; *SVV*, 1, no. 2 (February 1896), p. 37.

[419] From around 1892, the commemorative anniversaries for the Manchester Martyrs were dubbed 'Decoration Day', particularly in provincial newspapers in Munster, such as the *Irish Examiner*, *Kerry Sentinel*, *Southern Star*, and *Skibbereen Eagle*; see also Owen McGee, '"God Save Ireland": Manchester-Martyr Demonstrations in Dublin, 1867–1916', *Éire-Ireland*, 36, nos. 3–4 (2001), pp. 55–6.

[420] David W. Blight, *Race and Reunion: The Civil War in American Memory* (Cambridge, Mass.: Belknap Press, 2001), pp. 64–96. The *Nation* began reporting on Decoration Day in 1875, stressing Irish-American involvement in the commemorations; *Nation* 5 June 1875, p. 9 and 24 June 1876, pp. 2–3. In the 1890s, the commemorations were covered in the *BNL*'s column on 'Life in America'; see *BNL* 1 June 1891, p. 5; 31 May 1893, p. 5; 1 June 1895, p. 5; 1 June 1896, p. 6.

[421] *Northern Patriot*, 1, no. 8 (June 1896), pp. 120–1 and 124.

[422] *Northern Patriot*, 1, no. 9 (July 1896), pp. 138–40; *SVV*, 1, no. 6 (June 1896), pp. 116–17, and no. 7 (July 1896), 138–40.

[423] *Freeman's Journal*, 23 June 1897, p. 4; *SVV*, 2, no. 7 (July 1897), p. 129.

[424] *Northern Patriot*, 1, no. 7 (April 1896), p. 101.

The prototype for such grass-roots commemorative organization was a Fenian '98 Club that had been established already two decades earlier. In 1876 a group of Wexford men resident in Dublin formed a '98 Club which soon had 120 members, who met on a weekly basis. This inspired the founding of similar clubs in other cities in Ireland and further afield, including a particularly active club in Glasgow and another in Philadelphia, which raised funds for nationalist activities in Ireland. The Dublin '98 club organized in May 1877 a demonstration to mark the anniversary of the Battle of Oulart Hill in Wexford and the following year, despite local clerical opposition, its members erected a Celtic Cross memorial to the rebel priest Father John Murphy and his followers at the site of the outbreak of the rebellion in Wexford at Boolavogue (12 km north-east of Enniscorthy).[425]

These activities were indicative of wider popular interest in commemorating Ninety-Eight, which resulted in the erection of local monuments also in Newtownbarry, near Bunclody (18 km north-west of Enniscorthy), county Wexford, in 1875, and on French Hill, near Ballyheane (7 km south-west of Castlebar), county Mayo, in 1876.[426] Even though the original '98 Club in Dublin had declared that the 'determined, but brief effort of our Northern brethren' should not 'disappear with the oblivious past', the early attempts at publicly commemorating 1798 were not mirrored at the time in Ulster, where social forgetting remained the norm.[427]

As the centenary of 1798 approached, it seemed that the inhibitions of social forgetting in Ulster were to be finally overcome. Several '98 clubs were established in Belfast, as well as in various locations in Down, Antrim, and adjacent part of Derry, and these vigorously engaged in organizing and participating in commemorative events. Brimming with confidence, the *Northern Patriot* expressed the expectation that the commemorative initiatives would endure: 'we trust the '98 Clubs about being formed [sic] will become permanent in their respective centres, and that they will find plenty of work to do in the future.' While it lauded the 'Ulster patriots of the last century', the magazine curtly dismissed the inconvenient reality that 'large numbers of the friends and descendants of these men have taken shelter under the banner of British occupation' and rejoiced instead in the knowledge that 'there are still men in Belfast true to the memory of the teachings of the immortal United Irishmen.'[428] It was even fancifully hoped that the growing awareness to the memory of Ninety-Eight might make loyalists see the light and entice them to join nationalists in commemoration. This aspiration was expressed in a poetic appeal 'To the Presbyterians and Protestants of Ulster—Orange and Green':

> Your fathers were the first to rise
> In days of strife gone by,
> To guard the emerald banner,

---

[425] *Irishman*, 16 and 23 December 1876, p. 13, 30 December 1876, p. 12, and 23 June 1877, p. 5; *Freeman's Journal*, 21 May 1877, p. 2 and 30 September 1878, p. 7; see also Kinsella, '1798 Claimed for Catholics', pp. 146–8.

[426] See Séamas S. de Vál, *Bun Clóidí: A History of the District Down to the Beginning of the Twentieth Century* (Bunclody: self-published, 1966), p. 250; Beiner, *Remembering the Year of the French*, pp. 243 and 274–5.

[427] *Irishman*, 5 May 1877, p. 14.

[428] *Northern Patriot*, 1, no. 7 (April 1896), p. 101.

Or 'neath it bravely die.
Your northern hills are studded o'er
With martyred heroes' graves
Oh! can the sons of such brave sires
Still act the part of slaves?[429]

The triumphant rhetoric of revivalism gave the mistaken impression that the enthusiasm for public remembrance was universal and uncontested. In fact, its main proponents were limited to relatively small, albeit very devoted advanced nationalist circles.

The *Shan Van Vocht* has been rightly credited for its 'wide-reaching influence for Irish nationalists of the 1890s', but its ideological impact did not translate into vast numbers.[430] The combined readership of the *Shan Van Vocht* and the less successful *Northern Patriot* was actually quite limited, particularly when taking into account the overlap between readers who read both publications. Each magazine printed around 2,500 copies, however the police curbed their circulation by seizing copies at the Belfast port. Lists of subscribers to the *Shan Van Vocht* at its peak years of 1898–9 amount to some 350 names in Ireland and an additional 500 in America. When the *Shan Van Vocht* ceased publication in April 1899, its subscription list was subsumed into that of the *United Irishman* and in 1906 the list fed into *Sinn Féin*, both edited by the radical nationalist journalist Arthur Griffith. Even then, the subscribers' lists have been estimated at 'no more than a few thousand'.[431] These figures are considerably below those of the mainstream daily national newspapers and are also lower than the readership of much of the provincial press. To compare, according to figures compiled by Dublin Castle on the circulation of provincial newspapers *c.*1892, the nationalist *Belfast Morning News* reached 4,300 readers and the nationalist *Belfast Weekly Examiner* had a circulation of 11,500.[432] Magazines were often shared, so that the actual numbers of readers may have been somewhat larger, but in any case the northern radical newspapers that were dedicated to remembrance of the United Irishmen only reached a small proportion of the population of Ulster. In practice, very few of the 750,000 residents of Antrim and Down, and an insignificant fraction of the 300,000 Presbyterians among them, were directly exposed to the numerous items on 1798 published in the *Shan Van Vocht* and the *Northern Patriot*.[433]

The promoters of nationalist commemoration were aware that the memorial sites of the United Irishmen were, by and large, located in unionist strongholds and that the decoration of rebel graves would be perceived as an affront by loyalists. Out of concern that the district of Lisburn 'is hostile and anti-national', the party of men and women who laid a wreath in 1896 at an unmarked grave in Blaris churchyard, identified as the tomb of 'the martyred four'—soldiers of the Monaghan militia that had been executed

---

[429] *Northern Patriot*, 1, no. 6 (March 1896), p. 96.

[430] Karen Margaret Steele, *Women, Press, and Politics during the Irish Revival* (Syracuse, N.Y.: Syracuse University Press, 2007), p. 80.

[431] Virginia E. Glandon, 'The Irish Press and Revolutionary Irish Nationalism', *Éire-Ireland*, 16, no. 1 (1981): p. 25; Owen McGee, *The IRB: The Irish Republican Brotherhood from the Land League to Sinn Fein* (Dublin: Four Courts Press, 2005), p. 244.

[432] Legg, *Newspapers and Nationalism*, p. 127.

[433] *Census of Ireland for the Year 1901: Preliminary Report with Abstract of the Enumerators' Summaries* (Dublin: H. M. Stationary Office, 1901), pp. 13, table I (inhabitants in each county and province) and 14, table II (religious professions).

for taking the United Irish oath in 1797, made sure to arrive unannounced in the early hours of a Sunday morning, in order to avoid encountering local opposition. The commemorative visits that year to '98 sites mostly passed without causing commotion. Yet, when a deputation of the H. J. McCracken Literary Society made a return visit to Clifton Street cemetery in Belfast the week after Decoration Day, they were surprised to discover that the 'magnificent floral cross' that had been placed on the McCracken family grave could not be found. In declaring that 'such desecration deserves the strongest condemnation' and stating their belief that 'the parties who removed it will be yet brought to justice', the editors of the *Northern Patriot* failed to register that this theft was a warning that in the future open celebration of memory of 1798 would encounter resistance.[434] In the centenary, celebratory rituals of open remembrance would incur a hostile reaction—commemorating would be countermanded by decommemorating.

Generational change inevitably entails a loss of memory. 'The continuous withdrawal of previous participants in the process of Culture', according to the sociologist Karl Mannheim, 'serves the necessary social purpose of enabling us to forget'. Distinguishing between 'personally acquired' and 'appropriated' memories, Mannheim pointed out that 'if society is to continue, social remembering is just as important as forgetting'. It is therefore necessary to inquire 'in what social form remembering manifests itself' in order to understand 'how the cultural heritage is actually accumulated'.[435] The dynamics of social forgetting undermine the implied dichotomy between forgetting and remembering, allowing for private recollections to be transmitted below the radar. The frameworks—to use again the concepts of Maurice Halbwachs—that accommodated social forgetting in the generation that experienced the Turn-Out changed over time. Therefore, a historical, rather than a strictly sociological, approach is required to follow these developments. New conditions encouraged the retaining of recollections in private, while self-censorship was still exercised in public, even when fear of repression was no longer a concern.

Both Jan Assmann and Aleida Assmann have proposed that personal recollections are transmitted over three generations as a fluid 'communicative memory', through which grandparents pass on vivid narratives to the generation of their grandchildren, after which they are formulated into a more stable cultural memory.[436] This overly schematic model underestimates the influence of early formations of cultural memory and fails to adequately accommodate the regeneration of social memory. Studies of cultural memory tend to rely too heavily on the literary canon and on mainstream historiography, and therefore suffer from an unawareness of vernacular historiography, which is the key to unravelling less recognized manifestations of social memory. The professionalization of

[434] *Northern Patriot*, 1, no. 9 (July 1896), pp. 140–1. Interest in the graves of the soldiers executed at Blaris was revived by Bigger in an article titled 'Soldiers Four', which appeared in *SVV*, 1, no. 5 (May 1896), pp. 99–100. For remembrance of the executions see Chapter 1 above, pp. 58–9.

[435] See Mannheim's seminal essay 'The Problem of Generations', in Karl Mannheim, *Essays on the Sociology of Knowledge* (London: Routledge & Kegan Paul, 1952), pp. 276–322 (esp. 294–6).

[436] Jan Assmann, 'Communicative and Cultural Memory', in *Cultural Memories: The Geographical Point of View*, edited by Peter Meusburger, Michael Heffernan, and Edgar Wunder (Dordrecht: Springer, 2011), pp. 15–27; Assmann, 'Memory, Individual and Collective', pp. 210–24. For a sophisticated rethinking of 'communicative memory' see Harald Welzer, 'Communicative Memory', in *Cultural Memory Studies: An International and Interdisciplinary Handbook*, edited by Astrid Erll, Ansgar Nünning, and Sara B. Young (Berlin and New York: Walter de Gruyter, 2008), pp. 285–98.

the discipline of history depreciated local traditions of amateur scholarship, which had developed sophisticated methods of recording and interpreting the past. Over the nineteenth century, historians separated themselves from antiquarians and by the turn of the century the latter were no longer respected in academic circles. Nevertheless, antiquarians, who typically indulged a wide range of interests and recognized the value of vernacular sources, were far better equipped than historians, with their preference for archival documents, to uncover and appreciate folk history.[437]

The success of representations of cultural memory depended, to a certain extent, on their popular reception. Social memory often vetted cultural memory, rebuffing works that presumed to introduce artificial constructions of memory that did not match local expectations. Under scrutiny, the inventions of those traditions that took hold frequently turn out to be re-inventions of existing traditions. Once revived and brought out into the open, historical traditions could, after a while, lapse back into obscurity, where they were maintained less prominently. In this way, social forgetting was ultimately regenerated.

In Ulster, muted recollections were kept alive, even when out of the public gaze, partly because of the fascination with their inherent ambiguity. The unsettling nature of social forgetting defied the characteristic homogenizing tendency of collective memory. The complexity of hidden recollections was maintained by the collectors. The initial agents of regeneration—the pioneering collectors who documented the reminiscences of the generation of the Turn-Out—came from diverse backgrounds, whether they were conservative loyalists like Samuel McSkimin, nationalists like R. R. Madden, or liberal unionists like Classon Emmett Porter. The writers that came after them and repackaged the recollections of subsequent generations also held similarly contrasting positions, whether they were loyalists like William McComb, liberal unionists like W. G. Lyttle, or romantic nationalists like F. J. Bigger. Their passion and respect for traditions of a conflicted and uneasy past, which neither fitted the hegemonic meta-narrative of unionism nor the counter-hegemonic meta-narrative of nationalism, allowed these regenerators of tradition to penetrate the barriers of social forgetting. As shrewdly put by Bradford Vivian in a study of *Public Forgetting*: 'wading in the river Lethe might herald the rebirth rather than death of memory.'[438]

Towards the end of the century, with the arrival of the centennial anniversary of 1798, attempts to transcend social forgetting, and to bring the memory of the Turn-Out out into the light of day, unleashed political power struggles. Open remembrance was heavily contested. In turn, opposition to commemoration would stimulate further regeneration of social forgetting.

[437] See Guy Beiner and Joep Leerssen, 'Why Irish History Starved? A Virtual Historiography', *Field Day Review*, 3 (2007): pp. 67–81.
[438] Vivian, *Public Forgetting*, p. 47.

5

Decommemorating

The Turn of the Century

The passion for destruction is a creative passion, too!

Mikhail Bakunin, 'The Reaction in Germany'[1]

...there's no better way of forgetting something than by commemorating it.

Alan Bennett, *The History Boys*[2]

Before Maurice Halbwachs coined the term 'collective memory', his mentor Émile Durkheim had already grappled with the necessity for a society to attain a sense of continuity with the past, 'that is to say, of keeping alive their memory, by means of celebrations'.[3] Durkheim, who acknowledged that the memorial cult instituted by the French Revolution was short lived, had personally experienced the vigorous revival of the cult of the revolution by the Third Republic, from the inauguration of Bastille Day in 1880 to the celebrations of the centennial of 1789.[4] Centenaries and anniversaries, monumentalized through a spree of statuomania, were all the rage in turn-of-the-century Europe. The sociologist Paul Connerton maintained that 'if there is such a thing as social memory, we are likely to find it in commemorative ceremonies.'[5] Yet, behind such exuberant displays of remembrance often lie anxieties of forgetting.

The fin-de-siècle boom of public remembrance addressed a 'memory crisis' apparent in the intellectual writings of the period. It was felt that the rituals and customs through which the past had been traditionally remembered were destined to be swept away by modernity and that, for the sake of forging solidary, new civic rituals were needed to

---

[1] 'Die Lust der Zerstörung ist zugleich eine schaffende Lust!'; Jules Elysard [Michail Bakunin], 'Die Reaction in Deutschland: Ein Fragment von einem Franzosen', *Deutsche Jahrbücher für Wissenschaft und Kunst*, no. 251 (21 October 1842), p. 1002.

[2] Alan Bennett, *The History Boys* (New York: Farrar, Straus, and Giroux, 2006; orig. edn 2004), p. 25.

[3] Émile Durkheim, *The Elementary Forms of the Religious Life* (London: G. Allen & Unwin, Ltd, 1915), p. 428. See also Barbara A. Misztal, 'Durkheim on Collective Memory', *Journal of Classical Sociology*, 3, no. 2 (1 July 2003): pp. 123–43.

[4] Christian Amalvi, 'Bastille Day: From *Dies Irae* to Holiday', in *Realms of Memory: The Construction of the French Past*, edited by Pierre Nora, translated by Arthur Goldhammer (New York: Columbia University Press, 1996), vol. 3, pp. 117–59; Pascal Ory, 'Le Centenaire de La Révolution Française', in *Les Lieux de Mémoire*, edited by Pierre Nora (Paris: Gallimard, 1984), 1, pp. 523–60. See also Edward A. Tiryakian, *For Durkheim: Essays in Historical and Cultural Sociology* (Burlington and Surrey: Ashgate, 2009), pp. 89–114.

[5] Connerton, *How Societies Remember*, p. 71.

re-connect the mass societies of modern states with their national pasts.[6] Commemoration fervour was a transnational *zeitgeist*. It was reflected in a cult of centenaries in Britain and also stimulated the emergence of nationalist commemoration in Ireland.[7] However, public performance of memory was not always welcomed with open arms. In Ulster, commemoration had to contend with the constrictive inhibitions of social forgetting. Hostility towards open commemoration resulted in violent opposition, marking a phenomenon that can be labelled 'decommemorating'. While the targeting of sites of remembrance is most evident in the removal and destruction of monuments, decom-memorating can assume a range of forms that play into social forgetting by inhibiting celebrations of memory, as well as public displays of non-hegemonic counter-memory.[8]

The Diamond Jubilee of Queen Victoria was widely fêted in London and through-out the empire in June 1897.[9] To the dismay of nationalists, Victoria's sixty-year reign was also celebrated in Ireland. Speaking at a demonstration in Belfast, the Irish nationalist MP John Dillon indignantly exclaimed that 'we have no cause in rejoicing in this jubilee' and defiantly declared that 'the only centenary or anniversary which we can celebrate is the anniversary of the rebellion in '98.'[10] Throughout the following year, hundreds of centennial commemorative events in memory of 1798 were staged across Ireland and Irish diaspora communities in 1898. This was a forceful response to the Queen's jubilee and signified an open challenge to the dominance of British-Imperial memorial culture. The ubiquitous singing of 'The Memory of the Dead', a poem turned hymn that was adopted as the anthem of the centenary, gave the impression that all fears and hesitations to speak of Ninety-Eight had been fully overcome. It now seemed that social memory was unrestrained and irrepressible. In practice, the intro-duction of public rituals of remembrance in Ulster was contested on many levels. It was soon evident that silencing had not ceased and that social forgetting was far from eradicated. Commemorating was to be met with decommemorating.

INFIGHTING

Over previous decades, nationalists had become aware of the cultural capital that could be gained from investing in commemoration. Reclamation—or appropriation—of the public sphere was to a large extent achieved through massive memorial displays.

---

[6] Hobsbawm, 'Mass-Producing Traditions', esp. pp. 271–83; Richard Terdiman, *Present Past: Modernity and the Memory Crisis* (Ithaca and London: Cornell University Press, 1993).

[7] Roland Quinault, 'The Cult of the Centenary, *c.*1784–1914', *Historical Research*, 71, no. 176 (1998): pp. 303–23.

[8] The preference for the verbal noun 'decommemorating' is designed to emphasize the active process involved in various assaults on commemoration. For 'decommemoration' in modern Irish history see McBride, 'Memory and National Identity', p. 2; Yvonne Whelan, *Reinventing Modern Dublin: Streetscape, Iconography, and the Politics of Identity* (Dublin: University College Dublin Press, 2003), pp. 192–213.

[9] Meike Hölscher, 'Performances, Souvenirs, and Music: The Diamond Jubilee of Queen Victoria 1897', in *Mediation, Remediation, and the Dynamics of Cultural Memory*, edited by Astrid Erll and Ann Rigney (Berlin and New York: Walter de Gruyter, 2009), pp. 173–84.

[10] *Freeman's Journal*, 18 June 1897, p. 5. For the Diamond Jubilee in Ireland see James H. Murphy, *Abject Loyalty: Nationalism and Monarchy in Ireland during the Reign of Queen Victoria* (Washington, D.C.: Catholic University of America Press, 2001), pp. 269–74.

In Dublin, Fenians orchestrated well-attended funerary processions for the Young Irelander Terence Bellew McManus in 1861 and for the co-founder of the Irish Republican Brotherhood John O'Mahony in 1877. The Manchester Martyrs were commemorated annually, from the year of their execution in 1867, at large Fenian demonstrations.[11] Concurrently, constitutional nationalists participated in the memorial cult of Daniel O'Connell, attending in droves the laying of a foundation stone for a monument in his honour in 1864, the centenary of his birth in 1875, and, above all, the 'national festival' for the unveiling of the monument on Sackville Street in 1882. The erection in 1879 of a statue of William Smith O'Brien, a leader of the Young Ireland rebellion in 1848, located a monument associated with violent resistance to British rule right in the centre of Dublin. Elsewhere, memorials to the Manchester Martyrs, which were concentrated mainly in Munster, staked out a counter-hegemonic geography of republican sites of memory.[12] The popular rituals of nationalist commemoration established during these years reached new heights in the centenary of 1798.

The organizers of the centenary took pride in the programme's alleged inclusivity. The commemorations were supposed to be accessible to all those interested in remembering Ninety-Eight. In practice, the production of what claims to be a homogenizing collective memory is typically a contested enterprise. Performance of social remembrance in public places creates a market place of memory, in which organizations and individuals vie for dominance, scrambling to accrue for themselves the dividends of commemoration and to exclude others from enjoying its benefits. Close inspection of the workings of the 1798 centenary reveals the multiple conflicts that lurked behind the façade of professed unity.

Since the Parnell split of 1891, the Irish Parliamentary Party (IPP) was divided into rival factions that contended against each other: a minority of Parnellites, headed by John Redmond, faced a majority of anti-Parnellites. The anti-Parnellites were subdivided into followers of John Dillon, who from 1896 was elected chairman of the main anti-Parnellite body—the Irish National Federation (INF), and those who supported his principal opponent Timothy Healy, head of the People's Rights Association. Another anti-Parnellite, William O'Brien, initiated in 1898 an agrarian protest movement under the banner of the United Irish League (UIL). At the same time, separatist republicans, who rejected the parliamentary politics of Home Rule, were also split among themselves. The primacy of the main republican body—the Irish Republican Brotherhood (IRB)—was challenged by an attempt to introduce an alternative Irish National Brotherhood (INB), which was affiliated with the Irish National Association (INA). This rift echoed the schism a decade earlier within the Irish-American

[11] Garry Owens, 'Constructing the Martyrs: The Manchester Executions and the Nationalist Imagination', in *Images, Icons, and the Irish Nationalist Imagination*, edited by Lawrence W. McBride (Dublin: Four Courts Press, 1999), pp. 18–36; McGee, 'God Save Ireland'; Guy Beiner, 'Fenianism and the Martyrdom-Terrorism Nexus in Ireland before Independence', in *Martyrdom and Terrorism: Pre-Modern to Contemporary Perspectives*, edited by Dominic Janes and Alex Houen (Oxford and New York: Oxford University Press, 2014), pp. 199–220 (esp. 200–2 and 205–7).
[12] Judith Hill, *Irish Public Sculpture: A History* (Dublin: Four Courts Press, 1998), pp. 89–97, 102–4 and 114–18; Yvonne Whelan, 'Monuments, Power and Contested Space—The Iconography of Sackville Street (O'Connell Street) before Independence (1922)', *Irish Geography*, 34, no. 1 (2001): pp. 11–33 (esp. 20–7). For commemoration of O'Connell see Paula Murphy, *Nineteenth-Century Irish Sculpture: Native Genius Reaffirmed* (New Haven: Yale University Press, 2010), pp. 185–204.

Fenian movement Clan na Gael. Irish political nationalism at the turn of the century was clearly not a cohesive movement.

The rival political nationalist organizations competed against each other for a stake in the centennial commemorations, each trying to steer the programme towards furthering its own particular interests. Declarations of unity served as a smokescreen for makeshift alliances, which were intended to undermine and supplant contending organizations. Struggles over memory were conducted through drives for possession of, and exclusion from, entitlement to ownership of the past. While remembrance of Ninety-Eight was seemingly offered for the benefit of all, commemoration ceremonies were appropriated with a mind to prevent others from partaking in memorial rituals.

A national centenary movement was first initiated by the Young Ireland League (YIL), a Fenian front organization that encouraged the establishment of '98 clubs. In 1897, a 1798 Centenary Committee, chaired by the veteran Fenian John O'Leary, was formed in Dublin. Although constitutional nationalists were excluded from this republican-dominated body, Redmond, the leader of the Parnellites, maintained ties with the committee's secretary, Frederick (Fred) Allan, who conveniently happened to be both the secretary of the IRB Supreme Council and the editor of the Parnellite newspaper the *Irish Daily Independent*. To counter this development, Dillon, the main anti-Parnellite leader, toyed for a while with the possibility of aligning himself with a London-based Central Executive Committee for Great Britain, chaired by W. B. Yeats, which was associated with the rival Fenian INA organization. He soon relinquished this idea and instead set up an alternative anti-Parnellite United Irishmen Centennial Association, which accused the Fenian-Parnellite '98 Central Executive in Dublin— vilified, on account of its meeting place, as the 'City Hall gang'—of excluding the majority of Catholic nationalists. Outside of these wrangles, enthusiasm for the O'Brien's agrarian UIL movement, evident in the rapid spread of its branches alongside provincial '98 clubs, demonstrated the potential for grass-roots organizing of commemoration. The competition between the rival bodies on a national level was mirrored on a local level in Ulster, where nationalist commemoration had to contend also with violent opposition from loyalists.[13]

In contrast to the relatively unhindered emergence of nationalism in the South, unionist and Orange commemorative rituals continued to monopolize the public sphere in the North. Loyalists vigilantly resisted the intrusion of nationalist memorialization into Ulster. In the second half of the nineteenth century, delegations of northern Catholics travelled south to participate in memorial events in Dublin but were prevented from introducing corresponding commemorations in Belfast. In reaction to the laying in 1864 of the foundation stone for the O'Connell statue in Dublin, O'Connell was burnt in effigy in Belfast. Sectarian riots broke out in the streets, and passengers on trains returning from Dublin were attacked.[14] The authorities generally ruled in favour of loyalist objections to nationalist commemoration and prohibited nationalist demonstrations. Nonetheless, commemorative banners, which displayed

---

[13] Timothy O'Keefe, 'The 1898 Efforts to Celebrate the United Irishmen: The '98 Centennial', *Éire-Ireland*, 23 (1988): pp. 51–73.

[14] *Report of The Commissioners of Inquiry, 1864, Respecting the Magisterial and Police Jurisdiction Arrangements and Establishment of the Borough of Belfast* (Dublin: H.M.S.O., 1864); see also Boyd, *Holy War in Belfast*, pp. 44–89.

such slogans as 'Remember Orr' and portrayed images of Henry Joy McCracken and other United Irishmen, appeared regularly from the 1870s at Catholic processions on Saint Patrick's Day and Lady Day in Ulster.[15]

The Catholics of Belfast had refrained from holding a mock funeral for the Manchester Martyrs in 1867, but in subsequent years Fenian demonstrations in demand of amnesty for political prisoners picked up momentum in the town.[16] A ban imposed on commemoration of the Manchester Martyrs in 1890 resulted in arrests that caused 'a great deal of excitement' in the Catholic area of the Falls Road.[17] This euphemism for rioting (which had previously appeared in testimonies collected by the commissioners that investigated the Belfast riots in 1886) was indicative of increasing assertiveness.[18] The limits of preventing popular memorialization were soon exposed by the determination of local '98 clubs to hold centennial commemorations in Ulster, regardless of prohibitions, making it clear that the centenary of 1798 could not be quietly suppressed. Apart from the external opposition presented by loyalists, the success of commemoration of Ninety-Eight was threatened by internal divisions among nationalists.

The centennial programme was launched in Ulster on 14 October 1897 with a commemoration to mark the execution of William Orr. Just as memorialization rituals of Orr in 1797 had provided the schemata for the prememory—as well as the pre-forgetting—of 1798, the commemoration in 1897 created a prememory for the configurations of memory produced in 1898. Commemoration of Orr also foreshadowed some of the inherent conflicts at play during the centenary. Thomas Fitzpatrick, the house illustrator of the anti-Parnellite *Weekly Freeman*, depicted an imaginary portrayal of the event in a cartoon, which shows the nationalist parliamentarian John Dillon with the unionist leader Edward Saunderson, laying together a wreath inscribed 'From United Irishmen' at the pedestal of a broken monument to Orr (Fig. 5.1). The two politicians are clothed in the shades of the Irish republican tricolour, with white shirts, green jackets, and orange overcoats. They stand in front of an all-male crowd, one side of which rally behind Dillon and are clearly nationalists, as they hold a green banner labelled 'God Save Ireland' (a slogan associated with the Manchester Martyrs). Those situated behind Saunderson are presumably unionists (possibly even Orangemen), yet seem to have no qualms about standing beside a plain green banner.[19] This fanciful vision of political reconciliation on the terms of the largest faction of the Irish nationalist party had nothing to do with the discordant realities of the 1798 centenary in Ulster.

---

[15] 'Remember Orr' was first noticed on a banner at a Lady Day parade in Downpatrick in 1872; *Downpatrick Recorder*, 17 August 1872, p. 2; for subsequent appearances of the slogan see *BNL*, 17 August 1874, p. 3 and 7 August 1877, p. 3. A banner with the image of Henry Joy McCracken was displayed by nationalists from the Falls Road at demonstrations in Belfast; *Irishman* 7 October 1876, p. 230; *Nation*, 24 March 1877, p. 2. See also Neil Jarman, *Displaying Faith: Orange, Green and Trade Union Banners in Northern Ireland* (Belfast: Institute of Irish Studies, Queen's University of Belfast, 1999), p. 34.
[16] Catherine Hirst, *Religion, Politics, and Violence in Nineteenth-Century Belfast: The Pound and Sandy Row* (Dublin: Four Courts Press, 2002), pp. 102–3.
[17] *Freeman's Journal*, 24 November 1890, p. 6.   [18] *BNL*, 7 October 1886, p. 6.
[19] *Weekly Freeman*, 16 October 1897, supplement; see also Lawrence W. McBride, 'Visualizing '98: Irish Nationalist Cartoons Commemorate the Revolution', *Eighteenth-Century Life*, 22, no. 3 (1998): p. 109.

Fig. 5.1. 'Remember Orr!'

'William Orr, Judicially Murdered, October 14, 1797. Remember Orr', drawn by Thomas Fitzpatrick for the *Weekly Freeman*, gratis supplement, 16 October 1897. The cartoon of an imaginary commemoration of William Orr reflects the nationalist rhetoric of political reconciliation around the centenary, which masked intense rivalry and sectarian animosity.

Courtesy of the National Library of Ireland.

Police intelligence followed closely the preparations for the 1798 centenary and discovered that 'the modus operandi is to establish in numerous districts in the country local Committees who are placed in touch with a central body in Dublin or elsewhere.'[20] Northern nationalists had begun preparing for the centenary well in advance of many of their southern counterparts, but they had to contend with the aspirations of the Dublin '98 Central Executive to control provincial commemorations. The Dublin committee issued a call in April 1897 for the formation of '98 clubs in 'every town and parish in Ireland and in every district out of Ireland'. The top-down approach, which implied that Dublin would dictate the agenda for the centenary and that local committees would subserviently comply, was contested.[21]

By the end of 1897, Belfast had established nineteen '98 committees and clubs. Although this number was lower than the twenty-two committees and clubs in Dublin city, the Belfast clubs had more than twice as many paying members—3,005 to Dublin's 1,185. By May 1898, both cities had about twenty-eight clubs each, but, according to figures compiled by the police, Belfast membership had risen to some 5,000 whereas Dublin was only 1,400. Moreover, Belfast was the nerve centre of the most organized province in terms of centennial mobilization. At the beginning of 1898, Ulster had fifty-three clubs devoted to commemorating 1798 (compared to forty-nine in Leinster, twenty-six in Munster, and nine in Connacht) and this number would increase during the centennial year and reach sixty-eight clubs with 6,387 members, exclusive of Belfast.[22] Under pressure, the '98 Central Executive was obliged to recognize provincial representation and to accept delegates from Ulster. This local affiliation with the national organization in Dublin was disputed in Belfast.

The Belfast '98 movement had undergone a split already in 1896, when Alice Milligan and Ethna Carbery left their posts as editors of the *Northern Patriot*, the journal of the Henry Joy McCracken Literary Society, and established the rival *Shan Van Vocht*. Milligan later recalled that the *Northern Patriot* had been 'captured by opponents of advanced nationalism'.[23] This claim did not reflect the full picture. Their removal was debated in a heated exchange of letters, published in the *United Irishman*, which only implicitly referred to the existence of internal strife within republicanism, though this appears to have been the main cause for the break-up. Fred Allan, who was a central figure in the IRB had been appointed vice president of the McCracken Literary Society, in place of Milligan. Whereas Allan was amenable to cooperation with Parnellite politicians, Milligan and Carbery were associated with the rival Fenian INA and insisted on excluding representatives of the Irish parliamentary party.[24] They were supported by Henry Dobbyn, the president of the Belfast Independent Young Ireland Society, which

[20] RIC Inspector General's Confidential Reports for the month of February 1898, No. 15611/S, Chief Secretary's Office, Police and Crime Division (Special), TNA CO 904/68/9.

[21] *Daily Independent*, 14 April 1897; cited in McGee, *The IRB*, p. 249.

[22] Chief Secretary's Office, Police and Crime Division (Special), Summary of '98 Centenary Committees as of 31 December 1897, NAI CBS 15200/S; '98 Centenary Return of Clubs and Members by Provinces and Counties, 14 May 1898, NAI CBS 16235/S. See also Peter Collins, *Who Fears to Speak of '98? Commemoration and the Continuing Impact of the United Irishmen* (Belfast: Ulster Historical Foundation, 2004), p. 31; Matthew Kelly, *The Fenian Ideal and Irish Nationalism, 1882–1916* (Woodbridge: Boydell & Brewer, 2006), p. 113; Morris, *Alice Milligan*, p. 197.

[23] *Irish Press*, 23 November 1938, p. 10.

[24] *United Ireland*, 11 and 25 January and 1 February 1896, pp. 3, 2–3, and 3 (respectively). See also Morris, *Alice Milligan*, pp. 166–8.

had separated in 1892 from the main (IRB affiliated) Young Ireland Society. Dobbyn was the principal organizer of the INA in Belfast, which at the beginning of the centenary year controlled two '98 clubs with 450 members. However, his poor managerial and interpersonal skills drove the splinter Fenian organization into rapid declined. Its collapse in July 1898, left the Belfast republican scene entirely to the IRB, which by then controlled eight '98 clubs, with over 1,100 members.[25]

Republicans had taken the lead in preparing for the centenary in Ulster but, after quarrelling among themselves, they were soon outflanked by constitutional nationalists, who had come to realize the value of commemoration as a mobilizing force. In the autumn of 1897, anti-Parnellites guilefully seized control of the main northern '98 movement. This takeover was achieved through the manoeuvres of Joseph Devlin, Dillon's Belfast lieutenant. 'Wee Joe' Devlin came from a Catholic Belfast neighbourhood on the lower Falls Road and had previously been employed in an old Belfast pub, later known as Kelly's Cellars, which was said to have been a meeting place for United Irishmen in the 1790s. He worked there under the management of the Belfast whiskey distiller Samuel Young, a Presbyterian anti-Parnellite MP who claimed to be 'one of the few men living whose father had carried his pike and fought for liberty in '98' (he would live to the age of 96). Devlin had since made a name for himself as a journalist writing for established nationalist newspapers, the *Irish News* and the *Freeman's Journal*. In 1897, he founded the *Northern Star*, a 'nationalist democratic weekly' named after the organ of the United Irishmen, which appealed to a working class readership and brought him mass support.[26]

In September 1897, Milligan proposed that the membership of a newly formed Belfast and Ulster United Centenary Association should be limited solely to representatives of the '98 Clubs and literary societies. This veiled attempt to exclude the Irish parliamentary party from the organization of the centenary was quashed by a large majority of Devlin supporters.[27] Shortly afterwards, at the end of October 1897, Devlin, who claimed to represent nine-tenths of the nationalists in Belfast, was elected president of a Central Executive for Ulster, which was dominated by representatives of the anti-Parnellite Irish National Federation and of the Irish National League (officially a Parnellite organization, though the northern branches were, in practice, loyal to Devlin).[28]

In the Belfast municipal elections of 1897, Devlin mobilized the '98 clubs under his control to canvass for anti-Parnellite candidates. Fenians expressed their dismay at the 'determined attempt now being made by a political organisation to use the '98 Centenary movement as an election machine'.[29] In response, the more radical '98 clubs formed their own Ulster Provincial Council, which was affiliated with the '98 Central

[25] Summary of '98 Centenary Committees as of 31 December 1897, NAI CBS 15200/S; RIC District Inspector Report for June 1898, 16704/S, NAI CBS DICS Reports Box 5. See also Kelly, *The Fenian Ideal*, pp. 105n39 and 112; León Ó Broin, *Revolutionary Underground: The Story of the Irish Republican Brotherhood, 1858–1924* (Dublin: Gill and Macmillan, 1976), pp. 86–7.

[26] Hepburn, *A Past Apart*, p. 211; A. C. Hepburn, *Catholic Belfast and Nationalist Ireland in the Era of Joe Devlin, 1871–1934* (Oxford: Oxford University Press, 2008), pp. 40 and 51.

[27] *Freeman's Journal*, 3 and 10 September 1897, p. 6; *United Ireland*, 11 September 1897, p. 6. See also O'Keefe, 'The 1898 Efforts', p. 63; cf. Milligan's account of the meeting in Morris, *Alice Milligan*, p. 203.

[28] *Freeman's Journal*, 5 November 1897, p. 6; United *Ireland*, 6 November 1897, p. 3; see also O'Keefe, 'The 1898 Efforts', p. 64; McGee, *The IRB*, p. 253.

[29] *Daily Nation*, 28 September 1897, p. 2.

Executive in Dublin. James Stephens, the venerable co-founder of the IRB, was appointed nominal president and prominent northern republicans were elected to key roles (including Milligan as secretary).[30] When the Henry Joy McCracken Literary Society applied to the '98 Central Executive in Dublin to cooperate in the decoration of graves of United Irishmen, it was instructed 'to observe the guidance of the Ulster Provisional Council' (sic). John Clarke, the society's secretary, forthrightly rejected these terms:

> We absolutely refuse to have our policy manipulated and machined by this unrepresenta-
> tive Ulster Council. We are quite capable of performing our work without being led by the
> supposed genuine patriotic instrument of those who, through jealousy, imitated our work
> when founded, and some of whom long ago deprecated the commemorating of the
> memories of such men as Tone, Orr, and the heroine Betsy Gray.

Clarke added that 'the Council speaks for a very small proportion of the Nationalists of Ulster and Belfast, and that with the masses outside their sphere of influence will rest the success of the Centenary.'[31]

The bitter rivalries between constitutional and republican nationalists were not acknowledged in the official rhetoric of centennial organization, which was carefully phrased to maintain the pretence of harmony. Nationalist reportage was coated in self-congratulatory hyperbole. Each and every local event was hailed as a tremendously successful gathering of unprecedented numbers, so that it is difficult to determine accurate figures of participation in the meetings and to assess their real impact. Police assessments were sceptical of the centennial hype. In March 1898, the County Inspectors reported that 'there is a total want of general enthusiasm', in April they maintained that 'the work of the '98 Committees has in general been languid', and the commemorative events in May were described as 'displays of very feeble character'. The County Inspectors insisted 'without exception' in June that 'the '98 agitation is falling flat, and utterly fails to awaken any enthusiasm or even serious interest amongst the mass of the people.' The police clearly had an interest in downplaying the achievements of nationalists, but they were not entirely off the mark in detecting 'disunion and dissension in every direction'.[32]

The constant repetition of nationalist calls for unity reveals that disagreements actually continued on the ground. Moreover, the language of unity was employed deceptively to further partisan agendas. The *Northern Patriot* appealed for a union 'of all creeds and classes', yet its warning that 'no narrow-minded policy can carry a '98 commemoration' was implicitly aimed against the editors of the rival *Shan Van Vocht*.[33] Repeated denouncements of factionalism issued by Milligan and Carbery seem to express a heartfelt plea to come 'together in the bonds of brotherly union to do honour to the memory of the dead who died for Ireland'.[34] However, the identification of factionalism solely with the constitutional camp happened to serve the interests of a

---

[30] *Daily Nation*, 10 November 1897, p. 5.   [31] *Freeman's Journal*, 5 January 1898, p. 6.

[32] RIC Inspector General's Monthly Confidential Reports for February (February 15611/S), March (15900/S), April (16163/S), May (16944/S), and June (16699/S) 1898, Chief Secretary's Office, Police and Crime Division (Special), TNA CO 904/68/9, 144–5, 294, 429, and 567.

[33] *Northern Patriot*, 1, no. 11 (September 1896), pp. 165–6.

[34] *SVV*, 3, no. 1 (January 1898), p. 8. See Karen Steele, 'Editing out Factionalism: The Political and Literary Consequences in Ireland's "Shan Van Vocht"', *Victorian Periodicals Review*, 35, no. 2 (2002): pp. 113–32.

small republican splinter group, which was determined to exclude the representatives of the majority of Catholic nationalists and was also at odds with those republicans who were willing to cooperate with parliamentarians.

After the Central Council of the Belfast and Ulster '98 Centenary Association came under the control of anti-Parnellites, Devlin read out a letter from Dillon, commending, somewhat disingenuously, the invitation to 'all Nationalists, without regard to the sectional differences of to-day, to unite in honouring the memory of the men of '98, and to keep the '98 Centenary movement quite free of party politics'. A manifesto proclaiming that 'united and organized action is absolutely necessary' was circulated to all '98 clubs. It undertook to 'exclude no Irishman' and promised that 'the movement will be homogeneous, not split into fragmentary sections and sub-sections.'[35] Nonetheless, republicans remained outside of the main '98 movement.

Meanwhile, the cultural nationalist organizations that had enthusiastically come on board to celebrate the centenary were co-opted by rival political organizations. Fenians infiltrated the Ulster branches of the Gaelic Athletic Association (GAA), the growth of which was being promoted by the *Shan Van Vocht*.[36] Constitutional nationalists, for their part, gained influence over the Irish National Foresters, a society with a marked enthusiasm for parades, which had five '98 branches, with a combined membership of 840, and was particularly strong in counties Tyrone and Londonderry. As an additional counterbalance against republicans, Devlin revived the Ancient Order of the Hibernians (AOH), a Catholic fraternity that was supported by the clergy and which had origins in earlier secret societies, namely the late eighteenth-century Defenders and the early nineteenth-century Ribbonmen.[37] Francis Joseph Bigger, who was effectively the spiritual godfather of the centenary in Ulster, had to navigate his way through the minefield of internal divisions in order to remain on good terms with all sides. Being a close friend of Devlin, he insisted that the articles that he wrote for the more radical *Shan Van Vocht* would appear under the cover of pseudonyms. In effect, this charade was a gesture of mock secrecy, as the authorship of Bigger's contributions, typically signed with the initial B. or the pen-name ENREI, was unmistakable.[38]

Emerging out of a hotbed of intrigue, the 'remarkable commemoration' of William Orr at St Mary's Hall in Belfast on 14 October 1897, which marked the opening of the centenary celebrations in Ulster, was billed as a 'magnificent demonstration', but it primarily confirmed Devlin's ability as a canny local political operator to outmanoeuvre his rivals. Banners of 'Remember Orr' and 'Who Fears to Speak of '98' were waved in a street procession alongside the parliamentary slogan 'Ulster wants Home Rule'. Devlin and Dillon shared the platform with the independent-minded anti-Parnellite O'Brien and the alienated Parnellite Timothy Harrington. Tellingly, the Parnellite leader Redmond, who was heavily invested in the commemorations in Dublin and his native Wexford, was not invited to this seemingly united front of constitutional nationalism in

[35] *Freeman's Journal*, 31 December 1897, p. 5; *Irish Examiner*, 1 January 1898, p. 7.

[36] Dónal McAnallen, 'Michael Cusack and the Revival of Gaelic Games in Ulster', *Irish Historical Studies*, 37, no. 145 (2010): pp. 23–47.

[37] McGee, *The IRB*, pp. 253–4; Kelly, *The Fenian Ideal*, pp. 112–13. For the genealogy of the AOH see Tom Garvin, 'Defenders, Ribbonmen and Others: Underground Political Networks in Pre-Famine Ireland', *Past and Present*, 96 (1982): pp. 133–55 (esp. 134 and 138).

[38] Morris, *Alice Milligan*, pp. 174–6.

Ulster. In addition, the Catholic Association, a body run by Bishop Henry Henry of Belfast, who was believed to have the support of the rival anti-Parnellite Healyite faction, was kept out. Most significantly, Fenians were noticeably absent.[39]

The 'national celebration' of Orr, which, according to the Dillonite press, 'supplied an excellent inauguration for the '98 Anniversary', was in fact a display of exclusion.[40] In an astounding feat of appropriating memory, constitutional nationalists—who were ideologically opposed to separatist republicanism—proclaimed themselves heirs to the republican United Irishmen, while militant republicans—who were committed to continuing the revolutionary struggle of the United Irishmen—were prevented from attending the anniversary of the republican protomartyr. Moreover, the crowds that gathered in Belfast to commemorate the Presbyterian United Irishmen were mainly working class Catholics, most of whom would not have had a direct lineage to the rebels of 1798.

The unionist descendants of the Presbyterian insurgents baulked at the public memorialization of the rebellion and it was soon evident that commemoration of 1798 was 'causing no little annoyance to the loyalist faction in Ulster'.[41] Unionist anxieties that the centenary would be 'defiantly commemorated' were exacerbated by nationalist expectations that Americans would be 'coming over in great numbers to aid in the commemoration and to help to stir up ill will'.[42] Although the threat of a mass wave of heritage tourism did not materialize, as Irish-American interest in commemoration was overshadowed in 1898 by preoccupation with the developments of the Spanish–American War, loyalist aggravation would continue to rise until it reached a boiling point during the centenary.

Towards midnight on 31 December 1897, members of '98 clubs heralded the opening of the centenary year with torchlight processions through the main streets of towns across Ireland. There were some minor confrontations with Orangemen on the outskirts of Catholic quarters in Belfast. More strikingly, an attack by 'Orange rowdies' on the demonstration in Lurgan, county Armagh, offered an early indication that the hostility of loyalists to the commemorations in Ulster could lead to violence.[43] Setting themselves apart from the main nationalist procession, delegates from the '98 clubs affiliated with the republican Ulster Provincial Council held an alternative event on top of Cave Hill. There, they lit a bonfire and pledged 'never to desist from the struggle until Ireland is a nation', in a symbolic renewal of the separatist oath made there in 1795 by Wolfe Tone and his northern associates, McCracken, Russell, and Neilson.[44]

During the first months of the centenary year, constitutional nationalists and republicans refused to cooperate with each other. 'Stirring appeals for unity' were made at a large gathering of Fenian '98 clubs in Dublin's Phoenix Park on 13 March 1898, at which an Ulster platform was staffed by representatives of the republican Ulster Provincial Council.[45] Yet, the following month, an overture from Devlin's Belfast and Ulster United Centenary Association, which had realized that 'it will be impossible to have a demonstration of a fitting character in Belfast in honour of the

---

[39] *Freeman's Journal*, 15 October 1897, pp. 4–6; see also Hepburn, *Catholic Belfast*, p. 55.
[40] *Weekly Freeman*, 23 October 1897, p. 1.
[41] *Freeman's Journal*, 19 October 1897, p. 4.   [42] *BNL*, 15 May 1897, p. 3.
[43] *Irish News*, 1 and 3 January 1898, pp. 5 and 3 (respectively).
[44] *SVV*, 3, no. 1 (January 1898), p. 14.   [45] *Weekly Freeman*, 19 March 1898, p. 3.

memory of the men of '98 unless those working for that purpose come to some agreement as the how it should be carried out', was left unanswered by the Ulster Provincial Council.[46]

A settlement was finally reached on a national level in May 1898, with the formation of an amalgamated '98 Committee in Dublin. The 'complete absence of any sectional differences and the earnest desire by all to unite with the one patriotic object' was announced in June 1898 at a meeting in the Rotunda in Dublin, where it was decided that the main event of the centenary would be the laying of the foundation stone for a monument of Wolfe Tone at St Stephens Green, scheduled for 15 August.[47] Following the rapprochement between constitutionalists and republicans in Dublin, the way was opened for cooperation between rival nationalist groups in Belfast. Preparations for the commemoration of the northern rebellion in June therefore only commenced at the very last moment. Despite the constant talk of unity and the necessity to remember Ninety-Eight, a good part of the centennial year had been squandered by infighting.

In addition to the divisions on political lines, nationalist women were subject to particular exclusion and had to struggle to assert their right to take part in the commemorations. In August 1897, Milligan and Carbery were elected as representatives for Ulster on the republican '98 Central Executive in Dublin. Alongside Maud Gonne, who was a much admired figure in advanced nationalist circles, they were the only women on the executive.[48]

The favoured female speaker of the mainstream northern '98 movement was the author Margaret Pender, whose popular novel *The Green Cockade* (originally serialized in 1886–7) was one of several works of Ninety-Eight historical fiction set in Ulster to be re-issued for the centenary.[49] Complying with Victorian literary gender sensibilities, she respectfully signed her books 'Mrs. M. T. Pender'. Mention of her name, according to the *Northern Patriot*, was 'sufficient to bring a large audience together' and when she addressed the '98 clubs it was 'intimated that lady friends of the members would be heartily welcome'.[50] Milligan was considered more of a firebrand and she frequently complained about being excluded from meetings of constitutional nationalists.[51] In the context of the fin de siècle, the *Shan Van Vocht* was a 'New Woman' magazine, which challenged male dominance of the public sphere, and Milligan's editorial line has been recognized as 'implicitly feminist'.[52]

[46] *Freeman's Journal*, 8 April 1898, p. 6.   [47] *Freeman's Journal*, 21 June 1898, pp. 5–6.

[48] *SVV*, 2, no. 8 (August 1897), pp. 151–2.

[49] Mrs M. T. Pender, *The Green Cockade: A Tale of Ulster in 'Ninety-Eight* (Dublin: Martine Lester, 1898); Mrs Charles Montague Clarke, *Strong as Death: A Story of the Irish Rebellion* (Aberdeen: Moran & Co., 1898; orig. edn 1875). In addition to publishing Ninety-Eight fiction, the Scottish-Irish publisher James Joseph Moran also authored a collection of short stories about 1798 that includes 'Maureen's Find', which tells about a farmer's daughter saving rebels after the Battle of Antrim and suffering from yeomen brutality; J. J. Moran, *Stories of the Irish Rebellion, 1798* (Aberdeen: Moran & Co. and London: Simpkin & Co., 1898), pp. 111–31.

[50] *Northern Patriot*, 1, no. 12 (9 October 1896); *Freeman's Journal*, 5 November 1897, p. 6. See also Diane Urquhart, *Women in Ulster Politics, 1890–1940: A History Not Yet Told* (Dublin: Irish Academic Press, 2000), p. 91; Hepburn, *A Past Apart*, p. 12.

[51] See Morris, *Alice Milligan*, pp. 203–4.

[52] Catherine Lynette Innes, *Woman and Nation in Irish Literature and Society, 1880–1935* (Athens: University of Georgia Press, 1993), p. 134; Steele, *Women, Press, and Politics*, p. 58.

In an 'Appeal to the Women of Ireland', the female editors of the *Shan Van Vocht* demanded an active role for women in the centennial commemorations, even though (in absence of suffrage) they 'are not called upon to have any opinion whatever as to who has the right to speak for Ireland in the British parliament'.[53] Insisting that 'women should be patriots—never mere partisans', Milligan established an Irish Women's Centenary Union, designed as 'a secure and neutral ground' for 'Irish women working together on a high and patriotic platform above the strife and turmoil'. She maintained that 'in the North especially many women will be found willing to join in the '98 celebration whose husbands, or other male relatives, for business reasons, could not possibly do so'. Furthermore, she argued that 'the Government may find it expedient or necessary to forbid some of the demonstrations which the men's committees will organise' but 'no power of law exists to prevent the celebration of '98 in the form which the department under women's management is to be arranged.' The areas of activity that were identified as particularly suitable for women included the exhibition of relics and the 'care of the neglected and uninscribed graves', beginning with the erection of a memorial tablet for Mary Ann McCracken at her grave in Belfast's Clifton Street Cemetery.[54] These memorial activities corresponded to the types of philanthropy that were considered acceptable for women in late Victorian society. As Karen Steele observed, the *Shan Van Vocht* 'advocated politically subversive if socially conventional roles for women in 1890s Ireland.'[55] If the engagement of women in nationalist politics was a cause of unease for the nationalist establishment, unionists were even more troubled by this development.

The Irish Women's Centenary Union had emerged out of an Irish Women's Association, which was formed in Belfast in 1894 through the efforts of Milligan and Jennie Armour—the wife of the radical Presbyterian minister Rev. J. B. Armour of Ballymoney—and with the support of another progressive Presbyterian minister, Rev. Richard Lyttle of Moneyrea. Committed 'to work for the great end of self-government for Ireland', the Irish Women's Association offered liberal nationalist-minded women, both Protestant and Catholic, an equivalent to the Liberal Women's Unionist Association, founded in Belfast in 1886 by Isabella Todd. More specifically, it was supposed to counter the impressive achievements of the ladies committee of the Irish Unionist Alliance, which had recently organized a petition signed by thousands of women in opposition to Home Rule.[56]

Nationalist women's activism was met with hostility from liberal unionists. The *Northern Whig*, though it supported the extension of the franchise to women, vehemently denounced women's support of Home Rule.[57] During the centenary, three

[53] *SVV*, 2, no. 6 (7 June 1897), p. 104.

[54] *SVV*, 2, no. 10 (October 1897), p. 192. See also Innes, *Woman and Nation in Irish Literature and Society*, pp. 134–6; Virginia Crossman, 'The *Shan Van Vocht*: Women, Republicanism, and the Commemoration of the 1798 Rebellion', *Eighteenth-Century Life*, 22, no. 3 (1998): pp. 133–4; Morris, *Alice Milligan*, pp. 206–10.

[55] Steele, *Women, Press, and Politics*, p. 43.

[56] *Freeman's Journal*, 3 November 1894, p. 7 and 16 February 1895, p. 7. For unionist women organizations see Urquhart, *Women in Ulster Politics*, p. 49; Rachel Ward, *Women, Unionism and Loyalism in Northern Ireland: From 'Tea-Makers' to Political Actors* (Dublin: Irish Academic Press, 2006), p. 115; Noel Armour, 'Isabella Tod and Liberal Unionism in Ulster, 1886–96', in *Irish Women's History*, edited by Alan Hayes and Diane Urquhart (Dublin: Irish Academic Press, 2004), pp. 72–87.

[57] *Northern Whig*, 5 and 14 November 1894, pp. 5 and 4 (respectively); see also Morris, *Alice Milligan*, pp. 153–8.

ladies '98 clubs were active in Belfast—two of which were named after Mary Ann McCracken and the other after the county Down heroine Betsy Gray. Although the ladies '98 clubs honoured northern Protestant women, the possibility that female solidarity might be extended to unionists and facilitate joint remembrance of 1798 was ruled out, as the Ulster branch of the Women's Liberal Unionist Association declared in advance its opposition to the centenary.[58]

Ironically, remembrance of the United Irishmen was marred by multi-layered disunity, which impeded commemoration. A summation of the main centennial power struggles reveals the complexity of the conflicts that came into play. Frictions between periphery and centre emerged, as nationalists in Belfast were resolute on having their own say, rather than passively receiving directives from a committee in Dublin, or acquiescing to the demands of nationalist politicians in London. To complicate matters, the leading role of Belfast as the provincial centre driving commemoration in Ulster was contested. Commemorative initiatives that originated in the city were not always welcome in the countryside of Antrim and Down, where the organizers of commemorations were obliged to give heed to local sensitivities. Contrary to the rapid rise of the centenary movement in Belfast, by the end of March 1898, no '98 clubs had yet been established in county Down and not all of the seven clubs in Antrim were actually active. Other areas with a larger Catholic population, such as county Tyrone which boasted sixteen clubs, showed much more enthusiasm in commemorating the rebellion in 1898, even though there had been no insurrection there in 1798.[59]

Quarrels abounded between radicals and moderates, as republicans and constitutionalists battled against each other and between themselves, for control of provincial commemoration. Disagreements were also fuelled by gender discrimination, as the demand of radical women to be allowed an active role in the commemorations was perceived as a threat to patriarchal power structures. In addition to the multiple internal struggles, sectarian animosities between Catholics and Protestants, which were endemic in Ulster, pitted enthusiastic nationalist commemoration against truculent unionist opposition. In consequence of these conflicts upon conflicts, plans to dedicate monuments and publicly celebrate the memory of the United Irishmen encountered manifold difficulties. These seething tensions came to the fore in advance of the main centennial event in Belfast and erupted in May 1898 at an incident outside Ballynahinch, at the site identified as the grave of Betsy Gray.

ICONOCLASM

Towards the centenary, there was a resurgence of interest in Betsy Gray, the local county Down heroine of 1798. The phenomenal success of W. G. Lyttle's *Betsy Gray; or, Hearts of Down* had initiated a movement to erect a monument on the site in

---

[58] *BNL*, 15 May 1897, p. 3.

[59] Return of '98 Centenary Clubs on 31 March 1898, Chief Secretary's Office, Police and Crime Division (Special), NAI CBS 15984/S. Monthly police reports show that the first '98 club in Down was established in May and that by June there were four active clubs in the county; from around that time police reports repeatedly noted that only five of the seven clubs in Antrim remained active.

Ballycreen, nearby Ballynahinch, where she was believed to have been killed and buried, alongside her two male companions. Robert Fowler Walker, the proprietor of Walker's Hotel in Ballynahinch, identified a potential market in heritage tourism and placed an advertisement in Lyttle's book. He went on to become the treasurer of the subscription fund for the monument. The involvement of a prominent local figure such as Walker, who was a Commissioner for taking Affidavits and a member of the Church of Ireland, is indicative of Betsy Gray's wide appeal, which extended beyond Presbyterians.[60] Nationalists from further afield also discovered an interest in the '98 folk heroine.

In May 1896, the *Shan Van Vocht* published 'The Story of Betsy Gray', which described 'the pathetic tragedy of her cruel death by the hireling minions of England' in a style intended to 'make the coldest heart bleed with pity and indignation'. The article, probably written by Milligan, elevated the local county Down heroine to the supreme status of 'Ireland's Joan of Arc', proclaiming that 'her devotion to country and her bravery in battle are unsurpassed', and comparing her to such figures as the biblical warrior prophetess Deborah and the ancient Briton warrior queen Boadicea.[61] This hagiographic magnification entered into the nationalist lexicon. A St Patrick's Day special issue of the *Weekly Freeman*, dedicated to the 1798 centenary, hailed the 'Ulster heroine' as an 'Irish Joan of Arc'.[62] Comparisons to legendary heroines were repeated in subsequent years at nationalist gatherings, such as a speech on the 'Influence of the Irish Woman on the National Movement', delivered in 1906 by James Reidy, assistant editor of the *Gaelic American* newspaper, to the Brooklyn Gaelic Society and circulated as a pamphlet.[63] Betsy Gray was undergoing canonization as a national, rather than local, heroine.

From June through to September 1896, the *Northern Patriot* serialized 'The Heroine of Ardes' by Eblana, which was the pseudonym of Teresa J. Rooney, a popular Dublin writer of romantic historical fiction. It recounted the story of the rebellion in county Down up to the defeat at Ballynahinch and the subsequent death of Elizabeth Grey [Betsy Gray] at the hands of 'the myrmidons of the foreign power which was regaining its slippery grasp upon her country', comparing the outrage to the atrocities in Bulgaria and Armenia that featured in the press at the time.[64] Centennial '98 clubs were named after the heroine in such faraway places as Kildalkey in county Meath and Lahinch in county Clare, where a street was also re-named after her in the town of Kilrush.[65]

---

[60] Lyttle, *Betsy Gray*, 3rd edn (1894), ch. 41, p. 159n. Occupational and confessional details on R. F. Walker, who—like W. G. Lyttle—was in his early fifties at the time, can be found in *The Belfast and Province of Ulster Directory* (Belfast: James Alexander Henderson, 1896), pp. 67–8 and in the 1901 census. His good relations with Presbyterians is evident in a contribution to the manse fund of the First Ballynahinch Presbyterian Church; *BNL*, 29 June 1894, p. 7.

[61] *SVV*, vol. 1, no. 5 (1 May 1896), pp. 97–8.

[62] *Weekly Freeman*, 12 March 1898, supplement, pp. 1–2.

[63] *The Influence of the Irish Woman on the National Movement: Lecture Delivered by James Reidy, of New York, before the Brooklyn Gaelic Society, on Sunday Evening, March 18, 1906* (Brooklyn, N.Y.: s.n., 1906), p. 4; see also Mary C. Kelly, *The Shamrock and the Lily: The New York Irish and the Creation of a Transatlantic Identity, 1845–1921* (New York: Peter Lang, 2005), p. 67.

[64] *Northern Patriot*, 1, no. 8 (June 1896), pp. 116–17; no. 9 (July), pp. 130–1; no. 10 (August), pp. 146–7; no. 11 (September): pp. 162–3.

[65] *Meath Chronicle*, 11 June 1898, p. 3; *Freeman's Journal*, 1 March and 9 September 1898, pp. 5 and 7 (respectively).

A mare named Betsy Gray competed on race tracks, inadvertently bringing the heroine's name to the attention of a large public of sporting and gambling enthusiasts, who were not necessarily politically minded.[66] Betsy Gray's fame was also promoted abroad and featured in an article by Mary Barry O'Delany in a series on Irish martyrology published in *L'Irlande Libre*, Maud Gonne's 'Organ of Irish Nationalists in France', which was issued from the appropriately named address of Rue de Martyres in Paris.[67]

Northern nationalists began to regularly visit the site of the unmarked grave. It was located on the land of Samuel Armstrong, a Presbyterian farmer who could confirm for them the precise location, 'so there is no shadow of doubt as to where the grave of Betsy lies'. Armstrong had 'talked in his boyhood with the men who had assisted at the burial of the martyred dead' and could relate a 'touching episode hitherto unrecorded', which recalled how on the evening of the fateful day his uncle was taken by his mother to witness the mutilated corpses of Betsy and her companions, one of them 'still twitching in the last agonies of death'.[68] This story was an elaboration on a detail in Lyttle's novel, which told how a boy named Matthew Armstrong discovered the 'dead and mutilated bodies'. It also appeared in the book as a verse of a ballad:

> That night the murdered three were found,
> By Matthew Armstrong—then a lad;
> Who quickly running to his home,
> Related there his tidings sad.[69]

The oral affirmation provided by the local farmer is reminiscent of Alex Haley's fieldwork for his bestseller *Roots* (1976), which demonstrated that subaltern history could be recovered through oral tradition, though later research revealed that in Haley's interview with a local amateur *griot* [traditional history-teller] 'details of a story were made up or significantly embellished' so as to satisfy his expectations.[70] When Armstrong recounted family traditions to nationalist visitors, he indulged the anticipations of an eager audience, seeking authentication of the Betsy Gray legend.

The Betsy Gray burial site was among the 'Patriot Graves' visited on the first Decoration Day, 21 June 1896, by a party of women from Moneyrea, county Down, led by Rev. Richard Lyttle. Floral crosses were placed on the grave, one in honour of Betsy Gray by Milligan and Carbery and another 'in memory of the peasant heroes of Down', from the C. J. Kickham Society.[71] Grandiose aspirations to raise 'a statue of the noble and fearless maid, robed in her own beloved green, mounted on her charger and brandishing her patriot sword, as when she led the true hearts of Down to glorious battle' were set aside in order to achieve the more attainable goal of erecting a 'suitable

---

[66] See *BNL*, 24 February 1897; 7, 9, 10, 11 March 1898; 2 September 1898.

[67] *L'Irlande Libre*, 2, no. 7 (July 1898).

[68] *SVV*, vol. 1, no. 5 (1 May 1896), p. 98.

[69] Lyttle, *Betsy Gray*, chs 40 and 41. Matthew Armstrong is described as the uncle of Samuel Armstrong, the owner of the farm at the time the novel was written.

[70] Donald R. Wright, 'Uprooting Kunta Kinte: On the Perils of Relying on Encyclopedic Informants', *History in Africa*, 8 (1981): pp. 205–17; cf. Alex Haley, 'Black History, Oral History, and Genealogy', *Oral History Review*, 1, no. 1 (1973): pp. 1–25.

[71] *SVV*, 1, no. 7 (July 1896), pp. 139–40.

memorial of Irish granite'.[72] These plans came to fruition remarkably soon thanks to the unexpected appearance of a James Gray from London, who claimed to be a relative of the heroine and offered to finance the monument. The benefactor's proposal was readily accepted, even though his genealogical assertion that Betsy was the daughter of John and Rebecca Gray, Church of Ireland Anglicans from a townland in the parish of Garvaghy (later identified as Tullyniskey, 14 kilometres west of Ballynahinch), contradicted earlier traditions that linked the heroine with Killinchy (19 kilometres east of Ballynahinch), or alternatively with Six Road Ends (33 kilometres north-east of Ballynahinch).[73]

A modest monument, consisting of a 'polished oblong block, with margined sides resting on chamfered plinth, and surmounted with peaked terminal', was constructed in August 1896 and enclosed within iron railings. The choice of inscription tactfully avoided providing an interpretative text that might prove divisive and simply named the subjects of commemoration—'Elizabeth Gray, George Gray, William Boal, 13th June, 1798', while also endorsing on the reverse side the questionable pedigree of the sponsor—'Erected by James Gray, grandnephew of Elizabeth and George Gray, 1896.' The local appeal of this simple and uncontroversial design is apparent in the sale of cabinet photographs of the monument by the constructors at the Downpatrick and Newtownards Monumental Works (Fig. 5.2).[74] Nationalists were obliged to forgo their desires for a stirring inscription, which would have brazenly described the death of the heroine and her companions as 'foully murdered by Orange yeomen'.[75]

This monument stood out as the only centennial memorial dedicated to a heroine of Ninety-Eight. As pointed out by John R. Gillis in a wider context, 'national commemorations were largely the preserve of male elites' and consequently 'the history of real women was systematically forgotten'.[76] Contemporary sources tended to overlook the involvement of women in the 1798 rebellion and this neglect was continued in historiography.[77] Nonetheless, the presence of women amongst the rebels ignited loyalist fantasies. At Ballynahinch it was rumoured that 'a pair of very handsome women, who were fantastically dressed in green and other silks, one of whom they called the Goddess of Liberty and the other of Reason, both of which unhappy women were shot in the conflict.'[78] Although the participation of an Elizabeth (Betsy) Gray in the Battle of Ballynahinch cannot be positively corroborated, the near-contemporary

---

[72] *SVV*, 1, no. 5 (May 1896), p. 98.

[73] Killinchy was first mentioned as Betsy Gray's place of origin by Mary Ann McCracken and this location was endorsed by William McComb; Madden Papers, TCD 873/163; *McComb's Guide to Belfast*, pp. 130–2. The case for Six Road Ends was put forward by Lyttle, on the authority of Hans Gray Macartney, who claimed to be the son of a cousin of Betsy Gray and identified her father as Hans Gray of Granshaw [Gransha], near Bangor; Lyttle, *Betsy Gray*, ch. 1, fn. See also Colin Johnston Robb, 'Where Was Betsy Born' and H. J. Macartney, 'Betsy Gray's Birthplace', *Mourne Observer*, 18 and 25 October 1968, p. 10 (respectively); Lyttle, *Betsy Gray* (1968 edn), appendix, pp. 185–91; McCoy, *Ulster's Joan of Arc*, pp. 36–48.

[74] *BNL*, 22 August 1896, p. 3; *Down Recorder*, 22 August 1896.

[75] Letter by Robert Hanna in the *Nation*, 24 April 1897, p. 10.

[76] John R. Gillis, 'Memory and Identity: The History of a Relationship', in *Commemorations: The Politics of National Identity*, edited by John R. Gillis (Princeton: Princeton University Press, 1994), p. 10.

[77] See Dáire Keogh, 'The Women of 1798: Explaining the Silence', in *1798: A Bicentenary Perspective*, edited by Thomas Bartlett, David Dickson, Dáire Keogh, and Kevin Whelan (Dublin: Four Courts Press, 2003), pp. 512–28.

[78] *Freeman's Journal*, 16 June 1798, p. 3.

Fig. 5.2. Betsy Gray monument

Constructed in Ballycreen (near Ballynahinch) in August 1896, following a fundraising campaign initiated by the enthusiastic responses to Lyttle's novel, the monument to Betsy Gray and her two companions was destroyed in May 1898.

Originally published in the *Mourne Observer*, 5 July 1968 and reproduced by the National Library of Ireland with the newspapers permission.

memoir of Rev. Thomas Ledlie Birch noted that 'in scouring the country, the 22nd dragoons shot a number of fleeing rebels, among whom there was a young woman,' so that the story of her death was plausible.[79] Moreover, the attendance of 'a considerable number of females, chiefly servants, or the daughters or wives of cottiers or small farmers' at the rebel camp was later recalled by an eye-witness, James Thomson, who noted that 'it is said that two or three of them remained on the field, during the battle, submitting to their share of its labours and dangers, and performing as valiant deeds as the men.'[80]

In contrast to the limited documentary record, recollections of female participation in the rebellion were embroidered in folklore.[81] This social memory, however, was not reflected in the memorials of the 1798 centenary, best typified by the statues in Wexford of an anonymous pikeman. This iconic image was conceived by the Ulster-born sculptor Oliver Sheppard as a collective—essentially male—representation of the rebels.[82] Another emblematic form, common among the centennial monuments, was

[79] Birch, *A Letter from an Irish Emigrant*, p. 14.
[80] *Belfast Magazine and Literary Journal*, 1, no. 1 (1825), p. 57.
[81] Anna Kinsella, 'Nineteenth-Century Perspectives: The Women of 1798 in Folk Memory and Ballads', in *The Women of 1798*, edited by Dáire Keogh and Nicholas Furlong (Dublin: Four Courts Press, 1998), pp. 187–200; see also Beiner, *Remembering the Year of the French*, pp. 185–97.
[82] See John Turpin, 'Oliver Sheppard's 1798 Memorials', *Irish Arts Review Yearbook* (1990/1): pp. 71–80; John Turpin, '1798, 1898 & the Political Implications of Sheppard's Monuments', *History Ireland*, 6, no. 2 (1998): pp. 44–8; also John Turpin, *Oliver Sheppard, 1865–1941: Symbolist Sculptor of the Irish Cultural Revival* (Dublin: Four Courts, 2000), pp. 105–13.

the figure of Erin. Yet, this romantic female representation of Ireland, set in the mould of other such national monuments of allegorical maidens (e.g. Britannia, Germania, or Marianne), had little to do with local traditions of women rebels.[83] For this reason, the Betsy Gray monument had particular significance for the nationalist women involved in the commemorations in Ulster.

Members of the Irish Women's Centenary Union made an excursion to the site of the Betsy Gray monument on 21 September 1897. Among them, Milligan later recalled, was a 'shopkeeper from Falls Road, who had been maid to Miss Mary McCracken' and could recount 'anecdotes of "Ould Mary" and the Teelings'. In anticipation of additional visits, they raised a subscription to pay for a turnstile on the road, which would enable better access to the path that led to the site.[84] Visitors mainly came from Belfast, as nationalists in county Down were slower to organize and, by May 1898, only two 'fairly active' '98 clubs had been formed in the county.[85] According to the local unionist newspaper and a correspondent of the Belfast unionist press, the 'previously comparatively unknown' site was now 'visited by a good many people out of curiosity'. At first, it seemed that the sightseers were welcomed and that 'no distinction was ever made, and no visitor was ever asked to what particular political party he belonged.'[86] Yet, as the centenary progressed, the influx of commemorative tourists increasingly aggravated local residents.

East Down was an electoral division with a majority of 88 per cent Protestants.[87] Accordingly, it was a steadfast unionist constituency, represented in parliament from 1890, by the former Presbyterian minister James Alexander Rentoul, who was returned unopposed in three consecutive general elections.[88] In private, Rentoul was not averse to remembrance of 1798. He wrote in his memoirs that, once Home Rule was defeated, he could see no reason why 'Who Fears to Speak of '98', the song most associated with the memory of the United Irishmen, 'might not be sung in Unionist circles'.[89] However, such thoughts could not be expressed in public. Unionists considered the preparations for the centenary an obtrusive menace and complained that:

> The country is permeated with '98 Clubs; demonstrations are threatened; monuments to the memory of conspicuous rebels are proposed; thousands of visitors from other lands are coming to take part in the proceedings; and the Government sits in silence upon the fence.[90]

---

[83] Hill, *Irish Public Sculpture*, pp. 128–32; cf. Marina Warner, *Monuments & Maidens: The Allegory of the Female Form* (London: Weidenfeld & Nicolson, 1985).

[84] *SVV*, vol. 2, no. 10 (October 1897), p. 153. Four decades later, Milligan could vividly recall the visit, though she mistakenly dated it to 1898; *Irish Press*, 27 June 1939, p. 9.

[85] RIC County Down District Inspector's Report, Downpatrick, 1 June 1898, Chief Secretary's Office, Police and Crime Division (Special), TNA CO 904/68/462.

[86] *Down Recorder*, 7 May 1898; *Belfast Weekly Telegraph*, 7 May 1898, p. 7.

[87] *Census of Ireland for the Year 1891*, vol. 3, table XXIX ('Religious professions and sexes of the inhabitants of parliamentary divisions'), p. 560.

[88] Brian Walker, *Parliamentary Election Results in Ireland, 1801–1922* (Dublin: Royal Irish Academy, 1978), p. 342; Brian Walker, 'Landowners and Parliamentary Elections in County Down, 1801–1921', in *Down: History & Society*, edited by Lindsay Proudfoot (Dublin: Geography Publications, 1997), p. 319.

[89] James Alexander Rentoul, *Stray Thoughts and Memories*, edited by L. Rentoul (London: Leonard Parsons, 1921), p. 211.

[90] *BNL*, 28 April 1898, p. 5.

In particular, they frowned upon excursions of 'charabanc Nationalists' to sites associated with rebellion.[91] Consternation in the area of Ballynahinch intensified as noticeably 'large parties' of nationalists frequented the Betsy Gray monument and 'in the most audacious way decorated the grave with seditious emblems and mottoes'.[92] This public display of subversion was unacceptable to loyalists, even for those who still recalled in private that their own ancestors had participated in the rebellion.

The offence caused by commemorative visits did not only derive from political differences. The inhabitants of the Ballynahinch district were overwhelmingly Protestant (73 per cent), and the majority among them were Presbyterian (51 per cent).[93] The Sunday visits of Belfast Catholics, who availed of cheap weekend rail tickets, were perceived by many Protestants as a violation of the Sabbath. Strict observance of the Lord's Day had long been one of the tenets of Ulster Presbyterianism and this doctrine was strengthened in the evangelical revival which swept Ulster in 1859.[94] From its early days, the Ulster Railway Company encountered opposition from the Belfast Presbytery, which took a fervent stance against Sunday leisure travel, with one minister going so far as to declare that the railway 'is sending souls to the devil at the rate of 6d a piece'.[95]

Since Protestant evangelicalism in Ulster allied itself with unionism, attitudes towards secular activities on Sundays became a shibboleth that differentiated unionists from nationalists. A speaker at a convention of the Irish Nonconformist Unionist Association in 1888 lambasted the nationalist rallies held on Sundays, 'with the accompaniment of bands playing political and party tunes—often to the annoyance and disturbance of worshipping Protestants.'[96] Moreover, the nationalist sport events of the GAA, which were held on Sundays, were met in north-east Ulster with opposition that came to a head in 1898.[97] On the background of this pre-existing animosity, it was noted locally that, in response to the Sunday excursions to the Betsy Gray site, 'feeling is very strong on this subject in this neighbourhood, and the greatest indignation is expressed at this attempt to introduce a Southern Sunday into our quiet Northern district.'[98]

In offering meditations on the fate of monuments in times of transition, Sanford Levinson mused that 'perhaps the most important question is what happens to public space when the political and cultural cleavages within a given society are fully manifested.'[99] Samuel Armstrong, the farmer who owned the land, had been 'most courteous

[91] Collins, *Who Fears to Speak*, p. 43.
[92] *Down Recorder*, 7 May 1898; *Belfast Weekly Telegraph*, 7 May 1898, p. 7.
[93] According to the 1901 census, out of the 2,834 people in the Ballynahinch District Electoral Division, 1,438 were Presbyterians, 496 Episcopalians, 87 Methodists, and 18 'others', compared with 768 Catholics; *Census of Ireland for the Year 1901*, vol. 3, Part 2, table XXXIII ('Religious professions and education of the people by county districts and district electoral divisions'), p. 153.
[94] Andrew R. Holmes, *The Shaping of Ulster Presbyterian Belief and Practice, 1770–1840* (Oxford and New York: Oxford University Press, 2006), pp. 57–77. The official account of the 1859 revival is littered with references to the increase in Sabbath observance; Gibson, *The Year of Grace, passim*.
[95] Kevin Murray, *The Great Northern Railway (Ireland) Past, Present & Future* (Dublin, 1944), p. 4; W. A. McCutcheon, *The Industrial Archaeology of Northern Ireland* (Belfast: Great Northern Railway Company, 1980), p. 190.
[96] Hempton and Hill, *Evangelical Protestantism*, p. 175.
[97] McAnallen, 'Michael Cusack', pp. 33, 37–9, and 42.
[98] *Belfast Weekly Telegraph*, 7 May 1898, p. 7.
[99] Sanford Levinson, *Written in Stone: Public Monuments in Changing Societies* (Durham, N.C.: Duke University Press, 1998), p. 23.

to the strangers making a pilgrimage to this romantic spot on his property', and even delivered a short address at a commemorative ceremony in 1896, subsequently giving his permission for the monument to be placed there.[100] This largesse was not shared by his 20-year-old son Robert, who had inherited the farm by 1898. As disapproval of the visits of 'extreme Nationalists' spiralled in the neighbourhood, Robert Armstrong consulted a solicitor and decided to refuse permission of entry to the site of the monument, locking the gates, securing the fences, and notifying the police that 'he would prevent trespass'.[101] This act of exclusion set the ground for an inevitable clash.

On Sunday, 1 May 1898, a loyalist crowd from the surrounding area assembled at the train station, awaiting a confrontation with nationalists from Belfast, who were expected to arrive in great numbers, accompanied by music bands. It transpired that the dreaded visitors consisted of only twenty-two women—thirteen from the Mary McCracken '98 Centenary Club and nine from the Mary McCracken Decorative Club—escorted by five men from assorted '98 clubs. Although the Ballynahinch police force had received reinforcements from Downpatrick, they were unable to guarantee safe access to the monument. The women were obliged to stay behind, while the attempts of the men to lay wreaths at the site were thwarted by a substantial hostile mob (estimated by the police at 'about 150', though the press floated figures which ranged between 300 and 700). In the riot that ensued, the Betsy Gray monument was destroyed.[102]

It appears that unrest at the site occurred in two stages. Sometime between 30 April and 1 May, several hours before the visitors from Belfast arrived at the train station, the memorial was decorated with flowers placed by local nationalists. The inscription on a wreath in the figure of Erin, placed by 'the Nationalists of Ballynahinch', reflected on the sacrifice of local rebels: 'The blood of the heroes of Down has not been shed in a lost cause. Remember Monroe.' Another wreath, from 'the Nationalist ladies of Ballynahinch', was devoted exclusively to the heroine: 'Let the martyrdom, of Betsy Gray nerve us to be brave.' Within a short time, these decorations were disposed of by loyalist vigilantes, branded 'Orange sentinels' by the nationalist *Irish News*. Whereas some damage was caused to the memorial site in the earlier encounter between opponent local parties, the intensity of violence escalated to uncontainable frenzy later that day in the confrontation with the outsiders, during which the monument was smashed to pieces and its railings removed.[103]

The involvement of women was central to the incident. Their participation in a politically contentious event was apparently regarded a transgression of social norms by the locals. For the nationalist press, on the other hand, the disrespect showed to the

---

[100] *SVV*, 1, no. 5 (May 1896), p. 98; *Northern Patriot*, vol. 1, no. 9 (July 1896), p. 139.

[101] RIC County Down District Inspector's Report, Downpatrick, Co. Down, 11 May 1898; NAI CSORP/1898/2206 PQ; *Down Recorder*, 7 May 1898. The 1901 census lists Robert Armstrong aged 23.

[102] RIC County Down District Inspector's Report, NAI CSORP/1898/2206 PQ; 'Disturbances at Ballynahinch: Desecration of Betsy Gray's Grave', Intelligence Notes, B Series, no. 33 (May 1898), p. 24, TNA CO 903/6. For nationalist reports see *Irish News*, 2 and 3 May 1898, pp. 4 and 8 respectively [the second article was republished in the *Irish Weekly and Ulster Examiner*, 7 May 1898, p. 1]; *Anglo-Celt*, 7 May 1898, p. 3; *Freeman's Journal*, 3 and 7 May 1898, pp. 3–4 and 3 respectively; *Weekly Freeman*, 7 May 1898, p. 3. For unionist reports see *Belfast Evening Telegraph*, 5 May 1898 [republished in *Belfast Weekly Telegraph*, 7 May 1898, p. 7]; *Down Recorder*, 7 and 14 May 1898.

[103] Intelligence Notes, B Series, no. 33 (May 1898), p. 24, TNA CO 903/6; *Irish News*, 3 May 1898, p. 8; *Down Recorder*, 7 May 1898; *Irish Weekly*, 7 May 1898, p. 1.

visiting womenfolk who 'were hooted all the way on the return to the station', was inexcusable. The *Weekly Freeman* claimed, with some exaggeration, that the women had been 'threatened, insulted, and actually assaulted' in a display of blackguardism that went 'really beyond ordinary condemnation'. The sense of moral outrage was even more pronounced when juxtaposed with reminders of the villainy perpetrated against Betsy Gray at that very site.[104] Although the reportage referred only to male assailants, some loyalist women may also have been involved in the scuffle. It was later remembered that among the 'big powerful men' who wrecked the Betsy Gray monument, there was 'a big heavy woman, who was carrying a 16lb sledge hammer'.[105]

The visiting nationalists were resolute not to lose face. After they were repelled from the site of the monument, they determinedly headed into the town of Ballynahinch to celebrate mass at St Patrick's church, then proceeded on brakes and cars to make a tour of the 1798 battlefield sites, and returned for dinner at the Temperance Hotel, where a Boal and Gray '98 Centenary Club was established at a 'speedily convened meeting' of local nationalists. The *Irish News* could therefore boast of 'organised Orange rowdyism frustrated'.[106] Yet the extent of the havoc was undeniable. Nationalist papers offered lurid accounts of how the loyalist mob had 'burst into the graveyard, pulled down the headstone and railings that were around the grave, and decorated themselves with the flowers that were on the wreaths and wore them through Ballynahinch, shouting about the Pope, '98, and the Fenians from Belfast.'[107] The 'Orange rowdies' were reputedly not content 'to carry away parts of the broken memorial and flowers from the wreaths which were placed there during the morning' and 'their desecration went so far as to have mock pikes to plough into the grave of the heroes of '98.'[108] This somewhat Dionysian scene was satirized by Phil Blake, the illustrator of the *Weekly Freeman*, in a cartoon on 'Orange Rowdyism at Ballynahinch', which depicted a savage-looking Orangeman, adorned in wreaths and brandishing a cane, dancing on the grave of Betsy Gray (Fig. 5.3).[109] The vulgar carnivalesque character of this iconoclastic vandalism deliberately mocked the inherent self-reverence of commemoration.

In its essence, commemoration is self-interested. As put by the Northern Irish literary critic Edna Longley: 'Commemorations are as selective as sympathies. They honour *our* dead, not *your* dead.'[110] Longley also pointed out that 'rhetorical history', of the kind that flaunts exclusivist historical traditions, provokes 'rhetorical umbrage'— manifested as 'extreme readiness to be annoyed', which can lead to 'readiness to desecrate inscriptions, monuments, statues, headstones, wreaths and other memorials. Such actions counter-symbolically erase the Other's historical narrative, culture, territorial presence.'[111] Whereas commemoration is usually considered an expression of

---

[104] *Weekly Freeman*, 7 May 1898, p. 4; cf. *Freeman's Journal*, 7 May 1898, p. 3 (appears also in *Anglo-Celt*, 7 May 1898, p. 3).
[105] *Mourne Observer*, 19 July 1968, p. 9.   [106] *Irish News*, 3 May 1898, p. 8.
[107] *Irish News*, 2 May 1898, p. 4; reproduced also in *Freeman's Journal*, 3 May 1898, pp. 3–4.
[108] *Irish News*, 2 and 3 May 1898, pp. 4 and 8 respectively.
[109] *Weekly Freeman*, 7 May 1898, p. 4.
[110] Edna Longley, 'The Rising, the Somme and Irish Memory', in *Revising the Rising*, edited by Máirin Ní Dhonnchadha and Theo Dorgan (Derry: Field Day, 1991), p. 29.
[111] Edna Longley, 'Northern Ireland: Commemoration, Elegy, Forgetting', in *History and Memory in Modern Ireland*, edited by Ian McBride (Cambridge and New York: Cambridge University Press, 2001), p. 231.

ORANGE ROWDYISM AT BALLINAHINCH.

The mild and gentle Orangemen, after pulling down the railings around the grave of Betsey Grey, decorated themselves with wreaths.

Fig. 5.3. 'Orange Rowdyism at Ballynahinch'

A nationalist cartoon by Phil Blake mocked the riots that resulted in the destruction of the monument to Betsy Gray.

Published in the *Weekly Freeman*, 7 May 1898.

popular culture, for those who take offence and feel excluded from the festivities it is a flagrant *unpopular* culture. Hence, aggravated aversion to commemorating often produces an aggressive reaction in the form of decommemorating.

In decommemorating Betsy Gray, the various strands of centennial conflicts were enmeshed so that insiders—Protestant, and more specifically Presbyterian, loyalists from around Ballynahinch—objected to the celebration of the local heroine by outsiders—Catholic nationalists, and in particular republican women (who were not necessary Catholic), coming from Belfast. Heritage, as observed by David Lowenthal, 'foments conflict between rival claimants, rival visions of past and present, and rival views of truth and error'.[112] The conflict at Ballynahinch was not simply the outcome of efforts to deny remembrance but, at its core, was a struggle over ownership and appropriation of inherited memory.

Significantly, the Betsy Gray memorial was a public monument located on private property. Armstrong's decision to treat the visitors as trespassers was indicative of a more general attitude, which maintained that entitlement to the memory of Betsy Gray belonged first and foremost to the local community and that, in the polarized conditions of the centenary, outsiders were no longer welcome. The affronted visitors complained that their right of entry to the site had been arbitrarily withdrawn, but the local unionist press showed an understanding of the motivations of 'impulsive persons who regarded the virtual appropriation of the grave by the Nationalists as a piece of unwarrantable presumption'.[113] A local correspondent for the *Belfast Evening Telegraph* opined that 'the incident will have done good, however, if it teaches our Nationalist friends this lesson—not to presume too far on good nature, and to remember that we are living in a loyal and peaceable country.'[114] Competition over exploitation of the cultural capital of social memory had generated conflicting passions of 'commemorative possessiveness' and 'commemorative envy', to re-adapt terms introduced by Peter Novick in his study of Holocaust memory in American culture.[115] While an inside group zealously guarded its ownership of local traditions, insisting that they should be marked in a subdued and private form that corresponded to practices of social forgetting, an outside group assertively presented a claim to these traditions, with the intention of openly celebrating memory in public.

Nationalist politicians tried to get mileage out of the scandalous occurrence at Ballynahinch. William Redmond, Parnellite MP for East Clare (and younger brother of John Redmond), raised the matter in Westminster in a parliamentary query to the Chief Secretary, Gerald Balfour. He was joined in the short debate by Daniel Macaleese, anti-Parnellite MP for North Monaghan (and originally from Randalstown in county Antrim), who asked whether the 'police have the names of the miscreants who perpetrated this abominable outrage'. Redmond pressed on, demanding to know if the police would be instructed to 'make inquiries into what is regarded in the district as a sacrilegious outrage'. Balfour was unmoved by the sensationalist rhetoric and replied

---

[112] David Lowenthal, *The Heritage Crusade and the Spoils of History* (Cambridge and New York: Cambridge University Press, 1998), p. 227.
[113] *Down Recorder*, 7 May 1898.
[114] *Belfast Evening Telegraph*, 5 May 1898; republished in Belfast Weekly Telegraph, 7 May 1898, p. 7.
[115] Peter Novick, *The Holocaust in American Life* (Boston: Houghton Mifflin, 1999), p. 197.

that 'things will, no doubt, take their usual course.'[116] As far as the government was concerned, the matter was closed. Two months later, the amateur historian and anti-Parnellite MP for South Donegal John Gordon Swift MacNeill denounced the 'gross act of desecration' and condemned the Chief Secretary's 'mincing accounts' for 'endeavouring to condone the excessive loyalty of the ruffians who destroyed the tomb'.[117] Beyond these shrill statements, the politicians made little more of the events at Ballynahinch. Their attention was soon diverted to the many other commemorative celebrations that summer, so that the event was effectively forgotten on a national level. Even the *Shan Van Vocht*, which was largely responsible for sparking interest in the memorial site among nationalists, made no mention of the incident in its review of significant centennial events that had occurred in May.[118]

By contrast, the sheer audacity of how the monument had been wrecked ensured that it would be remembered locally. Among the first resolutions of the Gray and Boal '98 club, which had been established in Ballynahinch immediately after the riot, was to 'condemn in the strongest language the vandalism and blackguardism of the ruffianly horde'.[119] The denunciation of the 'cowardly and diabolical action of those who demolished the monument erected over the grave of Betsy Gray' was reiterated in subsequent meetings, such as a large demonstration in Edendariff, county Down (6 kilometres south of Ballynahinch), at the end of May 1898, so that recollection of the destruction was maintained through repetition.[120] It is worthy of note that this memory was not confined solely to the local nationalist community.

At first glance, the controversy over the memorial of Betsy Gray monument appears to signify clear intent on the part of local Presbyterian unionists, many of whose ancestors had been United Irishmen, to disassociate themselves from the memory of 1798. As put by Peter Collins, 'to most northern Loyalists she represented the misguided, or indeed traitorous, past of sections of their community and something to be exorcised rather than commemorated.'[121] In this view, the demolition of the monument at a time when nationalists were engrossed in flagrant remembrance represented a thorough purging of memory of the rebellion by those who now found its commemoration intolerable. However, such an interpretation underestimates the complexities entailed in the act of decommemorating.

The assumption that the obliteration of a monument marks an effacement of memory has been vigorously challenged by innovative scholarship on the destruction of statues in late antiquity, labelled by classicists '*damnatio memoriae*'. Peter Stewart pointed out that '*damnatio memoriae* was not exactly about the destruction of memory, though ancient sources insist that it was...what actually occurred was a highly symbolic, universal display of pantomime forgetfulness.'[122] Similarly, Charles Hedrick observed that '*damnatio memoriae* did not negate historical traces, but created gestures which served to *dishonour* the record of the person and so, in an oblique way, to

[116] *Hansard House of Commons Debates*, 12 May 1898, 4th ser., vol. 57, columns 1089–90; reported in *Irish Times*, 13 May 1898, p. 5; *North Down Herald*, 13 May 1898, p. 8.
[117] *Freeman's Journal*, 12 July 1898, p. 6.   [118] *SVV*, 3, no. 6 (June 1898), pp. 106–7.
[119] *Irish Weekly and Ulster Examiner*, 14 May 1898, p. 1.
[120] *Irish Weekly and Ulster Examiner*, 28 May 1898, p. 3.
[121] Collins, *Who Fears to Speak*, p. 43.
[122] Peter Stewart, 'The Destruction of Statues in Late Antiquity', in *Constructing Identities in Late Antiquity*, edited by Richard Miles (London and New York: Routledge, 1999), p. 167.

confirm memory. Thus it is more accurate to describe the attack as a *damnatio* than an *abolitio memoriae*.'[123] Whereas discussion of practices of *damnatio memoriae* in ancient Rome has often been limited to formal acts of censure, in practice there was a much wider range of informal 'memory sanctions'.[124] Likewise, the Betsy Gray monument was destroyed in a spontaneous riot, which was not orchestrated from above, despite allegations voiced in the nationalist press that held the leadership of the Orange Order responsible.[125]

As Stewart has shown for ancient Rome, 'the destruction of statues was only loosely subject to centralized control.' Although it is possible to distinguish, *pace* the Hungarian-German historian Thomas Pekáry, between official acts of proscribing monuments and spontaneous statue-destruction, even within the ostensibly mindless violence of 'statue-riots', patterns of recurring behaviour can be discerned. When irate crowds vent their rage by chanting and shouting, then topple a statue, mutilate it, drag it in public, and finally dispose of it in a symbolic negation of its symbolism, their uncoordinated iconoclasm presents a cohesive spectacle of sham oblivion, which actually does not signify the eradication of memory.[126] Defacement, as explained by the anthropologist Michael Taussig, enhances fascination and, through negation, unmasks a 'public secret', defined by Taussig as 'that which is generally known, but cannot be articulated'.[127] Therefore, decommemorating, being an outward expression of social forgetting, is misleading. It may seem to be an act of disassociation, but actually involves an unacknowledged form of attachment that implies subtle remembrance.

Similarly, the Presbyterians who took part in the smashing of the monument at Ballynahinch did not relinquish their hold on the memory of Betsy Gray. Seventy years after the destruction of the monument, 82-year-old James Mills, a Presbyterian who was said to have 'a very retentive memory', vividly recalled the outburst of commemorative possessiveness and commemorative envy that he had witnessed in his youth: 'They didn't like those people claiming Betsy and they decided to prevent the ceremony from taking place' (Fig. 5.4a).[128] From oral sources, documented in 1968, it transpires that the rioters, though intent on inhibiting further commemorative celebrations at the site, did not abandon their attachment to the memory of the local heroine. Even as they demolished the monument, they carried away keepsakes. In retrospect, it would be claimed many years later that 'vandalism by souvenir hunters led to the

[123] Charles W. Hedrick, *History and Silence: Purge and Rehabilitation of Memory in Late Antiquity* (Austin: University of Texas Press, 2000), p. 93.

[124] See Harriet I. Flower, *The Art of Forgetting: Disgrace and Oblivion in Roman Political Culture* (Chapel Hill, N.C.: University of North Carolina Press, 2006).

[125] *Weekly Freeman*, 7 May 1898, p. 4.

[126] Peter Stewart, *Statues in Roman Society: Representation and Response* (Oxford: Oxford University Press, 2003), pp. 267–99. Cf. Thomas Pekáry, *Das römische Kaiserbildnis in Staat, Kult und Gesellschaft, dargestellt anhand der Schriftquellen* (Berlin: Mann Verlag, 1985), pp. 139–42.

[127] Michael T. Taussig, *Defacement: Public Secrecy and the Labor of the Negative* (Stanford, Calif.: Stanford University Press, 1999).

[128] Recollections of James Mills of Antrim Road, Ballynahinch, whose family resided in 1898 in Ballymurphy, on the Ballynahinch-Hillsborough Road; he stated that he was 16 at the time, but according to 1901 census returns his age would have been 12. This account was confirmed by Edward Totten of Lisburn Street, Ballynahinch, who was raised in Ballycreen and, as a 14-year-old boy, had watched his uncle participate in the events from the vantage point of a nearby hill; *Mourne Observer*, 19 July 1968, p. 9.

(a)   (b)

Mr. Mills points to the letters ZABE on a slab of granite which was
once part of Elizabeth Gray's Grave.

Fig. 5.4. Decommemorating Betsy Gray

(a) Eighty-two-year-old James Mills of Ballynahinch pointing in 1968 to the remains of the Betsy Gray monument, which seventy years earlier he had witnessed being destroyed (*Mourne Observer*, 19 July 1968). (b) John Somerville of Ballycreen, whose father James composed in the Sixties a poem about Betsy Gray, points out the remains of the monument in 2003.

Photograph by Guy Beiner.

ruin of the grave.'[129] This attachment, which is redolent of the deeply ambivalent attitudes that David Freedberg has recognized as typical to the behaviour of iconoclasts in general, does not merely amount to the collecting of battle trophies but showed an underlying affection to the memorial of Betsy Gray.[130]

An 'In Memoriam' card, originally placed at the monument by the Henry Joy McCracken Literary Society, was afterwards kept by a local family, whose members apparently identified with its dedication 'In fond remembrance of Betsy Gray'.[131] Pieces of the railings that had surrounded the monument later adorned fences outside people's houses and a blacksmith in the nearby townland of Magheraknock made from the iron 'fancy horseshoes', which were distributed as mementoes and preserved locally.[132]

---

[129] *BNL*, 1 November 1976, p. 2; *Down Recorder*, 2 November 1976.

[130] David Freedberg, 'Iconoclasts and Their Motives', *Public*, 8 (1985): pp. 11–47; see also David Freedberg, *The Power of Images: Studies in the History and Theory of Response* (Chicago and London: University of Chicago Press, 1989), esp. ch. 14: 'Idolatry and Iconoclasm', pp. 378–428.

[131] In 1968, the card was in the possession of Elizabeth Irvine of Main Street, Ballynahinch, who had received it from her husband, Joseph; *Mourne Observer*, 9 September 1968, p. 9.

[132] In 1968, railings from the monument were still to be found outside the residence of Fred Bailie of Glassdrummond and one of the Betsy Gray souvenir horseshoes from William Reid's blacksmith

Chippings of the monument's granite stone were carried away and later taken abroad as souvenirs, presumably by emigrants or visiting tourists, so that, in the words of James Mills, 'there are pieces of the stones all over the world.'[133] Even after the monument was removed from the public domain, its fragments evidently continued to function as privately cherished *aides-mémoire*.

Moreover, a new edition of Lyttle's *Betsy Gray; or, Hearts of Down* was issued for the centenary and local sales of the book continued, regardless of the outburst of hostility that had resulted in the destruction of the monument. The *North Down Herald* promised its liberal unionist readership that:

> The story abounds in local incidents, never before published, but which have been handed down from father to son, and which are fresh in the recollection of the present generation. These must prove deeply interesting to those whose relatives took part in the stirring scenes of the Irish Rebellion of 1798, as well as to others, who by the winter fire, have heard, with paling cheeks and throbbing hearts, of the heroism and cowardice, the deeds of blood and vengeance, the wild adventures and hair-breadth escapes which marked that never to be forgotten period of Irish history.

Apparently local interest in traditions of 1798 continued unabated.[134] Yet, loyalists were careful not to exhibit their secretive sentimental affections to the memory of the Turn-Out. In public, they made sure to collectively take a firm stand against what was perceived as the abhorrent commemorative celebrations of Catholics. Police reports observed that 'feeling between Protestants and Catholics runs high' at Ballynahinch and that following the destruction of the Betsy Gray memorial 'many exciting incidents took place'.[135]

A fortnight later, violence erupted again. On 12 May 1898, the early release of two Protestants, who had been jailed for unruly sectarian behaviour, was celebrated by a crowd of over a thousand Orangemen, which greeted them at Ballynahinch train station and then paraded through the town to the sounds of flute and drum bands. This rambunctious demonstration ended with attacks on property of Catholics and an attempted assault on the police station.[136] In this bout of local rioting, which resulted in prosecutions and further unrest, loyalists attempted to re-assert their control over the public sphere, in the face of rising challenges posed by nationalists.[137] The nationalists of county Down, however, were unwilling to be silenced. On 22 May 1898, four bands and a crowd of six hundred people (which, according to the police, included 'no clergy or well to do people') assembled at Edendariff, near Ballynahinch, for a commemorative demonstration at which speeches were delivered by the nationalist politician Joseph Devlin and John Clarke of the Henry Joy McCracken Literary Society. The entire area

---

shop in Magheraknock was in the possession of Dr A. R. Hamilton; *Mourne Observer*, 13 September 1968, p. 10.

[133] *Mourne Observer*, 19 July 1968, p. 9.

[134] *North Down Herald*, 13 May 1898, p. 3. Advertisements for the new edition ran from 15 April to 27 May 1898, covering the period immediately before and after the wrecking of the monument.

[135] Police and Crime Division (Special), Inspector General's and County Inspectors' Monthly Confidential Reports, No. 16944 (May 1898), TNA CO 904/68, ff. 430, 461–2.

[136] 'Disturbances at Ballynahinch: Riot on May 12, 1898', Intelligence Notes, B Series, no. 33 (May 1898), pp. 24–5, TNA CO 903/6. See also *Down Recorder*, 14 May 1898; *Freeman's Journal*, 14 May 1898, p. 6; *Irish News*, 14 May 1898, p. 4.

[137] *BNL*, 31 May 1898, p. 7.

was 'well patrolled' by the Royal Irish Constabulary and the event passed peacefully.[138] Although public commemoration defiantly continued, the urge for decommemorating had not subdued.

ROWDYISM

While Ballynahinch remained a tinderbox, the flashpoint shifted to the centennial commemoration of the Battle of Antrim. As in Ballynahinch, the population of Antrim town was predominantly Protestant and unionist and, according to the 1901 census, only 18 per cent of the residents were Catholics. Like the other parliamentary constituencies in the county, Antrim South (to which the town belonged) consistently elected Unionist candidates. From 1885, it was represented by the Conservative-Unionist MP William Ellison-Macartney, who was returned unopposed in three consecutive elections.[139] Since this was clearly hostile ground for holding a nationalist commemoration, it was decided to relocate the anniversary of the battle away from its historical location to Belfast, which had not been the site of a battle in 1798 but was currently the power base of the northern '98 centennial movement.

The original plans for a procession through Belfast city centre, starting at Cromac Square, had to be changed after the municipal authorities demanded a last-moment re-routing of the commemorative march. The nationalist parade on 6 June 1898 consequently began at Smithfield and traversed through the Catholic neighbourhoods of west Belfast: it proceeded along the Falls Road and Milltown Cemetery, and ended with an assembly in Hannahstown, 8 kilometres out of city centre. This was an already established route for nationalist demonstrations, which had little to do with sites relating to the rebellion. It is unclear whether the organizers of the procession were even aware that United Irishmen had incidentally concealed arms in a cave near Hannahstown.[140]

Catholics in Belfast treated that Monday as a public holiday, many took the day off from work, and the streets in their neighbourhoods were decorated with green arches, banners, and flags. The *Irish News* beseeched 'every Nationalist who participates in the open-air demonstration to-day to be on his best behaviour' and argued that 'it would be a dishonour and a desecration of the memory of the men of '98 if any rioting were to occur.'[141] The 'monster procession and demonstration', which was considered the largest rally so far of the centenary, was attended by thousands, in spite of heavy rain (Fig. 5.5a). The dominance of Devlin's anti-Parnellite political machine was evident on the speaker's platform, from which Dillon delivered the main address alongside two members of his party—Michael McCartan, MP for South Down, and Jeremiah Jordan, MP for Fermanagh. Although this was supposed to be a unified nationalist event, the

[138] Telegram Reports from Ballynahinch to RIC Inspector General, Dublin Castle, 22 May 1898, NAI CSO/RP/1898/9100; *Irish Weekly and Ulster Examiner*, 28 May 1898, p. 3.

[139] *Census of Ireland for the Year 1901*, vol. 3, Part 1, table XXXV ('Population of the principal towns in the County of Antrim'), p. 168; Walker, ed., *Parliamentary Election Results*, pp. 326–7.

[140] See Pilson, *History of the Rise and Progress of Belfast*, p. 11; Lewis, *A Topographical Dictionary of Ireland*, 2nd edn, vol. 1, p. 200.

[141] *Irish News*, 6 June 1898, p. 4.

(a)

(b)

Fig. 5.5. '98 Centenary celebrations in Belfast

(a) Nationalist commemoration of the centenary was met with a violent bout of loyalist decommemorating. The centennial parade in Belfast, on 6 June 1898, took place in rainy conditions and was led
by Miss Lizzie McSorley riding on horseback, in what was considered an impersonation of the folk
heroine Betsy Gray (photograph taken prior to the outbreak of rioting). (b) On a ground level, the
commemorations were organized by local '98 clubs named after United Irish heroes, such as the
Jemmy Hope '98 Club, photographed in September 1898 outside their premises in Belfast.

leaders of the rival parliamentary factions, Redmond and Healy, did not attend and republicans were not represented. The nationalist press boasted that it was 'a peaceful and imposing display', yet the backlash of decommemorating that it provoked was anything but peaceful.[142]

Around noon, loyalist riots broke out in the Protestant neighbourhoods on the Shankill Road, resulting in violent clashes between loyalist mobs and police. By the evening, the unrest had spread into adjacent areas, leading to 'desperate rioting' around Peter's Hill, 'serious rioting' in Dover Street, a 'skirmish' in Durham Street, additional riots in Millfield and on North Street, the 'wrecking of Walmer Street' in south Belfast, stone-throwing in the west Belfast area of Broadway, and looting along the Donegall Road. Baton charges proved futile and, after 103 policemen sustained injuries, the military were sent in. The Inniskillen Dragoons ended up dispersing the mobs with their lances, though it took several days before peace and order were fully restored. The riots were then investigated by magistrates and debated in parliament. Thomas Joseph Campbell, a respected journalist of the *Irish News*, claimed that rioting could have been curtailed had the deployment of troops not been negligently delayed, a charge that was strenuously denied by the lord mayor of Belfast, Sir James Henderson. The scale of violence was compared in the press to the massive riots of 1886 (during which 32 people were killed and 371 were injured), even though the toll was nowhere as high. The main difference was that in 1886 loyalists protested against Home Rule and in 1898 the riots were motivated by an impulse of decommemorating.[143]

The misconduct of the loyalist rioters was denounced across the board, with notable differences in the attribution of blame. For the nationalist press the cause of unrest was clearly 'disgraceful conduct of Orange rowdies'.[144] Liberal unionist newspapers condemned the rioting, but also criticized the government for allowing 'a procession of would-be rebels to commemorate an abortive rebellion', which they perceived as a 'burlesque' of 'men celebrating a defeat as others celebrate a victory, and that, too, a defeat of men whom the demonstrationists could not in the remotest degree claim to represent.'[145] Conservative unionist papers were scathing in describing the 'damp weather, damp demonstrators, and damp speeches' as a '"Grate" Demonstration', which had irked loyalists and provoked the unwarrantable violence.[146] The divergence in ascribing responsibility for the outbreak of the riots is indicative of different attitudes to the centenary: nationalists refused to admit that their commemoration of rebellion was unacceptable to loyalists, liberal unionists opposed the commemoration but also seemed perturbed that Catholic nationalists had taken possession of the memory of the

---

[142] *Irish News* 7 June 1898 p. 6; *Freeman's Journal*, 7 June 1898, p. 5.

[143] The account of the Belfast '98 centenary riots and local responses draws on the coverage in a range of provincial and national newspapers, including *Banbridge Chronicle* (unionist), *Belfast Evening Telegraph* (unionist), *BNL* (unionist), *Freeman's Journal* (nationalist), *Irish News* (nationalist), *Irish Times* (unionist), *Irish Weekly and Ulster Examiner* (nationalist), *Newtownards Chronicle* (unionist), Newry edition of the *Dundalk Examiner and Louth Advertiser* (nationalist), *Northern Whig* (liberal unionist), *Ulster Echo* (liberal unionist), *Witness* (liberal unionist). See also Campbell, *Fifty Years of Ulster*, pp. 24–5. For the riots of 1886 see Boyd, *Holy War in Belfast*, pp. 115–73; Hirst, *Religion, Politics, and Violence*, pp. 174–82.

[144] *Irish News*, 7 June 1898, p. 6.

[145] *Witness*, 7 June 1898, p. 4; *Northern Whig*, 7 June 1898, p. 4.

[146] *Belfast Evening Telegraph*, 6 June 1898, pp. 3 and 5.

United Irishmen, and conservative unionists were even more blunt in branding the commemoration an offensive irritant.

A member of the 'Sandy Row Heroes' Orange lodge (L.O.L. 247) was furious with the report in the *Daily News*—which was repeated in many other papers—that 'the Orangemen are utterly lawless, and it is they who have disgraced the most populous city in Ireland'. He responded with a protest written in rhyme, which spelt out the 'lesson of '98', as seen by loyalists:

> Turn down the page of the story,
> Blot out its blood with tears;
> May its rancour be all forgotten
> In the peace of the coming years.[147]

Appearing as a parenthesis in a rather crude poem, these verses echoed the official Orange attitude to the centennial memorialization of 1798. The Grand Lodge of the Orange Order of Belfast had unsuccessfully tried to prevent the riots by passing resolutions which stated that 'it would be entirely contrary to the principles and character of the Loyal Orange Institution to interfere with any section of our fellow citizens in celebrating whatever event in their history commends itself to their good taste and deliberate judgment as deserving of public commemoration and honour' and called upon brethren to 'abstain from any attempts to molest the demonstration'.[148] These declarations were drafted by Rev. Richard Rutledge Kane, the grand master of the Orange Order in Belfast since 1885 and a central figure in Belfast loyalist politics, who forcefully advocated the obligation to forget 1798.

Rev. R. R. Kane was the Anglican rector of Christ Church in Belfast, and before that rector of Tullylish in county Down. He was active in several organizations that vigorously opposed Home Rule, including the long-established Belfast Conservative Association, the Ulster Loyalist Union (formed in 1886) and the Unionist Club movement (active in 1882–3).[149] His reputation as a fiery speaker at Orange demonstrations earned him among nationalists the pejorative nickname 'Roaring Kane'.[150] He gained notoriety during the Land War, when he was branded 'the shooting rector' for proposing that loyalist vigilantes should shoot priests and nationalist members of parliament in retribution for the assassinations of landlords.[151] Nevertheless, the *Shan Van Vocht* commended Kane for speaking out in favour of tenant rights in Ulster and considered him 'an Irishman first and a Unionist after'. Radicals apparently entertained an outlandish hope that Kane's occasional criticism of British mismanagement might be harnessed to win over his support for Irish separatism and that 'if the foundations of

---

[147] *BNL*, 11 June 1898, p. 7.

[148] *BNL*, 2 June 1898, pp. 4 and 5. The Orange resolutions were published also in other unionist newspapers, such as the *Belfast Evening Telegraph*, the *Weekly Telegraph*, and the *Larne Times*; see Collins, *Who Fears to Speak*, pp. 40–1; Hume, *To Right Some Things*, pp. 73–4.

[149] See obituaries in *BNL*, 21 November 1898, pp. 4–6. At a meeting of northern unionist clubs in Belfast in March 1893, Kane was said to represent a club 'consisting of 15,000 men—a number which would be raised to 30,000 before long'; *BNL*, 23 March 1893, p. 7.

[150] 'Roaring Kane', sometimes supplemented as 'Rampant Roaring Kane' or 'Ranting Roaring Kane', repeatedly appeared in references to Rev. R. R. Kane in the nationalist press from around 1883.

[151] *BNL*, 11 September 1880; Campbell, *The Dissenting Voice*, p. 308.

his belief are shattered we may live to see Dr. Kane in the national as he is now in the patriotic ranks.'[152]

In previous speeches, Kane had referred to the inability of Protestants to forget 1798, by which he meant the ingrained loyalist memory of sectarian atrocities in Wexford. Speaking on republican rebellions at a well-attended Twelfth demonstration in Ulster Hall in 1885, he informed his audience that 'they could not forget these periods of their history, because the rebel leaders of to-day were not ashamed to speak of '98', while Orangemen 'remembered them not for the purposes of exasperation and revenge, but in order that they might not lose sight of the fact that the struggle was for their people'.[153] In speeches at Orange events in 1889, Kane recalled the involvement of Ulster Presbyterians in the rebellion and noted their subsequent disillusion, which lead to conversion back to loyalism:

> In 1798 the Presbyterians of the North sympathised with the Roman Catholics of the South. Ballynahinch in the North sympathised with Wexford in the South, but when the men of the North found that the others were more intent upon slaying defenceless women and children they laid down their arms and returned to their allegiance.[154]

If in the past, memory of 1798 had proved useful for rhetorical purposes, come the centenary, Kane no longer recognized the usefulness of remembering the rebellion.

In a lecture on '1798: Its Lessons for Irishmen', which was delivered at Belfast's Clifton Street Orange Hall on 20 May 1898 and then circulated in print to Orange brethren, Kane expressed his 'deep regret that this subject should be forced upon our notice at the present time', stating that:

> It is a subject full of the most painful memories, calculated in a very great degree to stir up angry feelings, and it seems to me very surprising that our fellow countrymen, who are preparing to commemorate 1798 should not very much rather have that terrible year forgotten and forgiven than have attention focussed upon it.

Kane pointed out that 'the armed insurrection in the North was short lived and altogether inconsiderable.' He was, however, willing to concede that Ulster 'offers an instructive contrast to the rebellion elsewhere in 1798', as 'it was a rebellion prompted by patriotism and principles of philosophy and of government', which was untainted with the 'charge of bigotry and cruelty and unrestrained race and sectarian hatred' of the rebellion in the South. He went on to describe 'in thrilling language many of the outrages wrought by the rebels' in Wexford and to relate these atrocities to massacres of Protestants by Catholics in 1641 and 1689. Kane's conclusion was that remembrance of the rebellion should be entirely avoided:

> I greatly and deeply regret that these red pages, these bloodcurdling records, occur in the history of my country. Would to God that they could be blotted clean off the pages of Irish history. I greatly and deeply regret that our Nationalists or Roman Catholic fellow countrymen are capable of avowing their sympathy with such records and are actually prepared to commemorate such events by public and ostentatious demonstrations.[155]

---

[152] *SVV*, 1 no. 9 (September 1896), p. 179; vol. 2, no. 6 (June 1897), p. 111; vol. 3, no. 3 (March 1898), p. 56; vol. 3, no. 12 (December 1898), p. 230.

[153] *BNL*, 13 July 1885, p. 7.

[154] *BNL*, 31 October 1889, p. 7 (Newtownbutler, county Fermanagh); 12 November 1889, p. 7 (Antrim).

[155] *BNL*, 21 May 1898, p. 7.

This call for forgetting was endorsed by the unionist press.

In an editorial praising Kane's lecture, the *Belfast News-Letter* categorically stated that 'there was nothing in the rebellion that Irishmen of to-day have any real reason to be proud of' and that 'Ulstermen would gladly forget the mistake of 1798.' The problem, as seen by unionist spokesmen, was that 'Ulster wants to forget it all because Ulster is not proud of the rebellion, and Ulster is loyal. But we are not allowed to do so.' The centennial commemoration plans of 'ill-advised celebrants, who will not forget nor forgive' were considered 'a direct challenge from disloyalty to loyalty in the centre of loyalty.'[156] Along these lines, Kane argued that the riots in Belfast were 'exclusively due to the fact that a treasonable procession was permitted and patronized and assisted upon by the Executive Government of the country'.[157] Decommemorating was seen as an inevitable reaction to the sanction of commemorating in place of social forgetting.

Kane was not alone in advocating oblivion. Rev. Robert Stuart O'Loughlin, the rector of the Anglican parish of Shankill in Lurgan, county Armagh (just outside the north-west boundary of county Down), gave a lecture on 28 March 1898 to the Lurgan Church of Ireland Young Men's Society on 'The Rising of '98', which was shortly afterwards published in the *Lurgan Mail* and then issued as a penny pamphlet. O'Loughlin maintained that 'neither party was blameless, that many sad and bitter memories are connected with it, and that it would be well for the nation if they could safely be forgotten.' In this long and detailed lecture, which ran in print to eleven double-columned pages, the northern rebellion was only mentioned in a few brief sentences that described the engagements in Antrim and Down as 'small and insignificant'. Towards the conclusion, O'Loughlin rhetorically asked, 'would it not be well, if possible to tear this leaf out of the history of the country we all love?' and criticized the centenary for preventing such intentional forgetting:

> Throughout the length and breadth of the land commemorations are now being held; pilgrimages will be made to the site of those battlefields where lie buried the remains of those who fell. With these commemorations must come back other memories, which are bitter and fierce, which neither the stillness of death nor the softening influence of time seem capable of modifying or calming. The very mention of them seem like to a squirt of vitrol thrown in the face of vision to blind, distort and aggravate.[158]

The denial of forgetting through commemoration was considered an affront.

At a meeting of the County Antrim Grand Orange Lodge at the end of May 1898, Col. James Martin McCalmont, District Master of Larne and unionist MP for Antrim East, announced that 'they were threatened in the course of the next few days with having in their midst a series of processions commemorative of the rebellion of '98, which, he thought, would in the interests of Ireland, far better be obliviated from our memory.'[159] On the Twelfth of July, Rev. R. S. O'Loughlin, who was District Master of the Orange Order in Lurgan (L. O. L. no. 6), presided over a regional demonstration of Orangemen from neighbouring districts at Drumgor (3 km south-west of Lurgan) at which a resolution was passed which stated: 'It is a matter of great regret to us that a

---

[156] *BNL*, 21 May 1898, p. 4.   [157] *Belfast Evening Telegraph*, 8 June 1898, p. 5.
[158] Rev. R. S. O'Loughlin, *The Rising of '98* (Lurgan: L. Richardson, 1898), pp. 1 and 11. For biographical information see O'Loughlin's obituary in *Larne Times*, 3 March 1928, p. 10.
[159] *BNL*, 28 May 1898, p. 7.

section of fellow-countrymen has seen fit to commemorate the savage rebellion of 1798 . . . and we think the Government should not permit processions to be held commemorating abortive treason.'[160]

The repeated calls for deliberate forgetting offer a curious form of engagement with Ninety-Eight. Although distinguished Orangemen, who were Anglican—notably not Presbyterian—emphatically insisted that the rebellion should not be remembered, they did not refrain from talking about it. In fact, their references served to stir internal debates on 1798 amongst loyalists. After Rev. O'Loughlin delivered a lecture on 1798 at the Victoria Hall in Belfast in early May 1898 to great applause, this sparked a lively discussion and in the remainder of the meeting 'a number of views were exhibited of scenes in the Rebellion of '98.'[161] Craigs Orange Hall, near Ballymena, hosted on 27 June 1898 a lecture on the rebellion by Rev. Ralph B. Cooke, the rector of Dunaghy and Killagan, whose survey went beyond the standard loyalist narrative of atrocities in Wexford and also covered the rebellion in Ulster, showing detailed knowledge of local events in Antrim.[162] Orange audiences in Presbyterian areas apparently harboured an interest in the rebellion, regardless of their animosity to the commemorations.

James McFerran, a Presbyterian Orangeman, delivered on 11 May 1898 an 'interesting and highly instructive lecture on the Rebellion of 1798 and incidents of the battles of Randalstown and Antrim' at the Orange Hall in Antrim town. The lecture, which was 'given in the interests of working men', lasted for more than an hour and, according to the *Belfast News-Letter*, 'so attractive and entertaining was the subject that from beginning to end of the discourse no one wearied, but manifested the utmost interest and pleasure.' At the conclusion of the evening, it was resolved unanimously that it should be printed and 'sold at a reasonable price, and that all present should purchase copies of it.' The lecture was indeed published shortly afterwards as a booklet, priced at sixpence.[163]

McFerran wrestled with the memory of 1798. As a unionist, he could not condone the rebellion, but he openly admitted that 'some deeds done at the time were daring' and that 'the leaders showed some military skill, and many of the men they commanded considerable courage.' He stressed the catastrophic results of their futile efforts:

they were all eventually defeated, their leaders hanged, mutilated, and exposed; others imprisoned or exiled; others, whose offences were considered less aggravated, were subjected to floggings or compelled to wear the burning pitch cap, or any other conceivable torture the ingenuity of martial law could invent, in order to extract from unwilling witnesses evidence of the guilt of others, or where arms and ammunition might be found.

Accordingly, he objected to commemoration of 'these harrowing scenes':

better far to have no such celebrations to remind us of the folly and failure of 1798, of the organised rebellion, of the torturing cruelties deemed necessary by the military, of the many excellent lives foolishly thrown away, of the wringing of lively hearts by such separations as

---

[160] *BNL*, 9 July 1898, p. 6.   [161] *BNL*, 10 May 1898, p. 7.
[162] *Ballymena Observer*, 1 July 1898, p. 7.
[163] *BNL*, 14 May 1898, p. 7; James McFerran, *The Rebellion of 1798 and Sketches and Incidents of the Battles of Randalstown and Antrim* (Belfast: W. & G. Baird, 1898). McFerran's membership of the Orange Order can be confirmed from his participation some years earlier in a meeting of the County Antrim Grand Lodge at Larne; *BNL*, 21 May 1895 (his religion can be deduced from the 1901 census).

fathers from their families, or of Miss M'Cracken, when on the scaffold with her brother, refusing to leave him and repeatedly kissing him.

Yet, although McFerran maintained that many scenes depicting 'the misery of those days' are 'too affecting to relate', he prefaced his text with a hope that 'the centenary of the so-called "Turn-Out" of 1798' would 'prove interesting to many readers'. Despite the author's unionism, the detailed account of the rebellion in Ulster is largely sympathetic to the rebels.[164]

McFerran concluded that 'if a few of the restless and ambitious spirits, whose patriotic fervour compelled them to die for their country in 1798, when the outlook was dreary, were to visit Ireland again in 1898, who could describe their astonishment at the progress made.' Henry Joy McCracken, and by extension every other northern United Irishmen, was shown to be at heart a unionist, who 'would candidly admit that Belfast had got on better than he could have expected her to do alongside with Great Britain'.[165] A dismissive review in the *UJA*, most probably written by Bigger, stated that 'this is one of those delivered lectures that need not have been reprinted.' The review rightly identified that 'every single fact given—sometimes garbled' was taken, without credit, from sources that had been previously published in the journal, in particular Smith's *Memories of '98*, together with some information taken from Young's *Ulster in '98*.[166] McFerran's plagiarism actually showed that local traditions of Ninety-Eight compiled by antiquarians also fascinated loyalists.

Once the surge of decommemorative rioting had allayed and order had been restored to Belfast, friction returned to county Down for the anniversary of the Battle of Ballynahinch. Police reports from the locality noted that 'party feeling runs high' and the *Irish Weekly and Ulster Examiner* observed that 'since the memorable 1 May', when the Betsy Gray memorial was wrecked, 'the feeling of the Nationalists in this area has grown intense.'[167] By this stage, there were four fairly active '98 clubs in Down and their members were intent on commemorating the local insurrection, despite strong Orange opposition. Consequently, the centenary of Ballynahinch in mid-June became a stand-off display of commemorative competitiveness.

Colonel Robert Hugh Wallace, a prominent county Down Orangeman, who had previously declared to the Downpatrick Unionist Club that he 'would gladly blot out of the page of history' the embarrassing incidents of 1798, took preventive steps to hinder nationalist commemoration. Availing of his position as agent of the Montalto estate, Wallace leased the fields on which the battle had taken place to the master of the Orange lodge in Saintfield, so that entry could be denied to nationalists. In acknowledgement of this ruse, he was congratulated by the Orange leadership for having 'frustrated the wicked design of the other party'.[168] Barred from accessing the historical

[164] McFerran, *The Rebellion of 1798*, pp. 6–7.   [165] Ibid., p. 26.
[166] *UJA*, 2nd ser., 4, no. 4 (1898): p. 262.
[167] Police and Crime Division (Special), Inspector General's and County Inspectors' Monthly Confidential Reports, No. 16699 (June 1898), TNA CO 904/68/597; *Irish Weekly and Ulster Examiner*, 25 June 1898, p. 1.
[168] J. N. B. Blackwood, deputy grand master of the Orange Order in Ireland and Deputy District Master of No. 5 District, Saintfield, to Colonel R. H. Wallace, 1 January 1898, PRONI D1889/6/2 (also appears in D2223/21/14/5). Wallace's interpretation of 1798 was presented at a presidential lecture to the Downpatrick Unionist Club in 1894 in which he declared that 'those of us here this evening do not fear to speak of '98, but we do blush at the name'; *BNL*, 2 March 1894, p. 7.

sites of the battle, nationalists had to make do with attending a meeting of the local Gray and Boal '98 Club, while loyalists paraded through the town in celebration of the royalist victory over the rebels. In a symbolic appropriation of the local sites of memory, Union flags were placed on the courthouse and at the top of Windmill Hill and Edenavaddy, where engagements had taken place.[169] Commemorative possession and commemorative envy were clearly at play, as loyalists, who objected to the public commemoration of 1798, aggressively asserted control over the public sphere and held their own counter-commemoration.

On the weekend following the centennial of the battle, the succession of events that had occurred at the Betsy Gray memorial seemed to repeat itself at a nearby location. A party of nationalists from Belfast, headed by women from the Mary Ann McCracken club, visited Ballynahinch on Sunday 19 June 1898 to celebrate Decoration Day and were joined by several local pipe bands. Upon arrival, they set out to the nearby townland of Tievenadarragh (about 10 kilometres south-west of the town) with the intention of placing wreaths at the grave of a rebel named Brian McCormick, who, like Betsy Gray, was said to have come from Killinchy and to have been killed in cold blood by yeomen after the battle. The burial place had been confirmed by a Mr Boyd, who had excavated the grave and had allegedly discovered remains of a green uniform and buttons. Upon reaching the area, the visitors were confronted by a crowd of loyalists and were denied access to the site by the farmer who owned the land. In consequence, they were obliged to hold a demonstration at a distance. Once again, land ownership rights and mob intimidation were used to inhibit commemoration.[170]

The following month, the annual Orange celebration of 12 July offered loyalists an opportunity to outdo the commemoration of United Irishmen. Rather than treating the occasion as a time when contestations of remembering 1798 could be put aside, the anniversary of the Battle of the Boyne was dubbed that year 'the '98 Twelfth'.[171] Some 20,000 brethren of Orange lodges in county Down assembled for a 'monster demonstration' on Ednavaddy Hill, Ballynahinch, a historical site intentionally selected in order to mark the place where rebels had 'sustained a crushing defeat at the hands of the Royalist troops'. In explaining the choice of venue, unionist newspapers noted that the 'essentially Protestant' district had been upset when 'recently attempts have been made on the part of ultra-Nationalists to foment ill-feeling by placing a distinctive and peculiar construction on the battle of 1798, and traducing the British connection.' It was claimed that the Orange celebrations at Ballynahinch 'over-shadowed these abortive commemorations' and that, contrary to the accusations of rowdiness at previous events, 'everything was marked by the utmost order.' As a gesture of

Nonetheless, his draft manuscript for a history of Downpatrick, written *c*.1920, shows that he retained an interest in the rebellion; R. H. Wallace, 'Historical Collections Relating to Downpatrick', transcribed by R. W. H. Blackwood (1937), Wallace Family Papers, PRONI D1889/8/4 (pp. 33, 35, 55–8, 99–102).

[169] *Down Recorder*, 18 June 1898; *Newry Reporter*, 15 June 1898; *Newry Telegraph*, 16 June 1898.
[170] *Down Recorder*, 25 June 1898; *Irish Weekly and Ulster Examiner*, 25 June 1898, p. 1; see also Lyttle, *Betsy Gray* (1968 edn), appendix, pp. 179–81 (originally published in *Mourne Observer*, 20 Sept 1968, p. 9). My thanks to Roy Meakin, whose family owns the farm on which the gravesite is located, for sharing his photographs of the headstone of Brian McCormick; personal communication, 2 March 2016; see <www.oracleireland.com/Ireland/Countys/down/z-tievenadarragh.htm>.
[171] *Irish News*, 13 July 1898, p. 6.

triumphalist commemoration, a platform erected on 'a commanding position' exhibited a drum, which had been taken from rebels in 1798.[172]

Rev. Lewis Arthur Pooler, the Anglican rector of Downpatrick and Deputy Master of the Lecale No. 2 District Orange Lodge, gave the main address at the Orange celebration in Ballynahinch. He proposed a resolution expressing 'satisfaction that the rebellion of 1798 was not marked in the North of Ireland by the scenes of atrocity which characterised it in the South and West . . . and that the immediate result of the rebellion of '98 was the Act of Union'. Pooler proclaimed that 1798 in Ulster was an exclusively Protestant affair and that Catholics therefore had no right to engage in commemoration:

> Why the Romanist party should celebrate the rebellion in the North of Ireland he could not see. They had little or nothing to do with it. The night before the battle of Ballynahinch the Roman Catholics deserted; they would not face the dangers of the next day. They decorated the grave of Betsy Gray, but they had not the courage to fight beside her.[173]

In supporting the resolution, Rev. John McCracken of Saul Rectory in Downpatrick, who was also Chaplain of the Lecale No. 2 District Orange Lodge, commented on the transformation of rebels into unionists:

> If an inhabitant of Ballynahinch in 1798 could stand there that day, he would see great changes. He could see signs of industry and prosperity all around; he could see the descendants of the United Men in thousands praising God for the Union, and wearing Orange sashes; and he could see many a brave girl who would do a noble deed for her brother or a sweetheart, as the heroine Betsy Gray, who climbed the Ednavady Hill on the morning of 13th June, 1798.[174]

In this portrayal, which obliquely claimed the ancestry of the local rebel heroine, Rev. McCracken rehearsed an argument that he had heard Rev. Pooler make previously.

At a lecture on 'The Story of '98', delivered at Downpatrick town hall on 24 February 1898, Pooler had declared that 'to-day the descendants of the Protestant rebels of 1798 were all to be found on the side of England.' It appears that unionists were claiming the memory of both sides at the battle. The inventory of 'relics of that dark period' put on display at Downpatrick listed an indiscriminate mix of loyalist and rebel paraphernalia, including:

> swords, pikes, and flint guns, used in the battle of Ballynahinch, as well as a bullet found on the field; a blunderbuss, powder-horn, ammunition, cartridge, and flint cartouch; epaulettes of Inch Infantry, cross-belt and buckle of Down Volunteers, badges of Down Volunteers, Down Protestant Boys, Inch Infantry, Castleward Fusiliers, and Ballybidy Infantry; a copy of the London "Times" published in '98, and giving an account of the battle of Ballynahinch, together with the list of killed and wounded, and a volume containing the rules, regulations, and drill for the Volunteers and other forces published in 1798.[175]

[172] *BNL*, 14 July 1898, p. 6; *Down Recorder*, 16 July 1898.
[173] *BNL*, 14 July 1898, p. 6; *Down Recorder*, 16 July 1898. For biographical information on Rev. Pooler see L. A. Pooler, *Down and Its Parish Church* (Downpatrick: Down Recorder Office, 1907), p. 96; *Larne Times*, 6 October 1923, p. 5.
[174] *Down Recorder*, 16 July 1898. For the offices held by Rev. Pooler and Rev. McCracken in the local district of the Orange Order see *County Down Grand Orange Lodge Annual Report for the Year Ending 31st December 1898* (Downpatrick: Down Recorder, 1898), p. 16.
[175] *BNL*, 28 February 1898, p. 3.

Fig. 5.6. Orangemen marching in Ballynahinch

A photographic postcard of a Twelfth of July procession through Ballynahinch. The very areas which had once been sites of rebellion became, over the long nineteenth century, bastions of Orangeism.
© National Museum NI, Collection Ulster Museum (BELUM.W2011.1410).

When negating commemoration of the 1798 Rebellion, Orangemen were effectively seeking to repossess its memory for unionism (Fig. 5.6).

Towards the end of what had turned into a rambunctious summer, yet another round of sectarian riots broke out in Belfast, following the participation of nationalists in the main centennial event in Dublin on 15 August 1898 (which, as unionist newspapers pointed out, was deliberately scheduled on the Catholic holiday of Lady Day). Additional transport services were provided for that Monday and, according to figures provided by the Great Northern Railway, trains 'carried between nine and ten thousand excursionists from the North to Dublin'. Around 1,900 nationalists took a specially charted train from Belfast, though apparently some passengers fell prey to a 'curious fraud' and purchased counterfeit tickets that prevented them from travelling south.[176] The substantial presence of northerners was noticeable in the massive procession, choreographed by Fred Allan, which paraded through the streets of Dublin city centre and reverently passed by various sites associated with the United Irishmen.

At the end of the march, the crowd assembled at the top of Grafton Street, in front of St Stephen's Green, to witness a ceremony in which John O'Leary laid the foundation stone of a monument for Wolfe Tone. Significantly, the stone was quarried at McArt's Fort on Cave Hill and had been dedicated the previous week by Joseph Devlin at a large gathering of nationalists on the Falls Road in Belfast, which was 'marked by an outburst of popular enthusiasm'.[177] The choice to bring a foundation stone specifically from

[176] *Freeman's Journal*, 16 August 1898, p. 5; *Dundee Evening Telegraph*, 16 August 1898, p. 2; *Ulster Echo*, 16 August 1898; *Belfast Evening Telegraph*, 16 August 1898.
[177] *Daily Nation*, 11 August 1898, p. 6; *Freeman's Journal*, 11 August 1898, p. 5; *Irish News*, 11 August 1898, p. 5.

Ulster was a double tribute, which honoured the northern origins of the United Irishmen and also acknowledged the weight of Belfast in the national centenary organization. However, it was also an unconscious admission of the inability of northern nationalists to claim the Belfast cityscape, as it was clear that a monument to the founders of the United Irishmen could not be erected in Belfast.[178]

The 'record demonstration' in Dublin was designed to show that nationalists had achieved unity. O'Leary's participation embodied the republican cause, and the main speeches were delivered by the heads of both wings of the Irish Parliamentary Party, Dillon and Redmond. Words were also said by representatives of the Irish-American diaspora, Yeats spoke 'on behalf of the Irishmen of England', and William Rooney delivered a short speech in Irish in the name of the Gaelic League. Maud Gonne stood out among several women dignitaries on the platform, yet the prominent female representatives of the province of Ulster were noticeably absent. Neither Carbery nor Milligan—whose biography of Tone was commended by O'Leary in his speech—were invited to speak and their vital contribution to the centenary movement remained unacknowledged.[179] The professed aspiration for inclusivity clearly had its limits and the more radical promoters of commemoration in Ulster were pushed aside.

On the other hand, the presence of northern women, in particular the members of the Mary McCracken '98 Club, was visible in the parade through the streets of Dublin. The third section of the procession was entirely taken up by the Northern contingents, led by Devlin, and was estimated (with probable exaggeration) at around three thousand people. According to journalistic accounts, the Ulster clubs made a striking impression, which was even noted in the unionist and English press. They were specifically commended for the display of some seventeen imposing banners, which 'were of an exceptionally artistic and tasteful character' and portrayed the figures of heroic United Irishmen and scenes from the rebellion in Antrim and Down. Particular attention was drawn to the 'much admired figure' of a young lady on horseback, Miss Lizzie McSourley [McSorley], who was dressed in green, white, and gold (an outfit designed to match the flamboyant regalia of the Irish National Foresters), and was perceived, at least by some, as a personification of Betsy Gray.[180]

The colourful exhibition of provincial remembrance was, to a certain extent, misleading. Just as the praise showered by the *Freeman's Journal* on the 'Ulster turn out'—in reference to the large numbers of participants from the northern province— showed ignorance of the ambiguous connotations that this specific phrase carried in provincial folk history, many of those on parade may have been oblivious to the deep-rooted local traditions of the Turn-Out. Most of the Ulster '98 clubs in the procession came from the Catholic neighbourhoods of Belfast, with a few clubs arriving from

[178] James Loughlin, 'Creating "a Social and Geographical Fact": Regional Identity and the Ulster Question 1880s–1920s', *Past and Present*, 195, no. 1 (May 2007), p. 96.

[179] *Freeman's Journal*, 16 August 1898, p. 6; *Irish News*, 16 August 1898, p. 5. See also Morris, *Alice Milligan*, p. 206.

[180] *Daily Nation*, 16 August 1898, pp. 5–7; *Freeman's Journal*, 16 August 1898, pp. 5–7; *Irish News*, 16 August 1898, p. 5; *Weekly Freeman*, 20 August 1898, pp. 1–3. For identification of the woman on horseback as a personification of Betsy Gray see *SVV*, 3, no. 9 (September 1898), pp. 160–1. A review of newspaper coverage of the event appeared in *Irish News*, 17 August 1898, pp. 4 and 8. For hostile unionist accounts see *BNL*, 16 August 1898, p. 5; *Daily Express*, 16 August 1898, p. 2.

Catholic areas in counties Armagh, Tyrone, and Cavan. Tellingly, there were no clubs from Antrim in attendance and, though several prominent members of Down '98 clubs were present, only one club from the county marched in the procession. This was the Cloakey and Cochrane club from the Catholic district Newry, which proudly displayed a pike that had allegedly belonged to a Presbyterian rebel. A number of the northern clubs were even named after notable southern Catholic rebels, Father Murphy and Michael Dwyer, whose portraits were displayed on banners alongside northern rebels.[181] In this way, the Presbyterian United Irishmen, who in 1798 had turned out in Antrim and Down, were commemorated in 1898 mainly by Catholics from other areas of Ulster, most of whom did not have a direct personal connection with the rebellion. Theirs was an adopted, or transplanted, 'prosthetic memory', to borrow a term introduced in a different context in a study of American memory culture by Alison Landsberg.[182] The Protestant descendants of the northern United Irish rebels mostly shied away from the commemorations. For many of them, participation in a nationalist event was an anathema.

During the night, the trains that returned north from the commemoration in Dublin were stoned near Portadown. In advance of their arrival in Belfast, riots broke out between large crowds of nationalist Catholics, who had gathered by the train station on Great Victoria Street to greet the demonstrators on their return, and crowds of loyalist Protestants, who protested against their participation in the commemoration. Police charged the two groupings and tried to push each of them back into separate areas but found themselves outflanked and caught in between volleys of stone throwing. Violent confrontations broke out in the vicinity of the statue of Henry Cooke, a symbol of conservative-loyalist Protestantism. The windows of houses and businesses were smashed in nearby Wellington Place and College Street South, leaving several policemen injured. Sectarian riots also broke out in Lurgan, county Armagh, where members of the William Orr '98 Club were attacked on their way back home from Dublin. The nationalist press denounced the violence of 'Orange rowdies' and the unionist press responded in kind by detailing the rioting of nationalists.[183]

The *Belfast Evening Telegraph* sardonically wrote of 'Toners and Stoners', implying that the blame for the street violence lay with those who had gone to Dublin to commemorate Wolfe Tone and the 1798 Rebellion.[184] The *Belfast News-Letter* complained that 'the people who are glorifying the barbarity of their predecessors have the audacity to ask the Protestants to join in their orgies commemorative of deceit and treachery, rapine and incendiarism, cowardice and murder.'[185] Commemoration of Ninety-Eight was again construed by its opponents as an unpopular culture and displays of open remembrance were met with outbursts of decommemorating. However, the displays of 'rowdyism' were ultimately a futile attempt to stamp out the memory of 1798.

---

[181] *Freeman's Journal*, 16 August 1898, p. 5; repeated with illustrations in *Weekly Freeman*, 20 August 1898, p. 1. The participation of 'prominent men' from the Down clubs was noted in the RIC District Inspector's report for that month; TNA CO 904/69/39–40.

[182] Alison Landsberg, *Prosthetic Memory: The Transformation of American Remembrance in the Age of Mass Culture* (New York: Columbia University Press, 2004).

[183] *BNL*, 16 August 1898, p. 5; *Daily Nation*, 16 August 1898, p. 7; *Irish Weekly and Ulster Examiner*, 20 August 1898, p. 5; *Ulster Echo*, 16 August 1898.

[184] *Belfast Evening Telegraph*, 16 August 1898, p. 3.

[185] *BNL*, 23 August 1898, pp. 4–5.

At the close of the centenary year, a loyalist rejoinder to the centennial anthem 'Who Fears to Speak of '98?' appeared in the *Belfast New-Letter* under the heading 'Who Cares to Hear of '98?'. It expressed the unionist desire, which had been repeated over and over again during the commemorations, to do away with the memory of the United Irishmen:

> Let sleep the men of '98,
> Whose desperate deeds were well forgot;
> Since crooked things have been made straight,
> And clean wiped out full many a blot.[186]

The wish for oblivion was self-defeating. The very act of publishing a poem that referenced 'The Memory of the Dead' perpetuated remembrance of 1798 in an obscure form. Decommemorating effectively regenerated the mnemonic dynamics of social forgetting.

RESURGENCE

By the autumn of the centenary, after a ceremony on 4 September 1898 that marked the final defeat of the rebel forces at Ballinamuck in county Longford, the national commemoration programme had begun to wind down. Plans were scrapped for an exhibition of relics that would tie together the republican milestones of nationalist history—1798, 1803, 1848, and 1867—and the Central '98 Centenary Committee in Dublin authorized the return of the artefacts to their owners.[187] On a local level, the many relics of 1798 that had been put on display at various events around Ireland returned to serve as private *aides-mémoire*. At the same time, the sale of specially designed '98 centennial jewellery and miscellaneous memorabilia, which was advertised by the *Shan Van Vocht* and other nationalist newspapers, enabled also those who did not possess historical artefacts to take home souvenirs, which could function as private mementoes of the rebellion and its commemoration.[188]

The Belfast and Ulster United Centenary Association passed a resolution that the Belfast memorial for the United Irishmen would 'take the form of a public hall, to keep green the memories of M'Cracken, Neilson, and the other Northern leaders'. Though presented as an achievement, this decision actually signified the scaling down of the original, more ambitious, plans 'to erect a monument in the streets of Belfast to Henry Joy M'Cracken'.[189] Decommemorating had clearly taken its toll. In the wake of the destruction of the Betsy Gray monument and the violent centenary riots in Belfast,

[186] *BNL*, 27 December 1898, p. 7.   [187] *Freeman's Journal*, 12 September 1898, p. 2.
[188] See Steele, *Women, Press, and Politics*, p. 32; John Strachan and Claire Nally, *Advertising, Literature, and Print Culture in Ireland, 1891–1922* (Houndmills and New York: Palgrave Macmillan, 2012), pp. 66–7. The collections of the National Museum of Ireland host a range of badges from the '98 centenary: NMI HH:1939.41, 1941.12.4, 1948.3, 1948.32, 1948.35, 1971.7, 2013.80, 2013.82, and L.1478.6 (medallion). Other centennial souvenirs that demonstrate the domestication of memorialization include various commemorative handkerchiefs (NMI HH:1964.8 [also 1978.17 and 2013.77], 1936.98 [also 1944.222], 1954.5, 2013.422), mugs and bowls (NMI DC:1971.236; HH:1948.13, and 1969.3), and pottery figures of United Irish leaders, among them Henry Joy McCracken (NMI HH:1956.6).
[189] *Freeman's Journal*, 2 September 1898, p. 6; cf. 10 September 1897, p. 6.

northern nationalists had to concede their inability to erect monuments to Ninety-Eight in Ulster. Ultimately, even the reduced plans to dedicate a memorial hall to the United Irishmen did not come to fruition.

Towards the end of 1898, Joseph Devlin, president of the Belfast and Ulster United Centenary Association, was honoured with a banquet, at which the accomplishments of the centenary were extolled.[190] Lingering remnants of animosities from the centenary were still apparent. When the Central '98 Committee in Dublin initiated torchlight processions around Ireland on the New Year to mark the successful conclusion of the 1798 centenary, the Belfast '98 clubs 'dissociated themselves absolutely and entirely from the proceedings'. Their withdrawal signalled that the bitter competition between rival nationalist factions, which had stifled commemorative initiatives for most of the centenary, had not been entirely overcome. Nevertheless, the northern centenary movement took pride in having organized 'no less than 200 lectures upon Irish national subjects, a series of Irish songs and readings, and many social gatherings'. It was resolved that the activities of the '98 clubs in Ulster would continue, with the intention of channelling the enthusiasm that had been generated by the centennial commemorations towards further nationalist activism.[191]

That summer, a large nationalist demonstration, held in Belfast on 6 June 1899, was rightly perceived by loyalists as an attempt to renew public commemoration of 1798 and infuse it with current political content. The date had been selected for its close proximity to the anniversary of the Battle of Antrim and the main purpose of the occasion, as acknowledged by the nationalist leader Michael Davitt at an anti-Parnellite convention on the previous day, was to re-assemble the northern '98 clubs and recruit them into the United Irish League. Davitt reassured his audience that 'some of us hold the memories and the political creed of the band of brave revolutionists who founded the United Irishmen movement here in Belfast.' Joseph Devlin, the main nationalist organizer in Belfast, explained that over the last year they had engaged in 'the glorification of the memories' of 1798 and, calling upon his followers to 'commemorate in a larger and wider degree', announced that now 'the time for action had arrived.'[192]

The procession to Hannahstown in June 1899, which resembled the controversial centennial demonstration of the previous year, infuriated loyalists, who rallied for a counter demonstration. Although the Grand Orange Lodge of Belfast issued a manifesto that called 'upon every Orangeman and upon every true Protestant to abstain entirely from taking part', the riots that ensued were again labelled 'Orange Rowdyism' in the nationalist press. Among the scenes of 'serious disturbances' in the Protestant areas of north Belfast, 'terrible rioting' took place at Lodge Road and, following 'serious fighting', the Shankill Road was reported to be in 'a state of siege'. Several houses were wrecked and the military were called in. Dragoons charged the Protestant mob with fixed bayonets, in what seemed to be a replay of the centenary clashes.[193] Loyalist decommemorating was intent on stamping out the renewal of public commemorating of the rebellion in Ulster. The following month, at the Belfast celebrations of the Twelfth of July, effigies were gibbetted from chimney stacks with the ominous inscription 'The fate

---

[190] *BNL*, 11 November 1898, p. 6.   [191] *Freeman's Journal*, 2 January 1899, p. 2.
[192] *Freeman's Journal*, 5–6 June 1899, pp. 5–6.
[193] 'Belfast, Nationalist Demonstration, 6 June 1899, Riots &c.', Intelligence Notes, B Series, no. 38, TNA 903/6 5–10; *BNL*, 6 June 1899, p. 5; *Freeman's Journal*, 6 June 1899, pp. 5–6.

of all '98 rebels'. This lurid display of commemorative competitiveness, which was designed to both offend and intimidate nationalists, triumphantly evoked the brutal suppression of the rebellion in 1798 in order to symbolically stifle its commemoration in the aftermath of the centenary.[194]

In contrast to the self-congratulatory summations of the centennial commemorations in the nationalist press, which typically glossed over embarrassing displays of infighting, 'an independent observer' writing for the London newspaper the *Pall Mall Gazette* offered a critical assessment of the paralyses that allegedly afflicted the 'Commonplace Centenary':

> The effort to stage the centenary of 1798 as a great national demonstration was a failure, because it had not behind it the driving force of national enthusiasm. How could it acquire that enthusiasm when the rival elements associated in the work of organising the demonstration were dominated, on the one hand, by feelings of suspicion and fear, and, on the other hand, by an instinct of sheer contempt? ... It was because thousands of thinking, earnest, and self-respecting men revolted against all this mockery, because they held in contempt the hollow insincerity that tried to pass for undiluted and heroic patriotism, that they remained quiescent throughout the Centenary celebrations. These have now passed without leaving one enduring mark behind.

The author of this article cynically maintained that 'the sum total of the celebration of the Centenary of 1798 in Ireland has been the affixing of a few plain tablets to various houses in Dublin ... and the expression of an intention to erect monuments in different parts of the country—an intention which, in many instances, will never be realized.' He concluded that 'neither in literature nor in art, nor in the strengthening or beautifying of the national ideal, is Ireland, as I have said, one whit the better.'[195]

This scathing assessment cut through the hyperbole of centennial rhetoric, but failed to realize that, despite the acrimonious power struggles that had taken place, Irish nationalism was regenerated by the commemorations. The report of the police Inspector General for October 1900 noted a 'very serious wave of sedition which has spread over the country' and was attributed to the centenary:

> This seditious feeling was originally inflamed by the '98 demonstrations two years ago; which, though they had no practical result at the time, undoubtedly revived the old feeling of animosity to England, and awakened anew the sentiment of Irish independent nationality.[196]

The *modus vivendi* eventually reached between the rival nationalist parliamentary groups assisted in healing the Parnellite split that had crippled constitutional politics for the past decade. By 1900, the Irish Parliamentary Party was re-united under the leadership of John Redmond, with John Dillon as his deputy. In Ulster, Devlin mobilized the Ancient Order of Hibernians as an effective apparatus for organizing demonstrations that had first been tried out during the centenary.[197] Commemorative activism also invigorated separatist nationalists, who came together around the Sinn

---

[194] *BNL*, 13 July 1899, p. 5. [195] *Pall Mall Gazette*, 3 February 1899.

[196] Inspector General's Reports, October 1900, No. 23240/S, Chief Secretary's Office, Ireland; Police and Crime Division (Special), TNA CO 904/71/463–4.

[197] Hepburn, *Catholic Belfast*, pp. 90–9; see also Fergal McCluskey, *Fenians and Ribbonmen: The Development of Republican Politics in East Tyrone, 1898–1918* (Manchester: Manchester University Press, 2011), pp. 23–52.

Féin party, founded by Arthur Griffith in 1905. The 'very considerable revival of national feeling and sentiment' roused by the centenary of 1798 would be remembered as a formative experience in the political development of the young generation of radicals that would participate in the Irish Revolution.[198]

Bigger, who was the heart and soul of the northern centenary, was impervious to the setbacks of decommemorating. In the following decade and a half, he continued to tirelessly promote revivalist enterprises, plugging the memory of the United Irishmen throughout Ulster. The social gatherings at Ardrigh, his Belfast residence, remained a source of inspiration for local talents. Reporting on a visit to Ardrigh in 1913, Eleanor Roger Cox, an Irish-American poet originally from Enniskillen, described for the readers of the *Irish-American* the setting for the meetings, which were held among 'portraits of James Hope and Samuel Neilson and Henry Joy McCracken; while on the walls of the adjoining hall, pike and sword and gun of '98 still proclaim the undying gospel of Ireland's fetterless independence.'[199] Reminders of the rebellion seemed to hover above the writers, artists, and revolutionaries who attended Bigger's 'fireside school'.

Always out and about, Bigger promoted other venues for cultural revival. In 1904, he was involved in launching Feis na nGleann, a celebration of Irish language, music, dance, Gaelic sport, literature, and folk crafts in the Glens of Antrim.[200] He went on to establish another popular meeting place for cultural revivalists in 1911, when he purchased Jordan's Castle in Ardglass, county Down (10 kilometres south-east of Downpatrick). The medieval tower house was refurbished with antiquities and spuriously renamed Castle Shane, after one of Bigger's heroes—the Gaelic chieftain Shane O'Neill [traditionally known as Séan an Díomáis—'Shane the Proud']. It functioned as a prototype heritage centre, which—in the words of the contemporary nationalist historian Alice Stopford Green—would 'bring the people of Ardglass and the Lecale of Down into touch with the Irish past, and give them some conception of the historic background of their life'.[201] Historical pageantry at Castle Shane primarily featured quasi-Gaelic costumes, designed to evoke the heroes of the mythological sagas, yet dressing up as pikemen representing the rebels of Ninety-Eight was another common practice. The association of the place with the United Irishmen found inspiration in an

---

[198] Witness statement of Seán T. O'Kelly, President of Ireland, 5 March 1952, BMH 1,765/1, 19 and 65; see also Foster, *Vivid Faces*, pp. 42, 99–100, 194, 289, and 328.

[199] *Ulster Herald*, 30 August 1913, p. 6. See also Jeffrey Dudgeon, *Roger Casement: The Black Diaries, with a Study of His Background, Sexuality and Irish Political Life* (Belfast: Belfast Press, 2002), pp. 161–98.

[200] Eamon Phoenix, 'Francis Joseph Bigger: Historian, Gaelic Leaguer and Protestant Nationalist' and Eileen McAuley, 'The Founders of Feis na nGleann', in *Feis na nGleann: A Century of Gaelic Culture in the Antrim Glens*, edited by Eamon Phoenix et al. (Belfast: Stair Uladh, 2005), pp. 65–77 and 98–9 (respectively); see also Joseph McBrinn, 'The Peasant and Folk Art Revival in Ireland, 1890–1920, with Special Reference to Ulster', *Ulster Folklife*, 48 (2002): pp. 14–61 (esp. 36–8); Kirkland, *Cathal O'Byrne*, pp. 104–9; D. Roger Dixon, *Francis Joseph Bigger, 1863–1926: Ireland's Cultural Visionary* (Belfast: Belfast Education and Library Board, 2007), pp. 8–9.

[201] Alice Stopford Green, *The Old Irish World* (Dublin and London: M. H. Gill and Macmillan, 1912), pp. 149–57 (quotation from p. 151); Owen, *An Irish Chieftain of To-Day*, pp. 6–15; Eleanor Rogers Cox, 'Francis Joseph Bigger: His Work for Ireland. A Visit to Shane's Castle', *Ulster Herald*, 30 August 1913, p. 6; see also Hayward, *In Praise of Ulster*, 5th edn (1946), p. 116; Kirkland, *Cathal O'Byrne*, pp. 109–14; Roger Dixon, 'Francis Joseph Bigger of Belfast and Ardglass: Ireland's Cultural Crusader', *Lecale Review*, no. 6 (2008): pp. 52–3.

apocryphal tradition that Lord Edward Fitzgerald (whose family owned the property at the time) took refuge there when trying to avoid arrest in 1798.[202]

Bigger was also the patron and first president of the Ulster Literary Theatre (ULT), which was founded by Bulmer Hobson and David Parkhill, together with other members of the Ardrigh circle, in 1902, around the same time as the Irish Literary Theatre (which would evolve into the Abbey) was founded in Dublin. The ULT had stemmed out of a Protestant National Association, which championed 'the idea and principles of Wolfe Tone and the United Irishmen'. Bigger financed the theatre's journal *Uladh* (a title derived from the genitive case for Ulster in Irish).[203] To give a sense of purpose and direction, he contributed to the inaugural issue in 1904 an influential article on 'Art and Culture in Old Belfast', which identified the 'Athens of the North' of the 1790s as the golden age of Ulster's variant of romantic cultural nationalism.[204]

The recollection of the radical 'fellowship of freedom' that the United Irishmen had forged in Belfast between 'Protestant, Catholic, and Dissenter' was central to the revivalist construction of regional Ulster identity, which was offered as a cultural alternative to the polarized politics of the day. Although the 1798 centenary, which was supposed to be the apex of remembrance, had passed, Bigger vigorously continued to disseminate cultural memory of the northern United Irishmen at meetings in Ardrigh, celebrations of *feiseanna* [festivals] in the Glens of Antrim, gatherings at Castle Shane in Ardglass and through the activities of the Ulster Literary Theatre. This flourish of cultural creativity yielded a crop of literary production that included novels, plays, and poetry on the rebellion in Ulster.

Looking back at the Belfast which he had left behind, the author James Douglas, who moved to London in pursuit of a career as a newspaper editor and critic, published in 1907 his novel *The Unpardonable Sin*. The setting is the fictional 'Bigotsborough', in which a nationalist parade provokes loyalist rioting that closely resembles centennial decommemorating in Belfast. The place is described as 'a city which suffers from unsatisfied aspirations and baffled aims . . . it has lost its own past, and it is groping blindly after its own future.' [205] While some writers had to get away from the stifling morass of sectarianism and polarized politics, others refused to give in. Against all odds,

---

[202] Campbell, *Fifty Years of Ulster*, p. 282. For reference to pikemen in festivities at Castle Shane see Roger Casement's accounts of parties in September 1913 and New Year 1914; reproduced in Foster, *Vivid Faces*, 195–7.

[203] Eugene McNulty, *The Ulster Literary Theatre and the Northern Revival* (Cork: Cork University Press, 2008), pp. 61–5 and 80–2. See also Peter K. McIvor, 'Regionalism in Ulster: An Historical Perspective', *Irish University Review*, 13, no. 2 (1983): pp. 184–5; Marnie Hay, 'Explaining *Uladh*: Cultural Nationalism in Ulster', in *The Irish Revival Reappraised*, edited by E. A. Taylor FitzSimon and James H. Murphy (Dublin: Four Courts Press, 2003), pp. 119–31; Marnie Hay, *Bulmer Hobson and the Nationalist Movement in Twentieth-Century Ireland* (Manchester and New York: Manchester University Press, 2009), p. 15.

[204] F. J. Bigger, 'Art and Culture in Old Belfast', *Uladh*, 1, no. 1 (November 1904): pp. 11–12. Although late Georgian Belfast had enjoyed a renaissance of sorts, the notion of 'Athens of the North' was subject to exaggeration; see S. J. Connolly and Gillian McIntosh, 'Imagining Belfast', in Connolly, *Belfast 400*, pp. 22–4.

[205] James Douglas, *The Unpardonable Sin* (London: E. Grant Richards, 1907), p. 32 (the parade and sectarian riot is the theme of ch. 10). See also John Hewitt, ' "The Northern Athens" and After', in *Belfast: The Making of the City, 1800–1914*, edited by J. C. Beckett et al. (Belfast: Appletree Press, 1983), p. 81; John Wilson Foster, *Irish Novels, 1890–1940: New Bearings in Culture and Fiction* (Oxford and New York: Oxford University Press, 2008), p. 152.

Bigger's Belfast at the turn of the century was undergoing a northern literary revival, for which resurrection of the memory of United Irishmen was essential.

RECASTING AND PERFORMING

With Bigger's encouragement, James Owen Hannay, the Belfast-born Anglican rector of Westport in county Mayo wrote, under his pseudonym George A. Birmingham, *The Northern Iron*, arguably the finest of the 1798 novels set in Ulster. It first appeared in Dublin and London in 1907, with several editions and reprints coming out in the following years in Ireland, England, and America.[206] The author had received from his father, Rev. Robert Hannay, rector of St Anne's church in Belfast, an evangelical-Protestant unionist upbringing, which was reinforced by his maternal grandfather, Rev. William Henry Wynne, the rector of Moira in county Down, and interactions with his father-in-law, Rev. Frederick Richards Wynne, the Anglican bishop of Raphoe. As a writer, however, Birmingham irreverently questioned unionist politics and rejected evangelical puritanism. He was also critical of Catholic nationalism and his satire of the political involvement of priests incurred angry reactions in Mayo. Rather than conforming to a rigid political ideology, Birmingham formulated an independent-minded form of radicalism, manifested in his membership of the national executive of the Gaelic League and in articles that he wrote for Arthur Griffiths's newspaper *Sinn Féin*, which endorsed such causes as women's suffrage and the cooperative movement.

Birmingham gained literary repute with his popular humoristic fiction, typically set in the present day West of Ireland. Towards the publication of his '98 novel, the Irish publisher prepared the readers for 'an exciting story of action and adventure' that takes place in the historical past and is set in the North.[207] It was written following a holiday in Antrim and many of the scenes incorporated personal recollections of places familiar to the author from his childhood in Ulster. The book was dedicated to Bigger, in recognition of his vital assistance: 'You told me what I wanted to know, you corrected, patiently, my manuscript, and you have helped me to enter into the spirit of the time.'[208] In a review for the *Times Literary Supplement*, Virginia Woolf questioned the literary merits of 'drum and trumpet' historical fiction, yet she commended Birmingham for having 'a thorough grasp of his time and an enthusiasm for his subject which interest and satisfy'.[209] The bibliographer Stephen J. Brown maintained that 'seldom has a romance of almost breathless interest been so combined with a real picture of the times—not so much its costumes and manners and outward events, as the spirit that was abroad in those days and the stamp of men that they produced.'[210]

---

[206] George A. Birmingham, *The Northern Iron* (Dublin: Maunsel & Co., 1907). Further Dublin editions came out in 1909 and 1913 (Maunsel) and in 1910 and 1946 (Talbot Press); London editions came out in 1907 (Newnes) and in 1913 (Everett & Co.); a US edition came out in Baltimore in 1913 (Norman, Remington & Co.). An Irish language translation—*Iarann an Tuaiscirt*—was published in Dublin in 1933 (Oifig Díolta Foillseacháin Rialtais).

[207] *Daily Express* [Dublin], 25 November 1907, p. 6.

[208] Birmingham, *The Northern Iron*, dedication.

[209] *Times Literary Supplement*, 19 December 1907, p. 390.

[210] Brown, 'Irish Historical Fiction', p. 450; see also Brown, *A Readers' Guide to Irish Fiction*, p. 31; Stephen J. Brown, 'Novels of the National Idea', *Irish Monthly*, 48, no. 563 (1920): p. 257.

The title was taken from the prophet Jeremiah (a biblical source which fascinated Birmingham): 'Shall iron break the northern iron and the steel?'.[211] The protagonist Neal Ward is encouraged to join the United Irish struggle by his uncle, a hardened rebel who returns from America after participating in the War of Independence. Neal's father, Rev. Micah Ward, is a radical Presbyterian minister, modelled on Rev. James Porter and Rev. William Steel Dickson. The civil war nature of the rebellion is explored through Neal's friendship with Maurice and his love for Una, the children of Lord Dunseveric, a liberal Anglo-Irish peer. Dunseveric is shown to be humane, unlike the brutish Captain Twinely of the local yeomanry and the callous English commander General Clavering. He agrees with the need for reform but cautions Neal of the dire consequences of rebellion:

> I admit, and I always have admitted, the justice of the claims which your people make. There ought to be equality, full and complete, for you and the Catholics. There ought to be an end to the tyranny under which you suffer, but you are going the wrong way about getting your wrongs righted. Your rebellion, if there is to be a rebellion, can't succeed. You will be crushed. And Neal, lad, that crushing will be an evil business. It will be evil for you and your friends, but that's not all. It will be made an excuse for taking away the hard won liberty of Ireland.[212]

Actual United Irishmen, namely William Orr and Henry Joy McCracken, are mentioned in passing and James Hope is developed into a major character. For this purpose, the author read historical sources on Hope, provided by Bigger, and made an effort 'to understand what manner of man he was'. The radical republicanism of the United Irishmen and the liberal loyalism of Dunseveric are presented as equally chivalrous and patriotic causes. The conflict between these contradictory Irish ideologies, which runs throughout the novel, reflects Birmingham's own dilemma of being torn between unorthodox nationalism and liberal unionism.[213]

In the final chapter, Neal Ward, who escapes to America after the debacle at Antrim, returns to visit Ireland in the summer of 1800. He finds that, following the passing of the Act of Union, 'the country lay torpid and apathetic under the blow', and realizes that 'the society of United Irishmen was broken' and 'the Protestant gentry were frightened or bribed.' Yet, his father and James Hope refuse to emigrate to America, insisting that for them 'there is no other land except only this lost land.' In the finale, Birmingham subtly slips in a small, but telling, indication of his revisionist take on history. The fictional Presbyterian minister Rev. Micah Ward—like the historical Rev. Steel Dickson—returns from imprisonment in Fort George, where he was awarded by his fellow republican prisoners a book with a dedication, signed by four Catholics, six Presbyterians, and ten Anglicans.[214] This inflation of the proportion of the involvement of members of the Church of Ireland in the rebellion is indicative of Birmingham's

---

[211] King James Version, *Jeremiah* 15:12. The title of Birmingham's first novel, *The Seething Pot* (1905) was also taken from Jeremiah and he would later write a biography of the prophet titled *God's Iron* (1939).

[212] Birmingham, *The Northern Iron*, p. 57.

[213] See Masahiko Yahata, 'George A. Birmingham, *The Northern Iron* (1907) and the 1798 Rebellion', *The Harp*, 14 (1999): pp. 13–20.

[214] Birmingham, *The Northern Iron*, p. 317. See also Vance, *Irish Literature since 1800*, p. 140.

404   *Forgetful Remembrance*

attempt to find a place for himself and other Anglo-Irish Protestants in a shared history of 1798.

Whereas, Birmingham's novel, according to Stephen Brown, was 'without undue bias, yet enlisting all the reader's sympathies on the side of Ireland', Samuel Robert Keightley's *The Pikemen: A Romance of the Ards of Down*, published in 1903 in London and New York, showed a distinct 'Presbyterian-nationalist bias' (evident already from the illustration of pikes that adorned the book's cover).[215] It received praise in the English press for its vivid depictions of the rebellion and its gripping style. The *Spectator*, however, criticized its one-sidedness, 'symbolised by the green covers in which it is bound'.[216] Keightley, a barrister on the North-East circuit, had started off as a conservative and then moved towards liberal unionism and eventually joined with Rev. J. B. Armour of Ballymoney to support Home Rule. After becoming an advocate of tenant rights and land reform, he unsuccessfully ran for election in South Antrim (1903) and South Derry (1906) as a liberal unionist Russellite candidate, and was equally unsuccessful as a liberal candidate in South Derry (1910). He was knighted in 1912 for his efforts to moderate extremism in Ulster and, after a long retirement in Dublin, on his death in 1949 he was lauded as 'the last of the old school of Ulster Liberals'.[217]

Keightley had been writing historical fiction since 1894 and *The Pikemen* was to become his most celebrated novel. The story is presented as a personal narrative written in the United States by a Presbyterian minister, Patrick Stirling of Drenton, Sangamon County, Illinois, who is said to have emigrated after 1798 from Ardkeen in the Ards peninsula of county Down. It was written so convincingly that fictive details were later repeated by the *Newtownards Chronicle* as factual 'stirring incidents of '98'.[218] A review in the *UJA*, most probably written by Bigger, commended Keightley for his 'excellent knowledge of the period of which he writes, and a thorough grasp of local circumstances and the common dialect of the people', and noted that 'there is not a dry or uninteresting chapter throughout the book.' It was envisaged that the book would be of particular interest to 'those who are residing in the county in which the principal scenes described in the book are laid'. Yet, the recommendation to publish 'a cheaper and more popular issue of this work, so as to make its pages accessible to everyone' did not materialize.[219] A second edition appeared in London in 1905 and, like the original, was priced at six shillings, which made it too dear for many local readers in Ulster.

---

[215] Brown, *A Readers' Guide to Irish Fiction*, pp. 30–1.

[216] *Spectator*, 7 November 1903, p. 7. For examples of praising reviews see *Graphic*, 21 November 1903, p. 704; *Walsall Advertiser* 7 November 1903, p. 2. For the significance of the cover art; see Eileen Reilly, 'Beyond Gilt Shamrock: Symbolism and Realism in the Cover Art of Irish Historical and Political Fiction, 1880–1914', in *Images, Icons and the Irish Nationalist Imagination*, edited by Lawrence W. McBride (Dublin: Four Courts Press, 1999), p. 101n28.

[217] *Northern Whig*, 18 August 1949, p. 4. An indication of Keightley's early politics can be found in his lecture 'Why Am I a Conservative?', delivered in 1884 at the Derby Orange Hall to the Belfast Conservative Association; *BNL*, 31 October 1884, p. 5.

[218] *Newtownards Chronicle*, 18 August 1906, p. 8. A faux citation in the novel of a non-existent *History of the Rising in Down* by Patrick Stirling, supposedly published in Boston in 1831 (p. 250), has been mistakenly referred to as one of 'the most significant Ulster accounts of 1798'; Whelan, 'The Green Atlantic', p. 231.

[219] *UJA*, 2nd ser., vol. 4, no. 1 (January 1904): p. 44.

Keightley, who was resident at the time in Lisburn, was knowledgeable of local traditions of the 1798 rebellion, which 'still linger in the fireside history—the truest history in the world—of that eventful time'. He was concerned about the evanescence of memory: 'another generation, and the old traditions, the homely, household stories lingering faintly still along the hillsides and among the valleys of Down, will have gone for ever.'[220] The protagonist of *The Pikemen* becomes a rebel after being whipped by soldiers and is unable to let go of the memory of this injustice: 'There are injuries we can forgive with generous forgetfulness that buries the sting and the memory. But there are wrongs that cut too deep into the heart to die, and stand out for ever as landmarks in our lives.' At Ballynahinch, he is advised by a fellow rebel to stay out of harm's way, as 'we can't do without our historian later on.'[221] *The Pikemen* was designed to re-affirm and preserve in fictional form the history of the rebellion, as it appeared in social memory. It is grounded in the locality through its use of Ulster-Scots vernacular speech.

Similarly, a collection of interlocking stories titled *Ninety-Eight and Sixty Years After*, published in Edinburgh and London in 1909, was written in the dialect of 'Lowland Scots, which, until superseded in recent years by what might be called National School English, was the ordinary language of County Antrim Farmers, especially in such Scottish districts as those of the Braid and Clough Water.'[222] A couple of the stories had appeared previously in *Blackwood's Magazine* and were described by the *Irish Book Lover* as 'two of the best Ulster stories that have appeared for some years'. They were written by James Andrew Strahan, the recently appointed professor of Jurisprudence and Roman Law at Queen's University Belfast, who wrote fiction under the pseudonym Andrew James.[223]

Strahan's political trajectory ran in the opposite direction from that of Keightley. His grandfather was 'out' in 1798 and the family had remained liberals. An elder brother of the author, Dr Samuel Alexander Kenny Strahan, who died in 1902, was well known as 'an advanced radical and a staunch Home Ruler'. The author had run in 1900 as a Liberal candidate for South Islington, but had since become an avowed unionist. In an essay on Ulster history and politics, he justified opposition to Home Rule with reference to the changes in attitude that had taken place since 1798:

> Now the Protestants of Ulster find themselves perfectly free and perfectly contented and attached to the people of Great Britain, not merely by the Union, but by the stronger ties of a common race and a common religion, common traditions and common ideas, while they are separated from the Catholics of the South on every one of these points. That is shortly why they are now as anxious to maintain the British connection as they were before '98 to break it.[224]

---

[220] S. R. Keightley, *The Pikemen: A Romance of the Ards of Down* (London: Hutchinson & Co., 1903), foreword.

[221] Ibid., pp. 29 and 262 (respectively).

[222] Andrew James, *Ninety-Eight and Sixty Years After* (Edinburgh and London: William Blackwood and Sons, 1911), preface.

[223] Andrew James, 'Nabob Castle: A Legend of Ulster' and 'The Last O'Hara', *Blackwood's Magazine*, 181, no. 1096 (February 1907) and no. 1099 (May 1907): pp. 197–207 and 628–41 (respectively); *Irish Book Lover*, 1, no. 3 (October 1909): pp. 32–3.

[224] J. A. Strahan, 'The Rock of Fergus', *Blackwood's Magazine*, 207, no. 1245 (July 1919): pp. 387–400 (esp. 390 and 394). For the politics of the elder brother, S. A. K. Strahan, see *Northampton Mercury*, 28 February 1902, p. 7.

Unlike Keightley's *The Pikemen*, which was written primarily for nationalist readers, this collection of stories addressed the discomfiting memory of the Turn-Out among unionists.

The first set of stories in *Ninety-Eight and Sixty Years After* dwells on recollections of a second generation after 1798. The preface notes that 'most of the incidents related in "Ninety-Eight" actually occurred in the Rebellion in Ulster of that date. The characters are purely imaginary.'[225] Loyalists who had participated in the suppression of the rebellion are shown to be burdened with disturbing memories that could not be easily talked about. The narrator, an elderly schoolmaster, recalls that his father, who in 1798 was a sergeant in the yeomanry, 'never could talk o' the rising without greeting [crying] ower the woefu' things that he saw done, and sometimes helped to do, during that awfu' time'.[226]

Such stories would have traditionally been recalled orally within family circles:

> Femily history, in my father's young days, was ane o' the main factors in forming the characters and views o' a' men, frae the owner o' half a county to the poorest cattier; and mony o' the poorest cottiers kenned mair about their ancestors than do now not a few o' the latest made peers. It was the lang lonely winter e'ens by the fireside that did that. Then the father tauld his lads what his father had tauld him, and what his grandfather had tauld his father, and what his greatgrandfather had tauld his grandfather, and sae on. It wasna the great families alone that then had their traditions and their pedigrees—a' folks had them.

However, traditional transmission of social memory is said to be in decline in Ulster:

> But that's a' changed now, mair parteecularly in the towns. Naebody there kens [knows] or cares who his greatgrandfather was, or what he was; it's only when folks hae made a load o' money and wish to appear genteel that they inquire into the matter, and what they find out when they do inquire they generally say naething about. Folks' memories are gone; they mind naething o' their fathers' views and doings, and for that matter hardly anything o' their ain o' six months syne, and for a' that the newspapers and the music halls are to be thanked or itherwise.[227]

Despite the prevalence of reticence and the perceived indifference, it transpires that the countryside is haunted by ghosts of '98. Gothic fiction offered a compelling literary genre for expressing the troubling essence of social forgetting.[228]

According to the London *Daily News*, Strahan had 'written the best volume of stories we know on the northern aspect of the Irish Rebellion of Ninety-Eight' and 'his stories, most of the incidents in which are said to be true, read like narratives of real events told by the side of a country fire'.[229] Local readers shared this enthusiasm. When the author was invited as a guest of honour to the annual prize-giving event of the Ballymena

---

[225] Andrew James, *The Nabob: A Tale of Ninety-Eight*, notes and afterword by John Wilson Foster (Dublin: Four Courts Press, 2006), p. 7. For convenience, references are given to this more accessible modern annotated edition (in which the title has been changed).

[226] James, 'Galloper Starkie', in *The Nabob*, p. 13. In another story, the narrator reiterates this point: 'My father . . . till his dying day he couldna talk o' those awfu' times wi' out greeting' ['. . . he could not talk of those awful times without crying']; James, 'The Last O'Hara', in *The Nabob*, p. 35.

[227] James, 'Davie the Devil', in *The Nabob*, pp. 45–6.

[228] See Radvan Markus, *Echoes of the Rebellion: The Year 1798 in Twentieth-Century Irish Fiction and Drama* (Oxford and New York: Peter Lang, 2015), pp. 68–74.

[229] *Daily News* [London], 5 April 1911, p. 3.

Academy in 1916, he was praised by the Presbyterian minister Rev. Andrew Patton for his 'intimate knowledge' of the districts of Ballymena, Cloughwater, and the Braid and for his book, which the speaker admitted having 'read more than once' and could recommend for its 'thrilling stories of the Rebellion of Ninety-Eight'.[230]

The main villain is a notorious landlord, nicknamed 'the "Hangman," because he had dealt very faithfully with the rebels at ninety-eight'. After his death, he is better known as 'Galloper Starkie' since, 'according to popular tradition', his ghost is often seen riding through the neighbourhood.[231] A reviewer for the unionist *Daily Express*, who was originally from the locality in Antrim, could recall 'the terror infused into his young mind by the tales of those who had seen or heard him (or, at least, had known somebody who had seen or heard him).'[232] The concluding story, set around the turn of the century, reveals a vicious circle of unforgivingness, in which the ghost of the perpetrator is pursued by the ghosts of his victims. The 'Hangman's' inability to lie peacefully in his grave, until a resolution is finally reached, suggestively gives the lie to the notion that haunting memories can simply be put to rest.[233]

Gruesome depictions of the terror experienced by relatives of rebels reached new heights in the morbid poetry of Padric [also spelt Padraic] Gregory, who showed the most creative use of dialect in the early twentieth-century northern flourish of writing on 1798. Gregory was born to a Belfast Catholic family. His parents emigrated to the United States and he spent part of his childhood in New York and Durango, Colorado, before returning to complete his school education in Belfast, where he went on to become a noted architect of church buildings. His literary pursuits were driven by reverence for 'the words and airs of many fine old folksongs', which he considered 'worthy of being collected, properly patched, if absolutely necessary, and preserved'. Gregory's first collection *The Ulster Folk*, published in London in 1912, was dedicated to the leading dramatists of the Ulster Literary Theatre, Lewis Purcell [David Parkhill] and Rutherford Mayne [Samuel Waddell]. The poems are written as ballads in Ulster-Scots, which supposedly recycle 'some fragments—the beginnings, endings, and odd verses of many other songs'.[234]

Like contemporary revivalist folk song collectors across Europe, Gregory composed poetry in a folkish style that fused cultural regionalism with romantic nationalism. The *Northern Whig* commented favourably on this reinvention of tradition:

> Mr. Gregory does not hesitate to alter and adapt when it suits his purpose; a stray verse will suggest to him a new lyric; but at the same time he keeps the inspiration of the old. In this he follows the immemorial methods of folk-singers...Mr. Gregory has the traditional instinct, and, what is more important, a measure of the directness of the old singers. Consequently his lyrics are more than antiquarian experiments, the head under which one is inclined to rank most modern efforts in this style; they reflect a view of life which could only be expressed in the folk medium.[235]

---

[230] *Ballymena Observer*, 22 December 1916, p. 6.
[231] James, 'The Return', in *The Nabob*, p. 85.   [232] *Daily Express*, 11 May 1911, p. 5.
[233] James, 'Christmas Morrow', in *The Nabob*, pp. 124–5. See also Foster, *Irish Novels*, pp. 349–52.
[234] Padric Gregory, *The Ulster Folk* (London: David Nutt, 1912), introduction, pp. vii–x. For Gregory's early collections of Ulster folk songs see *Journal of the Irish Folk Song Society*, 14 (1914), pp. 32–6.
[235] Reproduced in Padric Gregory, *Old World Ballads* (London: David Nutt, 1913), p. 71.

As a Catholic nationalist, his writing in Ulster-Scots is particularly intriguing, given that this vernacular tradition is generally associated with Presbyterians and, more often than not, with those who held unionist views.

Gregory's *Old World Ballads*, published in 1913 and dedicated to W. B. Yeats, is divided into three parts: Scotch, Irish, and English. All four ballads in the Irish section are 'in the Ulster-folk dialect' (Ulster-Scots) and relate to 1798. 'The Wail of the Madwoman' is about a Scottish woman who travels to Islandmagee in county Antrim, with the intention of marrying her betrothed, but upon arrival encounters the horrific outcome of the suppression of the rebellion, which drives her insane:

> But the wee house he'd built was blazin' red!
> An' high, from the branch o' an oul' pine tree
> Swung my dear love, he was stark an' dead!
> An' his poor glassy eyes stared straight at me,
> So I laughed wi' the Yeos—right heartilie!

This depiction of a woman gone mad by witnessing atrocities revived a prevalent motif in early-nineteenth-century poetry on 1798, showing the continued influence of Edward Rushton's 'Mary Le More'.[236] In 'A Ballad of a Posthumous Child', set in Ballynahinch two months after the rebellion, the widow of a brutally executed rebel vows to pass on her rankling hatred to her new-born son:

> I'll tell him how his sire was killed,
> An' how whin only jist half-dead—
> The Redcoats stood, an' laughed, an' filled
> His squirmin' body wi' their lead.

'A Rebel's Wife' takes place in a cottage in Kilroot, county Antrim (just outside Carrickfergus), and opens with a powerful depiction of silencing:

> I was roped, an' gagged, an' cudnae speak,
> O my heart an' sowl wi' loathin' filled.

Immobilized, a bound man watches his brother's wife seduce and slay 'the Captain o' the Yeos, who'd killed her husband, a while afore'. In 'The Return of the Youngest Born', a son of a rebel from Carrickfergus takes cold-blooded vengeance on a yeoman who had terrorized his family.[237]

These poems had previously appeared in *Irish Freedom*, an IRB monthly launched in November 1910. Their re-publication was aimed for a more general readership. Reviewers, who took these compositions for authentic folk balladry, were mostly impressed. The London literary magazine *The Athenaeum* determined that 'in the Ballads of the Irish Rebellion of 1798, written in the Ulster-folk dialect, Mr. Gregory is at his best' and asserted that 'these ballads have successfully caught the old-world spirit.' The *Irish Rosary*, a Dominican monthly, claimed that Gregory 'has forced the reality of the horrors of 1798 upon the English-speaking world'.[238] The recently

---

[236] See Chapter 3 above, p. 184.

[237] Gregory, *Old World Ballads*, pp. 45–7 ('The Wail of the Madwoman'), 47–53 ('A Ballad of a Posthumous Child'), 54–5 ('A Rebel's Wife'), and 56–7 ('The Return of the Youngest Born').

[238] Reproduced in Padric Gregory, *Ireland: A Song of Hope, and Other Poems* (Dublin: Talbot Press and London: T. Fischer Unwin, 1917), 'Some Press Opinions on Mr. Gregory's Work' (un-paginated section at the end of the book).

founded Jesuit periodical *Studies* expressed satisfaction that the untold memory of the rebellion could now be addressed unflinchingly:

> who, for instance, in former times, dare speak or sing of '98 in Ireland? Few indeed: but now the sorrows of her people at that time, as at all other, are better known; their patience and wrongs are more taken into account, and the poets of Erin are returning to materials for ballad and drama unrivalled in the history of any other nation.

Gregory was praised for having 'caught the spirit of the time with unerring precision' and for showing how a ballad 'tells us more about '98 than many a page of dull history'.[239]

Encouraged by the positive reviews, Gregory wrote additional poems on the rebellion in Ulster. 'A Ballad of '98 Heroes', published in his 1917 collection *Ireland: A Song of Hope, and Other Poems*, is written in standard English and resembles the romantic nationalist poetry of Young Ireland rather than provincial vernacular poetry, though it still shows Gregory's signature fixation with atrocity:

> Here's to the Nameless Unnumbered Dead
> Who battled for Ireland's weal,
> Ne'er fearful of whirlwind showers of lead
> Or glittering lines of steel;
> And here's to the living whose hearts were wrung
> When they found themselves alone:
> Their women-folk strung,
> Or raped, or hung,
> Their babes on the dung-heap thrown.[240]

Whilst Gregory collected in the north-east 'old anonymous Ulster folk songs', considered 'too good to be permitted to be forgotten', he continued to compose in Ulster-Scots his own original poetry on the rebellion.

Gregory's new compositions were published in 1920 in *Ulster Songs and Ballads*. 'Molly Asthoreen', labelled 'a sorrow song of 1798', describes the pain of separation caused by forced emigration. In the poem 'A Rebel', a family from Islandmagee is obliged to watch the execution of the head of the family outside their house, in consequence of which his pregnant wife delivers a stillborn child and dies in labour. 'The Death o' Padraic' is yet another 'sorrow song of 1798' in which a woman laments the death of a lover, who was hung near Ballynahinch. In a poem on 'The Battle of Antrim', Gregory chose not to describe the fighting on the day, focusing instead on the grief of a woman, whose husband left 'tae MacCracken's bloody meet' and was brought back to her 'in a coul' clammy blood-stained windin' sheet'.[241] In all of these poems, the rebellion is recalled through the suffering of the relatives of the insurgents.

Gregory presented his own compositions as if they were revisions of folk poetry. A sympathetic critic, writing for the Dublin Catholic journal the *Irish Monthly* under

---

[239] *Studies*, 2, no. 7 (1913): pp. 364–5.
[240] Padric Gregory, *Ireland: A Song of Hope, and Other Poems* (Dublin: Talbot Press and London: T. Fischer Unwin, 1917), pp. 21–3.
[241] Padric Gregory, *Ulster Songs and Ballads* (Dublin: Talbot Press and London: Fisher Unwin, 1920), pp. 30–1 ('Molly Asthoreen'), 41–4 ('The Rebel'), 52–3 ('The Death o' Padraic'), 54–6 ('The Battle of Antrim').

the pen-name 'Bibliophile', described Gregory's work in terms of folklore collection and editing:

> He knew that a nation's childhood expresses itself poetically in folk-lore songs; that folk-lore could be found nowhere else but in the homes of people in outlying districts. He therefore adopted the method of Burns and became a snapper up of all folk-songs and fragments of folk-songs he could lay hold of in Co. Antrim and Co. Down, editing them, and where necessary, completing them.

Seen in this way, it appeared that Gregory's verses 'must be the product of many generations of faithful Irish narrators' and that his 'poetical gifts and love for folk-songs raise these traditional fragments to high levels in literature' so that 'the songs begin a new life in a new form', while still retaining the merits of 'perfect and unexaggerated' dialect.[242]

However, the impression of direct continuity with folk tradition was deceptive. Gregory's macabre verses, which revelled in horror, shed the subtlety and ambiguity that characterized vernacular poetry composed by the likes of James Orr and the 'rhyming weavers', who had actually experienced the ravages of the rebellion in 1798. The folk history of the Turn-Out is replete with descriptions of violence and terror and yet nothing compares to the stark outspokenness of Gregory's explicit imagery. In his yearning to express cultural trauma in its crudest form, Gregory did not hesitate to flesh out what had previously been left unspoken. Reticence, which was essential to social forgetting, was cast out. The Ulster public was not particularly responsive to this explicitness and Gregory's 1798 ballads, which were published in Dublin and London, did not enter into the local repertoire of folk tradition. His *Complete Ballads*, originally published in 1935, was re-issued in Belfast in 2013 by his grandson, Patrick Gregory, who felt that the poetry had been neglected and forgotten.[243]

It is instructive to compare Gregory's adopted use of dialect with the contemporary poetry of Adam Lynn of Cullybackey (5 kilometres north-west of Ballymena). Lynn came from a Covenanter background, attended a Presbyterian Sabbath School and became an evangelical member of the Church of Ireland, leaving a job in the textile industry to work as a missionary lay reader at the Shankill Parish in Lurgan. He wrote in the vernacular literary tradition of mid-Antrim and has been applauded for his 'vigorous and fluent Ulster Scots'. A biographical entry written by a local history society notes that 'his poems are rich and his use of rare words and quaint expressions, maybe difficult to understand if you were a stranger, but still appealed to the local people.'[244]

As a rule, Lynn's poetry, which was published in local unionist newspapers, avoided the awkward topic of 1798. Nevertheless, the subject appears, of all places, in the poem 'The Twalt O'July' [the Twelfth of July], written in 1903:

---

[242] *Irish Monthly*, 51, no. 601 (1923): p. 341.

[243] Padric Gregory, *Complete Ballads* (Belfast: Lagan Press, 2013), introduction by Eamon Hughes and preface by Patrick Gregory; see also accompanying website: <www.padraicgregory.com>.

[244] Adam Lynn, *Random Rhymes Frae Cullybackey* (Belfast: printed by W. & G. Baird, 1911), biographical notice (by James Loughridge), pp. iii–iv. See also Ivan Herbison, 'Beyond the Rhyming Weavers', *Études Irlandaises*, 38, no. 2 (2013): pp. 43–5; as well as the biographical entry on the website of the Cullybackey & District Historical Society; <http://cullybackeyhistory.co.uk/adam-lynn>.

Few o' us min' the turn-oot fecht
That taen place here in ninety-eicht,
A wud nae like tae be ower strecht,
Bit ye al' ken
The civil side had nae the weicht
Fur soger men.

Remarkably, a poem on Orange celebrations, which appeared in a volume published by subscription and made available for purchase at the offices of the *Ballymena Weekly Telegraph*, a provincial unionist newspaper, mentions that few people still remember [*min'*, deriving from the Scots *mynd*] the fighting [*fecht*] of the Turn-Out and notes that it is generally known [*ken*] that the rebels—who are referred to as 'the civil side'—did not have the means to overcome the military [*soger men*]. This passage deftly encapsulates the ambivalent nature of the social forgetting of 1798, by which it would seem that the rebellion was largely unremembered, and yet remains familiar all the same.[245]

Other unionist poets, though knowledgeable of local history of the rebellion, opted not to mention 1798 in their work. George Francis Savage-Armstrong—'the poet of Wicklow', who was educated in Trinity College Dublin and went on to become professor of History and English Literature at Queen's College Cork, took pride in his Ulster roots. His mother was the daughter of Rev. Henry Savage of Glastry in the Ards peninsula in county Down and, following the death of a maternal aunt in 1891, George adopted Savage as an additional surname. In editing the family papers, which were published just shortly after his death in 1906 as *A Genealogical History of the Savage Family in Ulster*, he became aware of local traditions of 1798.

It was remembered that a member of the family, Major Charles Savage, 'was three times down on his knees in the lawn of Ballygalget to be shot by the Rebels, and was three times liberated'. From John Rutherford of Portaferry, Savage-Armstrong heard reminisces of the rebel attempt to take the Market House, in an engagement known locally as 'The Battle of the Diamond' (in a nod towards the confrontation that signalled the foundation of the Orange Order four years earlier). The folklore he collected mainly recalled the plight of loyalists: 'For some time before the insurrection broke out loyal people in the Ards had a miserable time of it, and those who would not join in the movement were in danger of their lives, and had sometimes to sleep at night, with their families, in the fields.' However, he also encountered recollections that acknowledged the excesses of government soldiers and the tribulations of former rebels: 'After the insurrection was quelled many of the Rebels engaged in it fled to America. Some got pardoned and came home. Several houses in the country-parts were burned down by the soldiery by order of Government.' These traditions were not reflected in Savage-Armstrong's *Ballads of Down*, which were partly written in Ulster-Scots dialect. He preferred to generically praise the 'Men of Down' for their 'silent action' as a common collective, without touching on the divisive memories of the rebellion.[246]

---

[245] Lynn, *Random Rhymes*, pp. 45–7. An advertisement noted that 'copies to be purchased at the *Telegraph* office' (presumably the *Ballymena Weekly Telegraph*); *Ballymena Observer*, 3 November 1911, p. 6.

[246] George Francis Savage-Armstrong, *Ballads of Down* (London: Longmans, Green, and Co., 1901), pp. 173–5 ('Men of Down'); Savage-Armstrong, *A Genealogical History*, pp. 155–6, 241–2, 292, 318, and 361–2; Savage-Armstong Papers, PRONI D618/254.

W. B. Yeats found Savage-Armstrong's 'lacking in imaginative impulse', though he detected in the Irish poems some 'more or less interesting verse'.[247] The poet was faulted for not engaging with the literary revival and its reinvention of folk tradition.

By contrast, the poet Joseph Campbell, who wrote under the Gaelicized form of his name—Seosamh MacCathmhaoil, was a central figure of the northern revival and revered 'the Folk inspired utterance'.[248] Campbell addressed the memory of 1798 in a couple of his works, which described the plight of family members of rebels with considerable more restraint than the poetry of Gregory. Rather than wallowing in graphic depictions of brutality, he put an emphasis on fears and hesitations. The poem 'The Women at their Doors', published in Campbell's 1906 collection *The Rushlight*, described the anxieties of the womenfolk, who 'keened by their ashy fires till their faces were haggard and wan', as they waited for news of the men:

> For they knew they had gone to the trysting,
> With pike and musketoon,
> To fight for their hearths and altars
> At the rising of the moon![249]

Although Ninety-Eight is not explicitly mentioned in this poem, the historical reference is obvious from the allusions to pikes and to 'the rising of the moon'—the title of a popular ballad about the 1798 rebellion in the north-midlands, which was composed around 1865 by the Fenian poet John Keegan Casey ('Leo').[250]

Campbell, whose father (William Henry Campbell) was Catholic and mother (Catherine née Canmer) was of mixed Catholic and Presbyterian stock, was aware from his childhood of the sensitivities of remembering the rebellion:

> At home, there was scant mention of '98. Father, narrowed in his loyalties by Parnellite nationalism, then in a slough of disintegration, knew nothing of it. Mother, come of 'blackmouth' [Presbyterian] blood on her father's side, knew of it by family tradition, but she shunned it as a familiar topic. She would praise rebels hanged a hundred years ago, but feared revival of their intransigence in this day and age.[251]

As a regular attendant of Bigger's gatherings at Ardrigh, Campbell was inspired by the 1798 centenary. He was a cousin of Ethna Carbery and eagerly read articles on the rebellion published in the *Shan Van Vocht*. He also became acquainted with recollections that were documented by antiquarians, in particular Young's collection *Ulster in '98*. In 1912, Campbell skilfully re-adapted these traditions, while retaining their inherent ambiguities, in a one-act play titled *The Turn-Out*, which, as the name suggests, is steeped in references from folk history.

---

[247] W. B. Yeats, '"Noetry" and Poetry', *The Bookman*, no. 19 (September 1892): p. 182.

[248] Seosamh Mac Cathmhaoil [Joseph Campbell], 'The Music of the Folk', *Journal of the Irish Folk Song Society*, 1, no. 1 (April 1904): p. 2.

[249] Seosamh MacCathmhaoil [Joseph Campbell], *The Rushlight* (Dublin: Maunsel & Co., 1906), p. 32.

[250] John K. Casey, *A Wreath of Shamrocks: Ballads, Songs, and Legends* (Dublin: R. S. M'Gee, 1867), pp. 31–3; see also Zimmerman, *Songs of Irish Rebellion*, pp. 259–60; Beiner, *Remembering the Year of the French*, pp. 95–6.

[251] Joseph Campbell, 'Northern Autobiography', *Journal of Irish Literature*, 8, no. 3 (1979), p. 73; quoted in McNulty, *The Ulster Literary Theatre*, p. 43.

The drama takes place in the interior of a country cottage on the afternoon of the Battle of Antrim. It transpires that the head of the household, Jamey Maxwell, a linen-broker and farmer, has reluctantly set off, with his son Davey, to take part in the insurrection. Left at home, his wife Abbey, a Presbyterian, expresses her admiration for William Orr and her enthusiasm for the United Irish struggle, while their daughter Ruth, who admires the established church and derides Catholics, is weary of the consequences for the family, should their implication in the rebellion be discovered. Watty Bell, a duplicitous yeoman, arrives at their doorstep wounded from the battle and is mercifully treated for his wounds. In the concluding scene, he returns with a party of yeomen to burn down the house and arrest the father and son.[252]

Although Campbell's play faithfully captures the spirit of the local memory of the Turn-Out, and should have been produced by the Ulster Literary Theatre, it was written at an inopportune time. Northern loyalists, as explained by a contemporary polemicist writing under the name of 'An Ulster Protestant', were in an anxious state of 'Ulsteria', which cast dark shadows over the memory of Protestant involvement alongside Catholics in the United Irish rebellion.[253] The tensions of the Third Home Crisis, when Protestant unionists were mobilized in Ulster *en masse* to oppose the rise of a predominantly Catholic nationalism, discouraged public engagement with the troublesome memories of Ninety-Eight. Unlike the Irish Literary Theatre in Dublin, which famously produced in 1902 *Cathleen ni Houlihan*, a one-act play by W. B. Yeats and Lady Gregory set in 1798 in Killala, county Mayo, and described by Yeats, as 'the first play of our Irish School of folk-drama',[254] the Ulster Literary Theatre, despite the keen interest of its founding members in the memory of the United Irishmen, did not produce anything on 1798 in Antrim and Down. Consequently, Campbell's *The Turn-Out* was never staged.[255] It remained a neglected work of cultural memory that did not feed into social memory.

Conversely, a poem composed by Ethna Carbery had far-reaching impact on social memory. Carbery died unexpectedly from gastritis in April 1902, just shortly after the 1798 centenary, in which she had played a prominent role. She had just gotten married the previous year and was aged only 36 on her death. These tragic circumstances struck a chord with the general public and the nationalist papers published a gush of sentimental eulogies in her memory. Several weeks after she passed away, Carbery's bereaved husband, the author and folklore collector Seamus MacManus, published a collection of her poetry *The Four Winds of Eirinn*, which was received with great enthusiasm and all copies were immediately sold out. Ten editions appeared within a year and by 1905 the volume had gone through fifteen editions, arguably turning Carbery into the most widely read poet in Ireland. The volume included 'Rody M'Corley', a stirring ballad describing the last moments of a blue-eyed golden-haired young insurgent as 'he goes to die on the bridge of Toome today'. Republished in newspapers and countless songbooks, it became one of the most popular Irish rebel

[252] Joseph Campbell, 'The Turn-Out', *Irish Review*, 2, no. 18 (1912): pp. 317–35.

[253] An Ulster Protestant, 'Light on Ulsteria', *Irish Review*, 2, no. 15 (1912): pp. 119–20.

[254] *The Collected Works in Verse and Prose of William Butler Yeats* (Stratford-upon-Avon: Shakespeare Head Press, 1908), vol. 4, p. 242.

[255] See Norah Saunders and A. A. Kelly, *Joseph Campbell: Poet & Nationalist, 1879–1944* (Dublin: Wolfhound Press, 1988), pp. 59–60.

songs of all time. The incredible success of Carbery's memorable song brought the local '98 hero, who was formerly known only to very few people outside of the area of Toome in county Antrim, to the wider attention of nationalists throughout Ireland and Irish diaspora communities.[256]

Carbery's ballad 'Roddy McCorley' was originally written during the preparations for the centenary, when its titular hero was among the northern United Irishmen for whom the *Shan Van Vocht* organized commemorations. Starting with the first Decoration Day in June 1896, pilgrimages were organized to the site of McCorley's execution in Toome. Incidentally, the president of the C. J. Kickham Society, one of the main sponsors of these trips, was named Rodger 'Rody' McCorley and the fortuitous association with the executed hero was not missed on those who attended the commemorative events.[257] Several '98 clubs in the area of Toome honoured McCorley. A 'large and representative open-air meeting', held at Toome on 25 March 1898, was attended by two such clubs—one from Magherafelt, county Londonderry (9 kilometres west of Toome), and another from Newbridge, county Londonderry (2 kilometres west of Toome).[258] An additional Roddy McCorley '98 club was active in nearby Ballyscullion, county Londonderry (6 kilometres north-west of Toome). Because of its association with McCorley, Toome was designated as the focal point for regional commemoration and it hosted another large demonstration on 16 June 1898.[259]

Bigger, who was familiar with the sites of 1798 memory in Antrim and maintained that 'each has its own story of brave hearts, not yet fully recorded in any lasting way', proclaimed that 'amongst them all, none has a dearer memory than Rody MacCorly, who met his fate on the Bridge of Toome'. While he admired Carbery's 'stirring verse' and believed that 'every Ulster boy and girl should know it', he was intent on documenting surviving folk traditions of McCorley, in order 'to keep his memory green'. In June 1907, Bigger collected in Toome, the words of 'a popular ballad, still repeated in the district'. Although the metre does not match the rhythm of an early tune dedicated to Roddy McCorley, which was collected by the antiquarian George Petrie in 1833, the lyrics are rich in local detail and the style reflects the conventions of traditional Irish singing, suggesting that it is indeed an older folk song.[260]

Drawing on the details in the folk song, and supplementing them with scraps of information compiled from local sources, Bigger put together a biographical sketch of McCorley, which appeared as an article in the *Irish News*. The editor of the nationalist newspaper commended him on this achievement: 'It is an excellent thing to secure the local traditions that survive regarding the career of the men of '98 in their local districts,

---

[256] Seumas MacManus, ed., *The Four Winds of Eirinn: Poems by Anna MacManus ('Ethna Carbery')* (Dublin: M. H. Gill and Son, 1902), pp. 82–3. For a typical example of a nationalist eulogy and the consequent surge in demand for Carbery's work see *Freeman's Journal*, 3 April (p. 5), 25 April (p. 4), 23 May (p. 2), and 19 June (p. 4) 1902. For an early example of the poem's republication in a provincial newspaper see *Derry Journal*, 9 May 1902, p. 6.

[257] *SVV*, 1, no. 6 (June 1896), pp. 116–17 and no. 7 (July 1896), p. 140.

[258] *SVV*, 3, no. 4 (April 1898), p. 75.

[259] *Irish Weekly and Ulster Examiner*, 7 May 1898, p. 1 and 18 June 1898, p. 1.

[260] *Irish News*, 9 August 1907, p. 7. Bigger's original notes can be found in Bigger Papers, BCL Z271. See also Guy Beiner, 'The Enigma of "Roddy McCorley Goes to Die": Forgetting and Remembering a Local Rebel Hero in Ulster', in *Rhythms of the Revolt: European Traditions and Memories of Social Conflict in Oral Culture*, edited by David Hopkin, Éva Guillorel, and Will Pooley (Routledge: London and New York, 2017), pp. 327–57.

and as handed down by those amongst whom they lived, who conversed with them and saw them face to face.'[261] Bigger's Roddy McCorley essay re-appeared with an illustration in the popular national newspaper *Weekly Freeman* and was reproduced in part in the provincial newspaper the *Derry Journal*, as well as in the Irish-Australian newspaper the *Catholic Press*. It was also issued as a pamphlet.[262] Concurrently, an account of McCorley was collected by Robert Hanna, a resident of Belfast with an interest in 1798, from 90-year-old Hugh Lagan, the former gatekeeper at the demesne of the Marquis of Donegal.[263] The persistence of these older oral traditions was eclipsed by the overwhelming popularity of Carbery's more recent ballad. The general public was introduced to Roddy McCorley of the newly composed nationalist song, rather than how he was still remembered in oral traditions. By favouring revivalist compositions over local folk memory, national collective remembrance inadvertently contributed to provincial social forgetting.

At the same time, national remembrance also revived local remembrance. Following the success of 'Roddy McCorley', interest was aroused in other poems that Carbery had composed for the centenary. A long poem on Willie Nelson, a 16-year-old youth who was hanged in front of his mother's home in 1798, had originally been read out at an early commemoration of the Battle of Antrim in 1895, at which 'every stanza was listened to with breathless interest, and concluded with a burst of applause from the attentive hearers.'[264] Carbery utilized the memory of the execution as a rallying call for advanced nationalism:

> Remember Willie Nelson at the Dawning of the Day,
> When Freedom beckons from her height, and we have found the way
> That brave men fought and died to find on many a battle field,
> And taught us how to fight and die but never how to yield.
> Oh! Irishmen, when the signal comes again be ye gathered there,
> Be ye as ready to take your stand as ever your fathers were;
> Facing your foemen for Ireland's sake, sweep like a torrent down,
> And strike them a stronger, surer blow than that day in Antrim town.

The ballad of 'Willie Nelson' was originally printed as an illustrated broadsheet that was sold as a special supplement to the June 1897 issue of the *Shan Van Vocht* and which soon became a rare item.[265] Following the posthumous rediscovery of interest in Carbery's work, the poem was republished and cited in local newspapers and was included in an expanded 1918 edition of *The Four Winds of Eirinn*.[266] The publicity encouraged more open remembrance at the site of the hero's hitherto unmarked grave. Shortly after the poem 'Willie Nelson' appeared in the *Derry Journal* in 1905, the

---

[261] *Irish News* 26 August 1907, p. 7.

[262] *Weekly Freeman*, 7 September 1907, pp. 13–14; *Catholic Press*, 3 October 1907, p. 5; *Derry Journal*, 7 December 1908, p. 2; Francis Joseph Bigger, *Rody MacCorly: 'Who Fears to Speak of '98?'* (Belfast: s.n., 1907).

[263] *Newtownards Chronicle*, 14 August 1908, p. 8.

[264] *United Ireland*, 15 June 1895, p. 2. For the execution of Willie Nelson see Chapter 2 above, pp. 114–15.

[265] *United Ireland*, 26 June 1897, p. 13; *Willie Nelson* (Belfast: J. W. Boyd, n.d.). A copy of the broadsheet is held in Lily Williams Papers, NLI 8,286/1/3.

[266] *Derry Journal*, 23 May 1902, p. 7 and 7 June 1905, p. 2; *Fermanagh Herald*, 10 June 1905, p. 7; *Donegal News*, 20 December 1913, p. 2; *Ulster Herald*, 20 December 1913, p. 2; MacManus, ed., *The Four Winds of Eirinn* (1918), pp. 81–5.

epitaph 'The Ballycarry Martyr' was added 'as a sort of afterthought' to a roll of names on a tombstone in the graveyard of Templecorran, near Ballycarry.[267]

At one of the first meetings of Na Fianna Éireann, the nationalist youth movement founded by Bulmer Hobson and Constance Markievicz in 1909, the northern nationalist Patrick McCartan gave a lecture on 'The Boy Heroes of '98' and recited Carbery's 'Willie Nelson'. A Belfast *sluagh* (branch) was named after him, alongside *sluaighte* named after the more familiar heroes Henry Munro, Henry Joy McCracken, and Betsy Gray.[268] While Willie Nelson was presented as a role model for national youth, his mother was upheld by radical female writers, such as Markievicz and Helena Concannon, as an example for patriotic women. Alice Milligan later wrote 'The Dauntless Laddie', a poem in Ulster-Scots which recounts the tragedy of the execution from the point of view of the bereaved mother.[269] Nationalist preoccupation with the local hero influenced the Presbyterian, mostly unionist, community from which he hailed. The Ballycarry poet William Calwell, born in 1863 and known colloquially as 'Yankee Bill' for having spent time in the United States, strayed from his habit of writing on agricultural themes and penned sometime in the early decades of the century a poem on 'The Death of Willie Nelson', which was published anonymously as a pamphlet and recalled locally.[270]

Florence Mary Wilson's 'The Man from God Knows Where' is another poetic composition from the early twentieth century that achieved remarkable success and left an imprint on social memory. Wilson (neé Addy) had grown up in Lisburn, where her father, the Methodist industrialist Robert Charles Addy, was known as 'a devoted adherent of the Orange Institution'.[271] After marrying and converting to Presbyterianism, she lived in Bangor, county Down, and was a close friend of Alice Milligan, who encouraged her passion for writing. Around the turn of the century, Wilson wrote an unpublished short story titled 'The Man at the Well'. It tells of an English traveller encountering the ghosts of a rebel, who was hanged 'in the dark days after '98', and of his lover, who committed suicide and was disowned by her father, 'who prided himself on his unanswering loyalty to the British throne'. The story ends with the wayfarer

---

[267] *Belfast Evening Telegraph*, 24 November 1906; republished also in *Larne Times*, 1 December 1906, p. 9.

[268] *Freeman's Journal*, 12 October 1909, p. 10; *Donegal News*, 17 February 1912, p. 7 and 22 June 1912, p. 7; see also Marnie Hay, 'The Foundation and Development of Na Fianna Éireann, 1909–16', *Irish Historical Studies*, 36, no. 141 (2008), p. 61n62; Lauren Arrington, *Revolutionary Lives: Constance and Casimir Markievicz* (Princeton and Oxford: Princeton University Press, 2016), p. 60. A children's essay contest awarded a prize to a girl who recounted Willie Nelson's story; *Sunday Independent*, 17 September 1911, p. 9.

[269] Constance Markievicz, 'The Women of '98', *Irish Citizen*, 5 November 1915, p. 151; Mrs Thomas [Helena] Concannon, *Women of 'Ninety-Eight* (Dublin: M. H. Gill and Son, 1919), pp. 324–5; Alice Milligan *Poems*, edited by Henry Connell Mangan (Dublin: M. H. Gill, 1954), pp. 92–4.

[270] A copy of the undated pamphlet is held at the McClay Library, QUB; the ballad is reproduced in Avy Dowlin, *Ballycarry in Olden Days* (Belfast: Graham and Heslip, 1963), pp. 49–52. See also David Hume, 'Muskets on the Sabbath: Lessons from Local History', *The Glynns*, 38 (2010): pp. 10–18; David Hume and John W. Nelson, *The Templecorran Project: An Historic Guide to Ballycarry Old Cemetery* (Ballycarry: s.n., 1994), p. 17; Paul Callaghan, *Memories from the Farmyard* (Newtownards: Colourpoint Books, 2010), pp. 34–5. Renewed interest in Willie Nelson is evident in a ballad by an East Antrim singer, Randall Stephen Hall, and posted on the internet in 2012; <https://soundcloud.com/randall-stephen-hall/the-ballad-of-willie-nelson>.

[271] *BNL*, 6 August 1890, p. 5.

receiving advice from a local resident: 'Best, we should forget all about it. Treat it, if you will, as a strange dream with some basis in reality. Forget it. Forget it, I say.' [272] In writing fiction about 1798, Wilson was evidently well attuned to the allure of social forgetting.

'The Man from God Knows Where' appeared in a slim collection of Wilson's poetry *The Coming of the Earls and Other Verse*, which was published in Dublin in 1918 in at least two editions of 450 copies each. A note by the author identifies 'the "man" of this ballad' as Thomas Russell at the time when he toured Ulster to recruit United Irishmen, and explains the sobriquet: 'we will suppose he does not make his name or mission known in mixed company, or maybe does not suspect the possibilities underlying the dour reticence of the group of countrymen, though they afterwards gave a good account of themselves.'[273] Wilson was a regular visitor to Ardrigh. Her historical knowledge was informed by Bigger, who published in 1918 *Four Shots from Down*, a collection of short essays on local history, based on 'old traditions'. A section on Russell is illustrated with two drawings of his attempts to rally support for the rebellion, one of which is labelled 'The Man from God Knows Where' and portrays the opening scene of Wilson's poem, in which Russell visits a tavern—identified by Bigger as the Buck's Head in Annadorn, near Loughinisland, county Down. This account relied on 'stories told and believed . . . stories that have been burned into the hearts of the people of Down and further afield among the sea-divided Gael.' [274]

The nationalist poet and playwright Padraic Colum praised Wilson's poems for their 'winsome Ulster dialect, with their imaginative patriotism and their touch of the eerie', comparing her work to that of Alice Milligan and claiming that it exemplified 'the poetry of militant Irish nationalism'.[275] It appears that 'The Man from God Knows Where' circulated among republicans already prior to its official publication. It was a favourite of the trade unionist Sean Connolly, who would often recite it at separatist nationalist gatherings, most notably at an Emmet Anniversary organized in 1914 by the Wolfe Tone Memorial Association at the Rotunda in Dublin. After Connolly's death in the Easter Rising, the poem was recited by the balladeer Brian O'Higgins ('Brian na Banbha') at a concert of republican prisoners in Frongoch in 1916.[276]

Once published, 'The Man from God Knows Where' became an immensely popular public recitation, performed by nationalists on countless occasions. In subsequent decades, it was particularly associated with Cathal O'Byrne, a Catholic singer and

[272] Anne Colman typescripts of 'Florence Mary Wilson: The Collected Writings' (1994), Florence Mary Wilson Papers, Irish Linen Centre and Lisburn Museum. My thanks to the museum's research officer, Dr Ciaran Toal, for providing me with a copy.
[273] Wilson, *The Coming of the Earls*, pp. 7–10. See also *Irish News*, 9 November 1946; *Fermanagh Herald*, 17 October 1953, p. 3 [memoir of Florence Wilson by 'one who knew her']; John McLaughlin, 'Florence Wilson and The Man from God Knows Where', *Due North*, 1, no. 4 (2001): pp. 7–10; John A. McLaughlin, *One Green Hill: Journeys through Irish Songs* (Belfast: Beyond the Pale, 2003), pp. 111–18; Deirdre Armstrong, '"A Lady Who Has Written Much Admirable Verse": Florence Mary Wilson and the Man from God-Knows-Where', in *A Man Stepped out for Death: Thomas Russell and County Down*, edited by Brian S. Turner (Newtownards, County Down: Colourpoint Books, 2003), pp. 49–56.
[274] Francis Joseph Bigger, *Four Shots from Down* (Belfast: William Sweeney, 1918), pp. 46–50.
[275] Padraic Colum, 'Recent Irish Poetry', *The Nation*, 108, no. 2812 (1919), p. 833.
[276] *Irish Independent*, 3 March 1914, p. 6 and 11 September 1919, p. 4; *Kerryman*, 26 August 1916, p. 3.

Irish language enthusiast, who had been a constant participant in Bigger's soirées and was later 'known in every concert hall in Ireland for his famous recitation in the Co. Down dialect of that stirring Northern ballad'.[277] The ballad was set to music in the folk song revival of the Seventies and performed as a song by the Scottish folk group Five Hand Reel.[278] This acclaim offers yet another telling example of how revivalist poetry from the turn of the century instigated reinvention of tradition, while effectively diverting public attention away from local folklore.

Set apart from the familiar ballad, the lesser-known details of Russell's endeavours to stir rebellion in county Down were maintained in oral traditions that were still recounted in the late twentieth century.[279] However, folk memory was not insulated from outside influences. In 1955, a 48-year-old man in the Glens of Antrim told a folklore collector that he could 'remember the old people here saying that there was a Corkman in Glenariffe organising them for Ninety-Eight' and that his grandmother had referred to this stranger with a 'southern tongue' as 'The Man From God Knows Where'. Curiously, the storyteller insisted that this rebel was hung in Toome. The poems of Florence Mary Wilson and Ethna Carbery had evidently merged and filtered into local folklore.[280]

The Downpatrick local historian Richard Edward Parkinson later maintained that, as long as the tombstone that Mary Ann McCracken had erected for Russell remains intact, 'the story of Russell and his companions will not be forgotten.'[281] With Bigger's support, the gravestone was cleaned and decorated at a modest commemorative event in 1903, during the centenary of Emmet's Rising. It was noted at that time that 'the name of Thomas Russell is but little remembered outside the Northern district, where he chiefly worked.'[282] Efforts were made to commemorate also lesser-known local rebels executed in 1803, such as a David Porter of Antrim. An appeal was issued to the nationalist public, asserting that 'it is fitting that Catholics should not permit to sink into oblivion the memory of the brave Irish Presbyterians who risked liberty and life for the emancipation of their fellow countrymen in dark and evil days.'[283] Yet, the Ulster revival mostly focused on a select list of familiar United Irish leaders and did not reflect the wider democratic scope of vernacular historiography. The names of common rebels that were preserved privately in local traditions rarely attracted public attention.

In addition to northern literature entirely dedicated to the rebellion, recollections of 1798 also appeared as literary references made in passing. For example, the children's novel *The Weans at Rowallan*, published in London in 1905 to critical acclaim, recounts the adventures of five orphaned siblings growing up in an old run-down

[277] *Irish Press*, 26 July 1945, p. 3.

[278] Five Hand Reel, 'A Bunch of Fives' (Topic Records, 1979).

[279] Francis P. Gallagher, *A Blood Red Autumn: Thomas Russell and the Irish Rising of 1803* (Castlewellan, Co. Down: Fairythorn Press, 2003), pp. 7, 73, 78, 90, 97, and 99.

[280] Collected by Michael J. Murphy from Michael Leech, The Bay, Glenariffe, 14 January 1955; NFC 1384/158.

[281] See R. E. Parkinson, *The City of Downe from Its Earliest Days* (Bangor: Donard Publishing Company, 1977; orig. edn 1927), p. 106.

[282] Bigger Papers, BCL K6/G/11 (newspaper article titled 'the Grave of Russell' probably taken from *Irish News*, 21 October 1903).

[283] W. J. M. Flannagan, Belfast to F. J. Bigger, 26 October 1903, Bigger Papers, BCL K6/G/16; *Irish News*, 27 October 1903.

house in the Mourne Mountains of county Down. When visited by an English aunt, the children take her to a graveyard to see 'the tombstones of the rebels, with skull and crossbones on the top, and the grave of a great-uncle of theirs, who had been hanged at the time of the rebellion for deserting his friends'. The author, Kathleen Fitzpatrick, who was born and raised in Belfast, was clearly aware of the fascination in the Ulster countryside with rebel graves and with memories of informers.[284] Works written by authors from the south of Ireland showed less familiarity with vernacular history, as it was remembered in Ulster.

The Dublin-born suffragist, trade unionist, and peace activist Louisa ('Louie') Bennet started off as an aspiring fiction writer. Her second novel—*A Prisoner of his Word: A Tale of Real Happenings*, published in Dublin in 1908, is set in Ulster at the time of the United Irishmen. Giving testimony in 1921 to an American Commission on Conditions in Ireland, Bennet spoke of her upbringing in 'a strong Unionist family' and recalled that a visit to Belfast, where 'a friend of mine induced me to read books relating to the Wolfe Tone and Emmet time', provided the 'historical basis' for her conversion to radicalism.[285] In Bennet's fictional narrative, an English soldier named Ross Lambart spends several years in prison after he is inducted into the northern United Irishmen by Thomas Russell. He becomes enamoured with the radical Kate Maxwell and she extracts from him a promise to avenge the execution of her rebel brother Harry. Lambart, who is more of a radical in a fin-de-siècle sense, seeking 'spirituality in the prevailing materialism', comes to see the folly of armed rebellion. However, he is 'a prisoner of his word' and, on his release from prison, is obliged to assist Russell in the failed attempt to organize another insurrection in 1803. Although the characters of Harry and Kate Maxwell incorporate some aspects of stories told about Henry and Mary Ann McCracken, they are presented as the children of the Anglican rector of Ballynahinch, rather than Belfast Presbyterians. In fact, the prominence of Presbyterians among the rebels is not mentioned at all. The novel did not do well and failed to attract interest in Ulster, where its plot did not correspond with how the rebellion was remembered.[286]

The most popular form of cultural engagement with the memory of 1798 at the turn of the century took place in theatre houses, where Irish melodrama, a genre popularized over previous decades by the playwright and actor Dion Boucicault and his successors, such as Hubert O'Grady, was in full vogue. Boucicault's 1884 production of *Robert Emmet*, based on a script by the playwright Frank Marshall and first performed in Chicago, was a commercial failure. Nevertheless, this attempt at writing a historical play on a celebrated United Irishman inspired the English theatre manager and playwright James William Whitbread, who had recently relocated to Dublin and

---

[284] Kathleen Fitzpatrick, *The Weans at Rowallan* (London: Methuen & Co., 1905), ch. 15; re-issued as *They Lived in County Down* (London: Chatto & Windus, 1937), which went through several editions (1949 and 1963). For a review see *London Daily News*, 16 February 1905, p. 4.

[285] *Evidence on Conditions in Ireland: Comprising the Complete Testimony, Affidavits and Exhibits Presented before the American Commission on Conditions in Ireland* (Washington, D.C.: Bliss Building, 1921), pp. 1046–7.

[286] Louie Bennett, *A Prisoner of His Word: A Tale of Real Happenings* (Dublin: Maunsel & Co., 1908). See also R. M. Fox, *Louie Bennett: Her Life and Times* (The Talbot Press: Dublin, 1957), p. 16; Rosemary Cullen Owens, *Louie Bennett* (Cork University Press: Cork, 2001), pp. 6–7.

became in that year the lessee of the Queen's Royal Theatre on Brunswick Street [now Pearse Street], a venue on its way to becoming the 'home of melodrama'. Whitbread, as noted in an obituary in the *Era* (a weekly newspaper considered, according to the theatre historian W. J. MacQueen-Pope, 'The Actor's Bible'), 'made a speciality of Irish patriotic drama, dealing with Irish revolutionary movements of the past'.[287]

Whitbread wrote and produced a number of successful plays on the United Irishmen, which went on tour to theatres across Ireland and Britain, returning periodically for show in Dublin. These 1798 melodramas were mainly preoccupied with the rebellion in the South: *Lord Edward Fitzgerald or '98* (originally performed on 26 March 1894) depicted the attempts of the designated United Irish commander-in-chief to avoid arrest in various locations in Dublin; *The Insurgent Chief* (first performed on 31 March 1902 and advertised as a 'phenomenal success') told the story of the Wicklow rebel Michael Dwyer; and *The Sham Squire* (first performed on 26 December 1903) was about the Dublin informer Francis Higgins.[288] For the 1798 centenary, Whitbread produced the 'romantic Irish drama' *Theobald Wolfe Tone* (which opened to a packed hall on 26 December 1898). It followed the celebrated United Irishman on his travels from Dublin to France and ended with his embarkation on a French warship setting sail for Ireland.[289]

Henry Joy McCracken appeared in Whitbread's *Wolfe Tone* as a minor figure and was then elevated into the central character of *The Ulster Hero*, which premiered at the Queen's Theatre on 12 January 1903. The notably large audience responded with enthusiasm and—as observed by the correspondent of the *Irish Times*—the twists of the melodramatic plot were 'punctuated with wild applause, alternating with quite as wild hissing, groans, and laughter'. To the audience's delight, the dastardly informers Niblock and Hughes were played by particularly skilful actors, one of whom—Frank Breen from county Down—had a well-established reputation for villainous roles, and it was noted that 'their every move is noisily acclaimed'.[290] This response, as explained by the theatre historian Mary Trotter, was 'motivated by politics as well as by aesthetics', so that 'when the audience hissed Breen off the stage, they were really attacking

---

[287] *Era*, 21 June 1916, p. 10. For Boucicault's *Robert Emmet* and its influence on Whitbread see Deirdre McFeely, *Dion Boucicault: Irish Identity on Stage* (Cambridge: Cambridge University Press, 2012), pp. 169–72; Stephen M. Watt, 'Boucicault and Whitbread: The Dublin Stage at the End of the Nineteenth Century', *Éire-Ireland*, 18, no. 3 (1983): pp. 23–53.

[288] Séamus de Búrca, *The Queen's Royal Theatre Dublin, 1829–1969* (Dublin: Séamus de Búrca, 1983), pp. 20–1. For performances of *Lord Edward Fitzgerald* at the Queen's Royal Theatre see *Freeman's Journal*, 27 March 1894, p. 5; *Era* 31 March 1894, p. 11; programme for performance on 19 April 1897, NLI EPH E221; *Dublin Daily Nation*, 4 April 1899, pp. 5–6; the play's poster is reproduced in de Búrca, *The Queen's Royal Theatre*, p. 95. For *The Insurgent Chief* see *Era*, 5 April 1902, p. 7. See also Cheryl Herr, *For The Land They Loved: Irish Political Melodramas, 1890–1925* (Syracuse: Syracuse University Press, 1993), pp. 6–10, 48–53, and 83–170 (script of *Lord Edward Fitzgerald*); Christopher Fitz-Simon, *'Buffoonery and Easy Sentiment': Popular Irish Plays in the Decade Prior to the Opening of the Abbey Theatre* (Dublin: Carysfort Press, 2011), pp. 139–84.

[289] *Era*, 31 December 1898, p. 17; *Freeman's Journal*, 27 December 1898, p. 5; playbill from 1901 production reproduced in de Búrca, *The Queen's Royal Theatre*, pp. 21–3; promotion poster by David Allen & Sons (Belfast), NLI EPH F34. The script of *Wolfe Tone* is reproduced in Herr, *For The Land They Loved*, pp. 171–258.

[290] *Irish Times*, 13 January 1903, p. 6 and 17 January 1903, p. 18.

the imperialist villains whom he portrayed.'[291] Whitbread's theatrical productions essentially reflected the politics of the Irish Parliamentary Party.[292]

Melodrama, perhaps more than other forms of drama, requires viewers to suspend their disbelief. *The Ulster Hero* featured 'numberless hairbreadth escapes and thrilling encounters between the red and the green', pushing credulity to its limits: 'M'Cracken in one scene shoves a whole regiment of soldiers aside amid tumultuous applause from all sections of the house, and escapes to the hillsides.'[293] Reviewers, however, were willing to overlook such embroideries and to pretend that 'the piece deals in an exhaustive and lucid manner with the life and adventures of Henry Joy M'Cracken' and that his 'eventful career is traced with historical precision'. The scenery on the stage set, painted by the theatre's resident artist William W. Small with the help of photographs of sites in Ulster, was acclaimed as 'very realistic'. The atmosphere was further enhanced by the performance of music, both original and traditional, arranged by the Jewish maestro Philip Michael Levenston (a professor at the Royal Irish Academy of Music and leader of the Dublin Philharmonic Orchestra and the Vice-Regal Orchestra). All in all, the crowds who flocked to see the play were treated to 'an agreeable alternation of stirring incidents, emotional scenes, and bright, amusing comedy'.[294]

Unlike the uplifting conciliatory endings of the classic melodramas of Boucicault and O'Grady, the '98 plays typically concluded on a tragic note. The dramatization of the closing scene of *The Ulster Hero* was described by the correspondent of the *Freeman's Journal*: 'the brave Northern leader is seen upon the scaffold, on which also stands the hangman with the fatal rope. Then the curtain is lowered for a few moments, and when it is raised again the gallant soldier who has given his life for Ireland is seen lying dead beneath the grim instrument of his execution.' This tableau, which was 'calculated to fix itself on the imagination', was captured in an eye-catching poster prepared by the Belfast printers, David Allen & Sons, who specialized in producing promotional artwork for the theatre.[295]

Whitbread encouraged local playwrights to engage with the memory of the United Irishmen. In 1902, he announced a prize of £100 for 'the best original Irish drama— a drama to be composed upon that romantic and never-to-be-forgotten period of Ireland's history, the year 1798'. The competition was open only to authors 'born in Ireland, of Irish parentage and residing in this country.' The prize was awarded to Robert Johnston, a first-time writer with no previous stage experience, for his play *The Old Land* (first staged at the Queen's theatre on 13 April 1903).[296] Much of the success

[291] Mary Trotter, *Ireland's National Theaters: Political Performance and the Origins of the Irish Dramatic Movement* (Syracuse, N.Y.: Syracuse University Press, 2001), p. 65. One theatre-goer recalled that Breen was often 'received with howls of execration and catcalls-and sometimes had to retreat from an avalanche of missiles'; de Búrca, *The Queen's Royal Theatre*, p. 13.
[292] Ben Levitas, *The Theatre of Nation: Irish Drama and Cultural Nationalism, 1890–1916* (Oxford and New York: Oxford University Press, 2002), pp. 25–6.
[293] *Irish Times*, 13 January 1903, p. 6.
[294] *Dublin Evening Mail*, 13 January 1903, p. 4; *Era*, 17 January 1903, p. 7. A copy of the script is preserved in the Lord Chamberlain's Office, to which it was submitted in 1905 to get a license for a performance at the Metropole Theatre in Glasgow; J. W. Whitbread, 'The Ulster Hero', Lord Chamberlain's Plays, BL MS 1905/19N (Add. 65727). See also Watt, 'Boucicault and Whitbread', pp. 47–52.
[295] *Freeman's Journal*, 13 January 1903, p. 5; de Búrca, *The Queen's Royal Theatre*, p. 24.
[296] *Freeman's Journal*, 7 April 1902, pp. 4 and 6; *Era*, 23 April 1903, p. 11.

of Whitbread's productions can be attributed to his collaboration with Andrew Kennedy Miller, a Scottish actor who was appointed acting-manager of the Queen's theatre in 1899. The talented actors of Kennedy Miller's Very Capable Company of Irish Players performed the original productions of Whitbread's plays, and their performances were in great demand. According to the company's records, in 1903 alone, they appeared for eleven weeks at the Queen's Theatre in Dublin, five weeks at the Theatre Royal in Belfast, two weeks at each of the opera houses in Cork and Londonderry, as well as shorter engagements in smaller theatres across Ireland and tours of Britain.[297] Kennedy Miller died in 1906 and the following year Whitbread went into retirement in England.

A worthy successor was soon found in the actor and playwright Patrick John Bourke, who took on the management of Queen's theatre in 1909 and would also play parts in the plays alongside his brother-in-law, Peadar Kearney (who later gained fame as a republican revolutionary and song-writer). In reviving historical melodramas, P. J. Bourke collaborated with the director and playwright Ira Allen, who wrote a '98 play set in Wexford—*Father Murphy; or, The Hero of Tullow* (first performed by the Irish Amateur Theatrical Company at the Workmen's Club in Dublin on 17 November 1909 and staged at the Queen's theatre on 3 June 1912). The plays of Whitbread were repeatedly restaged, among them a new production of *The Ulster Hero*, directed by Allen and performed by H. J. Condron's company at the Queen's on 20 October 1919.[298] Bourke also wrote his own historical plays, which were performed with great success by his talented No. 1 Company of Irish Players, starting with the 'powerful historical drama of 1798' *When Wexford Rose* (originally staged on 4 March 1910).[299] He first tackled the northern rebellion with *Ulster in 1798*, subtitled *The Northern Insurgents*, which was first produced as a 'grand attraction for the national holiday' on St Patrick's Day 1912, with Bourke cast in the fictional role of Major Fox, Town Mayor of Belfast.[300]

Three and a half years later, Bourke's *For the Land She Loved*, a melodrama about the Ulster heroine Betsy Gray, premiered on 15 November 1915 at the Abbey Theatre as a benefit for the republican Defence of Ireland Fund (established by the advanced nationalist women's organization Cumann na mBan). The venue was the home of the Irish Literary Revival and its highbrow patrons looked down upon the more plebeian tastes of the audience that flocked in for the show. W. J. Lawrence, the Dublin correspondent for the British periodical *The Stage*, sardonically commented

---

[297] *Ballymena Observer*, 13 November 1903, p. 8; *Era*, 10 March 1906, p. 13. See also Christopher Fitz-Simon, 'Mr Kennedy Miller's Very Capable Company of Irish Players', Fourteenth Sir John T. Gilbert Commemorative Lecture (Dublin City Library and Archive, 24 January 2011), transcript available online: <www.dublincity.ie/story/mr-kennedy-miller-transcript>.

[298] *Freeman's Journal*, 21 October 1919, p. 4. The playbill for the 1910 production of Allen's *Father Murphy* is reproduced in de Búrca, *The Queen's Royal Theatre*; for the playbill of a 1913 production see Holloway Playbills Collection, NLI EPH E304.

[299] *Era*, 5 March 1913, p. 8 and 8 March 1913, p. 7. See also Herr, *For The Land They Loved*, pp. 53–6 and 259–310 (entire script of play). The original playbill is reproduced in de Búrca, *The Queen's Royal Theatre*; for the playbill of a 1913 production see Holloway Playbills Collection, NLI EPH E304.

[300] The original script of *Ulster in 1798*: *The Northern Insurgents* is preserved in fragmented form in Séamus de Búrca Papers, NLI MS 39,1601; reproduced in *Journal of Irish Literature*, 13, nos. 1 & 2 (1984): pp. 7–74. The playbill for the performance on 17 March 1912 is reproduced in de Búrca, *The Queen's Royal Theatre*.

that 'by sheer irony of circumstance, an Irish drama of the old, ollogical [sic], and cheaply made patriotic order, which the Abbey Theatre was instituted to kill, has had its first production at that theatre.' He complained that Bourke's play suffered from 'all the appalling inconsistency which marked the old school of Irish melodrama', but admitted that 'seemingly for that sort of play there is still a considerable public'. Lawrence's observation that *For the Land She Loved* 'was uproariously received by an audience of political extremists' was confirmed by Joseph Holloway, an avid theatregoer, who noted in his diary that the play 'is studded with patriotic sentiments, all of which the audience swallowed whole, and often became quite enthusiastic'.[301]

Under Bourke's directorship, melodrama had become associated with militant republicanism rather than constitutional nationalism. In 1914, when his play about Wolfe Tone *In Dark and Evil Days*, also known as *In Dark '98* (first performed on 24 November 1913), was running at the Queen's theatre, Dublin Castle ordered the removal of the posters. The depiction of the Franco-English naval battle in 1798 at Lough Swilly was apparently considered incendiary in the build-up towards the Great War.[302] The following year, when strict censorship was imposed on the advanced nationalist press following the outbreak of the war, the authorities were irritated by *For the Land She Loved*. P. J. Bourke's son, Seamus de Búrca, later recounted how the Abbey's manager, the Ulster dramatist St John G. Ervine, was summoned to Dublin Castle and reprimanded by the Chief Secretary for 'allowing such a piece of sedition to be shown'. Ervine, who could recall from his youth that performances of nationalist melodramas in Belfast often resulted in sectarian melees at which 'Orange corner boys' would throw shipyard rivets at the 'papists' in the galleries, barred Bourke from staging further productions at the Abbey. In response, the production of nationalist melodramas at the Queen's theatre increased.[303]

The 1798 plays antagonized Ulster unionists. Already in 1895, when Whitbread's *Lord Edward* was first performed at the Theatre Royal in Belfast, the *Belfast News-Letter* professed that 'no useful purpose can be served, in our opinion, by this dramatizing of incidents of this description.'[304] The plays, however, appealed to northern nationalist audiences, who were amused by the fanciful re-adaptations of historical narratives. Whitbread's *The Ulster Hero* was staged at the Derry Opera House on 19 January 1903, just one week after its Dublin premiere, and it subsequently went on tour to other northern venues, such as the Ballymena Town Hall (21 November 1903), before returning for another performance in Derry (28 November 1903). Whitbread incorporated in the play details from oral traditions compiled by Robert M. Young in *Ulster in '98*. In turn, Bourke's play *Ulster in 1798: The Northern Insurgents* borrowed heavily from

[301] W. J. Lawrence, 'Reviews of the Irish Theatre, Part Two', *Journal of Irish Literature*, 18, no. 3 (September 1989): pp. 11–12 (originally written 18 November 1915); Joseph Holloway Diary, entry for 19 November 1915, Holloway Papers, NLI MS 1823/969–972.

[302] For playbills of *In Dark '98* and *In Dark and Evil Days* (which was restaged on 26 May 1919) see Holloway Playbills Collection, NLI EPH E305 and EPH E371 (respectively). For claims of its suppression in 1915 see Seamus de Burca, 'The Queen's Royal Theatre 1829–1966', *Dublin Historical Record*, 27, no. 1 (1973), p. 16.

[303] *Irish Times*, 16 May 1980, p. 11 and 20 August 1982, p. 9; Kurt Jacobsen, 'An Interview with Seamus de Burca', *Journal of Irish Literature*, 13, nos. 1 & 2 (1984), p. 78; see also Chris Morash, *A History of Irish Theatre, 1601–2000* (Cambridge and New York: Cambridge University Press, 2002), pp. 114 and 153–4.

[304] *BNL*, 1 October 1895, p. 5.

George Birmingham's *The Northern Iron*, a novel which was informed by local history, though Bourke was mainly interested in its fictional characters. These local sources were changed beyond recognition to suit the familiar formulas of melodramas.

Bourke evidently consulted W. G. Lyttle's *Betsy Gray; or, Hearts of Down* (which had just been re-issued in a sixth edition, prepared and revised by Bigger) as the main source for the play *For the Land She Loved*, but he chose to completely rewrite the canonical story of the Ulster heroine as it had been preserved in folklore.[305] Betsy Gray is elevated from a common camp follower to the lover of the imaginary rebel leader Robert [rather than the historical Henry] Munro. In the final scene Betsy fights a duel with her villainous rival, the fictitious Lady Nugent, and is then quite literally caught between the swords of Munro and a British colonel. In this engagement, the soldiers retreat and their commander, General Nugent, is captured by the rebels, so that, when Betsy dies in the hands of Munro and is draped in a green flag, her sacrifice for Ireland turns the rout of the rebels at Ballynahinch into a symbolic victory.[306] This contrived sequence seems to have been over the top for northern audiences, who were acquainted with the traditions, which Lyttle's novel had popularized, that told of how Betsy Gray was killed, alongside her fiancé and brother, by yeomen in a side skirmish of little historical consequence.

In itself, the dramatization of the story of the local legend was considered acceptable. Back in the centenary, *Sweet Betsy Gray*, a play written by an amateur dramatist, P. J. Crawford, was performed at St Peter's Hall in Warrenpoint, county Down (5 kilometres south-east of Newry), to 'a very large audience, representative of every class and creed'. This community production, which was followed by a 'musical melange' of song and traditional dance that concluded with the singing of 'Let Erin Remember the Days of Old', was well received and impressions of the event could still be vaguely recalled fifty-five years later.[307] In contrast, Bourke's exaggerated nationalist reconfiguring of local tradition, which coincided with unionist mass mobilization against the third Home Rule bill, was not staged in Ulster.

Around the time when *For the Land She Loved* was first launched, Ulster unionists were intent on reclaiming the memory of Betsy Gray for their own political purposes. On 24 July 1913, the unionist leader Edward Carson presided over a rally of the North Down Division of the Ulster Volunteer Force (UVF), which consisted of some 2,000 members of unionist clubs from Bangor, Conlig, Donaghadee, Helen's Bay, Portaferry, Greyabbey, and Ballywalter. This demonstration took place at Six Road Ends, a location chosen for its identification in local tradition as the home of Betsy Gray. Carson, 'with characteristic thoughtfulness', paid a visit to an elderly woman (68-year-old Sarah Fletcher of Conlig), believed to be a relative of the heroine, from whom he received a copy of Lyttle's *Betsy Gray* novel, in which she had written 'a loyal message'.[308] This gesture of commemorative competition, in which unionists claimed ownership of

---

[305] Lyttle, *Betsy Gray*, 6th edn (1913). The nationalist journalist T. McGoran, whose series of 'Irish Readings' was circulated in the national and provincial press, republished information and excerpts from the book; *Sunday Independent*, 12 October 1913, p. 2; *Ulster Herald*, 13 December 1913, p. 16.

[306] P. J. Bourke, 'For the Land She Loved' (draft), Séamus de Búrca Papers, NLI 39,159; published in Herr, *For The Land They Loved*, pp. 311–59.

[307] *Newry Reporter*, 6 June 1898; *Warrenpoint Weekly*, 27 June 1953.

[308] *Belfast Evening Telegraph*, 25 July 1913, p. 3; *Belfast Weekly News*, 31 July 1913, p. 9. Mrs Fletcher can be identified by cross-referencing the 1911 census with information in a family letter;

the memory of a folk heroine identified with the United Irishmen, enraged Catholic nationalists. The nationalist press railed against the 'gross travesty of a symbol dear to Irish hearts', which in their opinion amounted to an 'outrageous attempt to associate the highest, and holiest in our country's history with the lowest and most ignoble movement in which any party in any clime were ever engaged'.[309]

On this background, as the escalating conflict in Ulster seemed to be moving towards a civil war between unionists and nationalist paramilitary organizations, a nationalist play on Betsy Gray could not be safely performed. Some years later, in 1920, Bourke staged at the Queen's theatre in Dublin a new production of *For the Land She Loved*, which was greeted with 'a rousing reception' from 'large and appreciative audiences'. This time, Ireland was on the verge of partition and Ulster was beset with sectarian violence. Once again, tensions between unionist and nationalists prevented the play from going on to tour to Ulster.[310]

The historical melodramas of J. W. Whitbread and P. J. Bourke clearly did not appeal to most Ulster Protestants. Consideration of unionist aversion of nationalist plays sharpens the distinction between cultural and social remembrance. In conditions of tense sectarian rivalry, the marked enthusiasm of Catholic audiences was a deterrent. Regardless of any intrinsic interest that the plays about the 1798 rebellion in Ulster might have had for northern Presbyterians, the dramatic productions were not reviewed in the unionist press. The relocating of Ninety-Eight to the stage substantially transformed historical traditions. Recollections of the Turn-Out were emptied of their inherent ambivalence and infused with explicit nationalist content, associated with the politics of Home Rule and separatism, which alienated liberal unionists. Paradoxically, the popular productions of cultural memory served to enhance social forgetting in Protestant Ulster.

HISTORICAL DISREGARD

Unlike creative writers, historians at the turn of the century showed relatively little interest in the rebellion in Ulster. The landmark academic history of the period was William Edward Hartpole Lecky's *History of Ireland in the Eighteenth Century* (originally included as part of his magisterial *History of England in the Eighteenth Century*), which was published as a five-volume cabinet edition in 1892 and reprinted in 1893, 1903, 1909, and 1913. Lecky responded to his predecessor James Anthony Froude, who had devoted to the United Irishmen the greater part of a volume of *The English in Ireland in the Eighteenth Century*, published in 1874. Froude's hostile account was heavily influenced by Musgrave's ultra-loyalist interpretation of 1798. In over a

---

K. Y. Sanders of Sandwich, Illinois, to George Macartney, 10 July 1891, Gray Family Papers, PRONI T1296/8.

[309] *Butte Independent*, 23 August 1913, p. 1; *Freeman's Journal*, 28 July 1913, p. 5 (appeared also on 2 August 1913, p. 6 in *Ulster Herald, Derry People and Donegal News, Fermanagh Herald, and Strabane Chronicle*) and 26 January 1914, p. 6; *Donegal News*, 9 August 1913, p. 4.

[310] *Dublin Evening Telegraph*, 27 April 1920, p. 2; *Irish Independent*, 27 April 1920, p. 6. A Photostat of the playbill preserved in Séamus de Búrca Papers, NLI 39,159 is reproduced in de Búrca, *The Queen's Royal Theatre*.

hundred pages on the rebellion, only five pages relate to the 'partial rising in Ulster', which he maintained was confined to a very small area and practically followed 'step for step the pattern of 1641'.[311] Lecky pointed out that 'Musgrave must always be read with suspicion when he treats of any question relating to Catholics', and yet he concurred with the frame of reference set by Musgrave and adopted by Froude, which attributed relatively little importance to the northern arena, and his chapter on 'The State of Ulster' considered the rebellion in Antrim and Down only in brief.[312]

Although Lecky was a southern liberal unionist, his work was considered the most authoritative history of the rebellion and was consulted by both nationalist and conservative commentators in the many centennial writings on Ninety-Eight.[313] F. W. Palliser, a lesser-known writer of Wexford origins, published in 1898 a history of *The Irish Rebellion of 1798*, which relied on Lecky and was praised for being 'dispassionate and unprejudiced'. Even though it did not offer new historical information, it was considered by the *Pall Mall Gazette* 'valuable to a generation that likes to take its history in a readily digestible form'. Unsurprisingly, in Palliser's work, the rebellion in Ulster does not warrant a chapter of its own and is covered briefly in just five pages (out of a total of 250).[314] While reliance on Lecky inadvertently perpetuated the neglect of Ulster, nationalist writers, who professed to go beyond Lecky, also fell short on this issue. *Ireland's Revolt in '98*, published by the Catholic historian Francis Tuite in 1898, allocated a short chapter of only two pages (out of 155) to 'Some Battles in Ulster'.[315]

The Dublin historian Cæsar Litton Falkiner, who was primed to be Lecky's successor, commented on 1798 in a couple of the essays in his *Studies in Irish History and Biography, Mainly of the Eighteenth Century*, published in 1902. He distinguished between Protestants—including among them Ulster-Scots Presbyterians—and Catholics in racial terms and maintained that the political identifications of unionists and nationalists were predetermined by time-old atavistic enmities:

> If the descendants of the men who drank to the memory of Orr and fought upon the field of Antrim and Ballinahinch are now, like the descendants of the Protestant United Irishmen of Dublin and the south, warmly attached to the connection with Great Britain, while the descendants of the Celtic and Catholic elements in the Irish Union remain inveterately opposed to that connection the difference can only be accounted for by that racial antagonism whose fires have survived for seven centuries and are unhappily still unextinguished.

Protestants, according to Falkiner, could not relate to the memory of their ancestors' involvement in the United Irish rebellion.[316]

---

[311] James Anthony Froude, *The English in Ireland in the Eighteenth Century*, vol. 3 (New York: Scribner, Armstrong, and Co., 1874), pp. 431–5; see also Ciaran Brady, *James Anthony Froude: An Intellectual Biography of a Victorian Prophet* (Oxford: Oxford University Press, 2013), 284–5.

[312] Lecky, *A History of Ireland in the Eighteenth Century*, vol. 4, pp. 416–24 (for reference to Musgrave see p. 419n1).

[313] See Kevin Whelan, *The Tree of Liberty*, pp. 173–4.

[314] F. W. Palliser, *The Irish Rebellion of 1798* (London: Simpkin, Marshall, Hamilton, Kent & Co., 1898), pp. 182–7; *Pall Mall Gazette*, 31 May 1898, p. 4; *London Evening Standard*, 12 August 1898, p. 2; see also *BNL*, 15 June 1898, p. 4 (reproduces praise from *Westminster Gazette* and the *Scotsman*).

[315] Francis Tuite, *Ireland's Revolt in '98, with Sketches of Prominent Statesmen and the Social Condition of the People* (Boston: Angel Guardian Press, 1898), pp. 50–1.

[316] Falkiner, *Studies in Irish History and Biography*, pp. 54–6.

In Falkiner's opinion, memory of the rebellion was essentially a southern Catholic ('Celtic') fixation:

> Not two generations, nor three, not sixty years nor a century, have availed to erase from the sombre memories of the Celtic population of Ireland the recollection of the events of '98. For them the lapse of time has scarcely served to soften a single animosity, or to obliterate the marks of racial and religious hate which the disorders of the Rebellion traced afresh in Ireland.

This sectarian preoccupation with the past, he believed, was driven by a 'peculiar attachment to memories of defeat and failure', which precluded oblivion of the failed rebellion among Catholics:

> Unfortunately for themselves, they have ever been as unable to forget as unwilling to forgive, and the contemplation of their own sufferings and misfortunes has continually a morbid attraction for them. They will allow neither the balm of time nor the oblivion of the grave to work their merciful alleviations. Contests which the victors have long ceased to remember, the vanquished cannot forbear to brood over.

In Falkiner's experience, 'the pathetic delight with which the Irish people love to indulge in the gloomy recollections of their abortive past' was 'never more powerfully exemplified than in the celebration of the hundredth anniversary of the Rebellion of 1798'. He observed that 'the popular press teemed with articles and paragraphs which, whatever might be thought of the reality of the commemoration as a serious political display, testified at any rate to the hold which the Rebellion and its incidents still retain upon the popular fancy.' Although he admitted that 'the cult of the Rebellion' had been initiated by Protestant Young Irelanders, Falkiner insisted that it had become an exclusively Catholic nationalist obsession, which did not take root in Protestant Ulster. Arguing that 'it is noticeable that the rising itself produced not a single heroic figure', he rejected likely candidates for memorialization from Wexford and Mayo and completely disregarded the United Irish leaders in Ulster.[317]

This neglect was challenged by Rev. James Barkley Woodburn in *The Ulster Scot: His History and Religion*. Woodburn, who at the time was the Presbyterian minister of Castlerock in county Londonderry (8 kilometres north-west of Coleraine), and whose brother was the Professor of Logic and Philosophy at Magee College, insisted that the divisions in Ireland were religious and not racial. His history, which was published in April 1914, just as the UVF was arming itself with weapons smuggled in from Germany in the Larne gun-running, attracted the attention of British and Irish reviewers interested in understanding the historical background to the Ulster Crisis. By December the entire run of the first edition, over a 1,000 copies, was sold out and a new, slightly enhanced, edition was issued in 1915.[318]

---

[317] Falkiner, *Studies in Irish History and Biography*, pp. 155–7 and 189.
[318] James Barkley Woodburn, *The Ulster Scot: His History and Religion* (London: H. R. Allenson Limited, 1914). For the publication of the second edition see *Derry Journal*, 5 April 1915, p. 8; *BNL*, 23 April 1915, p. 4. For biographical information see *Northern Whig*, 7 February 1940, p. 4; *Larne Times*, 10 February 1940, p. 2; Robert Ernest Alexander, *Fitzroy Avenue Presbyterian Church* (Belfast: s. n., 1949), pp. 33–4; Philip Orr, 'The Very Rev. Dr. James B. Woodburn (1922–1942)', in *Fitzroy— A River of Faith for 200 Years*, edited by Ken Newell (n.l.: n.s., 2008), pp. 55–68.

A quarter of a century earlier, on the background of the first Home Rule crisis, the Scottish historian John Harrison had written *The Scot in Ulster*, originally published as a series of articles in the Edinburgh newspaper the *Scotsman*. Scott devoted only a sentence to the northern insurrection, noting that 'when rebellion actually broke out in 1798, the struggle was not so severe in Ulster as it would otherwise have been, although much good blood was spilt of the Presbyterians of Down and Antrim.'[319] Woodburn, by contrast, addressed the topic in depth, with two chapters on the United Irishmen and another on the local rebellion, which made extensive use of earlier histories, in particular Latimer's *Ulster Biographies, Relating Chiefly to the Rebellion of 1798*.[320]

Woodburn, who had been ordained in Rostrevor, near Newry in county Down, and whose father had been the minister at Ballywillan, near Portrush in county Antrim, was very much aware that marks of the rebellion 'remain to this day' in the north-eastern counties. He acknowledged that:

> around the firesides of many a homestead in Ulster stories are still told by the people of the way in which their forefathers suffered and died in the battles of Ballynahinch and Antrim, and many are the anecdotes related of the thrilling escapes of the rebels when pursued by the soldiers flushed with victory.

In posing the rhetorical question 'how far was the Ulster Scot concerned in this rebellion?', he answered candidly that 'it is certain he was embroiled more deeply than most of the historians allow.' His account of the rebellion ends with a description of the harsh repression that followed:

> After the Government had stamped out the insurgents, they treated the people of the disaffected counties with great brutality and cruelty. The soldiers and the yeomen were let loose upon the inhabitants; they burnt the houses, devastated the country, and destroyed the property of the innocent as well as of the guilty, in their endeavours to hunt down the rebels. There is enough evidence to prove that they put many innocent people to death without a trial. Many others escaped to America, and some had to hide themselves until the danger blew past.

As a liberal unionist, Woodburn was willing to admit that bitter recollections of excessive use of violence by the forces of the Crown were deeply ingrained in social memory.[321]

The neglect of the northern rebellion was also challenged from a conservative point of view in the work of the historian of Orangeism, Robert Mackie Sibbett. Born and raised in Killycoogan, Portglenone, county Antrim (14 kilometres north-west of Ballymena), where he joined the local Orange lodge, Sibbett had travelled to America in the 1890s and returned home to a career in journalism. He worked at first for a local unionist newspaper, the *Ballymena Weekly Telegraph*, and then moved to Belfast, where he wrote for the principal unionist newspapers, the *Belfast News-Letter* and the *Belfast Telegraph*. A series of lengthy articles on the history of the Orange tradition, which originally appeared in the *Belfast Weekly News*, became the basis for his two-volume *Orangeism in Ireland and Throughout the Empire*, first published in Belfast in 1914. Although he made extensive use of Musgrave's history, among other loyalist sources,

---

[319] John Harrison, *The Scot in Ulster: Sketch of the History of the Scottish Population of Ulster* (Edinburgh and London: W. Blackwood and Sons, 1888), p. 96.
[320] Woodburn, *The Ulster Scot*, pp. 250–310.
[321] Ibid., pp. 306 and 310.

Sibbett attributed considerable importance to the 1798 rebellion in Ulster, which was surveyed in detail over three chapters that covered, in addition to the main battles in Antrim and Down, also minor encounters and skirmishes throughout county Antrim.[322]

Drawing on local loyalist memories, Sibbett referred to the rebellion as 'The Trouble', rather than the Turn-Out. His attitude was obviously hostile to the 'folly' of the United Irishmen. However, he recognized that they had enjoyed widespread popular support. He described the rebels in Ulster as 'a mixed body of Protestants and Roman Catholics, between whom there was no real bond of union, no real harmony of sentiment, no tie of friendship, and no feeling that could be called fraternal'. He openly acknowledged that among the rebels there was 'a considerable percentage of Presbyterians' and also claimed that 'various other Protestant denominations were more or less numerously represented in the ranks of the conspirators.' At the same time, he also pointed out that many Presbyterians had remained loyal.[323]

Most interestingly, subtle signs of ambiguity are interspersed between Sibbett's condemnations of the rebels. He reluctantly admitted that the military and yeomanry devastated the countryside, complaining that the blame was unjustly pinned on the Orangemen. In offering a somewhat strained apologia for these excesses, he argued that such actions are inevitable in wartime and that 'excited Loyalists' were responding to rebel atrocities.[324] Sibbett depicted the United Irish leaders as respectable 'men of good social position', who mostly acted honourably and showed courage.[325] Moreover, as a devout Presbyterian, he showed an empathetic understanding for why so many Presbyterians had rallied to the rebel cause:

> No one will seek to justify men in rising in revolt against their rightful Sovereign, but it can, at least, be urged in extenuation of the extremes to which Nonconformists, in particular, went when associated with the United movement, that their action was the inevitable result of long-continued exasperation . . . . It was no wonder, then, that, trampled upon at every turn, they determined to assert their own manhood and humiliate those whom they looked upon as their persecutors.[326]

In this history of Orangeism, the magnitude of the rebellion in Ulster is not dismissed, but presented as a temporary delusion so that 'in a few years, descendants of the men who fought and fell, in conflict with the Royal forces, or helped forward the revolutionary movement, were to be found among the best friends of law and order, and, in later times, standing in opposition to Home Rule and Papal tyranny.'[327] Though he maintained that it was no longer politically relevant, Sibbett considered the northern insurrection an undeniably memorable event.

Some local historians chose to reject social practices of disremembering. James W. Kernohan, who wrote in 1912 a history of Presbyterianism in the parishes of Kilrea and Tamlaght O'Crilly, was aware that 'in these days of consistent loyalty we are not always disposed to give due credit to the motives which prompted the United Irishmen in the movements that led up to the Rebellion of 1798', yet made a point of

---

[322] R. M. Sibbett, *Orangeism in Ireland and Throughout the Empire*, vol. 2 (Belfast: Henderson, 1914), pp. 44–74.

[323] Ibid., pp. 45–7.   [324] Ibid., pp. 59 and 67.   [325] Ibid., pp. 47–9.

[326] Ibid., p. 73.   [327] Ibid., p. 57.

mentioning the experiences of Ninety-Eight.[328] However, most unionist commentary on the history of Ulster sanctioned disregard. *Blackwood's Magazine* published in 1913 'The Wrongs of Ulster', a conservative historical survey, which opens with Froude's put-down of Ireland that 'as a nation they have done nothing which posterity will not be anxious to forget.' In this essay, the 1790s are only touched on in a single statement:

> Treason and disloyalty were connived at by the Government; and everywhere a spirit of disaffection prevailed, which finally found vent in that last frenzied effort of the Celts and Roman Catholics to extirpate the Protestants, the Rebellion of 1798, with all its accompanying horrors and atrocities.

As pointed out in a critical review, 'if its writer had meant to give a history of the Ulster Presbyterians, he would hardly have omitted all reference to Ulster's very prominent share in the rebellion of 1798'. The turning of a blind eye to the memory of the northern United Irishmen was evidently deliberate.[329]

Northern Protestant writers were engaged in 'the crystallisation of a provincial *mentalité*'. In this context, unionist historians promoted a distinct history of Ulster, which typically focused on events in the seventeenth century that pitted Protestants against Catholics, namely the Ulster Plantation, the 1641 rebellion, and the Siege of Derry (1688–9).[330] The radical attempt of the United Irishmen, as famously put by Wolfe Tone, 'to unite the whole people of Ireland; to abolish the memory of all past dissensions; and to substitute the common name of Irishman in place of the denominations of Protestant, Catholic, and Dissenter', did not fit this template.[331] Lord Ernest Hamilton's popular book from 1917, *The Soul of Ulster*, which has been described as 'a schematic and selective history of his native province', is exemplary of the emergent unionist historiography of its day.[332]

Hamilton promised to offer 'a glimpse into the secret soul of Ulster, so carefully screened from public gaze', which, due to an impenetrable culture of reticence, was largely imperceptible:

> It has been very truly said that the Ulster question is only properly understood by Ulstermen, residents in other parts of Ireland having, at the best, an incomplete grasp of the real deep-down issues. It may, I think, with equal truth be added that mere residence in Ulster is not in itself sufficient to lay bare the inner soul of the people, there being in the case of the native part of the population a very wide gap between their secret feelings and that which appears on the surface.

---

[328] James W. Kernohan, *The Parishes of Kilrea and Tamlaght O'Crilly* (Coleraine: Chronicle, 1912), pp. 67–8, see also pp. 30–2 and 38–40.

[329] C. W. C., 'The Wrongs of Ulster', *Blackwood's Magazine*, 193, no. 1167 (1913): pp. 47–8; Miriam Alexander, 'Irish History in English Magazines', *Irish Review*, 3, no. 25 (1913): pp. 42–3. For the origin of the quotation see Froude, *The English in Ireland*, vol. 1, p. 22.

[330] Ian McBride, 'Ulster and the British Problem', in *Unionism in Modern Ireland: New Perspectives on Politics and Culture*, edited by Richard English and Graham S. Walker (Houndmills and New York: Macmillan Press, 1996), pp. 7–9; Brian Walker, '1641, 1689, 1690 and All That: The Unionist Sense of History', *Irish Review*, no. 12 (1992): pp. 56–64 (esp. p. 58); Gillian McIntosh, *The Force of Culture: Unionist Identities in Twentieth-Century Ireland* (Cork: Cork University Press, 1999).

[331] *Memoirs of Theobald Wolfe Tone*, vol. 1, p. 64.

[332] Alvin Jackson, 'Unionist History (I)', *Irish Review*, no. 7 (1989): p. 63; Patrick Maume, 'Borders: Lord Ernest Hamilton (1858–1939), Race, Religion and Ulster Scots Identity in the Last Decades of the Anglo-Irish Union', in *Border Crossings: Narration, Nation and Imagination in Scots and Irish Literature and Culture*, edited by Colin Younger (2013), p. 122.

The author, whose father—the first duke of Abercorn—was twice Lord Lieutenant of Ireland, was schooled in the intricacies of Irish politics. Having triumphed in his own right over rival nationalist and liberal candidates in closely contested elections, going on to serve as a conservative unionist parliamentary representative for North Tyrone in the period between the first and second Home Rule crises (1885–92), Hamilton claimed to have 'perhaps had exceptional opportunities of getting occasional rather startling glimpses of the real soul of Ulster'.[333] His book came out during the Great War, when the decisions over the future of Ireland had been put on hold, and was hailed in the local unionist press as 'a book which certainly ought to be read by everyone who wishes to understand the intensity of feeling underlying Ulster's opposition to Home Rule'.[334]

In allocating an entire chapter to the 1798 rebellion, Hamilton professed that 'to the student of Irish Politics who looks below the surface, there is no episode in the history of the island more instructive, or that holds up a more minatory hand to the half-informed, than this rebellion.' Yet, unlike a near-contemporaneous history of Ulster by the conservative Anglo-Irish journalist Ramsay Colles, who covered 'the insurrectionary counties' in 1798, Hamilton ignored the insurrections in Antrim and Down. For a book that was supposed to be exclusively about the North, the discussion of the rebellion is surprisingly confined only to the South. The analysis essentially buys into Musgrave's skewed interpretation, whereby atrocities in county Wexford 'began to open the eyes of the Ulster Presbyterians to the precipice towards which they had been drifting' so that consequently 'the movement was dead, as far as the Ulster Presbyterians were concerned.' This postulation allowed Hamilton to recast 1798 as a reprise of the massacres of loyal Protestants by Catholic rebels in 1641, a topic that he addressed in depth elsewhere. His deceptive statement that ''98 and '41 were not forgotten' obscured the sleight of hand through which the rebellion in Ulster was completely absent from the *Soul of Ulster*.[335]

Hamilton's seemingly intimate history of the province embodied a subtle effort to repress memories of widespread Protestant—in particular Presbyterian—involvement in the 1798 rebellion. Ulster liberals were also susceptible to this impulse. Writing around the same time, the journalist James Winder Good, a former leading writer and assistant editor of the *Northern Whig* who had moved to Dublin to write for the constitutional nationalist *Freeman's Journal*, firmly rejected 'the modern Unionist view that the rising in the South opened the eyes of Northern Presbyterians to the folly of their republican dreams' and argued that the 'dragooning of Ulster' spurred the United Irishmen in Ulster to rebel. Nonetheless, Good's account of 'When Ulster Joined Ireland' mentioned 'the happenings in Wexford' but avoided explicit mention of the events of 1798 in Antrim and Down, leaving the northern rebellion undiscussed.[336]

---

[333] Ernest William Hamilton, *The Soul of Ulster* (New York: E. P. Dutton & Co., 1917), preface.

[334] *Larne Times*, 5 May 1917, p. 6.

[335] Hamilton, *Soul of Ulster*, pp. 89–106. Cf. Ramsay Colles, *The History of Ulster*, vol. 4 (London: Gresham Publishing Cpy Ltd, 1920), pp. 149–57. Hamilton wrote both historical non-fiction and fiction on 1641; see Ernest Hamilton, *The Irish Rebellion of 1641: With a History of the Events Which Led up to and Succeeded It* (London: John Murray, 1920); Ernest Hamilton, *Tales of the Troubles* (London: Unwin, 1925).

[336] James Winder Good, *Ulster and Ireland* (Dublin and London: Maunsel & Co., 1919), pp. 44–64.

Such omissions were the outcome of a deliberate act of disregard that effectively advocated collective amnesia of an inconvenient past.

RE-COMMEMORATING

At a more local level, antiquarian preoccupation with vernacular history of 1798 was vigorously encouraged by Bigger, whose efforts to stoke interest in the northern United Irishmen among amateur scholars did not cease with the centenary. He had previously led several field trips of the Belfast Naturalists' Field Club [BNFC] to sites of the rebellion, including visits to the grave of James Hope in Mallusk graveyard and adjacent sites (5 September 1891), the Massereene demesne and Antrim town (20 May 1893), '98 sites in the area of Ballymena (11 August 1894), and the grave of Rev. James Porter in Greyabbey (18 May 1895). These trips continued in the following years. On 2 September 1899, members of the club visited Ballynahinch, stopping at 'the wayside grave of a person who fell during the contests of 1798' and walking up to the ancient fort of Edenvaddy, where it was noted that it 'was last used for warlike purposes by the rebels of 1798, who fought at the Battle of Ballynahinch'.[337]

In preparation for a meeting of the British Association in Belfast in 1902, the BNFC issued *A Guide to Belfast and the Counties of Down and Antrim* to replace the previous guide from 1874, which had 'long remained a standard work of reference on the district, and lately it has gone out of print'. The historical section of the original edition had noted that 'considerable disturbances occurred in the counties of Antrim and Down in the Rebellion of 1798, and actions were fought at Antrim, Ballynahinch, and Saintfield'. But, there was no mention whatsoever of 1798 in the new volume, even though Bigger was one of the editors.[338] It was not that antiquarian interest in the local sites of rebellion had declined, in fact, just three years later the Royal Society of Antiquaries of Ireland held a field trip to Antrim, during which members visited several sites of 1798 memory, at Mallusk, Templepatrick, and Donegore (4 July 1905).[339] Yet, it was apparently considered inappropriate to refer to such a controversial episode of history in a general publication, which was intended also for outsiders, so that self-censorship was exercised.

By contrast, the *Ulster Journal of Archaeology* under Bigger's editorship remained a main platform for publications on local aspects of the rebellion (see Fig. 4.7a, p. 339). From the time of its revival in 1894 through to the centenary, the journal featured some fifteen articles on the topic. Subsequently, from 1899 till the end of the journal's second series in 1911, the *UJA* published another thirty-five articles, notices, and reviews with references to 1798. Additional items were in the pipeline. For example, Bigger slotted for publication, but didn't getting around to issuing, an article that

---

[337] *BNL*, 5 September 1899, p. 3 and 8 September 1891, p. 7; *Annual Reports and Proceedings of the Belfast Naturalists' Field Club*, ser. 2, vol. 4 (Belfast 1901), 10, 180–1, 270 and 544.

[338] Belfast Naturalists' Field Club, *A Guide to Belfast and the Counties of Down & Antrim*, edited by Francis Joseph Bigger, R. Lloyd Praeger, and John Vinycomb (Belfast: M'Caw, Stevenson & Orr, 1902); cf. Belfast Naturalists' Field Club, *Guide to Belfast and Adjacent Counties* (Belfast: M. Ward & Co., 1874), p. 191.

[339] *Journal of the Royal Society of Antiquaries of Ireland*, 5th ser., 35, no. 3 (September 1905): pp. 289–92.

would have showcased a curious traditional account that had been collected from a Mrs Larkin about a local Belfast hero nicknamed 'The Friar'. This unknown figure was mysteriously described as 'perhaps the most remarkable man in the North connected with the United Irishmen', yet 'he never rose to be a leader amongst them, his undoubted abilities being neutralised by—well his peculiarities. He is now forgotten, his name totally unknown even to the histories of the U. I. [United Irish] movement.'[340] The recovery of a seemingly forgotten past through publication of vernacular sources was a main antiquarian concern.

For Bigger and the acolytes who attended the social gatherings at his house—Ardrigh—the memory of Ninety-Eight was not merely a topic of academic interest. They were unwilling to accept the impositions of social forgetting in Ulster, which had become all too evident in the violent backlash of loyalist rioting during the centenary celebrations, and were intent on renewing public remembrance. In response to the coronation of Edward VII in 1902, Milligan cautioned against imitating loyalist protest: 'counter-demonstration which would take the shape of interference, conflict, and riot will be widely left out of the question. I have seen that sort of thing terminate with lamentable and fatal results.' Instead, she advocated for the revival of an annual Decoration Day, during which commemorative visits would be made to the graves of patriotic heroes, and admitted that 'since the '98 celebrations the custom has somewhat declined in popularity, but I think just now it would be singularly fitting to renew and extend it.'[341] Re-commemorating was considered the appropriate response to the threat of decommemorating.

Bigger was keen to follow in the footsteps of Madden, who had marked the graves of illustrious rebels, and energetically took upon himself to honour the graves of the northern United Irishmen. The memorial that Madden had erected for James Hope in the graveyard at Mallusk in 1847 had since fallen into disrepair and so in 1901 Bigger arranged for it to be re-cut and cleaned. New lines were added to the inscription. It now also honoured Hope's wife, Rose Mullan, who had been praised in the *Shan Van Vocht* as 'a valuable and courageous ally in her patriot husband's works'. In addition, the inscription mentioned two of their sons, who conveniently happened to have commemorative names that paid tribute to famous rebel leaders: Robert Emmet Hope and Henry Joy McCracken Hope. Bigger also arranged for the cleaning of the nearby grave of another son, Luke Mullan Hope, who was revered in radical circles for his editorship of the *Rushlight*, a Belfast republican magazine that had resuscitated the ideas of the United Irishmen for the duration of its short run, between December 1824 and September 1825. Looking with satisfaction at this commemorative restoration, which had been paid for by a relative of James Hope, Bigger combatively asked: 'How much more remains to be done?'[342]

In 1902, the Belfast antiquarian Robert May, a wood carver by trade, received notice that workmen engaged in altering premises on Church Lane had uncovered coffins and bones. These were rumoured to be the skeleton of Henry Joy McCracken, whose grave

[340] 'Future Papers for the Journal', *UJA*, 2nd ser., 10, no. 3 (July 1904): p. 144; Bigger Papers, BCL K2/A/12–13.

[341] *Derry Journal*, 29 June 1902, p. 3.

[342] *UJA*, 2nd ser., 7, no. 1 (1901), p. 64. For praise of Rose Mullan Hope see *SVV*, 1, no. 3 (4 March 1896), p. 51. For admiration of Luke Mullan Hope see *Northern Whig*, 12 March 1909, p. 10.

had originally been in that vicinity, though its location was long unknown. May assumed responsibility for the remains, which included arm and pelvic bones, as well as a skull. After examination, the skull was declared 'to be of a man of about 30 years of age or a little over, and to have more than the average brain capacity' and this statement was taken as sufficient proof to verify that this was the corpse of the United Irish hero. The remains were brought to Ardrigh, where they 'were reverently taken care of' by Bigger.[343] Disregarding doubts that were raised about the veracity of the quasi-forensic identification, the bones were reinterred beside the grave of Mary Ann McCracken in Clifton Street cemetery and a metal tablet was placed to mark the site as 'The Burying Place of Henry Joy McCracken'. While visitors took to placing flowers at the spot, at least one critic—the author of a series of newspaper articles on graveyards in Ulster, written under the pseudonym 'The Chiel' (and occasionally 'Belfastiensis')—argued that 'the person buried there cannot possibly be the great man of that name.'[344]

In 1909, Bigger erected a memorial on Mary Ann McCracken's grave, which noted that she had 'wept by her brother's scaffold'. May placed the additional remains in an oak coffer and added a sealed phial, which asserted that the bones 'from several circumstances are believed to be those of Henry Joy MacCracken' and assured that they had been 'reverently treated'. In absence of a separate memorial, commemoration of the leader of the Antrim rebels was quite literally buried under ground. An inscription added by a '98 Commemoration Association in 1963 to the granite surround of the grave was carefully phrased not to push the claim too far: 'In this grave rest the remains believed to be those of Henry Joy McCracken.'[345] The inconclusive formula marked the site of the grave with uncertainty.

Nearby, Bigger was determined to redress the prolonged neglect of the grave of the 'intrepid Presbyterian minister' Rev. William Steel Dickson, also located in Clifton Street cemetery, and complained that 'for well nigh ninety years this sacred spot had no memorial.' To make amends, he put up a stone slab as a 'permanent memorial', which recognized Dickson as a 'patriot—preacher—historian', but did not explicitly mention his membership of the United Irishmen, or his ordeal in 1798.[346] This somewhat elusive memorialization was considered fitting. In 1907, an article about Henry Joy McCracken in the *Irish News* had complained that 'no stone marks the grave'. Two years later, although there was still no monument in place, the nationalist newspaper expressed satisfaction with the recent commemorative developments,

---

[343] Robert May to F. J. Bigger, 11 May 1909, Bigger Papers, BCL K2/A/33; O'Byrne, *As I Roved Out* (1982 edn), p. 66. See also Edna C. Fitzhenry, *Henry Joy McCracken* (Dublin: The Talbot Press, 1936), pp. 156–7.

[344] The series 'The Silent Land' by 'The Chiel' appeared in the *Belfast Evening Telegraph* from 9 October 1906 through 1907 and was syndicated to local newspapers. For its questioning of the identification of the grave with Henry Joy McCracken, see *Belfast Evening Telegraph*, 12 October 1906, p. 6 and 6 November 1906, p. 6 (republished in *Larne Times*, 20 October 1906, p. 9 and 10 November 1906, p. 10).

[345] *UJA*, 2nd ser., 15, nos. 2/3 (1909): pp. 94–5; Heatley, *Henry Joy*, p. 47. Although Robert May dated the official reinterment to 12 May 1909, it appears that he had placed the bones in the McCracken plot some time earlier, as visits to the site of Henry Joy McCracken's grave were already noted in 1906.

[346] *UJA*, 2nd ser., 15, nos. 2/3 (1909): pp. 93–4.

concluding that 'it is work which should help to remind Ulstermen of much they are too foolishly and carelessly disposed to forget.'[347]

All of the memorials were carefully phrased—never explicitly mentioning 1798— and located in graveyards, rather than in prominent public places. Nonetheless, they represented a head-on challenge to social forgetting, which did not pass unopposed. At Toome in county Antrim, Bigger arranged for the cleaning of the McCorley plot in the old burying ground of Duneane, for which he received the consent of a John McCorley, who was identified as a grandnephew of the executed rebel. When the supposed remains of Roddy McCorley were discovered in 1852, there had been local opposition from the 'the Protestant or Orange element' to the reinterment, and the grave was consequently left unmarked. In 1909, Bigger placed there a gravestone, which was inspired by vernacular history. The inscription read: 'Rody Mac Corly, who died on the Bridge of Toome, Good Friday 1799, *Do Éirinn* [For Ireland]'. This epitaph accorded recognition to a symbolic date popularized in a local folk ballad, even though contemporary historical sources show that McCorley was actually executed on 28 February 1800. Folklore was given precedence over factual history. Meanwhile, Bigger tirelessly declared that 'there is still more to be done' and appealed for subscriptions in order 'to undertake more similar work'.[348]

Shortly afterwards, McCorley's graveside memorial, which had been paid for by local supporters, was broken. Once repaired, it was again attacked and this time efforts were made to conceal the broken pieces. Some forty years later, around 1947, a fragment was found at the bottom of a well in Cloghogue (1 kilometre east of Toome). Bigger dismissively attributed this outburst of vandalism to 'a small set of local intolerants having no general sympathy'. However, like the iconoclastic assault on the Betsy Gray monument in 1898, it signified local loyalist opposition to outsiders partaking in public commemoration of the 1798 rebellion, as opposed to more intimate traditions of folk remembrance, which were normally tolerated. The names of the people who had destroyed the gravestone were said to be known locally, but neither the Protestant rector, who was responsible for the churchyard burying grounds, nor the police, pressed charges and the memorial was not restored again. Unperturbed, Bigger persevered in his commitment to public commemoration and proposed the erection of a 'larger public monument' in the form of a Celtic cross to be raised by the site of McCorley's execution at Toome bridge. Although he assured the readers of the *UJA* that this initiative 'is not forgotten', the memorial was not erected in his lifetime.[349]

In spite of Bigger's ambitious intentions, additional commemorative initiatives remained unfulfilled. A committee was formed in Belfast around 1913, 'with the view of the erection in the near future of a suitable monument to the memory of William Orr'. One of the committee members—the veteran Fenian Robert Johnston—paid a visit to Orr's home area of Farranshane in county Antrim, where he met with 58-year-old Samuel Orr, a great-grandson of the United Irish protomartyr, and with several

---

[347] *Irish News*, 23 July 1907 and 17 July 1907; both articles appear as clippings filed in Bigger Papers, BCL K2/A.

[348] *UJA*, 2nd ser., 15, nos. 2/3 (1909), pp. 93 and 95. The actual date of execution is recorded in Kilmainham Papers, NLI MS 1200/262–3; also *BNL*, 4 March 1800, p. 3.

[349] Bigger Papers, BCL MS Z271; *UJA*, 2nd ser., 15, nos. 2/3 (1909), p. 93. For the discovery of the broken memorial piece see *Derry Journal*, 22 November 1950, p. 6.

nonagenarians from the neighbourhood, who were knowledgeable of local traditions. Johnston visited the old graveyard at Templepatrick and conducted 'a full inquiry and investigation of the grave in which William Orr is buried'. Even though the motto 'Remember Orr' was often repeated in nationalist discourse, the tombstone did not list his name, let alone allude to the tragic circumstances of his execution. Johnston noted that 'there is still some national feeling remaining in the District but there is a terrible effort being made to thoroughly West Britonize them at the present time.' He advised the inhabitants 'to let their watchword still be "Remember Orr"', however, his request for permission to erect a monument by the grave was met with hesitation.[350]

Six years later, Bigger decided to go ahead with the initiative to commemorate Orr. In 1919, he placed an order with the Belfast sculptors Purdy and Millard for a cross-shaped monument, but delivery of the limestone from a quarry in Galway suffered delays and ultimately failed to arrive. The Anglo-Irish War, also known as the Irish War of Independence, was raging and the plans to commemorate William Orr with a graveside memorial fell through.[351] The political circumstances had changed and the drive for re-commemorating had subsided for the time being.

During the Irish Revolution, several writers aspired to harness the memory of 1798 as a propaganda tool that would motivate nationalists to join the struggle for independence. Two radical female writers—Constance Markievicz and Helena Concannon—stand out for their upholding of women's involvement in 1798 as an example for female revolutionaries. Markievicz wrote 'The Women of '98', a five-part series, published weekly, from 6 November to 5 December 1915, in the *Irish Citizen*, the journal of the Irish Women's Franchise League, which was edited by Louie Bennett, who had already shown a literary interest in 1798. Upon outlining her sources, Markievicz mentioned memoirs, letters, and papers that 'have been examined by curious historians and their contents published', as well as ballads, 'passed on from mouth to mouth', and stories, 'told on winter nights round the turf fire, told reverently by old men whose fathers had been able to them what they themselves had suffered, and had seen happen in those glorious days.'[352]

As a girl growing up in a country house at Lissadell, county Sligo, Markievicz née Gore-Booth had met such a storyteller—'Mickey Oge', who was 'the oldest man in the district' and would recount the stories of his father's recollections from 1798 in the west of Ireland. This first-hand encounter with folk history had left a strong impression on her, yet in writing her essays she did not actually go out and collect folklore. Instead, she mostly relied on the traditions that had been documented over seventy years earlier by Madden, who had credited the preservation of recollections of the United Irishmen

---

[350] Robert Johnston, Lisnaveane, Antrim Road, Belfast, to Henry Dixon, 26 June 1913; Robert Johnston Papers, NLI 35,262/1.

[351] Bigger Papers, BCL PU 4/1–2.

[352] Constance Markievicz, 'The Women of '98', *Irish Citizen*, 6, 13, 20, 27 November and 4 December 1915 (quotation from 6 November, p. 150). See also Steele, *Women, Press, and Politics*, pp. 128–32; Mary P. Caulfield, 'Whenever the Tale of '98 is Told: Constance Markievicz, the National Memory and "The Women of Ninety-Eight"', in *Ireland, Memory and Performing the Historical Imagination*, edited by Christopher Collins and Mary P. Caulfield (Houndmills and New York: Palgrave Macmillan, 2014), pp. 87–100; Arrington, *Revolutionary Lives*, p. 118. For essential information on the journal see Louise Ryan, 'The "Irish Citizen", 1912–1920', *Saothar*, 17 (1992): pp. 105–11.

mainly to 'the fidelity of female friendship or affection on the part of their female relatives'. In referring to Ulster heroines, Markievicz repeated information from Madden (with some additional material from Teeling) on Mary Ann McCracken, including Mary Ann's account of Elizabeth Grey [Betsy Gray]. Among assorted anecdotes found in Madden's memoirs, she commended the willingness of the mother of Willie Nelson to sacrifice her son, as opposed to the fecklessness of the wife of Tom Armstrong, who supposedly pleaded with her husband to save his life by informing on his comrades (a legend that originated in a poem by Edward Rushton). These figures were embroidered and presented as role models for revolutionaries in 1916, including Markievicz herself. Four months after 'The Women of '98' appeared in print, Markievicz played an active part in the Easter Rising, for which she was handed a death sentence, which was subsequently commuted.[353]

The historian Helena Concannon wrote a more substantial study on *Women of 'Ninety-Eight*, which came out in Dublin in 1919, during the Irish War of Independence. Concanon née Walsh came from Magherafelt, county Londonderry (9 kilometres west of Toome in county Antrim), an area that saw United Irish mobilization in 1798. Her background was Catholic and nationalist—her father, the hotel proprietor Louis Walsh, had been a Fenian, Land League activist, and a supporter of the Irish parliamentary party, and one of her brothers, the solicitor Louis Joseph Walsh, was a constitutional nationalist who became a militant republican. She noted that 'for some reason (perhaps it was in part the long life and faithful heart of Mary McCracken and the influence she radiated around her) the North has kept a richer record of the sufferings and heroism of its obscurer women in '98 and '03, than other parts of the country.' In offering brief sections on several Ulster women, her information derived mainly from Madden and Teeling, alongside 'some very precious reliques' found in the issues of the *Shan Van Vocht* magazine, and additional insights provided by Bigger (mainly regarding Betsy Gray).[354] Nationalist readers, such as the Irish-Canadian Joseph Cyrillus Walsh, editor of the New York radical magazine *Ireland*, were quick to relate the book to the present struggle in Ireland and it received positive reviews in nationalist journals and newspapers. Though praised by Bigger in the *Irish Ecclesiastical Record*, Concannon's *Women of 'Ninety-Eight* did not attract the attention of Ulster Protestants, most of whom would have found its nationalist tone off-putting.[355]

---

[353] *Irish Citizen*, 6 November 1915, pp. 150–1 (Mickey Oge; Willie Nelson); 13 November 1915, p. 161 (Betsy Gray); 27 November 1915, pp. 177–8 (Mary Ann McCracken); 4 December 1915, p. 183 (Tom Armstrong).

[354] Concannon, *Women of 'Ninety-Eight*, pp. 68–102 (mother of Charles Hamilton Teeling), 165–85 (wife of Samuel Neilson); 215–40 (Mary Ann McCracken; see also p. 307); 259 (Teeling's sister); 259 (sister of Henry Hazlett); 297–8 (Betsy Gray), 306–7 (Teeling's fiancé), 307; 311 (a Miss Quinn); Rose Mullan Hope (320–2); 323–6 (miscellaneous Antrim traditions, including the mother of Willie Nelson). For correspondence between Concannon and Bigger see Bigger Papers, BCL CO 18 (especially letter nos. 3 and 8 regarding Betsy Gray).

[355] Joseph Cyrillus Walsh, *The Invincible Irish* (New York: The Devin-Adair Co., 1919), pp. 142–3; *Irish Monthly*, 47 (1919): p. 515; *Irish Book Lover*, 10, nos. 11–12 (1919): p. 108; *Irish Ecclesiastical Record*, 14 (1919): pp. 174–5; *Catholic Bulletin*, 9, no. 6 (1919): pp. 318–20 (also mentioned in no. 8, p. 408 and no. 9, pp. 486–7); *Tuam Herald*, 26 July 1919, p. 2.

A pamphlet history of *Ulster in '98*, published in Dublin around 1920, concluded that:

> Ulster is being used to dismember and disrupt the nation, but no bitterness we may feel for their sons' present anti-national attitude should make us neglect our duty to the memory of the Protestant Ulstermen who fought for Ireland in '98. We must keep green that memory for the time when the north-east breaking through the clouds of British-manufactured ignorance and prejudice, will learn to honour the United Irishmen themselves.[356]

In witness statements collected in the mid-twentieth century by the Bureau of Military History—an Irish state-sponsored body that documented recollections of veterans of the Irish Revolution—northern republicans remembered how they were inspired by the memory of 1798. As a youth of 20 years of age at the time of the centenary, the imagination of Patrick McCartan was ignited by literature on the United Irishmen that was smuggled into the seminary in Monaghan where he was studying. McCartan recalled how reading Alice Milligan's *Life of Theobald Wolfe Tone* 'gave me a solid foundation for my future convictions'.[357] Similarly, Bulmer Hobson, who was a leading member of the IRB before the Easter Rising, remembered in a published memoir how, as a schoolboy in Belfast during the centenary, 'a new fire was kindled when I learned about Tone and Russell and the Society of United Irishmen, and their activities in my native town.'[358]

Younger revolutionaries often attributed their radicalism to membership in the nationalist scouting movement Na Fianna Éireann, which had taught them about the legacy of the United Irishmen. In June 1913, the Fianna commemorated in Belfast the anniversary of Wolfe Tone's birth with a memorable pilgrimage to Cave Hill attended by six *sluaighte* [branches], of which four were named after '98 heroes from Ulster.[359] A half-century later, Ina and Nora Connolly—the Belfast-raised daughters of the socialist revolutionary leader James Connolly—dwelt on their membership in the Betsy Gray *sluagh*, and David McGuinness recalled the activities of other northern *sluaighte*, which honoured Willie Nelson, Henry Joy McCracken, William Orr, Rody McCorley, and Wolfe Tone.[360]

Several revolutionaries had entertained fancies that the 'the spirit of James Hope, Henry Joy McCracken and William Orr of old' would prevail and that Presbyterians would rally to join the fight for independence.[361] They found succour when Jimmie Hope, 'a grandson of Jimmie [James] Hope of 1798 fame, and an Independent Orangeman' joined the Dungannon Club, a republican organization established in 1905 and modelled on the Volunteers of the late eighteenth century, while also paying homage to the United Irishmen. The founders of the Dungannon Club, Bulmer Hobson and Denis McCullough, issued postcards that commemorated the battles of

---

[356] Diarmuid De Barra, *Ulster in '98: A Short Account of the Insurrection in Antrim and Down* (Dublin: Davis Publishing Company, n.d. [*c.*1920]).

[357] Witness statement by Patrick McCartan, originally of Tyrone, n.d., BMH 766/1–3.

[358] Hobson, *Ireland Yesterday and Tomorrow*, p. 2.

[359] *Irish News*, 26 June 1913; reproduced in Gaughan, *Memoirs of Senator Joseph Connolly*, p. 75n16.

[360] Witness statements by Ina Heron [née Connolly], 25 January 1954, BMH 919/74; Nora Connolly O'Brien, 21 July 1949, BMH 286/3–4; David McGuinness, 28 July 1950, BMH 417/2.

[361] Witness statements by Liam A. Brady of Derry, 1 May 1952, BMH 676/46; Patrick Rankin, originally of Derry, 16 April 1952, BMH 671/13–14.

Ballynahinch and Antrim and it was noted that several 'Presbyterian descendants of '98 men' came out in support of the club.[362] But this was scarcely the norm. A more typical reaction was that of Adam Duffin, a respectable liberal unionist businessman, related to the United Irishman William Drennan by marriage, who scoffed at the 1916 Rising, which he compared to a 'comic opera founded on the Wolf[e] Tone fiasco a hundred years ago'.[363] Throughout the turmoil of the revolutionary period, the vast majority of Ulster's Presbyterians remained loyal.

Commemoration of 1798 had been a significant stimulus for the 'Rising generation', but the enthusiasm of many of revolutionaries was curbed by the shock of their encounter with the brutal violence of guerrilla warfare. After hostilities ceased, disillusion sank in and popular interest in commemoration of Ninety-Eight plummeted.[364] Bigger was profoundly shaken by the events of 1916 and the years that followed. His friend the Sinn Féin activist Joseph Connelly, who travelled from Belfast to Dublin on Easter Sunday 1916 to take part in the rising and was subsequently jailed even though he hadn't actually taken part in the fighting, observed that 'the whole period must have been a nightmare of shock and apprehension to him.'[365]

Although Bigger was not a man of arms (apart from the antiquated weapons that he collected), many of the revolutionaries had been frequent visitors to his residence in Ardrigh and his activities were monitored by the police. A raid on the house nearly resulted in the arrest of Dennis McCullough, who at the time was president of the IRB supreme council and although he had not actually taken part in the rising went into hiding and was soon captured.[366] Above all, the trial and execution of Sir Roger Casement, who was a close friend and had shared an interest in 1798, caused Bigger considerable anguish. On the background of the release of the 'Black Diaries' and the controversial revelations of Casement's homosexuality, Bigger reputedly destroyed papers in his possession, possibly fearing that disclosure of the homosocial nature of the gatherings at Ardrigh might cause harm.[367] He was appalled by the outburst of sectarian violence on the streets of Belfast between 1920 and 1922. Labelled the 'Belfast Pogrom', it resulted in the deaths of some 500 people, who were predominantly

---

[362] Witness statements by Liam Gaynor, originally of Belfast, 21 October 1948 [Jimmie Hope], BMH 183/1–2; Denis McCullough, originally of Belfast, 11 December 1953, BMH 915/3. See also John Killen, *John Bull's Famous Circus: Ulster History through the Postcard, 1905–1985* (Dublin: O'Brien, 1985), pp. 24–5.

[363] Letter by A. Duffin, dated 25 April 1916; cited in Patrick Buckland, *Ulster Unionism and the Origins of Northern Ireland 1886–1922*, vol. 2 (Dublin: Gill and Macmillan and New York: Barnes & Noble, 1973), p. 20.

[364] See Heather L. Roberts, 'The Rising Generation and the Memory of 1798', in *Remembering 1916: The Easter Rising, the Somme and the Politics of Memory in Ireland*, edited by Richard Grayson and McGarry Fearghal (Cambridge: Cambridge University Press, 2016), pp. 155–67.

[365] Gaughan, *Memoirs of Senator Joseph Connolly*, p. 96.

[366] Special Branch Report on Sir Roger Casement, RIC Crime Department, 28 November 1914, TNA CO 904/194/46/15–16; Report of RIC Commissioner, Belfast, 1 May 1916, TNA CO 904/99/666. For McCullough's close call at Ardrigh see Roger Dixon, 'Heroes for a New Ireland: Francis Joseph Bigger and the Leaders of The '98', in *From Corrib to Cultra: Folklife Essays in Honour of Alan Gailey*, edited by Trefor M. Owen (Belfast: Institute of Irish Studies in association with the Ulster Folk and Transport Museum, 2000), p. 36.

[367] Dudgeon, *Roger Casement*, pp. 527 and 553–7. For Casement's interest in 1798 see Margaret O'Callaghan, '"With the Eyes of Another Race, of a People Once Hunted Themselves": Casement, Colonialism and a Remembered Past', in *Roger Casement in Irish and World History*, edited by Mary E. Daly (Dublin: Royal Irish Academy, 2005), p. 59.

unarmed Catholics from the districts immediately surrounding city centre.[368] It was later recalled that Bigger had witnessed such a killing outside his offices on Royal Avenue and was left stunned.[369]

For two decades, Bigger had been hard at work compiling materials for an intended series on the 'Northern Leaders of '98'. Determined to leave no stone unturned, he persistently corresponded with scores of contacts throughout the province and travelled to meet any person who was believed to have knowledge of relevant traditions, or who might own a relic from the period. The numerous accounts that he collected constituted a vast archive of social memory, as it was recalled at the turn of the century. His friend John S. Crone rightly asserted that 'no one alive knows more concerning the United Irishmen than F. J. Bigger.'[370] The source material was organized, after the fashion of Madden, into biographical memoirs of six pre-eminent individuals— William Orr, Henry Joy MacCracken, Henry Munro, James Hope, Samuel Neilson, and Thomas Russell. Before launching the series, Bigger appealed in January 1906 to readers of the *UJA* for any 'unpublished information or pictures'.[371] He repeated the call in a more targeted form in local papers, asking for example the readers of the *Lisburn Standard* for specific information on the local hero Henry Munro and promising that 'any manuscripts or other articles entrusted to me will be carefully preserved and returned.'[372]

The *Belfast Evening Telegraph*, under the proprietorship of Bigger's friend Robert Hugh Hanley Baird, endorsed the enterprise. The unionist newspaper reassured its predominantly working class readers that Bigger's 'intimate knowledge of the times and the places will render the work especially accurate, while the local and family traditions that are his, and the amount of original papers in his possession, will make the publication unique, and give it permanent value', not least because 'he has resided for most of his life close to the places associated with their actions, and is thoroughly familiar with every spot sacred to their memories.'[373] In May 1906, the inaugural volume *Remember Orr* came out with the Dublin publishers Maunsel & Co.[374] The *Belfast Evening Telegraph* commended the book, while acknowledging that it was 'probably impossible to write of these times and the stirring scenes they witnessed to the satisfaction of everybody, and Mr. Bigger's "Northern Leaders" will doubtless have its hostile critics.' The newspaper argued that 'whether readers agree with all the

[368] G. B. Kenna [Father John Hassan], *Facts & Figures of the Belfast Pogrom, 1920–1922* (Dublin: O'Connell Publishing Company, 1922); the label 'pogrom' is rejected in Alan F. Parkinson, *Belfast's Unholy War: The Troubles of the 1920s* (Dublin: Four Courts Press, 2004). For a mapping of deaths see Niall Cunningham, '"The Doctrine of Vicarious Punishment": Space, Religion and the Belfast Troubles of 1920–22', *Journal of Historical Geography*, 40 (2013): pp. 52–66.
[369] Interviews with Roger Dixon, Information Manager, National Museums Northern Ireland (Cultra, Holywood, Co. Down, 20 September 2011); Roland Spottiswoode, Ardrigh Books (Belfast, 17 July 2013).
[370] *Irish Book Lover*, 1, no. 3 (1909), p. 35.
[371] *UJA*, 2nd ser., 12, no. 1 (January 1906), p. 48.
[372] *Lisburn Standard*, 17 February 1906; clipping in Bigger Papers, BCL K3/H/23. Though considered a conservative newspaper, the *Lisburn Standard* showed an interest in local history and from 1917 to 1919 featured the series 'Some Extracts from the Records of Old Lisburn and the Manor of Killultagh', edited by James Carson, which also reproduced previously published traditions of 1798 (including the recollections of the renowned local historian Hugh McCall).
[373] *Belfast Evening Telegraph*, 27 February 1906, p. 3.
[374] Francis Joseph Bigger, *Remember Orr* (Dublin: Maunsel & Co., 1906).

conclusions of the author or not, the publication is one of considerable historical importance.' Complaining about 'the amount of ignorance that prevails in regard to these times and these men among the working classes', the editorial concluded that the reasonably priced booklets would 'bring the study within reach of the pockets of all'.[375]

Nationalists found unreserved inspiration in *Remember Orr*. Demonstrating the sincerest form of flattery, John Clarke, the former secretary of the Henry Joy McCracken Literary Society, also wrote a short memoir of William Orr, which was largely based on Bigger's work.[376] In glowing reviews, the nationalist press strongly recommended Bigger's booklet to its predominantly Catholic readership. The issue of the rest of the series, to be published in 'a limited edition made to order for 10s' and as individual 'popular shilling biographies', was highly anticipated.[377] Bigger, however, bid his time and did not rush to publish the other volumes.

Bigger continued to receive information from additional informants. Rev. Andrew James Blair, the Presbyterian minister at Ballynure, where Orr had been waked, wrote to express his appreciation for *Remember Orr* and added 'I wish I had met you before it was published as I think I could have added to your store of knowledge.' Richard Archer, who had provided illustrations and other titbits of information for the book, came back with queries and suggestions for minor corrections.[378] Meanwhile, Bigger didn't stop collecting sources for the other memoirs, pedantically aspiring to get to the bottom of each and every remaining puzzle. In 1910, he appealed again to the readers of the *UJA*, this time for help in locating a croppies' burial ground believed to be near May Street in Belfast. The existence of this site had been brought to his attention by the recently deceased dermatologist and antiquarian Henry Samuel Purdon (who had previously published in the journal an account of the Battle of Antrim that had been written by a relative of his, who had served in a British regiment in 1798).[379] As late as 1913, he received a manuscript of 'Notes Concerning Samuel Neilson', which had been dictated between 1889 and 1891 by Neilson's grand-daughter, Elizabeth Thomson, to her daughter.[380] Interest in the series remained strong and Bigger was approached by such distinguished figures as the author T. W. H. Rolleston, who wrote in 1915, asking to acquire the additional volumes.[381] Although Bigger completed the manuscripts for the five other memoirs, they remained unpublished.[382]

Following the dramatic events of 1916 and the Irish Revolution, the plans for issuing the 'Northern Leaders of '98' were shelved. In the Civil War that followed the War of

---

[375] *Belfast Evening Telegraph*, 25 May 1906, p. 3.

[376] 'Benmore' [Clarke], *Thoughts from the Heart*, pp. 35–41.

[377] *Irish News*, 16 May 1906; *Derry Journal*, 25 May 1906, p. 5 and 11 June 1906, p. 2; *Ulster Herald*, 26 May 1906, p. 3 (serialized also in the *Donegal News* and in the *Fermanagh Herald*, 26 May 1906, p. 3).

[378] Rev. Andrew James Blair, Ballynure, county Antrim, to F. J. Bigger, Bigger Papers, BCL BL4/1; Richard Archer to F. J. Bigger, 14 October 1924, BCL AR/2.

[379] *UJA*, 2nd ser., 16, nos. 1/2 (1910), p. 96. For the account of Battle of Antrim see *UJA*, 2nd ser., 8, no. 2 (1902): p. 96; Henry George Purdon, *Memoirs of the Services of the 64th Regiment (Second Staffordshire), 1758 to 1881* (London: W. H. Allen, 1882), pp. 33–4.

[380] T. W. H. Rolleston to F. J. Bigger, dated 1915; Bigger Papers, NLI 35,143.

[381] Bigger Papers, NLI 35,456/3.

[382] Bigger Papers, BCL K1 (James Hope); K2 (Henry Joy McCracken), K3 (Henry Munro), K4 (Samuel Neilson), K6 (Thomas Russell). For a cursory review see Dixon, 'Heroes for a New Ireland', pp. 32–5.

Independence, Bigger's nationalist acquaintances were bitterly divided between those who supported the Anglo-Irish Treaty brokered in 1921 and those who objected to it. The establishment of Northern Ireland, which officially devolved in 1922 on the basis of the basis of the Government of Ireland Act 1920 (10 & 11 Geo. 5 c. 67), partitioned the province of Ulster and separated the six north-eastern counties from the rest of Ireland. Partition shattered Bigger's vision of a vibrant Ulster as a distinct component of an independent united Ireland. From then on, he kept his nationalist views to himself, refraining from crossing the border into the Irish Free State and desisting from publishing articles in the nationalist press. In the new reality of Northern Ireland, Bigger's romantic blend of regionalism and nationalism had become a political anachronism.

On 9 July 1926, Bigger was awarded an honorary M.A. degree from Queen's University Belfast. At the conferment ceremony, the Professor of Modern History, James Eadie Todd, reviewed Bigger's 'lifetime of enthusiasms to researches in Irish archaeology and local history'. Todd attributed 'the ubiquity of his fame in Northern Ireland' to 'the fact that he had striven successfully to convey to the mass of his fellow-citizens what he himself felt with such intensity—that the record and remains of past life in Ireland constituted a precious communal inheritance in which each and all ought to be interested sharers'. Todd added that 'no man in these parts has given himself more generously to the task of maintaining for this, and for succeeding generations, a continuing interest in those fragmentary relics which had survived the violence of human hands and the corroding tooth of time.' Bigger's primary commitment to the memory of 1798, which did not suit the ethos of the new state, was left unmentioned and forgotten.[383]

Bigger passed away several months later, on 9 December 1926, and was buried in Mallusk graveyard, in close proximity to his hero, James Hope. His illustrious standing soon fell into obscurity. A few years later, readers of the local Antrim magazine the *Glensman* had to defend Bigger's reputation after the archaeologist Henry Cairnes Lawlor spitefully branded him a 'charlatan historian', whose work should be 'relegated to oblivion'.[384] This brief exchange, which concerned few members of the general public, did not touch on Bigger's preoccupation with the United Irishmen. The historian Donald Akenson described Bigger as 'the last Protestant to be able to reach out and touch the '98 Rising' adding that 'he had grown up listening to Carnmoney men whose fathers had been out in '98, and he had not permitted the confusions of the north's troubles to erase their words.'[385] This legacy was now out of tune and grating on loyalist ears.

In April 1971, Bigger's grave in Mallusk was damaged by an explosion. The local press maintained that this act vandalism was 'presumably the work of politically

---

[383] *Irish News*, 10 December 1926, p. 8; *Larne Times*, 18 December 1926, p. 5; Crone, 'Memoir', p. xxxiv–v.

[384] H. C. Lawlor, *Ulster: Its Archaeology and Antiquities* (Belfast: R. Carswell & Son, 1928), p. 145; H. C. Lawlor, 'Bun-na-Mairghie Friary: Ballycastle's Great Franciscan Link', *Glensman*, 1, no. 2 (November 1931), pp. 26–32. For responses see *Glensman*, no. 3 (December 1932), and no. 5 (February 1932), pp. 29 and 31; reproduced online: <www.ballycastlehistory.com/bun-na-mairghie-friary-by-h-c-lawlor.html>. See also Kirkland, *Cathal O'Byrne*, pp. 90, 109, and 117n16.

[385] Donald H. Akenson, *An Irish History of Civilization*, vol. 2 (Montreal: McGill-Queen's University Press, 2005), p. 565.

motivated ruffians indicating their hostility towards the memory of one of the most gentle scholars Ulster has known'. In what appeared to be an attempt to expunge remnants of memory tinged with romantic nationalism (with an inscription in Irish possibly being the immediate cause of offense), Ulster's great commemorator had been decommemorated (see Fig. 6.5, p. 506). At the same time, the nearby gravestone of James Hope, erected by Madden in 1847 and restored by Bigger in 1901, was left untouched. There were apparent limits to the assault on memory.[386]

Just as remembrance of William Orr had prepared the way for initiating social remembrance of 1798 and had also foreshadowed its forgetting—a dynamic which was labelled in an earlier chapter 'pre-forgetting', the publication of Bigger's *Remember Orr* preceded the failure to publish the rest of the 'Northern Leaders of '98', which heralded the return to dominance of social forgetting. The dynamics of memory and forgetting at the turn of the century constituted a cycle of commemorating, decommemorating, and re-commemorating. The revivalist activities of the last decade of the nineteenth century culminated with the effervescent commemorations of the centenary. In response, celebrations of memory in public were checked by a bout of hostile decommemorating. This aggressive reaction did not stamp out memory. On the contrary, decommemorating triggered a period of re-commemorating, which produced an impressive crop of literary works. Careful examination, however, shows that this gush of cultural remembrance was permeated with anxieties of forgetting. Seen as a long-term process, commemoration is not simply a triumphant celebration of collective memory and may prove to be an inconclusive series of contests that involve both remembering and social forgetting.

Overall, the lasting outcome of northern Ninety-Eight commemoration was limited. Commemorating took place under the constant apprehension of decommemorating and the few memorials that Bigger and his friends constructed were located in secluded graveyards. In Ulster, unlike the rest of Ireland, monuments to the United Irishmen were not erected in prominent public places. With the formation of Northern Ireland as a unionist entity, official proscription of memory associated with republicanism would be re-imposed. Reticence, rather than outspokenness, was back in the saddle.

---

[386] *Ulster Herald*, 17 April 1971, p. 8; *Irish News*, 7 April 1971, p. 1; *Irish Times*, 8 and 9 April 1971 pp. 9 and 11 (respectively). For the wider political context of this act of vandalism see Chapter 6 below, pp. 504–6.

6

Restored Forgetting

The Short Twentieth Century

Is there enough forgetfulness for them to forget?

Mahmoud Darwish, *Memory for Forgetfulness*[1]

And historians said that memorials helped classify society's memories and organize the collective memory and fight against oblivion in general and above all against specific oblivion, and that it was actually also a way of creating other forms of oblivion.

Patrik Ouředník, *Europeana*[2]

Practically all governments aspire to utilize collective memory as a tool for cementing hegemony. In particular, public remembrance is pressed in the service of new states, as they put down roots through commemoration. Memorialization bolsters the legitimacy of the state by projecting sovereignty over a geographical area into the historical past.[3] Territorial partition, however, complicates matters, as it introduces separate, mutually exclusive, memorial rituals into what had formerly been a unified space. Regimes that impose their authority on disgruntled minority populations which find themselves on the wrong side of partition typically suffer from insecurities, which are used to justify the proscription of counter-memories that undermine the official narratives propagated by the state. The prohibitions placed on historical traditions drive noncompliant memories underground, or into exile.[4] Partition, therefore, becomes a framework for social forgetting.

A Central-Eastern European example of partition, which was contemporaneous with the partition of Ireland, can serve to demonstrate how partitioned memories bolster social forgetting. When Arthur Griffith, the founder of Sinn Féin, wrote in January 1918 the preface for the third edition of *The Resurrection of Hungary*, an influential book in which he envisaged a resolution for the Anglo-Irish conflict along the lines of

---

[1] Mahmoud Darwish, *Memory for Forgetfulness: August, Beirut, 1982* (Berkeley: University of California Press, 2013; orig. edn 1995), p. 13.

[2] Patrik Ouředník, *Europeana: A Brief History of the Twentieth Century* (Normal, Ill. and London: Dalkey Archive Press, 2005), p. 119.

[3] For a classic case study see Yael Zerubavel, *Recovered Roots: Collective Memory and the Making of Israeli National Tradition* (Chicago and London: University of Chicago Press, 1995).

[4] This dynamic is particularly evident in the struggles over memory resulting from both the creation and partition of Yugoslavia. See Victor Roudometof, *Collective Memory, National Identity, and Ethnic Conflict: Greece, Bulgaria, and the Macedonian Question* (Westport, Conn.: Praeger, 2002); Pamela Ballinger, *History in Exile: Memory and Identity at the Borders of the Balkans* (Princeton: Princeton University Press, 2003).

the *Ausgleich* compromise that had created the Habsburg Dual Monarchy in 1867 (instead of Home Rule), he failed to realize that this political arrangement was on the verge of falling apart.[5] The partition of Austro-Hungary was formalized in the Paris Peace Conference, following the defeat of the Central Powers in the Great War, and its terms were dictated in the Trianon Treaty of 1920. In an iconoclastic outburst of decommemorating, driven by resentment to former policies of Magyarization, the secessionist states of the Czechoslovak Republic, the Kingdom of Serbs, Croats, and Slovenes (to be renamed Yugoslavia), and an enlarged Kingdom of Romania (after annexing Transylvania), rid themselves of the monuments and remaining symbols of the previous regime. In their place, new festivals celebrated national distinctiveness, and monuments commemorated separatist histories.[6]

Refusing to reconcile with the partition of the 'Lands of the Crown of Saint Stephen', the truncated Kingdom of Hungary under the regency of Admiral Miklós Horthy commemorated the loss of its provinces. The implied threat in the rhetoric and symbolism of irredentist remembrance, which proclaimed the aspiration to re-unite partitioned territories and appealed to nationalists across the border, pushed the neighbouring states to put restrictions on the cultural expressions of their Hungarian minorities and to forbid them from participating in the memorial culture of their ethnic homeland.[7]

Following partitions, histories of state formation are typically sanitized so that the violence through which sovereignty was achieved is left out of official collective memory. Nonetheless, recollections that challenge the legitimacy of the redrawn boundaries are preserved in conditions of social forgetting through oral histories and private rituals of commemoration. The silencing of traumatic memories and their persistence at a personal and community level can be seen in India and Pakistan, as well as in Cyprus.[8] Nowhere is this more obvious than in the proscription of the memory of the violence perpetuated during the partition of Mandatory Palestine in 1948.

Whereas Palestinians were left with painful memories of displacement, Israeli-Jews typically recalled their War of Independence as a heroic, and essentially virtuous,

---

[5] Arthur Griffith, *The Resurrection of Hungary: A Parallel for Ireland*, 3rd edn (Dublin: Whelan and son, 1918; orig. edn 1904), pp. ix–xii. For the original publication of Griffith's manifesto see Michael Laffan, *The Resurrection of Ireland: The Sinn Féin Party, 1916–1923* (Cambridge and New York: Cambridge University Press, 1999), pp. 3 and 17–19.

[6] Maria Bucur, 'Birth of a Nation: Commemorations of December 1, 1918, and National Identity in Twentieth-Century Romania', in *Staging the Past: The Politics of Commemoration in Habsburg Central Europe, 1848 to the Present*, edited by Maria Bucur and Nancy M. Wingfield (West Lafayette, Ind.: Purdue University Press, 2001), pp. 286–325; Dagmar Hájková and Nancy M. Wingfield, 'Czech(-oslovak) National Commemorations During The Interwar Period: Tomáš G. Masaryk and The Battle of White Mountain Avenged', *Acta Historiae*, 18, no. 3 (2010): pp. 425–52.

[7] Guy Beiner, '"No, Nay, Never" (Once More): The Resurrection of Hungarian Irredentism', *History Ireland*, 21, no. 3 (2013): pp. 40–4. See also Miklós Zeidler, *A Magyar Irredenta Kultusz a Két Világháború Között* (Budapest: Teleki László Alapítvány, 2002).

[8] Urvashi Butalia, *The Other Side of Silence: Voices from the Partition of India* (New Delhi: Penguin Books, 1998), pp. 347–41; Gyanendra Pandey, *Remembering Partition: Violence, Nationalism, and History in India* (Cambridge and New York: Cambridge University Press, 2001), pp. 175–205; Sukeshi Kamra, 'Engaging Traumatic Histories: The 1947 Partition of India in Collective Memory', in *Partition: The Long Shadow*, edited by Urvashi Butalia (Chicago: University of Chicago Press, 2015), pp. 155–77. For Cyprus see Rabia Harmanşah, 'Performing Social Forgetting in a Post-Conflict Landscape: The Case of Cyprus' (PhD: Graduate Faculty of the Dietrich School of Arts and Sciences, University of Pittsburgh, 2015).

victory and were reluctant to acknowledge atrocities perpetuated on their side.[9] From the foundation of the State of Israel, deliberate efforts were made to erase the vernacular landscape of the evacuated and destroyed Arab villages. Some villages were supplanted by Jewish communities, such as Ein Houd at the foot of the Carmel Mountains which was replaced with the artist colony Ein Hod, and others were left in desolation, such as Qula, near Ramla.[10] The prevention of Palestinians from commemorating in public the *Nakba* [catastrophe], through policies that critics have labelled 'memoricide', has been resisted through the cultivation of subaltern counter-memory.[11] Whereas most Jewish-Israelis embraced forgetting and readily opted for denial, the emergence of groups that seek to recognize Palestinian suffering, such as the NGO *Zochrot* [remembering], prompted the state to pass a law in 2011 that authorizes financial sanctions against public-funded bodies which host alternative commemorative ceremonies. In this way, memories that do not comply with hegemonic state memory have been officially forbidden.[12] Such prohibitions often stimulate defiance by non-conformists, who sustain proscribed memories.

On a micro-level, the larger scheme of a partition plan necessitates regional sub-partitions. The partition of Ireland entailed the partition of the historical province of Ulster. In creating distinct memorial rituals for six-county Northern Ireland, only selective use could be made of a legacy of provincial historical memory from the nine counties of Ulster, three of which were left to the Irish Free State. Instead, militant unionist opposition to the Third Home Rule bill during the Ulster Crisis of 1912–14, together with the memory of the decimation of the 36th (Ulster) Division at the Battle of the Somme in 1916—construed as a sacrifice for 'God and Ulster', were adopted as modern foundation myths for the new northern statelet.[13] By contrast, commemoration of the 1916 Easter Rising, which had become the foundation myth of independent

---

[9] Efrat Ben-Ze'ev, *Remembering Palestine in 1948: Beyond National Narratives* (New York: Cambridge University Press, 2011), pp. 63–123 (Palestinian memories) and 127–66 (Jewish-Israeli memories).

[10] Susan Slyomovics, *The Object of Memory: Arab and Jew Narrate the Palestinian Village* (Philadelphia: University of Pennsylvania Press, 1998); Susan Slyomovics, 'The Rape of Qula, a Destroyed Palestinian Village', in *Nakba: Palestine, 1948, and the Claims of Memory*, edited by Ahmad H. Sa'di and Lila Abu-Lughod (New York: Columbia University Press, 2007), pp. 27–51; see also essays by Rochelle Davis ('Mapping the Past, Re-creating the Homeland') and Lila Abu-Lughod ('Return to Half-Ruins') in that volume, pp. 53–104.

[11] Nur Masalha, *The Palestine Nakba: Decolonising History, Narrating the Subaltern, Reclaiming Memory* (London and New York: Zed Books, 2012); see also Tamir Sorek, *Palestinian Commemoration in Israel: Calendars, Monuments, and Martyrs* (Stanford: Stanford University Press, 2015).

[12] Budget Foundations Law, Amendment No. 40, *Reshumot* (Official Government Gazette): *Book of Laws*, vol. 2286 (30 March 2011), pp. 686–7 [in Hebrew]; see also Yifat Gutman, *Memory Activism: Reimagining the Past for the Future in Israel-Palestine* (Nashville, Tenn.: Vanderbilt University Press, 2017), pp. 90–112. For Israeli-Jewish engagement with the memory of the Nakba see Uri Ram, 'Ways of Forgetting: Israel and the Obliterated Memory of the Palestinian Nakba', *Journal of Historical Sociology*, 22, no. 3 (2009): pp. 366–95; Ronit Lentin, *Co-Memory and Melancholia: Israelis Memorialising the Palestinian Nakba* (Manchester and New York: Manchester University Press, 2010).

[13] Alvin Jackson, 'Unionist Myths 1912–1985', *Past and Present*, 136, no. 1 (August 1992): pp. 164–85. The construction of the memory of the Battle of the Somme was influenced by existing traditions of modern Irish memory; see Guy Beiner, 'Between Trauma and Triumphalism: The Easter Rising, the Somme, and the Crux of Deep Memory in Modern Ireland', *Journal of British Studies*, 46, no. 2 (2007): pp. 366–89.

Ireland, was strictly forbidden in Northern Ireland. More generally, all expressions of nationalist and, even more so, republican remembrance were deemed subversive.

The memory of the United Irishmen had no place in an official memorial culture that equated Ulster with unionist Northern Ireland and was ideologically opposed to cross-border cooperation. State support in southern Ireland for commemoration of the 1798 rebellion only exacerbated suspicions of creeping irredentism and strengthened the resolve to ban such commemoration in Northern Ireland. Yet, the ability of a state to control remembrance is inevitably limited, so that in practice memory and forgetting are never fully collective. The parameters of policies intended to dominate memory are partly determined by historical factors. From a long historical perspective, the attempts to inhibit public remembrance of the United Irishmen in Northern Ireland can be seen as a drive to restore social forgetting, which harked back to earlier attempts at silencing that had always been contested.

Prohibitions on commemoration of Ninety-Eight in Northern Ireland were seen as a form of cultural discrimination and would come up periodically in objections raised by northern nationalists and their liberal sympathizers. Just a few years after partition, the absence of memorials to the United Irishmen was incidentally discussed in the Northern Ireland parliament in May 1926, during the debates over an Ancient Monument Act. At the bill's second reading, William McMullen, Labour Party member for the predominantly Catholic constituency of Belfast West, declared that he saw 'no reason why somebody should not do something to perpetuate the memory of Henry Joy McCracken whether they agree with his exploits in leading at the Battle of Antrim or with his political views at that time or not'. He called upon the government 'to take these matters up and act in a spirit of impartiality'. At the bill's third reading, the veteran nationalist politician Joseph Devlin, who had recently lead the Nationalist party out of abstentionism and also represented Belfast West, announced that he 'would like to see a monument raised in this city to Wolfe Tone', suggesting that it should be erected on Cave Hill. To illustrate how monuments in Northern Ireland could have multiple meanings, Devlin pointed out the significance of Greyabbey, which was set to be preserved under the bill as a medieval monastic site, but was revered by nationalists for its association with the execution in 1798 of Rev. James Porter.[14]

Complaints of commemorative neglect made no real impact, as the opposition was left toothless in a political structure that virtually guaranteed that the majority Ulster Unionist Party (UUP) would form the cabinet, known as the Executive Committee of the Privy Council. One-party rule was consolidated with the abolition of proportional representation in 1929. Thirty years on, the ineffective calls of nationalist politicians for 'monuments erected at home to Tone and McCracken, two well-known Northern patriots' were still falling on deaf ears.[15] At a parliamentary debate on the rights of the Catholic minority in 1934, Northern Ireland's founding prime minister Viscount Craigavon (James Craig) admitted that he was 'very proud indeed to be Grand Master

---

[14] *Northern Ireland Parliamentary Debates*, vol. 7 (1927), p. 1363 (McMullen, 17 May) and p. 1472 (Devlin, 19 May). For a discussion of the act see Rev. W. P. Carmody, 'The Ancient Monuments Act, N.I., 1926, and Its Working', in *Proceedings and Reports of the Belfast Natural History and Philosophical Society for the Session 1929–30*, edited by Arthur Deane (Belfast: Northern Whig, 1931), pp. 1–10.

[15] Question posed by Cahir Healy to Minister of Finance Terence O'Neill; *Northern Ireland Parliamentary Debates*, vol. 43 (1958), p. 46 (21 October).

of the loyal County of Down' and professed that he was 'an Orangeman first and a
politician and Member of this Parliament afterwards'. At the same time, he insisted that
he 'was Prime Minister not of one section of the community but of all'. When queried
by George Leeke, nationalist MP for Mid Londonderry, about the apparent contradiction, Craigavon famously acknowledged that 'we are a Protestant Parliament and a
Protestant State.' This giveaway phrase, which filtered into popular memory as if he had
said 'a Protestant parliament for a Protestant people', seemed to encapsulate the
exclusivist ethos on which Northern Ireland was founded.[16]

The state endorsed unionist remembrance and awarded a privileged status to the
annual Orange commemorations of The Twelfth (12 July). Commemoration of
Ninety-Eight, on the other hand, was unacceptable, as memories of how the United
Irishmen had tried to bring Protestants and Catholics together in a common struggle
for an independent republic did not fit into official loyalist memorial culture. With
remembrance of the rebellion pushed out of the public sphere, social forgetting was
once more imposed from above.

PARTITIONED MEMORY

The parliament of Northern Ireland was officially opened by King George V on
22 June 1921. The King's speech, which was drafted by the Afrikaner former guerrilla
commander Jan Smuts, who had since become prime minister of the Union of South
Africa, called on Irishmen 'to forgive and forget' for the sake of reconciliation.[17]
Incidentally, the parliament had already held its first session a fortnight earlier, on
7 June, without anyone commenting that this happened to be the anniversary of the
Battle of Antrim. Forgetting was already in place.

Republicans, who were opposed to the new autonomous state, which remained
a constituent part of the United Kingdom, were left disappointed by the results of
the general elections held in May 1921 and were apprehensive about the political
implications of forgetting. In a letter published in a local nationalist newspaper, Kevin
Roantree O'Shiel—an unsuccessful Sinn Féin candidate for Fermanagh and Tyrone—
complained that 'our Protestant fellow-citizens voted for the partition and dismember-
ment of our common country' and 'in so doing they would seem to have forgotten
the splendid democratic teachings of their ancestors, those great Protestant patriots,
who unfurled for the first time the banner of the Irish Republic in 1798 and died for
it in hundreds on the bloody fields of Antrim, Randalstown, and Ballynahinch.'[18]
The sweeping support shown by Protestants for the UUP, which won two-thirds of
the votes and continued to retain its majority in subsequent elections, was denounced
by the opponents of partition as 'an insult to the memory of the United Irishmen . . . to
the memory of all that was clean and noble, aye, and heroic, in Antrim and Down
in 1798'.[19]

---

[16] *Northern Ireland Parliamentary Debates*, vol. 16, pp. 1091 and 1095 (House of Commons,
24 April 1934).
[17] *Irish Times*, 23 June 1921, p. 5.   [18] *Fermanagh Herald*, 18 June 1921, p. 8.
[19] From the speech of Rev. Peadar MacLoinsigh of Waterside, Derry, at a demonstration in county
Tyrone which was part of a larger campaign against partition; *Derry Journal*, 14 November 1938, p. 5.

Nationalists suspected of actively opposing partition were rounded up. A police raid on 17 June 1921 in the district of Greenan's Cross, near the border with county Monaghan, resulted in arrests, though 'no arms were found save an old rusted gun of the 1798 Yeoman pattern, which was taken from the house of a Presbyterian farmer.'[20] Such souvenir weapons from the time of the rebellion took on new meaning. Patrick McGrath of Belfast was sentenced in 1931 to three months in prison for 'possessing a revolver without a permit', regardless of the claim that this was an obsolete relic that had belonged to the family of Henry Joy McCracken. In all likelihood, the actual grounds for his incrimination was the discovery in his house of a copy of the militant republican magazine *An Poblacht*, which since 1926 had been banned under Regulation 26 of the Civil Authorities (Special Powers) Act. Owning up to remembrance of republicanism in the late eighteenth century was linked to subversive republicanism in the present.[21] The paranoia of the new regime struck deep and rubbed off onto the wider population. A teacher in a school in the Glens of Antrim exhibited three 'Queen Anne guns', which had been found by his pupils and were dated to 'the '98 fight', but, when the police made inquiries about the antiquated firearms, 'the master had them hidden away again and they never got them.'[22]

Amateur scholarly interest in 1798 was sustained under the lingering influence of Francis Joseph Bigger, who was still active in the early years of Northern Ireland. The Belfast Naturalists' Field Club continued to visit local sites of memory, organizing in 1923 an excursion to 'McCracken's Well' in Slemish, and a visit in 1925 to the 'Madman's Leap' (a gorge in the Redhall demesne associated with a legendary feat of a fleeing rebel) and the nearby grave of 'the young '98 rebel' Willie Nelson.[23] After Bigger's death in 1926, local historians continued to uphold his legacy. The members of the Larne Debating Society Rambling Club—popularly known as the Larne Ramblers—went in 1932 on an outing from Magheramorne to Kilroot (between Larne and Carrickfergus) and were guided by a devotee of Bigger—Dixon Donaldson of Dunoon, Islandmagee, who 'detailed the historical associations of the neighbourhood' and dwelled on the Turn-Out.[24]

Donaldson, the Presbyterian teacher of Kilcoan School in Islandmagee, was known for 'his retentive memory, his vivacious personality, and his provocativeness of debate', and for his 'keen interest in antiquarian and botanical matters'. Encouraged by Bigger, he had written, under the pseudonym Ben Magee, a series of articles on local history for the *Whitehead News and Ballycarry and Islandmagee Reporter*. These were collated in 1927 into a booklet titled *Historical, Traditional, and Descriptive Account of Islandmagee*, for which Donaldson credited Bigger as his 'guide and counsellor on all occasions'. A chapter on the Turn-Out made extensive use of previously published traditions, including accounts collected by Classon Porter that had appeared at the end of the

[20] *Anglo-Celt*, 18 June 1921, p. 1.
[21] *Irish Independent*, 1 September 1931, p. 5 and 2 December 1931, p. 10; *Irish Press*, 8 September 1931, p. 1. For the banning of expressions of republicanism see Laura K. Donohue, 'Regulating Northern Ireland: The Special Powers Acts, 1922–1972', *Historical Journal*, 41, no. 4 (1998): pp. 1089–1120.
[22] Childhood recollections of Pat McCambridge of Laney, county Antrim, recorded by Michael J. Murphy *c*.1953; NFC 1362/114.
[23] *Northern Whig*, 20 June 1923, p. 3 and 11 August 1925, p. 11.
[24] *Larne Times*, 1 October 1932, p. 3.

previous century in Young's *Ulster in '98*, as well as references found in McSkimin's *Annals of Ulster* (which was republished in 1906). Donaldson was also familiar with recollections of 1798 at first hand. His account of the execution of Willie Nelson notes that 'the present writer, on several occasions, has listened to a description of the execution from the lips of his grandfather, who, as a boy of 10 years, was an eyewitness, of the tragedy.' Donaldson showed evident sympathy for the rebels, but covered himself by stating that he had 'endeavoured to treat the subject on impartial lines and without any intention of political sentiment or bias'.[25] Local historians had to tread carefully when addressing Ninety-Eight in unionist Northern Ireland.

The extensive folk history collections that Bigger had amassed were later disseminated by one of his most devoted disciples, the Belfast Catholic raconteur and entertainer Cathal O'Bryne. Having mingled with literary talents at Bigger's gatherings in Ardrigh, O'Byrne went on to become a popular writer in his own right with 'Mrs. Twigglety's Weekend Letter'—a weekly column on everyday life in Ulster during the years of the Great War, published in *Ireland's Saturday Night* (a 'journal of general reading, football, cycling [and] athletics' launched by the owners of the *Belfast Telegraph*). He then joined the IRA in 1919 and was involved in smuggling arms from Belfast to Dublin, but was soon disillusioned by affairs in Belfast and emigrated in 1920 to America, where he raised money for the victims of the 'Belfast Pogrom'.[26] On his return to Belfast in 1928, O'Bryne gained renown as a performer of ballads, folk songs, and stories. Listings in the *Northern Whig* show that his regular appearances on a radio programme broadcasted in the Irish Free State in the mid-1930s were also heard in Northern Ireland.

From the late 1930s into the mid-1940s, O'Byrne published in the *Irish News* well over a hundred articles on the history and folklore of Belfast and its surroundings. He called attention to 'the memory of famous men who, despite the conspicuous role they played in national history, are often in danger of being forgotten', and in particular to the northern United Irishmen. These short pieces were compiled and republished in a book titled *As I Roved Out* (named after a well-known traditional song), which first appeared in 1946. O'Bryne sold copies from his home and the book was soon out of stock. In the year of the author's death, 1957, an abridged edition, which included only the Belfast material, was published by the Dublin printer Colm Ó Lochlainn, who's Three Candles Press specialized in folklore-related publications. The issue of a reprint of the original edition (1970), a facsimile publication of the second edition (1982), and several reprints (which came out in 1984, 1990, and 2000) attest to the book's lasting popularity.[27]

O'Byrne fashioned himself as an urban *seanchaí*—a storyteller and reciter of traditional lore [*seanchas*]. As such, he didn't put much effort into collecting folklore and instead specialized in retelling previously documented traditions. *As I Roved Out* was

---

[25] Donaldson, *Historical, Traditional, and Descriptive Account*, Preface and pp. 56–66 (a facsimile edition was produced by the Islandmagee Community Development Association in 2002). For brief biographical information see *Northern Whig*, 5 October 1931, p. 9; *Larne Times*, 15 July 1943, p. 4.

[26] Kirkland, *Cathal O'Byrne*, pp. 123–47 and 179–83.

[27] Cathal O'Byrne, *As I Roved Out: In Belfast and District*, 2nd edn (Wakefield: S. R. Publishers, 1970; reprint of 2nd edn, Dublin: Three Candles, 1957); Cathal O'Byrne, *As I Roved Out: A Book of The North, Being a Series of Historical Sketches of Ulster and Old Belfast*, 3rd edn (Belfast: Blackstaff, 1982; facsimile of orig. edn, Belfast: Irish News, 1946). See also *Irish News*, 14 November 1946 (republished in *Irish News*, 14 November 2015, p. 19).

dedicated to the memory of Bigger, 'whose erudition, generously shared, made the writing possible'. Practically all of the numerous anecdotes about the United Irishmen and 1798 that O'Byrne retold can be traced back to Bigger's collections, or to printed accounts found in Bigger's library. A reviewer in the *Irish Times* realized that 'these sketches contain little that is new to the student of Ulster in 1798, but here and there a modern reference—a visit to the grave of Betsy Gray, for example—makes them something more than the mere re-telling of twice-told tales.'[28] A closer inspection of this particular example can serve to demonstrate O'Byrne's method of writing.

From his piece on 'The Grave of Betsy Gray', it is apparent that O'Byrne had visited the site, but he stopped short of sharing his personal impressions. Instead, a good part of his account of Betsy Gray is taken verbatim from an article, which originally appeared in the *Shan Van Vocht* in 1896 (and was probably written by Alice Milligan) and another section is lifted from McComb's *Guide to Belfast* (including the misattribution of a quotation to McSkimin rather than Teeling). These sources are neither flagged nor credited, but woven seamlessly into the narrative, as if they are part of O'Byrne's own account. In another instance, O'Byrne recounted the story of a chance reunion thirty years after the Battle of Ballynahinch between William Fee, who was badly injured and left famished after escaping the battlefield, and a local man, who as a boy had saved Fee's life by providing him with a bowl of milk. Although he does not cite his source, it can be traced to Lyttle's *Betsy Gray*, from which it was taken almost word for word.[29]

O'Byrne's talent lay in making previously documented stories of vernacular history available to later generations of nationalists. *As I Roved Out*, a reviewer noted, 'could be lifted and read at intervals in a lifetime and still retain the joy in the heart of the reader'.[30] The bite-size stand-alone chapters, typically of three to four pages each, allowed readers to dip in and out at their convenience, without requiring too much rigour, and this seems to have contributed to their appeal. The book enjoyed widespread popularity, particularly among northern (and even more so Belfast) Catholics. Indeed, publications on Ninety-Eight often catered for a specific sectorial readership.[31]

Historiographical neglect of the rebellion persisted in the early years of Northern Ireland in the writings of professional historians. For example, the military historian Cyril Falls, the son of a unionist election agent in Fermanagh, alluded to the subject sparingly at the end of *The Birth of Ulster*, published in 1936. Falls laconically noted that 'the Irish Rebellion of 1798 left Ulster, outside Antrim and Down, practically untouched'. He then described the events in a single sentence: 'In the month of June the Presbyterian rebels were soundly beaten at Antrim and Ballinahinch, and that was virtually the end of the revolt in Ulster.' In the wider scheme of things, 1798 was construed as an insignificant aberration:

> From that time forward the Presbyterians of the north showed no sign of disaffection, and from the first day to the last not a single Presbyterian Yeoman violated his oath. Ulster's feet, after a moment's wavering, were set upon the path they have steadfastly followed ever since.

---

[28] *Irish Times*, 30 November 1946, p. 6.
[29] O'Byrne, *As I Roved Out*, 1982 edn, pp. 361–6; first published in *Irish News*, 18 and 28 April 1943, p. 2. Cf. *SVV*, 1 (1896), pp. 97–8; *McComb's Guide to Belfast*, pp. 129–32; Lyttle, *Betsy Gray*, ch. 37.
[30] *Irish Press*, 14 September 1967, p. 9.
[31] See also Kirkland, *Cathal O'Byrne*, pp. 198–205.

From a unionist point of view, the rebellion had left no lasting legacy and did not deserve to be remembered.[32]

Semi-official publications took time in catching up with the prevailing spirit of dismissing Ninety-Eight. The Ulster Tourist Development Association issued in 1925 a *Guide to Ulster*, which boasted of the unique features that 'combine to make this province the world's premier pleasure and health resort', mentioning among them that the countryside was 'steeped in legend and tradition'. The inventory of recommended tourist sites listed the village of Dunadry in Antrim, where 'Donegore Hill and Moat were the insurgents' rendezvous in the rebellion of 1798.' In county Down, the market town of Saintfield was described as 'the scene in 1798 of a brisk skirmish between the rebels and a company of York Fencibles, at which the Yorks were massacred'. More puzzlingly, a section on antiquities mentioned that the government had destroyed a number of castles in 1798, in what seems to be a mix-up with earlier rebellions.[33] Within a few years, when the booklet was edited into a more substantial publication, the few references to the rebellion were removed.[34] Another guide booklet, issued by the Ulster Tourist Development Association in 1927, was written by the dramatist and critic St John Greer Ervine. The proofs had been read and corrected by Bigger, just prior to his death, and Ervine poignantly remarked that Bigger had 'placed his countrymen in his debt by the patience with which he investigated their history, and the care with which he recorded local customs which, without his devoted work, would have faded out of their memories'. Nevertheless, the immediate forgetting of Bigger's life work was already evident in the absence of any reference to the heritage of the United Irishmen in Ervine's text.[35]

The official tourist guide book was revamped in 1934 and published as *Ulster for Your Holiday*. A forward was contributed by the Prime Minister, Viscount Craigavon, and the entries were rewritten by well-known writers, who exercised self-censorship on sensitive issues. A chapter on 'Belfast the Capital', written by the seasoned journalist Alfred (Alf) Stewart Moore, surveyed the city's history but ignored the United Irishmen. Moore had previously exhibited his knowledge of 1798 sites in a guide book that he had written in the beginning of the century, but he now chose to ignore these traditions. Similarly, the chapter on Down merely stated that the county is 'associated with Antrim in many of the more stirring episodes, such as the rebellion of 1798', without actually saying anything about the rebellion. The author, the naturalist and antiquarian Robert Lloyd Praeger, had included several references to 1798 in a guide book to county Down that he had written in 1898, but these were apparently no longer deemed suitable. A lengthy chapter on county Antrim, written by Alexander Riddell, included several brief references to the rebellion without providing too much detail: a description of the tomb of the poet James Orr in Ballycarry notes that 'he shared in the "Turn-out"'; the account of Ballymena acknowledges that 'the most exciting incident'

[32] Cyril Falls, *The Birth of Ulster* (London: Constable, 1998; orig. edn 1936), p. 243.

[33] *Guide to Ulster* (Belfast: William. Strain & Sons, Ltd, 1925); available online courtesy of 'Eddie's Book Extracts'; <http://freepages.genealogy.rootsweb.ancestry.com/~econnolly/books/ulster1925/index.html>.

[34] *Ulster for Your Holidays* (Belfast: Ulster Tourist Development Association, 1928); re-issued with slight changes as *Ulster: The Official Publication of the Ulster Tourist Development Association, Ltd* (Belfast: William Strain & Sons, 1929).

[35] St John Ervine, *Ulster*, 2nd edn (Belfast: The Ulster Tourist Development Association, 1927).

in the town's history 'was no doubt the battle which took place in its streets during the "turnout" of '98' (labelled 'a very "throughother" affair'); and Antrim town is recognized as 'the scene of a battle in '98' at which the insurgents were 'led by Henry Joy McCracken himself... a young and honest enthusiast of whom one can only speak with respect'.[36] This was as far as the official publication of the Ulster Tourist Development Association could go.

The new guide book, which was re-issued on an annual basis without significant changes, was lambasted in the *Derry Journal* for its 'significant silences'. These included: 'never a word mentioned about the most notable incidents in Cave Hill's history when Tone, Russell, and Neilson stood on its summit'; 'ne'er a mention of the fact that Drennan was one of the founders of the United Irishmen'; merely an oblique reference to William Orr, which failed to mention that his 'name was known and sung and revered throughout the native Province'; 'not a word about the splendid national tradition of which Rody M'Corley was the symbol'; 'silence about the gallant Henry Munro'; 'nothing said of Thomas Russell or his execution'; and 'we are told nothing of Betsy Gray or Jemmy Hope or the Rev. Warrick or the Rev. Dickson, nothing of Mary McCracken.' It was even pointed out that 'the national record, and the national work' of Bigger was 'inexcusably omitted'. This critique of reticence was not just about how Ulster's heritage was being presented to tourists. The nationalist reviewer was infuriated by the opinion of Rev. W. B. Naylor of the Omagh Education Committee, who considered the guide book 'a very compact and concise text book on Northern Ireland history and geography' and recommended that it should be adopted by schools.[37]

The absence of local Irish history—as opposed to British-Imperial history—from the curriculum was a sensitive topic for nationalists. In the late nineteenth century, Catholic educationalists had campaigned for the introduction of Irish history in the national schools and it now appeared that the battle had to be fought all over again in Northern Ireland.[38] In a parliamentary debate on education in 1928, John Henry Collins, Nationalist MP for Armagh (and soon to represent his home area of South Down), asked the Parliamentary Secretary to the Ministry of Education, John Hanna Robb, if he was willing to consider to 'teach the children in the Six County schools the history of the Six Counties themselves, and the history of the country from which they have been separated'. To make his point, Collins indignantly declared:

> I never saw in any national school book in Ulster the name of William Orr. Never did I see the name of Wolfe Tone, who has such historic associations with the Cave Hill here. Never did I see the name of William Drennan or his friend Rowan in any one of these school books.[39]

---

[36] *Ulster: The Official Publication of the Ulster Tourist Development Association*, Ltd (Belfast: William Cleland Limited, 1936; orig. edn 1934), pp. 47–68 (Belfast), 69–133 (Antrim, with references to 1798 on pp. 79–82 and 126–7), 155–220 (Down, with reference on p. 160); cf. Alf. S. Moore, *Belfast To-Day* (Belfast: The Nomad Press, n.d. [1909]), pp. 16 and 79; Robert Lloyd Praeger, *Belfast and County Down Railway Company Official Guide to County Down and the Mourne Mountains* (Belfast: Marcus Ward & Co., 1898), pp. 9 and 110.

[37] *Derry Journal*, 12 June 1939, p. 8.

[38] Margaret E. Smith, *Reckoning with the Past: Teaching History in Northern Ireland* (Lanham, Md.: Lexington Books, 2005), pp. 108–12; see also Beiner, *Remembering the Year of the French*, pp. 295–6.

[39] *Northern Ireland Parliamentary Debates*, vol. 9 (1928), p. 1363 (3 May).

The question, with its references to distinguished United Irishmen, was ignored.

Six years later, the nationalist leader Cahir Healy, who in his younger days had frequented Bigger's meetings at Ardrigh and was interned after Partition for engaging in republican activities, returned to query the avoidance of Ulster's history in the education system. In April 1934, he raised the 'question of school books', which 'ought to teach the child something about his own country and, particularly, the local places in which he moves and lives and has his being.' Healy argued that, by excluding the teaching of local history, the Ministry of Education does 'not give the children an opportunity of knowing their own country'. Robert Norman McNeill, an Independent Unionist, agreed with Healy, stating his belief that 'it is not for the good of the community even of Northern Ireland that the children of Northern Ireland are not taught something about the history and about the antiquities of this Province, going back as far as the days of Shane O'Neill, and the events which happened in Belfast in 1798 or thereabouts.' At this point in the debate, Samuel Fryar, the UUP representative for West Down, interjected '1690' [a reference to the victory of William of Orange at the Battle of the Boyne] as a correction to the allusion to 1798. From the ruling unionist point of view, if local history was going to be addressed it could only be officially sanctioned loyalist history, definitely not the United Irish rebellion.[40]

Some schools introduced Irish history into the classroom independently. Apart from Catholic schools with nationalist leanings, local history was taught in select Protestant schools, such as the Royal Belfast Academical Institute ('Inst'), which maintained a liberal tradition that stemmed back to its formation by former United Irishmen in 1810. Teachers, however, were hard pressed for suitable primers. Sections on 1798 in two new textbooks that came out in London—Ivor Jack Herring's *History of Ireland*, published in 1937 and Randall Clarke's *A Short History of Ireland*, first published in 1941—include only a couple of sentences on the rebellion in Ulster.[41] In the 1940s, the repeated requests of Catholic headmasters' and assistant headmasters' associations to include questions on Irish history in the state exams for secondary schools were rejected. When the need for teaching Irish history in the schools was again raised by nationalist politicians in the mid-1940s, it was met with a unionist counter-demand for a distinct Ulster history, which was approved by the Minister of Education, Samuel Herbert Hall-Thompson.[42]

For this purpose, the unionist historian and author Hugh Shearman was commissioned to write a thirty-two-page booklet on *Northern Ireland: Its History, Resources and People*. Published in 1946 by the state, 60,000 copies of Shearman's book were provided to all the schools that received public funding and another 25,000 copies were offered to the general public for sixpence each. The appearance of new editions in 1948, 1950, 1955, and 1962 testify to the demand for this textbook. The original version noted that 'the Ulster Protestant community took a prominent part in the movements for opposition and reform in Ireland, which incidentally culminated in

[40] *Northern Ireland Parliamentary Debates*, vol. 16 (1934), pp. 1012–13 (Healy), 1020 (McNeill and Fryar).

[41] Ivor Jack Herring, *History of Ireland* (London: John Murray, 1937), p. 132; Randall Clarke, *A Short History of Ireland from 1485 to the Present Day* (London: University Tutorial Press, 1948; orig. edn 1941), p. 61.

[42] Smith, *Reckoning with the Past*, 115–17.

the rebellion', without providing any actual information on the rebellion. This obscure allusion to 1798 was omitted in later editions.[43]

The choice to endorse a historian who claimed non-partisanship but showed one-sided sympathy for unionism was widely derided by the opposition. Edward (Eddie) Gerard McAteer, Nationalist MP for Mid Londonderry, denounced Shearman as 'a pseudo-historian' and Healy labelled him 'a sort of semi-official propagandist'. His history of Northern Ireland was described by Malachy Conlon, Nationalist MP for South Armagh, as 'a complete distortion'. Members of the Northern Ireland Labour Party added their condemnations, with Hugh Downey, the MP for Belfast Dock, calling Shearman's booklet 'a lying history' and Francis Hanna of Belfast Central referring to it as 'a very distorted document and one which no person would take seriously'.[44] This vehement criticism was disregarded and Shearman's historical writings continued to be favoured by the establishment.

In response to a parliamentary question on 'what standard works dealing with the history of Ulster are being used at present in all schools in Northern Ireland', Minister of Education Harry Midgley revealed in 1956 that, while 'teachers are given freedom to choose the books which they consider will be of greatest assistance to them in their work' (subject to the approval of the ministry), there was a list of officially recommended Irish history books. Unsurprisingly, all of these titles happened to be written by Protestant unionist authors, with Shearman featuring prominently. In fact, two more of his books were now published by the government and issued to grant-aided schools. Midgley ignored a question from Harry Diamond of the Irish Labour Party (and formerly of the Socialist Republican Party), who provocatively asked if the recommended histories acknowledge 'the fact that thousands of Protestant Ulstermen died fighting at Antrim, Ballynahinch and Saintfield for an Irish Republic'.[45] The allusion to 1798 touched on a sore spot. Earlier that year, Midgley, who had defected from the Commonwealth Labour Party to the UUP (where he was known as a hardliner), was taunted by nationalists in parliament that he had previously followed in the 'footsteps of the Presbyterian United Irishmen of 1798' (to which he humourlessly retorted that 'it is an absolute falsehood, and if not a manufactured lie at least a carefully distributed one').[46]

Unwilling to let the matter rest, Healy asked the minister at a follow-up question and answers session if 'he is not also aware that Irish history is practically under a ban or under censorship?'. Joseph Connellan, Nationalist MP for South Down, joined in and demanded 'information regarding the titles and numbers of Irish history books that have already been condemned by the Ministry in the schools'. Yet, unionists were

---

[43] Hugh Shearman, *Northern Ireland: Its History, Resources, and People* (Belfast: H. M. Stationery Office, 1946), p. 12 (cf. 1955 edn, p. 13); *Northern Whig*, 2 October 1946, p. 2 and 31 October 1947, p. 1. See also James Loughlin, *Ulster Unionism and British National Identity since 1885* (London and New York: Pinter, 1995), pp. 144–6; Stephen Howe, *Ireland and Empire: Colonial Legacies in Irish History and Culture* (Oxford and New York: Oxford University Press, 2002; orig. edn 2000), p. 101.

[44] *Northern Ireland Parliamentary Debates*, vol. 30 (1946), p. 3084 (McAteer); vol. 32 (1948), p. 696 (Healy), p. 1706 (Conlon), p. 3040 (Downey); vol. 33 (1949), p. 244 (Hanna).

[45] *Northern Ireland Parliamentary Debates*, vol. 40 (1956), pp. 2773–4 (13 November).

[46] *Northern Ireland Parliamentary Debates*, vol. 40 (1956), p. 546 (7 March). For Midgley's term as Minister of Education see Graham S. Walker, *The Politics of Frustration: Harry Midgley and the Failure of Labour in Northern Ireland* (Manchester: Manchester University Press, 1985), pp. 198–213.

unwilling to concede on this point. William Morrison May, the Unionist MP for the Ards in county Down, insisted that 'there is a distinction between history and mythology' and castigated the opposition that 'the sort of history which they want is not history at all as it does not consist of facts but folklore.' This statement reveals the utter disregard for vernacular history, which was dismissed as 'mythology' and 'folk-lore', in the crude sense of non-factual stories. Moreover, the narratives of popular history were considered politically dangerous. Joseph William Morgan, Unionist MP for Belfast Cromac, opined that 'it is very unwise in secondary schools to have a presentation of history which is not history at all but Republican propaganda.'[47] Healy, however, refused to give in to unionist recalcitrance and the following year asked May, who had been appointed Minister of Education, if he would 'consider the question of issuing a history of County Antrim in 1798 for the benefit of the children'.[48]

In 1968, the Minister of Finance (and former Minister of Education), Herbert Victor Kirk, announced that Shearman had once again been commissioned to write a history of Northern Ireland. This decision was met with regret by the nationalist MP for the county Down constituency of Mourne, James O'Reilly, who suggested instead 'a joint effort', whereby 'three or four historians holding different points of view could be induced to combine to write a real history.' Such multi-vocal sophistication was beyond the imagination of the government, which continued to promote a strict unionist history, purged of the episodes that it preferred to forget.[49] Shearman's new textbook, which was re-issued in a revised edition in 1970, emphasized the importance of the seventeenth century—noting that 'the events of this period have remained in the consciousness of Ulster men and women for almost 300 years'—but completely omitted any reference to 1798.[50]

Shearman was actually aware that the rebellion had long been remembered in the countryside. His own family tradition recalled how his grandfather used to visit an old woman, who 'was a centenarian and clearly remembered the soldiers coming in 1798'. Yet, when he wrote what may be his most successful book—*Ulster*, published in 1949 in the popular County Book Series, he deliberately presented the rebellion as 'a small affair', which merited no more than a sentence: 'Small bodies of the rebels in Ulster were defeated at Antrim and Ballynahinch in June, 1798, and the leaders were executed.' Shearman insisted that 'the small revolutionary republican element died out from among the Ulster Protestants' and asserted that its traces were no longer visible. When looking at Antrim town, 'you would hardly think that anything could ever happen there', let alone a battle in 1798.[51]

Shearman ended up working closely with the UUP. In 1972, he wrote on their behalf a propaganda pamphlet titled *27 Myths about Ulster*, which purported to refute all nationalist claims of injustice. With reference to history, he argued that 'Ulster has the most radical and progressive political tradition of any region in the British Isles' and

[47] *Northern Ireland Parliamentary Debates*, vol. 40 (1956), pp. 2837–8 (20 November).
[48] *Northern Ireland Parliamentary Debates*, vol. 41 (1957), p. 2387 (12 November).
[49] *Northern Ireland Parliamentary Debates*, vol. 69 (1968), pp. 1212 and 1216 (15 May).
[50] Hugh Shearman, *Northern Ireland* (Belfast: H. M. Stationery Office, 1970; orig. edn 1968), p. 17.
[51] Hugh Shearman, *Ulster* (London: R. Hale, 1949), pp. 127, 129, 197, and 274–5.

as proof he pointed to the contribution of Ulstermen to the American Revolution and the support given by northern liberals in the late eighteenth and early nineteenth centuries towards removing the political restrictions on Catholics. The United Irishmen were conveniently passed over.[52]

Despite official determination not to recognize the heritage of the United Irishmen, the government published in 1931 a selection of letters from the extensive correspondence of the United Irish poet William Drennan and his equally radical sister Martha McTier, making a major collection of primary sources available to the public. D. A. Chart, the Deputy Keeper of the Public Records Office of Northern Ireland (PRONI), was concerned that the budget allocated by the state might not be sufficient and appealed to the public for additional funds. The required sum was raised within a remarkably short time. Even though the list of subscribers includes names from the Irish Free State as well as from abroad, most of the support came from residents of Northern Ireland, who showed genuine interest in the neglected history of the northern United Irishmen.

As could be expected, the nationalist *Derry Journal* considered the publication of the Drennan-McTier Letters 'a literary event of very considerable interest'. Even more significantly, the *Northern Whig*, the main newspaper of liberal Presbyterians, cast its full support behind the project, endorsing Chart's appeal and subsequently treated its readers to extracts from the collection, billed as 'Glimpses of the United Irishmen'.[53] The government's backing has been described as 'a rare recognition of a safely remote republicanism', yet the fact that such a publication was so uncommon in official print indicates that the memory of United Irish republicanism was not all that safely remote.[54]

Although the Minister of Commerce, John Milne Barbour, acknowledged that the publication of the *Drennan Letters* was 'of great interest both for national and local history', it appears that the government had not fully thought through the implications of giving their blessing to this project. In offering congratulations, the Nationalist MP Connellan asked the Minister of Finance, Hugh MacDowell Pollock, 'was Dr. Drennan a Republican?', to which the minister, much to the amusement of the house, answered emphatically 'no'. Bothered by how a reference to 'the rebellious times of '98' sparked what seemed like a moment of camaraderie between members of the opposition and the government, the Independent Unionist MP John William Nixon 'began then to contemplate how at that time their ancestors were joined in a rebellion against the King's troops in this country'. Expressing concern that 'if this thing went too far we might have another coalition—and perhaps another rebellion', Nixon reminded the

---

[52] Hugh Shearman, *27 Myths about Ulster* (Belfast: Ulster Unionist Party, 1972), p. 12.

[53] D. A. Chart, ed., *The Drennan Letters: Being a Selection from the Correspondence Which Passed between William Drennan, M.D. and His Brother-in-Law and Sister, Samuel and Martha McTier, During the Years 1776–1819* (Belfast: H. M. Stationery Office, 1931); also *Derry Journal*, 23 October 1931, p. 10; *Northern Whig*, 17 and 25 October 1929, p. 6; 8 May 1930, p. 3, 23 October 1931, p. 11; *Irish Book Lover*, 19, no. 6 (November/December 1931), p. 162. For biographical information on Chart's career see Seán Magee, 'D. A. Chart 1878–1960: Archivist, Historian, Social Scientist', *History Ireland*, 11, no. 1 (2003): pp. 15–18.

[54] Nicholas Allen and Terence Brown, 'Publishing after Partition, 1922–39', in *Oxford History of the Irish Book*, edited by Clare Hutton and Patrick Walsh (Oxford: Oxford University Press, 2011), 5: *The Irish book in English, 1891–2000*, p. 79.

members that at Saintfield (by which he probably meant Ballynahinch) 'the King's troops walloped the rebels of Holywood and Comber, and of Windsor and Lisburn.'[55]

For their part, nationalist politicians never missed an opportunity of reminding Protestant unionists of their rebel backgrounds. They took relish in repeatedly referring to the United Irish ancestry of John Miller Andrews, prime minister from 1940 to 1943, who was the great-grandchild of William Drennan.[56] These taunts were intended to embarrass J. M. Andrews, who was grand master of the Orange Order in county Down and went on to become the grand master of the Orange Institution of Ireland and grand master of the Imperial Grand Council of the World. In private, however, unionists were not hostile to the memory of the United Irishmen. In a biographical memoir, John Clarke MacDermott (Baron MacDermott), who was Lord Chief Justice of Northern Ireland from 1951 to 1971, recalled how his father, minister of Belmont Presbyterian in Belfast and moderator of the Presbyterian Church in Ireland, would take the family on annual trips to Greyabbey and tell them 'the sad story' of how Rev. James Porter was executed for activities that fell 'far short of treason'.[57]

With the intention of attracting visitors to Northern Ireland, the Presbyterian historian of Orangeism Robert M. Sibbett wrote in 1928 a local history titled *On the Shining Bann*. Just as his *Orangeism in Ireland and throughout the Empire*, originally published in 1914 and re-published in 1939, discussed the northern rebellion in depth, this book also included a detailed chapter on the 'Days of the '98 Rebellion', followed by a chapter on the Emmet Rebellion. Although he was a conservative, Sibbett was aware of the ambiguities and complexities of the memory of 'the troubles associated with the '98 Rebellion'. He admitted that one of his own ancestors, a Protestant loyalist, was sheltered by a Catholic and noted that 'good offices such as this were confined to no side.' He recalled that as a child in Killycoogan, county Antrim (14 km north-west of Ballymena), he had heard two nonagenarian ladies 'discussing their experiences during that time' and recollecting how after the Battle of Antrim people hid in fields out of fear of reprisals from the dragoons. Sibbett observed that:

> The rebellion produced a great impression on the minds of simple, peace-loving country people, who long afterwards spoke of 1798 as 'a terrible time,' and on winter nights recalled by blazing hearth fires many scenes and incidents of those dark days illustrative of the dangers and trials through which they had passed.

On the Shining Bann, including the sections on the rebellion, was serialized in the local unionist newspaper the *Larne Times*.[58] There was an evident interest in traditions of Ninety-Eight.

In mid-Antrim, the unionist *Ballymena Observer* republished the ever-popular local history *Old Ballymena*, with chapters on 1798 appearing on a weekly basis from 5 November 1937 to 11 March 1938. A few months later, the unionist *County Down Spectator and Ulster Standard* serialized an article on a lesser known engagement

---

[55] *Northern Ireland Parliamentary Debates*, vol. 12 (1930), pp. 1069 and 1075–6 (7 May).
[56] *Northern Ireland Parliamentary Debates*, vol. 25 (1942), p. 752; vol. 29 (1945), p. 945; vol. 30 (1946–7), pp. 377 and 4295–6; vol. 32 (1948), p. 3656.
[57] J. C. McDermott, *An Enriching Life* (Belfast: self-published, 1979).
[58] Robert M. Sibbett, *On the Shining Bann: Records of an Ulster Manor* (Belfast: Baird, 1928), pp. 112–23 (quotations from pp. 113–14); *Larne Times*, 7 and 14 January 1928, p. 5.

in 1798 at Portaferry (near the southern tip of the Ards peninsula).[59] That year, the Belfast Museum exhibited artefacts associated with the rebellion, including relics that had belonged to Henry Joy McCracken. However, commemoration of the hundred and fortieth anniversary of 1798 was forbidden. Groups of republicans, who defied the ban had to be careful to avoid the Royal Ulster Constabulary. They were prevented on Easter week from entering the republican plot in Milltown cemetery, on the Falls Road in Belfast, but parties succeed in visiting the graves of McCracken and Steel Dickson in Belfast's Clifton Street cemetery, as well as the grave of James Hope in Mallusk, county Antrim.[60] The *Irish News* pointed out the irony, whereby it was 'unlawful for you to demonstrate at the grave of Henry Joy McCracken on Easter Sunday or any other Sunday', yet, with 'municipal encouragement', the museum in Stranmillis made it possible to 'do reverence to his uniform, his sword, his portrait and a wig containing a lock of his hair'.[61] Popular interest was purposely contained, so that it would not develop into fully fledged public commemoration.

BREAKING SILENCE

In spite of an official culture which effectively proscribed the memory of 1798, in the early decades of Northern Ireland there were rare moments in which the rebellion was in the limelight. On a few occasions, the United Irishmen made their way on to the Belfast stage. Gerald MacNamara (pseudonym of Harold Morrow) wrote in 1929 the aptly named play *Who Fears to Speak?*—a title that evoked Ingram's classic '98 poem 'The Memory of the Dead' and also hinted to the current conditions of renewed silencing. By then, MacNamara was one of the last remaining founding figures of the Ulster Literary Theatre still involved in Belfast's cultural scene. Although the original members of that group had participated in Bigger's gatherings at Ardrigh and were inspired by the memory of the United Irishmen, they did not get to stage plays on 1798. Two decades later, after partition had put an end to the aspirations of the northern literary revival to create a fusion between Irish nationalism and Ulster regionalism, MacNamara, with characteristic irony, poured his frustrations into a one-act 'tragi-farce'.[62]

In MacNamara's play, the fumbling antics of a tiny gathering of would-be revolutionaries, who meet in 1797 in Belfast under the guise of the 'Muddler's Club' (the actual name of a convivial society that was used by the United Irishmen as a front), make it clear that a rebellion in Ulster does not stand a chance. The United Irish leader Napper Tandy shows up and demonstrates his skill as 'a genius at disguising himself' by duping the conspirators twice over, first into believing that he is the dreaded Castlereagh and then that he is the notorious Major Sirr. Having exposed the gross incompetence of the northerners, Tandy takes his daughter, a passionate United

---

[59] *County Down Spectator and Ulster Standard*, 17 and 24 September 1938, p. 8; 1 October 1938, p. 10.
[60] *Irish News*, 18 April 1938 (reproduced in *Irish News*, 18 April 2007, p. 19).
[61] *Irish News*, 9 May 1938 (reproduced in *Irish News*, 9 May 2007, p. 28).
[62] Gerald MacNamara, 'Who Fears to Speak?', *Dublin Magazine*, 4 (1929): pp. 30–52 [republished in *Journal of Irish Literature*, 17, nos. 2 & 3 (1988): pp. 125–43]; see also McNulty, *The Ulster Literary Theatre*, pp. 219–20.

Irishwoman, and heads off to Wexford. The play was advertised in the *Northern Whig* and was performed at the Belfast Opera House before a crowded audience on 24 January 1929. A disapproving reviewer for the *Belfast News-Letter* found it all too confusing, commenting that 'there may be some subtle meaning in the play, but, if so, the subtlety is so extreme that a Belfast audience is not likely to discover it.' Indeed, after a very short run, MacNamara's *Who Fears to Speak?* passed away into obscurity.[63]

A more penetrating theatrical exploration of the dilemmas that the memory of the United Irishmen posed for society and politics in Northern Ireland came from less expected quarters, in the work of 'the shipyard poet', Thomas Carnduff. Born to a poor Presbyterian family in the Protestant working class neighbourhood of Sandy Row in Belfast, Carnduff's early biography is somewhat typical of many loyalist men in his cohort. He became an Orangeman (opting for the more radical offshoot of the Independent Orange Order), was a member of the Belfast Protestant Association, took part in the activities of the UVF, served in the Great War, and was a member of the 'C Specials', a reserve unit of the Ulster Special Constabulary which the new state mobilized against the perceived threat of Catholic nationalist insurgency. In consequence of repeatedly losing his employment at the Belfast shipyards, from the 1920s Carnduff began to write poetry, self-described as 'lines of mere doggerel' that developed into 'grammatical verse', which was published in various newspapers.

Carnduff's commitment to involving working class people in cultural activities resulted in the founding of the Belfast Poetry Circle in 1926 and the Young Ulster Society in 1936. By then, he felt that Northern Ireland was going through another literary revival. The foundation of the Belfast Repertory Theatre by Richard Hayward and J. R. Mageean, former members of the Ulster Literary Theatre, gave Carnduff his break as a playwright. His first major success was in 1932 with *Workers*, a play set in the Belfast shipyards, which was followed by other proletarian dramas—*Machinery* in 1933 and *Traitors*, about unemployment riots, in 1934. He then turned his gaze towards history.[64]

In searching for plebeian historical role models, Carnduff was enamoured by the weaver-poets who had participated in the 1798 rebellion—James Orr of Ballycarry and James Campbell of Larne—and collected materials for an essay on the 'Northern Ballads of '98'. Above all, he venerated the working class rebel hero James Hope, who, like himself, was also an amateur poet. Carnduff explained his reverence for the Presbyterian United Irishmen in a memoir:

> Incidentally, I myself belong to the same denomination, and have had the privilege of worshipping in several of the meeting places where these men worshipped in their day. The present congregations, though they may disagree with the principles these men upheld, neither deny nor dishonour their memory. . . . No participant in the turmoil of Irish history has left behind such a memory as this Templepatrick weaver [James Hope]. Monuments have been erected to greater figures in Irish history, but none to a greater man.

---

[63] *Irish Independent*, 25 January 1929, p. 8; *BNL*, 25 January 1929, p. 6. Advertisements appeared in the *Northern Whig* on 23 and 28 January 1929, pp. 5 and 3 (respectively).

[64] 'The Autobiography of Thomas Carnduff', in *Thomas Carnduff: Life and Writings*, edited by John Gray (Belfast: Lagan Press, 1994), pp. 57–117 (esp. 63–114); *Irish Press*, 27 November 1953, p. 6.

Apparently, memory of 1798 had not been entirely eradicated in hard-core Presbyterian loyalist communities.[65]

Despite being a unionist, Carnduff had no qualms about writing for the nationalist *Irish News* (using the pseudonym Carndhu), the southern *Sunday Independent* (under his initials), and later also for the *Irish Press* (signing with his own name). In an article from 1925 on 'Rebel Ulster', he contemplated the conundrum of how Belfast, 'the town which came so near uniting the Irish nation on two separate occasions in the eighteenth century'—a reference to the Volunteers and to the United Irishmen—'should now in the twentieth century stand square for partition'. He was adamant in characterizing 1798 as 'a rising of the Protestant peasantry, for, although there were Catholic contingents joined up in some places, the large majority of the rebels were Presbyterian rural and agricultural workers who had been living a hard, embittered life under the existing laws and the harsh treatment of the landlords.' Carnduff recognized that times had changed and that 'the old rebel strongholds of those days are now citadels of Unionism', yet he maintained that 'no true Ulsterman is ashamed to own that his ancestor had once taken up arms for what he thought then were the principle of liberty.' In his view, the memory of 1798 was still pertinent for unionists:

> There are no monuments to perpetuate the memory of the men who died, yet many of the Ulstermen who may don the Orange colours and hold beliefs that are antagonistic to the principles which our rebel ancestors fought for can still look back through the years and fervently hope that when our time comes to face the issue we may meet it in as heroic and unselfish a manner as our Fathers did in '98.[66]

This form of private remembrance did not require public commemoration.

Carnduff demonstrated the ongoing relevance of the memory of James Hope and the United Irishmen in *Castlereagh*, 'an historical play of the '98 rebellion' which he considered to be his 'supreme effort at playwriting'.[67] Produced by the Belfast Repertory Theatre in 1935, it was acclaimed in the *Northern Whig* as 'one of the most interesting Northern Ireland plays that has been seen for some time'.[68] Lord Castlereagh, the architect of the union between Great Britain and Ireland, was portrayed by Carnduff as a conflicted, and somewhat tortured, anti-hero. Derided by the populace for shedding his former radicalism, Castlereagh ruthlessly suppresses the United Irishmen, so that 'the British Empire may become greater in security, and my country take full share in the commonweal.' His disregard for the lower classes is challenged by James Hope, the champion of 'the common people who till the soil, who labour the looms, who carry your arms in battle'. Hope warns Castlereagh that 'the day is not far distant when your Lordship and those who rule with you will be subject to those people you now persecute.' The integrity and courage of Hope and the other leaders of the United Irishmen, who cannot be bought or intimidated, earn the reluctant respect of

---

[65] Thomas Carnduff, 'Castlereagh and James Hope, the Weaver', in Gray, *Thomas Carnduff*, pp. 131–3; Carnduff Papers, QUB 21/5/23 ('Northern Ballads of '98').

[66] *Sunday Independent*, 29 November 1925, p. 7. A revised version was published a decade later; *Irish Press*, 16 March 1935, p. 8.

[67] 'The Autobiography of Thomas Carnduff', p. 113.

[68] *Northern Whig*, 22 January 1935, p. 11.

Castlereagh, yet he remains adamant in his pig-headed determination to execute Rev. James Porter.[69]

Carnduff was attentive to folk history and on a visit Greyabbey was impressed by how 'the congregation still functions to perpetuate the memory and sacrifice' of Rev. Porter.[70] The reputation of Castlereagh was enjoying just then a historiographical revival, with which the playwright was not in the least concerned. The fastidious criticism of the unionist historian Harford Montgomery Hyde, author of the recently published *The Rise of Castlereagh* (1933), who complained that there was no evidence that Hope and Castlereagh had ever met, missed the point. Carnduff was not writing a factual history, but evoking folk memory to question the politics of class divisions in Northern Ireland.[71] The British theatre weekly *The Stage* commended *Castlereagh* as 'a fine effort to treat on the stage an always delicate subject in a manner that certainly pleased the two audiences', apparently referring to the play's popularity with both unionists and nationalists at the notably crowded performances in the Empire Theatre.[72]

Richard Hayward, who was responsible for the production and also took on the title role, opposite his wife Emma (who played Lady Castlereagh), received considerable praise. Hayward came to the play with personal knowledge of local traditions of Ninety-Eight, which he exhibited in his popular writings on local heritage. Hayward's *In Praise of Ulster*, which first appeared shortly after the staging of the play and went through numerous editions, was supposed to steer away from the controversial subjects of politics ('I shall say nothing in judgment, and no more than is historically essential') and religion ('shall say only what is necessary to make my book intelligible, and nothing at all in any kind of partisan spirit') and yet the book is replete with references to the United Irishmen. Similarly, in *Ulster and the City of Belfast*, published in 1950, Hayward refused to accept the official spirit of censorship and did not shy away from the topic of Ninety-Eight.[73]

Carnduff's career as a highly praised dramatist came to an end after the Belfast Repertory Theatre failed to secure a permanent theatre building and folded-up. In its place, some of the members went on to found the Ulster Group Theatre in 1940. Jack Loudan, one of the Group's playwrights, was particularly interested in 1798. Since, his first play was produced by the Ulster Literary Theatre in 1932, Loudan had established a reputation as a dramatist concerned with local issues. He was appointed organizer of

[69] Thomas Carnduff, 'Castlereagh' (typescript); Carnduff Papers, QUB 21/1/5. See also Connal Parr, *Inventing the Myth: Political Passions and the Ulster Protestant Imagination* (Oxford: Oxford University Press, 2017), 67–9. My thanks to Sarah Ferris, the literary executor of the Thomas Carnduff estate, for permission to consult the play and to the QUB Special Collections librarian Diarmuid Kennedy for providing me with a copy of the script.

[70] Thomas Carnduff, 'Porter of Greyabbey', in Gray, *Thomas Carnduff*, pp. 160–2.

[71] Montgomery Hyde to Thomas Carnduff, 27 March 1935; Carnduff Papers, QUB 21/10/2/1 H. For contemporary historiography see Philip Hughes, 'Castlereagh', *Studies*, 26, no. 102 (1937): pp. 249–66.

[72] *Stage*, 24 January 1935, p. 11. See also *Irish Times*, 28 January 1935, p. 2; *Northern Whig*, 22 January 1935, p. 11. Publicity materials for the original production are available at the Digital Theatre Archive of the Linen Hall Library, see Belfast Empire Theatre Collection, EM-0031 (poster); Mageean Collection, MG-0041 (programme).

[73] Richard Hayward, *In Praise of Ulster*, 5th edn (Belfast: William Mullan, 1946; orig. edn 1938), pp. 20–1, 31, 57, 59, 77, and 111; Richard Hayward, *Ulster and the City of Belfast* (London: Barker, 1950), pp. 32, 34, 46, 60, 61, 77, 84, and 100.

the Council for the Encouragement of Music and the Arts (CEMA)—the antecedent of the Arts Council—after its establishment in Northern Ireland in 1943. In this capacity, Loudan came to grips with the sensitive politics of culture in Northern Ireland, as he was required to find creative ways to resolve opposition in nationalist areas to the government's directive that the national anthem 'God Save the King' should be played at all events.[74] Writing about the United Irishmen in the past offered him a way of criticizing the narrow-mindedness of unionist cultural policy in the present.

Loudan, a Presbyterian from Armagh, claimed descent from Henry Munro, through his mother, Elizabeth née Munroe. He recalled that she would tell him stories about 1798 and 'tears would come to her eyes when she read *Betsy Gray and the Hearts of Down*'.[75] Although Loudan was familiar from childhood with the ballad 'General Munro' and had grown up admiring his ancestor, the leader of the rebels in Down, he first wrote a play about the more familiar leader of the rebels in Antrim. Loudan's *Henry Joy McCracken* was originally produced at the Ulster Group Theatre's home venue in Belfast, where it ran from the end of March to the beginning of May 1945.[76] Set in July 1798, the play relates the circumstances of the passing of McCracken's death sentence. Loudan admitted that 'all the speeches in the Court Scene are imaginary', as there were no trial records to consult and the brief contemporary newspaper account of the trial allowed considerable scope for creative re-imagining. The play's script pivots on the framing of McCracken by informers, who are paid to give false testimony that they had seen him at the Battle of Antrim. No thought was given to the fact that their notorious treachery was actually immaterial, as there is no denying that McCracken was at Antrim. The main issue of whether committing an unlawful act of rebellion in the name of patriotism justifies execution, or merits clemency, is evaded in favour of a run-of-the-mill denunciation of 'perfidious Albion', which appealed to nationalist sensibilities.[77]

Performances in Belfast, as noted by Dublin newspapers, attracted a notably 'mixed audience' of liberal Protestants and Catholics, who applauded Loudan's 'plea for tolerance and understanding among Irishmen'. The reviewer for the *Northern Whig* was impressed with how the play, in addition to explaining the motivations of the United Irishmen, also conveys 'the point of view of the British soldiers, who had a job to do in the putting down of outlawry and rebellion and even 'makes some of the soldiers, too, see the point of view of the Irish'. The nationalist *Irish Press* was delighted that 'a Belfast Presbyterian playwright has thought it right to remind his fellow-Presbyterians of their lead in the fight for Independence and for tolerance.'[78]

In the following decade, the Ulster Group Theatre ran into difficulties. Amateur drama groups stepped in to fill in the void, even though historical plays were considered

---

[74] Gillian McIntosh, 'CEMA and the National Anthem: The Arts and the State in Postwar Northern Ireland', *New Hibernia Review*, 5, no. 3 (2001): pp. 22–31; see also Joan Fitzpatrick Dean, *Riot and Great Anger: Stage Censorship in Twentieth-Century Ireland* (Madison: University of Wisconsin Press, 2004), p. 183.

[75] *Irish Independent*, 21 June 1963, p. 14.

[76] For the programme see Ulster Group Theatre Collection, Linen Hall Library, PG/HBP, f. 15; catalogued online as Digital Theatre Archive GR 0006.

[77] Jack Loudan, *Henry Joy McCracken: A Play in Three Acts* (Dublin: New Frontiers Press, 1946). The report of the trial and execution appeared in *BNL*, 20 July 1798, p. 2.

[78] *Irish News*, 4 April 1945; *Irish Press*, 16 April 1945, p. 5; *Irish Times*, 2 April 1945, p. 2; *Northern Whig*, 2 April 1945, p. 2.

expensive productions on account of the need for period costumes. The Rosemary Theatre Group exhibited 'competent individual performances' (in the opinion of the *Northern Whig*) when they staged Loudan's *Henry Joy McCracken* on 4 March 1955 at St Mary's Hall in Belfast and then went on tour with the play around Northern Ireland. Inspired by their success, the following year they produced Carnduff's *Castlereagh*.[79]

Taking a very different approach from his historical drama on McCracken, Loudan wrote in 1950 *A Lock of the General's Hair*, a sophisticated comedy that irreverently parodies remembrance of Ninety-Eight, while drawing on the author's own family traditions of Henry Munro. The play takes place on the background of heated elections in Armagh, in which rivalry between unionists and nationalists spills into sectarian aggression. The heiress of an impoverished Protestant gentry estate is approached by the curators of a national historical exhibition in Dublin for the loan of an heirloom—a lock of the hair of General Munro, which has been carefully preserved in the family for a hundred and fifty years. Such relics were in existence. Mary Ann McCracken devotedly retained locks of hair that she had taken from her brother before his execution, as well as from Samuel Neilson and James Hope and these were later carefully preserved by Madden (though a lock of hair from Wolfe Tone seems to have gone astray).[80]

In Loudan's play, a windbag politician from Dublin issues a torrent of nationalist rhetoric to justify his claim for the obscure souvenir:

> We've come here to do honour to the memory of a great Irishman. We've come here to resurrect a piece of living history. We've come here to show respect to a symbol of an unquenchable spirit, to an eloquent reminder of our historic past, to the reflected brilliance of imperishable history . . . This relic is the last living link with a man whose name will be ever enshrined in the memories of our people. This relic will remain through the ages as an example of the sacrifice and glory of the Irish race. This relic will be recalled . . . .

In response, an exasperated unionist politician, though embarrassed by his family's ownership of the relic, objects to it passing into the hands of nationalists. *A Lock of the General's Hair* is narrated by a journalist, reminiscent of Loudan in his earlier days, who criticizes the obsession with remembrance of the past:

> Having exhibitions. Displaying swords and guns and pieces of hair from the head of a man who was executed. Reminding the Irish how their ancestors killed each other. I think those were the things we should try to forget.

The confrontation is diffused when it is discovered that the domestic staff had mistakenly lost the precious lock of hair and replaced it with a tuft sheared from the buttocks of a dog. The last words are left to the journalist, who muses: 'Maybe most of the things we've fought about in Ireland weren't any more important than this. Maybe the wind of the years will come and blow them all away.'[81]

---

[79] *Northern Whig*, 5 March 1955, p. 5; Digital Theatre Archive, Miscellaneous Collection, Linen Hall Library MS-0156 (*Henry Joy McCracken* programme); Carnduff Papers, QUB MS21/14/5 (*Castlereagh* programme). See also Sam Hanna Bell, John Harold Hewitt, and Nesca Adeline Robb, eds, *The Arts in Ulster: A Symposium* (London: George G. Harrap & Co., 1951), p. 66.

[80] Madden Papers, TCD 873/335.

[81] Jack Loudan, *A Lock of the General's Hair: A Comedy* (Belfast: Carter, 1953).

Loudan's call for forgetting in a satirical work of cultural memory proved to be extremely popular with local theatre groups. After its Belfast debut with the Group Theatre in March 1953, *A Lock of the General's Hair* was staged across Ulster by the Omagh Players (1953), St Enda's Dramatic Company from Derry (1954), the Lifford Players in Donegal (1955), the Castlederg Parochial Players (1955), and the Enniskillen Convent of Mercy Past Pupils Drama Group (1957), as well as by the Metro Drama Group in Dublin (1955) and the more professional Stella Maris Players in Belfast (1960).[82] The play was originally intended as a radio drama and the scriptwriter Philip Rooney adapted it for Radio Éireann, which broadcast the play in 1954. The *Irish Times* recommended that it should be repeated 'here and now' and the play was indeed produced again for the radio in 1961.[83] Inquiries were made as to the possibility of adapting *A Lock of the General's Hair* into a film, but this initiative did not materialize.[84]

Radio turned out to be a media well-suited for producing short works of drama. Already in 1935, Radio Athlone broadcasted the second act of Carnduff's *Castlereagh* and in 1936 a commemorative programme for Robert Emmet included a children's play on the Ballycarry martyr Willie Nelson.[85] 'The Man from God Knows Where', a radio drama by Frank Conlon about Thomas Russell, featured on Irish radio in 1948 to mark the hundred-and-fiftieth anniversary of the rebellion and in 1952 Radio Éireann produced Loudan's *Henry Joy McCracken*.[86] Programmes broadcast from stations in independent Ireland were within wireless reception of most areas in Northern Ireland. State radio in Northern Ireland, however, was more reluctant to address the topic of 1798. This hesitation was partly redressed by the Ballymena-born drama producer Ronald Mason, who was undeterred by the tendency at the BBC to avoid political controversy.

Mason was committed to introducing to the general public the work of cutting-edge Northern Irish writers. Just shortly after he began to work at the BBC in 1955, he produced the radio drama *The Curate's Cloak* by Cecil Cree, a schoolmaster at Inchmarlo School in Belfast who had previously written a successful play for the Ulster Group Theatre. Cree's mother's family were from the townland of Ballykine, near Ballynahinch, and he had inherited an avid interest in the local history of the rebellion. He had originally intended to write about Betsy Gray, but, having come to the conclusion that the information about the legendary heroine was mostly spurious, Cree 'amassed enough evidence about other people and incidents in the rebellion to suggest a plot for a new play'. Recognizing that 'the 1798 rising was largely a Protestant affair in Ulster', while pointing out that it did not only concern Presbyterians, *The Curate's Cloak* is set in a Church of Ireland rectory near Lough Neagh, where a fugitive rebel takes refuge. The play captured the ambiguity of the Turn-Out, as described in a

[82] *Irish Press*, 2 November 1953, p. 4; *Ulster Herald*, 7 and 14 November 1953, pp. 8 and 2 (respectively); *Irish Independent*, 22 January 1955, p. 10; *Donegal News*, 21 May 1955, p. 2; *Ulster Herald*, 11 May 1957, p. 2; *Ulster Herald*, 27 March 1954, p. 2; *Fermanagh Herald*, 20 April 1957, p. 6; Digital Theatre Archive, Miscellaneous Collection, Linen Hall Library MS-0146; also TPA Group Theatre Press Cuttings, Linen Hall Library, TSB/Group/3, 11 March 1953.
[83] *Irish Times*, 6 February 1954, p. 10; *Tuam Herald*, 29 July 1961, p. 7.
[84] *Irish Press*, 27 March 1953, p. 1.
[85] *Derry Journal*, 15 February 1935, p. 8; *Irish Press*, 4 March 1936, p. 5.
[86] Radio Éireann transcripts, UCD P260/352; 11 June 1948, p. 5; *Irish Press*, 21 June 1948, p. 4. For Loudan's play see *Tuam Herald*, 23 August 1952, p. 6.

local newspaper: 'the rebellion has just been crushed and both the rectory and the parish are agonizingly divided as to the rights and wrongs of the whole affair.'[87] Mason later produced a television adaptation of *The Curate's Cloak*, which was broadcast on BBC in March 1961. This was a rare case in which vernacular history was given a prominent stage.[88] He then went on to produce a radio adaptation of Loudan's *Henry Joy McCracken* that aired on the BBC Home Service in 1965, more than a decade after it had been broadcast in the Republic of Ireland.[89]

At a 1955 meeting of the Historical Society of Trinity College Dublin, concerns were raised that history in Northern Ireland was being re-written in order to prove that Ulster had always been a distinct historical entity. When the discussion moved to consider popular interest in history more generally, Dr Charles Dickson claimed that 'nationalism in Ireland was in grave danger through the agencies of the cinema, radio and press', as opposed to the more earthly 'attachment to things of the past which nothing could weaken'.[90] Dickson, a non-subscribing Presbyterian from Dromore in county Down, was the grand-nephew of the Young Ireland revolutionary John Mitchel. He had acquired fluent Irish over the course of repeated visits to the Donegal Gaeltacht (Irish language speaking areas) and moved to Dublin. Though trained as a physician and employed as a senior medical officer in the civil service, Dickson was mostly known for his thoroughly researched writings on the history of the 1798 rebellion. He started off in 1944 with a biography of the Wicklow rebel Michael Dwyer, followed in 1955 by a history of the insurrection in Wexford, and in 1960 he wrote a history of the rebellion in Antrim and Down (which was published in Dublin and London, rather than in Belfast).

Advertised as 'an authentic account of the stirring events In the Counties of Antrim and Down in 1798', Dickson's *Revolt in the North* exhibited extensive use of archival sources, but, as pointed out by the historian F. S. L. Lyons, it amounted to 'a very badly constructed book'. More than half of the volume is taken up by a lengthy historical introduction, which runs to twelve chapters and goes all the way back to the Middle Ages and the Anglo-Norman conquest. Dickson then provided an additional five chapters of immediate background, before finally addressing the actual rebellion in Ulster, which is covered in just five chapters. Materials of considerable interest are left outside of the main narrative and instead crammed into thirty appendices, some of which include 'interesting personal narratives of the rising'.[91] A reviewer concurred that this ungainly structure 'makes few, if any allowances for the reader who expects narrative' and complained that Dickson 'takes the story out of history'.[92]

Nationalist readers were unperturbed by the structural flaws in Dickson's *Revolt in the North* and the *Cork Examiner* considered it 'a valuable addition to Irish historical

[87] *Lisburn Herald and Antrim and Down Advertiser*, 29 October 1955, p. 4; also *Northern Whig*, 24 October and 28 December 1955, pp. 2 and 3 (respectively); *Irish Independent*, 5 November 1955, p. 7. For Cree's acquaintance with traditions of 1798 from around Ballynahinch see *Mourne Observer*, 30 August 1968, p. 3 (reproduced in Lyttle, *Betsy Gray*, 1968 ed., p. 180).

[88] *Stage*, 9 February 1961, p. 9.   [89] *Ulster Herald*, 16 January 1965, p. 5.

[90] *Irish Times*, 26 November 1955, p. 11; *Irish Independent*, 28 November 1955, p. 9.

[91] Charles Dickson, *Revolt in the North: Antrim and Down in 1798* (Dublin and London: Clonmore and Reynolds, 1960); *Irish Times*, 2 January 1960, p. 8. For a sample advertisement see *Irish Press*, 17 June 1961, p. 10.

[92] *Irish Press*, 11 January 1960, p. 5.

literature'. The northern provincial press lauded it as 'a reference book of unusual quality, a history of more than ordinary interest'.[93] Interest was not limited to nationalists. A reviewer for the unionist *Belfast Telegraph* maintained that 'there is no doubt that this book will be read attentively by those who are interested in a little known portion of Ulster history' and that it would remind Presbyterians of 'our heritage of Scottish radicalism and sturdy desire for independence'.[94]

Several other Ulster-born writers living in independent Ireland also showed interest in the northern United Irishmen. The politician and former revolutionary Sean MacEntee, just prior to his election to Dáil Éireann [the Irish parliament] with the newly formed republican Fianna Fáil republican party, wrote in 1924 a parable on 'The Old Woman of Down'. MacEntee was born in Belfast, where he had been a member of the Gaelic League and the Ulster Literary Theatre. The story, presented as a personal recollection, tells of a youth from Belfast encountering an aged descendant of Betsy Gray, who reminiscences in a heavy Ulster-Scots dialect about the heroes of 1798. She bemoans how their cause was forsaken by southern nationalists:

> They forget a' aboot us—us that followed the Green, an' died for it at Antrim an' Ballynahinch, us that sufferit fer the 'Cause' as nivir ither folk in Irelan' sufferit. But they mauna [must not forget] . . . . they man' think o' us always if they want Irelan' tae be free.[95]

This cry against the forgetting of the rebellion was, in effect, a polemical denunciation of partition.

On the other side of the political divide left by the Irish Civil War, Ernest Blythe, Cumann na nGael minister of Finance in the Irish Free State, was also interested in the northern United Irishmen. Blythe was born in the Protestant area of Magheragall, near Lisburn in county Antrim, and as a child of about 10 had witnessed the centenary celebrations of 1798, which had made a strong impression. His Presbyterian mother, who claimed kinship with the United Irish protomartyr William Orr, told him stories about Betsy Gray and other United Irish heroes, and a distant elderly relative recounted to him recollections of how her father had been an insurgent colonel. His paternal grandfather, on the other hand was descended from a yeoman, so that he was well aware of the ambiguity of memories of Ninety-Eight. In 1935, the year Blythe became a director of the Abbey, the Irish national theatre hosted Thomas Carnduff's *Castlereagh*. As managing director of the Abbey, he commissioned in 1944 a production of Jack Loudan's *Henry Joy McCracken*, but this initiative apparently did not materialize.[96] Blythe, who later criticized the irredentist polices of the Republic of Ireland, never lost interest in 1798 and on a visit to Northern Ireland in 1963 attended an exhibition in the Newtownards church hall, at which he found on display relics associated with Betsy Gray.[97]

---

[93] *Cork Examiner*, 28 April 1960, p. 4; *Ulster Herald*, 27 February 1960, p. 9 (published also in *Donegal News*, 27 February 1960, p. 7).

[94] *Belfast Telegraph*, 27 February 1960; preserved in PRONI D4201/K/13 (Denis Barritt Papers, press cuttings).

[95] *Derry Journal*, 31 December 1924, p. 3; originally written for the *Irish Statesmen* (published also in *Meath Chronicle*, 21 June 1924, p. 8).

[96] *Sunday Independent*, 3 February 1935, p. 7; *Irish Times*, 19 February 1935, p. 8; *Irish Independent*, 19 February 1935, p. 10; *Stage*, 21 February 1935, p. 11. For the acceptance of Loudan's play see *Larne Times*, 6 July 1944, p. 2.

[97] Earnán de Blaghd, *Trasna na Bóinne* (Baile Átha Cliath: Sáirséal agus Dill, 1957), pp. 13–15; *Sunday Independent*, 7 July 1963, p. 12; interview with Earnán de Blaghd for the unfinished

The southern writer most preoccupied with the legacy of the northern United Irishmen was the London-born journalist Aodh de Blacam, whose family—the Blackhams—were an Ulster Protestant family from Newry. He Gaelicized his name, converted to Catholicism, and in 1914 moved to Ireland, where he worked as a propagandist for Sinn Féin and became an ardent supporter of Éamon de Valera. His popular book *The Black North*, first published in 1938 (and reissued in 1940, 1942, 1943, and 1950), offered 'an account of the six counties of unrecovered Ireland: their people, their treasures, and their history'. It was dedicated 'to Southerners who have not learned the history of the North and to Northerners who have forgotten it'.[98]

De Blacam maintained that the Presbyterians had an innate affinity to Catholic-Gaelic culture and that once they owned up to the forgotten heritage of their United Irish ancestry—the 'Other Hidden Ireland'—this revelation would inevitably lead them towards nationalist republicanism.[99] His thesis was encapsulated in an anecdote set in county Down ('Betsy Gray's county'):

> A youth of one of the most rigid Orange families was taken ill. He got *Betsy Gray* to read during convalescence. He had gone to bed a Unionist, he rose a Republican. In a few days, he had learnt the story of Down and Antrim in 1798.[100]

Ulster Protestants, according to de Blacam, lived in forgetful disavowal of the memories of Ninety-Eight, which were to be found under the surface in Belfast and throughout Antrim and Down.[101] De Valera, who was then Taoiseach [Irish prime minister], contributed a foreword to *The Black North* in which he confessed that as a boy he had harboured a special affection for Ulster, 'the land of the bravest deeds and the most gallant chivalry . . . the land of Henry Monroe, of William Orr and Henry Joy McCracken'.[102] Allusions to the rebellion in Ulster featured regularly in de Blacam's popular column in the *Irish Press* (the organ of De Valera's Fianna Fáil party), written under the pen-name 'Roddy the Rover'.[103]

George A. Birmingham's 1907 'heroic novel' *The Northern Iron*, which was serialized in 1935 in the *Irish Press*, was strongly praised by de Blacam and he also quoted extensively from the 'incomparable account' of the rebellion in S. R. Keightley's 1903 novel *The Pikemen*. Both these novels were re-published by the Irish government in Irish: Muiris Ó Catháin translated *The Northern Iron* in 1933 as *Iarann an Tuaiscirt* and Séamus Ó Ceallaigh translated *The Pikemen* in 1936 as *Lucht Pící a's Sleagh*.[104] The Irish government also published a Gaelic version of M. T. Pender's centenary novel *The Green Cockade*, translated in 1942 by Pádraig Mac Seághain as *An Cnota Glas*, and this

documentary 'The Survivors' (RTÉ, *c.*1965), online: <www.rte.ie/archives/exhibitions/1993-easter-1916/2017-survivors/610313-the-survivors-earnn-de-blaghd/>.

[98] Aodh de Blácam, *The Black North. An Account of the Six Counties of Unrecovered Ireland: Their People, Their Treasures, and Their History* (Dublin: M. H. Gill, 1950; orig. edn 1938), p. xi.

[99] Aodh de Blacam, 'The Other Hidden Ireland', *Studies*, 23, no. 91 (1934): pp. 443 and 450.

[100] de Blácam, *The Black North*, p. 156.

[101] Ibid., pp. 156–7, 161–4, 194–7, 210–14, and 233–57.   [102] Ibid., p. ix.

[103] *Irish Press*, 19 September 1931, p. 6; 18 January 1937, p. 8; 13 April and 16 September 1938, p. 8; 6 June 1939, p. 8; 13 July 1948, p. 4.

[104] George A. Birmingham, *Iarann an Tuaiscirt* (Baile Átha Cliath [Dublin]: Oifig Díolta Foillseacháin Rialtais, 1933); for the serialization of Birmingham's original English version see *Irish Press*, 4 August 1935, p. 4. S. R. Keightley, *Lucht Pící a's Sleagh* (Dublin: Oifig Díolta Foillseacháin Rialtaise, 1936); see also *Irish Examiner*, 6 October 1937, p. 4.

was adapted by Séamus Mac Ciarnáin into a six-part radio drama for Radio Éireann, which was broadcast from 26 June 1962.[105]

The Gaelicization of Ulster-Scots fiction, despite the absence of a language barrier preventing Irish readers from reading these novels in the original, is a striking demonstration of the desire of independent Ireland to take over the memory of the northern United Irishmen. In addition, the government published in 1938 an original Irish-language novel by the Antrim-born author Seán Mac Maoláin, *Iolar agus Sionnach* [Eagle and Fox], which focused on tensions between Catholics and Presbyterians in the preparations for the rebellion in Ulster.[106] The implied threat of cultural irredentism emanating from Dublin only exacerbated northern unionist antagonism towards the memory of the United Irishmen.

Nonetheless, pressures were mounting to permit open displays of remembrance. For the sesquicentenary of the rebellion in 1948, the authorities of Northern Ireland were willing, with hesitations, to tolerate public commemoration of the United Irishmen. The concerns of the government were not assuaged by the formation of a Belfast 1798 Commemoration Committee, which claimed to be 'representative of the citizens, irrespective of creed or political affiliations', but was in effect a body of republicans and socialists, chaired by the former IRA man Cathal McCrystal. Among its members were several prominent Presbyterian radicals, including the trade unionist Victor Halley, the labour activist Jack McGougan, and most notably the author Denis Ireland, who had a record of writing about the United Irishmen. In 1936, Ireland had published extracts from the memoirs of Wolfe Tone, in 1941 he established the anti-Partitionist Ulster Union Club to 'recapture for Ulster Protestants their true tradition as Irishmen', and in 1948 he was nominated to Seanad Éireann [the Irish Senate]. The oppositional politics of the members of the 1798 Commemoration Committee raised the suspicions of the unionist government, which felt that it had to take steps to 'prevent disorder arising from the processions and meetings'.[107] Although commemoration was permitted, it was to be monitored and kept out of central locations.

During the sesquicentenary of 1798, the northern nationalist readers of the *Irish News* were treated to a staple diet of articles on the United Irishmen.[108] In addition, the Belfast 1798 Commemoration Committee issued *Ninety-Eight*—'a booklet of short stories, biographies, articles, and ballads, published to commemorate the one hundred

---

[105] Margaret T. Pender, *An Cnota Glas* (Baile Átha Cliath [Dublin]: Oifig an tSoláthair, 1941); Séamus Mac Ciarnáin, 'An Cnota Glas', UCD P261/3380, RTÉ Box 121/1; see also <www.rte.ie/archives/2013/0312/376233-an-cnota-glas/> and <www.rte.ie/archives/exhibitions/1379-a-glimpse-into-rte-written-archives/374392-cuimhnigh-ar-orr/>.

[106] Seán Mac Maoláin, *Iolar agus Sionnach* (Baile Átha Cliath [Dublin]: Oifig Dhíolta Foillseacháin Rialtais, 1938). See also Alan Titley, *An tÚrscéal Gaeilge* (Dublin: An Clóchomhar, 1991), pp. 348–50; Philip O'Leary, *Gaelic Prose in the Irish Free State, 1922–1939* (University Park, Pa.: Pennsylvania State University Press, 2004), pp. 290–1.

[107] Northern Ireland Cabinet Papers, 8 September 1948, PRONI CAB 4/761/9 [MIC 686/35]; *Northern Whig*, 10 September 1948, p. 1; *Belfast Remembers* (film produced by the Belfast 1798 Commemorative Committee, 1948); see also Collins, *Who Fears to Speak*, pp. 65–6. For Denis Ireland see Risteárd Ó Glaisne, *Denis Ireland* (Baile Átha Cliath: Coiscéim, 2000), esp. pp. 69–79, 136–7, and 228; *Patriot Adventurer: Extracts from the Memoirs and Journals of Theobald Wolfe Tone, 1763–1798*, edited by Denis Ireland (London: Rich & Cowan, 1936); for the foundation of the Ulster Unionist Club see *Irish Times*, 22 February 1941, p. 8.

[108] For example: *Irish News*, 13, 16, and 27 September, 1 and 5 October 1948, p. 2.

and fiftieth anniversary of the Insurrection of 1798', edited by Seamus McKearney.[109] The committee, however, did not get its act together on time to mark in June the actual anniversary dates of the rebellion in Ulster. Instead, a commemoration was planned for September at 'Blitz Square', a bomb-damaged site off High Street (just opposite the location of the old Market House, where Henry Joy McCracken had been executed), but this event was banned.

The Minister of Home Affairs, Edmond Warnock (who incidentally was descended from an Antrim United Irishman) used the Special Powers Act to prevent commemorative meetings and processions in city centre. At the same time, decommemorating, in the form of protest rallies organized by the National Union of Protestants and the Ulster Protestant League, was also prohibited.[110] This injunction, which was extended to all events that year, apart from the commemoration of the Battle of Britain, unintentionally prevented a non-related parade of the Cumberland Loyal Orange Lodge (L.O.L. no. 685), whose chaplain happened to be the loyalist firebrand Rev. Ian Paisley. Warnock was criticized in parliament by fellow unionists for curtailing a loyalist event and only narrowly escaped further political embarrassment. While it was common practice to restrict nationalist activities, unionist demonstrations were supposed to be left unfettered.[111]

Barred from city centre, an inaugural 1798 commemoration, attended by about 500 nationalists, was held on the evening of 13 September 1948 at McArt's Fort, on top of Cave Hill (just outside the city boundary). Later in the evening, a second republican parade to Cave Hill featured four men dressed as pikemen, who accompanied a party with a green flag and an Irish tricolour. The brazen display of the forbidden republican flag and the singing of the Irish anthem 'A Soldier's Song' in Irish provoked angry reactions from unionists.[112] The commemoration continued with a week-long programme that included a rally at St Columb's Hall in Derry (12 September) and a concert in Belfast at St Mary's Hall (15 September), a popular venue for Catholic gatherings.[113] Alarmed at the sight of tricolours on the Falls Road, which were displayed alongside arches inscribed 'Remember 1798', the Belfast Corporation, decided to enforce a recommendation of the municipal Estates Committee and to revoke permission for a commemorative *céilidhe* (traditional music and dance event) at Ulster Hall. The event was banned after 'certain unionist and Protestant organizations planned occupying the hall to prevent the holding of the ceilidhe' and it was claimed that going ahead with the programme would 'result in disturbances'.[114]

[109] Seamus McKearney, ed., *Ninety-Eight* (Belfast: The 1798 Commemoration Committee, 1948).
[110] *Belfast Gazette*, 10 September 1948; *Irish Examiner*, 10 September 1948, p. 5; *Irish News*, 10 September 1948, pp. 1 and 2; *Irish Press*, 10 September 1948, p. 1; *Northern Whig*, 10 September 1948, p. 2; *Irish Independent*, 11 September 1948, p. 7.
[111] *Northern Ireland Parliamentary Debates*, vol. 33 (1949), pp. 667 and 679; Keith Jeffery, 'Parades, Police and Government in Northern Ireland, 1922–1969', in *The Irish Parading Tradition: Following the Drum*, edited by T. G. Fraser (Houndmills and New York: Palgrave Macmillan, 2000), pp. 87–9.
[112] *Irish Independent*, 14 September 1948, p. 3; *Irish News*, 14 September 1948, p. 1; *Irish Press*, 14 September 1948, p. 5; *Irish Times*, 11 and 14 September 1948, p. 1; *Northern Whig*, 11 and 14 September 1948, p. 1; Cal McCrystal, *Reflections on a Quiet Rebel* (London: Michael Joseph, 1997), pp. 121–2; Collins, *Who Fears to Speak*, pp. 69–70.
[113] *Irish News*, 13, 14, and 16 September 1948, pp. 1, 2, and 3 (respectively).
[114] *Donegal News*, 18 September 1948, p. 5; *Irish Examiner*, 14 September 1948, p. 5; *Irish Independent*, 14 September 1948, p. 3; *Irish News*, 13 September 1798, p. 1; *Irish Press*, 13 September 1948, p. 1; *Northern Whig*, 13 September 1948, p. 1.

The discriminatory cancellation of a lease taken out by nationalists on a public venue, which was regularly used by unionists, was successfully challenged in the High Court, where it was revoked by the Lord Chief Justice, Sir James Andrews (a unionist, who happened to be a great-grandchild of William Drennan). On 17 September some 1,600 people filled Ulster Hall 'to continue the celebrations in connection with the Rebellion of '98' in an atmosphere of 'complete gaiety'.[115] This festive display of cultural nationalism, complete with dance performances and the singing of patriotic songs, showed little regard to the catastrophic results of the rebellion. In order to restore a sense of solemn decorum, on the following day (18 September), graves of celebrated United Irishmen in the cemeteries of Clifton Street Belfast, Mallusk, and Templepatrick—identified by the 1798 Commemoration Committee as 'a few of our hallowed spots'—were decorated with wreaths.[116]

The final event of the sesquicentenary was a commemorative march down the Falls Road, through the Catholic neighbourhoods of west Belfast. On the afternoon of 20 September, contingents assembled at Smithfield and unfurled banners of Henry Joy McCracken, William Orr, James Hope, Wolfe Tone, Robert Emmet, and the Hearts of Down that had been preserved from the centenary commemorations in 1898. The banner of James Hope was carried by three of his descendants and 'several of the original pikes and swords used in '98 were carried by the men in the crowd.' Though this seemed to demonstrate continuity of remembrance from the time of the rebellion, pride of place was given to 'a car carrying several veterans of the 1898 Centenary Commemoration', which showed that for most of the Catholic participants, personal recollections only went back as far as half a century.

The procession concluded with a 'final '98 rally' in Corrigan Park, which was attended by 30,000 (including southern contingents from Dublin, Cork, Wicklow, and Carlow). Nationalist reportage claimed, probably with some exaggeration, that 'the parade drew thousands of Protestants as spectators' and McCrystal, chairman of the '98 committee, paid 'special tribute to that body of Protestants who were already forming the hard core for the final fight for freedom'. Evoking the ambitions of the centenary, the organizers announced that 'they hoped to see to it that every district of Belfast, Protestant and Catholic, had a '98 Commemoration Club.' There were, however, glaring disparities between the rhetoric of ecumenical inclusiveness and the sobering reality of sectarian divides. In practice, very few Protestants supported the commemorations and the desire to rekindle a movement on the scale of the centenary did not catch fire in Northern Ireland.[117] The passing of the Republic of Ireland Act in 1948, on the tail of the 150th anniversary of the 1798 rebellion, whereby independent Ireland declared itself a republic and opted to leave the British Commonwealth, antagonized unionists and resulted in Westminster enacting the Ireland Act 1949,

---

[115] *Evening Herald*, 16 September 1948, p. 1; *Irish News*, 16, 17, and 18 September 1798, pp. 3, 1–3, and 3 (respectively); *Irish Press*, 16, 17, and 18 September 1948, p. 1; *Northern Whig*, 15 September 1948, p. 1; see also McCrystal, *Reflections on a Quiet Rebel*, pp. 117–20; Collins, *Who Fears to Speak*, pp. 70–2.

[116] F. P. Carey, 'The Shrines of the Patriot Dead', in *Ninety-Eight*, edited by Seamus McKearney (Belfast: The 1798 Commemoration Committee, 1948), pp. 59–61; Collins, *Who Fears to Speak*, p. 73.

[117] *Irish Independent*, 20 September 1948, p. 5; *Irish News*, 20 September 1948, p. 1.

which re-affirmed partition.[118] There seemed to be no room for constructive dialogue between nationalists and unionists.

At the end of the sesquicentennial year, a statement issued by an All-Ireland '98 Commemoration Association expressed concerns that 'the very success of our Celebrations may be misleading.' It was acknowledged that 'monuments may become meaningless in the absence of popular knowledge of the events and of the men they were erected to commemorate' and that it was therefore necessary 'to reintegrate our national public opinion through the rebuilding of local public opinion, to recover and perpetuate the local history, and traditions commemorated by our local monuments'.[119] At one such local event in 1949, the historian Charles Dickson was invited to speak at a commemoration ceremony in Kilranalagh, near Baltinglass, county Wicklow, at which a monument was dedicated to Sam McAllister, a Presbyterian from Antrim. Traditions of this northern rebel—who, after the defeat of the rebellion in the Ulster, travelled south and joined the remaining rebels in the Wicklow hills, giving his life to protect their leader Michael Dwyer—had been remembered locally.

McAllister was recalled in a ballad composed in the early nineteenth century by the Wicklow poet Mrs Tighe, as well as in a short story by the popular author Gerald Griffin (in which he is nicknamed 'Antrim Jack') and in local folklore accounts.[120] The location of the grave, on which the memorial was erected, had been identified by Thomas Dornan, whose family had preserved the memory of the site for several generations (though their claim was disputed). The initiative to erect a monument was first proposed in 1902, but it had taken over half a century to come to fruition. Among the thousands who attended the Baltinglass ceremony in 1949 were about a hundred members of the Michael Dwyer Club of the Falls Road in Belfast, who carried with them a banner from the centenary, 'which had been kept in many places of hiding during the years'.[121] There were now numerous Ninety-Eight memorials in the South. However, in Northern Ireland—since the destruction of the Betsy Gray monument—there were still no public monuments to the United Irishmen.

On a visit to Northern Ireland in 1950, the Irish Minister for External Affairs, Seán MacBride, spoke at a GAA event in Toome. MacBride commented on the significance of the association of Toome with Roddy McCorley, who 'like most of the leaders of the United Irishmen, he too was a Presbyterian and was working not merely for the establishment of the Republic but also for Catholic Emancipation.' In this speech, the memory of McCorley was co-opted for the irredentist purposes of the Republic of Ireland and given an embellished history with current relevance (hinting at demands for

[118] Ian McCabe, *A Diplomatic History of Ireland, 1948–49: The Republic, the Commonwealth and NATO* (Blackrock: Irish Academic Press, 1991).

[119] Statement of the '98 Commemoration Association (1948) in the possession of Bernard Browne, former Chief Executive of Comóradh '98; reproduced in Collins, *Who Fears to Speak*, pp. 74–5.

[120] J. S. Crone to F. J. Bigger, 1 May 1905, Bigger Papers, BCL K1/A; 'Dwyer and M'Alister: A Tale of 1798', *Dublin Penny Journal*, 3, no. 129 (December 1834): p. 200; Richard Robert Madden, *The United Irishmen: Their Lives and Times*, 3rd ser., vol. 3 (Dublin: James Duffy, 1846), pp. 149–50 [account of James Hope]; Gerald Griffin, *Talis Qualis; or, Tales of the Jury Room*, vol. 3 (London: Maxwell & Co., 1842), pp. 73–125; E. P. O'Kelly, 'Historical Notes on Baltinglass in Modern Times', *Journal of the County Kildare Archæological Society*, 5, no. 5 (1908): p. 336; Pádraig Ó Tuathail, 'Wicklow Traditions of 1798', *Béaloideas*, 5, no. 2 (1935): pp. 154–88.

[121] *Irish Independent*, 22 August 1949, p. 7.

Catholic rights in Northern Ireland).[122] Later that year, a Roddy McCorley Memorial Committee began to raise funds for a monument in cooperation with the National Graves Association, a republican organization responsible for the maintenance of nationalist commemorative sites throughout the island.[123] The fundraising campaign was aimed exclusively at Catholics and included such events as a local production of the religious drama 'The Message of Fatima', which was performed in Toome Hall under the auspices of the Irish Graves Association.[124] General interest generated by the campaign is evident, for example, in the re-publication by popular demand of Ethna Carbery's famous ballad 'Roddy McCorley' in the local nationalist newspaper.[125]

On 13 September 1953, the hundred and fiftieth anniversary of Robert Emmet's rising was commemorated with a nationalist demonstration in Downpatrick, the site of the execution of Thomas Russell, attended by some 7,000 people. The rally was addressed by several nationalist members of the Northern Irish parliament, including Eddie McAteer, representative for Mid-Londonderry and chairman of the Anti-Partition League; James McSparran, representative for Mourne and President of the Anti-Partition League; and Joseph Connellan, representative for South Down and a regular contributor of articles on 1798 to the local nationalist press. The anti-partition message was strengthened by the participation of two prominent TDs (members of the Irish parliament), Sean McBride and Sean MacEoin. Houses in the Catholic neighbourhoods along the route of the parade were decked in republican flags. In protest of the police enforcing the ban on the display of tricolour flags at processions, a contingent of old IRA veterans was headed by a Loughinisland man with a flag of green and white, alongside a Downpatrick man holding a poster with the sardonic comment that 'orange is forbidden in the Six Counties'.[126]

The tricolour, which unionists perceived as an irredentist threat, was also banned at a Sinn Féin commemoration of the United Irish aborted rising in Newry on 14 September 1953.[127] Nonetheless, the republican flag was carried openly the following week at the head of a commemorative parade in the Catholic neighbourhood of Andersonstown in west Belfast.[128] In February 1954, the government gave in to pressures from hard-line loyalists and introduced a Flags and Emblems Act (1954 *c.*10), which empowered the police to remove any flag other than the Union flag when 'the display of such emblem may occasion a breach of the peace'.[129] The bill, which was

---

[122] *Derry Journal*, 10 July 1950, p. 1. [123] *Derry Journal*, 22 November 1950, p. 6.
[124] *Derry Journal*, 13 April 1951, p. 6. [125] *Derry Journal*, 21 March 1951, p. 2.
[126] *Derry Journal*, 14 September 1953, p. 1; *Irish Independent*, 14 September 1953, p. 7. For examples of articles by Connellan see *Fermanagh Herald*, 1 March 1948, p. 3 ('Newry Patriots of 1798'); 24 July 1948, p. 5 ('The Insurrection of 1798 and Its Causes'); 24 January 1953, p. 3 ('Seeds of the Republic in County Down').
[127] *Irish Independent*, 15 September 1953, p. 3.
[128] *Irish Independent*, 21 September 1953, p. 7.
[129] Flags and Emblems (Display) Act (Northern Ireland), 1954; <http://cain.ulst.ac.uk/hmso/fea1954.htm>; Dominic Bryan and Neil Jarman, 'Green Parades in an Orange State: Nationalist and Republican Commemorations and Demonstrations from Partition to the Troubles, 1920–1970', in *The Irish Parading Tradition: Following the Drum*, edited by T. G. Fraser (Houndmills: Macmillan Press and New York: St Martin's Press, 2000), pp. 103–4. See also Henry Patterson, 'Party Versus Order: Ulster Unionism and the Flags and Emblems Act', *Contemporary British History*, 13, no. 4 (December 1999): pp. 105–29.

clearly aimed against tricolours, was perceived by nationalists as an unjustified unionist prohibition.

A twenty-foot-high limestone Celtic cross monument in memory of the execution of Roddy McCorley at Toome was finally completed in 1954, half a century after it had been proposed by Bigger. The unveiling ceremony on 1 November 1954, which was attended by some five hundred nationalists, was closely monitored by the Royal Ulster Constabulary, who were charged with enforcing the ban on republican flags, though at some stage a tricolour was furtively unfurled. Rev. J. Mulholland, parish priest of Armoy and a native of Toome, presided over the commemorative event and Rev. J. Byrne, parish priest of Larne, performed the ceremony. An oration by Rev. Eamon Devlin, the curate of Donaghmore, commented on the state of remembrance: 'the memories of the men of '98 were still green among the countrymen. Even among the Presbyterian Unionist of to-day their memory was still green, but alas was fading rapidly.' Putting the blame on 'some sinister influence', which 'seemed to separate them from the glories of their forefathers'. Rev. Devlin candidly admitted that 'it is doubtful if one single Presbyterian from Drumaul, or from any other place, had come there that day to do honour to the memory of Rody McCorley.'[130]

The organizers of the memorial ceremony failed to realize that the dominant presence of Catholic priests at the memorial ceremony was in itself a deterrent for many Protestants. Showing a lack of self-awareness, which was characteristic of Catholic nationalist rhetoric, Rev. Devlin expressed the hope that the descendants of 'the Presbyterian patriots who suffered and died for Ireland in 1798' would eventually 'join us too in raising fitting memorials to their forefathers'.[131] In practice, Presbyterian communities shied away from public commemoration of their United Irish forebears. The official culture of Northern Ireland was hostile to the memory of Ninety-Eight and it would take an effort to coax people into speaking openly about hidden folk memories that had been masked by social forgetting.

UNPERCEIVED REMEMBRANCE

In the decades after partition, academic historians in Northern Ireland continued to show a general lack of interest in the United Irishmen. Over in England, F. H. Amphlett Micklewright, an Anglican curate at St Ann's church in Manchester who converted to Unitarianism, was elected a Fellow of the Royal Historical Society in recognition of a series of articles on the involvement of Presbyterian ministers in the 1798 rebellion, which were published in 1946–7 in the scholarly journal *Notes and Queries*. Under the influence of the Marxist historian Desmond Greaves, editor of the *Irish Democrat*, Micklewright became an anti-Partitionist and joined the republican Connolly Association. His study of radical Presbyterians made use of the standard historical sources, while faulting Teeling that he 'relied too greatly upon memory'. Micklewright was a long-time member of the Folklore Society and had a particular fascination with Scottish

---

[130] *Derry Journal*, 3 November 1954, p. 5; *Irish Times*, 1 and 2 November 1954, p. 1; *BNL*, 2 November 1954, p. 5; *Belfast Telegraph*, 1 November 1954; *Northern Whig*, 1 and 2 November 1954, pp. 4 and 5 (respectively). See also <www.roddymccorley.com/history of cross.html>.
[131] *Derry Journal*, 3 November 1954, p. 5.

folklore. He even met with the leading figure responsible for collecting folklore in Ireland—Seámus Ó Dúilearga, better known in English-speaking circles as James Hamilton Delargy. Yet, it did not occur to him that it might be worth considering the folk memory of the rebellion in Ulster.[132]

Charles Dickson dedicated his history of the *Revolt in the North* to Delargy, whom he admired as 'an Antrim glensman, an eminent folklorist'. Delargy, was born in Cushendall, county Antrim, and started primary school at nearby Glenariff, before his family moved south. Trained as a folklorist at University College Dublin (UCD), under the tutelage of Douglas Hyde and Oscar Bergin, Delargy was appointed Honorary Director of the Irish Folklore Commission on its foundation in 1935 and effectively managed its activities up to 1970, when it was integrated into the Department of Irish Folklore at UCD. Irish folklorists at the time showed a preference for long Gaelic tales (*scéalaithe*), mainly found in the remaining pockets of Irish-speaking communities in the West of Ireland. However, the Irish Folklore Commission, which received from de Valera's government initial funding to the symbolic sum of one hundred Irish pounds for each of the thirty-two counties of greater Ireland, was expected to extend its activities into Northern Ireland, to also cover English speaking areas, and not to neglect shorter forms of folklore that better reflect social history (*seanchas*).[133]

The main fieldworker entrusted with collecting folklore in Ulster was Michael Joseph Murphy, who was born in England and raised in Dromintree, south Armagh, near Newry and county Down (Fig. 6.1a). Both his father, Michael Murphy, and his mother, Susan Campbell, were storytellers, and a paternal great-grandfather, William Jordan [Liam Ó Sriodáin], was a Gaelic scribe and poet. Encouraged, among others, by Maud Gonne McBride, Murphy began to collect traditions in his home area at a young age and wrote in the 1930s articles for local and national periodicals. Following the publication of his first book, *At Slieve Gullion's Foot*, he was invited in 1941 to join the Irish Folklore Commission as a part-time collector and progressed to become in 1949 a full-time collector. Over a distinguished career that spanned four decades of fieldwork, Murphy wrote some 250 manuscript volumes of folklore accounts.[134]

The fieldworkers of the Irish Folklore Commission were equipped with *A Handbook of Irish Folklore*, written by the commission's archivist Seán Ó Súilleabháin in accordance with the folklore classification system developed in Uppsala, Sweden. It included a chapter on historical traditions, with a sub-section on 'The Rebellion of 1798', which instructed folklore collectors to inquire: 'Was your district actively connected with this

---

[132] F. H. Amphlett Micklewright, 'The Place of Presbyterians in the 1798 Rebellion in Ireland', *Notes and Queries*, 191, no. 1 (13 July 1946): pp. 2–7; no. 2 (27 July 1946): pp. 27–31; no. 3 (10 August 1946): pp. 57–60; also F. H. Amphlett Micklewright, 'Irish Presbyterians in the 1798 Rebellion', *Notes and Queries*, 192, no. 18 (6 September 1947): pp. 377–9. See also Gillian Hawtin, *F. H. Amphlett Micklewright (1908–1992): A Memoir* (Atlanta, London, and Sydney: Minerva Press, 1999), pp. 16–18 and 31–2.

[133] See Beiner, *Remembering the Year of the French*, pp. 35–48; Mícheál Briody, *The Irish Folklore Commission 1935–1970: History, Ideology, Methodology* (Helsinki: Finnish Literature Society, 2007), esp. pp. 129–49.

[134] *Irish Times*, 5 June 1996, p. 17; Bo Almqvist, 'Michael J. Murphy (1913–1996)', *Béaloideas*, 64/65 (1996): pp. 362–5.

(a)

(b)

Fig. 6.1. Collecting folklore on Rathlin Island

6.1a. Michael J. Murphy (1913–96) at this home in Dromintree, county Armagh (near Newry, county Down) *c.*1950. 6.1b. A photograph by Murphy of Peter McMullan of Rathlin and the pike he found in 1955. When the pike was found in the thatch of the house of the McMullan family on the lower end of Rathlin island, Michael J. Murphy, a full-time collector for the Irish Folklore Commission, was told that that there was 'no tradition anywhere on [the] Island' about pikes or pikemen. Yet, the following year, Murphy collected on the island several traditions of Ninety-Eight.

Courtesy of the National Folklore Collection, University College Dublin (photographs M011.25.00001 and K030.24.00001).

rebellion? In what way?'. Collectors were supposed to seek 'traditions about the men who fought' by pursuing specific lines of inquiry, asking about:

> local leaders; strength of the fighting men; equipment (detailed accounts of pikes, guns, and other weapons); preparations for the struggle; detailed accounts of fights, battles, sieges; smaller encounters and incidents; individual heroism; shootings, burnings, and other atrocities (pitchcaps, picketing, half-hanging); fate of captured men (death by hanging, shooting, transportation); fugitives; end of the rising. Detailed accounts of the activities of Croppies, Yeomen, Fencibles, Militia, Redcoats, and other bodies during the campaign. Parts played by the people and priests in struggle ... Songs and ballads about the rising.

A suggested list of heroic individuals, about whom stories should be specifically solicited, included several northern names: [Henry Joy] McCracken, Monroe [Henry Munro], Jemmy Hope, and Betsy Gray.[135]

Collecting folklore in the glens of Antrim in the mid-1950s, Murphy discovered that his questions awakened dormant recollections and soon realized that, under the surface, oral traditions of Ninety-Eight were very much alive. For example, from the winter of 1954 through to the summer of 1955, he met several times with 48-year-old Michael Leech ('Big Mick') of the Bay, Glenariff (3 km south of Cushendall) and it turned out that Leech had ancestors from Cullybackey (5 km north-west of Ballymena), who had been United Irishmen. When questioned on 1798, Leech found that 'things keep coming back to me: this talk started my memory.' Over the following months, he repeatedly came to Murphy with further recollections, each time remembering additional traditions about the rebellion. The return of repressed memories from the past was strikingly apparent when Leech suddenly recalled the details of a particularly gruesome story about 'the man they couldn't hang—they had to cut the shinnins of his neck, his body was that strong it supported him and the rope round his neck.' Murphy noted that Leech came to him 'one night in the downpours, unshaven, shouting', after he had suddenly remembered the man's name 'while shaving and kept repeating it lest he forget'.[136]

Once his memory had been jogged, Leech recalled many tales of Ninety-Eight that he had first heard from his grandmother and other elderly people in the area. The story of how a local rebel leader, Donal Delargy, blamed the blacksmith Cromellin of Cushendun of making 'bad pikes' and then 'led the pikemen against the Orangemen at Crebilly, near Ballymena'—for which he was flogged—had been preserved in an old ballad attributed to a local poet named Struthers Moore. Leech had heard his father recite the poem 'in the field when we were working' and could only remember fragments, confessing to Murphy that 'they come back into my head when something takes me in mind of them.' In absence of social frameworks for publicly recounting traditions of the rebellion, memory had been retained in fragmented form, but could still be pieced together.[137]

Recollection of traditions that seemed to have been long forgotten were occasionally triggered by the rediscovery of relics. In Rathlin Island (once known as Raghery), off the north coast of Antrim, memories of participation in the rebellion had been covered up. Already in the early nineteenth century, a story was told of how 'in the unfortunate

---

[135] Seán Ó Súilleabháin, *A Handbook of Irish Folklore* (Folklore Associates, Inc.: Hatboro, PA, 1963; orig. edn 1942), p. 533.
[136] NFC 1387/241; also NFC 1387/236 and 1389/189 ('things keep coming back').
[137] NFC 1384/153-159; also NFC 1365/284; 1387/229 and 234-9. NFC 1387/241; also NFC 1387/236 and 1389/189 (references to 'things keep coming back').

year 1798' those who were 'sworn to assist their mistaken neighbours on the mainland' were prevented from traveling after 'tremendous gales set in' so that no boat could leave the island 'till the misguided leaders of the rebellion in Ireland were subdued'.[138] When a pike was found in 1955 in the thatch of the house of the McMullan family on the lower end of Rathlin (Fig. 6.1b), Murphy maintained that there was 'no tradition anywhere on [the] Island' about pikes or pikemen and noted that an old islander, who had never heard of them, 'wanted to know what a pike was and what it was for'. Yet, the following year, Murphy collected in Rathlin several accounts about 1798, which recalled the designated signal that had been given for the island men to rise, that a local man named William [Bill] Curry had fought at the Battle of Antrim, and that a cave on the island had been a hideout for fugitive rebels.[139]

Along the north Antrim coastline, Murphy was told stories of military terror during the 'Time of the Croppies and the Yeos when the Presbyterians joined the Catholics'. Remembrance of oral traditions was assisted by recollection of colourful anecdotal details. For example, in November 1955 Murphy was told by a young barman in Ballycastle that 'he had heard local men in his bar a few years back talking on Ninety-Eight.' The clock on the Diamond [the town's main square] was said to have been left broken ever since a mother of a rebel cast a curse on it following the execution of her son. The story of the clock at Ballycastle breaking at the exact hour of execution had already been told to W. S. Smith in the late nineteenth century with reference to a man named McIlroy, who was believed to have been wrongly condemned to death.[140]

Indeed, it transpired that traditions that had been documented many years before could still be collected from living tradition in the mid-twentieth century. For example, Murphy heard in south Down a story of how the wife of a condemned rebel named Gordon from Templegowran swiftly rode to Belfast without stop and came back in the nick of time with a reprieve for her husband. The couple, who lived into their eighties, preserved the tail of the faithful steed as a relic. Unbeknownst to Murphy, the story that he took down in 1956 had previously been collected at the turn of the century by the local historian Francis C. Crossle, who in 1898 was given the souvenir tail, which he placed in glass frame and presented to the town commissioners of Newry.[141]

Around Burren, near Warrenpoint in south Down, Murphy heard vivid recollections of the terror unleashed in 1798 by the military, including particularly horrendous stories about the notorious Welsh cavalry unit known as the Ancient Britons. He uncovered subtle everyday practices of commemoration that recalled these misdeeds. For example, each of the Ryan families in the area had a tradition of naming one of their boys 'Willie', in memory of a young boy called Willie Ryan, who had been killed for no apparent reason by passing soldiers. The location of sites of atrocities was remembered

---

[138] 'Some Account of the Island of Raghery (Rahery) Off the Coast of Ireland, in the County of Antrim' *The Saturday Magazine*, 8, no. 251 (May 1836), pp. 209–10.

[139] NFC 1390/234 (finding of pike); 1432/277 (signal) and 283 (hideout); 1470/19 (William Curry).

[140] NFC 1413/22 (barman and clock); 1432/131 (clock) and 238–9 (terror); Smith, *Memories of '98*, pp. 71–2.

[141] NFC 1432/167; Francis C. Crossle, 'An Historic Tale: A Faithful Steed and a Devoted Wife', *The Open Window: An Annual of Literature and Popular Year Book*, 1900: p. 60. The souvenir has since been preserved in Newry; see Tony Canavan, *Frontier Town: An Illustrated History of Newry*, 2nd edn (Drogheda: Choice, 2009), p. 104; Anthony G. Russell, *Beyond the Battle: The Story of South Down and South Armagh in 1798* (Newry: The Newry and Mourne 1798 Commemoration Committee, 1998), p. 9.

in the vernacular landscape. Peadar J. Barry, a 58-year-old farmer from the townland of Corragh near Burren (7 km south-east of Newry), 'had heard the old people locally tell accounts of the time in Ninety-Eight when the Welsh horse came here'. He informed Murphy in 1956 that a family in Derryleckagh Wood were burned in their house and that 'there's a round circle there yet at the spot where nothing ever grows since.' Other local traditions recounted how a group of football players that had fled the soldiers took refuge in a barn, where they were all killed, and it was said that 'the blood was on the stones for ages and ages after.' Another resident of Corragh, Peter McGuinness, told Murphy that 'on stones around our place, you could see the dark stain.' Despite an official culture that did not accommodate public remembrance, a century and a half after the events, local memories of 1798 were apparently indelible.[142]

Murphy was a socialist republican, who later moved from Northern Ireland to live in county Louth. At a first glance, the folklore he collected in the 1950s seems to comply with standard expectations of how rebellions should be remembered by nationalists. He took down colourful tales of villainous red coats ruthlessly hunting down honourable rebels and brutalizing harmless civilians in 1798, alongside accounts of the Fenians and the more recent troubles of the Anglo-Irish War. This seemed to be just another popular version of commonplace nationalist history. Under closer inspection, it becomes apparent that the traditions of Ninety-Eight in Ulster had not lost their distinctive ambiguity.

Retelling a family tradition about a rebel ancestor and his comrade, who had taken refuge in the glens of Antrim, Michael Leech noted that he had heard that 'the priests would inform on them and tell the Catholics to inform.' It was recalled that a relative of the pursued United Irishman was 'mad at the informers that got him hunted' and organized a punitive raid on Catholics in Islandstown (10 km north-east of Ballymena). Leech explained that 'the attacks were inspired because Glens folk had informed on Ninety-Eight men, who were, of course, mainly Presbyterians.' Rose Emerson of Gortaclee, Cushendall added that the sectarian attacks on Catholics were stopped by 'a very well-up and prominent Protestant from beyond Ballymena'.[143] These local traditions, in which Catholics inform on Presbyterian rebels, and are then protected from reprisals by an Anglican, defy stereotypical narratives of Catholic rebels confronting Protestant loyalists. Although loyalist yeomanry in south Down were often accused of committing atrocities, it was recalled that Captain Hall's yeomen had intervened to stop the Welsh Horse from continuing a massacre.[144] Such accounts reflected the inherent ambivalence of the Turn-Out.

The impressive achievement of the Dublin-based Irish Folklore Commission in documenting a large volume of oral traditions under the directorship of Delargy, who hailed from Antrim, was viewed with envy in certain northern academic circles. The association of Irish folklore with Gaelic culture was jarring for unionists and it was 'felt that if folk material was to be collected in Northern Ireland the work should be done from Belfast rather than from Dublin'.[145] Emyr Estyn Evans, professor of

---

[142] NFC 1470/195-204. Traditions of 'The Bloody Britons' were also collected by Colin Johnston Robb; see *Irish News*, 3 June 1937 (reproduced in *Irish News*, 3 June 2006, p. 22).

[143] NFC 1387/238-9 (Leech) and 240 (Emerson).

[144] NFC 1470/199-202.

[145] E. Estyn Evans, 'Folklife Studies in Northern Ireland', *Journal of the Folklore Institute*, 2, no. 3 (1965), p. 355.

geography at Queen's University, Belfast, and a pioneer of archaeology and anthropology in Northern Ireland, rose to the challenge. Evans strongly disagreed with the political focus of Irish historiography. He considered the preoccupation of historians 'with the morbid phenomena of British rule in their country'—which he mocked as '1169 and all that done into academic prose'—to be 'confusing and repellent'.[146] He was also critical of the partisan narratives found in the popular histories upheld by loyalists and nationalists and asserted that 'we all have a lot of myths to forget.'[147] Instead, Evans believed that 'nothing less than the whole of the past is needed to explain the present, and in this difficult task we cannot afford to neglect the unrecorded past.'[148]

Casting their gaze on traditional rural practices, Evans and his acolytes showed a preference for ethnology–folklife, rather than ethnography–folklore. Their crowning achievement was the Ulster Folk Museum at Cultra Manor in Holywood, outside Belfast, which was established by act of law in 1958 and fitted into a wider pattern of open air folk museums that had come into vogue in post-war Britain (starting with the Welsh Folk Museum, opened at St Fagan's outside Cardiff in 1946). Both the inaugural director, George B. Thompson, and his successor, Alan Gailey, were trained by Evans. They maintained that traditions of vernacular architecture and material culture, which were believed to have ancient roots, were evidence of the uniqueness of Ulster within the isle of Ireland, and its position as a border region of Europe. By offering a model of 'common ground' that was shared by all the inhabitants of Northern Ireland, Protestants and Catholics alike, the folk museum was supposed to contribute to conflict resolution. Accordingly, the study of folklife tended to avoid mention of Ulster's ingrained sectarian animosities, effectively shying away from political history.[149]

In his search for cultural survivals from ancient times, Evans was aware that 'there have been opportunities, not only in this earliest period . . . but at other periods in Ulster history, at the end of the eighteenth century, for instance, when again extremes came together and sparked off a great cultural movement.' Yet, the essentially unionist theoretical framework that underpinned his landmark studies of Irish heritage discouraged Evans from explicitly engaging with the legacy of the United Irishmen. Although he maintained that a 'suspicion of external authority, especially of impersonal authority' was a persistent cultural trait in Ulster, which often resulted in 'difficulties of government', Evans was not particularly interested in historical traditions of sedition and rebellion.[150]

---

[146] E. Estyn Evans, *The Personality of Ireland: Habitat, Heritage and History* (Cambridge: Cambridge University Press, 1973), p. 5.

[147] E. Estyn Evans, *Ulster: The Common Ground* (Mullingar, Co. Westmeath: Lilliput Press, 1984), pp. 8–9.

[148] E. Estyn Evans, *Irish Folk Ways* (Mineola, N.Y.: Dover Publications, 2000; orig. edn 1957), p. ix.

[149] Anthony D. Buckley, 'Ethnology in the North of Ireland', in *Everyday Culture in Europe: Approaches and Methodologies*, edited by Máiréad Nic Craith, Ullrich Kockel, and Reinhard Johler (Aldershot and Burlington: Ashgate, 2008), pp. 167–8; Alan Gailey, 'Conflict-Resolution in Northern Ireland: The Role of a Folk Museum', *Museum International*, 44, no. 3 (1992): pp. 165–9; Diarmuid Ó Giolláin, *Locating Irish Folklore: Tradition, Modernity, Identity* (Cork: Cork University Press, 2000), p. 57; Mary Burgess, 'Mapping the Narrow Ground: Geography, History and Partition', *Field Day Review*, 1 (2005): pp. 123–5; Karine Bigand, 'How Is Ulster's History Represented in Northern Ireland's Museums? The Cases of the Ulster Folk Museum and the Ulster Museum', *E-rea*, 8, no. 3 (2011).

[150] Evans, *Ulster*, pp. 13–15. For a discussion of Evans's conceptualization of Ulster in unionist terms see Brian J. Graham, 'The Search for the Common Ground: Estyn Evans's Ireland', *Transactions of the Institute of British Geographers*, 19, no. 2 (1994): pp. 183–201.

When writing about the Mourne area in county Down, he noted that the 1798 rebellion 'had little effect' there, unlike the 'Irish districts'.[151] His other works did not even mention Ninety-Eight.

Together with the archaeologist Oliver Davies, Evans renewed the *Ulster Journal of Archaeology*, which had lapsed since Bigger's demise. The first issue of the new series, published in 1938, included an article on 'Lisburn and Neighbourhood in 1798' in which T. G. F. Paterson, the curator of the County Museum in Armagh, reproduced an extract from a loyalist memoir, written by the Orange yeomanry commander William Blacker. After that, no further items appeared on the rebellion. The lack of attention to the United Irishmen in the journal's third series, which continues till the present day, stands in stark contrast to the previous series, which under Bigger's stewardship had put an emphasis on recovering traditions of Ninety-Eight. Unlike the antiquarian folklorists of the turn of the century, the folklife scholars of Northern Ireland were disinterested in 1798 and were unconsciously complicit in social forgetting.[152]

The absence of a northern institution for collecting the oral traditions of Ulster remained a sore issue. Although Delargy and Evans maintained a cordial working relationship, there was a certain degree of tension between folklore and folklife studies, which reflected the wider political tensions between North and South. The all-Ireland brief of the Irish Folklore Commission was seen as an irredentist project and the Ulster regionalism in the work of Evans was seen as partitionist.[153] After hearing Delargy lecture to the Folklore Society in London in 1951, W. Cordner of Drumbo, county Down, proposed to the folklore and dialect section of the Belfast Naturalists' Field Club that there was a need for 'the formation of an organization which would pursue folklore studies in Ulster'.[154] The following year, a Committee on Ulster Folklife and Traditions—chaired by Evans—was formed in order 'to record local traditions for every townland in the province'. An appeal for government funding argued that 'Ulster cannot afford to be the only part of these islands that is neglectful of its traditions— traditions which are the living flesh of the bones and its great history.'[155]

The attempt to run a folklore collecting scheme in Northern Ireland was loosely modelled on the Irish Folklore Commission but did not benefit from the same level of state support. Its advocates used the familiar rhetoric of the imperative to salvage folklore from the ravages of modernity, pleading that 'the collection of the oral traditions of the people of the Six Counties of Northern Ireland is a work of great importance' since 'much of the oral heritage will have passed away for ever.' The Northern Ireland Tourist Board and the Ministry of Finance sponsored a single field organizer, Katherine M. Harris, to coordinate the project. Volunteer collectors were sent questionnaires on a wide range of folklore topics and it was expected that they would cover all the listed themes, writing their findings in notebooks. Noticing that the response was 'somewhat disappointing', Harris opted for a more individualistic, and less prescriptive, approach, which allowed the collectors to pursue their own particular interests.[156]

---

[151] E. Estyn Evans, *Mourne Country; Landscape and Life in South Down* (Dundalk: Dundalgan Press, 1951), pp. 210 and 211n8.

[152] T. G. F. Paterson, 'Lisburn and Neighbourhood in 1798', *UJA*, 3rd ser., 1 (1938): pp. 193–8.

[153] See Briody, The Irish Folklore Commission, pp. 290–6.

[154] *Northern Whig*, 11 October 1951, p. 4.   [155] *Larne Times*, 22 April 1954, p. 8.

[156] 'Questionnaires and Collectors', *Ulster Folklife*, 1 (1955): p. 7; K. M. Harris, 'Extracts from the Committee's Collection', *Ulster Folklife*, 4 (1958): p. 37.

The Committee on Ulster Folklife and Traditions issued in 1957 a collectors guide booklet, which more or less followed, in much reduced form, the outline of Ó Súilleabháin's *Handbook of Irish Folklore*. The foreword by Estyn Evans explained that 'the story of the kings and battles is in the history books, but the history of the countryside cannot be written unless we have the information we are now seeking.' In a brief section on 'Historical and Local Traditions', collectors were directed to inquire about ancient families, landlords, generals, saints, and clergymen and were then asked generally: 'do you know any stories about famous people or battles in your area?'. Rebels were not included. As a result, only one submission from Antrim and another from Down referred to 1798.[157]

A folklore notebook submitted by Miss A. M. Chestnutt of Gracehill, country Antrim (3 km west of Ballymena), dwelt on the experiences of the local Moravian congregation in 1798. The impact of the violent events of the rebellion and post-rebellion insurgency on this small community had been first recorded in the diaries of the Gracehill Moravian Church.[158] Nearly three decades after the rebellion, the recollections of an 'intelligent female' from Gracehill appeared in a Quaker history of 1798 (that shared the Moravian adherence to pacifism). A third edition of this popular history added in 1828 the recollections of Rev. C. Ignatius La Trobe, Secretary of the Moravian Missions. These personal accounts were republished several times over the nineteenth century.[159] The narrative submitted in 1959 to the Northern Ireland folklore scheme described how, when the rebellion arrived in 'Orange Antrim and Down', the 'Croppies' intimidated 'many neighbourhoods to demand money, and arms, and many innocent people were killed'. It recalled that the Moravian brethren of Gracehill, except from one individual, refused to join the rebellion, but still offered shelter to fugitive Catholic and Presbyterian United Irishmen from Ballymena, who feared government retribution.[160]

The Moravian account was presented as an oral tradition, suggesting that memory of 1798 had been retained in the neutral, though essentially loyal, community of Gracehill. Upon examination, however, it transpires that it had been copied verbatim, and without acknowledgement, from the text of a lecture on the history of Gracehill, given by Brother James Mitchell in February 1943. The lecture had been supplemented by archival material, provided by Brother John Berry and was made available locally in printed form, with 140 duplicated copies distributed in 1949 and a further 200 in 1950. It follows that the submission to the Northern Ireland folklore scheme was less an indication of the tenacity of oral traditions from the late eighteenth century than of the reception of local-community history in the mid-twentieth century.[161]

[157] Committee on Ulster Folklife and Traditions, *Ulster Folklife and Traditions: Collectors Guide*, with foreword by E. Estyn Evans (Cultra, Co. Down: Ulster Folk and Transport Museum, 1976; orig. edn 1957).

[158] *The 1798 Rebellion as Recorded in the Diaries of Gracehill Moravian Church* (Newtownabbey: Moravian History Magazine, 1998), pp. 7–20.

[159] Thomas Hancock, *The Principles of Peace Exemplified in the Conduct of the Society of Friends in Ireland, During the Rebellion of the Year 1798: With Some Preliminary and Concluding Observations*, 3rd edn, Part 2 (London: R. Clay, 1828; orig. edn 1825), pp. 40–2. This enhanced third edition was republished in London in 1838, 1839, 1844, and 1868 and was also published in the United States (appearing in Philadelphia in 1838 and in Boston in 1838 and 1843).

[160] UFTM V-12-5/11-13. My thanks to Linda Ballard, former Curator of Folklife, Collections and Interpretation at the Ulster Folk and Transport Museum, for granting me access to the notebooks.

[161] Reproduced in James Mitchell, *A History of Gracehill* (Gracehill: s.n., 1984; orig. edn 1977), pp. 24–5.

Conversely, another short entry on 1798 that appeared towards the end of Chestnutt's notebook included a local tradition about James Raphael of Galgorm (3 km west of Ballymena), who was killed at the Market House in Ballymena. As Raphael was a loyalist, the manner of his death could be recorded explicitly on his grave and indeed the family memorial at the old graveyard of Kirkinriola in Ballymena lists James as 'shot in Ballymena during the Irish Rebellion, 1798'. His death was mentioned in the mid-nineteenth century in the local history of *Old Ballymena* and was recalled again towards the end of the century in Rev. W. S. Smith's collection of 'Memories of '98'. Orange traditions subsequently recalled that Raphael was killed defending the Market House.[162] Chestnutt's account reflected the ambiguity of memories of internecine conflict in the Turn-Out, noting that 'it was never established who had done the deed' but it was 'generally supposed to be a man from the Braid, who was connected by marriage with Mr Raphael'.[163]

More in line with the expectations of the folklore scheme, William McMillan of the townland of Drumaghlis, near Crossgar, county Down (5 km east of Ballynahinch) submitted in June 1959 a notebook in which he claimed that he 'gave the true facts for I heard and seen a lot these last fifty years and more' and added that 'what I didn't know I got from older reliable people.' Commenting on 'the troubled times of 98', McMillan referred to the Battle of Ballynahinch and to the ambush at Saintfield, where rebels opened fire on a party of English soldiers in the York Fencibles. Although this incident was barely noticed in official history, its repercussions had apparently continued to plague the local community for some decades. McMillan was told by an old man that 'for years after this happened a man from Saintfield couldn't get a job in England on account of this tragedy.'[164]

In order to supplement the relatively slim volume of folklore accounts received from the volunteer collectors, an attempt was made to collect folklore through the schools, emulating the enormously successful School Scheme that the Irish Folklore Commission had conducted in association with the Irish National Teacher's Organisation during the school year of 1937–8. That folklore scheme had systematically covered the twenty-six counties of independent Ireland and yielded, among other subjects, extensive folk history accounts, with numerous traditions of Ninety-Eight. To facilitate the northern initiative, the Committee on Ulster Folklife and Traditions issued an abridged version of its guide for collectors, and asked teachers 'to allow the children to devote certain of their composition periods to local subjects'. The list of proposed subjects barely covered historical traditions and rebellions were of course not mentioned. Accordingly, the participating pupils in Northern Ireland did not submit any folklore traditions on 1798.[165]

---

[162] *Old Ballymena* (1857 edn), p. 34; *UJA*, 2nd ser., 1, no. 4 (1895): pp. 287–8; Brown, *Orangeism around Ballymena*, Part I, p. 12. For the Raphael family memorial see the entry on Kirkinriola on the website of the Braid Mid-Antrim Museum; <www.thebraid.com/pre-reformation-trail.aspx?title= kirkinriola>.

[163] UFTM V-12-5/46-47.   [164] UFTM V-16-2/25, 65 and 83–4.

[165] *Ulster Folklife and Traditions* (Belfast: Committee on Ulster Folklife and Traditions, n.d.); see also K. M. Harris, 'The Schools' Collection', *Ulster Folklife*, 3 (1957): pp. 8–13; K. M. Harris, 'Extracts from the Committee's Collection', *Ulster Folklife*, 4 (1958): pp. 37–49. Cf. Beiner, *Remembering the Year of the French*, pp. 54–9.

As opposed to the implicitly nationalist agenda of the Irish Folklore Commission, which encouraged documentation of historical traditions of Ninety-Eight, the Committee on Ulster Folklife and Traditions was clearly not geared to recording recollections of rebellion. Protestant unionists avoided the subject and northern Catholic nationalists were reluctant to trust a state-sponsored agency with their memories. Nevertheless, traditions missed by folklore collectors were still extant, often in fragmented form. The local historian Cahal Dallat, a schoolteacher in Ballycastle, county Antrim, recalled that in his youth, around the middle of the twentieth century, he heard numerous versions of a tradition about a fugitive United Irishman who took refuge in a cave at Port Calliagh, in the cliffs on the Antrim coast, and was provided with supplies by his sweetheart, until he could escape to Donegal and from there emigrate to America. Dallat noted that in different tellings of the story the name of the protagonist varied—Robert McNemaire, Robert McNair, Hughie McNair, or Hughie McMair—and he came to realize that this was a mechanism of concealing his identity, as 'even one hundred and fifty years after the event the matter was still "sub rosa".'[166]

In an article on 'a County Down incident of 1798', published in a local nationalist newspaper in 1950, a writer from Dromara stated that he 'has vivid recollections of sitting at the fireside, as a youth, on many a winters evening listening with delight to the recital of these tales':

> Some of them, or fragments of them, still survive in this area, from which contingents of 'United Men' went to join the Insurgents at the Battle of Ballynahinch. Few of them, however, have been recorded, except where they are commemorated in songs or ballads made by local poets or ballad makers—songs which, until quite recently, were much in favour at local gatherings, both private and public. Unfortunately, most of the old people who knew them have died out and only disconnected and varied versions of them now remain.[167]

The recounting of oral traditions about the rebellion was not limited to Catholic-nationalist areas. Occasional articles in provincial unionist newspapers reveal that folklore of the Turn-Out also persisted in the Presbyterian communities of north-east Ulster.

At a local level, 1798 was often recalled through the continued preservation of artefacts, identified as relics of the rebellion. For example, a table on which it was believed that an attempt had been made to resuscitate the corpse of Henry Joy McCracken was displayed from 1912 at the Londonderry Arms Hotel in Carnlough, county Antrim (18 km north of Larne, on the coastline). The proprietor, Mary Anne Rafferty, had inherited the table from her father, the owner of the Bambridge public house in Belfast, and would frequently retell the tradition behind the relic, up until her death at an advanced age in 1928.[168] Another souvenir table, on which it was said that Henry Munro had dined prior to his execution, was kept near Lisburn. It was housed at Ingram, the home of the Johnson-Smyth family, relatives of Rev. Snowden Cupples,

---

[166] Cahal Dallat, 'A Ballycastle Story of the 1798 Rebellion', *The Glynns*, 26 (1998): pp. 83–6. For brief biographical information on Dallat see *Irish News*, 4 August 2007, p. 3.

[167] *Fermanagh Herald*, 22 April 1950, p. 3.

[168] *Larne Times*, 14 July 1934, p. 6; see also Cahal Dallat, "'98 Rebellion in Glanarm and Glencoy', *The Glynns*, 27 (1999), p. 31. In 1967, the table was exhibited at the Ulster Museum; *Irish Times*, 25 August 1967, p. 11.

who ministered to Munro in his final hours.[169] The function of such *aides-mémoire* in retaining memory in conditions of social forgetting can be demonstrated with regards to the revival of remembrance of the '98 folk heroine Betsy Gray.

The church architect Denis O'Donoghue Hanna, a Protestant (Church of Ireland) liberal unionist from Belfast, recalled how as a child his father had taken him to a cottage near Six Road Ends in county Down, which was believed locally to have been the home of Betsy Gray. A 'weather-beaten old man', claiming to be a relative of the heroine, showed them various relics and recounted 'tales of hidden pikes, of spies, and the morning when the word went round, the United Irishmen were out, and the green flag was unfurled at Ballynahinch'.[170] The elderly man was probably George Gray McCartney [also spelt MacCartney], who together with his brother James had been photographed beside their collection of 1798 memorabilia in the late nineteenth century, at which time a postcard was made of 'Betsy Gray's Cottage' (Fig. 6.2).[171]

Hanna was left with a fascination of Betsy Gray and at the age of 17 (*c*.1918), still 'fervently in love with the memory of this girl', he visited the site known as her burial place, 'history-book in hand' (by which he probably meant Lyttle's novel *Betsy Gray*). In his book *The Face of Ulster*—published in 1952 in the popular Batsford *Face of Britain* series and reviewed favourably in the nationalist press—Hanna included several references to sites associated with the United Irishmen. He claimed that 'many

Fig. 6.2. Betsy Gray memorabilia

Late nineteenth-century photograph of George and James Gray Macartney outside 'Betsy Gray's cottage' at Six Road Ends, county Down, with a collection of memorabilia supposedly from 1798 that had been preserved in their family.

Courtesy of the Deputy Keeper of the Records, Public Record Office of Northern Ireland, MS T1295/2.

---

[169] *Lisburn Herald and Antrim and Down Advertiser*, 11 April 1953, p. 3.
[170] *Belfast Telegraph*, 20 July 1956, p. 4. For bibliographical information see Dictionary of Irish Architects; <www.dia.ie/architects/view/2376/HANNA-DENISO'DONOGHUE>.
[171] PRONI T1295/1-2. A photo of the postcard appeared in *Mourne Observer*, 11 August 1967, p. 4.

Irishmen who to-day consider themselves stalwart supporters of the British Empire, look over their shoulders with pride at the days of '98.' Upon discussing Betsy Gray, he wondered 'why Ulster has never raised a monument to her name'. This off-the-cuff reflection inadvertently revealed that the monument that had been erected half a century earlier and its destruction in an outburst of centennial decommemorating had already been forgotten. In absence of a public monument, carefully preserved relics served as *aides-mémoire* in more private settings.[172]

When George Gray McCartney passed away at the age of 72, in November 1916, the contents of his cottage—including heirlooms associated with Betsy Gray—were sold by auction, and Hanna's father purchased a set of six wooden chairs. Sensing the incongruity of keeping furniture from the home of United Irishmen in a household with a 'somewhat Redcoat family tradition', Hanna presented 'Betsy Gray's chairs' to Bangor Borough Council in 1956 and expressed the hope that 'the old cottage should be done up as a National Museum and the chairs go home again.' The premises had meanwhile fallen into neglect. A contemporary account noted that it was used to store farm implements and that 'the thatch has been roofed over with corrugated iron and the windows are missing.' The councillors debated the possibility of 'removing the remains of the cottage and having it re-erected' on the grounds of Bangor Castle, but concluded that this was not feasible.[173]

Bangor alderman Charles F. Milligan had also visited the cottage in his youth and had taken a photograph of its interior. He argued that members of the borough council should arrange for a local museum to preserve the relics associated with Betsy Gray, even if 'they might not agree with her political views'. The fact that local politicians in a unionist constituency were willing to consider the conservation of the folk heritage of the rebellion is in itself telling. Nevertheless, when the mayor of Bangor made a public appeal for the collection of these relics, the only item to be handed in was 'a muzzle loader used in the Irish Rebellion and believed to be in some way associated with Betsy Gray'. People were apparently unwilling to let go of the souvenirs in their private possession and put them on display.[174]

In 1954, when the unionist borough council of Enniskillen, county Fermanagh, decided to name a road bridge after Queen Elizabeth, nationalists protested and argued that it should be named instead after their revered Elizabeth—Betsy Gray. The local nationalist press lambasted the unionist *Impartial Reporter* for its ignorance in asking 'Who was Betsy Gray?' and tensions escalated in the lead up to the dedication of the new road by the Duke of Edinburgh, which had to be held under heavy police security. Commemorative competitiveness was apparent in repeated acts of vandalism that defaced signs with the official name, and nationalists made a point of referring to the

---

[172] Denis O'Donoghue Hanna, *The Face of Ulster: Antrim, Londonderry, Fermanagh, Tyrone, Armagh, Monaghan, Cavan, Donegal and Down* (London and New York: Batsford, 1952), p. 124; for other references to 1798 see pp. 7, 57, and 108. For nationalist reviews see *Ulster Herald*, 12 April 1952, p. 6; *Irish Press*, 13 May 1952, p. 4.

[173] *Belfast Telegraph*, 20 July 1956, p. 4; *County Down Spectator and Ulster Standard*, 28 July 1956, p. 4; *Irish Digest*, 60, no. 3 (September 1957): pp. 65–7; see also Dickson, *Revolt in the North*, p. 56.

[174] *County Down Spectator and Ulster Standard*, 20 May 1950, p. 9; see also McCoy, *Ulster's Joan of Arc*, pp. 51–3. For biographical information on Milligan see his memoir, written at the age of 87; Charles F. Milligan, *My Bangor from the 1890's* (Bangor: Spectator Newspapers, 1975).

place defiantly as the Betsy Gray Road.[175] In public, unionists adamantly opposed any public commemoration of 1798. However, in the unionist districts of county Down, the local heroine was still held in esteem.

By the 1950s, the nineteenth-century novels about 1798, even those that had been published in several editions, were no longer readily available. When visiting Ireland, 70-year-old Jane Bowden of Vancouver in Canada, an emigrant from the area of Ballynahinch whose grandfather—Rev. John Nicholson of Larne—had a been a chaplain to the rebels in Antrim, could not find a copy of McHenry's *The Insurgent Chief* or of Lyttle's *Betsy Gray*.[176] In August 1960, 'in response to many requests from readers near and far', the *Newtownards Spectator and Donaghadee Review*—a unionist broadsheet read in north-east county Down, decided to republish *Betsy Gray*. Although it appeared in a newspaper that had just given considerable coverage to the Orange celebrations of the Twelfth of July, the serialization of the popular '98 novel was prefaced by an anti-Partitionist, Rev. Albert H. McElroy, the Non-Subscribing Presbyterian minister of Newtownards.

McElroy, an early campaigner for Catholic civil rights, whose 'chosen legacy from the past was the spirit of '98', was an advocate of what he called 'that other Ulster Heritage, which some would like to suppress'. In 1953, he left the Labour party, which he found too conservative, to become chairman of the Ulster Liberal Association and President of the Northern Ireland Liberal Party. Three unsuccessful attempts to get elected for parliament did not diminish his commitment to breaking 'the Tory monopoly in the politics of Northern Ireland'. His preface to *Betsy Gray* argued that 'the memory of the men of '98 should underline the basic facts of life that there can never be rights without corresponding duties.' He was convinced that 'a new generation of liberal-minded young people' will reclaim the memory of Betsy Gray and 'march proudly to the long neglected graves of Porter, of Hope, of Henry Joy, of William Orr and of the legion of others who sacrificed their all in the age-old struggle for the cause of human freedom and dignity and true patriotism'.[177] McElroy's brazen rhetoric did not deter the unionist readership of the *Newtownards Spectator*. The *Betsy Gray* series ran from 12 August to 2 December 1960 and local journalists later recalled that it 'sent the circulation soaring'.[178]

One of many appreciative readers, Ernest Lowell, who had first read the book as a teenager, followed the weekly episodes and kept 'every copy of the story folded up and left past', noting that 'the people of Six Road Ends and surrounding district still cherish the name of Betsy Gray.'[179] Other enthusiastic readers shared their knowledge of local traditions and admitted that they kept relics of the rebellion in their homes.

---

[175] *Fermanagh Herald*, 27 November 1954, p. 4 [published on that date also in other provincial nationalist newspapers, including *Donegal News* and *Derry People and Tirconail News*]; 11 and 25 December 1954, pp. 5 and 3 (respectively); *Irish Press*, 24 April 1956, p. 1.

[176] *Larne Times*, 29 March 1951, p. 4.

[177] *Newtownards Spectator*, 12 August 1960, p. 7; also *Donegal News*, 30 December 1961, p.3; *Irish Times*, 23 November 1965, p. 1 and 11; 21 March 1967, p. 11; 29 November 1966, p. 8; 15 and 19 March 1975, pp. 11 and 13 (respectively).

[178] See the exchange of reminisces, posted in 21–22 January 2011 on 'TheCopyboys: The Weblog Site for Northern Ireland Retired Journalists'; <http://graham_mckenzie.typepad.com/thecopyboys/2011/01/mr-hack-no-94.html>.

[179] Ernest Lowry Papers, PRONI T2794/2.

Eddie Floyd, a retired postman from Kircubbin (16 km south of Newtownards), who was known to be 'deeply interested in the history of the Ards and Irish folklore for a long number of years', revealed that 'he has in his possession several relics of the Battle of Ballynahinch, including the sword which is believed to be the one cut down for Betsy Gray by the blacksmith, Mat McClenaghan' (Fig. 6.3a).[180] 'Betsy Gray's sword' had briefly been put on display in June 1908, at an exhibition of antiquities held in Belfast to mark the formation of the Presbyterian Historical Society of Ireland, but had since been kept out of public view.[181] The society would later acquire other artefacts associated with famous figures from 1798, including 'the pike wielded by the famous Jemmy Hope' and a dress sword that had belonged to Rev. Samuel Barber.[182]

H. J. Macartney of Bangor, whose grandfather had provided Lyttle with family traditions about Betsy Gray, wrote to express his appreciation for the novel's re-publication, noting that 'many people have asked me if I could procure a copy of the book, but I was unable to do so as it was out of print.' Macartney revealed that his family 'retains many of her possessions, including a set of Pewter plates which with other valuables were hidden in the well for safety when she and her brother George left home during the rebellion'. Although it had been rumoured that these artefacts had been taken to America, they were found to be in the possession of his niece, Elizabeth (Betsy) Gray McCartney, who still resided in the area.[183] Sometime afterwards, 'relics of Betsy Gray' were put on display at the Church Hall in Newtownards.[184] Loyalists were perturbed by the public attention showered on the memory of the rebellion. The year after the publication of the *Betsy Gray* series in the *Newtownards Spectator*, the Orange Order held in 1961 a 12 July celebration at Ednavady Hill, on the battlefield of Ballynahinch, offering a triumphalist demonstration of commemorative competitiveness.[185]

In consequence of the death of the nationalist politician Joseph Connellan in 1967, the *Frontier Sentinel and Down, Armagh and Louth Advertiser*, of which he had been editor, published posthumously his articles on 'Newry District and the Men of 'Ninety-Eight'.[186] Whereas this series appealed to a local nationalist readership, unionists in the area also continued to show interest in traditions of the rebellion. Jim Hawthorne, founding editor of the *Mourne Observer*—a unionist newspaper with a readership spread across south county Down—responded to 'many requests over the past few years' and decided in July 1967 to serialize Lyttle's *Betsy Gray* once again. In addition to reproducing the text of the novel, Hawthorne promised to include 'photographs of some of the relics, which are still to the fore, and of places mentioned'. This announcement heralded an ambitious local folklore collection project. The *Mourne Observer* made it known that it was 'interested to learn of relics or documents and of matters of local interest concerning the stirring events of '98.'[187] Subsequent issues repeatedly asked readers if their 'family has a story which has been passed down from the 1798 period'

---

[180] *Newtownards Spectator*, 26 August 1960, p. 7; also *Mourne Observer*, 18 October 1968, p. 10.
[181] *Journal of the Presbyterian Historical Society*, 4 (1908): pp. 142–3.
[182] Aiken McClelland, 'The Treasures of the Presbyterian Historical Society', *Bulletin of the Presbyterian Historical Society of Ireland*, no. 1 (December 1970): pp. 12–13.
[183] *Newtownards Spectator*, 9 and 23 September 1960, p. 5; also *Mourne Observer*, 16 August 1968, p. 9.
[184] *Sunday Independent*, 7 July 1963, p. 12.
[185] Ernest Lowry Papers, PRONI T2794/2 (p. 2).
[186] *Frontier Sentinel*, 26 August–25 November 1967.
[187] *Mourne Observer*, 7 July 1967, p. 1.

(a)

(b)

(c)

Fig. 6.3. Relics from Ballynahinch

6.3a. Eddie Floyd from Kircubbin, 6.3b. Miss N. Browne of Ballynahinch, and 6.3c. Wallace Mitchell of Corbet near Banbridge exhibiting weapons of the battle that had been preserved locally as treasured relics of Ninety-Eight. Originally published in *Newtownards Spectator*, 26 August 1960 (Floyd); *Mourne Observer*, 18 October 1968 (Browne), 28 July 1967 (Mitchell).

and put out reminders that the newspaper was 'still seeking information on historical facts and folklore relating to the 1798 period', stressing that 'original information concerning local folklore and relics' would be appreciated.[188] The popular response was overwhelming.

The *Mourne Observer*'s serialization of *Betsy Gray* commenced on 21 July 1967 and continued till 25 October 1968. The very same issue which launched this series on 1798 also devoted a full-spread page to the 'Great and Glorious "Twelfth"' and serialization of the novel continued alongside regular reportage on the activities of local Orange lodges. Constant reaffirmation of loyalism did not override interest in the memory of the rebellion. The chapters of *Betsy Gray* were supplemented with numerous accounts of local recollections submitted by readers, which made apparent the extent to which memories of the United Irishmen had been privately retained and kept alive by unionists.

Individuals from across county Down were photographed for the *Mourne Observer* with relics that had been preserved in their family. These featured an assortment of militaria, which was said to have seen action in the rebellion, and also included several apocryphal curiosities, such as 'the pistol believed to have been carried by Betsy Gray at the Battle of Ballynahinch'. Arthur Davidson of Spa, near Ballynahinch, posed 'with a military sword reputed to have been used at the Battle of Ballynahinch'. Miss N. Browne of Ballynahinch, whose father had 'collected items of historical interest', was photographed with two pikes and a cannon ball found near the battlefield (Fig. 6.3b). George Burrowes, a justice of the peace, showed two additional cannon balls that had been lodged in the thatch of his house in Drumhill, Ballynahinch. It turned out that James McKinney of Loughinisland (8 km south-east of Ballynahinch) kept a veritable museum of guns from the time of the rebellion. Wallace Mitchell of Corbet, near Banbridge (25 km west of Ballynahinch) brandished a 'well-preserved pike', which had been handed down from his great-grandfather, Joseph Richard Hooke, and was 'one of his mother's proudest possessions' (Fig. 6.3c).[189]

In the district of Saintfield, the correspondent of the *Mourne Observer* 'met dozens of people with a keen interest in the '98 period and with a remarkable knowledge of the Battle which took place there on 9th June 1798'. Mrs S. Grant showed him a sword and bayonet that her son Billy had found when playing in the area (he had since grown up and joined the Royal Ulster Constabulary). The garage owner J. Kinghan had 'inherited an interest in history from his late father' and owned 'a number of relics of the '98 period', including a flintlock pistol and gun. Several souvenir weapons were retained in the First Presbyterian Church in Saintfield, including a sword, gun, and pike head. The pike had been found in the thatch of an old house in Lessans (2 km north of Saintfield) and was given for safekeeping to Rev. Stewart Dickson, who was known as an unapologetic liberal. During his fifty-six years as minister of First Saintfield, Rev. Dickson (who passed away in 1949 at the age of 90) had refused to join the Orange Order and was held up as an example that 'Saintfield people don't change side overnight.'[190]

---

[188] *Mourne Observer*, 3 May and 19 July 1968, p. 9.

[189] *Mourne Observer*, 7 July 1967, p.1 (Davidson); 28 July 1967, p. 5 (Mitchell); 26 July 1968, p. 3 (Betsy Gray's pistol); 20 September 1968, p. 9 (McKinney); 18 October 1968, p. 10 (Browne and Burrowes).

[190] *Mourne Observer*, 19 April 1968, p. 3. For Rev. Stewart Dickson see *Northern Whig*, 3 June 1949, p. 5; *Mourne Observer*, 12 April 1968, p. 9.

Reflecting the complexity of the Turn-Out, not only rebel arms but also loyalist memorabilia was preserved, including items belonging to regular army units, militia, and the yeomanry.[191] Ambivalence is particularly apparent in controversy over recollections of the most notorious local atrocity committed by rebels—the burning of the house of Hugh McKee near Saintfield, in which twelve people perished. Loyalists refused to allow the killings to be forgotten. The key of the burned house was kept by Robert McKee of Carricknaveigh (4 km west of Saintfield). An article submitted to the *Mourne Observer* praised the victims for their steadfast loyalism and declared that 'McKee would be a True Blue today.' The author, who called himself 'The Student', used information from R. M. Sibbet's history of Orangeism to question the way in which the episode was described in the *Betsy Gray* novel and to claim that 'obviously not all United Irishmen were as noble as Lyttle would have us believe.' To another reader it seemed that this was an attempt 'to whitewash the unfortunate McKees', who had been targeted because of their involvement in counterinsurgency. He nonetheless distanced the act of retaliation from the people of the locality, insisting that 'most of those accused of the murder were not natives of the district.' In response, 'The Student' insisted that although McKee had provided the authorities with information, 'he was not by any means a "secret" or "sly" informer.' Clearly, this contested episode continued to trouble social memory.[192]

The *Mourne Observer* had promised its readers both 'stories of bravery' and 'of informers and treachery'. The most notorious of the informers was John Edward Newell of Downpatrick, described by Madden as 'the worst, the most thoroughly debased, the vilest of the vile'. Newell, who was fearful of giving evidence openly, eventually lost faith in his handlers and issued in 1798 an apologia for his activities as a 'celebrated informer'. He subsequently disappeared in mysterious circumstances, probably falling prey to an assassination by United Irishmen.[193] Local traditions would identify the place where Newell was supposedly shot as Holestone, near Doagh in county Antrim, and claim that he was buried near Templepatrick.[194] The *Mourne Observer* reassured readers that 'there are many instances of how nothing but ill-luck came to those who informed the military authorities of the plans of the United Irishmen.' In folk history, informers—such as Nicholas Maginn [Mageean] of Saintfield, who 'later took to drink and finally died in jail from his debts'—were duly punished by providence for their wrongdoings.[195] In reality, the misfortune of informers was often the outcome of social ostracizing.

Relying on the recollections of the local historian Hugh McCall, Lyttle described the comeuppance of the yeomen who had arrested the insurgent general Henry Munro: 'they afterwards became miserably poor, and the longest lived of the four died a pauper.' It was said that Billy Holmes, the man held responsible for disclosing Munro's hideout, 'was despised for his deceit, and denounced for his treachery, and he was held in scorn and contempt by people of every class and creed in his neighbourhood,

---

[191] *Mourne Observer*, 5 April and 18 October 1968, pp. 9 and 10 (respectively).
[192] *Mourne Observer*, 5 and 19 April 1968, pp. 9 and 3 (respectively) and 13 September 1968, p. 10.
[193] Edward Newell, *The Apostacy of Newell, Containing the Life and Confessions* [sic] *of That Celebrated Informer* (London: s.n., 1798); Madden, *The United Irishmen*, 2nd ser., vol. 1 (1843), pp. 347–50; Grimshaw, *Incidents Recalled*, pp. 34–5; see also Bartlett, *Revolutionary Dublin*, pp. 37–8.
[194] *An Phoblacht*, 13 August 1998.
[195] *Mourne Observer*, 30 August 1968, p. 3.

shunned in private life, and avoided in the Market Place'. The stigma of informing was remembered for generations and Lyttle claimed that the descendants of Holmes 'have the slur cast in their teeth'.[196] John J. McMullan of Clonvaraghan (10 km south-west of Ballynahinch) repeated to the *Mourne Observer* a story told by his granduncle, who had seen a beggar woman called Holmes castigated: 'go home for you betrayed Monro.' It was recalled that the family had eventually lost their land, which was considered the ultimate punishment in Irish rural culture, though 'an old-timer in Ballynahinch' soberly pointed out that 'people have been auctioned out of farms, and who are we to say that that particular incident influenced their destinies?'.[197]

In a public culture of social forgetting, vindictiveness was long retained in private and there was no forgiveness for relatives of those accused of betrayal. The family of James Little—a yeoman from Annahilt (8 km north-west of Ballynahinch) reputed to have been involved in the killing of Betsy Grey—'became most unpopular'. Hugh McCann of Drumkeeragh (5 km south-west of Ballynahinch) was told by his father, the local historian Terence McCann (born around 1850), that 'the Parishioners of Annahilt Church wouldn't sit in the same pew as the Littles, and that their children were stoned at school.' By the 1960s, the desecration of the Betsy Gray memorial in 1898 was remembered as a shameful deed and it was believed that 'many of the families of those men who played principal roles in the destruction of Betsy Gray's grave 70 years ago have also had bad luck!'[198]

In addition to collecting living traditions, the *Mourne Observer* series included 'Gleanings from the Robb Manuscripts', which showcased extracts from the writings of the local historian Colin Johnston Robb of Timpany, just outside Ballynahinch (and previously a resident of Loughall in county Armagh) (Fig. 6.4). Robb, a Church of Ireland Protestant, was an architect who specialized in church renovations. His passion for the past was sparked when as a young man, in the early twentieth century, he had 'heard his elders discuss the stormy events of '98'. His grandfather, who died in 1912, was familiar with traditions of the Battle of Ballynahinch, having personally known 'many descendants of those who fought in the battle'. Robb's interest in the rebellion was enthused by an acquaintance with Bigger, which inspired him to become an antiquary much in the same mould. Many of the traditions that he wrote about can be traced to sources collected by Bigger and, like his mentor, Robb would come to be recognized as 'a foremost authority on matters relating to the '98 and 1803 periods'.[199]

Over the course of six decades of free-lance journalism, Robb claimed to have 'written thousands of articles in the columns of the daily press and historical and archaeological journals'.[200] Even if this estimate is somewhat exaggerated, his actual output was undoubtedly impressive. He began publishing on 1798 already in the

---

[196] McCall, *Ireland and Her Staple Manufactures*, 2nd edn (1865), p. 129; Lyttle, *Betsy Gray*, ch. 38 ('The Betrayal of Munro').

[197] *Mourne Observer*, 30 August 1968, p. 3.

[198] *Mourne Observer*, 30 August 1968, p. 3; republished in Lyttle, *Betsy Gray*, 1968 edn, appendix, p. 162.

[199] *Irish Independent*, 18 June 1962, pp. 10 and 11 March 1976, p. 9; *Mourne Observer*, 12 July 1968, p. 5; *Down Recorder*, 23 April 1971, p. 3; *Irish Press*, 17 March 1976, p. 6. For additional bibliographical information see Dictionary of Irish Architects; <www.dia.ie/architects/view/4555/ROBB-COLINJOHNSTON>.

[200] *Down Recorder*, 9 October 1970.

Fig. 6.4. Colin Johnston Robb

Originally inspired by Francis Joseph Bigger, the local historian Colin Johnston Robb (1901–76) of Timpany, near Ballynahinch, was recognized as a leading authority on traditions of the Turn-Out, though his writings were mostly neglected by scholarly historians. Photograph originally published in *Mourne Observer*, 12 July 1968.

Reproduced by the National Library of Ireland with permission from the *Mourne Observer*.

1920s, but first made a mark in 1935 with an essay on Betsy Gray, which appeared in the *Irish News* under the pseudonym 'Lover of Reform' (an allusion to Robb's liberal politics). From then, till his death in 1976, he published numerous contributions on the rebellion in Ulster, including an essay in the sesquicentenary booklet issued by the 1798 Commemoration Committee in 1948.[201] In his writings, Robb was attuned to the intrinsic complexities and ambiguities of the memory of the Turn-Out. His great-great-grandfather, Captain James Robb, had been a yeomanry commander, while his

---

[201] *Irish News*, 13 June 1935, p. 4; Colin Johnston Robb, 'When the United Irish Society Was Born', in *Ninety-Eight*, edited by Seamus McKearney (Belfast: The 1798 Commemoration Committee, 1948), pp. 6–9. A scrapbook of undated articles by Robb relating to Ballynahinch and the 1798 rebellion is preserved in Aiken McClelland Papers, PRONI D3815/I/5.

brother, John Robb, had been a United Irish colonel, and according to family tradition the two siblings 'met in the heat of the battle in the market square of Ballynahinch'.[202]

In an article on the Battle of Ballynahinch from 1937, Robb explained that he had 'access to much historical data preserved in the muniment rooms of some well-known families, which have unreservedly been placed at the disposal of the writer'.[203] An article on Rev. James Porter, published in the September 1945 issue of *The Non-Subscribing Presbyterian*, stated that 'it is not our purpose to hackney the already published material, but to make public the contents of different original documents unknown to past historians.'[204] Nonetheless, a manuscript account that Robb acquired of the rebellion in the area of Larne, county Antrim, reveals the pervasive influence of printed sources on vernacular history, which is evident in references taken from the writings of Samuel McSkimin, Robert Magill Young, and Ethna Carbery.[205]

The extensive collections of local traditions scrupulously compiled by Robb included many curious items that had previously eluded other collectors. For example, he purchased in 1947 'the green dress worn at the Battle of Antrim in 1798 by Betty Haslet of Ballymena'. Elizabeth Haslet's father, the Presbyterian linen draper John Haslet, was known to be a United Irishman. The apocryphal story that 'she and her brother, Hood Haslet, were in the thick of the fight at Antrim and escaped' closely resembles the legend of Betsy Gray, though Betsy Haslet was said to have survived unharmed while Hood was later caught and severely flogged.[206] As Robb rarely provided a verifiable provenance for the unique items in his possession, his attribution of singular traditions to untraceable sources raises doubts concerning their authenticity. For example, he reproduced a portrait of Betsy Gray, claiming that it was a facsimile of a miniature painted by the informer Newell that had appeared in a booklet titled *Out in '98*, supposedly issued by Bigger in the 1920s. However, in absence of any record of such a publication, the attribution to Newell is questionable and it is unlikely that the image is indeed that of the heroine.[207]

Robb's work was largely ignored by academic historians. The antiquarian mode of history which he espoused did not fare well after the professionalization of Irish history in the 1930s. A new generation of local historians, many of whom held university postgraduate degrees, were reluctant to endorse publications without citations and rejected claims that were not thoroughly substantiated. The Armagh historian Monsignor Réamonn Ó Muirí, a long-time editor of the journal *Ulster Local Studies*, complained that Robb 'is always tantalisingly vague in his references'; the Saintfield historian Aiken McClelland pointed out discrepancies in Robb's writings; and Kenneth Robinson, a member of the Bangor Historical Society in county Down, asserted that

[202] *County Down Spectator*, 14 August 1937, p. 12; *Irish Independent*, 19 July 1946, p. 4; *Down Recorder*, 6 June 1971, p. 3.
[203] *County Down Spectator and Ulster Standard*, 14 August 1937, p. 12 (later re-published in revised form in *Down Recorder*, 11 June 1971, p. 3).
[204] Quoted in Samuel Bracegirdle, 'The Reverend James Porter of Greyabbey', *North Irish Roots*, 10, no. 1 (1999): pp. 20–2.
[205] 'The Oakboys, the Hearts of Steel the Volunteers and the United Irishmen of Larne and Neighbourhood', C. J. Robb Papers, PRONI D2095/18.
[206] *Irish Independent*, 22 May 1947, p. 6. Rev. Robert Magill recalled witnessing as a boy the flogging in Ballymena of Hood Haslet, who received 500 lashes; Young, *Ulster in '98*, p. 17.
[207] *Mourne Observer*, 5 July 1968, p. 5 (republished in Lyttle, *Betsy Gray*, 1968 edn, p. 159 and McCoy, *Ulster's Joan of Arc*, p. 6); Stewart, *Summer Soldiers*, p. 275n71; Séamas Ó Saothraí, *Heroines of 1798* (Bray, Co. Wicklow: Bray Heritage Centre, 1998), p. 36.

'Robb liked to mix his own imaginings with historical sources.'[208] Taking this criticism on board, an Irish-Canadian researcher writing about her ancestral home parish of Forkhill in county Armagh concluded that 'because Robb did not reveal his sources, his information cannot be considered reliable and cannot be incorporated into a scholarly study.'[209] Nonetheless, Robb contributed to the regeneration of tradition. In an article on Saintfield in '98', which had originally appeared in the 1920s and was republished in the unionist *Down Recorder* in 1971, he observed that 'the story of the events of 1798 are [sic] ever new and there has been a decided revival of interest by the younger generation of to-day.'[210] Through his many publications in the press, Robb was an active agent in this revival.

The 1967–8 *Betsy Gray* series proved to be so popular that immediately after its conclusion, the *Mourne Observer* issued a new edition of the novel with a forty-page appendix that included many of the additional items that had appeared in the newspaper. Since it was widely regretted that the novel 'has been virtually unobtainable for many years', its re-publication was received with appreciation across Ulster and it subsequently came to be considered the authoritative edition of the bestseller.[211] The book was prefaced by John Aiken McClelland, a curator and librarian at the Ulster Folk Museum and the former schoolmaster at Carricknaveagh Primary School (4 km west of Saintfield). As an enthusiastic local historian, Aiken McClelland was mainly preoccupied with Orangeism, yet he was a Presbyterian unionist who did not let his own membership of the Orange Order get in the way of his keen interest in traditions of 1798. Following his death in 1981, the *Mourne Observer* published the first issue of the Saintfield Heritage Society's journal, which included a short article by McClelland on the Battle of Saintfield, followed by a reading list on 'Saintfield and the '98', compiled by the Ballynahinch librarian Jack McCoy. This publication was intended to facilitate further local studies on the rebellion.[212]

Although still excluded from official state culture, memory of 1798 seemed to be on the verge of coming out in the open. But this was not to be the case. Following the outbreak of mass riots in 1969, Northern Ireland plunged into thirty years of violent civil conflict, known as the Troubles, which would reinforce reticence. Collecting folklore in south county Down in 1978, Michael J. Murphy recalled the accounts of Ninety-Eight that he had previously heard in the area. The persecution of Presbyterian republicans in the past now seemed to mirror the contemporary mistreatment of Catholic nationalists at the hands of the police and the army: 'and the Yeos and the Welsh Horse and Ancient Britons, harassing, intimidating, smash[ing] furniture and

[208] Réamonn Ó Muirí, 'Lt John Lindley St Leger, United Irishman', *Seanchas Ardmhacha*, 11, no. 1 (1983): p. 135; McClelland, 'Thomas Ledlie Birch, United Irishman', pp. 23n3, 26n10, and 31n34; Robinson, *Thomas Ledlie Birch*, p. 142.

[209] Kyla Madden, 'Ten Troubled Years: Settlement, Conflict and Rebellion in Forkhill, County Armagh, 1788–1798' (MA thesis: Department of History, Queen's University, Ontario, 1998), pp. vi. n8 and 97n69.

[210] *Down Recorder*, 4 June 1971, p. 3.

[211] *Derry People and Donegal News*, 23 November 1968, p. 9 (published also in *Fermanagh Herald*, *Strabane Chronicle*, and *Ulster Herald*). More recently, the 1968 expanded edition of *Betsy Gray* was made available online, courtesy of the <Lisburn.com> website (founded by Jim Collins): <www.lisburn.com/books/betsey_gray/betsy-gray1.htm>.

[212] *Saintfield Heritage*, 1 (1982): pp. 53–8. McClelland's essay drew upon a lecture that he had given in 1971; McClelland, *History of Saintfield and District*, pp. 6–9.

spilling crocks of milk, and inflicting injuries or fatalities with the current impunity'. Murphy's diary shows that he was disturbed by the sound of a low-flying helicopter, typical of British military involvement in Northern Ireland since the commencement of Operation Banner in August 1969. The present context of the Troubles quite literally impinged on remembrance of the past.[213] During these tense years, when talk of a republican rebellion could be misconstrued and associated with unlawful paramilitary activities, social forgetting reasserted its hold.

TROUBLED FORGETTING

Long before 1969, the term 'the Troubles' was already engrained in social memory as a familiar allusion to periods of strife. A Protestant family history of *Two Centuries of Life in Down, 1600–1800*, written in the early twentieth century, referred to the 1640s and the Cromwellian conquest of Ulster as 'the Time of the Troubles'.[214] Its author, John Stevenson, had previously translated the travelogue of the French émigré Chevalier de Latocnaye, from which he may have become familiar with the idiom, which had apparently entered popular parlance in the build-up to the 1798 rebellion.[215]

Travelling in the north-east of Ireland in 1797, de Latocnaye picked up on the term's colloquial use and repeatedly mentioned '*les troubles*' to describe the tense situation following the dragooning of Ulster under General Lake. He was struck by the ferocity of government intimidation that he encountered in Antrim. At the entrance to an inn in Newtownards, he read a notice warning the inhabitants that 'if any person fires again on the sentinel, orders will be given to burn the town.' From what he had heard en route, de Latocnaye expected to find Belfast 'on the eve of insurrection', but instead found its residents 'in a state of stupefaction the consequence of terror' and it seemed that 'it will be long ere the people of Belfast forget the terror.'[216] These apprehensions of brutal counter-revolutionary violence fed into the prememory that anticipated the memory of Ninety-Eight.

After the 1798 rebellion was suppressed, people began referring to the recent spate of violence as 'the Troubles'. In a letter to his brother in Pennsylvania, Henry Johnston of Loughbrickland in county Down (4 km south-east of Banbridge) wrote his recollections of the events that he had just witnessed:

> the low part of the county of Antrim was greatly involved in the Troubles, some killed in scrimmages with the military some tried and shot, some hanged and not ended yet . . . thank God the Troubles did not come just to our door, but much too near, one man out of this town was hang[e]d to [a] sign-post in Belfast.'[217]

[213] Journal entry for 22 April 1978, NFC 1925/5 and 9.
[214] John Stevenson, *Two Centuries of Life in Down, 1600–1800* (Belfast: McCaw, Stevenson and Orr, 1920), pp. 74–106.
[215] de Latocnaye, *A Frenchman's Walk through Ireland, 1796–7*, translated by John Stevenson (Belfast: McCaw, Stevenson, and Orr, and Dublin: Hodges Figgis, 1917).
[216] de Latocnaye, *Promenade d'un français dans l'Irlande*, vol. 3, pp. 281–2; for references to *des/les troubles* see 249, 283, 285, 289, 291, 293, 297, 298, and 300.
[217] Henry Johnston, Loughbrickland, County Down, to Moses Johnston, Northumberland, Pennsylvania, 11 May 1800, Johnston Family Papers, PRONI T3578/7; reproduced in Miller, *Irish Immigrants in the Land of Canaan*, pp. 37–8.

A few years later, Isabella Bryson of the parish of Bangor in county Down petitioned the Lord Lieutenant, seeking permission for her exiled husband to return home, as he had emigrated to America in June 1798, 'lest he might be induced to take any part in the troubles of those unhappy times'.[218]

As a euphemism, 'the Troubles' suited the culture of social forgetting. It was a characteristic understatement that obliquely designated a period of intense violence, while also masking the enormity of the carnage. The veteran rebel James Hope composed a satirical poem in which the rebellion appears as a divisive civil war from which England benefitted. The poem's title 'The Troubles' does not not give sufficient warning of its graphic depictions, which reveal the viciousness of the conflict:

> We fell to work, hammer and tongs,
> The Orange and Green both together,
> With sabres, with guns, pikes, and prongs
> Each party the other did leather.
> With slaughter we strewed the green plain,
> Our cannon the welkin made rattle,
> And furiously knocked out the brains
> Of men, women, children and cattle.[219]

The writers who documented the recollections of the generation that had lived through 'the Troubles' of 1798 made note of the use of the term and it subsequently entered into vernacular history.

Samuel McSkimin claimed that when Emmet's emissaries tried in 1803 to re-mobilize the United Irishmen, 'the "troubles" of that period were still fresh in the recollections of many'. Madden interviewed the elderly Israel Milliken, whom he described as 'a man not unacquainted with "the troubles" of that time'. The Lisburn historian Hugh McCall, who was acquainted with the family of Henry Munro, stated that the mother of the executed rebel general lived 'for many years after the "day of the trouble"'. A generation later, the widow of William Orr was described to Francis Joseph Bigger as 'a small, quiet, beautiful woman, who never took heart after the troubles'.[220]

In the nineteenth century, the term was adopted as a chronological landmark. Death notices published three decades after the rebellion noted that the deceased had lived through the 'troublesome period'. This formulation was used by the *Northern Whig* in an obituary for Luke Mullan Hope, the son of James Hope, which mentioned that as a young child he was left to be raised by a maternal uncle, hinting to the seldom-discussed repercussions of the rebellion for the dependents of rebels on the run, who had to leave their families to fend for themselves.[221] References could be more explicit in the case of loyalists. Reporting in 1831 on the death of James Edgar of Derry at the age of 86, the *Belfast News-Letter* acknowledged that 'he was for some time High Constable, particularly during the troublesome period of the rebellion of 1798.'[222]

---

[218] Robb family correspondence, PRONI T1454/3/1.
[219] Madden, *Literary Remains of the United Irishmen*, pp. 99–101.
[220] McSkimin, 'Secret History of the Irish Insurrection of 1803', p. 556; Madden, *The United Irishmen*, 2nd edn, 1st ser., vol. 1 (1857), p. 536; McCall, *Ireland and Her Staple Manufactures*, 2nd edn (1865), p. 134; Bigger, *Remember Orr*, p. 61.
[221] *Northern Whig*, 13 December 1827.
[222] *BNL*, 22 February 1831, p. 2.

498 *Forgetful Remembrance*

When Samuel and Anna Maria Hall travelled through Antrim in the 1840s, they heard recollections of events dated to 'a year, or maybe two, before the troubles'—described specifically as 'the ruction [insurrection] of 98'—and were also referred more generally to 'the times of the troubles'.[223] A description of the rebellion in Antrim, which appeared in a mid-nineteenth-century local history of 'Belfast as It Was', referred to the 'troubled times'.[224] Another variant of this term, used in the late nineteenth century, referred to 'the troublous times'.[225] Some decades later, 'the Troubles' would re-appear in the folk history of the early twentieth century in reference to the revolutionary period of the Anglo-Irish War and the War of Independence. The regeneration of the term made it a signifier for a cyclical notion of historical time, in which outbursts of violence recur periodically, each round carrying with it historical memories of previous bouts. In this way, memories of 1798 lay the ground for a subconscious prememory of the Troubles of the late twentieth century.[226]

Historians have not reached a consensus on the date on which the modern Troubles began. One possibility is the civil rights march from Belfast to Derry in the beginning of January 1969 that culminated with the notorious incident at Burntollet Bridge (4 January), which has been described by the historian Paul Bew—who retained personal recollections of the event—as 'the single spark that lit the prairie fire'. The march organized by People's Democracy, a radical offshoot of the civil rights movement, was continuously harassed by loyalist mobs and on its final leg the unarmed marchers were subjected to an extremely vicious attack. Dismay at the sheer incompetence of the Royal Ulster Constabulary in securing a non-violent protest, compounded with outrageous revelations that off-duty members of the auxiliary Ulster Special Constabulary ('B-Specials') had participated in the assault, exacerbated distrust in the ability of the security forces to protect the Catholic community and stimulated the resurgence of the IRA.[227] Less noted is that this formative event entailed an act of decommemorating 1798. The night before the march reached the village of Toome, on 1 January 1969, the Roddy McCorley monument was destroyed by explosives.[228]

The Toome Ninety-Eight memorial, which had been erected just a decade and a half earlier, was the only public monument for the rebellion in Ulster. Even though it was located near a police station, the culprits of the iconoclastic vandalism were not apprehended. It was fairly obvious to all concerned that the explosives must have been detonated by loyalist paramilitaries, yet the investigation was shelved, alongside

[223] Hall, *Ireland: Its Scenery, Character*, vol. 3, pp. 147 and 175.

[224] W. J. McMullan, 'Belfast as It Was, and as It Is (Chapter IV)', *The Ulster Magazine and Monthly Review of Science and Literature*, 2, no. 17 (May 1861): pp. 233–40.

[225] For example: O'Leary, *The Irish Widow's Son*, p. 8; M'Clintock, 'Beasts, Birds, and Insects', pp. 90–1; *The Belfast and Province of Ulster Directory* (Belfast: James Alexander Henderson, 1892), p. 220; *Some Recollections of Hugh McCall*, p. 171; S. Shannon Millin, *History of the Second Congregation of Protestant Dissenters in Belfast* (Belfast: W. & G. Baird Ltd, 1900), p. 48; Thomas Croskery, 'Narrative of My Life' (1883), R. W. H. Blackwood Papers, PRONI MIC 315/9, vol. 53, p. 3.

[226] For use of the 'The Time of the Troubles' in Irish folk history outside of Ulster see Beiner, *Remembering the Year of the French*, p. 128.

[227] Interview of Lord Bew by journalist Malachi O'Doherty, 3 August 2008; <https://malachiodoherty.com/2008/08/08/lord-bew-on-burntollet>. See also Bowes Egan and Vincent McCormack, *Burntollet* (London: L.R.S. Publishers, 1969), ch. 2.

[228] *Irish Press*, 2 January 1969, p. 1; *Irish Independent*, 3 January 1969, p. 9; *Irish Times*, 3 January 1969, p. 4; see also Bob Purdie, *Politics in the Streets: The Origins of the Civil Rights Movement in Northern Ireland* (Belfast: Blackstaff Press, 1990), p. 213.

several other similar cases. Months later, Austin Currie, the nationalist parliamentary representative for East Tyrone and a prominent civil rights organizer, joined James O'Reilly, nationalist member for Mourne, in condemning the apparent unwillingness of the authorities to expose what seemed to be a loyalist bombing campaign designed to destabilize the situation in Northern Ireland: 'To put it as mildly as I possibly can it seems decidedly peculiar that no arrests or prosecutions have resulted from the inquiries into these explosions.'[229]

When Rev. Ian Paisley, a principal advocate of loyalist opposition to the civil rights march, was asked by a reporter 'whether his followers should have blown up a memorial to a Presbyterian', he indignantly answered that 'Roddy McCorley was no Presbyterian. He was an Arian or a Unitarian.' This seemingly off-the-cuff reply echoed the hard-line nineteenth-century rhetoric of Rev. Henry Cooke, who had sought to stamp out the memory of Presbyterian involvement in the insurrection by distancing orthodox Presbyterianism from the United Irishmen. Nationalists responded by arguing that the rebel hero had been a Catholic. This identification was endorsed by the Presbyterian historians John de Courcy and Charles Dickson, as well as by Seamus O'Neill [Séamas Ó Néill], the northern-born professor of history at Carysfort College in Dublin, who published at the time several articles on 1798 in Ulster in the *Irish Press*. Although certain traditions seemed to support this case, the claim was ultimately unverifiable. McCorley was labelled in the nationalist press 'the Kevin Barry of 1798', with reference to a young republican revolutionary hero executed in 1920, who was also remembered in a popular ballad.[230] Rather than discouraging commemoration, loyalist decommemorating had stimulated the enthusiasm of nationalists to own the memory of the northern United Irishmen.

Three years before its destruction, the Roddy McCorley monument had been the site of a republican commemoration of the fiftieth anniversary of the Easter Rising. The choice to hold a parade with a contingent of IRA veterans at Toomebridge in 1966 drew a symbolic parallel between commemorations of 1798 and 1916. The binding of the memory of the United Irishmen with twentieth-century republicanism was an anathema to unionists, who were exasperated by commemoration of 1916.[231] The unionist politician David Trimble later argued that the Easter Rising was 'commemorated by an orgy of self-congratulation' and that 'the 50th anniversary of the [1916] rebellion started the destabilisation of Ulster.' The extent to which the triumphalist commemorations in 1966, which came to a climax with a military parade in Dublin, contributed to the outbreak of the Troubles in Northern Ireland remains a moot point.[232] On the other hand, critical attention has not sufficiently interrogated the radicalizing influence of the revival of interest in the memory of the United Irishmen around that time.

---

[229] *Northern Ireland Parliamentary Debates*, vol. 73 (1969), pp. 1671 and 1683 (18 June).

[230] *Irish Times*, 3 January 1969, p. 4; *Irish Press*, 6 January 1969, p. 9. For other articles on 1798 in Ulster published by Seamus O'Neill in 1969 see Irish Press 8 January, p. 11; 29 September, p. 9; 3 October, p. 11.

[231] Margaret O'Callaghan, ' "From Casement Park to Toomebridge": The Commemoration of the Easter Rising in Northern Ireland in 1966', in *1916 in 1966: Commemorating the Easter Rising*, edited by Margaret O'Callaghan and Mary E. Daly (Dublin: Royal Irish Academy, 2007), pp. 91 and 112.

[232] David Trimble, *The Easter Rebellion of 1916* (Lurgan, Co. Armagh: Ulster Society Publications, 1992), pp. 33–4. Cf. Roisín Higgins, *Transforming 1916: Meaning, Memory and the Fiftieth Anniversary of the Easter Rising* (Cork: Cork University Press, 2012), p. 111.

Wolfe Tone Directories were established in 1963 to commemorate the bicentenary of the birth of 'the father of Irish republicanism'. Jack Bennett, the secretary of the Belfast directory, edited a newspaper-style souvenir publication titled *Wolfe Tone Today*, which was printed in 12,000 copies, of which 3,500 were sold in Northern Ireland. Bennett was a member of the Communist Party of Northern Ireland, yet he worked as a journalist for the unionist *Belfast Telegraph*, while writing incognito (under the pseudonym Claud Gordon) a column for the southern nationalist *Sunday Press* and was also the Belfast correspondent for the republican newspaper of the English-based Connolly Association, the *Irish Democrat*. The complexity of Bennett's identity defies the standard differentiation between Protestant unionists and Catholic nationalists: he was a Protestant and the son of a senior officer in the Royal Ulster Constabulary, and was also an Irish language enthusiast and anti-Partitionist. For the Wolfe Tone commemorative publication, he brought on board several Presbyterian contributors, including the poet John Irvine, a former librarian at Queen's University Belfast, and the Orange historian Aiken McClelland, who was a librarian at the Ulster Folk Museum. Although Bennett sensed 'a changing atmosphere in the North', he regretted that 'there was a cold terror against Protestants with nationalist views' and complained that 'if a Protestant expressed those views he was rejected as a traitor.'[233]

The Wolfe Tone Society emerged in 1964 out of the bicentennial directories with the purpose of revitalizing Irish republicanism. In an article published in 1965, the radical Presbyterian minister A. H. McElroy (writing under the Gaelicized version of his name—Aodh MacElroy) argued that:

> it is not sufficient to make annual pilgrimage to the graves of the martyrs, to do homage and commemorate the heroes of yesteryear. Better by far to neglect the pilgrim journey and spend the time mastering the philosophy which motivated the actions of those whose memory we justly revere. Far too many lay their tributes at the shrine and leave as they came, empty of understanding of what deep motives impelled these men to give their lives for a cause they counted higher than life itself. There is no respect for the dead in remembering the manner of their death, while the cause for which they died lies buried in obscurity and forgotten by those who should keep it alive.

Rather than just making do with commemoration, a more active engagement with the legacy of the United Irishmen—with specific attention to the memory of the northern revolutionaries James Hope and Henry Joy McCracken—offered radicals inspiration for developing new forms of political action.[234]

In 1966, representatives of the Dublin, Cork, and Belfast branches of the Wolfe Tone Society held meetings to discuss strategies for non-violent activism in Maghera, county Derry (13 August), and in Belfast (28 November). The outcome of these deliberations was the formation in 1967 of the Northern Ireland Civil Rights Association (NICRA), which kick-started the civil rights movement. Although a few liberal Protestants supported this initiative, most prominently Robin Cole—former chair of Queen's University Young Unionists (affiliated with the UUP)—who was elected to

[233] *Irish Press*, 17 July 1963, p. 8; *Cork Examiner*, 30 July 1963, p. 7; *An Phoblacht*, 7 December 2000. Whereas John Irvine was a professed republican, Aiken McClelland was a liberal unionist and Orangeman.
[234] *An Phoblacht*, 1, no. 2 (November 1965), p. 6. This crudely produced newspaper (billed as 'the organ of Irish republican opinion') was produced by a Cork-based splinter republican group, headed by Jim Lane. See also Purdie, *Politics in the Street*, pp. 123 and 130–1.

the NICRA executive, loyalists were convinced that it was an IRA front. The association of civil rights exclusively with the plight of Catholics did not entice working class Protestants, who were apprehensive of how Catholic empowerment might tie in with the menacing ambitions of southern irredentism.[235]

Key figures in the Wolfe Tone Society were intent on making republicanism more appealing to Ulster Protestants. Roy Johnston—the son of a liberal Presbyterian from county Tyrone—published a controversial letter in the June 1966 issue of the Sinn Féin newspaper the *United Irishman* in which he objected to the reciting of the Rosary at commemorative events. Johnston argued that 'all commemorations should be non-sectarian' and should acknowledge 'the Protestant 1798 leaders in the North'.[236] This proposal annoyed some of the more devout Catholics in the republican movement. Cathal Goulding, the IRA chief of staff, had to suspend one of his senior officers, Seán Mac Stiofáin, who decided to censor Johnston's letter by stopping the distribution of the issue. More generally, the debates stirred by the revision of republican ideology stimulated a rift within the republican movement that ultimately resulted in the emergence in 1969 of the Provisional IRA (commonly known as the 'Provos'), which was initially headed by Mac Stiofáin with the support of Seamus Twomey, a Belfast Catholic who organized local defence in Catholic neighbourhoods during the riots of August 1969.[237]

Shortly after the Sinn Féin split, the Provisional republican movement established in 1970 its northern newspaper *Republican News*, which was initially edited by Jimmy Steele, a veteran Belfast republican. Steele was committed to promoting a cult of northern republican martyrdom. In 1936, he wrote the song 'Belfast Graves', which paid homage to northern IRA volunteers who had died in 1920–2 and associated their sacrifice for 'the cause of Ireland' with the memory of McCracken and Wolfe Tone. A decade later, he updated the song with another stanza, which honoured volunteers from Belfast who had died in the early 1940s in IRA operations, extending the continuity of republican martyrdom to cover 'every generation'.[238]

In the late-1950s, Steele edited for the National Graves Association a commemorative booklet on *Belfast's Patriot Graves*, which was enhanced in 1966 and re-issued as *Antrim's Patriot Dead 1797–1953*. Two of the contributors, Sean MacGoill [Mackel] and Seamus Clarke, made use of sources from vernacular historiography, such as the antiquarian writings of Bigger and the storytelling of Cathal O'Byrne, to compile short biographical entries on Antrim men that had been executed in 1798. This souvenir publication was sold as part of a fundraising campaign that resulted in the unveiling in

---

[235] Roy Garland, 'Protestant Fears & Civil Rights: Self-Fulfilling Conspiracies?', *History Ireland*, 16, no. 5 (2008): pp. 30–3.

[236] Sean Swan, *Official Irish Republicanism, 1962–1972* (n.l.: Lulu, 2008), pp. 188–9; Roy H. W. Johnston, *Century of Endeavour: A Biographical and Autobiographical View of the 20th Century in Ireland* (Dublin: Maunsel & Co., 2003), p. 196.

[237] Richard English, *Armed Struggle: A History of the IRA* (Oxford and New York: Oxford University Press, 2003), pp. 85–94; Johnston, *Century of Endeavour*, pp. 174–82; Matt Treacy, *The IRA 1956–69: Rethinking the Republic* (Manchester and New York: Manchester University Press, 2011), pp. 63–87 and 106–8; Robert W. White *Ruairí Ó Brádaigh: The Life and Politics of an Irish Revolutionary* (Bloomington: Indiana University Press, 2006), 117–18 and 138; Swan, *Official Irish Republicanism*, pp. 104–11; Anthony Coughlan, 'The IRA in the 1960s: Rethinking The Republic?'; <www.indymedia.ie/article/99779>.

[238] Following Steele's death in 1970, a stanza with his name was added to 'Belfast Graves' by Father Joseph Mullins; *Republican News*, 12 January 1973.

West Belfast's Milltown cemetery of a republican County Antrim Memorial (designed by MacGoill), which lists the names of thirty executed United Irishmen, alongside more recently killed members of the IRA.[239] The early issues of *Republican News* featured a series of articles on the Protestant patriots of 1798 and this theme was continued sporadically after Steele's death in August 1970, in the hope of attracting northern Protestants to the republican cause.[240]

The attempt of republicans to appeal to Protestants found few takers, given that the Provisionals presented themselves as the defenders of northern Catholics and engaged in acts of terrorism. Whereas militant Protestant youth responded to the resurgence of armed republicanism by joining loyalist paramilitaries, liberal Protestants were appalled by the violence that had been unleashed. Bob Cooper, a former chair of the Young Unionists who had become a co-founder of the liberal Alliance Party, refused to be taken in by the Provisional IRA's 'superb propaganda machine'. Cooper demanded that republicans be held accountable for their violent conduct and questioned the use of the memory of 1798 to justify atrocities:

> How many more Presbyterians are you going to kill in the name of Henry Joy McCracken? How many more members of the Church of Ireland are you going to murder in the name of Wolfe Tone? How many more Catholics are going to be slaughtered in the cause of Republicanism?[241]

Cooper left politics in 1976 and dedicated himself to combatting anti-Catholic discrimination as chairman of the Fair Employment Agency (FEA). At his funeral, he was eulogized by his Catholic colleague Oliver Napier, the first leader of the Alliance party, as 'one of those Presbyterians who most of us believed had been wiped out on the battlefields of Antrim and Ballynahinch in 1798'.[242]

Although the revival of republicanism was inspired by commemoration of the United Irishmen and intended to bring Protestants and Catholics together, Northern Ireland was to be radicalized along divisive sectarian lines. Republicanism was mainly supported by Catholics, who considered the United Irishmen their ideological forebears, even if their actual ancestors may have not participated in the 1798 rebellion. The iconic Provisional IRA hero Bobby Sands, who was OC [Officer Commanding] of the republican prisoners in the Long Kesh Detention Centre (also known as the HM Prison Maze, or the H-Blocks) and led the 1981 hunger strike, was a Belfast Catholic who admired the United Irishmen and was particularly fascinated with Roddy McCorley. He was so taken by Ethna Carbery's poem that he thought of inviting her to meet with the political prisoners, not realizing that she was long dead.[243] Sands wrote his own poem on 'Rodaí MacCorlai', Gaelicizing McCorley's name so as to identify him clearly with

---

[239] Seamus [Jimmy] Steele, ed., *Antrim's Patriot Dead 1797–1953* (Belfast: National Graves Association., n.d. [1966]), pp. 9–24 and 74–5. For a photograph of the Milltown memorial and the list of United Irishmen it honours see Murray and Cullen, *Epitaph of 1798*, p. 4.

[240] Richard Davis, 'The Manufacture of Propagandist History by Northern Ireland Loyalists and Republicans', in *Ireland's Terrorist Dilemma*, edited by Yonah Alexander and Alan O'Day (Dordrecht: Martinus Nijhoff Publishers, 1986), p. 150. For Steele see *An Phoblacht*, 2 June 2010. For examples of articles published after Steele's death see *Republican News*, 11 June 1972 (Betsy Gray) and 17 November 1973 (James Hope).

[241] *Irish Times*, 6 November 1971, p. 4. [242] *Irish News*, 20 November 2004.

[243] David Beresford, *Ten Men Dead: The Story of the 1981 Irish Hunger Strike* (Grafton: London, 1987), p. 99.

native-Irish stock, rather than with Ulster-Scots Presbyterians. Phrased in first person, it depicts the local hero as a champion of the 'common folk' and of 'those of no property'.[244]

The lionizing of United Irish heroes was not confined only to the Provisional republican movement. Republican Clubs, founded in the late 1960s and after the split affiliated with the Official IRA, were named after famous United Irishmen, such as Wolfe Tone, Henry Joy, McCracken, Jemmy Hope, and a particularly active William Orr and Betsy Gray club in Ballymurphy (a West Belfast Catholic neighbourhood that was hard hit by the Troubles).[245] The endorsement of rebel heroes by the IRA alienated unionist Protestants, including many of those whose ancestors had been rebels in 1798, and heightened the concerns of the authorities regarding commemoration.

Following on the tail of the Wolfe Tone anniversary, the bicentenary of the birth of Henry Joy McCracken, described as 'the father of Republicanism in the North East', was celebrated modestly in 1967. At a Dublin commemoration on 3 September in Kilmainham Gaol (where McCracken had been imprisoned for a while), a wreath was laid by a descendant of the McCracken family, Bill Meek, and short addresses were delivered by the journalist and folklore collector Seán Mac Réamoinn and the trade unionist Cathal O Seanain [Cathal O'Shannon], who was originally from Randalstown in county Antrim.[246] The Irish government, which did not send any officials to the ceremony, was heavily criticized for the decision of the Department of Posts and Telegraphs not to honour McCracken, as it had Wolfe Tone, with a commemorative stamp.[247] In a letter to the *Irish Times*, Frank Grogarty from Belfast pointed out the irony in the contrast between the indifference of the authorities in the Republic of Ireland and the decision of the Ulster Museum—'an institute subsidised by a Unionist Government'—to hold an exhibition of relics associated with McCracken.[248] According to Michael Agnew, the Acting Secretary of the Wolfe Tone Society, the McCracken exhibition at the Ulster Museum, which ran from 25 August to 30 September 1967, was 'a tremendous success with crowds to be found there on every day since it opened'.[249]

The Belfast Wolfe Tone Society published in June 1967 *Henry Joy McCracken and His Times*, a short biography of McCracken, written by the society's treasurer, Fred Heatley, a Catholic worker at the Harland and Wolfe shipyards. Heatley made use of the available written accounts and drew on traditions that had been previously documented in collections of vernacular history. In addition, he showed that folklore of 1798 was still being told. An appendix referred to an apocryphal tradition that Heatley had heard in Belfast, which claimed that McCracken was incarcerated for a while in a room in Pottinger's Court, where later a uniform was found hidden in a cavity in the wall.[250] The McCracken bicentennial publication was hailed in the *Irish Press* as 'a very

---

[244] Bobby Sands, *Prison Poems* (Sinn Féin Publicity Department: Dublin, 1981), pp. 57–9; republished in Bobby Sands, *Writings from Prison* (Mercier Press: Cork, 1998), 209–12.

[245] Collins, *Who Fears to Speak*, p. 76; Ciarán de Baróid, *Ballymurphy and the Irish War* (London and Sterling, Va.: Pluto, 2000; orig. edn 1990), pp. 32–3 and 36. For reports on the activities of the William Orr and Betsy Gray club see *Ulster Herald*, 14 April 1973, p. 9; *Donegal News*, 29 September 1973, p. 11; *Donegal News*, 15 December 1973, p. 7; *Irish Independent*, 14 January 1974, p. 22.

[246] *Irish Press*, 4 September 1967, p. 4; *Irish Times*, 4 September 1967, p. 11.

[247] *Irish Press*, 6 March 1967, p. 7; *Irish Independent*, 9 March 1967, p. 10; *Irish Times*, 23 March 1967, p. 9.

[248] *Irish Times*, 29 August 1967, p. 9.

[249] *Irish Press*, 4 September 1967, p. 9; *Irish Times*, 24 and 25 August 1967, pp. 8 and 11 (respectively).

[250] Heatley, *Henry Joy McCracken*, p. 54. For biographical information see *Belfast Telegraph*, 24 April 2017; *Irish News*, 26 April 2017; *Irish Times*, 24 April and 6 May 2017.

welcome pamphlet' and described in the *Irish Independent* as a 'comprehensive little book'.[251] A second edition came out in September. That month, representatives of the Wolfe Tone Society laid a wreath at the McCracken grave in Belfast's Clifden Street cemetery, symbolically staking a claim to be recognized as the rightful custodians of the memory of the heroic patriot.[252]

In an article published in the unionist *Belfast Telegraph*, Mary McNeill, a biographer of Mary Ann McCracken, presented Henry Joy McCracken in de-politicized universalist terms, as a 'champion of human dignity', and asked 'what happened to the non-conformist liberal tradition?'.[253] Nationalists tried to claim this tradition for themselves. The Irish National Foresters held a commemoration on 1 November 1967 at McCracken's grave, which was addressed by Rev. A. H. McElroy.[254] A few months earlier, McElroy had delivered a lecture in Newry on the 'Irish Nationalist Debt to Presbyterianism', declaring that 'he hoped and believed that one day Northern Protestants would rediscover the heritage of Presbyterian radicalism' and come to reject Partition.[255] The *Irish Independent*, soberly acknowledged that the exhibition at the Ulster Museum and the publication of articles on McCracken in both the nationalist and unionist press, 'does not mean that some Unionists are becoming Republicans; they are merely beginning to take a pride in local history'.[256]

The republican revival of interest in the United Irishmen did not pass unnoticed by loyalists. An irate reaction to the commemoration appeared in October 1967 in the *Belfast News-Letter* under the crude heading 'Henry Joy McCracken was stupid.' The writer, using the pseudonym Greenhill, argued:

> Only those Protestants who were suffering from mental ablepsy, or who were too deeply entangled in the [United Irish] movement, fought in the North. Of these McCracken was the chief, and he and others can only be described as traitors to their religion, and to their fellow Protestants.

In response, offended readers rushed to defend McCracken's reputation.[257] The increased preoccupation with the United Irishmen stirred by the Wolfe Tone bicentenary had evidently caused tension.

With the outbreak of the Troubles, the UVF—a loyalist paramilitary organization revived in 1966—launched a series of bombing attacks in the Republic of Ireland, some of which specifically targeted monuments.[258] Ten months after the destruction of the Roddy McCorley memorial, an explosion detonated at Bodenstown cemetery in county Kildare on 30 October 1969 destroyed the graveside memorial of 'the traitor Wolfe Tone' (as he was named in a UVF statement).[259] The Taoiseach Jack Lynch

[251] *Irish Press*, 8 July 1967, p. 4; 26 August 1967, p. 8.
[252] *Irish Times*, 1 September 1967, p. 9.
[253] *Belfast Telegraph*, 29 August 1967; McNeill Papers, PRONI D3732/3/2.
[254] *Irish Press*, 1 November 1967, p. 3.   [255] *Irish Times*, 21 March 1967, p. 11.
[256] *Irish Independent*, 4 September 1967, p. 3.
[257] Newspaper clippings, McNeill Papers, PRONI D3732/3/2.
[258] Jim Cusack and Henry McDonald, *UVF: The Endgame*, rev. edn (Dublin: Poolbeg, 2008), pp. 73–8.
[259] *Irish Independent*, 1 November 1969, p. 1; *Cork Examiner*, 1 November 1969, p. 1; *Irish Times*, 1 November 1969, pp. 1 and 9. For the UVF statement claiming responsibility see *Irish Press*, 3 November 1969, p. 1; *Irish Times*, 3 November 1969, p. 1; *Ulster Herald*, 8 November 1969, p. 10 (also published in *Strabane Chronicle* and *Fermanagh Herald*, 8 November 1969, p. 12).

denounced this vandalism as an 'outrage' and southern commentators struggled to make sense of the desecration of the memorial, unwilling to contemplate the possibility that a site that hosted at least three separate annual republican commemorations (by the Irish state, the Fianna Fáil party, and by the Official IRA) and was managed since 1945 by the republican National Graves Association, could in any way be considered offensive to loyalists.[260]

The *Irish Independent* was perhaps closest to the mark when it proposed in an editorial that the destruction could be read 'as a gesture of political tabernacle-smashing', while suggesting that it might also be seen as 'a redress for the feelings' aroused by the 1956–62 IRA border campaign, which had been 'carried out in Wolfe Tone's name'.[261] Re-commemorating commenced immediately and an appeal by the National Graves Associ-ation for funds 'to restore an even more worthy memorial' was reportedly met with donations from all over the island, 'including many from Northern Ireland'.[262] Within less than two years, in April 1971, a new memorial was dedicated with a republican ceremony that was presided over by the former IRA chief of staff Maurice Twomey.[263]

Loyalist decommemorating, which did not distinguish between constitutionalist and revolutionary nationalism, continued with attacks on iconic memorials in Dublin. Explosives caused limited damage to the O'Connell monument in city centre (27 December 1969) and to the Round Tower monument at O'Connell's grave in Glasnevin cemetery (17 January 1971), while the statue of Wolfe Tone outside Stephen's Green, unveiled by De Valera in 1967, was blown to pieces (8 February 1971) and required extensive renovation.[264] Of all the acts of loyalist decommemorating, perhaps the most symbolic gesture of suppressing remembrance of 1798 was the destruction of the gravestone of Francis Joseph Bigger in Mallusk cemetery on the night of 6 April 1971 (Fig. 6.5). As the *Irish Times* observed, in the violent context of the Troubles, 'it was a small incident among all the destruction, the maimings, the killings, but it was nonetheless a sad marginal commentary on the situation in the North today.'[265] The targeting of a memorial to a man who had dedicated his life to documenting traditions about the northern United Irishmen and to erecting monuments in their honour was in itself an audacious statement against open commemoration.

While the southern monuments that had been damaged were quickly repaired, conditions in Northern Ireland were adverse to restoration. Coincidentally, on the day that it was discovered that an explosion had damaged Bigger's grave, the committee that had undertaken to erect a new memorial for Roddy McCorley announced that, even though the trustees had been awarded £1500 in damages, 'it had been decided to postpone the unveiling in view of the present troubled state of the country.' Both reports appeared on the same page of the *Irish Times*, which wryly noted: 'Troubles hit Roddy McCorley memorial.'[266] The McCorley monument would eventually be

[260] *Cork Examiner*, 4 and 7 November 1969, pp. 1 and 10 (respectively).
[261] *Irish Independent*, 1 November 1969, p. 8.
[262] *Irish Press*, 4 and 27 November 1969, pp. 7 and 1 (respectively).
[263] *Cork Examiner*, 26 April 1971, p. 5.
[264] *Irish Independent*, 27 December 1969, p. 1; 18 January 1971, pp. 1 and 18; 8 February 1971, p. 1; *Irish Press*, 8 February 1971, pp. 1 and 5; *Irish Times*, 25 December 1969, pp. 1 and 9; 18 January 1971, p. 1; 8 February 1971, p. 1.
[265] *Irish Times*, 9 April 1971 p. 11.
[266] *Irish Times*, 8 April 1971, p. 9.

Fig. 6.5. Decommemorating F. J. Bigger

The gravestone of Francis Joseph Bigger in Mallusk cemetery was destroyed by explosives on 6 April 1970. The nearby gravestone of James Hope (erected by Madden in 1847 and restored by Bigger in 1901) was left untouched.

Photograph by Guy Beiner (2011).

rebuilt, yet Bigger's graveside memorial remained broken. In 1976 it was discovered that the shattered remains of the Betsy Gray monument outside Ballynahinch had been subject to vandalism (possibly by souvenir hunters) and that on the site, which for some time had been marked with a cairn, 'it seems like there is nothing at all to mark the spot.' It was acknowledged that 'there are many people in County Down who feel there should be a permanent memorial to one of the most dramatic times, and dramatic women, in Ulster's history.'[267] Yet no action would be taken. Decommemorating had, yet again, taken its toll and the violent climate of the Troubles hindered renewal of commemoration.

Meanwhile, other forms of cultural memory were coming into vogue. In the 1960s, the singing of 'rebel songs', an expression of social remembrance that had originally been performed guardedly, shed its inhibitions and featured more prominently in mainstream popular culture. The folk music revival, which had started in the United States in the forties and arrived in Britain in the fifties, became in the sixties a worldwide cultural trend and the increased demand for Irish traditional music generated a 'ballad boom', evident in concert performances, commercial recordings and

---

[267] *BNL*, 1 November 1976, p. 2; *Down Recorder*, 2 November 1976.

broadcasts.[268] The transitions between the local and the global are typified in the reception of *Irish Songs of Resistance*, a book written by the ballad singer, poet, and playwright Patrick Galvin (who would later settle in Belfast). Galvin's book presented, alongside historical notes, the words and music of fifty songs and had a section on 'The Great Rebellion of 1798 and its Aftermath' that included the Ulster ballad 'Henry Joy McCracken'. It was first published in 1955 in London by the left-wing Workers' Music Association (WMA)—the torchbearers of the revival in England—and shortly afterwards Topic Records, the label of the WMA, recorded an accompanying double album, on which Galvin performed a selection of the songs.[269] This publication was soon noticed across the Atlantic.

The following year, in 1956, an American edition of *Irish Songs of Resistance* came out with the Folklore Press, managed by the influential folksong collector and producer Kenneth S. Goldstein, and was immediately reviewed in *Sing Out!*, the magazine founded by Irwin Silber, Pete Seeger, and Alan Lomax to cater for the thriving New York folk scene.[270] A few years later, a second American edition, which emphasized on the cover that it includes guitar chords for the songs, proved to be extremely popular and was re-issued in numerous printings.[271] Galvin's work inspired the Smithsonian to record in 1956 the New York folklorist Wallace House singing 'Songs of the Irish Rebellion of 1798', including the Ulster ballad 'General Munroe'.[272] The same year, the Clancy Brothers and Tommy Makem recorded their first album *The Rising of the Moon: Irish Songs of Rebellion*, which was subsequently redone with new musical arrangements in 1959. Their commercial success opened the way for many other folk bands, such as the Dubliners and the Wolfe Tones, whose performances of traditional music were often associated with radical political statements on Northern Ireland.[273]

Fred Heatley commented in 1967 on the revitalizing influence of the folk revival, noting that the song 'Henry Joy', which he had known 'for many years', had 'of late times gained much in popularity at Irish folk concerts'. Although its provenance is unknown, the ballad may have originated in the early nineteenth century. It tells the story of the rebellion as seen by an 'An Ulster man' from the Antrim glens, who 'well remembered' following McCracken to Antrim town, where 'for Ireland's cause we fought', and then witnessing in Belfast how 'They have murdered Henry Joy.'[274]

---

[268] John O'Flynn, *The Irishness of Irish Music* (Farnham and Burlington: Ashgate, 2009), pp. 26–7.

[269] Patrick Galvin, *Irish Songs of Resistance* (London: Workers' Music Association, 1955), pp. 24–35; Patrick Galvin, *Irish Songs of Resistance*, 1 and 2 (Topic Records, 1956). For biographical information see *Irish Times*, 14 May 2011, p. 12; for the Workers' Music Association and Topic Records see Michael Brocken, *The British Folk Revival, 1944–2002* (Aldershot and Burlington: Ashgate, 2003), pp. 49–65.

[270] Ronald D. Cohen and Rachel Clare Donaldson, *Roots of the Revival: American and British Folk Music in the 1950s* (Urbana, Chicago, and Springfield: University of Illinois Press, 2014), pp. 90–1. For *Sing Out!* see Stephen Petrus and Ronald D. Cohen, *Folk City: New York and the American Folk Music Revival* (Oxford and New York: Oxford University Press, 2015), *passim*.

[271] Patrick Galvin, *Irish Songs of Resistance (1169–1923)* (New York: Oak Publications, 1962)

[272] Wallace House, *Irish Songs of Resistance* (Folkways Records, 1956), Galvin's influence is evident in the album's title and liner notes.

[273] Clancy Brothers and Tommy Makem, *The Rising of the Moon* (Tradition Records: 1956 and 1959); see also Susan H. Motherway, *The Globalization of Irish Traditional Song Performance* (Farnham and Burlington: Ashgate, 2013), pp. 142–4; O'Flynn, *The Irishness of Irish Music*, pp. 36–7.

[274] Heatley, *Henry Joy McCracken*, p. 59; *Folk Magazine*, 1, no. 1 (1967): pp. 20–1; Moylan, *Age of Revolution*, p. 83.

Following the rediscovery and revival of the song, it was performed and reinterpreted with the current political tensions of Northern Ireland in mind. Its lyrics appeared in 1966 in a collection of *Ballads from the Jails and Streets of Ireland* and were republished in other songbooks.[275] The song aficionado Andrew Rynne remembered hearing 'Henry Joy' performed at the Brazen Head pub in Dublin by Tony Murray, an IRA man recently released from the Curragh prison.[276]

Gerry Adams, a member of the Wolfe Tone Society who would become a leading figure in the provisional Sinn Féin movement, was working as a barman in the Duke of York pub in Belfast and recalled that some ballad singers 'sang quite republican songs, like "Henry Joy" but in general the ballad-singers avoided party songs as such'.[277] The Belfast folk song revival involved both Catholics and Protestants and was initially apolitical, preferring a shared regionalist notion of folk singing that corresponded with Estyn Evans' approach to folklife.[278] In 1955, the song collector Seán Ó Boyle recorded the singer Robert Cinnamond of Glenavy in county Antrim (18 km west of Belfast) perform some seventy songs, which included both 'Orange and Green party tunes'.[279] Yet, by the late 1960s ballad singing had become associated mainly with nationalists. 'Henry Joy' was recorded by several popular folk bands, including the Grehan Sisters (a trio from Roscommon), the Irish Rovers (founded by Ulster musicians who emigrated to Canada), and Tommy Makem—'the Bard of Armagh', and was memorably performed at concerts of the Dubliners by Ciarán Bourke, whose introduction to the song made specific connections with the conflict in Northern Ireland.[280]

The ballad 'General Munro', which had been collected in multiple versions in the nineteenth century, was similarly revived. The Belfast uillean pipe player Francis (Frank) McPeake, who as a child had been encouraged to play traditional music by Francis Joseph Bigger, recorded a version in 1952.[281] In 1966, the Dublin-born singer Michael 'Jesse' Owens, who had just established the first Irish singing club in New York, performed the ballad live on Telefís Éireann in a special episode of the current affairs TV programme 'Newsbeat', which compared Irish and American protest songs.[282] In the following decade 'General Munro' was recorded by a number of commercially successful singers, including the Dublin balladeer Declan Hunt, Andy Irvine of Planxty (whose mother's family came from Lisburn in county Antrim), and the Wolfe Tones, who made no secret of their republican sympathies.[283]

[275] Martin Shannon, ed., *Ballads from the Jails and Streets of Ireland* (Dublin: Red Hand Books, 1966), p. 22.

[276] Andrew Rynne, *The Vasectomy Doctor: A Memoir* (Cork: Mercier Press, 2005), p. 62.

[277] Gerry Adams, *Before the Dawn: An Autobiography* (London: Heinemann, 1996), p. 63.

[278] May McCann, 'Music and Politics in Ireland: The Specificity of the Folk Revival in Belfast', *British Journal of Ethnomusicology*, 4 (1995): pp. 51–75.

[279] David Cooper, *The Musical Traditions of Northern Ireland and Its Diaspora: Community and Conflict* (Farnham and Burlington: Ashgate, 2009), pp. 123–4.

[280] The Grehan Sisters' rendition was included in the collection *Here's to the Irish* (Transatlantic Records, 1968); Irish Rovers, *All Hung Up* (Decca, 1968); Tommy Makem, *The Bard of Armagh* (CBS, 1970). Ciarán Bourke's introduction to 'Henry Joy' at a concert in Hamburg in the 1970s can be heard at <www.youtube.com/watch?v=MF04VsJTJAk>.

[281] Francis McPeake, *The Rights of Man* (Folktracks, 1952).

[282] Newsbeat, presented by Frank Hall, 20 January 1966; <www.rte.ie/archives/2016/0119/761327-songs-of-folk-and-protest/>.

[283] Declan Hunt, *Songs of the Irish Rising—1798* (Outlet TOL, 1972); Planxty, *High Kings of Tara* (Tara Records, 1980)—from a session recorded around 1977; Wolfe Tones, *Belt of the Celts* (Triskel Records, 1978).

Commercialization influenced the local folk singing scene and performances of the ballad featured prominently in the Belfast revival.[284]

'Roddy McCorley' was another favourite of the folksong revival. Its authorship by Ethna Carbery a century after 1798 was obscured and the ballad was treated as if it had been transmitted seamlessly in oral tradition since the time of the rebellion. Introducing the song to an international audience, the Kingston Trio—an American group that signalled the rise to prominence of revived folk music—offered such an explanation: 'In Ireland, during their many revolutions, they always found someone to use as a hero. One of these men was Roddy McCorley . . . and although this was many years ago, they still sing this song about him.' The Clancy Brothers and Tommy Makem prefaced their performance of the song with an exegesis that inflated the role of the local outlaw hero: 'The history of Ireland is scarred by many rebellions. Roddy McCorley was the leader of one such revolution.' The Dubliners chose the song as the opener for one of their first recorded concerts.[285]

The rousing tune of 'Roddy McCorley' had previously been adapted into a march by the céilí bands that thrived in the Irish state in the forties and fifties.[286] However, this domestication of a rebel song was undermined when the air was adopted for the ballad 'Sean South', which honoured an IRA volunteer killed in a cross-border raid on the Royal Ulster Constabulary barracks in Brookeborough, county Fermanagh, on 1 January 1957. This new song, published within a week of South's funeral, soon became a staple at republican gatherings, much to the ire of the authorities on both sides of the border.[287] Its author, Sean Costelloe of Limerick, later claimed that he was informed by the Controller of Programmes of Radio Éireann that 'while the song is not banned officially, we see to it that it does not get played' (a charge that was denied by the broadcasting authority).[288] Nonetheless the song was recorded by the Wolfe Tones and became extremely popular.[289]

The folklorist Henry Glassie repeatedly heard 'Sean South' performed in traditional settings in county Fermanagh in 1972. Tellingly, one of the singers, referred to it as 'Rody McCrory' [sic]. This misnomer unwittingly revealed how the original song had been blurred and subsumed into its new reincarnation, so that the two had become practically indistinguishable.[290] Performances of 'Sean South' were in effect unconscious evocations of the memory of Ninety-Eight, while at the same time performances of 'Roddy McCorley' became tinged with an association of more recent republican

[284] McCann, 'Music and Politics in Ireland', p. 69.

[285] The Kingston Trio, *College Concert* (Capitol, 1962); The Clancy Brothers and Tommy Makem, *A Spontaneous Performance Recording* (Columbia/CBS, 1961); *The Dubliners in Concert* (Transatlantic Records, 1965). For the Kingston Trio see Cohen and Donaldson, *Roots of the Revival*, pp. 93–5 and 118–21.

[286] Fintan Vallely, *The Companion to Irish Traditional Music*, 2nd edn (Cork: Cork University Press, 2011), p. 428; for the rise and decline of céilí bands see pp. 45–9.

[287] Brian Hanley and Scott Millar, *The Lost Revolution: The Story of the Official IRA and the Workers' Party* (London: Penguin, 2010), p. 16. For Seán South see Kevin Haddick Flynn, 'Seán South of Garryowen', *History Ireland*, 15, no. 1 (2007): pp. 36–41; Des Fogerty, *Sean South of Garryowen* (Ireland: A. K. Ilen Co., 2006).

[288] *Irish Press*, 20 October 1971, p. 8; *Cork Examiner*, 23 October 1971, p. 3; *Irish Independent*, 24 October 1971, p. 22.

[289] Wolfe Tones, *Let the People Sing* (Dolphin Records, 1972).

[290] Henry Glassie, *Passing the Time in Ballymenone: Culture and History of an Ulster Community* (Philadelphia: University of Pennsylvania Press, 1982), pp. 294–6 and 818–19; Henry Glassie, *The Stars of Ballymenone* (Bloomington and Indianapolis: Indiana University Press, 2006), pp. 526–7.

paramilitary activity. The Belfast folk singers Tony Kearney and Geraldine McKeever recorded in 1974 the album *Hang My Country* in which 'Henry Joy' and 'Roddy McCorley' appeared alongside songs about the current conflict in Northern Ireland.[291]

In addition to reviving traditional songs, the 'ballad boom' also encouraged the writing of original songs in the same genre. Several new songs about 1798 were composed and performed locally. A ballad about Henry Joy McCracken was written in 1963 by Fintan Byrne and set to the air of 'The Flower of Sweet Strabane'.[292] In 1964, Eileen Keaney of Belfast (who was originally from Plumbridge, county Tyrone) won first prize in a ballad competition for another composition titled 'Henry Joy McCracken', which was written in the traditional 'come-all-ye' style and sung to another familiar air ('Patrick Sheehan' or the 'Glen of Aherlow'). It included verses that referred to previous silencing of remembrance:

> Where were the ballad-makers of Belfast in ninety-eight?
> Was it fear that stilled their sorrowing hearts this happening to relate?
> No song to keep his memory green, no chants to show the pride
> In our gallant Ulster Volunteers who for sweet justice died.[293]

As might be expected, the BBC in Northern Ireland refrained from broadcasting rebel songs. Silencing was set to make a return also in independent Ireland, as the authorities became apprehensive about the political use of folk songs.

On 8 March 1966 a militant republican group, operating independently from the IRA, committed a spectacular act of decommemorating when it blew up Nelson's Pillar, arguably the Republic of Ireland's most prominent remaining imperial monument, which was located just opposite the General Post Office, the central site for 1916 commemoration. The event was immediately celebrated in a number of songs. The Go Lucky Four, a group of Belfast schoolteachers, were quick to come out with the single 'Up Went Nelson' (sung to the air of 'John Brown's Body'), which immediately went to first place in the Irish music charts, while the Clancy Brothers recorded Tommy Makem's 'Lord Nelson' (mischievously sung to the tune of the Orange song 'The Sash my Father Wore') and the Dubliner's added to their repertoire 'Nelson's Farewell'.[294] The Irish government, determined to maintain control over commemorations of the Easter Rising and not to lose ground to republican extremists, issued a ban on the playing of rebel songs on Radio Éireann, for which it was strongly criticized.[295]

According to Section 31 of the Irish Broadcasting Authority Act of 1960, the minister in charge of communications could demand that the authority 'refrain from

---

[291] Tony Kearney and Geraldine McKeever, *Hang My Country* (Cuchulainn Records, 1974).

[292] Heatley, *Henry Joy McCracken*, p. 62.

[293] Ibid., p. 61; see also *Strabane Chronicle*, 7 November 1964, p. 2; Hugh Shields, 'Miscellanea from Eileen Keaney', *Ceol*, 2, no. 1 (1965), p. 9; Moylan, *Age of Revolution*; pp. 83–4.

[294] Go Lucky Four, *Up Went Nelson* (Emerald, 1966); Clancy Brothers and Tommy Makem, *Freedom's Sons* (Columbia, 1966); Dubliners, *Nelson's Farewell* (Transatlantic Records, 1966), also included in a recording of a life performance at the Gate Theatre: Dubliners, *Finnegan Wakes* (Transatlantic Records, 1966). See also Higgins, *Transforming 1916*, pp. 74–6 and 134; Donal Fallon, *The Pillar: The Life and Afterlife of Nelson Pillar* (Stillorgan, County Dublin: New Island Books, 2014), pp. 90–104 and 114–16.

[295] *Cork Examiner*, 24, 28, and 30 March 1966, pp. 12, 6, and 7 (respectively); *Irish Independent*, 24 and 31 March 1966, pp. 19 and 13 (respectively) and 1 April 1966, p. 17; *Irish Press*, 28 and 30 March 1966, pp. 9 and 3 (respectively).

broadcasting any particular matter'. These special powers were redefined in response to the Troubles. Gerry Collins, Fianna Fáil Minister for Posts and Telegraphs, issued a directive in 1971 to refrain from broadcasting 'any matter that could be calculated to promote the aims or activities of any organization which engages in, promotes, encourages or advocates the attaining of any particular objective by violent means.'[296] Subsequently, the controversial Section 31 could be used to prevent the playing of republican songs. The folk music collector Breandán Breathnach complained in 1972 that the policymakers at RTÉ (the Irish national broadcaster) were 'on their toes to ensure that no rebel songs are broadcast in any radio or television programme' and claimed that the ban had been extended also to songs of 1798.[297] In 1976, Conor Cruise O'Brien, Minister for Posts and Telegraphs in the Fine Gael and Labour coalition government, introduced an amendment to the law, which specified that the minister could suppress any matter that he deemed 'likely to promote, or incite to, crime or would tend to undermine the authority of the State'. Although the ban only applied to radio and television, newspaper journalists were also under pressure to exercise self-censorship and refrain from publishing items that might encourage militant republicans.[298]

The Troubles also brought a tightening of state control over the media in Northern Ireland. On 19 October 1988, Home Secretary Douglas Hurd announced a broadcasting ban, imposed on the BBC and on the Independent Broadcast Authority (IBA), which prohibited the airing of words of any member of a 'restricted organisation'. A list of ten such organizations included seven republican paramilitary, political, and cultural bodies, as well as three loyalist paramilitaries.[299] The UK and the Irish bans remained in effect till 1994, permitting censorship of utterances considered subversive both in the North and in the South. As republican violence was sometimes justified with reference to the historical example of the United Irishmen, references to 1798 could be seen as seditious statements and were implicitly discouraged.

Silencing was imposed on a street level through the interface of paramilitary intimidation and military surveillance. Terror and counter-terrorism played on each other, spreading distrust and discouraging open speech. An iconic IRA poster from the 1970s mimicked wartime propaganda in cautioning that 'loose-talk costs lives.' Illustrated with a daunting photo of a masked gunman, the poster issued strict instructions for self-censorship:

[296] Broadcasting Authority Act, 1960; Dáil Éireann Debate, Vol. 256 No. 7, p. 180 (4 November 1971).

[297] Breandan Breathnach, 'Montrose Music', *Ceol*, 4, no. 1. (January 1972), p. 24; cited in Harry White, 'The Need for a Sociology of Irish Folk Music: A Review of Writings on "Traditional" Music in Ireland, with Some Responses and Proposals', *International Review of the Aesthetics and Sociology of Music*, 15, no. 1 (1984), p. 8.

[298] Broadcasting Authority (Amendment) Act, 1976, article 16; see also Betty Purcell, 'The Silence in Irish Broadcasting', in *The Media and Northern Ireland: Covering the Troubles*, edited by Bill Rolston (Houndmills and London: Macmillan, 1991), pp. 51–68.

[299] Russell L. Weaver and Geoffrey Bennett, 'The Northern Ireland Broadcasting Ban: Some Reflections on Judicial Review', *Vanderbilt Journal of Transatlantic Law*, 22 (1989): pp. 1119–60; Ed Moloney, 'Closing Down the Airwaves: The Story of the Broadcasting Ban', in *The Media and Northern Ireland: Covering the Troubles*, edited by Bill Rolston (Houndmills and London: Macmillan, 1991), pp. 8–50; David Miller, 'The Media and Northern Ireland: Censorship, Information Management and the Broadcasting Ban', in *Glasgow Media Group Reader*, edited by Greg Philo (London and New York: Routledge, 1995), 2, pp. 45–75.

In taxis
On the phone
In clubs and bars
At football matches
At home with friends
Anywhere!
Whatever you say—
say nothing.[300]

The aphorism 'Whatever you say, say nothing' seemed to capture the spirit of everyday life during the Troubles. It was used by Seamus Heaney in 1975 as the title of a poem which bemoaned 'Northern reticence, the tight gag of place'.[301] The phrase also featured in a humorous song by the county Down balladeer Colum Sands, in which the chorus 'whatever you say, say nothing when you talk about you know what' mocked the paranoia and fear instilled by the Troubles. When the song was famously performed in concerts by Tommy Makem and Liam Clancy, audiences could both laugh at, and relate to, the streetwise advice of 'the less you say, the less you hear, and the less you'll go astray.'[302] In the precarious culture of reticence that prevailed, speaking of Ninety-Eight became awkward for those who did not want to be associated with the armed struggle of present-day republicanism.

The subtle ways in which the violent conflict influenced social forgetting can be demonstrated through a local poem about Ninety-Eight, from sometime in the mid-1960s in the townland of Ballycreen, where the folk heroine Betsy Gray was believed to have been killed and buried. It was composed by James Somerville, a Presbyterian farmer whose brother John was known for his knowledge of local history. According to family tradition, their grandfather had been present at Betsy Gray's burial. Drawing on long-standing memories, Somerville's poem recalled the plight of hard-working Presbyterian tenant farmers, who suffered under the yoke of exploitative rents, collected by 'the landlords and their muscle men', on top of the obligation to pay tithes to the Church of England, 'no matter what faith a man might hold'. Unwilling to submit to oppression, 'They rather chose the pike and sword / To right these wrongs or die.' It appears that the heritage of Presbyterian agrarian radicalism had not lost its edge. Somerville's poem shows that grievances from the time of the rebellion were still considered relevant in the mid-twentieth century:

The powers that be their force exploit
Unto this present day
For every pound to tenant lent
Twofold does he repay.

In addition to lamenting the death of 'brave Betsy of the wood and field', the poem reveals that the names of McCracken, Orr, Dickson, and Munro were 'honoured both now and then'.

---

[300] Reproduced in Marc Mulholland, *The Longest War: Northern Ireland's Troubled History* (Oxford and New York: Oxford University Press, 2002), p. 100.

[301] Heaney, *North*, 52–5.

[302] Colum Sands *Unapproved Road* (Spring Records, 1981); Makem and Clancy, *Live at the National Concert Hall* (Shanachie Records, 1983).

The Ballycreen Ninety-Eight poem was published in the *Mourne Observer* at the end of October 1968, just months before the outbreak of the Troubles, as part of the enthusiastic response to the serialization of Lyttle's *Betsy Gray*, which had encouraged Protestant readers in south Down to openly share their local traditions of 1798. Despite this climate of broad-mindedness, the poem was subtly revised in its adaptation to print. The untamed version that was recited in intimate settings, at local gatherings, and behind closed doors included additional verses that drew explicit parallels with current times. In one of the expurgated stanzas, the B-Specials [Ulster Special Constabulary, commonly referred to as the 'B Men'] were compared to the loyalist henchmen of 1798:

> The yeomen they are with us still
> Much changed we can allow
> Yet the same old hound with different spots
> They're called the 'B' men now.

Another stanza criticized the zealousness of ultra-loyalists, apparently alluding to Orange parades:

> And still the blind their banners waves
> Confused in every way
> And bow their heads to foreign Queen
> Subject's to display.

Such unorthodox verses could not be circulated in print, but were nonetheless recited orally in a unionist neighbourhood.

With the escalation of violence, political tensions ran high and many Protestants in the Ballynahinch area became supporters of Ian Paisley's hard-line loyalist Democratic Unionist Party (DUP), founded in 1971. After the *Republican News* suggested that 'Henry Joy, the Commander in Chief of the forces of '98, is one person both Nationalist and Unionist workers can be proud of', Paisley's *Protestant Telegraph* responded with characteristic invective. An article denouncing 'sentimental humbug' maintained that 'In the opinion of many, his [McCracken's] hanging was well deserved—not for his rebellion against the "Establishment" but for the betrayal of his fellow Presbyterians and for his joining with murdering papists.' Remonstrating against 'how an aura of romance and a halo of martyrdom has come to surround his name and his memory', the *Protestant Telegraph* asserted that 'no reason can be discerned to prevent his name stinking in the nostrils of every true Presbyterian as being a traitor and a renegade.' The Paisleyite prejudiced understanding of 1798 was that the Protestants, and in particular the Presbyterians, of Ulster had by and large remained loyal and the only ones to join the rebels were 'Arians' [Unitarians] and a few individuals 'of McCracken's peculiar character in whom the spirit of Presbyterianism and of conscience burnt but feebly'. The 'accepted myth of Harry McCracken' was said to be 'on a par' with the 'sentimental humbug' of the 'other myths' endorsed by republicans, such as Betsy Gray, who had also been lauded in the *Republican News*.[303]

In these polarized conditions, tolerance for the ambiguous recollections of the Turn-Out receded and performance of folk history became more risky. Accordingly, a *post*

---

[303] *Republican News*, 23 April 1972, p. 3 (McCracken) and 11 June (Betsy Gray); *Protestant Telegraph*, 4 November 1972, pp. 6–7; see Davis, 'The Manufacture of Propagandist History', p. 151.

scriptum was added to the local Ninety-Eight poem in Ballycreen, so as to vouch for the narrator's loyalty:

> Off the record whale hog rebel suits the theme.
> Betsy should have been at home
> Possibly strong boned country wench bossey,
> Big feet, buck teeth, Boles Gray should have died at B'hinch,
> That's where the battle was!

These verses, distinguished from the rest of the poem in their crude register and style, which in itself seems antiquated, and therefore suggests authenticity, were prudently designed to dissociate the reciter from the poem's seditious content. Betsy Gray was quite literally put in her place, as a woman who should have stayed at home, and her companions were discredited for running away from the battlefield. With this addition tagged on, the poem both evoked deep local memories of the rebellion and at the same time pretended to disown them, under the cover of a purposely deceptive veil of oblivion.[304]

Since militant republicans claimed to be the heirs of the rebels of 1798, militant loyalists were inclined to disremember the history of Protestant involvement in the United Irishmen. Gusty Spence, one of the senior figures in the revived UVF at the time of its establishment in 1966, recalled that as a youth he was taken by a Catholic acquaintance to the 1798 sesquicentennial parade on the Falls Road in 1948 and that he was surprised to discover that 'all the rebels in Belfast were Protestants.'[305] Loyalist paramilitaries were in effect 'Queen's rebels'.[306] Outlawed in Northern Ireland, they felt betrayed both by the Stormont regime and by the administration of British Direct Rule that replaced it on 28 March 1972, yet they refused to recognize the possibility that their predicament may have historical similarities with the republican rebels of the past.

An article that appeared in the UVF magazine *Combat* in 1974, written by 'an East Antrim Officer'—described as 'one who was reared in the staunch Orange Sixmilewater district of County Antrim and who has studied the history of the Protestant United Irishmen who once had strong support there', cautioned loyalists from identifying with the Protestant United Irishmen 'who like ourselves bitterly opposed, the interference of English politicians and overlords in the administration of their affairs'. The unnamed author recognized that 'today, we the loyalists, are classed as Protestant rebels. We are in the same situation as McCracken, Hope, Orr and Neilson were in 1798.' Nonetheless, he emphatically insisted that 'we must NEVER FOLLOW IN THE FOOT-STEPS OF THE PROTESTANT REBELS OF '98, we must never ally ourselves with the Republicans . . . We must stand alone and fight our own battles.'[307]

The independent historian and unionist politician Ian Adamson made an effort to integrate the 1798 rebellion into a loyalist sense of history. Adamson has been credited as the 'intellectual mentor of the UDA' for his contributions to the loyalist paramilitary's magazine *Ulster*, written under the pseudonym Sam Sloan—which adopted the

---

[304] Collected from John Somerville (the son of the author) on 24 August 2003, Ballynahinch, county Down; cf. *Mourne Observer*, 25 October 1968, p. 10.
[305] *Belfast Telegraph*, 3 April 1997.
[306] See David W. Miller, *Queen's Rebels: Ulster Loyalism in Historical Perspective* (Dublin: Gill and Macmillan, 1978).
[307] *Combat*, 1 April 1974, p. 3 (emphasis in the original).

surname of his maternal grandmother, who had told him family traditions of Ninety-Eight.[308] While imaginatively developing a far-fetched ethno-genesis for Ulster-Scots as 'the Cruthin', a supposed indigenous population that had been displaced and later returned to reclaim their birth right, Adamson found a place for the northern United Irishmen in this mytho-historical construction. In his narrative, the 'Presbyterian Cruthin of Antrim, Down and East Derry' idealistically rallied to the United Irish cause only to be let down by 'the lukewarm support from the Catholics, and [were] finally horrified by the stories of atrocity and massacre of Protestants' in the South. Consequently, 'the Cruthin; disgusted, dismayed and finally fearful of the new sectarian aspect of "Irish freedom," many joined the Orange Order, and with some reservation supported the Union of Great Britain and Ireland in 1801. This Union they have fought to maintain ever since.' Growing up in the townland of Conlig in county Down (2 km south of Bangor), Adamson had been raised on family traditions of his rebel descendant, Archibel Wilson, who was executed in 1798, yet such local folk memories were not openly celebrated by loyalists during the Troubles.[309]

An article in the *Orange Standard*, the official organ of the Orange Order, which apparently was not widely read by the membership, proposed in March 1988 that it might be acceptable to commemorate the Antrim and Down rebels of 1798, but this unorthodox suggestion was not pursued.[310] Nevertheless, at a grass-roots level, the notion that unionist Presbyterians could potentially retrieve their rebel ancestry seems to have gained some ground within loyalist circles. At a cross-community think tank facilitated in 1993 by Michael Hall, who brought together a small group of Protestant loyalists and Catholic nationalists to explore the notion of 'Ulster's Shared Heritage', a UDA leader from East Belfast with a county Down background argued with republicans over the ownership of the United Irishmen, asking 'how has [sic] these guys become the men of '98, and we're the men of '98?'.[311] Such claims were rarely, if ever, voiced in public.

Despite the repression of the memory of Ninety-Eight, traces of vernacular history could crop up in unexpected forms. 'The Ulster Girl', a seemingly innocuous song, performed by the Belfast band Platoon to the tune of Dan Hill's pop hit 'Sometimes When We Touch', became immensely popular among loyalists. It was first recorded around 1989 on the cassette *Songs of the U.V.F.*, which was presented as 'the first step on the long road of re-establishing the Loyalist tradition of recounting in song, stories of patriotism, courage sacrifice and resolve relating to our heritage of freedom and British way of life', and has since appeared on several CDs recorded by the band, all of which display paramilitary images on the cover. It is regularly included on compilations of loyalist songs and has also been recorded by other singers on the loyalist music

---

[308] Adamson, *Bangor, Light of the World*; Davis, 'The Manufacture of Propagandist History', pp. 153 and 174–5.

[309] Ian Adamson, *Cruthin: The Ancient Kindred* (Newtownards: Nosmada Books, 1974), pp. 86–7; Ian Adamson, *The Identity of Ulster: The Land, the Language and the People* (Belfast: self-published, 1982), pp. 49–53; see also Tom Paulin, 'At the Cape of Unhope', *Fortnight*, no. 192 (1983): pp. 21–2. For the execution of Archibel Wilson see Chapter 3 above, p. 161.

[310] See Howe, *Ireland and Empire*, p. 259n40.

[311] Michael Hall, *Ulster's Shared Heritage* (Newtownabbey: Island Publications, 1993); reproduced in Lee A. Smithey, *Unionists, Loyalists, and Conflict Transformation in Northern Ireland* (Oxford and New York: Oxford University Press, 2011), p. 179.

scene.[312] The song's popularity masked its origins so that it has been completely unnoticed that it is actually a re-adaptation of a Ninety-Eight ballad.

'The Ulster Girl' was written in 1973 by a loyalist prisoner in Crumlin Road jail, who used the initials J. McC. It opens with the stanza:

> An Ulster Girl in heart and soul, I love our dear old land,
> I honour those who in her cause lift voice or pen or hand,
> And may I die before I see this land we fought to save,
> In Rebel Hands and I at worst the mother of the slaves.[313]

These verses were unmistakably inspired by a poem that appears in Lyttle's *Betsy Gray* (and was possibly composed by Lyttle himself), which reads:

> An Irish maid in heart and soul
> I love the dear old land;
> Honour those who in her cause
> Lift voice, or pen, or hand.
> And may I live to see her free
> From foreign lord and knave;
> But Heaven forbid I'd ever be
> The mother of a slave.[314]

It is unclear if the author of the loyalist version was at all aware of his plagiarism or whether he was unconsciously drawing on a dim recollection of having previously read Lyttle's bestseller. Indeed, *Betsy Gray* was read with enthusiasm by loyalists. For example, the loyalist politician David Ervine of the Progressive Unionist Party (PUP), who had been a member of the UVF and served a five-year jail sentence in the Maze prison for possession of explosives, recalled that, when he was a teenager, his father had given him the novel to read.[315]

In a preface to the *Mourne Observer* edition of *Betsy Gray*, issued in 1968, Aiken McClelland wrote that:

> For many years after its first publication, this was a standard book in almost every County Down home, and though a vast number of books has been written about the Rebellion of 1798, many have gleaned their knowledge of the insurrection solely from Betsy Gray.[316]

Tony Stewart, an authority on the northern United Irishmen, confirmed that, even though Lyttle's *Betsy Gray* was dismissed by professional historians as a form of 'antiquarianism', among the general public 'for generations it had an honoured place in many an Ulster cottage alongside the Bible and Foxe's *Book of Martyrs*'. Stewart, a

---

[312] Platoon, *Songs of the U.V.F.* (n.d.); for the lyrics see *Songs of Honour and Glory as Performed by the Platoon Roadshow* (Belfast: s.n., 1998). See also Pietzonka, *And the Healing Has Begun*, p. 95; David A. Wilson, 'Ulster Loyalism and Country Music', in *Country Music Goes to War*, edited by Charles K. Wolfe and James Edward Akenson (Lexington, Ky.: University Press of Kentucky, 2005), pp. 192–207.

[313] Bill Rolston, 'Music and Politics in Ireland: The Case of Loyalism', in *Politics and Performance in Contemporary Northern Ireland*, edited by John P. Harrington and Elizabeth J. Mitchell (Amherst: University of Massachusetts Press, 1999), pp. 29–30.

[314] Lyttle, *Betsy Gray*, 1968 edn, pp. 99–100.

[315] Ed Moloney, *Voices from the Grave: Two Men's War in Ireland* (London: Faber and Faber, 2010), p. 316.

[316] Lyttle, *Betsy Gray*, 1968 edn, p. x.

Belfast Presbyterian, had a distinct memory of family gatherings at the house of an uncle, considered a bona fide unionist for having fought at the Battle of the Somme as a second lieutenant in the 36th (Ulster) Division. The uncle was originally from Killinchy in county Down and it was believed that 'some of his ancestors may have been "out" in 1798.' Stewart recalled how 'he would leap up and carry me off to his library to retrieve a much treasured copy of a work called *Betsy Gray, or Hearts of Down*' and would 'get quite emotional about her'.[317] Growing up just some years later in a Catholic neighbourhood in Belfast, Marianne Elliott, also an authority on the United Irishmen, observed that 'the short novel became a minor classic and I remember my father retelling the story as late as the 1960s and 1970s.' She recalled hearing in her childhood Ulster Presbyterians speak proudly of their rebel ancestors and realized that 1798 is a rare case of a 'history that Presbyterians share with Catholics', so that when it comes to remembering Betsy Gray 'both sides want to own her as a hero.'[318]

Even though the Troubles stifled remembrance of Ninety-Eight, the influences of the popular consumption of a shared vernacular history, which was of continued interest to both Protestant unionists and Catholic nationalists, was not entirely erased. Jay Winter, reflecting on the history of political silencing in the twentieth century, has drawn attention to the role of writers and artists, who 'occupy liminal positions within society, and sometimes manage to say the unsayable'. Their poetic license fulfils a social function, which can 'help us, perhaps force us, to hear the silences built into the language we use to describe the past'.[319] In defiance of the prevailing culture of silencing in Northern Ireland, it was up to small number of nonconformist writers to remind the public of the ambiguous legacy of the United Irishmen.

NONCONFORMISM

When in his 80s, the writer and folklorist Padraic Colum, who in his youth had been a key figure in the Irish literary revival, wrote five short historical plays in the style of the Japanese Noh theatre, a genre combining elements of drama, music, and poetry that had previously been utilized by W. B. Yeats for adaptations of Irish mythology. *Kilmore*, the last play in Colum's cycle, follows the deliberations of Henry Joy McCracken as he prepares to set off to lead the rebellion in Ulster. McCracken is shielded from an informer by the ghost of the Protestant Bishop William Bedell, who had earned the respect of rebels in 1642 by sheltering Catholic refugees. The play ends with the song collector Edward Bunting, a close acquaintance of the McCracken family, being charged by the ghost with preserving the legacy of those who have gone off to die in the 1798 rebellion. Written in 1965, Colum's 1798 play remained unpublished for a decade and half and has never been produced.[320] There were a few

[317] A. T. Q. Stewart, 'The Siege of Ulster', *Spectator*, 256 (11 January 1986): pp. 15–16 (republished as 'Why Loyalist Feeling of Betrayal Runs So Deep', in *Irish Times*, 14 January 1986, p. 8); A. T. Q. Stewart, 'The Ghost of Betsy Gray', in *1798 Rebellion in County Down*, edited by Myrtle Hill, Brian Turner, and Kenneth Dawson (Newtownards: Colourpoint, 1998), p. 251.
[318] Elliott, *The Catholics of Ulster*, p. 263; *Irish Times*, 28 January 1997, p. 15.
[319] Jay Winter, 'Thinking About Silence', in Ben-Ze'ev et al., *Shadows of War*, pp. 29–30.
[320] Padraic Colum, 'Kilmore', *Poetry Ireland Review*, no. 3 (1981): pp. 7–19. See also Zack R. Bowen, *Padraic Colum: A Biographical-Critical Introduction* (Carbondale: Southern Illinois

remarkable Northern writers who took upon themselves to revive the memory of the United Irishmen in Ulster, yet they too had to overcome inhibitions, which often impeded their work. The eminent poets John Hewitt and Seamus Heaney, for example, also wrote plays about Ninety-Eight that were neglected and forgotten. Social forgetting retained its hold, even over those who seemed determined to speak out.

John Harold Hewitt, described by the northern Catholic poet John Montague as 'the first (and probably the last) deliberately Ulster Protestant poet', is considered 'a father figure to Ulster's poets' of the late twentieth century.[321] He was raised in a unionist environment and recalled attending, at the age of 6, the county Down UVF rally addressed by Edward Carson in 1913 at Six Road Ends, a site chosen because of its connection with traditions of Betsy Gray and 1798.[322] Hewitt, who inherited his father's social radicalism, supported the Northern Ireland Labour Party and rejected mainstream unionism in favour of Ulster regionalism.[323] He found grounds for both his convictions—socialism and regionalism—in the heritage of Ninety-Eight.

Hewitt grew up on Belfast's Clifton Street, a neighbourhood where prominent United Irishmen had lived and in which some of them were buried. In ''98', an early poem written in 1930, he professed an intimate familiarity with the sites associated with the northern revolutionaries:

> I know well where William Orr,
> McCracken, Dixon, talked before
> those brief bought weeks of '98
> bore them away to brutal fate.[324]

Another poem, found in an undated notebook titled 'The Red Hand' (after the heraldic symbol of the province of Ulster), expresses admiration for Henry Joy McCracken's passionate ideological commitment ('ardor violent'), as opposed to the insipid unionist politicians of Northern Ireland. Hewitt was critical of the state funeral given to Carson at St Anne's Church, Belfast, on 26 October 1935, describing the outpour of unionist bereavement as 'hypocritical mourning for the cheated leader of a wrong cause'. Seeking more meaningful memorialization, he went that day to Mallusk to visit the grave of McCracken's faithful follower, the working class rebel James Hope.[325]

For Hewitt, Hope was one of the 'brave old pre-Marx Marxists of Ireland', his writings 'displaying a remarkably accurate analysis, even employing the very phrase,

---

University Press, 1970), pp. 23 and 88; Bernice Schrank and William W. Demastes, *Irish Playwrights, 1880–1995: A Research and Production Sourcebook* (Westport, Conn.: Greenwood Press, 1997), p. 73.

[321] *Irish Times*, 30 June 1987, p. 5; Gerald Dawe, 'Against Piety: A Reading of John Hewitt's Poetry', in *The Poet's Place: Ulster Literature and Society. Essays in Honour of John Hewitt, 1907–87*, edited by Gerald Dawe and John Wilson Foster (Belfast: Institute of Irish Studies, 1991), p. 218.

[322] John Harold Hewitt, *A North Light: Twenty-Five Years in a Municipal Art Gallery* (Dublin: Four Courts Press, 2013), p. 46. For the rally at Six Road Ends see Chapter 5 above, pp. 424–5.

[323] Aoileann Ní Éigeartaigh, '"No Rootless Colonist": John Hewitt's Regionalist Approach to Identity', in *Affecting Irishness: Negotiating Cultural Identity within and Beyond the Nation*, edited by James P. Byrne, Padraig Kirwan and Michael O'Sullivan (Oxford and New York: Peter Lang, 2008), pp. 121–41; Connal Parr, 'The Pens of the Defeated: John Hewitt, Sam Thompson and the Northern Ireland Labour Party', *Irish Studies Review*, 22, no. 2 (2014): pp. 147–66.

[324] Edna Longley, *The Living Stream: Literature & Revisionism in Ireland* (Newcastle upon Tyne: Bloodaxe, 1994), p. 114.

[325] Hewitt, *A North Light*, p. 43.

"war of the classes", to be popularised by Marx and Engels some years later.' In an essay on 'James Hope, Weaver, of Templepatrick', which was based on Madden's memoir and first published in 1941 in the socialist newspaper the *Northern Star* (a title that evoked the radical newspapers of the United Irishmen and of the Chartists), Hewitt asserted that 'no other life so epitomises that period of revolt from the inauguration of the United Irishmen to the defeat of Emmet. And no other participant so cut through appearance and illusion to the economic truth.' Hewitt called upon the 'socialists of Ulster' to mark Hope's birthday on 25 August with an annual pilgrimage to his grave, where they would 'make resolution that those ideas he spent a turbulent lifetime evolving become the very stuff and nature of their thought and activity'.[326]

In 1948, Hewitt contributed a slightly abridged version of his article on James Hope to the 1798 Commemoration Committee's sesquicentennial publication, but he disguised his authorship by adopting a Gaelicized version of his name—John McHugh—as a pseudonym.[327] He also chose to stay away from the contested commemorations of 1798 in Belfast and traveled instead to county Sligo to attend the reburial of Yeats in Drumcliffe churchyard.[328] That year saw the publication of his first major poetry collection *No Rebel Word.* Hewitt's protégé John Montague complained that the 'title does not do justice to the careful complexity of his lonely thought', as it 'seemed to suggest that he was a conservative in politics and language, alien to the Republic brought about by the Easter Rebellion and even to the 1798 Rebellion in his own beloved Antrim and Belfast'.[329] Hewitt had been careful to conceal his identification with the United Irishmen.

Around that time, Hewitt wrote the script of a play, provisionally titled 'The Parting of Friends' (after a traditional tune) and posthumously renamed *The McCrackens.* As pointed out by the county Down poet and critic Damian Smyth, it appears to have been written in response to Jack Loudan's play *Henry Joy McCracken.* Dissatisfied by Loudan's crude depiction, which left no room for ambiguity, Hewitt made use of vernacular history, drawing in particular on Madden's *The United Irishmen*, in order to show the range of opinions within northern United Irish circles, from the ideologically committed revolutionaries to those who were hesitant and chose not to join the insurrection. The play follows their deliberations and anxieties from 1795, as they resolve to prepare a rebellion, through to the dire consequences of their failure in 1798.

A final scene in Hewitt's play takes place in 1845 and addresses the anxieties of the last survivors over how they will be remembered. Madden, who has just visited the sites of the rebellion with James Hope, 'going over the ground to get places and times fixed' for his historical writings, pays a visit to the venerable Mary Ann McCracken. Both Hope and McCracken express their appreciation for Madden's 'great work', which 'should take up the task of rescuing the memories of valiant men from the infamous histories of privileged cupidity'. In turn, Madden affirms his belief that 'the heritage of

---

[326] John Hewitt, 'James Hope, Weaver, of Templepatrick', in *Ancestral Voices: The Selected Prose of John Hewitt*, edited by Tom Clyde (Belfast: Blackstaff, 1987), pp. 133–7; originally published in *Northern Star*, 2, no. 2 (April 1941). For the commemorative abridged version see McKearney, *Ninety-Eight*, pp. 33–4.

[327] McKearney, *Ninety-Eight*, pp. 33–4.

[328] W. J. McCormack, *Northman: John Hewitt (1907–1987), an Irish Writer, His World, and His Times* (Oxford and New York: Oxford University Press, 2015), p. 108.

[329] John Montague, 'An Ulster Tandem', *Irish Pages*, 3, no. 1 (2005): pp. 162–3.

honourable memory is one of man's greatest treasures' and McCracken is re-assured that 'the heritage is in safe hands.' Aware of the vagaries of heritage, Hope jokes that 'they'll be having coats in the museum we never wore and swords we never drew', giving voice to Hewitt's criticism of the abuse of official commemoration, as opposed to the more radical character of vernacular remembrance. Once completed, the manu-script of the play languished in obscurity and was not mentioned in Hewitt's notebooks and letters, or in the detailed diaries kept by his wife, Roberta Black Hewitt. Conse-quently, this remarkably sophisticated work of cultural memory did not make an impact on social memory.[330]

In 1951, Hewitt submitted to Queen's University Belfast a Master's thesis on 'Ulster poets, 1800–1870', which would be adapted in 1974 into the book *Rhyming Weavers and Other Country Poets of Antrim and Down*. He was interested in poets, such as James Orr and James Campbell, who had written vernacular verses in Ulster-Scots about their experiences in the 1798 rebellion and was aware that even the poetry of those who had opposed the United Irishmen, such as Francis Boyce, was still deeply affected by the insurrection. However, Hewitt prudently set the stating date for the subject of his dissertation after the rebellion and avoided mentioning the active involvement of James Hope (who was both a weaver and a composer of poetic verses) in the events of 1798 and 1803. When writing in 1953 about the poets in his ancestral parish, he chose to remain silent about their involvement on either side of the rebellion.[331]

Hewitt paid a personal price for his nonconformist politics. His promising career at the Belfast Museum and Art Gallery Belfast, where 'the sad, long-jawed painting of James Hope and the faded daguerreotype of Mary Ann McCracken proved themselves icons of greater charismatic power',[332] came to a halt after unionist members of Belfast City Council thwarted his appointment as director. He subsequently went into exile in England, taking up the post of director of the Herbert Art Gallery and Museum in Coventry from 1957 till his return to Belfast in 1972.

Hewitt's poetry has been credited for its grasp of remembrance and forgetting.[333] Less noticeably, he also took on board the northern culture of reticence, admitting in an autobiographical memoir that 'I had been schooled by living in Ireland for so long, to keep a discreet tongue in my head, never speaking to anyone of any confidential matter, unless the other man mentioned it first, or unless that I felt sure that he needed to hear it.'[334] As acknowledged by the critic Patricia Craig, he 'had the entire history of northern Irish literature at his fingertips' and commanded an incomparable knowledge of the writings of the United Irishmen and of the writers that had written about

[330] 'The Parting of Friends', John Hewitt Papers, Box 15, University of Ulster, Coleraine; John Harold Hewitt, *Two Plays: The McCrackens; The Angry Doves*, edited and introduced by Damian Smyth (Belfast: Lagan Press, 1999), pp. 13–71.

[331] John Hewitt, 'Ulster poets, 1800–1870' (M.A. thesis: Queen's University Belfast, 1951); McCormack, *Northman*, pp. 13 and 126–7. See also Chapter 3 above, p. 182n202.

[332] John Hewitt, 'No Rootless Colonist', in Clyde, ed., *Ancestral Voices*, p. 150; originally published in *Aquarius*, 5 (1972), pp. 90–5; see also *Belfast Municipal Museum and Art Gallery Bulletin*, 1, no. 2 (1949): pp. 29–30 and 32.

[333] Terence Brown, *The Literature of Ireland: Culture and Criticism* (Cambridge and New York: Cambridge University Press, 2010), pp. 170–7; Fran Brearton, 'Poetry and Forgetting: On Hewitt's "Neither an Elegy nor a Manifesto"', *The Poetry Ireland Review*, no. 104 (2011): pp. 81–7.

[334] Hewitt, *A North Light*, p. 207.

them.[335] Yet, he seems to have held back from engaging too openly with the topic. Hewitt's Ninety-Eight play, which may have been intended for radio, was left buried among his papers. It was only discovered some years after his death in 1987 and was first treated to a public reading in 1998, at the Eleventh John Hewitt International Summer School in Carnlough, county Antrim, but has never been staged.

The writer Sam Hanna Bell shared Hewitt's socialism and his advocation of regionalism. He felt unease with official unionist culture and considered himself 'a radical with a faint Nationalist colouration' and 'a nostalgic hankering for 1798', but was unwilling to become a fully fledged nationalist.[336] Bell had spent the formative years of his childhood in Raffrey, near Strangford Lough in county Down, before moving to live in poverty in Belfast. Though an autodidact, he became well versed in literature and history and, with the support of the poet Louis McNeice, was recruited in 1945 by BBC Northern Ireland. As a features assistant, Bell pioneered radio field recordings, producing programmes on 'the voices of men and women, describing their daily toil, their recreations, their hopes and troubles'. He worked with Michael J. Murphy to collect local folklore, which featured in the radio series *Fairy Faith* (1952) and in his book *Erin's Orange Lily* (1956). His characteristic broad-mindedness, which treated with respect all political traditions, was particularly evident in the production of the radio series *The Orangemen* (1967).[337]

A Man Flourishing, Bell's second historical novel, was published in London in 1973, re-issued in Belfast in 1986, and was also treated to a radio adaptation by Trevor Royle in 1988. It looks closely at the readjustments made by Ulster Presbyterians in consequence of the 1798 rebellion. The protagonist James Gaunt, a divinity student at the University of Glasgow, returns to visit his home in Ravara (5 km north-east of Saintfield) in the parish of Killinchy, county Down, just as the rebellion breaks out. He joins a party of United Irishmen, but their captain is reluctant to turn out and they disperse without participating in the Battle of Ballynahinch. Six of the would-be rebels are caught and summarily hanged, while Gaunt goes into hiding together with another United Irishman on the run, William Keane (whose character is based on a historical rebel from Belfast). They take refuge in the residence of a shady doctor, who has connections with the criminal underworld, and bide their time until they can escape to America.

Meanwhile, the home of James's sweetheart Katy Purdie is raided by a malicious yeomanry officer, Nugent Mullan, who brutalizes and humiliates the family members, even though they had chosen to remain loyal to the Crown. Once peace has been restored, James returns to marry Katy, puts aside his studies and devotes himself to the pursuit of commercial gain, forsaking his radical ideals. The experiences of 1798 later return to haunt the Gaunt household, when the former yeoman Mullan blackmails Katy and threatens to ruin her husband's reputation by revealing his involvement in the

---

[335] Patricia Craig, 'Finding Hope in the Weavers', *Fortnight*, no. 275 (1989): p. vi. See also Hewitt, 'The Northern Athens', pp. 71–82.

[336] Longley, *The Living Stream*, p. 114.

[337] Douglas Carson, 'A kist o'whistles', *Fortnight*, 290, supplement 'Radical Ulsters' (January 1991): pp. 2–3; Douglas Carson, 'The Antiphon, the Banderol, and the Hollow Ball: Sam Hanna Bell, 1909–1990', *Irish Review*, no. 9 (1990): pp. 91–9; Seán McMahon, *Sam Hanna Bell: A Biography* (Belfast: Blackstaff Press, 1999). See also brochure of the exhibition at the Linen Hall Library *Sam Hanna Bell: A Man Flourishing* (Belfast: BBC Archive Community Archive, 2009).

rebellion. Katy puts an end to this ordeal by murdering the villain, while allowing an innocent man (who incidentally had helped James hide after the insurrection) to be executed for the crime. James Gaunt, whose character may have been partly modelled on the Belfast merchant and banker William Tennent, goes on to become a pillar of Belfast society and is elected as a magistrate. He ends up colluding with his wife to send into exile his radical brother-in-law, who is involved in agrarian agitation. On their path to middle-class respectability and the accumulation of wealth, the couple show no scruples in their determination to bury the troublesome past.

By following the trajectory of a Presbyterian rebel who becomes a complacent unionist, Bell's *Bildungsroman* effectively traces the creation of a framework for social forgetting among the generation that had experienced the events. In time, 'James had discovered, to practise reticence about one's past' and, when 'the years, like tides, threw up fragments of a man's past', these troubling recollections had to be carefully concealed so that they would not be 'pieced together by the curious or the malicious'.[338] Publishers were reluctant to take on a book that dug so deep into Ulster's psyche. After being rejected by fifteen publishers, it was finally accepted by Gollancz, on the condition that the original manuscript would be substantially shortened. The final version could not avoid giving the impression that 'it had been cut down from a much larger undertaking' and consequently there were those who thought that '*A Man Flourishing* betrayed its great subject.'[339]

The observation of the literary critic Edna Longley that Ulster Protestant 'progressive bookmen' preferred 'to use 1798 rather than 1916 as a radical benchmark', and her suggestion that this choice 'may define difference from, rather than solidarity with, the Southern state', rings true for Hewitt and Bell.[340] The poet Seamus Heaney also espoused a form of Ulster regionalism, but, as a Catholic, did not feel a need to dissociate himself from southern Ireland. Heaney reflected indirectly on the jubilee of the Easter Rising in 1966 by composing 'Requiem for the Croppies', a sonnet about the 1798 rebels in county Wexford and their defeat at the Battle of Vinegar Hill. In spite of unionist hegemony in Northern Ireland, he sensed 'a new slight air of liberalism' that could accommodate a 'deliberately espoused nationalist Irish poem about the insurrection of 1798, which was the founding of Irish Republicanism'.[341]

'Requiem for the Croppies' would later acquire anthemic status among republicans, who interpreted Heaney's depiction of rebels 'shaking scythes at cannon' as a glorification of blood sacrifice, though this had not been the poet's intention. In 1968, Heaney, alongside the poets Derek Mahon and Michael Longley, and the singer David Hammond, participated in 'Room to Rhyme', a poetry reading tour funded by the

---

[338] Sam Hanna Bell, *A Man Flourishing* (London: Gollancz, 1973), quotation from p. 223. See also McMahon, *Sam Hanna Bell*, pp. 148–58; Richard Mills, 'Sam Hanna Bell, 1798 and the Death of Protestant Radicalism', in *New Voices in Irish Criticism*, edited by P. J. Mathews (Dublin: Four Courts Press, 2000), pp. 116–22; Markus, *Echoes of the Rebellion*, pp. 103–7, For similarities between Gaunt and Tennent see Wright, *The 'Natural Leaders'*, p. 43n155.

[339] James Simmons, 'A Man Flourishing' and Patricia Craig, 'Out of the Hands of Zealots', in *Fortnight*, 290, supplement 'Radical Ulsters' (January 1991): pp. 3–4; McMahon, *Sam Hanna Bell*, p. 151.

[340] Longley, *The Living Stream*, p. 114.

[341] Thomas C. Foster, *Seamus Heaney* (Dublin: O'Brien Press, 1989), p. 6. For Heaney's engagements with regionalism see Richard Rankin Russell, *Seamus Heaney's Regions* (Notre Dame: University of Notre Dame Press, 2014).

Northern Ireland Arts Council, during which Heaney's 1798 poem was recited to unionist audiences at various venues across Northern Ireland.[342] He later referred to these readings as an exercise of 'silence-breaking rather than rabble-rousing', through which he 'was trying to give voice to things that the culture in Northern Ireland did not admit'.[343] As noted by the literary scholar Heather Clark, Heaney attempted to 'subvert the Ulster code of silence through his poetry'.[344]

Heaney described his upbringing 'in an atmosphere that was full of the silent awarenesses' of belonging to the 'Papish rather than the Republican class', so that he was devoid of 'blistering Republican dogma' and 'knew very little about 1916', but 'knew a lot about 1798'. He recalled that when people gathered in his childhood home 'they would sing songs or recite poems about '98.'[345] Mossbawn, the family farmhouse in county Derry, was situated between Toome, with its associations of Roddy McCorley, and Castledawson, the seat of the Chichester Clarks (an Anglo-Irish family, of which James Chichester Clarke would become prime minister in 1969). This location seemed to Heaney to be 'a symbolic placing for a Northern Catholic, to be in between the marks of nationalist local sentiment on the one hand, and the marks of colonial and British presence on the other'.[346] Traditions of Ninety-Eight were part of the local culture and, in his youth, Heaney participated in an amateur production by the Bellaghy Dramatic Society of a play based on Lyttle's novel *Betsy Gray*, in which he played a blacksmith.[347]

After the outbreak of violence, Heaney notably stopped reading 'Requiem for the Croppies' in public.[348] Creative expression was curtailed by the Troubles, so that writing in Northern Ireland became marked by 'artistic silence and narrative breakdown in texts'.[349] In the introduction to his aptly named collection of critical essays *The Government of the Tongue*, Heaney recalled how his plans to record in 1972 a tape of poetry and songs with the singer David Hammond had to be put aside following a series of explosions in Belfast. It seemed inappropriate to sing as violence was raging around them.[350] Nonetheless, Heaney's familiarity with traditions of the rebellion in Ulster trickled into his poetry.

The depiction of Belfast in 1786 in 'Linen Town', a poem based on a print of a painting by Joseph W. Carey, looks forward to the execution of 'young McCracken' in

---

[342] Heather L. Clark, *The Ulster Renaissance: Poetry in Belfast, 1962–1972* (Oxford: Oxford University Press, 2006), p. 81.

[343] *Telegraph*, 11 April 2009 (interview with Sameer Rahim); *Guardian*, 27 May 2006 (interview with James Campbell).

[344] Clark, *The Ulster Renaissance*, p. 62.

[345] Monie Begley, *Rambles in Ireland and a County-by-County Guide for Discriminating Travelers* (Old Greenwich, Conn.: Devin-Adair, 1977), pp. 161–2; see also Dennis O'Driscoll, *Stepping Stones: Interviews with Seamus Heaney* (New York: Farrar, Straus, and Giroux, 2008), p. 135.

[346] *Irish Times*, 6 December 1975, p. 5 (interview with Caroline Walsh).

[347] Michael Parker, *Seamus Heaney: The Making of the Poet* (Dublin and New York: Gill and Macmillan, 1993), pp. 14 and 81; O'Driscoll, *Stepping Stones*, p. 92.

[348] *Irish Times*, 9 December 1997, p. 14.

[349] See Shane Alcobia-Murphy, *Governing the Tongue in Northern Ireland: The Place of Art/the Art of Place* (Newcastle: Cambridge Scholars Publishing, 2008), pp. 21–36.

[350] Seamus Heaney, *The Government of the Tongue: Selected Prose, 1978–1987* (New York: Farrar, Straus, and Giroux, 1989), p. xi.

twelve years' time.[351] The poem 'A Postcard from North Antrim' recalls how Heaney's friend Sean Armstrong, who was shot in the early days of the Troubles, would sing:

> . . . of Henry Joy McCracken
> Who kissed his Mary Anne
> On the gallows at Cornmarket.[352]

The poem 'At Toomebridge' is located 'where the rebel boy was hanged in '98', in a clear reference to Roddy McCorley.[353] Yet, despite his intimate knowledge of local vernacular history, Heaney's most notable confrontation with the northern reticence regarding 1798 in 'Requiem for the Croppies' purposefully focused on the South and avoided direct engagement with the rebellion in the North. The historian Tony Stewart deftly observed that the fact that 'our finest poet is more moved by the plight of the Wexford rebels [than] those of his native province says much about our present troubles.'[354] Heaney's supposed challenge of silencing was actually complicit with the practices of social forgetting, insofar as unionists were more comfortable, at least in public, in associating the rebellion with Catholics in Wexford than with Protestants in Antrim and Down.

'Requiem for the Croppies' was published in the poetry collection *Door into the Dark* in June 1969. When the sectarian violence of the Troubles erupted two months later, it seemed to Heaney that 'the original heraldic murderous encounter between Protestant yeoman and Catholic rebel was to be initiated again.'[355] That year, he read *The Year of Liberty*, a new history of the 1798 Rebellion by Thomas Pakenham, who wryly noted that 'strange chance which can make the most fervent nationalists of people of immigrant stock', pointing at how Henry Munro, 'a Protestant from Scotland', was elected commander-in-chief of the United Irish army in county Down.[356] Heaney became fascinated with the execution of the northern rebel leader and made several attempts to formulate his impressions in verse, drafting three poems on the subject: 'The Death of Henry Munro' (also titled 'Munro's comforters'), 'Munro to the Hangman', and 'Munro', which he originally thought to title 'Ulster Heritage' in order to flag the historical significance of 1798.[357]

Heaney's main historical source was an eyewitness account of Munro's execution that was written by William Blacker, a captain in the yeomanry and member of the Orange Order, who observed that 'some say the Popish portion of the rebels disliked going under the command of a Presbyterian' (although Munro was actually an Anglican). Blacker was openly hostile to the rebellion, yet he was clearly impressed by Munro's conduct:

---

[351] Seamus Heaney, *Wintering Out* (London: Faber and Faber, 1972), p. 38; based on J. W. Carey, *High Street and Old Market House, 1786* (c. 1903), housed at the Ulster Hall in Belfast. See also Helen Vendler, *Seamus Heaney* (Cambridge, Mass.: Harvard University Press, 1998), pp. 84–5.

[352] Seamus Heaney, *Field Work* (New York: Farrar, Straus & Giroux, 1979), pp. 19–20.

[353] Seamus Heaney, *Electric Light* (New York: Farrar, Straus & Giroux, 2001), p. 3.

[354] *Irish Times*, 10 October 1998, p. 52.

[355] Seamus Heaney, *Door into the Dark* (London: Faber and Faber, 1969), p. 24; Seamus Heaney, *Preoccupations: Selected Prose 1968–1978* (London: Faber and Faber, 1980), p. 56 ('Feeling into Words'; lecture given at the Royal Society of Literature, October 1974).

[356] Pakenham, *The Year of Liberty*, pp. 226–31; Seamus Heaney, 'Delirium of the Brave', *Listener*, 27 November 1969, pp. 757–9.

[357] Seamus Heaney Papers, NLI MSS 49,493/5 (1); MS 49,493/11 and 17 (18); 49,493/37/27, 28 and 29.

It is impossible to imagine anyone more cool and firm without anything of bravado. There was a barrel standing on the spot, on top of which he placed his shop-books, which he caused to be brought to him, and settled his accounts with several persons with as much apparent attention to business as if he had been in his own shop.[358]

To Heaney, this behaviour seemed typical of the down-to-earth business-like approach of Ulster-Scot Presbyterians. His fascination with the Ninety-Eight hero was given an outlet in 1970, when he was commissioned by the BBC to write a short play for the radio series 'Books, Plays, Poems', designed for schoolchildren.

Heaney's verse play *Munro* opens with a poetic depiction of Henry Munro's execution, followed by a singer performing stanzas of the folk ballad 'General Munro' (with which Heaney was familiar from the folk singer David Hammond). The play centres on an exchange between Munro, who believes that 'Sword, Bible and Purse' briefly facilitated 'a commonwealth where all was level', and General Nugent, who declares that 'Authority can smash wrong Bible, sword and purse' and chides Munro that 'Rebellion is not for the amateur.' The rebel hero is confident that his reputation will be saved by 'the ballad monger' and indeed verses of the ballad 'General Munro', which are interspersed throughout the play, appear at the conclusion, showing that the quelling of the rebellion will not stamp out its memory.[359] The play does not appear in the BBC listings in the *Radio Times* and it is unclear if it was broadcast. In any case, it remained obscure and did not make a public impact. Apart from one poem that was included in the play, Heaney did not get around to publishing his other compositions on Munro. In spite of his determination to confront the culture of silencing, his writings on the rebellion in Ulster, which were later played up by literary scholars, remained reserved.[360]

In the latter years of the Troubles, the poet and critic Tom Paulin contemplated the genealogy of radicalism that Hewitt and Heaney had traced back to the rhyming weavers and realized that the memory of the 'Lagan Jacobins'—an allusion to the northern United Irishmen—could be recovered through the vernacular resources of Ulster dialect.[361] Alert to the contradictions in Northern Irish Protestant culture and adverse to its official manifestations, Paulin identified with 'that strain of radical Presbyterianism, free-thinking Presbyterianism, which more or less went underground

[358] Reproduced in Paterson, 'Lisburn and Neighbourhood in 1798', pp. 196–8.

[359] Seamus Heaney, 'Munro', *Everyman*, no. 3 (1970): pp. 58–65. See also John Michael Bell, 'Compelling Identities: Nation and Lyric Form in Seamus Heaney' (DPhil: Faculty of English Language and Literature, University of Oxford, 1993), pp. 255–7; Richard Rankin Russell, 'Imagining a New Province: Seamus Heaney's Creative Work for BBC Northern Ireland Radio, 1968–71', *Irish Studies Review*, 15, no. 2 (2007): pp. 137–62.

[360] John Hobbs, 'United Irishmen: Seamus Heaney and the Rebellion of 1798', *Canadian Journal of Irish Studies*, 21, no. 2 (1995): pp. 38–43; August Gering, 'To Sing of '98: The United Irishmen Rising and the Ballad Tradition in Heaney and Muldoon', *Literature Interpretation Theory*, 10 (1999): pp. 149–79; John F. Healy, 'Seamus Heaney and the Croppies: 1798 and the Poet's Early Political Inclinations', in *Back to the Present, Forward to the Past: Irish Writing and History since 1798*, edited by Brian Coates, Joachim Fischer, and Patricia A. Lynch (Amsterdam and New York: Rodopi, 2006), 1, pp. 53–65.

[361] Tom Paulin, *Liberty Tree* (London and Boston: Faber and Faber, 1983), p. 68; see also Tom Paulin, *A New Look at the Language Question* (Derry: Field Day, 1983); John Harold Hewitt, *Rhyming Weavers & Other Country Poets of Antrim and Down*, 2nd edn (Belfast: Blackstaff, 2004), pp. vii–xii (foreword by Tom Paulin).

after 1798'.[362] He took issue with James Camlin Beckett, professor of Irish history at Queen's University Belfast, who in his seminal *The Making of Modern Ireland*, written in 1966 and re-issued in multiple printings, claimed that 'no matter on which side their forebears fought at Antrim or Saintfield or Ballynahinch', Ulster Protestants 'have long since sunk their differences in a common loyalty to the British connection'. Writing in 1983, Paulin argued that '"common loyalty" undoubtedly existed in 1966 but it is now a thing of the past.'[363]

Paulin's determination to recoup the lost legacy of the United Irishmen's radicalism is a recurring theme in his 1983 poetry collection *Liberty Tree*. In the poem 'Presbyterian Study', he finds that 'Memory is a moist seed' and that 'those linen saints, lithe radicals' still live on. Yet he acknowledges that:

> Hardly a schoolroom remembers
> Their obstinate rebellion;
> Provincial historians
> Scratch circles on the sand.

The poem 'Under Creon' describes his efforts:

> to find a cadence for the dead: McCracken,
> Hope, the northern starlight, a death mask
> and the levelled grave that Biggar traced.

Another poem, 'Father of History', notes how vestiges of historical memory, that are not commemorated by memorials, can be found in the collections of Belfast's Linen Hall Library, where the United Irishman Thomas Russell had been a librarian:

> I traced them to the Linen Hall stacks—
> Munro, Hope, Porter and McCracken;
> like sweet yams buried deep, these rebel minds
> endure posterity without a monument,
> their names a covered sheugh, remnants, some brackish signs.[364]

Paulin was not alone in his search for the memory of the northern United Irishmen. The playwright (James) Stewart Parker was on a similar quest of rediscovery and reclamation.

Parker came from an east Belfast working class Presbyterian background, belonging to what he described as 'an average Unionist family, without being hard line'. He had, according to Seamus Heaney, 'a sure grip on the folk wisdom and collective life of his home town and a natural sense of the northern downbeat'.[365] As an aspiring liberal writer with socialist tendencies, he identified with the non-sectarian and egalitarian ideology of the United Irishmen and had wanted to write about the northern leaders of the rebellion

---

[362] John Haffenden, *Viewpoints: Poets in Conversation with John Haffenden* (London: Faber and Faber, 1981), p. 58.

[363] Paulin, 'At the Cape of Unhope', p. 21; J. C. Beckett, *The Making of Modern Ireland, 1603–1923* (New York: Knopf, 1973; orig. edn 1966), p. 265.

[364] Paulin, *Liberty Tree*, pp. 13 ('Under Creon'), 32 ('Father of History'), 49 ('Presbyterian Study'). The allusion to Biggar probably refers to the antiquarian Francis Joseph Bigger rather than his cousin, once removed, the Home Rule parliamentarian Joseph Gillis Biggar.

[365] *Irish Times*, 3 November 1988, p. 8; *Sunday Independent*, 6 November 1988, p. 18.

since 1967.[366] In an article published in the *Irish Times* in 1970, Parker spoke out against the reinforcement of social forgetting following the outbreak of the Troubles:

> Nearly every day now in the North the plea goes out to 'forget the past.' Such advice is both impracticable and pernicious. On the one hand, you can't forget a nightmare while you are still dreaming it. On the other, it is survival through comprehension that is healthy, not survival through amnesia. Besides, the past is not a dead letter. The past is explosive cargo in everybody's family dresser.[367]

Nevertheless, over a decade passed before he would get around to addressing the elusive subject of Ninety-Eight in a remarkable work of drama.

Northern Star, Parker's most celebrated play, was named after the organ of the northern United Irishmen.[368] In coming to write 'an Ulster history play', Parker realized that 'our past refuses to express itself as a linear, orderly narrative, in a convincing tone of voice' and so he opted for 'a wide range of theatrical ventriloquism'.[369] The play presents a pastiche of dramatic styles that pays tribute to the history of Anglo-Irish theatre and its famous playwrights: George Farquhar and Richard Brinsley Sheridan, Dion Boucicault, Oscar Wilde, George Bernard Shaw, John Millington Synge, Sean O'Casey, Samuel Beckett, and Brendan Behan, while also showing the influence of Northern Ireland's working class Protestant playwrights, not least Thomas Carnduff. It is loosely structured around the Shakespearean concept of the seven ages of man, which, in its original phrasing in *As You Like It* (Act II, Scene VII), ends with 'mere oblivion'.[370] In a foreword to the play, Parker noted that 'so far as the "real" characters are concerned, they have been drawn from the marginalia of the historical record rather than its main plot' and it is evident that he made extensive use of sources from vernacular historiography, drawing in particular on the recollections compiled in Madden's *The United Irishmen*. Filtered through black humour, Irish history is presented as a cycle that 'just goes on, playing out the same demented comedy of terrors from generation to generation, trapped in the same malignant legend.'[371]

Instead of a conventional historical drama that takes place in a remote past, Parker was determined to 'write a play set in 1798 which was speaking directly to people

---

[366] Marilynn Richtarik, 'Living in Interesting Times: Stewart Parker's Northern Star', in *Politics and Performance in Contemporary Northern Ireland*, edited by John P. Harrington and Elizabeth J. Mitchell (Amherst: University of Massachusetts Press, 1999), p. 8.

[367] *Irish Times*, 6 March 1970, p. 11; republished in Stewart Parker, *Dramatis Personae and Other Writings*, edited by Gerald Dawe, Maria Johnston, and Clare Wallace (Prague: Litteraria Pragensia, 2008), pp. 38–41.

[368] Stewart Parker, *Plays*, vol. 2 (London: Methuen Drama, 2000), pp. 1–82; originally published in Stewart Parker, *Three Plays for Ireland* (Birmingham: Oberon Books, 1989). See also Parr, *Inventing the Myth*, pp. 147–8.

[369] Programme note for the original Lyric Players Theatre production of *Northern Star* (Belfast, 1984); cited in Marilynn J. Richtarik, *Stewart Parker: A Life* (Oxford: Oxford University Press, 2012), p. 256.

[370] *Times*, 26 September 1985, p. 17; Thomas Kilroy, 'From Farquhar to Parker', in the programme notes to the Field Day Theatre Company and Tinderbox Theatre Company production of *Northern Star* (Belfast, 1998); Anthony Roche, 'Stewart Parker's Comedy of Terrors', in *A Companion to Modern British and Irish Drama, 1880–2005*, edited by Mary Luckhurst (Malden, Mass. and Oxford: Blackwell, 2006), pp. 294–5; Richtarik, *Stewart Parker*, pp. 256–7.

[371] Parker, *Plays*, pp. xiv and 69; see also *Observer*, 6 October 1985, p. 21.

today'.[372] Accordingly, *Northern Star* is set in 'Ireland, the continuous past', a mnemonic timeframe which prompted the critic Fintan O'Toole to quip that 'there is no past tense in Irish history.' O'Toole later clarified that the play 'reminds us all the time that the events of 1798 are still being, literally, played out' and 'we are reminded that, in the theatre, the difference between the past and the present fades to nothing, and that people don't have to be alive to be our contemporaries.'[373] Convinced that 'in any play ancestral voices prophesy and bicker, and the ghosts of your own time and birthplace wrestle and dance', Parker revisited the failed United Irish attempt to offer an alternative to the divisive legacy of 'two islands (the "British Isles"), two Irelands, two Ulsters, two men fighting over a field'.[374]

On the forestage, Parker placed a lambeg drum (an icon of Protestant loyalist culture) alongside a bodhran (a symbol of Gaelic, and by extension Catholic, culture) and stipulated that these traditional musical instruments were to be 'played by members of the company, who may each play several roles in the action'. His instruction that 'a change of role may he accomplished merely by a change of hat, coat or wig' deliberately undermines the rigid separation between the 'two traditions' on which Northern Ireland was founded. In place of the standard dichotomy, Parker favoured a more fluid notion of interchangeable identities, based on memories of shared traditions, which make it clear that 'without the Protestants of the North, there'll never be a nation.'[375]

The play takes place in the interior of a farm labourer's cottage on the slopes of Cavehill, outside Belfast, and consists of a series of flashbacks in which Henry Joy McCracken reflects on the circumstances that led to the failure of the rebellion. His recollections culminate in a prison scene that is unmistakably resonant of the late twentieth-century Troubles. Three United Irish prisoners are forced to stand 'facing the back wall, leaning on their fingertips against the wall, feet splayed out, with hoods over their heads' and are exposed to ear-piercing 'white noise', before each of them in turn is thrown to the ground, pinioned with a baton across his throat, and interrogated. The dramatization of 1798 is designed to mirror present-day experiences in the 1980s.[376] Gliding on to the stage like 'ghostly figures', conjured up by McCracken's imaginary reckonings with the past, the United Irishmen in the play are in effect apparitions. Hence, *Northern Star* has been appositely described by Terence Brown as a 'ghost-haunted play'.[377]

The 'ghostly liminality' in Northern Star corresponds to a more general leitmotif in contemporary Irish drama, whereby 'the disturbing presence of ghosts' signifies

---

[372] *Sunday Tribune*, 29 September 1985, p. 19.

[373] Parker, *Plays*, p. 3; *Sunday Tribune*, 2 December 1984, p. 18 [reproduced in *Critical Moments: Fintan O'Toole on Modern Irish Theatre*, edited by Julia Furay and Redmond O'Hanlon (Dublin: Carysfort Press, 2003), pp. 33–5]; *Irish Times*, 12 October 1996, p. 37.

[374] *Irish Times*, 25 April 2008, p. 18.

[375] Parker, *Plays*, pp. 3 (stage instructions) and 58 ('the Protestants of the North').

[376] Ibid., pp. 78–80. See also see Eva Urban, *Community Politics and the Peace Process in Contemporary Northern Irish Drama* (Oxford and New York: Peter Lang, 2011), pp. 94–105; also Richtarik, *Stewart Parker*, pp. 257–8.

[377] Parker, *Plays*, p. 9; Terence Brown, 'Let's Go to Graceland: The Drama of Stewart Parker', in *The Cities of Belfast*, edited by Nicholas Allen and Aaron Kelly (Dublin: Four Courts Press, 2003), pp. 120–3.

'constant re-enaction of memories and traumas'.[378] Two of the characters are specific-ally designated as spirits. The 'future ghost of Jimmy Hope' comes back to tell McCracken, with due irony, that 'we hadn't the ghost of a chance. And it takes a ghost from the future times to say as much.' The appearance of a mysterious 'Phantom Bride' is both an ironic reconfiguration of Cathleen Ni Houlihan—the female repre-sentation of Ireland in a famous 1798 play written by W. B. Yeats and Lady Gregory in 1902—and the inversion of a traditional '98 ballad sung by Mary Bodle, the mistress of Henry Joy McCracken, in which 'every night pale bleeding', Harry's ghost 'comes for his promised bride'. After McCracken admits that he keeps 'seeing the most damnable things, shadows and moonshine', Bodle affirms that 'we're well used to the walking dead, we have more spooks than living bodies round these parts', and reassures him that 'there's no harm in seeing ghosts.' When McCracken and Hope part, they know that they will only meet again 'in the long memory of this town, the long dream'.[379] Parker invokes the shades of the historical United Irishmen, who, by coming back to haunt modern-day Belfast, disrupt social forgetting.[380]

Concerns of remembering and forgetting loom heavily. Bodle confesses that she cannot forget the horrific atrocities committed by the military that she has witnessed and McCracken tries to set her mind to rest by insisting that 'people do forget, though. They forget the facts that don't suit them.' Mary is despondent and regrets that 'they forget nothing in this country, not ever', but McCracken corrects her with even greater pessimism, pointing out that 'it isn't true to say they forget nothing. It's far worse than that, they misremember everything.' This pithy exchange epitomizes how Parker wrestled with the paradoxes of disremembering, as he tried to unravel memories of 1798 that had been co-opted by republican paramilitaries and renounced by unionists. Henry Joy McCracken's last words are drowned out and lost to posterity, but not by the trampling of horses, as described in the historical first-hand account given by Mary Ann McCracken to Madden. At the conclusion of the play, he is silenced by the loud beating of a lambeg drum—typical of Orange parades—as the lights fade to black in a symbolic depiction of the silencing and forgetting imposed by loyalist triumphalism.[381]

High expectations were set on the original production of *Northern Star* at the Lyric Theatre in Belfast, where it ran from 6 to 19 November 1984. The poet John Hewitt and the Catholic peace activist and journalist Ciaran McKeown were among those who believed that it would 'make a political difference in Northern Ireland'.[382] Parker hoped that 'the people watching will accept their share of responsibility for what has and is happening here in the North' and that they would realize, like McCracken, that 'the

---

[378] Emilie Pine, *The Politics of Irish Memory: Performing Remembrance in Contemporary Irish Culture* (Basingstoke: Palgrave Macmillan, 2011), pp. 152–70.

[379] Parker, *Plays*, pp. 48–50 (Bodle's song and the Phantom Bride), 52 ('the walking dead'), 58 ('ghost of a chance'), and 60 ('long memory'). The song 'Henry Joy McCracken' is a re-adaptation of the ballad 'Belfast Mountains'; see Fitzhenry, *Henry Joy McCracken*, pp. 158–9; Heatley, *Henry Joy McCracken*, p. 57; Moylan, *Age of Revolution*, pp. 81–2. For early broadsides of the original ballad see BOD Firth *c*.18(82); Johnson Ballads 2276. For the historical Mary Bodle, see Chapter 4 above, pp. 239–40.

[380] For 'spectral presence', in *Northern Star* see Markus, *Echoes of the Rebellion*, pp. 199–203.

[381] Parker, *Plays*, pp. 68 ('misremember everything') and 82 ('lambeg is loudly beaten'); cf. Mary Ann McCracken's account in Madden, *The United Irishmen*, 2nd ser., vol. 2 (1843), p. 495.

[382] Claudia W Harris, 'From Pastness to Wholeness: Stewart Parker's Reinventing Theatre', *Colby Quarterly*, 27, no. 4 (1991): p. 237.

destiny of the North lay ultimately in the hands of the people of the North.'[383] He was delighted with the Belfast premiere, which 'engendered real political controversy and debate and was extremely well attended'.[384]

While the response was 'electric in Belfast', Parker was disappointed by the lack of interest with which the *Northern Star* was met at the 1985 Dublin Theatre Festival.[385] Although applauded by the critics as 'a remarkable virtuoso achievement', the perform-ances at the Olympia theatre were poorly attended, resulting in box office losses. The organizers tried to lay the blame on the choice of venue, but the lack of enthusiasm in Dublin seems to have reflected a more general disinterest in the northern Troubles and a decline in the fervour of southern irredentism.[386] Back in Northern Ireland, the play's success at the 1985 Omagh Arts Festival in county Tyrone, where it filled the Townhall for two performances, may have been due, at least in part, to the leading actor Gerard McSorley (who played Henry Joy McCracken) coming from Omagh. Although a local critic found it 'very disappointing', these performances would later be remembered as 'an amazing tour-de-force'.[387] Parker died of cancer in 1988 at the age of 47. Despite all the accolades the play garnered, it would have to wait for the rebellion's bicentenary in 1998 to be revived. It appears that *Northern Star* had arrived on the scene too early to be fully appreciated. While the Troubles were still raging, the wider public was not quite ready for an open and sustained debate on the memory of 1798.

Nonetheless, literary output that recalled Ninety-Eight continued on a small-scale throughout the years of the Troubles. Whereas Sam Hanna Bell stands out as a major novelist willing to break public silence and engage with the topic openly, lesser-noticed juvenile historical fiction brought the rebellion to the attention of younger readers. *The Two Rebels* by the children's novelist Meta Mayne Reid was published in London in 1969, at the outbreak of the Troubles.[388] Praising the novel for bringing 'to life a unique time in Irish history, when the interests of the Catholic majority and the dissenters were at one against their exploitation by the ruling ascendancy', the radical *Irish Democrat* maintained that, on the background of the sectarian violence raging in Northern Ireland, the results of the failed outcome of the 1798 rebellion 'were never more evident than today'.[389] Robert Dunbar, an enthusiast of children's literature who originally came from Antrim, took upon himself to promote and 'resurrect' Reid's novel and a new edition came out in Dublin in 1994.[390]

The Two Rebels was dedicated to the memory of a great-grand-uncle, who had been 'out in the '98' and then escaped to America. Growing up in Yorkshire, Reid née

[383] *Irish News*, 15 November 1984; reproduced in Ophelia Byrne, *State of Play: The Theatre and Cultural Identity in 20th Century Ulster* (Belfast: Linen Hall Library, 2001), p. 130.

[384] Schrank and Demastes, *Irish Playwrights*, pp. 285–6; also *Irish Times*, 8 November 1984, p. 4; *Sunday Tribune*, 2 December 1984, p. 18.

[385] *Irish Times*, 31 January 1987, p. A9.

[386] *Irish Press*, 24 September 1985, p. 16; *Irish Times*, 24 September 1985, p. 10; *Times*, 26 September 1985, p. 17; *Sunday Independent*, 29 September 1985, p. 17; *Observer*, 6 October 1985, p. 21. For the lack of success at the Dublin Theatre Festival see *Irish Press* 3 and 4 October 1985, pp. 3 and 21 (respectively) and 8 November 1985, p. 7.

[387] *Ulster Herald*, 12 and 20 October 1985, pp. 4 and 20 (respectively) and 12 November 1988, p. 9.

[388] Meta Mayne Reid, *The Two Rebels* (London: Faber and Faber, 1969).

[389] *Irish Democrat*, April 1970 (no. 308), p. 7.

[390] 'The Children's Guru', *Books Ireland*, no. 208 (1997): pp. 281–2; Meta Mayne Reid, *The Two Rebels*, 2nd edn (Dublin: Poolbeg Press, 1994).

Hopkins was raised on stories of her Protestant parent's 'Planter' roots in county Londonderry. Her father had emigrated from Limavaddy and her mother from Coleraine, areas that had known strife in 1798. From her mother, in particular, she 'imbibed social history without knowing it and developed a strong sense of, and empathy with, the past'.[391] Reid later settled in Crawfordsburn, county Down (4 km west of Bangor), where loyalties had been divided during the rebellion and local traditions claimed that Henry Joy McCracken had taken refuge in the vicinity.[392] *The Two Rebels* tells of twins from a farm in county Derry, Andrew and Bess McIlroy, who assist their uncle and his friend, a scion of local gentry, as they hide after participating in the Battle of Antrim. The children are rewarded for their bravery with a gift of hidden treasure.

Legends of buried treasure from 1798, occasionally ignited by reports in the news of local discoveries, had long fascinated popular imagination. At the summer session of the Downpatrick assizes in 1860, it was revealed that a farmer had found a treasure trove of over seven hundred 'spade' guineas (a nickname that derived from the shovel-shaped shield, which appeared on gold coins minted between 1787 and 1799). It was widely believed that 'these guineas were secreted in the hiding place in which they were discovered during the eventful '98 year, by some person who fell in the Battle of Ballynahinch.'[393] A century later, a coroner's inquest into the discovery of twenty-eight gold guineas and another four half guineas pieces from the time of George III, found in 1954 in the wall of an old thatched house on a farm at Fourscore, near Glenavy in county Antrim (20 km south of Antrim town), suggested that 'one possible solution is that they were hidden about the time of the 1798 Rebellion by the then owner of the farm who feared for the safety of his savings.'[394]

Tom McCaughren's children's novel *The Legend of the Golden Key*, originally published in Dublin in 1983 and re-issued in 1988 and 2011, is premised on a search for gold coins hidden in 1798 near a castle in Antrim. McCaughren, the Security Correspondent for RTÉ, came originally from Ballymena in county Antrim. He had childhood memories of visiting Galgorm Castle in Antrim, but modelled the setting for his novel on Johnstown Castle in Wexford, finding inspiration from reports on the discovery of gold coins in an outhouse in county Wexford. Nonetheless, a mid-Antrim local history publication credited the novel for its 'measure of local colour'. The original edition included a note for teachers and over the years the novel was used as recommended reading for school projects and educational tours.[395]

McCaughren returned to write about the northern rebellion in another children's novel, *In Search of the Liberty Tree*, set in his native Ballymena. Availing of recollections documented in the nineteenth century by the antiquarians Rev. W. S. Smith and

[391] Ruth Baker, 'The Innocent Eye: Meta Mayne Reid, 1905–1990', *The Linen Hall Review*, 8, no. 4 (1991), p. 17.
[392] See Robin Masefield, *'Twixt Bay & Burn': A History of Helen's Bay & Crawfordsburn* (n.l.: Bayburn Historical Society, 2011), pp. 9, 12, 22, and 100.
[393] *Downpatrick Recorder*, 21 July 1860, p. 2.
[394] *Larne Times*, 20 May 1954, p. 9; *Lisburn Herald*, 22 May 1954, p. 3.
[395] Tom McCaughren, *The Legend of the Golden Key* (Cork: Mercier Press, 2011; orig. edn 1983), 'Introduction' and ch. 2 ('A Tale of '98'); *Irish Press*, 27 June 1983, p. 9; David Knox, '"On Writing Onions": A Reading of "The Legend of the Golden Key" by Tom McCaughren, in the Light of Some Recent Discussion of Children's Literature', in *Mid-Antrim: Articles on the History of Ballymena and District*, edited by Eull Dunlop (Ballymena: Mid-Antrim Historical Group, 1983), pp. 165–7.

Robert Magill Young and in the local publication *Old Ballymena*, which he noted was still to be found in the town, McCaughren weaved into the plot the exploits of local heroes, such as the rebel outlaws Thomas Archer and Roddy McCorley, the United Irish captain John Nevin and the loyalist Robert Davison. The *Irish Times* praised 'this most commendable book' for 'the author's ability to tread the political minefield of his subject matter'.[396] In Northern Ireland, these references to 1798 addressed to youth mostly passed below the radar.

A couple of northern Catholic writers, who moved to the South, wrote literary works in Irish on the rebellion in Ulster, which were published in Dublin. Séamas Ó Néill, who was born near Clough in county Down (12 km south-east of Ballynahinch) and educated in Belfast, went to teach in Dundalk (just south of the border) and finally settled in Dublin, where he taught history at Carysford College. He retained an interest in the northern United Irishmen, publishing articles on 1798 in the *Irish Press*. Ó Néill wrote the play *Faill ar an bhFeart* [Opportunity for a Miracle] about the United Irish hero Rev. James Porter, Gaelicizing the Presbyterian minister's name to Séamas Poirtéir. It was produced in 1967 at the recently opened Peacock Theatre for the Tenth Dublin Theatre Festival, with a descendant of Porter—Ormonde Waters—attending the opening night, but was considered 'something of a disappointment'. To critics it seemed that the drama 'petered out to its obvious ending' and the production was withdrawn after only eight days on account of poor attendance. The play's publication in an expensive hardback edition, sold for 9s 6d, was criticized for making the script inaccessible and beyond the reach of the few amateur drama companies willing to take on Irish language productions.[397]

The Irish language enthusiast Proinsias Mac an Bheatha [Francis McVeigh] was born in Belfast and raised in Killough, near Bangor in county Down. After Partition, his family relocated to Dublin, where he would find employment with the Customs and Mail service. Mac an Bheatha learned Ulster Irish from the Donegal authors Séamus Ó Grianna ('Máire') and Seosamh Mac Grianna, as well as the lexicographer Niall Ó Dónaill, and became a devoted campaigner for language revival. His literary output includes several notable works on 1798, including the historical novel *Cnoc na hUamha* [Cave Hill], published in 1978, a biography of James Hope (prefaced by the radical IRA veteran Peadar O'Donnell), published in 1985, and a long poem on Henry Joy McCracken that appeared in a collection in 1992.[398] These works, which were written in a high literary level and published in the Republic of Ireland, had a limited readership and made little, if any, impact on social remembrance in Northern Ireland.

---

[396] Tom McCaughren, *In Search of the Liberty Tree* (Dublin: Anvil Books, 1994) pp. 220–2 ('Historical Footnote'); *Irish Times*, 20 January 1995, p. 14.

[397] Séamus Ó Néill, *Faill ar an bhFeart* (Baile Átha Cliath [Dublin]: Sairséal agus Dill, 1967); *Irish Press*, 25 May 1967, p. 5; 7, 8, and 10 October 1967, pp. 4, 5, and 5 (respectively); 6 January 1968, p. 10; *Irish Independent*, 11 and 19 October 1967, p. 8 and 6 (respectively); *Sunday Independent*, 15 October 1967, p. 26: see also Markus, *Echoes of the Rebellion*, pp. 100–2. For Ó Néill's journalist writings on 1798 see above, p. 499n230.

[398] Proinsias Mac an Bheatha, *Cnoc na hUamha* (Baile Átha Cliath [Dublin]: Foilseacháin Náisiúnta, 1978); Proinsias Mac an Bheatha, *Henry Joy agus Véarsaí Eile* (Baile Átha Cliath [Dublin]: Coiscéim 1992), pp. 76–89. See also *Irish Press*, 30 November 1978, p. 8 [*Cnoc na hUamha*] and 11 January 1986, p. 9 [*Jemmy Hope*]; Titley, *An Túrscéal Gaeilge*, pp. 347–52; Markus, *Echoes of the Rebellion*, p. 103.

Irish language writers were not alone among northern Catholic authors in their choice to publish their work in the Republic of Ireland. Using the pen name Kathleen O'Farrell, Siubhán Ó Dubháin—a choral composer and novelist from Rostrevor in county Down—wrote *The Fiddler of Kilbroney* (1994), which was published by an independent publisher in Dingle, county Kerry. Ó Dubháin had been raised on stories from the time of 1798 told by her parents (William John and Cathleen Rose Farrell), some of them attributed to her grandfather's great-grandfather, Johnny 'leath-láimh' [one-armed] Fearon. The novel uses local traditions to imaginatively tell the story of the hedge schoolmaster and local rebel leader Thomas (Tom) Dunne, whose youthhood O'Farrell had covered in an earlier novel, *Kilbroney* (1992). Recommended by *Books Ireland* as 'escapist reading', *The Fiddler of Kilbroney*, which has been described as a 'post-revisionist' historical novel, downplays sectarian animosities in order to idealize the United Irish struggle.[399]

Northern authors seeking to take on controversial subjects, such as the memory of the United Irishmen, found a local outlet in Blackstaff Press, established in 1971 by Jim Gracey, a deputy librarian at the Linen Hall Library who had just recently launched with the local historian Aiken McClellan the journal *Irish Booklore*. With support from the Arts Council of Northern Ireland, Blackstaff specialized in the publication of studies by local writers on Ulster's history, literature, and folklore, giving a mouthpiece to silenced voices. On the background of the closing of minds that marked the Troubles, this progressive literary endeavour attracted hostility from paramilitaries. The offices of the press were repeatedly targeted by bombings, one of which destroyed some 30,000 books in 1974. The management, however, remained undaunted and in 1992 Blackstaff went on to win the coveted *Sunday Times* 'Small Publisher of the Year' award.[400]

Notable titles published by Blackstaff that recalled the heritage of 1798 include John Hewitt's *Rhyming Weavers and Other Country Poets of Antrim and Down* (1974; reissued in 2004 with a foreword by Tom Paulin), as well as new editions of Cathal O'Byrne's collection of folk history *As I Roved Out* (1982), Sam Hanna Bell's historical novel *A Man Flourishing* (1986), and Mary McNeill's *The Life and Times of Mary Ann McCracken* (1988), which, when it first came out in 1960, was praised by Hewitt as 'the best biography of an Ulsterman or woman to have come out in this century'.[401] Traditions of Ninety-Eight also appeared in local histories, such as Tony Canavan's history of Newry, *Frontier Town* (1989).

The platform that Blackstaff provided for nonconformist recovering of memory is typified in the publication in 1991 of *The Dissenting Voice* by Flann Campbell, son of

---

[399] Kathleen O'Farrell, *The Fiddler of Kilbroney* (Dingle, Co. Kerry: Brandon, 1994), pp. 335–6 (postscript referring to local traditions); Kathleen O'Farrell, *Kilbroney* (Dingle, Co. Kerry: Brandon, 1992); *Books Ireland*, no. 178 (1994): p. 175; *Irish Times*, 26 August 1994, p. 12; see also Markus, *Echoes of the Rebellion*, pp. 111–12. For folk traditions of Tom Dunn see Russell, *Beyond the Battle*, p. 14.

[400] *Irish Press*, 14 December 1972, p. 8; *Ulster Herald*, 25 December 1976, p. 3; *Sunday Independent*, 29 October 1978, p. 31 and 24 February 1980, p. 2. See also Jeremy Addis, 'A Decade of Dedication', *Books Ireland*, no. 59 (December 1981): pp. 226–7; Wesley McCann, 'Irish Booklore: A Retrospect', *The Linen Hall Review*, 3, no. 1 (1986): p. 15; Ian Kirk-Smith, 'Unpeeling the Parish', *Fortnight*, no. 306 (1992): p. 39.

[401] John Hewitt, 'The Longest Campaign', in Clyde, *Ancestral Voices*, pp. 126–32; originally published in *Threshold*, 5, no. 1 (Spring-Summer, 1961), pp. 58–64.

the Ulster poet Joseph Campbell, whose play *The Turn-Out*—written eighty years earlier—still remained unproduced. Having been raised in a radical Presbyterian household, Flann Campbell's polemical historical survey of 'Protestant Democracy in Ulster' called attention to the 'grave neglect of those liberals, nationalists and radicals, and later of ecumenicists and socialists' that were excluded from the 'conservative Protestant tradition'. He argued that 'comparatively little has been published, apart from a few incomplete accounts of the 1798 rising and the occasional specialized thesis, about those northern Protestants who were hostile to the dominant unionists' and noted that these exceptional theses complained of a 'conspiracy of silence', which 'overlooked, minimised or misrepresented' expressions of radicalism. *The Dissenting Voice* was an attempt to penetrate the 'collective amnesia' that had been perpetuated, according to the literary critic Terence Brown, by a false sense of Protestant unionist homogeneity, and to reveal an 'almost unconscious memory of the past' in which Ninety-Eight featured prominently.[402]

Campbell maintained that 'though the Croppies were compelled—by the sheer weight of military force—to capitulate, they were not willing, as subsequent history showed, to lie down for ever' and so 'the spirit of resistance went underground only to re-emerge when circumstances proved more propitious.' He identified two enduring legacies of the United Irishmen, 'one the stuff of poetry and ballads, the other more rooted in practical politics, which inspired future generations of Irish nationalists, both Protestant and Catholic'.[403] In *The Dissenting Voice*, he meticulously traced these influences through to the activities of such figures as Francis Joseph Bigger, Rev. Richard Lyttle, and Rev. James Armour. Whereas an academic-minded historian—Richard McMinn from Stranmillis College in Belfast—faulted Campbell for over-romanticizing Presbyterian radicalism and pointed out that the individuals he mentioned had not entirely been excluded from historiography, a local historian—Hugh Breslin from Strabane, county Tyrone—was more appreciative of Campbell's unravelling of the remarkable 'grip those few years in the 1790s still has on the popular imagination'.[404]

The historian Anthony ('Tony') Terence Quincey Stewart presented a different approach to recalling the northern United Irishmen, which was grounded in the intellectual tradition of liberal unionism rather than that of radical nationalism. Schooled at 'Inst'—the Royal Belfast Academical Institution (which had been founded by William Drennan and other Presbyterian radicals)—Stewart was dismayed that 'the Unionist establishment was trying to forget about the United Irishmen.' He completed in 1956 a Master's thesis, supervised by J. C. Beckett at Queen's University Belfast, on the 'remarkable transformation of political opinion in a relatively short time', whereby Presbyterians that had been 'distinguished for their liberalism and opposition to the English administration' later became 'distinguished for their conservatism and perfervid loyalty to the union'. Stewart complained that this topic 'has been strangely neglected by students of Irish history'. Although he would have liked 'to devote a good deal of space to the political thought of the tenant farmers who, when all is said and done, carried the pikes at Antrim and Ballynahinch', Stewart conceded that 'they left no

---

[402] Campbell, *The Dissenting Voice*, pp. 1–2; see also Terence Brown, *The Whole Protestant Community: The Making of a Myth* (Field Day: Derry, 1985), pp. 11–15 and 20.
[403] Campbell, *The Dissenting Voice*, p. 104.
[404] *Irish Historical Studies*, 28, no. 111 (1993): pp. 323–5 (McMinn); *Fermanagh Herald*, 9 May 1992, p. 4 (Breslin).

written memorials, except perhaps the depositions made by them when they were on trial.' Less inclined at the time to engage with folklore sources, his postgraduate study was 'concerned mainly with the articulate section of the Presbyterians'.[405] Stewart's interest in uncovering the legacy of the United Irishmen was originally prompted by the Ulster-born classicist Patrick Semple, former Dean of Arts at University College Dublin, who maintained that 'the time had come for Protestants to take up this history, that they had forgotten.' Yet, upon completion of his research, Stewart found that, in Northern Ireland's tight regime of social forgetting, no one was willing to publish his ground-breaking thesis. Although it remained unpublished, it was later remembered that 'when the Troubles began, foreign scholars queued to read it.'[406]

Stewart, who was appointed Reader of history at Queen's University, would be hailed as Northern Ireland's 'foremost historian' and its 'leading public intellectual during the darkest days of the Troubles'. He was particularly known as a 'spirited commentator' on the 'exigencies of the past and the present, and the connections between them'.[407] In his historical work, Stewart doggedly unravelled the origins of the Northern Irish conflict, attributing a pivotal role to 1798. His book *The Narrow Ground* (first published in 1977 and re-issued in 1989) included a chapter titled 'The Harp New-Strung', which showed that 'there can be no doubt that the Presbyterians were deeply implicated in the United Irish movement.' He pointed out that 'Presbyterians were not totally nationalist in 1798 and totally unionist in 1886', but concluded that 'in later times the conservative stratum was so obvious that the radical traditions inherent in Ulster Presbyterianism were completely forgotten.' Stewart's idiosyncratic, and often ironic, writing style was open to misinterpretation. To the author's utter astonishment, the ultra-loyalist Rev. Ian Paisley (who dogmatically refused to recognize the involvement of orthodox Presbyterians in the United Irishmen) held up a copy of *The Narrow Ground* in front of his congregation, declaring 'here is a great book which tells us the truth about the history of Ulster.' [408]

Stewart's *A Deeper Silence* (1993) offered an exploration of 'the hidden origins of the United Irish movement' in a book which, as Roy Foster pointed out, was 'full of paradoxes, quizzical inferences and small human ironies' and was also 'allusive, elliptical and sometimes obscure'.[409] Stewart drew on his intimate knowledge of Ulster history to explain what drove unionists to reject en masse the Anglo-Irish Agreement, signed on 15 November 1985 by Prime Minister Margaret Thatcher and Taoiseach Garret FitzGerald at Hillsborough Castle, county Down, in an unsuccessful attempt to bring an end to the Troubles. He considered their 'feeling of betrayal' to be consistent with

---

[405] A. T. Q. Stewart, 'The Transformation of Presbyterian Radicalism in the North of Ireland, 1792–1825' (M.A. thesis: Queen's University, Belfast, 1956), pp. v–vi.
[406] Hiram Morgan, 'A Scholar and a Gentleman', *History Ireland*, 1, no. 2 (1993), p. 56; *Telegraph*, 9 January 2011.
[407] See obituaries in *Belfast Telegraph*, 24 December 2010, p. 24; *Times*, 3 January 2011, p. 44; *Telegraph*, 9 January 2011; *Belfast Telegraph*, 3 February 2011 (also published in the *Independent*, 3 February 2011).
[408] A. T. Q. Stewart, *The Narrow Ground: The Roots of Conflict in Ireland* (London and Boston: Faber and Faber, 1989; orig. edn 1977), pp. 101–10. For Paisley's unwarranted endorsement see Tom Paulin, *Ireland & the English Crisis* (Newcastle upon Tyne: Bloodaxe Books, 1984), pp. 155–6 (originally published in the *London Review of Books*, vol. 4, no. 6, 1 April 1982, pp. 18–21); *Telegraph*, 9 January 2011.
[409] Stewart, *A Deeper Silence*; for Foster's review see *Times*, 25 February 1993, p. 35.

the attitudes that had driven Presbyterians to rebel in 1798.[410] Although faulted for being an apologist for partition, Stewart insisted on pointing out that the United Irishmen had not espoused the 'confessional nationalism which today divides rather than unites Ireland'.[411]

Blackstaff Press published in 1995 *The Summer Soldiers*, Stewart's history of the 1798 Rebellion in Antrim and Down, which, if just for the panache of its eloquent literary style, would supersede Charles Dickson's unwieldy *Revolt in the North* as the leading monograph-length study on the topic, even though it made limited use of archival sources available in Dublin. While both books were re-issued in 1997 in anticipation of the 1798 bicentenary, Stewart's *Summer Soldiers* garnered lavish praise and it was noticed that 'folk heroes pass through his pages.'[412] Northern readers could now engage with local historical traditions that had not been taught at school.[413] The author was inundated with letters from 'people whose ancestors had been out in 1798' and noted that 'none was hostile, and all were seeking more information.'[414]

In the bicentennial year of 1798, Stewart was recognized as the leading pundit on the northern arena and was given many platforms to address the history and memory of 1798 in Ulster. He delivered public lectures, including the Robert Allen memorial lecture to the Presbyterian Historical Society on '1798 and the Modesty of History' (a title that deliberately evokes a story by Borges), in which he argued that 'what people think happened in 1798 is, in one way, just as important for Irish history as what did happen' and cautioned that the past cannot be simply forgotten.[415] He appeared on radio and television, and contributed articles to newspapers and popular history publications. Stewart consistently called attention to unionist discomfort with appropriations of the Presbyterian United Irishmen by the 'authoritarian triumphalism' of Catholic nationalism.[416] His insistence that the rebellion in Ulster was essentially

[410] *Spectator*, 256 (11 January 1986): pp. 15–16; *Irish Times*, 14 January 1986, p. 8.

[411] Burgess, 'Mapping the Narrow Ground'; A. T. Q. Stewart, *The Shape of Irish History* (Belfast: Blackstaff, 2001), pp. 127–33. For a more general discussion of Stewart's historical approach see Arthur Aughey, 'Stewart on History', in *From the United Irishmen to Twentieth-Century Unionism*, edited by Sabine Wichert (Dublin: Four Courts Press, 2004), pp. 13–23.

[412] A. T. Q. Stewart, *The Summer Soldiers: The 1798 Rebellion in Antrim and Down* (Belfast: Blackstaff Press, 1995); for reviews see *New Statesman & Society*, 9, no. 385 (1996), p. 37; *Irish Independent*, 20 January 1996, Weekender p. 11; *An Phoblacht*, 29 May 1997 (calls attention to the limited use of the Rebellion Papers); Pádraig Ó Snodaigh, 'Who Dares to Speak?', *Books Ireland*, no. 208 (1997), p. 292 (notes the appearance of folk heroes). Cf. Charles Dickson, *Revolt in the North: Antrim and Down in 1798*, 2nd edn (London: Constable, 1997); for reviews see *Irish Examiner*, 6 July 1997, p. 33 (weekend supplement); *Irish Times*, 12 April 1997, p. 9 (weekend supplement).

[413] For example, after reading *Summer Soldiers*, David Adams 'learned of the sad fate of Henry Munro of Lisburn and other similar-minded townspeople, and the even sadder tale of Daniel Gillan, Peter Carron and the McKenna brothers, who were shot to death and buried at Blaris', realizing that his teachers had 'neglected to teach us anything about the history of Lisburn, where my school was located, or its surrounding area, within which I was born and grew up'; *Irish Times*, 25 April 2013, p. 14.

[414] Collins, *Who Fears to Speak*, p. 172.

[415] The text of the lecture is reproduced in James Seery, Finlay Holmes and A. T. Q. Stewart, *Presbyterians, the United Irishmen and 1798* (Belfast: Presbyterian Historical Society of Ireland, 2000).

[416] *Irish Times*, 7 February 1998, p. 4; *BNL*, 1 May 1998, p. 16; *Guardian*, 5 October 1998. Stewart's prominent bicentennial publications include: '1798 in the North', *History Ireland*, 6, no. 2 (1998): pp. 33–8; '1798 in Antrim and Down', in *The Great Irish Rebellion of 1798*, edited by Cathal Póirtéir (Cork: Mercier Press, 1998), pp. 72–82 [originally broadcast as a Tomas Davis lecture on RTÉ radio]; 'The Ghost of Betsy Gray', in *1798 Rebellion in County Down*, edited by Myrtle Hill, Brian Turner, and Kenneth Dawson (Newtownards: Colourpoint, 1998), pp. 251–7.

a different event from the other arenas of 1798 was, however, contested by other historians.[417]

The bicentenary of 1798 coincided with the signing on 10 April 1998 of the Good Friday (Belfast) Agreement, which promised to put an end to the Troubles and to resolve the Northern Irish conflict. The threat of irredentism was officially withdrawn with the amendment of articles 2 and 3 of the Irish constitution (approved over-whelmingly by referendum in May 1998). These were redrafted in order to reassure unionists that a United Ireland would only be attained through the consent of a majority of the Northern Ireland electorate, effectively endorsing the agreement's recognition of 'the birthright of all people of Northern Ireland to identify themselves and be accepted as Irish or British, or both, as they may so choose'.[418] In the new spirit of reconciliation, the policies that had repressed historical traditions that did not conform to a unionist ethos were to be removed, among them the prohibitions on commemoration of the United Irishmen. The gates were now open for popular engagement with a past that had previously been silenced. In addition to re-issuing Stewart's historical narrative of the rebellion, Blackstaff also published, to the benefit of amateur historians, a collection of contemporary accounts from the 1790s and a guidebook, which encouraged people to go and visit the sites of Ninety-Eight memory that had long been neglected.[419]

Since the foundation of Northern Ireland, for most of the twentieth century, traditions of 1798 had been subject to silencing. In 1998, with numerous bicentennial commemorative events being organized on a national and local level, it now seemed that social forgetting had run its course and that from now on the Turn-Out could be remembered openly, without inhibitions. However, the validity of this assumption would prove to be more complicated than it seemed. In a telling exchange published in the *Belfast Telegraph*, John Gray, the head librarian at the Linen Hall Library and chairman of the United Irishmen Commemoration Society (UICS), criticized Stewart's interpretation of the rebellion, as presented in two articles published in the same mainstream unionist newspaper. In response to the provocative heading of one of Stewart's pieces—'Don't dare to speak of '98', which cautioned against the co-option of the Presbyterian dissenting tradition by Catholic nationalism—Gray, who advocated cross-community commemoration and later complained about 'hostile public inter-ventions by key academics'—issued a heartfelt call to 'dare to speak of '98'.[420] Even as the United Irishmen were being commemorated in public, concerns of forgetting had not entirely abated. Public memorialization, for all its inherent self-confidence, may not succeed in eradicating deep-seated traditions of social forgetting.

---

[417] See for example Ruan O'Donnell, 'Contesting "Three Rebellions" View of 1798', in *Irish Democrat*, October 1998, p. 7; republished as 'Three Rebellions?—The Position of Ulster in 1798', in *Radicals and Revolutionaries: Essays on 1798* (London: Connolly Association 1998).

[418] *The Belfast Agreement* (Northern Ireland Office, 10 April 1998), Annex: 'Agreement between the Government of the United Kingdom of Great Britain and Northern Ireland and the Government of Ireland', Article 1 (vi); see also Gerard Hogan, 'The British-Irish Agreement and the Irish Constitution', *European Public Law*, 6, no. 1 (2000): pp. 1–11.

[419] John Killen, *The Decade of the United Irishmen: Contemporary Accounts, 1791–1801* (Belfast: Blackstaff Press, 1997); Bill Wilsdon, *The Sites of the 1798 Rising in Antrim and Down* (Belfast: Blackstaff, 1997).

[420] *Belfast Telegraph*, 4 and 5 June 1998 (Stewart) and 15 June 1998 (Gray). See also *Irish Independent*, 23 May 1998, special supplement, p. 5 (article by Stewart); John Gray, *Institutional Responses* (Belfast: Arts Council of Northern Ireland, 2011).

7

Post-Forgetting

Into the Twenty-First Century

> ...surely it is much more generous to forgive and remember, than to forgive and forget.
>
> Maria Edgeworth, 'An Essay on the Noble Science of Self-Justification'[1]

> I speak neither of avenging nor forgiving: for the only vengeance and the only forgiveness is forgetting.
>
> Jose Luis Borges, 'From an Apocryphal Gospel'[2]

When does social forgetting end? It is generally assumed that memory diminishes over time, as we move away from the remembered moment. The research of Hermann Ebbinghaus, the German psychologist who pioneered the experimental study of memory with the publication in 1885 of *Über das Gedächtnis*, provided the basis for what has become to be known as the 'forgetting curve', which charts rapid losses of retention that gradually decrease after a short initial period. Forgetting, in this approach, is a terminal condition of memory decline.[3] The applicability of Ebbinghaus's methodology, which relied on memorizing nonsense syllables, was questioned in 1932 by Frederic C. Bartlett, who argued that it created 'an atmosphere of artificiality', which stripped memory of any subjective meaning and examined 'isolated reactions' that do not relate to everyday circumstances. Bartlett, who was less concerned with the accuracy of recall, considered remembering as 'an effort after meaning' (akin to perceiving and

---

[1] Maria Edgeworth, *Letters for Literary Ladies; To Which Is Added, An Essay on the Noble Science of Self-Justification* (London: printed for J. Johnson, 1795), p. 28.

[2] 'Yo no hablo de venganzas ni de perdones; el olvido es la única venganza y el único perdón'; Jorge Luis Borges, 'Fragmentos de un Evangelio apócrifo' (no. 27) in *Elogio de la sombre* (Buenos Aires: Emece, 1969); for a bilingual edition, translated by Norman Thomas di Giovanni, see *In Praise of Darkness* (London: Allen Lane, 1975; orig. edn 1969), p. 109.

[3] Hermann Ebbinghaus, *Über das Gedächtnis: Untersuchungen zur Experimentellen Psychologie* (Leipzig: Duncker & Humblot, 1885), pp. 85–109 ('Das Behalten und Vergessen als Funktion der Zeit'); translated by Henry A. Ruger and Clara E. Bussenius as *Memory: A Contribution to Experimental Psychology* (New York: Teachers College, Columbia University, 1913), pp. 62–80 ('Retention and Obliviscence as a Function of the Time'). For reappraisals presented at the centennial Ebbinghaus Symposium see special issue of the *Journal of Experimental Psychology: Learning, Memory, and Cognition*, 11, no. 3 (July 1985); see also Henry L. Roediger, III, 'Remembering Ebbinghaus', *Contemporary Psychology*, 30, no. 7 (1985): pp. 519–23. Since Ebbinghaus, the 'forgetting curve' has been reproduced in different conditions.

imagining), which is constructed through social interaction.[4] As such, memory is not required to follow a predetermined path of decline towards oblivion, but can be reconstructed and effectively regenerated, keeping forgetting at bay.

It transpires that the vitality of social remembrance is not dependent on proximity to historical events. In fact, immediacy can even prove to be a hindrance, so that in some cases the conditions for popular revivals of historical memory only emerge at a temporal remove. To take a prominent example, the globalization of a transnational 'cosmopolitan memory' of the Holocaust towards the end of the twentieth century facilitated far more vigorous cultural remembrance of the *Shoah* than had been possible in the years immediately after the Second World War, when the atrocities perpetuated by the Nazi regime were not widely commemorated in public.[5] The inevitability of transience, described by the psychologist Daniel Schacter—an authority on memory and amnesia—as one of the fundamental 'sins of memory', needs to be rethought in order to take into account that memory not only wanes but can also wax.[6] At the same time, as shown in previous chapters, practices of social forgetting can also be regenerated and carried over to following generations through the transmission of traditions that maintain a long-lasting culture of silence in public, while retaining muted recollections in private settings. Rather than following the trajectory of a declining curve, the history of memory and forgetting might resemble more a sine graph, with recurring zeniths and nadirs, marking moments of public commemoration, when popular remembrance emerges into the open, and times when it recedes, as social forgetting is restored, only to be challenged again at a later period.

Academic and popular discourse from around the 1980s onwards has exhibited an obsessive preoccupation with collective-social-cultural memory, stimulated by anxieties of forgetting. As famously put by Pierre Nora, 'we speak so much of memory because there is so little of it left.'[7] This fixation, which has been labelled the 'memory boom', has had far-reaching cultural and political implications that have been studied in the growing literature of memory studies.[8] At the conclusion of the monumental collaborative study of French memory *Les Lieux de mémoire*, Nora realized that what had originally been envisaged as 'a counter-commemorative type of history' had ironically

---

[4] Bartlett, *Remembering* (for the critique of Ebbinghaus see pp. 4–7). The concept of 'effort after meaning' was first introduced in F. C. Bartlett, 'An Experimental Study of Some Problems of Perceiving and Imaging', *British Journal of Psychology*, 8, no. 2 (1916), pp. 231 and 261–5.

[5] Daniel Levy and Natan Sznaider, *The Holocaust and Memory in the Global Age*, translated by Assenka Oksiloff (Philadelphia: Temple University Press, 2006); see also Aleida Assmann, 'The Holocaust—a Global Memory? Extensions and Limits of a New Memory Community', in *Memory in a Global Age: Discourses, Practices and Trajectories*, edited by Aleida Assmann and Sebastian Conrad (Houndmills and New York: Palgrave Macmillan, 2010), pp. 97–117.

[6] Daniel L. Schacter, *The Seven Sins of Memory: How the Mind Forgets and Remembers* (Boston: Houghton Mifflin, 2001), pp. 21–40. As a caveat, Schacter acknowledged that forgetting can be stemmed 'by subsequent retrieval and recounting' and considered various methods for 'reducing transience'.

[7] Pierre Nora, 'Between Memory and History: *Les Lieux de Mémoire*', *Representations*, no. 26 (1989), p. 7.

[8] See Jay Winter, 'Notes on the Memory Boom: War, Remembrance, and the Uses of the Past', in *Memory, Trauma and World Politics: Reflections on the Relationship between Past and Present*, edited by Duncan Bell (Basingstoke and New York: Palgrave Macmillan, 2006), pp. 54–73; David W. Blight, 'The Memory Boom: Why and Why Now?', in *Memory in Mind and Culture*, edited by Pascal Boyer and James V. Wertsch (New York: Cambridge University Press, 2009), pp. 238–51.

been overtaken by commemoration. As in the previous fin de siècle, statuomania was once again all the rage. For Nora, the 'obsession with commemoration' at the end of the second millennium had become the sign of our times, marking a new 'Era of Commemoration', which 'has affected all contemporary societies that see themselves as historical'.[9]

Although Irish culture could boast of a rich inventory of memorial traditions, in catching up with the global mnemonic trend, Irish society had to overcome ingrained inhibitions of social forgetting, which may partly explain the delay in the arrival of commemorative fervour to the Emerald Isle. Notwithstanding the muted seventy-fifth anniversary of the Easter Rising in 1991, the 1990s developed into something of a commemorative decade.[10] A series of landmark anniversaries commenced in Northern Ireland with loyalist celebrations in 1990 of the tercentenary of the Battle of the Boyne that featured, among other events, a particularly large Twelfth parade through Belfast city centre.[11] This was followed by the bicentenary of the founding of the Society of United Irishmen in 1991, during which small-scale celebrations in Belfast signalled prospects for future memorialization.[12]

In the mid-1990s, commemoration escalated with the wide-ranging sesquicentenary of the Great Famine, which in the Republic of Ireland benefitted from extensive state support and in Northern Ireland (as well as in the Irish diaspora) was mostly commemorated through self-funded community projects.[13] The bicentenary of the 1798 rebellion signalled the apex of this burgeoning enthusiasm for commemoration. The politics of the peace process had created new arenas for public memorialization and the affluence of the 'Celtic Tiger' economy provided material means for the fulfilment of commemorative initiatives.[14] Commemorative zeal winded down with the more modest marking of the bicentenary of the passing of the Act of Union in 1800, which failed to capture popular unionist imagination. The commemorative decade ended with the anniversary of the rising of Robert Emmet in 1803, which in county Down

---

[9] Pierre Nora, 'The Era of Commemoration', in *Realms of Memory: The Construction of the French Past*, edited by Pierre Nora, translated by Arthur Goldhammer (New York: Columbia University Press, 1998), 3: *Symbols*, pp. 609–37.

[10] For official reluctance to commemorate the Easter Rising in 1991 see Declan Kiberd, 'The Elephant of Revolution Forgetfulness', in *Revising the Rising*, edited by Máirín Ní Dhonnchadha and Theo Dorgan (Derry: Field Day, 1991), pp. 1–20; for more detailed consideration see Mark McCarthy, *Ireland's 1916 Rising: Explorations of History-Making, Commemoration & Heritage in Modern Times* (Farnham and Burlington: Ashgate, 2012), pp. 312–34.

[11] See RTÉ News, 12 July 1990 (online: <www.rte.ie/archives/2015/0710/713964-battle-of-the-boyne-300th-anniversary>); *BNL*, 13 June 1990; Dominic Bryan, *Orange Parades: The Politics of Ritual, Tradition, and Control* (London and Sterling, Va.: Pluto Press, 2000), p. 121; Brian Mercer Walker, *A Political History of the Two Irelands: From Partition to Peace* (Houndmills and New York: Palgrave Macmillan, 2012), p. 173.

[12] See Collins, *Who Fears to Speak*, pp. 77–8; Michael Morgan, 'Belfast's Forgotten Bicentennial', *Études Irlandaises*, 17, no. 1 (1992): pp. 209–18.

[13] Emily Mark-FitzGerald, *Commemorating the Irish Famine: Memory and the Monument* (Liverpool: Liverpool University Press, 2013), esp. pp. 68–80, 98–101, and 158–60; see also Margaret Kelleher, 'Commemorating the Great Irish Famine: 1840s–1990s', in *Memory Ireland*, edited by Oona Frawley (Syracuse, N.Y.: Syracuse University Press, 2014), 3: *The Famine and the Troubles*, pp. 91–120.

[14] See Guy Beiner, 'Commemorating 'Ninety-Eight', in 1998: A Reappraisal of History-Making in Contemporary Ireland', in *These Fissured Isles: Ireland, Scotland and British History, 1798–1848*, edited by Terry Botherstone, Anna Clark, and Kevin Whelan (Edinburgh: John Donald, 2005), pp. 221–41.

focused on the failed attempt to mobilize the remaining United Irishmen in north-east Ulster and on the execution of Thomas Russell.[15]

Commemorations project the illusion that they are solely preoccupied with the past, when in fact they are very much concerned with the present, often with an eye to the future. The anthropologist Dominic Bryan, in a biting critique of the involvement of historians—as opposed to social scientists—in commemorations, pertinently argued that 'the nature of contemporary acts of commemoration is better understood by exploring the relationship between identity and contemporary politics rather than by examining the event being "remembered"'.[16] When approached in 1898 to contribute to the centennial commemorations of Ninety-Eight, George Bernard Shaw scoffed at the notion of 'assembling with other Irishmen to romance about 1798' and, with characteristic far-sightedness, proposed instead that Irishmen should 'apply themselves seriously to what the condition of Ireland is to be in 1998'.[17]

In 1998, the politics of the past in the present, and the implied expectations for a better future, were manifest in the bicentennial commemorations of 1798, which happened to coincide with the signing of the Good Friday Agreement. Previously, social forgetting had been sustained through conditions of prolonged conflict, which enforced a culture of silencing that effectively banished troubling memories from the public sphere. The peace agreement's promise to resolve the Northern Irish conflict stimulated a political climate in which 'telling stories' and 'facing truths' was seen as a necessary requirement for 'post-conflict transition'.[18] The introduction of conflict resolution arrangements along consociational lines, in which the rival sides were obliged to cooperate and to adopt a 'parity of esteem' towards each other's traditions, entailed an implicit promise of accommodating more open expression, through which unspoken legacies could be aired. This reckoning with the historical past was not only confined to recent memories of the Troubles. In light of the new spirit of rapprochement between northern Catholics and Protestants, and between North and South, remembrance of the United Irishmen acquired new cultural currency, which commemoration could capitalize on. The emergence of memory appeared to signal the descent of forgetting.

REMEMBRANCE AND RECONCILIATION

As in previous commemorations, remembrance of the protomartyr William Orr prefigured the anniversary of 1798. On 14 October 1997, a local Remember Orr

---

[15] *Irish News*, 26 August 2003, p. 10; Linda McKenna, 'Thomas Russell and County Down: Marking the Bi-centenary', in *Down Survey 2003* (Downpatrick: Down County Museum, 2003), pp. 41–4 (see also the bicentenary lecture by Marianne Elliott, pp. 31–40).

[16] Dominic Bryan, 'Ritual, Identity and Nation: When the Historian Becomes the High Priest of Commemoration', in *Remembering 1916: The Easter Rising, the Somme and the Politics of Memory in Ireland*, edited by Richard S. Grayson and Fearghal McGarry (Cambridge: Cambridge University Press, 2016), p. 24.

[17] George Bernard Shaw, 'In the Days of My Youth', in *M.A.P. [Mainly About People]*, 17 September 1898, pp. 324–5; reproduced in G. B. Shaw, *Sixteen Self Sketches* (London: Constable, 1949), p. 49.

[18] See Patricia Lundy and Mark McGovern, 'Telling Stories, Facing Truths: Memory, Justice and Post-Conflict Transition', in *Northern Ireland after the Troubles: A Society in Transition*, edited by Colin Coulter and Michael Murray (Manchester and New York: Manchester University Press, 2008), pp. 29–48.

society organized a memorial event at Templepatrick Old Presbyterian Church. This unabashed reclamation of memory by a Presbyterian community offered a prememory template for further bicentennial remembrance. The following year, on the same day, a commemoration for James Hope was held at that same venue.[19] It seemed as if the taboo on open remembrance of Ninety-Eight in Northern Ireland had been miraculously lifted.

The commonly felt notion that the bicentenary was an unprecedented novelty, as if for the first time the United Irishmen were being publicly memorialized in Ulster, was in itself a symptom of the pervasive reach of social forgetting, which obscured recollections of earlier commemorations. In advance of the bicentenary, a small group of local historians, urban conservationists and community organizers gathered in Belfast's Clifton Street Cemetery in October 1995 to unveil a plaque in honour of Henry Joy McCracken, which was presented as the 'first public memorial to the Society of the United Irishmen in the city where that revolutionary organization was founded'.[20] The extent to which this was truly a public memorial was called into question, as visits to the cemetery required an appointment with a caretaker. The marking of McCracken's supposed grave could therefore be described as 'a case of history locked away'. Moreover, the already existing memorials to United Irishmen buried in that very cemetery, which had been erected eighty-six years earlier by Francis Joseph Bigger, were ignored.[21]

The nationalist politician Seamus Mallon, deputy leader of the constitutional nationalist Social Democratic and Labour Party (SDLP), famously described the multi-party peace negotiations held in Belfast in 1998 as 'Sunningdale for slow learners', referring to a failed attempt in 1973–4 to introduce power-sharing to Northern Ireland, which met with massive unionist opposition.[22] A few years earlier, during a House of Commons debate in 1990 on anti-terrorist legislation for Northern Ireland, Mallon had argued about the significance of Presbyterian involvement in 1798 with David Trimble, who would go on to lead the Ulster Unionist Party (UUP) in the negotiations that resulted in the peace agreement.[23] To judge by the self-congratulatory statements made in the Irish parliament in 1998 during a debate on the 1798 bicentenary, or by the remarks of President Mary McAleese in her speech that year before the United States House Committee on International Relations, the Good Friday Agreement was seen by some as 1798 for *very* slow learners.[24] The bicentenary was envisaged as a time when the suppressed memories of northern Presbyterians that had gone underground in the wake of rebellion and had long remained obscure could be finally unveiled.

Disputes over ownership of the memory of Ninety-Eight mirrored the wrangling of the multi-party peace talks. Contenders from the different political sides were unwilling

[19] Collins, *Who Fears to Speak*, p. 81; *Belfast Telegraph*, 7 October 1997 and 16 October 1998; *An Phoblacht*, 23 October 1997.

[20] *Irish News*, 9 October 1995, p. 5; see also *History Ireland*, 3, no. 4 (Winter 1995), p. 6.

[21] *People*, 19 January 1997, p. 15. For earlier memorials at Clifton Street cemetery see Chapter 5 above, pp. 434–5.

[22] *Irish Times*, 2 April 1997, p. 4. Mallon's quip has been quoted extensively.

[23] 'Northern Ireland (Emergency Provisions) Bill, Second Reading', *House of Commons Debates*, vol. 181 (19 November 1990), cols 62–4.

[24] 'Bicentenary of 1798: Statements', *Dáil Éireann Debates*, vol. 493, no. 6 (13 July 1998), pp. 1439–51; *Irish Independent*, 25 June 1998, p. 14 (McAleese speech).

to leave the legacy of late-eighteenth-century republicanism in the hands of present-day republicans, who claimed to be its rightful inheritors. At the beginning of the bicentenary, a large republican demonstration held on 22 January 1998 near the battle site of Vinegar Hill in county Wexford, at which Sinn Féin president Gerry Adams delivered a keynote address, was berated by unionists for 'hijacking' the ideals of the United Irishmen and for 'trying, by any means necessary, to force them down the throats of people who are of a different religious persuasion to themselves'.[25] Unionists, who had discovered an interest in the participation of Presbyterians in the rebellion, complained that republicans had 'hijacked, twisted and distorted the history of 1798 for propaganda purposes' and this claim was endorsed by constitutional nationalists, such as the northern-born Irish senator Maurice Hayes (a former Town Clerk of Downpatrick), who argued that the provisional IRA had 'hijacked the true aims and ideals of the men and women of '98'.[26] In a society traumatized by years of terrorism, the notion of 'hijacked' memory, waiting to be rescued, was very much in the air.

On 18 April 1998, the SDLP held a conference at Springvale Training Centre in Belfast on the theme of 'Abolishing Past Dissensions: Perspectives for Social Democracy on the Bicentenary of the United Irishmen', which was addressed by the party leader John Hume. Advocacy for 'reclaiming republicanism' from militant nationalists was championed by Eamon Hanna, former SDLP general secretary and, up until recently, chairman of the United Irishmen Commemoration Society.[27] The following month, on 16 May 1998, a seminar on 1798 convened jointly by the Irish Association and the British-Irish Association at Hillsborough Castle included speeches by the British minister of state for Northern Ireland Paul Murphy and by the Irish Minister of State Seamus Brennan.[28] Even Ian Paisley's Democratic Unionist Party (DUP), which objected to the peace agreement, inadvertently referred to the United Irishmen when denigrating UUP leader David Trimble for his support of the peace accord. At an ultra-loyalist rally in Moigashel, county Tyrone, a poster read: 'What's the difference between David Trimble and Wolfe Tone? 200 years.' As noted by Ian McBride, the impact of the bicentenary was pervasive and 'no part of Ireland, not even the fundamentalist enclaves of Portadown, has been left untouched.'[29]

In the Republic of Ireland, an interdepartmental government committee responsible for commemoration, which was set up in 1994 for the purpose of promoting commemoration of the Great Famine, was required from 1997 to redirect its attention towards commemorating the United Irish rebellion. In preparing the ground for this change of historical focus, it was gingerly noted that 'Northern Ireland is a special case where sensitivity will be required in view of the different perceptions of the place of 1798 in history.'[30] The committee's mission statement, formulated in April 1997, put

---

[25] *Belfast Telegraph*, 20 and 28 January 1998; *Irish Times*, 19 January 1998, p. 14.

[26] *Belfast Telegraph*, 2 May 1998; *Irish Independent*, 23 May 1998, p. 48.

[27] *Belfast Telegraph*, 25 March 1998; Collins, *Who Fears to Speak*, p. 85; Eamon Hanna, 'Reclaiming Republicanism', in *The Republican Ideal Current Perspectives*, edited by Norman Porter (Belfast: Blackstaff Press, 1998), pp. 113–31.

[28] *Irish Times*, 30 May 1998, p. 44 (Weekend supplement); Collins, *Who Fears to Speak*, p. 90.

[29] *Independent*, 12 May 1998, p. 6; Ian McBride, 'The Anglophobe', *Times Literary Supplement*, no. 4986 (23 October 1998): p. 14.

[30] Stephen Lalor, '1798 Commemoration Discussion Document' (Department of the Taoiseach, August 1996), p. 7. My thanks to Dr Lalor of the Department of the Taoiseach (*Roinn na Taoisigh*) for

an emphasis on 'acknowledging that what happened in Dublin and Wexford was part of what happened in Antrim and Down' and on the need 'to acknowledge the Ulster dimension and particularly the contribution of the Presbyterian tradition, with its emphasis on justice, equality and civil liberty'. The work of the committee was identified by the Department of the Taoiseach as a 'project of significant national importance'. Accordingly, it was generously budgeted to the sum of 350,000 Irish pounds, much of which was made available to fund the bicentennial programmes of local groups and organizations that complied with the committee's mission statement.[31]

The Irish government launched its 1798 commemoration programme in January 1998. Taoiseach Bertie Ahern announced that 'the best way of all to crown the bicentenary and to fulfil some of the ideals of the United Irishmen would be to reach a new lasting and peaceful end to the conflict that has afflicted Northern Ireland in particular over the past 30 years.' Minister of State Seamus Brennan, chairman of the Government Commemoration Committee, confirmed that 'in recognition of the Ulster dimension and in a positive spirit of cooperation', funding had been made available for several commemorative events in Northern Ireland, including an exhibition at the Linen Hall Library in Belfast (January-February) and a five-day academic conference that commenced in the Ulster Museum and continued to Dublin Castle (19–23 May). Support was also allocated to the preparation of an education pack on 1798, which was to be distributed in schools both North and South.[32]

As the national history curriculum, which was introduced to Northern Ireland in 1991, did not consider the late eighteenth century a core period, 1798 had been left off the compulsory school history syllabus. However, a cohort of resourceful northern schoolteachers, who harboured a particular interest in the local history of the United Irishmen, had found ways to bring the subject into the classroom. Interested pupils were encouraged to take an A-Level history option on 'radical politics' that focused on the United Irishmen. Conferences organized through the Young Historian Scheme brought sixth-formers in contact with leading historians of the rebellion and school trips were organized to related historical sites.[33]

Some schools, such as Saintfield High School, availed of the bicentenary to run special programmes to mark the heritage of local involvement in the rebellion. Pupils in Moneynick and Duneane primary schools (between Toome and Randalstown) in county Antrim designed a gamebook, which made the Battle of Antrim accessible to younger children.[34] Nonetheless, an assessment of the historical knowledge of pupils,

allowing me unfettered access to files on the 1798 bicentenary and to Alice Kearney, Secretary to the Government Famine and 1798 Commemoration Committee, for sharing with me her recollections (Leinster House, Dublin, 2 November 2001).

[31] 'Commemoration Fund', in *Freedom of Information Act, 1997: Guide to the Functions and Records of the Department of the Taoiseach* (Dublin, 1998), section 16, article 3, p. 25; *Strategy Statement for the Department of the Taoiseach for the Years 1998–2000* (Dublin, 2001), pp. 18 and 43–4.

[32] *Irish Times*, 21 January 1998, p. 3. The speeches of Ahern and Brennan are reproduced in Collins, *Who Fears to Speak*, pp. 123–6. See also article by Brennan in *Irish Independent*, 23 May 1998, special supplement, p. 5.

[33] Collins, *Who Fears to Speak*, p. 79. For the reform of the history curriculum see Smith, *Reckoning with the Past*, pp. 143–6.

[34] *Saintfield High School Magazine* (1998), pp. 2 and 18; *Guide to the Sites Associated with the Battle of Saintfield* (Saintfield: Saintfield High School 1998); *The Battle of Antrim Gamebook* (Ballinful, Co. Sligo: Kids' Own Publishing Partnership, 1998).

based on interviews prompted by image cues—one of which was a 'photograph of a wall mural commemorating Mary Ann and Henry Joy McCracken, with added caption, Presbyterian leader of the 1798 rising, and his sister'—found that the United Irishmen were largely unfamiliar.[35] The bicentenary was supposed to mend this lacuna and to redress social forgetting.

Following the ratification of the Good Friday Agreement by dual referenda, held both North and South, the Taoiseach once more reiterated his belief that 'the best possible commemoration of the United Irishmen's struggle would be the consolidation of a stable and inclusive settlement in the North.' Ahern commended 'the willingness of the different traditions in Northern Ireland to take ownership of 1798 as part of our common heritage' and acknowledged that the Government Commemoration Committee had consciously 'highlighted the tremendous contribution of the Irish Presbyterian tradition'.[36] Questioning the smug attitude of southern politicians and of organizers of commemorative events, the historian John A. Murphy soberly pointed out that 'we still fear to speak of *all* the ghosts of '98'. Murphy perceptively observed that, while 'Northern Presbyterian unionists are by no means ashamed of the heroism and sacrifice of their republican ancestors at Ballynahinch and Saintfield', they 'regard their Insurrection as very different' and 'are also wary of being involved in southern-driven commemorations'.[37]

Bicentennial commemoration of 1798 in Northern Ireland was not dependent on external backing from the government of the Republic of Ireland, but was primarily propelled by home-grown, locally funded initiatives. Ecumenical commemorative programmes that reached across sectarian political divides received financial support from the Community Relations Council (CRC), which had been set up in 1990 to promote cultural diversity and encourage cooperation between Protestants and Catholics. Already in 1995, during a ceasefire that anticipated the breakthrough in the peace process, the unionist-dominated Belfast City Council established a multi-party committee to start planning for the upcoming bicentenary, indicating a new openness towards inclusive commemoration.[38]

The main driving force behind the northern commemorations was the United Irishmen Commemoration Society (UICS), which was founded in 1996 by dedicated enthusiasts, who five years earlier were active in celebrating the anniversary of the founding in Belfast of the Society of the United Irishmen. Among them were seasoned veterans of commemoration, like the local historian Fred Heatley, who had been involved in 1967 in the bicentenary of the birth of Henry Joy McCracken. By 1998, the UICS had a membership of 250, which brought together Catholics and Protestants. They organized a conference at the Linen Hall Library (7 November 1997), a lecture series with a distinguished line-up of professional and local historians, and tours to the sites of the rebellion in Antrim and Down, guided by local historian Bill Wilsdon.[39]

---

[35] Keith Barton and Alan McCully, 'History, Identity, and the School Curriculum in Northern Ireland: An Empirical Study of Secondary Students' Ideas and Perspectives', *Journal of Curriculum Studies*, 37, no. 1 (2005), pp. 91 and 115.

[36] *Dáil Éireann Debates*, vol. 493, no. 6 (13 July 1998), p. 1440; *Irish Independent*, 4 July 1998, p. 6.

[37] *Irish Independent*, 24 May 1998, p. 19.   [38] *Irish Times*, 21 July 1995, p. 15.

[39] Collins, *Who Fears to Speak*, pp. 79–83 and 90–8.

In addition to circulating a bi-monthly newsletter titled *'98 News*, the UICS issued a number of publications. UICS chairman John Gray authored *The Sans Culottes of Belfast*, a treatise, co-published with the Belfast Trades Union Council, on the tensions between the middle-class leadership of the United Irishmen and the rank and file of 'men of no property', which revealed complexities within the revolutionary movement that had not previously been discussed. The UICS also reprinted a facsimile edition of Bigger's *Remember Orr*. Originally published in 1906, this was the only volume of Bigger's series on the 'Northern Leaders of '98' to have appeared during the re-commemorative flourish that followed the centenary.[40] Although Bigger was honoured at an exhibition in the Belfast Central Library as 'a notable local antiquarian with a great interest in the 1798 rebellion and its aftermath', the manuscripts of his biographies of other United Irishmen remained unpublished in the library's special collections, outside of the public view.[41] There were apparent limits to bicentennial commemorative ambitions.

In promoting the bicentenary, the UICS was careful to circumvent the latent menace of stirring up commemorative envy with triumphalist displays of commemorative possession. Seeking to keep at bay outbursts of decommemorating, of the kind that had marred northern commemorations in 1898 and 1948, the committee refrained from organizing a major parade through the streets of Belfast. Instead, communities throughout Ulster were encouraged to come up with their own bicentennial programmes. The outcome was a bountiful crop of provincial grass-roots initiatives, which were supported by local authorities. In total, nineteen district and borough councils across Northern Ireland—spanning both nationalist and unionist constituencies—sponsored commemorations.[42] Considerable efforts were put into planning diverse activities that appealed to a wide range of audiences. The Down District Council, for example, established a Down District 1798 Bicentenary Committee that endeavoured to offer a 'balanced, suitable, dignified and appropriate cross-community programme of events', which was subsequently recognized as the 'largest programme of commemoration in the north' and would be partly repeated in 2003 for the bicentenary of the 1803 Rising.[43]

The noticeable participation in the bicentenary of academic historians, who published extensively on 1798 and were invited to give talks at numerous commemorative events, came under criticism. Roy Foster coined the scathing epithet 'commemorationist historians', alleging that they were 'retained by the government for the purposes

[40] John Gray, *The Sans Culottes of Belfast: The United Irishmen and the Men of No Property*, a *May Day Lecture* (Belfast: Belfast Trades Union Council and the United Irishmen Commemoration Society, 1998); Francis Joseph Bigger, *Remember Orr* (Belfast: United Irishmen Commemoration Society, 1998). The UICS produced four issues of *'98 News* (November 1997, February 1998, May/June 1998, November 1998); for select extracts see Collins, *Who Fears to Speak*, pp. 90–5.

[41] *BNL*, 9 June 1998, p. 13.

[42] The UCIS secretary, historian Peter Collins of St Mary's University College in Belfast, was awarded a fellowship from the Cultural Diversities Committee of the CRC to document the events of the 1798 bicentenary in Northern Ireland; see Collins, *Who Fears to Speak*, pp. 85–121. My thanks to Dr Collins for an interview in which he reflected on this experience (PRONI, 30 October 2001).

[43] *Irish Times*, 22 January 1998, p. 8; Elizabeth Crooke, 'Museums, Communities and the Politics of Heritage in Northern Ireland', in *The Politics of Heritage: The Legacies of 'Race'*, edited by Jo Littler and Roshi Naidoo (London and New York: Routledge, 2005), p. 65.

of commemoration' and compliantly produced works of 'commemorationist history' that downplayed sectarian violence to suit the politics of the peace process.[44] This somewhat conspiratorial thesis was developed with conviction by Tom Dunne, who claimed that the bicentenary—which he accused of consisting of *ceiliúradh* (celebration) rather than *comóradh* (commemoration)—idealized the United Irishmen and failed to appropriately recognize atrocities committed by rebels.[45]

The dispute mainly centred on Wexford—which had always been in the spotlight of historiographical controversies—and was less concerned with the rebellion's other arenas. Jay Winter, who has written about historical remembrance in other contexts, astutely observed that 'the contemporary memory boom is about history, to be sure, but historians are not its sole or even its central proprietors.' In calling attention to the social range 'of those who come together at sites of memory to recall particular aspects of the past', Winter pointed out that public commemoration is 'rarely the simple reflection of a fixed text, a script rigidly prepared by political leaders determined to fortify their position of power'.[46] Even if the Dublin-based professional historians 'involved in the repackaging and alterations of emphasis' (to use Foster's terms) shared with the Irish government a commitment to the peaceful resolution politics of the Northern Irish conflict, the extent of their influence on commemoration in Northern Ireland was limited.

Kevin Whelan, the most conspicuous of the southern historians involved in the 1798 bicentenary, was appointed part-time historical advisor to the government commemoration committee, in which capacity he drafted speeches for the politicians who attended commemorative events. His often-cited book *The Tree of Liberty* included a compelling survey of the 'politics of memory', in which Whelan maintained that the 'construction of collective memory is one of the primary tasks of the historian, and the nature of the project can be clearly seen in the shifting and contested meaning of 1798 after 1798'. This approach showed a reflective self-awareness to the role of historians in commemoration. However, the equating of collective memory with prominent works of historiography—which essentially mirrored a 'great man' approach to history—overlooked many of the more demotic manifestations of social memory found in vernacular sources. Though Whelan touched on the Presbyterian 'retreat from revolution', his analysis fell short of teasing out in detail the dynamics of social forgetting in Ulster.[47] More generally, in their publications and public talks, professional historians

---

[44] Roy Foster, 'Remembering 1798', in *History and Memory in Modern Ireland*, edited by Ian McBride (Cambridge: Cambridge University Press, 2001), pp. 67–94 [re-published, with very slight variations, in R. F. Foster, *The Irish Story: Telling Tales and Making It Up in Ireland* (London and New York: Allen Lane, 2001), pp. 211–34]; for a combative riposte see Thomas Bartlett, 'Sticking to the Past', in *Times Literary Supplement*, 25 January 2002, pp. 27–8.

[45] Tom Dunne, *Rebellions: Memoir, Memory and 1798* (Dublin: Lilliput Press, 2010; orig. edn 2004), pp. 84–107 and 205–21.

[46] Jay Winter, 'Sites of Memory', in *Memory: Histories, Theories, Debates*, edited by Susannah Radstone and Bill Schwarz (New York: Fordham University Press, 2010), pp. 314 and 322.

[47] Whelan, *The Tree of Liberty*, pp. 133–75; a reworking of the essay paid more attention to local material, see Kevin Whelan, *Fellowship of Freedom: The United Irishmen and 1798* (Cork: Cork University Press, 1998), pp. 121–41. Elsewhere, Whelan showed more sophisticated consideration of memory and forgetting in Ulster; see *1798: A Bicentenary Perspective*, edited by Thomas Bartlett et al. (Dublin: Four Courts Press, 2003), pp. 471–5.

showed little knowledge of provincial folk history outside of Wexford.[48] For all their authority and prestige, the academics from Dublin who were invited to speak at select community events in Northern Ireland could scarcely satisfy the palpable popular interest in how the rebellion in north-east Ulster had been remembered locally.

Organizers of provincial bicentenary events mainly relied on the dilettante knowledge of local historians. The Federation for Ulster Local Studies—an umbrella organization initiated in 1974—had seen its membership surge in recent years, with the number of member groups, which in 1981 had stood at forty-seven, nearly doubling to ninety-two. Towards the bicentenary, a special issue of its journal *Ulster Local Studies* was devoted to 'The Turbulent Decade: Ulster in the 1790s', and many of the affiliated societies became active in commemorating 1798 in their district.[49]

In county Antrim, for example, the main bicentennial publication of the Newtownabbey Borough Council—*The Liberty Tree*—was edited by Archie R. Reid of the Ballyclare and District Historical Society, with contributions from Charles McConnell of the Carrickfergus Historical Society, Robert (Bob) Armstrong of the Abbey Historical Society, Ernest (Ernie) McAlister Scott of Ballynure (a member of the Abbey, Ballyclare and Carrickfergus Societies), and from David Hume of the Templecorran Historical Society.[50] Hume, a prominent Orangeman (who was subsequently appointed executive officer for the Grand Orange Lodge of Ireland), also published that year a booklet on *The Spirit of 1798 and Presbyterian Radicalism in Ulster* in which he admitted that the legacy of the Presbyterian predominance in the northern rebellion 'presents today's Ulster Protestants with something of a dilemma'. Rather than continuing to 'ignore the events of 1798 in Ulster and try to sweep the role of the Presbyterians under the carpet', he argued that 'it is important, for history and for understanding, to analyse and clarify why the Presbyterians were the first republicans in Ireland.'[51]

As might be expected, writings on local history were not devoid of contemporary politics. In addressing the topic of 'Speaking of '98', Newtownabbey alderman Fraser Agnew, an independent unionist, reassured the members of his unionist constituency that they could participate in the commemorations by asserting that 'Republicanism or Separatism had nothing to do with the 1798 Rebellion.'[52] But for the most part, the focus was strictly on the past. The members of the Ballyclare and District Historical Society, in collaboration with the Abbey Historical Society and Larne Drama Circle, organized an evening at Newtownabbey's Courtyard Theatre (21 May), at which quotations from primary historical sources were used to retell the story of '1798 in

---

[48] Interviews with Prof. Tom Bartlett (University College Dublin, 18 September 2001); Prof. David Dickson (Trinity College Dublin, 11 September 2001); Dr. Dáire Keogh (St Patrick's College Drumcondra, 13 November 2001); Prof. Kevin Whelan (University of Notre Dame, Dublin campus, 9 October 2002).

[49] *Ulster Local Studies*, 18, no. 2 (1997). For the development of local historical studies in Ulster see Jack Johnston, 'The Federation for Ulster Local Studies', *Irish Historical Studies*, 23, no. 91 (1983): pp. 284–7; for updated information see <www.fuls.org.uk/thefederation.html>.

[50] Archie R. Reid, ed., *The Liberty Tree: The Story of the United Irishmen in and around the Borough of Newtownabbey* (Newtownabbey: Newtownabbey Borough Council, 1998).

[51] David Hume, *'To Right Some Things That We Thought Wrong': The Spirit of 1798 and Presbyterian Radicalism in Ulster* (Lurgan: Ulster Society Publications, 1998), pp. 37–8.

[52] Reid, *The Liberty Tree*, pp. 69–72.

the Six Mile Valley'.[53] At such local events, Presbyterian communities readily availed themselves of the opportunity to commemorate for the first time in public their traditions of the Turn-Out.

In county Down, the Newtownards Historical Society and the Upper Ards Historical Society assisted the Ards Borough Council to organize 'an exciting programme commemorating the 1798 Rebellion in the Ards'. Together with the local branch of the North of Ireland Family History Society, they compiled materials for a booklet that offered 'an examination of the local events and individuals'. It included an essay on 'The United Irishmen and their opponents in the Ards' by the local historian Trevor McCavery, who had previously covered the rebellion and the loyalist response in a popular history of Newtownards.[54]

Rev. William Desmond Bailie of Saintfield, the former minister of the Kilmore Presbyterian Church, who was known for his research on the involvement of Presbyterian ministers in the rebellion, teamed up with the Ballynahinch historian Horace Reid, who was recognized locally as an authority on the Battle of Ballynahinch (having published in the *Mourne Observer* from 1993 to 1995 a five-part series of articles on the topic). Together, Bailie and Reid assisted the South Eastern Education and Library Board (SEELB)—the public library service that covered the council areas of Ards, Castlereagh, Down, Lisburn, and North Down—in organizing exhibitions on the local rebellion.[55] Reid was also a member of 'The Hearts of Down 1998', a group of local historians associated with the Down County Museum who were committed to 'providing local people and other audiences with an opportunity to put the events of 1798 in County Down in context, to claim all aspects of their history, and to encourage discussion and debate'. In 1998, he gave talks on the legendary local heroine Betsy Gray, speaking at the Ulster Museum (28 June) and to the Tempo Historical Society at the Dooneen Community Education Centre (22 October).[56]

Rev. Finlay Holmes, the retired Magee Chair of Christian History at the Union Theological College in Belfast and a former Moderator of the Presbyterian Church in Ireland, had retained for many years a keen interest in the involvement of Presbyterians in the rebellion and in their gradual transition to unionism and Orangeism.[57] In 1998,

---

[53] Ibid., pp. 49–63; my thanks to Lindy Reid and to Dr Colin Reid for providing me with video recordings of *1798 in the Six Mile Valley* (dir. Archie R. Reid; self-produced, 1998).

[54] *The 1798 Rebellion in the Ards* (Newtownards: Community Relations and Ards Arts, 1998); Trevor McCavery, *Newtown: A History of Newtownards* (Belfast: White Row Press, 1994), pp. 91–102.

[55] Collins, *Who Fears to Speak* pp. 109; Horace Reid, 'The Battle of Ballynahinch: Anthology of the Documents', and W. D. Bailie, 'Presbyterian Clergymen and the County Down Rebellion of 1798', in *1798 Rebellion in County Down*, edited by Myrtle Hill, Brian Turner, and Kenneth Dawson (Newtownards: Colourpoint, 1998), pp. 123–46 and 162–86 (respectively); W. D. Bailie, 'William Steel Dickson', in *Protestant, Catholic and Dissenter: The Clergy and 1798*, edited by Liam Swords (Blackrock: Columba Press, 1997), pp. 45–80. For biographical details on Rev. W. D. Bailie see his obituary in *Down Recorder*, 8 April 2017.

[56] *Fermanagh Herald*, 14 October 1998, p. 19; Collins, *Who Fears to Speak*, p. 121; Horace Reid, 'The Legend of Betsy Gray', in *Fermanagh and 1798*, edited by Séamas Mac Annaidh (Dooneen: Tempo Historical Society, 2000), pp. 86–99; *When Down Was Up: Down County Museum Remembering the 1798 Rising* (Downpatrick: Down County Museum, 1998). My thanks to Horace Reid for an interview and informative tour of local 1798 sites (Ballynahinch, 21 September 2011).

[57] For articles by Rev. Holmes on the topic see 'Eighteenth Century Irish Presbyterian Radicalism and Its Eclipse', *Bulletin of the Presbyterian Historical Society of Ireland*, no. 3 (1973): pp. 7–15; 'United Irishmen and Unionists: Irish Presbyterians, 1791 and 1886', in *The Churches, Ireland, and the Irish:*

he was repeatedly invited to lecture on 'Ulster Presbyterians and 1798', a talk which ended with the observation that 'today, while there are Presbyterians who take pride in the fact that an ancestor carried a pike in '98, they would regard him as a crusader for a just society and not as an Irish nationalist, bent upon breaking Ireland's link with Britain.'[58] At an event titled '1798 Revisited' in Ballymena Town Hall (6 June), Holmes provided the wider historical context on the origins of the United Irishmen and Eull Dunlop of the Mid-Antrim Historical Group, together with Ivan Herbison, an authority on Ulster-Scot poetry, discussed the United Irishmen's local impact.[59] By drawing on the tireless enthusiasm of such local experts, provincial commemoration mostly rested on the authority of home-grown, rather than external, knowledge.

It was left to amateur historians to dig up references to oral traditions. In advance of the bicentenary, the genealogist Rob Davison appealed to the members of the North of Ireland Family History Society (NIFHS), an organization founded in 1979 and which had over a dozen branches for 'information on your ancestors who played any part in those momentous events—from whatever side of the conflict', asking them to 'delve into your family history for any connections with the "1798"'. Once material began to arrive, Davison repeated the call, seeking to tap into the 'collective knowledge of our many hundreds of members world-wide' and to gain access to some of the 'really interesting stories waiting to be told'. He acknowledged that 'it's fairly easy to follow up the family connections of the "personalities" of the Rebellion' (i.e. the more familiar heroes of Ninety-Eight, such as Rev. James Porter or Henry Joy McCracken) and stressed that he was more interested in collecting family traditions concerning 'the people on the fringes', while making sure to 'not forget those who remained loyal to the Crown, whether they were just citizens caught up in events or members of the Crown Forces, Militia and Yeomanry'. Family historians responded favourably, including the society's honorary president, John Bassett, who harboured a personal interest in the topic, admitting that several of his ancestors had 'played a minor part, as yeomen, in the Battles of Ballynahinch'. The fruits of this initiative were published in 1998 in two special issues of the society's journal *North Irish Roots*.[60]

Similarly, the journals of local history societies appealed to their readers for information on local traditions. For example, upon publishing 'A Ballycastle Story of the 1798 Rebellion', Cathal Dallat, editor of the *The Glynns*—the journal of the Glens of Antrim Historical Society—announced that he 'would welcome any stories or episodes

---

Papers Read at the 1987 Summer Meeting and the 1988 Winter Meeting of the Ecclesiastical History Society, edited by W. J. Sheils and Diana Wood (Oxford and New York: Blackwell, 1989), pp. 171–89; 'The 1798 Rebellion', in *Mid-Antrim: Articles on Ballymena and District*, edited by Eull Dunlop (Ballymena: Mid-Antrim Historical Group, 1991), Part 2, pp. 30–40; *Presbyterians and Orangeism 1795–1995* (Belfast: Presbyterian Historical Society of Ireland, 1996); 'From Rebels to Unionists: The Political Transformation of Ulster's Presbyterians', in *The Union: Essays on Ireland and the British Connection*, edited by Ronnie Hanna (Newtownards: Colourpoint, 2001), pp. 34–47. For biographical information see his obituary in the *Irish Times*, 2 August 2008, p. 12.

[58] The text of the lecture is reproduced in James Seery, Finlay Holmes, and A. T. Q. Stewart, *Presbyterians, the United Irishmen and 1798* (Belfast: Presbyterian Historical Society of Ireland, 2000).
[59] Collins, *Who Fears to Speak*, p. 101.
[60] Rob Davison, 'What Did Your Ancestor Do in the 1798 Rebellion?', and '1798 Up-Date', *North Irish Roots*, 8, no. 1 (1997), p. 30 and no. 2 (1997), p. 20 (respectively). 1798 featured in volume 9 (1998), nos. 1 and 2 (Bassett's admission appears in no. 1, p. 2).

of the '98 Rebellion connected with the glens of Antrim or north Antrim'.[61] The Ulster Historical Foundation, which was originally founded in 1956 at the direction of Prime Minister Basil Brooke and had since developed into a genealogical research agency, offered resources for independent scholars, outside of academia, to explore 1798. On the tail end of the bicentenary, the foundation published *Remembering All the Orrs* by Rob Foy of the Antrim and District Historical Society. Foy, who complained about inaccuracies in Bigger's *Remember Orr*, uncovered the lesser-known involvement in the rebellion of several other members of the Orr family, going beyond the familiar story of the protomartyr. Over the course of his research, he was assisted by aficionados of Antrim local history, who brought to his attention folk traditions, such as the reputed pedigree of the 'pike of William Orr' or the story behind the place-name 'Parade Field' in Groggan (4 km north-west of Randalstown), where the rebels had camped and held their prisoners.[62]

The emergence in Northern Ireland of popular interest in the United Irishmen was encouraged by the new political climate of conflict resolution. Mary Holland, the *Irish Times* correspondent for Northern Ireland, observed 'an extraordinary interest in 1798 right across the North' and noted that 'this must owe a lot to the coming of peace, which has provided space for both communities to look again at their most sacred traditions and at what is now needed to adapt them'.[63] The Farset Youth and Community Development Project, run by a group of activists committed to developing cross-community relations between Catholic west Belfast and Protestant north Belfast, published for the 1798 bicentenary a new edition of Madden's biography of James Hope, for which the unionist ideologue Ian Adamson wrote an introduction. Adamson professed that 'at a time when the two communities in Northern Ireland are hopefully approaching the end of their long nightmare and endeavouring to find a common ground between their differing though inter-related identities, it is especially useful to explore those periods of our history when appeals to a commonality of purpose were paramount'. Hence, he declared that 'no longer should the cry be: "Who dares to speak of '98?" We should *all* "speak of '98"'.[64]

EXHIBITING MEMORY

'Up in Arms', the main 1798 bicentennial exhibition in Northern Ireland, was curated at the Ulster Museum in Belfast. From April through August 1998, the museum put on public display some 300 historical artefacts and organized an accompanying pro-gramme of talks, lectures, and workshops, which was launched by Tony Worthington,

---

[61] *The Glynns*, 26 (1998): pp. 85–6.
[62] Foy, *Remembering All the Orrs*, pp. ix and 40. My thanks to William Roulston, Research Director at the Ulster Historical Foundation, and to Pamela Linden (née McIlveen) for facilitating a visit and allowing me access to their collections (19 September 2011).
[63] *Irish Times*, 16 April 1998, p. 16.
[64] *The Autobiography of James (Jemmy) Hope as Published in the United Irishmen: Their Lives and Times [Third Series, Vol 1, 1846] by R.R. Madden* (Belfast: Farset, 1998), p. 3 (emphasis in the original).

the Health and Education Minister at the Northern Ireland Office.[65] In addition to showcasing the museum's rich holdings, which originated in the antiquarian collections of the mid-nineteenth century, the exhibits also included items received on loan from other museums in Ireland. The exhibition in Belfast was designed differently from the major bicentennial exhibitions in the Republic of Ireland. 'Fellowship of Freedom' at the National Museum in Dublin, which was curated by Kevin Whelan, and the purpose-built permanent exhibition at the National 1798 Centre in Enniscorthy, county Wexford, placed 1798 in the international context of the Age of Revolutions. By presenting the radical ideology of the United Irishmen as an alternative to the polarization of modern Irish politics, these southern exhibitions put less of an emphasis on the violence of the rebellion. 'Up in Arms', on the other hand, portrayed the failed rebellion as a bloody civil war, which was 'the seed-bed of both unionism and republican nationalism'.[66]

In effect, the exhibition, which was sponsored by the CRC and by Belfast City Council, as well as by the unionist *Newsletter* and the nationalist *Irish News*, examined the rebellion as a foundational moment in the development of the present-day conflict in Northern Ireland. As such, it was seen as a follow-up to the Ulster Museum's exhibition 'Kings in Conflict', which marked the tercentenary of the Battle of the Boyne in 1990, and would become a precursor to the 2003 exhibition 'Conflict: The Irish at War', in which the museum surveyed the long history of conflict on the island and attempted for the first time to engage directly with the legacy of the Troubles.[67] The presentation of 1798 as a key for a deeper understanding of the origins of the Troubles signified a deliberate effort to harness public history in support of the peace process.[68]

According to attendance figures, the exhibition at the Ulster Museum attracted some 22,500 visitors, of which 1,500 were members of community groups involved in an outreach programme, funded by the EU Special Support Programme for Peace and Reconciliation and coordinated by the historian Jane Leonard, a specialist in the study of commemoration. In addition, over 7,000 members of community groups availed themselves of the linked activities and resources offered by the outreach programme, so

[65] *BNL*, 3 April 1998, p. 9; *Belfast Telegraph*, 3 April 1998; *Fermanagh Herald*, 15 April 1998, p. 32; *Irish Times*, 16 April and 13 June 1998, pp. 16 and 29 (respectively).

[66] Maguire, *Up in Arms*, p. 1; cf. Whelan, *Fellowship of Freedom*. See also Elizabeth Crooke, 'Exhibiting 1798: Three Recent Exhibitions', *History Ireland*, 6, no. 4 (1998): pp. 41–5; Thomas Cauvin, 'One Common Event, Two Distinct Narratives: Commemorative Displays in National Museums in Ireland and Northern Ireland in the 1990s', in *Great Narratives of the Past: Traditions and Revisions in National Museums*, edited by Dominique Poulot, Felicity Bodenstein, and José María Lanzarote Guiral (Linköping: Linköping University Electronic Press, 2011), pp. 587–96.

[67] Trevor Parkhill, 'The Curator as Interpreter, Interlocutor and Facilitator: The 1798 Exhibition and the Conflict Exhibition 2003', in *Effective Presentation and Interpretation in Museums*, edited by Marie Bourke (Dublin: National Gallery of Ireland, 2004), pp. 32–40; Trevor Parkhill, 'The Ulster Museum History Galleries and Post-Conflict Community Engagement', in *Ireland and Victims: Confronting the Past, Forging the Future*, edited by Lesley Lelourec and Gráinne O'Keeffe-Vigneron (Oxford and New York: Peter Lang, 2012), pp. 271–85.

[68] Greg McLaughlin and Stephen Baker, *The Propaganda of Peace: The Role of Media and Culture in the Northern Ireland Peace Process* (Bristol: Intellect, 2010), pp. 41–6; see also Trevor Parkhill, '"That's Their History": Can a Museum's Historical Programme Inform the Reconciliation Process in a Divided Society?', *Folk Life*, 41, no. 1 (2002): pp. 37–44.

that the exhibition had a wider impact.[69] The evident success of the outreach initiative was applauded by the Gulbenkian Foundation, which gave the museum its Best Education Project Award. Moreover, the exhibition's impressive 305-page catalogue, compiled by the museum's leading historian William Alexander Maguire and printed by the Mallusk-based firm Nicholson & Bass, was recognized as the 'Irish Print of the Year'.[70]

Reflecting on the achievements of the exhibition, Trevor Parkhill, the museum's Keeper of History, extolled its role as a 'neutral venue' that accommodated a 'shared history', which appealed to both nationalist and unionist visitors. One particularly memorable visit was organized in response to the murder by loyalist paramilitaries of Ciaran Heffron, a young Catholic student, and included over eighty people, Catholics and Protestants, from Crumlin in county Antrim (on the outskirts of Belfast). Yet, Parkhill also admitted that most of the visits 'remained single-identity in character', insofar as nationalist and unionist groups preferred to inspect the exhibition, and interpret its contents, separately. Remembrance largely took place within insular social frameworks, sustaining community, rather than inter-community social memory.[71]

The exhibition's centrepiece was Thomas Robinson's painting *The Battle of Ballynahinch* (originally titled *Combat between the King's Troops and the Peasantry at Ballynahinch*) (Fig. 7.1). The history of this iconic visual representation of the northern rebellion embodies the ways in which Ninety-Eight was initially remembered, then forgotten, and ultimately exhumed and re-adapted to new circumstances. Robinson, who lived for a while in Laurencetown, county Down, had moved in 1798 to Lisburn, where he completed his depiction of the main engagement of the rebellion in Down within four months of the event. Although the painting was advertised as 'a faithful representation of the field of battle and its scenes', it was purposely crafted as a loyalist visualization of how the victors wished the rebellion to be remembered, through the prism of its suppression.[72]

Bishop Percy of Dromore, who was intrigued by the drawing of Robinson's artwork, immediately spotted that it was modelled on Benjamin West's famous *The Death of General Wolfe* (which was painted in 1770 and popularized a few years later in an engraving by William Woollett), with the dying Captain Henry Evatt of the Monaghan Militia standing in for Major-General James Wolfe at the painting's focal point. The colour scheme, as pointed out by the art historian Fintan Cullen, is dominated by the red uniforms of the militia and the blue of the yeomen cavalry, which overshadow the green of the United Irishmen. The foreground is taken by General Nugent and his officers, overlooking in the far distance—as described by the *Belfast News-Letter*—the 'discomfiture of the rebels, and the burning of Ballynahinch', where 'the green standard is discerned amidst a multitude of routed insurgents.'[73]

---

[69] Trevor Parkhill, 'The Curator as Interpreter', p. 36.
[70] *BNL*, 8 and 15 December 1999, pp. 35 and 19 (respectively); for biographical information on W. A. Maguire see *Belfast Telegraph*, 8 April 2011, p. 26.
[71] Parkhill, 'The Ulster Museum History Galleries', pp. 274–5; *Irish Times*, 13 June 1998, p. A1.
[72] *BNL*, 6 November 1798, p. 3.
[73] *BNL*, 6 November 1798, p. 2; Lecky, *A History of Ireland in the Eighteenth Century*, vol. 4, p. 424n2 (Bishop Percy to his wife, 27 October 1798); Eileen Black, *Art in Belfast 1760–1888: Art Lovers or Philistines?* (Dublin: Irish Academic Press, 2006), pp. 6–10; Fintan Cullen, 'Radicals and

Fig. 7.1. 'The Battle of Ballynahinch' (1798)

The contemporary painting by Thomas Robinson (*c.*1767–1810) presented a triumphalist loyalist depiction of the battle, which became an iconic image of the rebellion in Ulster.

Image courtesy of OPW State Art Collection.

Robinson's painting was exhibited in November 1798 in the Exchange Rooms in Belfast at an exclusive showing intended for the wealthy elite, at which the admission price was a British shilling. The painting was then sold by raffle, with tickets priced at a guinea, and acquired by Lord Hertford, who displayed it as his house in Lisburn 'to be viewed . . . by all who were at the Battle of Ballynahinch, many of whom have their portraits drawn in it' (though the key, which identified the thirty portraits incorporated into the work, was subsequently lost). In the left corner can be seen the 'seizure of one of those deluded victims of civil contention', who is led to his execution, and, in the words of the *Belfast News-Letter*: 'a mixture of commiseration and contempt is discernible in the deportment of the yeomen performing that disagreeable office.'[74] The unnamed insurgent has been identified as the United Irish colonel Hugh McCullough [McCulloch] of Bangor, whose brother was fighting for the Crown in the Downshire Militia. Although McCullough suffered from an injury, contrary to standard regulations, he was dragged before a drumhead court-martial, which 'was instantly held upon him', and hanged from the sails of the local windmill.[75] *The Battle of Ballynahinch* is an unmistakably one-sided triumphalist depiction of the outcome of the rebellion.

Reactionaries: Portraits of the 1790s in Ireland', in *Revolution, Counter-Revolution, and Union: Ireland in the 1790s*, edited by Jim Smyth (Cambridge: Cambridge University Press, 2000), pp. 187–90.

[74] *BNL*, 6 November 1798, pp. 2 and 3 (advertisement); Maguire, *Up in Arms*, pp. 245–9.

[75] McCullough's execution was reported in letters to Lord Downshire from George Stephenson (13 June 1798) and William Hartigan (16 June 1798), Downshire Papers, PRONI D607/F/236 and 250; it was also described by Rev. Thomas Ledlie Birch in anon., *A Letter from an Irish Emigrant* (1799), p. 14.

By the mid-nineteenth century, as social forgetting prevailed and mention of the rebellion in public was discouraged, the whereabouts of the painting had become unknown and could not be recovered by antiquarians, who tried to track down its location.[76] It resurfaced in the mid-twentieth century, when the painting was acquired by a Dublin man who offered it for sale to the Belfast Museum and Art Gallery (the precursor of the Ulster Museum), but the protracted negotiations were stalled following the outbreak of the Second World War. Instead, Robinson's painting was acquired for a collection compiled by Douglas Hyde, the President of Ireland, 'of portraits and pictures of historical events, illustrative of the struggle of Ireland throughout the centuries to assert its nationhood and the right of its people to develop their own culture'.[77] While the unionist establishment was characteristically tardy in recognizing the historical significance of 1798, the portrayal of the rebellion in Ulster had quite literally been appropriated for the cause of nationalism.

Robinson's painting, which became the property of the Irish Office of Public Works, was housed in the National Gallery in Dublin and given on loan in 1998 to the Ulster Museum. In the promotional materials for the bicentennial exhibition 'Up in Arms', the image was cropped to show a more symmetrical struggle between the United Irishmen (represented by McCullough) and the forces of the Crown (his captors), which suited the exhibition's guiding concept of juxtaposing the rebellion with the counter-revolutionary struggle.[78] Throughout the exhibition, the curators made use of standard historical sources to reinterpret visual and material culture. Oral traditions were rarely, if at all, consulted so that the vernacular history of social forgetting was, by and large, excluded from the revised construction of an official cultural memory of Ninety-Eight.

Bicentennial exhibitions at local museums were more preoccupied with the experience of the rebellion on a ground level. For example, 'When Down Was Up', the exhibition that ran from 31 March to 30 November 1998 at the Down County Museum in Downpatrick, explicitly focused 'on how the lives of ordinary people in the area were affected'.[79] In these settings, vernacular history was somewhat better represented. Among the memorabilia associated with the insurgent general Henry Munro that was put on display at the bicentennial exhibition in the Lisburn Museum (March to December 1998) was the reputed key to his house (in front of which he was executed), and a commemorative bracelet said to contain a plaited lock of his hair.[80] While provincial exhibitions could not compete with the extensive collections assembled by the Ulster Museum, their relative advantage was apparent in the display of local heritage, which could be interpreted in accordance with folk, rather than official, history.

---

[76] *UJA*, 1st ser., vol. 2 (1854): p. 285 and vol. 3 (1855): p. 81.

[77] *Árus an Uachtaráin: Cnuasacht de Phictiúiri, Etc., Stairiúla . . . Collection of Historical Pictures, Etc* (Dublin: pr. Wood Printing Works, 1944), p. 41.

[78] Cauvin, 'One Common Event, Two Distinct Narratives', p. 591.

[79] When Down Was Up (Downpatrick: Down County Museum, 1998); M. Lesley Simpson, 'Down County Museum: Review of Collections and Activities', *Lecale Miscellany*, no. 16 (1998): pp. 99–103. My thanks to Linda McKenna, the Community Education Manager at the museum, for facilitating a visit and discussing the curating of the bicentennial exhibition (21 September 2011).

[80] My thanks to Brain Mackey, the museum's curator, for allowing me access to the 1798 exhibits and supplementary documentation, and for an interview on the bicentennial exhibition (Lisburn Museum, 23 September 2011).

The bicentennial exhibition at the Ballymoney Museum (21 April to 28 August 1998) featured several items that relate to the local United Irish hero John Nevin, who had been remembered in the neighbourhood through song and stories. These exhibits included Nevin's sword and one of the commemorative jugs that his family had commissioned following his death in 1806. For the bicentenary, the museum received from Peter Hutchinson of Melbourne a carved coconut embossed with silver, which, according to family tradition, had been presented after 1798 to the magistrate George Hutchinson by a convicted United Irishman, as a token of gratitude for commuting his death sentence to transportation. The uncovering of this unusual souvenir challenged local traditions, which recalled his responsibility for the hanging of United Irishmen. The unpopular magistrate was vilified in folklore as 'Bloody Hutchinson' and it was said that his ghost haunted Ballymoney's main street.[81]

When an authentic pike from 1798 could not be found for the bicentennial exhibition at the Ballycastle Museum, a replica was manufactured at local ironworks.[82] The small museum, however, could exhibit a remarkable series of visual representations of oral traditions that had been drawn at the turn of the century by Joseph William Carey, a founding member of the Belfast Ramblers Sketching Club and the Belfast Art Society, and an elected member of the Ulster Academy of Arts. Together with his elder brother John, who was also a painter, and in association with another artist, Ernest Hanford, J. W. Carey established in Belfast a graphic design office which provided illustrations of historical scenes for antiquarians. During the fin-de-siècle revival of interest in the United Irishmen, Carey sketched for W. S. Smith's *Memories of '98* a depiction of the Battle of Antrim. A variation of this drawing appeared in Robert M. Young's *Historical Notices of Old Belfast*, which also featured an illustration of the execution of Henry Joy McCracken. In addition, Carey drew several scenes from the life of William Orr for Bigger's *Remember Orr*.[83] Unlike these images, which were circulated in popular print and in time would be recognized as iconic images of the rebellion, the Ballycastle Museum acquired three of Carey's lesser-known paintings, which portrayed the fate of the local rebel Francis McKinlay [McKinley] of Conagher, as it was recalled in local folklore.

In 1898, hopes had run high that the American president William McKinley, who was the great-grandnephew of the United Irish rebel, would endorse the centennial of 1798 and perhaps pay a visit to his ancestral home in Antrim, but at the time he was preoccupied with the Spanish-American War.[84] In 1904, three years after McKinley was assassinated at the Pan-American Exposition in Buffalo, the president was hon-oured with tributes at the World Fair in St Louis, Missouri (which was officially organized to commemorate the centennial of the Louisiana Land Purchase of 1803). The Irish exhibition at that international exposition featured a reconstruction of the McKinley family's ancestral cottage, for which Carey painted three scenes pertaining to

---

[81] Beattie, *Ballymoney and the Rebellion 1798*, pp. 20–1 and 23–4. For Nevin see Chapter 2 above, pp. 120–1. Nevin's sword was subsequently selected for BBC's 'History of the World'; see <www.bbc. co.uk/ahistoryoftheworld/objects/yGTdMIZsQgSdClsgni38vg>.

[82] Cahal Dallat, 'Ballycastle in the 1798', The Glynns, 27 (1999): pp. 66–7.

[83] *UJA*, 2nd ser., 1, no. 2 (1895), p. 133 (republished in Smith, *Memories of '98*, frontispiece); Young, ed., *Historical Notices of Old Belfast*, pp. 187 (facing page) and 195; Bigger, *Remember Orr*, pp. 13, 36, and 41. See also Maguire, *Up in Arms*, pp. 241–2 and 250.

[84] See *Weekly Freeman*, 5 March 1898, p. 1; in *Derry Journal*, 11 March 1898, p. 7.

Francis McKinley and 1798: the burning of his home by yeomen, his execution at Coleraine, and the furtive burial of his reclaimed corpse in the old churchyard at Derrykeighan (8 km north-west of Ballymoney).[85] In contrast to Robinson's painting of the Battle of Ballynahinch, which presented the rebellion from the point of view of the triumphant military establishment, Carey's paintings reflected a subaltern counter-memory, which could not be put on canvas till many years after the event. The exhibition of these paintings in Ballycastle two centuries after the rebellion recalled the local experience of the Turn-Out, as it had been remembered in private. At the same time, it also evoked the public flaunting of this memory around the time of the centenary, before it once again went underground with the establishment of Northern Ireland.

While they were aware of the appeal of folklore, the curators of local exhibitions, who were in many cases local historians with postgraduate degrees, were influenced by the revisionist tendency to debase popular myths that had become pervasive in Irish academic historiography. They were therefore hesitant to validate their materials with information drawn from vernacular sources. Anthony Russell, chairman of the Newry and Mourne '98 Committee, prefaced the section on 'The Folk Memory of '98' in *Beyond the Battle*—a local history publication produced in conjunction with the bicentennial exhibition in Newry—with the cautionary note: 'Read with Great Care!'.[86] Folk history was generally kept at arm's length—its appeal was irresistible and yet two centuries of social forgetting had relegated oral traditions to the margins, so that doubts were cast on its inherent value.

Even though the bicentenary, which took place in a year of dramatic political developments, did not make front-page headlines, the media reported on the many commemorative events and provided running commentary. To a critic writing for the *Sunday Times*, it seemed as if 'hype and history are marching side by side' and the pertinent question was not 'who fears to speak of '98?' but 'who fears not to speak of '98?'.[87] The findings of historical research were brought to the attention of the general public in newspaper articles, some of which were written in the present tense in order to make the past seem more current. The '1798 Diary', written by the historian Ruán O'Donnell, used contemporary sources to present a detailed narrative that appeared in the *Irish Times* as weekly columns, which were collated into a book at the end of the bicentennial year.[88] The *Belfast Telegraph* reported on how the 'leading United Irishman Henry Joy McCracken was hanged yesterday in Belfast', as if the execution had just taken place, and the news reporter Steven Moore surveyed the rebellion in

[85] Walter Barlow Stevens, *The Forest City: Comprising the Official Photographic Views of the Universal Exposition* (Saint Louis: N. D. Thompson Publishing Co., 1904), entry on 'The McKinlay Cottage'; *Omaha Daily Bee*, 17 July 1904 (description by special correspondent); see also Elana V. Fox, *Inside the World's Fair of 1904: Exploring the Louisiana Purchase Exposition* (Bloomington: Authorhouse, 2003), 1.

[86] Anthony G. Russell, *Beyond the Battle: The Story of South Down and South Armagh in 1798* (Newry: Newry and Mourne 1798 Commemorative Committee, 1998), p. 21. My thanks to Anthony Russell for discussing with me his experiences in organizing the local bicentennial commemorative programme; Newry, 24 September 2011.

[87] *Sunday Times*, 31 May 1998.

[88] Ruán O'Donnell, *1798 Diary* (Dublin: Irish Times, 1998); for a review see *Irish Times*, 18 May 1999. For key entries on the rebellion in Ulster see *Irish Times*, 6 and 20 June and 20 November 1998 (all on p. 4).

Antrim and Down for the *Belfast News-Letter* in a series of articles that seemed to cover a present-day occurrence.[89] Such mock news reportage catered to the essential feature of commemoration—projecting a sense of reliving history in the present—so that Ninety-Eight was recalled in what the dramatist Stewart Parker had labelled 'the continuous past', an imaginative time-frame more suited to traditional vernacular remembrance than to modern sensibilities.

Living history was a central feature of bicentennial television productions, which made use of historical re-enacting to portray scenes from the rebellion with a sense of realism. Patrick Fitzsimons, founder of the productions company Clan Visions, filmed for UTV *News of the '98*, a series of short videos, mostly recorded in the Ulster American Folk Park (an open-air museum outside Omagh in county Tyrone), in which he played a modern-day journalist embedded in the events of 1798. Some of these reconstructions aroused controversy. A re-enactment of the execution of Henry Munro was called off, following claims that 'there were descendants around who might take offence'. Fitzsimons realized that 'in general, commemorations of 1798 are quite subdued' in areas where unionists were reluctant to see their 'rate-payer's money going into the celebration' of what was perceived as disloyalty.[90]

Moore Sinnerton, a filmmaker from Dunmurry (between Belfast and Lisburn), produced and directed for BBC Northern Ireland *The Patriot's Fate*, a two-part documentary on the rebellion in Ulster. The script was written by the Belfast-based historian Jonathan Bardon, who had previously covered the rebellion in brief in his *History of Ulster*, and was presented by the former Lebanon hostage Brian Keenan, who professed a personal fascination with 'the past, in the context of Ireland in general and the 1798 Rebellion in particular'. Although it was felt that the documentary was geared towards drawing a moral that could be applied to current politics, to the director's credit this was not done didactically. A journalist writing for the *Belfast Telegraph* concluded that 'there were so many conflicting themes north and south and so much brutality on both sides that perhaps it is best to salute the idealism and learn how violence perpetuates itself.'[91]

The documentary's choice of titles was deliberately evocative. The overall heading 'The Patriot's Fate' was taken from a verse of the ballad 'The Memory of the Dead', which asks 'when cowards mock the patriot's fate, who hangs his head for shame?', implying that it was no longer embarrassing to remember the heroes of Ninety-Eight. 'A Cordial Union', the title of the first episode, cited an early declaration of the Society of the United Irishmen, which called for 'a cordial union among all the people of Ireland', implying that this political message was once again relevant. The title of the second episode—'Not Quite Philadelphia'—has been commonly believed to be a historical quotation of Henry McCracken, but was actually taken from Stewart Parker's play *Northern Star*, in which the embellished character of McCracken sardonically comments on the failure of the rebels under his command to take Antrim Town, saying

---

[89] *BNL*, 4, 11, 12, and 13 June, pp. 14, 16, 22, and 11 (respectively); *Belfast Telegraph*, 18 July 1998.

[90] *News of the '98* compilation (dir. Patrick Fitzsimons; Clan Visions, 1998); *Irish Times*, 23 June 1998, p. 14.

[91] *The Patriot's Fate* (dir. Moore Sinnerton; Chistera Productions, 1998); *Belfast Telegraph*, 5 and 27 February 1998; *Irish Times*, 28 February 1998, p. 43; *An Phoblacht*, 5 March 1998. For Bardon's survey of the northern rebellion see Jonathan Bardon, *A History of Ulster* (Belfast: Blackstaff, 1992), pp. 232–6.

'have you ever been to Antrim, I mean it isn't exactly Paris, is it, it's scarcely Boston, it's not quite Philadelphia, is it?'.[92] Cultural memory had imperceptibly merged with history. When broadcasted on the BBC over two weeks in mid-February 1998, this television programme demonstrated the extent to which attitudes in Northern Ireland had changed, so that 1798 could now be aired on prime time.

In addition, historical programmes shown on the television channels of the Republic of Ireland were also available for northern viewers. Louis Marcus directed for the recently-opened Irish-language station Teilifís na Gaeilge (TnaG) the documentary *1798 agus Ó Shin* [1798 and Since], which was broadcast in April 1998. Marcus, who was particularly interested in the little-known history of Irish-speaking Protestants in Northern Ireland (which became the topic of his 2003 documentary *No Rootless Colonists: Na Gaeil Phrotastunaigh*), put an emphasis on the involvement of Presbyterians in the rebellion. The commentary purposely incorporated the voices of northern Presbyterian historians, in order to challenge what Marcus considered to be the 'simplistic myth' of Catholic nationalist history. A review in the *Irish Independent* praised the programme for 'its treatment of what happened in the decades after '98—explaining with real clarity how and why Presbyterianism became alienated from ideals it had once espoused with such passion and commitment'.[93]

RTÉ's *Rebellion*, the most extensive of the 1798 documentaries, was designed by its producer, Kevin Dawson, to be 'the centrepiece of the bicentennial commemorations' and was presented by the seasoned journalist Cathal O'Shannon. It was screened on RTÉ 1 in May 1998 in three hour-long weekly episodes and was subsequently issued commercially on videocassette. The *Irish Times* critic Hugh Lenihan found it to be 'an exemplary piece of historical television, drawing with great effect on international archives, first-hand written accounts and the analysis of modern historians'. It featured extensive dramatic reconstruction, alongside computer animation, and it also blended 'pictorial records of the period with astute sound-editing and a stirring musical score'. The historical advisors, Thomas Bartlett and Dáire Keogh, co-edited with Dawson an accompanying volume, which was written for a general readership as well as for schools. According to the *Irish Times*, it promised 'to be the definitive television offering on the subject for some time to come'.[94]

The directors of the three 1798 bicentennial documentaries attended in September 1998 an event in the National Museum at Collin's Barracks in Dublin, where they discussed the 'accuracy of film images'.[95] As Robert A. Rosenstone, among others, has shown, the seemingly realistic narration of history presented in documentary films is purposely constructed to appear authoritative.[96] The television documentaries on 1798

[92] Parker, *Plays*, p. 8.

[93] *1798 agus Ó Shin* (dir. Louis Marcus; Louis Marcus Productions and TnaG, 1998); *RTÉ Guide*, 10 April 1998, p. 14; *Irish Independent*, 18 April 1998, p. 32; *Sunday Business Post*, 19 April 1998, p. 33; see also Harvey O'Brien, *The Real Ireland: The Evolution of Ireland in Documentary Film* (Manchester: Manchester University Press, 2004), pp. 132–3.

[94] *Rebellion* (dir. Brian Hayes; RTÉ, 1998); *Irish Times*, 9 and 16 May 1998; Thomas Bartlett, Kevin Dawson, and Dáire Keogh, *Rebellion: A Television History of 1798* (Dublin: Gill & Macmillan, 1998); see also O'Brien, *The Real Ireland*, p. 133.

[95] *Irish Times*, 7 September 1998, p. 4.

[96] Robert A. Rosenstone, 'History in Images/History in Words: Reflections on the Possibility of Really Putting History onto Film', *American Historical Review*, 93, no. 5 (1988): pp. 1179–80; Paula Rabinowitz, 'Wreckage upon Wreckage: History, Documentary and the Ruins of Memory', *History*

relied solely on the authority of academic history and the select cadre of historians, who were repeatedly interviewed in all three programmes, gave little thought to provincial vernacular traditions. Together, they signalled a concerted effort to construct a popular-collective memory that corresponds with the dominant trend in historiography, to the exclusion of folk memories.

Towards the end of the bicentenary, in December 1998, an attempt was made to treat the memory of 1798 with iconoclastic humour. The Hole in the Wall Gang—a northern comedy group that had recently gained tremendous popularity with a satirical take on the Troubles in their television series *Give My Head Peace*—starred in a thirty-minute spoof titled *1798—The Comedy*. Ambitiously described by the producer, Jackie Hamilton, as 'a cross between Blackadder and Monty Python', the programme was supposed to be a pilot for a six-episode series—'The Comedies of Eire', in which the central character, Barry Simpson, would find himself entangled in iconic historical events, such as the Battle of the Boyne, the sinking of the Titanic, and the Easter Rising. The parodying of 1798 rebellion, however, was considered a dud and consequently the plans to make further comic historical episodes fell through. Ninety-Eight was apparently still considered by many members of the public a traumatic event that should not be remembered light-heartedly. That said, the programme ended with an apposite scene of forgetting. The fictional rebel Barry Simpson reconciles with his death sentence in the knowledge that he will be remembered by posterity, but his name is then misconstrued, so that—like many other 'common' rebels—he is ultimately consigned to oblivion.[97]

The cultural critic Fintan O'Toole observed that 'Irish artists have had difficulty with the legacy of 1798 because it disturbs both the Orange and the Green narratives—but can be appropriated by either.'[98] The bicentenary re-awakened interest in artistic interpretations of the rebellion that had fallen off the radar. Brian Ferran, the chief executive of the Arts Council of Northern Ireland, was invited in April to give a talk at the Ulster Museum on a sequence of paintings of the folk heroine Betsy Gray, which he had painted two decades earlier. In the midst of the Troubles, around 1976, Ferran—a Derry-born Catholic artist residing in Belfast—addressed the theme of Ninety-Eight through creatively reinterpreting the image of the local county Down heroine, stressing in the paintings her femininity and fragility. In these works, a red-headed Betsy Gray surveys scenes from the Battle of Ballynahinch, taken from Thomas Robinson's famous painting.[99]

and Theory, 32, no. 2 (1993): pp. 119–37; see also the essays on 'History and Television', in Marcia Landy, ed., *The Historical Film: History and Memory in Media* (New Brunswick, N.J.: Rutgers University Press, 2001), pp. 269–330.

[97] *1798—The Comedy* (Moondog Productions, 1998); *Belfast Telegraph*, 25 June and 2 December 1998. For the Hole in the Wall Gang and their take on the Troubles see Lance Pettitt, *Screening Ireland: Film and Television Representation* (Manchester and New York: Manchester University Press, 2000), pp. 186–8 and 204n50.

[98] *Irish Times*, 9 December 1997, p. 14.

[99] *Brian Ferran: Patterns and Parables, Paintings 1966–1996* (Dublin Gallagher Gallery, 1996). My thanks to Brian Ferran for providing me with a statement in which he reflected on his Betsy Gray paintings (2012), as well as images of the works and supplementary materials. For photographs of related paintings see Ferran's works in the Troubles Archive; <www.troublesarchive.com/artists/brian-ferran/work>.

Ferran's paintings were acclaimed in Dublin, where one of his imaginative portrayals of Betsy Gray received in 1978 the Douglas Hyde Gold Medal for the best painting with an Irish historical theme.[100] A review of Ferran's work in the *Irish Press* realized that the depictions of 1798 drew an 'analogy with today's situation in Northern Ireland' but failed to recognize the image of Betsy Gray.[101] The Belfast art critic Michael Catto later observed that most people outside of Ulster do not know her, which 'shows that some figure's become internationally famous and some remain parochial'.[102]

Ferran continued to experiment with reimagining the memory of 1798. In later paintings, he toyed with counter-factual notions of what would have happened if the rebellion had had a different outcome, depicting Betsy Gray on the winning side and in her old age, as an elderly stateswoman decorated with medals. The art historian Belinda Loftus likened his work, with its ironic distancing from nationalist romanticism of violence, to pop art, but it only attracted limited critical attention.[103] The bicentenary inspired Ferran to re-engage with Ninety-Eight. The following year, in December 1999, the Jonathan Swift Gallery in Carrickfergus hosted a solo exhibition of Ferran's new paintings, which the poet Michael Longley described as 'works of commemoration and celebration'. Among them was an image of a nude Betsy Gray with a Union flag wrapped around her. In the eyes of a reporter from *Belfast News-Letter*, it represented 'the ongoing spirit of resistance the painter would not have us forget' and the 'inheritance of ideals we could share'.[104] This unorthodox portrayal of Betsy Gray contrasted starkly with the folk history presented in W. G. Lyttle's late-nineteenth-century novel, which had popularized a more traditional romantic image of the local heroine.

Another artistic reinterpretation of Betsy Gray was offered by Moira McIver, a lecturer of Fine Art in the University of Ulster with a particular interest in the relationship between individual and public histories. Her exhibition *Portrait, Diary, Biography*, displayed in 2000 at the Ards Arts Centre in Newtownards, county Down, consisted of a fictional photographic portrait of the heroine and two monitor-based artworks, one showing a dramatized view of Betsy loading a musket and the other of her walking towards the Battle of Ballynahinch. This multi-media installation played on the dissonance between the scant historical information available and the bowdlerized speculations that had fuelled the legend in popular imagination. The implied suggestion that, in contemporary terms, Betsy Gray might be seen as a gunrunner accentuated the tension between her role as a Protestant heroine and a republican martyr.[105]

Vernacular representations of social memory—as opposed to the more refined cultural memory on display at art galleries—are particularly visible in popular expressions of street culture. By far the most familiar expressions of visual remembrance in Northern Ireland are the murals painted on the gable walls of houses (mainly in Belfast and Derry), a tradition that was noticeable in the 1920s in Protestant loyalist

---

[100] *Cork Examiner*, 16 September 1978, p. 10; *Irish Press*, 15 September 1978, p. 4.

[101] *Irish Press*, 24 October 1977, p. 4.

[102] Michael Catto, 'Making Sense of Ulster', *Art and Artists*, 14, no. 10 (February 1980), p. 13.

[103] Belinda Loftus, 'Mother Ireland and the Troubles: Artist, Model and Reality', *Circa*, no. 1 (1981), p. 11.

[104] *BNL*, 17 December 1999, p. 16; *Belfast Telegraph*, 18 December 1999.

[105] My thanks to Moira McIver for providing me with information and photographs of the exhibition (9 September 2012).

neighbourhoods (where it had originated already in 1908) and became widespread in Catholic nationalist neighbourhoods in the 1980s, from around the time of the 1981 republican prisoners' hunger strike protest campaign. Reflecting a build-up of commemorative competition between nationalists and unionists, hundreds of political murals, many of which sported historical themes, were painted and repainted during the Troubles.[106] However, in a curious reflex of social forgetting, 1798 was glaringly absent from murals during the Troubles. While unionists considered Protestant involvement in the rebellion a taboo that should be kept out of the public gaze, northern nationalists apparently also felt a measure of discomfort with ambiguous memories, which could not be simply portrayed. The United Irishmen did not fit easily in the canon of mythomoteurs chosen to be put on display and were therefore largely excluded from the public collective memory exhibited on murals. Scenes of 1798 only began to appear on murals as the Troubles winded down, but, even then, this was a relatively minor motif.[107]

Commenting on the scarcity of 1798 bicentennial murals in nationalist neighbourhoods, Derek Lundy deduced that the limited indulgence in visual displays of triumphalism might be a sign of confidence in the peace process. With reference to the slogan of the provisional IRA—*'tiocfaidh ár lá'* [our day will come], Lundy suggested that 'perhaps it was the restraint of a people who saw that the grafitto was right, that their time was, indeed, and finally, coming.'[108] Republicans, however, were intent on finding justification for their acceptance of the peace agreement by staking a claim on the legacy of the United Irishmen. For the bicentenary, a mural of *Na hÉireannaigh Aontaithe* [The United Irishmen] was painted on a house on South Link in Andersonstown, a Catholic neighbourhood in west Belfast Catholic. It showed a band of pikemen marching under a winged-maiden (angel) harp and the inscription 'It is new strung and shall now be heard', which was a subtle update—stressing the present moment—of the motto on the United Irish insignia: 'It is new strung and shall be heard.' The use of the Gaelic for the United Irishmen and the prominence of the harp, which has been recognized as 'a palimpsest of cultural memory' in Ireland, clearly marked the mural as an exponent of cultural nationalism.[109] Incidentally, the activists

---

[106] See Bill Rolston, 'Politics, Painting and Popular Culture: The Political Wall Murals of Northern Ireland', *Media Culture Society*, 9, no. 1 (January 1987): pp. 5–28; Bill Rolston, '"Trying to Reach the Future through the Past": Murals and Memory in Northern Ireland', *Crime, Media, Culture*, 6, no. 3 (December 2010): pp. 285–307; Alexandra Hartnett, 'Aestheticized Geographies of Conflict: The Politicization of Culture and the Culture of Politics in Belfast's Mural Tradition', in *Contested Cultural Heritage*, edited by Helaine Silverman (New York: Springer, 2011), pp. 69–107; Maximilian Rapp and Markus Rhomberg, 'The Importance of Murals During the Troubles: Analyzing the Republican Use of Wall Paintings in Northern Ireland', in *Visual Communication*, edited by David Machin (Berlin and Boston: De Gruyter, 2014), pp. 677–96.

[107] See Martin Forker and Jonathan McCormick, 'Walls of History: The Use of Mythomoteurs in Northern Ireland Murals', *Irish Studies Review*, 17, no. 4 (2009): pp. 423–65. For mythomoteurs see John A. Armstrong, *Nations before Nationalism* (Chapel Hill: University of North Carolina Press, 1982); the term has been embraced by the ethno-symbolism school of nationalism studies pioneered by Anthony D. Smith.

[108] Derek Lundy, *Men That God Made Mad: A Journey through Truth, Myth and Terror in Northern Ireland* (London: Jonathan Cape, 2006), p. 269.

[109] Forker and McCormick, 'Walls of History', pp. 436–7. For the significance of the harp see Mary Helen Thuente, 'Images of Irish Culture: The Origin and Significance of the Angel Harp', in *Back to the Present, Forward to the Past: Irish Writing and History since 1798*, edited by Brian Coates, Joachim Fischer, and Patricia A. Lynch (Amsterdam and New York: Rodopi, 2006), pp. 181–208 (image of the United Irish insignia on p. 183); Mary Helen Thuente, 'The Harp as a Palimpsest of

who commissioned the mural were probably unaware of the significance of the location as a site of oblivion—according to the local historian Joe Graham, the area of Andersonstown had originally been named Whitesidetown, after a local family that was dispossessed because of their associations with the United Irishmen.[110]

The Roddy McCorley Society, a local republican club that was formed in 1972 as a continuation of the earlier activities of the Andersonstown Republican Club, decorated an outside wall of its premises at Moyard House, on Glen Road in west Belfast, with a painting that reproduced J. W. Carey's iconic drawing of the Battle of Antrim (Fig. 7.2).[111] The location of the mural at this venue linked the rebellion in Ulster with the struggle of the provisional IRA. Inside the Roddy McCorley Society's clubhouse is a museum of the republican armed struggle, with rooms named after prominent United Irishmen. The commemorative garden outside the building has a bilingual memorial (Fig. 7.2), unveiled by Sinn Féin President Gerry Adams on 19 November 1995, which is 'dedicated to the memory of all Irish Men and Irish women who gave their lives in the 1798 rebellion and to all those who gave their lives for Irish freedom in every generation' ('do chuimhne na n-Éireannach uilig idir fhir agus mhná a thit in Éirí Amach 1798 agus igcuimhne achan duine, in ngach glúin, a fuair bás ar son saoirse na hÉireann').[112]

Whereas the murals in west Belfast placed the visual remembrance of Ninety-Eight squarely within the republican heartland, a more inclusive approach was taken in Ballynahinch. As part of an initiative to regenerate the town, a 'Murals Make Ballyna-hinch Beautiful' committee, chaired by Robert 'Brum' Henderson—former Managing Director of Ulster Television, commissioned a series of murals that would 'look back to the past in a pleasant way'. Under the direction of the artist Neil Shawcross (a resident of nearby Hillsborough), and through consultation with the local historian Horace Reid, artists were invited to draw large paintings of local historical scenes. The artworks were treated to protective layers of additional varnish, and then framed and hung on gable walls throughout the town. Among the images of 1798, which included a combat scene from the Battle of Ballynahinch, as well as depictions of the forging of pikes by the local blacksmith Matt McClenaghan and of the arrest of the intended leader of the United Irish army Rev. William Steel Dickson, the most striking was a painting by the Belfast artist Bill Gatt of a flame-haired Betsy Gray overlooking the battle, postcards of which were available for sale (Fig. 7.3). The local folk heroine, whose short-lived monument had been violently removed from sight in 1898, was commemorated in 1998 by having her image publicly displayed.[113]

Cultural Memory', in *Memory Ireland*, edited by Oona Frawley (Syracuse, N.Y.: Syracuse University Press, 2010), vol. 1: *History and Modernity*, pp. 52–65.

[110] Joe Graham, 'Myths, Legends and Facts on Olde Belfast', *Rushlight Magazine* (1998); online: <http://joegraham.rushlightmagazine.com/>.

[111] *An Phoblacht*, 26 June 1997.

[112] For information on the history of the society, its monuments and its museum see the Roddy McCorley Society website; <www.roddymccorley.com>. My thanks to Kevin Carson of the Roddy McCorley Society and to the history buff Jack Duffin for facilitating a visit to Moyard House (22 September 2011).

[113] *BNL*, 19 August 1997, p. 9 and 28 July 1998, p. 10; *Belfast Telegraph*, 28 July 1998; *Belfast Telegraph*, 26 October 2000; Albert Colmer, '"The 1798"—Remembered', *Lecale Miscellany*, no. 15 (1997), editorial; Collins, *Who Fears to Speak*, p. 110. For a photograph of the mural by Jonathan McCormick see CAIN Mural Directory, photograph no. 657; <http://cain.ulst.ac.uk/mccormick/photos/no657.htm#photo>.

(a)

(b)

Fig. 7.2. Roddy McCorley Society memorials

(a) Battle of Antrim mural. The Roddy McCorley Society clubhouse in Moyard House, in west Belfast, also functions as a museum and commemoration site for the Irish republican armed struggle. A mural outside reproduces a scene of the Battle of Antrim from a late-nineteenth-century painting by J. W. Carey.

Photograph by Martin Mellaugh © CAIN (<www.cain.ulster.ac.uk>).

(b) 1798 memorial. The plaque by the memorial in the commemorative garden was unveiled by Gerry Adams on 19 November 1995.

Photograph by Guy Beiner, 2011.

Fig. 7.3. Betsy Gray bicentennial mural

Bill Gatt's painting of Betsy Gray and the Battle of Ballynahinch was arguably the most striking of a series of murals put up in Ballynahinch for the 1798 bicentenary. Exposed to the elements, it was soon worn out and removed.

Postcard of mural, courtesy of Horace Reid (1998).

In the same spirit of regeneration, Down District Councillors Harvey Bicker of the Ulster Unionist Party (UUP), who ten years later would surprise his colleagues by joining the republican Fianna Fáil party, and Anne McAleenan of the nationalist SDLP jointly organized the competition 'A Ballad for Ballynahinch', which invited compositions of new songs relating to the local heritage of 1798.[114] Such artificial attempts to revive tradition had limited impact. During the bicentenary, traditional ballads of Ninety-Eight were often sung at commemorative events and were recorded by performing artists. Most notably, the Dublin balladeer Frank Harte and the traditional musician Donal Lunny issued the album *1798—The First Year of Liberty*, which included the popular Ulster ballads 'Henry Joy', 'General Munro', and 'Henry Joy McCracken'. The album also featured a performance of the lesser-known song about Roddy McCorley, which was collected by Francis Joseph Bigger, as well as the unfamiliar song 'Bold Belfast Shoemaker', about a northerner who 'enlisted in the train' and joined the rebellion in the South. The CD came with a 32-page booklet, with background historical information on the rebellion and details on the recorded songs, which promised to reveal 'what orthodox histories do not tell us; what those who suffered made of the events of 1798'. Harte earnestly advocated that 'these songs are the unwritten history' and should not be forgotten.[115] Yet, unlike the centenary flourish of songwriting, no new memorable songs were composed for the bicentenary.

---

[114] Collins, *Who Fears to Speak*, p. 109. For Bicker's subsequent defection to Fianna Fáil see *Irish News*, 23 February 2008, p. 1; *BNL*, 24 February 2008; *Irish Times*, 25 February 2008, p. 7.

[115] Frank Harte and Donal Lunny, *1798—The First Year of Liberty* (Hummingbird, 1998); *Irish Times*, 24 July and 15 August 1998, pp. 12 and 34 (respectively); see also obituaries of Frank Harte in *Independent*, 1 July 2005, p. 46; *Irish Times*, 2 July 2005, p. 12.

Although the bicentenary did not match the prolific literary flourish of the centenary, several northern poets and dramatists were inspired to write about 1798. The poet Medbh McGuckian admitted that her prior knowledge of the United Irishmen was lacking, as this was a subject that 'the school curriculum has avoided like the plague.' For McGuckian, who came from a Catholic area in north Belfast, 'learning the truth about the Rebellion was like a jigsaw puzzle falling into place.'[116] She was encouraged by Jane Leonard, the Outreach Officer at the Ulster Museum, to 'read up on the 1798 Rebellion with a view to writing a poem' and was influenced by the recent writings of historians, in particular Kevin Whelan. The result of her personal journey of discovery—which she described as her 'own enlightenment after a medieval ignorance'—was the publication in 1998 of the collection of poems *Shelmalier*. The title poem is named after a barony in county Wexford that is associated with rebels, a connection that became widely known through the popular ballad 'Kelly the Boy from Killane' (originally titled 'Kelly of Killane'), which was written for the 1798 centenary by P. J. McCall and was first published in 1911. This choice of title unwittingly echoed the common preference among northern Catholics to remember the rebellion in Leinster, rather than that of the Presbyterians in Ulster.[117]

McGuckian's *Shelmalier* collection opens with a quotation from James Hope:

> Physical force may prevail for a time . . . but there is music in the sound of moral force which will be heard like the sound of the cuckoo. The bird lays its eggs, and leaves them for a time; but it will come again and hatch them in due course, and the song will return with the season.[118]

These lofty sentiments, which in 1998 seemed to chime with the renunciation of paramilitary violence, were repeated by Bertie Ahern in a speech at the unveiling of memorial gardens on the Croppies Acre, a mass grave of United Irishmen executed in Dublin. The Taoiseach's speech, evidently drafted by Whelan, called for 'a process of commemoration and a retrieving of memories which have been deliberately suppressed'. It specifically referred to the Ulster Presbyterians, who 'were airbrushed out of the picture', and declared that 1798 is 'an event in the history of Presbyterians as much as in the history of the Catholics'.[119] Apart from quoting Hope in the epigraph, the United Irishmen are not mentioned explicitly in the poems of *Shelmalier* and, as noted by critics, the historical reference to the rebellion remains obscure throughout the volume. Despite being influenced by the bicentennial rhetoric of no longer fearing to speak of Ninety-Eight, McGuckian's poetry is beset with reticence.[120]

---

[116] Morris Sawnie, 'Under the North Window: An Interview with Medbh McGuckian', *The Kenyon Review*, 23, nos. 3/4 (2001): pp. 64–74.

[117] Medbh McGuckian, *Shelmalier* (Loughcrew, Co. Meath: Gallery Press, 1998). For the ballad see P. J. McCall, *Irish Fireside Songs* (Dublin: M. H. Gill and Son, 1911), pp. 39–40; Gaul, *Glory O!*, pp. 138–9. McCall also mentioned 'meadows of Shelmalier', in his '98 ballad 'Boolavogue' (originally titled 'Fr Murphy of the County Wexford'), which was first published in *Irish Weekly Independent*, 18 June 1898.

[118] Originally appeared in Madden, *The United Irishmen*, 3rd ser., vol. 1 (1846), p. 233.

[119] 'Unveiling at Memorial Garden at the Croppies Acre in Collins Barracks' (22 November 1998), Archived Speeches and Press Releases, Department of the Taoiseach; <www.taoiseach.gov.ie/eng/News/Archives/1998/Taoiseach's_Speeches_Archive_1998/Unveiling_at_Memorial_Garden_at_the_Croppies_Acre_in_Collins_Barracks.html>.

[120] For criticism of the vagueness regarding the connection to 1798 see the review by William Pratt in *World Literature Today*, 73, no. 4 (1999): pp. 744–5; see also also Eric Falci, *Continuity and Change in Irish Poetry, 1966–2010* (Cambridge: Cambridge University Press, 2012), pp. 96–100.

Ciaran Carson, who was raised in an Irish-speaking Belfast Catholic family and for over twenty years had been the Traditional Arts Officer of the Arts Council of Northern Ireland, before moving on to take up an academic post at Queen's University Belfast, addressed the memory of Ninety-Eight more expansively. During the bicentenary, Carson published a collection of seventy-seven sonnets, written in alexandrines, titled *The Twelfth of Never* (a playful reworking of the title of a popular love song famously recorded by Johnny Mathis, with cover versions by Cliff Richard and Donny Osmond). Carson drew on Irish ballad traditions to present what has been described as a 'dizzying bricolage of history, memory, and fantasy'. Among the many subtle allusions to various historical events, 1798—juxtaposed with 1998—stands out as the most significant date.[121]

The poem 'Rising of the Moon' takes its title from a famous '98 ballad, composed in the mid-nineteenth century by John Keegan Casey ('Leo'). With a whimsical nod to the time-old *aisling* genre of Gaelic poetry, Carson's poem recalls a meeting with 'an old colleen', who urges the poet 'to go out and revolutionize Hibernia' and leaves him among the 'People of No Property' (who turn out to be smokers of 'pipes of fragrant weed'). He returns to meet his mysterious lover in another poem titled '1798', in which he muses on the passage of time:

> Two centuries have gone, yet she and I abide
> Like emblems of a rebel song no longer sung.

In 'The Londonderry Air' (originally the title of a traditional tune to which the popular song 'Danny Boy' was set), a lover recalls her 'noble pikeman', who went out to war and did not return. The memory of the dead rebel is recalled:

> Like some strange seedling of the plant of Liberty,
> That breeds eternally beneath the Northern Star.

The poem '1795' retells the gist of Florence Mary Wilson's popular recitation about Thomas Russell, 'The Man from God Knows Where', and concludes with the scene of his execution at Downpatrick Jail. In 'The Year of the French' (a nickname for 1798 prevalent in the vernacular history of Connacht), the poet and his friends lie down outdoors, 'drugged with honied cakes of opium', and gaze at the stars, hallucinating about 'galactic battalions of those fallen in war'.[122] In Carson's distinctly playful style, as characterized by Matthew Campbell, the historical references are 'by turns oblique, metaphoric, allegorical and opaque'.[123] The memory of Ninety-Eight is present throughout the volume but always in an allusive form.

In 1998, Derek Mahon composed the poem 'Northern Star' (originally titled 'Starlight') in memory of the playwright Stewart Parker. It has been described as 'an acerbic lyric distillation' of Parker's historical play *Northern Star*, compounded with 'a bicentenary tribute to 1798'. The poem ends on a note of forgetting—'till all fade

---

[121] Neal Alexander, *Ciaran Carson: Space, Place, Writing* (Liverpool: Liverpool University Press, 2010), pp. 134–5.

[122] Ciaran Carson, *The Twelfth of Never* (London: Picador in association with The Gallery Press, 1999; orig. edn 1998), pp. 19, 39, 60, 71, and 82.

[123] Matthew Campbell, 'Ireland in Poetry, 1999, 1949, 1969', in *The Cambridge Companion to Contemporary Irish Poetry*, edited by Matthew Campbell (Cambridge and New York: Cambridge University Press, 2003), p. 18.

Forgetful Remembrance

oblivionwards', which corresponds to the silencing in the concluding scene of Parker's play, in which the dying speech of Henry Joy McCracken is interrupted by the pounding of a lambeg drum, 'drowning out any further words'.[124] Parker's *Northern Star* was revived for the bicentenary by the actor Stephen Rea. In 1980, Rea had been one of the founders of the Field Day Theatre Company, which endeavoured to create a new Irish cultural space—a 'fifth province'—that would transcend the binary oppositions of sectarian politics. Rea, who (like Mahon) came from a Belfast working class Protestant background, maintained that 'there is an amnesia amongst Protestants in this town about their part in the creation and preservation of so much of the culture of modern Ireland' and felt that, with the bicentenary of 1798, 'it could be that the context for *Northern Star* has finally come.' In retrospect, he realized that he 'was trying to get Belfast people to understand what 1798 was about, especially given the stifled and amnesiac memory of that pivotal experience in the life of the city'.[125]

Co-produced for the 35th Belfast Festival at Queens by Field Day and the Tinderbox theatre company (which was founded in 1988 to create 'challenging theatre not ordinarily seen in Belfast'), *Northern Star* was performed between 14 November and 5 December 1998 in the symbolically resonant settings of the First Presbyterian Church on Rosemary Street, a notably liberal non-subscribing Presbyterian congregation to which the McCracken family had belonged. Praising the 'riveting production' of the 'spine-tingling 1798 play', the *Irish Times* theatre critic Helen Meany sensed a bicentennial 'celebratory tone', which was manifested in 'reclamation of memory from sectarianism's selective amnesia and restoration of the place of Ulster Presbyterianism in the history of the United Irishmen's egalitarian ideals'.[126]

More generally, the bicentenary brought Ninety-Eight back on to Ulster stages, starting with plays that were nationalist in tone and moving on to less conventional productions. The programme of the Belfast Festival at Queen's in November 1997 included performances at St Kevin's Hall of the Dock Ward Community Theatre's play *Rebellion: The Henry Joy McCracken Story*, described by the theatre critic of the *Belfast News-Letter* as a 'curious and sometimes heartfelt mix of West End Musical, village pageant, socialist polemic, tableaux vivants and yearnings for liberty, fraternity and equality'. The playwright originally commissioned to write the drama, Ken Bourke, had opted to resign mid-way through a draft script following the declaration of a ceasefire by the Provisional IRA in July 1997, when he 'came to the decision that a play about a United Irishman, presented by a group from a republican area, would be more likely to get in the way of peace than to help it'. The play, as directed by Paddy McCoey, had an unmistakable nationalist hue and according to the *Irish Examiner* could just as well have been 'about the Belfast of our era'. A reviewer for the *Irish Times*

---

[124] Derek Mahon, *Collected Poems* (Oldcastle: Gallery Press, 1999); Hugh Haughton, *The Poetry of Derek Mahon* (Oxford: Oxford University Press, 2007), pp. 324–7.

[125] *Irish Times*, 7 November 1998, p. C1; Gibbons Luke and Whelan Kevin, 'In Conversation with Stephen Rea', *Yale Journal of Criticism*, 15, no. 1 (Spring 2002), pp. 11–12.

[126] *Northern Star by Stewart Parker* (Belfast: Belfast Festival at Queen's University Belfast, 1998); *BNL*, 16 November 1998, p. 14; *Guardian*, 18 November 1998, p. 12; *Irish Independent*, 20 November 1998, p. 10; *Irish Times*, 16 and 17 November 1998, pp. 19 and 14 (respectively). See also Ophelia Byrne, *State of Play: The Theatre and Cultural Identity in 20th Century Ulster* (Belfast: Linen Hall Library, 2001), pp. 130–3; Tom Maguire, *Making Theatre in Northern Ireland: Through and Beyond the Troubles* (Exeter: University of Exeter Press, 2006), pp. 63–6.

sardonically remarked that 'for all the palaver about McCracken being a symbol of inclusion . . . this was one deepgreen production.'[127]

More than half a century after its original performance in 1945, Belfast's Centre Stage Theatre put up 'a full-scale, meticulously costumed and generously staged production' of Jack Loudan's *Henry Joy McCracken*, which was performed in Belfast from 10 to 21 March 1998 and also toured provincial venues. What was considered by the *Belfast News-Letter* an 'unadventurous production' of Loudan's simplistic portrayal of the court martial of the United Irish hero seemed to suit the tastes of nationalist audiences, who found in it 'all the ingredients of British policy today: corrupt trials, executions, touts and collaborators'. The republican newspaper *An Phoblacht* was pleased 'to see the 1798 rebellion being commemorated in Belfast where to a greater extent the leadership and role of the Presbyterians in the struggle for Irish independence has been written out of so many histories'.[128]

The bicentenary was also studded with performances of small commemorative theatrical productions. John Gray, chairman of the UICS, adapted for a public reading Rev. James Porter's satirical collection of letters *Billy Bluff and Squire Firebrand*, a text that had long remained popular locally and which Gray believed could offer inspiration for both 'Christian and agnostic alike'. A performance by the Osborne Players in the Apprentice Boys' Memorial Hall in Derry was attended by a mixed audience of nationalists and loyalists, who greeted the play with 'guffaws and hoots of recognition'.[129] Local historian Philip Orr co-wrote with Bill Irvine, his former pupil from Downpatrick, *The Last Journey of Thomas Russell*, a one-man show on the death of Thomas Russell. It was staged in August 1998 at the Down County Museum, located in the building of the jailhouse in which Russell was executed, with the audience following the actor through the historical surroundings, and was considered 'a particular highlight' among the many local commemorative events.[130] The play (renamed *The Final Words of Thomas Russell*) was restaged for the bicentenary of Russell's execution in 2003 and was subsequently revived for the West Belfast Festival in 2005.

The Belfast-based Shibboleth Theatre Company went on tour with *The Turnout*, an irreverent reclamation of women's history that recalled Mary Anne McCracken, Betsy Gray, and the loyalist Peggy Gordon (remembered in local tradition as 'a huge masculine beggar-woman' who had single-handedly prevented rebels in Antrim town from capturing canons).[131] Ulster musicians Jane Cassidy and Maurice Leyden revived for the bicentenary a musical show of traditional and original songs on Mary Ann

[127] *BNL*, 21 November 1997, p. 16; *Irish Examiner*, 10 December 1997, p. 25; *Irish Times*, 26 November 1997, p. 12. See also Ken Bourke, 'The Play I didn't Write about Henry Joy McCracken (1997)'; <http://kenbourkeplays.blogspot.co.il/2011/11/play-i-didnt-write-about-henry-joy.html>.

[128] *Donegal News*, 6 February 1998, p. 27; *BNL*, 4 February, 6 and March 1998, pp. 10, 19, and 12 (respectively); *An Phoblacht*, 12 March 1998; *Strabane Chronicle*, 19 March 1998, p. 21.

[129] Walter Forde, ed., *From Heritage to Hope: Christian Perspectives on the 1798 Bicentenary* (Wexford: Byrne/Perry Summer School, 1998), preface. For the performance in Derry, as recalled by Eamonn McCann see *Hot Press*, 29 April 1998; Gayle Backus, '"Not Quite Philadelphia, Is It?": An Interview with Eamonn McCann', *Eire-Ireland*, 36, nos. 3 & 4 (Fall–Winter 2001), pp. 180–1.

[130] Interview with Philip Orr, Culturlánn (Belfast, 9 May 2013); see also Brian S. Turner, ed., *Down Survey 1998* (Downpatrick: Down County Museum, 1998), p. 47; *When Down Was Up: Down County Museum Remembering the 1798 Rising* (Downpatrick: Down County Museum, 1998).

[131] *Irish Times*, 10 October 1998, p. 2; *Sunday Times*, 11 October 1998. Shibboleth's *The Turnout* was staged in Northern Ireland in Antrim (16 May), Newtownabbey (1 June), Ballymoney (3 June),

McCracken (originally put together in 1987 and recorded on CD in 1995). It was performed at various local commemorative evenings, including a show at the 11th International John Hewitt Summer School in Carnlough, county Antrim, in August 1998. On that occasion, the script of Hewitt's neglected and unperformed play on the United Irishmen was read in public for the first time.[132]

The Yarnspinners—Antrim storytellers Liz Weir and Billy Teare, together with musicians Willie Drennan and Bob Spears—put together a folkish show that recounted in Ulster-Scots dialect the experiences of Presbyterians in 1798. It narrated the adventures of a fictional character, William Young, who gets caught up in the rebellion and in subsequent banditry. First performed in April 1998 at Belfast's Old Museum Arts Centre, additional gigs followed throughout the year at various venues. This was a first flush of a rediscovery of interest in the Ulster-Scots heritage of 1798, which was part of a wider Ullans (Ulster-Scots) revival stimulated by the peace process.[133]

The most original drama written for the bicentenary was Gary Mitchell's 'historical thriller' *The Tearing of the Loom*, which was performed at Belfast's Lyric theatre from 17 March to 4 April 1998. Mitchell, who has been described as 'the voice of working-class loyalism', came from the north Belfast Protestant neighbourhood of Rathcoole and was lauded by the *Belfast News-Letter* as 'the hottest penman in town'. Mitchell had not been taught about the United Irishmen at school yet immersed himself in the history of 1798 when he was commissioned to write the script for a bicentennial television drama about Wolfe Tone, titled *The Officer from France* (screened on RTÉ1 on 19 November 1998). Consequently, he 'began looking at 1998 from a 1798 perspective' and decided to address the memory of the rebellion in Ulster through a 'charged-up period piece about the early and lasting fragmentation of Protestantism in Northern Ireland', which, like the rest of Mitchell's oeuvre, offered a socio-political allegory on the present-day crisis of loyalism.[134]

Set in 1798 in Tandragee, county Armagh (near the border with county Down), *The Tearing of the Loom* opens with a horrific murder scene in which a fanatical grand master of the local Orange Lodge, Samuel Hamill, makes his son William garrotte a Catholic woman they had found praying beside the corpse of her slain husband. The rest of the action takes place in the interior of a cottage, where the master weaver Robert Moore tries to keep his family safe from the surrounding troubles but is obliged to confront his son David, who joins the Orangemen, and his daughter Ruth, who supports the United Irishmen. In this dark historical drama, all the protagonists are Presbyterians and 1798 is shown to be a vicious civil war, from which even those living in the rural periphery are not spared. By the end of the play, the young David Moore is mortally wounded and dies in disillusion, having participated in a sectarian massacre,

---

Sheskburn—near Ballycastle (5 June) and Downpatrick (13 June). For Peg Gordon see Young, *Ulster in '98*, p. 69.

[132] *BNL*, 3 August 1998, p. 14. For the original production of Cassidy and Leyden's 'Mary Ann McCracken' see <www.rte.ie/archives/2017/0714/890199-mary-ann-mccracken-celebrated/>. For Hewitt's play see Chapter 6 above, pp. 519–20.

[133] *BNL*, 24 April 1998, p. 17. For the Ulster-Scots revival see below, pp. 588–93.

[134] *BNL*, 6 and 12 March 1998, pp. 19 and 12 (respectively); *Belfast Telegraph*, 17 November 1998; *Irish Times*, 25 February and 14 November 1998, pp. 14 and 42 (respectively); Wallace McDowell, 'Staging the Debate: Loyalist-Britishness and Masculinities in the Plays of Gary Mitchell', *Studies in Ethnicity & Nationalism*, 9, no. 1 (2009), p. 93.

his sister Ruth commits suicide while tortured by Orangemen, and her lover Harry, an idealistic United Irishman, is dishonourably shot dead. The merciless perpetration of these heinous crimes resembles the blood-curdling murders of a sadistic loyalist gang known as the Shankill Butchers, which terrorized Catholic neighbourhoods in Belfast in the mid-1970s. Moreover, the two children die in full view of their grandmother, Anne, while the head of the household, Robert Moore, is left helplessly tied to his broken loom, the source of his livelihood and former pride, and cannot intervene to save his loved ones.[135]

Realizing that the play engages with issues that were pertinent for many Protestants in the wake of the Troubles, Steven King, political advisor to the UUP, warned that 'real unionists must keep loom fabric from tearing'. Critics, while recognizing that it was an 'extremely brave work', generally found that the playwright and the Lyric theatre were not quite equipped to deal with such sensitive historical materials.[136] Mitchell was toasted in Dublin, where he won an Irish Times/ESB Irish Theatre Award for an earlier play, but was branded a traitor by loyalists at home, who accused him of 'selling out'. A few years later, in 2005, Mitchell and his family were forced out of their home in Rathcoole and had to go into hiding, after loyalist paramilitaries petrol-bombed their house and blew up their car. These extreme acts of silencing prevented the playwright from writing for several years.[137] By focusing on violence perpetuated in 1798 by the Orange Order, *The Tearing of the Loom* called attention to troubling memories that had previously been avoided.

COUNTERING DISREMEMBERING

The most noticeable change of the bicentenary, in comparison to previous commemorations of 1798, was a willingness from within Orangeism to engage with the ambiguous legacy of the past. Despite a long history of disremembering Ninety-Eight in public, on an individual level at least some members of the Orange Order had retained a secret interest in the United Irishmen. Writing in 1960, the historian Charles Dickson shared his 'personal knowledge', as an Ulster Presbyterian, that 'there is many an Orangeman in the counties of Antrim and Down today whose proudest boast it is (in private) that his ancestor had a pike in his thatch in '98.'[138] In the run-up to the bicentenary, it seemed to the historian Richard Roche, chairman of the Dublin '98 Committee, 'opportune, albeit tendentious, to ask if there are many, or any Orangemen in those countries today who would be willing to admit (even in private)

---

[135] Gary Mitchell, *Tearing the Loom; and, in a Little World of Our Own* (London: Nick Hern Books, 1998), pp. 63–124. See also Urban, *Community Politics and the Peace Process*, pp. 106–29; Markus, *Echoes of the Rebellion*, pp. 115–20. For the Shankill Butchers see Martin Dillon, *The Shankill Butchers: The Real Story of Cold-Blooded Mass Murder* (New York: Routledge, 1999; orig. edn 1989).

[136] *BNL*, 19 March and 22 June 1998, pp. 12 and 14 (respectively); *Belfast Telegraph*, 2 April 1998 (Steven King); *Guardian*, 31 March 1998, p. 11; *Irish Times*, 18 March 1998, p. 13; *Times*, 24 March 1998.

[137] *BNL*, 10 February 1998, p. 7; *Belfast Telegraph*, 26 November 2005 and 12 May 2014; *Guardian*, 21 December 2005, p. 5; *Irish Times*, 1 December 2005, p. 11; *Irish News*, 10 January 2006, p. 8; *Observer*, 29 January 2006, p. 7.

[138] Dickson, *Revolt in the North*, p. 244.

that their ancestors were "out" in 1798'. Surprisingly, it turned out that 'in the north-east, many an Orangeman proudly boasts that his ancestors were "out in '98".'[139] Whereas in 1898 Orangemen fervently engaged in decommemorating, in 1998 at least some brethren of the Orange Order were keen in participating in commemoration and apparently did not fear any longer to speak of Ninety-Eight.

The mover and shaker behind this spirit of memorial rapprochement was Rev. Brian Kennaway, a Presbyterian minister and Convenor of the Education Committee of the Grand Orange Lodge of Ireland (GOLI). While accepting that 'the Orange Institution has always been a very conservative body' and that 'saying no comes naturally to Ulster Protestants', Kennaway and the self-described 'progressive and visionary' members of the Education Committee advocated from the early 1990s that 'something imaginative ought to be done to commemorate the bicentenary of the United Irishman's Rebellion of 1798.'[140] Their first initiative was to re-publish Orange historical narratives of the rebellion 'in order that the real story should be told'.[141] The *Orange Standard* reasoned that 'the Rebellion of 1798 has been a fertile source of story and song, fact, fiction and fantasy' and that it now 'needs to get the rational, logical and lucid examination it deserves free from the sentimental and emotional additions and amplifications of fiction of the rebellion'.[142] While denouncing nationalist mythologizing of Ninety-Eight, Orange history buffs were reluctant to contemplate that loyalists had also cultivated their own myths and did not undertake a critical revision of Orange historiography. It was subsequently pointed out that 'no substantial new Orange or Loyalist interpretation of 1798 seems to have appeared for the revolt's bicentennial.'[143]

In 1996, the GOLI Education Committee published *Murder without Sin*, extracts from a history of Orangeism by Robert Ogle Gowan, a Wexford Orangeman who emigrated to Canada in 1829. The selections from this text, originally published in Toronto in 1857, were introduced by the editor, schoolteacher Richard Whitten, as 'an unashamedly Orange account of the period 1791 to 1798 and as such should help the reader to become aware of the loyalist view of the rebellion in contrast to the many republican histories of 1798.' The booklet was severely criticized by historians involved in the commemorations for perpetuating a questionable loyalist myth that claimed that the initials M.W.S., which had been spotted on a rebel flag during the sectarian atrocity on Wexford Bridge, stood for 'Murder Without Sin, signifying that it was no sin to kill a Protestant'.[144] It seemed as if the ultra-loyalist historical interpretation of the rebellion, which stemmed from the influential writings of Richard Musgrave, was making a comeback.[145]

---

[139] *Irish Times*, 12 April 1997, p. 9 (weekend supplement) and 9 December 1997, p. 16.

[140] Brian Kennaway, 'Who Fears to Speak of '98: The Orange Contribution to the 1798 Commemorations', *Ulster History Foundation* (May 2000); reproduced in Collins, *Who Fears to Speak*, pp. 166–9. See also Brian Kennaway, *The Orange Order: A Tradition Betrayed* (London: Methuen, 2006), pp. 12–13.

[141] *Sunday Times*, 22 February 1998.   [142] *Orange Standard*, April 1998.

[143] Howe, *Ireland and Empire*, pp. 104–5.

[144] J. R. Whitten, ed., *Murder without Sin: The Rebellion of 1798 by Ogle Robert Gowan* (Belfast: Education Committee of the Grand Orange Lodge of Ireland, 1996); cf. Ogle Robert Gowan, *Orangeism: Its Origin and History* (Toronto: printed by Lovell and Gibson, 1859). For criticism of the reprint see *Irish Times*, 28 January 1997, p. 15 and 24 March 1998, p. 13.

[145] The interpretation of M.W.S. as 'Murder Without Sin' first appeared in a contemporary loyalist account written by George Taylor and was later propagated in the popular history by William H. Maxwell.

The following year, the Education Committee published *Sunshine Patriots*, extracts from R. M. Sibbett's *Orangeism in Ireland and Throughout the Empire* (originally published in 1914 and re-issued in 1939). Sibbett's more ambivalent narrative, which shows discernible sympathy towards the Presbyterian rebels, was presented by Kennaway as 'a balanced account of the events in the Counties of Antrim and Down, which led to the Battles of Antrim and Ballynahinch'.[146] There was a notably high demand for both these booklets, which were distributed by the county Antrim and county Down Grand Orange Lodges. 3,000 copies were sold of Ogle's text and another 5,000 of Sibbett's *Sunshine Patriots*, which was listed as recommended reading by the Department of Education for Northern Ireland.[147] Although the bicentennial Orange publications essentially reinforced loyalist prejudices, unionist readers were also encouraged to consider other ways of looking at the rebellion by reading additional literature on the subject, such as Lyttle's *Betsy Gray* and Stewart's *Summer Soldiers*.

In March 1997, Kennaway had a meeting in Leinster House (the parliamentary buildings in Dublin) with the Irish Minister of State for Finance Avril Doyle, who at the time was chairperson of the Government 1798 Commemoration Committee, in order to explore possibilities for the involvement of the Orange Order in the bicentennial commemorations. While stressing that 'the Orange Order was against the rebels', he acknowledged that 'the strands go back to both sides' and that 'it is said that the children of the men of 1798 became the leaders of the Orange Order in the next generation.'[148] Kennaway later explained that 'we are commemorating 1798 because of the elements of shared history, social justice and "disaffection".' Adopting the rhetoric of the peace process, he demanded a '"parity of esteem" in remembering all those who were involved', even including the lesser-known experiences of 'loyal Catholics' serving in the militia, who had participated in suppressing the rebellion.[149]

On the eve of the bicentennial, in December 1997, the Orange Order announced its intentions to stage re-enactments of the Battles of Antrim and Ballynahinch.[150] As preparations went ahead, brethren in county Down meanwhile organized in March 1998 a local exhibition at the Comber Orange Hall (5 km south-west of Newtownards) on the involvement of the district's Orange lodges in 1798.[151] The re-enactment of the Battle of Antrim on 6 June 1998, described as a 're-run of the Turn-Out', proved to be a

---

It was contested in the narrative of the rebel leader Joseph Holt, edited by the antiquarian Thomas Croker, who claimed 'from the best authority' that the initials stood for 'Marksman, Wexford, Shelmalier'; see Maxwell, *History of the Irish Rebellion*, pp. 153–4; Thomas Crofton Croker, ed., *Memoirs of Joseph Holt, General of the Irish Rebels, in 1798*, vol. 1 (London: Henry Colburn, 1838), pp. 89–90.

[146] R. M. Sibbett, *The Sunshine Patriots: The 1798 Rebellion in Antrim and Down* (Belfast: GOLI Publications, 1997); cf. anon. [R. M. Sibbett], *Orangeism in Ireland and Throughout the Empire*, 2nd edn (London: Thynne, 1939). For Sibbett's interpretation of 1798 see above Chapter 5, pp. 428–9 and Chapter 6, p. 458.

[147] Kennaway, *The Orange Order*, p. 195.

[148] *BNL*, 6 March 1997, p. 2; *Irish Times*, 4 and 6 March 1997, pp. 1 and 8 (respectively); *Sunday Times*, 2 March 1997.

[149] *Irish Times*, 5 December 1997, p. 8 and 3 March 1998, p. 12.

[150] *Belfast Telegraph*, 5 December 1997; *Irish Times*, 5 December 1997, p. 8.

[151] *Comber District Orange Lodge Exhibition of the Orange Institution Comber District Lodges 1798 Rebellion in Comber Orange Hall, Railway Street, Comber, 2–6 March 1998* (Comber District Orange Lodge, 1998).

popular event, which was massively attended. Lively commentary was provided by the local historian David Hall, a schoolteacher and member of the GOLI Education Committee. Hall had just published *A Battle Lost and Won*, a study of the Battle of Antrim, in which he maintained that its two-hundredth anniversary 'deserves the support of all of the people in our area'. He advocated that 'we should not "fear to speak of '98" but ensure that the courage, commitment and actions of all those who were involved in the bloody events of 1798 be remembered and respected, regardless of religious or political outlook.'[152]

Unlike England, where the Sealed Knot association began to re-enact the English Civil War in 1968, or the United States, where re-enactments of the American Civil War (first staged at the 1913 Gettysburg reunion) became popular in the centennial commemorations of the 1960s, Ireland had not previously developed a strong tradition of re-enacting living history. For the bicentenary commemorations in 1998, thousands of dedicated pikemen mobilized in county Wexford and its environs. These enthusiasts staged the battle reconstructions for the bicentennial TV documentaries and their presence in parades and re-enactments was noticeable at commemorative events throughout the country. Although the Government 1798 Commemoration Committee had intimated that the carrying of pikes, which was seen by officials as a display of militarism, should be discouraged, the popularity of this phenomenon turned out to be irrepressible. The Wexford pikemen were officially supposed to be apolitical, yet some of their leading figures, such as Bill Murray of the Carrigbyrne Pike Group—who presented a commemorative pike to Gerry Adams—openly supported Sinn Féin. The reluctance of pikemen to disband at the end of the bicentenary seemed to echo current deliberations on decommission of paramilitaries, which were seen as a stumbling block for the peace process.[153] Re-enactment of 1798 in Northern Ireland, however, assumed a different character on account of the involvement of unionists.

The Australian historian Stephen Gapps has described historical re-enactors as 'mobile monuments'. In his experience, the bicentennial re-enactment in 2004 of the defeat of the rebellious United Irish convicts at the Battle of Vinegar Hill in Sydney was a case of 'forgotten history finally staged as part of the national story'. Gapps maintained that such events 'open up avenues for more inclusive and historically accurate performances that allow less didactic and more open-ended forms of commemorative ritual'.[154] Somewhat surprisingly, the re-enactment of the Battle of Antrim was organized by the Ulster Heritage Museum Committee, which had close links to the Orange Order. At this event, Orangemen participated as re-enactors on both sides of the battle, playing the roles of yeomen and dragoons, as well as rebels. This was a way of publicly acknowledging an ambiguous lineage, which had previously not been spoken about.

---

[152] David Hall, *A Battle Lost and Won: The Battle of Antrim, 1798* (Antrim: self-published, 1998), p. 87; Collins, *Who Fears to Speak*, pp. 163–6.

[153] *Irish Times*, 22 and 23 June 1998, pp. 9 and 14 (respectively); *An Phoblacht*, 27 August 1998; *Wexford Echo*, 7 January 1999 and 7 August 2008. See also the documentary *Pike People* (dir. Angela Ryan; RTÉ, 2000); reviewed in *Irish Times*, 11 March 2000, p. 44.

[154] Stephen Gapps, 'On Being a Mobile Monument: Historical Reenactments and Commemorations', in *Historical Reenactment: From Realism to the Affective Turn*, edited by Iain McCalman and Paul A. Pickering (Basingstoke: Palgrave Macmillan, 2010), pp. 50–62; see also Stephen Gapps, 'Mobile Monuments: A View of Historical Reenactment and Authenticity from inside the Costume Cupboard of History', *Rethinking History*, 13, no. 3 (2009): pp. 395–409.

One such event seemed to suffice and instead of also re-enacting the Battle of Ballynahinch, as originally intended, the Orange Order crowned its bicentennial programme on 12 June 1998 with a commemorative dinner in the parliament buildings at Stormont, attended by dignitaries, including the Lord Mayors of Belfast and Dublin, as well as the heads of Irish universities, distinguished academics and leading journalists from all over the island. At an after-dinner lecture on 'The Lessons of '98', Brian Walker, Director of the Institute of Irish Studies at Queen's University Belfast, pointed out that 'the terrible violence of the rebellion tended to be forgotten', despite the enormous death toll that exceeded by almost tenfold the fatalities of the thirty years of the Troubles. Finding relevance to current issues in the peace process, Walker concluded that 'societies which fail to cope with problems of human rights and justice leave themselves open to violent challenge.'[155] While the event was widely praised, objections were raised by Joel Patton, leader of the militant Orange faction known as the 'Spirit of Drumcree'. This was an indication of growing opposition from hardliners within unionism to reconciliatory measures.[156]

By July 1998, the 3-year-old crisis at the Drumcree Church in Portadown, county Armagh, at which loyalists truculently resisted the re-routing of Orange marches away from the Catholic nationalist neighbourhood on the Garvaghy Road, had come to be seen as the 'Orange Order's last stand'.[157] Apart from a few individuals, such as the UUP MP Roy Beggs, who found parallels between the acts of opposition at Drumcree and 'the men from Donegore' who had rebelled in 1798, hard-line loyalists mostly disassociated themselves from the memory of the United Irishmen, which for them reeked of republicanism.[158] Escalating sectarian tensions played against the initiatives for cross-community cooperation that had been promoted by the peace process. Trenchant loyalists denounced participation in cross-border and ecumenical commemorations as a form of kowtowing to the politics of contemporary republicanism. Sensing that their work was being undermined and delegitimized by extremists, Kennaway and other key members of the GOLI Education Committee resigned, leading to the disbanding of the committee and the withdrawal of Orange readiness to engage in commemoration of 1798.[159]

Tony Stewart wryly observed that 'some Orangemen believed that what they were commemorating was the putting down of the Rebellion.' Despite the extent of the commemorations of 1798 in Ulster, 'the fact that Presbyterians actually looked back on it with pride was confusing' and, as Stewart pointed out, there were still 'some in both

---

[155] The lecture was subsequently elaborated into an essay on 'The Lessons of Irish History: The Continuing Legacy of the 1798 Rebellion and the United Irishmen'; Brian Walker, *Past and Present: History, Identity and Politics in Ireland* (Belfast: Institute of Irish Studies of Queen's University Belfast, 2000), pp. 29–77.

[156] *Irish Independent*, 1 June 1998, p. 7; *Irish Times*, 13 June 1998, p. 7; Kennaway, *The Orange Order*, pp. 201–3; see also Hiram Morgan, 'Interview: The Life of Brian', *History Ireland*, 8, no. 2 (2000), p. 46.

[157] See Dominic Bryan, 'Drumcree and "The Right to March": Orangeism, Ritual and Politics in Northern Ireland', in *The Irish Parading Tradition: Following the Drum*, edited by T. G. Fraser (Houndmills and New York: Macmillan Press and St Martin's Press, 2000), pp. 191–207; Chris Ryder and Vincent Kearney, *Drumcree: The Orange Order's Last Stand* (London: Methuen, 2001).

[158] For Beggs see Susan McKay, *Northern Protestants: An Unsettled People* (Belfast: Blackstaff Press, 2005; orig. edn 2000), pp. 102–3.

[159] Kennaway, *The Orange Order*, pp. 203–14.

communities in the North who, for different reasons, viewed the extent of Presbyterian involvement with some embarrassment'.[160] In advance of the bicentenary, the Heritage Lottery Fund rejected an application to support a plan for developing the site of the Battle of Ballynahinch on Windmill Hill into 'a focal point for the bicentenary commemorations', calling into question the historical significance of local 1798 heritage. An affronted SDLP representative on the Down District Council, Francis Casement, declared that 'every schoolboy in Ballynahinch knows that there are no such doubts'.[161] But the worthiness of memorializing Ninety-Eight became a moot point and the commemorative initiative was left unfulfilled.

Although the bicentennial commemorations were extolled as an unmitigated success, decommemorating was not entirely absent. Right from the beginning, even as the commemoration of William Orr in October 1997 seemed to peacefully usher in the bicentenary, conflict erupted in Rosslea, county Fermanagh. That month, loyalists protested against a monument to the 'Rosslea martyrs'—United Irishmen executed in Enniskillen on 12 October 1797 for having taken part in an arms raid six months earlier. The protestors were vexed by the overtly republican monument, which was also dedicated to local IRA volunteers who had died in various paramilitary actions in 1955, 1973, and 1988. A republican commemorative parade from Enniskillen to Rosslea lead by Sinn Féin politician Mitchel McLoughlin had to be re-routed on account of loyalist rioting. The following year, in October 1998, tensions were renewed in response to the unveiling of the monument.[162]

Unionists continued to harbour reservations about remembering Ninety-Eight. Even those willing to accept the commemorations were unwilling to tolerate explicit connections between the rebels of the late eighteenth century and the republican paramilitaries of the twentieth century. A monument to the Teeling family and their involvement in the United Irishmen, located between the Catholic nationalist neighbourhoods of Twinbrook and Poleglass in west Belfast, provoked loyalist ire. Erected by a group of volunteers, who named themselves 'the Teeling Group', it was unveiled in August 1998 by Joe Cahill, former chief of staff of the Provisional IRA, in conjunction with a nearby monument to the republican hunger striker Bobby Sands, which was unveiled by Gerry Adams. Repeatedly attacked and vandalized, the Teeling memorial was restored and re-dedicated in September 1999.[163] Decommemorating, and its correlative re-commemorating, were evidently making a return.

A Photographic Record of 1798 Memorials on the Island of Ireland and Beyond, compiled by the '98 enthusiasts Bill Murray and John Cullen of the Carrigbyrne Pike Group, reveals the remarkable extent of the bicentennial zeal for erecting

---

[160] Collins, *Who Fears to Speak*, p. 172.

[161] *Belfast Telegraph*, 4 September 1997; *BNL*, 23 December 1997, p. 11. Windmill Hill was subsequently acquired (alongside the historic Market House) by the Ballynahinch Regeneration Group with the intention of developing a commemorative park; *BNL*, 14 April 2000, p. 9 and 14 December 2000, p. 31.

[162] *Irish Times*, 13 October 1997, p. 11; *BNL*, 2 October 1998, p. 4; *An Phoblacht*, 8 October 1998; *Fermanagh Herald*, 25 February 1998, p. 6; *Irish Examiner*, 10 October 1997, p. 2; see also Collins, *Who Fears to Speak*, p. 81. For photographs of the monument taken in 2009 by Martin Melaugh see <http://cain.ulst.ac.uk/cgi-bin/AHRC/photos.pl?id=1413&mon=834>. For the events in 1797 see Denis Carolan Rushe, 'Rosslea and the United Irishmen', in *SVV*, 3, no. 4 (April 1898), pp. 71–2 and no. 5 (May 1898), pp. 82–3.

[163] *An Phoblacht*, 13 August 1998, 11 March and 7 October 1999.

monuments in memory of the United Irishmen, which, on an all-Ireland level, even surpassed the statuomania of the centenary. However, in Northern Ireland, the preferred form of memorialization was through plaques, rather than full-scale monuments, showing a general tendency for low-key commemoration.[164] The Antrim and District Historical Society put up a plaque on the Castle Wall to commemorate the Battle of Antrim. The clash at nearby Randalstown was mentioned on a plaque erected by Randalstown ARCHES—an association formed in 1995 and dedicated, as the acronym indicates, to 'Assisting Randalstown Community towards Harmony, Empowerment and Success'. Ballymena Borough Council similarly marked the Ballymena Town Hall, the site of the old Market House, which had seen fierce fighting between rebels and loyalists in 1798.[165]

Overall, memorialization of the rebellion in Ulster was patchy. The Down District 1798 Bicentenary Committee erected a plaque to commemorate the relatively minor Battle of Saintfield, but did not designate the site of the more substantial engagement in Ballynahinch.[166] Notably, a plaque was finally placed by the grave of the United Irish protomartyr William Orr in the old church graveyard in Templepatrick. In contrast, the supposed gravesite of Betsy Gray in Ballycreen near Ballynahinch, where a monument to the local heroine had been destroyed in 1898, remained barren.

The *Irish Times* complained in 1997 of the unavailability of accessible information on the 1798 landmarks in the North, stating the need for a 'small brochure', which would offer a 'map or guide' to the sites of memory.[167] This lacuna was more than adequately redressed with the publication of Bill Wilsdon's comprehensive guide to *The Sites of the 1798 Rising in Antrim and Down* and by the many local history publications that came out in the bicentennial year. In addition, places with connections to the United Irishmen were listed in the brochures for self-guided heritage walking tours, produced by local authorities and museums.[168] Consequently, Ninety-Eight became much more recognizable in the official cultural landscape. Nonetheless, most of the sites identified in vernacular historiography were not signposted and remained practically invisible to the unknowledgeable passer-by.

To a journalist reviewing the overwhelming volume of bicentennial programmes, it seemed that 'nobody fears to speak of '98'.[169] The impression that social forgetting had been expelled for good was, to an extent, an illusion. Commemoration demands constant maintenance and once commemorative fervour abated, the impermanence that marred the accomplishments of the bicentenary became apparent. Considering the 'life history of monuments' in general, Jay Winter concluded that 'public commemoration is both irresistible and unsustainable.' As the enthusiasm generated by commemoration inevitably fades over time, memorials are subject to a 'natural process of dissolution'.[170] Sometime after the bicentenary, the Down County Museum refreshed

---

[164] Murray and Cullen, *Epitaph of 1798*.   [165] Collins, *Who Fears to Speak*, pp. 100–1.

[166] For a photograph of the Saintfield plaque see <http://openplaques.org/organisations/down_district_1798_bicentenary_committee>.

[167] *Irish Times*, 8 May 1997, p. 15.

[168] See *Walk About Saintfield* (Downpatrick: Down County Museum, 1998), pp. 5–7; *Walk About Ballynahinch* (Downpatrick: Down County Museum, 1998), pp. 3–4, 6–7, and 10; *Historic Antrim and Randalstown Heritage Trail* (Antrim: Antrim Borough Council, 2000); *An Illustrated Guide to Ballymoney Old Church Graveyard* (Ballymoney: Ballymoney Borough Council, n.d.).

[169] *Irish Independent*, 11 April 1998, p. 6.   [170] Winter, 'Sites of Memory', p. 324.

its exhibitions spaces and removed a display of the killing of Betsy Gray, which had been designed in accordance with W. G. Lyttle's lurid description, complete with a gory severed hand. The mannequin used to represent the heroine was consequently demoted to the role of a female prisoner in an exhibition on the living conditions in the county Down gaol. 'Ulster's Joan of Arc' had once more disappeared from view.

The bicentennial murals in Ballynahinch were deceptively hailed as 'a lasting commemoration of the events in '98'.[171] However, murals in Northern Ireland, as shown by Jonathan McCormick and Neil Jarman, 'have a lifespan and a biography'. Among the different categories they proposed for understanding the demise of murals, the most basic is 'retirement', in consequence of decay. Such seemingly natural deterioration, which is largely determined by the quality of the materials used, has a cultural-political context since the neglect and unwillingness to undertake restoration is indicative of a decline of interest in the subject of the mural.[172] In all the bicentennial hype, it was little noticed that the scenes of Ninety-Eight displayed on the streets of Ballynahinch were not really murals, which by definition should be painted directly on walls, but were actually more fragile paintings on canvas that were affixed to walls. Exposed to the elements, the 'mural' of Betsy Gray was soon worn out and removed. The memory of the local heroine fell once more victim to decommemorating, even if the circumstances were less dramatic than the outburst of violence in the centenary.

The widely celebrated two-hundredth anniversary of the 1798 rebellion promised to put an end to a long history of social forgetting, but the burst of remembrance was not quite as pervasive as it seemed. The most glaring shortfall of the bicentenary was the failure to erect a prominent monument, in a central location, to the leaders of the northern United Irishmen. This absence, which repeated the let-down of the centenary, exposed the limits of representing ambivalent memory in the public sphere. Whilst the image of the bicentenary as a time of harmonious reconciliation, achieved through shared commemoration, matched the euphoria of the signing the Belfast agreement, moments of recurring crises in the following years of 'post-conflict' brought disillusion. From within the cracks in the peace process, signs of social forgetting made a reappearance.

DISPARITIES OF ESTEEM

The Good Friday Agreement guaranteed 'parity of esteem and of just and equal treatment for the identity, ethos and aspirations of both communities'.[173] This central principle of the peace accord reified a dichotomy between historical traditions associated with Protestants and those associated with Catholics, which were conceived as mutually exclusive entities. Hybrid 'plural identities'—to use the terms of Máiréad Nic

---

[171] Collins, *Who Fears to Speak*, p. 110.

[172] Jonathan McCormick and Neil Jarman, 'Death of a Mural', *Journal of Material Culture*, 10, no. 1 (March 2005): pp. 49–71.

[173] *The Belfast Agreement* (Northern Ireland Office, 10 April 1998), Annex: 'Agreement between the Government of the United Kingdom of Great Britain and Northern Ireland and the Government of Ireland', Article 1 (v). Additional references to 'parity of esteem' appear in 'Constitutional Issues', 1 (v); 'Strand One: Democratic Institutions in Northern Ireland', 5 (e); 'Rights, Safeguards and Equality of Opportunity', 4.

Craith—were regimented into essential 'singular narratives'.[174] The implementation of this model was ill-equipped to address complex traditions, such as the memory of Protestant United Irishmen who were allied with Catholics in rebellion against the Crown.

The power-sharing arrangements, which struck a symmetrical balance between Protestant unionists and Catholic nationalists, unintentionally depreciated the value of shared remembrance. Though intended to accommodate mutual respect, recognition of communal traditions stimulated inter-community competition and initiated a scramble for cultural capital.[175] Hence, parity of esteem proved to be a double-edged sword, which, on a ground level, nurtured partisan remembrance, fuelling feelings of commemorative possessiveness and commemorative envy that provided motivation for decommemorating.

This is not to say that there were no incentives for reaching across the divide. The Community Relations Council continued to foster explorations of 'common ground' and innovative local history projects could, on occasion, disrupt the reductive narrowing of heritage into binary oppositions.[176] Unionist disremembering and republican commemorative possessiveness were challenged by grass-roots activists, such as Michael Hall of the Farset Community Think Tanks Project, who held up 'the United Army of Ulster' as an example of 'a shared Ulster heritage'.[177] Yet, instances of silencing were still evident at a local level. In south Armagh—an area 'known for the fierceness of its enmities'—the journalist Susan McKay interviewed Willie Johnston, a liberal unionist Covenanter (member of the Reformed Presbyterian Church), who readily acknowledged that local Covenanters had joined the rebels in 1798. Johnston, however, was reluctant to speak about an incident in which the local history society had capitulated to threats and cancelled a talk on 1798 that was to be delivered by 'a Catholic priest with strong views about civil rights and state repression'.[178]

At least in some local authorities, the practices of shared commemoration initiated in the bicentenary continued to gather momentum. Belfast unionist city councillors had previously blocked proposals for a memorial to the United Irishmen, but in 1999, Bob Stoker, the UUP Lord Mayor of Belfast, unveiled a blue plaque for Henry Joy McCracken.[179] Blue plaques were erected by the Ulster Historical Circle for a number of other prominent northern United Irishmen, including Thomas McCabe and his son William Putnam McCabe (1998), William Drennan (2002), William Steel Dickson (2007), Thomas Russell (2009), James Hope (2014), as well as a generic plaque for the Society of the United Irishmen (2007).[180] Intent on having

[174] Máiréad Nic Craith, *Plural Identities—Singular Narratives: The Case of Northern Ireland* (New York: Berghahn Books, 2001); see also Catherine Nash, 'Equity, Diversity and Interdependence: Cultural Policy in Northern Ireland', *Antipode*, 37, no. 2 (2005): pp. 272–300.
[175] Roger Mac Ginty and Pierre Du Toit, 'A Disparity of Esteem: Relative Group Status in Northern Ireland after the Belfast Agreement', *Political Psychology*, 28, no. 1 (2007): pp. 13–31.
[176] Catherine Nash, 'Local Histories in Northern Ireland', *History Workshop Journal*, 60, no. 1 (2005): pp. 45–68. See also Máiréad Nic Craith, *Culture and Identity Politics in Northern Ireland* (New York: Palgrave Macmillan, 2003), pp. 163–88.
[177] Michael Hall, *Is There a Shared Ulster Heritage?* (Belfast: Island Publications/Farset Community Think Tanks Project, 2007), pp. 21–2.
[178] McKay, *Northern Protestants*, pp. 199–201.
[179] *Irish News*, 2 October 1999; *United Irishman*, January 2000, p. 8.
[180] *The Guide to the Blue Plaques in Ulster* (Belfast: Ulster History Circle, 2011); for updates see ulsterhistorycircle.blogspot.com.

McCracken commemorated by a more substantial memorial, Raymond Shearer, a member of the UICS, raised funds for a large bronze plaque, which was placed outside the masonic hall on Rosemary Street—in acknowledgement of McCracken's membership of the freemasons—and was unveiled in 2003 by the first Sinn Féin lord mayor of Belfast Alex Maskey in conjunction with the provincial grand master Bro. A. J. McKinley. Putting the celebration in perspective, the *Belfast Telegraph* pointed out that McCracken was 'as controversial now as he was on the day of his execution'.[181]

A blue plaque erected in memory of Mary Ann McCracken in 1999 described her as a social reformer, without mentioning her connections to the United Irishmen. A decade and a half later, in 2004, a bust of Mary Ann McCracken by the sculptor Elizabeth O'Kane was unveiled in Belfast city hall by the lord mayor Tom Ekin of the Alliance party. McCracken was chosen for this honour as part of a 'good relations strategy', which recognized that, 'although heavily involved in the 1798 United Irishmen rising, she was accepted by both communities afterwards because they acknowledged her as a dedicated champion of people's rights.' The plaque on the sculpture describes her as a 'fervent campaigner for the rights of Belfast's women, children and poor, for the abolition of slavery and the revival of Irish music, language and poetry'. It was considered more acceptable to remember Mary Ann McCracken as a benign philanthropist than as a radical revolutionary. Accordingly, there was no mention of her life-time devotion to her executed brother, who had led the rebels in Antrim.[182] All in all, despite the various commemorative efforts, Belfast was left without a proper monument to the United Irishmen. This shortfall lingered on as a sore point, which was brought up in letters to newspapers that repeatedly complained that no statue had been raised to Henry Joy McCracken in his home town.[183]

A discourse of commemorative competitiveness emerged in 2002 when the Progressive Unionist Party (PUP), which had a Protestant working class support base and links to loyalist paramilitaries, discovered an interest in the memory of Ninety-Eight. At an Ulster Day Parade (commemorating mass loyalist opposition to the Third Home Rule Bill) held in Ballymena in September 2002, Billy McCaughey—a prominent PUP activist—accused the UUP mainstream unionist establishment of having kept 'from public memory and commemoration the men who were executed on the Moat Hill in 1798'.[184] Moat Hill, the motte and bailey in Harryville, outside Ballymena, was remembered locally as the place of execution of members of Thomas Archer's band of outlaws, who had terrorized the neighbourhood by continuing popular resistance after the rebellion was suppressed.[185] As such, it had a particular fascination for McCaughey—nicknamed 'The Protestant Boy', who was a former

---

[181] *Irish News*, 10 October 2001, p. 12 and 5 February 2003, p. 9; *BNL*, 22 January 2003, p. 14; *Belfast Telegraph*, 5 December 2002, 4 and 6 February 2003. Around that time, Ken Dawson brought the connections between the United Irishmen and freemasonry to public attention; *Irish News*, 28 April 2003, p. 32. For scholarly consideration see Mirala, *Freemasonry in Ulster*, pp. 189–209.

[182] *Unveiling of the Bust of Mary Ann McCracken by the Lord Mayor, Councillor Tom Ekin and the Re-Naming of the Committee Rooms as the Conor Room and Lavery Room: Thursday 16 December 2004, City Hall, Belfast* (Belfast: Belfast City Council, 2004); *Irish News*, 17 December 2004, p. 12; *Belfast Telegraph*, 30 December 2004.

[183] See for example *Irish News*, 6 November 2007, p. 22 and 5 March 2009, p. 28; *Belfast Telegraph*, 1 November 2007.

[184] *Ballymena Times*, 22 September 2002.   [185] *Ballymena Times*, 14 September 2007.

member of the UVF's notorious 'Glenanne gang' and had served a sixteen-year prison sentence for murder.

McCaughey was one of several loyalist paramilitary ex-prisoners who professed an avid interest in local history, and in particular in the northern United Irish rebels. In 1998, the secretary of the PUP, Billy Mitchell—a member of the UVF who had served fourteen years in prison for paramilitary murders—participated in bicentennial debates, at which he made a point of stating that the recruiting base of the East Antrim Battalion of the UVF 'came out to a man in '98 in support of McCracken and the ideals espoused by the United Irishmen'.[186] These former gunmen were now committed to 'conflict transformation' through peaceful means and McCaughey urged for the need to 'educate our own constituency' about the history of Presbyterian involvement in the rebellion.[187]

After a loyalist Remembrance Day parade in Ballymena on 10 November 2002, members of the PUP visited Moat Hill and laid a wreath with the inscription: 'To commemorate dissenting Presbyterians. Faithful unto death in their fight for liberty and equality for all in 1798. They fought to right a great wrong.' PUP deputy leader David Rose explained that their purpose was 'to remember local men who died defending loyalist paramilitaries in 1798'. Rose, 'as a true loyalist thinker', professed his belief that 'Henry Joy McCracken would, I am sure, have been pleased to see the line reclaimed by its true inheritors.'[188]

These provocative statements infuriated republicans and nationalists. Denouncing McCaughey's claim as 'ludicrous', the Sinn Féin representative for north Antrim, Philip McGuigan, contended that 'for loyalists to stake a claim to the cause of the United Irishmen is rubbish'. Carmel Hanna of the SDLP fastidiously asserted that 'there were no "loyalists" among the rebels of '98' and that the 'loyalist paramilitaries' of the time were members of the Orange Order who opposed the rebellion. Re-affirming her own party's claim on memory, Hanna declared that 'the SDLP—alone of all the parties, north and south—were the only party which in the bicentenary year of 1798 sat down and considered in depth the implications of the sometimes uncomfortable legacy of the United Irish movement.'[189]

A torrent of irate letters to the *Irish News* accused the PUP of wanting 'to divide "United men" in death' and of desecrating 'the memory of men like Henry Joy'. A southern nationalist was baffled by Rose's attempt 'to portray McCracken and his colleagues as proto-loyalist'. A self-identified 'county Antrim Republican' expressed bewilderment that 'for decades people have remembered the brave Ulstermen as Presbyterian Irish nationalists/republicans, but Mr McCaughey now tells us we have all misunderstood their ethos and ideas.' An 'Uladh exile' from Sligo railed against 'the

---

[186] *Irish Times*, 7 September 1998, p. 10; see also McKay, *Northern Protestants*, pp. 52–9. For biographical information see Kate Fearon, *The Conflict's Fifth Business: A Brief Biography of Billy Mitchell* (Belfast: LINC Resource Centre, 2002); available online at <www.longkeshinsideout.co.uk/?p=1358>.

[187] *Irish News*, 13 November 2002, p. 4. For the turn to history among former paramilitaries see Carolyn Gallaher, *After the Peace: Loyalist Paramilitaries in Post-Accord Northern Ireland* (Ithaca: Cornell University Press, 2007), pp. 84–109.

[188] *Irish News*, 13 and 14 November 2002, pp. 4 and 8 (respectively) and 3 December 2002, p. 9. For biographical information on McCaughey see his obituary in *Ballymena Times*, 16 February 2006,

[189] *People*, 6 October 2002, p. 20; *Irish News*, 26 November, p. 9.

hijacking of Henry Joy McCracken' and Brian Kelly of the Socialist Workers Party, writing as 'a lifelong socialist and an historian', objected to the unionist attempt 'to claim Henry Joy McCracken for their own'. Another writer avowed that 'the PUP's attempts to distort the memory of Henry Joy McCracken and the other United Irishmen must be challenged.'[190] The commemorative envy of loyalists, who vied for a stake in the memory of Ninety-Eight, had been met with the commemorative possessiveness of nationalists, who considered themselves the rightful guardians of the United Irish legacy.

Responding to the critics, McCaughey accused 'those within contemporary Irish republicanism who would deny myself and others the right to commemorate the men of the Moat Hill' of having 'betrayed the cardinal principles of '98'. Rose insisted that 'Henry Joy was not a sectarian nationalist' and that 'loyalists haven't hijacked '98', which in his opinion deserved a place of honour in the loyalist 'history of the Ulster people'.[191] Trying to resolve the argument along consensual lines, Roy Garland—a member of the UUP who contributed a regular column to the nationalist *Irish News*, rehashed the bicentennial rhetoric that 'the most fitting tribute to the men of '98 would be a complete stop to coercion and violence for political ends and the building of a peaceful, inclusive society.' Art McMillen, a long-time activist in the 'official' republican Workers' Party, open-mindedly reasoned that 'there is no need for anyone to hijack Henry Joy because we all can share his memory.'[192] These overtures did not curry favour with exclusivists, who were keen on monopolizing memory for their constituency.

Controversy over commemoration returned to Antrim in 2004, when a bridge was constructed over the river Bann, as part of an 18-million-pound scheme for the Belfast-Derry motorway to bypass the village of Toome. The Sinn Féin representatives on the Antrim Borough Council, Martin McManus and Martin Meehan—a former member of the Provisional IRA, who had served eighteen years in prison—pushed for the new bridge to be named after the local Ninety-Eight hero Roddy McCorley. The neighbouring nationalist-dominated Magherafelt District Council passed a resolution in favour of the proposal. The SDLP, however, were disinclined to join forces with Sinn Féin. Donovan McClelland, the SDLP member of the Northern Ireland Assembly for South Antrim, advocated that the bridge ought to be named after the former party leader and Nobel laureate John Hume.

Billy McCaughey of the PUP believed that 'cross-community support existed to have the new Toome Bridge named after Roddy McCorley.' Alluding to social forgetting among unionists, McCaughey maintained that the Presbyterians of the area 'wouldn't beat the drum about that era of their history but scratch the surface deep enough and they would identify with it.' The unionist majority on the Antrim Borough Council, which consisted of UUP and even harder-line DUP representatives, did not buy into this argument and strongly opposed commemoration of Roddy McCorley. In an attempt to avoid conflict, the minister at the Northern Ireland Office responsible for

---

[190] *Irish News*, 16 and 26 November, p. 7; 6, 27, and 28 December 2002, pp. 8, 8, and 7 (respectively) and 1 February 2003, p. 7.
[191] *Irish News*, 2, 3, and 6 December 2002, pp. 7, 9, and 2 (respectively); 6 January 2003, p. 7.
[192] *Irish News*, 9 December 2002, p. 2 and 23 July 2003, p. 10.

regional development, John Spellar, announced that it would simply be named Toome Bridge, forgoing any commemorative intentions.[193]

Republicans were unwilling to back down. At an alternative dedication ceremony on Easter Tuesday 2004, attended by about a thousand people, signs were put up on the bridge and a plaque was erected, unofficially renaming it the Rodai Mac Corlai Bridge. Significantly, the protestors had opted for a Gaelicized version of the name, popularized in a prison poem by Bobby Sands, so that the memory of the United Irish hero was associated with Catholic nationalists rather than with Presbyterians. Rev. William McCrea, the DUP member of the Northern Ireland Assembly for Mid Ulster (and a former member of the loyalist vigilante group the Shankill Defence Association) demanded police intervention to 'remove any plaque erected'. After the signs were removed from the bridge, Martin Meehan announced that they 'will be replaced, and if they are taken down they will be replaced again and again', adamantly proclaiming that 'republicans and people in Toomebridge have a right to be consulted about what the new bridge here is to be called, and have a right to name it after their idol.'[194]

Commemoration of Roddy McCorley, which had previously been subject to decommemorating in 1852 (when a procession to rebury his supposed remains was obstructed), 1909 (when a graveside memorial erected by Bigger was smashed), and 1969 (when the monument in Toome was attacked) had once again been prevented (Fig. 7.4a).[195] The campaign to rename the new bridge at Toome was energetically promoted by the recently revived Roddy McCorley Society. Although there was a new Roddy McCorley monument in Toome (erected in the 1970s and touched-up for the bicentenary), the society took upon itself to try and restore the original monument, which had been unveiled in 1954 and was destroyed by explosives in 1969 at the beginning of the Troubles. The remaining ruins, still found on the site, were collected in November 2005 but were found to be beyond repair. Instead, a replica of the original Celtic Cross monument was constructed and unveiled on the grounds of Moyard House, the society's club in west Belfast, on 10 June 2007, to celebrate the thirty-fifth anniversary of the Roddy McCorley Society (Fig. 7.4). Decommemorating had resulted in repossession and re-commemorating.[196]

Bidding for ownership of memory was quite literally apparent in 2006, when members of Ógra Shinn Féin—the youth wing of Sinn Féin—disrupted the sale of republican artefacts at an auction in Dublin, protesting that 'historical items were in danger of being bought by foreign collectors.' This allegation was denied by Martin McManus, who attended the auction along with other members of Sinn Féin. McManus claimed that he had assisted a businessman to buy a William Orr memorial card, dating back to the protomartyr's execution in 1797, in order for it to be brought to Antrim and put on display. The material culture of Ninety-Eight remembrance, which over the years

---

[193] *BNL*, 16 March 2004, p. 5; *Irish News*, 11 February 2004, p. 1; 16 March 2014, p. 6; 15 April 2004, p. 10. For biographical details on Meehan see Joe Graham, *'Show Me the Man': The Martin Meehan Story* (Belfast: Rushlight Magazine, 2008).

[194] *BNL*, 6, 13, and 14 April 2004, pp. 6, 1 & 9, and 9 (respectively); *Irish News*, 5, 14, 15, and 16 April 2004, pp. 4, 3, 10, and 4 (respectively); *An Phoblacht*, 15 April 2004. For the poem 'Rodai MacCorlai' by Bobby Sands see Chapter 6 above, pp. 502–3.

[195] See above Chapter 4, pp. 284–5; Chapter 5, p. 435; and Chapter 6, pp. 498–9.

[196] *Irish News*, 11 June 2007, p. 6. See also the Roddy McCorley Society's account of the restoration at <www.roddymccorley.com/History of Cross.html>.

(a)

The Roddy McCorley monument at Toomebridge following the explosion.

(b)   (c)

Fig. 7.4. Decommemorating and re-commemorating Roddy McCorley

(a) The Roddy McCorley monument in Toome, unveiled on 1 November 1954, was destroyed by explosives on 1 January 1969. (b) A new monument was erected in Toome in the 1970s and touched up for the bicentenary. The ruins of the original monument were collected in November 2005 by members of the Roddy McCorley Society. (c) Unable to put them together again, they commissioned a replica, which was unveiled outside Moyard House, in west Belfast, on 10 June 2007.

The photograph of the destroyed monument appeared in *Irish Independent*, 3 January 1969; reproduced with the newspaper's permission by the National Library of Ireland. Photographs of the renewed monuments by Guy Beiner (2003 and 2011).

had been secretly kept in private possession, was being acquired by modern-day republicans who were keen on exhibiting it in their communities and on preventing such memorabilia falling into the hands of 'outsiders'.[197]

Meanwhile, bitter disagreements between the unionist parties and Sinn Féin resulted in the derailing of the peace process and the collapse of devolution. From October 2002, the Northern Ireland Assembly at Stormont, established in consequence of the Good Friday Agreement, was suspended and Direct Rule from London was restored. After a hiatus of four years, renewed multi-party talks in St Andrews, Scotland, brokered a new consociational agreement, signed by the Irish and British Government in October 2006. This resulted in new elections and the formation in March 2007 of a power-sharing government, led by former sworn enemies, with Ian Paisley of the DUP as First Minister and Martin McGuinness of Sinn Féin as Deputy First Minister.[198] While the more extreme unionist and nationalist parties were obliged to cooperate with each other in governing Northern Ireland, they still could not agree on a shared version of the past.

During a debate of the Transitional Assembly (which prepared the way for the election of a new assembly) on 4 December 2006, Gerry Adams held up the example of the United Irishmen:

> Most of those who were involved in that great enterprise were Presbyterians: people such as Samuel Neilson from Ballroney; Mary Ann McCracken and her brother Henry Joy McCracken, who was hanged in High Street in Belfast; Rev Sinclair Kelburn; Rev William Steele Dickson; Jemmy Hope, who was a Templepatrick man; Henry Monro from Lisburn; and John Robb from Ballynahinch.

Referring to a gathering that the DUP had recently held in Templepatrick, Adams went on to remind the unionist politicians of the legacy of local Presbyterian republicanism in 1798. Paisley responded to this 'interesting extract from republican propaganda history' by claiming that 'it is absolute nonsense and a perversion of history to be told that the Presbyterians of Northern Ireland were all lined up in an act to undermine proper democratic government and break the British link.' He insisted that orthodox Presbyterians were 'totally opposed to the rebellion' and that 'those who were named as Presbyterians were Arians or Unitarians.' This line, which had been consistently held by Paisley throughout the Troubles, was a return to the efforts of Rev. Henry Cooke in the early nineteenth century to disassociate Presbyterians from their prior history of radicalism and to effectively disremember 1798.[199]

While loyalists dissociated themselves from the memory of Ninety-Eight, conflicts between Sinn Féin and dissident republican groups that objected to the peace process were played out, among other arenas, through competition over ownership of historical memory. Militant dissidents asserted their claim to be the 'real' inheritors of the United Irishmen by staging commemorative demonstrations, which, in turn, aggravated loyalists. The intention of a William Orr Commemoration Committee to organize a parade in

---

[197] *Irish News* 17 April 2006 p. 8; *Sunday Times* 16 April 2006, p. 3 (Eire News section).

[198] Rick Wilford, 'Northern Ireland: The Politics of Constraint', *Parliamentary Affairs*, 63, no. 1 (2010): pp. 134–55.

[199] Proceedings of the Northern Ireland Transitional Assembly, *Official Report* (Hansard), vol. 21, 4 December 2006; *Irish Times*, 5 December 2006, p. 1. For Cooke's association of the memory of the rebellion with Unitarians see Chapter 3 above, p. 233.

Ballymena in August 2005 to commemorate the anniversary of the introduction of internment at the beginning of the Troubles, implicitly drawing a historical parallel between the incarceration of United Irishmen and of more-recent republicans, was met with threats from loyalists. The dissidents were intent to continue with the commemorative march despite requests from Sinn Féin to give in for the sake of peace. In the end, the Parades Commission—established in 1998 'to promote and facilitate mediation as a means of resolving disputes concerning public processions'—intervened and restricted the march to the nationalist Fisherwick estate, while riot police were dispatched to hold back some five-hundred loyalist protesters.[200] A repeat of the parade the following year was once again confined to the same residential area and the William Orr band was prohibited from playing music.[201]

A few years later, in 2010, a Henry Joy Commemoration Committee affiliated with the splinter group known as the Republican Network for Unity (RNU) began organizing annual parades, led by a Henry Joy McCracken Republican Flute Band, which marched through north Belfast, passed by the Clifton Street Orange Hall, and terminated at the graves of the United Irishmen in Clifton Street cemetery. In 2012, militant loyalist opposition to the McCracken parade resulted in three nights of rioting and the injury of numerous police officers. The return of violence was avoided in 2013, when the Parade Commission once again intervened, re-routing the parade and placing restrictions on the counter-demonstration. Although tensions were noticeable in following years, massive deployment of police forces (which far outnumbered the combined attendance of republican marchers and loyalist demonstrators) ensured that the parades in 2014, 2015, and 2016 passed peacefully.[202] However, the threat of violence was never far from the surface. In 2014, a loyalist mob, believed to be associated with the UDA, assailed a bus visiting 1798 sites in Antrim on a tour organized by the former Antrim Sinn Féin councillor Martin McManus as part of the west Belfast festival Féile an Phobail.[203]

In its commemorative possessiveness of the republican memory of Ninety-Eight, Sinn Féin waged a battle on two fronts: both against unionist disremembering and against dissident-republican commemorative envy. These dual conflicts surfaced in 2011, shortly after the newly elected Sinn Féin lord mayor of Belfast Niall Ó Donnghaile took office and decided to rearrange the memorabilia in the mayor's parlour. The removal of a number of portraits of members of the royal family and their replacement with the 1916 Proclamation of the Republic and a picture depicting the United Irishmen and the 1798 rebellion infuriated unionists. Less expectedly, complaints were also made by dissident republicans, among them the artist whose image of 1798 was being used—Brian Mor O'Baoigill, an Irish-American of Donegal

---

[200] *Belfast Telegraph*, 20 and 28 July, 2 and 3 August 2005; Ballymena Times, 4 August 2005. For background on the Parades Commission see Neil Jarman, 'From Outrage to Apathy? The Disputes over Parades, 1995–2003', *Global Review of Ethnopolitics*, 3, no. 1 (2003): pp. 92–105.

[201] *BNL*, 9 August 2006, p. 9; *Belfast Telegraph*, 9 and 10 August 2006; *Irish News*, 9 August 2006 p. 7.

[202] *Belfast Telegraph*, 3 September 2012, pp. 8–9; 15 and 16 August 2013; 1 and 11 September 2014; 23 and 24 August 2015; 29 August 2016, p. 19; *Irish News*, 1 and 3 September 2012, pp. 8 and 6 (respectively); 1 and 26 August 2013, pp. 12 and 6 (respectively); 21 August 2014, p. 5; 1 September 2014, p. 4; 29 August 2016, p. 7; 24 September 2016, p. 1; *Irish Republican News*, 23 August 2014; 3 September 2016.

[203] *Irish Republican News*, 9 August 2014.

parentage—who declared that he had 'created the poster to honour republican martyrs who fought for Irish freedom' and that he objected to its display in 'an office controlled and paid for by the UK'. The controversy was resolved the following year, when Ó Donnghaile's mayoral term came to an end and the original artwork was returned to its place.[204]

In 2008, the Ards Borough Council voted against a proposal to highlight the area's 1798 heritage in an application for a 'signature project' submitted to the Northern Ireland Tourist Board. The suggestion of alderman Kieran McCarthy of the Alliance party—a liberal party committed to a non-sectarian 'shared approach to the past'—that Betsy Gray should be publicly acknowledged as a local heroine was overwhelmingly rejected. Ten years earlier, during the 1798 bicentenary, the council had sponsored a commemorative programme that included numerous events. Since then, a book by the local historian Harry Allen, chairman of the Donaghadee Historical Society, had revived interest in the involvement of 'The Men of Ards' in the rebellion. Nevertheless, local unionist politicians now preferred to distance themselves from the memory of Ninety-Eight. The founding in 1998 of a Sinn Féin cumann (branch) in Ballynahinch named after Betsy Gray and the annual award by the GAA in county Down of a Betsy Gray Cup and Betsy Gray Shield in hurling—a sport associated with cultural nationalism—had contributed to what was perceived as nationalist appropriation of the heroine, which alienated unionists. UUP councillor Ronnie Ferguson dismissively referred to traditions of Betsy Gray as invented 'myth', noting that she 'only became famous 100 years afterwards when a book about her was published' (referring to Lyttle's popular novel). The SDLP councillor Joe Boyle, the lone nationalist representative on the council, could only regret that Ulster's 'Joan of Ards' (as she was dubbed in the *Irish News*) was 'not deemed to be worthy' of public remembrance.[205]

Even so, the local Ninety-Eight heroine was admired by individuals as 'the very heartbeat and soul of Co Down'. While admitting that 'the younger generation does not know who she was or what she represented', a resident of Lurgan recalled that 'within living memory the name of Betsy Gray has been revered in many a Presbyterian home and there may be paintings or plaques of her lying in attics.'[206] A unionist from Portadown passionately wrote to the *Irish News*, under the pseudonym Ultonian [native of Ulster], that Betsy Gray was 'a story that belongs to the Presbyterians of Ulster, a story that unionist Ards Borough Council should be proud of, a story unionists should promote, a story that should not be surrendered to Irish republicans'. Ultonian's assertion that 'unionists are the true inheritors of the spirit of Ulster 1798 and some of us are even proud to speak of '98' annoyed a nationalist reader from Newry, who wondered 'how can a unionist be a supporter of people like Wolfe Tone, Henry McCracken, Betsy Gray and others?'. In response, Ultonian defended his right 'to claim a heritage from the Ulster 1798 rebels' and argued that 'in terms of denominational ties, heritage and ethnicity the unionist Presbyterians of 2008 are the children of the Ulster rebels of 1798 and this is something to be cherished and

---

[204] *Belfast Telegraph*, 10 June and 13 October 2011, pp. 2 and 22 and 6 June 2012, p. 20; *Daily Mirror* (Ulster edition), 13 June 2011, p. 15.

[205] *Irish News*, 11, 18, and 27 September 2008, pp. 3, 22, and 9 (respectively); *An Phoblacht*, 2 October 2008. See also Allen, *The Men of the Ards*. My thanks to Harry Allen for an interview on his work (Donaghadee, 25 September 2011).

[206] *Irish News*, 28 October 2008, p. 23.

promoted.'[207] This attitude was reflective of a wider Ulster-Scots reclamation of Ninety-Eight that both defied republican commemorative possessiveness and rejected unionist disremembering.

In the same year that the Ards Borough Council turned its back on Betsy Gray, the Ulster-Scots Language Society—formed in 1992 for the protection and promotion of the Ulster-Scots language—issued in 2008 a new edition of Lyttle's *Betsy Gray*, which was praised on the society's website for the way it 'skilfully combines legend with local and social history'. An accompanying essay by Kenneth Robinson, erstwhile member of the Bangor Historical Society, described the novel as the ultimate monument to the local heroine. The *Mourne Observer* affirmed that 'two hundred years after those stirring events of the '98 Rising, the legend of Betsy Gray still refuses to die', while acknowledging that 'to this day arguments rage as to her origins, political significance, and even over her very existence.'[208] Significantly, the popular novel was associated with Ulster-Scots culture.

Since the 1990s, Ulster-Scots—also known as Ullans—had been undergoing a revival, marked by the establishment in 1995 of an Ulster-Scots Heritage Council that served as an umbrella organization for a plethora of clubs, bands, and language activists. Policies that advanced parity of esteem added impetus to the politicized reinvigoration of a provincial vernacular culture, which was identified with unionism and seen to be in competition with nationalist investment in Irish-Gaelic culture. In consequence of the Good Friday Agreement, two language agencies were formed in parallel: Foras na Gaeilge, to advance the Irish language both North and South of the border, and the Ulster-Scots Agency [The Boord o Ulstèr-Scotch], which, in addition to language revival, undertook in its mission statement 'to promote a wider awareness and understanding of the history of the Ulster-Scots'.[209]

In compiling a literary canon, advocates of Ulster-Scots could draw on a long list of regional authors, many of whom had contributed over the past two centuries to the vernacular historiography of 1798. They reclaimed the early works of writers who were members of the United Irishmen, such as William Drennan, Rev. William Steel Dickson, and (with the help of Madden) James Hope; contemporary local poets— the likes of Francis Boyle, Samuel Thompson, James Orr, and Mary Balfour; early-nineteenth-century novelists, such as John Gamble and James McHenry; late-nineteenth-century revivalists such as Lyttle and Bigger; through to late-modern writers, such as Thomas Carnduff, Sam Hanna Bell, and more recently Stewart Parker and Tom Paulin.[210] Responding to the new interest, the website of the Linen Hall Library added a section in dialect describing its Ulster-Scots collections ('the Ulster

---

[207] *Irish News*, 20 September 2008, p. 22; 24 and 29 October 2008, pp. 22 and 22 (respectively).

[208] W. G. Lyttle, *Betsy Gray; or, Hearts of Down: A Tale of Ninety-Eight* (Belfast: Ullans Press, 2008), p. 163; *Irish News*, 16 October 2008, p. 12; *Mourne Observer*, 22 October 2008; <www.ulsterscotslanguage.com/en/books/ulster-scots-novels/betsy-gray/>.

[209] Liam McIlvanney, 'Across the Narrow Sea: The Language, Literature and Politics of Ulster-Scots', in *Ireland and Scotland: Culture and Society, 1700–2000*, edited by Ray Ryan (Dublin: Four Courts Press, 2005), pp. 206–13; see also Katie Radford, 'Creating an Ulster Scots Revival', *Peace Review*, 13, no. 1 (2001): pp. 51–7; Máiréad Nic Craith, 'Politicised Linguistic Consciousness: The Case of Ulster-Scots', *Nations and Nationalism*, 7, no. 1 (2001): pp. 21–37.

[210] See Frank Ferguson, ed., *Ulster-Scots Writing: An Anthology* (Dublin: Four Courts Press, 2008).

Scots Clatter in the Lint Haw'), which could be traced back to the United Irishmen 'an the stoushie [commotion] o 1798'.[211]

In the early 1990s, folklore collectors documented Ulster-Scots place-names that recalled the rebellion, such as the 'hangin brae', which marked the execution place of Rev. James Porter in Greyabbey, or the 'Betsy Gray's fiel' [field].[212] Since then, interest had grown in 'The Turn-Oot', which was described by the language revivalist Philip Robinson as 'an Ulster-Scots Presbyterian revolt'. Robinson—the author of *A Grammar of the Traditional Written and Spoken Language*—wrote in dialect for the *Belfast News-Letter* a series of articles, 'which lifts the veil on why some Ulster-Scots rebelled in 1798', beginning with a piece on the veteran rebel James Orr—'the bard of Ballycarry'.[213] Renewed interest in the poetry of Orr sprung a campaign, run by the local historian David Hume and the Ballycarry Community Association, for the restoration of his long-neglected monument in Templecorran Cemetery, near Ballycarry. The monument was re-dedicated on 7 June 2014, on the anniversary of the Battle of Antrim—an event that Orr had recalled in verse in his celebrated poem 'Donegore Hill'.[214]

A number of Ulster-Scots revivalist organizations, which received state funding under the parity of esteem arrangements of the peace agreement, promoted the reclamation of Ninety-Eight. The Ulster-Scots Agency produced a series of leaflets on 'Great Ulster-Scots: People and Events in History', of which the second publication—issued in 2005—was devoted to Betsy Gray. Acknowledging 'great historical interest' in the subject, the agency's chief executive George Patton, conceded that 'we might never know the real facts of her life, her involvement in the uprising, and how exactly she died' but maintained that this uncertainty 'does not detract from her colourful and important place in local Ulster-Scots history'.[215] Reaching out to a younger generation, the agency prepared a series of six booklets of educational activities and corresponding teachers' manuals titled *Climb the Liberty Tree: An Exploration of the Ulster-Scots' Role in the United Irishmen's Rebellion of 1798*, which was intended for Key Stage 3 pupils (the first three years of secondary education). Despite these initiatives, a Belfast taxi driver, who identified himself as a concerned Ulster Scot, complained that 'the Ulster-Scots Agency website makes no reference to the 1798 rebellion', even though it was 'probably the most significant event in modern Ulster-Scots history'.[216] Sister revivalist organizations stepped in to fill in the perceived gap.

The Ulster-Scots Community Network (USCN)—established in 1995 'to promote awareness and understanding of the Ulster-Scots tradition in history, language and culture'—produced in 2013 the booklet *1798 an' a' That*. This publication paid tribute to the work of the recently deceased historian A.T.Q. Stewart by offering an

[211] <www.linenhall.com/pages/irish-and-reference>.

[212] Will McAvoy, 'Some Field Names in the Greyabbey District', *Ullans: The Magazine for Ulster-Scots*, no. 1 (Spring 1993); <www.ulsterscotsacademy.com/ullans/1/some-field-names-in-the-greyabbey-district.php>.

[213] Sandra M. Baillie, *Presbyterians in Ireland: Identity in the Twenty-First Century* (Basingstoke and New York: Palgrave Macmillan, 2008), p. 121; *BNL*, 27 October and 8 December 2001, pp. 28 and 22 (respectively). See also Philip Robinson, *Ulster-Scots: A Grammar of the Traditional Written and Spoken Language* (Belfast: Ullans Press, 1997).

[214] *Belfast Telegraph*, 4 January 2003 and 27 September 2014, p. 26; *Larne Times*, 1 June 2014.

[215] Catriona Holmes, *Betsy Gray: Heroine of the 1798 Uprising—Myth or Fact* (Belfast: Ulster-Scots Agency, 2005); Ulster-Scots Agency press release, 29 April 2005.

[216] *BNL*, 19 March 2014, p. 20.

examination of the formation of the Society of United Irishman (with an emphasis on the role of William Drennan) and providing an account of the 1798 rebellion. While considering the reasons for what Lecky had described as 'the defection of the Presbyterians from the movement of which they were the main originators', the booklet acknowledged that 'to this day, many solidly Unionist families in Antrim and Down remain proud to boast of ancestors "oot" in 1798, although to Unionists elsewhere this is often incomprehensible'.[217] Another USCN publication, *Herstory*, contained the 'profiles of eight interesting Ulster-Scot women', among them Betsy Gray and Mary Ann McCracken. A sequel, *Herstory II*, added an entry on the United Irish sympathizer Martha McTier née Drennan.

The Ulster-Scots Broadcast Fund (USBF)—set up 'to ensure that the heritage, culture and language of Ulster-Scots is expressed through moving image'—sponsored the production of *An Independent People*, a three-part documentary film on the history of Presbyterians in Ulster, which was broadcast on BBC Northern Ireland in March 2013. Presented by the journalist William Crawley—a former Presbyterian minister who professed a personal interest in the 'exploration of Ulster Scots history'—much of the second episode (titled 'Seeds of Liberty') was devoted to the northern United Irishmen.[218] The series was subsequently developed into an Ulster-Scot heritage package for tourists, consisting of DVDS, a booklet, and a guided tour.[219]

The Ulster-Scots revival also had a vibrant musical dimension, expressed through dances, marching bands, and folk songs. The Antrim traditional musician Willie Drennan formed in 1998 the collective of musicians Fowkgates [Culture]. With the help of the violinist John Trotter, this group evolved into the Ulster-Scots Folk Orchestra, an ensemble that recorded fourteen CDs and performed some eight-hundred concerts between 2000 and 2010. Their repertoire included two 1798-related ballads written by the guitar-player Bob Spears—one on Tom Archer (recorded on the 2000 album *A Clatter O Fowk*) and another on Betsy Gray (on the 2002 album *Endangered Species*), as well as the instrumental piece 'William Orr's Farewell' (on the 2004 album *Bringin It Thegither*). Their show 'Fae Lang Syne' (first performed in 2004) presented a musical history of the Ulster-Scots tradition, which deviated from standard unionist popular histories by attributing noted significance to the rebellion.[220] Consequently, scholars of traditional music came to realize that 'the songs of 1798 relate to the activities of the Ulster-Scots as much as to the Irish Nationalist community.'[221]

Faced with derision from nationalists who refused to acknowledge the linguistic validity of the Ullans dialect as a language-in-the-making, a dynamic of 'parity of

---

[217] *1798 an' a' That: Radicalism Revolt and Realignment* (Belfast: Ulster-Scots Community Network, 2013), p. 20. For the USCN see their website: <www.ulster-scots.com>.

[218] *Carrick Times*, 27 June 2012; *BNL*, 11 March 2013; *An Independent People* (dir. Brendan Byrne; Below the Radar, 2013); my thanks to producer Fiona Keene for providing me with DVDs of the series.

[219] *News Letter*, 22 January 2016; *Belfast Telegraph*, 25 January 2016.

[220] *Belfast Telegraph*, 12 December 2002; Cooper, *The Musical Traditions of Northern Ireland*, pp. 97–100; Willie Drennan, 'Fiddles, Flutes, Drums and Fifes', *Études irlandaises*, 38, no. 2 (2013): pp. 117–18; Gordon Ramsey, 'The Ulster-Scots Musical Revival: Transforming Tradition in a Post-Conflict Environment', *Études Irlandaises*, 38, no. 2 (2013), pp. 134–5. My thanks to Willie Drennan for providing me with recordings and accompanying information.

[221] Susan H. Motherway, *The Globalization of Irish Traditional Song Performance* (Farnham: Ashgate, 2013), pp. 96–7.

contempt' motivated Ulster-Scots activists to become even more productive. At the same time, they also had to overcome the condescension of fellow unionists who were not interested in this form of Ulster vernacular culture. At least some advocates of Ulster-Scots came to consider themselves torch-bearers of a 'third tradition', standing outside the standard dichotomy between the Irish nationalists who identified with Gaelic culture and the Ulster unionists who identified with British-English culture.[222] This noncompliant stance, which defied the duality of consociational politics, seemed to make traditions of dissent and rebelliousness all the more current. John Dean of the South Belfast Cultural Society, the organizer of the Belfast Ulster-Scots Festival—generally considered a loyalist celebration—recognized that the historical record of Presbyterian participation in the 1798 rebellion 'can be anti-British'.[223]

The flamboyant unionist politician John Laird, who had a reputation for being a hard-line loyalist within the UUP but considered himself 'a true Ulster liberal', enthusiastically championed the Ullans revival and served as chairman of the Ulster-Scots Agency from 1999 to 2004. Created a life peer in 1999, Lord Laird took pride in his family 'connections on both sides of the 1798 argument' and, in his typically eccentric fashion, saw no contradiction in celebrating Orangeism while commemorating the rebellion. On 12 July 2005, Laird marched in the Twelfth parade in Belfast dressed as an eighteenth-century redcoat, together with the brethren of the Royal York Loyal Orange Lodge (LOL 145)—a lodge originally formed from the ranks of the York Fencible Regiment that was stationed in Ireland to prevent the rebellion. The following month, Laird and the Royal York Orangemen participated as re-enactors in the filming of a dramatized documentary on the Battle of Saintfield, at which the fencibles had been ambushed by rebels and suffered heavy losses. The Orangemen played the roles of royalists and rebels.[224]

The amateur film *Brethren in Arms*, which was screened at the Queen's Film Theatre in December 2005, depicted the rebellion as a civil war, focusing on the conflicted story of the Birch family. The radical Presbyterian minister Rev. Thomas Ledlie Birch escaped execution for his participation in the rebellion thanks to the intervention of his brother George Birch, the commander of the Newtownards yeomanry, whose own sons had joined the rebels and one of them even died in action. According to the director and script-writer Vivien Hewitt, the film was designed 'to challenge many long held misconceptions about the '98'. She considered the 'strange scenario of Yorkshire Orangemen getting attacked by Ulster Presbyterians' to be 'one of those strange paradoxical events that many have forgotten about our history'. Lord Laird threw his weight behind the production and declared that he was 'very pleased to be part of something that celebrates and expresses the Ulster Scots culture in a positive way'.[225] For the sake of convenience, awkward folk traditions, which recalled that 'nothing

---

[222] Martin Dowling, 'Confusing Culture and Politics: Ulster Scots Culture and Music', *New Hibernia Review*, 11, no. 3 (2007), pp. 72–6.

[223] Cathal McCall, 'Political Transformation and the Reinvention of the Ulster-Scots Identity and Culture', *Identities*, 9, no. 2 (April 2002), p. 213.

[224] *Belfast Telegraph*, 12 July 2005; *BNL*, 20 August 2005, p. 3; *Sunday Tribune*, 19 November 2007, p. 19; see also John Laird, *A Struggle to Be Heard: By a True Ulster Liberal* (London: Global & Western Publishing, 2010), pp. 79–84.

[225] *BNL*, 20 August and 16 December 2005, pp. 3 and 30 (respectively).

could exceed the cruelty of the York Fencibles, both officers and men York Fencibles on local residents', were sidestepped.[226]

In following years, re-enactments of the Battle of Saintfield by Orangemen, along-side international living history groups, became a regular fixture of an annual Liberty Days festival. Launched in 2006, the Saintfield festival aspired to highlight the Ulster-Scots role in 1798. The 2006 programme included an amateur theatre performance of the play *Who Dares to Speak*, written by the festival organizer Vivien Hewitt. The drama recounted the local experience of rebellion through a fictional story, which was 'heavily based on the facts and community memories of those few June days in 1798 when the Ulster-Scots imagination caught fire'.[227] The battle re-enactments were supplemented with performances of traditional dance and folk music. Lord Laird, who showed up every year in period costume, explained that the celebration was 'about learning history and enjoying it at same time'.[228] Those who found the boisterous, and occasionally outrageous, antics of Laird and his associates excessive looked for more restrained ways of commemorating Ninety-Eight.

From 2007, the Saintfield Town Regeneration Committee (STRC), with help from the Down District Council, began to redevelop the area of York Island, a place name that marked the site where the York Fencibles were ambushed during the Battle of Saintfield. What had once been swampy terrain on a small island in the middle of a stream had since merged with the grounds of the cemetery of Saintfield's First Presbyterian Church. After the rebellion was suppressed, loyalists commemorated the dead officers with a memorial at Comber Parish church (12 km north-east of Saintfield), but, according to local folklore, most of the dead from both sides were buried in mass graves. Vernacular commemorative traditions were validated in the 1950s, when locals found on the battlefield two skeletons, as well as a sword and bayonet belonging to York Fencibles.[229]

The Regeneration Committee designated a section of the cemetery as a memorial garden with explanatory panels, prepared by the Saintfield Heritage Society, with the help of the Ballynahinch historian Horace Reid. An introductory sign placed the ideology of the United Irishmen in the context of the Scottish Enlightenment through reference to the locally educated philosopher Francis Hutcheson. The Saintfield 1798 Memorial Garden, which was opened on 10 June 2010, features a simple memorial consisting of an inscription carved on a rock: 'In Memory of the York Fencibles, Yeomen and United Irishmen who died at the Battle of Saintfield 9th June 1798.' This pluralistic commemorative formula was approved by all political parties, including Sinn Féin and the DUP. It offered an inclusive alternative to the more exclusivist political undertone of Ulster-Scots revivalism, which was seen as a partisan appropriation of the memory of Ninety-Eight.[230]

---

[226] *Mourne Observer*, 3 May 1968, p. 9.

[227] *Irish News*, 17 August 2006, p. 3. Highlights from the festival and scenes from the play are showcased in the video *Liberty Days Festival, 17th–19th August 2006* (filmed by Vivien Hewitt; Corish Productions, 2006).

[228] *BNL*, 27 August 2007 and 29 July 2008; *Ulster Star*, 1 August 2008.

[229] Stewart, *The Summer Soldiers*, pp. 187–8; Wilsdon, *The Sites of the 1798 Rising*, pp. 154–5.

[230] See information and photo gallery on the Discover Saintfield website: <http://discoversaintfield. com/saintfield-memorial-garden>. My thanks to Martyn Todd, former Recreation and Community Services Director in the Down District Council, for an interview (21 September 2011, Saintfield).

Under the directorship of the local historian David Hume, the 21st annual Broadisland Gathering in Ballycarry—'the longest established and largest Ulster-Scots festival in Northern Ireland'—added to its programme in 2013 a tour to the 1798 sites in east Antrim. The festival closed with a talk by the comedian Tim McGarry, a member of The Hole in the Wall Gang, which in 1998 had made the programme *1798—The Comedy*. McGarry was educated in St Malachy's College in Belfast, the oldest Catholic grammar school in Ulster, but also had Ulster-Scots ancestry which he was eager to explore.[231] Subsequently, McGarry and Hume collaborated in presenting the BBC radio series *The Long and The Short of It*, which investigated 'little-known Ulster Scots stories and well-known historical events from a new perspective'. An episode in the first series, broadcast in July 2014, was devoted to the 1798 Rebellion (focusing on the Presbyterian Ulster-Scots dimension), and an episode in the second series, broadcast in August 2015, was about Mary Ann McCracken (acknowledging her connections with the United Irishmen).[232]

A burgeoning provincial heritage industry picked up on popular interest in Ninety-Eight. Local festivals that were not directly associated with Ulster-Scots revivalism also came to incorporate related activities in their programmes. A Ballynahinch Harvest and Country Living Festival, sponsored by the Newry, Mourne, and Down District Council, was introduced in September 2014 and repeated two years later in 2016. The festival's events, held at the Montalto Estate and in the town's main square, featured re-enactments of skirmishes from the battle in 1798 and festival-goers were invited to interact with an actress impersonating the local heroine Betsy Gray.[233] The organizers of the festivities in Ballynahinch also arranged in June 2016 for a small-scale battle re-enactment in Antrim town, as part of an Irish Game Fair and Fine Food Festival sponsored by the Antrim and Newtownabbey Borough Council.[234]

In many cases, local commemorative initiatives renewed programmes from 1998. The Old Newry Society organized in 2010 a charity gala evening on the theme 'Beyond the Battle—Newry and the 1798 Rebellion', at which the local historian Anthony Russell gave a historical presentation which made use of materials that he had originally compiled for a bicentennial publication.[235] In these frameworks, living history was combined with educational activities. The Ballymoney Community Cohesion Project ran with the Ballymoney Museum in 2013 an educational programme on 1798 that included a visit to 'Humbert's Footsteps' in Killala, county Mayo, a colourful festival that commemorated the rebellion in the West of Ireland. Enthused by this experience, in June 2014, Ballymoney Borough Council sponsored a weekend of living history events. The programme, which was run in association with staff from the National 1798 Centre in Enniscorthy, included the handling of firearms from the period and demonstrations of how pikes were made by blacksmiths in preparation for the

[231] *Larne Times*, 4 September and 28 October 2013. For the festival's 2013 programme see <www.ulsterscotsagency.com/events/event/498/the-broadisland-gathering-ballycarry>.
[232] *Carrick Times*, 19 July 2014; *The Long and Short of It* (BBC Radio Ulster), series 1, episode 3 ('The 1798 Rebellion') and series 2, episode 6 ('Mary Ann McCracken').
[233] *Belfast Telegraph*, 20 and 24 September 2014; *Antrim Times*, 25 September 2014; *Ballymena Times*, 22 September 2014; *Down Recorder*, 6 May 2015; *Down News*, 28 September 2016; *Irish News*, 10 September 2016.
[234] *Ballymena Times*, 4 and 25 May 2016.
[235] *Newry Democrat*, 16 February 2010; *Newry Reporter*, 25 March 2010, p. 4.

rebellion, an experience that had been vividly recalled in local folk history traditions.[236] That year, the Down County Museum organized for the 2014 May bank holiday two days of living history events on the theme of 'Pikes and Prisoners' in 1798.[237]

New heritage trails in county Antrim continued a trend that had begun at the time of the bicentenary of identifying 1798 sites, which were subsequently marked around Antrim Town, Randalstown, Toome, Ballyclare, Ballynure, Doagh, and Mallusk.[238] In 2015, the pathways around the square in Gracehill were renamed 'The 1798 Walk' and it was decided to erect an obelisk inscribed with a local diary entry from 10 June 1798 in order to commemorate the part played by the Moravian settlement in the events of the time.[239] The revival of Ninety-Eight heritage also impacted Northern Ireland's provincial museums. Sentry Hill, the McKinney family house in the Antrim parish of Carnmoney, was purchased in 1997 by Newtownabbey Borough Council and in 2005 opened as 'the Province's newest, but oldest museum', going on to win in 2010 and again in 2014 the Sandford Award in recognition of the high quality of its educational programmes. Described as 'the most complete illumination anywhere of the life and broad-ranging interests of a middle-ranking Presbyterian farming family from the late 18th century almost to the present day', the exhibits at Sentry Hill showcase the collections of the nineteenth-century antiquarian William Fee McKinney, which include items from 1798, among them pikes and muskets used in the rebellion.[240] In Belfast, the Ulster Museum refreshed its modern history gallery in 2014. Several exhibits from 1798 that had been consigned to storage—including Henry Joy McCracken's sword and a lock of his hair, which had previously been preserved as a private souvenir—were put on display.[241]

In 2008, the Northern Ireland minister for Social Development Margaret Ritchie, an SDLP MP for South Down, unveiled four outdoor paintings of scenes from the history of the United Irishmen by the artist Michael O'Neill. These were exhibited on walls in the Cathedral Quarter's Four Corners, a regenerated historic area of Belfast in which the United Irishmen had previously met under the guise of the Muddler's Club.[242] Yet, despite growing awareness to the significance of 1798 heritage, Belfast city councillors had to put up a fight in 2015 against the decision of the Department of Environment to remove the protective listed status of Kelly's Cellars, an old pub which just a few years earlier, in 2007, was recognized with a blue plaque as a key meeting place of United Irishmen.[243]

---

[236] *Ballymoney Times*, 13 September 2013; 16 and 18 June 2014.

[237] *Down News*, 19 May 2014.

[238] *Antrim Borough Heritage Trails* (Antrim: Antrim Borough Council, 2007), pp. 8, 18, 19, and 25; *Mallusk Heritage Trail* (Mallusk Community Action Group, 2010), p. 3; *South Antrim Heritage Trail* (Newtownabbey Borough Council, n.d.), 4, 5, 7, 10, 14, and 16; see also guides for Ballyclare, Ballynure, and Doagh in the series *Heritage Walking Trails in Newtownabbey* (Newtownabbey Borough Council, n.d.).

[239] *Ballymena Times*, 25 May 2015.

[240] *BNL*, 1 April 1997, p. 11; *Irish Times*, 17 June 2000, p. 15; *BNL*, 11 August 2005; *Newtownabbey Times*, 25 April 2015; my thanks to custodian Wesley Bonar for facilitating a visit to Sentry Hill on 18 September 2011. For William McKinney's 1798 interests see Chapter 4 above, p. 326.

[241] *BNL*, 26 November 2014, p. 3.

[242] *BBC News*, 1 October 2008; *Daily Mirror*, 2 October 2008, p. 4 (Ulster edition).

[243] *Belfast Telegraph*, 20 February and 3 March 2015.

Apart from visual and material culture, renewed popular interest in remembrance of Ninety-Eight was also manifested in the performance arts. The Antrim Borough Council commissioned in 2010 an abridged adaptation of Jack Loudan's play *Henry Joy McCracken* that was produced through a collaboration of local amateur actors and the Centre Stage Theatre Company, which had previously staged Loudan's play for the bicentenary. The new shortened version—renamed *The Trial of Henry Joy McCracken*—was performed for the opening season of the Old Courthouse, a theatre located in Antrim town's Market Square. In 1798, McCracken had hoped to seize the courthouse building, in which a meeting of county magistrates assembled, and the failure of this half-baked scheme resulted in the inopportune killing of Lord O'Neill, an event which was deplored in loyalist memory. Hence, the 'atmospheric staged reading in period costume' that was performed at the newly renovated historic venue on 7 June 2010 was an evocative way of marking the anniversary of the Battle of Antrim.[244]

The Rough Magic Theatre Company went on tour in 2016 with a new production of Stewart Parker's *Northern Star*, which received rave reviews. It was directed—in the words of the *Irish Independent* critic—'with characteristic brio'—by Lynn Parker, a niece of the playwright who believed that his work 'has been horrendously ignored'. She had already made several attempts at grappling with the play—including an earlier production with Rough Magic in 1996 and a production with the students of the Lir academy in 2014—but felt that it was still 'unfinished business'. Significantly, the 2016 production coincided with the centenary of the Easter Rising and opened in April at the Project Arts Centre in Dublin, where the *Irish Times* observed that its 'chaotic riff on nationalism' had obvious 'resonances with contemporary commemorations of the 1916 Rising'. After a stopover in Glasgow, the play arrived in mid-May to Belfast's Lyric Theatre. Though more than three decades had passed since the *Northern Star* first premiered at the Lyric in 1984, Parker's historical drama—set in 'the continuous past'—had not lost its biting relevance. The *Irish News* found that its 'exploration of Henry Joy McCracken's attempt to square the eternal circle, and cycle, of conflict between Protestants and Catholics in a united Ireland is frighteningly topical'. For the reviewer of the *Guardian*, it seemed like the drama 'could have happened in Belfast last week'.[245]

Whereas new historical novels on the rebellion in Ulster had not been written for the bicentenary, this literary shortfall was redressed in subsequent years. Seán Ó Dúrois [John Dorrins], an Irish-language poet and author originally from England, published in 2003 *Rí na gCearrbhach* [King of the Gamblers], a sequel to his prize-winning novel *Crann Smola* [Tree Blight] from 2001. Set in mid-nineteenth-century Belfast, around 1860, the novel follows the adventures of a Protestant detective, William Watters, and his Catholic companion, Cameron, as they investigate an incident that turns out to be related to 1798. The setting implicitly shows that memories from the time of the rebellion continued to preoccupy the next generation after the events. However, the book's readership, regardless of its intriguing subject matter, was inevitably limited to

[244] *Antrim Times*, 1 April 2010; *Belfast Telegraph*, 29 May 2010, p. 30.
[245] *Irish Times*, 20 and 26 April 2016, pp. 12 and 7 (respectively); *Irish Independent*, 27 April 2016, p. 38; *Sunday Times*, 1 May 2016, p. 25; *Irish News*, 17 May 2016; *Belfast Telegraph*, 19 May 2016, p. 15; *Guardian*, 13 May 2016.

the small number of aficionados of detective fiction in the Irish language.[246] Conversely, a novel in English that was also set amid nineteenth-century recollections of the United Irishmen basked in the limelight. *The Mill for Grinding Old People Young* by Glenn Patterson, one of Northern Ireland's most popular contemporary writers, was selected in 2012 as the inaugural 'One City One Book' for Belfast. As such, the novel was vigorously promoted by the Arts Council of Northern Ireland, with copies distributed in cafés, bookshops, and bars, and was reviewed by the main Irish newspapers.[247]

In 2005, Patterson had organized an open letter of thirty writers in support of Gary Mitchell, when the playwright was hounded by loyalist paramilitaries for his outspokenness on issues that some Protestants would have preferred to have left forgotten.[248] Patterson's writing also became known for addressing sensitive issues from the past in order to re-assess northern Protestant identities. *The Mill for Grinding Old People Young* opens in Christmas 1897, on the eve of the centenary of 1798. Gilbert Rice, an 85-year-old distinguished Belfast industrialist, reminisces about his youth in the 1830s, when he was a clerk in the town's Ballast Office. Rice recalls his affair with a Polish barmaid, whose grandfather had visited Ireland and met Wolfe Tone. This romantic encounter unlocked clandestine recollections of 1798, which were extant in the early mid-nineteenth century but could only be talked about in whispers, or in confidential conversations.[249]

Patterson's protagonist is surprised to discover that his highly respected patron— whom he refers to as his grandfather, but who is actually a grand-uncle—had been associated with the United Irishmen and in private reveals to his ward that he is still troubled by disturbing memories. He confesses that he is unable to shake off the recollection of having seen a poor woman and her children searching in vain for her husband, who had been assassinated by United Irishmen under suspicion of being an informer. For present-day readers, this incident is unmistakably reminiscent of paramilitary murders during the Troubles that continue to upset life in post-conflict Northern Ireland. In particular, it is suggestive of the revelations that appeared in 2010 in *Voices from the Grave*—a book based on the controversial Boston College oral history tapes—regarding the disappearance in 1972 of Jean McConville, a widowed mother of ten who has been described as 'one of Belfast's stubborn ghosts'.[250]

The young Rice comes to realize that many of the prominent citizens of Belfast had been implicated in seditious activities in 1798 and, by accommodating to the new conditions of commercial prosperity under the Union, had repressed their recollections of revolutionary radicalism. In researching the novel, the author consulted a long list of local histories, including popular works of vernacular history, such as *McComb's Guide to Belfast* and Cathal O'Byrne's *As I Roved Out*, which allowed him to weave into the dialogues nuggets of folk memory that give a flavour of how Ninety-Eight was recalled locally.[251]

---

[246] Seán Ó Dúrois, *Ri na gCearrbhach* (Binn Éadair, Baile Átha Cliath [Howth, Dublin]: Coiscéim, 2003); see also Seán Ó Dúrois, *Crann Smola* (Baile Átha Cliath [Dublin]: Coiscéim, 2001).

[247] Glenn Patterson, *The Mill for Grinding Old People Young* (London: Faber and Faber, 2012); for reviews see *Irish Times*, 17 March 2012, p. 11 (Arts & Books supplement) and 2 April 2012, p. 12; *Irish Examiner*, 31 March 2012; *Independent*, 13 April 2012, p. 24; see also Caroline Magennis, 'Re-Writing Protestant History in the Novels of Glenn Patterson', *Irish Studies Review*, 23, no. 3 (2015), pp. 355–7.

[248] *Guardian*, 21 December 2005 p. 5.

[249] Patterson, *The Mill for Grinding Old People Young*, pp. 19–20, 120–2, and 127–8.

[250] Moloney, *Voices from the Grave*, pp. 128–9; *Telegraph*, 14 January 2012. For the Boston College oral history project see below, p. 612.

[251] Patterson, *The Mill for Grinding Old People Young*, pp. 213–17; for bibliographical sources see the 'Author's Note' on pp. 257–9.

Unlike Patterson's book, which was published by Faber and Faber and was primed for commercial success, other 1798 novels did not benefit from the marketing apparatus of a major publishing firm and languished unnoticed. Arthur Hamill, an Irish-American with mixed Catholic and Protestant Ulster ancestry wrote two novels about his paternal Ulster-Scot Presbyterian family in north Antrim, noting that 'the story is fiction, its genesis is a skeleton of fond memories, fleshed out by genealogical research and finally dressed in the clothing of history.' *A Place Called Tranquility*, which appeared in 2003, covered the late eighteenth century, culminating with the outbreak of the 1798 Rebellion. The sequel *Across the Saltwater Bridge,* which appeared in 2005, continues the narrative through the first half of the nineteenth century, following the consequences of the rebellion and eventual emigration. In recognition of their loyalty at the Battle of Antrim, the Hamills are mostly spared the ravages of the militia violence that terrorized the area after the rebel defeat.[252]

Hamill's second novel was written with help from the Ballyclare historian Archie Reid and the literary critic Patricia Craig, a resident of Antrim Town. Craig had read the prize-winning book *Rebellions* by the academic historian Tom Dunne about the history and memory of 1798 in Wexford and was inspired by its 'mixture of history and family history, autobiography and social comment'. She went on to explore her own hybrid family traditions.[253] Benefitting from the intimate knowledge of such local experts, Hamill's novels showed potential for arousing wider interest. But, as they were not distributed in bookshops and were not even available on loan at local libraries in Northern Ireland, these self-published books were passed by.

Another largely overlooked historical novel was published by Shepheard-Walwyn, an independent bookshop in South-West London. *Friend of Castlereagh* by John Alexander Stewart, an 82-year-old biographer and writer of historical fiction from Killinchy in county Down who had moved to London in 1950s, tells the story of 1798 through the fictional character of John Gray, a well-off tenant of Lord Castlereagh. Gray travels around Ireland, witnessing the insurrections in Wexford and Mayo, and encounters the consequences of the rebellion in Ulster during frequent visits to his home in Newtownards. Stewart made use of historical information, drawing in particular on a recently published biography of Castlereagh by John Bew, which he supplemented with local traditions that he recalled from growing up in the Ards. The Battle of Ballynahinch is described through the experience of a young Presbyterian rebel, Sam Shaw, who, thanks to Gray's intervention, narrowly escapes execution by court-martial. Although praised by Mark Bain, editor of the *Newtownards Chronicle*, for its 'great imagination' and 'great technique', the book's publication in 2013 did not attract much public attention.[254]

---

[252] Arthur R. Hamill, *A Place Called Tranquility: An Irish Story* (Bloomington, Ind.: AuthorHouse, 2003); Arthur R. Hamill, *Across the Saltwater Bridge* (Coral Springs, Fla.: Llumina Press, 2005); see also *Books Ireland*, no. 265 (March 2004): p. 66.

[253] Patricia Craig, 'To Scullabogue Backwards from Belfast: Against Sectarian Preconceptions', *Irish Pages*, 5, no. 2 (2008): pp. 134–52; Patricia Craig, *A Twisted Root: Ancestral Entanglements in Ireland* (Belfast: Blackstaff Press, 2012).

[254] John Stewart, *Friend of Castlereagh* (London: Shepheard-Walwyn, 2013); *Newtownards Chronicle*, 5 September 2013, p. 9. My thanks to Anthony Werner of Shepheard-Walwyn for supplementary information. For a main source of historical information see John Bew, *Castlereagh: Enlightenment, War and Tyranny* (London: Quercus, 2011).

By contrast, *The Star Man*, which was published in 2016 by Somerville Press—a relatively small publisher based near Bantry in West Cork—benefitted from high-profile publicity, which was at least partly due to the well-placed contacts of the author—Conor O'Clery, a distinguished journalist at the *Irish Times*. O'Clery was born in Belfast and grew up in Newcastle, county Down. As a youth, he had followed the *Mourne Observer's* serialization of Lyttle's *Betsy Gray* (1967–8), which left him with a life-long fascination with the local heroine and the rebellion in Ulster. He later recalled that, at the time:

> I had known little about the Battle of Ballynahinch, though I lived a few miles away. It wasn't commemorated locally, by either side. It was as if this bit of Irish history was too dangerous and contradictory to be disturbed.

Subsequently, he contemplated the conundrum at the heart of social forgetting, in an effort to fathom how the 'summer soldiers' of 1798 became 'the ancestors of today's Orangemen and unionists'.[255] In 1982, O'Clery published in the *Irish Times* an article on the Battle of Ballynahinch, which made use of the accounts of local traditions that had been sent to the *Mourne Observer* in response to the reprint of *Betsy Gray*, and pointed out that although the descendants of the Presbyterian rebels had become loyalists, 'pride in the exploits of Monroe and Betsy Gray and the Hearts of Down remains'.[256]

Covering the rebellion as it would have been seen by a contemporary newspaper man, *The Star Man* tells 'the true story of Willie Kean, journalist and rebel'. The historical Kean, a former clerk at the offices of the United Irish organ the *Northern Star*, had participated in the Battle of Ballynahinch and was arrested alongside Henry Munro. His name briefly gained fame after he escaped from Belfast's Provost prison on 2 July 1798, in consequence of which a general search was held and Colonel James Durham issued a proclamation warning that the house of anybody caught assisting him in his concealment 'will be burned and the owner thereof hanged'.[257] O'Clery considerably embellished Kean's character, adding an unrequited infatuation with Betsy Gray.[258]

The novel was acclaimed by Patricia Craig in the *Irish Times* as a 'deft blend of fact and fiction' and a reviewer in the *Sunday Times* praised it as 'sparkling history' that offers 'a vibrant mixture of the frolicsome and the horrific, leaving you with a feeling you've been dancing among the skulls'. The *Belfast Telegraph* got carried away and compared O'Clery's style to that of Ernest Hemingway.[259] The author promised a 'ripping yarn', unwittingly repeating praise that had been heaped on Lyttle's *Betsy Gray*, which a few years earlier had been described by the Ulster-Scots publisher Derek Rowlinson as 'a ripping good yarn, full of intrigue and incident' and 'an excellent way to acquaint yourself with the social history of the area and how folk spoke there not so very long ago'.[260] Yet unlike Lyttle's romantic novel, which was perfectly suited to

---

[255] *Irish News*, 8 September 2016; *Irish Times*, 9 September 2016.

[256] *Irish Times*, 10 August 1982, p. 10.

[257] *BNL*, 3 July 1798, p. 3; George Stephenson, Hillsborough, to Lord Downshire, 4 July 1798, Downshire Papers, PRONI D607/F/299. See also Madden, *The United Irishmen*, 3rd ser., vol. 1 (1846), pp. 390–1; Dickson, *Revolt in the North*, pp. 114, 154–5, and 200.

[258] Conor O'Clery, *The Star Man: The True Story of Willie Kean, Journalist and Rebel* (Dromore, Co. Bantry: Somerville Press, 2016).

[259] *Sunday Times*, 25 September 2016, p. 38; *Irish Times*, 10 October 2016; *Belfast Telegraph* 25 October 2016; see also David McConnell, 'A Brief Dream', *Dublin Review of Books*, no. 82 (2016); <www.drb.ie/essays/a-brief-dream>.

[260] *Mourne Observer*, 22 October 2008.

the sensibilities of its Victorian provincial readership, O'Clery's narrative lacks the literary creativity that can be expected of a modern-day novel and pales in comparison with some of the works of earlier authors who had wrestled with social forgetting and found inspirational ways to present Ninety-Eight to the readerships of their day.

O'Clery seems to have been oblivious to the appearance of his main character in earlier works of historical fiction. Kean had already featured in the first historical novel on 1798 in Ulster, Adam Douglass's *The Irish Emigrant* (1817). He was also a minor character in Sam Hanna Bell's novel *A Man Flourishing*, which thoughtfully reflected on the ambiguities of the rebellion, rather than just laud it in heroic terms. In Bell's irreverent adaptation, the protagonist James Gault goes into hiding with the fugitive Kean and learns that, like himself, Kean had joined the rebels but did not actually see action, leaving the reader with a healthy scepticism of received history.[261] It remains to be seen if *The Star Man*, despite its aesthetic simplicity and unsophisticated use of vernacular history, will appeal to twenty-first-century readers and impact social memory.

Rediscovered literary works from the past continue to fascinate readers. In 2006, Four Courts Press—a publisher of Irish academic books with a popular interest— issued a new annotated edition of *Ninety-Eight and Sixty Years After* by Andrew James (pseudonym of James Andrew Strahan), which since its original publication a century earlier had fallen into obscurity. Inexplicably, the editor of the new edition—the cultural historian and literary critic John Wilson Foster—took the liberty of changing the title of this work of vernacular literature and renaming it *The Nabob: A Tale of Ninety-Eight*, setting a precedent that would not have been acceptable for contemporary literary works by more-established authors, such as James Joyce's *Dubliners* (which dates back to around the same time). The Mid-Antrim Historical Group had previously republished this remarkable collection of short stories for the bicentenary, in order to facilitate 'critical evaluation', but the distribution of their crudely printed booklet was mostly confined to local history enthusiasts from the area. The book's re-issue in 2006 in a handsome new edition was made possible by the Ulster-Scots revival, which found interest in its use of vernacular dialect (elucidated in a glossary) as well as its reworking of local traditions. Foster stressed the ongoing relevance of the historical novel, which 'cautions us to see the violence and hatred as in remission', suggesting that they are 'not necessarily cured'.[262]

Books Ulster—an online antiquarian bookstore specializing in rare Irish books, established in 1997 in Bangor, county Down—published a new edition of Lyttle's *Betsy Gray* in 2015 which was issued both in print and electronic form. Realizing that 'in recent times copies of the book have been notably hard to find at a reasonable price', Derek Rowlinson of Books Ulster (who had previously been involved in the issue of the 2008 edition by Ullans Press) admitted that he 'was particularly keen to put this title back in print'. The author's great-grandson, A. G. Lyttle, expressed his delight that the re-publication of *Betsy Gray*, alongside other works by W. G. Lyttle, had made it possible

---

[261] An Hibernian [Adam Douglass], *The Irish Emigrant*, vol. 2, pp. 129–32 and 193–9; Sam Hanna Bell, *A Man Flourishing* (Belfast: Blackstaff, 1986; orig. edn 1973), pp. 22–51. For discussion of these novels see above, pp. 188–9 (Douglass) and 521–2 (Bell).

[262] Andrew James, *The Nabob: A Tale of Ninety-Eight*, Notes and Afterword by John Wilson Foster (Dublin: Four Courts Press, 2006); Andrew James, *Ninety-Eight and Sixty Years After* (Ballymena: Mid-Antrim Historical Group, 1998). See also Rory Brennan, 'Troublesome Fictions', *Books Ireland*, no. 291 (2007): pp. 16–17; *Canadian Journal of Irish Studies*, 32, no. 1 (2006): pp. 82–3. For the original edition see Chapter 5 above, pp. 405–7.

'for today's generation to discover the timeless charm of the fireside tale and the quaint dialect of the true Hearts of Down'. The newspaper of the Ulster-Scots Agency could proclaim with satisfaction that 'the legend of Betsy Gray simply refuses to die.'[263]

Popular interest of nationalists in historical materials has been catered for through the *Irish News* column 'On This Day', in which the historian Eamonn Phoenix regularly reproduces items from the newspaper's archives. What might seem like the regurgitation of old news amounts in effect to a thoughtful excavation of neglected sources for vernacular historiography. Many of the pieces selected for republication relate to the United Irishmen and Ninety-Eight. These reprints include articles by Cathal O'Byrne that were originally published in the 1940s and which already then had recycled local traditions previously collected by Bigger.[264] Whereas the writings of O'Byrne could also be found in his popular book *As I Roved Out*, most recently republished in 2000, Phoenix also republished more obscure articles by the local historian Colin Johnston Robb that were written around the same time. Robb's outstanding knowledge of 1798 traditions had been widely acknowledged in his lifetime but his reputation had since been forgotten.[265]

In 2004, Cathal O'Byrne was honoured by the Ulster Historical Circle with a blue plaque, unveiled by Phoenix, at the site of his former house in Belfast's Cavendish Street.[266] A few years later, in 2011, Francis Joseph Bigger was recognized as an 'Antiquary and Celtic Revivalist' on a blue plaque in Ballyvesey (near Newtownabbey), placed outside the Crown and Shamrock, which he had established in 1901 as a model roadside tavern for an Ulster Public House Association.[267] A blue plaque was erected in 2013 in Bangor for Wesley Greenhill Lyttle, who was recognized as a 'Writer and Entertainer', without specifically mentioning his most popular bestseller *Betsy Gray*.[268] This public recognition of major contributors to vernacular historiography tactfully elided explicit reference to the obsession with the memory of the United Irishmen that they had all shared. Acknowledgement was partial, leaving out key figures, such as Colin Johnston Robb, who remain neglected.

Though often seen as a lost preoccupation, antiquarian-style recounting of history, based on the collecting and publishing of local traditions, is still alive and thriving. The renewal of this practice is exemplified in the work of Joseph (Joe) Graham—self-dubbed 'The Belfast History Man'—whose publication *Rushlight* presents a cornucopia of Belfast local history 'warts and all', deliberately following the example of Cathal

---

[263] W. G. Lyttle, *Betsy Gray or Hearts of Down: A Tale of Ninety-Eight* (Bangor: Books Ulster, 2015); *Ulster-Scot*, 11 July 2015, p. 3.

[264] See *Irish News*, 7 June 2005, p. 23; 24 October 2008, p. 22; 6 August 2011, p. 15; 20 January, 31 March, 18 April, and 4 December 2012, pp. 19, 19, 17, and 17 (respectively); 20 April and 7 May 2013, pp. 21 and 17 (respectively); 14 November 2015, p. 19.

[265] See *Irish News*, 3 June 2006, p. 22; 5 April 2008, p. 20; 13 July and 19 December 2009, pp. 22 and 20 (respectively); p. 20; 18 June 2011, p. 15; 20 January and 16 June 2012, pp. 19 and 17 (respectively); 9 April, 7 and 24 June, and 20 November 2014, pp. 19, 24, and 17 (respectively); 22 September and 20 October 2015, pp. 19 and 21 (respectively). Cf. Cathal O'Byrne, *As I Roved Out: A Book of The North, Being a Series of Historical Sketches of Ulster and Old Belfast*, facsimile of 3rd edn (Belfast: Lagan Books, 2000; orig. edn 1946).

[266] *Irish News*, 18 October 2004, p. 7; *An Phoblacht*, 28 October 2004; see also Kirkland, *Cathal O'Byrne and the Northern Revival*, pp. 222–3.

[267] 'Blue Plaque for Francis Joseph Bigger—13 May 2011'; <www.ulsterhistory.co.uk/130511.html>. See also *Belfast Telegraph*, 16 February and 20 August 2016.

[268] 'Blue Plaque for W. G. Lyttle—17 December 2013'; <www.ulsterhistory.co.uk/171213.html>.

O'Byrne, whose writings Graham has hailed as the 'Bible of Belfast'. Graham grew up in the nationalist area of Ballymurphy in west Belfast, where he was raised on the stories of his father, who had a particular interest in traditions of 1798 and claimed kinship with the executed United Irish hero Walter (Watty) Graham of Maghera. In the early years of the Troubles, he edited and published several community-based republican magazines, namely *Ardoyne Freedom Fighter* (in a Catholic area of north Belfast), *The Vindicator* (in the lower Falls Road area of Clonard), *Scale* (in Ballymurphy), and *The Pike* (covering all of west Belfast), before establishing in 1972 *Rushlight*, which was named after the short-lived radical magazine published in 1824–5 by Luke Mullan Hope, the son of James Hope.[269]

Graham's *Rushlight*, which evolved into an online publication, has been widely recognized as an indispensable resource for the history of Belfast, and is consulted not only by nationalists. When searching for source materials for his historical novel, Glenn Patterson found that no other website is 'more eclectic or consistently informative'.[270] In an oration delivered at the grave of Henry Joy McCracken on 28 August 2011, Graham declared: 'Who fears to speak of '98...not I' and professed his commitment 'to speak and to proudly herald the events of 1798'. Accordingly, *Rushlight* features many items on Ninety-Eight, including the online re-publication of the autobiographical memoir of James Hope as taken down by Madden, offering open access to a key primary source for vernacular historiography.[271]

The sheer range of activities that have commemorated the 1798 rebellion in Ulster during the first decade and a half of the new millennium gives the impression that, despite setbacks, the rediscovery of memory initiated in the bicentenary had been successfully completed and the inhibitions of social forgetting have been finally overcome. Such an elusive notion of 'post-forgetting' is as nebulous as that of the wider concept of 'post-conflict'. Having devised political mechanisms to manage the conflict through consociational power sharing arrangements, reconciliation in Northern Ireland continues to stumble on the difficult issue of 'dealing with past'. Attention has focused on the memory of the recent Troubles, yet there are deeper memories lurking in the background, with recalcitrant undercurrents that surface in unexpected moments.

On 24 March 2014, a blue plaque for James (Jemmy) Hope was unveiled in Mallusk cemetery by Blanche McMordie, a direct descendant. Unlike another plaque erected that year in Carrickfergus for the mathematician Robert Adrain, which made no reference to his membership in the United Irishmen and participation in the rebellion, Hope was explicitly identified as a United Irishman and 'A Man of No Property'. The ceremony was attended by the UUP Mayor of Newtownabbey, Fraser Agnew, and representatives of the Ulster-Scots Agency, as well as local residents.[272] Within less than a month, the plaque was smashed (Fig. 7.5). Of more than 170 blue circle plaques erected over thirty years in Northern Ireland, this was apparently the first case of deliberate damage. The chairman of the Ulster Historical Circle, Chris Spurr,

[269] <www.rushlightmagazine.com>; see also Kirkland, *Cathal O'Byrne and the Northern Revival in Ireland*, pp. 199 and 222; Joe Graham, *Belfast Born, Bred And Buttered* (Belfast: Rushlight Publications, 2015).
[270] Patterson, *The Mill for Grinding Old People Young*, p. 259.
[271] <http://belfasthistory.rushlightmagazine.com/HenryJoyMcCracken.html>; <http://thejimmyhopestory.rushlightmagazine.com/>.
[272] *Irish News*, 25 March 2014, p. 13; *Newtownabbey Times*, 30 March 2014; see also 'Blue Plaque for Jemmy Hope—24 March 2014' (2014); <www.ulsterhistory.co.uk/240314.html>.

(a)

(b)

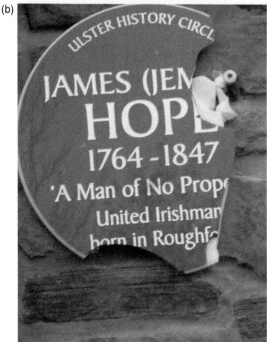

Fig. 7.5. Commemorating and decommemorating James Hope

(a) Chris Spurr (Chairman of the Ulster History Circle), Blanche Mordie (a direct descendant), and UUP Alderman Fraser Agnew (Mayor of Newtownabbey) at the unveiling of a blue plaque for James (Jemmy) Hope at Mallusk on 24 March 2014. (b) Within less than a month the plaque was smashed.

Photographs courtesy of the *Belfast News-Letter*.

condemned the vandalism as a 'form of censorship'. Yet, when asked for his thoughts on who might have been behind the act, Spurr could only speculate vaguely that 'it may be a hate crime', which 'had some kind of misguided sectarian motivation'. SDLP councillor Noreen McClelland branded the destruction 'pure vandalism' and Alderman Agnew maintained that it 'shows how much we have to do to educate the people who did this, to challenge their ignorance of their history and heritage'.[273] The attribution of this deliberate act of iconoclasm to mindless 'ignoramuses' failed to register that it falls within a tradition of decommemorating, which had long enforced silencing of Ninety-Eight in Ulster. Evidently, social forgetting, and its characteristic aversion to remembrance in public, had not been entirely dispelled. Indeed, once it has taken root, and after it has been repeatedly regenerated, social forgetting remains a historical factor to be reckoned with.

[273] *BNL*, 25 April 2014; *Belfast Telegraph*, 25 April 2014; *Newtownabbey Times*, 1 May 2014.

Conclusion

Rites of Oblivion

Life cannot go on without a great deal of forgetting.

Honoré de Balzac, *Cousin Bette*[1]

Blessed are the forgetful: for they 'will have done' with their stupidities too.

Friedrich Nietzsche, *Beyond Good and Evil*[2]

Is it at all possible to still talk of forgetting when, under scrutiny, it turns out that there are thousands of sources for a vernacular historiography of the 1798 rebellion in Ulster? The answer to this riddle requires a sharpening of the distinctions, which run like a thread through this study, between social forgetting and social, cultural, and collective memory. Forgetting, as the anthropologist Mary Douglas astutely pointed out, 'includes different kinds of selective remembering, misremembering and disremembering'.[3] In order to understand why these obscured forms of remembrance are often unnoticed, we must first return to the difference between *History* and *histories*, raised in the beginning of the introductory chapter, and home in on the neglected role of vernacular historiography as a key to the study of social forgetting.

Cyril Falls, in his 1936 classic *The Birth of Ulster*, referred to Antrim and Down in 1798 as 'practically untouched', a preposterous description, which is reminiscent of the *Hitchhiker's Guide to the Galaxy*'s definition of earth as 'mostly harmless'. Nevertheless, *The Birth of Ulster* retained its popularity over time. It was republished in 1973, and reappeared in 1996 in a new edition, which was issued in paperback in 1998. The neglect of Ninety-Eight remained uncorrected.[4] The bicentenary of the rebellion stimulated a publishing boom that produced an outpouring of 'Ninety-Eight Studies', in which Ian McBride found a 'startling omission' of references to the vernacular

---

[1] '*La vie ne va pas sans de grands oublis!*'; Honoré de Balzac, *La Cousine Bette* (Bruxelles: Melines, 1847), tome 3, p. 289. For an English translation by Sylvia Raphael see Honoré de Balzac, *Cousin Bette* (Oxford and New York: Oxford University Press, 1998), p. 460.

[2] 'Selig sind die Vergesslichen: denn sie werden auch mit ihren Dummheiten "fertig"'; F. W. Nietzsche, *Jenseits von Gut und Böse: Vorspiel einer Philosophie der Zukunft* (Leipzig: Druck und Verlag von C. G. Naumann, 1886), p. 163; translated by Judith Norman in Friedrich Wilhelm Nietzsche, *Beyond Good and Evil: Prelude to a Philosophy of the Future* (Cambridge and New York: Cambridge University Press, 2002), p. 110.

[3] Mary Douglas, 'Forgotten Knowledge', in *Shifting Contexts: Transformations in Anthropological Knowledge*, edited by Marilyn Strathern (London and New York: Routledge, 1995), p. 13.

[4] Cyril Falls, *The Birth of Ulster* (London: Constable, 1998; orig. edn 1936), p. 243.

historiography of the Turn-Out in Antrim and Down.[5] A decade and a half later, it was still possible for twenty leading experts to collaborate on an authoritative history of Ulster in which 1798 is covered in only two sentences and its legacy is left unmentioned, apart from an incidental comment noting that the United Irishman William Drennan later adapted his radical politics into a liberal civic unionism.[6]

This inattention is no mere oversight; it has a long history. The disregard shown by prominent historians for the northern arena of the rebellion—as opposed to the obsession with the rebellion in Wexford—was first advanced by Richard Musgrave immediately after the events and was widely shared by his contemporaries, even by his critics. For the most part, Musgrave's 'matrix of oblivion' retained its hold in subsequent historiography. Folk histories told a different story, but this was of little concern to those who wrote *History*.

By condescending to provincial vernacular history, academic historians buttress hierarchies of knowledge that marginalize popular traditions and berate them as 'myths'. Such traditions are not necessarily 'popular', in the sense of generally liked. Open remembrance of traditions that do not correspond to prevailing attitudes often incurs hostility. Silencing of unpopular voices can be enforced from above, by the establishment, as well as from below, by vigilantes. Sometimes, silencing is enforced from within, by members of the community who voluntarily safeguard taboos by holding their tongues when speaking in public. Such a culture of reticence, in which little is said out loud about controversial topics, does not signify that memory has been completely effaced. There is more to public forgetting than meets the eye.

It is commonplace to hear statements boldly asserting that 1798 was forgotten by the Presbyterians of Ulster, even though it is apparent that preoccupation with the memory of the rebellion never ceased (in fact, the very labelling of the event as 'forgotten' is in itself an indication that it is still recalled). This telling cognitive dissonance is the outcome of social forgetting, which upholds a façade of silence behind which recollections can be retained. Social forgetting is sustained by tensions between perceived public oblivion and muted remembrance in more private spheres. It is born out of anxieties, some of which preceded the events being remembered. Schemata of pre-forgetting, as in the clandestine commemorative traditions of the republican proto-martyr William Orr—a United Irishman who was executed before 1798—generates apprehensive remembrance, which, from the outset, is concerned that, without proper recognition, episodes may be forgotten. Inability to accommodate oppositional voices and to facilitate reconciliation, as in the curtailing of amnesty after the 1798 rebellion, pushes resentful memories underground. Practices of social forgetting offer a frame-work through which these counter-memories, which have been excluded from the public sphere, can be imperceptibly maintained.

Members of the generation who were obliged to keep quiet about their first-hand recollections of awkward historical events can experience 'postmemory angst'. In the twilight of their lives, some of them may feel an urge to break their silence, in order to get the record straight for posterity. At the same time, traditions of social forgetting can

---

[5] Ian McBride, 'Reclaiming the Rebellion: 1798 in 1998', *Irish Historical Studies*, 31, no. 123 (1999): pp. 395–410.

[6] Liam Kennedy and Philip Ollerenshaw, eds, *Ulster since 1600: Politics, Economy, and Society* (Oxford: Oxford University Press, 2013), pp. 41 and 231.

be regenerated and passed on from one generation to another, reinforcing reticence. The inbuilt ambiguity of disturbing memories that cannot be fully acknowledged has a particular fascination, which keeps them alive behind closed doors, or cloaked in veils of euphemism and obscuration.

If and when subversive memorial traditions, which were preserved discreetly, finally emerge into the open, this can result in a backlash of decommemorating that is intent on driving displays of social remembrance out of the public sphere, as in the violent reactions to the centenary celebrations of 1798 in Ulster. Such assaults can motivate re-commemorating, through which cultural revivalists—such as F. J. Bigger—return to claim for marginalized memories their rightful place under the sun. Yet, once enthusiasm for commemoration wanes, social frameworks of forgetting can be restored and silencing may return to inhibit public remembrance. This was the case after partition, when the memory of the United Irishmen did not suit the official ethos of Northern Ireland as a unionist state and public remembrance of 1798 was discouraged. We are therefore presented with a cycle of decommemorating, re-commemorating, and restored forgetting.

Social forgetting is a subtle form of remembrance, which creates ambivalent and multi-layered cultural memories. In themselves, representations of cultural memory are no guarantee for social remembrance. Just as neglected memorials that have ceased to accommodate commemoration no longer function as active sites of memory, a book that recalls an historical episode, but fails to attract the attention of readers, does not in effect facilitate remembrance. Some of the more obscure publications written about Ninety-Eight made little impact, while others were devoured. To a large degree, popular reception depended on how texts related to familiar traditions that were preserved underground, as in the remarkable success of W. G. Lyttle's best-selling novel *Betsy Gray*, which was essentially a literary reworking of folk history. These counter-memories can be widely shared, but they have no place in official collective memory. Therefore, this is not a history of monuments and when monuments are constructed, as in the case of the memorial for Betsy Gray in Ballycreen, they are soon targeted for decommemorating. When political conditions change, memorial traditions can be reclaimed and exhibited in public. It may then seem that forgetting has been conclusively overcome, as in the impression given by the widespread commemorations of the bicentenary of 1798. Social forgetting, however, proves to be tenacious and may just be biding its time, while waiting in the doldrums to make a comeback.

The history of these dynamics of generating, repressing, and regenerating social forgetting has been mostly missed by conventional historiography. As this study has shown for Ulster, attention to vernacular historiography presents another way of looking at history. This reconfiguration does not necessarily undermine the standard chronology and periodization of *History*, but it reprioritizes the focus of historical inquiry and broadens its scope. *Politics*—with a capital 'p' (in the sense of high politics)—is not the focus of attention, and, once removed from the centre stage, becomes a context for examining inconspicuous contestations that are found in everyday social and cultural activities. As an historiographical alternative, *lethehistory*—i.e. the history of social forgetting—follows how the past was perceived through the prism of less-noticeable memorial practices. Recognition of these traditions can contribute to a better understanding of some of the burning problems facing post-conflict Northern Ireland.

DEALING WITH THE PAST

Douglas Hyde cautioned in his manifesto for the Gaelic Revival—'The Necessity of De-Anglicising Ireland'—that 'Irishmen are sometimes prone to overstating as well as to forgetting.'[7] It is surprising how long forgetting has been neglected as a topic in Irish Studies, given its pervasiveness in literature and history. An Irish intellectual history of commentary on forgetting would nicely complement *Lethe*, Harald Weinrich's masterly survey of 'The Art and Critique of Forgetting'.

An alleged Irish propensity to muddle remembering and forgetting has become a cliché, if not a national stereotype. One of the reports on the centennial riots in Belfast in 1898 casually mentioned that Irishmen were disposed to 'forgetting everything they ought to remember and remembering everything they ought to forget'.[8] More than a half-century later, George Bernard Shaw, at the age of 93, wrote a short piece on 'The Wrong Sort of Memory' for the preface of his *Far-Fetched Tales*, in which he suggested that this anomaly may have political consequences, as 'on the whole the people who remember everything they ought to forget are, if given any authority, more dangerous than those who forget some things they had better remember.'[9]

The Anglo-Irish conflict has been described in terms of selective memory. The politician and agricultural reformer Sir Horace Plunkett opined that 'Anglo-Irish history is for Englishmen to remember, for Irishmen to forget.'[10] Whether or not this division of labour was followed through is another matter. A popular variant of the cliché on the peculiarity of Irish memory, which can be traced to the historian G. M. Young, and has also been attributed to the dean of Saint Paul's Cathedral William Ralph Inge, claims that 'the English never remember, and the Irish never forget.'[11] To this adage the Belfast-born Canadian author Derek Lundy—a descendant of the United Irish Presbyterian minister Rev. William Steel Dickson—helpfully suggested that 'we should insert the words "some things" after "remember" and "forget"', since 'forgetting is as necessary as remembering for a people to create a mythology of itself.'[12] The need to strike a balance between selective remembering and forgetting emerged as a main concern in post-conflict Northern Ireland.

In brokering the Good Friday Agreement, the British Prime Minister Tony Blair expressed the hope that 'now we can try to put our histories behind us, try to forgive and forget those old enmities.'[13] It was soon evident that the memories of the recent conflict could not be dismissed and that, to a large degree, the peace process depended on confronting the past. Blair established in 1998 the Bloody Sunday Inquiry, chaired

---

[7] Douglas Hyde, 'The Necessity of De-Anglicising Ireland', in *The Revival of Irish Literature*, edited by Charles Gavan Duffy et al. (London: T. Fisher Unwin, 1894), p. 125.

[8] *Irish News*, 9 June 1898, p. 8.

[9] George Bernard Shaw, *Buoyant Billions, Farfetched Fables, & Shakes Versus Shav* (London: Constable and Company, 1950), p. 94.

[10] Horace Curzon Plunkett, *Ireland in the New Century* (London: John Murray, 1904), p. 26.

[11] Young wrote 'what we could never remember, Ireland could never forget'; G. M. Young, *Victorian England: Portrait of an Age* (London and New York: Oxford University Press, 1936), p. 186; Dean Inge reputedly 'pointed out how difficult is the common government of a nation which never remembers and one which never forgets'; Shaw, *Buoyant Billions*, p. 94.

[12] Lundy, *Men That God Made Mad*, p. 14.

[13] *Guardian*, 27 November 1998, p. 11.

by Lord Saville of Newdigate, which, at the incredible cost of over 200 million pounds, took twelve years to produce a ten-volume report on the events of 30 January 1972, when British paratroopers opened fire on a civil rights demonstration in Derry. An official apology of sorts, issued by Prime Minister David Cameron on 15 June 2010, was intended to bring definitive closure to what had become a traumatic cornerstone of Catholic nationalist memory.[14] But remembrance did not come to an end and claims for historical restorative justice have not ceased.

Sir Kenneth Bloomfield, the Northern Ireland Victims Commissioner and former head of the civil service in Northern Ireland, produced in April 1998 a report titled *We Will Remember Them*, which thoughtfully contemplated the difficulties of remembering the Troubles in a deeply divided society. Bloomfield recognized that 'there is, in a sense, some substance in the argument that no-one living in Northern Ireland through this most unhappy period of its history will have escaped some degree of damage.' With this in mind, he recommended the erection of an inclusive 'central Northern Ireland memorial', as well the designation of an ecumenical 'Memorial and Reconciliation Day'.[15] The implementation of such generosity of spirit proved to be impractical. Irreconcilable disagreements on the identity of victims and perpetrators reinforced partisan 'hierarchies of pain and responsibility' that deny from others the right to speak out openly about their painful memories and to commemorate their loved ones.[16] Attempts to accommodate public remembering ran up against the recalcitrance of social forgetting.

Nationalist and loyalist communities erected their own separate memorials, which, through a 'process of appropriation and repudiation', purposely excluded sensitive subjects. Elisabetta Viggiani's study of post-conflict memorialization noted that 'there is no mention on memorial stones of the pain and death they [paramilitary organizations] inflicted on "the other side", intragroup assassinations or civilian deaths, accidentally caused within one's own community go unacknowledged.'[17] These embarrassing issues, which punctured self-gratifying communal narratives of valour and resilience, were to be forgotten; or, to be more precise, were to be recalled through social forgetting, as the bereaved families of the victims of such acts of violence were left to mourn in the privacy of their homes.

---

[14] Ann Rigney, 'Do Apologies End Events? Bloody Sunday, 1972–2010', in *Afterlife of Events: Perspectives on Mnemohistory*, edited by Marek Tamm (Houndmills: Palgrave Macmillan, 2015), pp. 242–61; Nevin T. Aiken, 'The Bloody Sunday Inquiry: Transitional Justice and Postconflict Reconciliation in Northern Ireland', *Journal of Human Rights*, 14, no. 1 (January 2015): pp. 101–23. For the development of social remembrance prior to Cameron's statement of apology see Brian Conway, *Commemoration and Bloody Sunday: Pathways of Memory* (Basingstoke and New York: Palgrave Macmillan, 2010).

[15] Kenneth Bloomfield, *We Will Remember Them* (Belfast: Northern Ireland Office, 1998), pp. 14 and 43–8 (articles 2.13 and 6.9 to 7.18); see also Kenneth Bloomfield, 'How Should We Remember? The Work of the Northern Ireland Victims Commission', in *Past Imperfect: Dealing with the Past in Northern Ireland and Societies in Transition*, edited by Brandon Hamber (Derry/Londonderry: INCORE/University of Ulster, 1998), pp. 50–5.

[16] Marie Smyth, 'Remembering in Northern Ireland: Victims, Perpetrators and Hierarchies of Pain and Responsibility', in Hamber, *Past Imperfect*, pp. 31–49.

[17] Elisabetta Viggiani, *Talking Stones: The Politics of Memorialization in Post-Conflict Northern Ireland* (New York and Oxford: Berghahn, 2014), pp. 77–9. For monuments erected during the years of the Troubles see Jane Leonard, *Memorials to the Casualties of Conflict: Northern Ireland, 1969 to 1997* (Belfast: Northern Ireland Community Relations Council, 1997).

Among the members of the public with whom Bloomfield consulted, there were those who 'argued strongly' for the establishment of a truth and reconciliation commission, which would bring out into the open disturbing memories that had previously been hushed.[18] The advocates of the transitional justice model of truth and reconciliation—which is most commonly associated with post-Apartheid South Africa, but has also been tried out in numerous other countries in Africa, Latin America, Asia, and even in Europe and Canada—often fail to notice its shortcomings, not least that 'truth commissions perpetuate silences just as frequently as they provide a forum for narrative.'[19] In any case, initiatives to introduce such a commission met with resistance in Northern Ireland, where it was seen, at least by some, to be 'too deep, too threatening'.[20] Unionists, in particular, have treated proposals for 'truth-telling' with marked distrust and, in the absence of agreement on an acceptable mechanism for truth and reconciliation, have made it clear that they would rather keep—as put by Kirk Simpson—their social memory 'locked in "cold storage"'.[21]

Since it is clearly not possible to conduct investigations on a similar scale to the Bloody Sunday Inquiry for the many other historical grievances that continue to unsettle the memory of the Troubles, 'truth recovery' was controversially delegated to the police. In 2005, a Historical Enquiries Team (HET) was set up as a special unit of the Police Service of Northern Ireland (PSNI) and was assigned responsibility for re-examining deaths from the time of the Troubles in order to provide answers to the unresolved questions of the victims' families. After an investigation report in 2013 found 'serious shortcomings' in the unit's work, the HET was replaced with a Legacy Investigation Branch, which has also come under criticism.[22] Although flaunted as an innovative 'home-grown' solution for transitional justice, the narrow brief of police investigations offers very limited scope for collecting 'hidden' narratives. Many people are reluctant to share their personal recollections with the law enforcement authorities.

The voices of victims have found outlets in support groups that receive funding from the state, as well as from the European Union. According to a report compiled in 2010 by the Northern Ireland Commission for Victims and Survivors, 'the victims and survivors sector has received in excess of £80 million since the signing of the Good

---

[18] Bloomfield, *We Will Remember Them*, pp. 37–8 (articles 5.36–5.37).

[19] Bill Rolston, 'Dealing with the Past: Pro-State Paramilitaries, Truth and Transition in Northern Ireland', *Human Rights Quarterly*, 28, no. 3 (August 2006), pp. 656–7.

[20] Brandon Hamber and Gráinne Kelly, 'Too Deep, Too Threatening', in *Assessing the Impact of Transitional Justice: Challenges for Empirical Research*, edited by Hugo van der Merwe, Victoria Baxter and Audrey R. Chapman (Washington D.C.: United States Institute of Peace Press, 2009), pp. 265–93.

[21] Kirk Simpson, *Unionist Voices and the Politics of Remembering the Past in Northern Ireland* (Houndmills and New York: Palgrave Macmillan, 2009), pp. 115–38; see also Patricia Lundy and Mark McGovern, 'A Trojan Horse? Unionism, Trust and Truth-Telling in Northern Ireland', *International Journal of Transitional Justice*, 2, no. 1 (2008): pp. 42–62; Cheryl Lawther, 'Denial, Silence and the Politics of the Past: Unpicking the Opposition to Truth Recovery in Northern Ireland', *International Journal of Transitional Justice*, 7, no. 1 (March 2013): pp. 157–77.

[22] Patricia Lundy, 'Exploring Home-Grown Transitional Justice and Its Dilemmas: A Case Study of the Historical Enquiries Team, Northern Ireland', *International Journal of Transitional Justice*, 3, no. 3 (August 2009): pp. 321–40; Patricia Lundy, 'Paradoxes and Challenges of Transitional Justice at the "Local" Level: Historical Enquiries in Northern Ireland', *Contemporary Social Science*, 6, no. 1 (February 2011): pp. 89–105; Patricia Lundy and Bill Rolston, 'Redress for Past Harms? Official Apologies in Northern Ireland', *International Journal of Human Rights*, 20, no. 1 (January 2016): pp. 104–22.

Friday Agreement.' It turns out that there are around fifty dedicated victim and survivor groups and at least another forty groups that work with victims among other activities.[23] In consequence of the encouraging of victims to tell their stories, Catholic nationalist communities have seen a growth of oral history and commemoration projects that openly challenge a perceived 'state-sanctioned forgetting'.[24] This development has stimulated Protestant unionists, particularly in the border counties, to break their silence and make a 'transition from private memories to public tellings', while still retaining gaps of silences in their narratives.[25] Storytelling has emerged as a powerful medium for dealing with the past in Northern Ireland.[26]

Consultations with community groups and individuals across Northern Ireland have repeatedly affirmed the value of storytelling as a form of individual remembrance that can be shared socially. Working under the assumption that 'for individuals and groups affected by the conflict forgetting the past is not an option, the wounds of the past will simply not heal by ignoring them', Healing Through Remembering—an NGO launched in 2001—conducted extensive consultations and collected 108 submissions that addressed the cardinal question of 'how should we remember the events connected with the conflict in and about Northern Ireland so as to individually and collectively contribute to the healing of the wounds of our society?'. Among the recommendations, which appeared in a report published in 2002, was the need for 'a collective storytelling and archiving process'.[27] Consequently, Healing Through Remembering formed a Storytelling Sub-Group, which carried out an 'audit of personal story, narrative and testimony initiatives related to the conflict'. The audit identified thirty-one storytelling projects that involve 'a broad range of individuals and organisations, who work for a variety of reasons and with a diverse set of outputs'. When taken together, these projects were seen to 'signify the development of a substantial body of experience and expertise on the facilitation of storytelling related to the conflict'.[28]

The role of storytelling as 'an important feature of any conflict transformation process' was also recognized by the Consultative Group on the Past, which was established in 2007 by the Secretary of State for Northern Ireland Peter Hain in order to 'consult across the community on how Northern Ireland society can best approach the legacy of the events of the past 40 years'. Chaired by Lord Robin Eames (the former Anglican Archbishop of Armagh) and Denis Bradley (a former

---

[23] *Comprehensive Needs Assessment: First Interim Report* (Belfast: Northern Ireland Commission for Victims and Survivors, 2010), p. 4; Kieran McEvoy and Pete Shirlow, 'The Northern Ireland Peace Process and "Terroristic" Narratives: A Reply to Edwards and McGrattan', *Terrorism and Political Violence*, 25, no. 2 (April 2013), p. 164.

[24] Patricia Lundy and Mark McGovern, 'The Politics of Memory in Post-Conflict Northern Ireland', *Peace Review*, 13 (2001): pp. 27–33.

[25] Hastings Donnan and Kirk Simpson, 'Silence and Violence among Northern Ireland Border Protestants', *Ethnos*, 72, no. 1 (March 2007): pp. 5–28; for early mobilizing of border Protestant victim groups see Graham Dawson, *Making Peace with the Past?: Memories, Trauma and the Irish Troubles* (Manchester and New York: Manchester University Press, 2007), pp. 233–87.

[26] Claire Hackett and Bill Rolston, 'The Burden of Memory: Victims, Storytelling and Resistance in Northern Ireland', *Memory Studies*, 2, no. 3 (September 2009): pp. 355–76; Margo Shea, 'Whatever You Say, Say Something: Remembering for the Future in Northern Ireland', *International Journal of Heritage Studies*, 16, nos. 4–5 (July 2010): pp. 289–304.

[27] *The Report of the Healing through Remembering Project* (Belfast: s.n., 2002), pp. 41–4.

[28] Gráinne Kelly, *'Storytelling' Audit: An Audit of Personal Story, Narrative and Testimony Initiatives Related to the Conflict in or About Northern Ireland* (Belfast: Healing Through Remembering, 2015).

Vice-Chairman of the Policing Board), the Consultative Group on the Past (which also included the Presbyterian minister Rev. Lesley Carroll and the former GAA footballer Jarlath Burns) found that 'there were various opinions on how and where an archive of stories could be held.' While 'many felt that archives of stories from all sides could provide a resource, accessible to the general public, from which all might learn to acknowledge the perspectives of the other side', there were others who 'preferred that archives should be private, or that story tellers should have control over who can hear their story'. The accepted view seemed to be that 'stories should continue to be collected locally but that a central archiving project should be established to collate them after this stage.'[29]

By 2013, it was generally felt that the peace process had reached an impasse on how to deal with the legacy of the past. The sense of frustration was exacerbated by an increase in dissident republican bomb threats and by mass loyalist riots, which were sparked by a decision taken by the Belfast City Council in December 2012 to reduce the number of days in which the Union flag would be flown over the City Hall. The political parties represented in the Stormont Assembly came together in July 2013 for multi-party talks, chaired by the US diplomat Richard Haass and the Harvard expert on international relations Meghan O'Sullivan. Months of negotiations produced a draft agreement, which included among its recommendations a proposal for the Northern Ireland Executive to establish an 'archive for conflict-related oral histories, documents, and other relevant materials from individuals of all backgrounds, from Northern Ireland and beyond, who wish to share their experiences connected with the conflict'. Oral history was recognized not just as a vehicle for the rehabilitation of individual victims, but as a vital cultural resource, and the familiar rhetoric of 'salvage folklore' was used to advocate the imperative to collect testimonies:

> Recording and preserving people's experiences—without judgment or prejudice regarding their experiences, political views, or professional or community affiliations—are necessary steps towards building a significant and comprehensive body of historical source material for future generations. Time is of the essence in this effort. Already, memories are fading and people are passing away. There are no second chances to record their memories. Each day of delay risks further losses at considerable cost to individuals and society alike.[30]

Even though it seemed that progress had been made, the Haass-O'Sullivan talks collapsed in December 2013, for which the blame was cast on the unionist parties, and the draft agreement was shelved.

Despite this setback, the proposal for an oral history archive remained on the political agenda. The following year, multi-party negotiations, which were chaired at Stormont by Secretary of State for Northern Ireland Theresa Villiers with the full support of the British and Irish governments, resulted in The Stormont House Agreement (SHA), signed in December 2014. Its section on 'The Past' determined that:

---

[29] *Report of the Consultative Group on the Past* (Belfast: Consultative Group on the Past Northern Ireland, 2009), pp. 32 and 97–8; see also Dawn Walsh, *Independent Commissions and Contentious Issues in Post-Good Friday Agreement Northern Ireland* (Cham: Palgrave Macmillan, 2017), pp. 119–47.

[30] *Proposed Agreement: An Agreement among the Parties of the Northern Ireland Executive on Parades, Select Commemorations, and Related Protests; Flags and Emblems and Contending with the Past* (Belfast, 31 December 2013), pp. 35–8.

The Executive will, by 2016, establish an Oral History Archive to provide a central place for people from all backgrounds (and from throughout the UK and Ireland) to share experiences and narratives related to the Troubles. As well as collecting new material, this archive will attempt to draw together and work with existing oral history projects.

The agreement stipulated that 'the sharing of experiences will be entirely voluntary and consideration will be given to protecting contributors, and the body itself, from defamation claims.' It also promised that 'the Archive will be independent and free from political interference.'[31] The practicalities of creating an official oral history archive proved more complicated than the legislators anticipated and the specified deadline was not met.

It was not made clear how a state-run archive, to be housed presumably in the Public Records Office of Northern Ireland (PRONI) and put under the directorship of the Deputy Keeper (who is a civil servant), would 'draw together and work with' the many independently established community-based oral history archives and how it could safeguard the collecting of contested oral testimonies from 'political interference'.[32] Moreover, provisions for 'protecting contributors' were not specified. This was a particular cause for concern in light of the ill-fate of the Boston College oral history project, which between 2001 and 2006 interviewed some forty former members of republican and loyalist paramilitary organizations but found that it could not stand behind the proviso that the testimonies would not be made public until after their death. Once it became apparent that the interviews contained sensitive information on illegal activities, including unsolved murder cases, the PSNI subpoenaed the Boston College tapes and subsequently arrested several political activists, including Sinn Féin president Gerry Adams (who was later released without charge).

This affair, which has become a cautionary tale for the ethics of oral history, demonstrated that it is not possible to speak with impunity about the past.[33] Unsurprisingly, the former manager of the Boston College oral history project—the highly respected journalist Ed Moloney—issued a call to boycott the proposed state archive, warning that 'any former member of any of the North's various paramilitary groups, either Republican or Loyalist who decides they wish to tell his or her story honestly, frankly and completely, would have to be completely insane to co-operate in any way with the Oral History Archive.'[34]

Oral history may not be able to carry the heavy responsibility that has been put on its shoulders and the expectation that storytelling will fulfil some kind of

---

[31] *The Stormont House Agreement* (London and Belfast: Northern Ireland Office, 2014), p. 5 (articles 22–4).

[32] Kieran McEvoy and Anna Bryson, 'Justice, Truth and Oral History: Legislating the Past "from Below" in Northern Ireland', *Northern Ireland Legal Quarterly*, 67, no. 1 (Spring 2015): pp. 67–90; Brandon Hamber and Gráinne Kelly, 'Practice, Power and Inertia: Personal Narrative, Archives and Dealing with the Past in Northern Ireland', *Journal of Human Rights Practice*, 8, no. 1 (March 2016): pp. 21–44.

[33] Donald A. Ritchie, *Doing Oral History*, 3rd edn (Oxford and New York: Oxford University Press, 2015), p. 68; Beth McMurtrie, 'Secrets From Belfast', in *Chronicle of Higher Education*, 26 January 2014; <www.chronicle.com/interactives/belfast>. See also Ted Palys and John Lowman, 'Defending Research Confidentiality "to the Extent the Law Allows": Lessons from the Boston College Subpoenas', *Journal of Academic Ethics*, 10, no. 4 (December 2012): pp. 271–97.

[34] Ed Moloney, 'Stormont Oral History Archive Must Be Boycotted' (28 September 2015); online blog: <https://thebrokenelbow.com/2015/09/28/stormont-oral-history-archive-must-be-boycotted/>.

quasi-psychoanalytical therapeutic function for society is questionable. The 'New Politics of Storytelling' have been criticized by Cillian McGrattan, who claimed that it fails to consider how stories 'are received in different ways by different segments, groups or individuals in a deeply divided society'. McGrattan raised the possibility that story-telling, because it is prone to bias and political manipulation, may actually undermine 'governmental aims to achieve a balanced, proportionate approach to the past'.[35]

History-telling is not new to Ulster and dealing with the past did not begin with the Troubles. The commentary of political scientists and sociologists on transitional justice shows little knowledge of folk history. The subtle but pervasive role of older historical traditions in shaping how the past is narrated is completely missing in the debates, which regularly refer to contemporary comparative cases, but lack a deeper historical perspective. In a book aptly sub-titled 'Haunted by History', McGrattan asked: 'if the politics of transition in Northern Ireland bear the hallmarks of a belatedness how then are we to approach what came before?'. His consideration of memory, politics, and identity realized that 'forgetting, like remembering, also has a history—and silences are as much imbued with political relevance and implications as public utterances and interventions.'[36]

Oral history in Northern Ireland operates within a culture of reticence. A study of community oral history archives found that 'deeply embedded fear and mistrust supports silences between communities and continues to inhibit the work of conflict transformation in Northern Ireland.' This observation seems to support the claim that 'archival activism' is required in order to ameliorate fears and overcome silences.[37] Another way of looking at this predicament might be to conclude that the pursuit of oral history needs to show more awareness of 'communicative silence', defined by Jay Winter as 'performative nonspeech acts' that 'transmit messages about distressing or suppressed incidents about which everyone knows but nobody speaks'.[38] The avoid-ance of open discussion of discomfiting episodes in the past conceals the subtle forms in which these very incidents are recalled and, in these conditions, traditions of vernacular history can perpetuate less-noticeable forms of forgetful remembrance. The long and complex history of social forgetting in Ulster has been mostly ignored. Those con-cerned with the current problems of Northern Ireland can benefit from consideration of the vernacular historiography of the Turn-Out, which shows how deeply disturbing memories can be tenaciously recalled over time, outside of official history and its archives.

Close examination of vernacular historiography entails the study of minutiae. Dwelling on the details of how numerous individuals from small localities in a provincial region of a relatively remote corner of Europe referred to a failed rebellion in the late eighteenth century may seem to some like navel-gazing. The poet Patrick

[35] Cillian McGrattan, 'The Stormont House Agreement and the New Politics of Storytelling in Northern Ireland', *Parliamentary Affairs*, 69, no. 4 (2016): pp. 928–46.

[36] Cillian McGrattan, *Memory, Politics and Identity: Haunted by History* (Basingstoke: Palgrave Macmillan, 2013), pp. 39 and 155.

[37] Michelle Moloney, 'Reaching Out from the Archive: The Role of Community Oral History Archives in Conflict Transformation in Northern Ireland' (PhD: Faculty of Art, Design, and the Built Environment, University of Ulster, 2014), p. 148.

[38] J. M. Winter, *War Beyond Words: Languages of Memory from the Great War to the Present* (Cambridge and New York: Cambridge University Press, 2017), pp. 201–2.

Kavanagh might have begged to differ. Kavanagh was convinced that 'parochialism is universal; it deals with the fundamentals.'[39] With this in mind, let us turn to consider the wider relevance of social forgetting, and how its study can contribute to a better understanding of dealing with the past in other societies, by briefly looking at some prominent twentieth-century European examples.

SOCIAL FORGETTING BEYOND ULSTER

Having surveyed over two centuries of *lethehistory* in Ulster, we can put aside the proverbial 'dreary steeples' of Northern Ireland and travel to the 'English Riviera' resort of Torquay. It is the mid-1970s and Basil Fawlty, the eccentric proprietor of a drab hotel, played to a tee by John Cleese, is clumsily attending to a group of German visitors, while suffering from a concussion. His instructive to the staff—'don't mention the War'—has become a legendary catchphrase. In a grossly exaggerated outpour of Freudian slips, Fawlty somehow manages to make a muddled reference to Nazis in almost every sentence he comes up with. The hilarious sequence of embarrassing utterances is peppered with recurring references to a yearning to forget the Second World War, at a time when United Kingdom (alongside the Republic of Ireland) had only recently joined the European Economic Community (the 'Common Market'):

> All in the market together, all differences forgotten, and no need at all to mention the war.... Oh, the war, oh, yes, completely slipped my mind, yes, I'd forgotten all about it.... oh yes, completely forgotten it, just like that... another one I can hardly remember .... So, it's all forgotten now and let's hear no more about it.[40]

For all its exaggeration, the skit masterfully illustrates how the desire to consciously repress unwanted memories, just barely a generation after the war, could result in awkward remembrance.

In his magisterial study *Postwar*, Tony Judt argued that Europe's astonishing recovery from the destruction and atrocities of the Second World War depended on forgetting, yet he also admitted that 'much was put out of mind that would subsequently return in discomforting ways.' It was therefore not a case of total oblivion but of 'a certain amount of selective, collective forgetting'. He was particularly taken by a quotation from the poet Hans-Magnus Enzensberger, who claimed that 'Europeans took shelter behind a collective amnesia.' For Judt, 'Enzensberger's phrase suggests a sort of passive collusion, an agreement not to discuss certain matters in public, as a result of which they become obscured in recollection.'[41]

The paradigmatic case for post-war forgetting is the 'Vichy Syndrome', the label Henry Rousso applied to the reluctance in France to face the uncomfortable history of

---

[39] Patrick Kavanagh, *Collected Prose* (London: MacGibbon & Kee, 1967), p. 283.
[40] John Cleese and Connie Booth, *The Complete Fawlty Towers* (London: Methuen, 1988), p. 155; *Fawlty Towers*, season 1, episode 6: 'The Germans' (BBC, originally aired on 24 October 1975).
[41] Tony Judt, *Postwar: A History of Europe since 1945* (New York: Penguin Press, 2005), pp. 61–2 and 808; Tony Judt, 'The Past Is Another Country: Myth and Memory in Postwar Europe', in *The Politics of Retribution in Europe: World War II and Its Aftermath*, edited by István Deák, Jan Tomasz Gross, and Tony Judt (Princeton, N.J.: Princeton University Press, 2000), p. 319n15.

collaboration with Nazi Germany, which disrupted the heroic myth of resistance that had been cultivated by Charles de Gaulle as a collective memory for the Fourth and Fifth French Republics.[42] Rousso realized that the denial of embarrassing wartime memories was not unique to France and that across formerly occupied Europe there was 'a more or less protracted period of official silence, repression, and forgetting'. He perceptively explained that this was 'a fiction, that is, a stance that, though adopted voluntarily by the state or public opinion, by no means indicates that individuals in reality forgot the crimes committed against people or the suffering they endured'. The breaking of public silence in the late 1960s opened the way to reclamation of memory. From the 1970s in Western Europe, and to a lesser degree from 1989 in Eastern Europe, Rousso observed that 'almost all European countries have witnessed a similar phenomenon of anamnesis', marked by fervent preoccupation with the problematic legacies of the war.[43] In France, the 'duty to remember'—*devoir de mémoire*—was adopted as a national ethos and reticence gave way to an 'obsession with Vichy'.[44] From a bird's-eye view, it would seem that the overall duration of post-war forgetting was short-lived, but closer inspection shows a more chequered picture, in which pockets of forgetting persisted within a flourishing culture of Second World War remembrance.

In a series of lectures, delivered in 1997 in Zürich on '*Luftkrieg und Literatur*' [air war and literature], which formed the basis for a book *On the Natural History of Destruction*, W. G. Sebald denounced the silence about the devastation caused by the wartime bombing of German cities. Although the bombings had been written about, Sebald argued that the so-called 'literature of the ruins' was:

> an instrument already tuned to individual and collective amnesia, and probably influenced by preconscious self-censorship—a means of obscuring a world that could no longer be presented in comprehensible terms. There was a tacit agreement, equally binding on everyone, that the true state of material and moral ruin in which the country found itself was not to be described.

In making a case for a 'persistent avoidance of the subject, or an aversion to it', Sebald overstated the extent of 'self-imposed silence', which he insisted was 'also typical of other areas of discourse, from family conversations to historical writings'.[45] The impression of collective amnesia derived from his disregard of family reminiscences and other recollections that had appeared in print. In reality, this was more of a case of social forgetting, in which counter-memories were marginalized. Shortly after Sebald's intervention, public silence was broken with the publication in 2002 of Jörg Friedrich's

---

[42] Henry Rousso, *The Vichy Syndrome: History and Memory in France since 1944* (Cambridge, Mass.: Harvard University Press, 1991).

[43] Henry Rousso, 'History of Memory, Policies of the Past: What For?', in *Conflicted Memories: Europeanizing Contemporary Histories*, edited by Konrad Hugo Jarausch and Thomas Lindenberger (New York: Berghahn Books, 2007), p. 29.

[44] Eric Conan and Henry Rousso, *Vichy: An Ever-Present Past* (Hanover: University Press of New England, 1998).

[45] W. G. Sebald, *On the Natural History of Destruction*, translated by Anthea Bell (New York: Random House, 2003; orig. edn 1999); Susanne Vees-Gulani, 'The Experience of Destruction: W. G. Sebald, the Airwar, and Literature', in *W. G. Sebald: History, Memory, Trauma*, edited by Scott D. Denham and Mark Richard McCulloh (Berlin and New York: Walter de Gruyter, 2006), p. 342.

Der Brand [The Fire], which evidently touched on a raw nerve and received considerable attention also outside the academy.[46]

Public silence also muted memories of the mass rape of women by the soldiers of the Red Army at the end of the war. The pervasiveness of sexual violations in Germany and Hungary was documented in personal testimonies and remembered in private, but it was a social taboo that was rarely talked about in public till the 1990s. The airing of these memories has been met with condemnation and denial in Russia, where the Soviet myth of 'The Great Patriotic War' is still vigilantly maintained as a sacrosanct collective memory.[47] In both these cases—the bombings and the rapes—silenced memories of suffering could demand public acknowledgement when phrased in the familiar language of victimhood. Over the second half of the twentieth century, remembrance of the trauma of victims—rather than the triumph of victors—emerged as the dominant paradigm of collective memory. The memory of the Holocaust has been at the centre of this development, relegating to its margins other memories that have not been given a similar public stage.

The primacy accorded to the Holocaust in public commemoration, which is apparent in countless memorials and cultural representations, has elevated the Shoah into a 'cosmopolitan memory' that has come to be regarded as a yardstick for commitment to universal human rights.[48] This broadening and de-contextualization of historical memory can also function as a transparent framework for social forgetting by overriding other memories. In Serbia, for example, state remembrance of the Holocaust, which was introduced as a gesture to placate the expectations of the EU, functioned as a 'screen memory' that was intended to silence troubling debates on the memory of atrocities committed during the Yugoslav Wars. In practice, silencing stimulated an array of secret practices—such as elusive storytelling—through which unsavoury aspects of the recent wars were remembered in private settings.[49]

Holocaust denial, described by Pierre Vidal-Naquet as the work of 'assassins of memory' and by Deborah Lipstadt as a 'growing assault on truth and memory', has not undermined the pre-eminence of Holocaust memory in the West.[50] The situation is less clear in the former communist countries of Europe, where denial re-appears in

---

[46] Jörg Friedrich, *The Fire: The Bombing of Germany, 1940–1945*, translated by Allison Brown (New York: Columbia University Press, 2006); see also Robert G. Moeller, 'On the History of Man-Made Destruction: Loss, Death, Memory, and Germany in the Bombing War', *History Workshop Journal*, 61, no. 1 (2006): pp. 103–34.

[47] James Mark, 'Remembering Rape: Divided Social Memory and the Red Army in Hungary 1944–1945', *Past and Present*, 188, no. 1 (August 2005): pp. 133–61; Norman M. Naimark, 'The Russians and Germans: Rape During the War and Post-Soviet Memories', in *Rape in Wartime*, edited by Raphaëlle Branche and Fabrice Virgili (New York: Palgrave Macmillan, 2013), pp. 201–19; see also Catherine Merridale, *Ivan's War: The Red Army 1939–1945* (London: Faber and Faber, 2005), pp. 322–35.

[48] Levy and Sznaider, *The Holocaust and Memory in the Global Age*.

[49] Lea David, 'Between Human Rights and Nationalism: Silencing as a Mechanism of Memory in the Post-Yugoslav Wars' Serbia', *Journal of Regional Security*, 10, no. 1 (2015): pp. 37–52; Jelena Obradović-Wochnik, 'The "Silent Dilemma" of Transitional Justice: Silencing and Coming to Terms with the Past in Serbia', *International Journal of Transitional Justice*, 7, no. 2 (July 2013): pp. 328–47.

[50] Pierre Vidal-Naquet, *Assassins of Memory: Essays on the Denial of the Holocaust*, translated by Jeffrey Mehlman (New York: Columbia University Press, 1992); Deborah E. Lipstadt, *Denying the Holocaust: The Growing Assault on Truth and Memory* (New York: Plume, 1993). See also Stephen E. Atkins, *Holocaust Denial as an International Movement* (Westport, Conn.: Praeger, 2009).

various forms.[51] Although governments in Eastern and Central Europe pay tribute to the memory of the Holocaust, national remembrance emphasizes shared victimhood under Nazi occupation, which is often seen as a prelude to a period of longer suffering under communism (in which Jews are considered to be disproportionately implicated).[52] By attributing blame for the Holocaust entirely to the Germans, official collective memory discourages public debate on local participation in the persecution of Jews. Revelations of the massacre of Jews by Poles in the village of Jedwabne, which disclosed memories that had been covered up locally by the perpetrators and their descendants, triggered hostile responses from Polish nationalists, who were unwilling to recognize these disturbing memories.[53] The heated controversies that raged over this incident hint at a wider social history of complicity in genocide, which for the moment cannot be officially recognized and remains masked by social forgetting.

Social forgetting is often misdiagnosed as collective amnesia and it takes more rigorous research to uncover the traces of private remembrance behind the scenes. It is generally assumed, for example, that official denial of the Armenian genocide in the Republic of Turkey eliminated all traces of memory of the atrocities in Anatolia. Allusions to historic wrongs have been branded threats to 'national security' and are prohibited under article 301 of the Turkish criminal code, which forbids any insult to 'Turkey, the Turkish nation, or Turkish government institutions', effectively preventing public discussion and publications on the genocide. This proscription, however, did not produce total oblivion. By calling attention to practices of 'silence and avoidance', Taner Akçam, has argued that there is 'a serious gap between the writing of official histories and society's ways of privately remembering and transmitting historical memories'.[54]

Akçam observed that notions of Turkish collective amnesia derive from a dearth of field research on how the genocide is actually perceived by various segments of Turkish society. Indeed, oral history interviews with elderly Turks and Kurds in Eastern Turkey reveal that the descendants of villagers who witnessed or participated in the events retained vivid memories of the persecution of the Armenians, which contradict official

---

[51] Florin Lobont, 'Antisemitism and Holocaust Denial in Post-Communist Eastern Europe', in *The Historiography of the Holocaust*, edited by Dan Stone (New York: Palgrave Macmillan, 2004), pp. 440–68; Michael Shafir, 'Denying the Shoah in Post-Communist Eastern Europe', in *Holocaust Denial: The Politics of Perfidy*, edited by Robert S. Wistrich (Berlin and Boston: Walter de Gruyter; Jerusalem: The Hebrew University Magnes Press, 2012), pp. 27–65.

[52] Alejandro Baer and Natan Sznaider, *Memory and Forgetting in the Post-Holocaust Era: The Ethics of Never Again* (London: Routledge, 2017), pp. 105–31.

[53] Jan Tomasz Gross, *Neighbors: The Destruction of the Jewish Community in Jedwabne, Poland* (Princeton: Princeton University Press, 2001); Antony Polonsky and Joanna B. Michlic, eds, *The Neighbors Respond: The Controversy over the Jedwabne Massacre in Poland* (Princeton, N.J.: Princeton University Press, 2004); Anna Bikont, *The Crime and the Silence: Confronting the Massacre of Jews in Wartime Jedwabne* (New York: Farrar, Straus, and Giroux, 2015). See also Barbara Törnquist-Plewa, 'The Use and Non-Use of the Holocaust Memory in Poland', in *Painful Pasts and Useful Memories: Remembering and Forgetting in Europe*, edited by Barbara Törnquist-Plewa and Niklas Bernsand (Lund: The Centre for European Studies at Lund University, 2012), pp. 11–27.

[54] Taner Akçam, *From Empire to Republic: Turkish Nationalism and the Armenian Genocide* (London and New York: Zed Books, 2004), pp. 226–42; see also Taner Akçam, 'Facing History: Denial and the Turkish National Security Concept', in Ben-Ze'ev et al., *Shadows of War*, pp. 173–80.

collective memory. By banning open commemoration at sites where evidence of atrocities has surfaced, the state created what Uğur Ümit Üngör called '*lieux de silence*', which are essentially sites of social forgetting.[55]

Behind the Iron Curtain, the communist governments of Eastern and Central Europe were determined to efface memories of popular opposition to their rule. Recollections of resistance were retained in private, under a veil of forgetting. An oral history of the children of the victims of government repression in Hungary that followed the failed revolution of 1956 demonstrated the clandestine ways in which painful memories were transmitted to 'the Second Generation of 1956ers'. These forbidden memories, which could not be uttered in public, were maintained and regenerated silently, in conditions of fear and anxiety.[56]

Official policies that imposed amnesia were defied by a sub-culture of counter-memory, sustained by dissidents through illicit writings in the *samizdat* press and in the publications of exiles. Milan Kundera, writing in France, famously nicknamed Gustav Husak—the communist leader of Czechoslovakia, who presided over the policy of 'normalization' that followed the suppression of the Prague Spring in 1968—the 'President of Forgetting'. Timothy Garton Ash explained the masquerade behind the public culture of forgetting, over which Husak presided:

> *Forgetting* is the key to the so called normalization of Czechoslovakia. In effect, the regime has said to the people: Forget 1968.... We do not ask you to believe in our fatuous ideology. All we ask is that you outwardly and publicly conform.[57]

Countless studies of memory quote Kundera's aphorism that 'the struggle of man against power is the struggle of memory against forgetting' without realizing the subtleties of social forgetting in which this struggle took place. Private remembrance was intertwined with displays of public forgetting, so that memory was not just opposed to forgetting, but was part of it.[58]

With the fall of communism in 1989, a wave of iconoclastic decommemorating swept across Central and Eastern Europe. The removal of public sculpture associated with the former socialist regimes heralded a complete transformation of heritage that seemed to promise an opening up of public memory.[59] In consequence of this change, social forgetting was inverted. The new museums that commemorate the communist era, such as the House of Terror in Budapest, depict communism as an oppressive foreign dictatorship, comparable to Nazism, and, by bolstering a spirit of shared victimhood, serve to conceal memories of the extent to which the local population

---

[55] Uğur Ümit Üngör, 'Lost in Commemoration: The Armenian Genocide in Memory and Identity', *Patterns of Prejudice*, 48, no. 2 (March 2014): pp. 147–66.

[56] Zsuzsanna Kőrösi and Adrienne Molnár, *Carrying a Secret in My Heart: Children of the Victims of the Reprisals after the Hungarian Revolution in 1956, an Oral History* (Budapest and New York: Central European University Press, 2003).

[57] 'Czechoslovakia Under the Ice', in Timothy Garton Ash, *The Uses of Adversity: Essays on the Fate of Central Europe* (New York: Random House, 1989), p. 62 [emphasis in the original].

[58] Milan Kundera, *The Book of Laughter and Forgetting*, translated by Michael Henry Heim (London: Penguin, 1983; orig. Czech edn 1978), p. 3.

[59] Monika A. Murzyn, 'Heritage Transformation in Central and Eastern Europe', in *The Ashgate Research Companion to Heritage and Identity* (Aldershot and Burlington: Ashgate, 2008), edited by Brian Graham and Peter Howard (Aldershot and Burlington: Ashgate, 2008), pp. 315–46.

had participated in these regimes.[60] The totalitarian nature of the communist states meant that practically everybody had been implicated in some way or another, but this cannot not be admitted in public.[61] In a new political climate, which has targeted former communists for recrimination, memories of varying levels of collusion with the state and the party have been withheld. The prerogatives of lustration, given to such bodies as the Institute of National Remembrance in Poland, became a political instrument of silencing, which could even be directed at former dissidents.[62] This created a new form of social forgetting, which has not yet been recognized as such.

In Western Europe, decolonization left an ambivalent legacy that was kept buried in social forgetting. In the initial post-war period, national memories mostly ignored postcolonial immigrant communities and state commemorations avoided embarrassing episodes from the colonial past. In the Netherlands, from the 1970s, after years of silencing and absence of commemoration, immigrants from the Dutch East Indies began to claim public recognition for the memory of the Japanese occupation during the Second World War. Their struggle encouraged immigrants from the West Indies (which had not been occupied) to demand recognition for their contribution to the war effort.[63] Elsewhere in Europe, other forgotten colonial memories were also coming out of the woodwork to unsettle collective memory.

Perry Anderson admonished Pierre Nora for the neglect of 'the entire imperial history of the country' in *Les Lieux de mémoire*.[64] Commenting on the glaring omission of colonialism and immigration from the history of memory, Ann Laura Stoler rejected the suitability of the term 'collective amnesia' and proposed instead the use of 'aphasia', which, by referring to 'an occlusion of knowledge' rather than 'ignorance or absence', signifies 'a dismembering, a difficulty speaking'.[65] Incidentally, Halbwachs began his study of collective memory with consideration of aphasia, from which he realized the need to communicate and share memory in social contexts.[66] The extension of the individual condition of aphasia to an entire society, which perhaps should be re-named 'social aphasia', has an affinity to the dynamics of disremembering and silence that facilitate social forgetting. It is not that recollections of colonialism were entirely absent, but that they were not spoken about openly or recognized officially.

Around the turn of the millennium, after several decades of silencing, the memory of the Algerian War returned to haunt French society and unsettle collective memory.

[60] Péter Apor, 'Eurocommunism: Commemorating Communism in Contemporary Eastern Europe', in *A European Memory? Contested Histories and Politics of Remembrance*, edited by Małgorzata Pakier and Bo Stråth (New York: Berghahn Books, 2010), pp. 233–46.

[61] Anne Applebaum, *Iron Curtain: The Crushing of Eastern Europe, 1944–1956* (New York: Doubleday, 2012), pp. 386–411.

[62] Marci Shore, *The Taste of Ashes: The Afterlife of Totalitarianism in Eastern Europe* (New York: Crown Publishers, 2013), pp. 311–22. See also Barbara A. Misztal, 'The Banalization and the Contestation of Memory in Postcommunist Poland', in *Heritage and Identity: Engagement and Demission in the Contemporary World*, edited by Marta Anico and Elsa Peralta (London and New York: Routledge, 2009), pp. 117–28.

[63] Gert Oostindie, *Postcolonial Netherlands: Sixty-Five Years of Forgetting, Commemorating, Silencing* (Amsterdam: Amsterdam University Press, 2011), pp. 91–100.

[64] Perry Anderson, 'Union Sucrée', in *London Review of Books*, vol. 26, no. 18 (23 September 2004), pp. 10–16.

[65] Ann Laura Stoler, 'Colonial Aphasia: Race and Disabled Histories in France', *Public Culture*, 23, no. 1 (January 2011): pp. 121–56.

[66] Halbwachs, *On Collective Memory*, pp. 43–5.

The public was rattled by revelations of torture by French troops, which brought out into the open the dark aspects of colonial rule that had hitherto been considered 'unspeakable'.[67] Closer to home, memories of the brutality with which the police had dispersed a pro-independence demonstration of Algerian migrants in Paris on 17 October 1961, an incident that had been downplayed by the authorities but was recalled within the French-Algerian communities as a massacre, also came to light.[68] Concurrently, the *Harkis*, former Algerian loyalist auxiliaries, who had been subject to 'triple silencing'—denounced in Algeria as traitors, disowned in France, and reluctant to talk about the horrific violence that had been directed against them—began to speak out about memories of their tribulations.[69] In addition, the *pied-noirs*—the repatriated settler population of French Algeria—also reconstructed their memories of decolonization as narratives of victimhood. Silenced memories were seeking a public voice.[70]

Campaigns of 'memory activism', run by immigrant communities and left-wing groups, claimed recognition for memorial traditions that had previously been transmitted in conditions of social forgetting. This open challenge to national collective memory was resisted by right-wing groups that were intent on reinforcing social forgetting through silencing. The controversies over the memory of French colonialism—which have been described as 'memory wars', but could just as well be labelled forgetting wars—have matched, and perhaps even superseded the controversies over remembrance of collaboration during the Vichy government.[71] This transformation of public memory and its relation to historiography became apparent in the trials of the former civil servant Maurice Papon.

In 1998, following what has been described as the longest trial in French history, Papon was found guilty of complicity with the Nazis in crimes against humanity. It was

---

[67] Joshua Cole, 'Intimate Acts and Unspeakable Relations: Remembering Torture and the War for Algerian Independence', in *Memory, Empire, and Postcolonialism: Legacies of French Colonialism*, edited by Alec G. Hargreaves (Lanham, Md.: Lexington Books, 2005), pp. 125–41; See also Jo McCormack, 'Social Memories in Remembering the Franco-Algerian War', *Journal of Social History*, 44, no. 4 (Summer 2011): pp. 1129–38; Raphaëlle Branche and Jim House, 'Silences on State Violence during the Algerian War of Independence: France and Algeria, 1962–2007', in Ben-Ze'ev et al., *Shadows of War*, pp. 118–26.

[68] Joshua Cole, 'Entering History: The Memory of Police Violence, October 1961', in *Algeria & France, 1800–2000: Identity, Memory, Nostalgia*, edited by Patricia M. E. Lorcin (Syracuse, N.Y.: Syracuse University Press, 2006), pp. 171–34; Jim House and Neil MacMaster, *Paris 1961: Algerians, State Terror, and Memory* (Oxford: Oxford University Press, 2006), pp. 216–309; see also Branche and House, 'Silences on State Violence', pp. 126–35.

[69] Martin Evans, 'The *Harkis*: The Experience and Memory of France's Muslim Auxiliaries', in *The Algerian War and the French Army: Experiences, Images, Testimonies*, edited by Martin S. Alexander, Martin Evans, and John F. V. Keiger (Houndmills and New York: Palgrave Macmillan, 2002), pp. 117–33; William B. Cohen, 'The *Harkis*: History and Memory', in *Algeria & France, 1800–2000: Identity, Memory, Nostalgia*, edited by Patricia M. E. Lorcin (Syracuse, N.Y.: Syracuse University Press, 2006), pp. 164–80; Enjelvin Géraldine and Korac-Kakabadse Nada, 'France and the Memories of "Others": The Case of the Harkis', *History & Memory*, 24, no. 1 (Spring-Summer 2012): pp. 152–77; Laura Jeanne Sims, 'Rethinking France's "Memory Wars": Harki Collective Memories, 2003–2010', 34, no. 3 (2016): pp. 83–104.

[70] Claire Eldridge, 'Blurring the Boundaries between Perpetrators and Victims: Pied-Noir Memories and the Harki Community', *Memory Studies*, 3, no. 2 (April 2010): pp. 123–36; see also Claire Eldridge, *From Empire to Exile: History and Memory within the Pied-Noir and Harki Communities, 1962–2012* (Manchester: Manchester University Press, 2016).

[71] See Jo McCormack, 'Social Memories in Remembering the Franco-Algerian War', *Journal of Social History*, 44, no. 4 (Summer 2011): pp. 1129–38.

proven that during his tenure as general secretary of the prefecture of Gironde under the Vichy regime, he had been responsible for the deportation of approximately 1,600 Jews from Bordeaux to the Drancy internment camp, from where they were sent on to death camps. During the trial, evidence emerged on his subsequent record as a colonial administrator who had authorized the use of torture in Algeria and of his role as Prefect of Police for Paris in the suppression of the October 1961 demonstration. As put by Richard Joseph Golsan, it had become a 'trial within a trial'—the memory of Vichy and the Holocaust had incidentally raised the spectre of Algeria. The following year, Papon lost a libel case against the historian and memory activist Jean Luc-Einaudi, who had accused him of responsibility for the massacre of demonstrators in 1961. The demand for historical information on what had happened at the demonstration resulted in the release of confidential archival files. It then transpired that some of the official records had been destroyed, and discovery of this cover-up served to reaffirm the value of unofficial personal recollections.[72]

By the turn of the millennium, it seemed that history, memory, and forgetting history were confronting each other in a Mexican standoff. Henry Rousso—the acclaimed author of the *Vichy Syndrome*—declined an invitation to give testimony at Papon's trial for his Vichy crimes, claiming that the judgement of history in the courtroom reflected a wider 'confusion between memory and history'. Rousso argued that the 'duty to remember' had lost its original sense of purpose and was now overused.[73] The duty to remember has been subject to growing academic criticism, which has taken its cue from the writings of the philosopher Paul Ricoeur on *Memory, History, Forgetting*. The sense that public obsession with memory had gotten out of hand and needs to be tempered could imply a duty to forget, but Ricoeur categorically negated such a possibility.[74] It is worth recalling that, in a healthy society, duties come with rights.

RIGHTS OF FORGETTING

In France, an 'official process of forgetting', in which the state tried for several decades to ignore colonial legacies, had been undermined by 'pressure to remember that past' from non-state actors.[75] When silenced memories of colonialism assertively emerged

---

[72] Wood Nancy, 'Memory on Trial in Contemporary France: The Case of Maurice Papon', *History & Memory*, 11, no. 1 (Spring-Summer 1999): pp. 41–76; Richard Joseph Golsan, *Vichy's Afterlife: History and Counterhistory in Postwar France* (Lincoln: University of Nebraska Press, 2000), pp. 2–4 and 156–80; House and MacMaster, *Paris 1961*, pp. 310–14. See also Joan B. Wolf, *Harnessing the Holocaust: The Politics of Memory in France* (Stanford, Calif.: Stanford University Press, 2004), pp. 159–88.

[73] Henry Rousso, *The Haunting Past: History, Memory, and Justice in Contemporary France* (Philadelphia: University of Pennsylvania Press, 2002); see also Richard J. Evans, 'History, Memory, and the Law: The Historian as Expert Witness', *History and Theory*, 41, no. 3 (2002): pp. 326–45.

[74] Ricoeur, *Memory, History, Forgetting*, pp. 418 and 456. See also Myriam Bienenstock, 'Is There a Duty of Memory? Reflections on a French Debate', *Modern Judaism—A Journal of Jewish Ideas and Experience*, 30, no. 3 (2010): pp. 332–47.

[75] Jan Jansen, 'Politics of Remembrance, Colonialism and the Algerian War of Independence in France', in *A European Memory?: Contested Histories and Politics of Remembrance*, edited by Małgorzata Pakier and Bo Stråth (New York: Berghahn Books, 2010), pp. 275–93.

into the public sphere, the authorities, as the guardians of national memory, stepped in to try and regulate this incursion of counter-memory. In 2005, the National Assembly passed a 'Law on Recognition by the Nation and National Contribution in Favour of the French Repatriates', which included a requirement that the high-school curriculum would 'recognise in particular the positive role of the French presence overseas, notably in North Africa, and give the history and sacrifices of the French army combatants from these territories the prominent place to which they are entitled' (article 4, paragraph 2).[76] The blatant attempt to enlist the teaching of history as an agent of historical revision, through which the state would impose a sanitized collective memory, was vigorously protested. After the Constitutional Council ruled that the contested article exceeded the jurisdiction of the law, it was repealed by President Jacques Chirac.[77]

The law on colonialism seemed to follow a tradition of previous memory laws enacted in France, which had prohibited Holocaust denial (the Gayssot Act of 1990), recognized the Armenian genocide (2001) and, perhaps more controversially, retrospectively defined slavery as a crime against humanity (the Taubira Act of 2001). These laws have been denounced by *Liberté pour l'histoire* [Freedom for History], an association of leading French historians, of which Pierre Nora is president.[78] Yet, distinctions can be drawn between these memory laws. The three earlier acts were laws against forgetting, which demanded recognition for atrocities that have been denied. By contrast, the original version of the law on colonialism stood out for explicitly prescribing a positive view on a contentious past. It effectively censured memories of atrocities that challenge the official national narrative and was therefore a law in favour of forgetting. Similar legislation has been passed in other states. An Israeli law prohibits commemoration of the Palestinian Nakba (2011); a Russian law against the 'Rehabilitation of Nazi Criminals' (2014) is designed to bar criticism of the Soviet Union's conduct during the Second World War; and, most recently, a Polish law forbids referring to Polish complicity in the Holocaust (2018). These laws, as argued by Yifat Gutman, are instruments of silencing, which even if not enforced have 'a chilling effect that in itself limits the forbidden views or actions from being expressed in public'.[79] The ability of such memory laws— which are essentially forgetting laws—to actually snuff out counter-memories is at best limited, but by driving troubling recollections outside of the public sphere they encourage the resurgence of social forgetting.

The attempt to orchestrate memory and forgetting through legislation has been particularly apparent in Spain, where the transition from Franco's authoritarian rule to democracy—commonly referred to as *la Transición*—was facilitated through a 'pact of

---

[76] 'Les programmes scolaires reconnaissent en particulier le rôle positif de la présence française outre-mer, notamment en Afrique du Nord et accordent à l'histoire et aux sacrifices des combattants de l'armée française issus de ces territoires la place éminente à laquelle ils ont droit'; *Loi n° 2005-158 du 23 février 2005 portant reconnaissance de la Nation et contribution nationale en faveur des Français rapatriés*, article 4, alinéa 2.

[77] Stiina Löytömäki, 'The Law and Collective Memory of Colonialism: France and the Case of "Belated" Transitional Justice', *International Journal of Transitional Justice*, 7, no. 2 (2013): pp. 205–23.

[78] For *Liberté pour l'histoire* see its website: <www.lph-asso.fr>. See also Michael Rothberg, *Multidirectional Remembering: Remembering the Holocaust in the Age of Decolonization* (Stanford, Calif.: Stanford University Press, 2009), pp. 267–70.

[79] Yifat Gutman, 'Memory Laws: An Escalation in Minority Exclusion or a Testimony to the Limits of State Power?', *Law & Society Review*, 50, no. 3 (2016): pp. 575–607.

forgetting' [*el pacto del olvido*], tacitly embodied in the spirit of the 1977 Amnesty Law. Contrary to a common claim, this political arrangement did not result in collective amnesia. Outside of the political domain, there was considerable cultural and social preoccupation with memories of the civil war, so that disremembering amounted to social forgetting.[80] The indictment in 1998 of the former Chilean dictator General Augusto Pinochet by the Spanish magistrate Baltasar Garzón has been identified by Omar Guillermo Encarnación as a watershed moment. The public debates that ensued picked up on the similarities between social forgetting in post-dictatorship Chile and Spain and resulted in the 'emergence of a vigorous movement devoted to the recovery of the forgotten historical memory'.[81]

The formation of the Association for the Recuperation of Historical Memory [Asociación para la Recuperación de la Memoria Histórica—ARMH], co-founded in 2000 by Emilio Silva and Santiago Macias (both grandchildren of people who were 'disappeared' during the civil war), signalled the end of the pact of forgetting. Mass graves of the victims of Franco's regime were identified by the ARMH through the use of vernacular history sources—oral and written testimonies—and this led to widely publicized excavations of corpses. The skeletons of the past had quite literally re-emerged to break the silence.[82] As Katherine Verdery has shown for Eastern Europe, the exhumation and reburial of bodies is a highly evocative act which can be readily politicized.[83] Indeed, the political consequences were soon felt in Spain.

In 2007, the Spanish Congress of Deputies passed a law that 'recognizes and broadens the rights and establishes measures in favour of those who suffered prosecution or violence during the Civil War and the Dictatorship'. [84] Commonly known as the Historical Memory Law [*Ley de Memoría Historica*], it decreed the removal of Francoist symbols from public spaces, promised provisions for victims and their descendants, and committed state support for the exhumation of graves. In addition, a Historical Memory Documentary Centre in Salamanca was established as an archive for the civil war and a number of museums and galleries curated exhibitions on the war. This move 'from realms of oblivion to realms of memory' seemed to lay to rest social

[80] Paloma Aguilar Fernández, *Memory and Amnesia: The Role of the Spanish Civil War in the Transition to Democracy*, translated by Mark Oakley (New York: Berghahn Books, 2002); cf. Joan Ramon Resina, 'Short of Memory: The Reclamation of the Past since the Spanish Transition to Democracy', in *Disremembering the Dictatorship: The Politics of Memory in the Spanish Transition to Democracy*, edited by Joan Ramon Resina (Amsterdam: Rodopi, 2000), pp. 83–126; Joan Ramon Resina, 'The Weight of Memory and the Lightness of Oblivion: The Dead of the Spanish Civil War', in *Unearthing Franco's Legacy: Mass Graves and the Recovery of Historical Memory in Spain*, edited by Carlos Jerez Farrán and Samuel Amago (Notre Dame, Ind.: University of Notre Dame Press, 2010), pp. 221–42.

[81] Omar Guillermo Encarnación, *Democracy without Justice in Spain: The Politics of Forgetting* (Philadelphia: University of Pennsylvania Press, 2014), pp. 132–57.

[82] Layla Renshaw, *Exhuming Loss: Memory, Materiality and Mass Graves of the Spanish Civil War* (Walnut Creek, Calif.: Left Coast Press, 2011). See also chapters by Antonius C.G.M. Robben, Ignacio Fernández de Mata, and Francisco Ferrándiz in Carlos Jerez Farrán and Samuel Amago, eds, *Unearthing Franco's Legacy: Mass Graves and the Recovery of Historical Memory in Spain* (Notre Dame, Ind.: University of Notre Dame Press, 2010), pp. 264–325.

[83] Katherine Verdery, *The Political Lives of Dead Bodies: Reburial and Postsocialist Change* (New York: Columbia University Press, 1999).

[84] *Ley 57/2007 por la que se reconocen y amplían derechos y se establecen medidas en favor de quienes padecieron persecución o violencia durante la Guerra Civil y la Dictadura.*

forgetting in Spain.[85] However, as noted by Mary Vincent, the reconstruction of collective memory through a 'renegotiation of the public narratives of the dictatorship and the Civil War' stopped short of addressing the historical political divisions, which were still in place, so that silence and forgetting were not fully overcome.[86]

Following the replacement in 2011 of the socialist government of José Luis Rodríguez Zapatero by the conservative government of Mariano Rajoy, state funding for the implementation of the Historical Memory Law was slashed. The new government also rejected the recommendations of the Expert Commission for the Future of the Valley of the Fallen, which had been established by the previous government to come up with proposals for the redesigning of Franco's triumphalist memorial site in Cuelgamuros for the dead of the civil war. In absence of state support, the exhumations of bodies continued through private non-governmental initiatives.[87] The demarcations between private and public remembrance had been re-opened for negotiation. With opponents of the Historical Memory Law calling for a return to the accommodations of amnesty, prospects for the restoring of social forgetting were once more on the horizon.

Reassessing the impact of his own work, Pierre Nora has spoken out against how the 'duty to remember', in becoming 'the defining mark of our era', has created a 'tyranny of memory'.[88] To critics, it seems that the 'memory crisis', which stimulated the turn-of-the-millennium 'memory boom' produced a surfeit of memory. In a scathing critique of the excesses of remembrance in today's world, David Rieff has come out 'in praise of forgetting'.[89] Finding fault in contemporary 'commemorative mania', Jean-Claude Guillebaud cautioned that 'an excess of commemoration may paradoxically lead to a lack of interest and obliteration' and called for a compromise to be found between 'the duty to remember and the right to oblivion' [*droit à l'oubli*].[90]

Posing the pertinent question of 'should we late moderns be advised to remember our past or forget it?', David Gross carefully weighed the advantages and disadvantages of remembering in comparison to forgetting and came out on the side of remembering. Borrowing from Theodor Adorno the concept of 'a remembrance of the forgotten', Gross maintained that:

> discarded things perhaps ought not to be neglected and forgotten just because they lost out to purportedly more advanced historical forces. In returning by means of memory to that which is different from the present, one not only pays respect to what has failed or been silenced but also acquires a standpoint from which to criticize the contemporary age.[91]

[85] Mikel Errazkin Agirrezabala and Rosa Martínez Rodríguez, 'Realms of Memory and the Recovery of the Historical Memory of the Spanish Civil War and Franco's Dictatorship (1936–2012)', in *Challenging History in the Museum: International Perspectives*, edited by Jenny Kidd et al. (Farnham and Burlington: Ashgate, 2014), pp. 149–61.

[86] Mary Vincent, 'Breaking the Silence? Memory and Oblivion since the Spanish Civil War', in Ben-Ze'ev et al., *Shadows of War*, pp. 47–67.

[87] Patricio Galella, 'Privatising the Search and Identification of Human Remains: The Case of Spain', *Human Remains and Violence: An Interdisciplinary Journal*, 1, no. 1 (2015): pp. 57–74.

[88] Pierre Nora, 'Memory: From Freedom to Tyranny', Address to the Israeli Academy of Sciences and Humanities, Jerusalem, 9 February 2016; online <www.youtube.com/watch?v=FTN9Uh56Xjw>.

[89] Rieff, *In Praise of Forgetting*.

[90] Jean-Claude Guillebaud, 'Entre mémoire et projet', in *La Mémoire, Pour Quoi Faire?*, edited by Alain Houziaux (Paris: les Éd. de l'Atelier, 2006), pp. 47–74.

[91] David Gross, *Lost Time: On Remembering and Forgetting in Late Modern Culture* (Amherst: University of Massachusetts, 2000), pp. 140–53 (quotation on pp. 149–50).

Another American historian, David Blight, wrote that 'even though we know the world is riven with too much memory, too much war, nationalism, and exploitation enacted in the name of some kind of memory, in the balance sheet of remembrance versus forgetting, it is far more dangerous to forget.'[92]

There is a prevalent conception that modernity (or perhaps postmodernity), despite its extravagant displays of memory, is steeped in forgetting. Andreas Huyssen was one of the first critics to describe the late twentieth century as a 'culture of amnesia'.[93] Paul Connerton argued that 'modernity has a particular problem with forgetting', which is apparent in 'the paradox of a culture which manifests so many symptoms of hyper-mnesia and which yet at the same time is post-mnemonic'.[94] This commentary has failed to take on board the implications of the cyber revolution.

Widespread use of digital communications and social media has diminished the distinctions between individual, social, cultural, and collective memory by creating 'networks that blur if not transcend the personal and the public, the individual and the social and the particular and the collective'.[95] Moreover, the balance between remembering and forgetting, as explained by Viktor Mayer-Schonberger, has undergone a paradigm shift:

> Since the beginning of time, for us humans, forgetting has been the norm and remembering the exception. Because of digital technology and global networks, however, this balance has shifted. Today, with the help of widespread technology, forgetting has become the exception, and remembering the default.[96]

The World Wide Web hosts what seems to be a limitless repository of cultural memory, which anybody can, at least in theory, contribute to and draw from. The promise of 'total memory', however, comes with an anxiety over 'loss of control over forgetting'.[97] The digitalization of memory threatens to turn us all into Funes the Memorious, ushering in an age in which everything will be remembered and it will not be possible to avoid undesirable recollections.

In conditions of unlimited global-digital 'web-memory' (labelled by one critic a 'globital age'), social remembering and forgetting have become functions of algorithm-based search technologies that mine data from users in order to customize the searches.[98]

---

[92] David W. Blight, 'The Memory Boom: Why and Why Now?', in *Memory in Mind and Culture*, edited by Pascal Boyer and James V. Wertsch (New York: Cambridge University Press, 2009), p. 240.

[93] Andreas Huyssen, *Twilight Memories: Marking Time in a Culture of Amnesia* (New York: Routledge, 1995).

[94] Connerton, *How Modernity Forgets*.

[95] Andrew Hoskins, 'The Mediatisation of Memory', in *Save As... Digital Memories*, edited by Joanne Garde-Hansen, Andrew Hoskins, and Anna Reading (Houndmills and New York: Palgrave Macmillan, 2009), pp. 27–43; see also Andrew Hoskins, 'Memory of the Multitude: The End of Collective Memory', in *Digital Memory Studies: Media Pasts in Transition*, edited by Andrew Hoskins (New York: Routledge, 2017), pp. 85–109.

[96] Viktor Mayer-Schèonberger, *Delete: The Virtue of Forgetting in the Digital Age* (Princeton, N.J.: Princeton University Press, 2009), p. 2.

[97] Andrew Hoskins, 'Archive Me! Media, Memory, Uncertainty', in *Memory in a Mediated World: Remembrance and Reconstruction*, edited by Andrea Hajek, Christine Lohmeier, and Christian Pentzold (Houndmills and New York: Palgrave Macmillan, 2016), pp. 13–35.

[98] Elena Esposito, 'The Forms of Web-Memory', in *Theorizing Social Memories: Concepts and Contexts*, edited by Gerd Sebald and Jatin Wagle (Abingdon and New York: Routledge, 2016), pp. 159–70; see also see Anna Reading, 'Memory and Digital Media: Six Dynamics of the Globital

In 2012 the European Commission published a draft European Data Protection Regulation that included a clause on the 'right to be forgotten and to erasure' (Article 17), which determined that individuals can request 'the erasure of personal data relating to them and the abstention from further dissemination of such'.[99] This principle was put to the test in 2014 in the lawsuit brought by Mario Costeja González against Google Spain in which the European Court of Justice upheld the right to be forgotten and ruled in favour of the plaintiff's request to remove links to a newspaper article concerning him. For Gonzalez this was a pyrrhic victory, as the details of his memorable case went viral and are unlikely to be forgotten.[100] More generally, the European deliberations initiated a global debate on the meanings of forgetting in a digital age.[101]

An historian's initial assessment of the possible outcome of allowing individuals to prevent access to digitally archived information in the public domain cautioned that, if such a right to be forgotten would be generally adopted, it 'would lead to the rewriting of history in ways that impoverish our insights not only into anecdotal lives (which is justified in a small class of recent cases) but also into the larger patterns and trends of history.'[102] These concerns are not all that novel. In determining the conditions of how and when documents should be made accessible, archivists have always had to wrestle with the dilemma of 'the right to social memory versus the right to social oblivion' and are often obliged to take into consideration personal requests for maintaining confidentiality.[103]

Discussions on the right to be forgotten are mainly concerned with conflicts between protecting privacy and the ability to freely construct one's own identity, on the one hand, and freedom of speech and the right of the public to know, on the other. By precariously walking a thin line between an inner duty to remember and a right to be outwardly forgotten, social forgetting offers another way to approach this dilemma. As this study has endeavoured to show, the desire for wilful forgetting produces rites of oblivion, which are in effect forms of unofficial remembrance that are discreetly performed alongside social memory in defiance of state prohibitions and social taboos.

Once we are aware of their existence, rites of oblivion can be found in many different societies. The discussion above provided some prominent European examples, which of course can be supplemented with examples from other areas worldwide. Rather than

Memory Field', in *On Media Memory: Collective Memory in a New Media Age*, edited by Mordechai Neiger, Oren Meyers, and Eyal Zandberg (Houndmills and New York: Palgrave Macmillan, 2011), pp. 241–52.

[99] *Proposal for a Regulation of the European Parliament and of the Council on the protection of individuals with regard to the processing of personal data and on the free movement of such data (General Data Protection Regulation)* (Brussels: European Commission, 2012), pp. 51–3 (Article 17 'Right to be forgotten and to erasure').

[100] *Guardian*, 14 May 2014.

[101] Meg Leta Jones, *Ctrl + Z: The Right to Be Forgotten* (New York and London: New York University Press, 2016); see also the essays in Ângela Guimarães Pereira, Alessia Ghezzi, and Lucia Vesnić-Alujević, eds, *The Ethics of Memory in a Digital Age: Interrogating the Right to Be Forgotten* (Houndmills and New York: Palgrave Macmillan, 2014).

[102] Antoon De Baets, 'A Historian's View on the Right to Be Forgotten', *International Review of Law, Computers & Technology*, 30, nos. 1–2 (2016): pp. 57–66.

[103] Inge Bundsgaard, 'The Question of Access: The Right to Social Memory Versus the Right to Social Oblivion', in *Archives, Documentation, and Institutions of Social Memory*, edited by Francis X. Blouin and William G. Rosenberg (Ann Arbor: University of Michigan Press, 2006), pp. 114–20.

surveying the dynamics of disremembering on a national scale, the case of social forgetting of the Turn-Out in Ulster suggests that provincial history allows for examination in greater depth. Just as Philippe Joutard could trace the transmission of traditions of the uprising of the Protestant Camisards in the Cévennes region of southern France from the eighteenth century through to present times,[104] it is evidently possible to study developments in social forgetting over long periods of time. Enduring traditions of social forgetting are more likely to be found in frontier zones, located on the margins of powerful states and empires, which have a history of local ethnic, religious, and political conflicts that has left troublesome memories. The reticence through which these memories have been obscured can be penetrated through engagement with vernacular historiography.

Historians have much to gain from developing an appreciation of vernacular historiography. 'Can the subaltern speak?'—the question with which Gayatri Chakravorty Spivak famously challenged postcolonial studies—is a *question mal posée*. For the sake of argument, we can put aside the question of whether the literate inhabitants of Ulster can be classified as 'subaltern'. After all, Spivak demonstrated her thesis through the example of Bhubaneswari Bhaduri—'a woman of the middle class, with access, however clandestine, to the bourgeois movement for Independence'.[105] Vernacular historiography makes it evident that people have always spoken, even if in whispers, about their past. The real question to be asked is can the historian listen?

[104] See Philippe Joutard, *La légende des Camisards: Une sensibilité au passé* (Paris: Gallimard, 1977); Philippe Joutard, 'Orality and Popular Revolts in Louis XIV's France: What Makes the Camisards Special?', in *Rhythms of Revolt: European Traditions and Memories of Social Conflict in Oral Culture*, edited by Éva Guillorel, David Hopkin, and William G. Pooley (Routledge: London and New York, 2017), pp. 171–97.

[105] 'Can the Subaltern Speak' was originally published in *Marxism and the Interpretation of Culture*, edited by Cary Nelson and Lawrence Grossberg (Urbana: University of Illinois Press, 1988), pp. 271–313; a revised version appeared in Gayatri Chakravorty Spivak, *A Critique of Postcolonial Reason: Toward a History of the Vanishing Present* (Cambridge, Mass.: Harvard University Press, 1999), pp. 244–311 (see esp. pp. 306–11).

Select Bibliography

MANUSCRIPTS

Belfast Central Library (BCL)
Francis Joseph Bigger collection
McAdam and Bryson manuscript collection
Newspaper cuttings

Bodleian Library, Oxford (BOD)
Broadside Ballads

British Library (BL)
Auckland Papers
Pelham Papers
Letters of Bishop Percy to his wife
Lord Chamberlain's Plays

Irish Linen Centre and Lisburn Museum
Florence Mary Wilson Papers

Kent History and Library Centre (KHLC)
Pratt Manuscripts

Linen Hall Library
Belfast Empire Theatre collection
Joy MSS
Lyric Theatre collection
Mageean collection
Miscellaneous theatre collections
Northern Ireland Political collection
TPA Theatre press cuttings
Ulster Group Theatre collection

Military Archives, Ireland
Bureau of Military History, Witness Statements

National Archives of Ireland (NAI)
Census of Ireland 1901/1911
Chief Secretary's Office Registered Papers
Crime Branch Special Records
Rebellion Papers
State of the Country Papers

National Library of Ireland (NLI)
Francis Joseph Bigger Papers
F. S. Bourke Papers
Séamus de Búrca Papers
Compensation Claims of Suffering Loyalists

Robert Emmet Papers
Ephemera collections
John Q. Graham Papers
Seamus Heaney Papers
Joseph Holloway Papers
Memoirs of Morgan Jellett of Moira
Robert Johnston Papers
Kilmainham Papers
Richard Musgrave Papers
Leon Ó Broin Papers
Teeling family correspondence
Lily Williams Papers

National Museum Northern Ireland (NMNI)
Ulster Folk and Transport Museum, folklore scheme notebooks

Public Record Office of Northern Ireland (PRONI)
1798 Rebellion miscellaneous related papers
Abercorn Papers
Anglesey Papers
J. B. Armour Papers
Denis Barritt press cuttings
Benn Papers
Bigger Family Papers
R. W. H. Blackwood Papers
Camden Papers
Castlereagh Papers
John Cleland Papers
Joseph Connellan Papers
Lenox-Conyngham Papers
Sharman Crawford Papers
Crosslé Family Papers
Capt. R. H. Davis press cuttings
Doak Family Papers
Dobbs Papers
Downshire Papers
William Drennan Papers
Duffin Family Papers
John Galt diary
Gosford Papers
Granard Papers
Gray Family Papers
Betsy Gray related photographs
Hill of Brook Hall Papers
Hobart Papers
Emigrant letters
John Kells Ingram Papers
Johnston (Johnson) Family Papers
Ker Papers
Leslie Papers
Ernest Lowry Papers

Lowry, Cleland, Steele and Nicholson Families' Papers
Lynn, Lawther and Houston Families' Letters
Massereene–Foster Papers
McBride Papers
McCance Family Papers
Aiken McClelland Papers
Henry Joy McCracken correspondence
McKee family (murder) Papers
Mary McNeill Papers
Morrow Papers
Nicholson deposited documents
Normanton Papers
Northern Ireland Cabinet Papers
William Orr Papers
Parks and Caldwell Papers
Pelham transcripts
Porter Family Papers
Classon Porter Papers (manuscript notebooks)
C. J. Robb (depositor) Papers
Robb and Bryson Family Papers
Russell Papers
Savage-Armstong Papers
Sheffield Papers
Shirley Papers
Tennent Papers
Wallace Family Papers
Aynsworth Wilson Papers
Col. J. B. Wilson (depositor) Papers
Young Family Papers

Queen's University Belfast (QUB)
Thomas Carnduff Papers

Royal Irish Academy (RIA)
Samuel McSkimin Papers

Trinity College Dublin (TCD)
Richard Robert Madden Papers

The National Archives, UK (TNA)
Charles Abbot, 1st Baron Colchester Papers
Home Office, Correspondence on Civil Affairs, Ireland
Home Office, Correspondence on Private and Secret Affairs
Home Office, Civil Service and Military Correspondence
Intelligence Notes, B Series
Royal Irish Constabulary, Crime Branch

University College Dublin (UCD)
National Folklore Collection, Main Manuscript Collection (NFC)
Radio Éireann transcripts

University of Ulster, Coleraine
John Hewitt Papers

Official Publications

A List of the Counties of Ireland, and the Respective Yeomanry Corps in Each County (Dublin: Dublin Castle, 1798)

A List of the Officers of the Militia and of the Yeomanry Cavalry and Volunteer Cavalry of the United Kingdom (1821)

Census of Ireland, British Parliamentary Papers (1891, 1901, 1911)

Dáil Éireann Debates

Dublin Castle Bulletins (1798)

House of Commons Debates (Hansard)

Journals of the House of Lords

Northern Ireland Parliamentary Debates (Stormont Papers)

Reports of the Secret Committees of Lords and Commons (1797)

Report from the Committee of Secrecy of the House of Lords of Ireland (1798)

The Report from the Secret Committee of the House of Commons in Ireland (1798)

Report from the Select Committee Appointed to Inquire into the Nature, Character, Extent and Tendency of Orange Lodges (1835)

Report from the Select Committee of the House of Lords, Appointed to Enquire into the State of Ireland in Respect of Crime (1839)

Ulster: The Official Publication of the Ulster Tourist Development Association, Ltd (Belfast: William Strain & Sons, 1925, 1929, 1934, 1936)

NEWSPAPERS

Aberdeen Daily Journal
Aberdeen Weekly Journal
American Monthly Magazine
Anglo-Celt
Antrim Times
Ballymena Observer
Ballymena Times
Ballymoney and Moyle Times
Banbridge Chronicle
Banbridge Leader
Banner of Ulster
Belfast Commercial Chronicle
Belfast Evening Telegraph
Belfast Gazette
Belfast Mercury
Belfast Morning News
Belfast News-Letter
Belfast Protestant Journal
Belfast Telegraph
Belfast Weekly News
Butte Independent
Carrick Times
Catholic Press
Catholic Telegraph
Coleraine Chronicle

Combat
Connaught Telegraph
Cork Examiner (Irish Examiner)
County Down Spectator and Ulster Standard
Daily Express
Daily Mirror
Daily Nation
Derry Journal
Derry People and Donegal News
Dover Express
Down News
Down Recorder
Downpatrick Recorder
Downshire Protestant
Dublin Evening Mail
Dublin Monitor
Dundalk Democrat
Dundalk Examiner and Louth Advertiser
Dundee Evening Telegraph
Enniskillen Advertiser
Era
Evening Freeman
Evening Herald
Fermanagh Herald
Finn's Leinster Journal
Free Press
Freeman's Journal
Frontier Sentinel
Glasgow Herald
Graphic
Guardian
Hampshire Advertiser
Independent
Irish Citizen
Irish Democrat
Irish Independent
Irish News
Irish People
Irish Press
Irish Republican News
Irish Times
Irish Weekly and Ulster Examiner
Irishman
Kerryman
Larne Times
Leitrim Observer
Limerick and Clare Examiner
Lisburn Herald and Antrim and Down Advertiser
Lisburn Standard
London Daily News
London Evening Standard

Londonderry Sentinel
Londonderry Standard
Loyalist News
Mayo News
Meath Chronicle
Morning Chronicle
Morning News
Morning Post
Mourne Observer
Nation
New Zealand Tablet
Newry and Belfast Standard
Newry Democrat
Newry Examiner and Louth Advertiser
Newry Herald and Down, Armagh, and Louth Journal
Newry Reporter
Newry Telegraph
Newtownabbey Times
Newtownards Chronicle
Newtownards Spectator and Donaghadee Review
North Down Herald
Northern Herald
Northern Star
Northern Whig
Observer
Orange Standard
Pall Mall Gazette
Pennsylvania Inquirer and National Gazette
The People
An Phoblacht
The Press
Protestant Journal
Protestant Telegraph
Republican News
Sheffield and Rotherham Independent
Sligo Champion
Southern Star
Spectator
Stage
Standard
Strabane Chronicle
Sunday Independent
Sunday Life
Sunday Times
Sydney Morning Herald
Telegraph
Times
Tuam Herald
Ullans
Ulster Echo
Ulster General Advertiser

Ulster Herald
Ulster Magazine and Monthly Review of Science and Literature
Ulster Star
Ulster Times
Ulsterman
Ulster-Scot
United Ireland
United Irishman
Vindicator
Walsall Advertiser
Warrenpoint Weekly
Weekly Freeman
Weekly
Western People
Wexford Echo
Witness

Literary Journals and Magazines
Ariel: A Literary and Cultural Gazette
Belfast Magazine and Literary Journal
Belfast Monthly Magazine
Blackwood's Magazine
Books Ireland
Bulletin of the Presbyterian Historical Society of Ireland
Catholic Bulletin
Dublin Penny Journal
Dublin Literary Gazette
Dublin University Magazine
Folk Magazine
Fraser's Magazine for Town and Country
Irish Book Lover
Irish Ecclesiastical Record
Irish Magazine, and Monthly Asylum
Irish Monthly Magazine
Irish Monthly
Irish Penny Journal
Irish Review
Journal of the County Louth Archaeological Society
Journal of the Presbyterian Historical Society
Journal of the Royal Society of Antiquaries of Ireland
L'Irlande Libre
Larne Literary and Agricultural Journal
Monthly Review
Newry Magazine; or, Literary & Political Register
Northern Patriot
Saturday Magazine
Shamrock
Shan Van Vocht
Ulster Journal of Archaeology
Walker's Hibernian Magazine

FILMOGRAPHY

1798 agus Ó Shin (dir. Louis Marcus; Louis Marcus Productions and TnaG, 1998).
1798 in the Six Mile Valley (dir. Archie R. Reid; self-produced, 1998).
1798—The Comedy (prod. Jackie Hamilton; Moondog Productions, 1998).
An Independent People (dir. Brendan Byrne; Below the Radar, 2013).
Brethren in Arms (dir. Vivien Hewitt; Lynx Productions, 2005).
News of the '98 (dir. Patrick Fitzsimons; Clan Visions, 1998).
Pike People (dir. Angela Ryan; RTÉ, 2000).
Rebellion, 3 episodes (dir. Brian Hayes; RTÉ, 1998).
The Patriot's Fate, 2 episodes (dir. Moore Sinnerton; Chistera Productions, 1998).

PRINTED SOURCES AND THESES

As the full list of books, pamphlets, articles and theses consulted (which runs to nearly 2,000 titles) is too lengthy to be reproduced, bibliographical details of items not listed below can be found in the footnotes.

'98 Centenary Committee, *The Story of William Orr* (Dublin: James Duffy, 1898).
anon., *A Brief Account of the Trial of William Orr, of Farranshane, in the County of Antrim* (Dublin: J. Chambers, 1797).
anon. [Publicola], *A Letter from a Father to His Son, a United Irishman, in the Barony of Ards, in the County of Down* (Dublin: n.s., 1797).
anon., *A Collection of Loyal Songs, as Sung at All the Orange Lodges in Ireland* (Dublin: printed by W. McKenzie, 1798).
anon., *Paddy's Resource: Being a Select Collection of Original and Modern Patriotic Songs Compiled for the Use of the People of Ireland* (New York: printed by R. Wilson, 1798).
anon., *The Beauties of The Press* (London: s.n., 1800).
anon., *County of Down Election, 1805: The Patriotic Miscellany: Or Mirror of Wit, Genius, and Truth, Being a Correct Collection of All the Publications During the Late Contested Election, between the Hon. Colonel John Meade and the Right Hon. Lord Viscount Castlereagh* (London: n.s., 1805).
anon., *The Orange Institution; a Slight Sketch. With an Appendix Containing the Rules and Regulations of the Orange Societies of Great Britain and Ireland* (London: J. J. Stockdale, 1813).
anon., *Journal of a Tour in Ireland, &C. &C. Performed in August 1804. With Remarks on the Character, Manner, and Customs of the Inhabitants* (London: Richard Phillips, 1806).
anon., *Ednavady; a Poetical Tale, founded on the Battle of Ballynahinch* (Belfast: printed by A. Mackay, 1822).
anon., *The Down Squib-Book, Containing an Impartial Account of the Contested Election for the County of Down, in May 1831, between Lord Arthur Hill, W. S. Crawford, Esq., and Lord Viscount Castlereagh. Also, the Addresses and Squibs Which Were Issued During This Interesting Struggle* (Belfast: Henry Lanktree, 1831).
anon., *Belfast & Its Environs: Or, Stranger's Guide*, new edn (Belfast: John Henderson and Dublin: James McGlashan, 1855).
anon., *Records of the General Synod of Ulster, from 1691 to 1820*, vol. 3 (Belfast: Presbyterian Church in Ireland, 1898).
anon., *The History of the Orange Order* (Toronto: William Banks, 1898).
anon., *The 1798 Rebellion as Recorded in the Diaries of Gracehill Moravian Church* (Newtownabbey Moravian History Magazine, 1998).
anon. [An Ulster Protestant], 'Light on Ulsteria', *Irish Review*, 2, no. 15 (1912): pp. 119–23.

A Physician [Alexander Maxwell Adams], *Sketches from Life* (Glasgow: W. R. McPhum and London: Simpkin, 1835).

Ian Adamson, *Cruthin: The Ancient Kindred* (Newtownards: Nosmada Books, 1974).

Ian Adamson, *The Identity of Ulster: The Land, the Language and the People* (Belfast: self-published, 1982).

Ian Adamson, *Bangor, Light of the World* (Belfast: Pretani, 1987).

Jean Agnew, ed., *The Drennan-McTier Letters*, 3 vols (Dublin: The Women's History Project in association with the Irish Manuscripts Commission, 1998–9).

Donald Harman Akenson and W. H. Crawford, *Local Poets and Social History: James Orr, Bard of Ballycarry* (Belfast: Public Records Office Northern Ireland, 1977).

Donald Harman Akenson and W. H. Crawford, *Between Two Revolutions. Islandmagee, County Antrim 1798–1920* (Hamden Connecticut: Archon Books, 1979).

Harry Allen, *The Men of the Ards* (Donaghadee, Co. Down: Ballyhay Books, 2004).

James Allen, *O'Halloran: Or, the Insurgent Chief, a Drama in Three Acts (Partly Adapted from the Novel of the Same Name)* (Belfast: D. Allen, 1867).

Benedict Anderson, *Imagined Communities: Reflections on the Origin and Spread of Nationalism*, rev. edn (London and New York: Verso, 2006).

Stuart Andrews, *Irish Rebellion: Protestant Polemic, 1798–1900* (Basingstoke and New York: Palgrave Macmillan, 2006).

W. S. Armour, *Armour of Ballymoney* (London: Duckworth, 1934).

Aleida Assmann, 'Memory, Individual and Collective', in *The Oxford Handbook of Contextual Political Analysis*, edited by Robert E. Goodin and Charles Tilly (Oxford and New York: Oxford University Press, 2006), pp. 210–24.

Aleida Assmann, 'Canon and Archive', in *Cultural Memory Studies: An International and Interdisciplinary Handbook*, edited by Astrid Erll and Ansgar Nünning (Berlin and New York: Walter de Gruyter, 2008), pp. 97–107.

Aleida Assmann, 'To Remember or to Forget: Which Way out of a Shared History of Violence?', in *Memory and Political Change*, edited by Aleida Assmann and Linda Shortt (New York: Palgrave Macmillan, 2012), pp. 53–71.

Jan Assmann, 'Communicative and Cultural Memory', in *Cultural Memories: The Geographical Point of View*, edited by Peter Meusburger, Michael Heffernan, and Edgar Wunder (Dordrecht: Springer, 2011), pp. 15–27.

Mary Balfour, *Hope, a Poetical Essay; with Various Other Poems* (Belfast: Smyth and Lyons, 1810).

Carol Baraniuk, 'James Orr: Ulster-Scot and Poet of the 1798 Rebellion', *Scottish Studies Review*, 6 (2005): pp. 22–32.

Carol Baraniuk, 'Setting His Own Standard: James Orr's Employment of a Traditional Stanza Form', *Journal of Irish Scottish Studies*, 1, no. 1 (2007): pp. 73–86.

Carol Baraniuk, 'The Leid, the Pratoe and the Buik: Northern Cultural Markers in the Works of James Orr', in *Affecting Irishness: Negotiating Cultural Identity within and beyond the Nation*, edited by James P. Byrne, Padraig Kirwan, and Michael O'Sullivan (Oxford and New York: Peter Lang, 2008), pp. 103–20.

Carol Baraniuk, *James Orr, Poet and Irish Radical* (London: Pickering & Chatto, 2014).

Jonathan Bardon, *A History of Ulster* (Belfast: Blackstaff, 1992).

John Barrow, *A Tour Round Ireland, through the Sea-Coast Counties, in the Autumn of 1835* (London: John Murray, 1836).

Thomas Bartlett, 'Repressing the Rebellion in County Down', in *1798 Rebellion in County Down*, edited by Myrtle Hill, Brian Turner, and Kenneth Dawson (Newtownards: Colourpoint, 1998), pp. 187–210.

Thomas Bartlett, 'Clemency and Compensation: The Treatment of Defeated Rebels and Suffering Loyalists after the 1798 Rebellion', in *Revolution, Counter-Revolution, and*

Union: Ireland in the 1790s, edited by Jim Smyth (Cambridge: Cambridge University Press, 2000), pp. 99–127.

Thomas Bartlett, 'Sticking to the Past', in *Times Literary Supplement*, 25 January 2002, pp. 27–28.

Thomas Bartlett, *Revolutionary Dublin, 1795–1801: The Letters of Francis Higgins to Dublin Castle* (Dublin: Four Courts Press, 2004).

Thomas Bartlett, Kevin Dawson, and Dáire Keogh, *Rebellion: A Television History of 1798* (Dublin: Gill & Macmillan, 1998).

Thomas Bartlett, David Dickson, Dáire Keogh, and Kevin Whelan, eds, *1798: A Bicentenary Perspective* (Dublin: Four Courts Press, 2003).

Keith Beattie, *Ballymoney and the Rebellion 1798*, 2nd edn (Ballymoney: Ballymoney Borough Council, Leisure & Amenities Dept., 1998).

John Beattie, 'The "Turn out" in Ballycastle, 8–9 June 1798', *The Glynns*, 42 (2014): pp. 41–8.

J. C. Beckett et al., ed., *Belfast: The Making of the City, 1800–1914* (Belfast: Appletree Press, 1983).

Guy Beiner, 'Commemorating "Ninety-Eight", in 1998: A Reappraisal of History-Making in Contemporary Ireland', in *These Fissured Isles: Ireland, Scotland and British History, 1798–1848*, edited by Terry Botherstone, Anna Clark, and Kevin Whelan (Edinburgh: John Donald Publishers, 2005), pp. 221–41.

Guy Beiner, *Remembering the Year of the French: Irish Folk History and Social Memory* (Madison: University of Wisconsin Press, 2006).

Guy Beiner, 'Between Trauma and Triumphalism: The Easter Rising, the Somme, and the Crux of Deep Memory in Modern Ireland', *Journal of British Studies*, 46, no. 2 (2007): pp. 366–89.

Guy Beiner and Joep Leerssen, 'Why Irish History Starved? A Virtual Historiography', *Field Day Review*, 3 (2007): pp. 67–81.

Guy Beiner, 'Modes of Memory: Forgetting and Remembering 1798', in *Memory Ireland*, edited by Oona Frawley (Syracuse, N.Y.: Syracuse University Press, 2010), vol. 1: *History and Modernity*, pp. 66–82.

Robert Bell, 'The Heart and the Altar', in *Tales and Selections from the English Souvenirs for MDCCCVIII* (Philadelphia: James Kay, Jr, 1828), pp. 58–72.

Sam Hanna Bell, *A Man Flourishing* (Belfast: Blackstaff, 1986; orig. edn 1973).

anon. [George Benn], *The History of the Town of Belfast with an Accurate Account of the Former and Present State; to Which Is Added a Statistical Survey of the Parish of Belfast, and a Description of Some Remarkable Occurrences* (Belfast: A. Mackay, 1823).

George Benn, *A History of the Town of Belfast: From the Earliest Times to the Close of the Eighteenth Century; with Maps and Illustrations*, 2 vols (London: Marcus Ward, 1877).

Louie Bennett, *A Prisoner of His Word: A Tale of Real Happenings* (Dublin: Maunsel & Co., 1908).

Efrat Ben-Ze'ev, Ruth Ginio, and J. M. Winter, eds, *Shadows of War: A Social History of Silence in the Twentieth Century* (Cambridge and New York: Cambridge University Press, 2010).

John Bew, *The Glory of Being Britons: Civic Unionism in Nineteenth-Century Belfast* (Dublin: Irish Academic Press, 2009).

Francis Joseph Bigger, 'The Northern Star', *Ulster Journal of Archaeology*, 2nd ser., 1, no. 1 (1894): pp. 33–5.

Francis Joseph Bigger, 'Grant of Pardon to a '98 Insurgent', *Ulster Journal of Archaeology*, 2nd ser., 4, no. 3 (1898): pp. 173–5.

Francis Joseph Bigger, 'Robert Anderson, the Cumberland Bard: Some Notes on His Connection with Belfast and Carnmoney, 1808–1818', *Ulster Journal of Archaeology*, 2nd ser., 5, no. 2 (1899): pp. 100–4.

Francis Joseph Bigger and Herbert Hughes, 'Some Notes on the Architectural and Monumental Remains of the Old Abbey Church of Bangor, in the County of Down (Continued)', *Ulster Journal of Archaeology*, 2nd ser., 7, no. 1 (1901): pp. 18–36.

Francis Joseph Bigger, 'Art and Culture in Old Belfast', *Uladh*, 1, no. 1 (November 1904): pp. 11–12.

Francis Joseph Bigger, 'Henry Munroe', *Ulster Journal of Archaeology*, 2nd ser., 11, no. 2 (1905): p. 96.

Francis Joseph Bigger, *Remember Orr* (Dublin: Maunsel & Co., 1906).

Francis Joseph Bigger, 'Notes and Queries', *Ulster Journal of Archaeology*, 2nd ser., 12, no. 1 (January 1906): p. 48.

Francis Joseph Bigger, 'Ulster Exiles on the Continent after '98', *Ulster Journal of Archaeology*, 2nd ser., 12, no. 1 (1906): p. 46.

Francis Joseph Bigger, 'Old County of Down Presentments', *Ulster Journal of Archaeology*, 2nd ser., 13, no. 3 (1907): pp. 109–16.

Francis Joseph Bigger, *Rody Maccorly: 'Who Fears to Speak of '98?'* (Belfast: s.n., 1907).

Francis Joseph Bigger, 'Memorials of the Patriot Dead: MacCorly, Dickson, MacCracken', *Ulster Journal of Archaeology*, 2nd ser., 15, nos. 2/3 (1909): pp. 93–5.

Francis Joseph Bigger, 'Beauties of the Press', *Irish Book Lover*, 1, no. 5 (1909): p. 56.

Francis Joseph Bigger, 'W. H. Maxwell', *Irish Book Lover*, 1, no. 11 (1910): p. 152.

Francis Joseph Bigger, 'Miscellanea', *Ulster Journal of Archaeology*, 2nd ser., 16, no. 1/2 (1910): p. 96.

Francis Joseph Bigger, 'The Old Barracks of Belfast', *Ulster Journal of Archaeology*, 2nd ser., 17, no. 1/4 (1911): pp. 74–8.

Francis Joseph Bigger, 'Andrew Mackenzie, the Bard of Dunover', *Irish Book Lover*, 3, no. 12 (1912): pp. 197–9.

Francis Joseph Bigger, 'Robert Gowdie', *Irish Book Lover*, 4, no. 3 (1912): pp. 53–4.

Francis Joseph Bigger, 'A Literary Relic of "Ninety Eight"', *Irish Book Lover*, 5, no. 3 (1913): pp. 43–5.

Francis Joseph Bigger, *Four Shots from Down* (Belfast: William Sweeney, 1918).

Francis Joseph Bigger, 'A Drogheda Schoolmaster: Rev. James Porter', *Journal of the County Louth Archaeological Society*, 5, no. 1 (1921): p. 37.

Francis Joseph Bigger, 'Rural Libraries in Antrim', *Irish Book Lover*, 13, no. 4 (1921): pp. 47–52.

Francis Joseph Bigger, 'James Porter (1753–1798), with Some Notes on "Billy Bluff" and "Paddy's Resource"', *Irish Book Lover*, 13, nos. 7 & 8 (1922): pp. 126–31.

Francis Joseph Bigger, 'The James Hope Monument', *Ulster Journal of Archaeology*, 2nd ser., 7, no. 1 (1901): p. 64.

anon., [Thomas Ledlie Birch], *A Letter from an Irish Emigrant, to His Friend in the United States: Giving an Account of the Rise and Progress of the Commotions in Ireland, of the United Irishmen, and Orange Societies, and of Several Battles and Military Executions* (Philadelphia: printed and sold at the book-sellers, 1799).

George A. Birmingham, *The Northern Iron* (Dublin: Maunsel & Co., 1907).

George A. Birmingham, *Iarann an Tuaiscirt*, translated by Muiris Ó Catháin (Baile Átha Cliath [Dublin]: Oifig Díolta Foillseacháin Rialtais, 1933).

Eileen Black, 'John Tennent, 1798–1813, United Irishman and Chevalier de la Legion d'Honneur', *Irish Sword*, 13 (1977–9): pp. 157–9.

Eileen Black, 'James Hope (1764–1847), United Irishman', *Irish Sword*, 14 (1980–1): pp. 64–8.

Robert Black, *Substance of Two Speeches, Delivered in the General Synod of Ulster at Its Annual Meeting in 1812* (Dublin: printed by Stewart & Hopes, 1812).

Allan Blackstock, *An Ascendancy Army: The Irish Yeomanry, 1796–1834* (Dublin: Four Courts Press, 1998).

Allan Blackstock, 'Pictures of the Past: Some Forde Documents', in *Down Survey 1998: The Yearbook of Down County Museum*, edited by Brian S. Turner (Downpatrick: Down County Museum, 1998), pp. 27–33.

Allan Blackstock, *Double Traitors? The Belfast Volunteers and Yeomen 1778–1828* (Belfast: Belfast Society & Ulster Historical Foundation, 2000).

Allan Blackstock, 'The Irish Yeomanry and the 1798 Rebellion', in *1798: A Bicentenary Perspective*, edited by Thomas Bartlett et al. (Dublin: Four Courts Press, 2003), pp. 331–44.

Allan Blackstock, 'Politics and Print: A Case Study', in *The Oxford History of the Irish Book*, edited by Raymond Gillespie and Andrew Hadfield (Oxford and New York: Oxford University Press, 2006), vol. 3, pp. 234–49.

Allan Blackstock, *Loyalism in Ireland 1789–1829* (Woodbridge: Boydell, 2007).

Allan Blackstock, 'Loyal Clubs and Societies in Ulster, 1770–1800', in *Clubs and Societies in Eighteenth-Century Ireland*, edited by James Kelly and Martyn J. Powell (Dublin: Four Courts Press, 2010), pp. 447–65.

Robert E. Blanc, 'James McHenry (1785–1845): Playwright and Novelist' (PhD: University of Pennsylvania, 1939).

F. S. Bourke, 'Musgrave's *Memoirs of the Different Rebellions in Ireland*', *Irish Sword*, 2 (1954–6): p. 298.

P. J. Bourke, 'The Northern Insurgents: Ulster in 1798', *Journal of Irish Literature*, 13, nos. 1 & 2 (1984): pp. 7–74.

Andrew Boyd, *Holy War in Belfast: A History of the Troubles in Northern Ireland* (New York: Grove Press, 1972; orig. edn 1969).

Andrew Boyd, 'The Life and Times of R. R. Madden', *Seanchas Ardmhacha: Journal of the Armagh Diocesan Historical Society*, 20, no. 2 (2005): pp. 133–54.

Andrew Boyd, *Montgomery and the Black Man: Religion and Politics in Nineteenth-Century Ulster* (Blackrock, Co. Dublin: Columba, 2006).

Francis Boyle, *Miscellaneous Poems* (Belfast: printed by D. & S. Lyons, 1811).

Samuel Bracegirdle, 'The Reverend James Porter of Greyabbey', *North Irish Roots*, 10, no. 1 (1999): pp. 20–2.

Peter Brooke, *Ulster Presbyterianism: The Historical Perspective, 1610–1970* (Dublin: Gill and Macmillan and New York: St Martin's Press, 1987).

John Brown, *Orangeism around Ballymena*, Part I (Ballymena: Mid-Antrim Historical Group, 1990).

Stephen J. M. Brown, *A Readers' Guide to Irish Fiction* (London: Longmans Green and Co., 1910).

Stephen J. M. Brown, 'Irish Historical Fiction', *Studies: An Irish Quarterly Review*, 4, no. 15 (1915): pp. 441–53.

Stephen J. M. Brown, *Ireland in Fiction: A Guide to Irish Novels, Tales, Romances, and Folk-Lore*, 2nd edn (Dublin and London: Maunsel & Co., 1919).

Stephen J. M. Brown, 'Novels of the National Idea', *Irish Monthly*, 48, no. 563 (1920): pp. 254–62.

William Bruce and Henry Joy, *Belfast Politics: Or, a Collection of the Debates, Resolutions, and Other Proceedings of That Town, in the Years M,DCC,XCII, and M,DCC,XCIII. With Strictures on the Test of Certain of the Societies of United Irishmen* (Belfast: H. Joy, 1794).

Samuel Burdy, *The History of Ireland, from the Earliest Ages to the Union* (Edinburgh: Doig and Sterling, 1817).

Mary Burgess, 'Mapping the Narrow Ground: Geography, History and Partition', *Field Day Review*, 1 (2005): pp. 121–32.

Fanny Byrne, ed., *Memoirs of Miles Byrne: Chef De Bataillon in the Service of France, Officer of the Legion of Honour, Knight of Saint-Louis, Etc.* 3 vols (Paris and New-York: Gustave Bossange et Cie, 1863).

C. W. C., 'The Wrongs of Ulster', *Blackwood's Magazine*, 193, no. 1167 (1913): pp. 30–48.

Paul Callaghan, *Memories from the Farmyard* (Newtownards: Colourpoint, 2010).

Thomas Camac, 'A '98 Gravestone', *Ulster Journal of Archaeology*, 2nd ser., 2, no. 3 (1896): p. 207.

Thomas Camac, 'The M'Kinleys of Conagher, Co. Antrim, and Their Descendants', *Ulster Journal of Archaeology*, 2nd ser., 3, no. 3 (1897): pp. 167–70.

Thomas Camac, 'The Parish of Derrykeighan (County Antrim) for Three Centuries', *Ulster Journal of Archaeology*, 5, no. 3 (1899): pp. 147–61.

A. Albert Campbell, *Notes on the Literary History of Strabane* (Omagh: Tyrone Constitution, 1902).

A. Albert Campbell, *Belfast Newspapers, Past and Present* (Belfast: W. & G. Baird, 1921).

Flann Campbell, *The Dissenting Voice: Protestant Democracy in Ulster from Plantation to Partition* (Belfast: Blackstaff Press, 1991).

James Campbell, *The Poems and Songs of James Campbell of Ballynure* (Ballyclare: S. Corry, 1870; orig. edn 1820).

Joseph Campbell, 'The Turn-Out', *Irish Review*, 2, no. 18 (1912): pp. 317–35.

Joseph Campbell, 'Northern Autobiography', *Journal of Irish Literature*, 8, no. 3 (1979): pp. 60–96.

Thomas Joseph Campbell, *Fifty Years of Ulster, 1890–1940* (Belfast: Irish News, 1941).

Tony Canavan, *Frontier Town: An Illustrated History of Newry*, 2nd edn (Drogheda: Choice, 2009).

Ethna Carbery, *Willie Nelson* (Belfast: J. W. Boyd, *c.*1897).

John Cardwell, 'The Legend of Ballylone Fort, in the County of Down', *Ulster Journal of Archaeology*, 2nd ser., 10, no. 2 (1904): pp. 90–1.

Denis Carroll, *The Man from God Knows Where: Thomas Russell 1767–1803* (Blackrock, Co. Dublin: Gartan, 1995).

Denis Carroll, *Unusual Suspects: Twelve Radical Clergymen* (Blackrock, Co. Dublin: Columba Press, 1998).

Ciaran Carson, *The Twelfth of Never* (London: Picador in association with The Gallery Press, 1999).

Joseph Carson, *Poems, Odes, Songs, and Satires* (Newry: printed by Morgan and Stevenson, 1831).

Mary P. Caulfield, 'Whenever the Tale of '98 is Told: Constance Markievicz, the National Memory and "the Women of Ninety-Eight"', in *Ireland, Memory and Performing the Historical Imagination*, edited by Christopher Collins and Mary P. Caulfield (Houndmills and New York: Palgrave Macmillan, 2014), pp. 87–100.

Thomas Cauvin, 'One Common Event, Two Distinct Narratives: Commemorative Displays in National Museums in Ireland and Northern Ireland in the 1990s', in *Great Narratives of the Past: Traditions and Revisions in National Museums*, edited by Dominique Poulot et al. (Linköping: Linköping University Electronic Press, 2011), pp. 587–96.

D. A. Chart, ed., *The Drennan Letters: Being a Selection from the Correspondence Which Passed between William Drennan, M.D. And His Brother-in-Law and Sister, Samuel and Martha McTier, During the Years 1776–1819* (Belfast: H.M.S.O., 1931).

Mrs Charles Montague [Marion] Clarke, *Strong as Death*, 3 vols (London: Tinsley Bros., 1875).

Mrs Charles Montague [Marion] Clarke, *Strong as Death: A Story of the Irish Rebellion*, 2nd edn (Aberdeen: Moran, 1898).

W. Clarke-Robinson, 'James MacHenry, Author of "O'Halloran," "Hearts of Steel," Etc., Etc.', in *Ulster Journal of Archaeology*, 2nd ser., 14, no. 2/3 (1908), pp. 127–32.

Brendan Clifford, *Belfast in the French Revolution* (Belfast: Belfast Historical and Educational Association, 1989).

Brendan Clifford, ed., *Billy Bluff and the Squire and Other Writings by Rev. James Porter* (Belfast: Athol Books, 1991).

Brendan Clifford, *Aspects of the Movement of United Irishmen* (Belfast: Athol Books, 1991).

Brendan Clifford, *Scripture Politics: Selections from the Writings of William Steel Dickson, the Most Influential United Irishman of the North* (Belfast: Athol Books, 1991).

Brendan Clifford, *Prison Adverts and Potatoe Diggings: Materials from the Public Life of Antrim and Down During the Years of Government Terror Which Led to the Rebellion of 1798* (Belfast: Athol Books, 1992).

James Coigly, *The Life of the Rev. James Coigly, an Address to the People of Ireland, as Written by Himself During His Confinement in Maidstone Gaol* (London: s.n., 1798).

Ramsay Colles, *The History of Ulster*, vol. 4 (London: Gresham Publishing Cpy Ltd, 1920).

Peter Collins, *Who Fears to Speak of '98? Commemoration and the Continuing Impact of the United Irishmen* (Belfast: Ulster Historical Foundation, 2004).

Maurice H. Fitzgerald Collis, 'Antrim Parish Church for Three Hundred Years', *Ulster Journal of Archaeology*, 2nd ser., 3, no. 2 (Jan. 1897): pp. 90–8.

Albert Colmer, '"The 1798"—Remembered', *Lecale Miscellany*, no. 15 (1997), cover.

Padraic Colum, 'Kilmore', *Poetry Ireland Review*, no. 3 (1981): pp. 7–19.

Committee on Ulster Folklife and Traditions, *Ulster Folklife and Traditions: Collectors, Guide* (Belfast: Committee on Ulster Folklife and Traditions, 1957).

Mrs Thomas [Helena] Concannon, *Women of 'Ninety-Eight* (Dublin: M. H. Gill and Son, 1919).

Paul Connerton, *How Societies Remember* (Cambridge and New York: Cambridge University Press, 1989).

Paul Connerton, *How Modernity Forgets* (Cambridge and New York: Cambridge University Press, 2009).

Paul Connerton, 'Seven Types of Forgetting', *Memory Studies*, 1, no. 1 (2008): pp. 59–71.

S. J. Connolly, ed., *Belfast 400: People, Place and History* (Liverpool: Liverpool University Press, 2012).

David Cooper, *The Musical Traditions of Northern Ireland and Its Diaspora: Community and Conflict* (Farnham and Burlington: Ashgate, 2009).

S. L. Corrigan, *A New and Improved History of the Rebellion in Ireland in the Year 1798, Abridged from the Most Authentic Sources: With an Appendix Containing a History of the Orange Association, &C.* (Belfast: James Wilson, 1844).

T. C. S. Corry, *The Battle of Antrim: A Reminiscence of 1798* (Belfast: J. Henderson, 1875).

T. C. S. Corry, *Irish Lyrics, Songs & Poems* (Belfast: D. & J. Allen, 1879).

Joseph Davison Cowan, *An Ancient Irish Parish, Past and Present: Being the Parish of Donaghmore, County Down* (London: David Nutt, 1914).

Patricia Craig, 'Finding Hope in the Weavers', *Fortnight*, 275 (1989): p. vi.

Patricia Craig, 'Out of the Hands of Zealots', *Fortnight*, 290, supplement 'Radical Ulsters' (1991): p. 4.

Patricia Craig, 'To Scullabogue Backwards from Belfast: Against Sectarian Preconceptions', *Irish Pages*, 5, no. 2 (2008): pp. 134–52.

Patricia Craig, *A Twisted Root: Ancestral Entanglements in Ireland* (Belfast: Blackstaff Press, 2012).

John S. Crone and F. C. Bigger, eds, *In Remembrance: Articles & Sketches, Biographical, Historical, Topographical, by Francis Joseph Bigger, M.A., M.R.I.A., F.R.S.A.I.* (Dublin and Cork: Talbot Press and Belfast: Mullan & Son, 1927).

Sean Cronin, *A Man of the People* (Dublin: The Worker's Party, 1998).

Elizabeth Crooke, 'Exhibiting 1798: Three Recent Exhibitions', *History Ireland*, 6, no. 4 (1998): pp. 41–5.

Thomas Croskery and Thomas Witherow, *Life of the Rev. A. P. Goudy, D. D.* (Draperstown, Co. Londonderry and Ballymena, Co. Antrim: Moyola Books and Braid Books, 1994; orig. edn 1887).

Francis C. Crossle, 'An Historic Tale: A Faithful Steed and a Devoted Wife. A Newry Relic of '98', *The Open Window: An Annual of Literature and Popular Year Book* (1900): p. 60.

Virginia Crossman, 'The *Shan Van Vocht*: Women, Republicanism, and the Commemoration of the 1798 Rebellion', *Eighteenth-Century Life*, 22, no. 3 (1998): pp. 128–39.

anon. [Eyre Evans Crowe], *Yesterday in Ireland*, vols 2–3 (New York: J. & J. Harper, 1829).

Isabel Rosborough Crozier, *William Fee McKinney of Sentry Hill: His Family and Friends* (Coleraine: Impact, 1985).

John A. Crozier, *The Life of the Rev. Henry Montgomery L. L. D., Dunmurry, Belfast; with Selections from His Speeches and Writings*, vol. 1 (London: Simpkin, Marshall and Co. and Belfast: W. H. Greer, 1875).

Daragh Curran, *The Protestant Community in Ulster, 1825–45: A Society in Transition* (Dublin: Four Courts Press, 2014).

William Henry Curran, *The Life of the Right Honourable John Philpot Curran: Late Master of the Rolls in Ireland*, 2nd edn, 2 vols (Edinburgh: Archibald Constable & Co. and London: Hurst, Robinson & Co., 1822).

Nancy J. Curtin, 'The Transformation of the Society of United Irishmen into a Mass-Based Revolutionary Organisation, 1794–6', *Irish Historical Studies*, 24, no. 96 (1985): pp. 463–92.

Nancy J. Curtin, *The United Irishmen: Popular Politics in Ulster and Dublin, 1791–1798* (Oxford: Clarendon Press, 1998; orig. edn 1994).

Nancy J. Curtin, 'Reclaiming Gender: Transgressive Identities in Modern Ireland', in *'A Nation of Abortive Men': Gendered Citizenship and Early Irish Republicanism*, edited by Marilyn Cohen and Nancy J. Curtin (New York: St Martin's Press, 1999), pp. 33–52.

M. D., 'To the Catholics of Ulster', *The Belfast Monthly Magazine*, 11, no. 62 (1813): pp. 255–7.

R. D., 'A Memorial of 1798', *Journal of the Cork Historical and Archaeological Society*, ser. 2, vol. 12 (1906): pp. 102–3.

Cahal Dallat, 'A Ballycastle Story of the 1798 Rebellion', *The Glynns*, 26 (1998): pp. 83–6.

Cahal Dallat, ''98 Rebellion in Glanarm and Glencoy', *The Glynns*, 27 (1999): pp. 21–32.

Cahal Dallat, 'Ballycastle in the 1798', *The Glynns*, 27 (1999): pp. 61–7.

Mary Damant, *Peggy: A Tale of the Irish Rebellion* (London: W. H. Allen & Co., 1887).

Francis Davis, *Earlier and Later Leaves; or, an Autumn Gathering* (Belfast: W. H. Greer; Dublin: W. H. Gill & Son; London: H. Washbourne, 1878).

Richard Davis, 'The Manufacture of Propagandist History by Northern Ireland Loyalists and Republicans', in *Ireland's Terrorist Dilemma*, edited by Yonah Alexander and Alan O'Day (Dordrecht: Martinus Nijhoff Publishers, 1986), pp. 145–78.

Rob Davison, 'What Did Your Ancestor Do in the 1798 Rebellion?', *North Irish Roots*, 8, no. 1 (1997): p. 30.

Rob Davison, '1798 up-Date', *North Irish Roots*, 8, no. 2 (1997): p. 20.

Rob Davison, 'George Casement and the United Irishmen', *North Irish Roots*, 9, no. 2 (1998): pp. 12–13.

Angélique Day and Patrick McWilliams, eds, *Ordnance Survey Memoirs of Ireland* (Belfast: Institute of Irish Studies in association with the Royal Irish Academy 1990–6), 40 vols, 2, 3, 6, 7, 8, 10, 12, 13, 16, 17, 18, 19, 21, 23, 24, 26, 29, 32, 35, 37.

Diarmuid De Barra, *Ulster in '98: A Short Account of the Insurrection in Antrim and Down* (Dublin: Davis Publishing Company, n.d. [*c.*1920]).

Aodh de Blacam, 'The Other Hidden Ireland', *Studies*, 23, no. 91 (1934): pp. 439–54.

Aodh de Blacam, *The Black North; an Account of the Six Counties of Unrecovered Ireland: Their People, Their Treasures, and Their History* (Dublin: M. H. Gill, 1950; orig. edn 1938).

Earnán de Blaghd, *Trasna Na Bóinne* (Baile Átha Cliath: Sáirséal agus Dill, 1957).

Séamus de Búrca, 'The Queen's Royal Theatre 1829–1966', *Dublin Historical Record*, 27, no. 1 (1973): pp. 10–26.

Séamus de Búrca, *The Queen's Royal Theatre Dublin, 1829–1969* (Dublin: self-published, 1983).

Franca Dellarosa, *Talking Revolution: Edward Rushton's Rebellious Poetics, 1782–1814* (Liverpool: Liverpool University Press, 2014).

Sergio Della Sala, ed., *Forgetting* (Hove and New York: Psychology Press, 2010).

William Steel Dickson, *A Narrative of the Confinement and Exile of William Steel Dickson, D. D., Formerly Minister of the Presbyterian Congregations of Ballyhalbert and Portaferry, in the County of Down, and Now of Keady, in the County of Armagh*, 2nd edn (Dublin: printed by J. Stockdale, 1812).

William Steel Dickson, *Retractations; or, a Review of, and Reply to, a Pamphlet, Entitled, 'Substance of Two Speeches, Delivered in the General Synod of Ulster at Its Annual Meeting, in 1812, by the Rev. Robert Black, Senior Presbyterian Minister of Londonderry. With an Account,' &C. &C* (Belfast: printed by Joseph Smyth, 1813).

Charles Dickson, *Revolt in the North: Antrim and Down in 1798* (Dublin and London: Clonmore and Reynolds, 1960).

Rev. A. H. Dill, Rev. James B. Armour, Rev. D. D. Boyle, and Rev. John Ramsay, *A Short History of the Presbyterian Churches of Ballymoney County Antrim* (Bradford and London: Percy Lund, Humphries & Co., 1898).

Roger Dixon, 'Heroes for a New Ireland: Francis Joseph Bigger and the Leaders of the '98', in *From Corrib to Cultra: Folklife Essays in Honour of Alan Gailey*, edited by Trefor M. Owen (Belfast: Institute of Irish Studies in association with the Ulster Folk and Transport Museum, 2000), pp. 29–37.

Roger Dixon, *Francis Joseph Bigger, 1863–1926: Ireland's Cultural Visionary* (Belfast: Belfast Education and Library Board, 2007).

Roger Dixon, 'Francis Joseph Bigger of Belfast and Ardglass: Ireland's Cultural Crusader', *Lecale Review*, no. 6 (2008): pp. 51–9.

Roger Dixon, 'Ulster-Scots Literature', in *Oxford History of the Irish Book*, edited by James H. Murphy (Oxford: Oxford University Press, 2011), vol. 4: *The Irish Book in English, 1800–1891*, pp. 73–80.

Gillian M. Doherty, *The Irish Ordnance Survey: History, Culture and Memory* (Dublin: Four Courts Press, 2006).

Dixon Donaldson, *Historical, Traditional, and Descriptive Account of Islandmagee* (s.l.: s.n., 1927).

Stephen Dornan, 'Beyond the Milesian Pale: The Poetry of James Orr', *Eighteenth-Century Ireland*, 20 (2005): pp. 140–55.

Stephen Dornan, 'Irish and American Frontiers in the Novels of James McHenry', *Journal of Irish and Scottish Studies*, 3, no. 1 (2009): pp. 139–56.

Stephen Dornan, 'Scots in Two Early Ulster Novels', in *Scots: Studies in Its Literature and Language*, edited by John M. Kirk and Iseabail Macleod (Amsterdam and New York: Rodopi, 2013), pp. 171–82.

James Douglas, *The Unpardonable Sin* (London: Grant Richards, 1907).

An Hibernian [Adam Douglass], *The Irish Emigrant: An Historical Tale Founded on Fact*, 2 vols (Winchester, Va.: John T. Sharrocks, 1817).

Avy Dowlin, *Ballycarry in Olden Days* (Belfast: Graham and Heslip, 1963).

John Borbridge Doyle, *Tours in Ulster: A Hand-Book to the Antiquities and Scenery of the North of Ireland* (Dublin: Hodges and Smith, 1854).

anon. [William Drennan], *Letters of Orellana, an Irish Helot, to the Seven Northern Counties Not Represented in the National Assembly of Delegates, held at Dublin, October, 1784, for Obtaining a More Equal Representation of the People in the Parliament of Ireland* (Dublin: J. Chambers & T. Heary, 1785).

anon. [William Drennan], *Fugitive Pieces, in Verse and Prose* (Belfast: printed by F. D. Finlay, 1815).

Willie Drennan, 'Fiddles, Flutes, Drums and Fifes', *Études Irlandaises*, no. 38–2 (2013): pp. 111–22.

W. H. Drummond and J. Scott Porter, *Sermons by the Late Rev. W. H. Drummond, D. D., M. R. I. A., with Memoir by the Rev. J. Scott Porter* (London: E. T. Whitfield and Edinburgh: Williams and Norgate, 1867).

John Dubourdieu, *Statistical Survey of the County of Down, with Observations on Means of Improvement; Drawn up for the Consideration, and by the Orders of the Dublin Society* (Dublin: The Dublin Society, 1802).

John Dubourdieu, *Statistical Survey of the County of Antrim, with Observations on Means of Improvement; Drawn up for the Consideration, and by Direction of the Dublin Society* (Dublin: The Dublin Society, 1812).

Jeffrey Dudgeon, *Roger Casement: The Black Diaries, with a Study of His Background, Sexuality and Irish Political Life* (Belfast: Belfast Press, 2002).

Charles Gavan Duffy, *The Ballad Poetry of Ireland*, 40th edn (Dublin: J. Duffy, 1869).

Charles Gavan Duffy, *Young Ireland: A Fragment of Irish History, 1840*–1850, 2 vols (London: T. Fisher Unwin, 1896).

Charles Gavan Duffy, *My Life in Two Hemispheres*, 2 vols (London: T. Fisher Unwin, 1898).

Eull Dunlop, ed., *Mid-Antrim: Articles on Ballymena and District*, 2 Parts (Ballymena: Mid-Antrim Historical Group, 1991).

Tom Dunne, *Rebellions: Memoir, Memory and 1798*, 2nd edn (Dublin: Lilliput Press, 2010).

Michael Durey, *Transatlantic Radicals and the Early American Republic* (Lawrence: University Press of Kansas, 1997).

Michael Durey, ed., *Andrew Bryson's Ordeal: An Epilogue to the 1798 Rebellion* (Cork: Cork University Press, 1998).

Michael Durey, 'Marquess Cornwallis and the Fate of Irish Rebel Prisoners in the Aftermath of the 1798 Rebellion', in *Revolution, Counter-Revolution, and Union: Ireland in the 1790s*, edited by Jim Smyth (Cambridge: Cambridge University Press, 2000), pp. 128–45.

Michael Durey, 'White Slaves: Irish Rebel Prisoners and the British Army in the West Indies 1799–1804', *Journal of the Society for Army Historical Research*, 80 (2002): pp. 296–312.

Michael Durey, 'Abduction and Rape in Ireland in the Era of the 1798 Rebellion', *Eighteenth-Century Ireland*, 21 (2006): pp. 27–47.

Michael Durey, 'Loyalty in an Age of Conspiracy: The Oath-Filled Civil War in Ireland 1795–1799', in *Unrespectable Radicals?: Popular Politics in the Age of Reform*, edited by Michael T. Davis and Paul A. Pickering (Aldershot and Burlington: Ashgate, 2008), pp. 71–89.

Eblana [Teresa J. Rooney], 'The Heroine of Ardes', *Northern Patriot*, 1, no. 8 (June 1896), pp. 116–17; no. 9 (July), pp. 130–1; no. 10 (August), pp. 146–7; no. 11 (September): pp. 162–3.

William Eden, *The Journal and Correspondence of William, Lord of Auckland*, vols 3 and 4 (London: R. Bentley, 1861).

S. E. [Samuel Edgar], 'A Letter to a Student at College', *Belfast Monthly Magazine*, 4, no. 19 (1810): pp. 95–9.

S. E. [Samuel Edgar], 'The Rejoinder of S. E.', *Belfast Monthly Magazine*, 5, no. 24 (1810): pp. 1–4.

E. [Samuel Edgar], 'Recollections of 1798', *Belfast Magazine and Literary Journal*, 1, no. 4 (1825): pp. 540–8.

Marianne Elliott, 'The Defenders in Ulster', in *The United Irishmen: Republicanism, Radicalism and Rebellion*, edited by David Dickson, Dáire Keogh, and Kevin Whelan (Dublin: The Lilliput Press, 1993), pp. 222–33.

Marianne Elliott, *The Catholics of Ulster: A History* (London: Allen Lane, 2000).

Astrid Erll, *Memory in Culture* (Houndmills and New York: Palgrave Macmillan, 2011).

Astrid Erll, 'Generation in Literary History: Three Constellations of Generationality, Genealogy, and Memory', *New Literary History*, 45, no. 3 (2014): pp. 385–409.

Astrid Erll and Ansgar Nünning, eds, *Cultural Memory Studies: An International and Interdisciplinary Handbook* (Berlin and New York: Walter de Gruyter, 2008).

Astrid Erll and Ann Rigney, *Mediation, Remediation, and the Dynamics of Cultural Memory* (Berlin and New York: Walter de Gruyter, 2009).

St John Ervine, *Ulster*, 2nd edn (Belfast: The Ulster Tourist Development Association, 1927).

E. Estyn Evans, *Mourne Country; Landscape and Life in South Down* (Dundalk: Dundalgan Press, 1951).

E. Estyn Evans, *Ulster: The Common Ground* (Mullingar, Co. Westmeath: Lilliput Press, 1984).

E. Estyn Evans, *Irish Folk Ways*, 4th edn (Mineola, N.Y.: Dover Publications, 2000).

Cæsar Litton Falkiner, *Studies in Irish History and Biography, Mainly of the Eighteenth Century* (London: Longmans & Co., 1902).

Cyril Falls, *The Birth of Ulster*, 2nd edn (London: Constable, 1998).

Charles Fanning, *The Irish Voice in America: 250 Years of Irish-American Fiction*, 2nd edn (Lexington: University Press of Kentucky, 2000).

Sean Farrell, *Rituals and Riots: Sectarian Violence and Political Culture in Ulster, 1784–1886* (Lexington: University Press of Kentucky, 2000).

Sean Farrell, 'Writing an Orange Dolly's Brae', in *Shadows of the Gunmen: Violence and Culture in Modern Ireland*, edited by Danine Farquharson and Sean Farrell (Cork: Cork University Press, 2008), pp. 90–106.

Frank Ferguson, ed., *Ulster-Scots Writing: An Anthology* (Dublin: Four Courts Press, 2008).

Frank Ferguson, 'Ulster-Scots Literature', in *Oxford History of the Irish Book*, vol. 4, edited by James H. Murphy (Oxford: Oxford University Press, 2011), pp. 420–31.

Frank Ferguson and Andrew R. Holmes eds, *Revising Robert Burns and Ulster: Literature, Religion and Politics, c.1770–1920* (Dublin: Four Courts Press, 2009).

K. P. Ferguson, 'The Volunteer Movement and the Government, 1778–1793', *Irish Sword*, 13, no. 52 (1978–9): pp. 208–16.

Samuel Ferguson, 'The Wet Wooing: A Narrative of Ninety-Eight', *Blackwood's Edinburgh Magazine*, 31, no. 193 (1832): pp. 624–45.

Samuel Ferguson, *Brief Biographical Sketches of Some Irish Covenanting Ministers Who Laboured During the Latter Half of the Eighteenth Century* (Londonderry: James Montgomery, 1897).

Ina Ferris, *The Romantic National Tale and the Question of Ireland* (Cambridge and New York: Cambridge University Press, 2002).

Henry M. Field, *The Irish Confederates, and the Rebellion of 1798* (New York: Harper & Brothers, 1851).

Edna C. Fitzhenry, *Henry Joy McCracken* (Dublin: The Talbot Press, 1936).

David Fitzpatrick, 'Instant history: 1912, 1916, 1918', in *Remembering 1916: The Easter Rising, the Somme and the Politics of Memory in Ireland*, edited by Richard S. Grayson and Fearghal McGarry (Cambridge: Cambridge University Press, 2016), pp. 65–85.

David Fitzpatrick, *Descendancy: Irish Protestant Histories since 1795* (Cambridge: Cambridge University Press, 2014).

Kathleen Fitzpatrick, *The Weans at Rowallan* (London: Methuen & Co., 1905).

Walter Fitzpatrick, ed., *The Manuscripts of J. B. Fortescue, Esq., Preserved at Dropmore*, vols 4 and 7 (London: H.M.S.O., 1892 and 1910).

W. J. Fitzpatrick, *The Life, Times and Cotemporaries of Lord Cloncurry* (Dublin: James Duffy, 1855).

W. J. Fitzpatrick, *The Sham Squire; and the Informers of 1798, with Jottings About Ireland Seventy Years Ago*, 6th edn (Dublin: W. B. Kelley and London: Simpkin, Marshall & Co., 1872).

W. J. Fitzpatrick, *Secret Service under Pitt* (London and New York: Longmans, Green, and Co., 1892).

Christopher Fitz-Simon, *'Buffoonery and Easy Sentiment': Popular Irish Plays in the Decade Prior to the Opening of the Abbey Theatre* (Dublin: Carysfort Press, 2011).

John Wilson Foster, *Irish Novels, 1890–1940: New Bearings in Culture and Fiction* (Oxford and New York: Oxford University Press, 2008).

R. F. Foster, 'Remembering 1798', in *History and Memory in Modern Ireland*, edited by Ian McBride (Cambridge: Cambridge University Press, 2001), pp. 67–94.

R. F. Foster, *Vivid Faces: The Revolutionary Generation in Ireland, 1890–1923* (London: Allen Lane, 2014).

J. H. Fowler, *William Orr* (London: Joseph H. Fowler, 1938).

R. H. Foy, *Remembering All the Orrs: The Story of the Orr Families of Antrim and Their Involvement in the 1798 Rebellion* (Belfast: Ulster Historical Foundation, 1999).

Oona Frawley, ed., *Memory Ireland*, 4 vols (Syracuse, N.Y.: Syracuse University Press, 2011–14).

Maeve Friel, *Here Lies: A Guide to Irish Graves* (Dublin: Poolbeg, 1997).

James Anthony Froude, *The English in Ireland in the Eighteenth Century*, vol. 3 (New York: Scribner, Armstrong, and Co., 1874).

J. G., 'Old Nanny Boyd—a True Narrative', *Dublin Penny Journal*, 2, no. 91 (29 March 1834): pp. 310–11.

Francis P. Gallagher, *A Blood Red Autumn: Thomas Russell and the Irish Rising of 1803* (Castlewellan, Co. Down: Fairythorn Press, 2003).

Patrick Galvin, *Irish Songs of Resistance* (London: Workers' Music Association, 1955).

John Gamble, *Sketches of History, Politics and Manners, Taken in Dublin, and the North of Ireland, in the Autumn of 1810* (London: C. Cradock and W. Joy, 1811).

John Gamble, *A View of Society and Manners in the North of Ireland, in the Summer and Autumn of 1812* (London: C. Cradock and W. Joy, 1813).

John Gamble, *Views of Society and Manners in the North of Ireland, in a Series of Letters Written in 1818* (London: Longman, Hurst, Rees, Orme, and Brown, 1819).

John Gamble, *Charlton; or, Scenes in the North of Ireland, a Tale*, 3 vols (London: Baldwin, Cradock, and Joy, 1823).

J. Anthony Gaughan, ed., *Memoirs of Senator Joseph Connolly (1885–1961): A Founder of Modern Ireland* (Blackrock, Co. Dublin: Irish Academic Press, 1996).

Liam Gaul, *Glory O! Glory O!: The Life of P. J. McCall* (Dublin: History Press Ireland, 2011).

Alice C. C. Gaussen, *Percy: Prelate and Poet* (London: Smith, Elder, & Co., 1908).

August Gering, 'To Sing of '98: The United Irishmen Rising and the Ballad Tradition in Heaney and Muldoon', *Literature Interpretation Theory*, 10 (1999): pp. 149–79.

Peter Gibbon, *The Origins of Ulster Unionism: The Formation of Popular Protestant Politics and Ideology in Nineteenth-Century Ireland* (Manchester: Manchester University Press, 1975).

John Gibney, *The Shadow of a Year: The 1641 Rebellion in Irish History and Memory* (Madison: The University of Wisconsin Press, 2013).

William Gibson, *The Year of Grace: A History of the Ulster Revival of 1859* (Edinburgh: Andrew Elliot, 1860).

Anon. [John Giffard], *Orange: A Political Rhapsody. Canto II* (Dublin: printed for John Milliken, 1798).

John Gifford, *A History of the Political Life of the Right Honourable William Pitt; Including Some Account of the Times in Which He Lived*, vol. 6 (London: printed for T. Cadell and W. Davies, Strand, 1809).

John Thomas Gilbert, ed., *The Manuscripts and Correspondence of James, First Earl of Charlemont*, 2 vols (London: H.M.S.O., 1894).

Peter Gilmore, '"Minister of the Devil": Thomas Ledlie Birch, Presbyterian Rebel in Exile', in *Ulster Presbyterians in the Atlantic World: Religion, Politics and Identity*, edited by David A. Wilson and Mark G. Spencer (Dublin: Four Courts Press, 2006), pp. 62–86.

Peter Gilmore and Kerby A. Miller, 'Searching for "Irish" Freedom—Settling for "Scotch-Irish" Respectability: Southwestern Pennsylvania, 1780–1810', in *Ulster to America: The Scots-Irish Migration Experience, 1680–1830*, edited by Warren R. Hofstra (Knoxville: University of Tennessee Press, 2011), pp. 165–210.

W. E. Gladstone, 'Plain Speaking on the Irish Union', *The Nineteenth Century*, 26, no. 149 (July 1889): pp. 1–20.

Henry Glassie, *Passing the Time in Ballymenone: Culture and History of an Ulster Community* (Philadelphia: University of Pennsylvania Press, 1982).

Henry Glassie, *The Stars of Ballymenone* (Bloomington and Indianapolis: Indiana University Press, 2006).

James Winder Good, *Ulster and Ireland* (Dublin and London: Maunsel & Co., 1919).

James Gordon, *History of the Rebellion in Ireland, in the Year 1798 &C., Containing an Impartial Account of the Proceedings of the Irish Revolutionists, from the Year 1782 Till the Suppression of the Rebellion* (Dublin: printed by William Porter, 1801).

Alexander P. Goudy, *Right Versus Might; or, Irish Presbyterian Politics Discussed. In Five Letters* (Londonderry: The *Standard*, 1852).

Ogle Robert Gowan, *Orangeism: Its Origin and History* (Toronto: printed by Lovell and Gibson, 1859).

Henry Grattan, *Memoirs of the Life and Times of the Rt. Hon. Henry Grattan*, vol. 4 (London: Henry Colburn, 1849).

Jane Gray, 'Folk Poetry and Working Class Identity in Ulster: An Analysis of James Orr's "The Penitent"', *Journal of Historical Sociology*, 6, no. 3 (1993): pp. 249–75.

John Gray, 'A Loyal Catholic Sermon of 1798', *Linen Hall Review* 4, no. 4 (Winter 1987): pp. 12–13.

John Gray, ed., *Thomas Carnduff: Life and Writings* (Belfast: Lagan Press, 1994).

John Gray, 'A Tale of Two Newspapers: The Contest between the Belfast News-Letter and the Northern Star in the 1790s', in *An Uncommon Bookman: Essays in Memory of J. R. R. Adams*, edited by John Gray and Wesley McCann (Belfast: Linen Hall Library, 1996), pp. 175–98.

John Gray, *The Sans Culottes of Belfast: The United Irishmen and the Men of No Property, a May Day Lecture* (Belfast: Belfast Trades Union Council and the United Irishmen Commemorative Society, 1998).

Alice Stopford Green, *The Old Irish World* (Dublin and London: M. H. Gill and Macmillan, 1912).

W. J. Green, *A Concise History of Lisburn and Neighbourhood: Comprising the Social, Industrial, Religious, and Educational Life of the People* (Belfast: T. H. Jordan, 1906).

Padric Gregory, *The Ulster Folk* (London: David Nutt, 1912).

Padric Gregory, *Old World Ballads* (London: David Nutt, 1913).

Padric Gregory, *Ireland: A Song of Hope, and Other Poems* (Dublin and London: Talbot Press and Fisher Unwin, 1917).

Padric Gregory, *Ulster Songs and Ballads* (Dublin and London: Talbot Press and Fisher Unwin, 1920).

Padric Gregory, *Complete Ballads* (Belfast: Lagan Press, 2013).

William Gregory, *The Second Edition of a Visible Display of Divine Providence; or, the Journal of a Captured Missionary . . . To Which Is Added, the Journal or Tour of the Author through the North of Ireland* (London: printed by J. Skirvern, 1801).

Brian Griffin, ' "Scallions, Pikes and Bog Oak Ornaments": The Irish Republican Brotherhood and the Chicago Fenian Fair, 1864', *Studia Hibernica*, no. 29 (1995): pp. 85–97.

William Grimshaw, *Incidents Recalled; or, Sketches from Memory* (Philadelphia: G. B. Zieber and Co., 1848).

Stephen Lucius Gwynn, *Ulster* (London and Glasgow: Blackie and Son Limited, 1911).

Kevin Haddick-Flynn, *Orangeism: The Making of a Tradition* (Dublin: Wolfhound Press, 1999).

Maurice Halbwachs, *Les cadres sociaux de la mémoire* (Paris: Félix Alcan, 1925).

Maurice Halbwachs, *La mémoire collective* (Paris: Presses universitaires de France, 1968; orig. edn 1950).

Maurice Halbwachs, *The Collective Memory*, translated by Francis J. and Vida Yazdi Ditter (New York: Harper & Row, 1980).

Maurice Halbwachs, *On Collective Memory*, translated by Lewis A. Coser (Chicago and London: University of Chicago Press, 1992).

David Hall, *A Battle Lost and Won: The Battle of Antrim, 1798* (Antrim: David Hall, 1998).

Gerald R. Hall, *Ulster Liberalism, 1778–1876: The Middle Path* (Dublin: Four Courts Press, 2011).

James Hall, *Tour through Ireland; Particularly the Interior & Least Known Parts, Containing an Accurate View of the Parties, Politics, and Improvements in the Different Provinces*, vol. 2 (London: printed for R. P. Moore, 1813).

Michael Hall, *Ulster's Shared Heritage* (Newtownabbey: Island Publications, 1993).

Michael Hall, *Is There a Shared Ulster Heritage?* (Belfast: Island Publications/Farset Community Think Tanks Project, 2007).

Mr & Mrs S. C. Hall, *Ireland: Its Scenery, Character, Etc.*, vol. 3 (London: Jeremiah How, 1843).

Arthur R. Hamill, *A Place Called Tranquility: An Irish Story* (Bloomington, Ind.: Author House, 2003).

Arthur R. Hamill, *Across the Saltwater Bridge* (Coral Springs, Fla.: Llumina Press, 2005).

Ernest William Hamilton, *The Soul of Ulster* (New York: E. P. Dutton & Co., 1917).

James B. Hamilton, *Ballymoney and District in the County of Antrim, Prior to the 20th Century* (Ballycastle: J. S. Scarlett and Son, 1958).

Thomas Hancock, *The Principles of Peace Exemplified in the Conduct of the Society of Friends in Ireland, During the Rebellion of the Year 1798: With Some Preliminary and Concluding Observations*, 3rd edn, Part 2 (London: R. Clay, 1828; orig. edn 1825).

Denis O'Donoghue Hanna, *The Face of Ulster* (London and New York: Batsford, 1952).

Eamon Hanna, 'Reclaiming Republicanism', in *The Republican Ideal: Current Perspectives*, edited by Norman Porter (Belfast: Blackstaff Press, 1998), pp. 113–31.

J. W. Hanna, 'An Inquiry into the True Landing Place of St Patrick in Ulster (Continued)', *Ulster Journal of Archaeology*, 2nd ser., 11, no. 2 (1905): pp. 71–6.

Philip Dixon Hardy, *The Northern Tourist; or, Stranger's Guide to the North and North West of Ireland* (Dublin: William Curry, Jr, 1830).

Philip Harwood, *History of the Irish Rebellion of 1798* (London: Chapman & Elcoate, 1844).

Marnie Hay, 'Explaining *Uladh*: Cultural Nationalism in Ulster', in *The Irish Revival Reappraised*, edited by E. A. Taylor FitzSimon and James H. Murphy (Dublin: Four Courts Press, 2003), pp. 119–31.

Marnie Hay, 'The Foundation and Development of Na Fianna Éireann, 1909–16', *Irish Historical Studies*, 36, no. 141 (2008): pp. 53–71.

Marnie Hay, *Bulmer Hobson and the Nationalist Movement in Twentieth-Century Ireland* (Manchester and New York: Manchester University Press, 2009).

Richard Hayes, 'Priests in the Independence Movement of '98', *The Irish Ecclesiastical Record*, 66 (1945): pp. 258–70.

Alethea Hayter, ed., *The Backbone: Diaries of a Military Family in the Napoleonic Wars* (Edinburgh: Pentland, 1993).

Harold Richard Hayward, *Ulster Songs and Ballads of the Town and the Country* (London: Duckworth, 1925).

Harold Richard Hayward, *In Praise of Ulster*, 5th edn (Belfast: William Mullan, 1946; orig. edn 1938).

Harold Richard Hayward, *Ulster and the City of Belfast* (London: Barker, 1950).

John F. Healy, 'Seamus Heaney and the Croppies: 1798 and the Poet's Early Political Inclinations', in *Back to the Present, Forward to the Past: Irish Writing and History since 1798*, edited by Brian Coates, Joachim Fischer, and Patricia A. Lynch (Amsterdam and New York: Rodopi, 2006), 1, pp. 53–65.

Seamus Heaney, *Door into the Dark* (London: Faber and Faber, 1969).

Seamus Heaney, 'Delirium of the Brave', *Listener*, 27 November 1969: pp. 757–9.

Seamus Heaney, 'Munro', *Everyman*, no. 3 (1970): pp. 58–65.

Seamus Heaney, *Wintering Out* (London: Faber and Faber, 1972).

Seamus Heaney, *North* (London: Faber and Faber, 1975).

Seamus Heaney, *Field Work* (New York: Farrar, Straus & Giroux, 1979).

Seamus Heaney, *Preoccupations: Selected Prose 1968–1978* (London: Faber and Faber, 1980).

Seamus Heaney, 'The Sense of the Past', *Ulster Local Studies*, 20, no. 20 (1985): pp. 108–15.

Seamus Heaney, *Electric Light* (New York: Farrar, Straus & Giroux, 2001).

Fred Heatley, *Henry Joy McCracken and His Times*, 2nd edn (Belfast: Wolfe Tone Society, 1967).

David Hempton and Myrtle Hill, *Evangelical Protestantism in Ulster Society 1740–1890* (London and New York: Routledge, 1992).

A. C. Hepburn, *A Past Apart: Studies in the History of Catholic Belfast 1850–1950* (Belfast: Ulster Historical Foundation, 1996).

A. C. Hepburn, *Catholic Belfast and Nationalist Ireland in the Era of Joe Devlin, 1871–1934* (Oxford: Oxford University Press, 2008).

Ivan Herbison, *Presbyterianism, Politics and Poetry in Nineteenth-Century Ulster: Aspects of an Ulster-Scots Literary Tradition* (Belfast: Queen's University, Institute of Irish Studies, 2000).

Ivan Herbison, 'Beyond the Rhyming Weavers', *Études Irlandaises*, 38, no. 2 (2013): pp. 41–54.

Cheryl Herr, *For the Land They Loved: Irish Political Melodramas, 1890–1925* (Syracuse, N.Y.: Syracuse University Press, 1993).

John Harold Hewitt, 'Portrait of a United Irishman' and 'A '98 Prelude', *Belfast Municipal Museum and Art Gallery Bulletin*, 1, no. 2 (1949): pp. 29–32.

John Harold Hewitt, *Two Plays: The McCrackens; the Angry Doves* (Belfast: Lagan Press, 1999).

John Harold Hewitt, *Rhyming Weavers & Other Country Poets of Antrim and Down*, new edn (Belfast: Blackstaff, 2004).

John Harold Hewitt, *A North Light: Twenty-Five Years in a Municipal Art Gallery* (Dublin: Four Courts Press, 2013).

Padhraig Higgins, *A Nation of Politicians: Gender, Patriotism, and Political Culture in Late Eighteenth-Century Ireland* (Madison: University of Wisconsin Press, 2010).

Judith Hill, *Irish Public Sculpture: A History* (Dublin: Four Courts Press, 1998).

Myrtle Hill, Brian Turner, and Kenneth Dawson, eds, *1798 Rebellion in County Down* (Newtownards: Colourpoint, 1998).

Catherine Hirst, *Religion, Politics, and Violence in Nineteenth-Century Belfast: The Pound and Sandy Row* (Dublin: Four Courts Press, 2002).

John Hobbs, 'United Irishmen: Seamus Heaney and the Rebellion of 1798', *Canadian Journal of Irish Studies*, 21, no. 2 (1995): pp. 38–43.

Bulmer Hobson, *Ireland Yesterday and Tomorrow* (Tralee: Anvil Books, 1968).

Mary Hobson, 'Some Ulster Souterrains', *Journal of the Royal Anthropological Institute of Great Britain and Ireland*, 39 (1909): pp. 220–7.

Andrew R. Holmes, 'Nineteenth-Century Ulster Presbyterian Perspectives on the 1798 Rebellion', *Irish History: A Research Yearbook*, 2 (2003): pp. 43–52.

Andrew R. Holmes, 'The Experience and Understanding of Religious Revival in Ulster Presbyterianism, c.1800–1930', *Irish Historical Studies*, 34, no. 136 (2005): pp. 361–85.

Andrew R. Holmes, *The Shaping of Ulster Presbyterian Belief and Practice, 1770–1840* (Oxford and New York: Oxford University Press, 2006).

Andrew R. Holmes, 'Presbyterian Religion, Poetry and Politics in Ulster, c.1770–1850', in *Revising Robert Burns and Ulster: Literature, Religion and Politics, c.1770–1920*, edited by Frank Ferguson and Andrew R. Holmes (Dublin: Four Courts Press, 2009), pp. 37–63.

Andrew R. Holmes, 'Presbyterian Religion, Historiography, and Ulster Scots Identity, c.1800 to 1914', *Historical Journal*, 52, no. 3 (2009): pp. 615–40.

Andrew R. Holmes, 'Covenanter Politics: Evangelicalism, Political Liberalism and Ulster Presbyterians, 1798–1914', *English Historical Review*, 125, no. 513 (2010): pp. 340–69.

Andrew R. Holmes, 'Professor James Thomson Sr. And Lord Kelvin: Religion, Science, and Liberal Unionism in Ulster and Scotland', *Journal of British Studies*, 50, no. 1 (2011): pp. 100–24.

Andrew R. Holmes, 'The Ulster Revival of 1859: Causes, Controversies and Consequences', *Journal of Ecclesiastical History*, 63, no. 3 (2012): pp. 488–515.

Andrew R. Holmes, 'Presbyterians, Loyalty, and Orangeism in Nineteenth-Century Ulster', in *Loyalism and the Formation of the British World 1775–1914*, edited by Allan Blackstock and Frank O'Gorman (Woodbridge: Boydell Press, 2014), pp. 125–44.

R. Finlay Holmes, *Henry Cooke* (Belfast: Christian Journals, 1981).

R. Finlay Holmes, 'United Irishmen and Unionists: Irish Presbyterians, 1791 and 1886', in *The Churches, Ireland, and the Irish*, edited by W. J. Sheils and Diana Wood (Oxford and New York: B. Blackwell, 1989), pp. 171–89.

R. Finlay Holmes, *Presbyterians and Orangeism 1795–1995* (Belfast: Presbyterian Historical Society of Ireland, 1996).

R. Finlay Holmes, 'From Rebels to Unionists: The Political Transformation of Ulster's Presbyterians', in *The Union: Essays on Ireland and the British Connection*, edited by Ronnie Hanna (Newtownards: Colourpoint, 2001), pp. 34–47.

Stephen Howe, *Ireland and Empire: Colonial Legacies in Irish History and Culture*, 2nd edn (Oxford and New York: Oxford University Press, 2002).

Robert Huddleston, *A Collection of Poems and Songs on Different Subjects*, vol. 2 (Belfast: s.n., 1846).

Herbert Hughes, 'General Munroe', *Journal of the Irish Folk Song Society*, 1, no. 1 (April 1904): p. 18.

David Hume and John W. Nelson, *The Templecorran Project: An Historic Guide to Ballycarry Old Cemetery* (Ballycarry: s.n., 1994).

David Hume, *'To Right Some Things That We Thought Wrong': The Spirit of 1798 and Presbyterian Radicalism in Ulster* (Lurgan: Ulster Society Publications, 1998).

David Hume, *Far from the Green Fields of Erin: Ulster Emigrants and Their Stories* (Newtownards: Colourpoint Books, 2005).

David Hume, 'Muskets on the Sabbath: Lessons from Local History', *The Glynns*, 38 (2010): pp. 10–18.

John K. Ingram, *Sonnets and Other Poems* (London: Adam and Charles Black, 1900).

Catherine Lynette Innes, *Woman and Nation in Irish Literature and Society, 1880–1935* (Athens: University of Georgia Press, 1993).

Iota [James Thomson], 'Recollections of the Battle of Ballynahinch by an Eye Witness', *Belfast Magazine and Literary Journal*, 1, no. 1 (1825): pp. 56–64.

Alvin Jackson, 'Unionist History (I)', *Irish Review*, no. 7 (1989): pp. 58–66.

Alvin Jackson, 'Irish Unionism and the Russellite Threat, 1894–1906', *Irish Historical Studies*, 25, no. 100 (1987): pp. 376–404.

Alvin Jackson, 'Unionist Myths 1912–1985', *Past & Present*, no. 136 (1992): pp. 164–85.

Alvin Jackson, *Ireland, 1798–1998: War, Peace and Beyond*, 2nd edn (Chichester and Malden, Mass.: Wiley-Blackwell, 2010).

Andrew James, *Ninety-Eight and Sixty Years After* (Edinburgh and London: William Blackwood and Sons, 1911).

Andrew James, *The Nabob: A Tale of Ninety-Eight*, Notes and Afterword by John Wilson Foster (Dublin: Four Courts Press, 2006).

John Moore Johnston, *Heterogenea, or Medley: For the Benefit of the Poor* (Downpatrick: James Parks, 1803).

Roy H. W. Johnston, *Century of Endeavour: A Biographical and Autobiographical View of the 20th Century in Ireland* (Dublin: Maunsel & Co., 2003).

Sheila Turner Johnston, *Alice: A Life of Alice Milligan* (Omagh: Colourpoint Press, 1994).

Thomas M. Johnstone, *The Vintage of Memory*, 2nd edn (Belfast: Quota Press, 1943).

Henry Joy, *Historical Collections Relative to the Town of Belfast from the Earliest Period to the Union with Britain* (Belfast: George Berwick, 1817).

P. W. Joyce, *Old Irish Folk Music and Songs* (London and New York: Longmans, Green, and Co., 1909).

P. W. Joyce, *English as We Speak It in Ireland* (London: Longmans, Green, and Co. and Dublin: M. H. Gill & Son, 1910).

S. R. Keightley, *The Pikemen: A Romance of the Ards of Down* (London: Hutchinson & Co., 1903).

S. R. Keightley, *Lucht Pící a's Sleagh*, translated by Séamus Ó Ceallaigh (Baile Átha Cliath [Dublin]: Oifig Díolta Foillseacháin Rialtais, 1936).

James Kelly, 'Select Documents XLIII: A Secret Return of the Volunteers of Ireland in 1784', *Irish Historical Studies*, 26, no. 103 (1989): pp. 268–92.

James Kelly, *Gallows Speeches from Eighteenth-Century Ireland* (Dublin: Four Courts Press, 2001).

James Kelly, *Sir Richard Musgrave, 1746–1818: Ultra-Protestant Ideologue* (Dublin: Four Courts Press, 2009).

James Kelly, 'Elite Political Clubs, 1770–1800', in *Clubs and Societies in Eighteenth-Century Ireland*, edited by James Kelly and Martyn J. Powell (Dublin: Four Courts Press, 2010), pp. 264–89.

Matthew Kelly, *The Fenian Ideal and Irish Nationalism, 1882–1916* (Woodbridge: Boydell & Brewer, 2006).

Brian Kennaway, *The Orange Order: A Tradition Betrayed* (London: Methuen, 2006).

Liam Kennedy and Philip Ollerenshaw, eds, *Ulster since 1600: Politics, Economy, and Society* (Oxford: Oxford University Press, 2013).

James G. Kenny, *As the Crow Flies over Rough Terrain* (Ballymena: s.n., 1988).

Daire Keogh, 'Christian Citizens: The Catholic Church and Radical Politics 1790–1800', in *Protestant, Catholic and Dissenter: The Clergy and 1798*, edited by Liam Swords (Blackrock: Columba Press, 1997), pp. 9–19.

Daire Keogh, *A Patriot Priest: A Life of Reverend James Coigly* (Cork: Cork University Press, 1998).

Daire Keogh, 'The Women of 1798: Explaining the Silence', in *1798: A Bicentenary Perspective*, edited by Thomas Bartlett et al. (Dublin: Four Courts Press, 2003), pp. 512–28.

James W. Kernohan, *The Parishes of Kilrea and Tamlaght O'Crilly* (Coleraine: Coleraine Chronicle, 1912).

John Killen, *John Bull's Famous Circus: Ulster History through the Postcard, 1905–1985* (Dublin: O'Brien, 1985).

John Killen, *The Decade of the United Irishmen: Contemporary Accounts, 1791–1801* (Belfast: Blackstaff Press, 1997).

Cecil Kilpatrick, ed., *The Formation of the Orange Order, 1795–1798: The Edited Papers of Colonel William Blacker and Colonel Robert H. Wallace* (Belfast: Education Committee of the Grand Orange Lodge of Ireland, 1994).

Thomas Kilpatrick, *Millisle and Ballycopeland Presbyterian Church: A Short History* (Newtownards: Henry Bros., 1934).

Anna Kinsella, '1798 Claimed for Catholics: Father Kavanagh, Fenians and the Centenary Celebrations', in *The Mighty Wave: The 1798 Rebellion in Wexford*, edited by Dáire Keogh and Nicholas Furlong (Dublin: Four Courts Press, 1996), pp. 139–55.

Anna Kinsella, 'Nineteenth-Century Perspectives: The Women of 1798 in Folk Memory and Ballads', in *The Women of 1798*, edited by Dáire Keogh and Nicholas Furlong (Dublin: Four Courts Press, 1998), pp. 187–200.

Richard Kirkland, *Cathal O'Byrne and the Northern Revival in Ireland, 1890–1960* (Liverpool: Liverpool University Press, 2006).

Alexander Knox, *A History of the County of Down from the Most Remote Period to the Present Day Including an Account of Its Early Colonization, Ecclesiastical, Civil, and Military Polity, Geography, Topography, Antiquities and Natural History* (Dublin: Hodges, Foster & Co., 1875).

L. [Alice Milligan], 'The Story of Betsy Gray: A Visit to Her Grave', *Shan Van Vocht*, 1, no. 5 (1 May 1896): pp. 97–8.

John Laird, *A Struggle to Be Heard: By a True Ulster Liberal* (London: Global & Western Publishing, 2010).

Stanley Lane-Poole, ed., *The Life of the Late General F. R. Chesney . . . By His Wife and Daughter* (London: W. H. Allen & Co., 1885).

W. T. Latimer, *A History of the Irish Presbyterians* (Belfast: James Cleeland and Edinburgh: R. W. Hunter, 1893).

W. T. Latimer, *Ulster Biographies, Relating Chiefly to the Rebellion of 1798* (Belfast: James Cleeland and William Mullan & Son, 1897).

W. T. Latimer, 'David Bailie Warden, Patriot 1798', *Ulster Journal of Archaeology*, 2nd ser., 13, no. 1 (1907): pp. 29–38.

W. T. Latimer, 'The Rev. Dr. Wm. S. Dickson at Keady', *Ulster Journal of Archaeology*, 2nd ser., 17, no. 1/4 (1911): pp. 95–6.

de Latocnaye [Jacques Louis de Bourgenet], *Promenade d'un français dans l'Irlande Orné de gravures en taille douce*, vol. 3 (Dublin: M. et D. Graisberry, 1797).

de Latocnaye [Jacques Louis de Bourgenet], *Rambles through Ireland; by a French Emigrant*, 2 vols (Cork: printed by M. Harris, 1798).

de Latocnaye [Jacques Louis de Bourgenet], *A Frenchman's Walk through Ireland, 1796–7*, translated by John Stevenson (Belfast: McCaw, Stevenson, and Orr and Dublin: Hodges Figgis, 1917).

Valentine Browne Lawless, *Personal Recollections of the Life and Times, with Extracts from the Correspondence, of Valentine, Lord Cloncurry* (Dublin: James McGlashan, 1849).

William Edward Hartpole Lecky, *A History of England in the Eighteenth Century*, 8 vols, vol. 8 (London: Longmans, Green, and Co., 1890).

William Edward Hartpole Lecky, *A History of Ireland in the Eighteenth Century*, New Impression, vols 4–5 (London: Longmans, Green, and Co., 1913).

Joseph Leerssen, *Remembrance and Imagination Patterns in the Historical and Literary Representation of Ireland in the Nineteenth Century* (Cork: Cork University Press in association with Field Day, 1996).

Joseph Leerssen, '1798: The Recurrence of Violence and Two Conceptualizations of History', *Irish Review*, no. 22 (1998): pp. 37–45.

Shane Leslie, *Doomsland* (New York: Scribner's, 1924).

Shane Leslie, *The Film of Memory* (London: Michael Joseph Ltd, 1938).

Daniel Levy and Natan Sznaider, *The Holocaust and Memory in the Global Age*, translated by Assenka Oksiloff (Philadelphia: Temple University Press, 2006).

Samuel Lewis, *A Topographical Dictionary of Ireland: Comprising the Several Counties, Cities, Boroughs, Corporate, Market, and Post Towns, Parishes, and Villages, with Historical and Statistical Descriptions*, 2nd edn, 2 vols (London: S. Lewis, 1847).

Rolf Loeber and Magda Loeber, *A Guide to Irish Fiction, 1650–1900* (Dublin: Four Courts, 2005).

Edna Longley, 'The Rising, the Somme and Irish Memory', in *Revising the Rising*, edited by Máirin Ní Dhonnchadha and Theo Dorgan (Derry: Field Day, 1991), pp. 29–40.

Edna Longley, *The Living Stream: Literature & Revisionism in Ireland* (Newcastle upon Tyne: Bloodaxe, 1994).

Edna Longley, 'Northern Ireland: Commemoration, Elegy, Forgetting', in *History and Memory in Modern Ireland*, edited by Ian McBride (Cambridge and New York: Cambridge University Press, 2001), pp. 223–53.

Jack Loudan, *Henry Joy McCracken: A Play in Three Acts* (Dublin: New Frontiers Press, 1946).

Jack Loudan, *A Lock of the General's Hair: A Comedy* (Belfast: Carter, 1953).

James Loughlin, 'Creating "a Social and Geographical Fact": Regional Identity and the Ulster Question 1880s–1920s', *Past and Present*, 195, no. 1 (May 2007): pp. 159–96.

Samuel Lover, ed., *The Lyrics of Ireland* (London: Houlston and Wright, 1858).

Derek Lundy, *Men That God Made Mad: A Journey through Truth, Myth and Terror in Northern Ireland* (London: Jonathan Cape, 2006).

Linde Connolly Lunney, 'Attitudes to Life and Death in the Poetry of James Orr, an Eighteenth-Century Ulster Weaver', *Ulster Folklife*, 31 (1985): pp. 1–12.

Adam Lynn, *Random Rhymes Frae Cullybackey* (Belfast: printed by W. & G. Baird, 1911).

W. G. Lyttle, *Betsy Gray; or, Hearts of Down: A Tale of Ninety-Eight* (Newcastle, Co. Down: Mourne Observer Ltd, 1968; orig. edn. 1888).

M. [Robert Shipboy MacAdam], 'The Archæology of Ulster', *Ulster Journal of Archaeology*, 1st. ser., 1 (1853): pp. 1–8.

J. M. [James Morgan], 'The Rebel's Grave', *Ulster Magazine*, 1, no. 1 (January 1830): pp. 9–12.

J. M. [James Morgan], 'Sketch of the Life of Thomas Russell, Who Was Executed for High Treason at Downpatrick, 21st October, 1803', *Ulster Magazine*, 1, no. 1 (January 1830): pp. 39–60.

Proinsias Mac an Bheatha, *Cnoc na hUamha* (Baile Átha Cliath [Dublin]: Foilseacháin Náisiúnta, 1978).

Proinsias Mac an Bheatha, *Henry Joy agus Véarsaí Eile* (Baile Átha Cliath [Dublin]: Coiscéim, 1992).

Proinsias Mac an Bheatha, *Jemmy Hope: An Chéad Sóisialaí Éireannach* (Cathair na Mart [Westport]: Foilseacháin Náisiúnta, 1985).

Séamas Mac Annaidh, ed., *Fermanagh and 1798* (Dooneen: Tempo Historical Society, 2000).

Seosamh MacCathmhaoil [Joseph Campbell], *The Rushlight* (Dublin: Maunsel & Co., 1906).

Michael MacDonagh, *The Viceroy's Post-Bag; Correspondence, Hitherto Unpublished, of the Earl of Hardwicke, First Lord Lieutenant of Ireland, after the Union* (London: J. Murray, 1904).

Brian MacDonald, 'Distribution of the *Northern Star*', *Ulster Local Studies*, 18, no. 2 (1982): pp. 54–68.

Brian MacDonald, 'The Monaghan Militia & the Tragedy of Blaris Moor', *Clogher Record*, 16, no. 2 (1998): pp. 123–43.

Robert MacGeagh, *Ulster's Apology for Being Loyal* (London: Cassell & Company, 1888).

William Lyon Mackenzie, *The Sons of the Emerald Isle; or, Lives of One Thousand Remarkable Irishmen Including Memoirs of Noted Characters of Irish Parentage or Descent*, 2nd edn (New York: Burgess, Stringer, and Company, 1845).

Thomas MacKnight, *Ulster as It Is; or, Twenty-Eight Years' Experience as an Irish Editor*, vol. 1 (London and New York: Macmillan, 1896).

Seumas MacManus, ed., *The Four Winds of Eirinn: Poems by Anna Macmanus (Ethna Carbery)*, new edn (Dublin: M. H. Gill, 1918).

Seán Mac Maoláin, *Iolar agus Sionnach* (Baile Átha Cliath [Dublin]: Oifig Dhíolta Foillseacháin Rialtais, 1938).

Gerald MacNamara, 'Who Fears to Speak?', *Dublin Magazine*, 4 (1929): pp. 30–52.

William James MacNeven, *Pieces of Irish History, Illustrative of the Condition of the Catholics of Ireland; of the Origins and Progress of the Political System of the United Irishmen; and of Their Transactions with the Anglo-Irish Government* (New York: Bernard Dornin, 1807).

Thomas MacNevin, *The History of the Volunteers of 1782* (New York: R. Martin & Co., 1845).

Thomas MacNevin, *The Lives and Trials of Archibald Hamilton Rowan, the Rev. William Jackson, the Defenders, William Orr, Peter Finnerty, and Other Eminent Irishmen* (Dublin: J. Duffy, 1846).

Breandán Mac Suibhne, 'Politicization and Paramilitarism: North-West and South-West Ulster c.1772–98', in *1798: A Bicentenary Perspective*, edited by Thomas Bartlett et al. (Dublin: Four Courts Press, 2003), pp. 243–78.

Breandán Mac Suibhne, 'Afterworld: The Gothic Travels of John Gamble (1770–1831)', *Field Day Review*, 4 (2008): pp. 62–113.

Breandán Mac Suibhne, ed., *Society and Manners in Early Nineteenth-Century Ireland by John Gamble* (Dublin: Field Day, 2011).

Richard Robert Madden, *The United Irishmen: Their Lives and Times*, 1st ser., 2 vols (London: J. Madden & Co., 1842).

Richard Robert Madden, *The United Irishmen: Their Lives and Times*, 2nd ser., 2 vols (London: J. Madden & Co., 1843).

Richard Robert Madden, *The Connexion between the Kingdom of Ireland and the Crown of England* (Dublin: James Duffy, 1845).

Richard Robert Madden, *The United Irishmen: Their Lives and Times*, 3rd ser., 3 vols (Dublin: James Duffy, 1846).

Richard Robert Madden, *The Shrines and Sepulchres of the Old and New World*, 2 vols (London: T. C. Newby, 1851).

Richard Robert Madden, *The United Irishmen: Their Lives and Times*, 2nd edn, 1st ser., 2 vols (Dublin: James Duffy, 1857–8).

Richard Robert Madden, *The United Irishmen: Their Lives and Times*, 2nd edn, 3rd ser. and 4th ser., 2 vols (London and Dublin: The Catholic Publishing & Bookselling Company and J. Mullany, 1860).

Richard Robert Madden, *The History of Irish Periodical Literature, from the End of the 17th to the Middle of the 19th Century, Its Origins, Progress and Results; with Notices of Remarkable Persons Connected with the Press in Ireland During the Past Two Centuries*, 2 vols (London: T. C. Newby, 1867).

Richard Robert Madden, ed., *Literary Remains of the United Irishmen of 1798 and Selections from Other Popular Lyrics of Their Times with an Essay on the Authorship of 'the Exile of Erin'* (Dublin: James Duffy, 1887).

Richard Robert Madden, *Antrim and Down in '98* (Glasgow: Cameron, Ferguson & Co., c.1900).

Thomas More Madden, ed., *The Memoirs (Chiefly Autobiographical) from 1798 to 1886 of Richard Robert Madden, M.D., F.R.C.S.* (London: Ward & Downey, 1891).

W. A. Maguire, 'Arthur McMahon, United Irishman and French Soldier', *Irish Sword*, 9 (1969–70): pp. 207–15.

W. A. Maguire, *Up in Arms: The Rebellion 1798 in Ireland, a Bicentenary Exhibition: Record of an Exhibition at the Ulster Museum, 3 April–31 August 1998* (Belfast: Ulster Museum, 1998).

Derek Mahon, *Collected Poems* (Oldcastle: Gallery Press, 1999).

Elizabeth Malcolm, 'A New Age or Just the Same Old Cycle of Extirpation? Massacre and the 1798 Irish Rebellion', *Journal of Genocide Research*, 15, no. 2 (2013): pp. 151–66.

Constance Markievicz, 'The Women of '98', in *Irish Citizen*, 6, 13, 20, 27 November and 4 December 1915.

Radvan Markus, *Echoes of the Rebellion: The Year 1798 in Twentieth-Century Irish Fiction and Drama* (Oxford and New York: Peter Lang, 2015).

R. L. Marshall, 'Maghera in '98', in *Presbyterianism in Maghera: A Social and Congregational History*, edited by S. Sidlow McFarland (Maghera: Presbyterian Church, 1985), pp. 174–8.

Robin Masefield, *'Twixt Bay & Burn': A History of Helen's Bay & Crawfordsburn* (s.l.: Bayburn Historical Society, 2011).

William Shaw Mason, *A Statistical Account; or, Parochial Survey of Ireland, Drawn up from the Communications of the Clergy*, 3 vols (Dublin: J. Cumming and N. Mahon, 1814–19).

William Hamilton Maxwell, *O'Hara; or, 1798*, 2 vols (London: J. Andrews and Dublin: Miliken, 1825).

William Hamilton Maxwell, *Stories of Waterloo, and Other Tales*, 3 vols, vol. 1 (London: H. Colburn and R. Bentley, 1829).

William Hamilton Maxwell, *History of the Irish Rebellion in 1798; with Memoirs of the Union, and Emmett's Insurrection in 1803* (London: Baily Brothers, 1845).

Dónal McAnallen, 'Michael Cusack and the Revival of Gaelic Games in Ulster', *Irish Historical Studies*, 37, no. 145 (2010): pp. 23–47.

Ian McBride, *Scripture Politics: Ulster Presbyterians and Irish Radicalism in the Late Eighteenth Century* (Oxford and New York: Clarendon Press, 1998).

Ian McBride, ed., *History and Memory in Modern Ireland* (Cambridge and New York: Cambridge University Press, 2001).

Ian McBride, 'Memory and National Identity in Modern Ireland', in *History and Memory in Modern Ireland*, edited by Ian McBride (Cambridge and New York: Cambridge University Press, 2001), pp. 1–41.

Ian McBride, 'Memory and Forgetting: Ulster Presbyterians and 1798', in *1798: A Bicentenary Perspective*, edited by Thomas Bartlett et al. (Dublin: Four Courts Press, 2003), pp. 478–96.

Ian McBride, 'Ulster Presbyterians and the Passing of the Act of Union', in *The Irish Act of Union, 1800: Bicentennial Essays*, edited by Patrick M. Geoghegan, Michael Brown, and James Kelly (Dublin and Portland: Irish Academic Press, 2003), pp. 68–83.

Lawrence W. McBride, ed., *Images, Icons, and the Irish Nationalist Imagination*, (Dublin: Four Courts Press, 1999).

Lawrence W. McBride, 'Visualizing '98: Irish Nationalist Cartoons Commemorate the Revolution', *Eighteenth-Century Life*, 22, no. 3 (1998): pp. 103–17.

Robert M'Cahan, *Tales from the Glens of Antrim* (Coleraine: Northern Constitution, 1923).

anon. [Hugh McCall], *Ireland and Her Staple Manufactures: Being Sketches of the History and Progress of the Linen and Cotton Trades More Especially in the Northern Province*, 2nd edn (Belfast: Henry Greer, George Phillips & Son, 1865).

anon. [Hugh McCall], *Some Recollections of Hugh McCall* (Lisburn: J. E. Reilly, 1899).

Tom McCaughren, *The Legend of the Golden Key* (Dublin: Children's Press, 1983).

Tom McCaughren, *In Search of the Liberty Tree* (Dublin: Anvil Books, 1994).

Trevor McCavery, *Newtown: A History of Newtownards* (Belfast: White Row Press, 1994).

Anna McCleery, 'Life of Mary Ann M'Cracken, Sister of Henry Joy M'Cracken', in *Historical Notices of Old Belfast*, edited by Robert M. Young (Belfast: Marcus Ward & Co., 1896), pp. 175–97.

Aiken McClelland, 'Thomas Ledlie Birch, United Irishman', *Proceedings and Reports of the Belfast Natural History and Philosophical Society*, 2 ser., vol. 7 (1965): pp. 24–35.

Aiken McClelland, 'A Link with the '98', in *Ulster Folk Museum Year Book 1966–67* (Cultra, Antrim: Ulster Folk Museum, 1968), pp. 14–15.

Aiken McClelland, 'The Treasures of the Presbyterian Historical Society', *Bulletin of the Presbyterian Historical Society of Ireland*, no. 1 (December 1970): pp. 12–13.

Aiken McClelland, 'Thomas Archer and His Gang', in *Ulster Folk and Transport Museum Year Book 1969–70* (Cultra Manor: Ulster Folk and Transport Museum Year Book, 1971), pp. 15–17.

Aiken McClelland, *History of Saintfield and District* (Saintfield: Anderson Trust, 1972).

Letitia M'Clintock, 'Beasts, Birds, and Insects in Irish Folk-Lore', *Belgravia: An Illustrated London Magazine*, 40, no. 157 (1879): pp. 87–95.

Letitia M'Clintock, 'An Actor in the Rebellion of 1798', *Belgravia: An Illustrated London Magazine*, 55, no. 218 (1885): pp. 185–93.

William McComb, *The School of the Sabbath, and Other Poems*, 2nd edn (Edinburgh: W. Oliphant, 1825).

William McComb, *The Repealer Repulsed! A Correct Narrative of the Rise and Progress of the Repeal Invasion of Ulster* (Belfast: William McComb, 1841).

William McComb, *McComb's Guide to Belfast, the Giant's Causeway and the Adjoining Districts of the Counties of Antrim and Down, with an Account of the Battle of Ballynahinch, and the Celebrated Mineral Waters of That Neighbourhood* (Belfast: William McComb, 1861).

William McComb, *The Poetical Works of William McComb* (London: Hamilton Adams, 1864).

W. J. McCormack, *Northman: John Hewitt (1907–1987), an Irish Writer, His World, and His Times* (Oxford and New York: Oxford University Press, 2015).

James McCormick, ed., *The 'Irish Rebellion of 1798', with Numerous Historical Sketches, Never before Published*, 2nd edn (Dublin: James McCormick, 1844).

Jack McCoy, *Ulster's Joan of Arc: An Examination of the Betsy Gray Story* (Bangor, Co. Down: North Down Borough Council Visitors and Heritage Centre, 1987).

Alexander McCreery, *Presbyterian Ministers of Killileagh: A Notice of Their Lives and Times* (Belfast: William Mullan, 1875).

Cal McCrystal, *Reflections on a Quiet Rebel* (London: Michael Joseph, 1997).

J. C. McDermott, *An Enriching Life* (Belfast: n.s., 1979).

A. McDowell, ed., *The Posthumous Works of James Orr of Ballycarry, with a Sketch of His Life* (Belfast: Francis D. Finlay, 1817).

Brendan McEvoy, 'Father James Quigley: Priest of Armagh and United Irishman', *Seanchas Ardmhacha: Journal of the Armagh Diocesan Historical Society*, 5, no. 2 (1970): pp. 247–68.

Andrew McEwen, *Zayda, and Other Poems* (Belfast: Lamont Brothers, 1846).

James McFerran, *The Rebellion of 1798 and Sketches and Incidents of the Battles of Randalstown and Antrim* (Belfast: W. & G. Baird, 1898).

W. O. McGaw, 'Notes on the Parish of Carnmoney, Co. Antrim', *Ulster Folklife*, 1 (1955): pp. 53–6.

Owen McGee, '"God Save Ireland": Manchester-Martyr Demonstrations in Dublin, 1867–1916', *Éire-Ireland*, 36, no. 3–4 (2001): pp. 39–66.

Owen McGee, *The IRB: The Irish Republican Brotherhood from the Land League to Sinn Fein* (Dublin: Four Courts Press, 2005).

Cillian McGrattan, *Memory, Politics and Identity: Haunted by History* (Basingstoke: Palgrave Macmillan, 2013).

Medbh McGuckian, *Shelmalier* (Loughcrew, Co. Meath: Gallery Press, 1998).

James McHenry, *The Bard of Erin; and Other Poems, Mostly National* (Belfast: Smyth & Lyons, 1808).

James McHenry, *Patrick: A Poetical Tale Founded on Incidents Which Took Place in Ireland During the Unhappy Period of 1798* (Glasgow: D. McKenzie, 1810).

James McHenry, *The Hearts of Steel: An Irish Historical Tale of the Last Century*, vol. 1 (Philadelphia: A. R. Pool, 1825).

James McHenry, 'The Outlaw of Slimish', *Philadelphia Monthly Magazine*, 2nd ser., vol. 1, no. 1 (1828): pp. 36–57.

James McHenry, *The Feelings of Age, to Which is Added the Star of Love*, 2nd edn (Philadelphia: Banks & Brother, 1830).

James McHenry, *The Pleasures of Friendship, and Other Poems*, 7th American edn (Philadelphia: Grigg & Elliott, 1836; orig. edn 1822).

James McHenry, *The Insurgent Chief; or, the Pikemen of '98: A Romance of the Irish Rebellion. To Which Is Added an Appendix, Containing Biographical Memoirs of the Principle Characters and Descriptive of the Scenery of the Work* (Belfast: John Henderson, 1844; orig. edn 1824).

R. H. McIlrath, 'Classon Porter: A Short Account of the Life and Work of a Nineteenth-Century Non-Subscribing Minister in Larne', *Ulster Local Studies*, 15, no. 1 (1993): pp. 13–37.

Liam McIlvanney, 'Across the Narrow Sea: The Language, Literature and Politics of Ulster-Scots', in *Ireland and Scotland: Culture and Society, 1700–2000*, edited by Ray Ryan (Dublin: Four Courts Press, 2005), pp. 203–26.

Gillian McIntosh, *The Force of Culture: Unionist Identities in Twentieth-Century Ireland* (Cork: Cork University Press, 1999).

Peter K. McIvor, 'Regionalism in Ulster: An Historical Perspective', *Irish University Review*, 13, no. 2 (1983): pp. 180–8.

Patrick Joseph McKavanagh, *Glenavy: The Church of the Dwarf 1868–1968* (Belfast: Irish News Ltd, 1968).

Susan McKay, *Northern Protestants: An Unsettled People* (Belfast: Blackstaff Press, 2005; orig. edn 2000).

Seamus McKearney, ed., *Ninety-Eight* (Belfast: The 1798 Commemoration Committee, Belfast, 1948).

Linda McKenna, ed., *Down Survey 2003: The Yearbook of Down County Museum* (Downpatrick: Down County Museum, 2003).

Andrew McKenzie, *Poems and Songs on Different Subjects* (Belfast: Alexander Mackay, 1810).

Felix McKillop, *Glenarm: A Local History* (Belfast: Ulster Journals, 1987).

Felix McKillop, *History of Larne and East Antrim* (Belfast: Ulster Journals, 2005).

John A. McLaughlin, *One Green Hill: Journeys through Irish Songs* (Belfast: Beyond the Pale, 2003).

William McMillan, *A History of the Moneyreagh Congregation, 1719–1969* (Moneyreagh: The Church Committee, 1969).

William McMillan, 'Presbyterian Ministers and the Ulster Rising', in *Protestant, Catholic and Dissenter: The Clergy and 1798*, edited by Liam Swords (Blackrock: Columba Press, 1997), pp. 81–117.

Richard McMinn, 'Presbyterianism and Politics in Ulster, 1871–1906', *Studia Hibernica*, no. 21 (1981): pp. 127–46.

W. J. McMullan, 'Belfast as It Was, and as It Is (Chapter IV)', *Ulster Magazine and Monthly Review of Science and Literature*, 2, no. 17 (May 1861): pp. 233–40.

Hugh McNeill, *The Annals of the Parish of Derrykeighan: From A.D. 453 to A.D. 1890*, 2nd edn (Ballymena: Mid-Antrim Historical Group, 1993).

Mary McNeill, *The Life and Times of Mary Ann McCracken 1770–1866: A Belfast Panorama*, 2nd edn (Belfast: Blackstaff Press, 1988).

Eugene McNulty, *The Ulster Literary Theatre and the Northern Revival* (Cork: Cork University Press, 2008).

Eugene McNulty, 'The Place of Memory: Alice Milligan, Ardrigh, and the 1898 Centenary', *Irish University Review*, 38, no. 2 (2008): pp. 203–21.

S. M. S. [Samuel McSkimin], 'Sketch of a Ramble to Antrim', *Belfast Monthly Magazine*, 2, no. 11 (1809), pp. 424–5; 3, no. 12 (1809), pp. 5–6; 3, no. 13 (1809), p. 105; 6, no. 32 (1811), p. 183; 8, no. 45 (1812), p. 265; 8, no. 46 (1812), p. 369.

Samuel McSkimin, 'Secret History of the Irish Insurrection of 1803', *Fraser's Magazine for Town and Country*, 14, no. 83 (November 1836): pp. 546–67.

Samuel McSkimin, *Annals of Ulster; or, Ireland Fifty Years Ago* (Belfast: John Henderson, 1849).

Samuel McSkimin, *History of the Irish Rebellion in the Year 1798; Particularly in Antrim, Down and Derry* (Belfast: John Mullan, 1853).

Samuel McSkimin, *Annals of Ulster: From 1790 to 1798*, new edn, edited by Elizabeth J. McCrum (Belfast: J. Cleeland and William Mullan, 1906).

Samuel McSkimin, *The History and Antiquities of the County of the Town of Carrickfergus, from the Earliest Records till 1839; Also, a Statistical Survey of Said County*, edited by Elizabeth J. McCrum (Belfast: Mullan & Son, James Cleeland, Davidson, and McCormack, 1909).

F. H. Amphlett Micklewright, 'The Place of Presbyterians in the 1798 Rebellion in Ireland', *Notes and Queries*, 191, no. 1 (13 July 1946): pp. 2–7; no. 2 (27 July 1946): pp. 27–31; no. 3 (10 August 1946): pp. 57–60; 192, no. 18 (6 September 1947): pp. 377–9.

David W. Miller, *Queen's Rebels: Ulster Loyalism in Historical Perspective* (Dublin: Gill and Macmillan, 1978).

Kerby A. Miller, *Irish Immigrants in the Land of Canaan: Letters and Memoirs from Colonial and Revolutionary America, 1675–1815* (New York and Oxford: Oxford University Press, 2003).

Kerby A. Miller, 'Forging the "Protestant Way of Life": Class Conflict and the Origins of Unionist Hegemony in Early Nineteenth-Century Ulster', in *Ulster Presbyterians in the Atlantic World: Religion, Politics and Identity*, edited by David A. Wilson and Mark G. Spencer (Dublin: Four Courts Press, 2006), pp. 128–65.

Kerby A. Miller, 'Ulster Presbyterians and the "Two Traditions" in Ireland and America', in *Making the Irish American: History and Heritage of the Irish in the United States*, edited by Joseph Lee and Marion R. Casey (New York: New York University Press, 2006), pp. 255–70.

Kerby A. Miller, '"Heirs of Freedom" or "Slaves to England"? Protestant Society and Unionist Hegemony in Nineteenth-Century Ulster', *Radical History Review*, no. 104 (2009): pp. 17–40.

Kerby A. Miller and Breandán Mac Suibhne, 'Frank Roney and the Fenians: A Reappraisal of Irish Republicanism in 1860s Belfast and Ulster', *Éire-Ireland*, 51, nos. 3 & 4 (2016): pp. 23–54.

Alice Milligan, *Life of Theobald Wolfe Tone* (Belfast: J. W. Boyd, 1898).

Alice Milligan, *Poems*, edited by Henry Connell Mangan (Dublin: M. H. Gill, 1954).

Charles F. Milligan, *My Bangor from the 1890's* (Bangor: Spectator Newspapers, 1975).

Seaton F. Milligan, 'Some Recent Cases of Remarkable Longevity', *Journal of the Royal Society of Antiquaries of Ireland*, 1, no. 3 (1890): pp. 232–9.

Seaton F. Milligan, 'Longevity', *Journal of the Royal Society of Antiquaries of Ireland*, 1, no. 5 (1891): p. 409.

Seaton F. Milligan, 'Some Recent Cases of Remarkable Longevity (Second Paper)', *Journal of the Royal Society of Antiquaries of Ireland*, 2, no. 3 (1892): pp. 224–36.

Seaton F. Milligan and Alice Milligan, *Glimpses of Erin: Containing an Account of the Ancient Civilisation, Manners, Customs, and Antiquities of Ireland* (London: Marcus Ward, 1888).

S. Shannon Millin, *History of the Second Congregation of Protestant Dissenters in Belfast* (Belfast: W. & G. Baird Ltd, 1900).

Richard Mills, 'Sam Hanna Bell, 1798 and the Death of Protestant Radicalism', in *New Voices in Irish Criticism*, edited by P. J. Mathews (Dublin: Four Courts Press, 2000), pp. 116–22.

Gary Mitchell, *Tearing the Loom; and, in a Little World of Our Own* (London: Nick Hern Books, 1998).

James Mitchell, *A History of Gracehill*, 2nd edn (Gracehill: s.n., 1984).

Ed Moloney, *Voices from the Grave: Two Men's War in Ireland* (London: Faber and Faber, 2010).

John Montague, 'An Ulster Tandem', *Irish Pages*, 3, no. 1 (2005): pp. 162–8.

Rev. Henry Montgomery, 'Outlines of the History of Presbyterianism in Ireland', *Irish Unitarian Magazine, and Bible Christian*, 2, no. 10 (1847): pp. 327–38.

Michael Montgomery, *From Ulster to America: The Scotch-Irish Heritage of American English* (Belfast: Ulster Historical Foundation, 2006).

Alf. S. Moore, *Belfast To-Day* (Belfast: The Nomad Press, n.d. [1909]).

S. J. Moore, *Memento of 'an Old Disciple'* (Ballymena: W. Erwin and Belfast: W. Mullan & C. Aitchison, 1874).

Thomas Moore, *Irish Melodies* (London: J. Power, 1821).

J. J. Moran, *Stories of the Irish Rebellion, 1798* (Aberdeen: Moran & Co. and London: Simpkin & Co., 1898).

Michael Morgan, 'Belfast's Forgotten Bicentennial', *Études Irlandaises*, 17, no. 1 (1992): pp. 209–18.

Catherine Morris, 'Becoming Irish? Alice Milligan and the Revival', *Irish University Review*, 33, no. 1 (2003): pp. 79–98.

Catherine Morris, *Alice Milligan and the Irish Cultural Revival* (Dublin: Four Courts Press, 2012).

H. Morris, 'Some Ulster Proverbs', *Journal of the County Louth Archaeological Society*, 4, no. 3 (1918): pp. 258–72.

John Morrison, ed., *The McIlwham Papers: In Two Letters from Thomas McIlwham, Weaver, to His Friend Mr James M'Neight, Editor of the Belfast Newsletter* (Belfast: William McComb, 1838).

Andrew Morrow, 'The Rev. Samuel Barber, A.M., and the Rathfrilan Volunteers (Continued)', *Ulster Journal of Archaeology*, 2nd ser., 16, no. 1/2 (1910): pp. 33–42.

Terry Moylan, *The Age of Revolution: 1776–1815 in the Irish Song Tradition* (Dublin: Lilliput Press, 2000).

Rosa Mulholland [Lady Gilbert], *Hester's History*, 2 vols (London: Chapman and Hall, 1869).

T. H. Mullin, *Families of Ballyrashane: A District in Northern Ireland* (Belfast: printed by News Letter Printing, 1969).

T. H. Mullin, *Coleraine in Georgian Times* (Belfast: printed by Century Services, 1977).

James Munce, *Poems*, 2nd edn (Glasgow: George Gallie, 1881).

Bill Murray and John Cullen, *Epitaph of 1798: A Photographic Record of 1798 Memorials on the Island of Ireland and Beyond* (Enniscorthy, Co. Wexford: Carrigbyrne Film Productions Ltd and The Carrigbyrne Pikegroup, 2002).

Richard Musgrave, *Memoirs of the Different Rebellions in Ireland, from the Arrival of the English*, 3rd edn, 2 vols (Dublin: Robert Parchbank, 1802).

Julie Louise Nelson, '"Violently Democratic and Anti-Conservative"?: An Analysis of Presbyterian "Radicalism" in Ulster, *c.*1800–1852' (PhD: Department of History, University of Durham, 2005).

Edward Newell, *The Apostacy of Newell, Containing the Life and Confessions of That Celebrated Informer* (London: s.n., 1798).

Pierre Nora, *Les Lieux de Mémoire*, 3 vols (Paris: Galimard, 1984–92).

Pierre Nora, 'Between Memory and History: *Les Lieux de Mémoire*', *Representations*, no. 26 (1989): pp. 7–24.

Pierre Nora, *Realms of Memory: The Construction of the French Past*, translated by Arthur Goldhammer, 3 vols (New York: Columbia University Press, 1996).

Gillian O'Brien, '"Spirit, Impartiality and Independence": *The Northern Star*, 1792–1797', *Eighteenth-Century Ireland*, 13 (1998): pp. 7–23.

R. Barry O'Brien, *The Life of Lord Russell of Killowen* (London: Smith, Elder, & Co., 1901).

Leon Ó Broin, *An Maidíneach: Staraí na nÉireannach Aontaithe* (Dublin: Sáirséal agus Dill, 1971).

Leon Ó Broin, 'R. R. Madden, Historian of the United Irishmen', *Irish University Review*, 2, no. 1 (1972): pp. 20–33.

Breandán Ó Buachalla, *Clár na Lámhsríbhinní Gaeilge i Leabharlainn Phoiblí Bhéal Feirste* (Dublin: An Clóchamhar Tta, 1962).

Cathal O'Byrne, *As I Roved Out: A Book of the North, Being a Series of Historical Sketches of Ulster and Old Belfast*, facsimile of 3rd edn (Belfast: Blackstaff, 1982; orig. edn 1946).

Cathal O'Byrne, *As I Roved Out: In Belfast and District*, reprint of 2nd edn (Wakefield: S. R. Publishers, 1970; orig. 2nd edn Dublin: Three Candles, 1957).

Margaret O'Callaghan, '"With the Eyes of Another Race, of a People Once Hunted Themselves": Casement, Colonialism and a Remembered Past', in *Roger Casement in Irish and World History*, edited by Mary E. Daly (Dublin: Royal Irish Academy, 2005), pp. 46–63.

Margaret O'Callaghan, '"From Casement Park to Toomebridge": The Commemoration of the Easter Rising in Northern Ireland in 1966', in *1916 in 1966: Commemorating the Easter Rising*, edited by Margaret O'Callaghan and Mary E. Daly (Dublin: Royal Irish Academy, 2007), pp. 86–147.

Conor O'Clery, *The Star Man: The True Story of Willie Kean, Journalist and Rebel* (Dromore, Co. Bantry: Somerville Press, 2016).

D. J. O'Donoghue, *The Poets of Ireland: A Biographical and Bibliographical Dictionary of Irish Writers of English Verse* (Dublin: Hodges Figges and London: Henry Frowde, 1912).

Seán Ó Dúrois, *Crann Smola* (Baile Átha Cliath [Dublin]: Coiscéim, 2001).

Seán Ó Dúrois, *Rí na cGearrbhach* (Binn Éadair [Howth], Baile Átha Cliath: Coiscéim, 2003).

Kathleen O'Farrell, *Kilbroney* (Dingle, Co. Kerry: Brandon, 1992).

Kathleen O'Farrell, *The Fiddler of Kilbroney* (Dingle, Co. Kerry: Brandon, 1994).

Timothy O'Keefe, 'The 1898 Efforts to Celebrate the United Irishmen: The '98 Centennial', *Éire-Ireland*, 23 (1988): pp. 51–73.

Patrick O'Kelly, *General History of the Rebellion of 1798: With Many Interesting Occurrences of the Two Preceding Years: Also, a Brief Account of the Insurrection in 1803* (Dublin: J. Downes, 1842).

James O'Laverty, *An Historical Account of the Diocese of Down and Connor, Ancient and Modern*, vols 1–3 (Dublin: James Duffy & Sons, 1878–84).

Con O'Leary [Peter McCorry], *The Irish Widow's Son; or, the Pikemen of Ninety-Eight: A Story of the Irish Rebellion, Embracing an Historical Account of the Battles of Antrim and Ballinahinch* (Boston: Patrick Donahoe, 1869).

Rev. R. S. O'Loughlin, *The Rising of '98* (Lurgan: L. Richardson, 1898).

Réamonn Ó Muirí, 'Lt John Lindley St Leger, United Irishman', *Seanchas Ardmhacha: Journal of the Armagh Diocesan Historical Society*, 11, no. 1 (1983): pp. 133–201.

Réamonn Ó Muirí, 'Father James Coigly', in *Protestant, Catholic and Dissenter: The Clergy and 1798*, edited by Liam Swords (Blackrock: Columba Press, 1997), pp. 118–64.

Séamus Ó Néill, *Faill ar an bhFeart* (Baile Átha Cliath [Dublin]: Sairseál agus Dill, 1967).

James Orr, *Poems on Various Subjects* (Belfast: Smyth & Lyons, 1804).

Jennifer Orr, '1798, before, and Beyond: Samuel Thomson and the Poetics of Ulster-Scots Identity', in *Revising Robert Burns and Ulster: Literature, Religion and Politics, c.1770–1920*, edited by Frank Ferguson and Andrew R. Holmes (Dublin: Four Courts Press, 2009), pp. 106–26.

Jennifer Orr, *The Correspondence of Samuel Thomson (1766–1816): Fostering an Irish Writers' Circle* (Dublin: Four Courts Press, 2012).

Jennifer Orr, 'Constructing the Ulster Labouring-Class Poet: The Case of Samuel Thomson', in *Class and the Canon: Constructing Labouring-Class Poetry and Poetics, 1750–1900*, edited by Kirstie Blair and Mina Gorji (Basingstoke: Palgrave Macmillan, 2013), pp. 34–54.

Jennifer Orr, *Literary Networks and Dissenting Print Culture in Romantic-Period Ireland* (Houndmills and New York: Palgrave Macmillan, 2015).

Seán Ó Súilleabháin, *A Handbook of Irish Folklore* (Hatboro, Pa.: Folklore Associates, Inc., 1963).

D. J. Owen, *History of Belfast* (Belfast and London: W. & G. Baird, 1921).

J. K. Owen, *An Irish Chieftain of to-Day* (Belfast: s. n., *c.*1911).

Thomas Pakenham, *The Year of Liberty: The Story of the Great Irish Rebellion* (London: Weidenfeld and Nicolson, 1997).

F. W. Palliser, *The Irish Rebellion of 1798* (London: Simpkin, Marshall, Hamilton, Kent & Co., 1898).

Stewart Parker, *Plays*, vol. 2 (London: Methuen Drama, 2000).

Stewart Parker, *Dramatis Personae and Other Writings*, edited by Gerald Dawe, Maria Johnston, and Clare Wallace (Prague: Litteraria Pragensia, 2008).

Trevor Parkhill, '"That's *Their* History": Can a Museum's Historical Programme Inform the Reconciliation Process in a Divided Society?', *Folk Life*, 41 (2002–3): pp. 37–44.

Trevor Parkhill, 'The Wild Geese of 1798: Emigrés of the Rebellion', *Seanchas Ardmhacha: Journal of the Armagh Diocesan Historical Society*, 19, no. 2 (2003): pp. 118–35.

Trevor Parkhill, 'The Curator as Interpreter, Interlocutor and Facilitator: The 1798 Exhibition and the Conflict Exhibition 2003', in *Effective Presentation and Interpretation in Museums*, edited by Marie Bourke (Dublin: National Gallery of Ireland, 2004), pp. 32–40.

Trevor Parkhill, 'The Ulster Museum History Galleries and Post-Conflict Community Engagement', in *Ireland and Victims: Confronting the Past, Forging the Future*, edited by Lesley Lelourec and Gráinne O'Keeffe-Vigneron (Oxford and New York: Peter Lang, 2012), pp. 271–85.

R. E. Parkinson, *The City of Downe from Its Earliest Days*, new edn (Bangor: Donard Publishing Company, 1977).

Connal Parr, *Inventing the Myth: Political Passions and the Ulster Protestant Imagination* (Oxford: Oxford University Press, 2017).

T. G. F. Paterson, 'Lisburn and Neighbourhood in 1798', *Ulster Journal of Archaeology*, 3rd ser., 1 (1938): pp. 193–8.

Glenn Patterson, *The Mill for Grinding Old People Young* (London: Faber and Faber, 2012).

James G. Patterson, *In the Wake of the Great Rebellion: Republicanism, Agrarianism and Banditry in Ireland after 1798* (Manchester and New York: Manchester University Press, 2008).

William Hugh Patterson, *A Glossary of Words in Use in the Counties of Antrim and Down* (London: English Dialect Society, 1880).

Tom Paulin, *Liberty Tree* (London and Boston: Faber and Faber, 1983).

Tom Paulin, 'At the Cape of Unhope', *Fortnight*, no. 192 (1983): pp. 21–2.

Tom Paulin, *A New Look at the Language Question* (Derry: Field Day, 1983).

G. K. Peatling, 'Who Fears to Speak of Politics? John Kells Ingram and Hypothetical Nationalism', *Irish Historical Studies*, 31, no. 122 (1998): pp. 202–21.

Mrs M. T. Pender, *The Green Cockade: A Tale of Ulster in 'Ninety-Eight* (Dublin: Martine Lester, 1898).

Mrs M. T. Pender, *An Cnota Glas*, translated by Pádraig Mac Seághain (Baile Átha Cliath [Dublin]: Oifig an tSoláthair, 1941).

George Pepper, 'Literary and Biographical Notices of Irish Authors and Artists: James Orr', *Irish Shield and Monthly Milesian*, 1, no. 12 (1829): pp. 449–57.

George Whitfield Pepper, *Under Three Flags; or, the Story of My Life as Preacher, Captain in the Army, Chaplain, Consul, with Speeches and Interviews* (Cincinnati: Curts & Jennings, 1899).

George Petrie, *Ancient Music of Ireland*, vol. 2 (Dublin: M. H. Gill and Son, 1882).

Eamon Phoenix, Pádraic Ó Cléireacháin, Eileen McAuley, and Nuala McSparran, eds, *Feis na nGleann: A Century of Gaelic Culture in the Antrim Glens* (Belfast: Stair Uladh, 2005).

James Adair Pilson, *History of the Rise and Progress of Belfast, and Annals of the County Antrim* (Belfast: Hodgson, 1846).

Francis Plowden, *An Historical Review of the State of Ireland, from the Invasion of That Country under Henry II to Its Union with Great Britain on the 1st of January, 1801*, vol. 2 (London: C. Roworth for T. Egerton, 1803).

Francis Plowden, *The History of Ireland from Its Union with Great Britain, in January 1801, to October 1810*, vol. 1 (Dublin: John Boyce, 1811).

Classon Emmett Porter, *Irish Presbyterian Biographical Sketches* (Belfast: The Northern Whig, 1883).

Classon Emmett Porter, *The Seven Bruces: Presbyterian Ministers in Ireland in Six Successive Generations* (Belfast: Northern Whig, 1885).

Classon Emmett Porter, *Congregational Memoirs: Old Presbyterian Congregation of Larne and Kilwaughter* (Larne: s.n., 1929).

James Porter, *Billy Bluff and 'Squire Firebrand; or, a Sample of the Times, as It Periodically Appeared in the Northern Star* (Belfast: s.n., 1797).

Patrick C. Power, *The Courts Martial of 1798–9* (Kilkenny: The Irish Historical Press, 1997).

Robert Lloyd Praeger, *Belfast and County Down Railway Company Official Guide to County Down and the Mourne Mountains* (Belfast: Marcus Ward & Co., 1898).

Henry George Purdon, *Memoirs of the Services of the 64th Regiment (Second Staffordshire), 1758 to 1881* (London: W. H. Allen, 1882).

H. S. Purdon, 'Battle of Antrim', *Ulster Journal of Archaeology*, 2nd ser., 8, no. 2 (1902): p. 96.

James Quinn, *Soul on Fire: A Life of Thomas Russell, 1767–1803* (Dublin: Irish Academic Press, 2002).

James Quinn, *Young Ireland and the Writing of Irish History* (Dublin: University College Dublin Press, 2015).

Archie R. Reid, ed., *The Liberty Tree: The Story of the United Irishmen in and around the Borough of Newtownabbey* (Newtownabbey: Newtownabbey Borough Council, 1998).

Horace Reid, 'The Legend of Betsy Gray', in *Fermanagh and 1798*, edited by Séamas Mac Annaidh (Dooneen: Tempo Historical Society, 2000), pp. 86–99.

James Seaton Reid and William D. Killen, *History of the Presbyterian Church in Ireland, Comprising the Civil History of the Province of Ulster, from the Accession of James the First*, 2nd edn, vol. 3 (London: Whittaker, 1853).

Meta Mayne Reid, *The Two Rebels* (London: Faber and Faber, 1969).

Thomas Reid, *Travels in Ireland in the Year 1822, Exhibiting Brief Sketches of the Moral, Physical, and Political State of the Country: With Reflections on the Best Means of Improving Its Condition* (London: Longman, Hurst, Rees, Orme, and Brown, 1823).

Marilynn Richtarik, 'Living in Interesting Times: Stewart Parker's *Northern Star*', in *Politics and Performance in Contemporary Northern Ireland*, edited by John P. Harrington and Elizabeth J. Mitchell (Amherst: University of Massachusetts Press, 1999).

Marilynn Richtarik, *Stewart Parker: A Life* (Oxford: Oxford University Press, 2012).

Paul Ricoeur, *Memory, History, Forgetting*, translated by Kathleen Blamey and David Pellauer (Chicago: University of Chicago Press, 2004).

Ann Rigney, *The Afterlives of Walter Scott: Memory on the Move* (Oxford: Oxford University Press, 2012).

Daniel Ritchie, 'Evangelicalism, Abolitionism, and Parnellism: The Public Career of the Revd Isaac Nelson' (PhD: School of History and Anthropology, Queen's University, Belfast, 2014).

Kenneth Robinson, *North Down and Ards in 1798* (Bangor: North Down Heritage Centre, North Down Borough Council, 1998).

Kenneth Robinson, 'Betsy Gray Revisited', *Journal of the Upper Ards Historical Society*, no. 24 (2000): pp. 8–13.

Philip Robinson, 'Hanging Ropes and Buried Secrets', *Ulster Folklife*, 32 (1986): pp. 3–15.

Frank Roney, *Frank Roney: Irish Rebel and California Labor Leader: An Autobiography*, edited by Ira B. Cross (Berkeley: University of California Press, 1931).

Charles Ross, ed., *Correspondence of Charles, First Marquis Cornwallis*, vols 2 and 3 (London: John Murray, 1859).

William J. Roulston, *Researching Scots-Irish Ancestors: The Essential Genealogical Guide to Early Modern Ulster, 1600–1800* (Belfast: Ulster Historical Foundation, 2005).

George Rudé, 'Early Irish Rebels in Australia', *Historical Studies*, 16, no. 62 (1 April 1974): pp. 17–35.

Edward Rushton, *Poems* (London: printed by J. M'Creery, 1806).

Edward Rushton, *Poems and Other Writings* (London: Effingham Wilson, 1824).

Edward Rushton, Jr, 'Biographical Sketch of Edward Rushton', *Belfast Monthly Magazine*, 13, no. 77 (1814): pp. 474–85.

Anthony G. Russell, *Beyond the Battle: The Story of South Down and South Armagh in 1798* (Newry: The Newry and Mourne 1798 Commemorative Committee, 1998).

Sean Ryder, 'Speaking of '98: Young Ireland and Republican Memory', *Éire-Ireland*, 34, no. 2 (1999): pp. 51–69.

William Sampson, *Memoirs of William Sampson* (New York: George Forman, 1807).

Bobby Sands, *Prison Poems* (Dublin: Sinn Fein Publicity Department, 1981).

Norah Saunders and A. A. Kelly, *Joseph Campbell: Poet & Nationalist, 1879–1944. A Critical Biography* (Dublin: Wolfhound Press, 1988).

John Savage, *'98 and '48: The Modern Revolutionary History and Literature of Ireland*, 4th edn (Chicago: Union Catholic Pub. Co., 1882).

George Francis Savage-Armstrong, *Ballads of Down* (London: Longmans, Green, and Co., 1901)

George Francis Savage-Armstrong, ed., *A Genealogical History of the Savage Family in Ulster* (London: Chiswick Press, 1906).

James Seery, 'Samuel McSkimin (*c.*1774–1843) Author of the History of Carrickfergus and Annals of Ulster 1790–1798', *Bulletin of the Presbyterian Historical Society of Ireland*, 27 (1998–2000): pp. 1–13.

James Seery, Finlay Holmes, and A. T. Q. Stewart, *Presbyterians, the United Irishmen and 1798* (Belfast: Presbyterian Historical Society of Ireland, 2000).

Hereward Senior, *Orangeism in Ireland and Britain 1795–1836* (London: Routledge & Kegan Paul, 1966).

Jim Shanahan, 'Fearing to Speak: Fear and the 1798 Rebellion in the Nineteenth Century', in *Fear: Essays on the Meaning and Experience of Fear*, edited by Kate Hebblethwaite and Elizabeth McCarthy (Dublin: Four Courts, 2007), pp. 31–46.

Jim Shanahan, 'Tales of the Time: Early Fictions of the 1798 Rebellion', *Irish University Review*, 41, no. 1 (2011): pp. 151–68.

Bernard Shaw, *Sixteen Self Sketches* (London: Constable, 1949).

Bernard Shaw, *Buoyant Billions, Farfetched Fables, & Shakes Versus Shav* (London: Constable and Company, 1950).

James J. Shaw, *Mr Gladstone's Two Irish Policies: 1868 and 1886, a Letter to an Ulster Liberal Elector* (London and Belfast: Marcus Ward & Co., 1888).

Hugh Shearman, *Northern Ireland: Its History, Resources, and People* (Belfast: H.M.S.O., 1946).

Hugh Shearman, *Ulster* (London: R. Hale, 1949).

Hugh Shields, 'Miscellanea from Eileen Keaney', *Ceol*, 2, no. 1 (1965): pp. 6–10.

Hugh Shields, 'Some "Songs and Ballads in Use in the Province of Ulster . . . 1845"', *Ulster Folklife*, 17 (1971): pp. 3–24 and 18 (1972): pp. 34–65.

Hugh Shields, *Narrative Singing in Ireland: Lays, Ballads, Come-All-Yes and Other Songs* (Blackrock: Irish Academic Press, 1993).

R. M. Sibbett, *Orangeism in Ireland and Throughout the Empire*, vol. 2 (Belfast: Henderson, 1914).

R. M. Sibbett, *On the Shining Bann: Records of an Ulster Manor* (Belfast: Baird, 1928).

R. M. Sibbett, *The Sunshine Patriots: The 1798 Rebellion in Antrim and Down* (Belfast: GOLI Publications, 1997).

Kirk Simpson, *Unionist Voices and the Politics of Remembering the Past in Northern Ireland* (Houndmills and New York: Palgrave Macmillan, 2009).

M. Lesley Simpson, 'Down County Museum: Review of Collections and Activities', *Lecale Miscellany*, no. 16 (1998): pp. 99–103.

Margaret E. Smith, *Reckoning with the Past: Teaching History in Northern Ireland* (Lanham, Md.: Lexington Books, 2005).

W. S. Smith, *Historical Gleanings in Antrim and Neighbourhood* (Belfast: Alex. Mayne & Boyd, 1888).

W. S. Smith, *Doagh and the 'First' Sunday School in Ireland* (Belfast: Alex. Mayne & Boyd, 1890).

W. S. Smith, *Memories of '98* (Belfast: Marcus Ward & Co., 1895).

Jim Smyth, *The Men of No Property: Irish Radicals and Popular Politics in the Late Eighteenth Century* (Basingstoke: Macmillan, 1992).

Jim Smyth, 'Anti-Catholicism, Conservatism, and Conspiracy: Sir Richard Musgrave's *Memoirs of the Different Rebellions in Ireland*', *Eighteenth-Century Life*, 22, no. 3 (1998): pp. 62–73.

Jim Smyth, ed., *Revolution, Counter-Revolution, and Union: Ireland in the 1790s* (Cambridge: Cambridge University Press, 2000).

Karen Steele, 'Editing out Factionalism: The Political and Literary Consequences in Ireland's "Shan Van Vocht"', *Victorian Periodicals Review*, 35, no. 2 (2002): pp. 113–32.

Karen Steele, *Women, Press, and Politics During the Irish Revival* (Syracuse, N.Y.: Syracuse University Press, 2007).

Seamus [Jimmy] Steele, ed., *Antrim's Patriot Dead 1797–1953* (Belfast: National Graves Association., n.d. [1966]).

John Stevenson, *Two Centuries of Life in Down, 1600–1800* (Belfast: McCaw, Stevenson and Orr, 1920).

A. T. Q. Stewart, 'The Transformation of Presbyterian Radicalism in the North of Ireland, 1792–1825' (M.A. thesis: Queen's University, Belfast, 1956).

A. T. Q. Stewart, *The Narrow Ground: Aspects of Ulster, 1609–1969* (London: Faber and Faber, 1977).

A. T. Q. Stewart, 'The Siege of Ulster', *Spectator*, 256 (11 January 1986): pp. 15–16.

A. T. Q. Stewart, *The Narrow Ground: The Roots of Conflict in Ireland* (London and Boston: Faber and Faber, 1989; orig. edn 1977).

A. T. Q. Stewart, *A Deeper Silence: The Hidden Origins of the United Irish Movement* (London: Faber and Faber, 1993).

A. T. Q. Stewart, *The Summer Soldiers: The 1798 Rebellion in Antrim and Down* (Belfast: Blackstaff Press, 1995).

A. T. Q. Stewart, 'The Ghost of Betsy Gray', in *1798 Rebellion in County Down*, edited by Myrtle Hill et al. (Newtownards: Colourpoint, 1998), pp. 251–7.

A. T. Q. Stewart, '1798 in Antrim and Down', in *The Great Irish Rebellion of 1798*, edited by Cathal Póirtéir (Cork: Mercier Press, 1998), pp. 72–82.

A. T. Q. Stewart, *The Shape of Irish History* (Belfast: Blackstaff, 2001).

John Stewart, *Friend of Castlereagh* (London: Shepheard-Walwyn, 2013).

J. A. Strahan, 'The Rock of Fergus', *Blackwood's Magazine*, 207, no. 1245 (July 1919): pp. 387–400.

T. D. Sullivan, A. M. Sullivan, and D. B. Sullivan, *Speeches from the Dock; or, Protests of Irish Patriotism*, 1st US edn (Providence: H. McElroy, Murphy, and McCarthy, 1878).

Liam Swords, ed., *Protestant, Catholic and Dissenter: The Clergy and 1798* (Blackrock: Columba Press, 1997).

Marek Tamm, ed., *Afterlife of Events: Perspectives on Mnemohistory* (Houndmills: Palgrave Macmillan, 2015).

W. C. Taylor, *History of the Civil Wars of Ireland, from the Anglo-Norman Invasion till the Union of the Country with Great Britain*, vol. 2 (Edinburgh: Constable, 1831).

Charles Hamilton Teeling, *Personal Narrative of the 'Irish Rebellion' of 1798* (London: Henry Colburn, 1828).

Charles Hamilton Teeling, *Sequel to Personal Narrative of the 'Irish Rebellion' of 1798* (Belfast: John Hodgson, 1832).

Thomas Thompson, "Memoir of the Late Mrs Thompson, of Heworth-Moor, near York', *The Wesleyan-Methodist Magazine*, 19 (December 1840): pp. 990–6.

A Belfast Man [A. H. Thornton], *Memoirs of the Rea Family: From the Period of the Irish Rebellion in 1798 Till the Year 1857* (London: s.n., n.d.).

Mary Helen Thuente, *The Harp Re-Strung: The United Irishmen and the Rise of Irish Literary Nationalism* (Syracuse, N.Y.: Syracuse University Press, 1994).

Mary Helen Thuente, 'Liberty, Hibernia and Mary Le More: United Irish Images of Women', in *The Women of 1798*, edited by Dáire Keogh and Nicholas Furlong (Dublin: Four Courts Press, 1998), pp. 9–25.

Mary Helen Thuente, 'William Sampson: United Irish Satirist and Songwriter', *Eighteenth-Century Life*, 22, no. 3 (1998): pp. 19–30.

Mary Helen Thuente, '"The Belfast Laugh": The Context and Significance of United Irish Satires', in *Revolution, Counter-Revolution, and Union: Ireland in the 1790s*, edited by Jim Smyth (Cambridge and New York: Cambridge University Press, 2000), pp. 67–82.

Mary Helen Thuente, 'United Irish Poetry and Songs', in *A Companion to Irish Literature*, edited by Julia M. Wright (Chichester and Malden, Mass.: Wiley-Blackwell, 2010), 1, pp. 261–75.

Martyn Todd, 'The Aftermath of 1798', *Saintfield Heritage*, 8 (2010): pp. 16–19.

William Theobald Wolfe Tone, ed., *Life of Theobald Wolfe Tone*, 2 vols (Washington: Gales & Seaton, 1826).

William Theobald Wolfe Tone, ed., *Memoirs of Theobald Wolfe Tone*, 2 vols, (London: Henry Colburn, 1827).

Francis Tuite, *Ireland's Revolt in '98, with Sketches of Prominent Statesmen and the Social Condition of the People* (Boston: Angel Guardian Press, 1898).

Brian S. Turner, ed., *Down Survey 1998: The Yearbook of Down County Museum* (Downpatrick: Down County Museum, 1998).

Brian S. Turner, ed., *A Man Stepped Out For Death: Thomas Russell and County Down* (Newtownards: Colourpoint Books, 2003).

Norman Vance, *Irish Literature since 1800* (London: Routledge, 2002).

Charles Vane, ed., *Memoirs and Correspondence of Viscount Castlereagh, Second Marquess of Londonderry*, vols 1–2 (London: Henry Colburn, 1850).

Bradford Vivian, *Public Forgetting: The Rhetoric and Politics of Beginning Again* (University Park, Pa.: Pennsylvania State University Press, 2010).

Edward Wakefield, *An Account of Ireland, Statistical and Political*, vol. 2 (London: printed for Longman, Hurst, Rees, Orme, and Brown, 1812).

Brian M. Walker, ed., *Parliamentary Election Results in Ireland, 1801–1922* (Dublin: Royal Irish Academy, 1978).

Brian M. Walker, *Sentry Hill: An Ulster Farm and Family* (Dundonald: Blackstaff Press, 1981).

Brian M. Walker, '1641, 1689, 1690 and All That: The Unionist Sense of History', *Irish Review*, no. 12 (1992): pp. 56–64.

Brian M. Walker, 'Landowners and Parliamentary Elections in County Down, 1801–1921', in *Down: History & Society*, edited by Lindsay Proudfoot (Dublin: Geography Publications, 1997), pp. 297–325.

Brian M. Walker, *Past and Present: History, Identity and Politics in Ireland* (Belfast: Institute of Irish Studies of Queen's University Belfast, 2000).

Brian M. Walker, *A Political History of the Two Irelands: From Partition to Peace* (Houndmills and New York: Palgrave Macmillan, 2012).

Colin Walker, 'A Bibliography of Presbyterianism in Irish Fiction, 1780–1920', in *Revising Robert Burns and Ulster: Literature, Religion and Politics, c.1770–1920*, edited by Frank Ferguson and Andrew R. Holmes (Dublin: Four Courts Press, 2009), pp. 165–92.

Eoin Walsh, *Watty Graham: Maghera Martyr* (Celbridge: printed by A. S. Donaldson, c.1955).

Mrs Ward, *Waves on the Ocean of Life: A Dalriadian Tale* (London: Simpkin, Marshall and Dublin: Moffat, 1869).

Ormonde D. P. Waters, 'The Rev. James Porter: Dissenting Minister of Greyabbey, 1753–1798', *Seanchas Ardmhacha*, 14, no. 1 (1990): pp. 80–101.

Charles Watson, *The Story of the United Parishes of Glenavy, Camlin, and Tullyrusk; Together with Short Accounts of the History of the Different Denominations in the Union* (Belfast: M'Caw, Stevenson & Orr, 1892).

James Watson, *Memorial of James Watson, Esq. Brookhill, with Notices of His Contemporaries* (Belfast: James Alex. Henderson, 1851).

Paul Weber, *On the Road to Rebellion: The United Irishmen and Hamburg, 1796–1803* (Dublin: Four Courts Press, 1997).

Harald Weinrich, *Lethe: The Art and Critique of Forgetting*, translated by Steven Rendall (Ithaca: Cornell University Press, 2004).

John Weir, *Irish Revivals. The Ulster Awakening: Its Origin, Progress, and Fruit, with Notes of a Tour of Personal Observation and Inquiry* (London: Arthur Hall, Virtue & Co., 1860).

Kevin Whelan, *The Tree of Liberty: Radicalism, Catholicism and the Construction of Irish Identity 1760–1830* (Cork: Cork University Press & Field Day, 1996).

Kevin Whelan, *Fellowship of Freedom: The United Irishmen and 1798* (Cork: Cork University Press, 1998).

Kevin Whelan, 'The Green Atlantic: Radical Reciprocities between Ireland and America in the Long Eighteenth Century', in *A New Imperial History: Culture, Identity, and Modernity in Britain and the Empire, 1660–1840*, edited by Kathleen Wilson (Cambridge: Cambridge University Press, 2004), pp. 216–38.

Yvonne Whelan, *Reinventing Modern Dublin: Streetscape, Iconography, and the Politics of Identity* (Dublin: University College Dublin Press, 2003).

anon. [George White], *Old Ballymena: A History of Ballymena During the 1798 Rebellion* (Ballymena: Ballymena Observer, 1857).

J. R. Whitten, ed., *Murder Without Sin: The Rebellion of 1798 by Ogle Robert Gowan* (Belfast: Education Committee of the Grand Orange Lodge of Ireland, 1996).

Sabine Wichert, ed., *From the United Irishmen to Twentieth-Century Unionism: A Festschrift for A. T. Q. Stewart* (Dublin: Four Courts Press, 2004).

Bill Wilsdon, *The Sites of the 1798 Rising in Antrim and Down* (Belfast: Blackstaff, 1997).

David A. Wilson, *United Irishmen, United States: Immigrant Radicals in the Early Republic* (Dublin: Four Courts Press, 1998).

David A. Wilson, 'John Caldwell's Memoir: A Case Study in Ulster-American Radicalism', in *Ulster Presbyterians in the Atlantic World: Religion, Politics and Identity*, edited by David A. Wilson and Mark G. Spencer (Dublin: Four Courts Press, 2006), pp. 104–27.

Florence M. Wilson, *The Coming of the Earls and Other Verse* (Dublin: Candle Press, 1918).

James Wilson, 'Orangeism in 1798', in *1798: A Bicentenary Perspective*, edited by Thomas Bartlett et al. (Dublin: Four Courts Press, 2003), pp. 345–62.

Thomas Witherow, *Historical and Literary Memorials of Presbyterianism in Ireland (1731–1800)*, 2nd ser. (London and Belfast: William Mullan and Son, 1880).

James Barkley Woodburn, *The Ulster Scot: His History and Religion* (London: H. R. Allenson Ltd, 1914).

C. J. Woods, 'R. R. Madden, Historian of the United Irishmen', in *1798: A Bicentenary Perspective*, edited by Thomas Bartlett et al. (Dublin: Four Courts Press, 2003).

Frank Wright, *Two Lands on One Soil: Ulster Politics before Home Rule* (Dublin: Gill & Macmillan, 1996).

George Newenham Wright, *A Guide to the Giant's Causeway, and the North East Coast of the County of Antrim* (London: Baldwin, Cradock, and Joy, 1823).

Jonathan Wright, *The 'Natural Leaders' and Their World: Politics, Culture and Society in Belfast, c.1801–32* (Liverpool: Liverpool University Press, 2012).

Julia M. Wright, *Ireland, India, and Nationalism in Nineteenth-Century Literature* (Cambridge and New York: Cambridge University Press, 2007).

Robert M. Young, *The Town Book of the Corporation of Belfast, 1613–1816* (Belfast: Marcus Ward & Co., 1892).

Robert M. Young, *Ulster in '98: Episodes and Anecdotes* (Belfast: Marcus Ward & Co., 1893).

Robert M. Young, ed., *Historical Notices of Old Belfast and Its Vicinity* (Belfast: M. Ward & Co., 1896).

Georges Denis Zimmerman, *Songs of Irish Rebellion: Irish Political Street Ballads and Rebel Songs, 1780–1900*, 2nd edn (Dublin: Four Courts Press, 2002; orig. edn 1966).

Index